"WORK HARD, STUDY . . .
            AND KEEP OUT OF POLITICS!"

ALSO BY JAMES A. BAKER, III

The Politics of Diplomacy:
Revolution, War & Peace, 1989–1992 (with Thomas M. DeFrank)

"WORK HARD, STUDY... AND KEEP OUT OF POLITICS!"

ADVENTURES AND LESSONS FROM AN UNEXPECTED PUBLIC LIFE

JAMES A. BAKER, III
with STEVE FIFFER

G. P. PUTNAM'S SONS
New York

G. P. PUTNAM'S SONS
Publishers Since 1838
Published by the Penguin Group
Penguin Group (USA) Inc., 375 Hudson Street, New York, New York 10014,
USA · Penguin Group (Canada), 90 Eglinton Avenue East, Suite 700, Toronto,
Ontario M4P 2Y3, Canada (a division of Pearson Penguin Canada Inc.) · Penguin
Books Ltd, 80 Strand, London WC2R 0RL, England · Penguin Ireland, 25 St
Stephen's Green, Dublin 2, Ireland (a division of Penguin Books Ltd) · Penguin
Group (Australia), 250 Camberwell Road, Camberwell, Victoria 3124, Australia
(a division of Pearson Australia Group Pty Ltd) · Penguin Books India Pvt Ltd,
11 Community Centre, Panchsheel Park, · New Delhi–110 017, India · Penguin
Group (NZ), Cnr Airborne and Rosedale Roads, Albany, Auckland 1310, New
Zealand (a division of Pearson New Zealand Ltd) · Penguin Books (South Africa)
(Pty) Ltd, 24 Sturdee Avenue, Rosebank, Johannesburg 2196, South Africa

Penguin Books Ltd, Registered Offices:
80 Strand, London WC2R 0RL, England

Library of Congress Cataloging-in-Publication Data

Baker, James Addison, date.
"Word hard, study . . . and keep out of politics!": adventures and lessons from an
unexpected public life / James A. Baker, III ; with Steve Fiffer.
p.   cm.
Includes index.
ISBN-13: 978-0-399-15377-8
ISBN-10: 0-399-15377-2
1. Baker, James Addison, date.   2. Baker, James Addison, date—Philosophy.
3. Statesmen—United States—Biography.   4. Cabinet officers—United States—
Biography.   5. United States—Politics and government—1981–1989.   6. United
States—Politics and government—1989–   7. Baker, James Addison, date—
Philosophy.   8. Civil service—United States.   9. United States—Politics and
government—Philosophy.   I. Fiffer, Steve.   II. Title.
E840.8.B315A3   2006   2006022305
973.92092—dc22
[B]

Published in the United States of America
10 9 8 7 6 5 4 3 2 1

TO THOSE PRESIDENTS OF THE UNITED STATES
WHO GAVE ME THE OPPORTUNITY TO EXPERIENCE
AN UNEXPECTED PUBLIC LIFE

CONTENTS

PREFACE

I WAS IN WASHINGTON, D.C., on January 20, 1953, the crisp, sunny day that Dwight David Eisenhower was inaugurated as our nation's thirty-fourth president. At the time, I was a twenty-two-year-old second lieutenant in the United States Marine Corps, on leave from nearby Quantico, Virginia. My fiancée, Mary Stuart McHenry, of Dayton, Ohio, was in town for a visit before I shipped out. I had joined the Marines' platoon leader officer program the summer after my junior year at Princeton, in part to keep from being drafted before I graduated. The Korean War was raging when I signed up, and I fully expected to be sent there.

Strolling down the street arm in arm on the day before the inauguration, very much in love, Mary Stuart and I were stopped by a well-dressed older gentleman. I was wearing my uniform. "Lieutenant," he said, "thank you for your service. I have a son who is a Marine second lieutenant in Korea. I'm wondering, would you and your lady like two tickets to the inaugural parade tomorrow?"

"Yes, sir," I said to our anonymous benefactor, "and thank you."

Mary Stuart and I showed up early the next day to claim our seats and discovered they were on the lip of Lafayette Park, directly across Pennsylvania Avenue from the White House and only a few yards downstream from the presidential reviewing stand. An estimated 750,000 people attended the inaugural festivities that day, and except for President Eisenhower, Vice President Richard Nixon, and the dignitaries and family members with them, we had some of the best seats in town.

As floats and marching bands streamed by, I clicked away with my 35mm camera. I still have the slides, including one of President Eisenhower and John Foster Dulles, soon to be sworn in as secretary of state, as they drove past, and another of a cowboy roping the president in the reviewing stand.*† Newspaper accounts said the parade lasted about four hours. I can't remember if we stayed until the end, but I doubt it. The dignitaries (and Mary Stuart) all wore heavy overcoats, but I had on only a light uniform jacket. Whatever the weather, however, it was a great experience. Mary Stuart and I had no idea what the months ahead might bring, but that day we were happy and thankful.

Twenty-eight years later another president-elect took the oath of office, this time on the terrace of the west front of the Capitol. I was privileged to attend both the inauguration ceremony and the parade that followed. This time, I didn't sit across from the parade reviewing stand, however; I sat *in* it. I was to be Ronald Reagan's White House chief of staff, charged with helping turn his ideas about the economy and defense into legislative and political realities. To those who knew me my first fifty years, my presence at this 1981 inauguration was as unexpected as my presence at Ike's, and I was just as surprised.

After my two-year tour of active duty with the Marines and three years of law school, I had dedicated myself to a career in a major Houston law firm. In my time away from the demands of the office, I

---

*Nothing like that would happen today, of course. After the assassination of President Kennedy and attempts on the lives of Presidents Ford and Reagan, White House reviewing stands are now enclosed by thick bulletproof glass.

†More than half a century later, my public service and political papers, as well as Dulles's, are stored on the same shelf at Princeton's Seeley G. Mudd Manuscript Library.

was more interested in serving a tennis ball than serving in a government job or a political campaign.

What finally blew my life off its more-or-less conventional course was a deep personal tragedy in early 1970. Afterward, a Republican friend invited me to get involved in my first political campaign—his losing bid for the U.S. Senate that same year. I threw myself into this new and exciting project, and if politics didn't exactly save my life, it certainly helped preserve my sanity. When Ronald Reagan was sworn in as president, that friend, George H. W. Bush, was sworn in as vice president. Later that day, he came up to me, smiling.

"Bake," he said, "who'da thunk it?"

WHO, INDEED?

Few have had the opportunity to serve six American presidents—two in the military and, decades later, three in senior government positions, then one more on several special projects. In my first book, *The Politics of Diplomacy: Revolution, War & Peace, 1989–1992,* I wrote in detail about how the world changed, dramatically and fundamentally, during my four years as secretary of state under the first President Bush. While revisiting some of those events in this second book, my aim here is to tell the story of my journey from Houston, Texas, to Washington, D.C., then around the world, and to share memories of the political campaigns, the presidential administrations in which I served, and the other offices I held.

But I hope to do more. I've now lived more than three-quarters of a century, some in private life, some in public service. I'm more at ease when I'm getting things done in the world of action than in stirring the ashes of the past and writing about what it all meant. Still, I've learned some lessons (often the hard way) and worked out some ideas about politics and public policy. While I'm telling the story of my life, of what happened, I'll also share a few of these lessons and ideas. But what I offer in this book are not grand theories; they are the lessons from one man's hard-won experiences during a long and varied life.

SOON AFTER Mary Stuart and I watched the inaugural parade of one of the great war leaders of the twentieth century, now my commander in chief, I shipped out from Quantico. The Corps sent me to the Mediterranean, not Korea. My months of service with the Sixth Fleet and the reinforced battalion of Marines that the United States maintains in the Mediterranean, even to this day, were not unpleasant and, obviously, were considerably less dangerous than even a few days in Korea. That bloody conflict occupies a hazy zone in our national consciousness between the glory of World War II and the disappointment of Vietnam, and is too often forgotten. It's something I never forget, however, because many of my classmates from Marine Corps Basic School—men I knew—sacrificed their lives on the Korean peninsula. I survived and they didn't, which still triggers a bit of guilt.

We have no say in choosing our parents. I was fortunate to grow up in Houston in a loving home under comfortable circumstances. Having gone away from home for two years of prep school, then on to Princeton, I entered the Marines as an immature young man. I left with more personal discipline and with a greater sense of purpose—the products of military training, of facing up to what it means to prepare for combat in time of war, and of losing young friends whose potential seemed so limitless.

As the old saying goes, "There is no such thing as a former Marine." Early in 1989, after I was sworn in as the sixty-first secretary of state of the United States, the commandant of the Corps paid a courtesy call. When General Al Gray walked into my seventh-floor office at the State Department with his four stars on each shoulder, I had to remind myself that I was no longer a second lieutenant who should stand and salute.

We had a very pleasant visit. "Mr. Secretary, I have a gift for you," the general said as he prepared to depart. He left a stack of small business cards with a military camouflage background. In the center of each card in large letters was, "James A. Baker, III, United States Marine." And under that, in very tiny letters, "and Secretary of State."

While in that office, I participated in the decision to dispatch Marines and other servicemen and -women to fight in the Gulf War. No matter how just the cause, it is a sobering responsibility to send Americans into combat, but it's a responsibility that, at times, must be met. To stand aside when America's core interests are challenged, as the nation was tempted to do after Vietnam, is dangerous.

In his inaugural address, President Eisenhower called for peace, but promised that America would remain strong. When President Reagan took his oath twenty-eight years later, he said the same thing. By then the Cold War had become a seemingly permanent feature of the second half of the twentieth century.

The payoff for four decades of American leadership and resolve came during the presidency of my friend George H. W. Bush. We saw the fall of communism in Eastern Europe and the Soviet Union. With the end of the Cold War, the principles of classical liberalism—personal, religious, and economic freedom, self-government, and the rule of law—prevailed against totalitarian ideology. There were other victories, as well, including the end of apartheid in South Africa and renewed hopes for peace in the Middle East. When those years ended, the United States was (and it remains) the world's sole surviving superpower.

Our geopolitical rival in the Cold War was the expansionist and nuclear-armed Soviet Union. Our adversaries today—transnational terrorist organizations and smaller nations with authoritarian rulers and nuclear ambitions—present different kinds of threats. Certain truths remain, however. As it has since World War II, the source of America's power rests in no small part on our ability to project strength responsibly around the world and our willingness to use that strength when necessary in furtherance of our values and interests.

My full-time career in public service ended with the inauguration of President Bill Clinton in 1993. In the previous thirteen years, I had served as White House chief of staff, secretary of the treasury, and secretary of state, and I had led presidential election campaigns. I was tired, and it was time to do other things—spend time with my family; write my diplomatic memoir; serve as senior partner for Baker Botts, my law firm, and as senior counselor for the Carlyle Group, a Washington-based private equity firm; help establish the James A. Baker III Institute for Public Policy as a first-rate think tank at Rice University; do some public speaking; submit the occasional op-ed piece on topics that interested me; and hunt, fish, and play golf.

In the years after 1993, however, I have been called off the bench several times. Kofi Annan asked me to try to help resolve a lingering dispute in Western Sahara, and candidate George W. Bush asked me to help preserve his 2000 presidential election victory in Florida, then to serve as his envoy or representative on several special projects—in 2003 and 2004, a mission to persuade countries to forgive a substantial share of the debt owed to them by Iraq; a trip to the former Soviet Republic of Georgia in 2004 to encourage my old friend Eduard Shevardnadze to support a free election; service in 2005 as cochairman with President Jimmy Carter of the Commission on Federal Election Reform; and a call later that year to chair the American delegation to Israel on the tenth anniversary of the assassination of my friend, the former prime minister of Israel, Yitzhak Rabin. More recently I agreed to serve as cochair of a bipartisan study group to make a forward-looking assessment of the situation in Iraq.

All but one of those summonses came after I had celebrated my seventieth birthday. All were unsought. None had a salary, except one that earned a dollar a year before taxes.* So why did I take time from my own affairs and the pleasures of private life to accept these commissions?

For several reasons, I suppose. For one, the projects were interest-

---

*However, federal law required that my law firm be paid for its work in the Florida recount effort in 2000.

ing. For another, I thought that each one had a worthy purpose or goal. The biggest reason, however, is that I simply felt a sense of responsibility. For the first few years of my adult life (except for my military service), I had largely left the burdens of public life to others. Then came my friendship with George H. W. Bush, my family's personal tragedy, and my unexpected life in politics and public service. Each of us, I learned, has the capacity to make the world a better place. All it takes is the dedication of some part of our time and talent to public service. This is a small price, really, for the privilege of being a citizen of our great nation. As a young man, I had sat on the sidelines; now I understood the importance of joining the parade.

"We must be willing, individually and as a nation, to accept whatever sacrifices may be required of us," President Eisenhower said in his inaugural address more than fifty years ago. Each citizen "plays an indispensable role," he said. "No person, no home, no community can be beyond the reach of this call," for "whatever America hopes to bring to pass in the world must first come to pass in the heart of America."

My hope is that this book will help the reader gain some appreciation for the importance of participation in public service and its corollary, politics, and also for the satisfaction that comes from giving both one's very best. For it is the promise of such participation by our citizens that is the best hope for our country's future.

ONE

"NUMBER ONE, I DON'T KNOW ANYTHING ABOUT POLITICS"

THE PRESIDENTIAL ELECTION was the tightest in a century. As the results came in, it was apparent that a small number of votes for my candidate or his opponent would swing the contest one way or the other. When I finally went to bed at 3:00 A.M., I was certain I would never see another race for president decided by such a narrow margin. Boy, was I wrong.

The 1976 race between Governor Jimmy Carter and President Gerald Ford was close. If there had been a shift of fewer than 5,600 votes in Ohio and 3,700 in Hawaii, Ford would have retained the presidency, winning the electoral vote while losing the popular election. But '76 now pales in comparison to the 2000 race between Vice President Al Gore and Governor George W. Bush. That one was decided by 537 votes in Florida and a 7–2 margin in the U.S. Supreme Court more than a month after the balloting. As most everyone knows, although Gore won the popular vote, Bush prevailed in the Electoral College.

In 1970, as a forty-year-old Houston corporate lawyer who had little interest and no experience in politics, I could never have imagined that I would be intimately involved in either of these presidential contests, much less both. Nor could I ever have dreamed that I would lead five successive presidential campaigns for three different candidates. At the beginning of 1975, I was still practicing law in my hometown. By that fall, I was in Washington, D.C., second in command at the Department of Commerce. And by the summer of '76, I was campaign chairman for the Ford-Dole ticket. Who'da thunk it?

Before losing narrowly to Carter, we had come back from a double-digit deficit after the conventions. Many observers believe that if Ford-Dole had been Ford-Reagan, we would have won. So why didn't Ford tap Reagan for the second spot and create a dream ticket?

The actor-turned-politician from California was the obvious choice. He had a huge core of supporters, and he was a great campaigner. Moreover, he had just missed getting the nomination himself at what turned out to be the last closely contested national convention in this nation's history.

President Ford was not happy that Governor Reagan had mounted such a strong challenge against a sitting president. But other nominees have chosen runner-ups after bitter contests, particularly if those runner-ups could improve the chances of victory in November. John F. Kennedy picked Lyndon Johnson that way. While the chemistry between Ford and Reagan was not good, that alone didn't impel Ford to bypass Reagan. Most accounts say there was another reason.

Early during President Reagan's first term, when I was his White House chief of staff, he and I discussed this. "You know, Mr. President," I said, as we sat together alone in the Oval Office one day, "if President Ford had asked you to run with him, he would have won, and you might never have been president."

"You're right," the president responded. "But I have to tell you, Jim, if he had asked, I'd have felt duty-bound to run."

"President Ford didn't ask you," I replied, "because we received word from your campaign that you would join him for a unity meeting only on the condition that he *wouldn't* offer you the vice presidency. And besides that, you very publicly shut down the movement by your supporters in Kansas City to draft you for the vice presidential nomination."

"Look," President Reagan said, "I really did not want to be vice president, and I said so at the time. But I don't have any recollection of telling anyone to pass a message to President Ford not to offer me the spot. If he had asked, I would have felt duty-bound to say yes."

I was shocked. How different history might have been. Given the intensity of their primary battle, Ford really didn't want Reagan as his running mate, but the president might have asked if he had thought Reagan would accept. And with a Ford-Reagan ticket in 1976, I think two presidential portraits might be missing from the White House walls today—those of Jimmy Carter . . . and Ronald Reagan.

This conversation about the vice presidency occurred early in President Reagan's tenure and was revisited several times over the years. As anyone who knew him well would attest, Ronald Reagan was completely without guile. What you saw was what you got. I have no reason to believe he wasn't being totally up front with me. Still, I must add here that a few years ago one of his close friends and advisers, former Nevada senator Paul Laxalt, told me that he still believes candidate Reagan made it clear in 1976 that he didn't want to be offered the second spot. But if, as President Reagan told me, he didn't tell anyone to pass on that message to the Ford camp, this would suggest his staff did that on its own. Why? Perhaps they knew he didn't want to be vice president, but would have felt he could not turn down a direct offer from the president. Or perhaps they simply reasoned that if a Ford-Reagan ticket had won, their man would have been too old to run for president in 1980 or 1984. (He wasn't, of course, and ran successfully in both of those years, although without having first served as vice president.)

MY ROLES as presidential campaign chairman and White House chief of staff would not have sat very well with another James Addison Baker, my grandfather. Nor would my view that all Americans should consider public service. A successful lawyer known as the "Captain," he admonished all who joined his firm to "work hard, study, and keep out of politics," which he viewed as a somewhat unseemly undertaking that really good lawyers left to others. He was an imposing figure who helped transform Houston from a regional cotton market and rail hub into a vibrant seaport and the capital of the U.S. oil industry. In the process, he turned a local law practice into a preeminent Texas firm that would later expand worldwide.

With due respect to the Captain, however, *not* keeping out of politics turned out to be one of the best decisions I ever made. Although my unplanned entry into public life was occasioned in part by personal tragedy, I found I had a strong predilection and passion for what the former *New York Times* correspondent Hedrick Smith called "the power game." Over the years, I witnessed the exercise of more power than I would have ever dreamed possible, but was often reminded (sometimes the hard way) to keep a sense of perspective about it all.

No one was better at keeping me humble than my mother, Bonner Means Baker. On my visits to Houston in the late 1980s and early nineties, she invariably asked: "Now, darling, tell me exactly, what is it you do?"

"Mom, I am secretary of state."

"Of the United States of *America?*"

"Yes, Mom."

"You don't mean it!"

Then she would add, "Well, you know, dear, if your father had lived, he would never have let you go to Washington."

My mother lived to the handsome age of ninety-six. She and my dad had tried to have children for thirteen years before I came along, so she doted on me and my younger sister, Bonner, when we finally arrived—me on April 28, 1930, and Bonner some eighteen months later. I talked baby talk until I was three or four years old, and I called my mother "Mamish." She was a warm, spirited, and elegant woman, not indifferent to fashion. I am still not sure whether her affectionate cross-examination of me in her twilight years stemmed from a failing mind or her enduring sense of humor.

Mother was only fifteen when she and my father, James A. Baker, Jr., met at a high school dance in Houston. It was love at first sight, she always said. They were engaged for five and one-half years. My dad wanted to be in a position to support his bride and, eventually, a family, but after he finished Princeton in 1915 and got his law degree at the University of Texas in 1917, World War I intervened. They married on August 4, 1917, about ten months before he shipped out as a young army lieutenant for the trenches of France. I remember Mother telling me that in his absence she comforted herself every day by repeating a verse from the 91st Psalm: "A thousand shall fall at thy side, and ten thousand at thy right hand; *but* it shall not come nigh thee."

Like my mother, Dad had a wonderful sense of humor and loved to joke, but he also had an austere demeanor and was a strict disciplinarian. And like his father, he, too, had a saying: "Prior preparation prevents poor performance." He called this the "Five Ps." It's a simple aphorism, the sort of thing adults tell children, then forget. People are often surprised to hear a man my age recite it, and without embarrassment. But this was a gift from my father that has helped me in one way or another almost every day of my adult life.

Dad was an intercollegiate wrestling champion and fine pole-vaulter while at Princeton. No doubt his training as an athlete and his military service reinforced his views about the importance of discipline and preparation, about doing your best in the fleeting time you are given on this earth.

Dad's fifth-year Princeton reunion book features the photographs of many classmates who never returned from the bloody battlefields of Europe. He came back, however, as an infantry captain and a genuine war hero. He once ordered some in his company to clear out an enemy trench. When they balked, he went in by himself, armed only with his .45-caliber service revolver, and captured two German soldiers. I had that pistol for many years until it was stolen, and I still have his World War I helmet and uniform.

My sister and I always addressed Dad with respect, but behind his back, my friends and I called him "Warden." He expected good manners, hard work, and deference to adult authority, and he regarded corporal punishment as a useful way to help us see the benefits of satisfying those expectations. The culture of the 1930s supported this approach. In those days, children did what their parents asked them to. Sometimes he spanked me. Occasionally, he would throw cold water on me in bed if I didn't get up when I should.

I'll leave it to the child-rearing experts to debate the pros and cons of this sort of upbringing, now considered old-fashioned and too harsh. All I can say is that he was a terrific dad. We had a wonderful relationship, I loved him dearly, and he set me on the right path. Many of my contemporaries had their lives ruined because their parents gave them too much money and too little discipline. That was never a problem in the Baker household.

Dad also loved to hunt and fish. From the time I was six, he and I spent many hours together in duck blinds. They are superb classrooms for teaching other forms of discipline, including the patience necessary to know exactly the right time to pull the trigger. After his love and his emphasis on the Five Ps, sharing his passion for the outdoors was Dad's greatest gift to me.

As a young competitive tennis player, I didn't question my father's orders to stay on the court after matches and practice backhand after backhand. Nor did I question his decision to send me across the country to Pottstown, Pennsylvania, to his alma mater, the Hill School. I didn't even protest when he told me to join his old undergraduate social fraternity at the University of Texas, Phi Delta Theta. Here I was *in law school,* twenty-four years old, just out of the Marine Corps, married with a child, and having to go through a Hell Week hazing in which college kids younger than I was poured raw eggs down my throat and made me sit bare-assed on a block of ice.

I didn't rebel. When I was growing up, our objective was to please our parents. Mother and Dad knew best, and we didn't argue with them. But we certainly didn't always do everything we were told. Like most teenagers, then and now, I broke curfew more than a few times.

One irony in my father's life is that he earned his military rank of captain in the most difficult way possible, but for my grandfather, "Captain" was an honorific title bestowed by a ceremonial Houston militia he joined in the late 1800s. After the Civil War, many prominent men in the South were forever known as "General Smith" and "Colonel Jones." My grandfather's militia was formed, I have heard, to give younger men a way to wear outlandish uniforms, join parades, conduct balls, and (not least) claim military rank of their own—all without the grim necessity of being actual soldiers.

I remember the Captain as a heavyset man who always smelled of cigars. He sat on the boards of many major banks, utility companies, and railroads, and represented them as a lawyer. Well known in Texas, he rose to national prominence in 1900 when he became the central figure in one of the most sensational scandals of his era.

In a New York murder trial, he proved that a butler and an unscrupulous lawyer had poisoned William Marsh Rice, a wealthy Texas merchant, with mercury and chloroform, then claimed Rice's fortune under a forged will. My grandfather had been Mr. Rice's lawyer, and his efforts restored the victim's original will, which endowed William Marsh Rice Institute, a "university of the first class" that Rice had chartered in Houston in 1891. Rice Institute (now Rice University) opened in 1912, and my grandfather served as its first chairman of the board of trustees for fifty years.

The Captain was the second James A. Baker in our family. The first, his father, was born in 1816 near Florence, Alabama, to Elijah and Jane Baker. Family lore says they descended from Scottish immigrants. They were part of the great migration of early Americans out of the thirteen original states to the unsettled forests and plains out west. They were, it seems, a well-educated family. In Alabama, James apprenticed to a lawyer and appeared to have prospects for a good career. In April 1852, however, he abruptly left for Texas, apparently in grief over the sudden death of his bride of less than two years. During the Civil War, he served as a judge. Afterward, he joined a small Houston law firm—the one that to this day bears his name, Baker Botts. He and his second wife, Rowena, are buried in Huntsville, Texas, not far from his friend General Sam Houston.

I will not pretend that I grew up under modest circumstances. My mother's father, J. C. Means, was in the timber, oil, and cotton business. He was not particularly successful, but the Bakers were reasonably well-to-do. Each generation had built on the success of the previous one. We lived in a nice two-story house near Rice University and belonged to two country clubs. The family owned a considerable amount of Houston real estate and made other good investments.

Still, I don't think my parents spoiled me. Dad was quite frugal. He understood that it was easier to spend a dollar than to make it. As a result, we didn't lead the stereotyped bigger-than-life Texas existence. No mansion. No big cars. And no big allowance for me. Dad invested most of his money. Yet he did spend, without hesitation, for his children's education or for things my mother wanted; material possessions for himself or his children were meaningless, something else I inherited from him. But I've become much better as the years have gone by and I have been able to accumulate some means of my own.

There were occasional extravagances in my childhood. Some were outlandish: when I was a young boy, my mother once had me dressed in a pink linen smock for a portrait by a member of the French Academy. Some were just plain fun: when the University of Texas played Texas A&M in football, the Captain often took us to the game in a private rail car arranged through one of his railroad clients.

There was one domain in which my father was willing to give me money. When I was a teenager, he said he would pay me $1,000 if I didn't smoke until I was twenty-one and another $1,000 if I didn't drink alcohol before that age. I didn't collect, though I managed to wait until I was eighteen for my first taste of hard liquor. I was not a habitual smoker until I went into the Marine Corps. At breaks in our training, the drill instructors would always say, "The smoking lamp is lit"—meaning it was okay to smoke. Most everyone did, so I did, too.

It's somewhat remarkable that I didn't start drinking the moment my parents dropped me off at the Hill School. My first year there was tough. I entered as a junior and didn't know anybody. Most classmates had already been there for two years and had established friendships. I was a new boy. All my friends were back in Houston. I even had to wear a beanie, and every time I put it on, it reminded me that I was not a part of the old boys' club.

By senior year, I was much more at ease. I was elected to the student government and captained the tennis team. I also made friendships that continue to this day. My grades were good, but not outstanding. Still, I managed to get into the university I wanted and that my father had attended: Princeton. Two centuries after it was founded by colonial Presbyterian clerics, it was still the destination of choice for many young American men of Scottish heritage, particularly those from the South.

As I said, I didn't really drink until I was eighteen, but I quickly made up for lost time during my first year at Princeton. Liberated from the constraints of prep school, I went wild. I became a member of both Princeton's Right Wing Club—so named because we spent much of our time using our right arms to hoist spirituous beverages—and 21 Club, another social organization with a similar mission. I also used my right arm to play tennis as cocaptain of the freshman team, but the team was loaded with nationally ranked players who were better than I was. The next year I gave up tennis and switched to rugby, in part because the rugby team went to Bermuda for spring break, and the tennis team went only to North Carolina. It was in Bermuda in 1950 that I met the girl I was later to marry, Mary Stuart McHenry, who was there on spring break from Finch College in New York.

My freshman and sophomore year grades reflected my membership in the social clubs. I ignored the Five Ps to such an extent that it is a wonder I didn't get five Fs and flunk out. By junior year, fortunately, I had matured a bit. I studied more, finding the classics (my minor) and history (my major) especially interesting.

My senior thesis covered the conflict within Britain's Labour Party in the 1930s and forties between two powerful members of Parliament, Aneurin Bevan, whom I saw as a "true socialist," and Ernest Bevin, a "social democrat." There was no love lost between these two men. When a British cabinet member declared that Bevan was his own worst enemy, Bevin said, "Not while I'm around."

I argued that the clash between Bevan and Bevin was a clash between idealism and realism. Those who know me will not be surprised that I favored the approach of the realist, Bevin, who served as Clement Attlee's foreign secretary. "Bevin was not interested in theories, but in practicalities," I wrote. "He knew that when men were unemployed they wanted bread and work, not an oration on the coming revolution. . . . Bevin believed in solving the problems of the present before tackling the problems of the future."

I had no interest or talent in science or math, but did have a fair grasp of history—an indicator that I might have an aptitude for the law. More important, however, I'd been brought up with the idea that Baker Botts was everything. I'd sat in my father's office as he worked, and had worked at the firm myself as an office boy.* That was my legacy. That was the history of my family.

"Practicing law is a wonderful lifestyle," Dad told me. "Although you'll never make really big money doing it, it's very satisfying." Still, this career path was not ordained. More than once Dad told me the choice was mine. "I'd never insist you be a lawyer." I even flirted with going to medical school, but that was before I took a job at St. Joseph's Hospital one summer as a teenager. My assignment was to hold the tray while stabbing victims and overdosed drug users threw up. I also had the opportunity to watch a baby being born and observe a surgeon cutting into a patient's chest cavity. All that blood! I quickly realized I didn't have the stomach or the aptitude to become a doctor.

In any event, I didn't have to make a decision by graduation day

---

*Another alumnus of the Baker Botts office-boy pool, hired many years later, was George W. Bush.

in the late spring of 1952. My immediate future was Basic School—the U.S. Marine Corps' officer training program—not law school. The government had started drafting young men out of college when the Korean War broke out in 1950. I wanted to serve, but I wanted to finish school first. It was too late to join an ROTC program at Princeton, and my tendency to motion sickness made it prudent not to consider the Air Force or the Navy.

The CIA seemed a possibility until I had an on-campus interview. "Would you have any problem jumping out of an airplane with a parachute behind enemy lines?" I was asked.

"You bet I would." End of interview.

Then I learned of the Marine Corps platoon leaders program. The deal: go to boot camp for six weeks each summer for two summers, and we'll give you a commission when you graduate. After that you'll have an obligation to serve on active duty for two years. I signed on.

In Basic School at Quantico, I was one of about five hundred second lieutenants. Our commanding officer told us that if we worked hard, we'd get our choice of duty station and military occupational specialty (MOS). I graduated at the top of the reserves in our class—behind a few regular Marine enlisted men picked to become officers. When it came time to hand out MOSs, the commanding officer told me, "We're going to put you where we put our best—platoon leader, MOS 0302—infantry officer."

"Major," I replied, "one reason I worked so hard is because I have a friend who graduated a year ago, and he talked to me about being a naval gunfire spotter, MOS 0840. That's what I really want to do." Spotters went in with the first wave of an amphibious invasion. They had a couple of jeeps, a few men, and some radio equipment, and their job was to deploy forward and direct the fire of naval ships supporting the operation. This was hazardous duty, as was leading a platoon, but I preferred it. I didn't want to be responsible for the lives of forty-four other people.

Although the major wasn't pleased by my request, he honored it. I thought I'd be going to Korea, and fifty-nine of the sixty officers in our class who received artillery MOSs went to Fort Sill, Oklahoma, for two weeks and then on to Korea. The sixtieth—me—ended up with the battalion of Marines the United States had kept deployed in the Mediterranean since the end of World War II. I was on a troop transport ship, the USS *Monrovia*, where the biggest danger was falling overboard as I perpetually heaved over the rail.

I was in the Mediterranean for six months. When I returned in November 1953, Mary Stuart and I were married in her hometown of Dayton, Ohio. After my discharge from active duty in 1954, we moved to a small apartment in Austin, Texas, where I entered law school on the GI Bill. I thought about applying to Harvard, but my father argued that the University of Texas was the best place to learn Texas law and establish connections with others who would be practicing in Texas. Again, I didn't question his counsel, which turned out to have been excellent.

During that initial year in law school, our first son, Jamie, was born. Nothing concentrates the mind like military service and being married with a child. Practicing the Five Ps to exhaustion, I made the law review and graduated with honors, but I wasn't much fun to be around.

We never considered settling anywhere except Houston. My family was there. So, too, was Baker Botts, the law firm where three James A. Bakers before me had hung their shingles.* I would have been happy to follow in their footsteps, but the firm had an ironclad antinepotism rule. My father was still practicing there, so I could not.

Thanks to my academic record and my name, the partnership considered making an exception for me, but eventually decided against waiving the rule. I was disappointed. Baker Botts was all I knew. In the end, however, their decision was the best thing that could have happened to me. Had I succeeded at a firm so closely identified with my father, my grandfather, and my great-grandfather, neither I nor any-

---

*Why am I James A. Baker, III, not IV? Because the numbering didn't start until I came along.

body else would have been able to say with certainty whether my success was based on my skills or my name. Going to another firm gave me a chance to sink or swim on my own.

That other firm was Andrews, Kurth, Campbell & Bradley. It was a smaller but also well-respected firm with a blue-chip roster of clients that included Howard Hughes. When I joined in 1957, the firm had thirty-five lawyers, and I was only the seventy-eighth to have been hired in the firm's fifty-five-year history. It was a wonderful place to work. The philosophy of the practice was collegial, we were proud of AK and its history, and we were loyal to the firm and one another.

"We're going to assign you to Harry Jones," said Mickey West, the firm's chief recruiter. "What an opportunity!"

And it truly was. The man who would become my mentor was warm, gentlemanly, brilliant, and pragmatic, the smartest practitioner I've ever known. In law school, I had briefed every case so thoroughly that I often got lost in the details. If not for Harry Jones, I might have followed the same dead-end path in my practice. He taught me to get to the heart of the matter.

I would sit across from him in his corner office while he read what I'd written. "Is there anything more on this?" he would ask in a non-threatening and professorial voice. The ability to separate the wheat from the chaff or, less delicately, to cut through the BS in a written memo or a face-to-face negotiation, not only served me well at the law firm, but has also been one of my strengths in politics and public service. I owe much of that to Harry Jones, a lawyer's lawyer.

In 1957, the practice of law was not as specialized as it is today. Andrews Kurth was just beginning to establish departments. In law school they told us that real lawyers tried lawsuits, so I asked to be assigned to the trial section. I soon found myself sitting second chair down at the courthouse as one of our lawyers tried a personal injury case. Our client was an insurance company bound by contract to provide a defense for its policyholder. It seemed obvious to me that witnesses were lying under oath and that nothing was being done about it. I didn't want any part of that, so I said goodbye to litigation and hello to a general business law practice—mergers and acquisitions, corporate and securities work, oil and gas, banking, and real estate.

As I approached forty, life was good. Our marriage flourished. Three more boys—Mike, John, and Doug—followed Jamie. We joined a couple of country clubs. And thanks to Mary Stuart, we could be described as a churchgoing family. My father was raised a Presbyterian. Mother had for a while been a Christian Scientist and for one year I went to Sunday school at her church. Dad was not a churchgoer, although he was a man of faith. He was a workaholic who spent Sundays at the office. On his way to work those mornings, and after that first year of Sunday school at Mother's church, he would drop Bonner and me off for Sunday school at First Presbyterian Church near his office in downtown Houston, to learn the hereditary faith of my Scottish forebears. After class, we'd join him at work.

I remember first getting a sense of fulfillment out of religion when I was at the Hill School. We attended chapel every day, and I found myself enjoying the hymns and learning a little how to pray. I was a nonobservant Christian in college and attended church only occasionally in the Marines and during law school.

Mary Stuart was a better Episcopalian than I was a Presbyterian, and when we married, I switched. I didn't think about it at the time, but my ancient Baker ancestors may have turned in their graves when I left the faith they had brought across the ocean from Scotland and went over to the "English" church they had spent so many centuries railing against. In Houston we attended St. Martin's fairly regularly. I found the services rewarding and eventually served on the vestry, the committee of lay members who help manage the parish, but my faith then was not nearly as important to me as it is now.

Like my father, my church on Sundays was often my law office. *Workaholic* is an overworked term, but it describes me during those first twelve years of practice. I made time for tennis and indulged my lifelong desire to escape to the country every once in a while to hunt and fish and clear my head, but Mary Stuart and I took very few real vacations.

Houston was my world, and I never dreamed of living anywhere else or doing anything besides being a lawyer. Politics was not in the picture. The most that can be said of me politically is that I voted . . . in some elections anyway. Oftentimes I did something else instead.

Texas still hadn't forgotten that Republicans were in office during Reconstruction, so like just about everyone else in the state at the time, I was a Democrat. And like many other conservative Democrats in the 1950s, when I voted, I voted for my party's candidates in local and state elections and for the Republican candidate for president. Mary Stuart was different. She came from a long line of Republicans in Ohio, and she remained active in the small Texas branch of her party, even serving as a precinct captain and often as a campaign worker for local candidates.

I sometimes wonder whether, if Mary Stuart had stayed healthy, I would have kept out of politics for my entire life. But in February 1968, she noticed a lump in her breast. Her doctor told her not to worry; the lump was most likely just mastitis, a side effect of being on birth control pills, which were relatively new at the time. "Come back if it persists," he said.

That summer we took a fishing trip into the mountains of Wyoming, camping at the same spot near the headwaters of the Yellowstone River where my father and I had camped to hunt elk twenty-four years earlier. By the end of the trip, Mary Stuart had lost all her stamina. The lump was now hot and red. Not too long after we returned, one of America's best surgeons, our friend Denton Cooley, performed a mastectomy. In the waiting room after the surgery, he didn't say, "She doesn't have a chance," but I sensed he was telling me to prepare for the worst. I was scared and depressed, but hopeful.

We were building a new home. Mary Stuart had designed it, and she continued to watch over construction. As the months passed, however, the cancer spread to her bones, and it was clear that she wasn't going to make it.

From the time I met her in Bermuda in 1950, I never dated anyone else. She was a gorgeous and bright woman, a devoted wife, and a loving mother.

We were close, but—whether out of fear or uncertainty or, more probably, concern for the other—we never talked openly about her real prognosis. She never told me she knew she was dying, and I never told her that I knew she was dying. That knowledge hung over us like a dark cloud in those last months. She did write me a goodbye letter. I found it after her death. Dated November 29, 1969, and addressed to "My dear sweet loving and lovable Jimmy," it reads in part:

> Though my time to die may not be far off, it is not now. I am not afraid. . . . My darling, it has been a beautiful life. We have been fortunate in so many ways. . . . Since the night I kissed you on the beach in Bermuda I have loved you more than anybody could ever love another body. The only thing that makes me sad about dying is leaving you and the boys. I often wonder what they will be like as grown men. Since they are half you they will have some good qualities in them. . . . God and I will watch over you and the boys and keep you safe. . . . Don't be sad. Rejoice and come to me someday.

My instinct from earliest memory has been to keep personal things personal. These few words reveal something about Mary Stuart's spirit that is worth sharing, however, not only for the sake of her children and grandchildren, but also as a model for others of how this young woman's faith gave her the courage to accept her own mortality so serenely.

When the house was just about finished, we took her over the threshold in a wheelchair. She never got to live in it. Within days, she had lapsed into a coma. The boys were ages seven, eight, thirteen, and fifteen. I never told them she was dying—a mistake I now profoundly regret.

Most nights while Mary Stuart was in the hospital, I had slept on a cot in her room. One evening, however, I went home for a shower and some rest in my own bed. The hospital called during the night and said, "You'd better come over here." When I arrived, Mary Stuart was breathing heavily. I held her in my arms, only the two of us, and I told her what a wonderful wife she'd been and how much I loved her. She made a little sound, and I like to think she heard me. She died a few hours later at 11:00 A.M., February 18, 1970. We had been married for sixteen years. The boys and I were devastated.

Eight months earlier, my tennis doubles partner had suggested that I file for the congressional seat he was vacating to run for the Senate. He and his wife were our good friends and had experienced their own tragedy with cancer in 1953, when their three-year-old daughter died of leukemia. I told him I was flattered, but given Mary Stuart's illness, there was no way I could do that.

After Mary Stuart died, that same friend suggested that I work on his senatorial campaign to take my mind off my grief. I thanked him for his concern and said there were two problems with that— "Number one, I don't know anything about politics, and number two, I'm a Democrat."

He chuckled. "We can take care of that second problem."

We did, and he put me in charge of the Houston area. I dotted the i's and crossed the t's, and we carried the county but lost statewide. Still, from that time forward, I was hooked on politics and forever linked with the candidate, George Herbert Walker Bush.

I first met the man I have called "George," "Bushie," "Mr. President," and now "*Jefe*" (the Spanish word for *chief* or *boss*) in 1959, when he moved his family (Barbara and their five children) and his business (Zapata Offshore Company) to Houston from Midland, Texas.

George and I shared a passion for tennis, and we became doubles partners at Houston Country Club—although I still preferred and continued to play singles. We were both extraordinarily weak servers, but George was excellent playing net and volleying, while I had very good ground strokes. We complemented each other nicely and won back-to-back club doubles championships in 1966 and 1967.

George and I would also play pickup games with the club pro,

Hector Salazar, and Hector's recruited partner of convenience. To me it was clear that Hector was playing just hard enough to take the match to three sets and make us believe we were almost as good as he. George was so competitive, so certain that we were elevating our game, however, that I'm not sure he ever quite realized we were being conned. George is genuinely personable, easygoing, and considerate of others—a truly wonderful human being—traits that come through in face-to-face meetings and on television. What sometimes doesn't come through is his competitive spirit and steely determination, which I first encountered on the tennis court and which strengthened him for success in business and politics.

Our friendship on the tennis court carried over to our homes. Mary Stuart and I occasionally entertained the Bushes and were frequent guests at their weekend barbeques. When he ran for office, Mary Stuart worked in his campaigns.

Lone Star Republicans were a lonely lot back in 1960. The state was overwhelmingly Democrat and had not elected a Republican statewide since Reconstruction. Some inroads had been made, however. At the presidential level, native son Dwight Eisenhower had carried the state in 1952 and 1956, thanks in part to a Democrats-for-Eisenhower movement led by Governor Allan Shivers.

Mary Stuart was undaunted by the strength of the opposition party or the weakness of her own. In 1958, she became our precinct's Republican chairperson and held the precinct's first-ever convention in our house. One other guy showed up! I served the two of them drinks while Mary Stuart conducted the meeting and did the paperwork.

Within a few years Republican prospects had brightened. In 1961, an obscure college professor and Democrat-turned-Republican, John Tower, won a special election against several vote-splitting Democrats for the Senate seat vacated by Lyndon Johnson when he assumed the vice presidency.

George Bush entered the fray the following year. Republicans afraid that the ultraconservative John Birch Society might take over the local party asked him to lead the county GOP organization for the Houston area. Two years later, he entered the statewide primary to become the party's candidate for the U.S. Senate. He won the nomination but lost the general election to the incumbent Democrat, Ralph Yarborough, who rode LBJ's long coattails in the 1964 presidential election.

George was undaunted. In 1966 he ran for a seat in the U.S. House of Representatives against a popular local district attorney, Frank Briscoe. In winning he became the first Republican congressman from Houston since Reconstruction.

I was not involved in George's first race for the Senate. In his campaign for Congress, however, I gave him some money, went to a few events, and voted for him. Still, I wasn't ready to call myself a Republican. In fact, I lent my name to the steering committee of a group of attorneys supporting Texas Attorney General Waggoner Carr, the candidate anointed by establishment Democrats in 1966 to recapture LBJ's old Senate seat from John Tower, the upstart professor. Thanks to an election-day boycott by liberal Democrats, however, Tower won again.

My political schizophrenia was often challenged by Mary Stuart and her Republican friends. One of those friends, Susan Winston, was married to a hunting buddy of mine, also a lifelong Democrat. "C'mon, you guys," Mary Stuart and Susan would tell us. "We know you vote Republican in the fall. Things aren't going to change until you get religion and convert to the GOP."

During his first term, George sat on the powerful House Ways and Means Committee. By 1968, he was on the short list of Richard Nixon's potential vice presidential running mates. When Nixon selected Spiro Agnew, George ran for reelection to Congress and won easily. Then, with his eyes on a higher prize, he gave up his safe House seat to run for the Senate again in 1970. This was the race in which I got my feet wet in politics, switching parties and coordinating the Bush campaign in Harris County.

George had backers far more powerful than I. Both President

Nixon and (privately) former President Johnson encouraged him. They sensed that the liberal Senator Ralph Yarborough, an outspoken critic of the Vietnam War, could be defeated by a moderate opponent. They were right, but unfortunately for George, that opponent ended up being Lloyd Bentsen, who beat Yarborough for the Democratic nomination and took the steam out of the "Anybody But Ralph" movement. Lloyd, a fine man who would become a friend of mine in later years, easily defeated George. Ironically, George, who had planned to run as the conservative alternative to the liberal Yarborough, found Bentsen portraying himself as the conservative alternative to an allegedly liberal Bush. George did carry Harris County, where both he and Lloyd lived, with 61 percent of the vote.

When I agreed to help George, I knew nothing about running a campaign organization. With the help of George's skilled campaign manager, Marvin Collins, I quickly learned that the operative word is "organization." The Five Ps proved invaluable.

For some time after Mary Stuart died, I was, quite simply, out of it. In addition to George, many others helped me cope. Harry Jones said, "You just take off whatever time you need." And I did.

Moving into that big house on Greentree Road that Mary Stuart had designed was painful. Less than three months after her death, I marked my fortieth birthday there with many of her friends and their husbands. Later they presented me with a portrait of her.

These same friends helped me find housekeepers. I use the plural because several did not work out. The boys didn't like one of them, and one of them liked me a little too much.

During these difficult months, I would come home from the law firm or the campaign, help the boys do their homework, get them to bed, have a drink to take my mind off things, have a second drink, and then maybe one or two more. I kept thinking that Mary Stuart might have survived if her doctor had diagnosed the cancer on her first visit, even though it was an aggressive malignancy.

Alcoholism runs on both sides of my family. Why didn't I succumb? In part because I always feel nauseated after three or four drinks. In part because I had my work—be it law, politics, or public service—to divert me. And in part because so many of Mary Stuart's friends, the wives of my friends—Fran Lummis, Mary Wilson, Kay Sharp, Susan Winston, Joanne Baker, Dossy Allday, Julia Wallace, and many others—rallied to our side, and were there in so many ways for my boys. Mostly, though, I owed it to those four boys not to succumb.

Susan Winston had her own worries during this period. Her marriage to my friend James (Jimbo) Winston ended, and she and her three young children endured some very dark days. The Winstons divorced, and in 1974 Jimbo died of pancreatitis. He was thirty-eight, the same age as Mary Stuart when I lost her.

About a year after Mary Stuart's death, I began to date. After going out with Susan, I never dated anyone else. Love blossomed out of friendship, and we married in August 1973.

Susan, eight years my junior, is the daughter of Jack and Mary Garrett. Her father, "Whispering Jack," was a well-known Texas rancher and rice farmer, and she grew up on a large ranch near Danbury, a tiny town near the Gulf of Mexico some forty miles south of Houston. He died on Christmas Eve of 2005. Her lovely mother died on January 31, 2004. Susan went to college at the University of Texas at Austin, where she studied a liberal arts program. She is a beautiful woman with great common sense, a wonderful spirit, and unwavering faith.

Susan had been a very close friend to Mary Stuart, but we had much in common beyond our love for Mary Stuart. We were both struggling single parents, and our combined seven children knew one another. We both loved the outdoors. And by this time, we both had an interest in politics—Republican politics. Susan's family had worked for the GOP when it was a dangerous thing to do.

We will always regret our big mistake in the way we went about getting married. We wanted to do it on my mother's birthday, August 6, because she kept encouraging us to marry. It had been a hard year for her. Dad, long incapacitated by Parkinson's disease, had passed away that May. Because Susan was Catholic and divorced, the Episcopal Church to which I belonged (and served on the vestry) refused to marry us. Fortunately, Dad's church, First Presbyterian, was willing. The minister, Jack Lancaster, a real man of God and a wonderful guy, performed the ceremony in the chapel. Only Susan and I were present—no family or friends. We had conspired to bring Susan's mother in from Danbury for lunch at my mother's house. We went there directly from the church to share our surprise. Both moms were ecstatic.

It was a different story with the seven kids. They were shocked. To them, the suddenness and secrecy of our marriage were close to family treason. We should have prepared them in advance. Our failure made the job of blending our families—difficult enough in the best of circumstances—much tougher. It took a while, but thanks to Susan's heroic efforts, we succeeded. My four (Jamie, Mike, John, and Doug) and her three (Elizabeth, Bo, and Will) soon became *our* seven. We added Mary Bonner in 1977. At this writing, Susan and I have seventeen grandchildren. We lost one of Jamie's girls—sweet Graeme, only seven years old—when she drowned in a neighbor's pool in 2002. She was a gift on loan to our family from God. Susan and I treasure the seven years she was with us, and her loss reminded us again how precious is our time with those we love.

At the time of our marriage, I was an acknowledged Republican. Participating in George's campaign for the Senate had awakened a sense of adventure and high challenge that was missing from the daily practice of law. I wasn't ready to quit the practice or run for office, but I was ready for something different. After the election, party leaders asked me to become state finance chairman.

This was, I knew, a thankless job. In trying to raise money for the party, I would be competing against committees seeking funds for two popular reelection candidates, President Nixon and Senator Tower. Candidate money is considerably easier to raise than party money, particularly for a party as weak as the Texas GOP was back then. Still, I accepted. I had to start somewhere.

Actually "somewhere" was everywhere. I had a small paid staff in Austin and many volunteers around the state, but I spent many a day driving to fund-raisers around our huge state and to party meetings in the capital. That's how I first got to know Senator Tower and Anne Armstrong, who had been a counselor for President Nixon and vice chairman of the Republican National Committee.

In 1972, I also coordinated the Nixon reelection effort in the fourteen-county Gulf Coast area of Texas. At George Bush's request, I organized a fund-raiser, and without using notes, the president gave a magnificent *tour d'horizon* on foreign policy. He seemed comfortable while speaking, but was clearly ill at ease in face-to-face meetings at the event. I remember his handshake as brief, formal, perfunctory.

We met a number of other times when I was in the Reagan and Bush administrations, and he periodically wrote me letters with suggestions on campaign strategies and foreign affairs. I was always respectful of him, but I find it hard to forgive him for betraying the country in the Watergate scandal. He lied to the American people, and with the release of his tapes in later years, his reputation fell lower and lower.

Watergate was traumatic, but in a way it demonstrated the strength and resilience of our system. The president's malfeasance was discovered, and within a relatively short time, by history's measure, he was gone. I wish we had just declared victory, thanked the Founders for their foresight, and moved on. Unfortunately, we tried to fix a system that, though imperfect (as all systems are and forever will be), wasn't broken. One thing we got in return was a generation of unaccountable independent counsels who investigated and attempted to criminalize every political controversy, a dreadful idea that was finally allowed to die a well-deserved death in 1999.

Nixon also betrayed the Republican Party and all of us who had worked hard for him, taken his claims of innocence at face value, and defended him in the early months of the scandal. He cost the party, as well as the nation, a great deal. After Watergate, Republicans suffered a political bloodbath. I will never forget my eldest son, Jamie, telling me right after Watergate broke that Nixon was behind it. I told him he and his hippie friends didn't know what they were talking about. The night Nixon announced he was resigning, Jamie called and said, "I told you so. But I'm proud to be an American, because the system worked."

When I was secretary of the treasury, Nixon wrote me to say he was giving up his taxpayer-supported secret service protection and would henceforth assume the cost personally. That was a noble thing to do. He deserves credit for opening relations with China, his serious efforts to disengage from Vietnam with honor, and other accomplishments, but I think his achievements will forever be overshadowed by the fact that he is the only president who has had to resign the office in disgrace.

In 1973, when Vice President Spiro Agnew resigned (also under a cloud), George Bush was on the short list to replace him as VP, a position that went instead to Gerald Ford. At the time, George was chairman of the Republican National Committee. Before that, he had served as our ambassador to the United Nations. Some say he would have preferred that President Nixon name him treasury secretary instead of sending him to the United Nations, but—much to George's disappointment—that job was given to former Texas Governor John Connally, a Democrat and a Nixon favorite.

When Nixon resigned on August 9, 1974, Vice President Ford took the oath of office as president. A poll of Republican officeholders put George on the top of the list to replace Ford as VP. I, along with many others, sent a telegram to Ford extolling my friend's virtues. Ford considered George but chose Nelson Rockefeller. George was asked to head our delegation in China, and he left for Beijing in 1974.

During this period, I decided it was time for me to do something different. The excitement of politics made me restless as a lawyer. I lacked Washington experience, but I had several things going for me. One was enthusiasm. I was ready for new challenges. Another was a work ethic grounded in the Five Ps. My father and the Marines had also taught habits of personal discipline that expressed themselves both in my personal behavior—polished shoes, neat suits, moderation in eating, drinking, and spending—and in my professional work. In addition, Harry Jones had taught me to organize and prioritize my work, to focus on what was achievable. To this day, I make lists— Point 1, Point 2—to organize my thoughts and my labors. I had also developed certain ways of dealing with colleagues and staff that would prove useful. (More about that later.) Finally, I was blessed with good health and stamina, which I always tried to preserve by exercising and getting outdoors as much as possible.

As a lifetime lawyer, my first choice for public service was the Justice Department, where I hoped to serve as assistant attorney general in charge of the civil division. In seeking such jobs, however, you don't call the White House; the White House calls you, and almost always after someone with clout has put in a good word. My interview with Attorney General Richard Kleindienst, scheduled for April 30, 1973, came courtesy of a good word from George Bush (although he never admitted it). The timing couldn't have been worse. Kleindienst resigned that same day, a casualty of Watergate. Goodbye interview. A few weeks later, I got a nibble about serving as the head of enforcement at the Environmental Protection Agency, but I wasn't interested.

Two years passed. I was still in Houston, still practicing law, raising seven children with Susan in the house on Greentree. But, having a close friend playing in the Big Game of politics and public service, I was growing ever more restless.

In June 1975 another opportunity presented itself. Again, thanks to George, I suspect, I was being considered for a high-level position. I met with Rogers Morton, who had recently replaced Fred Dent as secretary of commerce. Cabinet members are generally allowed to pick their own deputies, and Morton was looking for a number-two person with whom he would feel comfortable. Morton—a gentle giant from Kentucky, a wonderful man, and an outstanding public servant—interviewed several candidates for the spot, including some being pushed by the White House. A few days passed. Nothing.

I was on Interstate 10 between San Antonio and Houston, return-ing home from picking some of our kids up at summer camp. Check-ing in with my office from a roadside restaurant, I learned that Rogers Morton had called me. To learn my fate, I called the secretary of com-merce of the United States from a pay phone outside a Stuckey's restaurant.

"GOBBLERS AND HENS"

It's a pretty long way from a Stuckey's on Interstate 10 between San Antonio and Houston to the Oval Office, but there I found myself in mid-April 1976—not just sitting across from the president of the United States, but offering him advice. Nine months earlier, Rogers Morton had brought me to Washington as under secretary of commerce—the number-two position in the department. Now, President Ford and Ronald Reagan were in the middle of a close, contentious battle for the Republican presidential nomination. I had come to the White House to tell the president that his chances of winning the upcoming primary in my home state could increase dramatically if Secretary of State Henry Kissinger refrained from briefing the White House press before departing on a diplomatic tour of Africa.

The May 1 Texas primary could be pivotal. In the Illinois contest on March 16, Ford had soundly beaten Reagan to take a commanding lead in the delegate count. There was speculation that the challenger—whom I had met only once, four years earlier—might drop out of the race. "He'll survive until Texas," said John Sears, Reagan's campaign manager, "but if he loses there, he's out."

Kissinger was a carryover from the Nixon administration, and President Ford relied on him to maintain a steady course for U.S. foreign policy in the aftermath of Watergate and Vietnam. In 1976, however, he became a target of unhappy conservatives who viewed his policy of détente with the Soviet Union as appeasement, who were concerned about losing U.S. military superiority, and who opposed the Panama Canal Treaty and other initiatives. Reagan repeatedly accused the secretary of state of taking a defeatist posture toward the Soviet Union, of believing that the "day of the U.S. is past and today is the day of the Soviet Union," of "giving away our own freedoms." Real peace, Reagan argued, "does not come from weakness or retreat. It comes from the restoration of American military superiority."

Texas Republicans ate it up.

Kissinger was scheduled to make a two-week tour of Africa in late April and early May. When I learned that he planned to brief the press before leaving, I called Ford's chief of staff, Dick Cheney. "If you want to win Texas, you can't do this." Putting Kissinger on the air just before the primary was guaranteed to stir the political blood of the conservatives back home, I explained.

"Why don't you come over to the White House?" Dick suggested.

"Mr. President, I'm talking to you now as a Texan," I said after being seated in the Oval Office. "This would be devastating in the lead-up to the primary."

The president was rarely without his pipe. "Well, Jim"—puff, puff, puff—"Henry's done an extraordinarily good job"—puff, puff, puff—"and I think it's important that he tell the nation. It's very important to our foreign policy"—puff, puff, puff. "And you know, Jim," he added, "the *thinking* Republicans will understand my position on this."

"Mr. President," I replied, "with respect to this issue, there *are* no thinking Republicans in Texas right now."

Kissinger's pre-Africa press appearance with the president's blessing was probably one of several reasons why Reagan swept all ninety-six delegates in Texas and regained his momentum. It also didn't help that the president had tried to eat a tamale in San Antonio without first removing its corn-husk wrapper—a gastronomical gaffe that won headlines across the state. Or that nothing in Texas law prevented conservative Democrats from voting in the GOP primary. How bad was it? Even Senator John Tower was defeated in his bid to be a Ford delegate.

Shortly before the primary, I accompanied the president on a swing through Texas. On the flight back to Washington, he asked me to leave Commerce to work full-time in the campaign. One week later, I assumed the position of deputy chairman for delegate operations. My job was to keep Ford delegates in the candidate's camp and to win support from uncommitted delegates to the Republican National Convention in August. I took over the duties of Jack Stiles, Ford's long-time friend and congressional campaign manager, who had died in a car crash earlier that month.

In public service, titles are important for both symbolism and prestige, but they do not necessarily reflect the importance of your duties or how much influence you have. Presidents rely upon the people in whom they have the most confidence, regardless of title. Generally, these are the people who have been in the trenches with them—men and women who worked in the campaigns and helped win difficult elections. That's why—often to the dismay of some members of the cabinet with more prestigious titles—campaign workers who move to the White House staff are frequently the most important advisers to the chief executive.

Jockeying for post-election influence begins during the campaign. Titles tend to denote status, and higher-ups in a successful campaign can expect to get better jobs in an administration. The organization had several deputy chairmen, each with different responsibilities, but it was a prestigious title. Still, at first I felt that I was just another campaign hand, a delegate hunter. I would have preferred to stay at Commerce. As Rog Morton's alter ego and stand-in at cabinet meetings (and after he left, acting secretary of commerce for several months), I enjoyed dealing with the interesting and important issues that landed on my desk. Little did I know that the nomination fight would be settled on the floor of the convention and that the fortunes of Gerald

Ford and Ronald Reagan—and Jim Baker, to a certain extent—would eventually rest on who won the uncommitteds.

But remaining at Commerce was not an option. The president had already named Rog as chairman of the President Ford Committee (PFC), a title that *did* reflect Rog's power. He was in charge of the entire campaign. At Commerce, we had worked well together and liked each other. Now he asked the president to reassign me to the PFC. How could I say no to the man who had brought me to Washington in the first place? And even if I could have, I could not say no to the president.

BACK IN JUNE 1975, I received a letter from George Bush, then still in China. "Bake," it began, "I just got a call from Rog Morton querying me on you for under secretary of commerce. The job could be a good one and Morton would be good to work for in my opinion."

George was right on both counts. Rog was a terrific boss, as big-hearted as he was big in stature. Before coming to Commerce, he had served ten years as a congressman from Maryland, two years as chair of the Republican National Committee, and four years as secretary of the interior.

Although I was Rog's first choice for under secretary when he moved from Interior to Commerce at President Ford's request in May 1975, I was not necessarily the White House's. Reasoning that the appointment of a Reagan supporter to the number-two spot at Commerce might win points with conservatives, Don Rumsfeld, then White House chief of staff, lobbied Rog to offer the job to William Banowsky, president of Pepperdine University in California and GOP national committeeman from California. As I understand it, Rog went straight to President Ford and said, "No, Baker's the one I want."*

My visit with the president before the Texas primary was not my

---

*Soon after taking office, the Ford administration tried to head off a possible Reagan candidacy in an even more dramatic fashion, by offering the former California governor the top job at Commerce or Transportation, or the ambassadorship to the Court of St. James's. No luck.

first. Several months after I arrived in Washington, Rog poked his head into my office and said, "Jim, let's go over to the White House." When we got there, Rog instructed me to wait outside the Oval Office. Five or ten minutes passed. I busied myself reading. Finally the door opened. "Jim, come in here for a minute," Rog said.

I don't care how old you are or how much you think you have accomplished, walking into the Oval Office for the first time—or anytime, for that matter—to meet the president of the United States is a heady and humbling experience.

The door was held open by a man some ten years my junior, but far senior in the pecking order—Dick Cheney, Rumsfeld's successor and the youngest White House chief of staff in history. President Ford sat behind his desk. Rog sat in a nearby chair. Dick's chair was empty for the moment. He motioned for me to take it, and I thought, "Golly, the chief of staff is giving me his seat."

Rog introduced me to the president, who said something like, "Jim, we're certainly glad to have you on board." We exchanged a few more pleasantries and then discussed an issue of the day. I can't remember what it was, but I will never forget how gracious Dick was. It's a small thing, but powerful men and women in Washington, D.C., don't give up their seats. And the White House chief of staff, I came to learn, is potentially the second most powerful person in Washington, as long as the holder of that office remembers who is the boss.

First impressions count for a lot in Washington. Dick and I have worked together in several administrations. We do not always agree on policy—who does?—but the seeds of our long-lasting friendship were sown that day. That friendship extends far beyond Washington. Dick taught me everything I know about fly-fishing, and I still don't know half of what he knows.

Dick is an extremely bright, no-nonsense guy. He is very loyal to President George W. Bush, just as he was to the first President Bush and to President Ford. He understands that the people who go out there and take the risks and put their name on the ballot and get elected are the ones who have the right to exercise power.

When I was nominated for the position at Commerce, I told the *Houston Chronicle* that I hoped to help ease the problems that "government regulations and bureaucratic red tape" caused for businesses, particularly small businesses. President Ford had made this a priority. As a business lawyer for eighteen years, I'd seen many of those problems, such as the need to provide duplicate reports to different government agencies. "In some areas," I added, "governmental regulation is totally appropriate." I still believe that. The trick is to find the right balance, and that's never easy.

After I was confirmed by the Senate, Susan and I and five of our seven children moved to Washington. Jamie, my first son, was at Cornell, and Mike, my second, chose to stay in Houston to complete his senior year of high school and keep his place on the school football team.

Mike was a gifted athlete, the star of the Bush-Baker family football games (Turkey Bowls) we played after lunch every Thanksgiving Day. The other kids nicknamed him Conrad Dobler, after a tough offensive lineman ("I only bit one guy!") for the St. Louis Cardinals. Mike's football coach and family stayed with him in the Baker house on Greentree.*

Washington was (and still is) largely a one-industry town, but if you're in power it's a great place to live. While continuing to own our house in Houston, we lived in the northwest section of the District in a house rented from Alex Hufty. We might have preferred to enroll the kids in public school, but the system in the District at that time was in bad shape. As a result we found ourselves paying for private educations on a salary that was considerably lower than what I had earned at Andrews Kurth.

I am not looking for sympathy. It's bad form to ask for a job, then

---

*Mike has made his career with Smith International, a major Houston-based supplier of oilfield equipment and services. He also took on the extraordinarily difficult task of rearing two children as a single parent, something I don't think I could have done.

complain about the size of your paycheck. In addition, public service offers many important nonfinancial benefits. For one thing, the quality of life in Washington back then was better than in Houston—less traffic and less pollution. But many public servants make genuine economic sacrifices when they come to Washington. Fortunately, Susan and I were in a better position than most, in part because about that time, an oil play on a ranch I owned in South Texas provided us with a much-needed financial boost.

In Houston, our social life was organized around get-togethers with lifelong friends. In Washington, a city based on power and the perception of power, we found it more difficult to establish as many true friendships. You are extremely busy with your work and, further, you can never be certain whether people are attracted by your personality and character or by your title. With all the attention ranking public officials receive, it's hard to stay grounded. But you can be sure of this: the people who wouldn't return your phone calls before you went to Washington damn well won't return them after you go home.

Without a circle of old friends like those we had back home, we enjoyed far fewer backyard barbeques and endured far more official functions—where protocol determines almost everything. Your position at the table for an official luncheon or dinner (or for that matter a formal private party) is determined by your position in the government, and people pay attention to whether you are seated above the salt or below it.

Cabinet and subcabinet officials get invited to far more of these dinners and receptions than they can possibly attend. If you want to get all your work done—six and a half days a week at the office in my case—you have to learn to say no to the parties.

Of course, the work is what's important. A few weeks after I arrived at Commerce, I asked two of my top assistants, Frank Hodsoll and Jim Goyette, to present me some ideas for initiatives that might make a difference. I offer the following excerpts from the resulting "eyes only" memorandum because they express a guiding principle of policymaking: don't do anything without being aware of its political impact, especially during an election cycle. Frank and Jim listed five factors to consider in choosing initiatives. The first two are most instructive:

1. Interest in and usefulness of these actions in terms of good government to (a) the president, (b) the secretary, and (c) other key administration officials.
2. Public visibility and political impact of these actions.

At Commerce, I quickly learned that the power game is continually being played between departments within the executive branch. To illustrate, I have one word: *textiles.* In 1976, the State Department argued for the unlimited import of Chinese textiles into the United States. This policy would further former President Nixon's (and Secretary of State Kissinger's) earlier effort to open the door to the People's Republic, State argued. True enough. But the administration believed that our country's best economic interest was to pursue a more balanced approach that contained some protection for domestic textile manufacturers. Clearly, it was also in the best interest of the Ford political operation to avoid alienating the textile manufacturing states where important primaries between the president and Reagan loomed.

In late March the president flew to San Francisco to address the American Textile Manufacturers Institute. An advance draft of his speech was sent for comment to interested departments, including State and Commerce. At Commerce we were happy with language to allay the manufacturers' fears that cheaper Chinese textiles would flood American markets. The president intended to say that he was committed "to ensure that our domestic market is not seriously disrupted."

While we expected State to lobby for the removal of that language, the department had not weighed in when Ford took off for California.

At a meeting of the Economic Policy Board, Bob Ingersoll, the deputy secretary of state, had simply said that he didn't have the secretary's position yet. This was vintage Kissinger. A master at playing the power game, he knew that he who speaks last often speaks loudest. I figured that he would try to get the problematic sentence removed at the last minute—when it would be too late for us to offer a rebuttal. On the day of the president's flight, my suspicion was confirmed by Bob Hormats, an international economics specialist with the National Security Council. Kissinger planned to place a call to the president on Air Force One, Bob said.

I quickly called Cheney on the plane. He told me that Kissinger had already called and that the president had tentatively decided to remove the sentence. After hearing my argument, Dick agreed that at that time, politics should trump policy, and he persuaded the president to restore it.

A few days later, I met Kissinger—for the first time—at a State Department function. "Ah," he said in that distinctive voice of his, "so you're Textile Baker."

I guess that was better than being called "Goodbye-Kissinger Baker." In early April, the campaign asked me to attend a fund-raising event in Oklahoma, another important primary state where Reagan was strong. After my presentation, I was asked what role Kissinger would have if Ford won in November.

We were at a wealthy contributor's home. It was my understanding that no media were present, but just to be safe, I declared my remarks off the record, not for publication. I then said it was hard to imagine that Kissinger would serve in the next Ford administration.

As it turned out, reporters were present from both the *Oklahoma Journal* and the *Daily Oklahoman*. As Denise Donoho, a reporter for the *Journal* later wrote me, "We honored your request of confidence and apparently the *Daily Oklahoman* did not."

When I returned to Washington, I was not aware of this. Nor was I aware that Rog, now President Ford's campaign manager, had made similar remarks in California. Our unorchestrated comments had put the administration on the defensive and forced the president's press secretary, Ron Nessen, to tell the media that the president was not trying to ease Kissinger out of office.

After a ceremony in the White House Rose Garden, I finally learned what had happened. "Before you leave the White House, stick your head in Mr. Cheney's office," said Nell Yates, the president's secretary. The wire services had picked up the *Daily Oklahoman's* story featuring my speculation about Kissinger's future, and a solemn chief of staff showed me the clips. The State Department and the secretary were furious, Cheney reported.

This was my first major blunder on the job. It could have been my last. Presidents should never be forced to explain or correct the statements of those who serve them, particularly one as far down the pecking order as the under secretary of commerce. I told Cheney how sorry I was. "Don't worry," he laughed. "Just make it right with Henry." I called the secretary and begged his forgiveness, which he kindly gave me—but only after I had properly groveled in my apology to him.

Why did Cheney treat me so gently? I later learned that the White House had been impressed by my role in helping the president avoid a potentially big political problem with an issue that was hardly a household phrase: common situs picketing.

Common situs picketing is the picketing by a labor union of multiple employers at a job site because of the union's grievances against one employer at the site. Under federal labor laws, it is generally illegal. In December 1975, however, Congress—its ranks of Democrats swollen by the post-Watergate midterm election of 1974—passed legislation to make it easier for the unions to shut down multi-employer job sites. Now the president had to decide whether to sign or veto.

Within forty-eight hours of the bill's passage, I wrote a memorandum to Rog Morton and a letter to Jim Lynn, director of the Office of Management and Budget, explaining why it was imperative for the president to veto the bill. My eleven-point memo to Rog, which I knew would be forwarded to the White House, outlined the substantive problems with the bill. For instance, it would "strike hardest at small business and nonunion craftsmen and contractors, particularly minorities," I said. But I also laid out the political implications, with point one being this fairly blunt warning: "A failure to veto will be political suicide as far as the nomination is concerned."*

On January 3, 1976, the president vetoed the legislation. "I had hoped that this bill would provide a resolution for the special problems of labor-management relations in the construction industry and would have the support of all parties," he explained. "My earlier optimism in this regard was unfounded." This was the first veto he ever exercised. Secretary of Labor John Dunlop was so disappointed that he resigned and returned to his teaching post at Harvard.

When should a public official leave an administration over differences in policy? This is obviously a question each person might answer differently. One of my predecessors at State, Cyrus Vance, resigned in 1980 after Jimmy Carter authorized a military operation to free American hostages in Iran. Vance not only disapproved of the plan (which failed), but he also (justifiably) believed he had been ignored in the decision-making process. President Carter had made the determination after meeting with other advisers, principally Zbigniew Brzezinski, his national security adviser, while Vance was away for the weekend in Florida.

Although I never came close to resigning over a policy issue when I was at Treasury or State, there are times when it is appropriate to do so—when you can't in good conscience support a policy the administration asks you to carry out, or when, like Vance, you are not con-

---

*I was not alone in my call for a veto. Bill Simon, the treasury secretary, also opposed the bill. He and I were on the same wavelength so often that he once asked the president to let me leave Commerce and serve as his deputy. The president declined to do so. Bill was a true conservative, much admired by that wing of the party. Those conservatives who thought I was too moderate to serve President Reagan always ignored Bill's sense that he and I were in tune ideologically.

sulted about a significant issue in your portfolio. If you do choose to resign, you should do it in a way that is the least detrimental to the president and his administration. The president, after all, has given you the chance to serve.

At Commerce, I briefly worked under someone involved in one of the most spectacular cabinet resignations in history, Elliot Richardson. Elliot became commerce secretary on February 2, 1976. At the same time, Rog moved to the White House as a cabinet-rank counsellor to the president on domestic and economic issues and liaison to the President Ford Committee and the Republican National Committee. As noted, he would later become Ford's campaign chairman.

Immediately before replacing Rog, Elliot had been our ambassador to the United Kingdom. Before that, the Harvard-educated attorney served as secretary of health, education and welfare, secretary of defense, and—most famously—attorney general. In that latter position, he became the first victim of the "Saturday Night Massacre" in October 1973 when he chose to resign rather than to obey President Nixon's order to fire the Watergate special prosecutor, Archibald Cox.

Elliot was a wonderful man. This Boston Brahmin—who couldn't tolerate more than one drink—wasn't as earthy as Rog, but he was just as genuine. He once said that Washington was a city of cocker spaniels, meaning people who would rather be petted and admired than wield power. Maybe we hit it off because he knew I would rather wield power.

He was extraordinarily bright, so cerebral that he was sometimes difficult to understand. He often seemed to talk in riddles. In 1976, he wrote a book called *The Creative Balance: Government, Politics, and the Individual in America's Third Century.* I tried to read it but found it too esoteric to finish.

Politics, as the saying goes, ain't beanbag. It's a blood sport, featuring raw emotion and gutfighting. The intellectual is often at a disadvantage, but some have been successful. Elliot was one. He never considered himself too refined for retail politics and was never reluctant to stump for President Ford, whom he obviously admired.

I worked with Elliot for only three months before I left Commerce, reluctantly, for the PFC. The offices of our campaign headquarters at Eighteenth and L Streets were small and poorly furnished, as they should have been. A well-run campaign spends money on the things that will get its candidate elected, like television, not on amenities for the staff.

At the PFC, I reported directly to Rog, who had succeeded former Secretary of the Army Bo Callaway as chairman. In the weeks between Callaway's departure and Rog's arrival, Stu Spencer ran the PFC. Stu, a first-rate political consultant, had made a name for himself working for presidential candidate Nelson Rockefeller in 1964 and had cemented his reputation in 1966, when he and Bill Roberts helped orchestrate Reagan's win over Pat Brown for the California governorship.

Stu also worked on Reagan's successful campaign for reelection in 1970, but in September 1975, he joined the Ford effort. In time, he was appointed deputy chairman for political organization—the chief political strategist.

Stu was political, but he was not politic. At one point, he told Ford, "Mr. President, as a campaigner, you're no fucking good." The president was taken aback, but laughed it off.

Jack Stiles, my predecessor as delegate hunter, had reported directly to Stu. Although Stu and I worked closely together, I did not report to him. Initially, this was a source of tension. As time went on, however, we forged a strong relationship.

When I came to the PFC, there was no how-to manual on rounding up delegates, so I tracked down some good delegate hunters from past campaigns and picked their brains. Clif White, who engineered Barry Goldwater's remarkable drive for the Republican presidential nomination in 1964, and Dick Kleindienst, Nixon's man in 1968, were the most helpful.

Clif's advice went something like this: "You want to learn everything you can about these delegates. What makes them tick. What are their interests. What issues are important to them. Who are the personalities that are important to them. And then you want to get them to commit to Ford, if possible in a public way, not just tell you, 'I'll be there.' You want them nailed, so that it would be embarrassing for them to change."

Five days after moving to the PFC (and based largely on my conversations with White and Kleindienst), I sent Rog, Stu, and Roy Hughes, the deputy chairman for administration, a six-page, single-spaced memorandum titled "Proposed Delegate Management Operation."

"The primary results of the last ten days make it likely that the president and Reagan will go to the convention with neither having sufficient delegates for a first-ballot victory," I wrote—wrongly, as it turned out. As a result the delegate-hunting operation would be of vital importance and needed to be "promptly and carefully organized and implemented." I proposed that we keep dossiers on each delegate—"ours," "theirs," and "uncommiteds." I also offered a plan to divide the country into eleven regions, each headed by a regional chairman. Each state in the region would also have a chair, who should be a "knowledgeable party politician rather than [an] elected official who normally would be too busy to give us the time required." This is a cardinal rule of politics: party people will work their tails off for a candidate they like; elected officials have divided loyalties (their own careers always come first) and too many other demands on their time.

In the memo, I urged that the chairmen update the campaign two or three times a week on the status of delegates in their region, that the president set aside twenty to thirty minutes a day to call targeted delegates, and that we schedule caucuses with delegations in order to keep them "informed, plugged in, and fired up." "The worst thing that can happen to a politician is not to have someone to talk to," I wrote. "The next worst thing is not to know what is going on. Communication is the answer to both."

Twenty-nine states selected their delegates through primaries, while twenty-one chose them at state conventions. In all, 2,259 delegates would come to Kansas City. The magic number for the nomination was 1,130.

The race seesawed back and forth. After Reagan took Texas to put himself back in contention, Ford still led 232–183. Wins in Indiana, Georgia, and Alabama gave Reagan a brief lead, but by May 25, the count was Ford 732, Reagan 530, uncommitted 184. Ford stayed ahead through the end of the primary season on June 8. By then, however, only eleven of the twenty-one state conventions had been held, and Reagan was better organized in most. After the final state conventions on July 16, the *New York Times* called it 1,102–1,063 for Ford with ninety-four critical votes uncommitted.

Reagan's campaign manager, John Sears, saw it differently. On July 19, he said his man would come to Kansas City with 1,140 delegates, ten more than needed. Such projections, if credible, are important. When delegates perceive that one candidate has the nomination clinched, many will flock to his side. Everybody loves a winner. If Sears's numbers were even close to being accurate and if we couldn't hold those delegates committed to us and win enough of the uncommitteds, Gerald Ford would become the first sitting president to fail to hold his party's nomination since Chester Arthur.

NOT TOO MANY years ago, John Cabaniss, my protégé from the Andrews Kurth law firm in Houston, introduced me for a speech back home. "I realized on one of our spring turkey hunts that Jim Baker was destined for high office," John said. "There just has to be greatness in a man that can distinguish whether a wild turkey you are tracking is a gobbler or a hen by closely examining its droppings."

After the laughter stopped, he added: "The operative word there is *closely.*"

I didn't hunt delegates for President Ford exactly like wild turkeys, but almost. I began by sending out biographical questionnaires. Many delegates responded, and we filled in the blanks as best we could on those who did not. Here's an example, excerpts from a three-page, single-spaced bio we compiled on a delegate from the South who eventually committed to Ford.

> Engaged in practice of law continuously since 1951. Served on the Citizens Advisory Committee to juvenile court. . . . Active in Chamber of Commerce work. . . . Member of the Propeller Club of the United States. . . . American Legion, Young Americans for Freedom. Has been and probably would like to continue to be consulted on attorneys named as federal judges in [his state]. Practices extensively in federal courts.

The biography also included a detailed chronology of the delegate's involvement in Republican campaigns and activities, including information about local, state, and national candidates he had supported. For example: "1961, member Goldwater banquet committee which sponsored large and successful banquet honoring Senator Goldwater . . . long before Senator Goldwater was considered a presidential candidate."

We also kept a log of our contacts with delegates. In the case of our quarry mentioned above:

> 6/18/76—President sent him a thank you in response to letter of recommendation on behalf of [a candidate] for appointment to vacancy on the U.S. district court.
>
> 6/22—Per Jim Plummer: Will go for Ford on three conditions: If Ford does not veto the offshore oil revenue sharing bill; the vice presidential candidate is not unacceptable (Brooke/Percy); [and will not go for Ford if Ford challenges] Louisiana and Mississippi delegations [for not having] enough blacks, females, and young.
>
> 6/24—Baker: He needs lots of attention.

Whether the nomination would go to Ford or Reagan depended on the votes of about 150 swing delegates. Some were truly uncommitted. The rest backed either Ford or Reagan but not firmly. The contest would go to the outfit that did the best job of corralling its own herd while picking off strays from the other side.

It was my job to stalk the uncommitteds. Sometimes, however, they stalked me, and not always appropriately. I doubt that any of these pols were Latin majors, but clearly several of them understood the meaning of *quid pro quo*. If I had taken them up on their proposed deals, I well might have been *in flagrante delicto*. Two examples, and my responses:

> [A delegate from Missouri] offered through Peter Roussel [of the PFC] to deliver the uncommitteds in Missouri who do not like [Governor] Kit Bond if we would assure them they would have final say on patronage in the St. Louis area. I told Roussel not to discuss it with [the delegate]. . . .
>
> Party people had reported [that a delegate from Pennsylvania] wanted a federal job. He called me and asked for an appointment with Art Fletcher, [the deputy] assistant to the president [for urban affairs]. I refused to do it for him.

In all I had at least seventeen questionable contacts with delegates with their hands out. I remember that number because four weeks before the convention, I wrote a memorandum for the file ("Improper Suggestions from Delegates") that listed these incidents and the rest of them. For instance, a congressman from Colorado hinted we could get his vote if we promised to name him to the Federal Communications Commission; a delegate from the Virgin Islands wanted the new federal building named after him; and "a delegate from Brooklyn . . . issued a public statement saying he would sell his vote to the candidate who bids the most for it."

While we were scrupulous about making a record of improper

suggestions (and rebuffing them), we were otherwise plenty aggressive. For instance, we identified and assigned one key person as a "persuader" to approach each targeted delegate. It might be a public official, a party leader, or even a neighbor—anyone with enough personal influence to win or hold a commitment. The president would then follow up with a phone call and, in some instances, a face-to-face meeting.

Candidate Reagan also telephoned and met with key delegates, but Gerald Ford had a big advantage here. Imagine receiving a personal phone call at home from the president of the United States, asking for your help. Or being invited to a state dinner at the White House with President Ford and the leader of a foreign country. Or celebrating the nation's bicentennial on board the USS *Forrestal* in New York Harbor on July 4, 1976, as forty tall ships from around the world sailed past.

President Ford also met at the White House with entire state delegations. He was impressive at these events—gracious, humble, and articulate. No one who actually knew the president ever quite understood Chevy Chase's *Saturday Night Live* impersonation of him as a genial dolt who stumbled over doorsteps and big words. Unfortunately, the caricature—particularly the physical humor—took on a life of its own. Even the slightest misstep was taken as more proof that this graceful and athletic man, who had played on two national championship football teams at the University of Michigan and turned down offers from the pros, was, in fact, a bumbler.

President Ford personified all that is good about America, and he was comfortable with himself, popular with old friends on both sides of the aisle in Congress, admired and respected by his staff, and effective in private sessions with delegates. So why did he fail to win in 1976? The economy and the pardon of Richard Nixon were the principal reasons, but a contributing factor was that he was not television-friendly at a time when television had become the nation's window on politics. The president had a habit of pausing for several beats before he spoke. When the red light on a television camera would come on—

his cue to talk—he would not start speaking right away. This sometimes gave the mistaken impression that he was struggling to find the right words.

TV-friendly or not, this wonderful, lifelong public servant was absolutely the right person at the right time to heal the wounds of Watergate, to restore America's confidence in its government, and to bring the nation out of that terrible period. Pardoning the disgraced Nixon on September 8, 1974, was the right thing to do. The scandal "could go on and on and on, or someone must write an end to it," Ford said. "I have concluded that only I can do that, and if I can, I must. My conscience tells me that it is my duty not only to proclaim domestic tranquility but to use every means that I have to ensure it." By doing the right thing, however, he hurt himself in the polls, the primaries, and—ultimately—the election.

The average American might wonder whether it is proper for a sitting president to entertain delegates at the White House, just as Americans had concerns about President Clinton's inviting donors to stay overnight in the Lincoln Bedroom. After one delegation lunched with President Ford, reporters asked who had paid for the meal. Answer: The president had used personal funds.

Having led presidential campaigns five times from 1976 through 1992—and for three incumbent presidents—I have long been sensitive to these matters. The first rule, clearly, is to follow the law. We always took pains to do so. In late June 1976, I drafted guidelines "in connection with visits to Washington of delegates." We could not use government funds for "entertainment or political meetings or receptions at the White House," I wrote, but it was okay for delegates to attend state dinners and other official events, "as long as their presence does not alter the official nature of the event." Small gifts—cuff links, tie clasps, and the like—were okay if they were not purchased with government funds.

While I spent part of the summer of '76 at the White House with delegates, I spent most of the time at PFC headquarters working the phones and keeping in daily contact with regional and state chairmen, with our "persuaders," and with the delegates themselves. Spencer and I also flew around the country to meet delegates.

When the convention began, the *New York Times* published an article about our delegate operation under the headline, "'Miracle Man' Given Credit for Ford Drive." In Kansas City, the campaign picked up on the headline and gave me the code name "Miracle Man" for our walkie-talkie network. I earned that "sobriquet," the *Times* reported, by "having turned the most crucial phase of the Ford effort—the delegate hunt—from a failure into a success. . . . Others bugged the delegates on behalf of Mr. Ford. But they saved Mr. Baker for the soft sell on the hard cases."

I like recognition as much as the next guy, but delegate hunting is a team sport, and we had a great one—Jackie Fernald, Pete Roussel, Pete McPherson, Paul Manafort, Judy McLennan, Richard Mastrangelo, and others at headquarters, and many more in regional and state operations in the field. By the convention, we had a tremendous organization in place.

In politics, organization is much more important than people think. Texas pols have a term for a disorganized campaign: they call it a "goat rope" (as in roping goats, a figurative term for "chaos"). Without a smoothly functioning presidential campaign apparatus, the chairman would be forced to spend far too much time refereeing battles between players who are on the same team.*

PFC Chairman Rog Morton did have to referee one battle involving me. Some background: In 1966, Godfrey "Budge" Sperling, a Washington-based *Christian Science Monitor* reporter, started hosting breakfasts at which print reporters met for freewheeling on-the-record discussions with political newsmakers. Although Sperling re-

---

*Political operatives use a cruder term, also involving animals, for a campaign in which members of the same team spend most of their time fighting for turf and promoting themselves at the expense of their colleagues. They call that a "rat f—k."

linquished his duties as host in 2001 and retired from journalism in 2005, the breakfasts are now a Washington institution.

In 1976, I was asked to talk about the delegate hunt. I was eager to attend. The battle for the uncommitteds was being played out in the press; this was a chance to talk about our operation and delegate count. But the invitation created a furor within the campaign. Peter Kaye, head of the small PFC press operation, strenuously objected to my going.

Why? He told me I would be eaten alive by the veteran journalists, but I suspect the real reason was turf. The PFC press people wanted to keep tight control of what was said and by whom, but I didn't report to them. I was adamant about going, so I took my case to Rog, who gave his blessing.

The breakfast not only went smoothly but also contributed to our credibility. The Washington press corps certainly can eat you alive, particularly if you are ill-prepared or untruthful. In my early days at the campaign, however, no one seemed anxious to devour me. I was new to the Beltway, I was not a professional politician, and I came with a decent résumé: a successful lawyer in private practice with a good education who had done a respectable job as under secretary of commerce. Maybe they were just giving the new guy the benefit of the doubt.

As the summer progressed, however, the major reason that I had credibility with the press was simple: *I never lied to them.* I never claimed a delegate unless we had something from that delegate—a letter or a public statement, for example—that would support my claim.

Credibility is important in every political campaign, but it was essential in the too-close-to-call '76 nomination fight. Because reporters saw that the delegate counts we announced were accurate, not speculative, they could say, "Looks like Ford's got it," as we headed to Kansas City. This won support for us from some uncommitteds because it's human nature to side with the winner. (I believe the way we handled information about delegates also contributed to my generally positive relationship with the media in the eighties and nineties.)

The other side did not enjoy the same credibility. After Reagan campaign manager John Sears proclaimed on July 19 that his candidate had 1,140 delegates, I accused him of "blowing smoke." Four days later, I reported that we had picked up fifteen delegates from Hawaii and now counted 1,135 in our column—five more than we needed to win. The *New York Times* would later report:

> Some Ford operatives urged Mr. Baker to use razzle-dazzle to toss out numbers without names and claim delegates not yet confirmed and thus create a momentum in fiction that might lead to one in fact. He refused. . . .
>
> Unlike his counterpart in the Reagan campaign, where claims of 1,140 delegates—ten over the nomination—stood for weeks without evidence, Mr. Baker edged along slowly to the magic number, citing three delegates in Virginia or five in Hawaii—and handing out their names and addresses.
>
> The news media canvasses invariably confirmed the switches and, within a few delegates one way or the other, matched the Ford count and rebutted the Reagan count.

As we "edged along slowly," we knew that victory was not assured, even if we did reach the magic number by the beginning of the convention. By state law, some delegates had to vote for a particular candidate on the first ballot, but were free to go their own ways on procedural votes and, in some cases, on subsequent ballots for the nomination. We figured about twenty first-ballot Ford delegates might go Reagan's way on procedural matters.

Why was this important? Because unseating a president from your own party is hard to justify, unless he's perceived as a loser. Beating President Ford on procedural issues, the Reagan team believed, would create doubts in the minds of uncommitted delegates and some of our delegates, too. If Gerald Ford can't control his own convention, how can he defeat Jimmy Carter in November?

On July 26, Reagan made a desperate pitch for these swing delegates by naming a running mate, Senator Richard Schweiker of Pennsylvania. The senator was viewed as considerably to the left of Reagan, and Reagan's strategists believed he would broaden the appeal of the ticket in the general election. More important, they hoped that Pennsylvania delegates committed to Ford would switch to Reagan at the convention to show support for their home-state senator. This was possible but not probable. In football parlance, the Schweiker ploy was a Hail Mary pass.

The man who could make the ploy work or defeat it was Drew Lewis, President Ford's chairman in Pennsylvania. In 1974, he had managed his friend Schweiker's senate reelection campaign, but in 1976, Drew Lewis could not be moved. He not only remained loyal to Ford; he also prevailed on the Ford delegates to honor their commitments. (Drew would later serve as secretary of transportation for President Reagan before becoming CEO of Union Pacific Corporation.)

How confident was I that we had the nomination won when we arrived in Kansas City? Not totally. On the Sunday evening before the convention, I attended church with Susan. "If the count had been 1,250 for Mr. Ford, maybe that wouldn't have been necessary," I joked to the press.

THREE

"THE CLOSEST PRESIDENTIAL ELECTION YOU'LL EVER SEE IN YOUR LIFETIME"

VICE PRESIDENTIAL NOMINEES don't decide presidential elections. Americans vote for the top of the ticket. But it can be reasonably argued that in 1976, at least, the Republican nomination hinged on who the vice presidential nominee was . . . or was not.

As delegates were packing for their trips to Kansas City, Ronald Reagan's campaign strategist, John Sears, asked the party rules committee to force candidates to pick their running mates before the convention voted on a nominee. With Pennsylvania Senator Richard Schweiker already lined up for Reagan, Sears wanted to force Ford's hand. He reasoned that he could pick off some Ford delegates or undecideds who were alienated by whomever President Ford selected as his running mate. Aware of this, we opposed the proposal. So, too, did the rules committee, which we controlled. This forced a floor fight over what came to be known as Rule 16-C.

When the convention began on Monday, August 16, we knew the vote on 16-C would determine the nomination itself. And it did. The final count after the Tuesday night showdown was 1,189 no and 1,060 yes, with 10 abstentions. Sears's make-or-break gambit had failed by only 29 votes.

If I had been advising Reagan, I told reporters after the convention, I would have rolled the dice on a three-word proposal that was ideological, not procedural: "Fire Henry Kissinger!" That would have mobilized the Reagan troops, attracted some undecideds, and, more than likely, won support from a few of the president's supporters.

My suggestion about attacking Henry had nothing to do with my judgment of him or his policies. It was a purely political assessment. It would have been harder for President Ford to have kept his troops in line on a referendum over the controversial secretary of state.

I have always liked Henry and consider him a friend. When I sought his counsel before taking office as secretary of state in 1989, he offered lots of good advice. We come from very different backgrounds, but we are both realists—practitioners of realpolitik—and we generally see eye to eye on foreign policy issues, particularly those that demand national sacrifices. Values are important, of course, but we each realize that the American public will not long support a policy that cannot be explained in terms of hard national interests. We are both good bureaucratic infighters, too.

The vote on the nomination on Wednesday, August 18, was anticlimactic. Everyone knew Ford would win. Overnight, the uncommitteds committed, and a few soft Reagan delegates also joined the winning team. The president won 1,187 to 1,070, a narrow but decisive 117-vote margin.

From 1972 through 1996, I attended all seven Republican conventions. For sheer drama and excitement, 1976 stands alone. It was the last time either party actually picked its candidate on the floor. Candidates prefer to wrap up the nomination early, so they can spend more time and money against their general election opponents. I confess, however, that I am nostalgic for the days when the outcome was not preordained by state primary contests. Each election cycle, it seems, the primaries are earlier than last time, and a few key states always have disproportionate influence. Our system now virtually guarantees that the nominee will be known months before the party convention and that many states will have little or no say in the decision. The

Commission on Federal Election Reform that I cochaired with former President Carter in 2005 recommended having a series of regional primaries after the contests in Iowa and New Hampshire. That would be a good way to permit states that now have little say help decide who runs for our nation's highest office.

I do not suggest a return to smoke-filled rooms, but the modern system deprives us of something important. When the three major television networks first began covering the conventions in earnest in the early 1950s, the box in the living room drew Americans of all ages and political persuasions into the drama of self-governance. Seeing the system at work inspired many Americans to get involved. I wish we could find a way to reinvest major-party conventions with that same meaning and excitement. Nowadays, the selection of sixty-five teams to compete for the NCAA Men's Division I Basketball Championship seems to generate more excitement than the selection of the two nominees for the highest office in the most powerful nation on earth.

When John Kerry picked John Edwards as his running mate before the 2004 Democratic convention, the last vestige of suspense was drained out of the convention. By contrast, when Ford won the nomination in 1976, nobody—including the president himself—knew for sure whom he would select. As noted, he was under the impression that he should not offer the spot to Reagan. My choice, George Bush, was also out of the running.

George was conspicuously absent from politics in 1976. In January, he became director of the Central Intelligence Agency, a position he didn't seek. He hoped to run for president someday, and Langley seemed like a major detour, possibly a dead end, on the path to the White House. Would Americans ever accept a former spy chief as chief executive?

Before voting on the CIA nomination, Senate Democrats wanted President Ford to pledge that he would not ask George to be his running mate in 1976. Both Rogers Morton and I advised George not to take the post. George saw it differently. "It's an important position," he said, "and if the president wants me to do it, I'm gonna do it."*

There was speculation that the CIA appointment was engineered by Don Rumsfeld, then Ford's White House chief of staff. Rummy, who became secretary of defense after Ford fired Jim Schlesinger, was thought to have presidential aspirations of his own. If true, removing George from the scene could only have helped his chances.

After winning the nomination, Ford wisely sought Reagan's advice on possible running mates, among them John Connally, Howard Baker, Bob Dole, Bill Simon, Elliot Richardson, and William Ruckelshaus. Reagan favored Senator Dole, and after talking with his own advisers, Ford tapped the World War II hero as his running mate.

Anne Armstrong, then U.S. Ambassador to the United Kingdom, was also on the list. Had she been chosen, she would have been the first woman nominated by a major party to run on a national ticket. That would have been a big surprise in 1976, especially from our party. The face of the Kansas City GOP convention was largely white and male. While this demographic still predominates at our conventions, we now count considerably more women delegates and delegates of color. This is good for our party and our nation, and—not coincidentally— good politics.

After the convention, Ford advisers and campaign officials, including me, gathered at a retreat in Vail, Colorado, to plan the campaign against Jimmy Carter. In discussions to which I was not privy, a decision was made to replace Rog as chairman of the President Ford Committee (PFC). Rog had made a few mistakes during the primaries. Most notably, when Ford lost in Indiana, Alabama, and Georgia three

---

*In the end, George enjoyed his time as CIA director and did a great job in the office. "You restored America's trust in the CIA and the rest of the intelligence community," President Clinton wrote in 1999 when the Langley compound was named the George Bush Center for Intelligence. The experience also made George a better president, I think, because it enabled him to understand both the importance and the limitations of intelligence-gathering.

days after being humiliated in Texas, Rog had said, "I'm not going to rearrange the furniture on the deck of the *Titanic.*" At the same time, he permitted himself to be photographed in front of a row of less-than-full liquor bottles. To be fair to Rog, the press had joined in emptying those bottles. Furthermore, although few knew it, Rog was suffering from cancer.

Rumor had it that John Connally would replace Rog, who would then be given the largely ceremonial title of chairman emeritus. I was shocked when I learned that the president wanted *me* to take over day-to-day control of the campaign.

Chairman of the President Ford Committee was not a position I was seeking. I had been in Washington for less than a year. I really struggled with the question of loyalty to Rog, a wonderful man, now ill, who had been so good to me and had brought me to the capital in the first place.

The situation grew even worse when Rog's wife, Anne, a lovely woman and dear friend, heard about the offer. "Don't take it, Jim," she urged. "Tell him you can't do it."

"But, Anne," I said, "how can I turn down the president?"

If I hadn't thought it would hurt Anne even more, I would have told her that the decision to replace Rog had already been made. Even if I had turned down the president, he would have offered the chairmanship to somebody else. At least I could make certain Rog received the respect he deserved and the responsibility he wanted in his new role as chairman of a blue-ribbon steering committee for the campaign. When we returned to Washington from Vail, I refused to move into the large PFC chairman's office, insisting that Rog remain there.

The Ford-Carter contest in the year of our national bicentennial was historic on many levels. It marked the first chance Americans had to elect a president after Watergate. It was the only time one of the candidates was a sitting president who had not been elected to that office or, for that matter, to the vice presidency. And it was the last election in which Joe Garagiola played an important role.

I am only half-kidding when I mention Joe, the former catcher for the St. Louis Cardinals who parlayed his genial sense of humor into a career as a baseball broadcaster and television celebrity, eventually hosting NBC's *Today* show. His presence on the campaign trail symbolized the increased importance of television. By 1976, TV had not only penetrated our culture—almost every household had one or more sets—but had also begun to change the way most Americans thought about government and politics. The newspaper generation read about Watergate. The TV generation experienced it, through broadcast hearings and press conferences, and finally through the live resignation of a president, right there in the living room.

The post-Watergate campaign laws compounded the power of the tube. In *Marathon: The Pursuit of the Presidency, 1972–1976,* his comprehensive book on the 1976 election,* reporter Jules Witcover called the 1976 presidential race "ordination by television." In part this simply reflected the power of the medium, but it was also an indirect consequence of the new campaign-finance law passed by the Democratic Congress in 1974 in response to the fund-raising abuses of the 1972 Nixon campaign. In theory, both candidates Carter and Ford "voluntarily" accepted public financing of their general election campaigns. In reality, they had no choice, given the new limits on how much individuals and groups could contribute. (This decision had already been made by the time I took over.) Both campaigns got $21.8 million, but in return they could not accept private donations. As Witcover pointed out, this was "roughly one-third of what it had cost four years earlier" for Nixon's campaign against McGovern.

The spending limits forced each campaign to look for low-cost and no-cost strategies to sell its candidate to the public.† Television could

---

*This book, for which I was interviewed extensively, will refresh the memory of anyone interested in revisiting 1976. It refreshed mine.
†It also required us to assign a large tribe of lawyers and accountants to interpret the new law, comply with its detailed rules, and file reports with the Federal Election Commission.

reach millions, so the challenge for both campaigns was to win as much airtime as possible for as few dollars as possible. Twenty-four-hour cable news networks did not exist back then. The evening news on the three major networks—ABC, CBS, and NBC—drove the daily numbers. This begat a simple philosophy: orchestrate events featuring the president that the networks had to cover. If we wanted to emphasize the difference between our farm program and Carter's, for example, then send the president to a farm.

Televised debates—the ultimate reality television—also offered a way to reach tens of millions of Americans at a time. In his convention acceptance speech, the president said, "This year the issues are on our side. I am . . . eager to go before the American people and debate the real issues face-to-face with Jimmy Carter."

Here Ford was breaking the mold. He would be the first sitting president to participate in a broadcast debate with the other party's nominee. Comfortably ahead in the polls and reasoning that they had nothing to gain by giving their opponents a forum and credibility, Presidents Johnson and Nixon had refused to debate.

Free coverage was important, but both camps also recognized the importance of paid political advertising. For the last few days of the campaign, President Ford flew to key venues to do half-hour commercials in a talk-show format, not with his running mate, Bob Dole, but with a TV personality, Garagiola. Stay tuned for more about the "Joe and Jerry Show."

As chairman of the PFC, I appeared on television whenever the networks wanted me. We coveted the opportunity to push the Ford message without having to spend precious dollars. On September 12, 1976, a little less than one month after President Ford had won the nomination, I appeared on *Face the Nation*, where I was grilled on a range of issues (for which I had fastidiously Five P'd). Why was the president pursuing a Rose Garden strategy? Would he win any Southern states? What role would Reagan play in the campaign? And who the heck was James A. Baker, III?

"Do you go through Mr. Cheney to see the president on campaign issues, or do you have direct access?" I was asked by Bob Pierpoint.

"I have all the access to the president that I believe I require, Bob. Anytime I want to see the president, I can see the president."

I wasn't the only one surprised by my new job. On *Agronsky & Co.*, a forerunner of today's cable and network shows that feature pundits commenting on current political events, respected newspaperman Peter Lisagor characterized my appointment as "curious," given how little experience I had in national politics. On the same show, the conservative columnist James Kilpatrick acknowledged that I was a "competent technician" but deemed my ascension "startling." He wished aloud that Ford had brought in John Sears and other Reagan operatives.

The *Washington Post* reported my appointment under the headline: "Former Democrat, Political Neophyte Leads Ford Drive." The article described my style as "extremely low key" and "with an ever-evident sense of humor." Obviously, however, President Ford didn't appoint me because he liked my jokes. "Jim, as you know, was a very accurate counter in the pre-convention process," he said when he named me as chairman. "He demonstrated to me a very outstanding organizational capability."*

In a memo written early in 1975, well before he had even announced his candidacy, organizational ability was one of several characteristics the president had been advised to look for in a campaign manager. Among the other traits outlined in this memo, whose author was not identified: "1) Absolute loyalty to the president, even to exclu-

---

*I was not the only member of the Baker clan working for President Ford. Over the summer, my youngest son, Doug, then fifteen, volunteered as a grunt at PFC headquarters. That's probably where he got the bug for law, politics, and public service. When he grew up, he worked a few years as a lawyer in private practice, then served as executive director for the Houston Sport Authority. He also helped me in the 2000 Florida election dispute. In the first term of the Bush 43 administration, he was deputy assistant secretary at the Commerce Department. In the second term he moved to the White House as a special assistant to the president for homeland security.

sion, if necessary, of his own best interests; 2) the ability to make a decision. Indecisiveness to politicians is disastrous; 3) general knowledge of the political, business, and media worlds; 4) available on a full-time basis; and 5) a 'good guy' with few, if any, deep-seated adversaries."

Looking back from the perspective of five presidential campaigns, I would add one other essential characteristic: the willingness to look your candidate in the eye and give the bad news with the good. This is never easy.

About two weeks before the convention, Stu Spencer and Dick Cheney presented the president with a comprehensive, one-hundred-plus-page strategy notebook they had prepared with the help of a small group, most notably including Mike Duval, a valuable holdover from the Nixon administration. Although ever-changing circumstances prevented us from following it to the letter and the president always had the final say, this manifesto guided the campaign from August until November. My job was to implement it. Looking back on it today, I think it holds up as a good diagnosis of the problems the campaign faced and a good prescription for curing them.

The strategists began by offering a realistic assessment of the president's chances: "You face a unique challenge. No president has overcome the obstacles to election which you will face." In the greatest comeback in recent history, they noted, President Harry Truman trailed Thomas Dewey by only 11 points in August 1948. Ford, they predicted, would trail Carter by almost 20 points after our convention. (He was down by a staggering 33 percent margin—62–29, with 9 percent undecided—in the late July Gallup Poll, three weeks before Kansas City.)

This forecast proved pretty accurate. Thanks in part to a rousing acceptance speech that unified the convention and Republicans across the country, the president actually trailed by only 10 points in the first post–Kansas City Gallup Poll, 49 to 39, with 12 percent undecided. A week later, however, with the convention already fading from memory, the margin was back up to 15 percent.

Why was the president so far behind? In part because of a sluggish economy; in part because of the lingering effects of Watergate and the Nixon pardon; and, in part, according, to our polling, because Ford was frequently perceived as too partisan, particularly on the campaign trail. His national approval rating *declined* when he left the White House during the primary season.

I've learned that you really cannot, and should not try to, present a candidate as something he or she is not. You don't suggest a personality makeover or try to build a strategy around a false image. "Our campaign strategy has been developed around the president's actual strengths and aimed at Carter's actual weaknesses," our strategy document said. "We are not trying to change the president (style and substance); we are trying to change the voter's perception of the president and Carter."

Mistakes could be fatal. To avoid self-inflicted wounds, "the president must establish ironclad control over administration and campaign officials." This proved prophetic. In late September, it was reported that Secretary of Agriculture Earl Butz—a holdover from the Nixon administration—had told an offensive joke shortly after the convention that was derogatory to African Americans. President Ford instructed him to apologize, but did not publicly call for his resignation as many Republicans and Democrats demanded. With the controversy dominating the news and sidetracking the campaign, Cheney, Spencer, and I urged the president to jettison the secretary. The next day, October 4, Butz resigned.

"The president's campaign must be television oriented," said our strategy document. "We must change the perception of literally millions of voters, and this can only be done through the mass media." Many of our strategy points related to television. For example, the president was counseled: "Carefully plan, prepare, and execute all on-camera appearances. The president should be seen on television as in control, decisive, open, and candid." Also: "Use ads and advocates to compare the president's personal characteristics and experience with Carter's."

Other advice from the strategy memo reveals just how carefully a candidate is prepped for the campaign:

- Avoid self-deprecating remarks (I'm a Ford, not a Lincoln) and acts (being photographed with a cowboy hat).
- Avoid symbolic acts such as bill signings, submitting legislation, vetoes, and the like, which simply reinforce the perception of the president as part of the Washington establishment. . . .
- The president must not campaign for GOP candidates. This will seriously erode his support among independents and ticket splitters.
- In order to break the president out of the Washington establishment mold, we should launch an attack on the Democratic majority which has governed Washington for forty of the past forty-eight years.

Traditionally, presidential campaigns kick off after Labor Day, but normally the sitting president does not trail his opponent by double digits in August. After the convention, we had seventy-five days until the November 2 election. Ford did not have the luxury of relaxing for two weeks. He got in a few rounds of golf at Vail, but even that was squeezed into a working vacation.

The first order of business was to reorganize the operation. With the team in place, we could then develop a campaign blueprint based on the strategy notebook, post-convention developments, and the ideas of some campaign newcomers we had signed up. A five-page document, dated August 25 and titled "The President's Campaign," began with an important guiding principle that reflected the impact of Watergate: Pollster Bob "Teeter's data indicate that the 1976 election is a personality contest, not a battle of issues. Issues will be one of the determinants people use in sizing up each man."

Because "each candidate's style as perceived by the electorate [is] all-important," the campaign needed "to project the following characteristics." Reading the list of those characteristics must have transported Ford, the only Eagle Scout ever to serve as president, back to his youth. "Knowledgeable, solid, stable, decisive, compassionate, trust-worthy, future-oriented, experienced, and positive."

In discussing the Ford strategy in 1976, I do not mean to suggest that the campaign was bereft of substance. In fact, we were eager to engage the Democrats on the issues. We worked up a document—"Major Differences in Platform"—that contrasted the two parties' po-sitions on twenty-four topics. On energy, for instance, the Republican platform "eliminates price controls on oil and new sources of natural gas in order to increase the supply of oil and gas." The Democrat plat-form, on the other hand, "maintains 1975 oil prices and raises price ceilings on natural gas." The president would emphasize this differ-ence, particularly in the oil and gas producing states.

We focused our message on issues of the day. For each, the presi-dent would speak at a venue selected to yield coverage on the evening news. His surrogates—Senator Dole, cabinet members, high-profile supporters, members of the First Family, and I—would also push the same issue.

Then, as now, the press loved to play "gotcha" by finding contra-dictions in a candidate's statements or differences between what he and his surrogates were saying. How did we manage not to contradict one another? I still retain another thick document from the campaign that includes talking points on twenty-one issues of the day, from abortion to tax reform, from amnesty to drug abuse, from the economy to juvenile delinquency. Under "Older Americans," for instance, we said, "In his acceptance speech, the president reconfirmed his concern for the nation's elderly. 'We will ensure the integrity of the Social Se-curity system and improve Medicare.'" Below that, we listed four points about the president's proposals or accomplishments, including: "The president proposed a catastrophic health insurance program to limit the out-of-pocket amount older Americans must pay for medical and physicians' fees each year."

Every campaign with which I have been associated—and, I am confident, every opposing campaign—prepared talking points like these for the candidate and his surrogates. We also developed a dozen guidelines for these spokespersons. They included: "Two days travel per week per cabinet secretary, at least." "Emphasize travel to cities whose TV covers 70 percent of population" and "take it for granted people won't like [being addressed by a low-profile cabinet officer]— so have ready a list of very heavy hitters who aren't scheduled at all— supporters who can plug the perceived holes, and—even more—can nail Carter into a barrel when targets of opportunity arise. Our list of 'attackers' is: Mrs. Ford, Bob Dole, John Connally, Nelson Rockefeller, John Tower, Howard Baker, Rogers Morton."

We would have liked to include Ronald Reagan on this list. It is fair to say, however, that after the convention, the president and many of his supporters were not enamored of Reagan. It had nothing to do with the former governor's personality and everything to do with the fact that he had challenged and almost beaten a sitting president from his own party. At the same time, President Ford recognized that Governor Reagan could help him in some areas of the country.

While the president was at the White House and Dole and others were crisscrossing the United States, I was, for the most part, at the still-spartan PFC headquarters at Eighteenth and L Streets in northwest Washington. As chairman, I oversaw the activities of state chairmen and the deputy chairmen at the PFC, worked with the political people at the White House, and acted as a principal spokesman for the campaign with the print and television media.

There's no such thing as a typical day in a presidential campaign, except one that involves long hours, many meetings, and lots of telephone calls. On most days, I checked in by telephone with our paid state campaign chairs around the country and met in the office with our PFC deputies. Cheney, Spencer, Teeter, and I also devoted a good deal of time to figuring out how to allocate our limited resources and time.

In a race for the presidency, you are not dealing with one election; you are dealing with the electoral votes of fifty states and D.C.—i.e.,

fifty-one separate elections. Teeter's polling and reports from operatives in the field helped us target states for advertising and visits by
Ford or Dole.*

The PFC was theoretically governed by an executive committee
composed of me and other top officers of the campaign. I chaired the
meetings. My outline from one of the very first meetings, at 7:30 A.M.
on September 7, began with this note to myself: "Hold to forty-five
minutes." That was wishful thinking. I had put nineteen topics on the
agenda, among them PFC–White House coordination, campaign material distribution, coordination with Reagan staff, phone-bank operations, state organizations, president's schedule, and Democrats and
independents for Ford. All these and more were under my purview.

One thing we tried to do was create a better working relationship
between the PFC and the White House, which had not always seen
eye to eye during the primary season. Almost every day I would walk
over to the White House for strategy meetings with Cheney. White
House political appointees Mike Duval, Foster Chanock, and Jerry
Jones usually joined us. So did Jim Field, a young Cheney aide from
Rhode Island who served as liaison between Dick and me.

It didn't take long for the press to catch on to this pattern. Journalists began staking out our headquarters, following me with television
cameras on the walk, and peppering me with questions. I liked these
reporters, but the best way to get our message out was under controlled conditions, not impromptu walks down the street with micro-
phones in my face, so I started driving to the White House.

The presidential debates were also a topic of discussion at that

---

*The operatives' reports had to be taken with a grain of salt. During a campaign, everyone
believes the candidate should visit his or her state, yesterday, or the world will end. Everyone is an expert on strategy. Supporters sent the president stacks of letters and telegrams
on how to conduct his campaign. Many were referred to me. One of my favorites—from
a retired alternate delegate from Illinois—began in all caps: "GREAT BALLS OF GREEN
CHEESE, PRESIDENT FORD! WHY DO YOU LET CARTER GET AWAY WITH
HIS STATEMENTS ON UNEMPLOYMENT?"

September 7 meeting. The first ninety-minute Ford-Carter debate, sponsored by the League of Women Voters and moderated by veteran NBC newsman Edwin Newman, was held at the Walnut Street Theatre in Philadelphia on September 23. "The debates will overshadow all other presidential campaign activity," said the Vail campaign strategy document. "This activity must have the priority call on the president's time." And it did. Ford's preparation, led largely by Mike Duval, advertising guru Doug Bailey, and media consultant Bill Carruthers, began long before the first question was asked.

On September 15, Bailey sent Duval a two-page memo with a "debate thesis"—"'Winning the debate' will result from the president's seeing it not as a contest with Carter, but as an opportunity to communicate with the people, regardless of what Carter does—and a "debate strategy"—"The dominant fact of the debate will be that it is not between two candidates but between one candidate and the president." Seven guidelines followed, including these:

> The president should always stand, never using the stool. He
> should . . . take notes when Carter is making a strong point; ignore
> the cameras, always assuming they are on him.
> He should refer to him as "Mr. Carter." He should avoid any
> direct conversation with him. . . .
> The president should not cite congressional anecdotes. He
> should always be presidential by referring to the past two years.

A final guideline referred the president to an attached chart listing "seven points to be made, the type of question or comment which can be used to make them, and some memorable summary lines on each." Here is one example:

> Basic message to communicate: "With recovery of peace, economic
> stability, and trust, we can enter a new generation of freedom."
> When to use it: Questions on priorities; issues such as busing,
> government reorganization, equal rights, crime, education.

Key lines to use: "FDR's Four Freedoms are still valid. But today we must also seek freedom from government restrictions in our lives—freedom from Washington in our lives."

Carter arrived in Philadelphia for the first debate with a commanding 18 percent lead, but—thanks to an article from a most unexpected media source—momentum was beginning to shift our way. Three days before the debate, *Playboy* released a long interview with Carter.

"Christ said, 'I tell you that anyone who looks on a woman with lust has in his heart already committed adultery,'" Carter told his interviewers. "I've looked on a lot of women with lust. I've committed adultery in my heart many times. This is something that God recognizes I will do—and I have done it—and God forgives me for it. . . ."

Carter's statement was the perfect political gaffe. It hurt him with almost every voting group. His fellow Southern Baptists, for instance, were offended that he gave the interview without condemning *Playboy*'s role in what they saw as the coarsening of culture and weakening of traditional sexual morality. Some voters simply thought it was funny (in the sense of odd) for a presidential candidate to talk openly about his lustful thoughts. And others were troubled by what they saw as excessive religiosity. The episode cast doubt on Carter's judgment and political skills. Frank Irwin, a conservative Democrat from Texas, even printed bumper stickers saying, "God doesn't want you to vote for Jimmy Carter."

Meanwhile, we had to decide how to respond. It's inevitable on the painfully long campaign trail that a candidate will, at some point, say something controversial. The opposition then has to figure out whether it will gain more by speaking up or keeping quiet. The determining factor is often whether the press itself can be expected to keep the story alive, and on "lustful thoughts," reporters were doing just fine, thank you very much, without any help from us. Neither the president nor Bob Dole said a thing.

I accompanied the president to Philadelphia for the first debate.

Surprisingly, none of the panelists asked about the *Playboy* interview. Not surprisingly, neither candidate mentioned it.*

The first debate is best remembered, not for anything that was said but instead for its silence. With about eight minutes remaining, the sound system went dead while Carter was in the middle of a response. "The Great Cutoff," as the *Washington Post*'s Haynes Johnson called it, lasted twenty-seven minutes. While technicians tried to figure out what was wrong and fix it, the president and Carter remained standing on the stage. Neither said a word, and neither seemed to want to sit down.

President Ford eventually won the standoff. After about twenty minutes, Carter took his seat. Sound was restored a few minutes later. The first post–Philadelphia Gallup Poll suggested the president had won the debate, too. Carter's 18-point lead (54–36) was reduced to 8 (50–42).

A little more than a month later, with just days left in the campaign, a Harris poll showed the race was a virtual dead heat, with Carter leading Ford by only 1 point, 45–44. The tightness of the race was remarkable considering how far behind we had started, how difficult it was to overcome public concern about the Nixon pardon, and how many new and unexpected troubles came our way during the campaign.

Unbelievably, given President Ford's sterling reputation, one of our first big problems was fighting off an ethics charge. Watergate Special Prosecutor Charles Ruff was appointed by the administration's attorney general, Edward Levi—without prior notice to the president and in the heat of the campaign—to investigate whether, as a congressman, Ford had diverted campaign contributions for personal use. It

---

*Finally questioned about the interview in the third debate on October 22, Carter conceded that it had been a mistake. "If I should ever decide in the future to discuss my deep Christian beliefs . . . I'll use another forum besides *Playboy*." In interviews after he left office, President Carter admitted the interview had cost him a lot of votes.

was a bogus charge from the beginning, and Levi should never have referred it to a special prosecutor. In mid-October, Ruff announced there was no evidence of wrongdoing and closed the case. Nevertheless, the investigation badly hurt our campaign and was, in my opinion, inappropriate and unfair, a perversion of the political process, and a real sign of troubles to come from the post-Watergate independent counsels.

Another ethics question boiled up in the press while Ruff was conducting his investigation. John Dean, President Nixon's White House counsel who pled guilty to obstruction of justice in the Watergate scandal (he admitted paying the Watergate burglars to keep quiet), told reporters that Ford, as a congressman, had—at the behest of the White House—attempted to kill a 1972 House hearing on the Watergate burglary. At his vice presidential confirmation hearing, President Ford testified that he had opposed granting subpoena powers for the investigation but that he had not acted on behalf of the White House. (These events occurred well before the full implications of Watergate were evident.) Both Ford and the White House aide whom Dean cited as his source denied Dean's allegations, and—despite the hair-trigger post-Watergate spirit toward real or imagined impropriety—Ruff did not think the charges were worth investigating. Still, the damage was done. President Ford suffered guilt by association every time reporters wrote another story about Dean's baseless charge.

The Butz affair, another unexpected pothole on the campaign trail, resolved itself with the secretary's resignation, but two days later another key administration official spoke and the result was even more damaging. That official was President Ford himself.

During the second televised debate, the president painted himself into a corner while trying to defend the Helsinki Final Act, which he signed in 1975. It was an extremely important human rights document— among other things—but Jimmy Carter criticized it mercilessly. In defense, President Ford said the Soviets had kept their word and notified us about their military maneuvers. "In both cases where they've done so, there is no Soviet domination of Eastern Europe and there never will be under a Ford administration."

A follow-up question from Max Frankel of the *New York Times* gave the president an opportunity to correct his misstatement. But President Ford responded by citing two communist countries that in some sense had kept the Soviet Union at arm's length—Yugoslavia and Romania—and one other, Poland, that was clearly under the thumb of the Soviets. "I don't believe that the Poles consider themselves dominated by the Soviet Union," he said.

He was, of course, referring to the indomitable spirit of the Poles and other peoples of Eastern Europe—one of the major reasons for the collapse of the Berlin Wall some thirteen years later. And he was also stating a longstanding U.S. policy that refused to accept the legality of the occupation by the Soviets of Eastern and Central Europe after World War II. But it's one thing to have a policy and another to deny the facts on the ground, which is what he appeared to be doing.

At this stage in the campaign, we knew that to win we would have to carry most if not all of the northern and eastern industrial states. That's where the electoral votes were. That's also where the largest blocs of Polish Americans and others of Eastern European descent lived—the population most likely to be affected by the president's remarks.

What to do? Several of us met to discuss damage control. We decided that in the morning Cheney, National Security Adviser Brent Scowcroft, and I would go to the press to explain the president's statement—not an enviable task given the number of Soviet divisions stationed in Eastern Europe.

Interestingly, while both the Ford and Carter campaigns and the press immediately focused on the president's remarks about the Soviets and Eastern Europe, the public did not. Teeter's overnight polling of those who had watched the debate gave the president the win by a comfortable 11 percent margin. Then the newspapers hit the stands, the remark was rebroadcast on television, the pundits weighed in, and the Carter campaign focused on the assertion. Within forty-eight hours, polls revealed that a substantial majority of those who had watched the debate now believed Carter had won.

When you're wounded, you must stop the bleeding immediately. This is a guiding principle of politics. This gaffe had knocked us off message and threatened to keep us there for a long time.

Many of us advised the president to meet the press and clarify his remarks. Unfortunately, Henry Kissinger had called after the debate to tell the president what a wonderful job he had done, which reinforced Ford's view that he didn't need to do that. After all, we didn't officially recognize that the Soviets had any right to dominate Eastern Europe, and neither did the Eastern Europeans—at least in spirit. Only after it became clear to the president that his campaign was being sidetracked—six agonizing days later—did he speak up. "The original mistake was mine," he said. "I did not express myself clearly. I admit it."

That gave us something to work with, and I was soon happily pointing out to reporters that this was the first time in six weeks that the president had had to clarify any remarks, while candidate Carter was constantly revising what he had said. I cited six comparable Carter do-overs, including the famous *Playboy* interview.

Carter gaffes were in part responsible for the statistical dead heat the polls reflected on election eve. So, too, was the fact that voters not only liked Gerald Ford, but also saw him as presidential. The "Joe and Jerry Show" played a big part in reinforcing this perception.

The president and Garagiola had met earlier in the year and hit it off. The plan to team them together in six thirty-minute campaign infomercials was hatched at an October brainstorming session between Bob Teeter and consultant John Deardourff.

In modern baseball parlance, Garagiola pitched the president "cookies"—questions he could easily hit for home runs. I've long since forgotten these confections, but in *Marathon*, Witcover recounts a few of them, including: "Gosh, Mr. President, there sure are a lot of people worried about taxes, and just what are you going to do to help them out?" And, "How many world leaders have you dealt with?" These shows went over extremely well, with viewership well in excess of what we had expected.

By the time the polls opened on November 2, no one could predict the outcome with certainty. As our exit polling data trickled in, however, the picture began to look bleak. At about 5 o'clock in the afternoon, Cheney, Spencer, Teeter, and I presented the numbers to the president. He took the news stoically. As always, he was gracious. Before we left he even offered me a cigar.

"Thank you, but I don't smoke, Mr. President." After smoking cigarettes for years, I had stopped when Mary Stuart got sick, started up after she died, then quit again.

His voice reduced to a whisper by all the campaigning, the president said, "Maybe you might find some use for it."

For a time after the polls closed, it looked as if I might have reason to light it up as a victory cigar. The early results were better than our exit polling had predicted. As the spokesperson for the campaign on election night, I fielded questions from the press, monitored returns from our people in the field, and watched the television coverage from the Ford headquarters in downtown Washington. The president, his family, and several close friends—including Garagiola—watched from the residence in the White House.*

There is a telling photograph of Joe and Jerry, taken at some point during the evening. As the two friends sat together on a couch, the expressive Garagiola has his head buried in his hands. Beside him, the president calmly lights his pipe. Later Joe was reported to have said, "The president took all the news very calmly. I'd seen [Cardinals'

---

*The First Family was a real asset in the campaign. Because the president did not travel extensively until late in the campaign, appearances by Mrs. Ford and the children were very important. "Mrs. Ford is greatly respected because she is independent from the president," said our Vail strategy book. "We should not try to discourage this independence." We didn't, and Betty Ford, a classy woman, won a lot of votes for the president.

teammate] Enos Slaughter get more upset about an umpire saying, 'Strike two,' than Gerald Ford did when he realized he wasn't going to win a presidential election."

That realization didn't come until the early hours of Wednesday morning. In the end a shift of only a few thousand votes in Ohio (25 electoral votes) and Hawaii (4 electoral votes) would have given the victory to the president. Carter-Mondale won the popular vote by about 1.7 million ballots out of almost 82 million cast, 50 to 48 percent. In the Electoral College, where the magic number was 270, Carter-Mondale won 297 to 240. (A renegade elector from Washington gave Reagan one vote.) Not since Woodrow Wilson defeated Charles Evans Hughes by 23 electoral votes in 1916 had a race for president been so close.

As sunrise approached, I thought to myself, *How bizarre. Here you were a Democratic lawyer in Houston seven years ago, and now you've run a campaign for an incumbent Republican president, in what is obviously the closest presidential election you'll ever see in your lifetime.* That assessment held up for all of twenty-four years.

I also lit up the cigar the president had given me. For the next three or four years, until I kicked the habit, I smoked a cigar every night after dinner. Politics can be hazardous to your health.

Because the results were so close in so many states, we talked seriously about asking for one or more recounts. After thinking about it for a day or two, however, President Ford called us all together and said he had decided against it. "I lost the popular vote," he said. "It would be very hard for me to govern if I won the presidency in the Electoral College through a recount." He was right, of course.

Gerald Ford may have been calm about losing, as Garagiola reported, but that reflected the president's character, not indifference to the outcome. He was a strong competitor—all those who aspire to the presidency are—and he was a proud man. Still, he had a sense of perspective. His reputation was secure as the president who had helped our nation pull itself together after Watergate. Against great odds, he ran a strong campaign and almost pulled it off. Now he gracefully accepted the decision of the American people and prepared to move on.

As for me, I took satisfaction in having helped this wonderfully good man win his party's nomination and rally from 33 points down to come within an eyelash of recapturing the presidency. We'd given it a hell of a shot. In the end the Nixon pardon and concerns about the economy were just too much to overcome.

I also took solace from the many letters I received. Tom Brokaw, host of the *Today* show at the time, thanked me for demonstrating "class" in appearing on the program the morning after the election, and added: "I hope that you will take some consolation in knowing that the President Ford Committee conducted a masterful closing campaign. It was an effort of which you can be proud." And George Bush wrote: "Dear Bake: Nobody could have done any better—nobody!! The big thing is that you did it 'first class'—and you emerge with universal respect, your dignity intact. Just know we're awfully proud, Bushie."

ONE DAY during the campaign, I brought Susan and some of the kids over to the White House, and President Ford graciously invited us all into the Oval Office. Our ten-year-old son, Will, looked the place over, then said to the president, "Gee, you have a really pretty office. My daddy's office is really ugly."

The president laughed and said, "Well, son, if we win this election, your daddy will be getting a much prettier office."

Rumor had it the president planned to name me secretary of transportation. After the election, however, the only transportation I had to be concerned about was how to pack up the Baker brood and move it back to Houston. Andrews Kurth had an office waiting for me, and I took it, but resuming the practice of corporate law held little appeal for me. I knew I wouldn't be able to stay out of politics for long. The question wasn't whether I would run for office, but what office I would run for.

FOUR

"DOESN'T IT PISS YOU OFF?"

RUNNING FOR ATTORNEY GENERAL (AG) in Texas, as I did in 1978, was a far cry from running a presidential campaign. In this, my first (and only) bid for elective office, state dinners in the White House were out; potlucks in Rotary Clubs and barbeques in backyards were in. Over almost a year, I ate every variation of chicken imaginable. (In state politics there's no question about which comes first, the chicken or the ego.)

When I wasn't pressing my case at these gatherings, I was pressing the flesh on street corners and in supermarket parking lots. I had no advance team, and I didn't travel on Air Force One. My entourage, such as it was, usually consisted of two guys—Peter Roussel, a friend from Houston who had worked for George Bush, and Jim Cicconi, a recent University of Texas Law School graduate who had approached me one day on the street in Austin before I had announced and said he wanted to help. (Jim later served with distinction in the White House for George H. W. Bush and, afterward, helped set up the Bush Presidential Library and Museum. More recently, he was vice president and general counsel of AT&T before its merger with SBC.) The press rarely followed me.*

Susan rarely accompanied me. Her job was to stump in the areas I couldn't get to. She covered much of the state in our white Suburban with "Jim Baker for Attorney General" painted on the windows, stopping for coffees and teas organized by family and friends. Karen Jones, a young campaign worker, organized the trips and traveled with her, as did Susan's sister, Klinka Lollar, and other special pals. Much of the time Susan traveled with a portable crib in the back of the Suburban for our daughter, Mary Bonner, the newest Baker, born in Houston in September 1977.†

One hot summer afternoon I found myself in the Texas Panhandle. I saw a small crowd in a shopping center and went over to shake hands and distribute campaign literature.

"Hey, did anyone ever tell you that you look like Jim Baker?" one man said before I could introduce myself.

I was hardly a household name or face, but some people knew "Jim Baker" because I had frequently been on national television as President Ford's campaign chairman. "Yes," I replied with a smile. "Often."

---

*Back at our modest headquarters in Houston, my campaign manager, Frank Donatelli, led a small staff that included his wife, Becki, Carol Townsend, Frank Lavin, Lisa Stoltenberg, and Jan Naylor. (When I was White House chief of staff, Donatelli served as an assistant to President Reagan for political affairs. Today he is a prominent D.C. public affairs consultant. Lavin is under secretary of commerce. Naylor later served as deputy personnel director for Bush 41.) We were also blessed with any number of volunteers, one being my cousin Preston Moore.

†When I learned Susan was pregnant, I said, "Oh my goodness, we're gonna have another boy." "Jimmy, we are going to have a blue-eyed baby girl," she replied. When she went to the delivery room, I stayed behind, true to the old tradition that there are some places men just don't belong.

"Mr. Baker, you have a lovely baby girl," the nurse told me in the waiting room. "That is a really cruel joke," I told her, thinking Susan had put her up to it. But it was true. And the baby had blue eyes. I think it was God's providence that we had this lovely caboose to our train of eight children. She brought the Baker and Winston wings of our family closer together. Mary Bonner took her first steps in a press office in Brownwood, Texas, as Susan was giving an interview.

The guy never batted an eyelash. He looked straight at me and said, "Doesn't it piss you off?"

In those days, it was still hard to be a Texas Republican. In running for attorney general, I was attempting to do what no GOP candidate for statewide office—save Senator John Tower—had done since Reconstruction. Win.

George Bush and others had suggested that I should run for governor, but Dolph Briscoe, the incumbent, was an establishment Democrat, fairly conservative, and I didn't think I could raise enough money to beat him. My likely Democratic opponent for attorney general, former Texas House Speaker Price Daniel, Jr., was liberal enough to give a Republican a chance. It wouldn't cost nearly as much to run for AG, and I knew I was a better lawyer.*

Governor wasn't the only office I had been encouraged to seek. Before leaving Washington for Houston and the Andrews Kurth law firm a few weeks after the '76 election, some Ford supporters on the Republican National Committee (RNC) encouraged me to run for chairman of the RNC. I gave this serious consideration. When a Democrat holds the presidency, as Jimmy Carter would from 1977 to 1981, and Republicans control neither house of Congress, as was the case then, the RNC chair becomes de facto spokesperson for the party and, thus, a player.

I eventually withdrew my name for a couple of reasons. First, several other prominent politicians sought the position, and, as I told the press, I wanted to avoid being involved in "a knock-down, drag-out fight." Second, it's virtually impossible to run the party without being

---

*I eventually raised about $1.5 million. After the race, we had a deficit, but when George Bush received the vice presidential nomination in 1980, he wrote a fund-raising letter on my behalf. More money came in than was needed to pay off the debt, so I refunded the surplus to my contributors on a pro rata basis. Returning unspent campaign contributions is unusual but not unheard of. My father once told me how much he respected a former U.S. senator from Connecticut who had done the same thing in the 1950s—Prescott Bush, the father of my friend George. Even today people tell me, "You're the only politician who ever gave me any money back."

scarred politically. You have to be willing to make hard calls about what campaigns to support with funding and other tough issues. You can never please everyone, and if you're fair, you end up making more people mad than glad. Finally, although the White House privately encouraged me to run, President Ford did not want to endorse one candidate over the others.

As it turned out, not running was one of the best political decisions I ever made. Former Tennessee Senator Bill Brock won the chairmanship on, I believe, the third ballot and did a fine job. When the party reclaimed the presidency in 1981, President Reagan named him U.S. trade representative. Not bad. But Bill never became part of the president's inner circle, even when he served as secretary of labor in Reagan's second term.

When I returned to Houston, Bill Harvin, managing partner at Baker Botts, approached me about becoming a partner at the firm my great-grandfather had helped found. My dad was no longer alive, so the nepotism rule was not a problem. Getting my ticket punched at the family firm, albeit twenty years late, was appealing, but I declined. "I don't think I can do that, Bill," I said. "AK has been very loyal to me. They let me pursue this political agenda. I've got a lot of good friends still practicing there. It just wouldn't be right."

One of those friends was Harry Jones, the man who had taught me so much about practicing law and whom, nineteen years later, I still called "Mr. Jones." "Jim," he asked, "what do you think would have happened if President Ford had won?"

I would probably have been named secretary of transportation, I told him. "Wow," said this man whom I so admired, with genuine awe. "Secretary of transportation." I deeply regret that he did not live to see me serve as secretary of the treasury and secretary of state. He did live to see me run for attorney general, though, and lose.

In the Democratic primary, Mark White, a conservative protégé of Governor Briscoe, beat my opponent of choice, Price Daniel. This was a major upset, as Daniel—"Price, Jr.," in the idiom of Texas politics—

was widely expected to follow in the footsteps of his father, a legendary Texas House speaker, attorney general, governor, senator, and state supreme court justice. Young Daniel—descended on his mother's side from my great-grandfather's old friend Sam Houston—lost, in part because he was reluctant to spend money on TV during the primary. He figured, erroneously, that he would need it more when he faced me in the general election.

Just as George Bush had expected to run as the mainstream alternative to the liberal Ralph Yarborough in the senate race of 1970, I had expected to portray myself as the mainstream alternative to the liberal Daniel. And just as George's unexpected establishment Democrat opponent (Lloyd Bentsen) beat him, my unexpected establishment Democrat opponent (Mark White) beat me, 1,249,846 to 999,431.

Preston Moore recently reminded me that the race would have been a bit closer had I said yes to an offer made by leaders of a community organization that shall go unnamed here. They offered to deliver a large bloc of voters in return for a $5,000 check. "Walking-around money" for local political leaders was standard operating procedure in Texas politics, they said. I told them it wasn't SOP for me.

It was an odd election year. John Hill, a moderate,* upset Dolph Briscoe, a reasonably popular conservative governor, in the Democratic primary. This was an early sign that Texas conservatives were drifting away from their hereditary party. Bill Clements, a gruff Texas oilman, former Democrat with strong ties to John Connally, and former deputy defense secretary in the Nixon and Ford administrations, spent millions of his own money to win the governorship. With Texas Democrats still outnumbering Texas Republicans by a big margin, he almost drilled a very expensive dry hole. In the end, however, he squeaked by Hill, thanks to superb media, good organization, and a lot of crossover

---

*In a footnote to history, my daughter Mary Bonner married John Hill's grandson, Hunter Perrin, in 2005. They now live in Los Angeles, where Mary Bonner is an actress.

votes from conservative Democrats who regarded Hill as too liberal. Clements became the first GOP governor in Texas in 105 years.

Another Texas Republican also made his first bid for office in 1978. George W. Bush, then thirty-two, ran for Congress in a sprawling West Texas district that included Midland. That's where the Bushes lived when they first moved to the state. In the GOP primary, an opponent charged that "Junior" had "Rockefeller-type Republicans such as Karl Rove to help him run his campaign."

Rove "is a twenty-seven-year-old guy who works in my dad's office in Houston," George W. responded. "He has had nothing to do with my campaign. . . . I doubt he even supports Rockefeller." Junior won the primary but lost the general election to Kent Hance, a conservative Democrat.

Everyone knows what became of George W. Bush. Here's what became of Price Daniel, Jr. Devastated by his loss to Mark White, he returned home to Liberty, Texas. In January 1981, his wife shot him to death with a .22-caliber rifle, then beat the rap with Racehorse Haynes as her attorney. This story later showed up in a dreadful made-for-TV movie, a sad testament to a life and career that held such promise.

Another candidate, John Tower, retained his senate seat in '78. We ran into each other on the campaign trail one hot summer day in San Antonio and repaired for drinks to the old Menger Hotel. That's where in 1898 my hero Teddy Roosevelt recruited Texas cowboys of varying degrees of sobriety as Rough Riders to fight in the Spanish-American War. Over vodka martinis, Tower said, "You know something, Baker? This is a squalid business we're in."

"Speak for yourself, Senator," I replied. "I'm new to all this."

After losing my race, I still didn't find the business squalid. I wasn't disillusioned, but I was exhausted. So was Susan, who had attended so many campaign coffees on my behalf that she might have been mistaken for the Folgers Lady. We retreated to Florida for a little R&R.

We hadn't been vacationing for more than a day or two when George called. "Let's get going," he said. I knew what he meant.

George and I had talked many times since 1976 about the possibility of his running for president. I had promised to help if I were in a position to do so. Now he was ready to go.

Early on, George turned to me one day and asked, "Am I crazy to do this?" Even fellow Texans—who tend to admire bold action—were ridiculing him. "George, you don't mean you're gonna run against John Connally?" he was asked more than once.

Connally, a Texan's Texan who looked and sounded like central casting's idea of a president, had been planning a run for as long as George. John and I had crossed paths a few times over the years, but it wasn't until the Ford campaign of 1976 that I really got to know him. One of my duties at the Vail meeting where I was named Ford's campaign chairman was to host this fellow Texan (and fellow former Democrat). Over the next few months, the former Texas governor and U.S. treasury secretary was a great help to our campaign.

When I ran for attorney general, Connally made an appearance on my behalf at a fund-raising event in Fort Worth. Beforehand, he and his wife, Nellie, Susan and I, and Peter Roussel from my campaign staff were visiting in the hotel where the event was to be held. At one point, Connally stood up and in that deep, rich voice of his said, "Jim, if the ladies will excuse us, I'd like to have a word or two." We went into the next room. "Jim, I'm gonna run for president," he said, "and I hope you will help me."

I was never quite sure whether he asked because he was impressed by the job I had done for President Ford or because I was the only guy around who had run a Republican general election campaign for president in the last fifteen years and hadn't done jail time. Either way, I said I couldn't help. My first allegiance was to my friend George, I told him.

While the relationship between George Bush and Connally was always civil, it was never warm. I think George was disappointed when President Nixon appointed Connally as treasury secretary in 1971. It was largely at Nixon's urging that George had given up his safe seat in the House to run for the Senate against Ralph Yarborough. After that, George rightly believed he should have been rewarded with a cabinet position. The Connally family never considered George a real Texan and was, I think, somewhat envious that George, not John, eventually won the presidency.

Most of the business community supported Connally, which gave him credibility and a good source of campaign funds. (John was the only major candidate who turned down federal matching funds in the primaries, which, in theory, permitted him to raise and spend more money than other candidates.) Still, I told George he wasn't crazy to run, and I meant it. In my mind, he was the best-qualified candidate. He had what it took to be a strong campaigner and a fine president. After Nixon resigned in 1974 and the newly sworn-in President Ford was considering whom to nominate as his vice president, I had jotted down my thoughts on why George should be considered. Under the heading "Fit to be Pres.," I wrote: "Look at record in life—a record of success":

> Successful Yale—scholastically (Phi Beta Kappa) and athletically (capt. baseball team); war record—decorated—shot down; successful businessman; Congress—first Repub. from Houston—Ways and Means Committee as freshman; UN Ambassador; RNC—toughest job in country over last eighteen months.

In the four years since I had made those notes, George had added to his résumé, serving as our first liaison to China, then director of the CIA. (George's 1980 campaign slogan would be "A president we won't have to train.") My notes also included several other pluses, including:

> Age, geography (Conn. and Tex.), foreign affairs experience, admired by Repub. Party leaders in all sections of country, respect of those who knew him in Congress (both sides of aisle), reputation for honesty and integrity (above all), outgoing, articulate, intelligent, fair (votes convictions), competitive.

In addition to all this, he had many friends and acquaintances around the country, thanks to his family and business connections and his personal and political travels. George and Barbara's legendary Christmas card list was testimony that they never forgot anyone they had met.

Lest someone tag George as a loser because he had been beaten in two Senate races, I wrote: "Precedent for pres. losing race for Senate—William McKinley." (I later learned that our nation's twenty-fifth president had, indeed, lost two races, but for the House of Representatives in 1882 and 1890, not the Senate.)

Let's be frank about another reason George Bush ran in 1980. He was ambitious. So was I. Despite George's impressive résumé, however, he was a long shot; Ronald Reagan was the clear front-runner for the Republican nomination. But we believed we could win by using a model developed by another long shot, Jimmy Carter, in 1976. And if George made a credible run for the nomination but lost, there was always the possibility that he might be tapped for vice president.

I saw no downside. George was relatively young. He would turn fifty-six in 1980. Even if he lost, he would be only sixty in 1984. Going around the track is very important in presidential politics. The first time out, win or lose, you learn a lot. Besides, you've got to take your shot. Look at Bill Clinton in 1992. Big-name Democrats such as Lloyd Bentsen and Dick Gephardt saw George's 89 percent approval rating after the first Gulf War—the highest in the history of presidential polling—and decided to wait until next time. Clinton jumped in anyway and wound up becoming a two-term president.

After President Ford lost in 1976, George and I talked about taking that shot. On a 1977 trip to China, we quit talking generalities and started talking details. By the end of that year, we had set up a political action committee called the Fund for Limited Government. This was not exactly a campaign vehicle, but it was a legitimate way to raise money to pay for George's travel around the country. On these trips, he spoke about his philosophy of government and strengthened ties with local Republican leaders. By the time he formally declared his candidacy on May 1, 1979, he had already visited forty-two states.

I served as chairman of the fund even before I ran for attorney general. We operated out of a small office on Main Street in what had been the Houston Bank & Trust Company Building. We had a very small staff that included Jennifer Fitzgerald, George's assistant since 1974. Our first two hires were twentysomethings with lots of energy—a young man by the name of Karl Rove and a young woman named Margaret Tutwiler.

No one would ever wonder whatever happened to them. Karl, of course, later became George W. Bush's chief political strategist in runs for the Texas governorship and U.S. presidency. Margaret served as my assistant (her title was deputy assistant to the president for political affairs) when I was President Reagan's White House chief of staff and as assistant secretary for public affairs when I was secretary of the treasury and assistant secretary of state for public affairs when I was secretary of state. In the George W. Bush administration, she served with great distinction as ambassador to Morocco and then as under secretary of state for public diplomacy and public affairs. She is now an executive vice president of the New York Stock Exchange. To this day, I consider her one of my most loyal and capable advisers. She has incredibly sensitive political antennae and an uncanny feel for the way things will play in the press and with the public.

George and I got things going in earnest after my return from Florida. Before the end of 1978, we spooled up the Fund for Limited Government and created an exploratory committee that eventually became the George Bush for President Committee. We also started raising money. And we paid courtesy calls on both Gerald Ford and Ronald Reagan to advise them of George's intentions.

President Ford and George had always gotten along very well, and I still had great respect for the former president. "If you don't run, I would like to help George," I told him. He said he was uncertain of his plans, but he released me to work for my friend. Former Governor

Reagan was very friendly and thanked us for coming out to tell him of George's plans. He was noncommittal about whether he would run, but we believed he would.

This was not my first contact with Ronald Reagan. We first met— very briefly—when he spoke at a 1972 Nixon for President event I organized in Houston. Four years later, we crossed paths in the fight for the nomination during the primary season, and when he helped President Ford in the general election. I fondly remember one exchange we had. I was in my office at the President Ford Committee headquarters when Pete Roussel came running in.

"Bake," he said, "there's a guy on the phone who wants to talk with you. He says he's Governor Reagan."

"He's some kook, just get rid of him," I replied. (Campaigns get a lot of strange calls.)

"He really sounds like the governor," Pete said.

"Well, you don't think he'd be calling me, do you?"

"No, I don't. But it sure sounds like him."

So I picked up the phone. "Hello?"

"Howard?"

It was indeed Reagan, but he was trying to reach a different Baker—the senator from Tennessee, Howard Baker. Over the years, Howard and I became good friends. In the early eighties, my son Jamie worked on his staff when Howard was Senate majority leader. And this wasn't the last time someone confused Howard and me. We refer to each other as "O.B."—Other Baker.

In 1978, Reagan helped me campaign for attorney general. He headlined a fund-raiser in Lubbock at which we auctioned off hunting and fishing equipment.

George Bush spent more than three hundred days on political travel in 1979. Not me. An effective campaign chairman or manager doesn't need to go out on the road very much. Indeed, he shouldn't. His job is to plan the travel, name a good advance team for each visit, help organize the candidate's speeches and public statements, and manage the campaign finances—in short to administer the operation. It's grunt work, but it's necessary grunt work. It frees the candidate to be the candidate. (David Bates, a fine young man from Houston, traveled with George and did a first-class job.)

To better manage the campaign, I moved to the Washington area in January 1980. Susan and little Mary Bonner later joined me in a rented home in Alexandria, Virginia. (The other kids were either away in college or stayed in Houston for the time being.) I didn't immediately take a leave of absence from Andrews Kurth, but I did significantly reduce my partnership share. This resulted in my foregoing much of what I otherwise would have had of the largest payday in the firm's history—a big fee for fighting off ambitious tax collectors, spurious wills, and wannabe heirs to save the Howard Hughes estate for family members in Houston.

Running the primary campaign for a little known, underfinanced long shot would prove to be very different from running the general election campaign for a sitting president. The 1976 Carter model looked nothing like the 1976 Ford model. Still, there are certain characteristics common to all successful campaigns, the most important of which is organization.

The first step was to get the right people in place. George and I recruited his old Houston friend Bob Mosbacher to be finance chairman. Bob, who had served in the same role for President Ford's campaign, gave us instant credibility with Republican insiders and helped immensely as I recruited the rest of our core staff, most from the Ford campaign. Bob Teeter, Ford's pollster, joined us. So, too, did three talented operatives: David Keene, a dyed-in-the-wool conservative who had worked for John Sears; Rich Bond, a young Bush loyalist; and Pete Teeley, a very effective press aide for New York's liberal senator Jacob Javits, who had himself campaigned for President Ford. David served as political director, Rich was field director, and Pete was our press person. Others with the very good team we put together were David Sparks, Bill McInturff, Susan Morrison, Fred Bush, Joe Hagen, Jonathan Miller, Emily Ford, Alixe Glenn, Mary Ashmun, Rob Quartel, Tom Lias, and Betty Green.

It was not surprising that we were able to attract such good people. The American public may not have known or appreciated George Bush at the outset of the campaign, but he was well known and well liked by Republican insiders. They appreciated his service to the party and the nation, and knew that Ford also liked and trusted him.

Most of the other candidates would have been happy to have had these folks. In addition to Reagan and Connally, Senate Minority Leader Howard Baker, Senator Bob Dole, and Representatives John Anderson and Phil Crane joined the race. Although George often noted in his speeches that labels were for cans, not candidates, the consensus was that Reagan, Connally, Dole, and Crane were the conservatives, and Bush and Howard Baker the moderates.

At the beginning, George was an "asterisk in the polls"—a candidate with numbers so microscopic that they did not even show up in the polls. When he later cracked the polls, the campaign staff made some celebratory lapel pins that trumpeted our number, "3%."

As chairman of the RNC, George had inevitably bruised his share of GOP egos, but he also made a lot of friends and established valuable contacts. These friends and contacts helped us raise money and set up organizations in the critical caucus and primary states—particularly the early contests in Iowa and New Hampshire. Our strategy was to do so well in these venues that the cluttered seven-candidate field would quickly be reduced to two—Ronald Reagan and George Bush.

New Hampshire, historic site of the first primary of the season, had long been a make-or-break state. Until 1976, Iowa had not; candidates paid little attention to the state's caucuses, even though they came before New Hampshire's primary.

Jimmy Carter changed that. While opponents Birch Bayh, Fred Harris, Morris Udall, and Sargent Shriver focused on New Hampshire, the lesser-known governor from Georgia worked ceaselessly back and forth across the plains of Iowa. His unexpected victory there gave him momentum in New Hampshire. We knew an Iowa win would have the same effect for Bush.

Looking at the glass as half full instead of half empty—an essential trait for politicians—we believed George's low rank in the early polls was an advantage, not a disadvantage. If he won or even made strong showings early on, he would exceed expectations. In politics—and in governance, too—the name of the game is to do "better than expected." That's why a long shot who scores a strong second can sometimes win more press attention than a better-performing front-runner. In 1968, for instance, President Johnson polled the most votes in New Hampshire's Democratic primary, but his primary opponent, antiwar candidate Senator Eugene McCarthy, won the headlines by doing better than anticipated.

How does a little-known candidate become better known? Some Bush backers thought we should work the major media markets to win face time on television. This is what Connally and Howard Baker did. I disagreed. As I told a reporter early in the campaign, "To cure the name-identification problem . . . you have to win early, the same way Jimmy Carter did, and you can't win those early ones by standing in the lobby of the Waldorf-Astoria in New York."

Ronald Reagan liked to joke that George spent more days in Iowa than he, Reagan, had spent hours. George was a tireless campaigner. With Rich Bond running our operation on the ground, we scheduled appearances from dawn to dusk—on farms, at factories, in homes, and at rallies.

Retail politics takes time. Despite George's intense effort on the campaign trail (and a complementary wholesale effort: television ads that began airing in Iowa in early October), a November 28–December 1, 1979, poll by the *Des Moines Register* showed we trailed Reagan by 36 points—50 percent to 14 percent. The January 21 caucuses were only seven weeks away, and the front-runner looked unbeatable.

By this time, Maine and Florida had each held presidential "beauty contests." These were merely straw polls in advance of state conventions or primaries, not elections of delegates, but we took them seriously—and most other candidates did, too—as an important forum for trying to beat expectations.

Howard Baker was the favorite in Maine, a state in which Reagan was making no effort. He was also the candidate we had to knock out early because he and George were fishing from the same pond. We quietly engaged a young Maine state legislator named Josie Martin to run an under-the-radar effort. She did a masterful job, and in early November 1979, George shocked everyone by beating Baker in Maine. Several days later Reagan won the Florida straw poll convincingly, a blow to Connally, who had invested heavily there. Howard Baker and John Connally never recovered from these early knockdowns in straw polls for which no delegates were at stake.

Each party was to hold a debate in Iowa the first week in January. The much-anticipated Democratic showdown between President Carter and Teddy Kennedy never materialized. Citing the Iranian hostage crisis, the president refused to leave the White House. This put the spotlight on the GOP debate. We, too, had a no-show. On the advice of campaign manager John Sears, Reagan passed, the only Republican to do so.

During the final week, we sent out about *one million* pieces of mail and made thousands of telephone calls. None of our opponents matched this effort.

One hundred six thousand Republicans attended the caucuses, far more than ever before. The final preference vote was stunning: Bush upset Reagan, a candidate who had been running for president since 1968, a man who four years earlier had come close to wresting the nomination away from a sitting president. The count: Bush 33,530 (31.6 percent), Reagan 31,348 (29.5 percent). "Hell," said Charlie Black, one of Reagan's political operatives, "I didn't know it was gonna be a *primary.*"

In the afterglow of victory, an ebullient George Bush announced that he now had the "Big Mo"—momentum—heading into New

Hampshire. The weekly newsmagazines gave him extensive coverage, and dozens more reporters now clamored to travel on our rented campaign plane, an old nineteen-passenger turboprop Fairchild. (Unlike some other candidates, we never raised enough money to get a state-of-the-art airplane. For a long time George flew coach in commercial aircraft.)

George flew ahead in the polls, too. He had been down 19 points to Reagan in New Hampshire. Suddenly he was 6 points ahead. In the Puerto Rico primary, he whipped Howard Baker by 60 to 37 percent. He also took the lead in Florida (for a time) and built up sizable leads in Massachusetts and Illinois.

Still, as George has since acknowledged, the Big Mo boast was unfortunate because it raised expectations too high. We had every reason to be excited about the win in Iowa, but Reagan had hardly campaigned and we had barely beaten him. One week after the caucuses, *Wall Street Journal* reporter James Perry praised George's "organization and hard work." But, he added, "post-Iowa, Mr. Bush is so confident that he verges on cockiness." Cockiness is bad news for political candidates, and verging on it is nearly as bad as going all the way.

My first big opportunity to lower expectations came at a Sperling Breakfast shortly after Iowa. With the help of Pete Teeley, I jotted down some talking points for this meeting with the Washington press, including these:

> We would like to win New Hampshire and will do everything possible to do so. However, the reality is that N.H. is one of Ronald Reagan's strongest states. Combine that factor with the all-out efforts of Howard Baker and even John Anderson and you realize how difficult it will be. . . .

> After all the work that George Bush put into Iowa . . . his reaction to his victory was one of elation. It is a human quality that all of us have at one time or another. . . . Frankly, that was a week ago. The realities

are that he still remains an underdog, and he and the entire campaign staff realize that.

As we lowered expectations for New Hampshire, we also wanted to raise the public's image of George as a man of substance—the president you wouldn't have to train. In Iowa we had answered the question "George who?" Now, in New Hampshire, we had to answer, "George why?" We also wanted to stress the age difference between Bush (fifty-five at the time) and Reagan (sixty-nine). Our campaign literature featured pictures of George jogging, and he frequently went out for runs with the media in tow.

Teeter's polls showed that George needed to build a substantive base, to give voters a reason to back him other than the fact that he had won in Iowa. Bob, David Keene, and I all told George that he should be more specific on the issues. He wasn't quite as responsive as we hoped. After the campaign, George would tell reporters Jack Germond and Jules Witcover, "There was a feeling, well, now you've got to be more substantive, and I would argue with them: I think I am being substantive, I'm answering questions every day.... I just didn't see it. I'll readily concede at this point I may have been wrong. But I didn't feel any great need to do something different."*

The New Hampshire debates offered all seven candidates an opportunity to be substantive. I will wager, however, that few Americans remember the issues discussed at those events. What many do remember, however, is the following exchange between Reagan and moderator Jon Breen in Nashua on Saturday, February 23—three days before the primary. Reagan and Bush had agreed to a one-on-one debate that evening, but when Reagan took the stage, he argued that all candidates should be allowed to participate.

---

*Germond and Witcover's campaign journal, *Blue Smoke and Mirrors,* helped me recall a number of events from the 1980 campaign, as did George Bush's book, *Looking Forward.*

BREEN: Turn Mr. Reagan's microphone off.

REAGAN: I'm paying for this microphone, Mr. Green [*sic*].

Some observers believe this was the turning point in the campaign, that those seven words won the nomination for Reagan. That may be an exaggeration, but there is no question that it created momentum for him that was more real and sustainable than our Big Mo. And while all credit is due to Reagan for seizing the moment, I have to admit that we made our share of mistakes in New Hampshire.

Nashua was the second debate. Three days earlier all candidates had met in Manchester for a forum sponsored by the League of Women Voters. By this time, Reagan had pulled even with George in the polls. Stunned by the Iowa results, he was now campaigning with purpose and energy. Reagan also had the support of William Loeb, influential publisher of the state's largest newspaper, the *Manchester Union Leader*. George, an "oil man from Texas," was a "phony candidate" pushed by "the entire Eastern Establishment, the Rockefellers, and all the other power interests in the East," he thundered. Most viewers thought Reagan did better than George and the other five candidates in the Manchester debate, and by the twenty-third the race was no longer even. According to most polls, Reagan now held a double-digit lead. He was beginning to solidify his base, which was far larger than George's.

Although we were now trailing, we were excited by the prospect of the Nashua debate. This was to be Bush vs. Reagan, *mano a mano*. Our strategy from the beginning had been to engineer a two-candidate race. Still, it had not been our idea to leave the other candidates out. Jerry Carmen, Reagan's New Hampshire chairman, first broached the idea of a two-candidate debate. Hugh Gregg, our state chairman, quickly persuaded the *Nashua Telegraph* to sponsor the event. Why would the Reagan forces want to anoint George as their only serious challenger? Carmen later explained that he believed the debate would cut George down to size.

The other five contenders were not happy to be excluded. Dole complained to the Federal Election Commission (FEC) that the *Telegraph* was, in effect, giving the two invited candidates an illegal campaign contribution. The FEC agreed. When the Reagan camp then suggested that the two candidates split the cost, $1,750 each, Gregg refused, and those of us running the national campaign went along with him. This was a huge mistake.

The Reagan camp, having paid all the costs, then set an ambush, secretly telling the other candidates that if they came to Nashua, they might be included. Everyone showed up except Connally. He was going for broke in South Carolina. When Dole, Baker, Anderson, and Crane filed onto the stage of the Nashua High School auditorium as the debate was to begin, the majority of the 2,500 in the audience applauded. George and the *Telegraph*'s Breen stuck to their guns, however: as previously agreed, this was to be a two-man, not a six-man, forum.

As Reagan began to explain why he wanted to include the other candidates, Breen called for technicians to turn off his microphone. That's when Reagan hit it out of the ballpark.

The debate proceeded without the other challengers. As they left the stage, an angry Bob Dole came up to me and poked me in the chest. "Jim Baker," he said, "you'll regret this." (I worked very closely and effectively with Dole when I was chief of staff and in my cabinet posts. We were, and are, friends.)

Matters didn't get any better later. As Teeley told George a couple of days later, "The bad news is that the media are playing up the confrontation. The good news is that they're ignoring the debate, and you lost that, too."

Reagan had indeed "paid for this microphone," and we paid dearly for getting ourselves in a position where it mattered. His numbers rocketed. On primary day, he took 49.6 percent, Bush got 22.7 percent, and Howard Baker ran third with 12.1 percent. As I said, a candidate and a campaign manager learn a lot by going around the track that first time.

If there was a silver lining to New Hampshire, it was this: Howard Baker, John Anderson, and the others did even worse than we did. A week later, George rebounded to capture the Massachusetts primary. That same evening Reagan won Vermont. Baker, who finished poorly in each of these contests, dropped out. Connally was done four days later when Reagan crushed him in South Carolina.

Anderson held on longer. By finishing second in both Massachusetts and Vermont on March 4, he exceeded expectations and drew press attention away from the victors. His continued presence helped us to a certain degree because it made it more difficult for Reagan to paint George as the candidate of the left. But in the end, it hurt us worse than it hurt Reagan, because Anderson drew moderates who would otherwise have been more likely to vote for George.

Nineteen-eighty marked the first time I led the campaign of a candidate trying to win his party's nomination. When I had assumed the chairmanship of the Ford effort, he was already the party's choice. What does a campaign leader do from headquarters while his candidate is on the road during the primary season?

In addition to running the demanding day-to-day operation, I regularly offered George my counsel. A memo I sent him two days after Massachusetts and Vermont, "Reaction to March 4 Primary Results," is typical.

> You should be careful to stick to your position on Ford's statement that Reagan cannot win in November—i.e., you don't agree with that, but [you do believe] you would be a better candidate with a better chance to win.
>
> You should not refer to Anderson's showings in Massachusetts and Vermont as freakish or aberrations. This makes you look petty. It wouldn't hurt to even congratulate him on a good showing and [say] that it remains to be seen if he can do as well in states where the voting is primarily by Republicans, as it is in the vast majority of states.

I also coordinated George's campaign appearances. He was particularly effective on a series of campaign television broadcasts called "Ask George Bush." An April 8 memo to eleven members of our campaign staff offers a glimpse of the logistics for these events. For the four "Ask George Bush" telecasts in Pennsylvania, I spelled out everyone's duties. The goal was always to leave as little to chance as possible. We wanted a rested and prepared George Bush to meet a candidate-friendly audience that would ask candidate-friendly questions:

> John Morgan . . . is responsible for the buying of all required [television] airtime (after checking with me regarding cost).
>
> Red Caveney and Bob Goodwin, working with Dave Sparks, are responsible for securing the four locations . . . and all advance work.
>
> Each lead advance man . . . is responsible for lining up five or six articulate members of the audience to carry the Q&A at his event. Questions will be restricted to non-press members of the audience.
>
> Dave Gergen is responsible for writing the opening and closing remarks for George Bush for each telecast.
>
> Margaret Tutwiler is responsible for seeing that five hours are blocked out prior to each telecast for the following: one hour staff briefing on local issues; one hour jogging; one hour on site with [our television consultant] Bill Carruthers; and two hours off.

After Iowa, we had won only in Puerto Rico, Massachusetts, the District of Columbia, Maine, and Connecticut, but by late April all major candidates except Reagan and Bush had dropped out, and Pennsylvania offered the two-man matchup we had been looking for. We put everything we had into the April 22 primary—that's where the campaign charged that Reagan's plan to stimulate the economy with a tax cut was "voodoo economics"—and came away with a solid victory in the popular vote. Unfortunately, thanks to an odd "blind voting" system in that state, Reagan won more delegates and added to his commanding lead.

The conventional wisdom was that the loss in New Hampshire had put George off his game for a while. Perhaps. Again, this was his first trip around the track. By contrast, Reagan had run for president in both 1968 and 1976.

George is about the most competitive human being I have ever known. He does not like to lose, but as state after state went for Reagan, George never hung his head. Instead, he displayed the same determination he had shown at age eighteen, when instead of heading straight from prep school to Yale, he became a naval aviator in World War II.

Everything came together on May 20 in Michigan. I turned on the television that night expecting George's 57 to 32 percent landslide there to be the lead story, but ABC and CBS had a different take. They proclaimed George the winner in Michigan all right, but the big news, they said, was that by winning Oregon, Reagan had collected more than the 998 delegates needed for the nomination.

Three delegate-rich states—New Jersey, Ohio, and California—would hold primaries in two weeks on June 3. Reagan was way ahead in his home state, but George was strong in the other two. If the arithmetic was right, however—and it seemed to be—even if George won both New Jersey and Ohio, Reagan would still win the nomination. Now what?

We needed to raise about $500,000 to challenge in California. In light of the delegate projections, should we keep fighting? Could we? It would be "goddamn tough" to raise the money in California, I told reporters. At the same time, George told the *Washington Post* that without sufficient funds to contest California, campaigning in Ohio and New Jersey "might be an irrelevancy."

Washington Post staff writers Bill Peterson and David Broder reported that I said we were closing down operations in California. They quoted me as follows: "If you can't do California, then you can't argue to people that you still have a shot [at the nomination] in terms of the numbers. And once you concede that, why do you stay in?"

If I had it to do over again, I would have chosen my words more carefully. I didn't think through all the ways my remarks might be interpreted. It was obviously not my intention to throw in the towel. Only the candidate could do that. Nor was I trying to pressure George himself to call it quits. I was just answering questions honestly and being realistic about our prospects. In New Jersey, however, reporters were telling George, "Baker says you don't have anything going in California. Does this mean you're dropping out?"

George was furious, and I don't blame him. He wanted to know exactly what I had said. I had only talked about not having enough money on hand to compete in California, but I shouldn't have done it, I admitted, because it gave the impression that we had no choice but to pull the plug. The reality, of course, is that George had to decide soon whether to stay or go, but I hadn't done him any favor by talking so openly about our rocky financial position.

George had done a remarkable job in transforming himself from the pollsters' asterisk into the only legitimate challenger left standing. He had won Iowa and seven other contests. "The remarkable thing about Bush's candidacy is not that it failed, but that it kept going as long as it did," the *Post*'s Peterson wrote. I agree. And because it had kept going, George would be the only candidate besides Reagan with a significant number of delegates at the convention. This meant he had a good shot at becoming the party's vice presidential nominee.

Candidates for president should never create the impression that they are really running for vice president or would be happy to end up in second place. We had carefully followed this rule. It wasn't that difficult because George always said privately that he wasn't sure if he was interested in being vice president.

I now told George that it was time to decide and that I thought he would blow any chance of getting on the ticket if he ran a hopeless campaign much longer. Relations between the Bush and Reagan camps were already strained. Each candidate had tried to observe Reagan's Eleventh Commandment, *Thou shalt not speak ill of fellow Republi-*

cans, but opponents in a two-way race invariably rub each other the wrong way.

George decided to return to Houston to think about what to do. He talked at length with family members, close friends, and senior campaign staff. As I remember, senior consultant Vic Gold, Dave Keene, and I argued that he should withdraw. His family resisted. Neither they nor George wanted to disappoint supporters in Ohio and New Jersey. Nick Brady, who was running the operation in New Jersey, believed George could still win his state. Why not try to strengthen George's hand by picking up the delegates there and in Ohio?

For what? I asked. "You're the only person at the convention who's going to have any delegates," I said. "They have to start thinking who they're going to run with, and the longer you hang in if you don't have a mathematical chance of winning, the more you're going to hurt your chances." It went like that all weekend.

On the campaign airplane, Kenny Rogers's song "The Gambler" was sometimes played on the public address system. George and others had often joined the chorus, "You got to know when to hold 'em, know when to fold 'em." It's hard for a campaign manager to tell a candidate to fold 'em, particularly when that candidate is as competitive as George Bush, but I did not back down. On May 26, George announced he would stop campaigning and throw his support to Reagan. "I'm an optimist," he said, "but I also know how to count to 998."

George was a logical pick for vice president, but he was not Reagan's first choice. Nevertheless, he held a good hand. What other candidate had comparable delegate and party support at the convention, or a perfect résumé to balance the ticket?

At the convention, however, the answer switched from George Bush to a most surprising possibility, Gerald Ford. George's future suddenly depended on whether a former president might accept the role of vice president or, as Walter Cronkite suggested on the air, a "copresidency."

My future looked even more uncertain. I had managed two hard-fought battles to deny Ronald Reagan his party's nomination—one successful, the other not. I'm a realist, and realistically there was no room for James A. Baker, III, in the Reagan campaign or a Reagan presidency. It looked like time for me to fold 'em, too.

"I WANT TO TALK TO YOU BEFORE YOU GO BACK TO TEXAS"

GEORGE H. W. BUSH is nothing if not likable. Yet it has been reported that when the 1980 primary season ended, Ronald Reagan was not happy with George and did not want to select him as the vice presidential nominee. Let me set the record straight: *This is true.* At that moment, Reagan's preferred candidate for running mate was ABB—Anybody But Bush.

Why? After gracefully withdrawing from the presidential race and throwing his support to Reagan, George seemed the obvious choice. He was a proven vote-getter, the only other candidate who would arrive at the mid-July convention in Detroit with a significant number of delegates. He had a superb record of government service. As a Connecticut Yankee who had relocated to Texas, he balanced the ticket geographically, and he was perceived to be more moderate, politically, than Reagan. Selecting him would give the ticket credibility with undecided voters in the middle. But as Reagan biographer Lou Cannon writes, the governor thought George lacked spunk because he didn't stand up for himself in the school auditorium during the fight over whether to allow the other Republican contenders to debate.* The Bush campaign also lost points when it used the label "voodoo economics" for the policies that would later be known as Reaganomics.

"Lacked spunk"? George joined the Navy straight out of prep school, won his wings at eighteen, and flew fifty-eight combat missions. He parachuted out of a burning aircraft and was rescued by a U.S. submarine. He won the Distinguished Flying Cross. In business, he took the risks of entrepreneurship and started a thriving company. His résumé in politics and public service was replete with tough, high-profile positions. (I've listed his offices often enough in this book and won't do it again here.) Most recently, of course, he had entered the 1980 race as an overwhelming underdog and emerged as Reagan's only serious contender.

But at that time, these facts about the man seemed to matter little. Aware that the party's nominee held him in relatively low regard, both George and I thought he probably didn't stand much chance of winning a spot on the November ballot. We were even less hopeful when we learned that several prominent Republicans and members of the Reagan inner circle were lobbying for themselves or other strong candidates. Nevada Senator Paul Laxalt, one of Reagan's best friends and most ardent supporters, wanted the job. Senator Howard Baker and Congressman Jack Kemp were also apparently in the running. And Henry Kissinger, Alan Greenspan, Bryce Harlow, and others (including, it was rumored, the GOP chairman Bill Brock) pushed their own ABB candidate—the president many of them had once served, Gerald Ford.

Ford? To be sure, Republican polling revealed that a Reagan-Ford ticket in 1980 had the potential to be as appealing and successful as a Ford-Reagan dream ticket might have been in 1976. But the Ford crowd had another motive, the one everyone in politics shares:

---

*Cannon covered the White House for the *Washington Post.* His biographies—*Reagan: His Rise to Power* and *President Reagan: The Role of a Lifetime*—were excellent sources for researching this book.

ambition. If they could return their man to Washington, even in the number-two position, they would enhance their own chances of returning to power and influence.

At first, the odds of seeing Reagan-Ford bumper stickers appeared remote. The contentious battle for the 1976 GOP nomination had left both of these fine men with scars. They were anything but close. Moreover, Gerald Ford had been *president of the United States,* the most powerful man in the world. Traditionally, vice presidents were far removed from real power. The absurdity of having a former president come back as No. 2 became clear when I asked myself how I would address Ford. "Hello, Mr. President–Vice President"? Or was it, "Hello, Mr. Vice President–President"?

On his way to the convention, Gerald Ford stopped over in Omaha. By coincidence, I was there for a corporate board meeting, and he offered me a ride to Detroit. I hadn't heard any talk about his being considered for vice president, and we certainly did not discuss the subject. The flight was too short and the plane too crowded for much more than pleasantries. Even if we had been alone and I had known what was coming, however, I would not have broached the subject. Given my role in George's campaign, that would have been inappropriate.

But now, George's future was very much up in the air, and so was mine. Shortly after George withdrew in late May, I received a call from Reagan press secretary Lyn Nofziger. He asked if I were interested in serving as political director for the Reagan campaign.

As I have noted, titles are important. I did not presume to demand the position I had in 1976—campaign chairman. Governor Reagan had installed his trusted friend Bill Casey in that capacity. But for me to have accepted the title "political director" would have been quite a comedown for someone who had managed the campaign of a sitting president in the last election. I told Lyn I was interested in helping Reagan, but not in that capacity.

My role was still unresolved when I met with Casey in Dallas in late June. He was a Wall Street lawyer and former Securities and Exchange Commission chairman, but he hardly looked the part. Success may have gone to his head, but not to his wardrobe. When he wasn't rumpled, he was disheveled. Still, people paid attention when he spoke. They had to; he was a chronic mumbler. We talked about how to organize Reagan's effort against President Carter and how I might help the campaign.

At that time Jimmy Carter was 10 points behind Ronald Reagan in the polls. The soft economy, foreign policy failures (most notably the Iran hostage crisis), and the president's primary battles with Ted Kennedy were taking their toll. "But if anyone in your organization is wearing rose-colored glasses," I told Casey, "they're making a mistake. You can win this election, but it's going to be close."

I told him he was up against some tough, hard-nosed, capable politicians—accomplished gut-fighters who would do whatever they thought it would take to elect their guy. For all his problems, Carter had one big advantage, incumbency. He also had a campaign team that had been around the track. "They've got their act together," I said.

Governor Reagan had an advantage, too, one the Ford campaign did not have in 1976. As the party out of power, the GOP's convention would come first. "This gives us a head start in organizing and gearing up for the fall," I said.

"But don't expect to get much sleep until the election is over," I told Casey. "You're going to find incredible demands made on you and your time. You won't find enough hours in the day to do all you have to do." This is where I thought I could help. We discussed ways I could make his job easier, including by serving as a deputy chairman. He wasn't ready to make a decision, so we agreed to talk again later.

After we met, I sent him drafts of an organizational structure and budget based on our 1976 campaign, along with more ideas about strategy. He had not solicited this material. I wanted to help, but if the material also happened to remind him of my experience and expertise, so much the better. When the convention began on Monday, July 14, however, my role was still uncertain.

Reagan did not reveal his choice for vice president before arriving in Detroit. If he had, he would have removed all suspense from the proceeding. I'm all for injecting a bit of drama to win votes. That said, I offer this warning to any candidate who waits until the convention to name a running mate: make sure you have thoroughly vetted your choice (and that the press has done so, too) before making the announcement. We did not do that in 1988, the year George beat Michael Dukakis, and it was a mistake.

President Ford and I went our separate ways after we reached Detroit on Saturday, July 12. He stayed at the same hotel where Governor Reagan was headquartered, the Detroit Plaza. I joined George in the block of rooms we had reserved at the Hotel Ponchartrain. The Bush party was relatively small—Barbara and other family members, spokesman Pete Teeley, some other loyal campaign staffers, and a few friends, such as Dean Burch, an old Goldwater hand who had served in the Nixon and Ford administrations. Governors, other elected officials from the primary states where George had done well, and other prominent Bush delegates stopped by from time to time to pay their respects and talk about the one and only topic at conventions, politics.

President Ford's opening-day speech roused the delegates, pleased Governor Reagan, and created momentum for the possibility that Ford might be offered the number-two spot. This set off a series of closed-door meetings that did not conclude, literally, until the eleventh hour Wednesday evening.

Only the insiders know exactly how the Reagan-Ford courtship played out. Later reports said Bill Casey and Ed Meese headed a small group of Reagan loyalists who sat down with a Ford team led by Henry Kissinger and Alan Greenspan. One thing is clear, however: the talks would never have happened without a green light from Reagan.

Meanwhile, back at the Ponchartrain, we were not privy to the private meetings, but rumors were flying. Everyone claimed to have the inside story, so we hesitated to believe anyone. Besides, what could we do? About all George had scheduled during these long hours were a few delegation drop-bys, a duty he shared with other party luminaries, to motivate the troops for the fall campaign. On Tuesday morning, for instance, he met with the California delegation. Then it was back to the hotel to hurry up and wait.

On Wednesday evening, all hell broke loose. In an interview with Walter Cronkite, Ford laid out the general conditions under which he might be willing to take the second spot. He said that he would need "reasonable assurances" that his role would be substantive rather than ceremonial. Cronkite said this sounded like he was proposing a "co-presidency." Ford never used this word, but his failure to correct the anchorman led most viewers to believe that was exactly what he meant. By some later accounts, the former president's team had proposed that he would chair the National Security Council and have veto power over some appointments, which—if not exactly a copresidency—was pretty far down the road in that direction.

"As I watched that interview," Reagan wrote later, "it really hit me that we had some major problems with the idea: *Wait a minute,* I remember thinking, *this is really two presidents he's talking about.*" Still, negotiations continued as Wednesday evening wore on.

While Ford's remarks gave Reagan pause, they brought the floor alive. It now seemed that the dream ticket might soon be a reality. Reagan, the rumor went, would come to the convention center to make the announcement.

Meantime, George *was* on his way to the hall. He had one of the coveted prime-time speaking slots. He delivered a powerful speech, but the Ford story overshadowed his appearance.

Our mood in the Bush suite was not festive. Like those on the convention floor, we awaited the announcement of the once improbable, now seemingly inevitable, Reagan-Ford ticket.

Unbeknownst to us (and the delegates), the deal was not done. Reagan and Ford representatives were still trying to work out the details. Unable to reach agreement on the makeup of Ford's staff and its role, the parties broke off negotiations. Sometime between 10:30 and 11:30 P.M., Ford visited Reagan's suite. It's not going to work, he said. Reagan agreed.

I was not there for that meeting, obviously, but I was present for what happened next. Shortly after the Ford visit to Reagan, the phone rang in George's suite. I answered. Drew Lewis, who had been President Ford's man in Pennsylvania in 1976 and was now working for Reagan, was on the line. "Jim," he said, "Governor Reagan would like to speak to Ambassador Bush."

Was this a courtesy call to tell George that Reagan had selected Ford? Or was it the call we had been hoping for? Nobody was sure, although most in the suite suspected that the news would be bad.

After a brief exchange of pleasantries, George was silent as Reagan spoke. The tension built until George finally turned our way, smiled, and gave us the thumbs-up.

During the conversation, Reagan had asked George two questions, one general and one specific: Can you support my policy positions? And, can you support my position on abortion?

In his campaign literature, George had spelled out his position on that sensitive issue. "I am personally opposed to abortion. I am also opposed to a constitutional amendment that would override the Supreme Court decision, because there is a need to recognize and provide for exceptional cases—rape, incest, or to save the life of a mother. I oppose federal funding of abortion, with the exceptions noted above."

George and Reagan had a fundamental disagreement over whether to overturn *Roe v. Wade* with a constitutional amendment, but they agreed on several points. Both opposed abortion, personally. They also accepted that it was justified to save the life of the mother. (George would add cases of rape or incest.) And they both opposed federal funding for abortions, except in those cases.

Some of Reagan's more zealous backers may have hoped he would select a running mate whose positions on abortion and other social issues were identical to his own. The reality, however, is that just about the only way a presidential nominee and vice presidential nominee who had run against each other in the primaries could be in complete agreement on everything would be through cloning. The best No. 1 can realistically hope for, and unequivocally demand, is that No. 2 supports his policies. If in good conscience George could not have answered Reagan's two questions, "Yes, sir," he should have (and, I'm sure, would have) declined the nomination.

To put an end to the Ford rumors, Governor Reagan then went immediately to the convention hall to introduce his running mate. This broke the tradition that nominees were not supposed to appear on the podium until they were ready to give their acceptance speeches. "The roof almost came off," Reagan wrote later. "As George and I stood there together, it was almost as if we were putting the party back together again."

The next day, not surprisingly, the press honed in on their differences, real and imagined. This was to be expected. The two candidates had offered competing visions in the primaries. Any alliance between former adversaries is bound to raise questions. The goal now was to de-emphasize the issues that divided them and emphasize the ones on which they agreed.

When reporters asked George to state his positions on the Equal Rights Amendment (ERA) and abortion, he answered with language that could not be used to drive a wedge between the running mates or make news: "My view is that the big issues, the major issues in the fall . . . are going to be economic and foreign affairs. I oppose abortion and I'm in favor of equal rights." Note that he didn't say he supported the ERA, which Reagan opposed; he supported equal rights, as did Reagan. Nor did he say that he opposed the constitutional amendment on abortion that Reagan favored; he said, quite honestly, that he opposed abortion.

"I'm not going to get nickeled and dimed to death by detail," he said as the questions continued, adding that he would not "get bogged down in . . . permitting you to accentuate the differences with the governor during the campaign, which have been minimal."

The press also zeroed in on the point that George Bush, not Gerald Ford, was standing beside Ronald Reagan. "Isn't it clear then, Governor, that Mr. Bush was your second choice?"

"I think the situation is unique."

George was also asked if he was the number-two choice for the number-two spot. "It's unique," he echoed. "What difference does it make? It's irrelevant. I'm here."

In 2004, a perhaps even more "unique" situation arose when Democratic presidential nominee John Kerry spoke to Republican Senator John McCain about running as his vice president. After McCain declined, Kerry and the man he did choose, Senator John Edwards, faced questions similar to those faced by Reagan and Bush.

Would a Kerry-McCain ticket have been effective? Perhaps, because McCain appealed to the independents and ticket splitters who most likely made up most of the undecided voters in 2004. But having said that, it's important to remember that in presidential politics, people vote for the *top* of the ticket. Further, party switchers rarely do well. Case in point: John Connally.

In a brief speech accepting his nomination Thursday night, George endorsed the platform, compared Reagan to Eisenhower, encouraged Democrats and independents to vote Republican, and then got off the stage. This was Reagan's night.

Following a film about his life, the nominee walked onto the podium to a thunderous ovation. "Well, the first thrill tonight was to find myself, for the first time in a long time, in a movie in prime time," he joked.

Reagan hammered campaign themes that would take him to the White House and, afterward, provide a blueprint for his administration—repairing what he called "a disintegrating economy" and "a weakened defense."

"We're taxing ourselves into economic exhaustion and stagnation," he said, "crushing our ability and incentive to save, invest, and produce." The answer: tax cuts and better control of federal spending.

On defense, "the Carter administration lives in a world of make-believe," he charged, citing the Soviet invasion of Afghanistan, the Iranian hostage crisis, increased Soviet military spending, and the general failure of American leadership. His own priority, he said, would be "in working for peace, to ensure that the safety of our people cannot successfully be threatened by a hostile foreign power." "We know only too well that war comes not when the forces of freedom are strong, but when they are weak."

What was even more important than his views on the issues, however, was his soaring rhetoric. "It is impossible to capture in words the splendor of this vast continent which God has granted as our portion of His creation," Reagan said. "There are not words to express the extraordinary strength and character of this breed of people we call Americans." Language like this was balm to the spirit of a nation wounded by Vietnam, Watergate, and a fractured economy.

As the convention ended, it was clear what George would be doing for at least the next three and a half months. My future remained uncertain. Philip Uzielli, a great friend of mine from Princeton who died in August 2001, once told *Time* magazine, "Jimmy gets depressed whenever he faces the prospect of having to return to practicing law. He craves the action." To this charge, I plead guilty.

Reporters on the Reagan plane later fabricated phony book titles and attributed them to figures in the campaign. Showing that they understood my need to be where the action was, the title they picked for me was *Third Choice, The Only Campaign in Town,* by Jim Baker, referring to my serial support for Ford, then Bush, then Reagan. Ouch!

Among the other "books" was *Prospects for Nuclear Disarmament,* by Amy Carter. When people talk about the debate between Amy's father, President Jimmy Carter, and Ronald Reagan in 1980, they generally cite one famous line by each candidate. President Carter's came in response to a question about arms control. "I had a discussion with my daughter Amy the other day before I came here and asked her what the most important issue was," the president said. "She said she thought nuclear weaponry and control of nuclear arms."

Amy Carter had just turned thirteen. Her father's point, I think, was to suggest in an understated and indirect way that Reagan's views on nuclear disarmament scared children—an echo of the infamous "daisy commercial" Democrats used against Goldwater in 1964. What he did instead was feed a delicious straight line to the press, late-night comedians, and Reagan supporters. Remember the "Ask Amy" posters that popped up at rallies?

Reagan's memorable line had the opposite effect on his campaign. When Carter charged that Reagan had opposed legislation to create Medicare, Governor Reagan looked the president in the eye, sighed, and said, "There you go again."

Point. Set. Match.

I remember a different line from that evening of October 28, one uttered about an hour earlier. Governor Reagan and I were in his holding room at the Cleveland Music Hall, just the two of us. In a few minutes, he would take the stage for his only debate with President Carter—an event that could make or break his quest for the presidency. He was calm, almost serene. "Jim," he said as his stage call came near, "would you excuse me a moment. I want to have a word with the Man Upstairs."

I left the room with a deeper understanding of, and respect for, Ronald Reagan. He was, as I would see again and again, a man of faith who very privately, but very genuinely, drew his strength from a higher power. It was an extraordinary privilege to serve him, that night and for the next eight years.

That term of that service began a month or so after the convention. By then, George and I had agreed that, because of my prior general election experience with President Ford, I should work with Reagan, not Bush, if a suitable role and title could be found. Dean Burch would manage George's run for vice president.

Reagan officials told me they wanted me to work in the campaign, but not as a deputy chairman. Apparently Ed Meese, Reagan's long-time adviser and a deputy chairman himself, did not think the new kid on the block should have such an important title. After further conversations with Casey and others, I finally said, "Why don't you just call me a senior adviser and task me as you need to." This was acceptable to Meese. Soon, I was put in charge of debate negotiations and preparation.

The fictitious bibliography compiled by reporters also included a "book" authored by Casey: *The Man Who Never Was*. There actually is a book by that name about a famous ploy by the British military during World War II. This title, however, was meant to suggest that Casey was a clueless campaign leader.

I had some serious problems with Casey in years to come, but it was not fair to portray him as a cipher as a campaign leader. He had replaced John Sears early in the primary season to provide better organization, not strategy. Until Stu Spencer joined the campaign full-time about six weeks after the convention, however, strategy was the problem.

When Stu jumped to the Ford campaign in 1976, he fell out of favor with the Reagan camp. After Reagan got off to a slow start in August and lost his lead in the polls, several of us, including Mike Deaver, began to lobby for Stu's return. More important, Nancy Reagan wanted him back.

It was a great move. Stu hadn't changed at all since we had worked together on the Ford campaign. He still eschewed memos, still wrote most of his ideas on matchbook covers, and still had great political instincts.

In late August, we came up with a good way to use George's foreign policy experience to help the ticket, by sending him to China, where he had served as the U.S. liaison under Ford. The trip got off to a rocky start, however, when Governor Reagan publicly repeated his commitment to strengthening official relations between the United States and Taiwan. This created confusion about whether the Reagan campaign was supporting or undermining the Carter administration's 1979 joint communique between Washington and Peking that recognized the People's Republic of China and acknowledged that Taiwan was part of China. The Chinese government said Reagan had "insulted one billion Chinese people."

Quite naturally, he became angry at the press for picking apart his remarks on China and other issues. Sensing trouble ahead, I finally decided to offer my two cents' worth. In a letter dated September 4, 1980, I wrote, "Dear Governor Reagan:

> You have not asked for these comments and, having managed two presidential campaigns, I am well aware that the one thing a candidate receives too much of is unsolicited advice. However, it is critical that you be elected president . . . and I would not be discharging my obligations to you unless I gave you my advice when I feel strongly about a matter that could affect the outcome of the election.
>
> A general election for president is, of course, far different than a series of primaries. The attention of the entire country is focused upon the process continuously during September and October. The press scrutiny is intense and many times unfair. Each and every word is scrutinized by hordes of press for the slightest mistake. That simply is a fact, a fundamental rule of the game. And, the campaigns have to play the game by this rule.
>
> You are a tremendous campaigner and the best politician with television that I have ever seen. You are also a person of intense conviction and strong intellectual honesty. I happen to share with you a common political philosophy. . . .
>
> However, if you are to achieve a position to put your beliefs into practice, you will have to, for the next sixty days, be extremely careful about every statement which you make.
>
> Further, you have excellent relations with the press. Most of them like you. They do not like Jimmy Carter. This is a great

advantage. The press should not be blamed for picking your statements apart. They did this to Jimmy Carter in 1976 and, again, it is one of the rules of the game. . . .

Your political instincts are good. Your campaign organization is farther along than we were in 1976 and, in my opinion, you are going to win this election. Just remember that for the next sixty days, every word you say will be picked apart, or rather "nitpicked" apart. All you have to do is be aware of that, accept it, and otherwise be yourself.

This was not an easy letter to write. After signing it, I added a postscript by hand: "I've hesitated about sending this because I know you're inundated with advice. However, I'm confident you'll accept it in the spirit in which it is offered." My confidence was well placed. Ronald Reagan was comfortable enough with himself to listen to advice and even criticism from staff members he trusted. He knew the final decision was always his.

It also didn't hurt that on the same day I sent the letter, Spencer began traveling with the governor. From that point forward, the opportunities for on-the-fly, issues-oriented exchanges between the candidate and the media were kept to a minimum. At the same time, Reagan became less critical of the media.

A *Washington Post* poll on September 14 showed that Reagan had pulled even with Carter at 37 percent. John Anderson, running now as an independent, was at 13 percent.

I wrote my September 4 letter from our headquarters in Arlington, Virginia. I was stationed there with Casey, Meese, Bill Timmons, Clif White, and many others. In addition to Stu, Reagan was accompanied on the road by Lyn Nofziger, Mike Deaver, and Martin Anderson, an issues adviser.

My job as debate negotiator began in earnest after Labor Day. Jody Powell, President Carter's press secretary, who was among those with whom I negotiated, once described the process as "bluff and counterbluff, scheming, conniving, and hard-nosed horse trading." A debate negotiator's client, frankly, is his candidate, not the press and not some abstract ideal of how presidential debates should be conducted. The goal of the negotiator is to try to win a format and rules that play to his candidate's strengths and minimize his weaknesses. Staging can be just as important as format. Just as a movie director doesn't want a vertically challenged actor to appear shorter than his leading lady, for instance, a debate negotiator doesn't want his candidate to appear shorter than the opponent.*

Many Reagan advisers doubted he would do well in a debate. They feared that he might misspeak and sound less than presidential. When I came on board, they told me that unless our candidate fell significantly behind in the polls, we would prefer staying out of any debates.

I disagreed. The Great Communicator would do well, I believed. My well-founded show of faith in the candidate was, I think, an important factor in Reagan's later decision to find a major role for me in his administration.

In 1980, the League of Women Voters lacked the presumptive mandate to sponsor presidential debates that the Commission on Presidential Debates now enjoys. The league had, however, sponsored the 1976 Ford-Carter debates. Without consulting the candidates, the organization proclaimed that it would sponsor three presidential debates in 1980.

And what of John Anderson? The league said that he could participate if he averaged at least 15 percent in the major polls. Anderson was hovering around that figure, so it appeared that he would be eligible for the first debate on September 21.

---

*All three of my candidates—Ford, Reagan, and Bush 41—were taller than their opponents, so we always held a bargaining chip on height. Each time, we let the other side adjust the podium, add a riser, or do something else to compensate, but we always got something good in return. I have a short anecdote about the Dukakis negotiation, but I'll save it until later.

The timing of the league's announcement couldn't have come at a better time for us. It shifted press attention from other issues to President Carter's refusal to participate in a debate that included Anderson. Polls showed that the third-party candidate was drawing more voters from Carter than from Reagan, and the president apparently didn't want to give Anderson any greater stature or to expose himself to a two-on-one attack from opponents with the common goal of removing him from office.

President Carter's decision to boycott the first debate was a magnificent gift to our campaign, because the league went ahead with a two-candidate event. I proposed, not totally in jest, that we place an empty chair on stage to symbolize the chief executive's absence. That didn't happen, of course, but the setup offered Ronald Reagan and John Anderson free airtime to explain why they would be better presidents than the one who hadn't bothered to drive forty-five miles from the White House to the Baltimore Convention Center.

Prior preparation was essential to prevent a poor performance. Republican Senator John Warner and his wife at the time, actress Elizabeth Taylor, graciously loaned Governor Reagan their large country estate in Wexford, Virginia, as a base of operations. We turned the garage into a replica of the stage in Baltimore.

Some critics have portrayed Ronald Reagan as an empty suit whose only skill was reading lines. Nothing could be further from the truth. He was a hard worker and a voracious reader who understood the importance of this first debate and did his homework. I generally presented that homework to him in the form of a briefing book prepared by David Gergen, Martin Anderson, and Richard Allen. Nancy Reagan, fiercely protective of her husband, strongly suggested we avoid giving him overly lengthy memos. He was most adept at digesting material that was already reduced to its essence.

We had agreed with the Anderson campaign on a one-hour debate in which each candidate would have two and a half minutes to respond to a panelist's question, then the other candidate would have one minute and fifteen seconds for rebuttal. We found the perfect stand-in to help our candidate practice—a bright young Republican congressman from Michigan who had previously served on Anderson's staff, David Stockman. He joined us at Wexford and did a terrific job in our mock debates. Among the "journalists" asking questions were John Tower, Alan Greenspan, Jeane Kirkpatrick, and Howard Baker.

Casey, Meese, Deaver, Gergen, TV consultant Bill Carruthers, and Frank Hodsoll, an aide from my days at the Commerce Department, took notes and made suggestions. Stockman later wrote about my role in the mock debates. "Jim Baker looked like the efficient production foreman, with a pencil behind his ear," Stockman said. "He cussed a blue streak and told off-color jokes. . . . He had a way of moving things along, of pointing to the ceiling and spinning his arm around in a 360-degree circle, saying, 'Let's go, let's move it.'"

Reagan made his share of mistakes during these run-throughs, as does every candidate in preparing for presidential debates. These mock debates are always harder than the actual ones because the stand-in candidates and panelists ask the toughest questions they can come up with, and the candidate has to work impromptu. That's why we practiced long hours and filmed the sessions for in-depth postmortems. When the night of the debate arrived, Ronald Reagan was confident. So was I.

Both candidates acquitted themselves well and, of course, nobody thought the absent president had won. Anderson set the tone with the very first question of the night.

"What politically unpopular measures are you willing to endorse, push, and stay with that might provide real progress in reducing inflation?" asked Carol Loomis of *Fortune* magazine.

"It seems to me that the people who are watching us tonight . . . are truly concerned about the poor rate of performance of the American economy over the last four years," the congressman replied. "Governor Reagan is not responsible for what has happened over the last four years, nor am I. The man who should be here tonight to respond to those charges chose not to attend."

Teddy White, the legendary chronicler of presidential campaigns, said this debate marked the turning point of the election, but I believe the Carter-Reagan debate in Cleveland just one week before the election was more important. Despite Reagan's solid performance against Anderson, the head-to-head debate between President Carter and Reagan almost didn't materialize because some Reagan advisers still didn't trust our candidate.

Reagan had no fear of debating Carter, but he relied on his advisers to determine whether the event would help the campaign. Many at our headquarters, including the well-respected Dick Wirthlin, still opposed a last-minute face-off against the president. Polling suggested that the election was already going our way, they argued. In their view, a debate couldn't help us much, but it might hurt badly if the governor said something akin to former President Ford's remarks about Soviet domination of Eastern Europe. Stu Spencer and I were among the few advisers in the pro-debate camp.

I didn't think we had done a good enough job defining our candidate. He was still seen by many as a mere actor who could not be trusted with our nation's nuclear arsenal. A good debate would reassure people that he had the intelligence and judgment to be president, we argued. He was also more likable than Carter, and after years in television, he understood the medium better than any other political figure at the time.

Stu and I saw one other advantage. Once debates are announced, they tend to freeze the campaign. It's difficult for a candidate who is trailing to pick up ground while prepping for a debate. Carter, who was slightly behind, probably wouldn't see his numbers move until after a debate—and then, of course, only if he won.

Our campaign's greatest fear was an October surprise that could thaw a frozen campaign in a hurry. Just as Democrats in 2004 thought the incumbent administration might apprehend or kill the terrorist leader Osama bin Laden just before the election, Republicans in 1980 thought the incumbent administration might suddenly make a deal to bring home the fifty-two kidnapped American hostages who had been held by Iranian militants since November 4, 1979. An honorable resolution of the hostage crisis would have been welcomed by all Americans, including candidate Reagan, but there's no doubt that it would have given the sitting president a huge boost. Eleventh-hour resolutions of long-running crises may invite widespread cynicism, but they are almost impossible to challenge politically.

Knowing that the release of the hostages would in all likelihood give President Carter a dramatic lift, we wanted the Carter-Reagan debate to take place as close to the election as possible. This would give our candidate one last chance to make his case. If a release came after the debate, we would be out of luck.

On October 16, both candidates spoke at the annual Al Smith Dinner in New York City. Our man came off as warm and charming. The president didn't. This helped move the no-debate faction among Reagan advisers to consider letting the nation see a side-by-side display of the two candidates' personalities. At a meeting the next morning, the brain trust and the candidate discussed the pros and cons of a two-man debate.

We were already leading in enough states to win the electoral vote, but there were still too many undecideds. Our colleagues finally agreed with Stu and me that if the timing could be worked out to our advantage, a debate could help our candidate.

On October 17, the league invited the two candidates to a debate in Cleveland on October 28. Anderson, who had dropped below 10 percent in the polls, was not invited. We accepted the idea of a two-candidate debate, but reserved judgment on the time and place.

On October 20, Dean Burch, Bill Carruthers, and I met in Washington with representatives from the league and the president's campaign (Jody Powell and my fellow Texan, campaign chairman Bob Strauss). We agreed that the league would pick the moderator and panelists, that the debate would run ninety minutes, and that the format would allow for follow-up questions.

We could not, however, agree upon a date. "We really like November third," I told the press later. "About 10 percent of the people make up their minds on election eve; let them make their decision on the basis of the debate." An election-eve debate could become an American tradition, I suggested.

Carter's representatives pushed for the earliest possible date, October 26. They didn't like the election-eve idea because it wouldn't let candidates correct mistakes before the next day's voting. Perhaps, I countered, but it would also give the media less opportunity to influence voters by declaring a winner. (Remember this was before the proliferation of the cable news channels. The instant analysis we take for granted today was not quite so instant twenty-six years ago.)

Truth be told, I was much less interested in establishing an American tradition than I was in getting the best date (meaning the latest possible date) for my candidate. We met again the next day and compromised. The debate would be in Cleveland on the day the league had originally proposed, October 28.

Reagan again prepared at Wexford. Stockman rejoined us, this time impersonating President Carter. There were a few new faces, too, including the conservative columnist George Will. He served as a mock reporter-panelist. In his columns, George had long made it clear that he supported Reagan, but at the time he did not disclose his role in preparing for the October debate. Another Reagan supporter, William Safire of the *New York Times,* turned down our invitation to help at Wexford. Whether it is proper for a political columnist to assist a candidate without revealing it to his readers, is, I suppose, a matter of conscience or editorial policy. Whatever the answer, it wasn't our problem. We were glad to have George's help.

I must wrestle with my own conscience, however, over something else that happened well before the debate with President Carter had been agreed to. At our campaign headquarters in Arlington, Virginia,

Bill Casey handed me a notebook. I looked it over, saw that it contained debate-briefing material for President Carter (as opposed to strategic or tactical matter), and then passed it on to David Gergen and our debate preparation group. Stockman later said the book helped teach him to answer questions as Carter might. He also said Carter's answers during the debate mirrored the material in the book.

Casey did not tell me how he had come into possession of the book and I did not ask. There were only a few possibilities. Someone in the Carter campaign could have provided it. Someone from our campaign could have stolen it. Or someone outside either campaign, but sympathetic to Reagan, could have found it and passed it on to Casey, perhaps after it was misplaced by a Carter staffer. The first possibility seemed most likely. It was no secret that many people in the Carter administration were dissatisfied with the president.

The story of the briefing book did not become public until 1983, when Laurence Barrett of *Time* magazine mentioned it in his book about the early years of the Reagan administration, *Gambling with History*. "Foul play," said many from the Carter campaign. Congress and the FBI initiated inquiries.

President Reagan and all in his administration, including me, cooperated fully with these investigations of what became known as Debategate. I said that Casey had given me the book and that I had no knowledge of how it had come into his possession.

Casey, who was then director of the CIA, told a different story. He said he did not recall seeing the briefing book and claimed he would have remembered if he had given it to me. (Bill Casey died of brain cancer in 1987. It's enough to say now that his memory was not operating at 100 percent of capacity when he gave those answers.)

At one point there was talk of strapping Casey and me up to lie detectors to determine how the book had come into the campaign's possession. That didn't happen; the investigators settled for affidavits. I was glad. I was telling the truth, but I feared that someone who headed the CIA would know how to game a polygraph examination.

After a yearlong investigation, a House subcommittee published its findings in a May 1984 report that found Casey less than credible and corroborated my version after hearing from an aide whom I had told in 1980 about receiving the material from Casey. (In a separate three-page report several months earlier, the Justice Department said it had not uncovered credible evidence of a crime.) In Washington, D.C., a good reputation can quickly become a bad one. Until the report was released, my credibility and reputation for truth-telling were in question, and that disturbed me.

"Baker was fastidious about propriety," Barrett wrote in his book. I was and still am. As an unnamed White House official would tell Lou Cannon during the investigation: "Here's a person who writes his own $700 check when he has a door cut in his White House office and makes a big deal of reporting every gift." And as President Carter's own campaign manager Bob Strauss said, "But I'll tell you, anything Jim Baker says, I would judge to be true. There isn't anyone in American politics whose ethics I place higher than Jim Baker's."

I wasn't responsible for obtaining the briefing book, and I told the truth. But should I have asked Casey where he got the book? Should I have refused to pass the material on to those preparing Reagan? These are legitimate questions. In hindsight, my answer to both questions is yes.

House Speaker Tip O'Neill and President Reagan were good friends who rarely agreed on the issues. One thing they did agree on, however, was that the briefing book did not change the result of the 1980 election.

Going into the debate, Reagan was slightly ahead. He then won the debate, not because of any prepared answers, but because he made no major mistakes, softened his image on defense issues, and came across as the more appealing candidate.

I admire Jimmy Carter for his faith and sincerity. While I do not agree with all he has done, particularly in lobbying other nations not to support a UN resolution to use force to kick Iraq out of Kuwait in

1990, I believe he has handled his post-presidency well and been a force for good in many ways. At the dedication of the Reagan Library in 1991 and at the 1994 groundbreaking for the James A. Baker III Institute for Public Policy in Houston, his remarks about me offered good evidence that he appreciates the fundamental difference between a political adversary and a personal enemy. Considering how hard I worked to defeat him in 1976 and 1980, I'm very grateful for that. In 2005, I had the pleasure of serving as cochair with him on the highly productive Commission on Federal Election Reform, which recommended a number of very useful ways to improve the administration and security of U.S. elections. (I'll say more about that later.)

The first question to Reagan was exactly the one we needed to defuse concerns about our candidate's call for a U.S. military buildup and a less accommodative stance toward the Soviet Union. "You have been criticized," said Marvin Stone of *U.S. News & World Report,* "for being all too quick to advocate the use of lots of muscle—military action—to deal with foreign crises. Specifically, what are the differences between the two of you on the uses of American military power?"

"I believe with all my heart," Reagan replied, "that our first priority must be world peace, and that the use of force is always and only a last resort when everything else has failed. . . . And to maintain that peace requires strength."

Perfect.

After the debate, polls showed a sharp drop in the percentage of Americans who were concerned that Reagan might lead the nation into war.

"There you go again" was not Reagan's only memorable line that night. Another came in his closing statement. "Are you better off than you were four years ago?" he asked. For too many Americans, unfortunately, the answer was no.

Reagan's margin of victory a week later surprised all of us. He won forty-four states and carried the Electoral College 489–44. The popular vote split 50.5 percent for Reagan, 41 percent for Carter, and 6.6

percent for Anderson. America had embraced the California governor and wanted to give his ideas a chance.

On the day after the election, President-elect Reagan called me in my hotel room at the Century Plaza. "I want to talk to you before you go back to Texas," he said. When I relayed this news to Susan, she broke into tears.

"PRESIDENT REAGAN DOESN'T LIKE YES MEN. WHEN HE SAYS NO, WE ALL SAY NO"

IT WAS TWO DAYS after the 1980 presidential election. I had just walked up to the door of Ronald and Nancy Reagan's home in the Pacific Palisades section of Los Angeles, reluctant to knock. Inside, the next president of the United States was meeting with Bill Casey, Mike Deaver, Ed Meese, and others.

Ronald Reagan had won the election on the strength of his ideas about how to make America a better place. Now he had asked me to serve as his White House chief of staff because he wanted a Washington insider—someone with hands-on experience in our nation's capital—to help him turn those ideas into reality. At this moment, however, I felt much more like an outsider. The other men in the meeting were the president-elect's close friends, two of whom he had relied on for many years. I, on the other hand, was not only a newcomer but also a former adversary who had fought hard, twice, to deny him the presidency. *"What are you doing here?"* I asked myself as I hesitated at the door.

Ronald Reagan quickly spotted me through the window and rescued me from my momentary paralysis. "What are you doing out there, Jim?" he asked with a smile as bright as the California sunshine. "Come on in."

Some of Ronald Reagan's supporters would have been happier if I had stood outside that door for the next eight years. He was their hero. I was the enemy, as they saw it—someone from the dark side, lacking credentials as a loyalist to the man or his ideas.

They weren't afraid to make their feelings known. Not long after the announcement of my appointment, Pete Teeley sent me a memo about a phone call from Pam Curtis, with whom we had worked in the 1976 Ford campaign. She had bumped into Donald "Buz" Lukens, a Republican state senator from Ohio who had served as a regional political director (RPD) for the Reagan campaign. Teeley reported:

> Curtis said Lukens is bad-mouthing JAB [James A. Baker] in incredible fashion all over town. He is apparently attempting to organize the RPDs to make a stand against what has been happening in terms of building this administration, including the White House staff.
>
> He is furious at JAB ... for the fact that this administration does not reflect the thinking of the New Right, nor is it putting in key positions right thinkers. He went on to call Ed Meese a "dumb shit" and [an] "incompetent" who cannot organize or manage [and] who has sold out to JAB....
>
> When asked by Curtis if he was repeating all this around town, he replied, "I'm telling you and everyone else I run into. JAB is nothing more than a representative of the Eastern liberal establishment, and this is nothing more than a George Bush administration comprised of retreads from the Nixon and Ford administrations...."
>
> Lukens ... promises to "make life miserable for JAB, Meese, and Bush."

Lukens started out disliking me for ideological reasons, but it quickly turned personal. He wanted to be appointed as the White House congressional liaison, but I passed him over for Max Friedersdorf, who had vastly more experience (he had worked for presidents Nixon and Ford) and was better qualified.

Political loyalty was important, of course, but competence mattered to me, not just whether each job applicant had been with the Gipper from the first step of his long march to Washington. Many Reagan loyalists saw this as a betrayal of their champion and their cause, and they were angry. They were the winners, they thought. Why weren't they getting all the spoils?

Two weeks before the inauguration, I talked to several critics and tried to answer their complaints. It had been my idea, I said, to appoint Lyn Nofziger, a longtime Reaganite, as the White House political director (over opposition from some other longtime Reagan advisers). I also pointed out that I had recommended several RPDs, including Lee Atwater, for important positions in the administration. "I'm a political animal—believe in political loyalty," I wrote in my notes.

What few of the critics could bring themselves to accept was that the crime that so offended their ideological and political sensibilities— placing a prototypical Ford-Bush Republican in a high position in a Reagan administration—had been committed by none other than their beloved leader, Ronald Reagan. Why? For the same reasons he had already accepted me as a campaign adviser: he trusted me to get things done, and he was comfortable enough in his own skin to accept help from any quarter. He didn't need and didn't much like sycophants. "Ronald Reagan doesn't like yes men," we would say, tongues planted deeply in our cheeks. "When he says no, we *all* say no."

Reagan also had enough confidence in his own leadership to know that no one could hijack his presidency. He understood (as did I) that my power would be vicarious, derived entirely from the office of the president. The chief of staff truly holds what is potentially the second most powerful job in Washington, but the rule to remember is that the power comes from the position not the person. The chief of staff is what the title says—*staff*.

Reagan's open-mindedness reflected more than self-confidence.

Contrary to public perception, he was much more a pragmatist than an ideologue. Yes, he had strong convictions and principles, but he was willing to compromise to get the best deal he could. "Jim," he would often tell me as we discussed strategy, "I'd rather get eighty percent of what I want than to go over the cliff with my flag flying."

By contrast, many of his less pragmatic followers hated compromise. To them, it was better to lose everything than to give an inch. They didn't understand how the system works. Pragmatism without principles is cynicism, but principle without pragmatism is often powerless. To turn ideas into policies, a leader must be prepared to fight hard—yes—but also to accept victory on the terms that can be won, even when they are short of perfection. That's the reality of politics. My leader called me to his service because he wanted to change things, not die trying, and he thought I could help.

President Reagan understood what many of his followers did not: that it's more important for the chief of staff to be competent and loyal than to be a so-called true believer (although I had a lot more faith in his ideas than I was given credit for, and that faith grew stronger over the years). He also understood that one of the most important tasks of a White House chief of staff is to look at policy questions through a political prism. After watching me at work in 1976 and 1980, he apparently believed I could do this.

The president-elect offered me the post at a private meeting in the Century Plaza Hotel in Los Angeles on the morning after the election. Almost everyone expected him to tap Ed Meese as chief of staff—including Ed—but I was not surprised. Stu Spencer and Mike Deaver had tipped me off.

Stu and Mike tell slightly different stories about how the offer materialized.* Mike says that over drinks one night about ten days before

---

*My recollection of the events leading to my appointment as chief of staff and my early days in office has been aided by two books by longtime friends—*Behind the Scenes*, by Mike Deaver, and *The Acting President*, by Bob Schieffer and Gary Paul Gates.

the election, he and Reagan were discussing appointments. Reagan said he assumed Meese would be his chief of staff. Ed, a staunch conservative with degrees from Yale (BA) and the University of California, Berkeley (JD), had caught Reagan's eye as a law-and-order deputy district attorney in Alameda County during the Berkeley demonstrations in 1964. After winning the governorship in 1966, Reagan named him legal affairs secretary. Within a few years, Ed was the governor's executive secretary, chief of staff, and chief policy adviser.

Mike says he told Reagan that "Ed would be more valuable in another role." He then suggested me for chief of staff because I knew Washington so well.

"Jim Baker. That's an interesting thought," Reagan responded.

Mike says he later spoke with Reagan confidante Bill Clark about how to head off a problem with Meese if I got the job he had expected. Clark suggested naming Meese chief counsel to the president. Mike passed this idea on to Reagan, who liked it.

In the Spencer version, Stu floated my name a week or two before Mike did, at a dinner in Dallas with Ronald and Nancy Reagan. His reasoning was the same as Mike's: that Washington was not Sacramento and that Reagan would need someone who knew the ropes in Washington. Nancy Reagan agreed.

Mike, Stu, and Nancy had watched Meese over many years and concluded he was better suited for a different position. They saw, as I would later see, that Ed was a wonderful human being, someone whose word you could take to the bank, and a superb policy analyst. He was not, however, a cross-the-t's, dot-the-i's kind of guy—the kind needed in the chief of staff's office. If he had a failing, it was that he took on too many projects and sometimes didn't finish what he started. Even his friends in the administration sometimes referred to his briefcase as the black hole. Once something went in there, it often would never come out again. But he was excellent at synthesizing policy options for Reagan.

Mike and Stu evidently discussed the idea for the first time shortly after the convention. As my stock rose in the Reagan campaign, what had been a wild idea gradually turned into a plausible alternative. Stu approached me first, and Mike joined the discussion later. I told them I would be willing to give it a try if asked, but that I doubted Reagan would want to appoint Ford's delegate hunter and campaign chairman and Bush's campaign chairman as his chief of staff.

Stu and Mike figured that the more the Reagans talked with me, the more they would warm to the idea of naming me to an important position, so they arranged for me to sit with the couple on the campaign plane, to brief them. Mike may even have set up a few Reagan-Baker dinners. Nancy Reagan soon became an ally and lobbied her husband to appoint me.

Susan was proud that I was being considered for chief of staff, but she was not enthusiastic about my taking the job. She feared that I would be so busy that neither she nor the children would ever see me. That's why she cried after that election night phone call from Reagan. She knew, as did I, that the offer was probably coming.

Before going to meet the president-elect, I had breakfast with Meese. We talked about working together under Reagan. Although I said nothing about our titles, I assumed—wrongly, as it turned out—that Reagan had already told him I would be chief of staff.

"I hope you can work with Ed," the president-elect told me when he and I met in his suite a little later. He reminded me that Meese was his friend and had served him well over the years.

I said I was sure that we could get along and suggested that Ed's position carry an impressive title, such as counselor to the president, and that he have cabinet rank. Even though Reagan seemed to like this idea and all the other pieces were falling into place, I asked for a little time to think about the offer. The arrangement would work, I explained, only if both Ed and I understood and accepted the other's powers and duties.

After meeting with me and then breaking the news to Ed that he would be counselor to the president rather than chief of staff, Reagan held a press conference that Susan and I attended. He didn't talk about staff appointments. After the event, however, he did address Susan's concerns about losing me to the job. He pulled her aside, put his hands on her shoulders, looked her in the eye, and said, "Your husband is not going to work fourteen hours a day in my White House. I don't believe in that. I believe in my people spending time with their families. Jim will be home at six o'clock every evening."

My wife is a woman of deep Christian faith. She had been praying for guidance, and this assurance came as an answer. She agreed that I should accept the post. Unfortunately, whatever the president may have believed about his people going home at night, the demands of my office were so intense that it was a very rare evening, indeed, that I got out of the office by six.

Ed was now slated for a major role in the White House, but the boundaries between us were still unclear. My solution was to draft a memorandum to sort out our respective powers and responsibilities. As far as I know, this sort of thing had never been done before, but it was a good, lawyerly way to mark our territory at the beginning. That way, we could spend our time working together for the president, each on his own portfolio, rather than quarreling over who was on first. Ed, also a lawyer, liked this approach, and on November 13 we each initialed the document. (We initialed it again on November 17 after adding handwritten amendments.) A copy appears on the opposite page.

When President-elect Reagan made the staffing announcement on November 14, the *New York Times*'s Hedrick Smith reported that "longtime associates of Mr. Reagan" said his plan was "to do most of his policymaking with an inner circle of his cabinet." This would require "a top-level adviser and cabinet coordinator [Meese] free of the day-to-day management of the large White House operation headed by a chief of staff [Baker]."

One book says I "euchred" Meese into signing the agreement, leaving him with "a nice title and a beautiful office and little else." Yes,

11/13/80

A/e213
6420921
6709161

MEESE	BAKER
Counselor to the President for Policy (with cabinet rank)	Chief of Staff

Member Super Cabinet Executive
Committee (in absence of The
President preside over
meetings) *and V-P*   *as per published articles*

Member Super Cabinet Executive
Committee

Participate as a principal in
all meetings of full Cabinet

Coordination and supervision of
White House Staff functions

Coordination and supervision
of responsibilities of The
Secretary to the Cabinet

Hiring and firing authority over
all elements of White House
Staff

Coordination and supervision
of work of the Domestic
Policy ~~council~~ and the
National Security Council

With Meese coordination and
supervision of work of OMB,
CEA, CEQ, Trade Rep and
S&T

With Baker coordination and
supervision of work of OMB,
CEA, CEQ, Trade Rep and
S&T

Participation as a principal
in all policy group meetings
~~of full Cabinet~~

Participation as a principal
in all policy group meetings

Coordination and control of
all in and out paper flow
to the President and of
presidential schedule and
appointments

*attend any meeting
which Pres. attends - w/ his
consent*

Preside over meetings of
White House Staff

Operate from office customarily
utilized by Chief of Staff

11/19/80
OK -
OK

*attend any meeting Pres.
attends - w/ his consent.*

I wound up controlling the press and legislative operations (among other levers of power), but Ed retained his position as President Reagan's top policy adviser and head of the Domestic Policy Council. In addition, National Security Adviser Dick Allen reported to him. The president and Ed were also longtime friends, and that gave him a degree of access and influence that no memorandum could ever diminish.

The third member—with Ed and me—of what soon came to be known as President Reagan's "troika" was Mike Deaver, assistant to the president and deputy chief of staff. He was a smart and talented guy, a great manager, and a genius at providing rich visuals—whether in the Oval Office or out in the country—to complement the Great Communicator's marvelous speeches. At the same time, by his own admission, he was not terribly interested in the details of policy. Most important, perhaps, he enjoyed the confidence of the Reagans, particularly the First Lady.

Ed was the only one of the troika to have cabinet rank. That didn't bother me or, as far as I know, Mike. For the most part, cabinet meetings are staged show-and-tell events. The real business of the White House is accomplished in small meetings, usually in the Oval Office.

For advice, presidents turn to people they trust, not to bureaucracies. The most heavily relied-upon advisers, generally, are those who have been with the president in the trenches of electoral politics. Traveling together, planning, taking fire and returning it, tending each other's wounds, and finally winning—these shared experiences teach the candidate who can think clearly under pressure, who can get things done, and who can be trusted. When this team comes off the road, the personal bonds are tighter than anything that can be depicted or even hinted at in an organizational chart. The members of the troika—particularly Ed and Mike, due to their years of loyal service—had that bond with their president.

Proximity is also a major determinant of power in the White House. The important business of the executive branch in Washington goes through the Oval Office. When President Reagan would turn and ask, "What do you think?" Ed, Mike, and I were usually there in the room to hazard an answer. The cabinet officers usually were not.

To help President Reagan turn his ideas into realities, I needed control of the staff working with Congress on our legislative agenda, looking after the president's political interests, getting out the message (the press office and speechwriters*), scheduling the president's time, advancing his events, and managing the operation of the White House.

Keeping up with all of this was an administrative challenge of the first order. I hired a young staffer named John Rogers, three years out of college, gave him a great title—assistant to the president of the United States for management and administration of the White House—and crossed my fingers. What a find! He ran the place like he had been doing it all his life, then followed me to Treasury (assistant secretary) and State (under secretary for management). John's flawless stewardship of these agencies gave me the freedom that every executive needs, to focus on the big picture. When I left public service, John helped me with the creation of the James A. Baker III Institute for Public Policy at Rice University. He is now an officer and a member of the management committee at Goldman Sachs.

I took the large office traditionally occupied by the chief of staff, just down the hall and around a corner from the Oval Office in the southwest corner of the West Wing. Meese moved into the office in the northwest corner that had been occupied by President Carter's national security adviser, Zbigniew Brzezinski. Deaver occupied a small dining-room-turned-office closer to the Oval Office. My quarters were not as finely appointed as others, nor was the view as good, but they fulfilled my prime objective: I wanted space where I could host and, therefore, run staff meetings.

President Reagan, by the way, also appreciated that when it comes

---

*In my opinion, the best presidential speechwriter who ever worked in the White House—at least since Lincoln—was Ronald Reagan himself. Until he became president, he wrote all his speeches. Only the constraints of time prevented him doing that in office. Even then, however, he had a fearsome red pencil.

to offices at least, size matters. When he turned seventy on February 6, 1981, the White House staff held a surprise party for him in my office. We were just past two weeks after the inauguration, and the president had not yet been down the hall to see where I worked. "Jim," he said, "this is a *big* office." Then, with the timing of a great actor, he added, "But it's not *round!*"*

Under the Meese-Baker memorandum, I was also responsible for controlling and coordinating "all in-and-out paper flow to the president" and "all presidential schedules and appointments." Except in emergencies, cabinet members were asked to request appointments with the president twenty-four hours ahead of time.

Under our handwritten addendum of November 17, Ed and I could walk into the Oval Office at virtually any time. This meant we were usually present when the president talked with cabinet members and other dignitaries. It also meant that I could walk in when Ed met with the president, and he could walk in when I was in the Oval Office. The president, of course, had the right to keep us out, but I don't think that ever happened. What did happen, however, is that Ed and I sometimes met privately with the president, without the other's knowledge.

A popular myth about the first Reagan administration is that I blocked Ed's efforts to persuade the president to push legislation on school prayer, busing, abortion, and other social issues. That simply wasn't true. Even before taking office, the president had stated clear goals for the first year—to reduce taxes, cut the rate of growth in government spending, and strengthen the U.S. military. We recognized that he would enjoy a brief honeymoon with Congress and the American people. This was the time to push the core Reagan agenda. The Carter

---

*Vice President Bush took former Vice President Mondale's office next door to the chief of staff's office. National Security Adviser Dick Allen, who reported to Meese, got an office in the basement of the West Wing, a remote location that did not bode well for him. In retrospect, layering the national security adviser from the president may have been a mistake. Bill Clark, a closer friend of the president's, assumed a more prominent role in the administration when he replaced Allen. Unlike his predecessor, Clark had Oval Office walk-in rights, just as Meese, Deaver, and I did.

administration had wasted its honeymoon by sending far too much legislation to the Hill. President Clinton would later get his administration off on the wrong foot by raising the issue of gays in the military before he had built a consensus for his legislative program. If President Reagan had immediately introduced legislation on controversial social issues, he would almost certainly have weakened—possibly even destroyed—support for his all-important tax, spending, and defense initiatives. At least that's how he felt, and he was right.

One of my major responsibilities was to protect the president. The chief of staff is, among other things, a catcher of javelins aimed at the president—by political adversaries, by the press, and—surprisingly, perhaps—by members of his own political party. Those last kind come in from close range and are usually unexpected.

I also had to protect the president from traps, and one of the surest signs of one being laid were the apparently innocent words, "Oh, by the way, Mr. President..." They usually sounded in the doorway at the end of a cabinet meeting or a meeting with lawmakers. Someone would linger a bit, then pretend to have an afterthought. "Oh, by the way, Mr. President, my brother-in-law Fred would make a great appointee for the Rutabaga Commission." Or "How about supporting my bill to help mass transit in Houston?"

Maybe the petitioner was a friend or political supporter. Maybe he hoped the president was too tired to resist, or that the president would agree to avoid ending a positive meeting on a negative note. Whatever was going on, however, this was obviously not the way decisions should be made. My job was to grab an elbow, say, "We'll be happy to look at Fred's résumé (or your pet legislation) and get back to you," and escort Trapper John out the door.

This preserved the president's freedom. We would consider the appointments in due course, and the president could then decide what to do as part of a coherent plan, not on a first-come, first-served basis. It would also give me time to investigate the political implications of the request.

This is just one form of javelin-catching and trap-dodging. (There are others.) They are necessary, but they win no popularity contests for a chief of staff. That was not my concern, however. I just wanted to help the president succeed.

And the real test of presidential success (and best measure of his power) is whether his policies are enacted into law. We knew from the start that winning passage of the Reagan agenda would be difficult in 1981. Republicans controlled the Senate, where the other Baker—Howard—now served as majority leader, but Democrats ruled the House under a formidable speaker, Boston's Tip O'Neill. Like the president, Tip was a good-natured Irish American with a penchant for salty jokes. The two men genuinely enjoyed sharing drinks and swapping stories, but Tip opposed most of the president's agenda and didn't plan to do him any favors.

Enter the Legislative Strategy Group (LSG), which I formed and chaired. Initially created to implement the policies formulated by Meese's policy councils, the LSG quickly evolved into a policymaking group itself. This was inevitable. For one thing, legislative strategizing inevitably morphs into policymaking, because legislative battles are fought in real time. Success requires flexibility and the ability to make changes on the fly. We could never halt the proceedings to consult every policy guru in the White House. When a key senator needs a couple of tweaks to get a bill through committee, the White House political team needs authority to say yes or no, even if the amendments have significant policy implications. The only policymaker who can be consulted at times like these is the one who counts—the president.

Meese was a member of the LSG. This was one reason it worked so well. The group gave him a way to influence the team's on-the-go work. Other key members were David Stockman, director of the Office of Management and Budget; domestic adviser Martin Anderson; congressional liaison Max Friedersdorf; and my deputy, Dick Darman.

The LSG met in my office virtually every day. The group was the brainchild of Darman, whom I first met at the Commerce Department in early 1976. He arrived there before his mentor at the time, Elliot

Richardson, who was returning from his post as our ambassador to the United Kingdom to replace Rog Morton as secretary of commerce. Dick was an extraordinarily bright and able student of government who could direct traffic through the intersection of policy and politics as well as anyone I ever met. A graduate of Harvard College and Harvard Business School, Dick had worked for Richardson in several departments during the Nixon administration. After serving with me in the White House, he accompanied me to the Department of the Treasury as deputy secretary. He is perhaps best known as head of the Office of Management and Budget from 1989 to 1993 under President George H. W. Bush. Dick is still a good friend.

The best way to succeed in high office in Washington, I believe, is to surround yourself with strong, bright, and hardworking assistants. As chief of staff, I recruited the best I could find. A leader who is afraid of hiring strong people is usually a leader on a glide path to failure. My senior aides were Dick Darman as staff secretary; press secretary Jim Brady and his deputy, Larry Speakes; John Rogers, administration; Elizabeth Dole, public liaison; Fred Fielding, White House counsel; Max Friedersdorf, congressional liaison; David Gergen, communications; Pen James, personnel; Lyn Nofziger, politics; Rich Williamson, intergovernmental affairs; and Margaret Tutwiler, my indispensable executive assistant, who later headed the White House Office of Political Affairs and served as spokesperson at the departments of both Treasury and State. Margaret's grasp of politics and press relations was better than anyone I ever met, and I owe much of whatever success I achieved in public service to her on the political side and Darman on the policy side.

Dick and Margaret aren't shrinking violets, and neither were my other staffers. This resulted in spirited, sometimes contentious, one-on-ones and group meetings with the boss. I wanted straight talk, and these people gave it to me. In the end, this helped us make better decisions.

After the election and the Meese-Baker agreement, I was put in charge of the White House transition team for my area of responsibility.

Meanwhile, we had a team—Gergen, pollster and adviser Dick Wirthlin, and others—working on a strategic plan for the president's first one hundred days in office. That group actually started research before the election on the first terms of Presidents Franklin Roosevelt, Eisenhower, Kennedy, Nixon, and Carter. We wanted to know what had worked and what hadn't.

The group's report began with charts that summarized each president's activities during the first one hundred days in several categories, such as travel, press conferences, and meetings with foreign leaders. Under "Constitutional Responsibilities," for example, we saw that Eisenhower and Kennedy had delivered State of the Union addresses within days of taking office. FDR, Nixon, and Carter had waited a year, and President Reagan decided to do the same.

Under "Domestic Affairs—Meeting with Various Groups," a chart summarized how often the presidents had met with their cabinets, congressional leaders, governors, mayors, and representatives of their political party—even whether they entertained the Supreme Court. FDR, for instance, usually met with his cabinet every Tuesday and Friday. Ike had fourteen cabinet meetings during the first one hundred days. Nixon and Carter usually held weekly meetings. As for JFK: "One [meeting] on 1/26. Preference for individual meetings with cabinet members; on 4/11 says cabinet meetings a waste of time."

Behind the charts were chronologies of each president's first one hundred days. For example, on January 21, the day after his inauguration, President Carter "pardoned everyone who violated military Selective Service Act between 8/4/64 and 4/28/73 (military personnel evading the Vietnam draft); announced nominations of ten people for posts in the State Department . . . ; hosted small inauguration reception for some Democratic National Committee members."

Based on the report and Wirthlin's polling, we developed a day-by-day schedule for the pre-inaugural week and the first three weeks of the Reagan presidency. During the week leading up to the swearing-in, for instance, we planned "emphasis on hard work in preparation for presidency; push story of the Reagan economic inheritance; Iran hostage policy announcement; and . . . unannounced visits to Washington memorials, mix with crowds."

During the first week, we planned an "emphasis upon new leadership coming into office; show decisive break with past, fresh hope for future; set brisk but not frantic pace; begin building constituencies support (e.g., blue collar)." We also developed an action agenda for the president to implement these goals. On January 22, for instance, the president would issue "directives to department heads re: fraud and waste and cutting costs."

Like Jimmy Carter in 1976, Ronald Reagan had run as an outsider who criticized the Washington status quo. Unlike Carter, however, we made plans to extend an immediate olive branch to Congress. On January 23, according to our plan, the president would host a breakfast for the GOP leadership and have dinner with Tip O'Neill. On January 25: "Super Bowl—invite in top congressional leaders (including a few Democrats) to watch on big screen, White House family theater."

During the transition period, I tracked down former chiefs of staff and asked for their advice, just as I had asked former delegate hunters and campaign managers for advice before assuming those positions. The counsel I received from my predecessors ranged from the practical to the philosophical to the personal. Notes from my conversation with Dick Cheney filled four legal pages. His suggestions included:

- Restore power and authority to the executive branch.
- Orderly schedules and orderly paper flow [are] way you protect the president. Most valuable asset in D.C. is time of Ronald Reagan.
- Keep a low profile. Talk to press always on background. If you become a major public figure you lose credibility, feathering your own nest rather than serving the president.

Dick also told me to "be an honest broker. Don't use the process to impose your policy views on people." I highlighted that advice, and it served me well during my four years in the White House. I had my own opinions on most important issues—particularly on the politics of doing something about them—and understood, as well, that some issues were not important enough for presidential attention. That said, the president was best served when all sides got a fair hearing in the White House, and that's what I tried to provide.

Dick's predecessor Don Rumsfeld, like a true CEO, presented me with a twelve-page primer that he had written four years earlier, "Rumsfeld's Rules for the Assistant to the President." The first and last notations were the same: "Don't play president." Other advice:

- Assume that everything you say and do will be on the front page of the *Washington Post* the next morning and conduct yourself accordingly.
- Don't take the job or stay in it unless you have, in understanding and fact, the freedom to tell [the president] what you think and feel on any subject with the bark off.
- Obviously, always tell the full truth. If you screw up, tell him and correct it.
- Force responsibility down and out. Find problem areas, arrange them in groups, assign them, and delegate. All the pressure is to do the reverse, to take more and more responsibility yourself.
- Don't get or let the White House or the president get paranoid about the press or Congress or leaks. Relax. Understand the inevitable interaction among institutions.

Rumsfeld also included some valuable personal tips: "Don't be consumed by the job or you will lose your balance. Maintain and tend your mooring lines into the world, your family, friends, neighbors, people out of government. That balance is critically important to your performance. Help your staff, children, and friends to understand that you are still the same person, despite the publicity, good or bad . . . and don't forget it yourself."

As White House chief of staff, I was in a position to help my friend

George Bush stay in the loop more than some past vice presidents. But I was working for Reagan now, not Bush—his principal opponent in the bruising primaries—and my first loyalty would be to the president. Any appearance that my real goal was only to help my old friend would have been inappropriate. I wasn't about to do that. Even the *appearance* that I was more closely aligned with Bush than Reagan would have undermined my effectiveness.

George was present—along with Casey, Meese, and Deaver—at the meeting I attended at the Reagans' home two days after the election. One topic was cabinet selection. We were joined by the president-elect's close friend and confidante Senator Paul Laxalt, and by Pen James, a private-sector headhunter who would run the White House personnel office. Pen had already begun putting together a short list of candidates for each position.

During the transition, James, Meese, Deaver, and I met every day at 5:00 P.M. in my office to go over candidates for key positions such as deputy or assistant secretaries. We would then discuss our recommendations with Reagan, and he would make the final decision.

Reagan tentatively selected General Al Haig as secretary of state. Al had a heck of a résumé. He had just returned from serving as Supreme Allied Commander of NATO. Before that he had combat experience in Vietnam and a stint as an aide to Henry Kissinger. In the last days of the Watergate crisis, he served as White House chief of staff for Richard Nixon.

Before offering the post to Al, the president-elect wanted assurances that he would not use it as a base of operations to run for the presidency, as rumors suggested. In early December, he had told Meese, Laxalt, Allen, and me that he did not want to be president. Furthermore, he said, no one interested in running for president would want to be secretary of state. Too many occupants of that office, he suggested, have been scapegoated by their presidents. That satisfied Reagan, and he soon nominated Haig for the position.

On January 20, 1981, a bit more than a month later, Susan and I sat on the inaugural platform as Ronald Reagan took the oath as our nation's fortieth president. We later watched the parade from the presidential reviewing stand in front of the White House. As bands, dignitaries, and floats crept past, I showed Susan the area under the bare trees in Lafayette Park, just across the street and to the left, where Mary Stuart and I had shivered through the 1953 parade twenty-eight years earlier.

Inauguration day was memorable for other reasons, as well. Moments after President Reagan took office, Iran freed the hostages taken more than fourteen months earlier. While work crews swept Pennsylvania Avenue after the parade, Mike Deaver and I went to Ed Meese's office. We probably talked about the president's response to this momentous event. It's also likely that we lifted a toast to our new administration and the bright possibilities ahead. Suddenly and unexpectedly, Al Haig walked in. He said he had a proposed National Security Decision Directive (NSDD) he wanted the president to sign.

Talk about bad timing. We were still in formal attire. We hadn't even unpacked our briefcases. And here was Al Haig, not yet confirmed by the Senate, with a twenty-page document no one—including the president—had yet seen, proposing to put the secretary of state—that is, Al Haig—in charge of crisis management for the administration. Ed told Haig that we needed comments from Secretary of Defense Weinberger, CIA Director Casey, and National Security Adviser Allen before we could put something this important on the president's desk.

This did not sit well with Al. In his diplomatic memoir, *Caveat: Realism, Reagan, and Foreign Policy,* he suggested that he had an earlier understanding with the president about lines of authority that was now in danger of being reversed. Striking specifically at Meese, Haig wrote: "Surely the President did not want his counselor editing communications from the cabinet, or muddying presidential instructions."*

Instructions? President Reagan had given us none about this document. But as Al Haig and others would soon learn, the president did want communications to his office—including those from cabinet officers—to be vetted, if not edited, by Ed and me. Management 101. This presented a real problem for Al. He thought the president relied far too heavily on the White House staff, whom he later referred to as "a bunch of second-rate hambones."†

Just ten weeks after President Reagan took office, tragedy struck. Without warning, senior White House staff, the cabinet, and the vice president were forced to consider a variant of the question Haig had posed: in a crisis, who's in charge here?

---

*When I later served as secretary of state for George Bush, 41, the scope of my authority was defined by something considerably more powerful than a National Security Decision Document—the confidence and friendship of the president.
†After a thorough review, President Reagan signed NSDD No. 3 on December 14, 1981. It put a "Special Situation Group, chaired by the vice president," in charge of crisis management. In 1988, Al Haig ran unsuccessfully against that same vice president for the Republican presidential nomination.

SEVEN

"SPARED FOR A PURPOSE"

I WAS IN THE White House mess having lunch when Press Secretary Jim Brady dropped by my table and said it was time to leave. It was March 30, and the president was scheduled to speak to 3,500 AFL-CIO members at the Washington Hilton. I had planned to attend.

"I just can't go," I said. "I've got too many things going on today."

Mike Deaver went in my place. After the event, he was at the president's side as the entourage exited the VIP entrance at the lower level of the hotel at 2:25 P.M. to return to the White House. It was a warm and breezy day, the sidewalks were wet from a light drizzle. The president had been in office seventy days.

As the president walked toward his car, "the press started asking their usual questions," Mike recalled later. "I turned and moved [Jim] Brady up because he was the press secretary. I took three steps. Then the first shot went over my shoulder. I knew what it was. I ducked down with the help of a Washington policeman. I smelled the powder. I never saw the gunman."

In less than ten seconds, that unseen gunman, John Hinckley, Jr., twenty-five, fired six hollow-nosed bullets from his .22-caliber revolver. It sounded like firecrackers—*pop, pop, pop*—the president said later. One bullet hit police officer Thomas Delahanty in the neck. Another struck Secret Service agent Tim McCarthy in the stomach as he rushed between the president and the shooter. A third hit Jim Brady over the left eye and entered his brain. And although nobody, including Ronald Reagan, realized it at the time, another bullet ricocheted off the president's limousine, cut into the president's chest, ripped into his left lung, and embedded itself there, inches from his heart.

Jerry Parr, head of the Secret Service detail, shoved President Reagan into the black Lincoln limousine and told the driver to head for the White House. Parr radioed ahead. Shots have been fired, he said, but the president was not hit. About that time, the president began coughing up blood. Parr immediately ordered the driver to divert to nearby George Washington University Hospital.

The car arrived there about 2:35. Flanked by Secret Service agents, the president walked into the emergency room under his own power. Once inside, however, his legs gave way and he suddenly collapsed. With the help of agents, a paramedic carried him into a private suite in the ER and gave him oxygen.

Meanwhile, David Gergen burst into my office with the news that shots had been fired, but in those first confused moments, neither he nor anyone else we could find knew exactly what had happened or whether the president had been injured.

Ed Meese joined me in my office. Now Deaver called. After the shooting, he had jumped into a limousine and followed the president. This was the first contact between the hospital and the White House. Brady and at least one agent had been hit, Mike said, and doctors had found a small bullet hole in the president's coat. Dr. Daniel Ruge, the White House physician, was also on the line. He told us the president had lost an enormous amount of blood. The bad news was getting worse.

Meese and I agreed that we should get to the hospital ASAP. Before we left, I received a phone call from Secretary of State Al Haig. I told him what I knew and said I was on my way to the hospital. Vice President Bush was in Texas. Haig said he would set up a White House command post with key cabinet members—Secretary of Defense Cap Weinberger, Secretary of the Treasury Don Regan, Attorney General William French Smith, CIA Director Bill Casey, and National Security Adviser Dick Allen. I told Haig he would be my point of contact, and he said he would call the vice president.

Haig arrived at the White House a few minutes after 3:00 P.M. Meese, Speakes, Lyn Nofziger, and I were already on our way to the hospital, about six blocks away—siren wailing, lights flashing.

When we arrived the president winked at us from behind his oxygen mask. "Who's minding the store?" he asked. His greeting to Nancy was just as light: "Honey, I forgot to duck," a line borrowed from Jack Dempsey. But there was nothing funny about the way he looked. He didn't appear to be in danger of dying, but his appearance shocked me. In my two-plus months on the job, I had been impressed with the president's vigor, a testament to his natural good health and active outdoor lifestyle. Now he was ghostly pale. "Doctors believe bleeding to death," Speakes wrote in his notebook. "Can't find a wound. Think we're going to lose him. Touch and go."

The doctors worked fast. They soon found the wound, a small slit in the side of the president's chest under his left arm. Now we knew for certain: Ronald Reagan had been shot. The bullet, flat as a dime, was lodged in his left lung, which had collapsed. At 3:25 P.M., one hour after the shooting, he was wheeled into surgery to try to stop his massive internal bleeding.

As commander in chief, the president is always accompanied by officers and equipment to communicate with the U.S. military. Potential threats to national security don't take time off for weekends, vacations, or—in this case—an attempt to assassinate the president of the United States. A White House team quickly set up a command center at the hospital. Presidential aides Dave Fischer and Helene von Damm staffed it. They were joined by the military aide who always traveled with the president and kept the "football," the black bag containing the codes the president would need in case of a nuclear exchange with the Soviet Union. We would later learn that Hinckley was a disturbed young man, acting alone. In those first minutes, however, it was not clear that something larger and more ominous had not happened.

Under Section 3 of the Twenty-fifth Amendment to the Constitution, the president is empowered to declare his own disability and transfer power to the vice president, as acting president. If the president is in no condition to declare his own disability, Section 4 says the transfer can be effected by a majority vote of cabinet members and the vice president. Congress approved the amendment in 1965 in the aftermath of the Kennedy assassination. The amendment was ratified in 1967, but had never been invoked for presidential succession. (It was invoked twice in the 1970s on vice presidential succession, first to replace the disgraced Spiro Agnew, then to replace Gerald Ford as VP when Nixon resigned as president.)

Meese and I had seen President Reagan at the hospital. With the vice president in Texas, we decided, it would be difficult to transfer power to George Bush during the surgery. More important, we didn't think the transfer was medically required, even though the president would be under anesthesia. Our decision would be second-guessed in the days to come and would rightfully lead to the development of more specific White House guidelines in later years.

When President Reagan was anesthetized for colon cancer surgery in 1985, he did transfer power to the vice president under Section 3. Why didn't we use Section 4 to do so in 1981? In part (and primarily) because doctors told us that the president would be able to make decisions, save for the brief period he was under anesthesia. In part because it was essential to send a clear message to the world: *Despite the assassination attempt, the government is open for business, and the president is in charge.* And in part, frankly, because I was sensitive to the fact (and knew George Bush would be, too) that many Reagan loyalists—mindful that we had campaigned against President Reagan in the primaries—still questioned our allegiance to the president. Unless it was absolutely necessary, they might view the transfer as something just short of a Bush-Baker *coup d'etat*. For these reasons, I think we made the right call at the time. Furthermore, we knew that the transfer could always be made later if, say, complications arose during surgery. By then, Vice President Bush would be back in Washington. There was no harm in waiting.

Back in the situation room in the West Wing basement, Haig, other cabinet members, and White House aides crowded around television screens. They were getting some of their information about the shooting like everyone else in America, from network news reports. They were soon joined by White House counsel Fred Fielding, who had taken it upon himself to prepare documents to transfer power under the Twenty-fifth Amendment if worse came to worst.

Haig later wrote that he thought Fielding's timing was premature and that the preparation of documents was ill advised. Dick Darman's reaction was even stronger. It was out of order to discuss the transfer of power in this manner, he said, taking possession of Fielding's papers. He then called me at the hospital. I agreed with him. The White House counsel reported to me and should not have raised the issue without consulting me. Dick put the documents in his office safe.

At the hospital, the hours passed quickly and are blurred in my memory. I spent most of my time with Meese, Deaver, Nofziger, and other White House staffers. We were all running on adrenaline. For me, it was triggered by three emotional shockwaves—first when I was told of the shooting; then when I saw the president, pale and injured, in the emergency room; and again when I watched him being wheeled away to the operating room. We were all trying to figure out what had happened, what needed to be done, and how to do it. For me, that meant a lot of time on the telephone, primarily with the situation room and my staff back at the White House, but I also fielded several incoming calls from others.

At one point, I remember being in the small hospital chapel with

Mrs. Reagan. We prayed for our country, for the president, for Jim Brady, for the injured officers, and for guidance in responding to this ordeal. I don't remember our exact words, but here's a good summary: "Lord, please help us!"

Meanwhile the press clamored for information. The nation—indeed, the world—wanted to know what had happened and what it all meant. Even before we had the answers ourselves, we needed to share what we knew. In a situation like this, silence fuels anxieties and rumors outrun facts. I briefed Nofziger and Speakes, then sent Speakes to deal with reporters at the White House.

The televised press conference did not go well. Watching from the situation room, Allen and Haig were concerned, understandably, that Speakes, trying too hard to be precise, had left the erroneous impression that the country was not being defended and that no one was running the government. In fact, Weinberger had ordered Strategic Air Command pilots to their bases, and the cabinet and the troika, soon to be joined by the vice president, were quickly coming to grips with the situation.

"This is very bad. We have to do something," Allen said.

Haig agreed. "We've got to get him [Speakes] off."

The secretary of state and national security adviser then bounded up the stairs to the press room. Red-faced, perspiring, and near breathless from the run, Haig briefed reporters on the president's condition and the status of our military. He then offered to take questions. One of his answers would haunt him for a long time.

> *Reporter:* Who is making the decisions for the government right now?
>
> *Haig:* Constitutionally, gentlemen, you have the president, the vice president, and the secretary of state, in that order, and should the president decide he wants to transfer the helm, he will do so. He has not done that. As of now, I am in control here, in the White House, pending return of the vice president and in close touch with him. If something came up, I would check with him, of course.

As Haig himself would later admit, "I am in control here" was an unfortunate choice of words. He also conceded that his physical appearance made him look anything but "in control" and that he should have caught his breath before trying to reassure the nation that all was well. He also famously misstated the line of presidential succession. Under legislation passed in 1947, the speaker of the House and president pro tempore of the Senate follow the vice president. The secretary of state follows them.

In his diplomatic memoir, *Caveat*, Haig sometimes spoke critically of the White House staff. He thought we had too much power, were too protective of the president, and distracted the president from more important foreign policy issues by keeping the focus on a narrow domestic agenda. Early on, for example, he believed that we stymied his efforts to deal aggressively with Central America. (He once suggested solving the Cuba problem by turning the island nation into "a [expletive deleted] parking lot.")*

Before the assassination attempt, the president had decided to accept a crisis management plan that Meese and I had developed. Furious that the vice president rather than the secretary of state was to be put in charge of operations in emergencies, Haig openly criticized us at a congressional hearing.

It's fine to disagree on policy, but it's better to do it privately with the president rather than publicly before Congress. Haig threatened to resign a number of times over the next year. After each such threat, he would eventually cool down, but he never seemed to learn that President Reagan liked team players better than Lone Rangers and did not respond well to management by ultimatum.

Despite the tension between the White House staff and the secretary of state, Meese and I did not fault Haig for his conduct on the day

---

*Haig was at least partly right. In the early months of the administration, we did try to keep Central America on the back burner. We didn't want to distract attention from the president's critical tax and spending reforms.

the president was shot. At a press conference on March 31 and on ABC's *Nightline* on April 1, we were invited to join the Haig-bashing. Instead, we defended the secretary's actions, and I will defend them now: Al Haig served the country well on March 30, 1981; at a very difficult time for our nation, he assured the people—on balance and despite the gaffe—that all was well.

At about 6:15 P.M., I returned to the White House. Vice President Bush was expected to land at Andrews Air Force Base at 6:30. As we waited, I briefed those in the situation room. The surgeons had found the bullet in the president's lung, I reported, but according to the doctors he was in good condition and would make a full recovery.

The vice president arrived at about 7:00 P.M. He had the sensitivity and presence of mind to land his helicopter at the Naval Observatory, the vice president's official residence, and drive to the White House. Setting down on the South Lawn would have sent two negative and inaccurate messages—that the president was no longer in charge and that the vice president was.

As we discussed national security issues and the agenda for the next twenty-four hours, Dr. Dennis O'Leary, dean of clinical affairs at George Washington University Hospital, said in a televised news conference: President Reagan "has a clear head and should be able to make decisions by tomorrow, certainly." And with that, we breathed long-deferred sighs of relief.

The details of what happened next have slipped my memory. I suspect I worked at my desk, conferred with my immediate staff, tried to pick up where I had left off a few hours earlier, returned calls, prepared for the next day, then went home to Susan.

That's how I worked. I would go to my desk every day and cross all the t's and dot all the i's, then I'd go home. I ran presidential campaigns that way and served presidents that way. I never thought too much about history in the abstract sense. In the back of my mind, I knew the things I was involved in were important; that's one reason I enjoyed public life so much. If I had a theory of history, it was: that if we worked hard and worked smart, we could win each day's battles, and that if we won each battle, we would win the war. To the extent I had a larger theory, it was that history is shaped by human actions and reactions.

I still believe that, by and large, but March 30 taught me how fragile it all is, how unanticipated events can change the course of history in an eyeblink. The administration had been in office a bit more than two months. We were still getting our sea legs. Now the voyage had almost ended before it ever really began. All of President Reagan's great accomplishments lay ahead. What if the president had died on the operating table? What if he had been disabled?

And what if the president had never been shot? Looking back, I wonder if this long and emotional day didn't play some role in focusing the administration on what was important. I know that it strengthened my resolve to make every day count. It also reminded me of a lesson of my faith: we are responsible for doing our best here on earth, but at the end of the day, God is in charge, and on March 30, 1981, He spared Ronald Reagan.

The day after the shooting was not a typical day at the office. On a typical day, I arrived at the White House at about 7:00 A.M. A car picked me up at my home about thirty minutes earlier. My driver was Ernie Caldwell of the U.S. Army, a true gentleman and dedicated public servant, who could always be counted on for efficient services, utter discretion, and a smile that would warm the coldest mornings. After more than twenty-five years, he still drives me when I'm in Washington, now as an employee of Baker Botts.

On my way to the office, I read the White House news summary, prepared overnight by the press office and distributed early each morning to the president, senior White House staff, and cabinet members. At the office, I caught the top of the morning network news reports and read full accounts of what I considered the important stories mentioned in the White House summary. The *New York Times,* the *Washington Post,* the *Wall Street Journal,* the *Washington Times* (after it was founded in 1982), and the *Early Bird* (the Pentagon's sixteen-page news summary) were on my desk when I arrived. I discussed problem stories with Margaret Tutwiler, my executive assistant (who had great instincts about whether to respond, and how), and later with the press secretary, who would handle the response.

My first office project each day was to prepare an agenda for a meeting with Meese and Deaver and (with some sensitive items being deleted) for a general staff meeting afterward. This checklist didn't take long. I always prepared a draft the day before, as I worked. All I had to do in the morning was rewrite and update it. This list and the meetings that followed were examples of the Five Ps in action. (Somewhere, Dad was smiling.)

At 7:30 A.M., Meese and Deaver would gather in my office. Over breakfast, we would go over the agenda I had prepared. Ed and Mike would bring additional items to the table. We generally discussed scheduling, media coverage, and the legislative agenda for the day.

This was an example of the troika at its best. We worked together to serve the president, notwithstanding our differences of opinion and the natural tensions that sometimes developed. This approach to sharing responsibility worked well for President Reagan. It gave him a functional administrative system to keep things moving, plus a useful way to hear competing views on important issues. With the troika, President Reagan had a darn good first term. The second term, without the troika, was in many ways not as successful.

Ed, Mike, and I worked hard to develop a story line for each day. A good economic report, for instance, proved our programs were working, while a bad economic report only showed the need to adopt our programs or stay the course on programs already in place. At one level, this approach may offend logic, but it makes perfect sense under the logic of politics. Ronald Reagan was trying to change the direction of the country. To succeed, it was critical not to lose momentum or be blown off course by events, by politics, or by the press. When the headlines were favorable, we raised our sails; when they were unfavorable, we tacked into them. We believed in what we were doing, and we wanted to succeed.

At 8:00 A.M., Meese, Deaver, and I would go to the Roosevelt Room for a meeting with the president's assistants and deputy assistants, some of whom reported to me, others to Meese (from the policy shops) or Deaver (responsible for the East Wing—the First Lady, scheduling, advance work, and the military office). I chaired the meeting. We talked about most of the same issues the troika had discussed earlier, plus issues from the floor. If senior staff had something useful to say, we wanted to hear it. (One other group I headed, the White House Legislative Strategy Group, did not have regularly scheduled meetings. It was on call to meet when the need arose, sometimes with only an hour's notice.)

We also presented the day's story line to the communications director and the press secretary. To keep everyone in the administration on the same page in telling this story, the press secretary would then hold daily conference calls with spokespersons for the cabinet departments.* We didn't want other agencies out in front of the White House on issues, so at 9:15 A.M., the White House press secretary always held the day's first media briefing. In 1984, we would also coordinate our theme of the day with the president's reelection campaign.

Our initial daily meeting in the Oval Office was always triggered by a call from Kathy Osborne, the president's personal secretary. "The president is in," she would say. This was our cue to gather our papers and head down the hall.

The daily presidential meeting with we three top advisers was my

---

*After Jim Brady was shot, Larry Speakes assumed his duties but, in deference to Jim, not his title. We were intent on making life as good as possible for Jim and his wife, Sarah. Less than three weeks after the shooting I approved continued use of the White House car for Sarah; continuation of the secure military signal phone in Jim's room at the hospital; continuation of his salary (which would otherwise have stopped when he did not return to work after forty-five days); and investigation of the best way to set up a trust fund for the Brady family.

idea, supported by Mike and Ed. When I was named chief of staff, Stu Spencer said, "Listen, Jim, you call the president every day. It's not his style to contact you or to contact others. But he'll want you to call him every day." I went beyond that, gaining the president's approval for these start-of-the-day meetings.

Most days, Ronald Reagan was awakened about 7:00 A.M. While eating breakfast with Nancy, he read the White House news summary and the newspapers. Some newspapers didn't like his policies, but he still wanted to know what they were writing. The president was so genial and had such an uncanny ability to put people at ease that reporters couldn't help but like him personally. This was also true of many of his political opponents and some foreign leaders who didn't agree with his policies.

Out of his deep respect for the institution of the presidency, President Reagan also reversed the 1970s trend toward informality in the White House. It's been reported many times, but bears repeating: he would not remove his suit jacket in the Oval Office. The room where Lincoln, Wilson, FDR, Truman, and other predecessors had confronted the most profound national issues was to him not simply a place to get the day's business done; it was a sacred place, embodying the ideas of freedom and self-government that framed America's history. The only proper attitude, he believed, was one of deep respect, even reverence. Wearing his jacket was a small thing, easy for cynics to mock, but President Reagan was right and the cynics were wrong.

The session in the Oval Office was devoted to matters carried forward from the troika's 7:30 meeting and the larger White House senior staff meeting, except for routine stuff that the president and vice president didn't need to be bothered with. At 9:30, the national security adviser joined us and gave his daily briefing to the president. The vice president, Meese, and I stayed for this unless we had other commitments. At about 10:00 A.M., I would usually return to my office or accompany the president to his next event.

I tried to work at my desk as much as possible, but I would also attend presidential press conferences, accompany the president to events both inside and outside the White House, sit in on important Oval Office meetings (particularly including meetings with the congressional leadership), and participate in cabinet meetings. (Under my bargain with Meese, I sat at the cabinet table, not in the back row with staff.)

The good news for Susan and my family was that the president was true to his word: he didn't force me to work fourteen-hour days. The bad news was that I put in that many hours anyway. As a workaholic with an endless list of things to do, I saw no other way to get the job done. The Five Ps have their price.

I knew from experience and from conversations with previous chiefs of staff how important it was to maintain good relationships with Congress and the press. A simple rule helped me do that. Before going home each night, I returned every phone call from reporters and lawmakers. I wasn't always eager to talk with yet another reporter about yet another hot story or another congressman on the prowl for a quid pro quo that I couldn't provide, but I wanted the overnight call slips to be on their desks, not mine. And I didn't mind leaving a signal that I was still at the office working after they had gone home.

Each evening the president received the next day's schedule. The schedule might include meetings with foreign heads of state, congressional leaders, cabinet secretaries and other administration officials, business and community leaders, old friends, and, of course, the troika. Schedules from a typical month, October 1981, reveal that the president met with—among many, many others—representatives of the National Association of Broadcasters, the prime minister of Mauritania, Governor Pete du Pont of Delaware, Budget Director David Stockman, and eighty-three-year-old character actor Regis Toomey, a pal from Hollywood.

President Reagan also met regularly with a bipartisan group of congressional leaders. Here's a secret: members of Congress generally don't come to the White House to engage the president in deep conversations about policy issues. Those discussions take place with the president's aides. What lawmakers usually want with the chief executive is simple face time—a handshake, a drink, and a bit of socializing. That way they can tell the press or the people back home, "I was talking yesterday to the president, and he told me . . ."

Sometimes, of course, congressional leaders might come to the Oval Office loaded for bear on a particularly contentious issue, such as foreign policy in Central America. On those occasions, there might be a good deal of give-and-take, *but in the Reagan White House, the atmosphere always remained friendly.* Twenty-five years ago, it was still possible to be political adversaries without becoming personal enemies. You could disagree agreeably.

Rank partisanship is both undignified and unproductive. It's also shortsighted. The best way to persuade someone to see things your way is to start by trying to see things his way. You need to understand and respect the political imperatives that guide his action, then to deal with both the person and his politics in a civil and respectful way. I learned as a corporate lawyer that, more often than not, negotiators who worked in this way could find a common path that served the needs of both sides. President Reagan was a master at doing this; he told me he had cut his teeth as a negotiator when he was president of the Screen Actors Guild.

Why are things more contentious today? I'm not really sure. I hesitate to blame cultural factors because I don't claim to be a cultural critic. I also don't want to sound like another old geezer who thinks kids today don't measure up. I will say, however, that President Reagan's and President Bush's upbringing—mine too, for that matter— put a higher value on courtesy and civility than on unfettered self-expression. It was the same for Tip O'Neill and many other old-line traditional Democrats. Maybe that has something to do with it, and maybe not. Another possible reason for the loss of the old spirit of comity was the independent counsel law, which created a perverse incentive for politicians to try and win political arguments by getting their opponents indicted.

Many of the president's Oval Office meetings with visiting dignitaries began with photo opportunities for the press. While photographers and TV cameramen got their pictures and footage, the president and his visitor would joke with each other and banter with the press, usually about light and inconsequential topics. Before his meeting with the president, however, Archbishop Desmond Tutu bulldozed past the president's statement that this was a photo-op with no questions and thoroughly trashed the administration's South Africa policy.

Smelling conflict, a reporter at a different photo-op the next day asked President Reagan: "What about your meeting with Tutu?" The president got a big laugh and totally defused the situation when he looked down at his hands, then slowly replied: "Tutu? So-so." (The first President Bush incorporated the Tutu story into the lovely eulogy he delivered at Ronald Reagan's funeral in 2004. He got a big laugh too.)

President Reagan preferred to have at least one hour each day for personal business. He would take care of paperwork and visit with staff (often regaling us with stories). He also read his briefing material.

I quickly learned how to present briefing material to the president: *briefly*. Ronald Reagan was much more interested in the big picture than in the details, a big-idea man who left the fine points to others. Ironically, however, he was almost too diligent for his own good. If you gave him a long memo or a thick briefing book, he would read every word of it and waste a lot of valuable presidential time on staff-level material. It was better to brief him orally or in short memos.

President Reagan's reputation for having a lack of interest in details led some people to think he was not intelligent. They were wrong and made a big mistake in this underestimation of him. First of all, his radar quickly picked up the signals from friends who patronized him and adversaries who thought they could outsmart him, which put both groups at a disadvantage in dealing with him. Second, lowering expectations about his intelligence gave him an opportunity to exceed those expectations, which he did, time after time.

President Reagan also liked to write letters. He had a private mailbox at the White House, the number of which he could give to anyone. Letters in that box went directly to him, not through the system. He also received hundreds of pieces of mail each week through the correspondence unit of the White House. He could not read or answer all of them, but he believed hearing from ordinary citizens kept him in touch with the mood of the country. He replied to a surprisingly large number of his citizen correspondents, often taking mail with him on the weekend to the presidential retreat at Camp David. A soft touch, he sometimes sent personal checks to individuals with stories of medical or financial hardship.

Unless he had an engagement, the president ate lunch in the Oval Office or the small adjacent study. On Thursdays, he lunched with the vice president. In any administration, it's almost a given that those close to the president, and sometimes the president himself, will view the vice president as a competitor. Often the staffs of the top two officials compete more than they cooperate. Because the vice president had battled the president for the nomination and candidate Reagan originally had doubts about asking his primary opponent to join the ticket, the table was set, so to speak, for a tense relationship—one that could have lasted for four years or more.

It did take the two men a while to get to know each other, but after the first three or four months, Ronald Reagan developed total confidence in George Bush. Without reservation, I can say that George was the perfect vice president. He understood the role. He knew, for example, that it was better to speak privately to the president about differences of opinion than to voice those differences in meetings. Speaking up in groups would inevitably generate leaks to the press about the president and vice president's being at odds over one thing or another.

I helped facilitate this relationship by supporting the idea that they should have as many opportunities as possible to spend time together. The president grew increasingly fond of George and valued his counsel. Although their backgrounds were vastly different, they were both comfortable with themselves and respected each other. Neither had anything to prove to the other. They could let their guard down and talk freely about whatever was on their mind.

When the president was in town, Wednesday afternoons were reserved. He often took this time to go horseback riding at the Marine Corps base in Quantico, Virginia, my old military training ground. He loved horses and kept a sign on his desk that said, "There's nothing better for the inside of a man than the backside of a horse." Knowing that I was a Texan who also liked horses, the president often invited me to join him. Sometimes he would also ride with his close friend Senator Paul Laxalt. We would ride for an hour or more through the lovely Virginia woods, usually at a slow pace. I used a western saddle and rode in blue jeans and cowboy boots, but the president preferred an English saddle, jodhpurs, and polished riding boots. Our conversations on the trails were mostly personal. If I had business to discuss, I would usually save it for the helicopter ride back to the South Lawn.

A riderless horse with boots placed backward in the stirrups is a tradition in presidential funeral processions. For President Reagan's funeral, however, the symbolism was especially powerful. I had seen him wear those boots, or ones just like them, many times.

Remembering Ronald Reagan, the horseman, reminds me of a story. If it's not true, it should be.

The president was visiting Queen Elizabeth II at Windsor Castle. Like him, she was an avid and accomplished rider, so the staffs arranged for a horseback tour of the grounds. After the obligatory photo-op, the monarch and president rode away, the queen in front. A few minutes later, however, Her Highness's poor steed—suffering perhaps from a bad batch of oats—began to expel gas in a remarkably rhythmic way with each step, step, step across the English countryside.

Elizabeth the Second—by the grace of God, queen of the United Kingdom of Great Britain and Northern Ireland and her other realms and territories, head of the commonwealth, and defender of the faith—was suitably mortified. "Oh, dear, Mr. President," she said, "I'm so sorry."

"Quite all right, Your Majesty," the president replied. "I thought it was the horse."

The president often directed his wit at his own alleged frailties in a way that charmed his friends and disarmed all but the most humor-impaired critics. There was lots of talk, for example, about his falling asleep in meetings.* "Someday," the president joked to one Oval Office visitor, "people will say, 'Ronald Reagan slept here.'" After a U.S. fighter plane shot down two Libyan jets one night, controversy erupted because the president had not been awakened. "I've laid down the law, though," he joked later at a dinner for White House correspondents. "From now on . . . no matter what time it is, wake me . . . even if it's in the middle of a cabinet meeting."

At 5:00 P.M. the president would usually leave the office for the residence, a brief, traffic-free commute. He generally took work home with him. He and Nancy would get into their pajamas, eat dinner, and watch the television news. After dinner he would read—he was a voracious reader—and do paperwork. I only occasionally made evening visits to the residence, but I can testify that President Reagan and the First Lady spent their free evenings in pajamas. Why not?

Ronald Reagan's devotion to Nancy was genuine and inspiring. They truly were best friends, and very much in love. He treasured her counsel, which almost always served him well. She had a good political nose and was the one who could get him to make hard political choices, particularly about personnel. I still can't get over the fact that when Don Regan was chief of staff he hung up on her during an argument. This was not only rude, but suicidal. He didn't last much longer.

Nancy Reagan had a fierce desire to protect her husband's health from a stressful schedule and his psyche from critics, be they in the

---

*As far as I could see, the president was always as alert as the rest of us, except for one well-publicized meeting with Pope John Paul II after we'd flown overnight to the Vatican.

press or in politics. She could be a grand ally when we were trying to persuade the president to do something. Mike Deaver, who had her trust, played an indispensable role in these efforts.

As has been reported, the president's close relationship with Nancy did not carry over to all his children, at least while I served him. He was probably not unique among many public figures in this regard. High officials are often too busy or single-minded to spend as much time with their children as they might, and a distance sometimes develops.

It is not for me to psychoanalyze the president I served. I am just happy to know that during his final years, Ronald Reagan reconciled with his children and they with him. At his funeral, the devotion of his surviving children, Michael, Patti, and Ron, was apparent to me and the nation.

While relations between the president and some of his children may at times have been distant, this does not mean he didn't enjoy children. My daughter, Mary Bonner, was three when I became chief of staff. The president took great delight in having her visit the Oval Office or Camp David, even when she once turned to Susan as the adults reached for their dinner forks and loudly announced, "Mommy, we haven't said grace!" The president, laughing, promptly gave a blessing. Another time he taught Mary Bonner how to dive into the pool at Camp David—a lesson that featured beautiful flips, jackknives, and swan dives from the diving board. The president, then past seventy, was showing off his decades-old lifeguard skills to impress a little girl. He also impressed her parents.

AFTER THE assassination attempt, the president, the vice president, senior staff, and cabinet agreed that it was essential to demonstrate that Ronald Reagan was still in command. While he was in the hospital, we couldn't replicate a day at the office. We could, however, demonstrate that the president was conducting business as usual.

On the morning after the shooting, Meese, Deaver, and I met with the president a little after 7:00 A.M. He was sitting up in bed, brushing his teeth. He may have lost half his blood the day before, but he never lost an ounce of his sense of humor. "Hi, fellas," he said smiling. "I knew it would be too much to hope that we could miss a staff meeting."

With the world watching, we couldn't. The president had been scheduled to sign a bill canceling an increase in dairy price-support payments. He did so now, albeit with a shaky hand.*

That afternoon I briefed the press. I gave more details about the shooting; explained that Meese and I had decided it was not necessary to invoke the Twenty-fifth Amendment; played down rumors of tension between Haig and Weinberger in the situation room; supported Haig's conduct during the crisis; and reported that when the president learned that a bullet had entered Jim Brady's brain, tears welled up in his eyes and he said, "Oh, damn! Oh, damn!" Earlier that day, I had also attended a White House cabinet meeting. George Bush presided, but sat in the vice president's chair, not President Reagan's. He wanted to make it very clear that he was not taking over the presidency.

One thing that didn't get much press was the president's post-operative infection. It was very serious, frankly, and we may have come closer to losing him from the infection than from the shooting itself.

Our routine didn't vary too much over the twelve days the president spent in the hospital. Meese, Deaver, and I moved our daily breakfast meeting to the hospital cafeteria, then met with the president afterward. George sat in for him at White House meetings, but deferred all major decisions to the president.

He, in turn, signed legislation, made appointments, and weighed in on pressing matters. He also agreed with my recommendation that we formally review who did what, when, in the White House during the

---

*The president later inscribed a copy of that bill to me. "Dear Jim," he wrote, "having signed this bill lying down the day after [the assassination attempt] . . . with your pen, I thought you might like to have it as a memento. Actually it proves there wasn't much of a pause in our operation. Oops! That reads like a pun. Ron."

crisis. I appointed Darman to lead the study and recommend necessary policy changes.

As the president grew stronger, he was eager to return to the White House. When Senate leaders visited him in the hospital, he said he feared that his economic program, still being debated by the Congress, would lose momentum if he stayed in the hospital too long. The symbolic hundred-day mark, April 29, was fast approaching.

He returned home on April 11, wearing a bulletproof vest under his cardigan to be on the safe side. On the advice of doctors and at the insistence of the First Lady, he remained in the residence for the next ten days or so, except for periodic trips to the Rose Garden for sunshine and fresh air. The president also spent a few hours each day working in the Oval Office. We continued to hold our 9:00 A.M. meetings with him, and the national security adviser continued to brief him.

Surviving the attempt on his life had a profound effect on Ronald Reagan. More than once, he told the troika something like this: "Fellas, I feel like I've been spared for a purpose; the rest of my days here on earth belong to Him, with a capital *H*." "Perhaps having come so close to death," he wrote later, "made me feel I should do whatever I could in the years God had given me to reduce the threat of nuclear war; perhaps there was a reason I had been spared."

On April 24, less than two weeks after returning to the White House, the president sent Soviet leader Leonid Brezhnev two letters— one formal, one personal. The formal letter restated the president's well-known public position, that the Soviet Union's arms buildup in recent years exceeded its defensive needs and suggested a desire to achieve military superiority.

The second draft of the president's personal note, in his own handwriting, was given to me by President Reagan. It has been displayed at the James A. Baker III Institute for Public Policy at Rice University and is now at Princeton University with the papers of my public and political service. It reveals the Reagan I knew—a thoughtful and pragmatic student of history, a human being and leader who was secure enough to bare his concerns about the future to a tough geopolitical adversary. No speechwriter, image-maker, handler, or foreign policy expert had anything to do with this draft. Here, as with so many other of Ronald Reagan's communications, he proved again that the best writer on the White House payroll was the president himself. The people of the world "want the dignity of having some control over their individual destiny," he wrote. "They want to work at the craft or trade of their own choosing and to be fairly rewarded. They want to raise their families in peace without harming anyone or suffering harm themselves.... [Mr. Secretary,] should we not be concerned with removing the obstacles that prevent our people from achieving these simple goals?"

I saw the drafts and knew what the president was doing, but he didn't consult me about content, nor did I volunteer any advice. At the time, I was a brand-new White House chief of staff with zero foreign-policy experience.

The president ended the Soviet grain embargo, but unfortunately the unilateral gesture didn't work. Brezhnev did not agree to join in meaningful and constructive dialogue. A summit wasn't in the cards in the near future, he wrote back. He also accused the United States of starting the Cold War and chided President Reagan for telling the Soviet Union how to run its affairs.

Brezhnev was right. President Reagan was lecturing him. The letter was warm and personal, all right, but it was also Reagan 101: a sermon that basically said the Soviets had it wrong on economics, politics, and international relations, and that the United States had it right. It's as if the president thought maybe Brezhnev didn't know this stuff and that if he just heard it, he'd come to his senses.

To foreign policy sophisticates, the president's approach was naive. But history has proven otherwise. Events have validated President Reagan's view of how to deal with the Soviet Union. Only two months earlier, he had charged in a press conference that the Soviets "reserve unto themselves the right to commit any crime, to lie, to cheat, in order to" further their cause. And in his famous 1982 speech to the British Parliament, he would label the Soviets an "evil empire," destined for "the ash heap of history."

What the Brezhnev letter demonstrates is the side of Ronald Reagan that is less well known—his willingness to take a unilateral gamble for peace and his interest in communicating directly and personally with the Soviet leadership. Before Ronald Reagan left office, he would work directly with another Soviet leader, Mikhail Gorbachev, to lay the foundation for an end to the Cold War. The letter to Brezhnev was an important first step in that direction.

The assassination attempt did more than change Ronald Reagan, the man. It changed his presidency. At the time, his ambitious economic plan was stuck in Congress. (His speech to the AFL-CIO union group on March 30 was an attempt to drum up support.) His bravery, dignity, and humor during the crisis, however, were admired by virtually all Americans and gave him enormous political capital. Over the next four months, he used that goodwill and his own enormous skills as a communicator to push the most far-reaching set of tax and spending policy reforms since the New Deal. Would he prevail? And if he did, would his reforms save the economy . . . or wreck it?

EIGHT

"A REFORMED DRUNK"

"JIMMY, DARLING," my ninety-one-year-old mother, Bonner Means Baker, said plaintively, "you didn't really say those things, did you?"

Being honest is the right thing to do and the best way to keep out of trouble, but this time I made an exception to spare my wonderfully Victorian mother the heartache of knowing that her sweet Jimmy sometimes used salty language.

"Of course not," I said.

The truth is that I had said "those things." It was the spring of 1986, and President Reagan's former budget director, David Stockman, had quoted me all too accurately in his new book, *The Triumph of Politics.**

"A different Jim Baker was now sitting two feet away," he wrote about our meeting of November 12, 1981. "His whole patented opening ritual had been completely dispensed with. No off-color joke. No casual waltz around his big office before he sat down. No jump shot that resulted in the arched flight of a paper wad across the room and

---

*Stockman's book helped refresh my memory about what happened in 1981.

without fail into the wastebasket. This time it was all business, and his eyes were steely cold."

That was bad enough, but here's what really upset my mother:

"My friend," he started, "I want you to listen up good. Your ass is in a sling. All of the rest of them want you shit-canned right now. Immediately. This afternoon.

"If it weren't for me," he continued, "you'd be a goner already. But I got you one last chance to save yourself. So you're going to do it precisely and exactly like I tell you. Otherwise you're finished around here."

Baker continued his verbal thrashing without blinking an eye. "You're going to have lunch with the president. The menu is humble pie. You're going to eat every [expletive-deleted] spoonful of it. You're going to be the most contrite sonofabitch this world has ever seen."

Three months before, the president had signed into law the most sweeping overhaul of federal tax and spending policies since the Great Depression. The true author of Reaganomics was Reagan himself, but David Stockman was the numbers man, the technician who had turned the president's ideas into legislative proposals.

What put the young budget director in the hot seat was "The Education of David Stockman" in the December 1981 issue of the *Atlantic Monthly*. At first, none of us saw the trouble it would bring. Not Ed Meese or his deputy Craig Fuller, not Treasury Secretary Don Regan, not my deputy Dick Darman, and not me. If we had, we would never have begun our Legislative Strategy Group (LSG) meeting two days earlier—Stockman's thirty-fifth birthday—by giving him a framed copy of the magazine cover. We even autographed the darn thing.

The laughing stopped, however, when critics began cherry-picking quotes out of the article to cast doubt on the president's economic package. They said it showed that Stockman knew in advance that the tax and budget cuts were based on guesswork and would neither balance the budget nor restore the economy, and that the administration's confidence in supply-side economics was a sham. Democrats had a field day. Stockman was guilty of "one of the most cynical pieces of performance by a public official perhaps since the Vietnam era," said Senator Gary Hart of Colorado.

Stockman quickly labeled the article "wrong and grossly misleading." Later he was even more plainspoken: "I hadn't worked around the clock for seven months to enact the Reagan Revolution because I thought the supply-side tax cut was a scam."

The article was based on taped interviews with William Greider, then an assistant managing editor at the *Washington Post,* now as I write—no surprise—a writer for a hard-left political magazine. Greider was an old friend and intellectual adversary, Stockman would explain. They had begun meeting on Saturday mornings in January so the budget director could test the president's budget and tax plans, and the thinking behind them, against the reporter's skepticism. Stockman later said he had hoped to "convert" Greider and, through him, "the establishment opinion makers" at the *Post.*

In addition to the naïveté of giving no-holds-barred interviews to Greider, Stockman made three mistakes. He didn't set clear ground rules, except that nothing would be written until the legislative battles were over. He had a loose tongue. And he foolishly trusted his friend to report the substance of what was said, not the sloppy language. For instance, Stockman once said low- and middle-bracket tax cuts were a "Trojan horse" for high-bracket tax cuts. Critics took this as a confession that the administration had tricked Congress and the American people. It was really a comment about legislative strategy, and it was factually wrong. From day one, Ronald Reagan insisted on cutting taxes across the board, not as a cynical excuse to help better-off Americans, but because it was the fair thing to do.

Stockman had betrayed the administration, Meese and Deaver told the president at our regular 9:00 A.M. meeting. Furthermore, the story wasn't going away. The networks had hammered us for two straight nights, less about what the article said (in my opinion) than what Democrats said it said. But, no matter. Stockman had to go, they said.

Unfortunately, he didn't have a lot of friends in high places. Like an emergency room doctor, he was often required to deliver bad news. He was also impatient—sometimes a tad arrogant—with anyone who didn't "get it" or who disagreed with him. And it didn't help, frankly, that this former campus radical, divinity school grad student, and Democrat-turned-Republican was barely older than our own kids.

I was the lone holdout. Stockman was smart and articulate. He worked hard and was a super-hawk on balancing the budget. As I wrote in the last chapter, I always believed in surrounding myself— and the president—with the best possible advisers, and Stockman was clearly the best man for this job.

I also knew throwing Stockman overboard would be portrayed as an admission that the administration was guilty as charged. He had made a terrible mistake, I told the president, but it would be better to give him a chance to repent and stay on the team. Invite him to lunch, listen to what he has to say, then make up your mind, I suggested.

When the president agreed, I knew Stockman would probably survive. Ronald Reagan was a soft touch. He was perhaps the only person in Washington who had as hard a time firing someone as I did. Screw up and I'll chew you out, no extra charge for the language that bothered my mother. But I also believe in second chances. Maybe it's because my career in Washington would have ended almost as soon as it started if President Ford or his chief of staff, Dick Cheney, had fired me for predicting that Henry Kissinger would not be in a post-election Ford cabinet.

I had also made mistakes of my own as chief of staff. Three months earlier, for instance, I told a reporter I thought the president would reduce the size of the current proposal for an increase in the defense budget. The next morning, President Reagan and I were having breakfast alone in California when Secretary of Defense Cap

Weinberger called to complain. "Don't do that again," the president lectured me afterward. He was right. I had spoken out of turn. It was a good lesson.

Shortly after I set up Stockman's lunch date, I called him to my office and reminded him the menu was humble pie. "Let me repeat something just in case you didn't get the point. When you go through the Oval Office door, I want to see that sorry ass of yours dragging on the carpet."

The way the press reported it the next day, it was the president, not me, who let Stockman have it. "My visit to the Oval Office for lunch with the president was more in the nature of a visit to the woodshed after supper," Stockman told reporters.

Not so, as it turned out. In his book, Stockman said the president's eyes grew moist. "Dave, how do you explain this?" Stockman said his reply "meandered off into a total digression." But when the unhappy young man offered to resign, the president said no. "I need your help."

The White House then issued a press release saying the president "stated unequivocally that he would not tolerate any attempt to mislead the American people" and "that the policies of this administration were being pursued ... in good faith on the basis of the best evidence and judgment possible."

This formally distanced the White House from the most serious charges against Stockman. The next step was to show that the president still supported him. How? "Only on a not-for-attribution basis was an official willing to give Reagan's reason for rejecting Stockman's resignation," the *Washington Post*'s Lee Lascaze wrote later. "He said the president is satisfied Stockman can and will support Reagan's programs; that Stockman is needed and his remarks do not affect the economic program; that Stockman 'is an extraordinarily capable public servant.'"

Sound familiar?

I often spoke to journalists on a not-for-attribution basis. One essential task of the White House chief of staff—as Dick Cheney, Don Rumsfeld, and others told me—is to spend a lot of time explaining the president's policies to reporters. This is called backgrounding and is very different from leaking. Leaking is when you put out unauthorized information to undermine the president's policy or drive the policy debate on an issue the president has not yet settled. Or when you say something for no other purpose than to skewer someone else.

When Don Regan took over as chief of staff, he said he couldn't believe I had spent so much time with the press. All his statements would be on the record, he said. To each his own, I suppose, but he didn't do himself, the president, or the public any favors by refusing to talk privately with journalists. This was another illustration of why individuals who have been principals, such as governors and CEOs (Regan ran Merrill Lynch), generally have a hard time as chief of staff. It's hard for them to think and act in a secondary role. As chief of staff, you hold what is possibly the second most powerful job in Washington, but nobody elected you. You're still staff. All your power is vicarious from the president. Forget that for one minute, and you're in trouble!

Like Don Regan, some media outlets today want everything on the record and say they will limit what they will take on background. So be it. The approach in the Reagan and Bush administrations was simple: if you don't like the rules, don't come. The press is so competitive, particularly with the modern proliferation of news outlets, that I doubt any reporter can really afford to stay away from good sources that other journalists are tapping.

I learned how to get along with the press during presidential campaigns. One ironclad rule: on or off the record, never lie. If I couldn't answer a question, I'd just say I wouldn't comment. Reporters knew I worked for the president and would explain things his way—call it spinning if you wish—but they also knew they could trust, factually, what I told them.

Another thing that worked in my favor was the perception that I was a moderate voice in a conservative administration. I'll leave it to journalists to explain why they are, as a group, more comfortable with public officials on the left and in the middle than with those on the right. Whatever the reasons, this served me well and, through me, the president.

The fact is, I am a Texas Republican. We are a fairly conservative bunch, even among other Republicans. My reputation as a moderate probably stemmed from my pragmatism. I resisted efforts to broaden the administration's agenda to include every item on the Republican wish list, particularly some social issues that would have distracted us from the president's main goals of strengthening the economy and re-building the military. The Carter administration tried to do too many things at once. That was a big mistake, even when the president's party controlled Congress. With the House solidly controlled by Democrats in 1981, we had even less room to chase every good idea that came along. To accomplish anything, we had to pick our fights and put all our energy into winning them.

Some of Ronald Reagan's more ideological supporters thought I kept the president from following his better instincts. "Let Reagan be Reagan!" they proclaimed. All I can say is that they overestimated me and underestimated their president. He was a strong-willed man with clear principles and firmly held views, not a puppet in the hands of staff. Besides, I wasn't the only adviser who wanted to give priority to strengthening the economy and national defense. Meese, Deaver, and Nancy Reagan did, too.

The Reagan-Stockman meeting was big news and, as I had hoped, the focus of the stories shifted. Now it was about what the president said to his budget director, not what the budget director said to a re-porter. The hungry news beast fed on this personality-driven story for a day or two, then moved on, sniffing as always for something new.

WHEN THE HISTORY of the last half of the twentieth century is written, the Stockman flap, justifiably, will be only a footnote. The real story was the revolution in economic policy in that fateful year of 1981.

Ronald Reagan won the presidency because the American economy was broken. He said he knew how to fix it, the voters believed him, and he did what he promised.

In the seventies, an unprecedented combination of high inflation and high unemployment —"stagflation"—put people out of work and hammered living standards. The sum of these two indices was called the "misery index," and when it reached 12 percent in 1976, it helped Jimmy Carter beat President Ford. Now the index was more than 20 percent. The once-mighty U.S. economy actually shrank in 1980. *Newsweek* said President Reagan had inherited "the most dangerous economic crisis since Franklin Roosevelt took office forty-eight years ago." Watergate and Vietnam also cast doubt on our ability to control larger events at home or abroad. By 1980, Iranian militants held American hostages in Tehran and Soviet tanks rumbled across Afghanistan.

The worst part is that no one seemed to know what to do. We tried wage-and-price controls—mandatory under Nixon, "voluntary" under Carter (as long as your company wanted government contracts)—but quickly discovered the old lesson about fixing prices: it creates shortages. Hello, gasoline lines. The famous Keynesian tradeoff between inflation and unemployment also failed, and we got both. Economic pessimists said we needed to accept the "limits of growth" and learn to get along with less. Even President Carter saw "an erosion of confidence in the future that is threatening to destroy the social and political fabric of America."

All during this period, Ronald Reagan—as governor of California, commentator, and presidential candidate—preached economic optimism. The key to prosperity, he believed, was economic freedom. If government would just get out of the way, American workers and investors would do the rest. The elements of what came to be known as Reaganomics were lower taxes, reduced government spending (except for defense), fewer regulations, a sound dollar, and free trade.

Meanwhile, a handful of economists, editorial writers, and politicians (including Stockman) were pushing something called supply-side economics. They said high marginal tax rates created a perverse incentive for American workers and businesses to slow down, work less, and invest in tax shelters, not productive enterprises. Cut the confiscatory rates, they said, and people will work harder and invest more. This was consistent with Ronald Reagan's larger set of ideas, so he and the supply-siders embraced each other as natural allies.

Traditional Republicans believed many of the same things, but put a higher priority on balancing the budget. This set up a primary fight for the soul of the GOP, and if George Bush was anything, he was a traditional Republican. "Voodoo economics" was his campaign's label for the idea that we could dramatically cut taxes and balance the budget at the same time.

The mandate for Ronald Reagan was a mandate for Reaganomics. Now came the hard part, turning the candidate's ideas into law—a job that would consume most of my waking hours in 1981. The outline of the plan was set in the campaign. It would be built around three annual 10 percent tax cuts. We would then have to control spending to put the government on a course toward a balanced budget. (Critics who later said we never intended to balance the budget were dead wrong. We started down that road with genuine confidence and enthusiasm.)

The federal budget process is peculiar. Cuts are not necessarily cuts. They are measured, not against the previous year's spending, but against a baseline of future spending under existing law. If the federal subsidy for widget manufacturers is set to grow by 10 percent, for example, a 5 percent "cut" will still leave the beneficiaries ahead of the game. We tried to cut a few programs below existing levels, but most of our cuts were intended to slow down the runaway train of federal spending, not to throw it into reverse. The federal budget grew during every year of the Reagan presidency.

But Stockman had more ambitious cuts in mind. Early in the game, he identified $40 billion in potential first-year reductions. Much more would be needed to balance the budget, he said, but this was a good start. Cabinet officers went along. At that point, Stockman understood their budgets better than most of them did. They also knew this is what the president wanted. And frankly, cutting the budget is an easy principle to support; what's hard is doing it.

Democrats were in a bind. Existing policies simply weren't working, and the president had carried many of their states and congressional districts. Still, most Democrats were unwilling to undo the programs their party had put in place over the past four decades, and they were far from powerless. They controlled the House by more than 50 votes. If they stuck together, they could obviously block the president's program. There was an opening, however, if we could win the Boll Weevils.

They were the remnant of the once-powerful bloc of conservative Democrats who ruled the Solid South, plus a few like-minded party members from other parts of the nation. As their party moved steadily to the left on economic, defense, and social issues, these forty or so conservative lawmakers occasionally voted with Republicans. We would need them.

Thanks to the president's coattails, Republicans controlled the Senate for the first time in decades. GOP senators supported their president and they could read the election returns, but they also worried about budget deficits, and—like Democrats—were not happy about cutting programs they had backed in the past.

We had a two-part strategy. Ronald Reagan was one of the finest public speakers in presidential history. Using his tremendous skills as a communicator and capitalizing on his popularity, particularly after the assassination attempt, he made repeated televised appeals to Congress and the American people. Every time he spoke, he moved the needle on public and congressional opinion. I've never seen anything like it, and I doubt anyone else has, either.

Meanwhile, the Legislative Strategy Group did the grunt work.

This was a good example of how—contrary to popular belief at the time—Meese and I regularly worked together for the benefit of the president. We settled our differences in LSG meetings, counted

My grandfather Captain James Addison Baker, and the advice I obeyed for forty years. After that—two out of three aren't bad. The Captain was an important figure in the history of Houston, the Baker Botts law firm, Rice University, and my childhood memories. I keep this newspaper photomontage from the late 1930s on a wall by my desk. (BAKER COLLECTION)

My father, James Addison Baker, Jr., during World War I. (BAKER COLLECTION)

My mother, Bonner Means Baker, with me and my sister Bonner in the late 1930s. (BAKER COLLECTION)

Bonner and me at summer camp in the Texas Hill Country. (BAKER COLLECTION)

My first inaugural: My fiancée, Mary Stuart McHenry, smiles at me as she waits for Eisenhower's 1953 inaugural parade to begin. We got there early to claim seats directly across from the White House. (BAKER COLLECTION)

Eisenhower was riding past us when I took this shot. (BAKER COLLECTION)

With the Marines, 1953. I was a lieutenant on active duty for two years—below, as a naval gunfire spotter—then rose to the rank of captain in the Reserve. (BAKER COLLECTION)

Mary Stuart at the beach in North Carolina before I shipped out with the Sixth Fleet. (BAKER COLLECTION)

In early 1970, I entered politics for the first time as Harris County chairman for George H. W. Bush's Senate campaign. This was the day we opened our local headquarters—and I gave my first political speech. (BAKER COLLECTION)

Briefing the press as President Gerald Ford's delegate hunter in the contest with Governor Ronald Reagan for the 1976 Republican presidential nomination. (MARTY LA VOR)

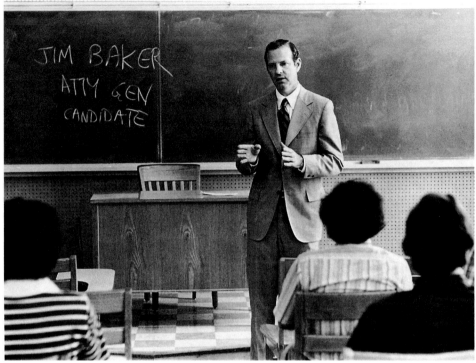

My one and only race for political office, in 1978 for Texas attorney general.
Here I'm speaking at LBJ's alma mater, Southwest Texas State University.
(DON ANDERS, TEXAS STATE UNIVERSITY)

Jim Baker is an independent, tough, dedicated man who'll make a great Attorney General for Texas.

Jerry Ford

As I campaigned across Texas, I handed out this small "push card" to potential
voters. (JASON LYONS COLLECTION)

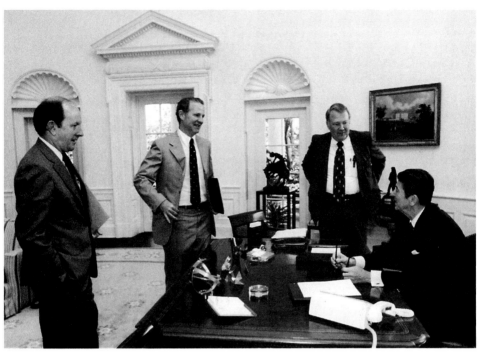

As Ronald Reagan's chief of staff. Every morning during his first term, the "troika"—Michael Deaver, Ed Meese, and I—briefed the president. (WHITE HOUSE PHOTOGRAPH)

Aboard *Marine One* with the president. This helicopter trip was taken on March 25, 1981, five days before he was shot. (WHITE HOUSE PHOTOGRAPH)

Vice President Bush arrives in the White House situation room after the shooting. To the left, Richard Allen, Ed Meese, and Martin Anderson. To the right, Alexander Haig and me. (WHITE HOUSE PHOTOGRAPH)

At George Washington University Hospital, nine days later. Even while recuperating, the president continued to sign legislation and conduct staff meetings. (WHITE HOUSE PHOTOGRAPH)

May 28, back at work in the cabinet room. Caspar Weinberger and I share a light moment with the president. Behind us, Alexander Haig, Richard Allen, and Bill Clark seem to have something else on their minds. (WHITE HOUSE PHOTOGRAPH)

With the president on *Air Force One*, 1982. (WHITE HOUSE PHOTOGRAPH)

A somber White House meeting on October 23, 1983, the day the Marine barracks in Beirut were bombed. Clockwise from left: Ed Meese, General John Vessey, Caspar Weinberger, Vice President Bush, President Reagan, George Shultz, Deputy CIA Director John McMahon, and me. The man with his back to the camera is probably Bud McFarlane. (WHITE HOUSE PHOTOGRAPH)

In the Oval Office, August 1984. I had two major responsibilities now—serving as chief of staff and running the president's reelection campaign.
(WHITE HOUSE PHOTOGRAPH)

Celebrating the end of the campaign with champagne aboard *Air Force One.*

And celebrating the second inauguration with Nancy Reagan. Nancy was always an ally.

In January 1985, Don Regan and I swapped jobs. He took over as White House
chief of staff and I became treasury secretary. (WHITE HOUSE PHOTOGRAPH)

Attorney General William French Smith swears me in as secretary of the treasury.
Barbara Bush, President Reagan, and Susan witness the ceremony.
(WHITE HOUSE PHOTOGRAPH)

Three key members of my inner circle at both the White House and Treasury: Margaret Tutwiler, Dick Darman, and John Rogers. (BAKER COLLECTION)

With President Reagan, as he names Alan Greenspan to succeed Paul Volcker as Fed chairman. (WHITE HOUSE PHOTOGRAPH)

A new president, George H. W. Bush, meant a new job for me. In January 1989, two months after I helped defeat his vice-presidential bid, Texas senator Lloyd Bentsen graciously introduced me to the Senate Foreign Relations Committee for my confirmation hearing as secretary of state. (*THE NEW YORK TIMES*/JOSE R. LOPEZ)

Chief Justice William Rehnquist administers my oath of office, while Susan holds a family Bible and President Bush looks on. (WHITE HOUSE PHOTOGRAPH)

Serving as secretary of state for my friend was the pinnacle of my public career. At top, with him and Treasury Secretary Nicholas Brady at the 1989 G-7 Economic Summit in Paris. Below, at a NATO summit meeting in Brussels.

June 1991. Hope for peace was high when Yitzhak Rabin took office as prime minister of Israel.
(BAKER COLLECTION)

With our troops in the Saudi desert, November 1990, in the run-up to Desert Storm.
(GREG ENGLISH/GETTY IMAGES)

August 1992. Resigning from the State Department to return to presidential politics was one of the hardest things I've ever had to do.
(DAVID AKE/GETTY IMAGES)

our votes, developed strategies, then fanned out to do the necessary cajoling, hand-holding, and trading. Max Friedersdorf headed our very capable Office of Congressional Relations, which included, among others, Ken Duberstein and M. B. Oglesby, but everyone in the administration pitched in. When called on, which was often, even the president would work the phones. It was a helluva team.

President Reagan gave his first televised speech on the economy from the White House on Thursday, February 5, sixteen days after taking the oath of office. Some in our ranks wanted to use campaign-style rhetoric to attack the tax-and-spend Democrats. But the president woke up at 4:00 A.M. and massaged the text to make it more conciliatory. He was, after all, the president now. He would call on both parties to act responsibly and work together to fix the economy.

The speech won rave reviews. So too did a second televised address to a joint session of Congress on February 18. We thought about using this appearance to deliver a full state of the union address, as Eisenhower and Kennedy did early in their administrations, but decided instead to focus exclusively on our number-one issue, the economy.

President Reagan entered the chamber to great applause, then outlined the most revolutionary economic program in at least half a century. He called it "America's New Beginning: A Program for Economic Recovery." Individual income taxes would be cut by 10 percent a year for three years, as promised, and business would get faster depreciation rules. By then, Stockman had worked up about $49 billion in itemized savings for fiscal year 1982, with $44 billion more in "future savings to be proposed." The president ordered cabinet secretaries to postpone the effective dates for hundreds of new federal regulations and put Vice President Bush in charge of a cabinet-level task force on regulatory relief. And he pledged to support the Federal Reserve System in its fight against inflation.

Tax and budget cuts were clearly centerpieces of Reaganomics, but other elements were important, too. Within nine days of being sworn in, for instance, the president had deregulated crude oil prices, shut down a standby wage and price regulatory program, and set up the regulatory oversight process—all by executive order.

A little more than a year later, the president commissioned Peter Grace to lead fellow business executives in an internal management review of federal programs. The Grace Commission recommended more than 2,500 ways to reduce the number of federal employees, eliminate redundant publications, cut travel costs, and otherwise streamline federal agencies and improve their management and financial systems.

President Reagan told the joint session he wanted to balance the budget by 1984. The written version of his plan boldly predicted that economic growth would reach 4 or 5 percent by 1986 and that inflation would fall to less than 5 percent. He challenged Congress to move quickly. "The people are watching and waiting," he said. "They don't demand miracles, but they do expect us to act."

The president was interrupted by applause sixteen times, and he drew an extended ovation when he said, "Let us act together." Stockman went to the Hill the next day to explain the nuts and bolts of the program. The game was on.

But when the Senate Budget Committee started marking up the plan, we immediately had a problem. Chairman Pete Domenici and other GOP senators wanted to protect a lot of existing programs, so they threw out the administration's laundry list of spending cuts and penciled in a one-year freeze on the cost-of-living adjustment for Social Security. Stockman said I went into "red alert" when I heard about this. He was right. I arranged for the president to visit the Hill. By making it a test of loyalty, he talked the GOP senators into taking Social Security off the table.

In early April—the president was then in the hospital—the Senate adopted our budget resolution, pretty much without any changes. A test vote went our way 59–41, with sixteen Democrats, and the resolution was adopted 88–10. For a brief moment it looked all too easy, but our troubles were just starting.

The next problem was Stockman's "future savings to be proposed," a multibillion-dollar item that came to be known as the "magic asterisk." We wanted to show it on the budget documents as a spending cut, out of respect for our plan to announce additional cuts in coming weeks, but Senator Domenici refused. He posted it as a deficit and, predictably, the Senate Budget Committee revolted and voted down the plan 12–8. The senators' appetite for budget cutting wasn't strong to begin with, and the hint of a big deficit gave them a reason to take to the sidelines. The president's plan was in trouble in the Senate.

Over on the House side a furious battle was under way for the hearts and minds of the Boll Weevils. The president invited the Democrats for breakfast in the East Room in early March. I remember it well. The meeting ended with effusive declarations of support for our plan. The only problem was the first priority for many Boll Weevils was deficit reduction, not tax cuts. For us, it was a package deal.

Winning uncommitted or wavering House members is not much different from winning uncommitted delegates. The power of the presidency—certainly one as popular as Reagan's—is hard to resist, so the president regularly invited key Democrats to the Oval Office, to state dinners, even to Camp David. The White House Office of Public Liaison, headed by Elizabeth Dole, effectively organized public-sector support.

The counterattack from Democrats was strong and visceral. The Congressional Black Caucus accused the president of jeopardizing programs that were lifelines for poor people. "Reagan is reverse Robin Hood, robbing the poor and giving to the rich," said a Democratic congressman from Illinois. On May 7, Democratic constituencies—the organized poor, the elderly, farm workers, and people with disabilities—were bused into Washington for a "National Day of Mourning."

Everybody's welcome to his opinion, but the fact of the matter is that we had no intention of touching the big social programs—Social Security, Medicare, and Medicaid. We did propose to cut some smaller programs in education, training, unemployment, and social services, most fairly recent in origin, and mostly by consolidating overlapping programs into block grants and tightening eligibility standards. We also tightened up retirement, disability, and benefit programs for federal workers, railroad employees, coal miners, and veterans—ancient programs that, frankly, were long overdue for a good scrubbing.

A lot of the criticism was not about the merits of our proposals, however; it was personal. Critics said we were out to help the rich at the expense of the poor. Well, I never knew a less class-conscious guy than Ronald Reagan. He himself came from humble beginnings. He loved to correspond with Americans from all stations of life, and he treated them all with unfailing dignity and respect. He honestly believed that the best way to help the poor—and all other Americans—was to strengthen the economy. He also believed that many social welfare programs did more harm than good for their supposed beneficiaries. The success of the 1996 welfare reform bill—post-Reagan Reaganomics, signed by Bill Clinton—proves he was right, in my opinion. President Reagan sympathized with genuine deprivation. "Those who, through no fault of their own, must depend on the rest of us—the poverty stricken, the disabled, the elderly, all those with true need—can rest assured that the social safety net of programs they depend on are exempt from any cuts," he said. And he meant it, as David Stockman learned again and again in his endless search for budget-cutting targets.

Democrats knew the president had a mandate for change, so they set about crafting a Reagan-lite plan with a one-year tax cut and modest spending reductions. Jim Jones, the Oklahoma Democrat who headed the House Budget Committee, worked up the proposal, and it tempted some Boll Weevils. On one Sunday talk show in April, Jones even floated the idea that the president was ready to compromise. Still recovering from the assassination attempt, the president replied the next day: "No compromise!"

The path forward was a substitute bill drafted by Phil Gramm, a second-term Boll Weevil congressman from Texas, and Ohioan Delbert Latta, a senior Republican, both members of the Budget Committee. Except for some sweeteners for key Boll Weevils, it was almost identical to the administration's bill.

On April 28, nine days before the House vote, Ronald Reagan returned to the Hill for his first nationally televised address since the assassination attempt. A thinner president—accompanied by the heroic Jerry Parr, head of his Secret Service detail—entered the chamber to a wild ovation that lasted several minutes. He first thanked the nation for "your messages and flowers and, most of all, your prayers, not only for me but for those others who fell beside me."

Then he said the American people had sent a message in the 1980 election, but now were losing patience. "Six months is long enough. [They] want us to act, and not in half measures." "The old comfortable way is to shave a little here and add a little there," he said, alluding to the Jones bill. "Well, that's not acceptable anymore." Only the bipartisan Gramm-Latta budget resolution would restore the American economy.

Tip O'Neill threw in the towel before the climactic May 7 House vote. "I can read Congress," he said. "They go with the will of the people, and the will of the people is to go along with the president." Sixty-three Democrats joined the GOP to pass Gramm-Latta 253–176. (The tired but happy LSG had expected about forty Democrats to cross over.) A *Washington Post* headline the next day said it all: "Shattered: Democratic Coalition Falls to Pieces on First Test with Reagan." When the Senate approved the budget resolution a few days later, the Reagan revolution appeared to be unstoppable.

Then we shot ourselves in the foot.

The issue was Social Security, the system to provide retirement income for older Americans, plus a cornucopia of other benefits. By 1981, it was financially unsound. Within two or three years, everyone knew, revenues from payroll taxes would not cover the monthly rounds of checks. A major overhaul was needed, and reasonable minds disagreed about how to do it. Unbeknownst to those of us in the West Wing, Stockman had decided to squeeze billions of dollars of "future savings to be proposed" out of the program.

Whoever first called Social Security the third rail of American politics got it exactly right. Every time a policymaker says "Social Security" and "reform" in the same sentence, the Social Security lobby rises up—and damn the consequences for the younger generation, the economy, the budget, and Social Security itself. The reality is that old folks vote, and Congress pays attention to constituents who vote.

Just two days after House passage of Gramm-Latta, the White House received an administration task force report on Social Security. Former Senator Richard Schweiker—the president's 1976 running mate, now secretary of health and human services (HHS)—headed the task force. Stockman was an influential member. The report recommended major reforms, including stiff new penalties for retiring before sixty-five—penalties that would go into effect with little warning on January 1, 1982.

Uh-oh!

At an Oval Office meeting on May 11, Schweiker, Stockman, and domestic policy adviser Martin Anderson pitched the president hard. These experts understood the numbers, but they hadn't adequately considered the political implications. If we appeared to be cutting Social Security benefits to balance the budget, we would face a political disaster. Later, Anderson, Ed Meese, Jack Svahn (the Social Security commissioner), and others quickly led the president through a black binder of recommended options. To my distress, the president agreed with them without taking the matter under advisement as he usually did. Our success on the budget resolution may have encouraged him to shoot for the moon on this issue, which he had talked about for years. The proposal would be released the next day.

Heading off trouble or limiting damage before it occurs is always better than trying to clean up a mess afterward. In a contentious later afternoon meeting with Schweiker and Stockman, I engineered a pre-

emptive damage-control plan to present the new Social Security proposal as an HHS response to a congressional inquiry, not as a White
House initiative. I also recommended that the site for the release be
Baltimore, where the Social Security administration was headquartered. That would put as much distance as possible between the proposal and the president.

Back in my office, Schweiker was very exercised as he told Dick
Darman and me that he had been a U.S. senator! He knew Congress!
He had worked all of this out! All he had to do was take the first step,
and key Democrats would embrace the proposal! "If that's the case,
why not make a bipartisan announcement?" we asked. He said that he
knew what he was doing and that the president was on board.

As I feared, the blowback from the announcement was hot and
heavy. Republicans complained about being blindsided, and Democrats, still smarting from their budget defeat, blistered us. Even though
the plan was never formally put on the table, the Senate preemptively
voted against it 92–0. And that was that. Social Security was off the
front pages, but at significant cost to our legislative momentum.*

Unfortunately, the system still needed repair. Stockman revived
the issue in September. This time, the president said he wanted to address the nation on television. In my view, we were setting ourselves
up for a repeat of the Social Security debacle in May, so I asked the
Republican leaders in the Senate and House—Howard Baker and Bob
Michel—to come to the Oval Office and tell the president what they
had both told me, that we didn't have a prayer of passing a major overhaul of Social Security in either house. The big tax and budget fights
had left Congress with battle fatigue, they said.

The president was not easily convinced, but when Howard sug-

---

*There was a silver lining to all of this. We used the incident to get the president to agree that
from now on, all significant policy proposals involving Congress had to go through the Legislative Strategy Group before they reached the Oval Office. The effect of this was to better
protect the president, but also to transfer much of the policymaking process from the cabinet council system overseen by Ed to the legislative system overseen by me.

gested appointing a blue-ribbon committee on Social Security, he agreed to think about it. That's an idea we had already been kicking around. Later that year, the president and congressional leaders—all genuinely concerned about the national retirement system—agreed to "take the issue out of politics" by putting it in the hands of a commission appointed by the leaders of both parties.

Was this a case of "not letting Reagan be Reagan"? Not at all. Once the president understood that overhaul wouldn't fly in Congress, he had no hesitation about doing what had to be done to save Social Security. This was the pragmatic "Reagan being Reagan."

In December, the House, the Senate, and the White House each named five members, and the White House appointed Alan Greenspan to head the group. Over the next year, it met secretly in the basement of my D.C. home on Foxhall Road. One of my favorite members was Daniel Patrick Moynihan. The brilliant and personable senator from New York, an academic-turned-politician, was a big man with an even bigger intellect, a man with a thirst for knowledge and a thirst for, well, other things.

One afternoon my son Will Winston, seventeen, answered the doorbell. "Come right in, Senator."

"Thank you, sir. Thank you very much," Moynihan said. "I want to tell you something: you look exactly like your father." (Will was too polite to say I was his stepfather, not his biological father.)

"Is there someplace where a man could get a drink in this house?"

"Yes, sir," Will replied. "We've got coffee, Cokes, ginger ale, iced tea . . ."

"No, son, I mean a *real* drink."

Will had seen adults imbibe before. This was how he learned that for some folks, cocktail hour begins earlier than 6:00 P.M.

But Moynihan was a better public servant with a drink or two under his belt than most others with none. His knowledge of Social Security was exceeded only by his passion for saving it. I treasure my memories of working with him, then sharing laughs and drinks (real ones) with him afterward. When I left public service, he wrote one of the nicest letters I received.

The Greenspan Commission was a great success. It worked out a genuine compromise between those who wanted to increase taxes and those who wanted to reduce benefits.

Because the commission included Republicans and Democrats selected by the White House and the leadership of both houses of Congress, it provided political cover for Congress to make these hard decisions. The 1983 reforms put Social Security on a sound footing for more than three decades (on a cash-flow basis) and about sixty years (with the trust fund).

As I was writing, President George W. Bush proposed new reforms for Social Security. My opinion, for what it's worth, is that the system does not face a crisis today but that the president's proposed personal accounts made sense on their own merits. There's no great risk (and considerable upside) in personal accounts that are designed correctly. An "ownership society"—having assets to pass to heirs—is a good way to give all Americans a stake in our economic system.

At the same time, personal accounts won't cure the future solvency problem. There is no easy way to do that. The best way would be to get the leaders of both parties together privately to work out a solution, as we did in 1983. It'll be hard, and perhaps impossible, to do what needs to be done unless both parties agree not to use the issue as a political battering ram.

Can we do that? I'm not sure. The nation is evenly split today, and relations between the parties are poisonous. It's not like when I first went up in 1975 and throughout the 1980s, when it was still possible—even after Watergate—to "disagree agreeably," where your political adversary was not necessarily your political enemy, and where genuine friendships were forged across party lines.

The reason we put Social Security on the back burner in 1981 was to focus on tax and spending issues. By mid-June, however, it was clear we had a big problem. Gramm-Latta had instructed Congress to come back with $36 billion in spending cuts, but hostile Democratic chairmen produced a budget bill that was "riddled with gimmicks," not real savings, Stockman told the president. So the administration did something unprecedented. We wrote our own budget bill, Gramm-Latta II. This offended congressional Democrats and not a few of our own supporters. They saw this as a challenge to the prerogatives of Congress as an equal branch of government.

A week out, we didn't have the votes. We had lost many budget-balancing Boll Weevils and also faced possible defections from "Gypsy moths"—moderate-to-liberal Republicans, mostly from the Northeast, who often voted with the Democrats. While the LSG horse-traded, the president worked the undecideds by telephone. The key vote came on a June 25 motion to keep Gramm-Latta II off the floor. Thirty-one Democrats sided with us, and we won 217–210. The Senate approved its version of the budget bill in mid-July, and a final bill passed both houses in late July.

All the while, we were fighting on a second front for tax cuts. Dan Rostenkowski, powerful chairman of House Ways and Means, wanted nothing to do with our three annual 10 percent cuts, and what Danny wanted (or didn't want), Danny usually got. More than one pundit declared the president's plan dead. Even supporters lost heart. We'd be lucky to come away with a one-year cut for low- and middle-income taxpayers, commentators said. But, as I mentioned earlier, the president's dramatic April 28 speech changed everything. Suddenly, almost overnight, the momentum began to shift. Stockman says this is when I started playing poker with the tax bill. He's right, but I was playing the hands I was dealt in meetings with Regan, Meese, and other members of the LSG.

The only way to win was to deal. To hold the Boll Weevils, for instance, we reduced the first year's cut to 5 percent and delayed it for nine months. Rostenkowski answered with a 15 percent cut over two years. President Reagan acknowledged, tongue in cheek, that the Democrats' bill might do more for the average guy and gal, *if they planned to live for only two more years.* The principal sponsors of our bipartisan plan were Barber Conable, a respected Republican moderate from New York who later headed the World Bank while I was serving as treasury secretary, and Kent Hance, a Texas Democrat who won his congressional seat in a 1978 race against George W. Bush. The fight between Rostenkowski's bill and Conable-Hance was less a battle of ideas, sadly, than a bidding war over tax breaks, but that was the price for the cuts the president wanted. That's also how we got indexing of federal income tax rates to prevent "bracket creep," the stealth tax hikes that result from inflation, and an immediate reduction of the 70 percent marginal tax rate on investment income to 50 percent, which was more than we had originally hoped for.

As the vote approached, the LSG worked overtime. The showdown in the House would not be on the bill itself, but on a motion to substitute Conable-Hance for the Rostenkowski bill. To hold Republicans, we arranged for each of four soft Gypsy Moths to receive a high-level phone call. We also identified friendly lawmakers to give post-speech statements supporting the president and talked about having some converts step forward after the vote on the motion to create a sense of momentum.

Thanks to our hard work and a final speech by the Great Communicator on July 27, we won the key vote by 238–195. Forty-eight House Democrats supported the president. Jim Jeffords was the only Gypsy Moth who flew away.* Two days later, the Senate passed its version by voice vote. The headline in the *Washington Post* read, "Reagan Triumphant on His 3-Year Tax Cut Bill."

On August 13, the president signed the historic legislation at a morning press conference at his California ranch. The budget bill "represents $130 billion in savings over the next three years" and the tax bill will cut $750 billion over the next five years, he said. Together, "they represent a turnaround of almost a half century of a course this

---

*This is the same Jim Jeffords who left the GOP early in George W. Bush's first term and helped the Democrats regain control, temporarily, of a closely divided Senate.

country's been on and mark an end to excessive growth in government bureaucracy, government spending, [and] government taxing."

WE DIDN'T celebrate long. Ten days before the signing ceremony, in fact, Stockman had called a White House meeting to tote up the numbers. We hadn't won all our proposed budget cuts, many "future savings" still remained "to be proposed," the tax cut was larger than we had estimated, and the nation was slipping into a recession. For these reasons, Stockman said, we were looking at minimum deficits of $60 billion for each of the next four years, maybe even $100 billion. We were stunned. If these numbers held up, the goal of a balanced budget was out the window.

There has been a lot of finger-pointing about who knew what, and when. That's one reason the *Atlantic* article hit us so hard in November. But I didn't have much interest then, and don't now, in the blame game or the excuse game. I also don't believe in going on the battlefield after the fighting is over and shooting the wounded. The fact is that the president could not hope to accomplish the goals of his first administration (not to mention winning a second term) unless he maintained his political viability, and that absolutely required him to win these battles over spending and taxes. We didn't have enough votes—and couldn't get them—for 100 percent of the spending reductions the president wanted, and we were forced into a bidding war over the tax bill. When the dust settled in August we found ourselves staring at a huge deficit. Now we had a problem we needed to try to solve.

Stockman suggested a "September Offensive" to keep up the momentum of budget cutting. We knew it would be tough. More cuts in discretionary spending would be hard for Congress and the public to stomach. Defense had been off limits, but Stockman argued that it needed a second look. I agreed. We made a serious run at the president, but—after having won big increases in the defense budget—he was reluctant to pare them back, and Defense Secretary Weinberger was a masterful bureaucratic infighter. We won modest reductions, nothing substantial. Looking back now at the success of the Reagan-Bush defense policy—"peace through strength"—it's clear that the investment in defense paid big dividends.

Both parties in Congress had simply lost their appetite for major spending cuts. So had a lot of cabinet officers and, in his own way, the president. The September Offensive soon fizzled. We could be proud of the budget cuts of 1981, but we would never again repeat that success.

The recession hit hard in the fall of 1981 and continued for more than a year. The downturn hurt the GOP in the '82 midterm elections. Critics blamed Reaganomics, but the budget and tax plans didn't even go into effect until October 1, 1981, and it would be another year before the first 10 percent tax cut kicked in. The real problem was the Fed's shock therapy to stop inflation. This was something that had to be done, but it happened so quickly that it knocked the wheels off the American economy and messed up our economic assumptions. Still, the president never blinked. Inflation was the cruelest tax of all, he said, and he never leaned on the Fed—as some presidents had—to back off.

Despite the recession, we had to try to do something about the deficits. We had campaigned on cutting taxes by $500 billion over five years, but had actually cut them by $750 billion. In early 1982, Meese, Deaver, Stu Spencer, and I—with the support of Nancy Reagan—tried to persuade the president to raise taxes to recoup some of the cuts beyond the $500 billion campaign target. We could do it without touching the '81 rate cuts, we said, but the president didn't want to do it. "I'd rather be criticized for a deficit than for backing away from our economic program," he wrote in his diary.

After months of wrangling with Congress over the budget and getting nowhere, Meese, Deaver, and I tried one more time in the late spring of 1982. The president listened, then took off his reading glasses and threw them down on the Oval Office desk. "All right, goddammit," he said. "I'm gonna do it, but it's wrong." The resulting

Tax and Fiscal Responsibility Act of 1982 was designed to raise about $98 billion in business and excise taxes over three years. As promised, we didn't touch the '81 rate reductions. The president later said he regretted capitulating.

I SOMETIMES call myself a "reformed drunk" on Reaganomics. Even though I was a traditional conservative, not a supply-sider, when I joined the administration, I worked my butt off to put the president's economic program in place. At the same time, I always worried that Stockman and other pessimists might be right about budget deficits leading to hyper-inflation, intolerable interest rates, and economic decline.

Well, the pessimists turned out to be wrong and Ronald Reagan, economics major at Eureka College, former movie actor, and eternal optimist, turned out to be right. The economy started growing in November 1982 and hasn't stopped yet, except for slowdowns in 1990–1991 and 2001 that were modest by historical standards. When the final tax cuts went into effect in 1984, the economy grew more than 7 percent. That was the best year since 1951, and it hasn't been matched since. Inflation averaged close to 10 percent in the Carter years; under Presidents Reagan and George H. W. Bush, it fell to 3 percent. All told, more than nineteen million new jobs were created during the Reagan-Bush years. And while we never balanced the budget, we dramatically increased tax revenues—despite the tax cuts!—and slowed the rate of growth in federal spending.

What appeared radical in 1981 is now conventional wisdom. No serious politician in the last twenty years—not one—has openly proposed restoring the failed tax policies of the 1970s. The success of Reaganomics and its British counterpart, Thatcherism, also discredited central planning, state ownership, excessive regulation, and heavy taxation worldwide. Today, even China, Russia, and India have liberalized their state economies.

Does this mean that deficits don't matter? Of course not. I still object to running a credit card on the next generation. But the deficits of the eighties, though unfortunate, did less harm than the tax cuts did good. The green-eyeshade crowd said we would have a meltdown. Instead, thanks to Ronald Reagan, our economy boomed.

In the 1990s, Robert Rubin took up the mantle of "fiscal discipline," first as a Clinton adviser, later as treasury secretary. Bob was one of the stars of the Clinton cabinet. I have great respect for him and consider him a friend, but I disagree strongly on this issue. He used "fiscal discipline" as an argument for raising taxes, as Democrats did in 1993. But tax hikes without spending restraint never balance the budget because Congress always spends the new money, and more.

Did President Clinton's "fiscally responsible" 1993 tax bill trigger the prosperity of the 1990s? No. Despite the downturn in 1990–1991, the economy had already been growing smartly for two years before that bill was passed. Let me repeat: you simply cannot deal with deficits with taxes alone, unaccompanied by spending restraint. President Reagan said it best. "Deficits aren't caused by too little taxing, they are caused by too much spending." He was so frustrated at the end that he believed the only way to control the budget was with constitutional amendments to force Congress to balance the budget and give the president a line-item veto.

We never conquered the deficit in the Reagan-Bush years, but our tax cuts triggered what has now turned out to be more than twenty-four years of sustained, noninflationary growth, punctuated only by the two modest slowdowns I mentioned. It's a great legacy, and I'm proud to have had a part in it.

THE WEEKEND AFTER the Stockman–*Atlantic Monthly* incident (Nancy was out of town), the president and I flew to Texas to hunt turkeys on the Winston Ranch near San Antonio, acreage owned by my stepchildren's paternal grandfather—James ("Dear Father")

Winston.* The president, Jerry Parr, and I put on camouflage outfits, then went out with shotguns to wait in the brush for our Thanksgiving dinners to walk by.

Turkeys are smart as hell and have the sharpest eyesight and hearing of any game I've ever hunted. With border patrol officers, Texas highway patrolmen, and Secret Service agents rattling around behind us, we really didn't have much of a chance. Finally, however, a small flock came within range. Unfortunately, they were all hens. (Male turkeys—gobblers—are blacker and larger and have beards.) It fell to me to tell the president it was not legal to shoot them. He was disappointed, but he got his revenge when he signed a photograph of the hunting party. "Jim, see me smile? Of course this was *before* the hunt."

Despite his empty game bag, however, the president clearly enjoyed the outing, probably for the same reasons he enjoyed riding horses and chopping wood. Every now and then, it's good to trade your burdens for a few hours in the sunshine and fresh air. Even when the turkeys don't cooperate, there's nothing quite like a day in the woods to refresh your spirits.

THE FIRST YEAR of the Reagan presidency ended on a somber note, due to the bad economy. We nevertheless had a sense of satisfaction about what we had accomplished. The president "has the best legislative record of any incoming president since Lyndon Johnson," I told reporters at the time. And we were confident, none so much as the president, that better days lay ahead.

My next three years as chief of staff were filled with dramas of

---

*My sons, Bo and Will, had the privilege of cohosting the event with their grandfather. It was quite an experience. The White House staff took control of the house, did the cooking, and served meals on presidential china that had been lugged down from Washington. In addition, the president slept in the master bedroom. "This is the first time I ever felt like a guest in my own house," Dear Father said later. True to their upbringing, both Bo and Will still hunt and fish every chance they get. Bo is now a businessman in the central Texas town of Boerne. Will served in the U.S. Army's Special Forces. He lives in Dallas and works for an oil and gas company.

their own, but nothing that quite matched the excitement and historic importance of that first year. By the end, it was time to move on. At first, I sought another position in the White House. When that didn't work out, I flirted with the possibility of a private-sector job. But as the president's first term drew to a close, I was still unsure what I would do.

Then a member of the cabinet approached me with an unexpected proposition. The president gave it his blessing, and I left the White House for a new job in the administration. Years later, President Reagan would write, with perhaps a bit of understatement, that this move had "created some problems."

NINE

"CATCHING JAVELINS"

ON JULY 12, 2003, the United States Navy commissioned a magnificent nuclear-powered Nimitz-class aircraft carrier, the USS *Ronald Reagan*, at the Norfolk Naval Station in Virginia. Nancy Reagan attended the Saturday ceremony, as did Susan and I and many others who had served and loved the fortieth president. Vice President Cheney delivered the keynote speech, and Mrs. Reagan, as the ship's sponsor, proudly gave the order to "man our ship and bring her to life!"

While we were in Norfolk, Susan and I went to dinner with Mike Deaver and his wife, Carolyn. By chance we were seated near a table that included Ed Meese and his wife, Ursula; former National Security Adviser Bill Clark and his wife, Joan; and former U.S. ambassador to the United Nations Jeane Kirkpatrick. After looking over at that formidable group, Mike smiled at me and said, "Some things never change."

I could only laugh. Ed Meese is a wonderful guy for whom I have genuine affection, notwithstanding differences we may have had during our service to President Reagan. Bill Clark and I weren't as close, but I respect his public service.

Ed, Bill, Mike, and I fought several battles side by side during the first term. In August 1982, for example, we all helped persuade the president to convince Israel's Prime Minister Menachem Begin that the bombing of West Beirut should be stopped. (The air strikes, which targeted six thousand armed PLO members holed up in civilian neighborhoods, had killed and injured many innocent bystanders.) As one might expect of those working in a high-powered environment like the White House, however, we also had our disagreements. That night in Norfolk, Mike was alluding to two well-publicized occasions in 1983 when we were divided as we were in the restaurant—Baker and Deaver on one side, Meese and Clark on the other. Had the second of these two clashes turned out differently, the president might well have avoided the Iran-Contra scandal in his second term.

Clash number one took place on September 14, 1983, and also involved Lebanon. Mike and I were in a car on our way to lunch when he told me that Clark, with Meese's support, had prevailed upon President Reagan to authorize an FBI investigation of a recent leak about U.S. policy in that war-torn Middle Eastern country. A presidential memo, which I believe was inspired by Clark, approved the use of polygraphs on, among others, everyone present at National Security Council meetings on Lebanon three days earlier. Anyone refusing to cooperate was to be subject to immediate dismissal.

Although I was not the leaker, I think Clark considered my side of the White House to be suspect. It was no secret in the White House that I often spoke with reporters, but Clark failed to recognize that I always spoke on background, which, as I have already explained, is important for the chief of staff to do and is far different from leaking. More important, Vice President Bush and Secretary of State George Shultz (who had replaced Al Haig fourteen months earlier) had also attended the meetings. Calling their integrity into question by strapping them to a lie detector would be humiliating to them, demoralizing to others on the Reagan team, and politically disastrous for the president. It would, of course, also be unconstitutional to try to dismiss the vice president, an elected official.

This plan was also inconsistent with a national security directive signed by the president six months earlier. As best I can remember, it gave the White House counsel's office authority to recommend use of polygraphs in investigations of leaks of classified and sensitive information at the White House. And since the counsel's office reported to me, that meant I had the ultimate authority to go to the president on this issue.

I told our driver to turn around.

As we headed back to the White House, I could imagine what had probably happened. Because of his long association with Ronald Reagan, Bill was a more powerful national security adviser than Dick Allen, the man he replaced in January 1982. Dick had reported to Ed Meese, but Bill reported directly to the president. Bill had probably used his Oval Office walk-in privileges to complain, legitimately, about yet another leak that undermined the administration and to persuade the president to take drastic action. Like other presidents, Ronald Reagan hated leaks and was often frustrated that he could not stop them. The president also trusted Bill, his chief of staff as governor of California, particularly so after Ed seconded the idea of using polygraphs. Based on what happened a few hours later, I'm confident I could have headed off this misadventure if I had been there at the time.

Returning to the White House, I was one unhappy chief of staff. I could just see the headlines: "President Orders Bush, Shultz, Others to Take Lie Detector Tests." What credibility would we have with others if it appeared that we didn't even trust one another? Democrats would have a field day. Political cartoonists would fall to their knees and give thanks for an early Christmas present. I stopped in my office and picked up a copy of the directive that gave me authority to recommend White House polygraphs.

The president was having lunch with the vice president and the secretary of state. Ordinarily, I would not have interrupted them, but this was no ordinary situation. "Mr. President," I said, handing him the directive, "here's the paper you signed that says the chief of staff has authority to recommend when we do this in the White House. Do you really mean to strap your vice president and secretary of state to a lie detector?"

The whole thing was a surprise to Bush and Shultz. I don't remember his exact words, but Shultz told the president something to this effect: "If you want me to take a polygraph, you might also want to get yourself a new secretary of state." I suggested that I, too, might leave. The vice president agreed that lie detectors were a bad idea.

As the implications of this decision sank in, the president was obviously troubled. "Bill shouldn't have done this," he said. "Let's get the fellows together and kick it around." He then withdrew the order, pending further discussion.

The "fellows"—the vice president, the attorney general, Clark, and the troika—met a short time later. It was an acrimonious meeting. We kicked the idea around, and we kicked one another. I didn't object to the investigation, I said, just to the mandatory polygraphs. Bill suggested I was afraid of what the lie detector might reveal. Not true! I was worried about the impact on the president's image and on his team's morale. I was also, truth be known, not happy that Clark and Meese had tried to usurp for themselves, without a word to me, authority and responsibility that had been specifically assigned to the chief of staff. After listening to everyone, the president reversed himself. "This is not the thing to do," he said. And that was that. The FBI investigated but never identified the leaker.

This flap led to another barely civil war within the White House. To all appearances, it was just a high-stakes game of musical chairs that bruised a couple of egos (mine included). But it also set in motion the events that produced one of the few stains on the legacy of Ronald Reagan.

Here's what happened. Clark, worn down by the responsibilities of serving as national security adviser, was already contemplating a return to civilian life or another government post. The polygraph incident reinforced his desire to move on.

Enter Jim Watt, secretary of the interior and a member of the "let

Reagan be Reagan" crowd. He was an outspoken proponent of developing our federal lands (responsibly, he believed) and, as a consequence, a lightning rod for most environmentalists. Our polls showed that he would be a liability when the president ran for reelection in 1984, but Ronald Reagan was nothing if not loyal. As the Stockman affair revealed, a Reagan appointee had to go a long way to reach the point of no return.

Watt reached that point on September 21, 1983, when he told a U.S. Chamber of Commerce breakfast that a commission reviewing his department's coal leasing program had "every kind of mix you can have. I have a black, I have a woman, two Jews, and a cripple."

I don't condone what Jim said and we weren't particularly close, but he was a fine and decent man. As he was recruited for the job, he had leveled with the president: "The day may come when you will have to let me go." Now that day had come, and he was quick to offer to leave.

Clark saw Watt's departure as an opening and volunteered to move to the Interior Department. Good idea, said the president. The First Lady, who evidently felt that what Clark had done in the polygraph incident had embarrassed her husband, agreed.

I also liked the idea. Too often the national security adviser was off doing his own thing and encouraging the president to spend time on matters and appearances unrelated to the plan of the day or the plan of the week. These diversions were costly. They made the administration appear unfocused and uncoordinated and made the job of prioritizing our objectives very difficult. This had not been the case with Dick Allen, who reported to Meese rather than to the president.

Clark's penchant for secrecy and his desire to exercise total control over some foreign policy issues also created problems. He once persuaded the president to send Jeane Kirkpatrick, our UN ambassador, on a fact-finding trip to Latin America. Trouble was, neither Bill nor Jeane had cleared the mission with the cabinet officer who ostensibly had the lead on foreign policy, Secretary of State George Shultz. This was an example of a classic problem that has plagued many administrations: the White House national security adviser's bypassing the responsible agency (in this case, State; sometimes Defense) and "going operational" on a sensitive foreign policy or security issue. When I learned that the mission had not been cleared with the secretary of state, I told the president. He was shocked and told Clark to get Shultz's approval.

With the 1984 campaign approaching, Deaver and I wanted to avoid the kind of internal conflicts that inevitably occur when the political side of the White House and the national security side are not singing from the same hymnal. The best way to assure coordination rather than competition is for the national security adviser and chief of staff to work well together. So it occurred to Mike and me (who worked very well together): what if I moved to the national security adviser's office and Mike, who had served as deputy chief of staff for more than two and a half years, took my job?

My status in the White House had long been grist for the rumor mills. For more than a year, newspapers had reported that I was thinking about leaving the White House. Their "sources" said, variously, that I was tired of the internal strains in the White House, frustrated at my inability to persuade the president to cut the deficit, gripped by "end of the day weariness," and hungry for political advancement—to U.S. attorney general, some office in Texas, or, my all-time favorite, a run for the presidency in 1988. The *Dallas Morning News* floated that one in March 1982, then reported that "Baker responded with an expletive when the prospect of a presidential bid was broached to him." Hell yes I did! I worked for a president who planned to run again and a vice president who was likely to run after that. Whatever ambitions I may have had weren't built around fantasies about one or both of them turning their back on a second term or being defeated.

My principal motivation for wanting to leave the chief of staff's job in October 1983 was "none of the above." Rather I wanted to help Ronald Reagan function more efficiently as a chief executive and get reelected. That said, I won't deny that I thought a change would do me good. Yes, working in foreign policy and national security would be challenging and might prove helpful, though not essential, if I later were offered a shot at a cabinet job. And, yes, I was beginning to wear down.

From the beginning, I knew from talking to former White House chiefs of staff that the job would be brutal. When the president offered the chief of staff position in 1980, I told him it was best done in two-year stints. He agreed. By late 1983, I was already well past my original departure date.

The White House is at the very center of the political process by which our nation governs itself, and the chief of staff is at the very center of operations in the White House. The job is to get things done for the president while catching political javelins that come from all directions. It's important and it's fun, mostly. But to borrow a line from a country song, it surely tires your mind.

One thing that tired my mind was the never-ending chorus from the right about letting Reagan be Reagan. In July 1981, for example, when the president nominated Sandra Day O'Connor to the Supreme Court, Howard Phillips, head of the Conservative Caucus, complained that from the outset, "the administration has been staffed by country-club conservatives who have contempt for social conservatives." M. Stanton Evans, a syndicated columnist, was happy to name names. In the January 29, 1983, issue of the weekly conservative journal *Human Events*, he wrote a piece titled "Time for Jim Baker to Resign." I was a "likable fellow," he said, but "spectacularly ill-fitted to a crucial role in an administration allegedly seeking a conservative revolution in our politics. Baker is about as qualified for such a job as I would be to play left tackle for the Dallas Cowboys."

Evans was considerably gentler than Clymer Wright, a Houston conservative activist who had supported Reagan over Ford in 1976. In a May 1982 letter, he said I was undermining and sabotaging the president's efforts. He attached several news articles to prove his point.

Usually I am thick-skinned about such criticism. What people like

Clymer Wright (who was anything but a likable fellow) failed to realize, however, was that in undermining me, they were really undermining Ronald Reagan. To win votes for the president on the Hill, I needed to approach members of Congress from a position of strength. If they doubted for one minute that I enjoyed the president's full confidence and support—that I spoke for him—they would have no reason to listen to my arguments, trust my promises, or ponder my ever-so-gentle hints about what might happen if they voted the wrong way.

Reagan being Reagan, he promptly replied to Wright. "Yes, there is undermining of my efforts going on, and, yes, there is sabotage of all I'm trying to accomplish," the president wrote. "But it's being done by the people who write these articles and columns, not by any White House staff member and certainly not Jim Baker. . . . Don't join their group, Clymer—you are helping them with their sabotage.

"I'm in charge," the president continued, "and my people are helping to carry out the policies I set. No, we don't get everything we want and, yes, we have to compromise to get 75 percent or 80 percent of our programs. We try to see that the 75 percent or 80 percent is more than worth the compromise we have to accept. So far it has been."

Mike and I knew that Ed Meese, Bill Clark, and others would oppose a job switch that put the two of us in charge of both the National Security Council and the rest of the White House.* So, first things first, we ran the idea by a handful of people whose counsel we trusted and whose support we would need—Vice President Bush, Secretary of State Shultz, Stu Spencer, and, of course, the First Lady. All were in favor. Now it was time to go to the president. He listened to our pitch, looked at who was in our corner, thought it over, and okayed the plan.

---

*Time has clouded my memory of the details of what the *New York Times*'s Hedrick Smith called "the staff coup that failed." Revisiting Smith's book *The Power Game,* and Lou Cannon's *President Reagan: The Role of a Lifetime* helped me reconstruct the events. I trust their accuracy on this episode because both interviewed me about the "coup" way back when.

D-Day was Friday, October 14, the day after the president had announced that Clark would be leaving the National Security Council to replace Watt at the Interior Department. Mike and I thought we had orchestrated the schedule so that nothing could go wrong. After lunching with Shultz, the president would go to the situation room for a one o'clock meeting of the National Security Planning Group (NSPG)—the highest-ranking members of the NSC, chaired by the national security adviser. Participants generally included the vice president, secretary of state, secretary of defense, CIA director, chairman of the joint chiefs of staff, and the troika (although on this day Mike and I decided it would be prudent not to attend).

Under our plan, the president would announce to the NSPG that he was appointing me to succeed Clark, and Deaver to succeed me. We would then give the press office a release about the switch. At four o'clock, the president would make an appearance in the briefing room and announce the personnel changes to the press. He would then head off to Camp David for the weekend.

Timing is everything, and our timing failed us. Instead of being in the situation room at one o'clock, as scheduled, the president was in Mike's office going over his NSPG remarks. This was to be Clark's last meeting, and when the president failed to show, Bill came upstairs to fetch him. We should have accompanied them. On the way to the situation room, the president told Clark about the planned changes. From what I understand, Clark betrayed no emotion, but did ask the president to postpone the announcement until the two of them could talk. The president obliged him.

Notes get passed at White House meetings all the time. Some are frivolous, distractions from the tedium of meetings that won't end. When my pal George H. W. Bush was president and I was secretary of state, he would pass notes asking if I might be available for an all-too-rare game of golf or tennis. Once he even asked if I thought a visiting head of state was responsible for the unpleasant odor in the room. (Was George telling the truth, I always wondered, or only trying to cover his own backside?)

Other notes are more substantive. In the situation room on this day, Clark sent Meese, Casey, and Weinberger notes asking them to stick around and meet with him and the president. They all are reported to have argued vigorously against the changes, with Jeane Kirkpatrick loudly joining the chorus. Apparently Clark also volunteered to stay at the NSC and suggested that I take his job at Interior. The president said this wouldn't work because I owned oil and gas interests back home. He knew this because I always declined to participate in White House decisions on energy issues.

Mike and I didn't know the president was meeting with the four horsemen of our apocalypse. When he failed to return upstairs on schedule, however, Mike tracked him down. At this point, to mix a couple of metaphors, we could see the handwriting on the wall, which said: your goose is in the oven and the thermostat is set on high.

When he came back, the president told us that there was opposition to the plan and that he wanted to think about it over the weekend. "Mr. President," I said, "I don't want to be a problem for you. If there's that much opposition, let's forget it." Mike took it much more personally. He thought the president's hesitancy reflected, in part at least, a lack of confidence in him as a potential chief of staff.

The president did review the decision over the weekend. Some say his thinking was aided by calls ("Don't do it!") from critics recruited by Clark, et al. On Monday morning he told us he had decided against the switch. He later said he did it to avoid friction among the cabinet and White House staff. By the end of the day, he had named a new national security adviser—Bud McFarlane, who had served on the staff of the Senate Armed Forces Committee under Senator John Tower, as counselor in the Haig State Department, and as the president's special representative in the Middle East.* Bud was clearly a compromise choice. Casey had lobbied strenuously for Jeane Kirkpatrick. The less hawkish Shultz, however, strongly opposed her, and the president

---

*Things later went south for Bud, but I always liked him and worked well with him. On Iran-Contra he just took a wrong turn trying to do what he thought was the right thing.

didn't want "bad chemistry" (as he wrote later) between these two high-ranking officials.

Disappointed as I was, I decided to stay put as chief of staff for the time being, but to keep my eyes open for opportunities outside the administration. Why? The rodent-related expletive I used earlier to describe a certain form of political infighting again comes to mind. Sometimes it's not much fun. It wasn't fun for the president, either. "Jim took it pretty well," he wrote in his diary, "but Mike was pretty upset. . . . It was an unhappy day all around."

Seven years later, former President Reagan reflected in his autobiography on the impact of that hassle: "My decision not to appoint Jim Baker as national security adviser, I suppose, was a turning point for my administration, although I had no idea at the time how significant it would prove to be."

How so? One hyphenated word: Iran-Contra. The president was suggesting that if I had been his national security adviser—rather than Bud McFarlane and Bud's successor, John Poindexter, a retired admiral—the scandal that rocked the administration during its second term might never have happened.

That trouble began on Bud's watch in 1985, when Iran secretly made a request to buy weapons from our government. An embargo against such a sale was in place, but Bud asked the president for authority to talk to the Iranians. His reasoning: the sale would lead to better relations with Iran and, quite possibly Lebanon, where Iranian-backed terrorists were holding seven U.S. hostages. The president had long made it clear that he would not deal with terrorists, but he was, as I've already stated, a very sentimental man.

That same sentimentality led him, I believe, to approve the arms-for-hostages gambit. He also sincerely believed that dealing with Iranian moderates—the administration never dealt directly with terrorists—might influence the direction Iran would take after the death of Ayatollah Khomeini. Casey also favored the deal, but the president probably should have known it was a bad idea from the fact that Shultz and Weinberger, who rarely agreed on anything, both gave it a thumbs-down. In the end, however, sentiment trumped good sense, and McFarlane was authorized to make overtures to the Iranians.

In time, talk turned to action. Israel sold several million dollars' worth of U.S. weapons to Iran, and the U.S. sold replacement weapons to Israel. Then under Poindexter, millions of dollars from the arms sales were diverted to the anti-communist Contras in Nicaragua, who were attempting to oust the Russian- and Cuban-backed Sandinista government from power. This diversion, it was argued at the time, violated the Boland Amendment, a congressional mandate that restricted U.S. involvement in Nicaragua. Regardless of whether it did or did not violate that legislation, however, the White House was running an off-budget foreign policy project outside the agencies, outside the system of congressional oversight, and in conflict with both congressional and stated White House policies.

From beginning to end, Iran-Contra was wrong, a textbook example of what can happen when the White House "goes operational." The White House isn't always right, State and Defense aren't always right, and Congress isn't always right. But policies developed through the rough-and-tumble of politics—within the administration, between the administration and Congress, and in a continuing dialogue with the American people—are more often right than wrong. Bypassing these institutions and processes put dangerous weapons in the hands of known terrorist sponsors, drove up the market price for hostages, and weakened rather than strengthened the case for helping the Contras. Iran-Contra crippled the administration and it hurt our nation, at home and abroad.

One of the worst injuries, ironically, was the commissioning of Independent Counsel Lawrence Walsh to investigate. He spent millions of dollars proving the obvious, then cynically influenced the 1992 elections. (I'll have more to say about that later.) McFarlane, Poindexter, and Oliver North (an NSC staffer)—the architects of Iran-Contra—were convicted of crimes, along with several other lower-level players. But

Walsh also went after Weinberger and, through innuendo, President George H. W. Bush, neither of whom was ever credibly alleged to have had anything to do with the operation itself. George was right to pardon Weinberger, McFarlane, and four other Iran-Contra figures in December 1992. And the nation was right, finally, to let the independent counsel law expire in 1999 after it became apparent, even to Democrats, that on balance, independent prosecutors and the "gotcha" politics associated with trying to get them appointed did more harm than good.

As George said in 1992, the Walsh prosecution reflected "a profoundly troubling development in the political and legal climate of our country: the criminalization of policy differences. These differences should have been addressed in the political arena without the Damocles sword of criminality hanging over the heads of some combatants. The proper target is the president, not his subordinates; the proper forum is the voting booth, not the courtroom."

Amen.

President Reagan approved the arms deals with Iran, but insisted he had no knowledge of the diversion of funds until Ed Meese, then attorney general, uncovered an Oliver North memorandum about the scheme. Subordinates who knew of his ardent support for the Contras took it into their own hands to arm them, the president said. Had he been asked to approve such action, he wrote later, he would have refused. I believe that. I also admire what he did when he found out. "There are reasons why it happened," he said, "but no excuses. It was a mistake." And he ordered his administration to cooperate in the investigation.

Would Iran-Contra have happened on my watch as national security adviser? It's easy and potentially self-serving, I suppose, to say I don't think so. Hindsight is always perfect. I also have sympathy for the folks who tried in good faith to do what they thought was right, then had it blow up in their face. But the fact is, they messed up. Iran-Contra was wrong and it wasn't likely to work. The fantasy upon which all the other fantasies were constructed was that no one would ever know. But, as Secretary Shultz warned at the time, you can't do something on this scale in Washington, D.C., and keep it secret. From the start, Iran-Contra had the potential—no, the near certainty—of blowing up and damaging the reputations of, among others, the president of the United States. And that's exactly what happened.

Unfortunately, I never got a chance to weigh in. As secretary of the treasury during this period, I still sat on the National Security Council, but as I would later learn, Poindexter made it a point to exclude me from meetings at which the arms-for-hostages deal was being discussed. He said he knew I would object, perhaps because at a June 1984 NSPG meeting I was quoted by Shultz and Casey as saying that the United States government may raise and spend funds only through an appropriation of Congress. Poindexter later apologized for having kept me in the dark. "John," I said, "that was the biggest favor you could have done for me." But not for President Reagan.

What I *might have done* about Nicaragua as national security adviser can perhaps be measured against what I *actually did* when I took office as secretary of state in January 1989. The Sandinistas were still in power, the Contras were still fighting, and Congress was still locked in a fierce struggle over U.S. policy. I knew we would never solve this foreign policy problem until we removed it from the domestic political debate. So we negotiated a bipartisan accord on Central America, an agreement between congressional Democrats and Republicans,* calling for an election that both sides in Nicaragua would pledge to respect. When the Sandinistas were voted out of power—much to their surprise—they honored the election results, thanks in large part to the efforts of former president Jimmy Carter, with whom the administration worked closely and effectively.

---

*I've often said that my first major negotiation as secretary of state was not with a foreign power but with the Congress of the United States.

. . .

DURING THE AUTUMN of 1983, I was presented with an intriguing job possibility outside the administration: commissioner of Major League Baseball. Bowie Kuhn was about to retire, and Bud Selig, major shareholder of the Milwaukee Brewers and head of the search committee to find a new commissioner, approached me about the position. We talked in my home on Foxhall Road, then sat down with legendary trial lawyer and political insider Edward Bennett Williams, co-owner of the Baltimore Orioles and Washington Redskins. Despite his evident interest in seeing me take the job, Williams doubted I would accept. "Jim, you're not going to do this," he said, "because President Reagan is going to put you in his cabinet." It was a prophetic remark, although I had no reason to think so at the time. Anyway, it soon became clear to me that the baseball owners did not want to vest their commissioner with real authority on labor contracts, TV rights, and other big issues, so I withdrew my name. I wasn't looking for a ceremonial job. *Washington Post* columnist George Will, a big baseball fan, said I should have taken the job if I ever wanted to run for president because more people would know my name as baseball commissioner than as a cabinet officer.

When the story got out, Jack Ohman, political cartoonist for *The Oregonian,* created a three-panel masterpiece. It was prefaced by the words: "White House chief of staff James A. Baker III may become the new major league baseball commissioner. His experience?"

Panel One read, "Takes abuse well," and showed a pitcher from the "New Right" firing a baseball off my noggin. "BONK."

Panel Two read, "Has practical experience dealing with prima donnas and egomaniacs, as he will likely encounter in the form of players and team owners," and showed me talking with four men in baseball uniforms: Clark, Meese, Bush, and Shultz.

The final panel read, "Has both fielding and hitting experience." Here I was shown fielding reporters' questions with a "No comment" and hitting Bill Casey over the head with a bat. "THOK."

. . .

SOME WROTE at the time that I was driven from the White House by pressure from the family residence. The First Lady blamed me, so the story goes, for President Reagan's poor performance in the first 1984 presidential debate against Walter Mondale. I was reported to have been demoralized by her alleged tongue-lashing, to have seen this as another example of how the Reagans failed to appreciate me, and to have decided then and there, enough is enough. Like so many Washington stories, however, this makes for good gossip but bad history.

If you look at the results of Reagan vs. Mondale, it's hard to believe that the president's team could have been too worried. Running on a strong record with an improving economy against an opponent who admitted he would raise taxes, the well-liked president was reelected with 58.8 percent of the popular vote and won a staggering forty-nine out of fifty states and 525 out of 538 electoral votes. Yet it *is* true that after the first presidential debate in Louisville, we were somewhat worried* . . . and that some of the blame was laid on my doorstep.

Let's go back to early October 1984. As chief of staff, I was effectively in charge of the reelection effort and of the debate negotiations and preparation. Darman was my principal deputy. For the most part, we followed the successful script of 1980. Again, we gave the president briefing books, and again, David Stockman played the role of his opponent in full-scale ninety-minute rehearsals.

Unfortunately, the president was off his game at the first debate in Louisville. In his own words, he began okay but "flattened out." This was evident in his closing statement. Instead of reminding voters of our campaign theme—"Morning in America"—with his usual eloquent paean to our nation and his vision of an even better tomorrow,

---

*One reason we were concerned is that the GOP had lost twenty-six House seats in the November '82 midterm elections. That was the political price we paid for an economy that had then not yet turned around. By coincidence, the Reagan boom began that very same month, which set up the big victory for the president in 1984.

he got bogged down in minutiae. Morale was not high in our camp after the debate, but I was honest with reporters. This was not one of the Great Communicator's better efforts, I said.

We knew what was coming: that nasty three-letter word, *age*. Newspapers asked if the president was too old to serve another four-year term. Worse, the television network news trotted out footage of the president falling asleep in the Vatican in June 1982 after an all-night flight from Washington to Rome.*

But it wasn't age that did in the president in Louisville. Uncharacteristically, he had not done his homework, the only time I ever witnessed such a failure. It's really important in a presidential debate to open strong and close strong. Candidates generally memorize their closing statements. If you review the tape of that debate, however, you'll see that the president didn't do that, and after a confusing back-and-forth exchange with the moderator about how much time he had, he lost his train of thought.

Nancy Reagan didn't see it that way, and who can blame her? She loved her husband dearly and was accustomed to seeing him perform smoothly. After the debate, she expressed her concerns to Deaver, Stu Spencer, and Paul Laxalt, a close friend of the Reagans and general chairman of the campaign. Paul said he had reservations about the way the president had been prepared, or, in his eyes, over-prepared. "He was brutalized by a briefing process that didn't make any sense," Paul said publicly. "It filled his head with so many facts and figures that he lost his spontaneity and his visionary concepts."

That put the blame squarely on the staff, with Darman (whom Laxalt disliked) being nominated as the scapegoat. Deaver and

---

*He deserved a nap. On that same trip, the president and Pope John Paul II met for almost an hour in the Vatican library and set in motion what *Time* magazine later called "a clandestine campaign to hasten the dissolution of the communist empire." Their short-term goal was to help protect the Solidarity movement from a military crackdown, but their ultimate aim was nothing less than the liberation of Eastern Europe. The deaths of President Reagan in 2004 and Pope John Paul II in 2005 reminded us of how much we owe these two great men.

Spencer suggested that I should fire him, but I refused. "Look," I said, "if he's the problem, I'm sure I'll hear about it from the president himself. If he orders me to fire anyone, I'll do it." Of course, I was fairly certain that wouldn't happen. I am aware that the president later said he was "overtrained," but in interviews at the time, he refused to blame staff. And in his conversations with me at the time, the president took personal responsibility for his poor performance.

In the days that followed, both the staff and friends outside the campaign worked to restore the president's confidence. It seemed to work. For good measure, just before he took the stage for the second debate in Kansas City on October 28, I handed the president a note that called to mind his successful debate against Jimmy Carter four years earlier. "Chuckle again and have fun out there," I wrote.

He had fun with at least one question. The *Baltimore Sun*'s Henry Trewhitt reminded the president that John F. Kennedy had gone with little sleep for several days during the Cuban missile crisis, then asked, "Is there any doubt in your mind that you would be able to function in such circumstances?"

"Not at all, Mr. Trewhitt," the president replied, "and I want you to know that also I will not make age an issue of this campaign. I am not going to exploit for political purposes my opponent's youth and inexperience."

Everyone laughed, including the fifty-six-year-old Walter Mondale. From that point on, our campaign never looked back.

Did I resent the criticism directed at Darman and me? Yes. Was it the final straw that caused me to leave the chief of staff position? No. In my mind, I was already out the West Wing door. I just didn't know what new door I would be entering. In serving four years as chief of staff, I had caught about as many javelins as I could, and Susan wanted me to find a job that would allow me to come home at a regular hour.

SHORTLY AFTER I got into the office on November 16, 1984, just ten days after the election, Treasury Secretary Don Regan chewed my ear off in an expletive-filled telephone call. He was furious about a *Washington Post* article detailing some of his remarks at the previous day's cabinet meeting and assumed that someone on the White House staff had been the source. After he hung up, he sent a letter of resignation to the president. I told the president about the letter, which I knew he would not want to accept, and said I would sit down with Don and straighten things out. I then went over to Treasury to make nice with the former Merrill Lynch chairman, who was one of the president's favorite cabinet members.

We quickly and calmly resolved the matter—ex-Marine to ex-Marine—then Don asked me to stay for lunch. As we visited, he sensed that I was one tired guy. "You're right," I said. He later wrote that he surprised himself with his response. He certainly surprised me. "We should swap jobs," he said.

I had already given some thought to serving in the cabinet, if President Reagan should ask, but the "no vacancy" sign was up at what would have been my top four choices—State, Treasury, Defense, and Justice. I'd had no reason to believe Regan was interested in leaving the second-ranking cabinet department. But now . . .

"Do you really mean that?" I asked.

"I guess I do."

"Well, watch out. I may just take you up on it."

"When you're ready to talk, I'll be here," he said.

I wasn't ready to talk until I had consulted my own troika—Susan Baker, Dick Darman, and Margaret Tutwiler. Dick, as he so often did on issues of policy and personnel, boiled everything down to a sharp one-page analysis of the upside and downside of the proposed move. In a way, he provided the same service to me that I had provided to others, first as a business lawyer, then as a political and policy adviser. He helped sort out the issues, offered an independent perspective, and gave good advice. Margaret, in turn, helped me analyze the prospective benefits and costs. I relied heavily on her political instincts—using "political" in the broadest sense—and good judgment. Finally, Susan's common sense and grounding in faith and family helped me keep things in perspective.

All three liked the idea of moving to Treasury, and after I weighed their advice, I did too. As soon as I made the decision to move (if the president approved), I felt an excitement that I hadn't felt since the day I was asked to serve as chief of staff. I was ready for a new challenge.

On November 30, 1984, Don Regan and I lunched at Treasury. The biggest item on his plate was tax reform, and I had a lot of questions. Near the end of the lunch, I told him I was ready to switch, if he was serious and if the president liked the idea. He asked for a few days to think it over.

"We need to get Deaver involved," I said before I left. "We could never do this without telling Mike." Why? First of all, as a courtesy. Mike had wanted to be chief of staff. He was now about to leave the administration to work as a lobbyist, but he still deserved to be told. And second, because Mike was the best person to talk to the First Lady about the switch.

Darman and I put together a plan to win Deaver's support. "It's time for a change," our memo said, because both Regan and Baker "are tired of their current jobs and have spent a fair amount of political capital in them [and] both would be reinvigorated by the shift, as would the administration." The plan would put me, "our top legislative negotiator," in charge of "the difficult tax simplification fight," we wrote. And it would put Regan, "our top economic policy maker," in charge of "the difficult job" of reducing the budget deficit. In addition, we argued, the succession "would be respected by most internal and external factions, senior cabinet officials, financial markets and the international community, and . . . would be enjoyed by the president."

I mentioned the idea to Deaver, and Darman followed up with him. Deaver then talked to the president. Because the president knew both Regan and me so well, we hoped he would say yes rather quickly. "Leaks could stimulate conflict, which could destroy one of the main benefits: infusion of momentum," we cautioned. After checking, Mike told us the president liked the idea and Nancy was on board, too.

On January 7, 1985, Deaver, Regan, and I met with the president in the Oval Office. "I've brought you someone your own age to play with," Mike said, smiling. The president truly enjoyed Regan's company. They were close in age, they were both Irish Americans, and they both loved a good joke. I also reminded the president about our discussion four years ago about how it would be best if I served just two years as chief of staff. He laughed and gave the switch his blessing. The announcement was made the next day.

LOOKING BACK on my time in the White House, a few dos and don'ts come to mind. The most important, as I've already mentioned, is to remember that all your power as chief of staff is vicarious through the president. Nobody elected you; you're staff. Powerful, yes, but staff nonetheless.

Understand what the president wants, then help him get it. If you think he's wrong, tell him, but always respect and carry out his decisions. On contentious issues, be an honest broker so he hears all sides (and all sides know they have been heard). Make the trains run on time so he doesn't have to worry about the small stuff. Husband the president's power, and your own, by using it wisely. Don't start more fights than you can win, and win the ones you start. Success builds on success.

Surround yourself with the best people you can find. You can't do this job without help. Give loyalty and demand loyalty. Delegate. Expect performance. When you get it, show appreciation.

Politics ain't beanbag, but there's no reason to be uncivil. Disagree agreeably. Listen respectfully. Treat everyone, allies and adversaries alike, with dignity. Return telephone calls. Count the votes. When you're ahead, call the question. When you're behind, work harder. If you can't get everything you want, get what you can. When you can't win, fall back and fight another day.

Respect the press and get to know reporters. Talk to them, on background most of the time, but on the record when necessary. Help them understand the administration's position. And never lie to them.

. . .

I WILL ALWAYS treasure my memories of those times and my good fortune in being able to work at the right hand of Ronald Reagan. He was a wonderful man, a lovely human being, and without doubt one of our greatest presidents. He refreshed the nation's spirit, rebuilt our economy, and—more than any other president before him—hastened the collapse of communism. The vast majority of the American people loved him. Even the media, which disliked so many of his policies, could not dislike him as a person. It's good to see that history is beginning to treat him with the respect and honor he so richly deserves.

For me, however, four years in the White House were enough. It was time to do some prior preparation to prevent poor performance at Treasury.

TEN

"JIMMY, YOU'RE MASSAGING ME"

MEASURED BY my new responsibilities, the move from the White House to Treasury was a long journey. Measured by the tape measure, however, it was only a few hundred feet. The Treasury building faces the East Wing of the White House, across East Executive Avenue. The Greek Revival building with its thirty great stone columns is one of the most majestic in Washington, befitting Treasury's role as the second-oldest executive department (after State) established by Congress in 1789.

You can see a picture of the building on the back of a ten-dollar bill. On the front is Alexander Hamilton, the first treasury secretary and one of the most brilliant of the Founders. Against great opposition, he had the good sense to pay off the nation's Revolutionary War debts dollar for dollar, not at a steep discount as his critics urged. With this one act, the new American government secured its financial reputation. To do this, Hamilton had to make a deal with Southern lawmakers to build the new federal capital in the South. That's how the District of Columbia came to be located between Virginia and Maryland.

I took my official oath of office as Hamilton's successor, the sixty-seventh secretary of the treasury, from a White House notary public in the basement of my D.C. home on Foxhall Road just after noon on Sunday, February 3, 1985. Susan was in Houston, so Mary Bonner, then seven, held the Bible.* Longtime friends from Houston, Will and Fran Lummis, served as witnesses. Five days later, I had a ceremonial swearing-in by Attorney General William French Smith in the Oval Office with Susan holding the Bible and my family, Barbara Bush, and President Reagan as witnesses.

At the time, of course, the pundits wrote less about "Team Baker Goes to Treasury" than about "Regan and Baker Switch Jobs." A political cartoon by Pulitzer Prize winner Tony Auth showed the "Gipper" addressing a huddle of football players, including one labeled "Secretary of the Treasury" and another "Chief of Staff." "OK guys. It's halftime," the president says. "I want you all to exchange jerseys."

The jersey exchange was also a source of interest, possibly even concern, on Capitol Hill. At my two-and-a-half-hour confirmation hearing before the Senate Finance Committee eleven days before my official swearing-in, Senator Russell Long asked if the relationship of the treasury secretary, chief of staff, and president was "going to be the same." This was important because President Reagan wanted to streamline our federal income tax system, and Long—ranking Democrat on the Senate committee that would oversee that project—was curious about how the job switch would affect the working relationship between the White House, Treasury, and Congress. I assured him

---

*As chief of staff, I would often take Mary Bonner with me to the White House, particularly when I worked on weekends. She added a delightful irreverence to the proceedings, as in the fall of 1981 when the president and I prepared to depart by helicopter one day from the South Lawn. Three-year-old Mary Bonner was kicking the leaves outside the diplomatic entrance. As he passed, the president bent down to say hello. "Hi there," she replied, still kicking the leaves, "you old silly." This grandfatherly relationship between our nation's oldest president and one of his youngest admirers grew warmer each time she visited him in the Oval Office or at Camp David. When we told her four years later that I would serve as secretary of the treasury, she burst into tears. "You're leaving the White House, and I won't get to see the president again!"

that Don and I had worked closely for four years and would continue to do so. Moreover, I would still be a member of the Legislative Strategy Group.

A very detailed tax reform plan was already in play. Three weeks after President Reagan won reelection in November, Treasury had laid out a plan to simplify and restructure the federal income tax system. Don was a major architect of the plan, and had I remained chief of staff, I would have been the major architect of the strategy to get the bill passed. Now the two architects were changing places.

"We must, on a bipartisan basis, bring greater fairness to the American tax system and make it simpler," I told the senators. Malcolm Wallop, the Republican senator from Wyoming, was not impressed.

"Jim, let me add my words of admiration and affection for you in wishing you well as you go forward," he said.

I enjoy "words of admiration and affection" as much as the next guy, but when you appear before congressional committees—which you do often as a cabinet officer—kind words are often a warning signal. Having unburdened himself of the obligatory niceties, Senator Wallop set about his real work, which was to torch my opening statement.

"I am particularly glad that you are still chief of staff of the White House and not coming to us green from Wall Street," he said, "because I would assume then that you had written, and not somebody in Treasury, the opening statement which you gave, which I really would have to define as a sort of tapioca, which is an indefinable thick fluid surrounding equally sweet squishy lumps, and when you have finished it, you have found it totally unsatisfying."

When the laughter subsided, Malcolm continued. My opening statement, he said, was "just full of platitudes and devoid of definition. You know, like 'bringing greater fairness to the American tax system.'"

I don't recall if I wrote those platitudes myself, but I certainly approved them. I never delivered a speech that I hadn't written myself or thoroughly vetted. And, yes, my remarks were short on definition and long on motherhood, apple pie, and, if you wish, tapioca. Better to serve that menu at breakfast than to eat crow for lunch.

Confirmation hearings are not the proper forum for detailed policy agendas. The more specific you are, the greater the chance that your words will come back to haunt you. Some political opponent or reporter will dig up the transcript or videotape of the hearing and point out that you said one thing last year and another thing last week, never mind that circumstances may have changed. People start calling you a flip-flopper, and you spend all your time explaining the past, not getting things done in the here and now. Cabinet nominees should say enough to show that they support the president's agenda and understand the issues, then—when questioned about details—promise to "get back to you on that, Senator."

And get back we did. The November tax plan had been written by technicians with a tin ear for politics. When I got to Treasury, we worked with Congress and the White House, and in May 1986 the president offered a new plan with plenty of details—no tapioca here— to reform the system. Our goals were to simplify the tax code, broaden the tax base, and reduce rates while maintaining "revenue neutrality"— neither increasing nor decreasing the overall tax revenues of the U.S. Treasury.

But it wouldn't be easy. Every time the federal government tinkers with tax policy, you can count on interest groups showing up to influence the tinkerers. The corridor outside the Senate Finance Committee room was known as Gucci Gulch, in honor of the fashionable wardrobes and fancy footwear of the lobbyists gathered there. We had a fight on our hands.

And what a fight it was! From the day Don Regan laid out the first tax reform proposal until President Reagan signed the bipartisan Tax Reform Act of 1986 took almost two years. This turned out to be the greatest domestic achievement of the president's second term. One knowledgeable reporter later called it "the most extensive overhaul of the federal tax system since the income tax was created in 1913." The

story of how, against great odds, that remarkable legislation was enacted shows how Washington works—or can work—when a president
provides leadership on an issue that is ripe for change. It also offers a
glimpse into the styles of President Reagan, Speaker of the House
Tip O'Neill, House Ways and Means committee chairman Danny
Rostenkowski, Don Regan, and other players.*

Some background first. Tax reform was not a new idea. A thicket of
tax preferences had swallowed our tax code. It's easy to criticize those
preferences now, but they were put there, one by one, over the decades
to protect Americans, first one group then another, from the punishing
rates in our tax code, once higher than 90 percent for some unfortunate taxpayers, believe it or not.

In the language of journalism and retail politics, we needed to
"close loopholes" that favored "special interest groups." President
Reagan would talk that way, and sometimes I would, too. But I rarely
used those terms with members of Congress. They tend not to react
well when you call their favorite tax preference a "loophole" and their
political friends "special interests."

President Reagan first called for tax reform in his 1984 state of the
union speech. "I am asking Secretary Don Regan for a plan for action
to simplify the entire tax code, so all taxpayers, big and small, are
treated more fairly," he said. "I've asked that specific recommendations . . . be presented to me by December 1984."

We would use the election year to build public support for the
principle of reforming the tax system. There would be plenty of time in
the second term to deal with the messy details. It's the same approach
that worked for tax cuts in 1980 and 1981—offer a big idea in the campaign, win a mandate in the election, then push the legislation through
Congress.

---

*I am indebted to *Showdown at Gucci Gulch: Lawmakers, Lobbyists, and the Unlikely Triumph of
Tax Reform,* by Jeffrey Birnbaum and Alan Murray, *Wall Street Journal* reporters, for re-
freshing my memory of these events. It should be clear to anyone reading their book that
I was one of their behind-the-scene sources.

The wild card was how Walter Mondale, the Democratic nominee in 1984, might respond. Two Democratic lawmakers, Senator Bill Bradley and Representative Dick Gephardt, had pushed a serious tax reform bill in 1982. What if Mondale campaigned on tax simplification, took the issue away from us, and trumped our December '84 target date? Fortunately for us, however, he preferred to fight a rearguard action against the highly popular Reagan tax cuts. "Mr. Reagan will raise taxes," Mondale predicted (erroneously), "and so will I. He won't tell you. I just did." So much for the wild card.

The tax reform plan offered by Don Regan's Treasury had a lot to recommend it. For instance, it would have cut the fourteen different individual tax brackets (the highest being 50 percent) to just three. But the proposal would also have raised business taxes by about $150 billion over five years to help pay for individual rate reductions. For a president who viscerally opposed high corporate taxation, this was too much. The business lobby was not amused, and neither were GOP lawmakers. The only endorsements we got were from liberals like George McGovern and Ralph Nader. The plan was DOA. Don acknowledged as much when he said as he introduced it, "This thing is written on a word processor. It can be changed."

Bad choice of words. Tax reform is so tough that everyone knows it will be subject to a lot of give-and-take in the legislative process. But the only way to win is by laying out a plan you are willing to defend, then defending it as you work for principled compromises. Saying "it can be changed" on the same day you introduce a plan is like throwing blood in a shark tank.

When the plan was announced, I was in a peculiar position. Eleven days earlier, Don and I had first discussed the possibility of switching jobs, but we hadn't made a final decision. If we did decide to swap and the president approved, I would be selling reform, not as chief of staff but as secretary of the treasury.

Looking at the Treasury proposal solely as chief of staff, responsible for getting the president's proposals through Congress and for looking out for his political well-being, however, I didn't like what I saw. So I arranged for the proposal to be unveiled by Don at Treasury, not by the president at the White House. The White House then issued a terse statement saying President Reagan would withhold judgment until he had studied the plan. Translation: it's a good thing it was written on a word processor.

But President Reagan didn't abandon his tax reform vision. "We have cut tax rates by almost 25 percent," he said in his 1985 state of the union address, "yet the tax system remains unfair and limits our potential for growth. Low-income families face steep tax barriers that make hard lives even harder." He praised the Treasury plan ("excellent"), but instead of calling for its passage, he said only that its "principles will guide the final proposal we will ask you to enact.... I am instructing Treasury Secretary James Baker—I have to get used to saying that—to begin working with congressional authors and committees for bipartisan legislation conforming to these principles."

Back to the drawing board.

By then, my staff was in place, starting with a core group that migrated across the street with me from the White House. Dick Darman served as deputy secretary. Margaret Tutwiler was assistant secretary for public affairs. And John Rogers, the president's assistant for management and administration, came over as assistant secretary for management.

We also recruited an impressive group of others: George Gould (a founder of Donaldson, Lufkin & Jenrette) as under secretary for domestic finance; David Mulford (a Regan Treasury holdover) as assistant secretary for international affairs; and Bob Kimmitt (a West Pointer who had served in Vietnam and on the National Security Council staff in President Reagan's first term) as general counsel. Bob followed me to State and served with distinction as the No. 3 official in the department. He now serves as deputy secretary of the treasury in George W. Bush's administration. Don Chapoton, a tax lawyer with Baker Botts, served as assistant secretary for tax policy and helped immeasurably with the nuts and bolts of reform.

Darman also hired a bright young Harvard law grad named Bob Zoellick to serve as a staff aide. A friend of mine later described Bob, who was famous for his yellow legal pads with neat hand-lettered points lists, as "the best prepared guy in the room." He and I quickly hit it off. Bob worked his way up through a series of posts at Treasury, including executive secretary to the department, deputy assistant secretary for financial institutions policy, and counselor to the secretary. Like Darman and Tutwiler, he later followed me to George H. W. Bush's presidential campaign in August 1988, and after that to the State Department. In President George W. Bush's first term, he served as U.S. trade representative. He is now deputy secretary of state for Secretary of State Condoleezza Rice.

Finally, I also had the good sense to take Caron Jackson to Treasury as my executive assistant. She is an administrative wizard. In the White House, at Treasury, and at State—and afterward, working for me in the private sector—she always made sure that everything that needed doing got done, and done right.

One thing that took some getting used to in my new job was that I no longer had the daily, even hourly, contact with President Reagan that I had enjoyed as chief of staff. Generally speaking, cabinet officers need appointments to see the president, so my walk-in privileges were gone. Still, anytime I needed face time, I could expect to get it, thanks to my years in the trenches with President Reagan in the 1980 and 1984 elections and as chief of staff. But that was a privilege I was careful not to abuse. I also understood that the president's White House advisers—Don Regan and others—would have the last word after I left the room. Proximity is power. The dynamics had changed and I would have to change with them. At the same time, I got along quite well with Congress, the press, and the interest groups. Treasury was an important portfolio, and most folks understood that I had a special relationship with the president and enjoyed his confidence.

Before I went to the president on tax reform, however, I would need a plan that stood a fighting chance in Congress. Cleaning up the tax code is one of those good-government ideas that almost everybody supports in principle. The problem is translating principle into policy. To lower rates substantially in a revenue-neutral way, for instance, requires that a lot of tax preferences be eliminated to offset the rate reductions. If you think that's easy, look at your own tax return. Consider giving up your standard deduction or personal exemption. Or your itemized deductions for mortgage interest, state and local taxes, or charitable contributions. Which ones would you send to the chopping block? The usual answer, to repeat a very old joke, is: "Don't tax me; don't tax thee; tax that fellow behind the tree."

To make the math of tax reform work, and the politics, the "guy behind the tree" in 1985 and 1986 would turn out to be American business. To get individual rates down substantially, we would need to go after business preferences. The first Treasury proposal would have done this, of course, but it overshot the mark. The trick now would be to work with both parties in Congress to figure out what was doable.

The key to bipartisan consensus was Danny Rostenkowski, the veteran Chicago Democrat who chaired Ways and Means. The GOP-controlled Senate would later present its own challenges, but nothing would ever even get to the Senate that had not already been blessed by Danny in the House. He supported tax reform, but he was also a cautious realist who had no interest in joining a doomed crusade. "Danny," I would tell him, "we can do this." To which he would reply, "Jimmy, you're massaging me."

It was possibly Danny's concern with being massaged that led him to stay away from the private meetings Dick Darman and I organized in February to craft a bipartisan bill. This was the same strategy the administration had used for Social Security in 1983—convening a small number of leaders from both parties with agency experts to write a bill everyone could live with. Our group included Bradley and Gephardt, sponsors of the 1982 Democratic tax reform proposal; Senator Bob Kasten and Representative Jack Kemp, sponsors of a GOP counterproposal in 1984; Senate Finance chairman Bob Packwood and the committee's ranking Democrat, Russell Long; and John Duncan, the ranking Republican on House Ways and Means. If these key players could reach a compromise, maybe we could get tax reform through the gulch before the lobbyists had slipped on their Guccis. Unfortunately, however, this approach failed. Without Danny's participation and endorsement a compromise bill stood no chance, and Danny was neither participating nor endorsing.

So what to do? We quickly convened another group, the tax policy experts at Treasury, to craft a bill. In *Gucci Gulch,* reporters Jeff Birnbaum and Alan Murray accurately captured the flavor of these gatherings, which "set a very different tone" from the way my predecessor had operated.

> The meetings were frequently held on Saturdays, a practice that Regan nearly always avoided. Baker would show up in casual corduroys and pick a seat on the side of the table (unlike Regan, he seldom sat at the head). He propped his cowboy boots on the table, crammed a wad of Red Man chewing tobacco in his mouth, and placed a large plastic cup in front of him.... Where Regan avoided all talk of politics, Baker talked about little else. He had scant patience for the theoretical presentations of [Treasury tax experts Ron] Pearlman and [Charles] McClure. He would lean back and spit in his cup or scratch his nose and then demand, "What are we hearing on that one?" or "Who's working against it?"

Pearlman, assistant secretary for tax policy, and McClure, his deputy, were brilliant guys who knew the tax code inside and out. They were also the same guys who had put together the original doomed proposal. I was happy to stir a pinch of political realism into their idealistic recipes.

One day a member of our Treasury team, Manley Johnson, complained that another team member was slow to get him the numbers he needed to make some important projections.

"Manley," I said, "this reminds me of the Easter back in the sixties when my four Baker boys got four fluffy little yellow ducklings that you couldn't tell apart. That night we put the ducks in a big cardboard box in the kitchen, with a light bulb to keep them warm. Before the sun came up, unfortunately, one went to duck heaven. When the boys ran into the kitchen the next morning, Jamie, the oldest, said, 'Poor Dougie. His duck died.' Doug—at six, the youngest—tearfully bought the story. 'Yeah,' he said, 'my duck died.'

"I'll bet you feel like Dougie did," I said to Manley.

He laughed and nodded.

"Well, you're not gonna have to wait for those numbers anymore," I said. And he didn't, after I had a considerably saltier talk with the offender about not ducking his number-crunching responsibilities.

I got a few talking-tos myself. Business executives, association leaders, and heads of charities lined up at my doorstep. They were all in favor of fairness and simplicity for taxpayers, they said. They just wanted to make sure that our package didn't hurt *their* interests. I knew we were in trouble when some of the president's, and my, friends in the oil and gas industry launched a campaign to send back the Eagle pins they had been awarded for making big contributions to the '84 campaign.

We didn't hear nearly as much, frankly, from the great majority of Americans who would benefit from lower individual rates. You see the same thing in fights over free trade. Open markets help most everyone by increasing overall economic growth. But "everyone" doesn't have a lobby in Washington. Instead, the political heat—and it's intense— comes from industry and labor groups that will be hurt. That's when politicians become statesmen, by doing the right thing anyway. And we were trying to do the right thing on tax reform.

I presented our plan to the president toward the end of May. He tweaked it, then offered it to the nation in a twenty-minute televised address on May 28. "We call it America's tax plan because it will re- duce tax burdens on the working people of this country, close loopholes that benefit a privileged few, [and] simplify a code so complex even Albert Einstein reportedly needed help on his 1040 form . . ."

A family taking the standard deduction would pay no taxes on the first $12,000, he said. Above that, individual income would be taxed in just three brackets—15 percent, 25 percent, and 35 percent. The top corporate rate would be cut to 33 percent from 48 percent. To make up for lost revenues—that is, to maintain "revenue neutrality"—we would limit or do away with scores of tax preferences, including deductions for business meals (the famous "three-martini lunch"), state and local tax deductions, the investment tax credit, the oil depletion allowance (except on marginal wells), and so on.

Rostenkowski delivered the Democrats' response to the president's address. Nowadays, such replies from the opposition party (whether Democrat or Republican) are all too predictable. They begin with lip service about working with the president, but quickly devolve into a criticism of virtually everything he has just said.

Danny's response was different—"a strong, if qualified endorsement," as the *Washington Post* characterized it the next day. "Every year politicians promise to make the tax code fair and simple, but every year we seem to slip further behind. . . . But this year there's a difference. . . . It's a Republican president who's bucking his party's tradition as protectors of big business and the wealthy. . . . If we work together with good faith and determination, this time the people may win."

It wasn't all sweetness and light, however. Danny later groused to reporters that we had worked up the president's plan without consulting him. And he and his staffers were less than thrilled the next day when they saw the details of the proposal.

Okay, we said, draft your bill, then we'll work on a compromise. We hoped the Democrats would have something ready before Congress recessed in August. To our dismay, however, Danny insisted on running his hearings well into the fall. He was serious, I believe, about wanting to give everyone a say, but it was frustrating nonetheless. Too often, congressional hearings are held to score political points and win thirty-second sound bites back home. But then, that's our system. Call it "just politics," if you wish, but politics is the basis of our democracy. At their best, congressional hearings can also highlight important public policy issues and help educate the public.

BY LATE NOVEMBER, Danny was finally ready to schedule a committee vote on his markup of the president's bill. Dick Darman and I went over to the White House on Friday the twenty-second to brief the president and get our marching orders. We thought it was a routine visit, but it turned out to be the start of a near-death experience for tax reform. And congressional Democrats weren't to blame. It was the White House, itself.

The president, who had returned the day before from a meeting with Mikhail Gorbachev in Geneva, was very tired but listened carefully. Others present that day were Don Regan and Dennis Thomas, who was to Don as Darman was to me. We weren't in love with the bill, but—though far from perfect—it would broaden the tax base and bring down rates. Furthermore, we told the president, Danny's markup was also written on a word processor. Keep the process moving, we counseled, and encourage Republican House members to support the bill. Our party controls the Senate. We can fix it there.

The president, always a pragmatist, agreed and promised to do two things before the day was out. He would call Congressman Duncan, the ranking Republican on Ways and Means, to urge him to support the bill. He would also write letters of support to the other Republicans on the committee.

Neither step was taken. No phone call. No letters. Why? Dennis Thomas had not objected to the plan at the meeting with President Reagan. But afterward, we learned, he told Don Regan that the bill had little support from leading Republicans in the House. That was true. Regan and Thomas then apparently persuaded the president to remain neutral, at least for the time being. Proximity is power, and tax reform had just been proximitied into the ditch.

When I learned of this Friday evening, I was furious. This might very well mean the end of tax reform. Wavering Republicans had no reason to support the Democrats' markup if the president himself was unwilling to go public with an endorsement.

There's a protocol to handling these problems. First, Darman called Thomas. No satisfaction there. Then I got on the line and tried to get Regan. Again, no satisfaction. Tired, like the president, from the Geneva trip, he was home resting.

By then, it was about ten o'clock. The only way to get this straightened out, I thought, is to go to the top. I reached for the telephone to call the president in his private quarters. I would wake him up and tell him what his chief of staff had done and how tax reform was dead without the president's support... and... and...

Then I had second thoughts and put the receiver down. As I later explained to the authors of *Gucci Gulch*, life was too short. I'd try to fix this some other way.

Instead of calling the president, I paid a late-evening call on Rostenkowski on Capitol Hill. I told him President Reagan thought the new version was a positive beginning. "He will call on House Republicans to support it in its present form," I said. We had problems with certain provisions, I added, but hoped our concerns would be addressed in the Senate. In a late-night session of Ways and Means, the Democrats made the bill somewhat worse, particularly the deductions for state and local taxes. Rosty then called a surprise voice vote. Republicans on the committee were upset, but the administration—represented by Dick Darman—did not object. If we did not get a bill out of committe, tax reform was dead. The bill was voted out of committee about 1:00 A.M. It was ugly, but we had what we needed, which was a live bill. Now we had to get it through the full House, then on to the Senate to be fixed.

Fresh from a good night's sleep, President Reagan, we trusted, would give his support to the tax bill, warts and all, in his weekly Saturday morning radio address to the nation. That didn't happen. Okay, a statement on Monday would do. Then Thomas told Darman that Tuesday was a better bet. But there was nothing on Tuesday, either.

We kept pressing the White House for action, and the White House kept putting us off. Danny tried to telephone the president, but his call was not returned. The president appeared willing to let tax reform die, some newspapers reported. And, as feared, the White House's silent treatment gave cover to House Republicans who didn't like the bill. The White House was signaling, in effect: "The president doesn't care, so you don't have to, either."

I'll never know exactly why this happened, but the president later blamed some of his second-term troubles on his isolation in the Oval Office and on Don's "oversized ego," mistreatment of staff, and appetite for power. "Don thought of himself as a kind of 'deputy president' empowered to make important decisions involving the administration," the president wrote in his memoir. "Although I only found out about it later, he resisted having others see me alone and wouldn't forward letters or documents to me unless he saw them first. In short, he wanted to be the *only* conduit to the Oval Office, in effect making the presidential isolation . . . more complete."

Perhaps Don put up the roadblock because he was unhappy about having had his Treasury's tax plan pushed aside and the Baker Treasury's plan advanced in its place. I'll never know for sure. What I do know is that Don was hearing from a lot of people—business groups and Republican lawmakers—that we were going too far, too fast with tax reform. If Don agreed, this was odd, to say the least, because the first Treasury plan had gone further and faster than the version in Ways and Means. Whatever the reason, by late November 1985, the White House was inexplicably withholding public support for even the principle of tax reform.

On December 4, the White House finally issued a statement. The president thinks the legislative process should go forward, it said. Talk about damning with faint praise. This all but invited a GOP revolt.

By this time, Republicans on Ways and Means had fashioned their own bill. It was more business friendly. It also didn't have a chance in hell of passing the Democrat-controlled House. In response, the

White House sent another bad signal: the president would not choose between Danny's proposal and that of the Republicans.

Two days later, however, President Reagan got back on board. Frankly, I can't remember what caused the turnaround. *Time* magazine said I was able to convince Nancy Reagan of the growing threat to her husband's top domestic priority of his second term. I'm also almost certain I talked to the president and told him directly that White House indecision and neutrality were about to kill tax reform. At any rate, that's how I normally would have operated. In his Saturday morning radio address of December 7, President Reagan finally settled the question. He called on the House to pass the bill and let the Senate have a go at it. He then sent every House member a letter supporting the bill.

By then, unfortunately, the momentum had gone too far in the wrong direction. Trent Lott, then a Mississippi congressman, rallied GOP opposition and won a test vote 223–202. Only fourteen Republicans supported their own president. GOP congressmen had "voted to humiliate the man who had led them to victory," Tip O'Neill told the press.

The president *was* humiliated, and angry. The White House hadn't seen the rebellion coming, nor had I. We both *should* have, however, in light of the White House's bizarre actions—or inaction—of the previous three weeks, but what was done was done. We now had to play catch-up.

Prodded by Danny, the speaker agreed to schedule another vote, but on one very big condition: President Reagan had to promise him personally that at least fifty Republicans would vote for the package. We had until 8:00 P.M. on December 16 to round up the votes, he said. I left his office with a sick feeling. The game might very well be over.

Although we didn't think so at the time, Tip probably did us a favor by setting the tight deadline. He forced the administration to act quickly and, more important, to focus. And at this point, the only person who could save President Reagan's tax reform was President Reagan himself. He wanted to, and he did.

For a multitude of reasons, presidents rarely travel from the White House to Capitol Hill to meet lawmakers on their own turf, but Ronald Reagan—who had already come to Congress once to save the 1981 tax bill—came again. On the afternoon of December 16, about six hours before Tip's deadline, he sat down on the Hill with House Republicans. (My best memory is that I accompanied him.) By our count, he started with somewhere between thirty-five and forty supporters.

Earlier that day, the president had attended a memorial service at Fort Campbell, Kentucky, for 248 servicemen who had died when their plane crashed in Newfoundland. He began the meeting by asking the congressmen to join him in a silent prayer. "This took the sting out of our bite," Trent Lott later told Birnbaum and Murray.

But not entirely. After the president asked for their support, several House members unloaded. Their opposition was based on a combination of principle (they thought it was bad legislation) and pocketbook politics (why had the president thrown in his lot with that rascal Rostenkowski to take down our friends' tax breaks?).

The president listened patiently, then assured the critics that he would veto any bill that didn't include the major items on their wish list. But there wouldn't be a chance to fight, he pointed out, if the bill didn't make it to the GOP-controlled Senate.

The president's remarks struck a chord with one of the more prominent holdouts, Henry Hyde, an influential conservative congressman from Illinois. When he came over to our side, a handful of colleagues followed. A secret ballot at the end of the meeting showed that we had forty-eight votes.

Could we count on these forty-eight to go public? Could we find at least two more? We assembled a team in the office of my old friend, House Minority Leader Bob Michel, and started working the phones. It took a lot of calls and a lot of horse-trading. I even agreed to come stump for one representative. A breakthrough came when we persuaded Bob and another influential Republican, Jack Kemp, to sign up.

At six o'clock, I phoned Regan to tell him we'd reached our goal and that the president should call the speaker with the news. O'Neill was not immediately available. The 8:00 P.M. deadline came and went with no word from him. Four frustrating hours passed before the men talked. Why so long? I suspect the speaker just wanted to play us a bit before he closed the deal.

Trent Lott and his allies did not go gently into the night. They kept working their votes, so I set up a boiler-room operation on the Hill to hold ours. Henry Hyde helped man the phones, as did Guy Vander Jagt, my buddy from the Gerald Ford campaign, now an influential minority member of Ways and Means.

Was it unusual for a cabinet member to play politics like I did here, at least so publicly? The answer is yes. I rolled up my sleeves and got involved in the grunt work because of the importance of the issue, because of what it meant politically to the president, and because I knew how to do it. I had spent four years as chief of staff shepherding legislation through Congress on behalf of Ronald Reagan. And let's face it: I also knew that if we lost, my reputation and effectiveness would have taken a big hit.

Shortly before the vote, Tip O'Neill gave an excellent speech in support of the bill. Seventy Republicans—far more than we had counted on twelve hours earlier—joined 188 Democrats on a second test vote. We were on our way. Later that evening, the bill itself passed the House on a voice vote.

There would be several more bumps in the road over the next ten months. In April, for example, Senate Finance Chairman Bob Packwood of Oregon personally saved tax reform in the Senate. He had asked senators what it would take to win their votes. They answered with a shopping list of tax breaks they wanted to protect. The resulting business-as-usual approach was a disaster. Bob saw what was happening, scrapped the bill, and started from scratch. The White House supported his new version, and in June the Senate approved it 97–3. Pat Moynihan reportedly called it "the most ethical event I've ever seen in this place." The conference committee took two agonizing months. By late September, however, each house was ready to vote on a final bill.

On September 23, I delivered public remarks about tax reform at the White House. First I read aloud from old headlines about the president's package being "in trouble" or "in limbo" or "a loser" or "moribund" or "down for the count." Then I recited a little ditty called the "Tax Reform Shuffle."*

> *They said tax reform was dead. Now it's alive.*
> *Here's its story. It began in '85.*
> *We drew up a plan, and sent it out in May,*
> *But the special interests said, "Ain't no way!"*
> *Rosty started hearings before the fall;*
> *They were Gucci-to-Gucci in the hall.*
> *December came, reform was off the track,*
> *So to the Hill rode the Gipper to bring it back.*
> *Chorus: All along it's been a big tussle,*
> *But we keep doing the Tax Reform Shuffle.*

Both houses approved the final bill on September 27. Unbelievably, we had pared the brackets from fourteen to two—15 percent and 28 percent. We won the $2,000 personal exemption and increased the standard deduction for married couples to $5,000, both indexed for inflation (as were the brackets). These provisions, together with the earned income tax credit, meant that a family of four would pay no taxes on the first $15,380 of income. We limited some deductions and eliminated many others, including deductions for many work-related expenses and for interest on most personal loans. (Mortgage interest on the principal residence was still deductible.) Business lost the investment tax credit, full deductions for business meals and entertainment, and other tax breaks. In return the top corporate rate was reduced to 34 percent, from 48 percent.

---

*I had no luck finding out who wrote this piece. It was obviously someone with a keen eye and a wonderful sense of humor.

On October 22, President Reagan signed the legislation on the South Lawn. I was on the podium, along with Danny Rostenkowski and other key players. "When I sign this bill into law," the president said, "America will have the lowest marginal tax rates and the most modern tax code among the major industrialized nations." He thanked everyone who had helped pass the bill, including "my two incomparable secretaries of the treasury, Don Regan and Jim Baker. I feel like we just played the World Series of tax reform," the president said, "and the American people won." As I watched the ceremony—even now as I look back—I was amazed that we had pulled it off. It was something of a miracle, frankly.

My pride about the Tax Reform Act of 1986 is tinged with sadness. The code today is as complex as ever, perhaps worse. We wiped the blackboard fairly clean in 1986, but this only encouraged Congress to come up with a new generation of preferences. As it became harder and harder to pass spending bills, Congress turned to "tax expenditures" and used the IRS to reward favored constituencies by reducing their taxes. That's a bad idea for a lot of reasons, not the least of which are that it junks up the code and forces Congress to tax the majority of taxpayers more heavily to finance benefits for the few.

Marginal rates were pushed back up to 31 percent under President George H. W. Bush (who famously traded the tax hike for congressional spending cuts), then to almost 40 percent under Bill Clinton (who liked to use the tax code for social engineering on savings, education, and other issues). President George W. Bush has gotten the top rate back down to 35 percent, which helped our economy recover from the 2001 recession and from 9/11, but with all the new preferences in the tax code, it'll be hard to cut the rates any lower.

Like President Reagan, President Bush 43 has also announced a second-term goal of reforming the tax code. He has one big advantage, GOP control of both houses of Congress, but for many reasons—including his decision to give his unsuccessful effort to reform Social Security a higher priority—it will be a tougher fight now than it was back in 1986, and it was plenty tough back then. I wish him well. A more sensible tax code would do a lot to help our economy.

The tax-reform fight—and particularly the White House's weeks of indecision in late 1985—revived talk that President Reagan was a puppet of his staff. As troubled as I was by what happened, I still don't believe that. Every president has eighteen thousand things coming at him. It is the staff's job to prioritize his time. For instance, it would be very rare for a president to telephone the ranking member of Ways and Means unless his staff recommended it as part of a White House legislative game plan, then set up the call. Any president who goes down in the weeds to handle that kind of detail himself will lose control of his presidency. In that sense, every president is to some extent hostage to his staff, and President Reagan was no different. The White House staff certainly let him down on the tax-reform fight, but it was more likely the result of political indecision or confusion, in my opinion, than of cynical manipulation. Once the president understood what was going on, he stepped up and personally saved tax reform.

There has also been talk that the president exhibited symptoms of early stage Alzheimer's disease in his second term, based, for instance, on his responses to Iran-Contra and his stumbling over some facts in a 1985 interview with the *Wall Street Journal.* Well, I wasn't at his side every day, as before, but every time I was in his presence or talked to him by telephone during the second term, he was alert, capable, and vibrant. When the president announced in 1994 that he suffered from Alzheimer's and had begun "the journey that will lead me into the sunset of my life," I was deeply saddened and genuinely shocked.

AS RONALD REAGAN'S second term drew near its end, I was again approached about suiting up in a different jersey (albeit one I had worn before), this time by George H. W. Bush. I agreed, and we went to the president. One might have expected the outgoing president to give his immediate blessing to this request by his vice president and treasury secretary. To our great surprise, however, he resisted.

ELEVEN

"IF THAT'S WHAT YOU WANT, GEORGE, THAT'S WHAT WE'LL DO"

IN APRIL 2005, I celebrated my seventy-fifth birthday in Houston with family and friends, more than six hundred in all. The size of the event was a subject of intense diplomatic negotiations with Susan and others. I reluctantly agreed to a large party on three conditions: first, that the occasion be used to raise money for the James A. Baker III Institute for Public Policy at Rice University (more about the institute later); second, that it be casual; and third, that all speeches be short.

The birthday celebration, held under a huge tent on the Rice campus, raised almost $4.5 million for the institute. The theme was western. I wore a beige cowboy-style shirt with button-down pockets, brown pants, a big silver belt buckle with two eagles on it, well-worn but highly polished cordovan cowboy boots, and a narrow-brim felt Stetson in a style favored by Texas ranchers and businessmen.

Country-western star Clay Walker, a Texas native, sang "Happy Birthday," then provided music for an evening of dancing. I'm a big fan of country music. I don't collect recordings or keep up with the latest releases from Nashville (or anyplace else), and when I was courting age, I danced to big band swing and listened to Frank Sinatra and Tony

Bennett. These days, however, I usually tune my satellite radio to George Jones, Conway Twitty, Tammy Wynette, Loretta Lynn, Merle Haggard, and the others, particularly as I drive south from Houston on hunting trips. I like the human-interest stories in country music ("D-I-V-O-R-C-E," "Hello, Darlin'," "Don't Come Home A-Drinkin' with Lovin' on Your Mind"); the humor ("I Miss You Only on Days That End in Y"); and the themes ("When they're runnin' down our country, hoss, they're walkin' on the fightin' side of me"). I'm just *comfortable* with that kind of music. For one thing, I haven't met a country singer yet who is ashamed to sing about friends, family, country, and faith. Even the cheatin' and drinkin' songs usually have a moral.

The Baker family knows something about other kinds of lyrics. In 1985, Susan encouraged Tipper Gore to join her, Pam Howar, and Sally Nevius in forming the Parents Music Resource Center (PMRC). The goal of their group was to educate parents about the sick lyrics in popular music, primarily rock and rap, that glorified violence, drug use, suicide, murder, and other criminal behavior. The group did not set out to censor recordings, as some charged. Instead it urged the record industry to put warning labels on records with "explicit lyrics or content" so consumers, young and old, would at least know what they were buying.

In response to the PMRC, a U.S. Senate committee began investigating rock music in September 1985. Within two months, the Recording Industry Association of America had agreed to label explicit albums. This is similar to the motion picture industry's rating system and the one adopted by the cable television industry.

Tipper and Susan became good friends during this mission and remain so today. Both testified before the committee. So did several recording artists, most notably Frank Zappa of the long-defunct rock band Mothers of Invention. The PMRC was a "group of bored Washington housewives," he said, who wanted to "housebreak all composers and performers because of the lyrics of a few." He even mocked Susan's Texas accent. This was mild, however, compared to *Hustler* magazine, which awarded Susan and Tipper their coveted Assholes of the Month Award.

Zappa needn't have been so concerned. The rating system didn't silence anybody. If you think it did, just scan your radio dial today and listen to some of the outrageous music that debases women, promotes drug use, and glorifies violence. Thank goodness only a few stations play it.

Truth is, Susan was never out to housebreak composers, and she was anything but a bored Washington housewife. When she wasn't running the ever-lively Baker household—try organizing life for eight children—and advising me daily on the hard decisions I brought home from work, she always lived out her Christianity by giving food, clothes, and other material comfort to "the least of these." She was involved with food banking in Washington and Houston, then in 1983 cofounded the National Alliance to End Homelessness, which she serves today as cochair.

Public service is not all glamour and fun. It's tough, but it is toughest on spouses and children because the public servant generally works very long hours and is totally absorbed in the job and the important issues of the day. Legislators spend many days away from home to campaign in the home state or district. Long hours at work make it difficult to help the spouse with family problems. The spotlight of public scrutiny falls not just on the public figure but also, and sometimes unfairly, on the family. If your child gets caught speeding, it's a family problem. If an officeholder's child does the same thing, it can be a national story. A lot of families crack under the strain of public service. Susan is a strong woman. I was blessed, and our children were blessed, to have her in charge of our home.

The speeches at my birthday party were, thank goodness, brief. Even if he had wanted to, George Bush 41 couldn't have spoken for long. He had a bad case of laryngitis, but I will always treasure his scratchy remarks that evening. He characterized me as "a man to whom friendship means everything." True. He also said that I was "a man without whom I would not have become president of the United States." Maybe.

IF TWO other presidents—Nixon and Reagan—had had their way, I might not have been able to help George make his run for the presidency against the Democrats' Michael Dukakis in 1988. A history refresher first.

George's path to the White House started with the '88 Republican primaries. Although he was a two-term vice president and the clear front-runner, seven candidates lined up against him—Bob Dole, Jack Kemp, Pat Robertson, Howard Baker, Al Haig, Don Rumsfeld, and Pierre "Pete" du Pont. The race did not begin well. George finished third in the Iowa caucuses. No surprise that Dole won. He was from neighboring Kansas and, as Senate majority leader, was good at delivering for Midwest farmers. But few expected televangelist Pat Robertson to take second place. He did a good job of getting his supporters to the Iowa caucuses.

The flight from Iowa to New Hampshire, the first primary state, was glum, but George kept his composure, campaigned hard, and regained momentum by winning there, just as Ronald Reagan had done eight years earlier. George then won sixteen out of sixteen primaries on Super Tuesday, March 8. That sewed it up.

Former New Jersey senator Nick Brady chaired the Bush effort. Lee Atwater was campaign manager. George's chief of staff, Craig Fuller, pollster Bob Teeter, finance chairman Bob Mosbacher, and media expert Roger Ailes were also members of the brain trust. Within the campaign, they were called the "Gang of Six," or "G-6." I watched it all from the sidelines at Treasury. Every once in a while I was asked to contribute my two cents' worth to the campaign. Generally, however, I tended to my knitting at Treasury and George and the G-6 tended to the campaign.

Because of my long friendship with George and my experience in running presidential campaigns (including his in 1979–1980), conventional wisdom was that I would resign from Treasury before the party convention in mid-August to run the fall general election campaign. But Richard Nixon thought that was a bad idea. On May 15, the former president said in a letter to George that it "would be a serious mistake" for Baker to "take a leave of absence" and join the campaign. "The antis in the media would take it as a lack of confidence in your ability to win and too much deference to Reagan," Nixon advised George.

Interesting. Having entered the Reagan administration with the reputation of being the vice president's man, I was now seen, at least by the politically savvy Nixon, as the president's guy.

George had obviously asked Nixon for his opinion about my taking on the fall campaign. Nixon's reference in his letter to a "leave of absence" reflected perhaps how much things had changed after Watergate. By 1988, no cabinet official could just take a leave, as opposed to resigning from government, to run the presidential campaign of another cabinet or constitutional officer. Even if a way could have been found to do it legally, a leave of absence would have given the Democrats a political club.*

Nixon's counsel notwithstanding, George approached me to run his fall campaign. The G-6 had not functioned as well as he had hoped. Without one acknowledged leader who spoke with authority and credibility for the candidate, differences of opinion were difficult to settle. I was happy where I was, frankly, and the prospect of resigning my cabinet post left me with mixed emotions. Don't get me wrong, however. There was never really any doubt about whether I would do it. This wasn't just a campaign; it was my friend's campaign.

I believed in George. He had one of the best résumés in the history

---

*If I had left government when I resigned as secretary of state to lead George's campaign against Bill Clinton in 1992, new ethics-in-government laws would have prohibited my even talking to those with whom I had served in the cabinet. That's why I stayed in government and became White House chief of staff and senior counselor to the president.

of presidential politics—great education, military hero, successful businessman, respected congressman, party chairman, UN ambassador, head of the CIA, envoy to China, and the most active and engaged vice president in American history in one of the most successful administrations in American history. Even more impressive was the flesh-and-blood George Bush that I knew so well, a man who embodied honor and decency. They say that integrity is doing the right thing when nobody knows. It's also doing the right thing when the only person who knows is your friend. And in our countless hours of playing tennis or golf, shooting quail and dove, downing Otto's barbeque, visiting each other's families, and doing both politics and public service together, I never saw him cut a corner or do anything disreputable. He always went by the book.

I also owed George, personally and professionally. He and Barbara stood by me and the boys when Mary Stuart died. They were the last outside the family to visit her in the hospital. Afterward, they welcomed Susan and her children into our circle of friendship. He led me into politics and public service, then helped me by example and with advice to do my jobs at Commerce, the White House, and Treasury.

And yes, I also knew that if George won, there would probably be something in it for me. But we never discussed it. We were both conscious—very conscious—of the fact that it was illegal to promise anyone a job in exchange for campaign help.

Of course I would help George. We wanted to do it the right way, however, and that meant we needed President Reagan's blessing. But when I approached the boss about resigning from Treasury and moving to the campaign, he politely said no. "You can be more valuable by staying here and keeping the economy on course," he said.

"It doesn't look to me like this is gonna fly unless *you* talk to the president," I told George, who promptly did so and, I believe, got the same response. Sensing George's disappointment, however, the president suggested that we talk it over one more time. Shortly thereafter, President Reagan, Nancy, George, and I gathered in the living quarters on the second floor of the White House. The president listened to

George's pitch, then said, "If that's what you want, George, that's what we'll do. It just occurred to me that Jim might be more valuable as secretary of the treasury."

Over the past seven and a half years, I had walked in and out of the Reagan White House countless times, always as a member of the team. As I departed that day, however, I had a real sense of separation, of moving on. I would be back a few more times for the goodbyes, of course, but if I returned in January, it would be to a Bush White House—an old and familiar setting for an exciting new act in the great drama of American history. Imagine walking into the Oval Office and seeing your best friend behind the desk! At the same time, I could not deny a quiet sadness as I shook hands with President Reagan that day and walked away, symbolically transferring my loyalty from one great president to the friend who could, and would, be another.

George and I had a lot of work ahead of us, but first I needed to wrap things up at Treasury. On August 5, I submitted my letter of resignation, effective August 17, the day before George would formally accept the party's nomination at the convention in New Orleans.

I thanked the president for giving me the opportunity to serve and for entrusting me with such great responsibilities. "In seeking to advance your vice president's candidacy, I [can] best help insure the survival of your legacy and assure that your remarkable contributions are extended on toward the twenty-first century," I wrote. I wanted him to know that we would be running *on* his legacy, not *against* it.

The letter in which the president accepted my resignation "with mixed feelings" is among the most important keepsakes from my life in government. In part, it's typical end-of-service boilerplate about a departing officer's "solid record of accomplishment and extraordinary service to the American people." But, as usual, the president knew how to touch the heart.

> I was somewhat surprised to learn of your grandfather's admonition to "work hard, study, and keep out of politics." His view represented a healthy strain of American skepticism about the potential pitfalls of

involvement with politics. But in your career you have set an important example: You have clearly demonstrated that the best of the political arts can be combined with first-class professionalism in the
effective pursuit of America's interests.

After the markets closed on August 5, President Reagan and I appeared in the White House press room to announce my resignation
and the nomination of Nick Brady, then cochairman of the investment firm Dillon, Read & Company, to succeed me. "You've been a secret of our success," the always-gracious president said to me in front
of the assembled reporters. "Now, Jim, go do it for George."

Federal Reserve Board Chairman Alan Greenspan issued a statement calling me "one of the most effective secretaries of the Treasury
in the nation's history" and "a tough act to follow." At that point Alan
had been in office less than a year. The summer before, he had replaced
the highly respected Paul Volcker. Alan is one of the great legacies of
the Reagan years and was reappointed again and again by presidents of
both parties. As I write, he has just retired after almost nineteen years
in office. (I will interject here to ask: what has America done to be so
fortunate as to have two such outstanding men as Paul Volcker and
Alan Greenspan to lead our central bank? Both deserve enormous
credit for our nation's prosperity over the past quarter century.)*

Besides looking back at my time at Treasury, the press looked
ahead to my role as campaign chairman. In a front-page story, the
Washington Post's David Hoffman wrote that I was assuming "command

---

*Hobart Rowen, veteran reporter on economic matters for the *Washington Post*, summed up
my legacy in a column on August 11. "Baker has been a dominant international presence,
perhaps the most influential U.S. Treasury Secretary of modern times. . . . Baker's arrival
at the Treasury had a positive effect on the global economy."

In the appendix to this book, readers may read about our successful efforts to stabi-
lize international currency exchange rates and negotiate the Canada-U.S. Free Trade
Agreement, and also about "Black Monday," the day in October 1987 that the Dow Jones
Industrial Average dropped 22 percent.

of the deeply troubled presidential quest ... at the outset of a critical two-week period in which Bush hopes to climb out of a distant second place in the polls and use his national convention to more clearly define his goals and identity. ... Many Republicans have also concluded that Bush needed a strong manager to replace the diffuse organization running his campaign. With Baker's arrival, campaign sources said the so-called 'G-6' ... would now lapse."

A presidential campaign needs strong organization and a way to make decisions quickly. The best way to do that is with a leader who can get things done *now*, not with a committee that can get things done *after* a meeting that takes two hours to organize and two more to conduct. Still, "lapse" was too strong a word to describe what happened to the G-6. On the same day I announced my resignation, George and I met with about thirty top people in the campaign. He told them I would be in charge, but I assured them that I had no intention of reinventing the wheel. Atwater, Ailes, Teeter, Fuller, Mosbacher, and the others had done good work and would continue to play important roles through November, I said.

I already had some ideas about strategy. The slow start in the polls didn't alarm me. (Early polls tell you what you need to know to win a campaign, not whether you will win it.) Nor did the critical stories about the campaign operation. (That could be fixed.) The biggest problem, in my view, was structural. It may sound trite, but it's true that "change is the only constant in politics." If you can't portray your candidate as an agent of change, he will have a tough time winning.

That's one reason it's hard for any political party to win the presidency a third time after having held power for eight years. Since the Twenty-second Amendment (limiting chief executives to two elected terms) was ratified in 1951, no party had held the Oval Office more than two successive terms. In peacetime, at least, voters usually want a change.

As the perfect vice president, George had served the Reagan presidency superbly, but at significant cost to his image as a man with his own ideas. One thing in Nixon's May 15 letter to George was correct. From now on, he needed to be seen as his own man, not just as President Reagan's vice president. He could not expect to win by totally piggybacking on the prior administration, even one as successful as the Reagan presidency. He needed to say how he would change things for the better. This had to be done carefully, however, because new ideas could sound like implied criticism of the old order, prompting questions about why he didn't do something about the issue when he had a chance.

Al Gore would later have the same problem. President Clinton's reputation was tainted by personal scandal, so Al had a particularly tough call to make—whether to enlist a great campaigner who was still popular with the party's base or to cut the cord. Al separated himself from his president, in part by refusing Clinton's help on the stump and in part by embracing a more aggressively liberal agenda. I think he made a mistake on both counts. Bill Clinton wouldn't have helped much in the reddest states or hurt much in the bluest ones, but in a race as close as the one in 2000, he could have made the difference in the states that were the closest.

The GOP convention in New Orleans promised to be a big snore. George had bagged the nomination months earlier. His acceptance speech would be covered, but to restless reporters, it was already old news before it happened. Political conventions once featured brutal floor fights over the nomination. Now, however, primaries were the true battlefields of presidential politics, with conventions serving only to formally tie up the loose ends. They had become media events, useful for rolling out the candidate, stirring the party faithful, and—most important—reaching through the television to give voters a chance to get to know the candidate.

Unfortunately, we had little to offer the media, other than President Reagan's political valedictory on the first night of the convention and George's speech on the last night. If we didn't gin up more excitement, George would be presented to the nation through the jaundiced filter of journalistic boredom. The one big mystery we had left, of course, was selection of a vice presidential nominee. As the convention began, George still hadn't picked his running mate. If we played it right, that would add some drama, or so we thought.

Well, we didn't play it right, but we got the drama anyway. The star was James Danforth Quayle and the plot was about whether his wealthy family had or had not pulled strings to get him in the Indiana National Guard during Vietnam.

Before I tell the story, however, let me get one piece of old baggage out of the way. Despite it all, Dan Quayle was a good choice in 1988. The Bush-Quayle ticket went on to win every state but ten. What more could any vice presidential candidate have delivered? Dan worked hard in the campaign and, more important, served effectively and honorably as vice president, just as he had as a senator from Indiana. How we messed up was in not announcing the selection until we got to the convention.

Vice President Bush publicly introduced Dan Quayle as his choice on the second day of the convention, Tuesday, August 16, after taking a cruise on the Mississippi in the paddle wheeler *Natchez*. Minutes earlier the ever-playful presidential son, George W., had boarded the boat with a sign reading, "Dad, you can tell me!"

For perspective, remember that no matter how much noise the parties make at their summer conventions about the running mate, voters almost uniformly ignore vice presidential nominees in deciding how to vote in November. The office is of the utmost importance constitutionally, but often of little consequence in swaying voters.

Before the convention, George had narrowed his choices to five men and one woman. Alan Simpson (Wyoming) and Pete Domenici (New Mexico) brought strong credentials from the Senate, but Simpson was pro-choice—a position that was anathema to most Republican delegates—and Domenici took himself out of consideration a few days before the convention. That left four possibles. Bob Dole and Jack Kemp had opposed George in the primaries. Picking either of them would have echoed what Ronald Reagan did in 1980, which was to select a worthy adversary from the primaries. Elizabeth Dole, Bob's wife, had served most recently as transportation secretary. Dan, the junior senator from Indiana and less well known than the others, was good-looking, conservative, and, at forty-one, a generation younger than the sixty-four-year-old presidential nominee—a real advantage, some of us thought.

As the convention approached, most pundits predicted a Bush-Dole (Bob, that is) ticket, despite the pair's sometimes contentious relationship during the primaries. Bob made no secret about wanting the nod. He told reporters he had left a two-word message on his answering machine: "I accept." He still had his pride, however. A few weeks before the convention he told me he would do whatever George wished, even pull out of contention, but he would not "grovel" for the nomination. I couldn't understand why Bob thought George would want his running mate to grovel, but I promised to pass it along.

George may have made the vice presidential decision alone, but he asked friends and family members for advice. I was still at Treasury at the time, but he apparently met with his other top advisers on August 6 and August 12. The only time I remember weighing in was on a Wyoming camping trip with George in mid-July. In our shared tent in the wilds of the Shoshone National Forest, he went through the list one night, and I gave him my thoughts. I don't recall the details, but I remember that I thought Bob Dole and Dan Quayle were the most logical choices.

Dole was a proven leader, a man with experience and the gravitas to serve as vice president or president. On the other hand, he had shown a tendency in the 1976 presidential election and the 1988 primaries to make controversial statements. It has been reported that I expressed reservations about his ability to run a well-coordinated campaign and to serve as an effective number-two man. I don't recall ever doing so. In fact, I have always admired Bob and his service to our country. He and I worked well and closely together when I was at the White House, the Treasury, and State.

I remember being impressed by Quayle's positives, and he had strong backing in Ailes, Teeter, and Brady. He was young, handsome, and conservative, and he came from the heartland. But I also thought he was a little green, politically. For the record, I don't believe any of us knew about the National Guard issue.

George had one more source of information, a most important one—background checks by Bob Kimmitt, an old hand from the Ford administration, the Reagan White House (national security staff), and the Baker Treasury (general counsel). I had recommended him. He was a good man for a tough job, supercompetent and absolutely trustworthy.

Background checks are a necessary evil of modern political life. They are intended to keep unqualified or corrupt candidates out of high federal offices, but their most important role, if we're honest, is to prevent embarrassment for the person making the nomination. You may be better qualified than any other person on earth for the job for which you've been nominated, but if you've ever consulted a psychiatrist, hired a gardener from Tijuana, failed to withhold from your nanny's paycheck, or worked for (or invested in) an unpopular company, you're probably toast. A lot of well-qualified candidates simply won't submit to the process. It's intrusive and time-consuming; it tears down hard-won reputations on account of youthful indiscretions; it makes journalistic mountains out of ethical molehills; and it fuels partisanship. Who needs the grief? A lot of good people still endure it, thank goodness, but the process can give opportunists an advantage over better-qualified candidates with rough edges.

I wonder how many of our nation's Founders would have failed federal background checks. "Mr. Hamilton, when you started paying the old continental debt, didn't a lot of the money go to your rich friends at the Bank of New York, which you helped organize?"

George told the press that no one other than Kimmitt would see the results of the background checks. He kept his word. I never saw them, and I don't know of anybody else (other than George and Bob) who did. I admire George's concern for the privacy of the people under consideration and Bob's absolute sense of discretion about the sensitive information he handled. By keeping the information away from his political advisers, however, George might have missed an opportunity to head off the trouble that lay ahead. That's not to say that any of us would have spotted it. Who knows? But more review might have increased the chances that at least one person would have seen what was coming. (Of course, it could also have resulted in damaging leaks.)

The best way to avoid this sort of thing, however, is not through background checks; it is to select nominees who have already had a run at national politics, high-profile senate or gubernatorial races in states such as New York, California, Florida, or Texas, or federal appointments requiring Senate confirmation. You can be sure that the backgrounds of these kinds of candidates have been vetted by the toughest possible investigators—their opponents and the press. Bad news usually outs. Candidates who can deal with it survive. Those who can't are swept away, as Democratic front-runner Gary Hart was in mid-1987. Donna Rice and the *Monkey Business* ruined his chances, not only for the White House, but also for being considered as Dukakis's running mate. Another benefit of this approach is that it can give the candidate a laboratory for appraising the hopefuls' talents for winning votes or for serving in public office. The downside of limiting the universe of possible vice presidential nominees to experienced pols or appointees, obviously, is that it eliminates a lot of very good people from consideration.

The way to handle a proposed vice presidential nominee who has not been tested in national or big-state politics or high appointive office—and I have the obvious benefit of hindsight—is to float the name a few weeks before the convention and let the games begin. By opening gavel, the candidate will have run the gauntlet of press scrutiny or opposition research, or have dropped out. This approach wouldn't necessarily work in a contested convention and, unfortunately, it eliminates the drama of dropping the name at the convention. But it would pretty well guarantee that the news from the convention would not be dominated by questions about the vice presidential selection. If you do it the other way (as we did) in, say, New Orleans, be prepared to spend your time in the press room knocking down stories rather than at Galatoire's knocking down oysters.

If George had limited his consideration of potential candidates in this way, however, Dan would not have been selected. And if George had floated the Indiana senator's name a few weeks earlier, the National Guard question would probably have come up earlier and allowed the campaign to deal with the issue beforehand. Either way, the selection wouldn't have blown up the way it did on the second day of the convention.

Why did George make the decision alone, then hold the choice so close to the vest? Well, he had been vice president for eight long years. The office is hard on its occupants. "Cactus Jack" Garner, FDR's first vice president (a Texan), said the position wasn't worth a pitcher of warm spit. George would sometimes repeat an old Mark Twain joke about two brothers. "One went to sea and the other became vice president. Neither was heard from again." I think he wanted to use the selection of his running mate to step out of the shadows and assert his authority as leader of the party.

On our Tuesday flight to New Orleans aboard Air Force Two, George told Teeter, Fuller, and me that he'd made up his mind, but he didn't tell us which candidate he had picked. He also told us he wanted to make the announcement that day, not later in the convention as planned.

The first person (other than Barbara) to learn of the decision was President Reagan. He had given his emotional political farewell the night before. As usual, the speech was a masterpiece. He reminded the misty-eyed delegates of all he and they had accomplished together on their "national crusade to make America great again." "While our triumph is not yet complete, the road has been glorious indeed."

He reminded Americans how much their lives had improved since 1980, with sixty-seven months of economic growth and years of foreign-policy successes. Responding to the theme of the recent Democratic convention—"time for a change"—he answered, "Well, ladies and gentlemen . . . we are the change."

Then he handed off the baton to candidate Bush with skill and grace.

"Go out and win one for the Gipper!" he concluded.

The delegates answered with a thunderous demonstration for the man they would always love and revere.

Great start.

The next day, President Reagan departed, and George arrived to stake his claim to the nomination. A well-publicized handshake at Belle Chase Naval Air Station marked the passing of political command. During their photo-op on the tarmac, George leaned over and shared his secret with the man he would succeed.

As soon as we got back to the hotel, George told me his choice. George first telephoned all the unsuccessful candidates, then told me to get Senator Quayle on the phone. George then told Dan that he was his first and only choice.

Our schedule that day called for us to take the *Natchez* down the Mississippi to the Spanish Plaza in downtown New Orleans. Quayle was instructed to meet us at the dock. The announcement didn't go off well. Veteran reporters Jack Germond and Jules Witcover described the scene this way:

> Quayle was absolutely giddy with happiness, grabbing his benefactor by the shoulder and repeatedly hugging his arm, gamboling around the platform like the jackpot winner on a television game show. The bizarre scene was reminiscent of the memorable moment at the 1972 Republican national convention in Miami when entertainer Sammy Davis, Jr., came up behind President Richard Nixon and gave him a full-blown bear hug. . . . Bush himself looked on a bit thunderstruck at the display of juvenile enthusiasm he had unleashed.

I was standing in the audience. I was surprised by, but only mildly concerned about, Dan's excess exuberance.

Would that Quayle's enthusiasm had been our only problem. Until now the national press had had little reason to scrutinize his personal story or public record. But two negative stories quickly surfaced. One was about a 1980 golfing vacation. Dan and two congressmen had briefly shared a cottage with Paula Parkinson, a blond lobbyist who would later display her wares in *Playboy*. That one faded quickly. The other, about the National Guard, had more legs. Within hours, it was attracting all the ink and TV time we had counted on for George's official rollout as nominee.

There's a phenomenon, pack journalism, where reporters compete to outdo one another on a story, and that happened here. It's not always fair, because information that is inconsistent with the storyline sometimes gets short shrift. Still, the reporters were doing their jobs and we had to do ours.

The connection between military service and the American presidency is strong. Our first president was a general. So were Andrew Jackson, Ulysses S. Grant, Dwight Eisenhower, and several others. Every president from Harry Truman to Ronald Reagan served as a military officer, and George H. W. Bush, if he won, would extend that list. The U.S. president is commander in chief of the most powerful military force on earth, and voters seem to prefer candidates with command experience. In addition, millions of Americans have served in the military. They identify with candidates who, like them, have sacrificed and, in some cases, risked their lives for our nation.

That's why I think the military records of recent presidential and vice presidential candidates have become such important issues. In 1992, questions were asked whether candidate Bill Clinton had dodged the draft. More recently, similar questions have been raised about President George W. Bush's Air National Guard service and the legitimacy of Senator John Kerry's combat medals in Vietnam. These subjects arouse passion and are capable of moving elections.

That's why in 1988 we clearly had to answer the questions about Dan's service. He had served honorably in the Indiana National Guard, but the real question was whether he signed up in 1969 to avoid serving in Vietnam and, more to the point, whether his prominent family had used its influence to move him up the waiting list.

At a Wednesday morning press conference, a reporter asked Quayle why he had opted for the Guard. After explaining his desire to get married and go to law school, Quayle added, "I did not know in 1969 that I would be in this room today."

Uh-oh. Our candidate had just provided a new definition of "selective service."

By now, it was clear that we'd be hammered in the Thursday morning papers. There was nothing we could do about that. Our goal was to get ahead of the story (or put it to bed) before George gave his acceptance speech that night.* That's when he would step out from the shadow of the great president to whom he had been so loyal and reveal his own vision for the country. We wanted Friday's headlines to be about our candidate for president, not our candidate for vice president.

We needed to do three things. The first was dig up the facts. The second was to disclose them. (The worst thing with a negative story is for it to dribble out in installments.) And the third was make it clear that, despite it all, George was standing by his selection.

While the delegates at New Orleans's Superdome were nominating George, I met with my gang of strategists and operatives, including Dick Darman, Margaret Tutwiler, Lee Atwater, Bob Teeter, Craig Fuller, Stu Spencer (who would manage Dan's campaign), Jim Lake (our communications director, who would also work with Quayle), Bob Kimmitt, and political specialists Paul Manafort and Charlie Black.

First, we needed to know what Kimmitt had uncovered in his

---

*A good place to read more about how the campaign responded to the National Guard issue is *Whose Broad Stripes and Bright Stars,* by Jack Germond and Jules Witcover, which helped me remember who did what, and when, during those hectic days in August.

background checks. My focus was not, however, on assessing whether anything went wrong with the vetting process and, if so, who was to blame. There wasn't time for that. Besides, as I've already said, the blame game serves little purpose. The real issue is always what to do about a problem, not what you can dig out of the ashes of the past about who knew what, and when.

After our meeting, I called Dan and told him we needed better answers to the questions the media were asking. I then sent Darman and Kimmitt to his suite to get those answers. They reported back that he truthfully didn't know or remember the relevant particulars. Not good enough. We made several calls over the next few hours to National Guard officials and politicians from Indiana. We even woke up Dan's father to ask what he remembered.

As dawn approached, we still didn't have all the answers, but it appeared that Dan's father had, indeed, made a call or two to help his son get in the Guard. Three hours later, I got out of bed to make the talk shows. At each interview, the message was that we would have more to say about Dan's military record later in the day and that George Bush had complete confidence in his running mate.

As the day wore on, we considered several scenarios short of dropping Dan from the ticket, which was never in the cards. He could hold a press conference. (Bad idea.) He could deliver a speech to explain his Guard service. (Slightly better.) Or we could do the talking for him. (Even better.)

On Thursday evening, shortly before George was to deliver his acceptance speech, Fuller, Teeter, and I each appeared on a different television network to lay out what we had discovered. "There's nothing to hide," I said, disclosing what we knew so far—that Dan's father had made telephone calls to help his son get in the Guard but that Dan hadn't received preferential treatment.

Quayle's brief acceptance speech was also orchestrated. We added a few sentences, including this one: "I served six years in the National Guard and like millions of Americans who have served in the Guard and serve today, I'm proud of it." We also gave the press pool a few minutes with Dan before the speech.

George and Dan spent the day after the convention in Dan's hometown, Huntington, Indiana. When reporters asked about Dan's military record, he answered with the information we had pieced together. Yes, he'd asked for his father's help. And, yes, a family friend—a retired Indiana National Guard officer who worked for one of his family's newspapers—had made a few calls. There was nothing wrong with that, he said.

Questions about Dan's military record didn't seriously sidetrack the campaign. One reason is that the head of the ticket was a certified World War II hero. Another is that on the last night of the convention, George single-handedly changed the direction of the campaign.

TWELVE

"IF YOU'RE SO SMART, JIMMY, HOW COME I'M VICE PRESIDENT AND YOU'RE NOT?"

GEORGE REGAINED THE SPOTLIGHT with his acceptance speech—
the speech of his life. It is now best remembered for the phrases it
added to our lexicon: "kinder, gentler nation," "one thousand points of
light," and, darn it, "Read my lips: no new taxes." But it was much more
than that—substantively, politically, and personally. It revealed to the
nation the George Bush whom I knew and respected, a modest man
with the experience to serve as president, with deeply held values, and
with a clear and inspiring vision of the role of government in the lives
of Americans and the role of Americans in the world.

At their mid-July convention in Atlanta, the Democrats had tried
to define George as a wimp, and worse. Actually, "define" is too polite
a word. They ridiculed him, both as a public figure and as a human being. If that's how they wanted to play their hand, more power to 'em.
The irony, however, is that many of the same people who jumped from
their seats to cheer these mean-spirited attacks would later whine
about George's campaign being too negative. For what it's worth, I
think the sharp anti-Bush rhetoric at their convention hurt the Democrats with undecided voters.

Ted Kennedy, whose party had rejected his presidential hopes in 1980, taunted the vice president. The senator read a laundry list of what he deemed shortcomings of the Reagan years. After each one, he asked: "Where was George?" Soon the delegates joined the refrain. "Where was George? Where was George?"*

Keynoter Ann Richards, the Texas treasurer—who would win her state's governorship in 1990, then lose it four years later to a young baseball executive named George W. Bush—was even more acerbic. "For eight straight years, George Bush hasn't displayed the slightest interest in anything we care about," she said. "And now that he's after a job he can't get appointed to, he's like Christopher Columbus discovering America.... Poor George. He can't help it. He was born with a silver foot in his mouth."

California congressman Tony Coelho, the House majority whip, told the audience George was blue blood, not blue collar. Noting that the vice president was then on a fishing trip with me in Wyoming, he quipped that I had accompanied him "in case George is too squeamish to bait his own hook."

Coelho got one thing right. We were in Wyoming. I had made plans to go trout fishing with my pal, congressman Dick Cheney. When Dick had heart-bypass surgery, I suggested to George that he and I go. He trailed Dukakis by as much as 17 percent in some polls and was down in the dumps. I figured the trip would invigorate us both for the coming campaign and would also spare my friend from having to endure the Democratic convention. (When we returned George joked to reporters that the beauty of the wilderness is that "you don't have to listen to Teddy Kennedy.")

Accompanied by Steve Mealey of the U.S. Forest Service, director of the Shoshone National Forest and a friend of mine from prior fly-

---

*In 2003, the Bush Library Foundation honored Ted Kennedy with the George Bush Award for Excellence in Public Service in a ceremony at the Bush Library. George himself handed the award to the senator. This generosity toward an old political foe speaks volumes about the man George Bush.

fishing trips with Cheney, we packed into the wilderness by horseback along the North Fork of the Shoshone River in northwest Wyoming. The Shoshone National Forest borders Yellowstone National Park. The trip did wonders for both George and me. We talked a little business, but not much, and we enjoyed the unhurried rhythm of riding our horses, fishing, eating our catch, sleeping, then doing it all again the next day. The sight, sound, and smell of the mountains, the woods, and the streams invigorated our spirits. And as a bonus, we avoided the ear pollution of the other party's convention. When we returned, we were refreshed and ready to roll!

In his convention speech, George hit all the marks. To connect with the audience in the Superdome and around the nation, George cast himself as the underdog and used self-deprecating humor ("I'll try to hold my charisma in check").

Much of the speech was a triumphal account of what the Reagan-Bush administration had accomplished, and George firmly embraced the Reagan legacy. "For seven and a half years I have helped the president conduct the most difficult job on earth," he said. "The most important work of my life is to complete the mission we started in 1980."

George made it clear, however, that he brought his own ideas and his own sensibility to the table. That's where "kinder, gentler" came from. "Let's be frank," he said. "Things aren't perfect in this country. There are people who haven't tasted the fruits of the expansion.... And, you know, it doesn't do any good to debate endlessly which policy mistake of the seventies is responsible. They're there and we have to help them."

After eight years in the shadows, George also set out to define himself, to answer—in an indirect and gentlemanly way—the ad hominem attacks from the Democratic convention. George explained his philosophy this way:

> At the bright center is the individual. And radiating out from him or her is the family, the essential unit of closeness and of love....

From the individual to the family to the community, and then on out to the town, the church, and the school, and, still echoing out, to the county, the state, and the nation—each doing only what it does well, and no more....

I am guided by certain traditions. One is that there is a God and He is good, and His love, while free, has a self-imposed cost: we must be good to one another....

Does government have a place? Yes. Government is part of the nation of communities—not the whole, just a part. And I do not hate government. A government that remembers that the people are its master is a good and needed thing.

George also spotlighted his differences, philosophically and political-ically, with the Democratic candidate, Michael Dukakis—a bright, hardworking, and, by all accounts, personable man who served as gov-ernor of Massachusetts. Dukakis had a great résumé and one that played well against George's. Son of Greek immigrants. Swarthmore under-graduate. Harvard Law School. Military experience in Korea. A long, successful career in state politics with some interesting policy initia-tives such as no-fault auto insurance. All capped by a well-earned vic-tory in the Democratic primaries over Gary Hart, Richard Gephardt, Al Gore, and civil-rights leader Jesse Jackson.

And yet the fact of the matter is that when the Democrats nom-inated Michael Dukakis, they all but elected George Bush. No mat-ter how many reporters and editorial boards referred to him as a moderate—and no matter that he presented himself as a nonideolog-ical centrist—he was in fact a classic Democratic liberal in the mold of George McGovern and Walter Mondale. Pick any topic—defense, the death penalty, tax policy, you name it—he was off to the left. The more the American people knew about him and his core beliefs, the less likely they would be to vote for him for the simple reason (which even in 2004 still seemed to baffle some Democrats) that the great majority of Americans don't agree with those policies. Eight years of Republican peace and prosperity made it even harder to pitch the liberal agenda.

What would make Dukakis even easier to beat, however, was that his campaign apparently didn't understand the importance of *symbolism* in American life and American politics. He had vetoed a bill in the 1970s that would have required teachers in the Massachusetts public schools to lead students in reciting the Pledge of Allegiance. I'm confident the governor loved his country, but this act gave voters reason to doubt. His campaign also demonstrated a severe lack of political imagination about how to deal with the issue. Every time we served the issue, he volleyed it straight back into the net.

The Dukakis pitch was that he was "competent," not ideological. The problem with that approach, however, is that the American people weren't looking—and they never have looked—for a technocrat-in-chief. They were looking for someone who could also lead and inspire them, as President Reagan did. In his speech, George blew Dukakis away on this point. "Competence is a narrow ideal," he said in New Orleans. "Competence makes the trains run on time but doesn't know where they're going. . . . The truth is . . . this election is about the beliefs we share, the values we honor, and the principles we hold dear."

"I . . . may not be the most eloquent," George said, "but I learned . . . early that eloquence won't draw oil from the ground. I may sometimes be a little awkward, but there's nothing self-conscious in my love of country." Then he ended the speech by leading the convention in reciting these words: "I pledge allegiance . . ."

Thanks to George's great speech, we got our convention bump and more. Immediately after New Orleans, polls showed Dukakis 49–Bush 46. We were still behind, but we were headed in the right direction.

THE 1988 CONVENTION is memorable to the Baker family for another reason wholly unrelated to politics. At the end of our stay in New Orleans, former PepsiCo CEO Don Kendall, a loyal and generous Republican, told me he was off to his ranch in Wyoming.

"I'm a jealous wreck," I told him. I had fallen in love with Wyoming in 1944 when my father took me there as a fourteen-year-old to hunt elk. For some time Susan and I had wanted a place in the Mountain West, and we had begun actively looking after I moved to Treasury in 1985. The fishing trip with George in July had only reinforced my hunger for blue skies, big mountains, sagebrush, and trout streams.

I had a great helpmate in Susan. She was reared on a ranch, loves the outdoors as much as I do, and welcomed the notion of having a retreat away from Washington and Texas. Whenever we had free time—which we occasionally did at Treasury, unlike at the White House—we'd go looking for a place in Idaho, Montana, or Wyoming. We even made a bid on a place near Tom and Meredith Brokaw's ranch in Montana. I'm not sure why, however. It was remote and beautiful, but had no river or creek, although there were some streams nearby that I might have been able to fish. What I really wanted was a ranch that was remote and offered both hunting and fishing.

Kendall told me he'd keep his eyes open and let me know if he heard of anything. Two weeks later he called me at campaign head-quarters. "I think I've found a place that you might like," he said. It was a 1,600-acre ranch an hour and a half south of Jackson Hole in the Wind River Mountains and about twelve miles from the metropolis of Boulder, Wyoming, population seventy-five. It had had only three own-ers since it was homesteaded in the early 1900s. "But," said Kendall, "it's not gonna last long. You better get out here if you're interested."

What timing! "I can't go," I said. "We're just starting a presidential campaign. But I'll send Susan."

She flew out and back in one day. To help me visualize the place, she climbed a big rock formation left by the glacier that had scoured out the valley that covered about one-third of the ranch. From that vantage, she took enough photographs to provide a panoramic view. I loved what I saw—a beautiful place nestled in the western foothills of the Wind River range, surrounded on three sides by wilderness, with a wonderful mountain-fed trout stream. It was also home to an abun-dance of game.

We quickly bought it, sight unseen by me, which was very much out of character with my usual cautious approach to a matter like this. Then we learned the eternal truth about what happens when a man and woman fall in love with a piece of land that is still just like God made it. They don't own it; it owns them. We are in the truest sense stewards, privileged to hold it for a while, obligated to protect it.

I swear by prior preparation, but this was one time when it was better to be lucky than good. Susan and I love Silver Creek Ranch. The fishing is great. We catch and release four kinds of trout from the stream, but eat the rainbows and cutthroats that we have stocked in some small spring-fed ponds that we built on the place. We hunt elk, antelope, and deer, but don't allow any hunting of the moose, black bear, and mountain lions that roam the ranch and surrounding wilderness.

I was also luckier than good when I bought a South Texas ranch in the late 1960s. My dad loved hunting and fishing, but as the frugal descendant of Scottish ancestors, he never considered paying good money to buy land of his own. "I've seen too many of my land-poor friends ruined by the Depression," he would say to me when I would plead with him to get a place where we could hunt together. "The last thing I need is a pile of rocks somewhere!"

After Dad became ill, I managed his affairs under a power of attorney. He had some U.S. government bonds that paid only 1.5 percent. When they matured in 1969, I used the proceeds—with my mother's approval—to buy 1,350 acres of prime hunting land near Pearsall, Texas. In time, I would inherit the acreage. I named it "Rock Pile Ranch," its name to this day.

Mary Stuart died shortly after I bought it. Following her death, that piece of South Texas brush land became a source of great comfort and joy for me and our four sons.* In addition, there have been at

---

*In his spare time, my third son, John, runs the ranch for the family. He developed his street smarts and common sense by running his own oilfield service company for several years, then he joined Hollywood Marine, a Houston-based company that operated tanker barges. It was later acquired by Kirby Corporation, for which John now works.

least four oil and gas plays on the property. Lease bonuses and royalties have paid for the ranch many times over. That money also helped offset the significant loss of income I suffered when I quit practicing law and went into politics and public service. Silver Creek Ranch has also appreciated in value. As I said, it's better to be lucky than good!

Why are the outdoors so important to me? Part of it is nostalgia. When I was six, my dad started taking me hunting. I still feel his presence when I am in a duck blind or tracking an elk. I hope Silver Creek and Rock Pile have planted the same kind of memories in the hearts and minds of my own children and grandchildren.

Part of it is just the need to escape. The more complicated my life got, the more I needed simplicity. Anytime I could slip away from the State Department to Silver Creek Ranch for a day or so to stand in that cold mountain stream with a fly rod in my hand, I'd get well in a hurry.

For me, it is spiritually refreshing to go into nature and see the glorious evidence of God's handiwork. The sun rising over the mountains through the east window of our cabin, then setting across the rolling sagebrush plains to the west. A bull moose suddenly appearing behind me on the grassy bank of the creek where I am fishing, then scaring me to death as I hear it jump loudly into the water and cross the creek. A bunny feeding among the wildflowers Susan planted in the front yard, ready to fly under the cabin in an instant if our English cocker spaniel, Josh, picks up its scent. Noisy hummingbirds fighting for space at the feeders. A majestic herd of elk cresting a ridge, eyeing the human interlopers below, then galloping away. Pronghorn antelope running effortlessly through the sage. A lumbering black bear, the "ghost of the forest," suddenly and noiselessly materializing at last light as I photograph it from my ground blind twenty yards away. Millions of stars wheeling overhead in the vastness of the universe, undimmed by artificial light.

SOMETIMES there is a lull after the party-in-power's convention in mid-August and before Labor Day, the customary date for kicking off presidential general-election campaigns. Candidates catch their breath, and their staffs retreat to organize and set strategy for the big two-month push. Trailing so badly in the polls going into New Orleans, however, we knew we could not afford the luxury of taking ten days or two weeks off. After George's terrific acceptance speech, we had what George once referred to as the Big Mo, and we weren't about to let it dissipate. We planned to run hard until November 8, and that's what we did.

I spent most of my time at our D.C. headquarters on Fifteenth Street. Our goals were to be prepared for everything that might come our way and to leave nothing to chance. For instance, we kept up with the Dukakis ad buys in major markets, so we would always know where his campaign was fighting and where it had surrendered. In addition, we had to provide leadership and resources to the small army of national, regional, state, and local volunteers who wanted George to be president and who, before the campaign was over, would contact millions of voters by telephone and mail.

Craig Fuller, George's vice presidential chief of staff, traveled with the candidate. Two or three times each day, he would touch base with me by telephone. George and I also talked fairly often. Headquarters had to stay in close touch with the candidate and his road team to coordinate events, pass along information (we had wire-service tickers in the office), and receive intelligence from the field. Stu Spencer traveled with Quayle, but that didn't work out as well as we had hoped. Dan thought he was being overmanaged.

In *Whose Broad Stripes and Bright Stars,* their book on the 1988 election, political reporters Jack Germond and Jules Witcover wrote: "The Republican campaign was quintessentially shallow but dramatically effective." Yes, it was effective. George won 53.9 percent of the popular vote, forty states, and 426 electoral votes. It doesn't get much more effective than that. But to say it was shallow was just as wrong as these two normally accurate political reporters were when they said in 1979 that George's campaign for president peaked on the day he announced. To say that our campaign was shallow presumes that the American people could be fooled by campaign smoke and mirrors, and that's not true. They knew exactly what they were doing when they elected George. They were extending the Reagan revolution for one more term and giving George a chance to move it in new directions. They also knew that George was better qualified to serve as president and better reflected their principles and values.

Some have characterized the general election in roughly the following manner: George H. W. Bush, a decent man, wanted to win the presidency so badly that he allowed himself to be manipulated by his managers. Instead of running a positive campaign based on the candidate's obvious credentials and vision, these critics say, Bush's handlers ran one of the most negative campaigns in history. Rather than putting forth a clear picture of his presidency, they add, Bush spent most of his time posing for pictures and attacking Dukakis. Moreover, the issues he did choose to talk about had little relevance to the lives of most voters. Two examples: the Pledge of Allegiance and Massachusetts's prison-furlough program.

My response to this is that the analysts couldn't delegitimize the numbers on the scoreboard, so they tried to take the victory away on style points. "Well, he may have won, but wasn't it just awful! No mandate for George, not after the way his campaign behaved!"

Let's set the record straight, first on the question of manipulation. This came to a head when *Time* magazine's October 3 edition ran a cover featuring me and John Sasso, Dukakis's manager. "It's the Year of the Handlers," read the headline. The article described me as a "backstage puppeteer" who controlled Bush just as I had controlled Reagan. I was miffed and George was, too.

As I've already pointed out, President Reagan was his own man. So, too, was George H. W. Bush. Did he rely on me and others for advice and counsel? Of course. That was my job. He may have placed more confidence in me than most other candidates did in their campaign managers. So what? It made sense. We had been friends for more than thirty years and we understood and trusted each other, but this hardly made me a puppeteer. Look at one of the most important appointments George made. He named John Sununu, the former governor of New Hampshire, as his chief of staff, despite my lobbying for Craig Fuller. I could fill this chapter with other examples of George's overruling me and his other advisers.

Having the world think that you are a candidate or president's alter ego actually has certain advantages. As I've previously written, proximity is power. But there are disadvantages, too. In '88, it seemed as if every time campaign advisers couldn't persuade George to do something, they begged me to work on him. Once Roger Ailes and others on the staff asked me to urge George to go after Dukakis more aggressively. I exploded. "Do it yourselves," I said. "You're not the ones who have to go in, deliver the message, then listen to him say, 'If you're so smart, Jimmy, how come I'm vice president and you're not?'"

As I wrote earlier, Michael Dukakis was a bright, honorable man. He evidently represented the values of the people who had elected him, but he was running now for president of the United States, not president of Massachusetts. And it was George Bush, not Michael Dukakis, who better reflected the values of the majority of Americans. The goal of the Bush-Quayle campaign was to drive home that point. George did so by explaining his positions on issues ranging from defense to disabled rights, from the environment to energy, and, yes, from prison furloughs to the Pledge of Allegiance. Those who insist that he was short on specifics should review the many detailed issues papers we released.

But there's also a place in politics for going after the other guy. It is, after all, a contact sport, and has been since at least John Adams and Thomas Jefferson. And going after your opponent is also an appropriate part of politics in a free society. Think about it: what better way is there to explain how your candidate is right than to show how the opponent is wrong? I make no apologies for going after Dukakis on prison furloughs, the Pledge, or anything else. He led with his chin on a lot of these issues, and we used them to take him out.

As for the idea that these issues had "little relevance to the lives of most voters," that's baloney. In our nation, the flag and our other symbols serve to unite us, despite our many differences (including our political differences). The vast majority of Americans love this country, and they want their children to love it. The Pledge is a useful ceremony for planting love of country—patriotism—in the hearts of our children.

One thing that disturbed our critics was that the Pledge had never before come up as an issue in presidential politics. That's true, as far as I know, but the reason is simple: Dukakis was the first major candidate for president who thought it was important to veto a bill on reciting the Pledge.

Some describe what we did as "going negative." A better term would be to say that we were showing the "contrasts" between the candidates, a fair tactic as long as the ads were factual, and ours were. Did those "contrasts" reflect negatively on our opponent? Yes, they did. Factual contrast ads are used all the time in political campaigns today, and there is no reason they should not be.

How do you get your own message across and drive home the differences between your candidate and his opponent? In 1988 and for some time before and since, the answer has been relatively simple: use the airwaves. Most voters form their opinions of presidential candidates from what they see on television. As campaign manager, it's not your task to worry about whether that's a good thing or a bad thing; your job is to deal with that reality.

Nowadays, television viewers can follow candidates twenty-four hours a day on cable networks and the Internet. Speeches, rallies, town hall forums, and other appearances are covered, many times live and in their entirety. Cable pundits pontificate hourly. In 1988, our job was somewhat simpler. Most Americans relied then on the evening news broadcasts by the three major networks. We devoted ourselves to trying to get positive coverage every night on ABC, CBS, and NBC—preferably at the beginning of the broadcasts when the most people were watching.

With few exceptions, the top network reporters and anchors (who often double as the editor responsible for selecting stories) are bright, savvy men and women who know when they are being spun. But they also know that they only have a minute or two to tell most stories and that television is a medium that depends on pictures. A presidential campaign is an eight-hundred-pound gorilla; it can't easily be ignored, and neither can the visuals and sound bites it generates.

When I was Ronald Reagan's White House chief of staff, we tried to steer coverage toward our story of the day. Mike Deaver brilliantly choreographed those events, scheduling the president to appear before the perfect backdrops for appealing visuals that the networks could hardly ignore. In the Bush campaign of '88, the troika of Roger Ailes, Bob Teeter, and Lee Atwater planned the visuals, which were executed by an experienced team of advance men and communications specialists.

It is not a stretch to say that we probably would not have won that year without any one of these three named individuals. Each one brought different skills to the campaign. Media consultant Roger Ailes, who has gone on to an extraordinarily successful career as chairman, CEO, and president of Fox News, was indispensable in planning and implementing our advertising strategy. He also helped prepare the candidate for the presidential debates.

Bob Teeter was recognized as one of the nation's foremost political pollsters. He practically invented the tracking poll, which is to old-fashioned spot polls as movies are to photographs. With Lee Atwater, he was also one of our principal political strategists, a reprise of his role in the 1976 Ford campaign. In later years, his polls would appear on *NBC News* and in the *Wall Street Journal*. Sadly, he died from cancer in June 2004. He was a wonderful friend, and I miss him.

Lee Atwater, who died from a brain tumor at age forty in 1991, was our able campaign manager.* He received, and deserved, much of the

---

*My daughter Elizabeth Winston Jones worked for Lee in the '84 campaign and did a terrific job. She later earned a law degree. Today her energy and talents are being put to good use as a wife, mother, and active volunteer in Houston.

credit for our win. I first met him in 1980 when Senator Strom Thurmond called me at the office of the Reagan transition team to recommend him for the White House staff. I hired him for the political office, where he did an excellent job. In 1984, he was our White House liaison with the campaign in the Reagan reelection landslide. After the 1988 election, he served until his death as chairman of the Republican National Committee. When he became ill, he underwent a spiritual conversion. "My illness helped me see what was missing in society was what was missing in me: a little heart, a lot of brotherhood," he wrote shortly before he died. He lived not far from me in D.C., and as his disease progressed, I visited him both in his home and at the hospital.

These men were artists whose job was to listen to what the voters were saying (through the polls), then to try to craft messages that would work on television and help influence the public's perception of their candidate. Does this mean that image trumps substance in evening news stories? I think most campaigns, and most broadcasters, hope that image *complements* substance.

Consider how we rolled out George's position on the environment. On August 31, he raised the issue in a photo-op in up-for-grabs Michigan. (Again, anyone—voter or reporter alike—who wanted more details was always welcome to read candidate Bush's position papers.) The next day he went to Dukakis's home state and took the media on a boat tour of Boston Harbor. Pointing to the floating garbage, he questioned the governor's "competence" in dealing with the pollution. All three networks gave the tour extensive airtime. One network described the event as "floating political theater."

Exactly.

By comparison, some of Dukakis's photo-ops were poorly conceived. The most damaging came on August 13. To provide visuals for a foreign policy speech he had given early that day, he traveled to a General Dynamics plant in Michigan and donned an oversized combat helmet with built-in earphones and "Mike Dukakis" stenciled across the front. Then he rode around in the open hatch of a sixty-eight-ton

Abrams M1A1 battle tank,* smiling and waving to reporters like a kid on a carnival ride.

There's no kind or gentle way to say this: Dukakis looked goofy. The photo of that event has to be one of the most damaging in political history. Watching this, I remembered one of the "don'ts" in the campaign manual we gave President Ford: don't ever put on a hat that makes you look silly.

In case anyone missed the incident on the evening news, we put the footage into a television ad. "Michael Dukakis has opposed virtually every defense system we developed," the announcer said, mentioning seven instances from new aircraft carriers to the stealth bomber. All the while, the on-screen candidate bounced around, incongruously, in the giant tank. "Now he wants to be our commander in chief. America can't afford that risk."

We were charged with distorting Dukakis's position. My answer is that we did nothing more than take an image his campaign had created and put it on the air with factual commentary about how he had opposed or criticized most of the new weapon systems and defense initiatives of the Reagan administration.

We were also criticized for a commercial about the Massachusetts program that granted unsupervised weekend furloughs to convicts. The program started under Dukakis's Republican predecessor, but the governor wholeheartedly supported it and during his first term proudly vetoed a bill to keep first-degree murderers locked up. In 1987 a furloughed murderer named Willie Horton stabbed and tortured a Maryland couple, then raped the young woman. The outraged people of Massachusetts collected seventy thousand signatures for a referendum to end the program. When the legislature passed a fur-

---

*Three years later in Kuwait, Abrams tanks got their first real combat test against Saddam Hussein's much-vaunted tank corps. The Abrams has night vision, can fire while moving over rough ground, and can find targets over the horizon. Iraqi tanks were being killed by a foe they could not even see.

lough ban by a veto-proof majority, Dukakis signed the bill, but reluctantly. Meanwhile, Horton was put away for two life sentences by a Maryland judge who made a point of criticizing Massachusetts for letting him loose.

We developed a thirty-second commercial to nail Dukakis for his support of furloughs for convicted murderers. It showed a long file of men in prison garb (every one of them white) exiting and entering prison through a revolving door. The narrator said Governor Dukakis's "revolving-door prison policy gave weekend furloughs to first-degree murderers not eligible for parole. While out, many committed other crimes, like kidnapping and rape." This text was superimposed over the images: "286 escaped...and many are still at large." "Now Michael Dukakis says he wants to do for America what he's done for Massachusetts. America can't afford that risk." This ad, too, was factual and effective.

Unfortunately, a second prison furlough commercial came out about the same time. It differed from our spot in two big ways. First, it included a photo of Willie Horton, who was not pictured or mentioned in our ad. Horton was an African American, and the commercial immediately drew criticism for what some considered a not-so-subtle attempt to play on racial fears. I found the commercial offensive and said publicly that the Bush campaign deplored it and wanted it off the air. Second, the Bush-Quayle campaign did not produce this commercial; the National Security Political Action Committee did, and it was wholly independent of our organization.

Skeptics accused the Bush team of coordinating with a not-so-independent political action group to produce the inflammatory ad, so we could then repudiate it and enjoy the best of two worlds. In other words, we were accused of using a two-track system to get an outside group to do our dirty work for us.

I have three responses. First, as far as I know—and I was campaign chairman—we had nothing to do with that ad. Second, given the uproar that followed, I'm fairly sure it did us more harm than good.

Third, I truly deplored the Horton ad. I condemned it then and I condemn it now.

As in the two Reagan campaigns, I was responsible for negotiating the debates on behalf of our campaign. Across the table was Paul Brountas, a respected Boston lawyer who was my counterpart as Dukakis's national campaign chair. I started with the better hand. George was now ahead in the polls, and Dukakis, a skilled speaker, needed the debates more than George, who by his own admission was not the world's most eloquent guy. (At New Orleans, he joked that he was prone to turn "make my day" into "make my twenty-four-hour time period.")

At the beginning, Brountas came on strong. He wanted three presidential debates, one devoted exclusively to foreign affairs and one to domestic policy, plus one for the vice presidential candidates. He also wanted the candidates to be able to direct questions to each other. And he wanted the debates to begin as soon as possible.

I thought we couldn't get away without debating, but that's not exactly the way I played it. The American people expect and deserve televised face-to-face meetings of the candidates. Refusing to debate gives your opponent a wonderful political issue, as President Carter found out in 1980. But I told Brountas we were willing to do only what had been done in the previous two elections. In '80 and '84, there were just two presidential debates, and the candidates did not ask questions of each other. I also turned down his timetable. We wanted the debates to come later in the campaign, between September 25 and October 15. Why? Because debate preparation freezes the campaign. I hinted that if they held fast to their position, I might stop negotiating altogether and blame the Dukakis camp for being unreasonable. End result: two presidential debates within our timetable.

Had I been bluffing when I suggested I might stop negotiating? As I later told Michael Kramer of *Time* magazine, "Let's just say that whatever edge they thought they had, they convinced themselves they didn't have it."

We did agree to Paul's demand that the debates be ninety minutes instead of one hour. We also agreed that Dukakis, who was considerably shorter than Bush, could stand on an unseen riser behind his podium, but we had a lot of fun before giving in. "This race is for the presidency of the United States! Do you mean to tell us that if your man wins and has to go face-to-face with the leader of the Soviet Union, he's going to ask for a riser to stand on?" we asked.

We prepared for the debates as in previous elections. After George studied his briefing books, we held mock debates at the vice president's residence. The sessions were not without their light moments. Darman, our Dukakis stand-in, came to one wearing a tank-crew helmet.*

You can prepare a candidate all you want for a debate. When he stays up too late the night before the big event, however, all bets are off. That's what happened before the first debate at Wake Forest University on September 25. PBS's Jim Lehrer moderated, and both sides got in their licks. All in all, nothing unexpected or particularly memorable came of the debate, but most observers scored it for Dukakis.

George didn't get a good night's sleep. By one account, the vice president had been up searching for Spikey, his granddaughter's missing stuffed animal. Whatever the reason, George left the stage disappointed in himself, but confident he would do much better in the second debate.

The vice presidential debate was sandwiched in between the two

---

*Among the others who helped prepare George were Roger Ailes, Margaret Tutwiler, Bob Goodwin, Jim Pinkerton, Debbie Steelman, Lee Atwater, Craig Fuller, Bob Teeter, Vic Gold, Sheila Tate, and Dennis Ross, the campaign's foreign policy adviser who would later serve under me at the State Department.

In the Dukakis camp, D.C. attorney Bob Barnett played the role of Bush. He later helped both Clinton and Gore prepare for their presidential debates by standing in for their GOP adversaries. He also served as my lawyer and literary agent for *The Politics of Diplomacy* and this book. Small world.

presidential debates. On October 5, Dan Quayle and Dukakis's running mate, Texas senator Lloyd Bentsen, met in Omaha. Dan was asked several questions about his qualifications to be president. "I have as much experience in Congress as Jack Kennedy did when he sought the presidency," Dan replied.

Quayle had used this line on the campaign trail, but his team warned him against invoking Kennedy's name in the debate. Comparing yourself to one of the other team's icons is inherently risky. Bentsen responded with one of the most memorable and devastating lines in debate history, obviously scripted beforehand. "Senator, I served with Jack Kennedy. I knew Jack Kennedy. Jack Kennedy was a friend of mine. Senator, you're no Jack Kennedy."

To this day, I'm still not sure that Lloyd truly was a friend of Kennedy's. Four years later, Tom Brokaw reported that a search of the Kennedy Library failed to turn up "much evidence Lloyd Bentsen knew John Kennedy very well." Friend or not, the audience ate up Bentsen's riposte. So did the media. It dominated coverage of the debate and, for that matter, coverage of the vice presidential candidates for some time. Lloyd's verbal comeback was such a success, politically, that it's almost bad form to point out that the same folks who thought our campaigning was too rough didn't seem to mind this cheap shot.

Lloyd's insult wasn't fair to Dan, but I don't hold any grudges. Politics is politics. Furthermore, I knew Lloyd Bentsen. I served with Lloyd Bentsen. Lloyd Bentsen was a friend of mine. The reason he was even in the Senate is that he had beaten George for the seat in 1970. Like George, Lloyd was a decorated combat veteran of World War II (he flew B-24s out of Italy), a former three-term congressman, and a successful Houston businessman. He turned out to be a fine senator, well respected on both sides of the aisle, a moderate Democrat of the sort that, while not extinct, is far too rare in today's politics. Two months after the bitter 1988 race ended, Lloyd graciously introduced me to the Senate Foreign Relations Committee for my confirmation hearing as secretary of state. This was a perfect example of the old way of doing things—fighting like hell in the campaign, then working together across party lines to do the public's business. Lloyd later served ably as President Clinton's first secretary of the treasury.[*]

The second presidential debate on October 13 in Los Angeles produced an equally memorable moment. Moderator Bernard Shaw, a CNN anchor, began by asking Dukakis a shocker: "Governor, if Kitty Dukakis were raped and murdered, would you favor an irrevocable death penalty for the killer?" Dukakis replied without an ounce of passion, as if he were discussing the weather.

> No, I don't, Bernard. And I think you know that I've opposed the death penalty during all of my life. I don't see any evidence that it's a deterrent, and I think there are better and more effective ways to deal with violent crime. We've done so in my own state. And it's one of the reasons why we have had the biggest drop in crime of any industrial state in America, why we have the lowest murder rate of any industrial state in America. But we have work to do in this nation.

He then went on to pledge more international cooperation to combat drugs and more attention to early childhood education on the dangers of drugs.

It's too much to say that I knew right then that the race was over, but it would be hard to lose to someone who couldn't manage to get visibly angry about the rape and murder of his wife. The American public identifies with crime victims. In a way that is difficult to explain but easy to understand, his lack of passion and his overintellectualizing a simple, human question essentially proved everything we had said about his being soft on crime.

In his rebuttal, George seized the moment. His syntax may have meandered, but his core beliefs didn't.

---

[*]Sadly, Lloyd suffered a stroke in 1998 and was in a wheelchair for the last eight years of his life. He died in 2006. I was honored to be a pallbearer at his funeral.

Well, a lot of what this campaign is about, it seems to me, Bernie, goes to the question of values. And here I do have, on this particular question, a big difference with my opponent. You see, I do believe that some crimes are so heinous, so brutal, so outrageous, and I'd say particularly those that result in the death of a police officer, for those real brutal crimes, I do believe in the death penalty, and I think it is a deterrent, and I believe we need it.

George's clear win in that debate was a sign of what was to come, despite a strong push by Dukakis in the final days of the campaign. Still, I never stopped worrying, even as we piled onto airplanes late Monday, November 7, to fly to Houston. One of my rules is never to claim victory until the votes have been counted. Polls can be wrong. It's better to assume the worst and try to do something about it than to assume the best and get blindsided.

Susan and I voted, then I spent most of the day on the telephone. When nothing more could be done, we went out for a Mexican food dinner, then drove over to the home of Charles and Sally Neblett to join the Bush clan in waiting out the election returns. Before George and Barbara moved to Washington in 1980, they had lived next door to the Nebletts. Charles, a neurosurgeon, was an old college pal of Susan's. In the 1990s, he would operate on both Susan and me (twice) to cure spinal disk problems.

By election day all polls, ours and the media's, pointed to a solid Bush-Quayle victory, but I never stopped worrying, first about one state, then another. Other people who were there that night remind me that I was the last to accept that George would win, much less by a landslide. "We need to wait on Michigan," I recall saying. As the others began to celebrate, they joked about my caution. "NBC, ABC, and CBS have called it, but Baker's still out."

The numbers kept getting better and better, of course, and finally, tired but elated, I accepted the outcome. George Bush—war hero, successful businessman, dedicated public servant, my friend—would, indeed, be the forty-first chief executive of the United States, the first sitting vice president since 1836 to be elected to the Oval Office. As events over the next four years would richly demonstrate, our nation had just elected the right man for the right job at the right time.

"Congratulations, Mr. President," I said at last.

George won because he offered the three most important things American voters look for in a president—someone who shares their vision of America, someone with whom they are comfortable, and someone who can lead. These provide the structure on which every successful presidential campaign is built. Everything else, including questions about the issues, important though they are, must hang on that framework.

All too often, I think, the other side sees voters as a collection of discrete interest groups to be picked off, one by one, with government programs—teachers with this, trial lawyers with that, farmers with something else. From this perspective, the first real measure of a candidate is found in the scope and generosity of his programs. When that approach fails, as it did in 1988, the instinct of the losers is to blame the political adversary for tricking the American people. The fact is, however, that people have passions for things greater than themselves and greater, certainly, than government programs.

Late Tuesday night, George, Barbara, and the rest of us motorcaded to Houston's cavernous George R. Brown Convention Center to share the moment with thousands of happy supporters and, through television, with the American people. Country singer Crystal Gayle had warmed up the crowd. Many were hometown friends who had worked for George in every campaign since his first race for Congress back in the 1960s. His appearance at the podium, decorated with a giant replica of the facade of the White House, set off wild applause and cheers. When it subsided, George spoke.

"I have just received a telephone call from Governor Dukakis," he said, "and I want you to know that he was most gracious."

The crowd already knew its man had won, but news of the concession sparked another round of celebration. Susan and I joined with joyous applause and countless handshakes and hugs with the Bush family and others on the large stage.

"We can now speak the most majestic words that democracy has to offer," George continued—"'the people have spoken.' Now we will move again for an America that is strong and resolute in the world, strong and big-hearted at home."

It was an intoxicating moment, doubly so for me because of what George had said to me immediately after his election was assured. "I want your appointment as secretary of state to be the first appointment I announce," he said, "and I want to do it at tomorrow's press conference."

My responsibilities for the campaign were over.* Now I had to get ready for what would be the most exciting and demanding four years of my professional life. But prior preparation for that new challenge would have to wait a few days. Susan and I had a new (and, for me, yet unseen) ranch in Wyoming we needed to visit.

---

*When the campaigns ended—in 1980, 1984, and now 1988—my focus would always shift from electoral politics to public service. In 1999, I attended a conference at Lake Como, Italy, with Democratic political operative Bob Shrum. He had just helped Ehud Barak win election as prime minister of Israel. When Bob was asked what Barak might do about the peace process, he said, "You ought to ask Jim Baker that question, because I just do campaigns. He does campaigns and governing." That's true, and I've always thought it was important, if possible, to have had political experience with the president you serve. It secures your political bona fides within the administration and, more important, gives you a political perspective on public policy issues, which is always helpful in getting things done in government.

THIRTEEN

"FROM 'FENCING MASTER' TO 'FOXTAIL'"

AT THREE MINUTES past noon on January 20, 1989, a left-handed George Herbert Walker Bush raised his right hand and took the oath of office as the forty-first president of the United States. As this solemn act of constitutional succession unfolded, Susan and I stood not far behind George and his family. Patriotic red-white-and-blue bunting snapped in the brisk northeasterly wind. The moment was rich in symbolism, linking our nation's past and future in a simple and elegant ritual. I reflected on the responsibilities ahead and the path that had led me to this place.

Twenty years earlier, James Addison Baker, III, was a thirty-eight-year-old Houston lawyer, a little restless perhaps, but otherwise content to carry on the family tradition of providing legal advice for banks, oil companies, and other business clients. Then, all too quickly, my wife Mary Stuart died, followed three years later by my father. I was left with a broken heart, four confused and distraught young boys, and new questions about what to do with my life. Since then, providentially, Susan and her children had come along to form a new family, and George* had talked me into trying my hand at politics and public service. Now my friend was president. I was days away from becoming his secretary of state, the sixty-first in a line of succession that began with Thomas Jefferson in 1790.

After the inauguration ceremony, George and Barbara escorted Ronald and Nancy Reagan through the majestic space of the Rotunda and out the east side of the building. After the usual hugs and handshakes, the former commander in chief—ever the showman and model president—drew himself erect, saluted his successor, military style, then climbed aboard the waiting Marine helicopter. It lifted, circled to give its passengers a last look at the White House, their home for the last eight years, then disappeared over the trees en route to Andrews Air Force Base. This was a graceful end to a great presidency, but for all of us who had worked alongside this wonderful man for so many years, unavoidably sad. I could not hold back my tears.

President Reagan left behind what George called in his inaugural address "a moment rich with promise." Paradoxically, much of that promise rested on the troubles of the world's other nuclear superpower, the Soviet Union, which suffered from a failed ideology, a moribund economy, and a dispirited people. With his new policies of perestroika (economic reform) and glasnost (openness), Mikhail Gorbachev had signaled that change was needed and would come, but what specific type of change? "Our most powerful foe, the Soviet Union, so aggressive a decade ago, is undergoing an ideological soul-searching of historic proportions," I said in my confirmation hearing. Managing the decline of Soviet power would be our biggest challenge. If we succeeded, the prospects were indeed rich with promise—for

---

*To maintain the flow of the narrative of this book, I refer to my friend as "George." After he won the Oval Office, however, I always called him "Mr. President," just as I did Presidents Ford, Reagan, Carter, and Clinton, and just as I do President George W. Bush. The office deserves that respect, even from the occupant's close friends. I still call him "Mr. President" when others are present, but when we're by ourselves or with close friends, I call him "*Jefe*," which is Spanish for "boss" or "chief."

democracy, economic freedom, and personal liberty. If we failed, the Cold War might well end with a bang rather than a whimper.

I sounded the same theme at my swearing-in ceremony seven days after the inauguration. "We are entering a new era of international relations, one that's filled with more than its share of promise, but perhaps more than its share of perils as well," I said. As the new president looked on, Susan held the Bible and Chief Justice Rehnquist administered the oath in the East Room of the White House. Our eight children were there, along with many members of our extended family. At ninety-four, my mother was unable to travel to Washington for the ceremony, but I called her right afterward to tell her about it.

"This is a very special occasion for me," George said, "because as you all know, Jim and I have been friends a long time, going back perhaps more years than either of us would care to admit." He concluded with some of the kindest words I have ever received: "Those of you who are here today—Jim Baker's family, closest friends—know something that many other people will soon learn for themselves: Jim Baker will be a great secretary of state."

"I hope that in foreign policy, we're going to make a better team than we oftentimes did on the tennis courts in Texas," I replied.*

The forty-three months I would serve as secretary of state were, indeed, marked with promise and peril. The world as we had known it for all our adult lives changed entirely. No administration since the post-war 1940s had faced any more consequential issues. It was a time of fundamental change. I have already told this story in *The Politics of Diplomacy*, published in 1995. It is a 672-page account, sometimes hour by hour, of my time as secretary of state. I cannot repeat that full story here. Instead, I will tell how the Cold War ended and Eastern Europe and Central Asia were liberated, then how our administration led an

---

*One price of public service at this level is that during his presidency, George and I rarely played tennis or golf, or got away on hunting and fishing trips. When we did take time to relax together, we found ourselves talking business. The pressures of the Oval Office are omnipresent. A president clocks in on Inauguration Day and clocks out four or eight years later. In between, there's almost no escaping the weight of presidential responsibility.

international coalition to victory in the first Gulf War and, afterward, advanced the prospects for peace in the Middle East. I will also explain why the Bush foreign policy and defense team was so successful and offer some thoughts on a few of today's foreign policy issues.

My first task upon taking office was not to deal with the Soviet Union, the Middle East, or any other international hot spot, however; it was to work out a modus vivendi with the department I would head. State was established in 1789 as the Department of Foreign Affairs, the nation's first government agency. Two centuries later, befitting our nation's leadership role in world affairs, it was large and powerful, with posts in more than two hundred locations around the world and in every time zone on earth.

In shorthand, it was called simply the "Building." That term refers literally, of course, to the eight-floor behemoth, covering two and a half city blocks in the Foggy Bottom section of the District of Columbia, that houses the State Department. Metaphorically, however, it refers to the elite foreign service officers and career staff members who so effectively administer our nation's foreign policy, year in and year out, as administrations come and go. Our nation is fortunate to have the services of these talented and hardworking men and women, and I am grateful for the support they provided me.

But George Bush had won the presidency and with it the right and responsibility to make foreign policy. No doubt, he was prepared for the task, thanks to his years of service in the United Nations, the Central Intelligence Agency, China, and the vice presidency. In addition, he had surrounded himself with a foreign policy and national security team of individuals who had worked together for years, who actually liked one another (and, thus, got along well), and who brought an impressive array of skills to the table—Dick Cheney (President Ford's former chief of staff) at Defense, Brent Scowcroft as national security adviser (a post he also held in the Ford administration), Colin Powell (national security adviser in President Reagan's second term) as head of the Joint Chiefs of Staff, and me at State.

Behind closed doors, this group would bump heads plenty of

times. We were all strong-willed men, dealing with terrifically important issues. With the rarest of exceptions, however, we sang from the same hymnal in dealing with foreign leaders, Congress, the agencies, and the press. We also didn't leak. George demanded a tight ship, and, of course, he was right to do so. Disunity signals confusion and lack of resolve; unity signals clarity and strength of purpose. These are important assets in politics, diplomacy, and—if worse comes to worst—in a military conflict. As sorry as I am to say it, the scrimmages between State and Defense in the first four years of the George W. Bush administration hurt the president and made it more difficult for him to win public, congressional, and international support for U.S. foreign and security policy, particularly for U.S. operations in Iraq.

The knock on me was that I lacked foreign policy experience. That was not quite true. I had had some terrific mentors-by-example (Ronald Reagan and George Bush) and unparalleled on-the-job training. Serving as White House chief of staff gave me daily exposure to foreign and security policy issues. As treasury secretary, I worked closely with foreign finance ministers and central bankers on international economic issues. All eight years, I attended National Security Council meetings. And in the ten weeks before the inauguration, I gave myself a crash course in international relations, once again following my father's adage that "prior preparation prevents poor performance." As things turned out, however, not having held an office with primary responsibility for foreign or security policy may have helped more than it hurt. With no vested interest in old policies, or the battles to formulate them, I had greater flexibility in dealing with the revolutionary changes of 1989–1992.

I brought other assets to the job, including a strong relationship with Congress and the press. I also understood the inextricable linkage of politics (in its broader sense) and policy, not just domestically, but also internationally. Political constraints inevitably shape the outcome of any negotiation by defining what is possible and what is not. With a nod to Clausewitz, diplomacy is the continuation of politics. This understanding came from my years in electoral politics and public service, but it was also grounded, I think, in my experiences negotiating deals and working out disputes as a business lawyer.

My biggest asset, however, was simply this: I was George's friend and he was mine. We had a degree of trust and loyalty that transcended anything that could be represented by the lines and boxes of an organizational chart. He also made clear that mine was the first chair on international affairs. "As secretary of state, he will be my principal foreign policy adviser," George said. That, and the fact that I had been his political campaign manager, meant that no one in the administration was going to come between the president and his secretary of state. When foreign officials talked with me, they knew I was speaking for the president. I also had the freedom, as a friend, to tell George exactly what was on my mind without worrying about offending the boss. By setting up his cabinet this way, then backing me when the going got rough, George avoided the destructive turf battles that characterized the Nixon, Carter, Reagan, Clinton, and George W. Bush administrations. We were the exception to a very unfortunate rule.

I told interviewers in January that I intended to be the president's man at the State Department, not State's man at the White House, a statement that certainly got the Building's attention. And I staffed the seventh-floor executive offices with a formidable and close-knit team of Baker loyalists, most of whom had followed me over from Treasury or the campaign. One was Robert Zoellick, the brilliant policy analyst one journalist called my "second brain." (Ever since, I've accused Bob of telephoning the reporter and yelling, "Second! Second!") He would serve as department counselor and gatekeeper for my in-box. Another was Dennis Ross, a specialist on the Middle East and the Soviet Union, who would serve as director of the policy planning staff. He was an idea man with good common sense, and he was very laid-back. I didn't hold it against him that he had at one time been a liberal Democrat (and maybe still was!). He later served as special envoy to the Middle East in President Clinton's administration. Margaret Tutwiler—

Nixon once told me she was "tough and smarter than a shithouse rat," excellent qualities for a political adviser and spokesperson—would be assistant secretary for public affairs and spokesperson for the department.

The second-ranking position in the department, deputy secretary, went to Lawrence Eagleburger. I had not worked with him before, but for more than thirty years, he had served the nation with distinction as a foreign service officer, assistant to Henry Kissinger, ambassador to Yugoslavia, and high-level appointee in the Reagan State Department. Robert Kimmitt, who had served in the Reagan White House and with me at Treasury, was the third-ranking official as under secretary for political affairs, and Janet Mullins (whom I had met in the campaign) served very ably as assistant secretary for congressional affairs. I could always count on this group to run the shop and manage problems while I traveled or worked on special initiatives, and to help with those initiatives. Collectively, they and the regional assistant secretaries (most of them, career diplomats) would serve as my brain trust.

Of course, I also had the help of my invaluable executive assistant, Caron Jackson—always at the office when I arrived, always there when I left. My extensive travels (more than 750,000 miles to more than ninety countries) were successful because of the organizational skills and formidable protective presence of Karen Groomes, as well as Lynn Dent and Pat Kennedy. Kim Hoggard ably assisted Margaret Tutwiler with press, and John Rogers joined us later as under secretary for management.

On a typical day, my security detail* would pick me up about 7:00 A.M. I would review my schedule in the ten-minute ride between home and the Building. Over breakfast, I would read intelligence reports, press clips, and the *White House News Summary*. At least twice a week, I

---

*With the move from Treasury to State, my Secret Service code name changed from "Fencing Master" to "Foxtail." Susan was "Featherweight," and Mary Bonner, our only child still living at home, was "Footnote."

would go over to the White House for freewheeling talks with the president. I had walk-in rights to the Oval Office, and I would also go to the White House whenever the president met with a foreign leader. On a good day, I would get home about 7:30 or 8:00 P.M., but good days (in that sense) were rare. Formal dinners and other social events for visiting dignitaries claimed many evenings. As secretary of state, I usually had to attend, but I sometimes slipped away early. I needed my sleep.

On international trips, my old Boeing 707 had a private stateroom that allowed me to rest in flight. I occasionally used the sleep aid Halcion to help me rest. When that plane hit the ground in a foreign capital, it was the United States of America calling. Even a hint of fatigue or jet lag might reflect badly on my country, interfere with my concentration, and diminish the sense of authority—what the military calls "command presence"—that is an important, though generally unacknowledged, part of diplomacy. From the moment I stepped off the plane until the moment I stepped back on, I represented the United States of America, and I wanted to embody our nation's strength and spirit in my own dress, demeanor, and vitality.

My family paid a heavy price for my public service, particularly when I traveled. One of the hardest moments came in April 1991. While I was on a diplomatic mission, my mother died in Houston, just short of her ninety-seventh birthday. Susan reached me with the news in the office of Yitzhak Shamir, the Israeli prime minister. I still regret being away from her so often in her last years. In 1995, I co-dedicated *The Politics of Diplomacy* to "my wonderful mother, whose love and support gave me wings to fly."

The twin tyrants of any executive are the in-box and the calendar. Secretaries of state are particularly susceptible to schedule overload. Almost every foreign dignitary who visits Washington wants face time. If you are too generous with your availability, you will become a ceremonial figure, not an effective one. If you are too restrictive, however, you may offend someone who doesn't need offending. You also miss opportunities to develop personal relationships with heads of government and their ministers, which is an important part of the job.

Sometimes events overruled the calendar. That happened spectacularly on November 9, 1989, as I hosted an eighth-floor luncheon for Philippine President Corazon Aquino. Toward the dessert course, an assistant passed me a note saying East Germany's communist party chief, Günter Schabowski, had just announced that the border points between East and West Germany were being opened.

It took a moment for this news to sink in. For twenty-eight years, totalitarian East Germany, a Soviet satellite state, had locked its people behind the concrete and barbed wire of the Berlin Wall and a separate fence along the main border between East and West Germany. Guards in watchtowers, the dreaded *Grenzschutzpolizei* (Grepos), had orders to fire on anyone who ventured into the death strips—two hundred yards wide in some places, lighted with floodlights, cut in places by deep ditches, armed with mines and trip wires, sometimes patrolled by vicious dogs. Now, suddenly, the gates were open! The Berlin Wall was falling! With some emotion, I read the note aloud, then we toasted the moment—the symbolic beginning of the end of the Cold War. As I write, I can see a segment of that wall, a monument that today sits outside the window of my office at the Baker Institute on the campus of Rice University.

My entire adult life had been defined by that conflict, which began immediately after the German surrender in World War II. The Soviet Union, our ally of convenience, refused to liberate Poland, Hungary, Czechoslovakia, the eastern sector of Germany, and the other countries it had occupied. Instead, Moscow installed puppet governments backed by secret police and the Red Army. Worse, the Soviets began trying to expand their reach into Greece, Turkey, and elsewhere.

In 1946 Winston Churchill warned that an "Iron Curtain" had descended across Europe. The next year, the U.S. ambassador in Moscow, George F. Kennan, famously recommended a policy of "long-term, patient but firm and vigilant containment of Russian expansionist tendencies." The outcome, he predicted forty-two years before the event, would be "either the break-up or the gradual mellowing of Soviet power." In 1949, policy became program when the United States and its Western allies established the North Atlantic Treaty Organization (NATO) to guard against Soviet expansion into Europe. The Cold War was officially under way.

As this happened, I was a teenager focused more on making grades, playing tennis and rugby, and chasing girls—not necessarily in that order—than on U.S. foreign policy. In 1950, however, the East-West conflict ceased to be an abstraction for me and other draft-eligible young men. Between my sophomore and junior years at Princeton, North Korea invaded South Korea. The Cold War had suddenly turned hot. That is how I wound up serving from 1952 to 1954 as a young Marine officer, much of the time with the Sixth Fleet in the Mediterranean. I was a bit player in a very large world drama.

In time, the fighting stopped in Korea, but the East-West conflict continued. President Reagan posed the central question to the British Parliament in 1982. "Must civilization perish in a hail of fiery atoms?" he asked. "Must freedom wither in a quiet, deadening accommodation with totalitarian evil?" The answer, he said, is that if we stayed the course, the Soviet Union would simply fail. It was destined, he predicted, for the "ash heap of history." This was a stunning thing for any president to say, much less one sometimes derided as a former movie actor, but events would prove that he had a better understanding of the realities of the Cold War than many of his critics.

President Reagan believed passionately in "peace through strength," which is why he put defense off limits during the budget-cutting wars of 1981. His policy might be called "containment-plus." He wanted to roll back Soviet beachheads in Afghanistan, Nicaragua, and elsewhere and push for victory—peaceful victory—in the Cold War. In June 1987, he laid down this historic challenge at Berlin's Brandenburg Gate: "General Secretary Gorbachev, if you seek peace, if you seek prosperity for the Soviet Union and Eastern Europe, if you seek liberalization, come here to this gate. Mr. Gorbachev, open this gate! Mr. Gorbachev, tear down this wall!"

Immediately after the Bush administration came into office, we initiated a top-to-bottom review of policy toward the Soviet Union. From the start, we understood that we would have two historic responsibilities. The first was to exercise leadership to see that the Cold War ended peacefully. The other, equally important, was to set a new course for the post–Cold War era.

Until then, the U.S. had hedged its bets on whether glasnost and perestroika represented genuine change or merely a fresh coat of paint on a rotten structure. Against the advice of some who mistrusted Gorbachev and preferred to wait and see (with an emphasis on *wait*), George decided on an activist policy. We would take the Soviets at their word (but test their rhetoric), while engaging them and trying to move them in directions that advanced our national interests.

In April, George announced trade and financial aid in support of Poland, where a Solidarity-inspired liberalization program was already under way. This was a crucial signal that, despite Moscow's disapproval, we would support communist countries that took steps to move toward political, economic, and personal freedom. In mid-May, George spoke of going "beyond containment," toward a policy of integrating the Soviet Union into the community of nations. At the same time, he said our response would be determined by the actions of Moscow, not by its promises; by reality, not by rhetoric. And in late May, he made clear what one of those actions had to be. "Nowhere is the division between East and West seen more clearly than in Berlin," he said. "And there this brutal wall stands as a monument to the failure of communism. It must come down!"

My job as our nation's chief diplomat was to communicate with Soviet leaders about our desire for warmer relations and, at the same time, to push for concrete steps toward liberation of the captive nations of Eastern Europe. I made my first personal contact in March 1989, shortly after the administration and Congress reached a bipartisan accord on policy toward Nicaragua. If the Soviets would stop sending arms and other support to the Sandinistas and would back free and fair elections, I told Soviet Foreign Minister Eduard Shevard-nadze, the United States would honor the results. He agreed. With this step, Central America ceased to be an issue in both our domestic politics and geopolitically, and the Shevardnadze-Baker understanding on Nicaragua set a pattern for U.S.-Soviet cooperation on a host of larger issues.*

I had met Shevardnadze near the end of the Reagan administration. He was an old-school politician from Soviet Georgia, a year older than I was and distinguished by his long white hair, sharp eyes, and gentle manner. George Shultz, my predecessor at State, told me this was someone I could do business with, and he was right. Over the months, Eduard and I would meet again and again.

A climax of sorts came in late September 1989. With domestic turmoil mounting in the Soviet Union, I invited Shevardnadze for one-on-one talks in Jackson Hole, Wyoming—the first time an official of the Soviet Union was allowed anywhere in the United States other than Washington and New York. Over three days and nine formal meetings at a lodge in the shadow of the Tetons, we made good progress on chemical weapons, arms control, and other East-West issues. Between sessions, we would speak informally about the growing strains inside the Soviet Union and other sensitive issues. At the end, I gave him a pair of cowboy boots (symbolic of the venue) to commemorate the talks, and he gave me an enamel picture of Jesus Christ. "You see, even we communists are changing our worldview," he said.

It was in this pristine and glorious setting that Eduard and I developed a personal friendship—a friendship that would prove invaluable in the tumultuous days ahead. His candor made it clear to me that the Soviets were feeling their way, gingerly, toward economic and political

---

*Fortunately, the Sandinista's Daniel Ortega lost the election to Violeta Chamorro. Former President Jimmy Carter persuaded the Marxist leader to leave office peacefully.

liberalization, but I was also struck by how little they appeared to understand the difficulties of achieving either. On Eastern Europe, particularly, the Soviets were being driven by events they did not fully comprehend and could not fully control. On the flight to Jackson Hole on my military aircraft, Shevardnadze said something about East Germany that may have foreshadowed what was to come: "It is not up to us to solve this problem; it is up to them. If I were in their shoes, I'd let everyone who wants to go, leave."

Only seven weeks later, Shevardnadze's wistful musing became reality. The Berlin Wall fell and East Germans left by the thousands. (Others, knowing they *could* leave, decided to stay.) After my lunch with President Aquino that day, I rushed to the White House. All afternoon and into the night, George and I watched live broadcasts of young Berliners dancing atop the hated barrier and chipping pieces away as souvenirs.

The fall of the Wall was a triumph for the U.S.-led Western alliance—a vindication of a policy put in place by the Truman administration, of four decades of bipartisan support for our nation's Cold War policies through nine administrations, of "peace through strength," and of George's decision to engage the Soviet Union and promote the liberation of Eastern Europe. It was also a delicate moment, particularly for Gorbachev and Shevardnadze. In rejecting the use of force to keep the Soviet empire together, they were on the side of the angels. But would hard-line elements in their government and military accept this public humiliation or try to do something about it? The Soviets had sent tanks to crush revolts in East Germany in 1953, Hungary in 1956, and Czechoslovakia in 1968. Now Gorbachev worried aloud that a "chaotic situation may emerge with unforeseeable consequences." This was not a threat, in our judgment; it was a warning. The stability of both the Soviet Union and the region were at risk.

George decided to respond in a deliberate and low-key manner. We must not overreact, he said. That is why we did not dance, rhetorically, on the ruins of the Berlin Wall. Our cool response that day and afterward puzzled many observers and was criticized by some in the D.C. press corps, but it created trust and goodwill in Moscow and helped with the difficult negotiations to follow.

Would East and West Germany now unite as one country? If so, on what terms? Would the Soviets permit a unified German state to remain in NATO, the military alliance that protected the West against Soviet aggression? Six parties participated in the negotiations under a "Two-Plus-Four" structure designed by my close advisers in the State Department. The "Two" were East and West Germany. They would settle "internal" issues. The "Four" were the occupying powers after World War II—the Soviet Union, the United States, France, and Great Britain. They would have a voice on "external" issues.

Beginning in January, I flew to Europe repeatedly, first to push the Two-Plus-Four concept, then to participate in the negotiations. We faced deep concerns and, indeed, initial resistance—not only from the Soviet Union but also from France and Britain—about the implications for Europe and the world of reconstituting the state responsible for two of the bloodiest wars of the century.

Despite this, and the fact that we had only a very narrow window of opportunity to get it done, the outcome was an almost-unqualified success. On October 3, 1990, West Germany annexed the East, and the new enlarged state continued as a member of both the European Community and NATO.* This would never have occurred without U.S. leadership. We framed the talks, kept them on course with endless telephone calls from the Oval Office and State, flew again and again to Europe for meetings, and helped settle disagreements on borders and other issues in sensible ways. As the president would later write, we

---

*After unification, prosperous West Germany embraced the poverty-stricken East with unparalleled generosity. Unfortunately, the East's legacy of communist rule—a decrepit infrastructure, widespread environmental pollution, a dysfunctional economy, and a people whose spirits had been deadened by life in a police state—has proved very difficult to overcome. These difficulties contribute even today to Germany's economic and political troubles.

accomplished "the most profound change in European politics and security for many years, without confrontation, without a shot being fired, and with all Europe on the best and most peaceful terms."

Germany was just one story. Within weeks after the Berlin Wall fell, all Soviet satellite states in Europe were free. Within twenty-six months, the Soviet Union itself would implode, releasing the former republics of the Soviet Union in Eastern Europe and Central Asia to go their own way. Except in North Korea, Cuba, and China (in an attenuated form), communism simply melted away, ending the deadly illusion of the twentieth century that took the lives of uncounted millions and impoverished those who survived, both materially and spiritually. Communism as a governing philosophy is as dead as the divine right of kings.

None of this happened spontaneously, however. As with German unification, I logged tens of thousand of miles on the 707 that served as my second office (and home), landing in capital after capital and negotiating, first with one leader then another, to push events in the right direction. One ten-day trip in early 1992 took me from Germany to Moldova to Armenia to Azerbaijan to Turkmenistan to Tajikistan to Russia to Uzbekistan. I could have been an explorer for *National Geographic,* except that I was not out to see mountains, rivers, and wildlife. Much to our surprise and the surprise of many, the Soviet Union was gone forever, and I was trying to influence the newly independent states of Central Asia to deal responsibly with the Soviet nuclear weaponry on their soil, to adopt political and economic reforms, and to engage in a positive way with the United States.

At every stop, I was greeted like royalty, showered with gifts, feted with the best national food and drink. After years of forced isolation, these fledgling nations were starved for contact with America and eager to establish good relations. The most dramatic moments came in Albania, then the poorest country in Europe, which had been misruled for decades by Enver Hoxha, a hardcore Stalinist. Men, women, and children lined the streets in Tirana, eager to touch, even kiss, my car.

People hung from every window and lined every roof. Between a quarter and a half million people—more than the whole population of the city—packed the square. "USA! USA! USA!" they chanted. "Bushie! Bushie! Bushie!"

"On behalf of President Bush and the American people," I said when I could finally speak, "I come here today to say to you: *freedom works!*" The Albanians went berserk.

That was a better crowd reaction than the polite applause George had received for the same two-word phrase in his inaugural address. But that is because after more than two hundred years, Americans treated political, economic, and personal freedom as part of the natural order of things. Albanians knew better: freedom is precious, and they owed theirs to the American people. Why? Because the American people—by their political choices and through their taxes and their military service—had accepted the same burden after World War II that the "greatest generation" had borne during the war, which was to risk all to protect others.

Something that put it all in perspective occurred on the very day the Wall fell. About 5:00 P.M. in Washington—six hours later in Bonn— German Foreign Minister Hans-Dietrich Genscher telephoned me. Before he came on the line, however, his secretary, speaking in a thick German accent, said this:

"God bless America! Thank you for everything, sir!"

"DON'T WORRY. Nothing's going to happen."

That was Shevardnadze's reply on August 2, 1990, to my concern about whether the Iraq army would invade its tiny neighbor, Kuwait. He and I were meeting in Irkutsk near Lake Baikal in Siberia, the largest body of fresh water in the world. He was reciprocating for my invitation to Jackson Hole nearly a year before. Our agenda included arms control, conventional forces reduction in Europe, and conflicts in Afghanistan and Cambodia—the sorts of things two superpowers talk about as they move to stand down from long years of conflict. We also planned to do some fishing.

What was really on my mind that day, however, were reports of Iraqi troops massing on the Kuwaiti border. Even though Shevardnadze seemed certain nothing would happen, I suggested that he check with Soviet intelligence. Iraq was a client state of the USSR. Surely the Arabists back in Moscow would know what was going on.

If they did, they did not tell their foreign minister. "Saddam would not be so foolish," Shevardnadze assured me after lunch, referring to Saddam Hussein, the Iraqi dictator. Later that day, however, Iraq's army poured across the border. The invasion and occupation of Kuwait, virtually defenseless, proved notable for their gratuitous brutality—torture, mutilation, and rape.

Before learning of the invasion, I had already flown from Siberia to Mongolia, the latest stop on the Baker freedom-and-democracy tour. When the news reached me, I cut the visit short and immediately headed for Moscow. Once again, events had overwhelmed the calendar.

The fall of the Berlin Wall was richly symbolic, but in my opinion the Cold War actually ended nine months later. With me standing by his side in a Moscow airport on August 3, 1990, Shevardnadze announced that the Soviet Union would join the United States to condemn the invasion and impose an arms embargo on Iraq. "This aggression is inconsistent with the principles of new political thinking and, in fact, with the civilized relations between nations," he said. It was a remarkable moment. In the past, the United States and USSR would have faced off across the geopolitical chessboard. Now we were together on the same side.

It is difficult to know quite why Saddam Hussein invaded Kuwait. An eight-year war with Iran had wrecked Iraq's economy. Perhaps that is what tempted him to try to plunder the oil wealth of Kuwait. He might also have imagined that the end of the superpower rivalry had created a power vacuum in which a weakened Soviet Union would not stop him, nor would an irresolute United States. In any event, he was wrong, at least about America. "This will not stand, this aggression against Kuwait," George Bush said on August 5. The only issue from then on was whether Iraq would go peacefully or would be forced out at gunpoint.

Under international law, the United States did not need the permission of the United Nations to liberate Kuwait. Chapter 51 of the UN charter gave the Kuwaitis an inherent right of self-defense against territorial aggression, and the UN's core doctrine of voluntary collective security meant the United States could answer the call of the Kuwaiti government-in-exile for help. George had once served as U.S. representative to the United Nations, however, and he knew that if we could win a Security Council resolution authorizing the use of force to eject Iraq from Kuwait, our task would be easier. It would then be the "international community" versus Iraq, not just the United States and a few other countries. He also appreciated that we might use a UN resolution to leverage or embarrass a hostile U.S. Congress into supporting the effort. And he understood that it would be useful in winning political support, domestically and internationally, for whatever had to be done.

We started on the day of the invasion with a unanimous Security Council resolution—even Cuba voted yes—that condemned Iraq's action, demanded withdrawal, and imposed economic sanctions. This was the beginning of a program of coercive diplomacy designed to isolate Iraq from the world community and cause enough pain, diplomatically and economically, to force withdrawal. In coming weeks, the UN resolutions would grow stronger and stronger, with the Soviet Union providing crucial support at each stage.

In November we asked the Security Council to approve the use of force, albeit delicately, through the euphemism of "all necessary means." I met personally with all my Security Council counterparts, at one point traveling to twelve countries in eighteen days, in an intricate process of cajoling, extracting, threatening, and occasionally buying votes. I celebrated Thanksgiving Day in Sanaa, Yemen. The administration also began banging the tin cup to win international financial support for the posting of U.S. military forces to the region and, if necessary, for war. And win it we did, to the tune of about $50 billion. This pretty much wiped out congressional objections to the cost of the effort.

One of the oddest moments in my diplomatic career came when I authorized Lieutenant General Howard Graves* to explain our war plans against Iraq, a Soviet client state, to Shevardnadze. The combined air and ground campaigns would take no more than three months, the general said. Privately, however, we believed three or four weeks would do it, largely because Iraq's Soviet-built tanks and other armaments were so thoroughly inferior to U.S. weaponry. Shevardnadze, a realist, soon agreed that a military solution might be necessary, but Gorbachev initially resisted and later agreed only reluctantly. To the end, he kept alive the hope that Saddam could be talked into pulling out of Kuwait.†

The United States chaired the Security Council meeting of November 29, 1990, so I wielded the gavel. To add weight to the proceeding, we had persuaded most of the other fourteen members to send their foreign ministers, not their UN representatives. I started by reminding the ministers how the League of Nations had responded halfheartedly and ineffectually to Haile Selassie's desperate plea for help when Italy invaded Ethiopia in 1935. That failure doomed the

---

*General Graves, a fellow Texan, represented the Joint Chiefs of Staff on my trips. He was an extraordinarily fine man who later served five years as superintendent of West Point and four years as chancellor of Texas A&M University System, then—sadly— succumbed to cancer in 2003.

†Diplomacy had its lighter moments. In a September meeting, I showed Gorbachev a small package I had been given with Saddam Hussein's picture on the outside and a condom on the inside. The legend said, "For big pricks who don't know when to withdraw." Gorbachev and Shevardnadze roared when they heard the translation, and Gorbachev promptly pocketed the trophy. The story to this point was in *The Politics of Diplomacy*, but not Gorbachev's reply. "Making love with a condom is like licking sugar through a glass," he said.

League and set the table for further aggression by Germany, Italy, and Japan. "History has now given us a second chance," I said. "With the Cold War now behind us, we have the chance to build the world envisioned by the founders of the United Nations. We have the chance to make this Security Council and this United Nations true instruments for peace and justice..."

The Security Council vote for Resolution 678 was twelve for, two against (Cuba and Yemen), with China abstaining. It gave Iraq until midnight, January 15, 1991, to withdraw unconditionally. After that, member states would be authorized "to use all necessary means... to restore international peace and security in the area."

This was only the second time the United Nations had ever authorized the use of force to protect a member state from aggression. The first was the Korean Conflict, and the only reason the United Nations could act in 1950 was because the Soviets walked out and did not use their veto. In 1990, by contrast, the Soviets voted with the United States.

Even after the Security Council acted, however, Congress was still reluctant to support the use of force. Many lawmakers wanted to give economic sanctions more time. The administration was convinced, however, that the only way to make sanctions work was to set a firm deadline for withdrawal, backed with a mailed fist. "We did not stand united for forty years and bring the Cold War to a peaceful end in order to make the world safe for the likes of Saddam Hussein," I told one committee. On January 12, 1991—just three days before the withdrawal deadline set by the Security Council—the Democrat-controlled Congress grudgingly gave the president authority to wage war under the UN resolution. A shift of just three votes in the Senate, which voted 52–47, would have meant defeat.

Before pulling the trigger, we made one last attempt to avoid war—a head-to-head meeting in Geneva on January 9 between me and Tariq Aziz, the foreign minister of Iraq. "Our objective is for you to leave Kuwait," I told him. "That's the only solution we'll accept." If it came to war, I said, the Iraqis would face "devastatingly superior firepower." I also warned him of severe reprisals for using chemical or biological weapons. "This is not a threat," I said, "it's a promise."

Aziz obviously had no authority, except to try to talk us into delaying the inevitable. He spoke with forced bravura ("war doesn't frighten or intimidate Iraq") and striking fatalism ("I hope you won't miscalculate our capability to endure the costs of war"). Iraq was a victim, he argued, and the Arab world would rise up against U.S. aggression. More than six hours after we began, we shook hands and parted, each certain that war was inevitable.

On January 16, the U.S.-led coalition launched air attacks on Iraq. In mid-February, the Iraqis—sensing now that they would never enjoy their plunder—set the rich Kuwaiti oil fields afire, an ecological and financial disaster of unimaginable proportions. After weeks of allied air strikes, military ground operations began on February 24. One hundred hours later the war was over. The Iraqis never had a chance. Secretary of Defense Dick Cheney, JSC Chairman Colin Powell, and General Norman Schwarzkopf, the field commander of Operation Desert Storm, designed a brilliant campaign, and the men and women of the coalition forces, most of them American, implemented it almost without a hitch.

For years, the question I was most often asked about Desert Storm is why we did not remove Saddam Hussein from power. There were many reasons, as I wrote in 1995 in *The Politics of Diplomacy*. A coalition war to liberate Kuwait could then have been portrayed as a U.S. war of conquest. Furthermore, even if Saddam were captured and his regime toppled, American forces would still have been confronted with the specter of a military occupation of indefinite duration to pacify a country and sustain a new government in power. The ensuing urban warfare would surely have resulted in more casualties to American GIs than the war itself, thus creating a political firestorm at home. And as much as Saddam's neighbors wanted to see him gone, they feared Iraq would fragment in unpredictable ways that would play into the hands of the mullahs in Iran, who could export their brand of Islamic fundamentalism with the help of Iraq's Shiites and quickly transform themselves into a dominant regional power. Finally, the Security Council resolution under which we were operating authorized us to use force only to kick Iraq out of Kuwait, nothing more. As events have amply demonstrated, these concerns were valid. I am no longer asked why we did not remove Saddam in 1991!

Am I implicitly criticizing President George W. Bush for having done twelve years later what his father's administration declined to do in 1991? No, I am not. Iraq's continued violation of UN resolutions and its expulsion of weapons inspectors in 1998 prompted the Clinton administration to adopt regime change in Iraq as U.S. policy—a policy President George W. Bush also followed. After the 9/11 terrorist attacks, U.S. patience with Saddam Hussein finally ran out. By 2003, the Iraqi dictator had thumbed his nose at UN resolutions for twelve years, turned the UN's oil-for-food program into a cesspool of corruption (what one critic called an "oil-for-palaces" program), and continued to abuse his own people. Every intelligence service in the world, including those in Russia and France, also believed—erroneously, it now appears—that Iraq still possessed weapons of mass destruction. I do not doubt that President George W. Bush in acting militarily against Iraq weighed the concerns we considered in 1991. He simply decided that the costs I had described in 1995, though real, were justified in 2003. That's why the buck stops in the Oval Office.

In an August 2002 op-ed column in the *New York Times* seven months before hostilities began, I argued that "the only realistic way to effect regime change in Iraq is through the application of military force, including sufficient ground troops to occupy the country (including Baghdad), depose the current leadership and install a successor government." But "it cannot be done on the cheap," I counseled. The right way to proceed, both politically and substantively, I said, was to seek a Security Council resolution requiring Iraq to "submit to intrusive inspections anytime, anywhere, with no exceptions, and authorizing all necessary means to enforce it." If Saddam employed his usual "cheat-and-retreat" tactics (as he subsequently did), I argued, we should then act to remove him from power.

I also warned that winning the peace would be difficult and potentially costly—"politically, economically and in terms of casualties." "We will face the problem of how long to occupy and administer a big, fractious country and what type of government or administration should follow." "Unless we do it the right way," I wrote, "there will be costs to other American foreign policy interests, including our relations with practically all other Arab countries (and even many of our customary allies in Europe and elsewhere) and perhaps even to our top foreign policy priority, the war on terrorism." The costs could be reduced, I said, "if the president brings together an international coalition behind the effort. Doing so would also help in achieving the continuing support of the American people, a necessary prerequisite for any successful foreign policy."

In January 2003, the James A. Baker III Institute for Public Policy and the Council on Foreign Relations published a joint study entitled *Guiding Principles for U.S. Post-Conflict Policy in Iraq.* "There should be no illusions that the reconstruction of Iraq will be anything but difficult, confusing, and dangerous for everyone involved," the report said, warning that a long-term U.S. occupation "will neither advance U.S. interests nor garner outside support." The working group recommended that the Iraqi army be preserved, not disbanded, to serve as a guarantor of peace and stability, and declared that it was "wishful thinking" to suggest that Iraqi oil revenues would be sufficient to pay for post-conflict reconstruction.

President George W. Bush did, in fact, win a unanimous Security Council resolution in November 2002, demanding that Iraq comply or face serious consequences. To help its most steadfast ally, Tony Blair, prime minister of the United Kingdom, the administration later sought a second resolution that would have defined "serious consequences" to mean the use of force. The Security Council, led primarily by France, balked. In retrospect, it was a mistake to have sought the resolution without first knowing that we could get the votes to pass it. Better to have just put our own interpretation on "serious consequences" and gone ahead without trying and failing to get a second resolution. I wrote in February 2003 that the United States could not permit itself to be held hostage by the lowest common denominator of opinion on the Security Council. Acting in reliance on the first UN resolution and congressional authority, the United States led a coalition of the willing into battle against Saddam Hussein's army in March 2003, winning quickly, decisively, and predictably.

Unfortunately, the formulation and implementation of policy in the lead-up to, and aftermath of, the war were negatively affected by substantial and continuing turf battles between the State Department and the CIA on one side, and the Defense Department and the vice president's office, on the other.

The Defense Department made a number of costly mistakes, including disbanding the Iraqi army, pursuing de-Baathification too extensively (and thereby prohibiting many qualified Iraqis from serving in a successor Iraqi government), failing to secure weapons depots, and perhaps never having committed enough troops to successfully pacify the country. One thing is for sure: the difficulty of winning the peace was severely underestimated.

Despite the troubles that have followed, however, the Iraqi people are better off now than under their murderous dictator. In polling released while I was writing, seven in ten Iraqis said their lives were going well and two-thirds expected things to improve in the year ahead. Once again, sacrifice by America and its allies has brought down a totalitarian government and delivered a degree of hope for political, economic, and personal freedom to an oppressed people. But the costs to our nation—primarily in terms of sacrifice by brave young Americans and their families, but also the economic, diplomatic, political, and military costs—are very real and canot be ignored.

Those costs will have been worth paying, however, if we can promote progress toward representative government and individual freedom for many countries and people of the Middle East. The jury is still out on whether we will succeed, although Iraq has held democratic elections, as have the Palestinians, notwithstanding that the results in each may prove unfavorable to U.S. interests. In addition, the "Cedar Revolution" has ended the twenty-nine-year Syrian occupation of Lebanon, and Libya has given up its weapons-of-mass-destruction programs.

Regardless of one's views about the wisdom of going to war in Iraq, what is important today to our country's international political, diplomatic, and military credibility is that we find a way to manage the endgame effectively and successfully. The "Lebanonization" of Iraq through a descent into sectarian fragmentation and violence, or an Iraq that erupts into full-blown civil war, or an Iraq with a government hostile to America—each would be an extraordinarily undesirable result for the United States, the region, and the world. Unfortunately, the jury also remains out on whether these outcomes can be avoided.

At the urging of members of Congress, a bipartisan group (the Iraq Study Group) was formed on March 15, 2006, to make a forward-looking and fresh assessment of the situation in Iraq and to provide Congress and the administration with insights and advice. I was named cochair of the group, along with Lee Hamilton, former Democratic chairman of the House Foreign Affairs Committee. The administration welcomed the effort. As I write, the Iraq Study Group has just begun its work.

IN THE GULF WAR, Israel and some of Iraq's Arab neighbors, including Syria, found themselves on the same side for once, however uncomfortably. The administration wanted to capitalize on the momentum created by this first-ever experience with regional cooperation in the Middle East and on the goodwill generated by the unselfish leadership of the United States in dealing with Saddam Hussein.

"We must now begin to look beyond victory and war," the presi-

After the White House. Behind me is the most beautiful building on the Rice University campus, in my opinion—James A. Baker III Hall, home of the Baker Institute for Public Policy. (GITTINGS)

With Ed Djerejian, founding director of the Baker Institute, at an event in the mid-1990s. (RICE UNIVERSITY)

President Bush 41 and I escort Russian president Vladimir Putin for an appearance at the Baker Institute. (AFP/GETTY IMAGES)

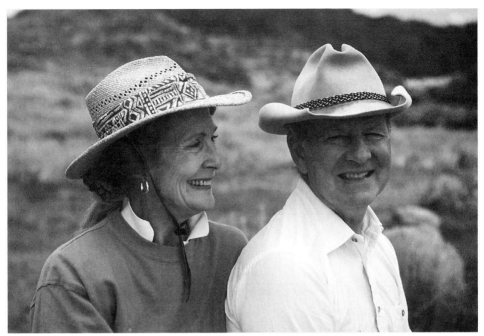

The stresses of life fade in a hurry when Susan and I spend time at our Silver Creek Ranch in Wyoming. (WALLY MCNAMEE/CORBIS)

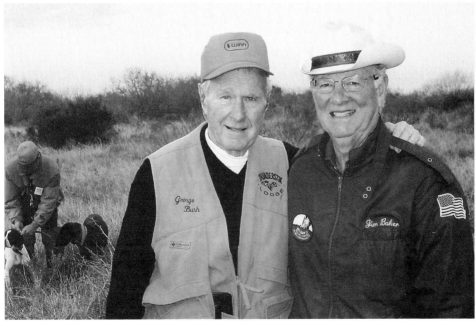

"Forty-one" and I now have the freedom to hunt quail, play golf, and laugh about how much fun we have had through almost fifty years of friendship. (BAKER COLLECTION)

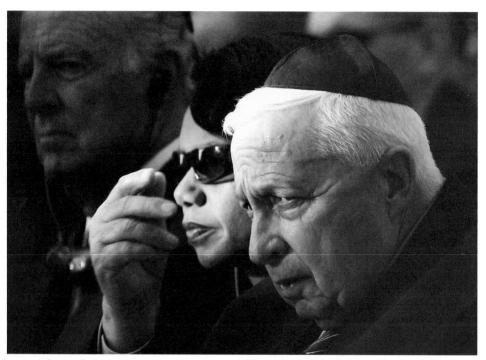

The tenth-anniversary commemoration in November 2005 of the tragic assassination of Yitzhak Rabin reminded me, Condoleezza Rice, Ariel Sharon, and others of what might have been if the great champion of peace had lived. (POOL/GETTY IMAGES)

December 2003: After my first round of visits to foreign capitals—Paris, Bonn, London, Moscow, and Rome—to win Iraqi debt relief, I reported to President Bush and then national security adviser Condoleezza Rice. (GETTY IMAGES)

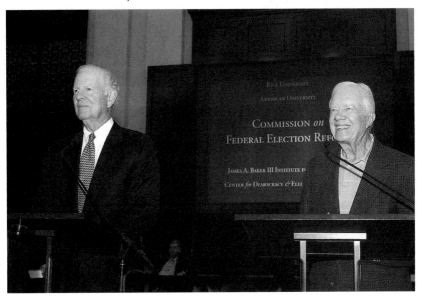

Serving as cochair of the Federal Election Reform Commission in 2005, with former President Jimmy Carter. (RICE UNIVERSITY)

A press conference during the Florida 2000 election dispute: I'm explaining the problem with "hanging chads."
(JEFF KOWALSKY/GETTY IMAGES)

On inauguration day January 2001, George W. Bush graciously invited me to join him and his father in the presidential reviewing stand. (REUTERS/CORBIS)

The extended Baker-Winston family—children, spouses, and grandchildren—vacationing together in New Mexico in 2004. (BAKER COLLECTION)

The tragic drowning of my seven-year-old granddaughter, Graeme Baker, in 2002 prompted her parents and me to support enhanced safety measures for pools and spas.
(BAKER COLLECTION)

With Wendell, Leola, and James Otis in July 2005—and you'll just have to read the last chapter of this book to learn why! (DARRELL HANCOCK)

dent said on the day the fighting stopped. "We must meet the challenge of securing the peace." This was more than post-conflict happy talk. We wanted to stabilize the balance of power in the region, prevent a resurgence of Iraqi power, reduce U.S. reliance on oil from the Middle East, and revive the Arab-Israeli peace process. In short order, most of our proposals—for example, a Mideast development bank—died for lack of support, but we refused to give up on efforts to promote peace between Arabs and Israelis.

We wanted the leaders of Israel and its Arab neighbors—Syria, Jordan, and Lebanon—plus representatives of the Palestinian people (but not the Palestinian Liberation Organization) to sit down across the table and start a conversation about peace. Whatever the outcome, this would break the Arab states' taboo of that time against talking peace with Israel because to do so would recognize, at least implicitly, Israel's right to exist. Almost everywhere, I was met with delays, refusals, evasions, unreasonable demands, broken commitments, and endless lectures about the untrustworthiness of the other side, not to mention policy initiatives such as aggressive Israeli settlement activity in the Occupied Territories that almost seemed designed to scuttle the project. Syrian president Hafez al-Assad, for instance, demanded that the United Nations sponsor the event. Reasonable? Not really. It was a way of trying to torpedo the conference. He knew very well that Israel would never participate in anything sponsored by the international body that famously resolved in 1975 that "Zionism is racism."*

In all, I made eight trips to the Middle East before all parties agreed to the conference. Each diplomatic mission was marked by its own frustrations, but the payoff was sweet. On October 30, 1991, Presidents Bush and Gorbachev hosted the opening ceremonies in Madrid's splendid Royal Palace. The meetings that followed were stiff

---

*With administration leadership, that resolution was revoked in December 1991. "To equate Zionism with the intolerable sin of racism is to forget history and forget the terrible plight of the Jews in World War II and indeed throughout history," President Bush said at the time.

and formal. The principals offered neither handshakes nor eye contact, and their public statements were canned and predictable. Nevertheless, Madrid was a success. Its enduring legacy is simply that it happened at all. After forty-three years of bloody conflict, the ancient taboo against Arabs talking with Israelis was dramatically broken. Like the walls of Jericho, the psychological barriers of half a century came tumbling down. Within two years, Israel had signed a treaty with Jordan and the Oslo Accords with Palestinians. It was a period of great hope, and I take a measure of pride in having contributed to the prospects for peace in that troubled region.

Sadly, that period of hope ended in November 1995 when Yitzhak Rabin, prime minister of Israel, was assassinated by a hardcore right-wing Israeli who opposed Rabin's peace efforts. Yitzhak and his wife, Leah—both deceased now—hosted Susan and me as guests of the government of Israel after I left office as secretary of state.* We still miss these dear friends. To honor them in the most appropriate way possible, we have established the Yitzhak Rabin Fellowship in Middle East Peace and Security at the Baker Institute. In November 2005, at President George W. Bush's request, I led the American delegation to the ceremonies marking the tenth anniversary of Yitzhak's death.

On Tuesday, September 11, 2001, I was in my office at Baker Botts in Washington, D.C. Later that morning, I was scheduled to speak at a Carlyle Group investors conference. Word that an airplane had hit the north tower of the World Trade Center in New York probably reached me around 8:50 A.M.

Early reports were confused. A light plane had struck the tower. Or maybe it was an airliner. It was surely an accident. Or was it? No one was certain. At 9:37 A.M., however, we watched the television in horror

---

*The U.S. ambassador to Israel at the time was Edward Djerejian, who soon would be the founding director of the James A. Baker III Institute for Public Policy.

as a large commercial airliner flew directly into the south tower. Not long afterward, both towers collapsed and, with them, any doubt about whether the strikes were intentional.

About this time, my daughter Mary Bonner called. "Are you and Mom all right?" she asked. "Don't worry, darling. We're fine," I said. But as we talked, I saw a big plume of black smoke rise in the distance, from across the Potomac. We would later learn that a third hijacked airliner had hit the Pentagon. To add to the confusion, the air was quickly filled with wailing sirens, the *thump-thump-thump* of helicopter rotors, and sonic booms as fighter planes scrambled to defend against whatever else might come.

My speaking event was scheduled for 10:45 A.M., and—not sure whether it would be canceled—I arrived early and chatted with John Major, the former British prime minister. We were on the same program. Our topic: "World Affairs Overview."

The conference was soon canceled, however, and I returned to my office and the continuing television coverage. That afternoon, I gave telephone interviews to Peter Jennings, Tom Brokaw, CNN, Fox, and many others. It was now clear that the United States had been struck by terrorists.

American interests had been hit before. The Marine barracks in Lebanon in 1983, the Khobar Towers in Saudi Arabia in 1996, and the USS *Cole* in Yemen in 2000 all come to mind. But 9/11 was different. It brought death to our own soil, it targeted innocent civilians, the scale was larger than anything that had gone before, and it was an unambiguous act of war against our nation. Like Pearl Harbor and the fall of the Berlin Wall, 9/11 marked with finality the end of one era of history and with awful clarity the beginning of another. Events in Madrid, London, Moscow, Bali, Casablanca, Riyadh, and elsewhere would later confirm that terrorism was a global threat that demanded a global response. By virtue of its military power, economic strength, and international preeminence, only the United States could lead that effort—in direct military action, joint law enforcement, and intensified sharing of intelligence. The new administration, not yet in office for a full year, was called to action and would forever be defined by its decisive leadership, at home and abroad, in the months and years that followed.

Terrorism is best defined, I think, as the intentional killing of civilians to achieve a political end. It is a tempting weapon for stateless radical groups that lack the resources to fight conventional wars. But it is doubly dangerous when those groups seize control of a state, as the Taliban and al Qaeda did in Afghanistan before the 2001 attacks on America. Except when terrorists come to ground, as in Afghanistan, conventional military tools are of little use. You cannot target a cruise missile on a meeting of terrorists in a Hamburg apartment complex. What is needed instead is good intelligence, international cooperation, national confidence, strong leadership, and realism about the possibility that, despite it all, dedicated terrorists will succeed now and again in killing the innocent. Most of all, there must be a determination not to let acts of terrorism weaken our resolve.

As I write more than five years later, America has not been attacked again inside its own borders. By that measure, the administration's 9/11 policies have succeeded. Realists, however, should understand that the costs of our defense are high and the terrorists, though weakened, have not yet been defeated.

In time, America and its allies will prevail, just as we prevailed in the Cold War and in World War II. We have firefighters, police officers, and medical personnel who will rush into burning buildings and sacrifice their lives to save others. We have air passengers like those on United Flight 93 who will rise from their seats and fight hijackers with their bare hands. We have troops who will go where asked and do what is needed with skill and professionalism unmatched in military history. And we have a people whose generosity in helping others around the world is wondrous to behold. No nation so blessed will be defeated by a small band of hate-filled killers of innocent men, women, and children.

. . .

ANOTHER ISSUE that emerged after George and I left office was the dilemma of failed states—territories where governments cease to function, the rule of law breaks down, and competing warlords and their private armies of thugs seize power. This is what happened in Somalia, for instance, and later in Liberia, the Congo, and elsewhere. The proper response of the developed world to these political, economic, and human train wrecks is yet to be settled. George H. W. Bush probably had the right idea in sending soldiers on a limited mission to deliver humanitarian aid in Somalia. When President Clinton later escalated the mission to nation-building, however, the cost of going up against the warlords—Black Hawk down!—proved to be higher than he or the American people would easily tolerate.

One other feature of our post–Cold War foreign policy, sadly, is a deterioration in our nation's relationships with many other countries. At the end of the first Bush administration, America was the most-admired nation on the face of the earth. That began to erode in the late 1990s, interrupted briefly by the outpouring of world sympathy after 9/11. Today, it is probably safe to say that majorities in most countries oppose our policies and distrust our motives. Some of this loss of confidence from the highs of the end of the Cold War and the first Gulf War was inevitable. As the world's sole remaining super-power, we occupy a uniquely preeminent place in world affairs. This sets up natural anxieties, resentments, and jealousies, and makes it all the more important that we exercise our power in as understated and collaborative a way as our national interests permit. It will take many years to repair the international loss of trust in our motives, but we must do our best to do so, and as I write, that effort is under way.

SO MANY THINGS happened during my tenure as secretary of state that I can barely mention them, much less do them justice. Besides the end of the Cold War, victory in the Gulf War, and efforts to promote Arab-Israeli peace, we dealt with Tiananmen Square, Panama, the end of apartheid in South Africa, ethnic warfare in the Balkans, and many other challenges. A second Bush administration would have brought more, and I have no doubt that George would have handled them as well as those he faced in the first term, which is to say, very well indeed. My hope and expectation, frankly, was to remain in office as secretary of state and continue to help him. In July 1992, however, he asked me to run his reelection campaign, and I could not say no to my friend. My resignation as secretary of state was effective August 23, 1992, and my farewell was the most emotional speech I have ever given. After all we had accomplished, it was hard to leave the best job I'd ever had. Once again, however, I felt a duty to leave the world of public service and return to the world of electoral politics.

FOURTEEN

"THE ONE CONSTANT IN POLITICS IS CHANGE"

As AFTERNOON TURNED to evening at the Gerald R. Ford Museum in Grand Rapids, George Bush took the microphone to fight for his presidency. In five days, American voters would go to the polls. Michigan was in play, and he could not win reelection without it. "The choice before the American people," he said, "is a vast difference on experience, philosophy, and, yes, character."

The president was not a naturally gifted stump speaker (he admits as much), but as I listened that day in October 1992, he was on his game—buoyant, smiling, assertive. I was running the campaign, a reprise of my role in 1988, but this was the first time I had traveled with him in 1992.

Despite having served with distinction as president, George was the underdog. With the Cold War over and the world largely at peace, foreign policy leadership, his biggest political asset, was yesterday's news. As often happens after a period of conflict, America was turning inward. A mild nine-month recession in 1990–1991 had created an opening for Bill Clinton, the politically gifted governor of Arkansas. He exploited it skillfully, especially here in the Industrial Belt. For weeks George had trailed by double digits. In the last week or ten days, however, he had closed to within one or two points in some major polls. We were still behind, but for the first time in the campaign, we were moving.

Clinton had exaggerated our nation's economic troubles for political purposes, George told the Grand Rapids audience. His voice betrayed few signs of long days on the road and a gathering cold. "The only way they can win is to convince America we're in a recession," he said, but the economy had actually grown for the past eighteen months—at a rate of 2.7 percent in the third quarter alone.

"Four more years! Four more years! Four more years!" the crowd chanted.

George was absolutely right. The recession was over. The economy was growing. So successful was the Democratic mantra, echoed by a sympathetic press, however, that many people erroneously believed that America was in a deep recession on election day. On this issue, perception had not caught up to reality, and it still hasn't.

Clinton's track record in Arkansas did not inspire confidence, George said. The state was "fiftieth in environmental quality . . . fiftieth in per capita spending on criminal justice . . . forty-sixth on teacher salaries, and forty-fifth in overall well-being of children." "And in the debate the other night he says, 'I want to do for America what I've done for Arkansas.' No way! No way!"

Then came the delicate character issue. George Bush—war hero, family man, successful businessman, veteran public servant—had a hard-won reputation as an honorable man, even among most Democrats. By contrast, polls showed that many voters were still uneasy about Clinton. (The complaint that character should be off-limits in a campaign for the American presidency is both absurd and not historical. What could be more important?)

"I do not believe you can be president of the United States and try to be all things to all people," George said.

In the Gulf War, for instance, "we had to mobilize world opinion and then make a very difficult decision to send someone else's son or daughter into combat. And what did Bill Clinton say? He said, 'Well, I agree with the minority [the Democrats in Congress who voted *against* giving the president authority to use force], but I guess I would have voted with the majority.'"

"The thing that bothers me is there is a pattern of deception.... You cannot lead by misleading."

"Bush! Bush! Bush!"

The president had been worked over pretty good in the campaign, not only by the Clinton campaign, but also by H. Ross Perot, the on-again, off-again third-party candidate. Seeing George counterpunch was fun. As he spoke, I chatted with Ann Compton of ABC News about George's surge in the polls. Ann could sense my optimism. I don't remember her exact comment, but it was something like this: "You all seem to be upbeat now, but in a day or two you're not going to be so happy."

She would not elaborate, so I filed her strange remark away and moved on. George had an interview that night, then we were on to Missouri, excited by the possibility of pulling off the biggest late-surge upset since Truman beat Dewey.

I HAD KEPT out of sight for much of the campaign. For one thing, running a campaign requires spending most of the time taking care of business in the office, not lighting up the television screen. But early on, I also got boxed in and had to keep somewhat of a low profile to avoid hurting my candidate.

How did that happen? Well, let's begin at the beginning.

In mid-July of 1992, President Bush and his son Jeb—later a two-term governor of Florida—joined me, Susan, and my son Jamie for a few days of fishing at our Wyoming ranch. As in 1988, George wanted to get away from the Beltway during the Democratic convention. Better to refresh himself for the battle ahead than listen to four days of Bush-bashing. George trailed Clinton by serious double digits, and we knew that gap would get worse with Clinton's inevitable convention bounce.

Perot, a controversial Texas billionaire, was also a worry. His backers had already gathered enough signatures to put him on the ballot as a third-party candidate in twenty-five states, and that number was sure to rise. Starting with a *Larry King Live* appearance in February, he had parlayed a series of folksy talk-show appearances into an antiestablishment movement. As late as June 2, he led both major-party candidates in some polls and, unfortunately for us, was drawing far, far more voters from Bush than from Clinton.

Perot probably decided to run for president for a number of reasons. Only he really knows what they were. In my view, however, one of them was that he disliked George Herbert Walker Bush. The trouble started when Perot decided that live American prisoners of war were still being held in Vietnam. He wanted to go over there, look for them, and bring them home. The war had ended about a decade earlier and there was no evidence the Vietnamese still held any of our troops (and none have shown up since), but Perot was adamant. I think he had a meeting with President Reagan about this. The president then ordered a complete review of the situation by our defense, intelligence, and security apparatus, which reported that there was no basis to believe the Vietnamese still held any American POWs. It would be a mistake for Perot to go over there, President Reagan decided.

George and I met with the president in the Oval Office to discuss how to break the news. "I'm willing to tell Perot," the president said, "but I don't really know him. Maybe you Texans can tell him." As chief of staff, it was usually my job to deliver bad news, but I also barely knew the man. The vice president stepped up. "I know him very well," George said. "He's supported me in the past. I'll be glad to tell him."

When George called, however, the hot-tempered Perot apparently blamed the messenger for the message. From that day on, it seemed that he hated George. Sometimes it got ugly . . . and bizarre. During the campaign, for instance, he accused the Bush camp of planning to sabotage a daughter's wedding—a ludicrous charge, notable both for the number of times Perot repeated it to nodding TV interviewers and for the total absence of any credible evidence that it ever occurred.

At Perot's request, he and I once met privately at my D.C. home. All I remember is that he was full of conspiracy theories, including the wedding story. Two days later, details of the supposedly secret meeting appeared in the press. He also came by to see me at the site of the first presidential debate that fall, shortly before the three-way event was to begin. I still don't know why!

But Ross Perot was the last thing on my mind when I went to the ranch in July. All I wanted was a little R&R. A few weeks earlier, I had worked long hours with the Russians in Lisbon, London, and Washington to finish the START II agreement. Finally, on June 16, President Bush and Russian President Boris Yeltsin announced an accord to reduce the number of nuclear warheads on both sides to the lowest levels in more than twenty years and to eliminate all land-based missiles with multiple warheads. It was a landmark achievement in both nuclear arms control and normalization of relations with the new Russian Federation. (The formal treaty was signed in January 1993.) I would soon head to the Middle East to try to restart peace talks after a change of government in Israel. All I wanted to do in Wyoming, however, was wade out into Silver Creek, plant my feet on the rough gravel bed, and drop a fly line over the big brown trout that lurked in the eddies of its cold mountain waters.

George had other ideas. One morning he asked Jamie and Jeb to leave us alone in the cabin. He told me his campaign was not going the way he wanted it to and asked me to leave State and try to put it back on track.

I have said it before, and I will say it again here: I did not want to leave the State Department and run another presidential campaign, but I immediately said yes. George was my president and my friend. He had made me secretary of state. We had accomplished a lot together and, given the chance, I believed, we would accomplish more. I also thought I could help him against his tag-team opponents. The only real issue was when to start. George and I agreed that I would close up shop at State and officially take over the campaign on August 23, immediately after the GOP convention in Houston.

IT IS TRUE, as popular history reminds us, that the president came out of the 1991 Persian Gulf War with an 89 percent approval rating. Those kinds of numbers never hold up, however, and by 1992 he was flying into heavy headwinds.

One big problem was that Republicans had occupied the White House for almost twelve years. This was four years beyond the normal expiration date for party control. For fourteen election cycles over fifty-six years—Eisenhower to George W. Bush—the natural order has been two terms for Republicans, two for Democrats, two more for Republicans, and so on. There have been only two exceptions to this powerful trend—Carter (four years, because things were not going well) and Reagan and Bush (twelve, because they were). To win, we would have to extend twelve years to sixteen.

Then there were the media. I respect the press, acknowledge its important role, and get along well with journalists. It's an open secret, however, that the great majority of political reporters and editors vote—and think—Democratic. In 1992 they were clearly ready for a change.

This is not to minimize Bill Clinton's achievement. He came from a family of modest means, but parlayed a good mind into an undergraduate degree from Georgetown, a law degree from Yale, and a Rhodes scholarship at Oxford. Then he returned home to Arkansas and worked his way up to the governor's mansion. In 1992, he had the courage to run against George when more prominent Democrats demurred, and he ran a good race. Only in America.

Over the years, I've had the opportunity to spend a fair amount of time with him. He's brilliant, charming, engaging, and politically savvy. Even when you're in a crowded hall with him, Susan and I have noticed, he has that rare ability to make you feel as if you are the only other person in the room.

Still, George Bush was the right man for the job in 1992, just as he was in 1988. The world had changed dramatically between 1988 and 1992. It would continue to change from 1992 to 1996. America's post–Cold War foreign policy was necessarily a work in progress. We still needed a chief executive like George, who understood these issues so well, had a successful security and foreign policy team in place, and enjoyed good relations with world leaders, old and new. The Arkansas governor, by contrast, had no serious experience in international affairs. He finessed this point in the campaign by simply agreeing with George on most foreign policy issues, or differing only modestly.

He did speak up on one foreign policy issue with domestic overtones—the North American Free Trade Agreement then under negotiation with Canada and Mexico. To his everlasting credit, he supported free trade against the wishes of some important constituencies of his own party. Perot, on the other hand, bitterly charged that Mexico would siphon jobs from the United States with a "giant sucking sound." He was wrong, but he convinced many voters that their jobs were at risk. Clinton split the difference. He promised to support NAFTA, but only after it was amended to protect jobs and the environment. By putting a little paint on George's policy, he could claim it as his own. This was a good example, by the way, of how Perot and Clinton sometimes delivered one-two punches against their common adversary.

GEORGE'S REQUEST THAT I run his campaign against Bill Clinton and Ross Perot was not a huge surprise. What happened next was. As the Democratic Convention drew to a close, Perot dramatically dropped out of the race. (In October, of course, he would dramatically drop back in.) "Now that the Democratic Party has revitalized itself," he said, "I have concluded that we cannot win in November." His theory was that no candidate in the three-way race would get a majority of the electoral votes, leaving the race to be decided by rank-and-file Democrats and Republicans in the House who would never support him.

Out in Wyoming, we weren't buying that reason. Neither were many of Perot's people. Some disappointed supporters said their man didn't like the intense personal scrutiny attendant to a run for the presidency and had buckled under the pressure. "I thought he had more guts," said Dick Peters, vice chairman of the Arizona Perot campaign.

Whatever the reason, Perot's withdrawal set off a political tug-of-war. "Big Voter Block Is Cut Adrift; Bush and Clinton Rush to Court the Disaffected," read a front-page headline in the *Washington Post*. Clinton was in a better position to make his pitch. Only hours after Perot's announcement, he would have a nationwide audience for his acceptance speech. George, on the other hand, was virtually incommunicado at the ranch.

George was fishing when the news broke. I rushed down to the creek and said, "You need to call him right now. Tell him you share his principles and values, and hope he will support you." I handed George a satellite telephone and he placed the call from the middle of the Wyoming sagebrush.

George then phoned a statement to the White House press corps, stationed about seventy-five miles away in Jackson Hole. That did not work too well. The audio quality was too noisy for use on the air. Even if the sound quality had been good, however, there were no pictures, and if you've read this far, you know that television needs pictures.

With time running out, we bused the press two hours out to the ranch. Reporters shot video of George's statement in front of the foothills of the Wind River Range and quickly relayed it to satellite uplinks for the evening news. This worked. George's remarks were picked up on all three networks, with pictures. "I have a message for anyone who supported Ross Perot and anyone who identified with the frustration that brought them together," George said: "I heard you."

. . .

IF I WERE in the business of writing political fortune cookies, I would put this message in a lot of them: "The one constant in politics is change." The electorate wants to know that a candidate, even an incumbent, is an agent of change, someone who will make things better. This was a particularly salient point in 1992. George understood this: "You want action and you want change, and to anyone who wants to block change, I say, 'Get out of our way and let America move forward once again.'"

There was one obvious way for George to demonstrate that he was a change agent: by replacing his running mate. Dan Quayle was not a problem in 1988. Despite the distraction caused by his nomination, the ticket won forty states. By 1992, however, Dan had become a liability in George's uphill fight for reelection.

A second fortune cookie might read: "Politics is perception." Dan suffered—unfairly in many ways, but to a degree that could not be ignored—from a negative image among voters at large. He still had the strong support of many in the party, but Bob Teeter's polls showed that the verdict with too many voters was "no sale."

Teeter said George would fare much better with undecided voters if he replaced Quayle with Colin Powell, Dick Cheney, me, or any number of other prominent Republicans. (For the record, I would never have been a serious option. The Constitution says a state's presidential electors may not cast their votes for both a presidential and vice presidential candidate from the same state as themselves.)

There were some private meetings within the campaign's inner circle to consider whether an effort should be made to encourage the vice president to leave the ticket. One thing was clear, we decided: Dan could not be removed against his will. That would be bad politics, suggesting panic and disarray, and would be seen, wrongly in my opinion, as an admission that it had been a mistake to pick Dan in the first place. It would also give critics an opening to criticize George. "Don't you understand? Quayle is not the problem. You're the problem." What was needed was to persuade the vice president to remove himself from the ticket and exit gracefully, stage right.

Easier said than done. It was no secret that Quayle wanted to run for president in 1996. He had worked hard and honorably to advance the goals of the administration. No scandal had touched him. Why should he allow himself to be pushed out?

I won't speak for George, but I think it's fair to say he would have accepted Dan's decision if the vice president, on his own, had concluded that the best way for George to be seen as an agent of change (and thereby give us a chance to win) was to take himself out. At one point, it was even suggested that Barbara Bush give Dan a nudge. No way, George replied. Looking back, he was right. She would have been seen as a courier for the president. Ditto for George W. In the end, George would neither send a signal to Dan nor authorize anyone else to do so.

When rumors of the "Dump Quayle" movement surfaced, Dan did not take the hint. "If I thought I was hurting the ticket, I'd be gone," he said in one interview. "I want George Bush reelected." At the same time, he insisted he was not a drag on the ticket. "I've been tested," he said. In late July, George cut off speculation by telling reporters that Dan's spot on the ticket was "certain." And that was that. Afterward, Dan campaigned hard and did a great job against Al Gore in the vice presidential debate. Still, the biggest favor he could have done for the president—and the country, in my opinion—would have been to graciously take himself off the ticket.*

---

*Something Marilyn Quayle said when Dan threw his hat into the ring for the 2000 GOP presidential nomination still disturbs me. She called George W. Bush "a party frat-boy type," "a guy that never accomplished anything; everything he got Daddy took care of." These remarks were offensive enough in their own right, but doubly so from the wife of a man who was himself the object of equally inaccurate personal criticisms, and who was plucked from relative political obscurity by the father of the man she was criticizing. I know for a fact that these remarks did not endear her to the Bush family.

. . .

ON AUGUST 13, 1992, I gave one of the most difficult speeches of my life. "I have decided to resign as secretary of state, effective August 23, to work with the president to help develop a second-term agenda that builds on what has been achieved and that fully integrates our domestic, economic, and foreign policies," I told the foreign service officers, career civil servants, and political appointees gathered in the Dean Acheson Auditorium at Foggy Bottom. For one rare time in my public life, I struggled to maintain my composure. But looking out at all the dedicated men and women who had served and would continue to serve their country so capably and so loyally and reflecting on what we had done together, I became quite emotional.

I was less emotional when I addressed the American people in the same speech. Here, my first goal was to make the point that there were "contrasting philosophies" and "sharp differences" in the approaches of George Bush and Bill Clinton. My second goal was to enunciate the president's philosophy, as simply as possible. "We should build on the fundamentals of lower tax rates, limits on government spending, greater competition, less economic regulation, and more open trade that can unleash tremendous private initiative and growth," I said. "But I think that in the nineties government can add to this growth program by building opportunity and hope for individuals, families, and communities."

The analysis began almost instantly. The *Washington Post*'s David Broder had some nice things to say about me . . . and a few questions.

Years ago, when he was President Reagan's chief of staff, Baker was described in this column as "the most capable unelected official Washington has seen in years." Nothing in his later service in the Treasury and State departments would cause me to revise that judgment. There is no one in either party I'd rather see working for the U.S. government than Jim Baker.

His return to the White House will improve morale in the administration and the Republican Party. His masterful speech at the State Department yesterday was the most coherent and persuasive case for Bush's presidency that anyone—including the president—has offered.

Still, there are reasons to wonder—from the country's point of view—about the costs and benefits of this shift. It takes Baker away from day-to-day diplomacy at a time when his personal efforts, particularly in the Middle East, seem on the verge of bearing fruit. That is clearly a loss.

One can also question whether Baker brings to the task an understanding of how much America has changed in the past four years and why the voters are so sour on Bush. Baker is as much an Establishment man as the president, a polished Princetonian, a wealthy lawyer whose skill lies in dealing with other power brokers, domestic and foreign.

Although he referred in his speech to the "anxiety and anger" in the American people, he has not heard the voices of the jobless engineers and construction workers or the complaints of taxpayers who see all too clearly the costs of paralysis in Washington. He can read the polls, but I wonder if he can feel the fear and frustration that Bush so far has failed to address.

I won't address the question of the costs and benefits to the nation of my move back to the White House, except to say that my successor as secretary of state, Larry Eagleburger, was a consummate professional who kept the department on course and moving ahead. As to whether I could understand the "anxiety and angst" of the unemployed and feel the "fear and frustration" of the voters, there's really no answer I can give that would satisfy critics. But I'll point out a few things Broder overlooked.

Yes, George and I were brought up in accomplished (and loving) families, we both had good educations, and we both succeeded in our careers. So what? Each generation of mothers and fathers wants its children to have better opportunities than the last generation, and George and I were the beneficiaries of the hard work, discipline, and frugality of our ancestors. Because of our advantages, we were also taught that we had special responsibilities to others. Furthermore, our faith instructed us that all men and women were created in the image of God and were equal before God and man, clothed in dignity and deserving of respect. It is also worth remembering that many of America's great leaders, starting with George Washington, were Establishment men.

THE BIGGEST MISTAKE our administration made in 1992 was not following up "Desert Storm," the successful war to eject Iraq from Kuwait, with "Domestic Storm," an economic revitalization program that we could have built a reelection campaign around. George could have capitalized on his strong approval ratings from the first Persian Gulf War to engage Congress in a political battle over fundamental economic policy.

Why didn't that happen? My understanding is that Dick Darman, head of the Office of Management and Budget, suggested the idea, but that other advisers assured the president that the economy was turning around, that no dramatic federal action was needed, and that voters would soon see that things were better. And things were, in fact, better, although this did not become fully apparent until after the election.

The recession began shortly before Iraq invaded Kuwait in August 1990 and ended shortly after the U.S.-led coalition ejected Iraq from Kuwait in February 1991. It was part of a worldwide downturn that was nastier than anything we experienced here.

When the recession ended in early 1991, growth resumed. Unfortunately, voters accustomed to the glory years of the 1980s were disappointed by the more routine growth of 1991–1992. Worse, the Rust Belt and some other hard-hit regions stayed down while the rest of the country moved ahead. All of this created an opening for Clinton and Perot—one warm, the other brusque, both claiming they could fix a broken economy. Just by talking about the issue, they scored points with voters, even though their answers (big tax increases and in Perot's case, magic-wand budget cuts) were wrong and simplistic.

The federal debt was a legitimate issue, however. President Reagan had sharply increased federal revenues, but Congress spent the money faster than it came in. While Clinton and Perot talked about deficit control, George had actually tried to do something about it. In 1990, he agreed to higher taxes as part of a complex budget deal. This would have been controversial enough, but it was double trouble for George because it broke his 1988 pledge—"Read my lips: no new taxes."

I was at State at the time, but I remember thinking George's agreement to higher taxes, even conditioned on spending cuts, might present a political problem. And it did, with our Republican base, which accounted for some of George's weakness in the early primaries. By the summer of 1992, however, the question was not what we coulda or shoulda done about Domestic Storm or the deficit issue, but what we would do now.

WHEN PRESIDENT BUSH announced that I would return to the White House as chief of staff and senior counselor, he said that I would be in charge of integrating foreign, economic, and domestic policy and formulating the plans for how such policies would be implemented in a second Bush term. Rumors circulated that instead of going back to State if the president were reelected, I would be given a "super-cabinet" post. This led to silly-season editorials and columns in several newspapers, including one in Peoria: "If Baker is as good as the president thinks, maybe he should be chief of the country, not just chief of staff."

These comments did not sit well with me or anyone else in the Bush camp. One aide referred to speculation about my role as "the copresidency problem." The notion was preposterous, but puffing up my role was an indirect way for critics to imply that voters should be concerned about George. Perceptions were what counted, and the best way to manage them, he and I decided, was for me not to keep too high a profile—a decision for which I was later criticized by some.

The mid-August GOP convention was in Houston. To stay out of the spotlight and gather myself for the campaign, I hung out the "Gone Fishin'" sign and repaired to Wyoming for a couple of days. I came back for the final two days of the convention and helped a little with George's acceptance speech, but limited my public appearances to a prayer breakfast and the closing session.

When I officially took over as chief of staff on August 23, I was accompanied from State to the White House by what some referred to as my "plug-in unit." Margaret Tutwiler became communications director. Bob Zoellick assumed the role of deputy chief of staff. Dennis Ross became a top foreign policy adviser to the president. And Janet Mullins became assistant to the president for political affairs. All reported to me.

It has been written that these folks were unenthusiastic about making the move. Maybe, but such feelings did not affect their commitment to the president or their performance in their new roles. We hit the ground running and had little time to catch our breath until the election.

Back in the West Wing, I occupied the same office that I had as President Reagan's chief of staff. Each day at 7:30 A.M., I met with Margaret, Bob, Dennis, and Janet. Darman, press secretary Marlin Fitzwater, and national security adviser Brent Scowcroft regularly joined us, as did campaign officials Bob Teeter and Fred Malek. Oftentimes, Mary Matalin, Charlie Black, and others with the campaign would join us.

A top priority was creating a message of the day or issue of the day, and making sure that both the White House and the campaign got that message across. One goal was to set up "quick-turnaround" systems so the president could move from place to place and issue to issue effectively and swiftly. We also spent time on major policy initiatives and speeches for the days ahead.

Whether in the daily message or a major address, we encouraged George to make several points. First, he needed to show that he truly cared for people and felt their pain. (He did, of course, but he was not a hugger, physically or rhetorically, and Clinton was.) Second, for the reasons I have already discussed, he needed to be seen as an agent of change. Clinton and Perot said they would shake things up. For George, it was a bit trickier. Granted, the economic reforms he was proposing were not as radical as those of his opponents, but that was good. Our proposed remedies were tried and true. As mentioned, we also tried to make Clinton's character an issue. Looking back, we were unsuccessful.

One successful thing I did was call George's and my old friend Robert Mosbacher of Houston, to help with fund-raising. Bob had served as national finance chairman for the 1976 Ford campaign, then for George in 1988. In between, he served for a period as chairman of the Republican National Committee. As George's secretary of commerce, he saw that the 1990–1991 recession had left the nation in a sour mood and that many voters thought George was out of touch with that mood. Bob lobbied hard, but fruitlessly, for the administration to follow up Desert Storm with a domestic economic program that would demonstrate the president's concern about, and intention to address, the problem. He was right but unsuccessful. By the time I took over the campaign, Bob was back in private life. He initially resisted my plea to help with fund-raising. "Listen, buddy," I said, "if I can resign from State for George, you can come out of retirement for one more campaign." He did, of course, and with great results.

We believed the presidential debates would offer our best opportunity to overtake Clinton. (Underdogs always need the debates more than front-runners, and we were the underdogs this time.) But we knew the Arkansas governor would be a formidable adversary. He was almost congenitally articulate (although he sometimes tended to ramble—and ramble and ramble) and he was also trained to think on his feet. George (as he acknowledges) is a better do-er than debater. Still, he worked hard in our mock debates, and we had reason to hope he might hit a home run.

It didn't help that Ross Perot had reentered the fray in early October and would get equal time with the two major-party candidates. As a talker, he was no Bill Clinton, and he lacked George's substance, but he could be counted on for comic relief. In 1980, candidate Reagan had been very happy to team up with independent John Anderson to hammer the incumbent president Jimmy Carter. This time George would face that same two-on-one dynamic.

Under these conditions, George performed admirably in the first debate at Washington University in St. Louis on October 11. He stressed his experience in foreign affairs and outlined his program for economic renewal. By most accounts, the debate was a draw. We didn't hit a home run, but there would be two more chances.

Unfortunately, one line that George delivered in St. Louis that night thrust me back into the spotlight. "What I'm going to do," he declared, "is say to Jim Baker when this campaign is over: 'All right, let's sit down now. You do in domestic affairs what you've done in foreign affairs, be kind of the economic coordinator of all the domestic side of the House, and that includes all the economic side, all the training side, and bring this program together.'"

This was a total surprise to me. He never hinted to me that he intended to do this. When asked in the post-debate spin session about the president's plans for me, I said he had not "defined what it was specifically" that my responsibilities would be. Over the next couple of days, the press and the opposition paid more attention to me and less to the president than either one of us liked. Clinton spokesman George Stephanopoulos, grinning, asked publicly whether *I* planned to announce a role for *Bush* in a second term.

In mid-October, we tentatively planned for me to give a speech in Detroit on our economic program and, secondarily, to fill in the blanks about what the president had in mind for me in a second Bush administration. But the more he and I thought about it, the more we were convinced that I should not give the speech. The attention needed to be on the president, and on September 10, he used Detroit as a forum to outline the "Agenda for American Renewal," his detailed economic plan.

In the third debate, October 19 at Michigan State University in East Lansing, Bill Clinton won laughter and applause when he made an issue of my role.

> In the first debate, Mr. Bush made some news. He'd [previously] said Jim Baker was going to be secretary of state, and in the first debate he said, no, now he's gonna be responsible for domestic economic policy. Well . . . I'll make some news in the third debate. The person responsible for domestic economic policy in my administration will be Bill Clinton. I'm gonna make those decisions . . .

"Well, that's what worries me," George replied, earning a well-deserved round of laughter of his own.

I SAID EARLIER that George had been worked over pretty good in the campaign. Al Gore was the attack dog on one issue, the so-called "Iraq-gate" scandal. Hardly anyone remembers it now, but it was a big deal that October, a twofer designed to knock George down a peg or two on foreign policy and to sully his reputation. It was based on two things. First, federal agents discovered in 1989 that the Atlanta branch of an Italian bank had partially financed Saddam Hussein's arms buildup. Second, early in our administration we tried to improve our relations with Iraq (a country we had helped in its long war with Iran) with trade credits, primarily agricultural. Unfortunately, the policy had failed, as policies sometimes do. "The objective was to try to include Iraq in the family of nations," I said when my name was linked to pushing agricultural loan guarantees for Iraq through the bureaucracy. "That's what we did. You can argue in hindsight, but that was the policy."

Critics conflated the two events—the genuine bank scandal and the unsuccessful policy of trying to engage Iraq—to create an imaginary political scandal. Al Gore's job was to keep it in the news that October, and he handled his assignment with what appeared to be genuine enthusiasm.

Iraqgate "involves the biggest bank fraud, it involves $2 billion of the American taxpayers' money that we're stuck with," Al said. "It involves the decision by George Bush to arm Saddam Hussein and to lead him to miscalculate and launch a war that never should have taken place and would not have except for the poor judgment and bad foreign policy of George Bush, and he ought to be held accountable for it."

This was not the first time the Baker and Gore names had been linked (and it would not be the last). In 1985, Susan Baker and Tipper Gore helped found the Parents Music Resource Center to fight for the labeling of violent and obscene music. They have been friends ever since. If you were to visit the room in our home that serves as Susan's office today, you would see a silver-framed picture of Al Gore, Susan, and me watching Mary Bonner and Kristen Gore in a lacrosse game at National Cathedral School. It is inscribed: "I will always cherish our friendship. With love, Tipper."

I got to know Al about the same time our wives became friends. When I was secretary of the treasury, I joined a Christian prayer group on Capitol Hill. Al, who was then in his first term as a senator, was also a member. Among the others were senators Mark Hatfield, Sam Nunn, Lawton Chiles, Paul Tribble, and Pete Domenici. Our group was totally bipartisan. It included Democrats and Republicans, liberals and conservatives.

We would meet once a week, usually in Pete's office, for forty-five minutes or so. First we would read a short Scripture. Business and politics were off limits, but we would then talk about whatever else was on our minds or troubling us. At the end, we would have a short prayer and go about our business. These meetings comforted us, created a circle of friendship, and reminded us of something that everyone—high-ranking public officials included—needs to remember: we are all subject to a higher power. One important rule was that nothing said in the room was ever to leave the room, and it did not.

This was part of a worldwide small-group movement coordinated by a remarkable man named Doug Coe. His organization also sponsors the nondenominational Prayer Breakfast in Washington each February. The small-group meetings were designed to help create a "family of friends" organized around the teachings of Jesus. I continued to attend as secretary of state, both in Washington and abroad, and even helped establish groups in Germany and Japan.

I've been around long enough to know that politics ain't bean-bag, but I was extremely disappointed that Al would accuse President Bush (and me, indirectly) of what appeared to be criminal behavior. "George Bush is presiding over a coverup significantly larger than Watergate," he said again and again.

That always stuck in my craw. There are certain rules in politics, and one of them is that you never accuse anyone, much less the president of the United States, of breaking the law unless you can back it up with something more than innuendo.

After the campaign ended, Iraqgate more or less evaporated. Writing in *Atlantic Monthly*, the highly respected *National Journal* columnist Stuart Taylor, Jr., delivered this postmortem:

> One staple of Washington life is the phony scandal: a conflagration of bogus accusations and intimations of criminality and sleaze, fanned to an inferno by the media and partisan enemies of the accused, only to finally fade away for lack of evidence.
>
> It's a bipartisan phenomenon. The classic of the genre was "Iraq-gate," aka the Banca Nazionale del Lavoro (BNL) scandal. Not to be confused with Iran-Contra (a real scandal), Iraqgate was whipped up in 1992 by Democratic congressional investigators, sloppy journalists,

and a partisan federal judge. It erupted into thousands of newspaper articles and a gaggle of network television specials, turning President Bush's greatest triumph—his victory over Saddam Hussein in the 1991 Persian Gulf War—into a political liability....

These charges were false. All of them.

One other controversy boiled up in 1992. Over the summer there were rumors that Bill Clinton had renounced his citizenship to avoid the draft while he studied in England. Newspapers filed freedom-of-information requests to see his passport files. Our campaign group heard about the requests and talked about them in mid-September, but did nothing. On September 30, the State Department, acting on the freedom-of-information requests, checked its files and found no such renunciation. Unfortunately, staffers there tried to call some individuals then working at the White House.

The State Department's inspector general, Sherman Funk, investigated and recommended that an independent counsel be appointed. That was ridiculous, but Attorney General William Barr—who had done the right thing in refusing to ask for an independent counsel on Iraqgate—seemed to cave in to demands from the media (principally the *Washington Post*) and didn't have the guts to say no this time. As a result, an independent counsel was named on December 14, one day before expiration of the law authorizing such appointments. Three years and millions of dollars later, the independent counsel, Joseph diGenova, issued a final report that found no criminal wrongdoing. His staff's report on Sherman Funk's investigation was "one of the most chilling accounts of government incompetence I have ever read in my life," diGenova said. His conclusion: no independent counsel should ever have been appointed, and the government owed an apology to the White House aides who were the subjects of the investigation. In fact, he apologized by name to the White House and State Department staffers targeted by the investigation, and some of them later won financial settlements from the government.

. . .

PRESIDENT BUSH'S appearance in Grand Rapids on Thursday, October 29, was perhaps the high point of the campaign. Despite everything, he had closed the gap to a point or two and was in position to pull a major upset. He was smiling as he campaigned, and by some accounts, Bill Clinton was not.

Then came October 30. After six years of investigations, Lawrence Walsh, the independent counsel in the Iran-Contra investigation, picked the Friday before Tuesday's presidential election to indict Caspar Weinberger, President Reagan's secretary of defense, for allegedly lying to Congress. It was a legal missile with a political warhead, fired straight into the heart of the presidential election and clearly timed to try to destroy President Bush.

What was wrong with the indictment? Let me count the ways. First, it was a rehash of an earlier charge that had already been thrown out of court. Second, this flimsy new indictment was, itself, thrown out exactly six weeks to the day after it was filed. Why? Because the statute of limitations had run on the alleged crime, a point that a serious prosecutor might well have considered beforehand. Third, the indictment did not charge Cap with *participating* in Iran-Contra. Every scrap of evidence in the investigation showed that Caspar Weinberger *vigorously opposed* that misguided adventure from beginning to end. Walsh knew this. Instead, he indicted one of the most honorable men who ever served in our government for allegedly lying to Congress, a charge that the respected cochairmen of the Iran-Contra committee, one a Democrat, one a Republican, said was inconceivable. Fourth, the Weinberger indictment was handled by James Brosnahan, a major contributor to Democratic campaigns, including the Clinton campaign.

Fifth, and most egregiously, the indictment quoted from Cap's diary to suggest that George Bush himself had favored the proposed arms-for-hostages deal with Iran at a January 1986 White House meeting.

This bit of text, a few words fished out of thousands of pages of evidence, was pasted into the document for one reason and one reason only, which was to smear the president. It had *nothing whatever* to do with the indictment of Weinberger. (Walsh later conceded—with his typical lack of grace—that he had no evidence that George had ever violated any criminal statute.) The purpose was to cast doubt, not on George's sworn testimony about Iran-Contra, but on his *public* statements. In other words, the purpose was obviously political and, it seemed to me, a clear abuse of prosecutorial discretion and simple decency.*

The indictment was a godsend for the Democrats. An extraordinarily detailed three-page rapid response from the "war room" of Clinton's Little Rock headquarters—released almost immediately, but dated one day before the indictment was even filed (an "error," his office later said)—called it "the smoking gun showing that George Bush lied to the American people about his role in the arms-for-hostages affair." Suddenly the issue that had helped move the polls our way, concerns about the opponent's character, lost traction. The press spent the entire weekend asking George what he knew and when he knew it. And that was that. Ann Compton turned out to be right. One day after George's strong performance in Michigan, we were "not so happy."

George fought back, but vainly. "Being attacked on character by Governor Clinton is like being called ugly by a frog," he said at one point.† Nothing in the indictment contradicted his deposition testimony "under oath, under oath," he protested again and again, a point that would be confirmed in Walsh's final report. But it was too late. We never caught up with the story.

---

*A federal appeals court would later chastise the prosecutor for smearing others. His final report "repeatedly accuses named individuals of crimes, although in many instances the individual was never indicted, if indicted was never convicted, or if convicted the conviction was reversed," the judges said.

†George later received a complaint about this statement from the Worldwide Fair Play for Frogs Committee. He apologized . . . to the frogs.

. . .

WOULD WE HAVE won if Lawrence Walsh had not tossed his stink bomb into the American political process? Who knows? Even as the polls tightened the week before the election, we were always behind. All I know is that on Thursday before the election we had a chance and on Friday we didn't.

There were three big reasons that we lost, however, and I have already mentioned two. One was that Republicans had held the White House for twelve years, and both voters and the press were tired and ready for change. The other was the administration's failure to follow Desert Storm with Domestic Storm, an economic revitalization program.

The third was Henry Ross Perot. On his best day, he had no chance to win the presidency, but he succeeded spectacularly as a spoiler. His 18.9 percent of the popular vote was the best showing by a third-party candidate since Teddy Roosevelt's 1912 Bull Moose candidacy split the Republican majority and allowed a politically weaker Democrat to win the White House. Back then, it was Woodrow Wilson. This time, it was Bill Clinton.

The Democrats won 43 percent of the popular vote and Bush-Quayle took 37.4 percent. The electoral vote was 370–168 for the Democrats. I believe about two-thirds of Perot's supporters were natural Republican voters who would have supported George in a head-to-head race. If I'm right and if Perot had never entered the race, George might have won more than 50 percent of the popular vote and— applying the same two-thirds/one-third split on a state-by-state basis— he might have won the Electoral College, too.

"WHEN YOU WIN, your errors are obscured; when you lose, your errors are magnified," George said in a radio address five days after the election. "But as for what has passed, I can only say that it was my administration, my campaign, I captained the team, and I take full responsibility for the loss. No one else is responsible. I am responsible."

That was George Bush at his best—a general, wounded himself, thinking only of his troops. That's what character looks and sounds like.

In truth, of course, all in the campaign shared responsibility for the loss, and in view of my position in the campaign, my share was greatest. There are no mulligans in campaigns, but I've sometimes wished for a "do-over" on some of our decisions. Still, we did our best as we understood it at the time. We just lost, and losing is not easy.

In the aftermath, emotions were raw. Some critical words indirectly came my way, primarily over whether I should have done more talk shows and interviews. By one account I was "the invisible man." Maybe I should have been more public and out front. All I can say is that at the time, as I've written above, the president and I discussed the issue more than once and we both believed that it would be better for me to say less and him to say more.

Fortunately, time helps heal the pain of losing. George and I and our families are bound by a lifetime of deep friendship. These days, he, Barbara, Susan, and I enjoy time together on the golf course, hunting quail, or just remembering old times. As I write, Susan and I have just returned from visiting them in Kennebunkport.

On January 20, 1993, William Jefferson Clinton was inaugurated as our nation's forty-second president. That morning, Susan and I joined George, Barbara, the Quayles, and a few others for one last time in the Blue Room. I had already cleaned out my White House office. Bill and Hillary Clinton and the Gores soon dropped in for the traditional pre-inaugural coffee. Hillary assured me that the new administration was determined to work with Republicans. We then rode in a motorcade to the Capitol for the peaceful transition of power that is the hallmark of our great democracy. After the ceremony, Susan and I joined George, Barbara, and other Bush friends and staffers on Air

Force One for the flight back to Texas and a welcome-home rally at the airport.

We were all sad and weary. The initial pain of seeing my friend lose the presidency—like being hit in the stomach with a baseball bat—had now dulled a bit. Between election day and inauguration day, we had all adjusted to the new reality. What might have been was not to be.

For me, the excitement and responsibility of public service began to slip away shortly after the election. I still attended to my duties, but fatigue settled deep into my bones. I'm sure George went through the same experience on some levels. Truth be told, I also felt an enormous sense of relief. After running for attorney general of Texas, leading five presidential campaigns, serving four years-plus as White House chief of staff, and serving almost four years each as secretary of the treasury and secretary of state, I was simply worn out.

Soon after the election, Vernon Jordan came by my home to discuss the transition. Twelve years later, he and I would negotiate the terms of the 2004 presidential debates between President George W. Bush and Senator John Kerry. Warren Christopher headed the Clinton transition team, and I worked with him to achieve a smooth handoff. In a twist of history, Chris would soon be appointed secretary of state, then of course we would meet again in Florida in November 2000.

Unlike many of my colleagues in the Reagan administration, I never got Potomac fever. My view is, when it's over, it's over, and the best place to go is back home. D.C. is a wonderful place to live when you're in power, but it's a one-industry town and, for me at least, not a particularly good place to live when you're out of power. Susan and I remained in Washington until Mary Bonner graduated from National Cathedral School, but there was never any doubt that we would come home for good after she got her diploma.

Still, what a grand experience it all was! The only thing I miss is not having had another four years as secretary of state. I think we could have accomplished a lot that did not get accomplished. For one thing, my good friend Yitzhak Rabin was elected prime minister of Israel in June 1992. I would like to have worked with him to promote peace between Arabs and Israelis.

Sadness and weariness were natural as our time in office came to an end, but George was not one to mope, and neither was I. We were going home to Texas, to families and friends, to new opportunities and responsibilities. George would soon turn to the important work of setting up his presidential library, writing about some aspects of his public life, and pursuing a long-deferred dream—skydiving.

As for me, I had a few plans of my own.

FIFTEEN

"I DON'T MISS WASHINGTON"

BY THE CALENDAR, presidential transitions occur in the fall and winter. For the triumphant administrations-in-waiting, however, it always feels like springtime. The air is sweet with enthusiasm and ideas. Profiles of top executive branch nominees bloom like flowers on fertile newsprint. Rivers of wisdom flow from the high peaks of the big talk shows.

Almost unnoticed in all the excitement, at least when the White House changes hands from one party to the other, is the operation of an iron law of politics: for each high-spirited newcomer, one weary officeholder from the outgoing administration is packing files and memories in cardboard boxes, saying goodbye to colleagues and power, and looking for a new job. In late 1992, one of those weary officeholders was me.

I would soon be sixty-three, and my first project would be to repair the family finances. I had spent my prime years, so far at least, on a government payroll. Susan and I were certainly well-off when we came to Washington in 1981, but not, contrary to popular belief, extremely wealthy. Over twelve years, we had seriously tapped our family savings to pay living expenses and educate children. To top it off, Mary Bonner was still at home working on her SATs and college applications.

Finances were not the only consideration. I also had an obligation to history, I thought, to write a diplomatic memoir. In addition, Rice University had a proposal that deserved serious consideration. At a personal level, my wonderful family needed attention. Our children had grown up and moved away while, too often, I was not at home. Now I had grandchildren to spoil, with more to come. In my closets were golf clubs, hunting paraphernalia, and fishing equipment to dust off and put to their natural and intended uses. And lurking in the back reaches of my mind was the idea that maybe, just maybe, I had one more presidential campaign in me, this one for myself.

But first I needed to find work. Offers came almost immediately. They always do for high public officials who leave office. Multinational banks, major law firms, and Fortune 500 companies today operate in global markets, subject to the laws, regulations, and taxes of many nations, and vulnerable to disruptions—some swift, others slow-moving—in their economic and geopolitical environments. Cabinet officers and other top officials generally have useful experience in steering through these heavy currents.

Some prospective employers wanted me to stay in Washington and lobby our government. This was definitely out. The decision to return to Houston was unshakable, and I long ago had decided I would never lobby on policy, personnel, or anything else. A former high-ranking Republican senator had showed up in my office at Treasury one day with a client in tow who wanted permission for his company to do business with Libya at a time when that was a definite no-no. It was not a happy experience. I respect the decisions of others to take offices on K Street, but it was not for me.

When the right opportunity finally knocked, fortunately, I found Bill Barnett of Houston on the other side of the door. We had met at the University of Texas School of Law in the mid-fifties. Thanks to the alphabetic seating chart, he and I were near neighbors in the class-room. Together, we sweated out the dreaded calls to recite cases.* Bill and I became friends and later worked together on the law review.

Now, more than thirty-five years later, Bill was one of the first visi-tors to my White House office after the November election. Thanks to his talent, hard work, and integrity, he was one of the most highly re-spected attorneys in Houston. More to the point, he was also managing partner of the law firm, today known as Baker Botts, that my great-grandfather James Addison Baker had helped build more than a cen-tury earlier. That's where the "Baker" in the firm name came from. Both my grandfather (Captain James Addison Baker) and father (James Ad-dison Baker, Jr.) had worked there, and my son, Jamie (James Addison Baker, IV), was now a partner. After law school, I would have joined the firm myself, but fortunately, as I've written, the firm's nepotism policy blocked my path back then.

Bill proposed that I enter the firm all these years later as senior partner. Even though Jamie was there, nepotism was no longer a prob-lem. Either Baker Botts had decided that the policy ran downhill, not uphill or—more likely, perhaps—determined that it did not apply to former secretaries of state. I had other offers, of course. Al Ebert and John Cabaniss, two old friends, invited me to return to Andrews Kurth, the respected Houston firm I joined immediately after law school. In 1976, I had refused an earlier job offer from Baker Botts because An-drews Kurth had been so good to me and because a lot of my contem-poraries still practiced there. By 1992, however, most of them had moved on. Other major firms from New York, Washington, and Hous-ton also came to see me. But Bill offered something none of the others could ever match—an opportunity to have my ticket punched at the one law firm that carried my family's DNA.

---

*"And now, Mr. Baker, Mr. James . . . Addison . . . Baker . . . the . . . Third, please recite the facts of *Ghen v. Rich*, the issue presented, and the holding." I had been in the Marine Corps, but when my property law professor, Corwin Johnson, a former FBI agent, called my name, I felt more like a mouse tied to a cat by a very short string.

For decades, Baker Botts had been a strong regional law firm, primarily serving local banks, railroads, and energy companies. In recent years it had gone national, with offices in New York, Washington, and elsewhere. The firm was now building a strong international presence. In part, this was to serve the energy companies in Houston as they fanned around the globe to search for oil and gas, but Baker Botts was also finding new clients overseas. The liberalization and integration of the world economy created a demand for American lawyers, and the firm had positioned itself to compete for the work.

I told Bill I would not lobby, draft legal documents, handle routine business negotiations, or serve on the management committee. "I have managed everything I ever want to manage," I said.

No problem, Bill replied. My role would be that of a graybeard, a special resource, an adviser to the firm and its clients on big or unique problems. As I write, for instance, I am overseeing an investigation— called for by a federal agency—into safety issues at a large energy company in the refining business. I have also corresponded occasionally with foreign governments to sort out controversies involving Baker Botts clients in those countries. Sometimes my letters help; sometimes they don't. (My no-lobbying rule does not apply to foreign governments.) I do advise the firm's lawyers and clients on strategies for dealing with Washington, but I never lobby our federal government on their behalf. In some ways, I have served much the same function at the firm that my great-grandfather, the first James Addison Baker, did late in his career. Even after he withdrew from active practice, it was later written, "his judgment was relied on." One more point: when Baker Botts recruited me, it did not go unnoticed, obviously, that my presence at the firm might help attract new clients.

There is also a tradition among big law firms of supplying candidates as directors for important clients, and I agreed to serve on the boards of two public companies. Why so few? Because being a director of a public corporation today is time-consuming work and carries weighty responsibilities. Too many former public figures overload themselves with board appointments, and I did not want to make that mistake. I no longer serve on the two boards I accepted, but to this day I am still fending off a lawsuit in which I am a defendant just by virtue of once having been a board member. This is something that, unfortunately, goes with the territory in today's litigious society.

Baker Botts gave me two offices, one in Washington and one in Houston, each staffed with two assistants. Until Mary Bonner graduated from National Cathedral School in 1994, Susan and I kept a home in Washington, and I worked primarily at the D.C. office, where I was assisted by Bridget Montagne, who had worked for George H. W. Bush when he was president, and Caron Jackson. In recent years, however, I have spent most of my time in Houston.

My able executive assistant in the Houston office today is Charlotte Cheadle. The two sides of her personality are symbolized by her size (small) and her dog (a rottweiler). Ninety-nine-point-nine percent of my callers, correspondents, and office visitors—the polite and reasonable ones—deal with Ms. Petite, a modern Texas woman. When I hear that unmistakable low growl from the direction of her desk, however, I know she is talking to the other one tenth of one percent. I'm happy to report, though, that she hasn't bitten anyone yet.

Now let me do a little growling myself. The practice of law today is very different from when I started. Computers, instant communications, and overnight deliveries changed everything, generally for the better. I remember going to the office with my dad in the forties and fifties, and watching his secretaries—first Mollie Jones, then Virginia Cooper—bang out long real estate contracts on a manual typewriter, with carbon paper for the copies. In my early years of practice, we had electric typewriters, but everything else was about the same.

Not all the changes since then are so welcome, however. The practice of law today has to a large extent ceased to be a true profession and become a business. It has to be that way, I suppose, when firms are so big and far-flung that the partners in New York, say, may not even know those in Hong Kong.

But firm size is not the only factor in the decline of professionalism. I blame greed, advertising, and the almost-total breakdown of respect, even in the courts, for lawyer-client confidentiality. Attorneys have special responsibilities to their profession that should always transcend the contract, case, or controversy at hand—responsibilities such as truthfulness, loyalty to clients, respect for law, and a common code of ethics. One of the great pleasures of my time at Baker Botts has been to work with lawyers, young and old, who still think the way I do.

One more rule I laid down before joining Baker Botts was that I would never keep or report hours, even though for most attorneys that is probably a necessary evil of practicing law. When I showed up for work on my first day, however, Jamie escorted me to my office, and there on my pristine desk was one equally pristine copy of the red, hardbound timekeeping diary the firm issues to new lawyers.

I opened it to March 12 and made two entries: "9:00 A.M., arrived for first day at Baker Botts, found time book on desk; 9:12 A.M., resigned from Baker Botts." Then I sent it to Jamie.

The book was a joke, of course, and so was my resignation. My years at Baker Botts have been satisfying beyond measure, personally and professionally. I hope and believe I have repaid the favor of being invited into the firm.

ANOTHER FINANCIAL opportunity was the Carlyle Group, now one of the world's largest private equity firms. Back in 1992, however, the five-year-old D.C.-based outfit was much smaller. In fact, when David Rubenstein, Bill Conway, and Steve Norris came to see me after the election, their goal was to create a fund of $100 million. They thought I might be able to help. Today the firm manages more than $30 billion and operates out of offices on three continents.

I had never met the Carlyle executives before, but two friends of mine who had worked with David Rubenstein in the Carter White

House said they were good guys. One endorsement came from Bernie Aronson, a former speechwriter for President Carter, later assistant secretary of state for inter-American affairs while I was secretary of state. Another was from Bob Strauss, a longtime eminence in the Democratic Party, but also a good friend of mine and the president's, who had served in the Bush administration as ambassador in Moscow.

Carlyle raises money from what it calls "high net worth individuals" (in plainer English, very wealthy people) and from private institutional investors, including large pension funds. The firm then invests that money in going concerns, start-up ventures, real estate, and the like. In most cases, it acquires a majority interest in the target companies. Carlyle is private, so it does not publish its results, which vary from investment to investment. Overall, however, the firm has been extraordinarily successful in generating good returns for its investors.

I agreed to become senior counselor to Carlyle, a post I held until my retirement in April 2005 at age seventy-five. As with Baker Botts, I set boundaries, particularly about lobbying, and I refused to solicit funds directly from potential investors. Typically I would be asked to speak to groups invited by Carlyle—usually at an overseas conference, sometimes in the United States—about economic, political, or geopolitical issues. Later, Carlyle representatives would pitch the invitees on investment opportunities at the firm. I also advised Carlyle on international business and political issues and, in some cases, introduced the firm to key figures in the countries where it wished to do business.

Carlyle promised it would never do anything to embarrass me, and it never did, except once. When I was serving as President George W. Bush's special envoy on debt relief for Iraq, a Carlyle representative— unbeknownst to me—was apparently talking to the Kuwaitis about engaging a consortium of Carlyle and other firms to help collect and manage the reparations owed to Kuwait by Iraq. That was improper. When I first heard about it, I called David Rubenstein, and the proposal was dropped almost before the sun went down.

The best evidence of my continuing respect for Carlyle is that, even though I am probably still dollars short of most of the other high-net-worth individuals who invest with the firm, I still commit investment dollars there when I can.

About the same time, I also signed up with the Washington Speakers Bureau to handle my public appearances. Like me, most folks on the circuit are "formers"—former public officials, former business executives, formers from the worlds of sports and entertainment. But personalities from the news media often hit the road while they still have day jobs on television or in print. I figured speaking was something that should be done soon, because name recognition usually decays rapidly for public figures who are not regularly in the news. Susan said I needn't worry about that, however, because my experience enabled me to speak on numerous topics—politics, foreign policy, economic policy, and public service.

In a way, we were each partly right. More than thirteen years after I left full-time public service, I still get quite a few speaking invitations, though fewer than in years past. The honoraria are still generous, and welcome, and speaking to interested people about interesting topics is not a hard way to earn a living. Still, I am not sure I would go as far as Jack Kemp, the 1996 GOP vice presidential candidate, who once nicknamed it "white collar crime."

Another opportunity came eight years after I left Washington. Despite my general reluctance to serve on corporate boards, I made an exception in 2001 for the privately held King Ranch, a Texas legend.

At first I declined. "I don't do boards," I said when Julia Jitkoff first approached me. Julia is a longtime friend, a talented painter and sculptor, a descendant of the ranch's founder, Captain Richard King, and—as I soon learned—a gifted recruiter.

"Would it make any difference if I told you that directors have the same rights to hunt on the ranch that family members do?" she replied.

Asking a hunter if he would enjoy access to the King Ranch is like asking an art lover if he wants a key to the Metropolitan Museum. At almost 900,000 acres, the ranch is larger than Rhode Island. The experience of hunting there is as close as possible to what Spanish and Anglo pioneers might have enjoyed centuries ago, and Native Americans before that.

"Where do I sign up?" I asked.

I also agreed over the years to serve on a number of nonprofit boards. Both Princeton University, my alma mater, and Rice University invited me to serve as trustee. (I would be the second James A. Baker on the Rice board, after my grandfather, Captain Baker.) I have also served on boards or held honorary positions at Howard Hughes Medical Institute in Chevy Chase, Maryland, and St. Luke's Hospital and the M.D. Anderson Cancer Center in Houston.

Early on, I also signed up—briefly—with Enron, but not as a board member. It was the hottest energy company in town, perhaps in the country, when I returned to Houston, and Ken Lay recruited Bob Mosbacher and me as consultants. Susan thought it was a really bad idea, but after thirteen and one-half full years and three part-time years in politics and public service, we needed to make some money, so I accepted anyway. I helped write a few reports and occasionally met with company officers about international projects they were trying to win.

It was an underwhelming experience. I remember telling both Susan and Mosbacher after about six months, "I just don't understand how this company works." What threw me was seeing the present value of a long-term power contract posted as current earnings when the contract was signed and before either party had even begun to perform. "It doesn't seem to me there's any way to grow the company except to keep putting these kinds of deals on the books," I said. Another problem was that corporate executives won big bonuses by signing these contracts, regardless of whether the transactions were good or bad for the company. My misgivings never crystalized into a clear understanding of the troubles that lay ahead, much less their magnitude. Still, I was not unhappy when my relationship with Enron ended by mutual agreement after two years, in February 1995.

. . .

In my spare time, I wrote a book.

President Bush's and my primary responsibility in office was to see that the Cold War ended without bloodshed and left behind a world that was peaceful, prosperous, stable, and congenial to U.S. interests. We succeeded. My obligation out of office, I believed, was to create a detailed and accurate record of what happened, for the benefit of historians, public officials, journalists, and other interested readers.

I started my research on *The Politics of Diplomacy* shortly after I left government, and the book was published in the early fall of 1995. It was hard work. I've done my share of writing over the years—in school, in law, in politics and public service, in columns and speeches, and for a while after leaving office as a columnist for the *Los Angeles Times* Syndicate—but long-form composition was more demanding than anything I had ever done before. It gave me a new respect for those who scribble, scribble, scribble for a living.

I wanted to put down in black and white exactly what happened during my tenure as secretary of state, as gleaned from contemporaneous records. Writing everything, immediately and in detail, would head off later revisionism, I thought. My first priority was to create a historical record; my second, to sell books—an approach that undoubtedly caused heartburn for my publisher. I had a lot of help with the project, of course, from many individuals, all of whom are credited in the book.

The Politics of Diplomacy was reasonably well received by academics and the foreign policy establishment, but was not—I am sorry to say—wildly popular with general readers. In my desire to create a complete record of those tumultuous years, the book grew and grew, to 672 pages. That may be why one hardback printing satisfied the demand for the book, which can be found today in most full-service libraries. Previously owned copies, to borrow a euphemism from the used-car business, are also available in specialty bookstores and on the Internet.

I'm sorry *The Politics of Diplomacy* was not a best seller, but I'm very proud of it, nonetheless. It testifies to the vindication of American leadership under both Democrats and Republicans, beginning after World War II with Dean Acheson's generation and climaxing four decades later with mine. It tells how to effectively organize the foreign and security policy apparatus of the United States government. And of the liberation of hundreds of millions of men, women, and children in Eastern Europe and Central Asia; of the triumph of democracy, free markets, and the rule of law; of the dramatic and peaceful end of the superpower nuclear threat; and of freedom for Kuwait and new hopes for peace in the Middle East. And at a personal level, *The Politics of Diplomacy* is also one man's testimony to the privilege of having served as our nation's secretary of state in a time of war, revolution, and peace.

ANOTHER PROJECT, an unexpected one, also presented itself as I prepared to leave office. Charles Duncan, then chairman of the Rice University board of governors, and George Rupp, president of the university, asked to see me. This was November 1992, about the same time that Bill Barnett was talking to me about joining Baker Botts. "We are thinking about setting up a public policy institute bearing your name at Rice University," they said. "Would you have any problem with that?" Political science professor Ric Stoll had come up with the idea, they said, and the board and president liked it.

So did I. What an honor! After all, my grandfather, Captain James A. Baker, had been instrumental in founding Rice University. He drafted the school's charter, then famously proved that a devious butler and crooked lawyer had murdered William Marsh Rice in hopes of taking his estate under a forged will. Rice's money was used as an endowment to set up what was then called the Rice Institute. For the first fifty years, Captain Baker was chairman of the board at Rice, and one of the university's residential colleges is named for him. Now the Baker legacy at Rice would be extended in a new and unexpected direction, and today many Rice faculty are engaged in the institute's public policy research and programs.

I had no problem with the idea, but I did have two conditions. One was that I not be asked to raise the money. (In time I expected to be asked to help with fund-raising, and I was. I just did not want to be obligated to say yes.) The other was that the institute not grant degrees. This was Dick Darman's suggestion. By offering a master's degree in public policy, say, the institute could soon be expected to get crossways with other elements of the university over money, professors, courses, space, and prestige. By standing outside the formal academic process, however, the institute could work cooperatively, not competitively, with the Rice faculty and university administration. And that is exactly how things have worked out, I am happy to say. We are seen to be an integral part of Rice University.

In a speech on March 31, 1993, I laid out my vision for the institute— to "draw together statesmen, scholars, and students" and to "build a bridge between the world of ideas and the world of action." (Those words would later be inscribed on the north face of the building that today houses the James A. Baker III Institute for Public Policy.)

Charles Duncan made an extraordinarily generous cornerstone gift, and thanks to the support of friends of Rice University (and mine) around the nation and the world, we soon had enough money for a building, a staff, and our first research fellows. Our original goal was $30 million, and to date we have raised more than $75 million. Space does not permit me to list our donors, but their names are written on my heart.

We broke ground for the building in October 1994. All four former U.S. presidents participated in the ceremony—Gerald Ford and George H. W. Bush (in person), Jimmy Carter (by teleconference hookup), and Ronald Reagan (by taped message). As far as I know, this was the last time President Reagan ever spoke in public.

James A. Baker III Hall was dedicated in 1997. I am biased, of course, but to me it is far and away the most beautiful building on a very beautiful campus. The style echoes the Italian Renaissance, with Byzantine elements and other features from the eastern Mediterranean. Administrative and academic offices are arranged around a central commons that extends upward three stories to a skylighted roof. The commons seats about four hundred for speeches and conferences. Our international conference center seats another 130 and offers state-of-the-art communications equipment for simultaneous translations and broadcasts over the Web or by television.

The institute will continue to thrive after I pass from the scene, I believe, because of the quality of its work, its nonpartisan spirit, its strong base of financial support, and—most of all—its association with a world-class university. We now have fifteen endowed fellowships, most from the world of action, others from academia. Our fellows have included the former head of Israeli military intelligence and the former head of NASA. Most important, however, our scholarship and recommendations on domestic and foreign policy are widely respected.

Founding Director Edward P. Djerejian deserves enormous credit for our success. Before being recruited by our search committee, he served thirty-three years in the foreign service, including stints as assistant secretary of state for the Near East and ambassador to Syria, both while I was secretary of state, and ambassador to Israel under President Clinton. Besides his leadership of the institute and its first-class staff, he is an authority in his own right on Mideast policy, and particularly on Arab-Israeli relations and our nation's public diplomacy in the region.

Ed's wife, Françoise Djerejian, has drawn on her longtime experience as the spouse of a career diplomat in making many essential contributions to the institute's success, including serving as its de facto curator. And she has done it all with her usual quiet elegance.

IN THE FIRST YEARS after leaving public service, I was obviously very busy working at Baker Botts and Carlyle, writing the book, starting the Baker Institute, and handling the other projects I have mentioned. Because of this activity and the fact that I was pretty well worn out by my thirteen years in politics and government service, I did not find the transition from public figure to private citizen to be all that difficult. Coming home was, in fact, quite enjoyable. I did what I wanted to do, when I wanted to do it, and I no longer had to open the papers first thing every morning to see what nasty things were being said about me or my president.

I never regretted being out of the political centrifuge, which continued to spin quite nicely, I noticed, without any help from me. My only real regret is about what was *not* accomplished—some things, particularly in foreign policy, we might have gotten done with another term. I treasure my opportunities to serve this wonderful country of ours, but I don't miss Washington, and I don't miss being in government.

FOR TWO OR THREE YEARS, my name popped up regularly on talk shows and in newspaper stories and columns about the 1996 presidential race. And the fact of the matter is, I thought very seriously about running.

There is a certain audacity in imagining yourself in the Oval Office, but audacity, if we're honest, is one of the job requirements. There were a lot of entries on the positive side of the ledger. I had the résumé. I knew how our government worked. And I knew the job of the presidency about as well as it can be known without ever having held the office. I also had gotten along well with representatives, senators, foreign heads of state and government, and many in the media.

Having led five presidential campaigns, I also knew politics firsthand. My name identification was way up in the eighties, and my approval/disapproval numbers were strong. I am pretty sure I could have raised the money. I had many friends around the country, thanks to my work with the five campaigns and my service to three presidents. The 1996 GOP primaries were certain to be contested, but I enjoy competition.

But there were a lot of negatives, too. I was still dog tired. As my strength and spirits returned, I invested them heavily in the projects I have mentioned, and I was happy. Day by day, the idea of exposing myself to the rigors of a campaign for president became more and more unattractive.

Serious candidates in an open race for the nomination must start work at least two years ahead of election year. For me, that would have meant beginning in January 1994, just one year after having left office. Hello, Iowa and New Hampshire. Hello, living out of suitcases on the road. Hello, rubber-chicken dinners and nonstop events. I just wasn't ready for that.

Then, too, I would be sixty-six in 1996. Presidents Reagan (sixty-nine when he took office) and Bush (sixty-four) showed that senior citizens can run and win, but they had both run before (Reagan more than once), and George was a two-term vice president. Presidential politics is really more of a young man's game (and someday soon, I'm sure, a young woman's). President George W. Bush was sworn in at fifty-four, Clinton at forty-six, Carter at fifty-two. You've got to really want it, to have that legendary "fire in the belly." I didn't. As a rule, running for president is just not something a person does for the first time when he's already eligible for Social Security.

The best thing to say about any presidential ambition on my part is this: for two years, I did not rule out the possibility, but I also never really pushed the start button. Campaigning for the White House was something to think about, not a plan and certainly not an obsession. Even when I was out campaigning for GOP candidates in the fall of 1994, the buzz from those who would have supported me was I probably wouldn't run myself. Susan and I talked about it often, and I discussed it with a number of other friends and advisers. In the end, we just concluded it was not something we wanted to do.

Could I have won? Who knows? If I had run, I would have run hard, but I'm not sure I could have defeated Senator Bob Dole in the primaries. And even if I had captured the Republican nomination,

President Clinton would have been hard to beat. A corollary of the rule I mentioned earlier—about how rare it is for one party to maintain control of the White House longer than eight years—is that history shows that it is equally difficult to unseat a sitting president after only four years.

While the GOP sweep of the 1994 midterm elections exposed President Clinton's vulnerabilities, the nation in 1996 was prosperous and largely at peace. The federal deficit was also declining, thanks to the post–Cold War peace dividend, congressional budget discipline (which, sadly, has since evaporated), and the continuation of the economic boom that began in November 1982 and was fueled in the 1990s by the liberalization of the world economy. President Clinton's personal troubles still lay ahead, and he was, as I've said, a gifted politician. He easily won reelection against Bob Dole.

Let me say here that my relationship with President Clinton has always been cordial and respectful. In his first term, he invited me to speak in the East Room with him, President Carter, and Secretary Kissinger, in the final push to win congressional support for the North American Free Trade Agreement. I also helped his administration win ratification of the Chemical Weapons Convention, which our administration had negotiated. In 1995, President Clinton invited me to be a member of the official American delegation to the funeral of Yitzhak Rabin, but I had just had back surgery and could not fly. Later, however, I flew with President Clinton on Air Force One to attend the funeral of King Hassan II of Morocco. For some time, the former chief executive has had a standing invitation to speak at the Baker Institute.

I am not given to regrets about things political, and today I have no regrets about not having run for president. Susan and I just decided against doing that at our age and stage in life. I did try to help Bob Dole's campaign, first by giving a political foreign policy speech with a little red meat in it at the 1996 GOP National Convention in San Diego, and later by consulting with Bob and his running mate, Jack Kemp, about debate strategy.

My decision not to run for president liberated me. I would never again return to full-time government service, but if the telephone were to ring with other opportunities for public service, I would now be more available to listen.

And, indeed, the telephone did ring.

KOFI ANNAN, secretary-general of the United Nations, called in 1997. "Would you be willing to help us with the conflict over Western Sahara?" he asked.

Western Sahara is the last decolonization issue on the UN docket. When Europe carved up Africa in the nineteenth century, Spain claimed this territory on the northwest coast of the continent, which became known as Spanish Sahara. It is a desert, about the size of Wyoming, and originally peopled by the Sahrawis—once-nomadic Arabs and Berbers.

After decades of conflict and pressure by the UN, Spain withdrew in 1975. Neighboring Morocco from the north and Mauritania from the south quickly claimed the territory. The International Court of Justice, while it recognized that both protagonists had claims that did not affect the decolonization of the territory or the principle of self-determination, failed to settle the issue of sovereignty. Mauritania pulled out under pressure in 1979, leaving Morocco in possession, but in a running battle with a Sahrawi group and government-in-exile known as Frente Polisario.

The UN brokered a cease-fire in September 1991 under a settlement plan designed to lead to a referendum of self-determination that would allow the people of Western Sahara to choose between integration with Morocco or independence. The cease-fire, however, left thousands of Sahrawis in Algerian refugee camps, both sides holding prisoners of war, and the Polisario awaiting the promised referendum. For six years, little progress had been made, Kofi said, but the parties might finally be ready for some kind of resolution. What was needed, he said, was an experienced mediator to help them. As U.S. secretary of state, I had helped resolve international disputes, and I felt an obligation to try to use that experience in this conflict.

I signed on as an unpaid volunteer. Kofi named me as his personal envoy, won the support of the Security Council, and backed the project with all necessary resources, including the help of the undersecretary-generals in charge of political affairs and peacekeeping, and of Anna Theofilopoulou, a UN senior political officer with expertise in this issue. For the next seven years, we worked to find a political solution to give the people of Western Sahara a shot at self-determination.

I first met privately with the government of Morocco, the Polisario, and two other interested parties, Algeria and Mauritania, then arranged a number of meetings of those four parties, the first in June 1997. In all, we met fourteen times on three continents.

I also toured the region several times and developed a real sympathy for the humanitarian costs of this frozen-in-time conflict. Despite the harsh conditions in which they lived, the Sahrawi people had exercised a degree of democracy, maintained a high literacy rate, and never resorted to terrorism. At the same time, my relations with Morocco had always been good, going all the way back to the 1980s when, as treasury secretary, I assisted King Hassan in obtaining satellite photography to help in building a huge sand wall, or berm, as part of Morocco's military efforts against the Polisario.

As the years passed, however, my frustration grew. There were small victories—persuading the parties to talk face-to-face; winning the release of some prisoners of war; resuming efforts to develop a voter list; and maintaining the UN-monitored cease-fire—but never any real progress on the big issues. The animosity and mistrust were too great, and both parties had a winner-take-all mentality that ruled out compromise. More often than not, my requests for new proposals or comments from the parties were met with silence, reiteration of their hardened positions, or harsh rhetoric. As long as I saw any hope, however, I stuck with it, working through one failed approach after another.

Toward the end, the Security Council voted 15–0 to support a "Peace Plan for Self-Determination for the People of Western Sahara" that I had crafted in response to the Council's earlier request that I make one last effort to develop a political solution that provided for self-determination. It called for a transitional period of limited autonomy for Western Sahara. Morocco would retain military authority and control of foreign policy, and its flag would still fly over Western Sahara. After an appropriate number of years, the United Nations would conduct a referendum, with the electorate being all bona fide residents of Western Sahara, not just those covered by the ancient Spanish census (the proposed electorate under the 1991 settlement plan) or the voter list developed by the UN. This would have given a voice to all Moroccans who had moved into Western Sahara during the occupation.

Surprisingly, even that plan was not acceptable to Morocco. It had won the war, occupied the territory, and suffered few if any negative consequences for having done so. Why should it agree to anything? The answer, which Morocco continues to reject, is that unless it finds some way to resolve the issue, it will never receive the imprimatur of international legitimacy for its occupation of Western Sahara. Fortunately for Morocco, however, and unfortunately for many Sahrawis, this conflict involves a remote and barren land, and a small group of very poor people. As a result, the dispute has never really engaged the attention of a busy world, and very few countries are willing to use up any political chits to help settle it.

"The UN will never solve the problem of Western Sahara without requiring that one, or the other, or both of the parties do something they do not wish to voluntarily agree to do," I told the Security Council more than once. Despite the continuing impasse, however, the Security Council was never willing to move beyond calling for settlement to be based on a never-yet-achieved consensus of the parties.

I kept at it until 2004, then resigned. I had given it my best shot and it now was time to give someone else a chance. I still think often of the people in the camps—victims of forces beyond their control, never returning home, largely forgotten—and of many others living unhappily under occupation in Western Sahara itself.

IN 1998, George W. Bush won a landslide second term as governor of Texas. I had known him since he was maybe twelve or thirteen years old, when his family moved to Houston and I began to play tennis with his father. I always liked him, but I wouldn't have taken a bet in the late fifties or early sixties that he might ever be a governor, much less a candidate for president. (Heck, I wouldn't have taken a bet at that time that his father would ever be president.) Almost four decades later, however, it made perfect sense.

In the old days, the Bush and Baker families often got together after Thanksgiving lunch. The two dads, George's four boys (George W., Jeb, Marvin, and Neil) and my four (Jamie, Mike, John, and Doug) would repair to a vacant lot at the end of Greentree Road in Houston to play what we called the Turkey Bowl. It was touch football, but the touching sometimes looked a lot like tackling.

It's no secret by now that George W. was the cutup in the Bush family. His younger brother Jeb was always more serious. Many of us thought that maybe, just maybe, Jeb would be the one to carry on the Bush family tradition in politics.

In 1978, George W. and I both decided to run for public office: I for attorney general of Texas, he for Congress from a large West Texas district that included his childhood home, Midland. We both lost, of course, but the experience would later prove useful for both of us.

George W. ran that year against Kent Hance, a conservative Democrat, who would later become one of the congressional Boll Weevils who supported President Reagan's 1981 tax and spending cuts. Hance won by painting George as an Eastern establishment kind of guy, someone who had actually attended—gasp!—Yale University. It's hard to explain Whiffenpoofs and Skull and Bones to Texas rednecks.

George W. took this as a lesson about maintaining his roots, and he would never again be out-Texaned. Although he was born in New Haven while his father attended college there after World War II, young George spent his childhood in Midland, a wild and woolly oil town, and absorbed the spirit of his home state in his bones.

In the 1980s, George W. took a more active interest in his father's campaigns and became a sort of enforcer. He got to be good friends with Lee Atwater, his father's campaign manager in the 1988 primaries. When the vice president asked me to come over to run the general election campaign, Lee was distraught. He took it as a demotion, a downgrading of his role. George W. helped me persuade him that it was for the best—that my friendship and prior experiences with the candidate would help the campaign and that I would respect Lee's position in the campaign. And I did. Lee came to all my morning meetings and played a very important role. George W. was not directly involved in the day-to-day decisions or the overall strategy. It later became clear to me, however, that he was keeping up, absorbing what was going on, and developing a political acumen of his own.

At some point during this period, George W. had turned his life around. By then, he had a wonderful wife, Laura, and two beautiful daughters. He quit drinking, started attending Bible classes, and became much more serious about his family, business, politics, and life in general. I sensed that something was different, but I was not around him much and might have been slow to recognize the full implications. I don't recall discussing this development with his father or mother.

Others may be cynical, but to me, George W. Bush is living testimony of the power of faith to change lives. He went on to serve as managing partner for an investor group that bought the Texas Rangers baseball team and did a good job building a new stadium and upgrading the team (although I'm sure he'll always regret trading Sammy Sosa).

In 1994, George W. ran for governor against Ann Richards, the salty Democrat who made the famous crack at the Democratic Convention in 1988 about father George's being born "with a silver foot in his mouth." Even though Texas was known to be trending Republican, few commentators thought George W. stood much of a chance against a reasonably popular sitting governor.

We had a big fund-raiser for him in Houston. I had just gotten out of public service myself, and people were still talking about me as a possible presidential candidate, so I was a pretty good draw. We raised a lot of money. George W. went on to beat Governor Richards, 53–46 percent, in an extremely well-run campaign.

His big three advisers were Karl Rove, the campaign strategist; Karen Hughes, his communications director; and Joe Allbaugh, his campaign manager. I didn't know Karen or Joe at the time, but Karl and Margaret Tutwiler were the first two people I hired for the political action committee I set up in 1979 as a vehicle for George H. W. Bush's pre-campaign activities. Karl left to work for the Republican Party about the time we folded that committee into the 1980 presidential primary campaign, and I had little contact with him again until 1994. By then, he had mastered Texas politics and become the go-to Republican political consultant in the state.

George W. did a great job as governor, especially on taxes (he cut them), crime (more money to fight drugs), welfare (work requirements), and education (more testing). Democrats still controlled the Texas legislature, and he developed a genuine friendship with legislative leaders from that party, Bob Bullock and Pete Laney. In 1998, he won reelection with 69 percent of the vote against a McGovern-style liberal.

When George W. started preparing for his possible presidential run, a steady stream of policy advisers, political consultants, and GOP heavyweights began flowing into Austin to test his intentions and offer advice and help. I was not among them, and that was okay with me.

"The reason you didn't see him in my campaign was not because of a family feud or anything," George W. said later. "It was more that we were trying to give the indication that we were moving forward in a way, away from my father's generation and into my own."

That's exactly what happened and exactly what should have happened. If he really wanted to be president, Governor Bush should not be seen as a clone of his father. That ruled me out for any public role, much less running the campaign or being seen as part of an administration-in-waiting. It was important that George W. be perceived as his own man, not as a stalking horse for a restoration of Bush I. We had had our turn. Now it was his.

George W.'s one exception was picking Dick Cheney, his dad's defense secretary, as his running mate. I knew and respected Dick and thought he was a very good pick. He was not seen as a Bush family loyalist in quite the same way I was, and was young enough to be considered more of George W.'s generation than his father's. Of course, he proved to be a good campaigner and a loyal and influential vice president.

I helped the campaign in modest ways, but quietly and for the most part privately. At different times, Don Evans, the governor's close friend, campaign chairman, and chief fund-raiser, and Joe Allbaugh—all six feet, four inches, and 275 pounds of him—came to see me in Houston to talk about organization and strategy. I also did a couple of small fund-raisers, one in Alaska.

What did I think about the campaign? Well, Bush-Cheney ran a good one. The only mistake, I think, was spending the last few days in California, which they really never had a chance of winning, instead of, say, Florida. But twenty-twenty hindsight is a luxury reserved for the aftermath of a campaign, not something that is ever available in real time.

Gore-Lieberman had a lot of trouble getting organized, but from the convention on it also did a pretty good job. Vice President Gore's biggest mistake, I thought, was in distancing himself too far from the president. Bill Clinton might have helped Gore win in a number of states, any one of which could have given him the electoral votes he needed to win.

In general, however, I was just a bystander in 2000. I told George W. Bush I would do what I could to help, but it would not have been good for him if I had had a major role in the campaign.

. . .

ON ELECTION DAY, November 7, 2000, Susan and I camped out in Austin's Four Seasons Hotel, along with Dick and Lynne Cheney and several hundred other friends and family of the candidates. Early that evening, Susan and I watched television in the crowded hotel ballroom. A while later, a few of us— including, I think, Jack and Joanne Kemp, Trent and Tricia Lott, and Bob and Betsy Teeter—joined the Cheneys in their suite. From the beginning, it was clear that it would be a long night.

Dick was bone weary. Even as his fate was being sorted out in election counting rooms across the nation, he kept nodding. "Go take a nap," we finally said, and he gave up and slipped away to his bedroom. A restless George W. Bush and his family, including his father, were gathered in the governor's mansion a short distance away to watch election results and prepare for what might come.

Florida was the make-or-break state. A few minutes before 8:00 P.M. Eastern time—7:00 P.M. in Austin—the networks called Florida for Al Gore. There were two problems with this. First, people were still voting in the panhandle section of Florida. Second, it was not an accurate call.

The projections came from the Voter News Service, a consortium of the commercial and cable networks that conducted exit polls in each state, then fed the information into a computer model for that state. In past years, the projections had almost always been right, but Florida 2000 proved to be an exception. The Bush campaign quickly issued a statement quarreling with the call, and by 10:00 P.M. Eastern time, all networks had backed down and put the state back in the undecided column.

Finally, at 2:16 A.M. Eastern time, Fox News Channel called Florida for Bush, and the other networks quickly followed. A few minutes later, Vice President Gore telephoned Governor Bush to concede. That was the traditional signal that it was all over but the shouting, so Susan and I went back to our room, got our stuff, and headed down to the hotel lobby. Buses were lined up to take guests to the bunting-draped podium near the state capitol where Governor Bush would accept Gore's concession and address his own supporters and the nation.

But it was raining like hell, I had a terrible cold, and all Susan and I had for cover was one dinky umbrella. As much as I wanted to see the speech, I told Susan I didn't want to stand in the rain, so we decided to go back up to our room and watch the festivities on television.

As everyone knows by now, there was no public concession. While Al Gore was being driven to a rally in Nashville for the speech, aides told him the Bush lead in Florida was down to a few thousand votes and falling. He quickly telephoned George W. to retract his earlier private concession. "Our campaign continues," Gore's campaign chairman told the waiting crowd. Shortly afterward, the networks backed down once again. Too close to call, they said, finally getting it right. Florida was still in play.

That was one twist of the road farther than my seventy-year-old, fever-ridden body was willing to travel, so I gave up, went to bed, and fell asleep. It was a little after 3:00 A.M. local time, I think.

When I awoke a few hours later that morning, I felt a little bit better, but Florida and the election were still up in the air. Susan and I packed and flew back to Houston, as originally scheduled. As we drove into town from Hobby Airport, we told our driver to drop me at the office, then take Susan home. And that's when the cell telephone in the car rang. It was Don Evans. "If the governor asked you to go to Florida to represent him in the vote recount, would you be available?"

SIXTEEN

"GOOD EVENING, MR. PRESIDENT-ELECT"

I WAS IN the Bush-Cheney headquarters in Tallahassee, Florida, late on the night of Tuesday, December 12, 2000, when the United States Supreme Court handed down its decision in *Bush v. Gore*. The offices were filled with lawyers and staff members who had worked by my side since early November in the dispute over Florida's electoral votes. We anxiously jumped from channel to channel as reporters struggled to read the opinion on the air and figure out what it meant. Meanwhile, our lawyers flipped through their faxed copies of the document. The answer hit us all about the same time. What it meant was that five heart-stopping, up-and-down weeks of legal and political conflict in Florida were over.

A few minutes later, Governor George W. Bush called me from Austin, Texas, and I answered with a smile.

"Good evening, Mr. President-Elect."

Around me, the room exploded in cheers.

At some point, Don Evans's cell phone rang. The governor's long-time friend and campaign chairman had sweated out the Supreme Court watch with me in Tallahassee. "It's Big Time," Don said. "He wants to talk to you."

"Big Time" was George W.'s running mate, Dick Cheney. He had won his nickname at a campaign rally a few months earlier when, unaware that their mikes were open, George W. had leaned over and whispered to him that a *New York Times* reporter in the crowd was an "asshole." "Yeah, big time," Cheney replied.

"Jim, congratulations," said the vice president–elect and an old friend of mine. "Only under your leadership could we have gone from a lead of 1,800 votes to a lead of 150 votes."[*]

On his call, Governor Bush thanked me for helping him in Florida. It was a team effort, I replied. In turn, I thanked him for his leadership and confidence in me.

A bit more than five weeks later, the president-elect again showed his gratitude by seating Susan and me in very prominent seats on the platform for his inauguration (and later in the president's box on the parade route). When we arrived for the swearing-in, Secret Service agents whom we knew from the Reagan and first Bush administrations shook our hands and escorted us to our places.

As Susan and I waited, Vice President Gore and Tipper descended the aisle to their front-row seats.

"Hello," Tipper said cheerily to Susan.

She acknowledged me somewhat more coolly perhaps. "Oh, hello."

"Hi, Jim. How are you?" Al said more evenly.

"Fine, thank you, Mr. Vice President," I responded.

President and Senator Clinton soon followed. He stopped on the way down, motioned me from my seat just off the aisle, and whispered, "You were good in Florida. Really good."

After the ceremony, he stopped again. "I told those people that if they continued to play by the Marquess of Queensberry rules, you were gonna beat their brains out," he said sotto voce.

---

[*]Robert Zelnick's book *Winning Florida: How the Bush Team Fought the Battle* helped refresh my memory about the election dispute. Another good source is *Deadlock: The Inside Story of America's Closest Election,* by the staff of the *Washington Post.* And for a deeper look at the legal issues along with some fine humor, see Judge Richard Posner's *Breaking the Deadlock.*

And thus in a couple of quick comments, he took a shot at the Gore camp, which had not used him in the campaign in the way he probably should have been used, and flattered me for being on the winning side. At the same time he implied that the reason his side lost was because it played by the rules in a way that our side did not.

With all due respect to the forty-second president, the two major reasons we won in Florida were actually much simpler. First, George W. Bush and Dick Cheney had more votes. They had more votes on election day, more votes when the dispute ended thirty-six days later, and more votes every day in between. And although this was legally irrelevant, Bush-Cheney also had more votes in the media recounts that followed.

Second, the law was on our side. I'll explain this in a moment. For now, just remember that we won every significant case in Florida at trial or on appeal. The purpose of my going to Florida was to *preserve* the Bush-Cheney victory, not to take it away from the other side. The idea that Florida was stolen is a fantasy that says more about the people who believe it than about what really happened.

But I'm getting ahead of myself. Let me back up and tell the story from the beginning—how and why I got involved, how the Bush-Cheney operation in Tallahassee was organized, why we fought the legal battles the way we did, how we ultimately prevailed, and what lessons were learned.

GOING TO FLORIDA was the last thing on my mind as I crawled out of bed in Austin, Texas, early Wednesday, November 8. When I went to sleep in the wee hours that morning, I didn't know who had won Tuesday's presidential election—George W. Bush or Al Gore. When I awoke, the race was still up in the air.

A few things were clear. For one, Al Gore had a national popular-vote majority that would eventually reach about 540,000 votes. With Florida, New Mexico, Wisconsin, Iowa, and Oregon still in limbo early Wednesday, however, neither candidate could claim victory where it mattered—in the Electoral College. Unless George W. picked up all the smaller states (and he didn't), whichever candidate took Florida's twenty-five electoral votes would be the next president. And Governor Bush led there by only 1,784 votes out of almost six million cast. Florida law mandated a statewide machine recount in races where the margin was less than one-half of one percent. This one certainly qualified, and the machines started retabulating the ballots early Wednesday.

Susan and I didn't see any reason to hang around Austin, so we flew home, as scheduled. At the same time, postelection battle plans for Florida were being laid in both Nashville and Austin, and the early advantage, we would soon learn, had already gone to Gore-Lieberman.

A team of about seventy experienced Democratic lawyers and political operatives lifted off from Nashville early that morning, headed to the Florida capital, Tallahassee. The Democrats had also done good research before November 7 on the election laws in Florida and other potential toss-up states, so when that plane hit the ground, the Gore team could come out swinging, not looking for the nearest legal library.

Before sunrise, the Bush campaign had also instructed its general counsel, Ben Ginsberg, to head for Tallahassee, but he was unable to get into the air until about 10:00 A.M. Ben had good contacts in the Florida bar and a good grasp of the state's election laws, but he was just one guy going into battle against a cadre.

Later that morning, the Democrats named Warren Christopher, seventy-five, to represent Gore-Lieberman in Florida. In many ways, it was a good move. He had served as President Clinton's first secretary of state. Before that, he had led the search that selected Bill Clinton's running mate, Al Gore. Now he was senior partner of the prestigious law firm of O'Melveny & Myers. Warren (or "Chris," as his friends call him) was a serious, capable, and trustworthy man who was seen to be "above politics"—instant gravitas in a double-breasted suit.

Chris is a real gentleman and fine public servant, and he has always treated me with perfect respect and courtesy. In 1993, for instance, he lent me an office at the State Department, along with full access to department files, classified and unclassified, as I was writing *The Politics of Diplomacy*.

The Democrats' appointment of Warren Christopher—a septuagenarian former secretary of state and a big-firm lawyer—to represent them in Tallahassee may have influenced the Bush camp's decision to ask me—a septuagenarian former secretary of state and a big-firm lawyer—to represent the Republicans. Tit for tat. The biggest difference between Chris and me was that he had not been a political animal in the same sense that I had. That's probably why Gore-Lieberman also sent campaign chairman Bill Daley of Chicago to Florida.

I first heard of the Christopher appointment when Don Evans called my car shortly after Susan and I had touched down in Houston. "We've been talking about you up here," he said, adding something like this: "If the governor asked you to go to Florida to represent him in the vote recount, would you be available?"

"Yes," I replied.

One reason for the request, I think, is that I fit the job description of what Bush-Cheney needed at that point: an experienced lawyer with extensive political and media-relations experience. Another factor, obviously, was my special relationship with the Bush family. Without George H. W. Bush, I would never have even dreamed of working in the White House or serving in the cabinet. *El Jefe* never asked me to help his son, but I owed it to my dear friend to try.

Another old friend, fellow Texan Bob Strauss, later tried to talk me out of taking the assignment. He's a Democrat, but I've never held that against him. He's a wonderful person and a brilliant political strategist.

"Jim," he said, "you're going to get hurt by this. Florida is going to be a tough legal and political brawl that will be very emotional with both sides. It could diminish your aura as a statesman."

What could I say? Florida was not the Middle East and fighting over vote recounts was not a high-level diplomatic mission, but in my view helping to preserve the integrity of a presidential election was plenty important. It certainly never once crossed my mind to say no. My aura as a statesman would just have to take its chances.

I also told Bob there was one other reason I wanted to help Governor Bush in Florida. I still hadn't forgotten the outlandish charges about the imaginary scandal, Iraqgate, that Al Gore had leveled against Bush 41 and me in 1992. (Susan often speaks of the need to be more forgiving. I confess falling short of her ideal here, but give me points for another virtue—honesty.)

Confirmation of my appointment came shortly after that first contact. I don't remember who called this time—I believe it was Governor Bush—but I do remember the message: please go to Florida ASAP!

The first thing I had to do was clear my calendar, including a long-planned hunting trip in Great Britain with George H. W. Bush. He went on to England, and one of my tasks while he was there was to take his daily calls, chew him out for having a good time while I worked, and brief him on what was happening in Florida.

I also tried to call Warren Christopher to arrange a meeting. I knew his executive assistant, Kathy Osborne, very well. She had once served as President Reagan's personal secretary. When I asked, however, she quite properly refused to tell me where Chris was. I later learned he had flown, or was flying, to Nashville to talk to Al Gore and his advisers, en route to Florida.

About 2:00 P.M., George W. Bush's campaign manager, Joe Allbaugh, arrived from Austin in a private jet the campaign had arranged. I boarded with the one suitcase Susan had packed for my trip. The plane quickly lifted off and set a course for Florida. Meanwhile the campaign announced to the press that I would represent Bush-Cheney in Florida. The purpose was to checkmate the Christopher announcement in the same news cycle.

JOE AND I ARRIVED in Tallahassee about 4:00 P.M. local time. Our hotel would be our home away from home for the next week and a half, after which we were evicted in favor of guests with longstanding reservations for the Florida–Florida State football game. In that city on that weekend, the Seminoles-Gators rivalry easily trumped a mere presidential election dispute. After we were kicked out of the hotel, we moved into apartments.

The first thing I needed to do was some serious "prior preparation to prevent poor performance," starting with an inventory of where our side stood. What did Florida law say? How many people did we need and how many did we already have? What other assets would we need?

I quickly hooked up with Ben Ginsberg, and we had our first sit-down with Florida Republicans Wednesday evening in the conference room of Al Cardenas, state GOP chairman. At the time, I didn't know Ben very well. I quickly learned, however, that he was a first-class party general counsel with good instincts, organizational skills, and contacts.

Only a handful of lawyers and political types attended that first meeting, including Barry Richard, a really good lawyer who happened to be a Democrat and whose expertise in Florida election law would prove indispensable, and Frank Jimenez, acting counsel to Florida Governor Jeb Bush, George W.'s younger brother.

Jeb had rightly recused himself from direct participation, as governor, in the dispute, but he was still available to us as an information source and a strategist. In the days to come, I would often seek his counsel.

All of us in that first meeting were acutely aware that the Democrats' head start in getting lawyers and other workers into the field had given them a big advantage. The Republican Party had put observers in place for the mandatory county-by-county statewide recount, but we did not have a full team of battle-ready attorneys, media people, and political types at our headquarters, as the other side did.

One bit of good news was that the early numbers in the mandatory recount didn't look too bad. The next day, however, several hundred votes evaporated. I began to think Bush-Cheney might fall behind in the mandatory recount before it ended, but we never did.

As I've said, we had two big advantages, both of which were immediately evident. One was being ahead in the vote count. It seems almost silly to have to remind people that elections are about votes and that the candidate with the most, wins. But in all the subsequent controversy about pregnant chads, voter intent, and all the rest, that simple point was constantly in danger of being lost. By the time the mandatory recount was over, our lead was down to 300 votes. Whether it was 300 votes or 300,000, however, the outcome would be the same. It would be enough to win.

The second big advantage was that the law was on our side. Given all the controversy that followed, this may be difficult to believe, but events proved that we were right. Once the mandatory recount was over, I don't think there was ever any serious doubt on either side that if Florida law as it existed on November 7 were followed to the letter, Bush-Cheney would be certified as the winners. The essence of the legal problem faced by the other side was how to prevent that from happening.

As the days wore on, we developed one other advantage—organization. It began at the top with Governor Bush. He delegated the day-to-day management of Florida to me, and we developed a strong chain of command under him.

I reported directly to the candidate, not to the campaign staff in Austin or to anyone else. There was never any question about that. After all, I had been around since George W. Bush was twelve or thirteen years old, had served as his father's closest political adviser and secretary of state, and had run several presidential campaigns.

In turn, I quickly set up my own brain trust in Tallahassee, featuring some of the usual suspects from my days in government—among them, Bob Zoellick to serve as my right-hand man on strategy and message, and Margaret Tutwiler to handle communications. There were important additions from the Bush-Cheney campaign, particularly Joe Allbaugh, and still others with whom I had worked in the Reagan or Bush 41 administrations, like John Bolton and Josh Bolten.

Each morning, I would have a private telephone conversation with George W. and Dick, just the two of them. No staffers were involved on either side. I passed along information and made recommendations about the major issues, but never bothered them with the small stuff. They listened, then made any decisions I needed made. After that, we generally had an open conference call with key staff members in both Tallahassee and Austin.

This is how I had conducted business in the White House, at Treasury, and at State—by dealing directly with the president, then acting on his personal authority to implement his decisions. Thus, when I spoke, I always spoke for the president and everyone knew it. True leaders are always good delegators. In a strong organization, that's the way it has to work, and that's the way it worked in Florida.

George W. had the ability to listen to advice, then make up his own mind what to do, and he was good at delegating. This was especially important in Florida because of the complex legal issues, the dozens of separate legal challenges around the state, and the fast pace of events. "Any questions you have about what's happening in Florida, I would ask you to refer those to Jim Baker," he told the press on November 10. "Secretary Baker is in charge of that process."

Al Gore, on the other hand, was apparently more of a micromanager. This may have served him well in Congress and when he was vice president, but it probably hurt him in Florida. It likely spread him too thin, distracted him with peripheral issues, and created competition within his own ranks for his time and attention.

One decision I suspect he would like to have back was replacing the respected constitutional scholar Larry Tribe at the eleventh hour with David Boies, a trial lawyer, for the final oral argument before the U.S. Supreme Court. This was exactly the sort of decision a principal— especially a principal who was not a lawyer—should have delegated, not made.

And speaking of lawyers, we may have started behind, but we soon built an instant law firm with an all-star staff, a physical base in Tallahassee, and, thanks to computers and other equipment installed by Joe Allbaugh, virtual support from sympathetic attorneys around the country. Some good lawyers simply showed up in Tallahassee looking to help. Among them were prominent Democrats or former Democrats such as Griffin Bell (President Carter's attorney general) and John Hill (former attorney general of Texas and chief justice of the Texas Supreme Court). But I recruited many others on the legal team.

With the possible exception of Ted Olson, the brilliant trial and appellate lawyer I tapped to argue Governor Bush's case in the U.S. Supreme Court, few readers probably remember (or ever knew) the names of these talented men and women.* Among many, many others, our team included Barry Richard (mentioned earlier); George Terwilliger, deputy attorney general in the first Bush administration; Washington attorney Michael Carvin; and Chicago trial lawyers Phil Beck and Fred Bartlit.

Several of my partners from Baker Botts also migrated to Florida during this period, notably Kirk Van Tine, who coordinated much of our legal research, and trial lawyers Daryl Bristow and Irv Terrell, each of whom handled major cases. (Terrell and Beck had each successfully gone head-to-head in litigation with David Boies, Gore's chief lawyer. I wanted them on our team to share the lessons they had learned in battling him.) Others were Bobby Burchfield, Marcos Jimenez, Ken Mehlman, Tim Flanigan, John Bridgeland, Ken Juster, Alex Azar, and Bill Kelley.

I had no problem getting all these people to sign on. My biggest problem was slotting them into the project in ways that would take full advantage of their talents. These were first-chair attorneys, top partners from some of the best firms in the country. Most dropped big cases to come to Florida and do whatever needed to be done, even work they might ordinarily have delegated to associates.

Every day we had to make tough calls. Do we contest this Gore

---

*Less than a year later, Ted's wife—a brilliant attorney and writer—Barbara Olson, died on the hijacked airliner that hit the Pentagon on September 11, 2001. What a great loss for him, their friends, and the nation.

move? Do we initiate this move for Bush-Cheney? Do we file in this court or that court? Our brilliant, competitive, and strong-willed lawyers often held different views on how to proceed and *who* would proceed (that is, handle the case). But it was out of this vigorous clash of opinions that we developed our successful legal strategies. Zelnick later quoted Ginsberg as saying, "This was the biggest group of egos not flexing their egos I've ever been associated with." For those five-plus weeks in Florida—if I may say so—I was privileged to serve as managing partner of what might have been the finest law firm in America.

If most people can't remember our lawyers, many surely remember the name of Gore's lead attorney, David Boies of New York, one of the nation's best trial lawyers and a genuine legal celebrity. He was no doubt assisted by a strong team, but he was spread pretty thin. Arguably, at least, handling most of the high-profile cases himself—in state and federal courts, and in trials and appeals—was too much for one person, no matter how talented.

Our usual approach, by contrast, was to send fresh players into every game, not to rely on one traveling superstar. Exceptions were Florida election-law expert Barry Richard, who represented us in several different state court contests, and Olson, who worked most of the federal cases. In general, however, our lawyers had narrow, specific assignments. Some wrote briefs for particular cases in federal court. Others argued one case or maybe one element of one case in state court. Big law firms are organized on the principle of division of labor, and that's how we organized our legal team in Florida.

I wrote no briefs and argued no cases myself. It had been a long time since I had practiced law at that level, and anyway I could not have competed with the exceptional talent around me. I did review some documents, ask questions, and occasionally suggest a line of legal argument, but my real job was to recruit, organize, and make assignments, then to listen to the debates on tactics and strategy and decide what we should do, subject always, of course, to the instructions of our client in Austin. To be done well, this work had to be handled by an experienced lawyer, not by the principals and certainly not by campaign advisers.

Florida is largely remembered as a legal battle, but in my opinion it was every bit as much a political battle, and we may have understood this point better than the other side. That's why we put so much effort into setting up a communications and press operation in Tallahassee, rather than relying solely on the campaign's existing (and excellent) press apparatus in Austin. It was vital to our ultimate success that we controlled both the messengers and the message on what was happening in Florida.

One of my first calls was to recruit Margaret Tutwiler as our press person in Tallahassee. She worked well with reporters and was simply the best person I knew at designing a communications strategy. She had done it for me at the White House, at Treasury, and at State, and now she would do it in Florida.

I resisted pressure to get overly involved in the daily televised battles of the talking heads. In part, I didn't want to use myself up. That's why we brought in a number of respected Republican surrogates—among them, Bob Dole, Christie Todd Whitman, Fred Thompson, Arlen Specter, and Marc Racicot—to communicate our daily messages to the press. Remember, too, that I was in Florida as a former secretary of state to put a patina of statesmanship on a political dispute. I didn't want to go out there every day as a sort of hired-gun pol, despite what some of the Bush-Cheney advisers in Austin might have wanted. Governor Bush, of course, was properly reserved for blockbuster statements to the nation, not for the daily give-and-take.

One surrogate we didn't get was Colin Powell. After the Democrats tried to throw out some overseas military ballots, we asked him to speak up for the right of our troops to have their votes counted, but he demurred. He was in line to be George W.'s secretary of state, and I think he wanted to stay above the fray.

I regret that he did not come to Florida. My own political work for Ronald Reagan and George H. W. Bush never did me any harm when it came to being confirmed by the Senate for cabinet posts, and it considerably improved my standing with the presidents I served. Coming to Florida might well have strengthened Colin's relationship with George W. Bush, which in turn might have helped him in the first-term battles for influence and power in the administration.

Another reason I resisted going out there every day, however, is that in dealing with the press, oftentimes less is more. I am not sure the Gore team understood this. They had too many people speaking for the campaign at the same time, not always with a common message. Their lawyers, in particular, were always ready to talk whenever a reporter stuck a microphone in their face. Good manners, perhaps, but not always good politics. By limiting my appearances, I was able to fill the room with reporters every time I called a press conference, which was fairly often. A couple were after midnight.

I think we were more disciplined. We coordinated our message and we coordinated our messengers. With rare exceptions, no one spoke to the press except me, the principals, and our surrogates, always with well-thought-out statements and talking points. This kept the press focused on the message we wanted to convey.

As we fought to maintain good order on the legal, political, and media battlefields, the GOP state headquarters building—recently named the George Bush Republican Center (after Bush 41)—was a scene of creative chaos. Lawyers and other workers had quickly overwhelmed the resources of our hosts. I had a nice office but some had to share space, sometimes in shifts. Many lawyers and legal assistants worked together in the conference room. Legal research, briefs, and other documents were stacked on the floors, and those stacks grew until no one quite remembered what was in them, then fell over. Extension cords snaked around corners and down halls in search of electricity for computers, fax machines, television sets, and copiers. And everywhere there were people—people working in every cranny of the building, people bumping into one another, people installing equipment, people clicking away on keyboards, and people talking, talking, talking. The intensity grew until we could bear no more, then it grew again.

. . .

BEFORE MY AIRPLANE ever hit the tarmac in Tallahassee, local Gore supporters had filed the first two lawsuits in Florida, demanding either a *revote*—a do-over—in Palm Beach County or a court-ordered re-allocation of the votes. They blamed a badly designed butterfly ballot for confusing many would-be Gore voters.

These lawsuits were a joke. For one thing, there was no way to change the date of an election set by the U.S. Constitution. A local trial judge quickly and correctly threw the plaintiffs out of court. Still, the cases offered a near-perfect illustration of the dynamics of the Florida election dispute, with its unique interplay of public relations, politics, and law.

On day one, every network was carrying angry interviews about the butterfly ballots and other real or imagined voting problems. Some of this was genuine, I'm sure, but Democrats clearly orchestrated many of the protests. (In fairness, both sides organized rallies and protests.) The Democrats' purpose, I believe, was to delegitimize the Bush-Cheney victory and set the stage for intervention by the courts. Even though local Democrats, not the Gore campaign, filed the but-terfly cases, Bill Daley, Warren Christopher, and others publicly em-braced the charge that the Palm Beach County ballot was illegal. On Friday, November 10, I spoke about the butterfly ballot and, to use a phrase from an old lawyers' joke, I pounded the law.*

> There's a rule of law to be followed in all elections. The state of
> Florida has established legal procedures to design, approve, publish,
> and if need be to protest ballots before the election. The [butterfly]
> ballot was designed by a Democratic elections supervisor. She ap-

---

*How do you win a case? When the law is on your side, pound the law; when the facts are on your side, pound the facts; and when neither the law nor the facts are on your side, pound the table. The other side was pounding the table, in my opinion. From Novem-ber 10 onward, we pounded the law.

proved it. The Democratic Party did not question it before the election. This butterfly-type ballot was used in recent elections in the same county and under the same rules and, again, the Democrats did not complain. . . . Our lawyers have confirmed the legality of this ballot. And we have with us here today . . . copies of the relevant Florida statutes if you would like to have them.

The butterfly ballot cases illustrate what the rule of law is all about, which is playing by the rules as they existed *before* the game was played, then living with the results, good or bad. This is the same principle, by the way, that says you can't go to court to collect a debt if you file your lawsuit after the deadline set by the statute of limitations. It is unjust, in some sense, for a deadbeat debtor to get away without paying, but it would be an even greater injustice to change the rules after the event. The law is full of deadlines and technicalities and procedures, and if we purport to live under the rule of law, we have no choice but to respect them, even when they hurt us.

"Butterfly ballots" was a warm-up bout. The main event started on Thursday, November 9, when Bill Daley announced that the Gore campaign would request a hand count of ballots in Palm Beach County and three others: Volusia, Miami-Dade, and Broward.*

Obviously, Al Gore didn't invite me to represent him in Florida or to play Monday morning quarterback, but I will say this: his decision to seek manual recounts in four heavily Democratic counties rather than all sixty-seven counties was a big mistake. It undermined his otherwise effective public relations slogan—"count every vote"—and gave us the moral high ground on that issue.

There was debate in our camp on how to respond. Some team members believed we should call for hand recounts in pro-Bush counties or for a full statewide hand recount, but these folks, in my opinion, were not seeing the big picture. First off, political strategists in the

___

*I later joked that after arriving in Florida, I learned that the state has sixty-three counties . . . and four *re*counties!

state advised me that there weren't many places where we could expect to get a bounce. Secondly, I worried about the fact that most of those counting the ballots were Democrats. At the very least, there would be, as I put it to the press, "the opportunity for mischief." The final and most important reason for not seeking a recount, however, was that recounts are for losers, and we had won.

We were still ahead, unofficially, by 300 votes when the mandatory statewide machine recount ended on Friday, November 10, and my position was, "Hey, it's over." Even though two-thirds of the state elections supervisors were Democrats, I told reporters, Bush-Cheney had prevailed. All that was left was to count the overseas ballots, and they traditionally favored Republican candidates. "We will vigorously oppose the Gore campaign's efforts to keep recounting over and over until it happens to like the result," I said.

In answer to a question, I reminded reporters of another close race. "I'm particularly drawn back to the memory of 1976, when I was in the room and many, many people were arguing to President Ford that he should insist upon a recount, because he was only some seven thousand votes or so down in Ohio. . . . And he said, 'No. . . . That's not what would be good for the country.'"*

I'll come back in a moment to our legal efforts to block the recounts, but, as everyone knows, they went forward. Human vote counters began holding machine ballots up to the light, twisting in their seats, squinting, trying to read the minds of voters based on whether tiny rectangles of paper were dangling or hanging or dimpled or pregnant. There were absolutely no uniform standards for this process. At times, the rules changed in the middle of the counts. It was chaos from beginning to end—what we in Texas would call a "goat rope." To try to protect against the excesses of creative counting, we had senior

---

*My memory was a bit off. As noted in chapter one, a shift of fewer than 5,600 votes in Ohio would have moved the state to the Ford column, but we would also have needed to turn just under 3,700 votes in Hawaii.

people—including John Bolton and Frank Donatelli—sitting in the chad rooms for days and days.

This is where Katherine Harris, the elected secretary of state of Florida (and a Republican), became a familiar figure to America's television viewers. Each county was supposed to certify its results to her office on November 14, exactly one week after the election. With the hand recounts just getting under way, however, the four counties obviously could not meet that deadline. Under legal pressure, she announced on November 14 that Bush-Cheney led by 300 votes, but postponed formal certification to November 17, subject only to counting the overseas ballots and to the possible acceptance of late returns that could be legally justified. Two days later, however, the Florida Supreme Court ordered that the hand recounts could continue, pending its decision on whether they were legal. By then, Miami-Dade had simply given up, so we were down to three counties.

Shortly after arriving in Florida, Zoellick, Allbaugh, and I went to see Katherine Harris. She would soon be subjected to some vicious ad hominem attacks by both the Gore team and members of the press. Secretary Harris was obviously very bright, but I sensed that she was uneasy about the position into which she had been forced by circumstances, almost to the point of being paralyzed. She wanted to do what the law required, and we made the case that the law required her to certify the election at a specific time and in a specific manner, which basically meant sooner rather than later. For her own sake, we also advised her to get the best legal help she could, which she did. I understand that Gore representatives also visited her to make their case, as was perfectly appropriate.

The next stop was the Florida Supreme Court. By then, the absentee ballots had come in and the Bush-Cheney lead had grown to 930 votes. Oral arguments were set for November 20 and the opinion came down the next day. It was an outrageous piece of judicial overreaching. In complete disregard of the statutory law of Florida and of Article II, Section 1, of the United States Constitution ("Each State shall appoint, *in such Manner as the Legislature thereof may direct,* a Number of Electors . . . "), the court extended the deadline set by the legislature for the ongoing recounts to Sunday, November 26, twelve days after the deadline set by Florida statutes.

"For the first time since his arrival in Tallahassee," Robert Zelnick wrote later, Baker "looked his age as he read a statement attacking the court's decision." Absolutely. I was worn out, angry, and worried.

> Today, Florida's supreme court rewrote the legislature's statutory system, assumed the responsibilities of the executive branch, and sidestepped the opinion of the trial court as the finder of fact. Two weeks after the election, that court has changed the rules and invented a new system for counting the election results. One should not now be surprised if the Florida legislature seeks to affirm the original rules.

The court said it was guided by "the will of the people, not a hyper-technical reliance upon statutory provisions." That's the sort of lawyer talk that sounds impressive until you think about it. The best expression of "the will of the people" on this subject, after all, was the statute enacted by lawmakers elected by the people. And "hyper-technical reliance upon statutory provisions" is another name for what this court had just trampled into the dust—the rule of law. "It is simply not fair, ladies and gentlemen," I said, "to change the rules, either in the middle of the game or after the game has been played."

WHEN I WAS treasury secretary, I became friends with Lawton Chiles, the Democratic senator from Florida who chaired the Senate Budget Committee. We both loved to hunt wild turkeys. Our friendship continued after I left Washington in 1993, and we would sometimes hunt together at my ranch in Texas and at various places in Florida.

In 1994, Lawton was elected governor of Florida. He defeated Jeb

Bush, who was making his first run for the office. Lawton ran a tough campaign—many thought it was too negative—focused mostly on Social Security, which is a federal issue, not a state issue. After that, it wasn't particularly popular with the Bushes for anybody to be friends with Chiles, but the Chiles-Baker relationship had been struck up long before Jeb ran for governor, and it survived.

On one trip in Florida, Lawton and I were joined by his close friend Dexter Douglass, a silver-haired lawyer who served as the governor's general counsel. Dexter was a colorful humorist and lively conversationalist. In short order, I learned two important things about him. One was that he was a liberal Democrat, big time. The other was that one of his jobs was to recommend candidates to Lawton for appointment to the Florida Supreme Court. I think he may have recommended five of the seven justices on the court.

At the time, I didn't think any more about it. In November 2000, however, that memory helped shape the Bush-Cheney legal strategy, which was very, very simple. The only way to deal with the Florida Supreme Court, I believed, was to go over its head.

I told the Dexter Douglass story in the first meetings with my brain trust in Florida to help explain why I thought we needed to file a federal lawsuit. "If we don't get into federal court," I said, "we'll be as dead as a doornail."

Some of them argued with me. They thought Florida was a state issue and that the federal courts would be reluctant to intervene, but I insisted we try anyway. I also recommended that course to Governor Bush. He agreed, and on Saturday, November 11, Ted Olson filed our motion in U.S. District Court in Miami for an injunction to stop the manual recounts. We argued that the recounts violated both the due process and equal protection clauses of the Fourteenth Amendment because they gave too much latitude to the men and women who were counting the ballots and because all Florida voters were entitled to have their votes counted in the same way.

It's important to understand that our purpose in going to the federal courthouse was not to *overturn* the election. Our purpose, rather, was to *preserve* a lawful Bush-Cheney victory by stopping the election results from being changed by a subjective recount system without uniform standards, which we believed was both wrong and unconstitutional.

We took a lot of flak for filing the lawsuit, some of it from Republicans. I got a real earful, for instance, when I called my friend, former Missouri senator Jack Danforth, to ask him to be our lead counsel in federal court. Jack is well liked and well respected across the political spectrum and has a spotless reputation for integrity. He was a former Missouri attorney general, a man Dick Cheney had recommended as W's running mate, and an ordained Episcopalian priest. I thought he would lend instant stature to our federal case.

Jack was vacationing in Cancun when I asked him to sign on. Instead of a yes, I got a lecture, the essence of which was: if you go to court and lose, you're going to ruin Bush's career; he's young enough to run again sometime, but not if he's seen as having challenged a presidential election in court. When I reported this to Bush and Cheney in Austin, we decided to look elsewhere. That's when I recommended Ted Olson, who went on to do a superlative job for us in the federal courts, including two successful appeals to the U.S. Supreme Court.

Our first shot at the federal courts went nowhere. On November 13, a district judge ruled against us. Two days later we appealed to the 11th Circuit Court of Appeals, and on November 17 that court upheld the lower court. The recounts would continue.

These defeats didn't come as a surprise. The 11th Circuit said we had not exhausted our remedies in state courts and, with the recounts just beginning, had not demonstrated a substantial threat of irreparable injury. We were disappointed, of course, but our case had been dismissed without prejudice, which meant we still had a foot in the federal courthouse door.

Three days later, the Florida Supreme Court conducted oral arguments on the recount issue. This was the hearing that led to the November 21 opinion I have already described as outrageous. The first few seconds of the Gore-Lieberman oral arguments were fairly memorable to me.

"Mr. Chief Justice, members of the court, I'm here to introduce the speaker today who will argue the case for us, Mr. David Boies from the state of New York."

It was a routine introduction, except for one thing. The man who introduced Boies, who sat at the table with Boies, who was sometimes referred to as Boies's right-hand man, was none other than Dexter Douglass. He was introducing his new Yankee friend to the very justices he had helped place on the court. I felt like a stranger at somebody else's family reunion.

I've already said all I need to say about the Florida court's decision to extend the deadline for the recounts to November 26. I resisted the temptation back then to assign political motives to the seven justices, and I'll resist it now. I assume they honestly believed they were doing the right thing, which just happened to be what Gore-Lieberman wanted. What they really did by changing the rules in the middle of the game, however, was to give our side a new and stronger case for the U.S. Supreme Court. I quickly met with Ginsberg, Olson, Zoellick, Terwilliger, Carvin, and others to decide what to do next. Some of them were not optimistic that the Supreme Court would take an appeal of the Florida decision, and, in any event, estimated our odds of winning at no better than fifty-fifty. Maybe we should just keep going with the recount suit, some suggested, to avoid putting the high court in the posture of overruling a state court. The calendar was also a factor. There were only five days until the Florida Supreme Court's new deadline for certification. Was it realistic to expect the U.S. Supreme Court to grant our petition, hear arguments, and rule that quickly? If not, the recount would be over before a decision could be issued.

I listened, then decided we should go forward. For one thing, I liked our chances. For another, we simply needed to try in every way possible to get into federal court. Once again, Governor Bush gave us a green light, and on November 22, our lawyers asked the U.S. Supreme

Court to review the Florida Supreme Court's decision. The state court had violated a federal statute by changing the deadline for certifying the election, we argued. In doing so that court had also violated Article II of the U.S. Constitution, which gives state legislatures authority to determine how presidential electors are chosen. We also argued that the selective recounts and random counting rules violated the due process and equal protection clauses.

On November 24—to the surprise of many, including some of my colleagues—the high court agreed to hear our case. Now what? To paraphrase the famous Groucho Marx line about club membership, we now had to decide whether we wanted to have anything to do with a court that would have us. The November 26 deadline was now only two days away, and it was beginning to look as if we would still be ahead when the recounts were completed. What could a victory in the U.S. Supreme Court add to a certified victory at the ballot box? One word, I argued: *legitimacy.*

We presented Governor Bush with a memorandum listing "reasons for dropping the case" and "reasons for continuing the case." Among the reasons for dropping: "If we lose the case after eking out a narrow win in the vote count, Gore will be seen as scoring a big victory, which he will use to lend momentum and legitimacy to his contest challenges in Florida courts." Among the reasons for continuing: "A Supreme Court win might remove the basis for Gore's election contest.... Furthermore, as long as the case is pending, the Florida Supreme Court is likely to be more careful in contest proceedings."

Governor Bush quickly decided he wanted us to continue. Why? One word: *legitimacy.*

On November 26, Secretary of State Harris certified Bush-Cheney as the winner by 537 votes. In Tallahassee we drafted a speech for the governor to claim victory and call on Gore to end his fight. In Austin, however, the Bush team reportedly thought the language "too arrogant." Governor Bush delivered a kinder, gentler version. "Now that the votes are counted, it is time for the votes to count," he said.

In *Winning Florida,* here's how Zelnick describes my remarks to the press that same evening: "The speech may have been 'too arrogant' to be delivered by the next president of the United States, but, with a few modifications it seemed just right for a tough old political strategist slugging it out in Florida but wishing he were off somewhere abbreviating the lives of pheasants."

Unfortunately, Vice President Gore did not accept the certified results and concede. In a nationally televised speech on November 27, he vowed to press onward. In what surely was the one of the oddest remarks of the thirty-six-day dispute, the man who had asked for selective recounts in just four heavily Democratic counties said, "That is all we have asked since election day: a complete count of all the votes cast in Florida." We were all pretty tired by then, so maybe "complete count of all the votes" was just a slip of the tongue.

Certification changed the legal landscape entirely. George W. Bush had now officially won. From this moment, Gore-Lieberman were no longer *protesting* the election count; they were *contesting* a certified election and seeking to overturn it. This created two enormous problems for the Democrats. For one thing, the burden of proof would be much higher, requiring evidence of fraud or some other serious wrongdoing or of some monumental irregularity or inaccuracy significant enough to change the statewide results. The second problem was that the Florida Supreme Court's extension of the recount deadline to November 26 had chewed up so much time that there weren't many days left for the contest. Both camps and all courts were working on the assumption that the election had to be resolved by December 12 to meet a statutory federal "safe harbor" deadline for settling the names of Florida's electors.

The United States Supreme Court heard our case on December 1. Olson argued the case and did an excellent job. I stayed away. I had been in the Reagan and Bush administrations when some of the justices were appointed. My presence was unnecessary, and it could have been distracting. Some might even argue, inappropriate.

The next day, distinguished and folksy Circuit Judge N. Sanders

Sauls kicked off a three-day quickie trial in Leon County to hear the Gore contest. Boies gave it his best shot, but on December 4, Judge Sauls ruled against Gore-Lieberman on every issue, without exception. That same day, the U.S. Supreme Court vacated the Florida Supreme Court decision of November 21. And elsewhere, we were soon to win cases filed in Florida courts by the Democrats to challenge absentee ballots and overseas ballots. For a couple of days, Bush-Cheney was running the table.

But the Democrats still refused to concede, and once again the Florida Supreme Court saved their bacon. On December 8, the justices voted 4–3 to reverse Judge Sauls's decision and ordered something that Gore-Lieberman had not even asked for, a *statewide* manual recount of so-called undervotes—those ballots the machines registered as not having voted for any candidate for president. This decision will be reprinted in law books for decades to come as an example of what appellate courts are *not* supposed to do.

Wearily, wearily, wearily I trudged to the microphone to explain, yet again, that the Florida court had overstepped its boundaries, this time by (among many other things) overruling Judge Sauls's findings of fact that there was no evidence of fraud or other serious wrongdoing. Appellate Law 101 says appeals courts are supposed to deal with the law, not—except in rare instances—with the facts, which are settled in lower courts.

In a scorching dissent, Florida Chief Justice Charles Wells explained the true nature of this opinion. "The majority's decision to return this case to the [trial] court for a count of the undervotes from either Miami-Dade County or all counties has no foundation in the law of Florida as it existed on November 7, 2000, or at any time until the issuance of this opinion," he wrote.

Amen, brother. That's the sort of thing we had been saying since November.

"I have a deep and abiding concern that the prolonging of judicial process in this . . . contest propels this country and this state into an unprecedented and unnecessary constitutional crisis," Chief Justice Wells said.

There's no point in my saying much more about the decision, because the U.S. Supreme Court promptly stayed the Florida court's order, then vacated it in *Bush v. Gore*, the famous late-night decision of December 12. By a 7–2 vote, the high court held that the recount ordered by the Florida Supreme Court was unconstitutional because the lack of uniform counting rules violated the equal-protection clause of the U.S. Constitution. Let that sink in. Seven out of nine justices agreed with Bush-Cheney on the issue of constitutionality. Critics who say the case was "really 5–4" are talking about a second vote on a subsidiary matter, the remedy—what to do about the Florida Supreme Court's outrageous decision. Referring to December 12, the federal statutory safe harbor deadline, a majority of the court said, "That date is upon us, and there is no recount procedure in place under the State Supreme Court's order that comports with minimal constitutional standards."

It was over.

Yet again, the law was on our side. And yet again, we still had more votes than the other side—537 to be exact.*

The next day, I flew back to Houston and, despite some fairly serious fatigue, dropped by my office at Baker Botts. Dozens of lawyers and staffers flocked down to my end of the hall to welcome me home.

"Did you ever think you might lose?" someone asked.

"Every day I thought it was possible," I replied. "Every day."

---

*One subject I chose not to write much about in this chapter is the so-called "nuclear option." A very strong argument can be made that under the U.S. Constitution, the Florida legislature simply could have named a slate of electors and put an immediate end to ongoing court battles. There was a lot of talk about this possibility, and we did a fair amount of legal research on it. On December 12, the Florida House actually approved a slate of twenty-five pro-Bush electors, but the Senate never acted.

I don't think Governor Bush would have authorized us to try to win Florida's electors by legislative fiat rather than through the votes of the people of Florida. Having lost the popular vote by more than 500,000 votes, he understood very well how hard it would have been to govern if he won the White House that way.

. . .

FLORIDA WAS an unsettling experience for the American people. I hope we never have to go through anything like that again. It was equally unsettling to the world at large. As the legal battles dragged on, I received telephone calls from several present and former prime ministers and foreign ministers with whom I had worked as secretary of state. "What's happening to your country?" they asked. "Can't you even conduct an election?" In part this was simple curiosity, but there was also a whiff of anxiety about the uncertainty of who would be president of the sole remaining superpower.

"What's happening," I replied, "is that our system is working. This is a very emotional issue for the American people, but on both sides, I think, we are handling it with dignity and pursuant to the rule of law. And whatever else may be happening, we do not have tanks in the street." For a few callers, I added a zinger: "as might have been the case, were this to have happened in some other countries."

I meant what I said about dignity. In a dispute as important and contentious as Florida, it was inevitable, given human nature, that some things would be said outside the boundaries of civility and that other things would be done that, in hindsight, might have been done differently. What is striking, however, is how few those incidents were and how quickly they have faded from mind.

That tone was set early. Two days after the election, I met with Warren Christopher. As we touched gloves, neither of us suggested that a settlement could be negotiated. One candidate was bound to win and the other was bound to lose. There was no middle ground, even for experienced negotiators. But we agreed that the contest would be conducted in an honorable and dignified way on both sides. That's what both sides did, by and large, and I salute Chris and his colleagues. Al Gore's gracious concession speech deserves special acknowledgment. It helped our nation accept the legitimacy of the outcome.

One great benefit of having done things in the right way and in accordance with the rule of law—and it would have been the same for Al Gore, had he won—is that the American people were more willing to accept the outcome and move on. Some didn't, of course, but that was also inevitable, given the intensity of feelings on both sides.

Even the Florida Supreme Court finally had second thoughts about the process it set in motion. "Upon reflection," the court wrote in a little-noted December 22 opinion, "we conclude that the development of a specific, uniform standard to ensure equal application and to secure the fundamental right to vote throughout the State of Florida should be left to the body we believe best equipped to study and address it, the legislature."

A bit more of that sort of judicial restraint early on, and the Florida recount exercise would have unfolded very differently.

After all the visiting lawyers, political operatives, and reporters had packed up and gone home, two different media-sponsored organizations conducted statewide recounts of the Florida ballots. Here's what the *New York Times* reported on November 12, 2001:

> A comprehensive review of the uncounted Florida ballots from last year's presidential election reveals that George W. Bush would have won even if the United States Supreme Court had allowed the statewide manual recount of the votes that the Florida Supreme Court had ordered to go forward.

> Even under the strategy that Mr. Gore pursued at the beginning of the Florida standoff—filing suit to force hand recounts in four predominantly Democratic counties—Mr. Bush would have kept this lead, according to the ballot review conducted for a consortium of news organizations.

In a separate study, the *Miami Herald* and *USA Today* said that if the recount called for by the Florida Supreme Court's final opinion of December 8 had been implemented—the opinion the Supreme Court declared unconstitutional—Bush-Cheney would have widened their lead to more than 1,600 votes from 537 votes.

I'm sometimes asked if I think I tarnished my reputation by going into the trenches of the Florida election dispute. This is a way of suggesting that maybe Bob Strauss was right, that going to Florida had "diminished my aura as a statesman."

My answer is that Florida was a unique and historic event in the political life of our nation, and I'm proud to have been able to play a successful part in it. It was tough on both sides, but defending the rule of law and preserving a legitimate victory in a presidential election are important and satisfying tasks. Politics and public service are two sides of the same coin. There is nothing disreputable about doing politics if you do it with dignity and play by the rules. It is, after all, through politics that our leaders achieve the right to practice public policy or statesmanship.

One of the big lessons of Florida is that candidates must abide by the rules in place on election day. A corollary is that if you don't like those rules, you should try to change them before the next election. We can always do better next time. That's one reason I agreed to serve with former President Jimmy Carter in 2005 as cochair of a bipartisan Commission on Federal Election Reform. More on that in the next chapter.

Election 2000 also generated a lot of talk about doing away with the Electoral College and electing our presidents by popular vote. That will never happen, and it shouldn't. The Electoral College was part of the grand bargain by which the Founders induced the states to give up some of their sovereignty and become part of the United States. As part of that compromise, the small states won disproportionate influence in the U.S. Senate (each state, regardless of size, gets two senators) and in electing our presidents. The Founders wanted our presidents to have broad appeal among many states, not one-sided political majorities in a handful of big states. Even if you disagree with the theoretical and historical arguments, however, there is no practical

way to get rid of the Electoral College. That would require a constitutional amendment ratified by a significant number of the small states,
which ain't gonna happen.

The media also learned a few lessons in humility, thanks to their
erroneous election-night calls on Florida. The call for Gore was made
before the polls had even closed in the Florida panhandle, which is
strong Republican territory. Most fair-minded people would agree
that this hurt the Bush-Cheney ticket. Some potential voters simply
stayed home after they heard the race in their state was over. Given
the obvious importance of Florida in the Electoral College and the
closeness of races in Iowa, New Mexico, Oregon, and Wisconsin—all
within one percent—it is also reasonable to speculate that the early,
erroneous call may have influenced the results in those states.

The media exercised more caution and restraint in the 2004 presidential election. Still, as memories fade and competitive pressures
mount, it's fair to ask what we might do within the limits of the First
Amendment to avoid adverse effects from early or erroneous reporting of results in future elections. The most obvious answer—to forbid
journalists to call the races until all the polls have closed—is probably
unconstitutional. One other possibility might be for the states to
arrange polling schedules so that voting would end everywhere at the
same time. But even that would not prevent early birds from calling
the whole thing, based on exit polls, or prevent erroneous calls based
on erroneous exit polls, as happened in 2000. It's a real conundrum. It
may just boil down to hoping that journalists will recognize and embrace a special obligation on their part to let our elections play out
naturally, without doing anything that would undermine the integrity
of the process. It's the right thing to do, and they ought to do it.

We also need to keep a sense of perspective about Florida. Having
a presidential election with more than 105 million ballots decided by
fewer than a thousand votes in one state was a rare event that exposed
flaws in our election laws and voting systems. We can certainly do better, and I think we will. But if that ever happens again, I suspect that

no matter what reforms we have made, the losing side will find more than a thousand votes to complain about. No system is or ever will be perfect.

Finally, the biggest lesson of Florida was that the system worked. Despite all the turmoil, as I told the foreign leaders, there were no riots and no tanks in the streets. We Americans may take the peaceful transfer of power for granted, but measured against the standards of history, Florida testifies to the strength of our constitutional democracy and our faith in the rule of law.

THE BUSH-KERRY presidential race of 2004 was close, but not as close—thank heavens—as 2000. Still, when America went to bed on election night, Senator Kerry had not conceded. Whoever won Ohio would win the presidency. There was talk that the Democrats might protest the vote in that state, which the networks had called for Bush.

I was on the way to the dentist the next morning when I got a call from Andy Card, President Bush's White House chief of staff. My heart stopped. "Please, Andy," I thought, "don't ask me to go to Cleveland."

SEVENTEEN

"MR. PRESIDENT, THIS IS NOT THE FIRST TIME I'VE DONE THIS"

"MR. SECRETARY," asked Andy Card, "would you mind calling Vernon Jordan to see if he would encourage Senator Kerry to concede?"

I've known Andy since 1979 or 1980, when he signed up to help organize Massachusetts for George H. W. Bush's first presidential run. He was a Republican state legislator back then, still in his early thirties. Andy came to Washington in the mid-1980s and through hard work, telling it like it is, and fierce loyalty, climbed the ranks in the Reagan and Bush 41 White House staffs to become secretary of transportation.

In November 2004 he was White House chief of staff for President George W. Bush, the same office I once held for Presidents Reagan and Bush. I'd worked with him a lot over the years, admired him, and regarded him as a friend. He had a low-key style, but was very effective and had President Bush's full confidence. When his tenure in the office extended longer than my own four-plus years, I joked that he had taken my place as the longest-serving chief of staff in the past fifty years, except for Eisenhower's Sherman Adams (who resigned in disgrace) and Nixon's H. R. Haldeman (who ended up in prison).

I've also known Vernon Jordan a long time. He's a mover and shaker in Washington with close ties to the Democratic Party, a deep friendship with Bill Clinton, and a wonderful sense of humor. We both try not to treat our political adversaries as enemies. Right after Governor Clinton won the 1992 election, Vernon came to my house to start talks about the presidential transition. He and I are both past presidents of Washington's Alfalfa Club, the only function of which is to hold one dinner each year to poke fun at ourselves and our national leaders.

In September 2004, Vernon and I negotiated the terms of the Bush-Kerry and Cheney-Edwards debates. Both of us had experience at this, and our talks were amiable and efficient, done mostly by telephone. Going in, the biggest issue was how many debates to have. As always, however, almost all other details of the event were also in contention. Would the candidates sit or stand? Where would the podiums be located? Who would ask questions? Would the candidates be permitted to address each other? Would there be warning and stop lights to keep the candidates within their time limits? (Senator Kerry initially didn't want them. His fallback position was that the lights should not be visible to the television audience.)

I proposed the following to Vernon: "You're gung ho for three debates, and we would probably prefer two, since our candidate is president and has a lead in the polls. I'm absolutely convinced that we can say we'll do only two and won't have to pay a political price. But I want to know if your side would be willing to give us everything we want on format, subject matter, duration, warning lights, and so on, if the president were to agree to do three."

Vernon's first reply was, "Well, I don't know." But after we had feinted back and forth for several days, he said, "Yeah, we'd be willing to do that."

I proposed this idea in a meeting in the White House residence with the president, Karl Rove, and Karen Hughes. The president was not eager to do three debates, initially, and Karen favored just two.

President Clinton had given Bob Dole only two, which would have been good precedent for saying no to more. But Karl and I supported three if we could get everything else we wanted.

"Mr. President, this is not the first time I've done this," I said. "I remember times when I was darn glad my candidate had another debate to make up for a poor performance in an earlier one."

He listened, then agreed. "Okay, if we get everything we want on the other issues."

As it turned out, the third debate was President Bush's best performance. He hit a home run. But you never know in advance how these things will turn out. I thought our bargain was a good one, and it certainly worked out well this time, but it could have bitten us in the tail.

After Vernon and I had tied up all the loose ends, we repaired to the bar of New York's Waldorf-Astoria to seal the agreement with martinis. Our conversation drifted back to 2000. "It's too bad what happened in Florida," we agreed, perhaps for different reasons. Then we began to muse. What if either candidate, Bush or Kerry, lost the popular vote and also lost the electoral vote by a narrow margin? Would it be appropriate for him to ask for recounts in one or two states—other than the recounts mandated by state law—to try to reverse the outcome in the Electoral College? I didn't think that would be appropriate, nor did Vernon. At that point, of course, we were just two guys nursing our drinks, not representatives of our candidates.

Which brings me back to my telephone call from Andy Card.

It was Wednesday morning, November 3, 2004, the day after the presidential election. I was on my way to the dentist. To all appearances, Bush-Cheney had defeated Kerry-Edwards by healthy margins in both the popular and electoral votes. The networks had called the election for the GOP, and they were right this time. George W. wound up with 50.6 percent of the popular vote (Kerry took 48.1 percent) and 286 electoral votes to Kerry's 252.

On Wednesday morning, however, Senator Kerry had yet to concede. He had his eyes on Ohio and its twenty electoral votes. When the counting ended that morning, the president was leading there by about 136,000 votes. The senator was said to be holding out hope that uncounted provisional ballots could give him the Buckeye State, which in turn would give him the Electoral College and the presidency.

Provisional ballots are those cast by voters whose names do not appear on the registration rolls at the local polling stations—for example, because of an administrative error. The top state election official estimated the number as high as 175,000 (which later turned out to be about 20,000 too high). Under state law, it would be November 13 before these ballots had been verified and tallied. If Senator Kerry wanted to wait out that process before conceding, we were in for a long wait.

Andy Card was the public face of the Bush-Cheney campaign on Wednesday morning. "We are convinced that President Bush has won reelection with at least 286 electoral votes," he told supporters, but "President Bush decided to give Senator Kerry the respect of more time to reflect on the results of this election."

Andy's call to me to see if I would ask Vernon Jordan to encourage his candidate to concede was clear evidence that in politics as in diplomacy, there are back channels.

"Sure," I said, "I'll give him a call. It took a while to track Vernon down by telephone. When I reached him, he was on the eleventh tee at Augusta National Golf Club, home of the Masters tournament. He didn't say he would or would not talk to Senator Kerry, but my suspicion is that he either weighed in or was about to when the senator called President Bush to concede at about 11:00 A.M. Eastern time.

That concession was absolutely the right thing to do. Senator Kerry had lost the popular election by almost three million votes and Ohio—after the provisional and overseas ballots were counted—by almost 119,000. There was no plausible way for him to have reversed the outcome.

George W. Bush won the 2004 election for a number of reasons. In large part it was a referendum on his leadership in the aftermath of the terrorist attacks of September 11, 2001. I also believe the debates helped him, on balance. Another big reason was simply that our side did a much better job of organizing and getting our voters to the polls. Turnout was more than 122 million, up about 16 percent from 2000, and the sixty-two million votes cast for the president broke the prior record by about eleven million.

I certainly didn't see this coming. On election day, I was in Washington, D.C., for a board meeting of the Howard Hughes Medical Institute. When I arrived back in Houston that afternoon, I was given the results of several exit polls that didn't look good for the president. I mentioned my concerns to Margaret Tutwiler. She happened to talk to Lynne Cheney later that day, and before long Dick Cheney was on the telephone to let me know the exit polls were wrong, as indeed they turned out to be. The more things change . . .

I LEFT full-time public service in 1993 after working for three great American presidents—Ford, Reagan, and Bush 41—each a man of character and each of whom left our nation in far better shape than he found it. An unexpected pleasure of later years has been adding a fourth name to that list, although in a more limited role.

Early in his first administration, President George W. Bush asked me to let him know each time I came to Washington, and I do. When it's convenient for him (and it usually is), he asks that I drop by for a private visit at the White House. I usually stay about thirty to forty-five minutes. We discuss whatever is on his mind—sometimes foreign or economic policy, sometimes politics, sometimes personnel. He wants me to be candid and frank, and I am. This idea that he is overly sensitive to critical comment is not accurate, as far as I'm concerned. And despite what a lot of pundits may imagine, I always speak for myself, not as a conduit from the president's father or anyone else. Finally, what I learn in confidence in those visits to the Oval Office stays in the Oval Office.

On a couple of occasions I have been asked by the president, or by the vice president on the president's behalf, whether I would consider a full-time position in the administration. I know how demanding and all-consuming these kinds of jobs are, however, so my reply in each case was the same: "I am extremely honored by the suggestion, but at my age and stage of life I do not think this is something I should do." Discussing the details of these inquiries would break my rule about respecting presidential confidences.

In addition to negotiating the ground rules for the debates in the 2004 election, I have taken other special assignments at the president's request—a diplomatic mission to former Soviet Georgia, a mission to win forgiveness of Iraqi debt, and service as cochair of the Carter-Baker federal election reform commission. At the request of members of Congress and with the approval of the White House, I recently agreed to cochair a bipartisan study group to conduct a forward-looking assessment of the situation in Iraq. In addition, I led presidential delegations to the twenty-fifth anniversary commemoration of the Solidarity movement in Poland and events commemorating the tenth anniversary of the assassination of Israel's prime minister, Yitzhak Rabin.

EDUARD SHEVARDNADZE was foreign minister of the Soviet Union during most of my tenure as secretary of state. We worked side by side as the Berlin Wall fell, Germany was reunited, Eastern Europe and Central Asia were released from Soviet domination, and an international alliance formed to liberate Kuwait from Iraq. Thanks to Eduard, the Cold War ended more quickly, more peacefully, and in a more orderly fashion than it otherwise might have. For that, he will have an honored place in history.

When it was all over, he went home to Georgia—a small country bounded by Russia, the Black Sea, Turkey, Armenia, and Azerbaijan. His countrymen called him back there after their experiment with freedom dissolved into chaos and internal violence. The elegant and soft-spoken man known to his countrymen as "Grandfather" or the "Silver Fox" had a reputation for honesty and hard work, and, serving as acting chairman of the state council, he quickly restored a degree of stability. Three years later Georgia adopted a new constitution and elected Eduard president.

In one of my last acts as secretary of state, I flew to Georgia in 1992 to show support for my old friend. A civil war was still raging. I could hear gunfire from the government guesthouse where I stayed, which had been the home of Joseph Stalin's infamous KGB chief, Lavrenty Beria. Tens of thousands of Georgians rallied in Freedom Square, and my diplomatic security agents nearly swallowed their walkie-talkies when Eduard and I went down to address the crowd amid all the burned-out buildings. Things were more peaceful when I visited again as a private citizen in 1994.

The Shevardnadze years in Georgia were mixed, at best. At times the economy showed signs of life, but Eduard had to fight hard to preserve the territorial integrity of Georgia against tremendous pressure from Russia and other neighboring countries. Eduard never succeeded in eradicating corruption—a fight that, in a twist of history, he had begun as a Soviet apparatchik in the 1960s, also without much success.

In addition, an estimated 260,000 Georgians were driven out of their homes by violence in outlying regions, much of it sparked by ethnic discord. And thousands more, many of them well-educated young adults, fled to Europe to find work.

Through it all, Eduard was steadfastly pro-Western, and the United States reciprocated with economic aid, diplomatic support, and low-level military support. In 1997, he visited the United States (and the Baker Institute). "Georgia's future security," I wrote at the time, "is important to America's security" because Georgia occupied a strategic location between the vast oil and gas resources of the Caspian Sea and international markets in the West.

No wonder, then, that the United States cared what happened in Georgia's tumultuous parliamentary elections of November 2003 and the presidential election that would come early the next year. Liberal reformers had substantial political support for taking Georgia in a new direction, but they feared that irregularities that had been evident in past Georgian elections would deprive them of their victory.

That's when the White House and State Department asked me to visit my old friend to impress upon him how important it was that the elections be free and fair. To lend authority to the undertaking, I was appointed as a special presidential envoy (SPE), without salary or benefits. On the flight to Georgia in early July 2003 on one of the White House's Air Force jets, I worked out a set of election guidelines—we called it "Scorecard for Georgian Elections"—with my traveling team, Elizabeth Jones, assistant secretary of state for European and Eurasian affairs, Matt Bryza from the National Security Council and Julie Fisher, the State Department's desk officer for Georgia. We were joined on the ground by the U.S. ambassador, Richard Miles. Among other things, we called for equal access to the media, independent election observers, and most important, perhaps, the rejection of violence by all sides.

It was not pleasant to tell an old friend how to run his nation's business, and we knew that fair elections would not necessarily go his way. As always, however, Eduard was gracious and did the right thing. "America has been providing Georgia with invaluable assistance since the very first day of its independence," he would say later, "and therefore [has] the moral right to give us friendly advice." He quickly signed the guidelines, as did the opposition. As far as I know, Eduard's government implemented the guidelines, except in those provinces that were out of its control.

That November, exit polls showed that the opposition had won, but for several days the election commission refused to certify the results. Tens of thousands of Georgians took to the streets in what came to be known as the Rose Revolution. Just as he had done at the end of the Cold War, Eduard refused to use force to preserve the old order. He held out a few days, then, facing the inevitable, he resigned.

Less than a year later, he lost his beloved wife, Nanuli. They had been married fifty-three years. Today he is writing his memoir. I still have a big warm spot in my heart for this man and his family. I had told him many times, as a friend, that life after politics was good and that he should not stay too long. Sadly, I am afraid, that is what he did. But he will be treated well by history for his refusal to support the use of force to keep the empire together when he was foreign minister of the Soviet Union.

LESS THAN two weeks after the Shevardnadze resignation, President Bush announced that I had accepted another assignment as special presidential envoy, this one concerning Iraq. "Secretary Baker will report directly to me and will lead an effort to work with the world's governments at the highest levels, with international organizations, and with the Iraqis in seeking the restructuring and reduction of Iraq's official debt," the White House announced on December 5, 2003.

The first administration contact about this mission came from Condi Rice, then the president's national security adviser, in October 2003 while I was at my Wyoming ranch. Earlier that same year, the U.S.-led military coalition had invaded and occupied Iraq. A necessary first step in rebuilding the devastated country was to get rid of the billions of dollars of Iraq's debt to other countries.

Saddam Hussein's government had borrowed far more money from other governments—an estimated $120 billion or more—than the people of Iraq would ever be able to repay. Much of it went for tanks and missiles, billions more for palaces and luxuries for the governing elite. After debt repayment, no money would be left over for humanitarian relief or to rebuild schools, hospitals, utility systems, and other infrastructure. And a financially crippled Iraq, like the Weimar Republic after World War I, would almost certainly guarantee permanent instability in Iraq. One more point: from a U.S. perspective, every dollar of debt relief would potentially be one less dollar that the American taxpayer might have to be asked to pay toward reconstruction.

My debt-relief mission covered only government-to-government (or sovereign) debt, not the billions more that Iraq owed to private companies or the reparations the Security Council had ordered Iraq to pay Kuwait after the first Gulf War. The idea was that I would do a reprise of my tin-cup tour in the fall of 1990, when I went from capital to capital soliciting pledges of financial support for a military campaign to liberate Kuwait. This time, however, I would be asking governments to write off their Iraqi debts.

Condi suggested that I operate through the Treasury Department. "For this to work," I replied, "I have to be seen as a representative of the president." That meant that my office, if I had one, had to be in the White House, that I needed to report directly to George W. Bush, not to a cabinet officer, and that I should meet with prime ministers and other foreign heads of government, not with their finance ministers.

All this was agreed to, and I was again appointed as special presidential envoy. This time, however, I was actually put on the roster of the White House as its lowest-paid employee at one dollar per year, before taxes. I also had to take a drug test, which, fortunately, I passed. With me standing by in the Oval Office, the president then telephoned Jacques Chirac, Gerhard Schroeder, and other government leaders and asked them to see me.

The president and I also talked about strategy. I don't recall the exact words, but my main point was that this would be a delicate mission, in view of the opposition of many creditor nations—France, Germany, and Russia in particular—to Operation Iraqi Freedom. There was no reason to think they were in a mood to do us any favors.

"Regardless of our disappointment with the way we were treated by longtime allies, however, we can't let that disappointment cloud our judgment," I said. "These alliances have meant a lot to us through the years, and now we're up against a situation where we need them if we're going to rebuild Iraq. So I want to be able to go to them and say that we're reaching out." The president agreed, and I later used this in my talking points with foreign leaders.

On Monday, December 15, an Air Force 757 from the fleet available to the White House picked me up in Houston for a four-day trip to France, Germany, Italy, Great Britain, and Russia. I was delighted to get one of the big birds, usually reserved for the vice president, the secretary of state, or the secretary of defense. It had excellent facilities for staff, communications, and most of all, sleep, that vital friend of the successful diplomat. Traveling with me were the indispensable Gary Edson, deputy assistant to the president for international economic affairs and deputy national security adviser; Larry Greenwood, deputy assistant secretary of state; Clay Lowery, deputy assistant secretary of the treasury; and Sean McCormack, press spokesman from the National Security Council, all of whom offered superb support.

Our strategy was simple. *The president values our historic alliance and is grateful that you have received me. Our countries have had disagreements about Iraq, but we are reaching out and asking you to help the Iraqi people rebuild their country. These debts can never be repaid. By forgiving them, we simply accept that reality and move on, which will lift a dark shadow from Iraq's future. What the president seeks is your agreement to the principle of a substantial reduction in your country's debt in Iraq. We also seek your commitment to settle this matter quickly, in 2004.*

One thing I would not do, however, is talk numbers. The details could be settled by finance ministries. My job was to create momentum by winning commitments on very generous *words* at the political level that would translate into very large *numbers* at the technical level.

My meetings with President Chirac and others went remarkably well. In a joint statement, France and Germany pledged "substantial" reductions in the debts owed them by Iraq and urged other nations to do the same. Great Britain and Italy, both coalition allies, also gave their support. Russia agreed to consider the matter. Later that month, Japan raised the bar by agreeing to forgive the "vast majority" of its debts. China refused to be pinned down publicly, but privately assured me of a "big, big reduction." On a later trip to the Middle East, Qatar and the United Arab Emirates quickly signed on. Because of special circumstances, however, Kuwait (reparations) and Saudi Arabia (a dispute over whether payments were loans or grants) did not come to terms, and last I heard negotiations with these two countries were still ongoing. I also talked to leaders of several other countries by telephone.

By December 2004, a year after we started, the Paris Club—a consortium of nineteen industrialized countries that have worked together since the 1950s to help over-indebted countries—had agreed to an across-the-board reduction of *a minimum of* 80 percent, which was a new record for that organization. (The previous high, I have been told, was 67 percent.) Some creditors wrote off even more. The United States, for instance, forgave every dollar Iraq owed us—$4.1 billion. If this was not the largest debt-relief operation in history for a single nation, it was certainly one of the largest. Iraq's finance minister, Adil Abd al-Mahdi, called it "the second liberation of Iraq." And from my point of view, it also demonstrated how much good the developed nations can accomplish when they work together.

As I WAS putting this book to bed in early 2006, another opportunity for service on Iraq came my way. I was asked to cochair a bipartisan study group on Iraq. Our assignment: to make a forward-looking assessment of the situation there. The group was formed at the urging of members of Congress, but the White House welcomed it and agreed to help with travel, access to documents, and other assistance. (Anyone who has read this far knows I would not have taken this assignment without White House approval.)

My cochair is former congressman Lee Hamilton, a Democrat, who chaired the House Foreign Affairs Committee. He now heads the Woodrow Wilson International Center for Scholars, which will assist with the project, along with the United States Institute of Peace, the

Baker Institute, the Center for Strategic and International Studies, and the Center for the Study of the Presidency.

I don't have any illusions about the difficulty of the task. My hope is that we can develop insights and advice that will be helpful to the administration and to Congress, and that will benefit our country. To me, this study group has much the same mission as the Social Security commission in 1983. That group worked out a bipartisan consensus on a set of commonsense policies that helped Congress and the administration put aside considerations of political advantage and do what was best for our country on a very difficult and contentious issue. My hope, my prayer, is that the Iraq Study Group can do something similar.

IN THE 2000 Florida presidential election recount dispute, I objected strenuously to changing the rules in the middle of the game, not to the idea that election reforms might be needed. But those reforms should come by legislative action between elections, I believed, not by letting courts rewrite the rules while the votes were being counted.

In late 2004 I was challenged to put up or shut up on election reform. The call came from Ken Mehlman, head of the Republican National Committee. After the 2000 election, a commission headed by former presidents Jimmy Carter and Gerald Ford had recommended a package of election-law changes, some of which were enacted by Congress in 2002. Now President Carter wanted a new bipartisan commission to push for additional reforms, and unfortunately, President Ford no longer traveled.

This was not something I was eager to do, but I told Ken I would consider it. The commission would be a private undertaking, not anything official, and we were winning elections, not losing them, so I wondered why the administration cared about it. "Because," Karl Rove told me later, "President Carter will find a Republican who will be willing to serve, and we want someone on our side who won't get rolled."

I still hadn't made up my mind in January 2005 when I attended a White House dinner in honor of George H. W. Bush and Barbara Bush's sixtieth wedding anniversary. President Bush 43 sort of settled the issue for me, however, when he pulled me aside and said, "Thanks for being willing to do this federal election reform commission with President Carter."

"You're welcome, Mr. President."

I'm glad I accepted. Working as cochair with President Carter turned out to be a pleasure. We have had our political and policy differences in the past, and I'm sure we'll have more in the future, but he's a man of integrity who deserves credit and respect for promoting free and fair elections around the world, personally and through his Carter Center. In 1990, for instance, he worked with our Republican administration in connection with the elections in Nicaragua that replaced Daniel Ortega with Violeta Chamorro, ending more than a decade of violent conflict in that Central American nation. But for President Carter's moral authority, I doubt that Ortega would have accepted the results and stepped down.

We held hearings at American University, the Baker Institute, and the Carter Center. I was concerned that the commission would turn into a philosophical debating society, then make a bunch of pie-in-the-sky recommendations. That didn't happen. The report came out in September 2005, and it was a good one.*

"Americans are losing confidence in the fairness of elections," President Carter and I wrote, "and while we do not face a crisis today, we need to address the problems . . ." Our goals were to improve the administration of our elections, enhance their integrity, and increase voter participation.

The commission had eighty-seven recommendations. The big four, I think, were asking voters to present driver's licenses or other

---

*My assistant on the project was John Williams, a former political reporter for the *Houston Chronicle*. His writing skills, practical experience covering elections, and hard work with the commission staff had a lot to do with how well things turned out.

photo IDs when they show up to vote, improving our system for registering voters, turning elections over to nonpartisan administrators, and requiring electronic voting machines to print paper records that can be audited. The commission also asked states to do more to register potential voters and to supply IDs without cost for people who lacked driver's licenses.

States should take responsibility for the accuracy and integrity of their voting lists, we said—local officials do it now—and all state lists should be linked together through a national computer, so a prospective voter would need to register only one time.

Other recommendations included four regional presidential primaries; a request that the media wait until voting ends in all forty-eight contiguous states before projecting the results anywhere; and the enfranchisement of ex-felons who have done their time, except registered sex offenders and those convicted of capital crimes. That last one was something I would not have proposed myself, but I accepted it as part of the overall package.

All in all, the Commission on Federal Election Reform turned out to be a positive experience—practical in its aspirations, bipartisan in its spirit and approach, successful in its outcome.

In 2005, President George W. Bush also asked me to lead the presidential delegation to the twenty-fifth anniversary commemoration of the Solidarity movement in Poland. What a pleasure it was to renew old acquaintances (Lech Walesa, Bronislaw Geremek, Václav Havel), to reflect on how the spirit of Solidarity had transformed Poland and was still at work in peaceful democratic movements like the Rose Revolution in Georgia, and to read to the assembled dignitaries President Bush's letter of greeting.

Later that year, I also led the presidential delegation to the ceremonies commemorating the tenth anniversary of the assassination of Israel's prime minister, Yitzhak Rabin. If anything, this event was even more emotional, because Yitzhak—architect of the Oslo accords, advocate of peace, Nobel laureate—was also my friend. The ceremony at his grave on Mount Herzl in Jerusalem reminded us all of what he had done and, even more, what he might have done if he had not been cut down.

I saw and visited with many acquaintances and colleagues from the old days—among them, Ariel Sharon, Ehud Olmert, David Levy, Benjamin Netanyahu, and Eytan Bentsur. I had dinner one evening with Olmert, Condi Rice, and Sharon. "Tell the prime minister," I joked to Ehud, "that this is the only time I've ever come to Israel and he has not announced the creation of a new settlement." Ehud translated my remark to Prime Minister Sharon, who smiled and replied in English: "That's because I've used that trick before."

The irony, of course, is that Sharon, who long resisted the peace process, had now become a peacemaker himself. How sad, then, that he would be disabled by a severe stroke two months later. Time's winged chariot . . .

EIGHTEEN

"A SINGLE BLUEBELL"

IT'S A TRADITION in the news business to prepare obituaries for prominent people before the event, and reporters also like to get their interview stories ready ahead of time. That's why my office telephone lit up in early June 2004. Ronald Reagan had been ill for almost ten years. Now word had spread that it was just a matter of time before Nancy lost Ronnie and our nation lost one of its greatest presidents. Journalists wanted my memories of the man and reaction to his death. Hour by hour, the list of press inquiries grew, but I didn't return the calls. I had nothing to say. One of my rules, rarely violated, is not to give past-tense interviews about anyone who is still alive. To me, it seems inappropriate.*

President Reagan's illness had cut him off from his friends long before death took his body. For years, however, I had made a point of visiting Nancy most every time I was in Southern California. Seeing her,

---

*In the years before President Reagan's death, I put one or two retrospective interviews in the can, but only because Nancy approved of my doing so, along with others who had served the president.

even for a few minutes, was my way of communicating love and respect, and it always refreshed my spirit.

My last conversation with the president came three days before his eighty-third birthday at a February 1994 gala in his honor. I don't recall what we talked about—probably just social chitchat—but he was in great spirits. His political soul mate, Margaret Thatcher, spoke that night, and he always delighted in her presence. "It is an honor and a joy to be here with you to celebrate the forty-fourth anniversary of your thirty-ninth birthday," she joked.

A bit more than eight months later, President Reagan supplied a taped message for the groundbreaking ceremony of the Baker Institute. In the excitement of the moment, I failed to notice what is now evident to me. His speeches usually soared, even for routine events. On this day, however, his words fluttered to the earth, never quite taking wing.

Exactly sixteen days later, on November 5, 1994, he announced that he suffered from Alzheimer's. "At the moment, I feel just fine," he wrote, but he understood the burden his family would bear. "I only wish there was some way I could spare Nancy from this painful experience."

"When the Lord calls me home, whenever that may be," he concluded, "I will leave with the greatest love for this country of ours and eternal optimism for its future. I now begin the journey that will lead me into the sunset of my life."

On Saturday, June 5, 2004, Margaret Tutwiler telephoned to say the president had passed away. He was ninety-three. I was deeply saddened, but I took consolation in knowing that his suffering, and Nancy's, had ended, and that he was in a better place.

Now I could talk, so I went to my office at the Baker Institute and gave interviews until nine or ten that night, then got up early the next morning for a couple of Sunday talk shows. Each contact with reporters was coordinated through the White House, at its request.

I repeated the Reagan story to all who cared to hear it. "Restored America's pride . . . made everybody feel good . . . completely without guile . . . big-picture president . . . stuck to his principles . . . changed the world." And Nancy "has handled these final difficult years with dignity and grace."

I also mentioned that the Washington of Ronald Reagan's time was a more civil place than today. Political adversaries then were not treated as personal enemies. The president could fight all day with Tip O'Neill over public policy, then sit down with him over drinks that evening and share a laugh.

Early Wednesday, June 9, Susan and I caught a ride to Washington with George and Barbara Bush on the White House airplane sent to fetch the forty-first president and his first lady. That afternoon, President Reagan's coffin arrived from California and was pulled slowly up Constitution Avenue to the U.S. Capitol on a horse-drawn caisson, followed by a riderless horse.

Shortly after George, Barbara, Susan, and I arrived in Washington, we went by the Capitol Rotunda to pay our respects. The flag-draped coffin—brightly spotlighted, framed by a military honor guard—rested alone in that vast space on the same catafalque (I am told) used for President Lincoln. In a ceremony there a few hours earlier, Vice President Dick Cheney had eulogized President Reagan as a gentle man— "If Ronald Reagan ever uttered a cynical, or cruel, or selfish word, the moment went unrecorded"—and a powerful figure in history—"It was the vision and will of Ronald Reagan that gave hope to the oppressed, shamed the oppressors, and ended an evil empire." As we walked down the steps of the Capitol afterward, I wept. My emotions were still in turmoil when Susan and I went to sleep that night in the Lincoln Bedroom, guests of the forty-third president.

As thousands of mourners streamed through the Rotunda to pay their respects the next day, Susan and I accompanied George 41 and Barbara on a visit to Nancy at Blair House. We said all the right things, I am sure, but the fact is that she comforted us more than we comforted her. Nancy was a source of strength for her Ronnie. And as she accompanied him to Washington one last time—and later back to California— her love and devotion were a source of strength for us all.

The agency in charge of state funerals is the Military District of Washington, a unit of the U.S. Army, which worked out the details with the family well ahead of time. Mike Deaver had coordinated much of the planning for Nancy. Everything was prearranged, tightly scripted, and beautifully done. The staging would have delighted the former actor, I think. He was playing a leading role in a vast national drama, this one about love, remembrance, and heroism, an old pro hitting his marks one last time.

On Friday, Susan and I traveled in the president's motorcade from the White House to the National Cathedral for the memorial service. We entered in a Secret Service "security package" after most others—including all former presidents except 41—had been seated, which was a bit embarrassing.

Former senator Jack Danforth, an ordained Episcopalian minister, officiated. The text of the homily for President Reagan was based on the Sermon on the Mount, "'You are the light of the world. A city set upon a hill cannot be hid,'" Jack said. "For him, America was the shining city on a hill."

George H. W. Bush delivered one of the eulogies. "As his vice president for eight years, I learned more from Ronald Reagan than from anyone I encountered in all my years of public life," he said. "I learned kindness [and] I also learned courage."

Margaret Thatcher, present for the funeral service but not well, spoke by prerecorded tape. While "others hoped, at best, for an uneasy cohabitation with the Soviet Union," she said, "he won the Cold War—not only without firing a shot, but also by inviting enemies out of their fortress and turning them into friends."

As the former British prime minister's distinctive voice filled the cathedral, she sat quietly, head bowed. In the chair immediately to her right was one of the friends she had in mind, Mikhail Gorbachev, invited (like her) as a special guest of the Reagan family.

"For the last years of his life, Ronnie's mind was clouded by illness," she said. "That cloud has now lifted. He is himself again—more himself than at any time on this earth. For we may be sure that the Big Fella Upstairs never forgets those who remember Him."

The outpouring of love and affection, and deep respect, for this former president—in the ceremonies and on the street—was overwhelming. His supporters had always loved him, but now everyone, including some of his old detractors, had come to realize something that those of us who worked with him knew about his character, his integrity, and his performance as president.

Even members of the media, many of whom had abhorred his policies, could never bring themselves to dislike him as a person. And now that he was gone, many journalists and commentators, to their credit, admitted the obvious—that he had changed the nation and the world for the better.

I've had a lot to say, pro and con, about the impact of television on American politics and public life, but an event like this one demonstrates the power of the medium to unite our country around shared experiences, this time in celebrating the life of a great president and mourning his passing.

I owe my career in politics and public service to my friend George H. W. Bush, but I also owe it to President Reagan. Who else would have had the confidence, the comfort in his own judgment, to hire the campaign chairman for two political rivals as White House chief of staff? How was I fortunate enough to serve this wonderful man for eight years? My life was forever changed by his one generous decision to invite me into his administration, and I tried every day to be worthy of that honor. I loved him dearly.

That's one of the things I told Nancy at Blair House the day before. After everyone else had said their goodbyes, I lingered a bit. "Nancy, I want to tell you one more time," I said, "how appreciative I am for having had the opportunity to serve the president."

"We're very grateful," she replied, my hands in hers, "for what you did for us."

I left the room in tears.

. . .

AFTER THE memorial service, I waited for my ride in a group at the side entrance of National Cathedral, along with President Carter and Rosalynn, President and Senator Clinton, Senator Kerry, and others. I think George and Barbara were there, too. I was talking with Rosalynn when someone grabbed me from behind, turned me around, and gave me a big hug and kiss. My osculatory partner was none other than Teresa Heinz Kerry, wife of the presumptive Democratic nominee for president. She and her first husband, Senator John Heinz, were friends of Susan's and mine before his death in a 1991 air crash. This was the first time we had seen her in years, and she was as vibrant as ever. Although he didn't kiss me, John Kerry was also very friendly. I didn't know the incident had been caught on camera until my friends kidded me about it later.

After the ceremony, George, Barbara, Susan, and I rushed back to Houston. Forty-one was turning eighty, and a long-planned party for him was scheduled for Saturday night in Minute Maid Park. The next day, he went skydiving over the Bush Library in College Station, Texas—a stunt that made me wonder whether he was aching for his own funeral!

A FRIEND later told me he was fascinated by the aftermath of President Reagan's funeral. Cameras followed some dignitaries as they left the cathedral, and he was struck by the sight of former national leaders and world leaders setting off down the sidewalk by themselves, without fanfare, destined in all likelihood to fade into the crowd.

I was not surprised by this. When I was President Reagan's chief of staff back in the early eighties, I saw my counterpart from a former administration walking down Pennsylvania Avenue. Once he had been at the center of American public life. This day, however, he was by himself—no reporters, no security, no trappings of power—just a solitary man, unnoticed, alone with his thoughts. Ever after, that mental picture served to remind me of the impermanence of power and place.

Three things helped me stay grounded during my years in the spotlight—my family, my friends, and my faith. I've talked about my family throughout the book, and will return to that subject. But for my friends, of course—and in particular George H. W. Bush, but also Gerald Ford, Rog Morton, Dick Cheney, Stu Spencer, Mike Deaver, and Bob Teeter—most of this book would have been blank pages. I have only alluded, however, to the role of faith, and I want to say more about this.

I had been a churchgoer and a regular participant in small-group worship, but the first time I spoke openly about my faith was at the National Prayer Breakfast in 1990. Of all the speeches I've ever given, the transcript for this one is the most requested.

Many believe faith is more difficult for those in public life. For me, at least, the exact opposite was true. Living in the centrifuge of politics encouraged, even demanded, spiritual growth. That life was certainly exciting and, in many ways, satisfying. But power can also be intoxicating and addictive. "Power tends to corrupt, and absolute power corrupts absolutely," Lord Acton said, and I think that's true. I've felt the temptation myself, and it's unsettling.

In addition, temporal power is fleeting. I cleaned out my desk in January 1993 and became a private citizen. Like the lonely chief of staff I had spotted on Pennsylvania Avenue so many years before, all my titles now had "former" in front of them. As my public prominence diminished, I also discovered that I could stand on busy street corners and walk through airports without being recognized. This was liberating in a way, but also—truth be told—disquieting.

Power has its satisfactions, but inner security and the deepest kind of personal fulfillment are not among them. It is only through a relationship with God, not by our actions here on earth, that life has real meaning. And for me, at least, a life of faith does not come easily. I have to work at it.

One blessing of faith is that you can see God's handiwork in the events of your life. When I was secretary of state, for instance, a great revolution swept Eastern Europe and the former Soviet Union. As the Berlin Wall fell, dictators were toppled, the Soviet Union collapsed, and communism was consigned to President Reagan's "ash heap of history," it was hard not to see the profound influence of the religious beliefs of those who were freed from tyranny. I do not discount the role of human agency or the powerful economic and political causes of this revolution, but I believe it also had a spiritual source.

I'll never forget my September 1989 meetings in Wyoming with former Soviet Foreign Minister Eduard Shevardnadze. He and I ended our very productive round of negotiations with an exchange of gifts. I gave him cowboy boots. He gave me an enamel picture of Jesus teaching the people. "You see, even we communists are changing our worldview," he said.

He was right. Communism had denied the very existence of God and treated individuals as servants of the state, but the political revolution that swept Eastern Europe and the former Soviet Union brought with it a resurgence of faith. Individuals were affirmed as children of God, each equally worthy of respect, free to choose, and responsible for their choices.

Václav Havel, then president of Czechoslovakia, said his country's democratic revolution was a moral event, restoring the faith, compassion, humility, and forgiveness that communism had opposed. It was no accident that the churches of Eastern Europe played such an important part in these political changes. Despite decades of oppression, the people of God maintained their integrity as custodians of the faith and guardians of the dignity of individual men and women.

There was a lesson for the United States in these events. Lech Walesa, the hero of a free Poland, once said, "Americans were drifting away from spiritual values as they become richer." "Sooner or later," he said, "we will have to go back to our fundamental values, back to God, the truth, the truth which is God." This is a useful reminder, I believe, that the great political experiment of the United States was, and continues to be, a great spiritual experiment as well. President Kennedy had this in mind, I think, when he closed his inaugural address with these words: "here on earth God's work must truly be our own."

MY INSTINCT as a young man was to go it alone. I loved my friends, but I was slow to accept their help in getting through life. If you were strong enough, if you prepared carefully enough, and if you worked hard enough, I believed, you could do it all yourself. Self-reliance meant never admitting you needed help. If you suffered pain, you endured it. If you had problems, you solved them.

The truth, however, is that we can't do it alone. We need each other. Friends are especially important in times of personal distress. I've written about how I lost my first wife, Mary Stuart, to cancer when she was only thirty-eight. My friends helped save my life. They were there with me at her bedside during the last days. There to help our four boys—heartbroken, scared, confused. And there to stand with Susan and me as we put two families together at a very difficult time in the lives of our seven children.

My public career was a monument to the friendships I made along the way. I also developed close relationships with many of the young people who worked with me. We formed a team, and their judgment, creativity, hard work, and loyalty were responsible for much of what we accomplished together. That's why I have mentioned so many of them in this book, and I wish there was room to mention many others. In the end, however, we do not choose our friends because of what they can do for us. They are the people we love and trust, and whose company we enjoy.

MY OTHER ANCHOR has always been my family. My mother, Bonner Means Baker, taught me—by precept and example—many of the values that have guided me. I will always treasure her memory. That's why I dedicated my first book, in part, "to my wonderful mother, whose love and support gave me wings to fly."

The other dedication went to "my great-grandfather, my grand-father, and my father, the three generations of James Addison Bakers whose belief in God, integrity, and hard work gave me a remarkable heritage that inspired me." It's hard to explain what it means to carry the same name as such accomplished men. From childhood, I was simply expected to succeed. I was also given the love and support to allow me to do well in life. Without this legacy, I doubt that I would have ever had the education, the experiences, or the confidence my public life demanded.

I'm not sure I did as well for my own children as my father and grandfather did for me. I loved them all dearly, but when they were young I worked hard in my big-firm law practice and left most of the child-rearing to Mary Stuart. We were a happy family, but I wish I had spent more time with the boys.

One of the biggest mistakes in my life was not telling them how ill their mother was. Another was surprising them three years later with my marriage to Susan. My four and Susan's three knew one another beforehand, so that helped with the blending, but it was a rough time for all of them—losing one parent through death or divorce, dealing with the disloyalty (from a child's perspective) of the remaining parent's remarriage, then sharing that parent's attention with other children.

The family name that was such an asset to me sometimes proved to be a burden for my children. They were the fifth generation of a dis-tinguished family, with a father whose name was often in the news-papers. It was natural for them to wonder, I suspect, whether their best would ever be good enough. "Why can't we just be a normal family?" one child wondered aloud.

Some in our family struggled with alcohol and drug abuse during their teen and early adult years. We had the resources, thank God, to help them find the treatment they needed, and we are very proud of how they have put their problems behind them.

It was Susan who ran the car pools to four different schools and countless after-school activities, bought the groceries, kept the chart in the kitchen to determine which teenager got the station wagon on which night, and explained why Daddy wasn't home. The way I knew it was time to get up many mornings was when I heard the *whack, whack* of her knees hitting the floor to pray for our family.

The joy of my life is that those prayers were answered. When our family gathered for Thanksgiving about eight or ten years ago, I asked everyone to say in one sentence what they were thankful for. "I'm thankful," one of my sons said, "that my parents didn't give up on me." I want to say to our children—for the world to hear—how thankful and proud I am to be their father and stepfather.

In MID-MAY of 2002, I found myself tromping through the woods of northwestern Alabama with a group of distant cousins I had never met before. They were descendants of Mary Jane Baker, a sister of the first James Addison Baker, who had married a James Carroll and produced a large family that still has its roots around Florence, Alabama. We came into a small opening that showed evidence of a lot of fresh work with axes and weed trimmers, and there—amid thirteen small American flags pushed into the ground to decorate the site for my visit—I saw the gravestone of our common great-great-grandfather, Elijah Baker, 1792–1845. Hunters had recently found it, and my cousins had reclaimed it from the encroaching forest.

Later that day, I told this story in a commencement speech at the University of North Alabama in Florence. "We are all embedded in history," I told the graduates. "It shapes us. It defines our opportunities. And it challenges us."

The first James Addison Baker and four brothers left Alabama in the early 1850s and planted themselves in Huntsville, Texas. James

Baker's first wife had died early, and he was probably looking for a fresh start. He soon met and married Rowena Crawford, the principal of the Huntsville (Texas) Female Academy, and that's how my Baker ancestors wound up in Texas.

It's an interesting story, one I have heard repeated all my life. My family scrapbooks contain old handwritten genealogies that trace our history back to Elijah Baker (and trace some branches even further back), but I've never really been much of a genealogy buff myself. What I take from family history is the idea that we did not invent ourselves. The past lives in us and we are, individually and as a nation, the beneficiaries of untold generations of love and toil and sacrifice. It is our responsibility, in turn, to pass on these same values to future generations.

IN *The Politics of Diplomacy*, I wrote that President George H. W. Bush characterized our friendship "as a big brother–little brother relationship." "I think that's a fairly accurate description," I said in the book, "and one that I consider quite a compliment."

Well, according to genealogist William Addams Reitwiesner, George and I are not brothers; we're long-lost cousins. Reitwiesner makes this claim on a Web site—"Ancestry of George W. Bush"—that my staff ran across while doing research for this book. The site traces the Bush family history to colonial America and beyond. At the end of his genealogical database, Reitwiesner reports that two of George's remote ancestors are also mine—Richard Cocke and Mary Aston. They lived in Henrico County, Virginia, in the 1600s. One son (Richard, Jr.) was George's ancient grandpa, and another (William) was mine.

I've always been suspicious of far-out claims of kinship and there's no way for me to judge the accuracy of Reitwiesner's work, other than to say that the bottom of his twelve-generation chart of my ancestry is consistent with Baker family records. My staff asked him about his sources, and he said two of Captain James A. Baker's sisters (my great-aunts) had joined the Daughters of the American Revolution, "and their lines take Mr. Baker back to pre-revolutionary Caroline County, Virginia. From there," he said, "it's trivially easy to make the connection to the Cockes and Astons that the Bushes descend from."

Is it true, then, that I am a distant cousin of my close friend, my tennis partner, the man who led me into politics and public service? All I can say is that the Bush-Baker family connection is such a perfect story that I plan to believe it until someone proves it ain't so. Maybe I'll drop *Jefe* and start saying *cousin*.*

IT RAINED on the cold November day in 2004 that I was supposed to give an outdoor speech in the Oakwood Cemetery in Huntsville, Texas. That's where my great-grandfather, the first James Addison Baker, is buried, along with his friend Sam Houston, the general who won Texas independence, served as its first president, then—after annexation—as U.S. senator and governor. The Texas Historical Commission had authorized a marker for my great-grandfather's grave, and I was invited to attend the ceremony to install the marker and say a few words.

Susan and I got out of our car and started walking to the cemetery under a dripping umbrella, when we were stopped by a very tall, attractive gentleman, who approached from the other direction. I had never seen him before.

"How do you do, sir?" he said, extending his hand. "My name is James Baker."

---

*I am less confident in, but intrigued by, the possibility that I also share common ancestry with Thomas Jefferson. In reviewing the Bush-Baker connection, my researcher (who is not a genealogist) noticed that one branch of my ancestral family, the Blands, traced back to Richard Bland and Elizabeth Randolph. This is something my family has known, or at least claimed, for many years. My researcher said it appeared plausible to him that Elizabeth Randolph was the daughter of William Randolph and Mary Isham, Thomas Jefferson's maternal grandparents. If it's true, the sixty-first secretary of state would be a distant cousin of the first one.

"That's interesting," I said, playing along. "My name is James Baker, too."

"I know," he replied. "I have followed your career for a long time. I'm your cousin."

His name was James Otis Baker. Though born nearby, he had lived most of his life in Los Angeles. He quickly introduced me to his brother, Wendell Baker, who still lived in Huntsville.

I wasn't sure whether to take them seriously, but they seemed genuine in their assertion of kinship. In my remarks a few minutes later, I introduced my children and other relatives who were present at the event. Then, not quite knowing if I myself were serious, I introduced my "just-discovered cousins."

James Otis and Wendell Baker—handsome African-American men—smiled as the crowd turned to identify them.

Afterward, a woman warned me to be careful. "That Wendell Baker is an agitator," she whispered.

"WHAT ARE these called?"

It was Sunday, July 3, 2005, and I was driving through the woods just southwest of Huntsville with my newfound cousins, James Otis, eighty-six, and Wendell, eighty-two. Out the window, I spotted a beautiful flower.

"They're called bluebells," Wendell said.

"May I pick one?"

"Pick as many as you want."

Jesse Baker was James's and Wendell's father, and their family still owned the sandy-soiled acreage and the old home place—off "Baker Road"—where Jesse and his wife, Fannie Willis, had farmed and reared their children. Jesse's father was Andy Baker, my grandfather's first cousin. Andy had had a relationship with an African-American woman named Emma Curtis, which made James and Wendell my third cousins.

They had told me about Andy and Jesse that rainy day the preceding November when I first met them, but they mistakenly thought "Andy" was a nickname for Robert Baker, a brother of my grandfather. They also invited me to attend the biennial reunion of Jesse Baker's descendants. I accepted, and that's how I came to be riding through the woods with them on a hot Sunday afternoon in July, eight months later.

Susan and I had arrived at Wendell's home about an hour earlier, along with two of our sons, John and Mike, and Mike's daughter Mary. (Some of my Houston Baker cousins showed up later.) It was a lovely brick residence on a large green lot shaded by towering pines. The living room walls were covered with scores of family pictures—formal portraits, wedding pictures, graduation shots—including one of a smiling Jesse Baker in a suit, tie, and hat. It was similar in style to the photographs of my grandfather when he was young.

I had had the family connection researched, and I explained what I had learned to James Otis and Wendell. "Your great-grandfather was Gabriel Baker," I told them. "Judge James Addison Baker and Gabriel were sons of Elijah Baker, whose grave I saw when I went to speak at a graduation ceremony at the University of North Alabama in 2002. My great-great-grandfather, Elijah, was also your great-great-grandfather."

Gabriel had a son named Andy, I said. He was born in 1864, one year before the Civil War ended, and he would have been about twenty-three when Jesse was born in 1887. According to research done by Dr. Bernadette Pruitt, a history professor at Sam Houston State University, Andy acknowledged his son, wanted him to have the Baker name, and (by one account, which Wendell disputes) helped provide for Jesse until adulthood. (I have no way of knowing who is right about the question of support, but I hope Andy did that.)

When he grew up, Jesse farmed cotton and vegetables with mule-drawn plows, bought and sold land, and cut pulpwood and timber, James Otis and Wendell told me. "Everybody worked for my dad in the summer. He'd buy the land just to get the trees off it. And if he ran out of money, the bank wouldn't bounce his check."

Jesse had eleven sons and daughters, they told me. One was Herbert, who married a beautiful woman named Mackie. As a boy, I actually knew her. She worked for my grandfather, Captain Baker, and lived with her husband in Houston in a house behind the Captain's residence. The Houston Bakers "didn't know who she was," Wendell said. "We laughed about it."

My grandfather might well have known about Jesse because Andy is buried in the same cemetery plot with Captain Baker, who was his cousin. I don't know whether Mackie's employment was merely a coincidence or happened because she was married to a grandson of Andy Baker. One thing's for sure, however: no one ever told me or others of my generation of Houston cousins anything about this other branch of our family.

At the reunion, I couldn't help thinking about how much things had changed since my grandfather's day, and for the better. In the early 1890s, Captain Baker and other Houston leaders wrote a charter to establish what is now Rice University as a first-class institute for the "white inhabitants of Houston and Texas." That kind of overt discrimination seems foreign to us now, but it was standard back then and evidently what the founder, William Marsh Rice, dictated. University trustees went to court in 1963 and got the racial restrictions eliminated.

Wendell and Jesse told me with pride about their accomplished family and in-laws. Teacher. Lawyer. Judge. Social worker. Entrepreneur. Health inspector. First African-American deputy sheriff in Harris County. Mathematician. Jazz prodigy. Network budget officer. Vice president at Disney–ABC Television Group. Marriage to a son of James Lawson, the intellectual architect of the nonviolent civil rights movement. (Lawson "is the guy who got Mandela out of prison and he is the one who taught Dr. King the power of nonviolence," Wendell said.)

As for Wendell's being an agitator—"and a troublemaker, too," he added cheerfully—that stemmed from civil rights work, including the registration of black voters throughout East Texas in the early 1960s and the peaceful racial integration of Sam Houston State University.

Wendell explained his motivation this way: "I said to myself, 'I have served in the army to defend America.' I said, 'We've been good citizens. We're taxpayers. We're a productive family. Hell, I'm not going to take it.'"

One of his most fascinating stories was how he helped lead a movement in 1961 to throw African-American support to Republican senatorial candidate John Tower. Conservative Anglo Democrats had locked African Americans and Mexican Americans out of the party, according to Wendell, and anointed a candidate he and other minority leaders regarded as a racist.

"Boy, we wiped 'em out. We put John Tower in there," he said. And afterward, "calling Tower was just like calling my brother. He'd pick up the phone and say, 'What do you want?' We got blacks appointed to all sorts of offices."

I told Wendell and James Otis about having the support of several African-American leaders, including Barbara Jordan and Mickey Leland, when I ran for attorney general as a Republican against a conservative Democrat in 1978. "Barbara Jordan," Wendell said wistfully. "She understood."

Wendell then passed around a copy of his book, *If Not Me, Who? What One Man Accomplished in His Battle for Equality.* It's a fascinating read, including an appendix at the end filled with his aphorisms. "Make changes, but use the system to do it." "Compromise, but never when you get nothing." "Results count; excuses don't!"

In telling these political yarns, Wendell and I were not ignoring the likelihood that we had spent most of our political careers on different sides of many important issues. We were just doing what we should have done, which was to start our relationship on the basis of what we had in common, not what we might disagree about. At our ages, we'll probably never get around to the other stuff anyway, and it doesn't much matter whether we do. We did our part. The rest belongs to younger generations.

James Otis sat quietly while his younger brother told political stories, interjecting only once that I should have run for president. "I'll tell you, you did a good job," he said. "You know how to go and talk to people. You straightened out things."

On the way to the reunion, I had stopped by the family cemetery in Houston and copied the inscription off Andy Baker's gravestone. I now read it to his grandchildren. "They who knew him best will bless his name and keep his memory dear while life shall last." He never married, I told them. Jesse was his only child.

The reunion itself was wonderful. It was held a mile or so away at the home of one of Wendell's sons, Bruce, in and around a beautiful hardwood-shaded home down the hill from the main road. Out front, he displayed an old disk harrow, a symbol of his family's heritage.

When I arrived, barbeque was sizzling on big cookers, kids were running everywhere, and probably 150 relatives were swapping stories and studying a large board that displayed their family history. James Otis and Wendell introduced me to their sister, Leola. They were the last living children of Jesse Baker.

The day brought a swirl of emotions. A year ago, this branch of my family was unknown to me. Now Susan and I were being accepted with open arms and sweet spirits. I was profoundly moved by this experience and pleased to have had the opportunity to learn about them and to reminisce with them about our mutual great-great-grandfather.

James Otis quietly shared memories of his beloved wife with Susan. Baker relatives came by, one by one, to shake hands, explain how they fit into the family, and welcome us. We posed for group photographs. Jokes were told. Children ran past, kicking up dust and wondering who these old people were. In these ways, two families acknowledged and embraced each other, becoming one family, quietly and happily.

Reverend Chris Bell, a great-grandchild of Jesse Baker, blessed the meal. "Holy Father," he said, "thank you for another opportunity for fun and fellowship, and for all those who have come such a long way. . . . Bless this food, Father God, that it would be a nourishment to our bodies. In the name of Jesus, Amen."

Our hosts pushed us to the head of the line, and Susan and I stacked our plates with brisket, sausage, ribs, potato salad, beans, tomatoes, onions, and sliced bread. Then we went inside Bruce's home to enjoy our feast. In her lovely strawberry blond hair, Susan wore a single bluebell.

APPENDIX

·————————·

"Item One on Our Agenda Was the Dollar"

W HEN I RESIGNED from Treasury in 1988, my letter to the president said three of his second-term economic initiatives "will be widely judged to have lasting significance." One, of course, was tax reform. Another was a new system of multilateral economic policy coordination we set in motion. And the third was a free-trade agreement between Canada and the United States. I've described the tax reform battle in chapter ten. Now I want to say a few words about the other two items on that list, international economic policy coordination and the trade agreement with Canada. I'll also discuss Black Monday, that day in October 1987 when the stock market fell 508 points. I want to write about these issues because today we face many of the same challenges to U.S. and world prosperity that confronted us in 1985–1988. Our answers to those problems then, I think, hold important lessons for what might be done today.

The first of these subjects, international economic policy coordination, is a good-government catchphrase that, unfortunately, causes some people's eyes to glaze over. It shouldn't. The failure to understand its importance caused U.S. policymakers to pull up the drawbridges after World War I. We tried to insulate America from economic problems elsewhere in the world and keep whatever growth we could generate to ourselves. But those policies did exactly the opposite of what we had hoped. International trade and capital transfers dried up, and with them, economic growth. The isolationism and protectionism of that era actually helped cause the Great Depression and arguably set the stage for World War II. In other words, we got it wrong.

After World War II, however, we got it right. Victorious in war once again, the United States decided not to try to go it alone. Instead, we would cooperate to rebuild postwar economies. Under our leadership, forty-four nations signed the Bretton Woods agreements in 1944, setting up the International Monetary Fund and the World Bank. The dollar was pegged to gold and other world currencies were pegged to the dollar. Soon thereafter, the General Agreement on Tariffs and Trade (GATT) was put in place to promote free trade. These agreements provided a foundation for postwar global prosperity.

I wasn't worried about another Great Depression when I took my oath of office in February 1985. The Reagan tax cuts and the Fed's successful war on inflation—down 10 points since 1980—had set the American economy afire. As the U.S. economy grew, so did the world economy. What concerned me was how to *maintain* this prosperity in the face of unsustainable, and growing, global economic imbalances. We confronted an overvalued dollar, measured against other currencies, and a trade imbalance that favored the Japanese, Germans, and other trading partners at the expense of U.S. manufacturers and exporters. These two economic problems, in turn, had created a big political problem—a protectionist fever in Congress that grew hotter each time Honda or Mercedes won another customer from the Big Three or another pop economist wrote about the inevitable triumph of Japan, Inc. Would we return to the failed go-it-alone policies of the post–World War I era? Dick Darman (at the time, deputy treasury secretary) and I quickly concluded that the best way—and perhaps the only way—to solve these problems was to work more closely with the finance ministers and central bankers of other major economies.

Item one on our agenda was the dollar. For years, relative world currency values had been set by the market. Sometimes they fluctuated wildly on the foreign exchanges. This made it difficult for governments, companies, and investors to make long-range plans. A business could do everything right, then be ruined by a sudden overnight move in exchange rates. And the disparity between the strong dollar and weak foreign currencies gave foreign competitors a big advantage over companies in the United States. This contributed to our growing trade deficit and sparked demands for high tariffs, import quotas, and other protectionist measures.

An analogy may help explain the problem. In the early days of our nation's history, we had a multitude of currencies—paper issued by the Continental Congress, bills printed by the states, notes from private banks, even foreign bills and coins. Shopkeepers had to be mathematical geniuses to price a loaf of bread. The dollar eventually prevailed, thanks in no small part to the work of Alexander Hamilton. We now have a single national currency that makes it easy to buy, sell, and invest in markets from Maine to California, with perfect confidence in the medium of exchange and with no internal currency risk.

While there is no practical way to establish a global currency to provide the same benefits worldwide—and I was not advocating doing so—we knew we could move in that direction if we could stabilize the relative values of the major national currencies. The only way to achieve that stability, however, would be to coordinate the underlying economic fundamentals of the countries that issued these currencies. And doing that would require, in turn, a process for macroeconomic policy coordination among those countries. That *process* is what we created, beginning with the Plaza Accord in 1985.*

---

*A good account of this can be found in *Managing the Dollar: From the Plaza to the Louvre,* by Yoichi Funabashi.

The first Reagan administration's policy toward the dollar was invariably described by commentators as "benign neglect"—letting our currency wander where it will. I'm not sure that's a fair description, but, fair or not, the problem wasn't nearly as acute from 1981–1984 as in 1985. To win White House support to change this policy, we adopted a top-down strategy. There is truly only one decision-maker in the executive branch of the U.S. government, so all we needed was an okay from the president. To make sure we got it, however, I would have to sell Don Regan on the idea. Remember, he and I had traded jobs. His focus now as White House chief of staff, rather than treasury secretary, was more political and less economic. He agreed that we had to find a way to beat back the protectionist sentiment in Congress and that our plan offered the best way to do that. The president liked the idea as well, and with his approval we were in a position to go forward without telling anyone else. And we didn't. A leak would have destroyed or diminished the effectiveness of what we were planning.

Of course, we also needed the support of Federal Reserve Board Chairman Paul Volcker. At one of our regular weekly meetings, I told him what we were considering. He had been on record since early 1985 in favor of correcting the overvalued dollar, so he liked the idea, but he questioned whether I would be able to get the administration to change its dollar policy in such a fundamental way. He was strongly of the view, which I shared, that the dollar's decline must be orderly, not precipitous.

Treasury then made quiet contacts with the finance ministries of the four other major currency countries—Germany, Japan, the UK, and France. On first hearing about what we were considering they too were skeptics, but as the summer of 1985 wore on, they began to realize that we were serious. Our leverage with them was that if we didn't act first, the protectionists in Congress would throw up trade barriers. Auto makers and other industries were pounding the desks at the White House, Treasury, and Congress, demanding that something be done to save them from foreign competition, and Congress was listening. By late summer, top foreign economic officials had begun to see that we were serious.

To our great relief, news of these quiet contacts never leaked. On our side, we kept the circle very tight—the president and his chief of staff, the Fed chairman and his top assistant, and at Treasury, Darman, David Mulford (assistant secretary for international affairs), Margaret Tutwiler (assistant secretary for public affairs), and me. Our foreign counterparts evidently did the same. All that was needed now was a face-to-face meeting of the finance ministers and central bank governors of the five countries to agree on the actions to be taken by each toward coordinating their underlying economic policies.

That came on September 22, 1985, in the Gold Room of New York's lovely old Plaza Hotel. All participants had managed to arrive secretly in New York for the Sunday afternoon meeting. We picked that day because financial markets would be closed. We didn't tell the press until the meeting was under way. (Once alerted, they showed up in droves. The room was packed.) By the end of the day, we had agreed on what came to be known as the Plaza Accord. The public communiqué described the risks to the world economy in these words:

> The U.S. current account deficit together with other factors is now contributing to protectionist pressures which, if not resisted, could lead to mutually destructive retaliation with serious damage to the world economy: world trade would shrink, real growth rates could even turn negative, unemployment would rise still higher, and debt-burdened countries would be unable to secure the export earnings they vitally need.

Ministers and governors "stand ready to cooperate more closely to encourage" exchange-rate adjustments, the communiqué said. And in a masterful use of understatement, it added that "exchange rates should play a role in adjusting external imbalances." The word "intervention" was never used, but in a separate document, a "nonpaper" that was not

made public, participants agreed to sell dollars and buy other currencies to adjust the relative values of the currencies—that is, to lower
the value of the dollar against other currencies.

The results were spectacular. Despite strong resistance from traders,
the dollar dropped against other currencies, quickly and substantially,
but in an orderly way. In his January 1986 state of the union address,
President Reagan signaled our satisfaction with the Plaza Accord and
our commitment to continue working with our trading partners to stabilize exchange rates.

Plaza was about more than just currency adjustments. It also established the principle (and for a while, at least, the practice) of multilateral economic policy coordination. Among other things, the United
States undertook to control the fiscal deficit, Japan agreed to stimulate
domestic demand and open its borders to more imports, Germany said
it would reduce the size of its public sector and remove "rigidities"
(read, "excessive regulations") that inhibited the labor and capital
markets, and all signatories promised to fight protectionism.

Critics say the United States later reneged on its deficit-reduction
pledge. All I can say is that we made the promise in good faith and
did our best to implement it. In December the president signed the
Gramm-Rudman-Hollings Act, which slowed the rate of growth of
federal spending. Other signatory countries also fell short on their
commitments. What was important, however, is that we were all trying
to coordinate our policies. Each country was subject to political constraints that made it difficult to put all the desirable policies fully into
practice. Just because implementation of the Plaza Accord was not perfect, however, does not mean that the agreement itself was not good. It
was clearly successful in forestalling potential protectionist legislation
in Congress.

In early 1986, Treasury even pushed for international coordination of monetary policy to drive down interest rates. Central bankers
resisted. They didn't want finance ministers, mere politicians, telling
them what to do. Some understandings were reached, however, and in-

terest rates began to fall as central bankers responded to calls for coordinated action.

In time, concerns grew that the dollar might have fallen too far. This led to the Louvre Accord of February 22, 1987. While Plaza was a onetime agreement to deal with a specific set of circumstances, Louvre was more ambitious. It aimed to *institutionalize* the process of coordination of economic policies to stabilize world currencies within an agreed, but unpublished, set of ranges. Like Plaza, it worked. Deputy finance ministers began to meet monthly, finance ministers less frequently, to work out common policies, and the dollar headed north. By the fall of 1987, I publicly referred to the possibility of looking at "a basket of commodities, including gold," to stabilize our currencies on the basis of what economists called "purchasing power parity."

The effects of macroeconomic policy adjustments often are not visible for many months. By 1987, however, the U.S. current account deficit—which the Plaza communiqué had cited as evidence of trouble in the global economic system—had begun to fall. In 1991, it reached zero. Talk in Congress about erecting trade barriers never completely died away, but it subsided. The Reagan economic boom continued, and the world economy grew with it.

Multilateral coordination of economic policy is very difficult politically for all countries involved, but that is no reason not to make the effort. After I left Treasury in 1988, the process continued of its own momentum for a short time, then fell dormant. In President Clinton's second term, Robert Rubin briefly revived it to deal, successfully, with the East Asian economic crises. Otherwise, and sadly, the process largely ended with the Reagan administration.

The need for aggressive economic policy coordination today is, if anything, more acute now than in 1985. The U.S. current account deficit that worried us so much in 1985 was only 2.7 percent of GDP. In 2005, it reached 6.4 percent. Even China is starting to bid for high-profile U.S. assets—shades of "Japan, Inc."—and, all too predictably, protectionist sentiments are strong and growing in Congress. The U.S. current account deficit together with other factors is now contributing to protectionist pressures which, if not resisted, could lead to mutually destructive retaliation with serious damage to the world economy: world trade would shrink, real growth rates could even turn negative, unemployment would rise still higher, and debt-burdened countries would be unable to secure the export earnings they vitally need.*

Furthermore, the United States is now, for the first time, about to start paying debt service on its net investment debt position. In other words, for the first time we have less total U.S. investment abroad than foreign investment here. If something isn't done, that net debt service—payable to China, Japan, and other creditor countries—will approach $200 billion a year in another couple of years.

There are only two ways out of this problem, as I see it. One is through the mechanism of a U.S. recession, which would come at a terrible cost to both the U.S. and global economies, and is, of course, unacceptable. The other is through another round of aggressive international economic policy coordination, which could over time reduce imbalances. Unfortunately, the prospects for coordination now are not good. The United States today has a policy, not quite "benign neglect," of hoping the dollar will fall, but not saying or doing much about it. Our trading partners appear to be less interested in currency stability than in maintaining their trading advantages against the United States. Also, they generally view the dollar as too weak, not too strong—exactly the reverse of 1985. Finally, there is widespread resistance in Europe and elsewhere to following U.S. leadership on many issues. This is not a happy picture. We should not be indifferent to these risks to the global economy, nor should our trading partners.

THE THIRD MAJOR economic accomplishment of President Reagan's second term, after tax reform and international economic policy coordination to defeat protectionism and stabilize exchange rates, was

---

*In case you didn't catch it, I lifted this sentence word for word from the twenty-one-year-old Plaza Accord. Sadly, it is even more true today than it was then.

the Canada–United States Free Trade Agreement. It went into effect on January 1, 1989, and removed many trade barriers between the United States and its largest trading partner. More important, perhaps, it served as a model for the North American Free Trade Agreement (NAFTA), which went into effect five years later and made Mexico, Canada, and the United States the world's largest trading bloc.*

The catalyst for the agreement with Canada was the election of a conservative government headed by Brian Mulroney in 1984. Like President Reagan, he passionately believed in free trade and had the political courage in the face of significant domestic opposition to try to erase tariffs and other barriers to the movement of goods between Canada and the United States. The ultimate agreement was a testament to the vision, courage, and political will of these two great leaders.

Trade liberalization is as close to accepted gospel as anything in economics. It holds that free trade between any two countries makes both more prosperous, even if one is dominant in all sectors. Politically, however, free trade is always a tough sale. The reason is that the benefits are diffuse (everybody shares to some extent in the general increase in prosperity), but the costs are specific and painful (some industries and labor groups invariably suffer when import tariffs and quotas are removed). Beneficiaries of trade liberalization are usually quiet, but victims scream and politicians listen, which makes it easy to rail against free trade (as Ross Perot did in the 1992 presidential election). That's why efforts to liberalize the world trading system through the General Agreement on Tariffs and Trade (GATT) and, later, the World Trade Organization (WTO) have stretched over many decades. Countries impatient with this slow pace have independently formed regional trade blocs, such as the European Community (forerunner of

---

*Two good references are *Free Trade: Risks and Rewards*, edited by L. Ian MacDonald, and *Building a Partnership: The Canada–United States Free Trade Agreement*, edited by Mordechai Kreinin.

the European Union) or signed bilateral trade agreements, such as the one Prime Minister Mulroney and President Reagan wanted.

The agreement almost didn't happen. Negotiations were protracted, painful, and more than once on the verge of complete collapse. Initial talks began in 1984 while I was still White House chief of staff and went on for years. Still, with just days to go before the midnight, October 3, 1987, deadline for submission to Congress, no agreement was in sight.

The deadline was set under "fast-track" legislation that authorized the negotiations. If we met the deadline, Congress would have to vote up or down on the agreement as a whole and not pick it apart with amendments. If we missed it, however, the agreement was as good as dead.

As the deadline approached, President Reagan asked me to take over as point man for U.S. negotiators and gave me a simple mandate: if a deal is at all possible, get it! With only two days left, I telephoned Derek Burney, Mulroney's chief of staff, with a plan for resuming negotiations. "This was a critical move in itself," Burney wrote later. "We knew we needed someone like Baker to make it happen."

The next day we started through the agreement, point by point, in a high-level meeting in the Treasury conference room. I was ably assisted throughout these negotiations by Peter McPherson, who by then had replaced Dick Darman as deputy secretary of the treasury. (Peter later served as president of Michigan State University.) I have participated in many negotiations in my career, but few that compared in complexity and contentiousness with these. There was a lot of thunder and lightning as old controversies were fought one last time and new ones brought to the table. Meanwhile, teams of lawyers in another building were sweating over language to satisfy Canada's biggest sticking point—a mechanism to enforce the agreement. In the last hours before the deadline, Burney and I worked out the final details in my office.

Successful negotiation requires a sense of political limits. For this agreement, that meant sensitivity to the political dynamics in both Canada and the United States, two democracies where interest groups are varied and vocal, and power is divided and diffuse. I spent a lot of time gauging congressional opinion and cultivating bipartisan support from friends of free trade on Capitol Hill. I also had to educate myself on the political constraints faced by the Canadians. For instance, it was a no-no in Canada to give up trade and investment barriers designed to protect their culture against Americanization. The principle was okay with us, but to the Canadians, "culture" was a very elastic concept. It seemed that whatever they wanted to protect, they called culture. I finally told them, more for effect than anything, "Fine, okay, let me tell you what is cultural in the United States—automobiles!" That seemed to encourage them to become less elastic about what was culture and what wasn't. Even today, however, Canadians are still "protected" from seeing too many American movies or sitcoms on television.

Getting the agreement ratified in the U.S. Congress was no picnic, but the Canadian ratification fight almost brought down Mulroney's government. National elections were called in 1988, and only after his party won could we be certain that our deal would stick.

One thing that I will never forget about President Reagan is his political courage in going on the offensive on trade and investment liberalization. Remember that at the same time we were seeking to knock down trade barriers with Canada, powerful protectionists in Congress were threatening punitive legislation against our major trading partners. Instead of playing defense, however, President Reagan snatched the ball and ran the other way. We turned the debate from narrow questions of advantage for one industry or another and from near-xenophobic attacks on our trading partners to broader questions of our national interest.

The agreement was a huge success. Trade between Canada and the United States more than doubled in the decade after it went into effect. The result: higher economic growth, more jobs, and better wages in both countries.

The deal with Canada also prepared the way for NAFTA, a trade agreement that today covers more than 425 million people. After George Bush 41 became president in 1989, he worked with Prime Minister Mulroney and Mexico's President Carlos Salinas to bring Mexico into the trade zone. Negotiations went more quickly this time, primarily because of the lessons learned in the Canadian round. President Bush signed the agreement in December 1992. "We've committed ourselves to a better future for our children and for generations yet unborn," he said.

The next administration inherited the task of winning congressional ratification. I salute President Clinton for having the political courage to do so, despite strong opposition from labor unions and other constituencies within his own party. On November 2, 1993, fifteen days before Congress would vote NAFTA up or down, he organized a bipartisan show of support for the trade pact in the White House East Room. I attended, along with former president Carter, five other former secretaries of state, five other former treasury secretaries, eight Nobel laureates, and Paul Volcker. Former presidents Bush, Ford, and Reagan issued statements of support. (As I said, trade liberalization is as close to accepted gospel as anything in economics.) In my remarks to the distinguished attendees that day, I said, "Our task . . . is to persuade Americans that they have nothing to fear from NAFTA . . . Working together on a bipartisan basis, we must expose the fact-fudging, the fearmongering, the prophets of protectionism who are playing on the doubts of the American people." The House passed NAFTA by 234–200 and the Senate by 61–38, with Republicans providing more votes than Democrats.

Over the past decade, NAFTA has been a resounding success. Trade among the three signatory countries has more than doubled. The economies of Mexico and Canada have grown more than 30 percent and the economy of the United States has grown about 40 percent. Wages and productivity are up in all three countries. The strong U.S. economic expansion of the 1990s owes a great deal to NAFTA, I think, and the trade pact clearly helped Mexico weather a currency crisis, consolidate free-market reforms, and strengthen its democracy.

What we still lack, however, is the long-dreamed-of FTAA—Free Trade Area for the Americas—uniting South, Central, and North America in one trade zone. Immediately after NAFTA went into effect, prospects looked good. President Clinton convened the first Summit of the Americas in Miami in December 1994 to announce plans for "a free trade area that stretches from Alaska to Argentina." It would be in place by 2005, he said. More than thirty heads of state from Latin America endorsed the plan, then went home to wait, expectantly, for negotiations to begin.

What President Clinton lacked, however, was the same fast-track authority from Congress that had made it possible for Presidents Reagan and Bush to put in place the two earlier trade agreements. He could have gotten that authority in 1995. Unfortunately, however, he waited until 1997 to ask for it. By then, opposition within his own party had hardened. Lacking critical support from Democrats, President Clinton became the first president since President Ford to be turned down on a fast-track vote. He tried again in 1998, but seemingly not wholeheartedly. His personal troubles had erupted earlier that year. The House would vote on an impeachment resolution later that year and he apparently hesitated to alienate fellow Democrats in the run-up to the midterm elections.

President Clinton's decision not to go for fast-track authority in 1995 was arguably the biggest mistake of his presidency. Why? Because nothing would have done more for economic growth for all the countries of this hemisphere, including the United States, than to have been part of a free trade agreement for the Americas. And the opportunity we had to get there at that time was lost. Now Asians and Europeans are cutting free trade agreements with many countries of South America while Uncle Whiskers is left sitting on the sidelines. This is a real tragedy.

George W. Bush has resumed the movement toward hemispheric

trade liberalization with the Central America–Dominican Republic Free Trade Agreement of 2005. My former adviser, Robert Zoellick, queued up that project as U.S. trade representative in the forty-third president's first term. In the absence of real progress on liberalization of world and hemispheric trade, he also won bilateral free-trade agreements with a number of U.S. trading partners, including Morocco and Australia. We've also signed deals recently with Chile, Peru, and Colombia. Unfortunately, however, the all-important FTAA is still just a dream, not a reality.

As I HAVE SAID, the U.S. economy exploded into a frenzy of growth under President Reagan, thanks to tax cuts, tax reform, free trade, and stabilization of the dollar. There were some dark days along the way, however. One came on "Black Monday," October 19, 1987.

In all my years of public service before then, I had never taken a real boondoggle overseas trip. Things were going so well in 1987, however, that I decided to do just that when the king of Sweden, Carl Gustaf, invited me to hunt elk with him.*

I was scheduled to depart for Stockholm on Sunday, October 18. Signs of trouble appeared the week before, although I didn't regard them as particularly serious at the time. From the end of 1984 through the late-August peak in 1987, the Dow Jones Industrial Average had gained a stunning 127 percent. Since then, it had been drifting down. The Wednesday before I left, the downtrend accelerated as bad trade figures set Congress to talking about protectionism.

On Thursday, I tried to calm the market in a press briefing at the White House. We weren't about to go into a recession, I said, but I complained about the plans of the Bundesbank (Germany's equivalent of our Federal Reserve) to hike interest rates. On Friday, the market declined again.

---

*What the Swedes call "elk," we call "moose."

Before my Sunday departure, I appeared on *Meet the Press*. Again I criticized the Bundesbank. "We will not sit back in this country and watch surplus countries jack up interest rates and squeeze growth worldwide on the expectation that the United States somehow will follow by raising its interest rates," I said. Then I boarded a plane and flew to Europe, visions of majestic Swedish elk playing in my head.

When I landed, my official host, the Swedish minister for finance, Kjell-Olof Feldt, met me at the foot of the stairs. His face was white as a snowcapped glacier on a mountain peak, and he could hardly speak. "The market closed down five!" he said. I was puzzled. What's wrong with a five-point drop in the market? "No, no!" he said. "Five hundred!"*

The Dow Jones Industrial Average had dropped 508 points in one excruciating day, losing about 22 percent to close at 1738, the second-biggest one-day percentage decline in history. I went to my room in the government guesthouse for visiting dignitaries and started working the phones. I don't remember all the details, but I quickly learned that my Treasury staff had frantically been trying to reach me. I also called the White House to get a briefing from former senator Howard Baker, who had succeeded Don Regan as chief of staff. I also talked to officials at Treasury and the finance ministers of Germany, Japan, the UK, and—if I'm not mistaken—France. This was a global crisis, I was told, and we had to consider the possibility that it was just beginning. After spending the entire night on the telephone, I flew to London the next morning and caught the Concorde home.

Back in Washington, I went straight to a meeting in my office at Treasury with Alan Greenspan, Howard Baker, George Gould (our under secretary for domestic finance), Robert Zoellick (Gould's assistant at the time), and others. By then, it appeared that the markets were beginning to stabilize, but we couldn't be sure they wouldn't drop again. The

---

*Almost the same thing happened to Alan Greenspan when he landed in Dallas to deliver a speech. Over the summer, he had succeeded Paul Volcker as Fed chairman. Alan immediately hopped a plane back to Washington.

most important thing, we decided, was to reassure investors. John Phelan, who headed the New York Stock Exchange at the time, did a great job by instituting emergency procedures to let trading resume without getting out of control. We all agreed that it was important to inject huge amounts of liquidity into the system, and this is exactly what Alan then did and would continue to do. Alan also issued a statement that affirmed the Fed's "readiness to serve as a source of liquidity to support the economic and financial system." This permitted investors to borrow to cover their positions, which prevented a cascading series of defaults that could have brought down banks and investment houses. In addition, the president issued a statement to reassure the public.

There was one more aftershock—an 8 percent drop on October 26—then the crisis ended almost as precipitously as it had begun, with little impact on either exchange rates or long-term economic growth. It hurt a lot of people, clearly, and raised disturbing thoughts about where the economy might be headed. Despite Black Monday, however, the Dow Jones ended 1987 with a 2 percent *gain* for the year, then went on to post solid gains in eleven of the next twelve years.

I'm not sure why Black Monday occurred and won't try to speculate. The president appointed former New Jersey senator Nicholas Brady to head a task force to investigate the meltdown. At the time, he headed Dillon Read, a prominent Wall Street firm, and he later succeeded me as treasury secretary. The task force report in January 1988 mentioned several contributing factors, including overvaluation of the market, a negative investor psychology that took root the preceding week, concern about our fiscal and trade deficits, worries about protectionist legislation and antitakeover legislation (Ways and Means had just okayed a bill to eliminate the tax deduction for interest on borrowed money in corporate takeovers), automatic program trading by computers in the big investment houses, the failure of market specialists to serve as buyers of last resort for securities they managed, and capacity problems at the exchanges (they simply couldn't handle the flood of sell orders).

The report also mentioned my remarks to the press about Germany and exchange rates. I still have difficulty believing my remarks contributed to the sell-off, and I absolutely don't believe they triggered it. What I said then wasn't substantially different from other statements I had made to the press. Still, if I had it to do over, I wouldn't say the same thing. One lesson I learned at Treasury is that even the most innocent remarks about the dollar or other economic issues could provoke investors to buy or sell, almost blindly, in response.

A number of market reforms were installed after Black Monday, including restrictions on program trading and "circuit breakers" to halt trading and allow investors to cool off after significant drops in the market. They seem to have helped. In addition, I believe our ongoing efforts to stabilize the dollar probably prevented the crisis from being worse. While the dollar lost value during this period, it did so in an orderly way and did not plunge with the securities market. I think this helped restore confidence. We've had several other significant one-day sell-offs—including two 500-plus-point drops in the late 1990s and two 600-plus drops in the early 2000s, one of which came on the day the market reopened after 9/11—but nothing like 1987, as a percentage of total market value.

The big lessons, I think, are that we survived that dark day, that it didn't trigger a depression (or, for that matter, a recession), that the economy was healthy and kept growing without significant damage, and that the market recovered and prospered as investor confidence returned.

P.S. I never did see the king of Sweden, much less an elk.

ACKNOWLEDGMENTS

Writing a book—I learned with *The Politics of Diplomacy* and relearned with *Work Hard, Study . . . and Keep out of Politics!*—is a team sport, especially for someone whose writing career was long on contracts, diplomatic statements, and points lists, and short on writing for a general audience.

My quarterback was collaborator Steve Fiffer. Steve is a professional writer and editor with fourteen other books to his credit. He researched my story from public sources and my files, interviewed me for hours, and churned out first drafts that I then edited into my own voice. He may be a Baby Boomer, a Yankee (by way of Evanston, Illinois), and a Democrat, but he did an honest and very fine job for his client, a septuagenarian Texas Republican. And one of the great pleasures of working on the book was getting to know Steve and his wife, novelist Sharon Fiffer.

My second collaborator was my former policy assistant and speechwriter, Darrell Hancock. Darrell originally authored first drafts of many of the later chapters of this book and helped research and fact-check the entire manuscript. Without his expertise, judgment, advice, and talent, this book would not have happened.

Neil Nyren at Putnam did his usual expert job of editing and was particularly generous in his understanding of my inability to complete the work as rapidly as I had originally agreed.

And of course, my editor in chief was Susan, never shy about telling me when I got something wrong, ever helpful in suggesting ways to improve the book.

Margaret Tutwiler offered invaluable advice, as usual, including reading drafts of chapters for accuracy and refreshing my memory of events.

I was fortunate that Dick Darman was willing to review parts of the manuscript and help me in confirming facts and reminding me of things that I had forgotten. My great friend Otis Carney, a talented and prolific writer himself, reviewed much of the manuscript and offered many helpful suggestions, in spite of the fact that he was ill with terminal cancer.

Many people consented to be interviewed by my collaborators, beginning with President George H. W. Bush and including Robert Mosbacher, Stuart Spencer, Peter McPherson, Gary Edson, Preston Moore, Caron Jackson, Peter Roussel, Frank Donatelli, Anna Theofilopoulou, and James and Wendell Baker.

My researchers and I also relied on a number of fine books, magazine articles, and newspaper accounts of my years in politics and public service, many of which are mentioned in the book.

A number of people constantly encouraged me to write this book—too many to mention here. The recurring theme of their arguments was: you've written about your State Department experiences as a statesman, but you've also had other experiences in public service and in politics that very few other people have had; you need to write about those. Susan was one who encouraged me to write. Another was David Paton, my college roommate and lifelong friend. Two others were Ed Djerejian, founding director of the Baker Institute, and his wife, Françoise, who also assisted Steve and Darrell in accessing my files and in selecting photographs for the book.

My staff—Charlotte Cheadle, John Williams, and Catherine Duke of Baker Botts—contributed in ways too numerous to mention. So, too, did Joe Barnes of the Baker Institute.

Others who were helpful were my attorney Bob Barnett, and Dan Linke and Dan Santamaria of Princeton University's Seeley G. Mudd Manuscript Library, where my political and public service papers are stored. I also received valuable assistance from Fannie Richard, Wendell Baker, Jr., Wistar Morris of the Miller Center of Public Affairs, Maggie Cryer, formerly with the Baker Institute, and researchers Anne Hong, Alexandra Joseph, Cornelia van Amerongen, Marina Powell, and Jessica McBride.

Every memoirist is, I suppose, faced with the question of whether to kiss and tell. For me, the answer was easy: I would not violate the principles by which I gained and held the trust of Gerald Ford, George H. W. Bush, Ronald Reagan, George W. Bush, and many others, and by which I served them. I love and respect the presidents I served, and anyone who thinks James Addison Baker, III, might turn on them in his old age must have another James Addison Baker, III, in mind.

Many quotations in the book came from my memory, not from a written record. (Most quotations in *The Politics of Diplomacy*, by contrast, came from detailed transcripts and notes taken by State Department stenographers.) Although some quotations in this book may not be word for word, I believe all of them convey the substance of what was said.

To the trout, quail, and turkeys whose lives were spared because I had to work on this book when I might otherwise have been in the field or on the stream, go forth and multiply. I'll be back.

Finally, everyone says this, but I certainly mean it: Credit those I have mentioned above for their help in keeping errors out of this book, and blame me for those that may have slipped through my defenses. They are, I assure you, unintentional.

INDEX

BUTLER'S LIVES OF THE SAINTS

NEW
CONCISE EDITION

PAUL BURNS

LITURGICAL PRESS
Collegeville, Minnesota

www.litpress.org

First published in North America in 2003 by the
LITURGICAL PRESS
St John's Abbey, Collegeville,
Minnesota 56321

ISBN 0–8146–2903–2

Biblical quotations are taken from the New Revised Standard Version of the Bible, copyright 1989, Division of Christian Education of the National Council of the Churches of Christ in the United States of America, published by Oxford University Press, Inc., 200 Madison Avenue, New York, New York 10016.

Library of Congress Cataloging-in-Publication Data
Butler, Alban, 1711-1773.
[Lives of the saints]
Butler's lives of the saints / Paul Burns– New Concise Ed.
    p. cm.
  Includes bibliographical references and index.
  ISBN 0–8146–2903–2 (alk. paper)
  1. Christian saints–Biography. I. Burns, Paul. II. Title.

BX4655.3.B88 2003
282′.092′2–dc21
[B]

2003041637

Typeset by YHT Ltd, London
Printed and bound by MPG Books Ltd, Bodmin, Cornwall

CONTENTS

Contents

Contents

INTRODUCTION

The present volume is designed to present a concise account of one saint (or "blessed") for each day of the year from among those featured in the new twelve-volume *Butler's Lives of the Saints* published by Burns & Oates and The Liturgical Press between 1995 and 2000. It therefore stands in the same relation to that edition as Michael Walsh's "Concise Butler's" (1985, new revised edition 1991) does to the previous general revision of *Butler's Lives* made by Donald Attwater in the 1950s and updated in 1964. It differs from that volume in including "blessed"—those beatified but not, or not yet, canonized—as well as "saints" in the full meaning of those canonized by the Catholic Church. Canonization itself was originally a decision of a local church or council, in response to popular demand. It was officially reserved to the papacy from about 1200, though local "saints" were still recognized as such.

Those accepted into the Roman Martyrology, first compiled by Cardinal Baronius in the sixteenth century, were held to be "equivalently" canonized. The inclusion of blessed as well as canonized saints here is sanctioned by the new Roman Martyrology published by the Vatican in 2001, the first revision since 1956. This is an implicit recognition that beatification is the most important step in the process. Before they reach that point, candidates will have been declared first "servants of God" and then "venerable" as a result of diocesan and curial investigation into the sanctity of their lives. As a general rule, when a saint is included in the Universal Calendar of the Roman Catholic Church (as revised in 1969), he or she is accorded the entry here. Inclusion in the Universal Calendar means that devotion *should* be paid to that saint, as opposed to the devotion that *may* be paid to those who are not included. When there is no official universal commemoration (the majority of days, at just under two hundred in the year), the selection aims to take the following criteria into account: interest for the English-speaking world; an emphasis on newer canonizations and beatifications; a wide geographical spread; and a fairer gender division. These last two reflect the declared policy of the papacy of Pope John Paul II, which has, at the time of writing, produced over four hundred and fifth new saints and some one thousand three hundred blessed.

From an early date, records were kept of the date of martyrs' deaths. Christian thinking saw this date as their "birthday into heaven," and this was when Christians gathered to remember and honour their martyrs, and later other holy men and women. These did not, however, die on conveniently spaced dates: some days have a plethora of deaths of major figures, others very few from any period and none of outstanding significance. In some cases here, then, entries have been transposed from an actual date of death to a nearby "vacant slot." When this has been done, it is noted in the introductory paragraph(s) preceding each month's entries.

The selected list of other familiar names at the end of each month gives those names in the new Roman Martyrology (in Latin only, as I write) that can reasonably be said to be current in English-speaking countries. They are offered as suggestions for baptismal, or confirmation, names for children born on these days and also as a suggestion that we might especially remember anyone we know called by these names in our prayers on that day. They represent less than a quarter of the names in the Roman Martyrology, but readers are unlikely to know anyone named Archelais, Asclas, Bassian, Blathmac, Catellus, Cosconius, and the like, or to want to name their babies after them (please, parents, do not be tempted!). Many of the names here, especially where there are a larger number of male names on a particular day, are those given to converts, especially in Asia.

Butler's original purpose, expressed over two hundred years ago, remains the basic inspiration: "Example instructs without usurping the authoritative air of a master. ... In the lives of the saints we see the most perfect maxims of the gospel reduced to practice." This may seem obvious today, but Butler in his day was in fact being a pioneer in this approach to the saints. They were earlier seen principally as intercessors, members of the "Church triumphant" to whom we in the "Church militant" prayed for help. While this aspect is certainly still a strong aspect of popular piety (and was the main emphasis in liturgical prayers at least until Vatican II), Butler's approach and changing times have led to a greater emphasis on achievement and less on the miraculous in saints' lives. Women feature more often than in traditional collections, most selected equally for their achievements. As Kathleen Jones has written in her *Women Saints: Lives of Faith and Courage* (1999):

> Traditionally, women saints have been classified as virgins, matrons and widows—that is by status rather than by their own achievements [classifications abandoned in the new full *Butler's Lives*]. Yet we do not write of "St Jerome, bachelor," or "St Peter, married man," and if a male saint became a widower, we assume that the loss was his private affair, not a description of his personality. Women have been treated by ascription, men by achievement; but a holy life is essentially a matter of achievement. Women do not become saints by being somebody's wife, somebody's daughter, or somebody's mother. They become saints by the way in which they deal with the problems of living.

A contemporary version of Butler's thesis is provided by the theologian Jon Sobrino, writing from El Salvador:

Stories from the past shed light on those of the present but are also, in turn, illuminated by these. The first and foremost story, in effect, is always real life. The narrative of Jesus' life sheds light on our lives, but it is also true that ours shed light on his. The base communities express this simply by seeing present-day lives that resemble Jesus' and telling their story. As [Gustavo] Gutiérrez rightly says: "Calling to mind, for example, the life and death of a man of our time such as Archbishop Romero is telling, faithfully and creatively, the life and death of Jesus in the Latin American present" (*Christ the Liberator*: Maryknoll, NY, 2001, p. 249).

This element of "telling, faithfully and creatively," has always been present in writing Lives of the saints. "Faithfully," of course, has not always meant ideas of historical accuracy that do not predate the nineteenth century. "Creatively" has often included rereading the "life and death of Jesus" as presented in the Gospels into the lives of particular saints: one thinks of the period in the wilderness, miracles of healing, and years of preaching attributed to so many. Saints are presented as faithful to the spirit of Jesus, and if in the process they come to mirror his life, this is natural enough. Today we have more care for "historical accuracy" and generally also have far more information and so fewer gaps to fill. Perhaps we need to take care not to lose the element of storytelling. Lives of the saints are still an important way of retelling the story of Jesus, and if we do not keep doing this, Christianity will have no meaning for most people. Theology and christology, with their vocabulary of natures and persons, procession and the like easily lose sight of the reality of the life and death of Jesus of Nazareth. The saints show what following him means, in almost as many ways as there are canonized and beatified individuals. Their lives and the Lives written (or told) about them bring us back to the essential narrative—without which there can be no salvation. They are not just a pious add-on for those given to daily devotion; they are a basic component of the faith of the Church as a whole.

The principal source for this book is the twelve volumes of the new full edition of *Butler's Lives of the Saints* (1995–2000), and my first thanks are to the revisers of those volumes (other than January and February, for which I was responsible) for permitting me to paraphrase entries written by them. They are: Dame Teresa Rodrigues, OSB (March); Peter Doyle (April, July, and October); Dr David Hugh Farmer (May); Prof. Kathleen Jones (June and December); John Cumming (August); Sarah Fawcett Thomas (September and November). This single volume is designed to be a popularization of—and, let me hope, an introduction to—that considerable work, and it does not pretend to fresh research, except for those (few) entries that deal with beatifications since it was completed. Most entries here are shorter than those in the full edition; some are longer and here other publications have proved useful: Kathleen Jones' *Women Saints* (1999), for Agnes, Mary of the Incarnation (Barbe Acarie), and others; *Lives of the Saints You Should Know*, vol. 2 (1996), by Margaret and Matthew Bunson, for the entry on Kateri Tekakwitha. In May, the quotations from the *Navigation of Brendan* (16th) are taken from E. C. Sellner, *Wisdom of the Celtic Saints* (1993); the entry on St Dunstan (19th) owes much to Douglas Dales, *Shepherd and Servant: The Spiritual Legacy of Saint Dunstan* (2001); the stories about Godric of Finchale (21st) and animals can be found in Helen Waddell, *Beasts and Saints* (1934; new edn. 1995); quotations from Bede's *Ecclesiastical History of the English People*, in the entries on John of Beverley (7th), Augustine of Canterbury (27th), and elsewhere, are from the translation by Leo Sherley-Price (revised edn. 1990); the words of Joan of Arc (30th) are translated from Bernard-Marie and Jean Huscenot, *Paroles de Saints* (1994). In June, the quotations from Eusebius' *History of the Church* in the account of the martyrs of Lyons and Vienne are taken from the Penguin Classics translation by G. A. Williamson (revised edn. 1989); that from Adomnán of Iona's *Life of St Columba* is from the translation and edition by Richard Sharpe (1995); the Prayer of St Ephraem is translated from the French text in Olivier Clément, *Trois Prières* (1993); information on the development of the Camaldolese Congregation (St Romuald; 19th) is taken from Peter Day, *Dictionary of Religious Orders* (2001); quotations from Bede's *Ecclesiastical History of the English People* are from the translation by Leo Sherley-Price, revised by R. E. Latham (1968). In September, quotations from Bede in the entry on St Theodore of Canterbury are, as usual, taken from the 1990 Penguin Classics edition, translated by Leo Sherley-Price; Kathleen Jones' *Women Saints* has again proved useful, particularly for the entries on St Hildegard of Bingen (4th) and Catherine of Genoa (15th) but also for comments on Paula in St Jerome (30th). In October, once again I am indebted to Kathleen Jones for the entry on St Pelagia the Penitent (8th) and to the Penguin Classics edition of Bede for quotes relating to St Cedd (26th). I have deliberately not looked at corresponding entries in Michael Walsh's *New Concise Butler's Lives* ... (new edn., 1991) or Robert Ellsberg's *All Saints* (1997) for fear of unconscious plagiarism, but I am grateful to both as predecessors. Further back in time, Donald Attwater's (1959) revision of Henry Sebastian Bowden's (1877) *Miniature Lives of the Saints* deserves mention as a begetter, and I have occasionally followed Attwater's technique of extracting a relevant quotation and putting it at the end of the entry in order to leave a more historical "Life."

JANUARY

The Church's Universal Calendar dedicates the first day of the year to Mary as Mother of God, and this is followed in the full edition of *Butler's Lives of the Saints*, in which Mary is commemorated on her various feasts throughout the year. Here, following a strict "one saint per day" formula, she will feature on the date of her "birthday into heaven," 15 August, the Feast of the Assumption. Generally, January saints and blessed are presented on the day they feature in the new Roman Martyrology, which is the anniversary of their death. However, holy people did not conveniently space out their "birthdays into heaven" day by day, so some days have more than one major figure and others have none, requiring some adjustments here.

On the 12th, St Margaret Bourgeoys, Canada's first saint, has been chosen over either of two very strong monastic candidates (and attractive figures) from earlier times, St Benedict Biscop and St Ailred of Rievaulx. On virtually every day, the saint chosen died on that actual day. St Wulfstan is moved forward two days from his (new) date of the 20th, which is given to the first West African to be beatified, Bd Cyprian Michael Iwene Tansi. The 25th is properly The Conversion of St Paul, and he shares 29 June with St Peter as the major feast commemorating the two great pillars of the Church; as it would be impossible to give them both anything like adequate treatment in the same entry in this work, however, Paul is considered here, with 29 June reserved to St Peter. Bd Joseph Freinademetz is moved forward one day, from the 28th (St Thomas Aquinas) to the 29th. St Alban Roe and his companion Bd Thomas Reynolds were executed on 21 January according to the reformed Gregorian calendar then in use in England, and the new Roman Martyrology restores them to that date (which here belongs to St Agnes); St Alban is here moved forward one day from his Benedictine feast-day, the 31st, which belongs to St John Bosco.

1

St Odilo of Cluny (962–1049)

The great monastery of Cluny, near Mâcon in the Burgundy region of eastern France, stands at the forefront of so much reform and innovation in the history of the Church that Odilo, one of its prominent early abbots, seems an appropriate figure to pick from the saints commemorated on the first day of the year.

Cluny was founded in 910 by a duke of Aquitaine named William the Pious. Its first abbot was Berno of Baume, who set high standards of observance. His successor was St Odo, and under his rule the reform spread widely in southern France and into Italy. Odo was followed by Aymardus, then Majolus, and then Odilo, who was thus the fifth abbot.

He entered the monastery at a young age, was made coadjutor in 991, and was elected abbot only three years later. His rule as abbot was marked by an expansion of the Cluniac reform throughout western Christendom and an increase in devotion, especially to the Blessed Virgin Mary. Monasteries that embraced the reforms were made directly dependent on Cluny, which helped administrative efficiency but departed from the Rule of St Benedict and so led to the historical division between Cluniac monks and Benedictines.

Odilo was severe with himself and in his government, but gentle with others and especially toward the poor, going so far as to melt down the monasteries' precious vessels and ornaments to raise funds to help relieve a famine in 1006. He was also a man of peace and established the "Truce of God" or "Peace of God," periods when local warring warlords who ravaged the lands agreed to abstain from fighting. These periods, originally the sacred seasons of Christmas and Easter, were then extended to Advent and Lent, then to every Friday, Saturday, and Sunday, so encompassing a considerable portion of the year. This truce eventually spread through most of the provinces of France.

One innovation of his is still observed throughout the Church—the commemoration of All Souls on 2 November. He started this as an observance for the monks of Cluny and all the other communities in the Cluniac family, requiring them, on the day following All Saints, to pray for deceased monks. The practice soon grew into the custom of saying three Masses for the souls in purgatory and was officially extended to the whole Western Church in 1748. After the First World War it developed into a universal observance, with one Mass being said for a particular person or group, one for all the dead, and one for the pope's intentions.

Odilo's rule as abbot lasted for fifty-six years. During this time he travelled widely, spreading the Cluniac reform. He made several journeys to Rome, also visiting the abbey of Monte Cassino. He was responsible for considerable building works at Cluny itself, especially for the church and cloister, which he found in wood and left in marble. He died while visiting the monasteries under his control, on 1 January 1049. Cluny itself is now a ruin, the result of the ravages of the French Revolution, when the buildings were sold to a local builder, who blew up the church to make the stone more accessible for quarrying. At one time this church had been the largest in Christendom until the rebuilding of St Peter's, and it was influential in spreading many features, especially stone vaulting, more fire-resistant than wooden beams, and carved portals, of which the finest surviving example is perhaps that at Vézélay. Cluny also played a major role in the development of Gregorian chant and illuminated manuscripts.

Today, the nearby Taizé Community draws many thousands of mainly young people to the area each year and has a worldwide influence through its teaching, music and prayers, not entirely unlike that of Cluny in Odilo's time.

❖

Why would we doubt that our offerings for the dead bring them some consolation? Let us not hesitate to help those who have died and to offer our prayers for them.

St John Chrysostom, homily on 1 Corinthians, cited in *The Catechism of the Catholic Church*, 1032

2

St Basil the Great (329–379)

The "Cappadocian Fathers"—Basil, his lifelong friend Gregory Nazianzen, commemorated with him today, and his younger brother Gregory of Nyssa (see 10 Jan.)—were immensely influential in the development of monastic spirituality in both East and West and vital figures in the struggle between orthodox doctrine and Arianism, which took up so much time and energy at the early ecumenical councils. Of the three, Basil was outstandingly the socially concerned man of action.

He was born into a wealthy and saintly family in Caesarea, the capital of the Roman province of Cappadocia (now eastern Turkey). His paternal grandmother, mother, father, one sister, and two brothers are all venerated as saints. He received the education proper to a young man of his social standing at Constantinople and then Athens, returning to teach rhetoric in Caesarea. The influence of his sister, St Macrina, seems to have diverted his course from that of potential prominent lawyer to the religious life. He was baptized and set off on a tour of monasteries in Syria, Palestine, Egypt, and Mesopotamia to study the religious life at first hand. On his return he settled at Pontus, where Macrina, his widowed mother, and several other women were living as a religious community. Basil gathered disciples around him, and so formed the first monastery in Asia Minor. He lived in this way for five years only, but in that time he produced the "long" and "short" Rules, which were to become known to St Benedict and through him permeate monastic life in the West, as well as being directly influential in the East.

He left the monastery to become a hermit with his brother, Gregory, but was summoned out of his solitude by Archbishop Eusebius of Caesarea to refute the teachings of Arius. Eusebius then became jealous of his success, so he retired to his hermitage once more. Gregory seems to have persuaded him to return to Caesarea, where he effectively governed the diocese for five years. He was then elected to succeed Eusebius on the latter's death in 370. A model administrator, he soon won the support of the fifty suffragan bishops over whom he exercised authority as "metropolitan." He gave away his family inheritance for the sake of the diocese, organized soup kitchens for the poor in times of famine, and built a vast hospital complex just outside the gates of Caesarea, known as the Basiliad and regarded as one of the wonders of the world. The land on which it was built was donated by the Arian emperor in the east, Valens, who had originally wanted Basil banished (or converted to Arianism) but was impressed by his adamant refusal to compromise. This was based on his reflections on the source of Church and State authority, which convinced him that there was a limit to the Christian duty of obedience to the State, a vital insight at a time when Christianity was in danger of losing its way by becoming the official religion of the Roman Empire.

Basil died on 1 January (the date on which his feast is still kept in the East) in 379. He had given monasticism a theological content and transformed it into an intellectual movement from the popular and evangelical movement it had been before. He saw monks simply as Christians seeking the most effective way to salvation through observing the gospel commandment to love one another. His monasteries had schools attached, to prepare children either for the monastery or for life "in the world" outside it. His monks took part in all the social activities of the Church, in which he himself had been such a pioneer. His teaching was that individuals are formed for the spiritual life not in isolation but by integration into an ideal society.

In the West, he is venerated as one of the Four Greek Doctors of the Church. This reflects the decisive nature of his interventions on trinitarian theology in the debates with Arianism over the divinity of the Son and definition of the place of the Holy Spirit. It was he who formulated the classic definition of the Trinity as three Persons in one Nature. He is also venerated as one of the patron saints of Russia.

Do you, Basil, there also welcome me in your dwelling, when I have departed this life; that we may live together and gaze more directly and perfectly at the holy and blessed Trinity, of which here on earth we have been granted but fleeting glimpses.

from the funeral oration for Basil preached by St Gregory Nazianzen

3

St Genevieve of Paris (about 422–500)

Genevieve, though piously presented as poor, probably came from a wealthy Gallo-Roman family. She took the veil of a dedicated virgin at the age of fifteen. After the death of her parents she lived with her godmother in Paris and devoted herself to an energetic course of charitable works—to the point where she aroused envy and perhaps the fury of merchants who saw her giving away goods that they might have sold. She was supported by St Germanus of Auxerre, who at one point laid his hand on her head (ordaining her deacon?) and at another sent her blessed bread as a mark of his esteem.

Her charity and energy brought her to prominence during the siege of Paris by the Franks, which reduced the population to starvation. Genevieve is reputed to have led an expedition up the Seine by boat to Troyes, coming back laden with grain to relieve the famine. From this point on she was an inspiration to the people of Paris. At her request they built a church in honour of St Dionysius, or Denis (see 10 Oct.), and it was her bravery and exhortation that made the people stay and pray rather than flee before the advance of Attila the Hun—who turned away and marched on Orleans instead. She may have been influential in persuading King Clovis of the Franks to become a Christian, and she is said to have inspired him to begin building the church of SS Peter and Paul in Paris. She was buried there, and the fame of miracles worked at her tomb spread all over France, so that the church became known as St Genevieve's.

Belief in the power of her intercession was apparently confirmed most spectacularly in 1129, during one of the epidemics of ergotism ("burning fever" or "holy fire," brought on by eating rye bread infected by the ergot fungus) that ravaged many parts of Europe during the Middle Ages. This epidemic abated after the casket containing Genevieve's bones was carried in solemn procession to the cathedral. Pope Innocent II visited Paris the following year and ordered an annual procession to commemorate the miracle. When Paris became capital of France, her importance increased. Her church was rebuilt in the neoclassical style in the eighteenth century, but secularized in the French Revolution as the Panthéon, a shrine to its heroes. Genevieve's shrine was destroyed, but devotion to her continued, and Puvis de Chavannes painted frescoes of her life around the Panthéon in 1877. Besides being patron saint of Paris, she is invoked against drought as well as flooding and other disasters. Her part in assuring the safety of Paris led to her being proclaimed patron of French Security Forces, a title confirmed by Pope John XXIII in 1962.

4

St Elizabeth Ann Seton (1774–1821)

Born just two years before the United States won its independence, she is the first native-born American citizen to be canonized. Both her parents belonged to prominent non-Catholic families in the then colonies, and she was born Elizabeth Ann Bayley on 28 August 1774. Her father, Dr Richard Bayley, was a distinguished physician and professor of anatomy at King's College (which later became Columbia University) and the first health officer of New York City. Her mother, daughter of the rector of the Episcopal church of St Andrew's on Staten Island, died when Elizabeth was only three, leaving her to be educated—well, if eccentrically—by her father. Her upbringing left her with a deep desire to devote herself to nursing the sick, especially the sick poor.

At the age of twenty she married William Magee Seton, a wealthy young shipping merchant, and the couple went on to have two sons and three daughters. Elizabeth had the means to put her youthful ideals into practice and founded an organization called the Society for the Relief of Poor Widows with Sick Children, which caused her to become known as "the Protestant Sister of Charity." Then disaster struck: William lost many of his ships in the Napoleonic wars, and his business went bankrupt. He then developed tuberculosis and took Elizabeth to Italy to seek a cure in a sunnier climate, but he died there in December 1803. She stayed on in Italy for some months and returned to the States determined to become a Catholic, being received in March 1805 in the face of unrelenting opposition from her family and desertion by her friends.

In dire financial straits, she tried running a school and then a boarding house for boys in New York. She was rescued by a priest from Baltimore, who invited her to open a school for girls there. This opened in June 1808 and flourished. Elizabeth, feeling herself supported by God, gathered a group of like-minded women around her and contemplated starting a religious Congregation. She took her first vows in March 1809 and in June that year moved her school and infant community to nearby Emmitsburg, to what became known as the Stone House. The school took in poor children without charging for tuition, and Mother Seton, as she was known from then on, trusting in God's help, rapidly developed her Congregation, which became known as the Daughters of Charity of St Joseph.

By 1812 their numbers had grown to twenty. They opened a home in Philadelphia in 1814 and an orphanage in New York three years later. By the time of her death in 1821, there were twenty houses spread across the country.

She and her Congregation are rightly regarded as founders of the parochial school system. Their work has spread to South as well as North America, to Italy, and to mission territories; they staff hospitals, child-care institutions, homes for the aged and disabled, and schools at every level. Elizabeth Ann Seton was beatified by Pope John XXIII in 1959 and canonized in the presence of over a thousand Sisters of her Congregation in 1975. Her body lies in the chapel of the National Shrine in the provincial house of the Daughters of Charity in Emmitsburg, Maryland.

[I do] realize it—the protecting presence, the consoling grace of my Redeemer and God. He raises me from the dust to feel that I am near Him, He drives away all sorrow to fill me with his consolations—He is my guide and friend and supporter. With such a guide can I fear, with such a friend shall I not be satisfied, with such a supporter can I fall?

Elizabeth Ann Seton, in *Elizabeth Seton: Selected Writings*, edited by E. Kelly and A. Melville (1987)

5

St John Neumann (1811–1860)

John's father was German and his mother Czech. He was the third of six children, born in Prachatitz in Bohemia, now half of the Czech Republic, then part of the Austrian Empire. He went to school first in Prachatitz and then, at the age of twelve, in Budweis (of beer fame). He was a bright boy with a special talent for languages and seemed destined for the priesthood. In 1831 he entered the diocesan seminary in Budweis, from where he went on to theological studies at the Charles Ferdinand University in Prague.

He was due to be ordained in 1835, but the elderly bishop of Budweis considered that he had enough priests and cancelled the ordinations for that year. This was the spur for John to put his missionary dreams into action. He sailed for the United States, where he was ordained by the bishop of New York the following year. He worked tirelessly for four years in the Buffalo–Rochester area, ministering to German immigrants and to Native Americans. He was, however, working very much on his own and felt the need for a community. The Redemptorists had recently arrived in the United States, and after meeting their superior, John was accepted into the Congregation.

He began his novitiate in Pittsburgh in 1840 and took his vows two years later. The fact that he spoke eight languages made him an ideal preacher among immigrant communities, and he was in great demand in both Pitts-burgh and Baltimore. His religious superiors in Europe recognized his holiness and zeal by appointing him vicar of all the Redemptorists in America. He worked tirelessly for causes such as the education of African-American chil-dren, became an American citizen, and in 1852, much to his surprise, was appointed fourth bishop of Philadelphia. His friend Francis Patrick Kenrick, recently appointed from there to be archbishop of Baltimore, had, it turned out, placed his name on the *terna*—list of three candidates—sent to Pope Pius IX.

Philadelphia was a sprawling diocese with a polyglot population and a large debt. With, perhaps, a touch of desperation at the task ahead of him, John took as his episcopal motto *Passio Christi, conforta me!*—"Passion of Christ, strengthen me!" He set about putting his apostolic zeal to good effect: he built schools and churches, completed the cathedral, introduced new devotions, and founded a Congregation of religious Sisters to staff the crowded schools, the population of which doubled during his short time as bishop. He somehow also found time to write two German Catechisms. He was overtaxing himself to an impossible extent, and he collapsed in the street and died on 5 January 1860, at the age of only forty-eight. He was buried in the Redemptorist church of St Peter in Philadelphia, which has come to be known as the "National shrine of St John Neumann." He was declared Blessed by Pope John XXIII in 1963, but John died before the ceremony could be carried out, so he was actually be-atified by Pope Paul VI, who also canonized him in 1977.

6

St Raphaela Mary Porras (1850–1925)

Rafaela Porras y Ayllón was born near Córdoba in the southern Spanish region of Andalusia on 1 March 1850. Her father, mayor of the small town of Pedro Abad, caught cholera through nursing the sick during an epidemic and died when Rafaela was four. Her mother died when she was nineteen, leaving her and her elder sister, Dolores, in charge of the household. The two sisters decided to become nuns. They could have had no idea what was in store for them as they became caught up in a web of religious hostility.

A certain Fr Ortíz Urruela, who had at one time studied in England under Bishop Grant of Southwark, had invited the Society of Mary Reparatrix to Córdoba, and the sisters were received into its convent there. But the bishop of Córdoba, Mgr Ceferino González, resented the community's presence and ordered them out of the diocese. They left sixteen novices behind, with Sr Rafaela in charge of them. He then announced that he had drawn up a new Rule for them, quite different from the one they had intended to vow themselves to. Rather than submit to something alien to them or face being returned to their homes, the novices decided to escape. With the connivance of Fr Ortíz, they fled by night to Andújar, some forty miles east of Córdoba, where he had arranged for them to be sheltered by the nuns who ran the hospital. Both the diocesan and the civil authorities tried to evict them, but both failed: the bishop discovered that he had no jurisdiction over them in canon law, since they were not a canonically constituted Congregation (for which he had himself to blame). Fr Ortíz had time to appeal to church authorities in Madrid on their behalf before dying suddenly. A Jesuit named Fr Cotanilla invited them to Madrid, where they were allowed to settle. Rafaela and Dolores eventually made their solemn profession in the Congregation that took the name of Sisters of Reparation of the Sacred Heart in 1877.

For a time things went relatively smoothly. The Congregation grew, opening other houses in Spain and spreading to other countries, including England and the United States, where its members worked in schools and organized retreats. In 1886 it was granted Vatican approval and changed its name to Handmaids of the Sacred Heart of Jesus. Then Rafaela and her sister quarrelled: Rafaela had been elected superior general at the time of the approval, but Dolores, now Mother María del Pilar, objected to her administrative methods and led a faction against her, forcing her to resign in 1893, whereupon she took over as superior general.

Rafaela accepted this with complete humility and for the remaining thirty-two years of her life lived simply in the Congregation's house in Rome, where she did the housework and took no office whatsoever until she was appointed mistress of novices when Dolores was removed from office. For the spirited escapee and determined foundress this cannot have been easy, but she bore it all with courage and charity: she is on record as saying, "God wants me to submit to all that happens to me as if I saw him there commanding it." She died on the Feast of the Epiphany, 1925, and was beatified in 1952 and canonized by Pope Paul VI in 1977.

7

St Raymund of Peñafort (about 1175–1275)

Raymund began his extraordinarily long and productive life in Catalonia sometime between 1175 and 1180, so was probably between ninety-five and ninety-nine when he died. His family was descended from the counts of Barcelona and related to the kings of Aragon. He was a brilliant student at Barcelona, where he was teaching philosophy by the age of twenty. Around 1210 he went to Bologna to take doctorates in both Civil and Canon Law.

Bologna was then one of the leading emerging universities, and among those attracted by its reputation was Dominic of Guzmán (see 8 Aug.), founder of the Order of Preachers, who was to die there in 1221. Raymund is likely to have known him or at least to have been influenced by him, and he joined the Dominicans eight months after Dominic's death.

He had returned to Barcelona in 1219 and spent his time between study and preaching aimed at the conversion of Moors (who still occupied large portions of Spain) and Jews (who had flourishing communities there). In 1230 Pope Gregory IX summoned him to Rome to be his confessor. He enjoined on Gregory the duty of acting promptly on all petitions presented to him by the poor. He was commissioned to use his expertise in canon law to gather all the "Decretals"—decrees issued by popes and councils since they were last collected by Gratian in 1150—into one body. There were over two thousand of them, and the task took three years and produced five volumes, which became the foundation of a Code of Canon Law that was to last until a new Code was promulgated in 1917. His work formed a major link between the Middle Ages and modern times. Exhausted by this great work, he retired once more to Barcelona.

He refused the archbishopric of Tarragona, pleading that he preferred his life of solitude, study, and preaching, but in 1238, when he was already over sixty, he was chosen to be the third master of the Dominicans, following the death of Jordan of Saxony (see 13 Feb.). He spent a very active two years visiting the houses of the rapidly growing Order on foot and making revisions to its constitution. One of these was that superiors should be able to resign their post voluntarily with good reason, and in 1240 he availed himself of this provision on the grounds that he had reached the age of sixty-five—still the official "retirement age" in many countries.

He did not exactly retire, however: his remaining thirty-four years encompassed preaching and working for the conversion of the Moors, encouraging St Thomas Aquinas (see 28 Jan.) to write the *Summa contra Gentiles*, establishing friaries, some actually on Moorish territory, and instituting the study of Hebrew and Arabic. In his final days King Alfonso of Castile and King James of Aragon came to receive his blessing. He died in Barcelona on 7 January 1275 and was canonized in 1601. His greatest achievement was in the field of canon law, but legends surrounding him—such as that he sailed from Majorca to Barcelona in half an hour, using only his cloak for a boat and sail and his staff as a mast—suggest that his energy made him a more dashing personality than his academic career might suggest.

8

St Wulsin (died 1005)

Wulsin, whose name is also spelt Wulfsin or Wulsige, was a monk at Glastonbury under St Dunstan (see 19 May), who restored Benedictine monastic life for men in England and went on to become archbishop of Canterbury. The monasteries he restored or founded were closely dependent on the royal family for protection against local lords and were notable for the integrity and learning of the abbots chosen to lead them, of whom Wulsin was typical. Dunstan is said to have "loved [Wulsin] like a son with pure affection." He was bishop of London for two years, during which time he acquired land and restored the abbey of Westminster, advising King Edgar to place Wulsin in charge of the monks there. Wulsin was appointed its first abbot in about the year 980.

In 992 or 993 he was moved again, to Sherborne in Wessex, then one of the largest dioceses in the west of England, where the cathedral was administered by secular canons. Wulsin seems to have intended from the start to make radical changes. In 998 he obtained a charter from King Ethelred ("the unready") authorizing him to eject the canons and install Benedictine monks in their place. So the cathedral of the diocese was from then on also an abbey church, and it was usual in such cases for the bishop of the diocese to be abbot as well. So Wulsin held both offices, though the abbey would have been administered by a prior: he is on record as warning his monks that the combination of both offices in one person would cause difficulties in the future. The magnificent *Sherborne Missal*, produced at the abbey in about 1400, has an illustrated page for his feast-day, in which he is shown receiving black-robed monks with his right hand while dismissing canons wearing white fur tippets with his left. The canons are then shown being received into a sumptuous building by a bishop—possibly St Osmund at Old Sarum, the precursor of Salisbury Cathedral—so they were not exactly cast into outer darkness.

In keeping with the tone of Dunstan's reform, Wulsin was energetic in spreading the ideals of the monastic renewal far and wide. The principles of the good life as embodied in the Rule of St Benedict were applicable to other priests and to lay people too, and were arousing considerable interest among rural priests and their parishioners. As a monk, Wulsin was accustomed to writing in Latin, which would have been lost on many of the audience for his pastoral letters, but he had the good sense to employ a scholar named Aelfric, then abbot of the nearby monastery of Cerne Abbas, to translate a pastoral letter dealing with matters of clerical duty, observance, and conduct into English.

He also set about developing Sherborne Abbey in keeping with the architectural and musical reforms emanating from Cluny (see 1 Jan.). He built a huge porch at the west end, with a musicians' gallery let into the thickness of the wall. This was subsequently pulled down; its foundations were discovered in the course of a nineteenth-century restoration, but all that remains of Wulsin's west wall is the south door. He was evidently regarded at least locally as a saint from soon after his death. His remains were moved to a prominent shrine in the abbey when building work had progressed to a point where they could be worthily received, in about 1045 or 1050. This "translation" is also recorded in the *Sherborne Missal*, for the Mass of 28 April, where the remains of another local saint, Juthwara, said to have been murdered by her brother, are shown being moved with his. His memory was brought back vividly to life in 1998, when Sherborne organized a festival to celebrate the millennium since the coming of the Benedictines.

A bishop and confessor of noble blood in the city of London, and for because he was given unto virtue in youth, his friends put him into Westminster, where he was abbot, and after that bishop of Sherborne, a man of hard life great perfection and many miracles.

description of Wulsin in the Martyrology compiled by Wynkyn de Worde, the great printer who took over Caxton's business in London and ran it successfully until his death in 1535

9

St Adrian of Canterbury (died 709 or 710)

The main source of information on Adrian (or Hadrian), as for most of his contemporaries, is the *Ecclesiastical History of the English People* by the Venerable Bede (see 25 May). In Chapter 1 of his Book Four he writes:

> On the fourteenth of July in the above-mentioned year [664], when an eclipse was suddenly followed by plague ... Deusdedit the sixth archbishop of Canterbury died. ... The see of Canterbury was then vacant for a considerable time, until Wighard, an English priest with great experience in church administration, was sent to Rome. ... On his arrival in Rome, where Vitalian was ruling the apostolic see, Wighard explained to the pope the reason for his journey; but shortly afterwards he and nearly all his companions fell victim to a plague that broke out at the time.

Deusdedit had been the first Englishman to occupy the see of Canterbury, and his death, so closely followed by that of Wighard, who had been picked to succeed him by King Egbert of Kent and King Oswy of Northumbria, left the pope with a considerable problem. Making "careful enquiry," he consulted the abbot of a monastery near Naples, Hadrian, who was "a native of Africa … very learned in the scriptures, experienced in ecclesiastical and monastic administration, and a great scholar in Greek and Latin"—who, in other words, seemed to be the ideal candidate. Adrian, however, considered himself unfit for such high office and proposed instead a monk named Andrew, who "was considered worthy of a bishopric by all who knew him," but Andrew too excused himself, on the grounds that his health was not up to the job. Pope Vitalian asked Adrian to think again, and this time he proposed "a monk named Theodore … learned both in sacred and in secular literature, in Greek and in Latin, of proved integrity, and of the venerable age of sixty-six." (Adrian had considered himself too young for the post.) So Vitalian agreed to consecrate Theodore, who was indeed to prove an excellent choice, "but made it a condition that Hadrian himself should accompany him to Britain, since he had already travelled through Gaul twice on various missions and had both a better knowledge of the road and sufficient men of his own available." He was also to act as a sort of theological watchdog, making sure that Theodore, who came from Tarsus in the east, did not introduce "into the Church which he was to rule any Greek customs which conflicted with the teachings of the true faith." Theodore was a simple monk but was rapidly ordained and consecrated bishop, setting out, with Adrian, on 27 May 668.

Adrian arrived some time after Theodore, having been detained for a time in France by Ebroin, "mayor of the king's palace" and effective ruler of the Frankish kingdom, who suspected him of dubious political intrigue to his disadvantage. But he realized that Adrian was innocent and eventually allowed him to cross to Britain. In Canterbury, Theodore "appointed him abbot of the monastery of blessed Peter the Apostle … for when he left Rome the apostolic Pope had instructed Theodore to provide for him in his diocese."

For the next twenty-one years Adrian accompanied Theodore on visits to every part of the island. He also made his monastery (later named St Augustine's) a major seat of learning, teaching Greek, Latin, Roman law, scripture and patristics, poetry, and astronomy. Its students, drawn from all over Britain and also from Ireland, included many future bishops and archbishops. Among these was Aldhelm, who became the first bishop of Sherborne and who declared that the teaching there was superior to anything available in Ireland. Adrian carried on teaching for almost twenty years after Theodore's death, dying probably in 710. "Never," declares Bede, "had there been such happy times as these since the English settled in Britain." Perhaps something of his character can be glimpsed in the fact that many of the "miracles" for which his tomb became famous worked to the benefit of boys in trouble with their masters.

10

St Gregory of Nyssa (about 330–395)

The younger brother of St Basil the Great (see 2 Jan.) was educated by Basil and their sister, Macrina, which suggests that their parents died while he was young. He studied rhetoric, became a professor, and was married by the time Gregory Nazianzen persuaded him to place his intellectual prowess at the service of the Church. Apparently at Basil's suggestion, he was elected bishop of Nyssa, in Lower Armenia, in 372. Nyssa was a hotbed of Arianism, and Gregory lacked Basil's administrative and diplomatic skills in dealing with theological adversaries who were quite capable of furthering their cause by underhand means. He was accused of embezzling church funds and arrested by the governor of Pontus. He escaped from captivity, which his enemies saw as an admission of guilt, but did not return to his see until 378. Shortly after this, Basil died, soon followed by Macrina.

He may have lacked some skills, but his intellectual gifts, shown in his numerous writings against Arianism and in support of orthodoxy, soon caused him to become known as the "common mainstay of the Church." He was sent on missions to counter heresy in Palestine and Arabia, and was the chief proponent of trinitarian doctrine at the First Council of Constantinople in 381, which safeguarded the true humanity as well as divinity of Christ. And as Christ is truly one person in two natures, Mary is truly *theotokos*, "God-bearer," Mother of God. His reputation remained high for the rest of his life, but then gradually works originally by him were attributed to others (authors were not given to asserting their "moral rights" over a text in those days) and his stature was less appreciated. It was not until the second half of the twentieth century that investigations by a number of scholars, including Hans Urs von Balthasar and Jean Daniélou, brought to light just how much the Church owes to him.

Developing the work of Basil and Gregory Nazianzen, he provided a mystical basis for monasticism that formed a bridge between Clement and Origen and the flowering of the high Middle Ages. He was steeped in the Greek and Roman classical philosophers, but made his own entirely Christian and bib-lically- based synthesis of their work. His meditations, through a series of biblical commentaries and a second series of spiritual works aimed more directly at the monastic life, start with an intuition drawn from a passage from the Bible or the Fathers, move through his own personal philosophical reflections, and finally unfold in a return to the Bible. Being Christian is, for him, imitating God as revealed in Christ, and this imitation assimilates us to what God actually is. Life is a conflict between sin and the will of God; learning is the ability to distinguish between good and evil; its source is the word of God as received in the tradition of the Church; the place where its effects can best be put into effect is the cenobitic (communitarian) life within the bosom of the Church. He is now seen as a precursor and inspirer of Pseudo-Dionysius, whose remarkable mystical works (gaining extra credibility from long being attributed to Paul's disciple) were a direct influence on St John of the Cross (see 14 Dec.) and most medieval and later mysticism.

Just as he who looks at the sun in a mirror, even if he does not fix his eyes on the sky itself, nevertheless sees the sun in the mirror's brightness, so you also, even if your eyes could not bear the light, possess within yourselves what you desire, if you return to the grace of the image that was placed in you from the beginning.
Gregory of Nyssa, *Oration on the Fifth Beatitude*

11

St Paulinus of Aquileia (about 726–804)

Aquileia, whose relative size and importance have declined considerably since Paulinus' time, lies in what is now the Friuli-Venezia Giulia region of north-eastern Italy, north of the Gulf of Trieste. Paulinus was born there to a farming family and managed to combine working on the family farm in his youth with becoming famous as a professor of grammar. This brought him to the attention of the emperor Charlemagne, who in around 776 invited him to his court at Aachen, where he became one of the circle of intellectuals responsible for what has become known as "the Carolingian Renaissance." Charlemagne also gave him the anomalous (because there are no patriarchs in the Western Church other than the pope) title of Patriarch of Aquileia.

The court school at Aachen was directed by Alcuin, who came there from the cathedral school of York a few years after Paulinus, for whom he always expressed great respect. It developed into a sort of academy, with regular meetings to discuss important topics and to exchange learning, poems, and even riddles. Its importance can be seen in Alcuin's "General Admonition" of 789, laying out fundamental reforms in Church and State designed to promote lasting peace and order in both.

Paulinus was instrumental in tempering the severity of the emperor's missionary efforts, which generally consisted of forced conversion at swordpoint. Paulinus objected to baptizing "barbarians" before they had received instruction. Charlemagne respected his learning and teaching and sent him on a series of journeys to attend the synods he was convening to stamp his rule on western Europe. At that of Frankfurt in 794, Paulinus claimed for Charlemagne the right to a say in theological as well as political matters, so laying the foundations for a "Christian empire." He praised Charlemagne as *"rex et sacerdos,"* "king and priest," contributing to a decisive shift in power from pope to emperor. Charlemagne came to see the papacy as coming under his responsibility and could lecture Pope Leo III on his duties in terms similar to those used by Pope Gregory the Great two hundred years earlier addressing the Frankish kings.

Theological controversies also involved Paulinus. He helped resolve the "adoptionism" debate (over whether Christ should be seen as the adoptive son of God), and to define the "procession" of the Holy Spirit from the Father and the Son—the *Filioque* question that was later to split the Western Church from the Eastern. In 796 he presided at the Synod of Bavaria, held to define missionary methods. Here his pastoral vision came to the fore: conversion, he insisted, was God's work, not human, so instruction should be in terms that "rough and unreasoning people" could understand, not based on fear. Several of his books and sermons have survived, and in these he is concerned with the duties of king and nobles. Here he was instrumental in forming a specifically lay, as opposed to clerical, conscience. He also addressed clerics, insisting that their pastoral effectiveness—through making sermons intelligible to the "simple faithful" and conducting sacramental rites properly—was more important than their own inner spirituality. This pastoral legacy may well be seen today as more valuable than his—inevitably time-conditioned—contributions to politics and trinitarian theology.

12

St Margaret Bourgeoys (1620–1700)

Margaret's family came from Troyes, on the River Seine upstream from Paris—and where St Genevieve (see 3 Jan.) sailed to in search of grain to relieve the famine in Paris. Her father was a wax-chandler there, and Margaret was the sixth of twelve children. She sought to enter the religious life when she was twenty, but for some reason she was rejected by both the Carmelites and the Poor Clares. A priest, Abbé Gendret, told her to take this as an indication that she was destined for an unenclosed religious life and formed a group of "extern Sisters" with Margaret and several other young women, who taught children in the poor districts of Troyes for several years. This initiative was, however, discouraged by the religious authorities. At the time, this was only to be expected: it was only a few years since the papal Bull *Pastoralis Romani Pontificus* had decreed that Mary Ward's embryonic Institute of the Blessed Virgin Mary was to be "suppressed, extinct, uprooted and abolished." "Galloping girls"—as her I.B.V.M. Sisters were called—were not a required feature of the ecclesial scene, and what Margaret was to call her *vie voyagère*, "travelling life," was not far from this.

Her opportunity to follow her missionary calling came when the governor of the French settlement of Ville-Marie in Canada (then just a fort, now the city of Montreal) came to visit his sister in the Augustinian convent in Troyes in 1652. He was looking for a schoolmistress, and Margaret accepted the post. She landed at Quebec in September 1653 and reached Ville-Marie a month later. For the first few years she helped the two hundred people living in the fort, looking after children, working in the hospital, and gradually becoming the life and soul of the little settlement. Convinced of the importance of families, she concentrated on the education of women. She opened her first school in 1658, with twelve pupils, taught by herself and an assistant. From the following year she made herself responsible for welcoming and looking after young women sent out from France with a royal dowry to enable them to marry and so build up the population of the colony. She had the foresight to see that future growth would require more teachers and made a return visit to France, coming back a year later with three young women recruits. The school did grow rapidly, along with the colony, especially when the fort began to develop into the town of Montreal after the Iroquois War of 1667. Margaret was back in France looking for more teachers from 1670 to 1672, when she received civil authorization for her work from King Louis XIV.

She had always planned a religious community, and she and her fellow-teachers were canonically formed into the Congregation of Notre Dame by the first bishop of Quebec, Mgr Laval, in 1676. He, however, held to the official line and wanted them to be an enclosed community. Margaret had a different vision, based on her experience in Troyes, but was unable to gain approval for it, despite another journey to France to seek ecclesiastical approval. In 1683 their convent was destroyed by fire, worsening their already desperately poor situation. Mgr Laval tried to persuade them to amalgamate with the Ursulines, but Margaret held out. It was not until 1698 that twenty-four Sisters were allowed to make their simple profession as members of a separate Congregation, and by that time Margaret, aged seventy-eight, had ceased to act as superior.

Her foundation had already made progress, despite hardships and opposition. A first boarding school was opened in 1673, and a first mission school for Native American children three years later. Two young Iroquois women joined the community in 1679, as did Lydia Langley, the first New England girl to become a nun. She had been captured by Abenaki Indians, then ransomed in Montreal, where she became a Catholic. After the Iroquois massacred everyone not protected by the fort of Ville-Marie in 1689, Mgr Laval's successor relaxed his opposition to the point of allowing the Congregation to start a school in Quebec. The number of its schools was eventually to reach over two hundred.

Margaret, the first schoolmistress of Montreal, was an indomitable pioneer, an example of unfailing courage and of devotion to her children, her community, and all those with whom she came into contact. She overcame early rejection and continued disapproval from Church authorities to make her vision reality. She resigned as superior in 1693, and from that point on her health declined until her death on 12 January 1700. She was beatified in 1950 and canonized in 1982, thereby becoming Canada's first saint. She is venerated as "Mother of the Colony" and as co-foundress of the Church in Canada.

13

St Hilary of Poitiers (about 315–367)

Hilary is one of the great figures of the decades following the conversion of Constantine and the Church's adaptation from—periodically—persecuted minority to official State religion. He is roughly contemporary with St Basil the Great (see 2 Jan.) and occupies as prominent a place in the Western Church as Basil does in the Eastern. Born into a wealthy pagan family of Poitiers, in central south-western France, he became an orator, married, and had a daughter, Afra. His studies brought him into contact with the scriptures, and he was converted and baptized in 350. While he was possibly still a layman, the Christian people of Poitiers chose him as their bishop: it was more usual to select bishops from among the priests or deacons of a place, but not unknown to choose a layman of good repute. Hilary accepted and was plunged into the confused period of theological controversy and endless synods that followed the Council of Nicaea in 325.

Orthodoxy was being shaken by Arius' teaching "that the Son was created out of non-being, that there was a time when he did not exist, that his nature was capable of good and evil, that he is a creature and created." Theology being then inseparable from politics, the controversy threatened to split the empire, so Constantine summoned a council to settle the question. This met at Nicaea in Phrygia (part of modern Turkey) in 325, defined the doctrine that the Son was "of one being" with the Father, and excommunicated Arius, whose views nevertheless continued to gain ground in the East. When Constantine's son Constantius, who had ruled the eastern empire, became sole emperor, he promoted Arianism, against the pope. Hilary avoided two synods convoked in Gaul by the emperor to get the French bishops to support Arius but had to attend a third, at which he refused to sign a pro-Arian document. He was exiled to Phrygia but apparently travelled and resided there in reasonable comfort, and he used the three years he spent in exile to compose a treatise on the Trinity, another on synods, and a historical work of which only fragments remain.

In 358 Pope Liberius effectively capitulated to the emperor's views, leaving Hilary as virtually sole champion of orthodox belief in the West. Two synods, one for the East and one for the West, were proposed, with the purpose of making all the bishops support a compromise formula, that the Son was "of like nature" to the Father. The Western bishops, who assembled at Rimini, on the Adriatic coast of Italy, threw this out and insisted on holding to the formula of Nicaea, "of one being." But the Arian faction managed to trick the emperor into not allowing the bishops to return to their sees until they had signed a quite different document, which Hilary (still in exile and so unable to attend the Rimini synod) called "the Sirmium blasphemy"—Sirmium being the city where the eastern synod was held. The Arians then persuaded the emperor that Hilary was more of a nuisance to them in exile in Phrygia than he would be back in Gaul, so Constantius sent him home.

His journey back, through the Balkans, Italy, and Toulouse became something of an orthodox campaign, as he made converts all along the way. He received a hero's welcome in Poitiers, from where he and his former pupil Martin of Tours made Gaul a bastion of orthodox belief. He summoned all its bishops to a synod in Paris in 361, at which he made them sign their allegiance to the Nicene Creed in full. In 364 he presided over a synod of Italian bishops in Milan, the purpose of which was to depose its Arian bishop, Auxentius. But Auxentius managed to persuade the pope—falsely—of his orthodoxy, and Hilary had to be content with expressing his views in a book, "Against Auxentius." He died in 367, not yet sixty but worn out by his travels, exile, and struggles.

He was venerated as a saint while he was still alive. Many of his writings have survived: they earned him the title of "Athanasius of the West," and St Jerome (30 Sept.) called him "the trumpet of the Latins against the Arians." His work was wider and more eirenic in scope than this, however, as he sought to interpret the East to the West as well as the other way round, as in his treatise "Concerning the Faith of the Eastern Church." His major surviving work is on the Trinity, and part of a treatise on miracles came to light as late as 1887, together with some poems and hymns, which make him the earliest writer of Latin hymns. He was declared a Doctor of the Church in 1851, and his feast-day traditionally marks the beginning of the Hilary Term (spring semester) at Oxford and Cambridge Universities and in the British law courts.

Anyone who fails to see Christ Jesus as at once truly God and truly man is blind to his own life: to deny Christ Jesus, or God the Spirit, or our own flesh, is equally perilous.

from St Hilary's *Treatise on the Trinity*

14

St Sava of Serbia (1174–1237)

Sava was the youngest of three sons of Prince Stephen I, who established Serbia as a State independent from Byzantium and made his family, named Nemanya, the ruling dynasty. At the age of seventeen, Sava joined one of the monasteries on Mount Athos, and in 1198 his father abdicated his throne and joined him there. Together they set up a new monastery for Serbian monks, named Khilandari. This became a focus for Serbian religious and secular culture, and it still survives as one of the seventeen "ruling monasteries" on Mount Athos. Sava was appointed abbot and was known for his gentle manner in training young monks.

He returned to Serbia in 1206 in order to try to settle a quarrel over inheritance between his two brothers, Stephen II and Vulkan. He took several monks from Khilandari with him, and they found Christianity in Serbia at a low ebb, with few clergy, mainly ignorant, and lax practices mixed with paganism. Sava and his monks set out to re-evangelize the country; he settled at the monastery of Studenica, from where he established smaller satellite monasteries from which his monks could engage in pastoral and missionary work.

The Church in Serbia had been governed from either Constantinople or Ohrid in Bulgaria; the religious leaders in both regarded the Serbs as barbarians and neglected the care of their churches. Sava and his brother, King Stephen II, saw that if the Church was to develop it would need its own hierarchy. Stephen sent Sava to Nicaea to argue this case with the emperor, Theodore II (who was, conveniently, related to the Nemanya family), and the patriarch, Germanus I, who had taken refuge there from the Crusaders, who had seized Constantinople. The emperor supported the Serbs' cause and persuaded an unwilling patriarch to ordain Sava as bishop, whereupon he appointed him metropolitan of the new hierarchy with his archbishop's see at Zica, where he built a church.

Sava returned via Mount Athos, where he collected up a number of books that had been translated there, including a Psalter and a Ritual translated by him, and gathered more monks to aid in his campaign to re-educate and reorganize the Church in Serbia. In a gesture that could be seen as asserting a measure of independence, he crowned his brother as king, despite the fact that he had previously been crowned by the papal legate. He established bishoprics, built monasteries and churches, and worked tirelessly to reconvert the half-

Christianized Serbs. By the time he was fifty he had reformed the religious life of his country and sealed the dignity of its rulers. He had also played a major part in the development of Serbian literature through the composition in the vernacular of two Rules for his monastery at Studenica, a *Life and Office* of his father (who had been canonized as St Simeon—his name in religion at Mount Athos—in 1216), and the *Laws of Simeon and Sava*, which provides a valuable insight into the conditions of life in Serbia at the time. In his later years he made two journeys to Palestine, and he died in Bulgaria on his way back from the second.

He is regarded as the patron saint of the Serbs and as the author of their separation from Rome and adherence to (Greek) Orthodoxy—a powerful contributory factor to conflict and hatred in the Balkans over many centuries. Nevertheless, he personally should be seen as a potentially healing rather than divisive figure. He is venerated in Roman Catholic Croatian dioceses as well as in Orthodox Serbian ones and features as St Sava *Prosvtitely*, "the Enlightener," in several Latin calendars.

15

Bd Arnold Janssen (1837–1909)

Arnold was the second of eight children born to Gerhard Johann Janssen and his wife, Anna Katharina. The family home was in Goch, a small town near the Rhine in the diocese of Münster, now just inside Germany over the border with Holland. His father was involved in farming and transportation; his mother looked after the numerous children and the farm animals and devoted what time she could to prayer. The atmosphere in the family was intensely religious. Arnold was obviously a bright boy, and when a middle school was opened in Goch in 1847, its first principal persuaded his parents to send him there. He progressed from there to the diocesan minor seminary, then to Borromeo College in Münster, and then to Bonn University, from where he returned to Münster to study theology. He was ordained priest in August 1861.

He spent the next ten years teaching mathematics and natural sciences in Germany, but he felt increasingly drawn to mission activity, which was at the time forbidden in Germany under the cultural revolutionary laws promulgated by Chancellor Bismark. Arnold therefore looked to nearby Holland, where he was able to buy an old inn at Steyl, on the banks of the Meuse. He converted this into his own seminary, devoted to training priests for the missions, in 1875. It started with nine students and had grown remarkably five years later, with Arnold continuing to build, using money "already there, in the pockets of the good people who will give it to you at the proper time." The community took the form of a religious Order as the Society of the Divine Word.

Arnold was a pioneer in the use of mass-circulation printed material in evangelization. In 1874 he had started the "Little Messenger of the Sacred Heart" to promote his ideas, and at Steyl he set up a press to print it, soon adding another magazine, *Stadt Gottes* (City of God), which still flourishes as the highest-circulation illustrated Catholic magazine in Germany. The printing works expanded, and he added Divine Word Missionary Brothers to the priests in order to man them. By 1900, they outnumbered the priests. The aim of the Order was defined, at its first general chapter in 1886, as "proclamation of the word of God on earth, through missionary activity . . . in the first place [among] the non-Christian peoples especially in the Far East." The first two missionaries had been sent to Hong Kong in 1879, and one of them, Joseph Freinademetz, was to be martyred (and beatified with Arnold Janssen himself; see 29 Jan.). Others followed, and the Divine Word missions spread throughout China, to Japan and other Asian countries, and widely in Latin America. In 1876, the Sisters of Divine Providence, who had been expelled from Germany, took refuge at Steyl, initially to cook and do the laundry. But soon they had applicants who wished to work in the missions, and so the Holy Spirit Missionary Sisters were formed, in 1892.

One of Arnold's convictions, clung to sometimes in the face of ecclesiastical opposition, was that missionaries needed to be learned in the natural sciences in order to understand what they found. This led to the publication of the journal *Anthropos*, for studies in ethnology and linguistics, with a corresponding Institute, the members of which are Divine Word missionaries from all over the world.

When the Prussian government reversed Bismark's policies, it offered Arnold the exclusive right to establish mission seminaries and do mission work in German colonies. The resulting expansion led to new foundations in Germany. Shortly before his death, he extended his mission to the United States, where St Mary Mission Seminary was built in Techny, Illinois, near Chicago. This was followed in 1922 by Bay St Louis Seminary, which has produced well over a hundred African-American priests, of whom six have gone on to become bishops.

Arnold died on 15 January 1909 and was promptly referred to as a saint by Pope Pius X. He was beatified by Pope Paul VI on World Mission Sunday in October 1975. The press at Steyl has continued to grow, embracing modern printing technology to pursue its founder's aim.

16

Bd Joseph Vaz (1651–1711)

The recent (1995) beatification of Joseph Vaz sets the seal of church approval on a style of mission activity that has not always been the hallmark of Christian evangelists: free of political or economic manipulation, untainted by cultural imperialism, respectful toward non-Christians, and relying solely on personal sincerity and charity. His background is the very imperialist struggles between the Portuguese and Dutch in colonial Asia. Through an arrangement with the papacy known as the *Padroado*, the (Catholic) Portuguese crown enjoyed extensive jurisdiction over local churches established there in the sixteenth century. In the following century most of Portugal's Asian possessions were seized by the (Protestant) Dutch, and Catholic missionaries fled or were expelled.

Joseph Vaz was born in Goa, one of the few Portuguese enclaves left. His family belonged to the Brahmin caste and were Catholic converts. He was ordained in 1676 and found himself caught up in struggles between Rome—now appointing vicars apostolic in Asia since Portugal could no longer fulfil its responsibilities—and Portugal, still clinging to its rights under the *Padroado*. Joseph refused to become embroiled in these quarrels and so gained the reputation of being a true *sanyasi*, a holy ascetic, with people of all religions, but not with the Portuguese ecclesiastical authorities in Goa, who accused him of disloyalty.

As a "native," he was barred from the mainstream religious Orders, who confined their candidates to those of European blood. He therefore joined a group of Goanese clergy who were seeking to form their own Congregation. He was elected their superior and established the community on the Oratorian model. He had, however, long been concerned by the plight of Catholics in Ceylon (now Sri Lanka), where the Dutch East India Company controlled the ports and allowed no Catholic priests to land on the island. So he resigned as superior and, with a former family servant named John Vaz, managed to make his way there in disguise. They arrived sick after a dreadful crossing and were rescued from death by a woman who brought them a little rice gruel every day.

He could then only beg for a living, but the rosary he wore round his neck brought him protection by established Catholic families, who found him a safe haven. Then the Dutch increased their anti-Catholic measures, flogging the most prominent Tamil Catholics to death and forcing Joseph to take refuge in the still independent Buddhist kingdom of Kandy. His luck turned when, after a spell in prison, the coming of the monsoon rains after a long drought was attributed to his prayers. He sent John back to Goa with a letter asking for help, and volunteers from the Goan Oratory began to arrive. Since they worked dressed usually as coolies and could blend in with the local population, they managed to exercise their ministry even beyond the borders of Kandy without being caught by the Dutch authorities. Joseph expected them to master the two vernacular languages, Sinhalese and Tamil. He himself composed hymns and prayers in both. The missionaries supported themselves, Buddhist-style, on alms alone, and such was the response of their flock that they were able to give surplus rice to the poor, making, at Joseph's insistence, no distinction between Catholics and those of other faiths.

He was revered by the Buddhists, especially for his care of the sick during an epidemic of smallpox. His work even reached the ears of Pope Clement XI, who offered him a bishopric. He refused this, fearing that papal recognition would enrage the Portuguese authorities in Goa and make them prevent any more missionaries from being sent to Ceylon. By the time of his death, on 16 January 1711, there were seventy thousand Ceylonese Catholics, of whom forty thousand were former Catholics whose faith had been revitalized and thirty thousand fresh converts. The Goan Oratory continued to provide the island with missionaries until it was suppressed by an anti-Catholic Portuguese government in 1834. The cause of his beatification was started just two years after his death but met with a number of procedural (political?) obstacles, and it was not until 1995 that he was declared blessed, by Pope John Paul II during a special papal visit to Sri Lanka.

It is simply a matter of the way of the cultural tradition in which the faith is presented. If we cling to the past, we simply become irrelevant. If we have the courage to change, then the message comes through in a way that is meaningful to people. That is the hope.
    Bede Griffiths, OSB

17

St Antony of Egypt (about 251–356)

Antony is described as an abbot, and as the first monk. He was the most famous of the *abbas* of the Egyptian desert, who were not elected superiors, as modern abbots are, but were simply those who had been tested by long years in the desert. St Athanasius, who knew him, wrote a Life of him, and this became one of the most popular books in medieval monastery libraries, thereby making Antony the inspiration for countless monks.

Antony's parents were wealthy landowners and Christians; they died when he was about eighteen or twenty. He was then struck by the words from the Gospel of Matthew: "If you wish to be perfect, go, sell your possessions and give the money to the poor ... then come, follow me." This was not too "harsh" a saying for him, and he followed it quite literally. Having sold or given away all his possessions, he became the disciple of a local hermit. When this proved not a strict enough way of life, he retired farther into the desert for another twenty years. Eventually he emerged and founded monasteries, or collections of hermits' huts. He also took part in a disputation with the Arians in Alexandria, supporting Athanasius, after which he retreated again to a remote hut on top of a mountain. But even there, disciples sought him out, asking for a "word of wisdom." These "words" were collected and included in the "Sayings of the Desert Fathers," endlessly repeated, translated, copied, and published, as recently in Thomas Merton's *Wisdom of the Desert*.

The teaching these sayings embody can be summed up as "flight from the world." With the end of major persecutions at the beginning of the fourth century, many devout Christians saw extreme asceticism as a substitute for martyrdom, and went voluntarily into the deserts into which they had previously been driven by the Roman authorities. But the "desert" was also in one's nature: it was a spiritual place where one faced up to one's own demons. (This is perhaps the origin of the "Temptations of St Antony" beloved of late medieval painters. Antony himself, in fact, said that the demons could not be visible and could be given "body" only inside oneself.) Conquering one's demons where they are strongest—in solitude—is to win the final victory over them and so earn the right to teach others.

Antony's spiritual teaching has come down in a number of surviving letters, which confirm much of the material in Athanasius' Life as authentic in tone. He emerges as above all a teacher of charity, with strictness of principle softened by gentleness of application. Despite his quest for solitude, he saw relationships with others as the key to the spiritual life: "If we gain our brother, we gain Christ; but if we scandalize our neighbour, we sin against Christ."

He is said to have visited St Paul the Hermit, who had preceded him in this way of life, at the age of ninety. Paul told him that he had been sent by God to bury him and asked him to fetch the cloak Athanasius had given him, in which to wrap his body. Antony went to fetch this and returned to find Paul dead and two lions digging his grave. When Antony himself died, apparently at or around the age of one hundred and five (a tribute to moderation in diet and a healthy climate), he was buried secretly on top of his mountain, but his remains were disinterred a few years later and taken first to Alexandria and then to Constantinople. In the eleventh century, according to a Western version of events, the emperor gave them to the French count Joscelin, who took them to

France. This version is not accepted in the East, and the story may belong to the scramble for relics at the time of growth in pilgrimage: Antony was famous through Athanasius' Life, and his relics would be a considerable possession. They were claimed by La-Motte-Saint-Didier in the Isère region of France, which was renamed Saint-Antoine-en-Dauphiné.

They soon brought him fresh fame as a healer: two noblemen claimed to have been cured of ergotism (see St Genevieve, 3 Jan.), which was also known as St Antony's fire, through his intercession, and founded the Hospital Brothers of St Antony in gratitude. As incidences of ergotism spread during the twelfth and thirteenth centuries, their numbers grew, until they were running three hundred and sixty hospitals. When the epidemics later declined, so did their numbers, until they died out in 1803. His attributes and patronages derive from these Hospitallers rather than from his actual life or from Athanasius. They wore black cloaks with a T-shaped cross on them, representing a walking-stick, presumably as a tribute to the great age to which Antony lived; they rang bells to announce their alms-seeking missions, and they kept pigs: a stick, bell, and pig all appear in depictions of St Antony. The pigs have made him the patron saint of butchers and of brush-makers (from hogshair bristle); because he supported himself by making rush mats, he is also patron of basket-weavers; because of his association with ergotism, he is invoked against skin diseases. In Eastern Churches he is revered as "first master of the desert and pinnacle of holy monks."

Abbot Antony taught Abbot Ammonas, saying: You must advance yet further in the fear of God. And taking him out of the cell he showed him a stone, saying: Go and insult that stone, and beat it without ceasing. When this had been done, St Antony asked him if the stone has answered back. No, said Ammonas. Then Abbot Antony said: You too must reach the point where you no longer take offence at anything.
    The Wisdom of the Desert (1997 edition, pp. 57–8)

18

St Wulfstan (about 1009–1095)

Wulfstan was born in Warwickshire in the English Midlands and was educated by Benedictine monks, first at nearby Evesham and then at Peterborough. He trained for the priesthood as a member of the household of Bishop Brihteah of Worcester, but after his ordination he took the unusual step of refusing a richly endowed living and instead joined the Benedictines in the priory adjoining Worcester Cathedral. There he first taught children in the school run by the monks, and after holding various other offices he was appointed prior in 1050. Twelve years later the see of Worcester became vacant when the bishop was appointed to York: previous incumbents had been allowed to hold both sees, but the papacy had decided that this plurality was no longer appropriate. Papal legates advised King Edward the Confessor that Wulfstan would be a suitable appointment; the king and his council agreed, and he was duly consecrated.

He was still also prior but carried out his dual responsibilities admirably. He was the first bishop on record to make a systematic visitation of all the parishes in his diocese. He encouraged church building and undertook a rebuilding of Worcester Cathedral—not totally successfully: only the crypt and a few walls of his building survive, the remainder having succumbed to fire and the collapse of the central tower in 1175.

Edward the Confessor, who had spent some years in exile in Normandy, saw the Church in England as remote from continental reform movements and replaced Anglo-Saxon bishops and other ecclesiastics with Normans. Edward died in 1066, Harold seized the throne, and Wulfstan was caught up in the struggle for the succession and the further division between "old" and "new" factions in the Church following Harold's death and William the Conqueror's victory at the battle of Hastings. William was supported by the papacy, and monastic bishops were generally more supportive of Continental-style reform (enforced by Lanfranc, archbishop of Canterbury from 1070) than were secular ones. Wulfstan was one of the first bishops to make his submission to William. This political move was embroidered into a legend involving Edward the Confessor's tomb (see below).

After a dispute between the provinces of Canterbury and York was resolved to Canterbury's advantage by Pope St Gregory VII, Worcester became a suffragan bishopric of Canterbury, and Wulfstan was instrumental in carrying out Lanfranc's reforms there. He had in fact already introduced most of them, including strict insistence on clerical celibacy. He was responsible for a major social reform when his preaching persuaded the merchants of Bristol to stop the trade in slaves sent from there to the Vikings in Ireland. He defended the castle of Worcester for William in the barons' uprising of 1074, and again against the Welsh in 1088, this time for William II, but he was more than a typical medieval "warrior" bishop. He was renowned for his generosity to the poor, making sons of gentleman being educated at the priory school wait on poor people at table.

By the time he died he had been bishop for thirty-two years, during which he had been a major force for peace, calm, and reform not only in his diocese but also in a troubled and war-torn Church and nation. A cult soon developed at his tomb, which William Rufus had covered in gold and silver (which Wulfstan would have been more likely to give to the poor), and later kings, especially John and Edward I, had a great devotion to him, the latter more on account of his defence of Worcester against the Welsh than for his more truly Christian qualities.

❖

Summoned by the Norman Archbishop Lanfranc to resign his see, as being too simple to govern it, Wulfstan refused: he had, he declared, received his pastoral staff from King Edward by authority of the Apostolic See, and to him alone would he resign it. Thereupon, it is said, he went up to the king's tomb and placed his staff upon it, saying, "Take this, my master, and deliver it to whom you will." The staff remained embedded in the stone; no force would dislodge it. So Lanfranc reinstated him in his see, and bade him ask his holy master King Edward to restore him the staff. Wulfstan did so, and the staff yielded to his hand at once; and all praised God who is wonderful in his saints.

Bowden

19

St Macarius the Elder (about 300–390)

This Macarius is also known as the Egyptian, or the Great, to distinguish him from St Macarius of Alexandria, who died just four years after him. As a young man he drove camels carrying the form of salt used for embalming or mummifying bodies, called *natron*, from its source, the Wâdi 'N Natrûn. His story is not unlike that of St Antony of Egypt (see 17 Jan.) but has enough personal elements to make him worth including only two days later. He first answered a call to the ascetic life by becoming a "village hermit," devoting himself to prayer and supporting himself by weaving rush baskets, like Antony before him. The story of how he eventually moved to the desert of Skete is a cautionary tale appropriate to an age of widespread teenage pregnancy. It is recounted among the "sayings" of the Desert Fathers:

> When I was young and lived alone in my cell, they took me against my will and made me a cleric in the village. And since I did not wish to remain there, but fled to another village where a pious layman helped me out by selling my work, it happened that a certain young girl got herself into trouble and became pregnant. And when her parents asked who was responsible for it, she said: "That hermit of yours committed this crime." [Her parents beat him and made him provide for her, and he meekly gave in.] And I said, "Well, Macarius, now you've got yourself a wife, you will have to work harder in order to be able to feed her." So I worked day and night in order to make her a living. But when the poor thing's time was up, for several days she was tormented by labour pains and could not bring forth her child. And when she was asked about it she said, "I pinned the crime on that hermit when he was innocent. For it was the young man next door who got me in this condition." ... Hearing this, and fearing that people would come and bother me, I quickly made off and came to this place.

This happened when Macarius was about thirty years old, and the story shows him as having achieved a high degree of the peace of soul that hermits sought to achieve by self-denial. He was ordained priest ten years later, probably as a result of a visit he made to St Antony (fifteen days away on foot), who persuaded him to accept ordination since there was no Eucharist being celebrated in Skete. He spent a further fifty years in the desert, becoming the revered elder of all the hermit-monks in Skete. He was evidently a great spiritual master, to judge from the considerable body of writing attributed to him, a popularizer rather than an original thinker, drawing on the mystical and spiritual teachings of Gregory of Nyssa (see 10 Jan.). He gives practical directions as to how the community should be organized, on a basis of mutual help, with manual work appreciated but not allowed to encroach on the prayers of others—basing himself here on the gospel story of Martha and Mary. He dwells on the significance of Jesus washing his disciples' feet to show the pre-eminence of work in the service of others. In general, he combines St Gregory's intellectual originality with a certain folk wisdom and common sense deriving from the collective experience of the early monastic community in Skete, where the teaching of the "sayings" attributed to the *abbas* (and, less often, the *ammas*) formed the basis for the way of life, rather than a fixed Rule.

He was almost certainly banished to the Nile Delta when the emperor Valens expelled all monks who supported the orthodox, as opposed to Arian, doctrine concerning the two natures in Christ, around 374, but was reinstated by popular demand. He died at an age almost as advanced as that of Antony, another tribute to personal and climatic virtues. (There is no record of hermits in Ireland, where this way of life was much copied, living to a comparable age.)

Once Abbot Macarius was on his way home to his cell from the marshes, carrying reeds, and he met the devil with a reaper's sickle in his path. The devil tried to get him with the sickle, and couldn't. And he said: I suffer great violence from you, Macarius, because I cannot overcome you. For see, I do all the things that you do. You fast, and I eat nothing at all. You watch, and I never sleep. But there is one thing in which you overcome me. Abbot Macarius said to him: What is that? Your humility, the devil replied, for because of it I cannot overcome you.

The Wisdom of the Desert, pp. 50–51

20

Bd Cyprian Michael Iwene Tansi (1903–1964)

The first Nigerian, or indeed West African, to be beatified was born in south-east Nigeria in 1903. His parents followed the traditional religion of the Ibo people, but his father died while he was young, and his mother sent him to be educated by the Irish Holy Ghost Missionaries. He was baptized when he was nine, adding the baptismal name Michael to his given name Iwene, studied to become a teacher, and was appointed headmaster of St Joseph's when he was only twenty-one. He was then drawn to the priesthood and was ordained in Onitsha Cathedral in 1937.

In 1939 he started a new parish, where one of his catechumens was a boy who was later to become Cardinal Arinze, who has said that Fr Michael, the first priest he knew, was, "under God," his inspiration and that he "wanted to be like him." He was a brilliant preacher, ascetic in his personal life, and a great community leader, setting an example for building a weekly boarding school by treading mud bricks himself. He confronted supposedly spirit-possessed members of a secret society with a stick and the words, "The spirit has been confronted by a more powerful Spirit," and he was unusually forthright in condemning corruption among the wealthy and powerful. His long-felt desire, however, was to become a contemplative monk, and there were no monasteries for these in Nigeria,

In 1950 he was accepted by Mount St Bernard Abbey, near Leicester in England, and took the name Cyprian in religion. The original intention was that he and any other Nigerian postulants should eventually return to Nigeria to found a monastery there, which would depend on Mount St Bernard as its motherhouse. But these plans were not put into effect, largely through lack of money, and in 1953 Cyprian and another Nigerian, Fr Clement, both made the decision to stay at Mount St Bernard. Though ordained priests, they had to go through the full training process as novices, which included working in winter fields very much colder than anything they had experienced in Nigeria.

Fr Cyprian's reputation for holiness in his home country brought him frequent visitors, to whom he would expand on the contemplative life. In the community he was "quiet ... conscientious ... self-effacing and thinking of others." By 1959 he was suffering from a recurrence of an old stomach ulcer and was an invalid for two years. In 1963 plans for an African foundation finally began to take shape, but it was to be in Cameroon, not in Nigeria. Despite his disappointment at this, Cyprian was due to go there as novice-master, but his health was failing. He was able to celebrate the Silver Jubilee of his ordination in December 1963, but an aortic embolism led to his death in Leicester Royal Infirmary on 20 January 1964, as he was preparing for an operation on his stomach.

The then Fr Arinze was determined that his memory should be perpetuated and began collecting documentation of his life with a view to instituting a diocesan process in 1974. The bishop of Nottingham waived the normal right for this process to be held in the diocese in which he had died, ceding this to the archdiocese of Onitsha, and it became an African process, formally opened in 1984. The promoter general of the Trappist Order suggested that Fr Cyprian's remains should be brought back to Nigeria, and when they were, a remarkable cure of an apparently terminally ill young woman was attributed to his intercession. He was declared venerable in 1995 and beatified in Onitsha in 1998. Cardinal Arinze declared that his beatification sends a clear message to African Christians that "Saints are ordinary men and women from your own villages." At Mount St Bernard a wall statue of him has been put up in the abbey church.

When we see others as brothers and sisters, it is then possible to begin the process of healing the divisions within society and between ethnic groups ... We must be convinced that each of us, according to our particular state in life, is called to do no less than what Father Tansi did. Having been reconciled with God, we must be instruments of reconciliation, treating all men and women as brothers and sisters, called to membership in the one family of God.

Pope John Paul II, homily at the Mass for the beatification of Fr Tansi, 22 March 1998

21

St Agnes (perhaps 292–305)

Agnes, according to stories circulating about a hundred years after her death, was a beautiful thirteen-year-old Christian girl from a wealthy Roman family. Many suitors sought her hand in marriage, but she rejected them all, saying that her only spouse was Christ. She was dragged before statues of gods and told to sacrifice to them; she refused and was then ordered by the prefect to become a vestal virgin (serving in the temple of Vesta); again she refused, so she was stripped naked and exposed in a brothel, whereupon her hair instantly grew to cover her. The prefect's son tried to rape her and was struck blind (or even dead in some versions) but was restored by her prayers. She was finally condemned to death by burning and was dragged out to die in this way in the Stadium of Domitian, now the Piazza Navona, where a church named after her stands.

She is not just a legend, as is proved by the marble tomb erected for her by her parents on the Via Nomentana, some two miles outside the walls of Rome. She was evidently venerated there not long after her death. Before the end of the fourth century, Pope St Damasus I composed an inscription for her tomb; this was then lost for many centuries, but it was rediscovered under the floor of the church on the site during restoration work in 1792. St Jerome, who was Damasus' secretary for three years, wrote that "The life of Agnes is praised in the literature and speech of all peoples, especially in the churches, she who overcame both her age and the tyrant, and consecrated by martyrdom her claim to chastity." St Ambrose preached a sermon about her and wrote a hymn, which became very influential in the growth of her fame. This suggests, probably correctly, that she was not burned but stabbed in the neck with a sword, the normal Roman method of execution. The great Spanish-Roman poet Prudentius gathered this and other stories circulating about her into a hymn, which then became the basis for further development of her story.

Her extreme youth seems to have been discarded in artistic representations. In the procession of virgins in the mosaics of St Apollinare Nuovo in Ravenna she comes fourth and has a lamb at her feet. The lamb came from the similarity of her name (which actually came from the Greek *agneia*, meaning "pure") to *agnus*, the Latin for lamb, also a symbol of purity in the imagery of the Book of Revelation. This led to her association with the wool used to make the *pallium* (woollen collar) sent by popes to archbishops around the world. Every year on her feast-day two lambs are brought into her church on the Via Nomentana (St Agnes outside the Walls) and blessed. They are then taken out and kept until they are ready to be sheared. Their wool is then laid on the high altar of St Peter's on the feast of SS Peter and Paul (29 June), then taken to be woven to make these signs of archbishops being united to the see of Rome.

She became extraordinarily popular in the Middle Ages, together with other virgin saints, such as Barbara, Dorothy, Margaret of Antioch, and others, many of whom have now been relegated to the status of myth. They prove the enduring value attached to virginity through the ages. It signifies power to resist—men, authority, the world—rather than just the rather more docile concept of "purity." It has been suggested that nothing of her story is true and that it was all simply attached to a play on the word *agneia*. That there was a historical figure, a girl who was killed, began to seem more rather than less likely in sceptical modern times, however, when the body of a young girl, headless, was found in a reliquary under the church on the Via Nomentana in 1605. This was again excavated and measured in 1901: the body would seem to the right size for a girl of twelve or thirteen. A head was found in the Lateran

Palace the following year: the teeth suggested a child of about twelve. (The separation of the head from the body was a practice of the time, intended to provide two focuses for veneration, and does not indicate that she was beheaded.) The head is now venerated in the church in the Piazza Navona, on the supposed site of her execution. Historical or legendary, however, she remains an abiding symbol and powerful focus of veneration.

22

St Vincent Pallotti (1795–1850)

One of ten children (of whom five died in infancy) born in Rome to Paolo Pallotti and his wife, Maria Maddalena de Rossi, Vincent had decided by the age of fifteen that he wanted to be a priest. He was ordained in 1818 and awarded a doctorate in theology and philosophy two months later. He taught theology at the Sapienza College for the next ten years. He then decided to renounce the prestige of an academic career and also that of a "career priest" advancing through the parish system, in order to concentrate on a purely spiritual pastoral ministry.

He lived at a time of great change in urban society as a result of the industrial revolution, and he saw that a new type of ministry was needed to reach people. In 1835 his ideas took shape in the "Pious Union [later the Society] of the Catholic Apostolate," which included both clerics and lay people, aiming to renew the apostolic spirit in the Church: "An evangelical trumpet calling all, inviting all, awakening the zeal and charity of all the faithful of every state, rank and condition to serve the Catholic Apostolate as it is instituted by Christ in the Church." The union included a group of priests who devoted themselves full time to its aims; they became the Congregation of the Catholic Apostolate. The use of the term "apostolate" offended some bishops, who thought it should be reserved to those who claimed descent from the apostles, and it was not until a century after Vincent's death that this controversy was resolved in the context of a new understanding of mission and apostolate. Next came a group of women religious, brought into being to look after girls orphaned in the cholera outbreak of 1837. They formed into the Sisters of the Catholic Apostolate, later the Pallottine Missionary Sisters.

In Rome, Fr Vincent became close friends with the future Cardinal Wiseman, and even effectively told him to open a college in England for the foreign missions. Wiseman passed this counsel on to Herbert Vaughan (later to be the third cardinal-archbishop of Westminster), who put it into effect with the founding of St Joseph's Missionary Society at Mill Hill. Wiseman in turn advised Pallotti to recruit John Henry Newman, then a convert studying in

Rome, into the Union. This did not happen, but the acquaintance led to Pallotti taking a deep interest in the foundation of the London Oratory and the progress of the missions in London. He was appointed rector of the church of Santo Spirito dei Neapolitani in Rome where poor people flocked to hear his sermons, again arousing resentment among senior clerics. He had the ear of Pope Pius IX, and from him obtained full canonical status for the Society, with all the privileges granted to regular Orders and Congregations.

In the year of revolutions, 1848, when Pius IX was forced to flee from the Papal States in disguise to escape an anticlerical mob in the newly proclaimed Roman Republic, Vincent took refuge in the Irish College in Rome. From there he issued a stream of letters of advice to lords spiritual and temporal, lamenting the evils of the time. By the time Pius was restored with the aid of French troops the following year, Vincent was in poor health and felt that he was dying. He put all the affairs of the Society in order, contracted pleurisy, and died on 22 January 1850.

Development of the Society after his death was initially slow, but by 1900 there were thirty houses in eight countries. The Missionary Sisters spread to England, Poland, Switzerland, and the USA, and the Pallottine Fathers have some two thousand members worldwide. They arrived in the USA in the first decade of the twentieth century and are now engaged in every type of missionary activity. Pallotti's great achievement, however, lies in his mobilization of the energies of lay people in mission. It was only with the establishment of Catholic Action in the early twentieth century that his prophetic voice was truly appreciated throughout the Church. Pope John XXIII, who canonized him in 1963, said that "the foundation of the Society of the Catholic Apostolate was the starting-point in Rome of Catholic Action as we know it today."

Vincent Pallotti anticipated a discovery by almost one hundred years. He discovered in the world of laypeople a great capacity for good work. This capacity had been passive, dormant, and timid, unable to act. Vincent Pallotti has awakened the conscience of the laity.
Pope Paul VI

23

St Ildephonsus of Toledo (died 667)

The Church in Spain entered on a period of relative power and of intellectual, spiritual, and pastoral development following the conversion of the Visigothic king Recared from the prevailing Arianism to orthodox Catholicism. Recared was hailed as a new Constantine at the Third Council of Toledo in 589. He established his capital in Toledo, which was also the ecclesiastical capital, the only city in the West to fulfil both functions. Its archbishop had the right to summon national councils and to summon other bishops to make five-yearly visits to him. Toledo retains the primacy of Spain to this day.

Ildephonsus came from a distinguished family and eventually succeeded an uncle, also canonized, St Eugenius of Toledo, as archbishop. He had become a monk at an early age, and was appointed abbot of the community he joined, at Agalia, near Toledo. As abbot, he attended councils of Toledo held in 653 and 655. His uncle died in 657, so he was archbishop for nine years only. His period in office saw increasingly close links between Church and State, a condition that was to recur throughout subsequent Spanish history, not always to the advantage of either. In this way, he helped to develop a "medieval" concept of the relationship between Church and State several hundred years in advance of its time.

His greatest contribution to the life of the Church was in the sphere of devotion. He may have been a pupil of St Isidore of Seville, and he certainly carried on that great master's intellectual and spiritual work. He increased veneration of Spanish saints, while at the same time promoting a special devotion to the Virgin Mary, which might be seen as a national characteristic ever since. His "Book of the perpetual virginity of Mary" became a landmark in the cult of Mary in Spain and beyond. Sentences from it were copied into Books of Hours for many centuries, and a whole body of work was written in imitation of it, so that much of what has been attributed to him is more probably "school of Ildephonsus." He was also deeply concerned with the education of the laity and wrote a treatise especially for "ordinary" baptized people rather than for the religious elite who gathered around monasteries.

His devotion to Mary gave rise to legends and determined the way he was later represented in art. In one popular story Our Lady herself appeared to him seated on his own bishop's throne and holding out a chasuble to him as a gift. This passed into many twelfth- and thirteenth-century collections of legends about Mary, and also became the subject of paintings by El Greco (who lived and worked in Toledo from 1577 to his death), Velázquez, and others.

Virgin Mother of God, may I cleave to God and to you, wait on your Lord and on you, serve your Son and you: Him as my maker, you as the mother of my Maker; Him as the Lord of Hosts, you as the handmaid of the Lord; Him as my God, you as the mother of my God.

Prayer of St Ildephonsus

24

St Francis de Sales (1567–1622)

This great bishop and spiritual writer was born in what is now Switzerland, then the independent duchy of Savoy. He was the eldest child in what was eventually to be a large family, belonging to the lesser nobility. He was sent to Paris to study rhetoric, philosophy, and theology when he was fifteen and already determined to become a priest, contrary to the wishes of his elderly and stern father. He returned home after six years to find his father planning a career for him as a soldier or, failing that, a lawyer. After six months he went away to university again, this time to Padua, from where he emerged with a brilliant doctorate in law in 1591.

He met the Benedictine bishop of Geneva, who had been forced out of that city when it became a Calvinist stronghold and was living in nearby Annecy. The bishop was so impressed with Francis' intellect that he told him that if he was ordained he would certainly eventually become a bishop. Francis was too humble by nature to let this influence him, but he still felt the call and faced up to his father, who accepted his son's decision with bad grace. He was ordained in Advent 1593, by which time he had already become famous as a preacher and been appointed to the provostship of Geneva, a post ranking second to the bishop.

Greater demands were, however, soon made of him. He and his cousin Louis were chosen by the bishop to win back for Catholicism the poor and mountainous district of Chablais, south and east of Geneva, which had swung between Catholic and Protestant in seemingly endless dynastic and religious wars. In 1591 the Calvinists had reoccupied it and driven out all Catholic priests. Francis toiled at the task for four years, in danger from cold, violent Calvinists, ordinary ruffians, and even wolves. His father had not forgiven him and refused him any financial help. By the end of four years, during the last of which he had been seriously ill, he was able to celebrate High Mass before a crowd of thirty thousand and put on processions and a mystery play.

He travelled to Rome in 1598 to be appointed coadjutor bishop of Geneva. There he met Robert Bellarmine (see 17 Sept.), the Oratorian Juvenal Ancina, who became a close friend, and the future Pope Paul V. On his return (with the appointment as coadjutor for some reason unconfirmed) he conceived a grandiose scheme for a "Hostel for all the arts and sciences" in the middle of the Chablais district. It was never built as such, but he was to put the principles underlying it into practice in his ministry. Over the next few years he struggled with the religious and political affairs of the diocese and the duchy and also made his mark at the French court in Paris, where the convert king, Henry IV, called him "a gentleman" and offered him a rich bishopric if he would stay in France, to which Francis replied, "Sire, I have married a poor wife and I cannot desert her for a richer one." On his way back to Geneva he learned of the bishop of Geneva's death, which meant that he would take over as bishop.

He was consecrated on the feast of the Immaculate Conception in 1602 and set about bringing a diocese of some four hundred and fifty parishes into line with the reforms of the Council of Trent. His main weapons were to be preaching, which he did tirelessly; education of the clergy, with all candidates to the priesthood examined by him personally; and writing, through a series of lengthy letters. He acquired a reputation—possibly undeserved—for severity when he suppressed Valentine cards. It is perhaps ironic, then, that the rest of his life was to be transformed by a great love—a spiritual one, certainly, but his meeting with a young widow, Jeanne-Françoise Frémyot, known to history as St Jane Frances de Chantal (see 12 Dec.) proved to be a fruitful meeting of hearts and minds to a degree rarely encountered. It was to produce a new religious Order and a remarkable correspondence, and to console them both in depression and disaster. The first of the latter came when Francis' youngest sister, whom he had sent to live with Jeanne and her children, died of a fever at the age of fourteen. Francis wrote to Jeanne expressing his grief in a letter that contains a phrase that has come to serve as his motto: *Je suis tant homme que rien plus*, "I am so much a man as to be nothing more."

Francis was becoming convinced that anyone could serve God in any walk of life, but that this required an elevation of the spiritual aspirations of the many, not a reduction in those of the few. A series of spiritual exercises he devised for the wife of a cousin developed into his best-known book, the *Introduction to the Devout Life*. It became an immediate bestseller, going into several editions in French and being translated into several languages, including English, within a few years. It in fact puts across a very demanding ideal and addresses the concerns of the leisured classes, despite being addressed to "those ... obliged to lead outwardly at least an ordinary life."

Jeanne de Chantal had been making a regular annual visit to him, and by 1610 he had decided that she must move to Annecy and start a new Order. A house was found, and the Order of the Visitation of Mary came into being. Despite having its critics (among them, most probably, those who saw the foundation as a means of keeping Jeanne near him), the Order prospered and spread, cultivating the new inner-directed spirituality embodied in Francis' teaching. It was approved by the pope in 1618, on condition that the Sisters accepted enclosure. (This was just thirteen years before the Vatican condemnation of Mary Ward and her "galloping girls.")

Francis remained endlessly busy with visiting parishes, preaching, and fresh political disputes and debates over the proper spheres of Church and State power. In 1613 he visited the shrine of St Charles Borromeo, who had been canonized three years earlier, and he wept over the Shroud of Turin when it was publicly unwound in a ceremony at which he preached. His spiritual counselling of the Visitation nuns led to the book he really wanted to write, the *Treatise on the Love of God*, which also became a solid success in several languages, though not on the scale of the *Introduction*. (After his death, a collection of his homilies to the nuns was published in a pirated edition, to Jeanne de Chantal's fury.)

By this time he was famous and regarded as a living saint. In Paris, where he went to pursue marriage negotiations for the duke of Savoy's daughter, great crowds flocked to hear him preach. He met the man known as "Monsieur Vincent," the future St Vincent de Paul (see 27 Sept.), and established a deep friendship with Angélique Arnaud, later the Jansenist abbess of Port-Royal. He still wrote twenty or thirty letters a day, many of them long; he preached constantly, yet somehow found time for prayer. His health was now failing, with problems associated with high blood pressure. An arduous and, as it turned out, unnecessary journey over the Alps to Turin, at the pope's request, almost killed him. Another journey, this time in winter to Avignon at the duke of Savoy's request, finally did. He had a last meeting with Jeanne in Lyons on his dreadful journey back and then suffered a stroke. Asked by a nun for a last word of advice, he wrote HUMILITY three times on a piece of paper. He was canonized in 1655, declared a Doctor of the Church in 1877, and named patron saint of writers and journalists in 1923.

My advice ... is that we should either not utter words of humility, or else use them with sincere inner feeling that matches our outward words. Let us never lower our eyes except when we humble our hearts. Let us not appear to want to be the lowest unless we want it with our whole heart. I take this rule to be so general that I allow no exception to it.

St Francis de Sales, *Introduction to the Devout Life*

25

St Paul (died about 64)

What we know of Paul comes from his own Epistles and from the Acts of the Apostles, neither of which is designed to be in any way "biographical" in a modern sense: the letters are theological in purpose and only incidentally autobiographical, while the author of Acts (Luke) presents the story of Paul as the second part of his Gospel. Furthermore, the later letters are now generally taken to be attributed to Paul rather than written by him, which makes them less useful as a source of information about the later part of his life.

He is at pains to stress the exemplary and zealously Jewish nature of his upbringing. He writes in Greek but is clearly at home in Hebrew. He is generally thought to have been born about 4 BC in Tarsus and to have been educated in Jerusalem: Acts speaks of him sitting at the feet of the distinguished Rabbinic teacher Gamaliel. It then refers to his conversion in the context of the stoning of the first martyr, St Stephen (see 26 Dec.), of which he (still named Saul) approved. The famous story of the "road to Damascus" appears only in Acts, where it is repeated in three differing versions, whereas Paul himself refers to it only indirectly. Whatever happened, its consequences were seen as crucial for the development of the early Church. Stephen's death can be dated with some certainty to the year 36. The descriptions of the event in Acts may well be based on earlier stories, and the writer's concern is with calling rather than with conversion.

After his conversion, Paul withdrew to Arabia to pray—for three years, he says, though the "three" may be symbolic rather than accurate. He then went to Jerusalem and spent time with Peter, after which he began to travel and preach the message that Jesus was "the Messiah and the Son of God." This message aroused such hostility among the Jews (for whom calling Jesus "Son of God" was blasphemy) that Paul retired to his home town of Tarsus (in what is now southern Turkey) for safety. His own account indicates a long period of fourteen years before he went to Jerusalem again. What then took place has come to be referred to as the Council of Jerusalem and is generally placed in the year 49. Essentially, Paul persuaded Peter that Gentiles should be admitted to the Church without previously being converted to Judaism and without having to comply with Jewish dietary and other laws. He thus opened up the missionary effort to the Gentile world and brought in what has been called the "second age" of the Church, which was that of the continuation of his mission in the cultures descended from classical Greece and Rome. This was to last until the "true universalization" of the Church's mission at the Second Vatican Council of 1962–5.

His famous journeys—including being let down in a basket from the prison walls in Damascus and being shipwrecked on Malta—around the eastern and central Mediterranean are split into three in Acts, but this may be less historical than to press home a point: that Paul was three times rejected by the Jews, three times turned to the Gentiles, and three times claimed that this fulfilled the prophecies of the Old Testament. He is said to have done this first at Antioch in Asia Minor, then at Corinth in Greece, and finally in Rome itself. His missionary activity in fact finished in Jerusalem, where Roman soldiers took him into protective custody when a hostile crowd was threatening. He appealed to the emperor on the grounds that he was a Roman citizen and was taken to be tried in Rome. This enabled Luke to provide a satisfying end to the story of how the gospel spread from Jerusalem to the capital of the great empire.

Paul's call to be an apostle and his subsequent teaching shifted Christianity from a Jewish sect to a world religion. This is a huge claim, and to exaggerate it by saying that he "invented" Christianity, as some have done, would be going too far. Paul's whole teaching is rooted in the experience of Jesus Christ crucified and raised from the dead, and what he expresses with unique vividness is rooted in the primitive Church. His great themes are the Kingdom of God, conversion, revelation, the centrality of the cross, the universal application of Jesus' message, justification through grace, and love as fulfilment of the Law. These have provided the basic material for virtually all subsequent Christian theology.

Exactly how and when he died in Rome is uncertain. He seems to have been kept under a fairly mild regime of house arrest, which allowed him to communicate with the Jewish community in Rome. He was then released for a time and re-arrested. He was executed at Tre Fontana, in the year 64 or 65. As a Roman citizen, he would have had the privilege of being beheaded instead of suffering one of the more barbarous forms of judicial execution used on non-citizens. The belief that he died on the same day as St Peter probably arose from their shared feast-day. His body was buried where the basilica of St Paul without (outside) the Walls was built in the fourth and fifth centuries. The original stood until it was destroyed by fire in 1823; it was rebuilt to the same plan and reopened in 1854. Paul is the patron saint of Greece and Malta, as well as of the Cursillo movement and, by implication, of all forms of Catholic action. Today's feast now marks the closing day of the Week of Prayer for Christian Unity.

Now as he was going along and approaching Damascus, suddenly a light from heaven flashed around him. He fell to the ground and heard a voice saying to him, "Saul, Saul, why do you persecute me?" He asked, "Who are you, Lord?" The reply came, "I am Jesus, whom you are persecuting."
Acts 9:3–6

26

SS **Timothy** and **Titus** (First Century)

The New Testament contains two letters addressed to Timothy and one to Titus, the three being referred to collectively as the Pastoral Epistles. They are said to be from Paul, but this is a convention used to impart authority to their writers, who are almost certainly unknown. They date from around the end of the first century or the early years of the second, long after Paul's death, and cannot be relied upon to provide biographical information about the persons to whom they are addressed. This does not mean that nothing can be known about these. Both are referred to in the Acts of the Apostles and in letters certainly written by Paul, indicating that they were connected with him.

In Acts, Timothy is described as "the son of a Jewish woman who was a believer; but his father was a Greek . . . well spoken of by the believers in Lystra and Iconium" (16:1–2). In 2 Timothy 1:5 we learn that his mother's name was Eunice and his grandmother's Lois and that both were Christians. Paul took him as a companion and had him circumcised to make him acceptable to Jewish Christians. He went with Paul to Macedonia and from there came to Corinth, arriving at the time Paul was turning his back on the Jews and resolving, "From now on I will go to the Gentiles" (Acts 18:6). Paul then sent him back to Macedonia, with Erastus, while he himself stayed on in Asia (19:22). He was later in Greece with Paul and others and returned to Syria by way of Macedonia after a plot against them (20:4). Later tradition, recorded by the historian Eusebius, made Timothy bishop of Ephesus, and "Acts of St Timothy," written in Ephesus in the fourth or fifth century, gives an account of his martyrdom. This document is the earliest reference to it, but its sober tone indicates that it has at least a basis in historical fact. It claims that he was killed by pagans for opposing their festivals at a feast of Dionysius in which participants carried a club in one hand and an idol in the other, ready weapons with which to beat Timothy to death. His supposed relics were transferred to Constantinople in 356 (perhaps after "Acts of St Timothy" was written), and cures at his shrine became a common experience.

Titus accompanied Paul on the journey to Jerusalem that led to the debates that came to be known as the Council of Jerusalem (see Gal. 2:1ff). There Paul won the day, arguing that Gentiles should not be subjected to the Mosaic law before becoming Christians. In accordance with this, he did not insist that Titus, who was a Greek, should be circumcised. Titus went to Corinth to encourage the Corinthians to give as generously to the support of the communities as their poorer brethren in Macedonia were doing. He was later urged to come to Nicopolis and was then sent to Dalmatia, after which he seems to have stayed in Ephesus. He is believed to have been the first bishop of Crete, where he had to deal with a population the letter to him describes as "always liars, vicious brutes, lazy gluttons" (Titus 1:12). There are further stories about him in a fictitious "Acts of Titus," supposedly written by the "Zenas the lawyer" referred to in Titus 3:13. His body was supposedly buried at Gortyna in Crete; the head was detached and taken to Venice in 823.

Both are called "loyal child in faith" in the letters addressed to them. Timothy is sent to the Corinthians to remind them of Paul's "ways in Christ" (1

Cor. 4:7). Paul describes him to the Thessalonians as "our brother and co-worker for God" (1 Thess. 3:2), and he tells the Philippians that they will find "no one like him who will be genuinely concerned for your welfare" (2:20). Titus is described in similar terms: Paul tells the Corinthians that he is his "partner and co-worker in your service" (2 Cor. 8:23) and that "since he is more eager than ever," he is going to them of his own accord (8:16). Less can be gleaned of their characters from the letters addressed to them, but in general the writers are expecting them to be wary of new ideas, of the influence of rich people in their communities, and of the leadership exercised by women. They are being urged not to go against the grain of patriarchal Greco-Roman society: hence the insistence, especially in 1 Timothy, on the subjection of women, children, and slaves to their masters, an attitude not characteristic of the letters actually written by Paul, but here given his authority and so handed down through generations.

27

St Angela Merici (about 1470–1540)

Angela came from a family of farmers on her father's side and of lesser nobility on her mother's. She was born in either 1470 or 1474, the fifth of sixth children, of whom four died young, closely followed by both parents. She was then cared for by the family of an uncle who lived on the banks of Lake Como in northern Italy. Accounts of her childhood make her pious, rebelling against the fashions of the age, devoted to the legend of St Ursula, and the recipient of a vision showing a great company of virgins and other saints coming down from heaven to her. They included a dead sister, who invited her to form a great "Company of Virgins," which was what Angela had actually done by the time the account was written.

She became a Franciscan tertiary and spent some years as a companion to a widowed friend, back in her home town of Desenzano. With a group of other young women, many of them also Franciscan tertiaries, she then formed a sort of "support group" for unmarried girls in the area. The venture flourished, and she was invited to open a similar one in the larger city of Brescia. There she developed acquaintances among the leading families of the city and became the focus of a group of devout women and men. In 1494 Brescia had been invaded by Louis XIII of France; at first, at least the aristocracy collaborated, but the merchant classes eventually rose up against the French. This led to terrible reprisals in 1512, when troops under Gaston de Foix slaughtered, it is said, ten thousand of the seventy-five thousand inhabitants in a single day. For the next five years it was fought over by French, Venetians, and Spanish, creating chaos and deprivation on a vast scale. This was the climate in which Angela pursued her mission.

She went on pilgrimage to the Holy Land and on the way, in Crete, was mysteriously struck blind. She insisted on completing the journey, but she could only listen to her companions' descriptions of places she could not see. On the return journey, in the same place, she just as mysteriously recovered her sight. Her work became widely known: she was received in audience by the pope and invited to move to Rome, but she saw her calling as attending to local needs. Young women who neither married nor joined religious Orders—and convents were mainly places for the aristocracy to dump surplus daughters—had nowhere to go except into prostitution or menial service. Angela, personally austere but still capable of enjoying the company of aristocrats, devoted herself to these young women, effectively re-creating the "social class of virgins" (L. Fossato) revered in the early Church, seen as relating primarily to Christ out of free choice, not from failure to secure husbands. Angela and her helpers grew into a "Company," echoing the contemporary foundation of the Company of Jesus. Its "members" had to join freely, seeing themselves as acquiring a dignity that would be the envy of empresses, queens, and duchesses.

A structure gradually emerged, and on military lines. The "first daughters" still lived with their families but met together for instruction, gathered into groups by district under the command of a "virgin-mistress." These were older women, often widows, who were responsible for the physical, economic, and moral welfare of their "virgins." Any problems they could not handle were referred upward to four "widow-matrons" or "colonels" chosen from among the aristocracy of Brescia. Angela herself and some companions moved together into a house near the church of St Afra in November 1535, and the foundation of the Congregation of the Ursulines is generally dated to this move, though formal papal approval dates from 1544.

She had many supporters but also made enemies, especially among the upper classes, who suspected her of attempting to lure their marriageable daughters away from prestigious alliances. But she won through, with absolute confidence that her work would last. And so it has: the Ursulines are now the largest teaching Order in the Church and active worldwide. In her *Testament* she left her followers the precious message that their strength lay in unity: "There is only one sign that is pleasing to the Lord, that of loving and being united to one another."

Angela died on 27 January 1540, just before the opening of the Council of Trent. (Had she lived a generation later, she might well have found her unenclosed Congregation blocked by the Inquisition.) Her body lay unburied for thirty days while canons of St Afra quarrelled with those of the cathedral over where it should be buried. It was not until 1768 that a reliable account of her life was written, and she was canonized in 1807.

❖

She had such a hunger and thirst for the salvation and good of her fellows that she was disposed and most ready to give not one, but a thousand lives, if she had had so many, for the salvation even of the least. ... With maternal love, she embraced all creatures.

from the "Declaration of the Bull" establishing the Ursulines as a religious Congregation, issued by Pope Paul III in 1544

28

St Thomas Aquinas (1225–1274)

This great medieval theologian and philosopher died at the early age of forty-nine, leaving a body of work that would have taken three normal lifetimes to compose. He was born mid-way between Rome and Naples, near the small town of Aquino, of which his father was count. He started his schooling at the nearby Benedictine abbey of Monte Cassino, but war between the emperor and the pope, in which his family sided with the emperor and the Benedictines with the pope, led to his removal at the age of fourteen, whereupon he studied for a further five years at the new university of Naples.

At Naples he was drawn to the Dominican Order, founded twenty years earlier, largely on account of the scholarship its members were already demonstrating in university circles. Despite being locked in a castle and tempted with a courtesan by his parents (who considered that the mendicant Dominicans could not offer the same career prospects for their son as the established Benedictines), he joined the Order in 1224. He studied under Albert the Great (see 15 Nov.), first at Paris and then at Cologne. The Dominican house of Saint-Jacques in Paris was where the brightest Dominican students were sent, and the university was in a ferment of new learning, largely revolving around the rediscovered works of Aristotle. Thomas was in the forefront of commentary on him in the light of Jewish and Islamic commentaries and so helped to make Paris outstanding in European intellectual life. He was ordained priest during his time in Cologne, where Albert prophesied that "the lowing of this dumb ox"—Thomas was physically large and spoke little—"would be heard all over the world."

He was appointed to a lectureship in Paris in 1252, and four years later, at the early age of thirty-one, he was made a master of theology, which imposed the threefold task of lecturing, disputing, and preaching. He encountered quite ferocious opposition, mainly from the leader of the secular clergy, William of Saint-Amour, who saw the mendicant Orders and their poverty as heralding the arrival of the Antichrist. Thomas and his Franciscan contemporary Bona-venture (see 15 July) composed replies to the tracts attacking them. Before he left Paris, Thomas began work on the *Summa contra Gentiles*, undertaken at the request of Raymund of Peñafort (see 7 Jan.), who wanted an authoritative text to help combat the Moors and Jews in Spain. In 1264, at the request of Pope Urban IV, he composed the office for the new feast of Corpus Christi, and some of the magnificent hymns he wrote for this are still in use.

After three years as master in Paris, Thomas was called to Italy, where he taught at several places, including Orvieto, Viterbo, and Rome for the next ten years. In Rome he lectured at the recently opened university of the Roman Curia, completed the *Summa contra Gentiles*, and began work on the vast *Summa theologica*. He then returned to Paris for three years, where he was appreciated at court as well as at the university and was a frequent guest of King (later Saint) Louis IX. The Dominicans recalled him to Italy in 1272, to reorganize their house of studies at Naples. There, while saying Mass one day, he had some sort of visionary experience that caused him to stop work on the *Summa theologica* and declare that he was done with writing, as "All I have written seems to me like straw compared with what I have seen and what has been revealed to me." He gave no further details of the experience (which could have involved a minor stroke) to anyone.

Pope Gregory X summoned him to take part in the Council of Lyons in 1274. He set out on what would have been a long and arduous journey, but after only a few hours he suffered a major stroke. He was taken to the castle of Maenza, which belonged to a niece, and then at his request transferred to the monastery of Fossanuova, where he died on 7 March. (His feast-day was, unusually, moved from the day of his death to today, which actually marks the day on which his relics were eventually interred in Toulouse in 1368, in the calendar reform of 1969.)

His writings are too extensive in number, scope, and achievement to be presented here in any meaningful summary. He insisted that the Christian faith rests on reason and that therefore the object of philosophy as well as of theology is God, while both must recognize that "the ultimate human knowledge of God is to know that we do not know God." God is always greater. His influence has increased rather than diminished over the centuries. He was canonized in 1323 by Pope John XXII, who showed considerable understanding of his teaching, but his system of thought remained one of several. He was highly praised at the Council of Trent, and in 1567 the Dominican Pope St Pius V declared him a Doctor of the Church, and he is generally known as the "Angelic Doctor." But it was not until three hundred years later that "Thomism" was made an officially established system, which led to the dominance of "neo-Thomism" in Catholic philosophy and theology until the Second Vatican Council. Both have since been freed from what had become a straitjacket, enabling his achievement to be seen more as a "model" than as a rule. But he himself was more than a towering intellect: he was an exemplary religious and was observed to reach ecstatic states in contemplative prayer. His work sprang not so much from a disputatious disposition as from his own experience of following Christ, nourished by deep spiritual reading and reflection. He is the patron saint of Catholic schools, colleges, and universities, of their teachers and students and, by extension, of education in general, so he has been adopted by booksellers as their patron also.

29

Bd Joseph Freinademetz (1852–1908)

Joseph came from a poor family in the Tyrol district of Austria and originally spoke the local dialect, Ladino. He was obviously a very bright child, needing more than the local school could offer, and a philanthropic local weaver found him a place in a German-speaking school in the cathedral city of Bressanone. He moved on from there to the Imperial Grammar School and then to the cathedral choir school, where he learned Latin, Italian, and some French. He then progressed to the diocesan seminary, being ordained in 1875. Finding life as a parish priest too easy, he wrote to Arnold Janssen (15 January), who came to see him, secured his bishop's permission to take him for his Divine Word Missionaries, educated him for the task at Steyl, and sent him as one of the first two from the Congregation to go to China.

Joseph and his companion, Johann Baptist von Anzer, were blessed on their way by Pope Leo XIII and reached Hong Kong on 21 April 1879. The Divine Word missionaries were assigned an area of South Shantung, and after re-learning Chinese twice to make himself understood locally, Joseph embarked on a wandering mission to the peasant population. Catholics in the area had been reduced by persecution to some one hundred and fifty in number. Through dressing like the peasants, trying to understand them, and obviously loving them (while largely ignoring the aristocracy) Joseph had a thousand catechumens by 1888, spread over some thirty villages.

Foreign missionaries in China relied on protection—often more military than diplomatic—from European powers, which enjoyed "concessions" of land wrung from the Chinese along the seaboard. They were either tolerated or persecuted, depending on the attitude of the local mandarin. Joseph and his companion saw that if Christianity was not to be forever the "religion of the Europeans" there had to an indigenous priesthood. In 1885 Anzer was summoned back to a general chapter in Steyl, leaving Joseph as administrator of the region and so less able to travel. Anzer returned as a bishop and appointed Joseph pro-vicar and administrator of several districts. By now several more

Divine Word missionaries had come to join them. They built a seminary, and the first two Chinese priests from it were ordained in 1896.

Widespread persecution broke out with the "Boxer Rebellion" of 1900, though South Shantung was not as badly affected as some areas. Joseph was forced to flee at one stage, but he returned and managed to restore order. He was appointed first provincial, responsible for the religious life of all the missionaries in his province. The Boxer Rebellion was put down, Western influence in China grew, and the number of converts increased. But Joseph was clear-sighted enough to see that growing westernization was a threat to the missions. He had come to identify with the Chinese and despised the European adventurers whom he saw as undermining the values of the country: "The greatest scourge for us, as well as for the Chinese, are the crowds of morally inferior Europeans without any religion who swarm all over China," he wrote.

Anzer had gone back to Europe once more, leaving Joseph as his vicar. The day after an audience with the pope, Anzer died suddenly in Rome. Joseph was not appointed as his successor, to general surprise and his relief. In 1907 the new bishop left him as provincial and administrator while he went on a visit to Europe, but Joseph's health had been ruined by his efforts during an outbreak of typhus, and he died on 28 January 1908.

A popular movement for his beatification soon began in his native Tyrol. A one-time pupil of his in the Chinese seminary, Cardinal Tien, wrote of him: "Of all the missionaries of China I know of no holier one than Fr Freinademetz. He was all things to all men." He was, above all, a friend to the local people who loved them and admired them and saw that the future of Christianity in China depended on Chinese virtues and Chinese leaders. Pope Paul VI beatified him with Arnold Janssen on World Mission Sunday, 19 October 1975. His example is more relevant than ever since Pope John Paul II has apologized to the Chinese people for mistakes made by Western missionaries in the past.

30

St Alban Roe (1538–1642)

Alban Roe (or Rouse, Rolfe, or Rosse) was born to Protestant parents and christened Bartholomew. He studied for a time at Cambridge University, but his religious education there failed to provide him with answers to questions asked of him by an uneducated Catholic named David, whom he visited in prison in order to show him "the errors and absurdities of his religion." He withdrew from this encounter confused, read books and contacted Catholic priests, and eventually became a Catholic and sought to be a priest.

Study for the priesthood then meant studying overseas, and Bartholomew was sent to the English College established at Douai in northern France. Like all students, he was required to take an oath never to disturb the peace of the college; he seems to have found three years the limit for tolerating this, as in 1611 he was sent back to England, accused of misleading the young and questioning the decisions of superiors. Early in 1613 he joined the Benedictine community at Dieulouard in Lorraine (which was to move to England as the founding community of Ampleforth Abbey in Yorkshire in 1802).

The missionary spirit of the English monks at Dieulouard was much to his liking. He was professed in 1614, taking the name Alban in religion, and was shortly sent on the English mission. His superiors considered him "thoroughly qualified by a long practice of all religious virtues for the apostolic functions." He spent less than three years as a missioner in England before being captured and thrown into Maiden Lane prison in London. He spent five years there and was then released and banished under pain of death should he return to England. This he did a few months later, and again he spent three years on the mission before being arrested once more. This time he was imprisoned in St Albans, the terrible prison in which he had earlier started his conversion process.

Mercifully, he was transferred to the Fleet prison in London, where conditions were easier and from where he was able to carry out the most fruitful period of his ministry. Over the next sixteen years he preached inside and outside the prisons, and many were converted through his words. He also became known as a great teacher on prayer and translated works on prayer for his own use and that of others. He was often seriously ill but had a cheerful disposition that saw him through: he was even accused of unbecoming activities such as drinking and gambling, but was more charitably credited with becoming increasingly cheerful as the prospect of gaining heaven drew nearer.

He was eventually transferred to the more severe Newgate prison and brought to trial for treason in 1642. He attempted to avoid being tried by a jury, so that others would not be involved in responsibility for his death, but it was a jury that brought in the inevitable guilty verdict. He thanked them "for the favour which he esteemed very great and which he had greatly desired." He and Thomas Reynolds were dragged together on a hurdle to Tyburn, and Alban encouraged his companion (who was eighty-two years old, in poor health, overweight, and understandably not inclined to be so cheerful) to the last. They gave one another absolution, and Alban also ministered to three criminals who were to die with them, joking the while. According to an eyewitness, his was a "death showing joy, contentment, constancy, fortitude and valour." They were allowed to hang until they were dead. Both Alban and Thomas were beatified in 1929, and Alban was canonized as one of the Forty Martyrs of England and Wales on 25 October 1970.

31

St John Bosco (1815–1888)

This pioneer of modern education methods was born in Piedmont (now in north-western Italy) in the year of the Treaty of Vienna, which tried to establish a new order after the Napoleonic wars, and lived through the age of revolutions, Marx, Italian reunification under Garibaldi, and changing and often acrimonious Church–State relations. His illiterate but devout and commonsensical mother prepared him for his First Communion and, when he later told her of his intention to become a priest, commented, "If you have the misfortune to get rich, I shan't set foot in your house again." Fortunately for them both, he never did, and she was able to become one of his main helpers in his later life.

He received an excellent formation in Turin, and after his ordination in 1841 he began, influenced by St Joseph Cafasso (23 June), to devote himself to looking after the needs of those who were flocking into the rapidly industrializing city looking for work. Thousands of young people were roaming the streets with no pastoral care, on a course that would land them in prison. John Bosco made them his special concern. The virulently anticlerical government of Turin closed all religious houses in 1855, but "Don" (as he became universally known) Bosco gathered his abandoned boys into what he called an "Oratory," thereby evading these laws. He developed a "total dedication" approach to his charges, expressed in all-day Sunday outings with a full agenda of Mass, work, and games. The Oratory acquired a house, his mother came to help, and it was soon housing six boys—a number that was eventually to grow to over eight hundred.

But lodging was not enough: the boys had to be under constant good (his) influence, which meant finding occupation for them. Don Bosco started opening workshops: one for tailors and shoemakers in 1853, soon followed by a book-bindery, a joinery, a printing works, and an iron foundry. He was regarded as either subversive of the parish and political order or mad, or both. Other clergy came to join him and so formed the nucleus of the new Congregation that had been taking shape in his mind. During a cholera epidemic in Turin in 1854, in which thousands died, he formed his boys into teams to carry the sick to hospital and the dead to mortuaries. Not one of them died, and he acquired a reputation as a miracle-worker: he had told all his boys that they would be spared as long as they trusted in God—and washed their hands with the vinegar he gave each of them after handling the sick and dead. An apparently prophetic dream about "great funerals at court" led him to write to the king warning him not to sign the law closing religious houses. The king took no notice, and four members of his family died within a few months, whereupon he virtually accused Don Bosco of causing their deaths by super-natural means and signed the law.

Don Bosco somehow found time to write: he produced histories of the Church and of Italy, several biographies and a series of educational textbooks, including a simple explanation of the metric system. One of these was in its 118th edition by the time of his death. His educational methods are now generally regarded as old-fashioned, but there is no questioning the basic impulse that lay behind them: total love and dedication. He divided human needs into four foundational spheres: home, school, Church, and society; in these, everyone experiences belonging, learning, meaning and social inter-action. All these needs must be met if people are to be happy and fulfilled.

In his day he earned such respect that he was able to form his Salesian Congregation despite the laws prohibiting religious Orders and even with the help of the anticlerical minister who had devised them. His devotional pre-ferences were very much of his time: he ardently believed that "we have to believe and think as the pope believes and thinks," and he was a great pro-moter of the new devotion to the Sacred Heart of Jesus: he was largely responsible for raising funds to build the church of the Sacré Coeur in Montmartre, Paris, a major symbol of that devotion.

He is the first known saint in history to submit to a press interview, at which journalists seem typically to have concentrated on his supposedly supernatural powers: his comment was that he did what he could and trusted in God and the Blessed Virgin to do the rest. He was also the first to take a stand at a major exhibition, when in 1884 the National Exhibition of Industry, Science and Art featured "Don Bosco: Salesian Paper Mill, Printing Works, Bindery and Bookshop." Those who expected well-intentioned clerical amateurism found themselves looking at a thoroughly professional presentation of the complete process of book manufacturing.

The Congregation was founded in 1854; by the time Don Bosco died thirty-four years later it had almost eight hundred members, with thirty-eight houses in Europe and twenty-six in America. Today it numbers some seventeen thousand, working in one hundred and thirteen different countries. A parallel Order for women grew just as rapidly, as did a lay organization of "Salesian Cooperators." Don Bosco is recognized as one of the great "social saints" of all time, even if he has been criticized (as Mother Teresa was a century later) for being an activist in limited areas rather than trying to reform society as a whole, as his contemporary Karl Marx was attempting to do. He said that political action belonged to "more educated" Orders, while "We go straight to the poor."

Virtually the entire population of Turin lined the streets for his funeral. He was canonized on Easter Sunday 1934 by Pope Pius XI, who as a young priest had visited him almost fifty years earlier. A national holiday was declared in Italy for the day following his canonization, a unique tribute.

I have promised God that until my last breath I shall have lived for my poor young people. I study for you, I work for you, I am also ready to give my life for you. Take note that whatever I am, I have been so entirely for you, day and night, morning and evening, at every moment.
   St John Bosco

Other Familiar English Names for January

1. Felix, John, Joseph, Justin, Mary, Peter, Vincent, William
2. Basil, Charlotte, Frances, Madeleine, Martha, Rose, William
3. Daniel, Jenny, Florence, Valerie
4. Angela, Ann, Elizabeth, Gregory, John, Thomas
5. Charles, Edward, Emily, Francis, John, Mary, Peter, Roger, Stephen
6. Andrew, Charles, Felix, John, Julian, Peter
7. Ambrose, Crispin, Joanna, Mary, Matthew, Teresa
8. Albert, Edward, George, Laurence
9. Agatha, Alix, Antony, Julia, Mary
10. Anne, John, Peter, Paul, William
11. Bernard, Peter, Thomas, William
12. Aelred, Antony, Benedict, Bernard, Francis, Martin, Mary, Peter
13. Dominic, Godfrey, Joseph, Lucy, Peter, Veronica
14. Felix, John, Peter
15. Francis, James, John, Paul, Peter
16. James, Joanna, Priscilla
17. John, Julian, Rosalind
18. Andrew, Beatrice, Carol, Christine, Felicity, Francis, James, Margaret, Mary, Monica, Paul, Victoria
19. Antony, Henry, Susannah
20. Benedict, Fabian, John, Sebastian
21. Edward, Nicholas
22. Antony, Dominic, Francis, George, Joseph, Laura, Mary, Matthew, Vincent, William
23. Paul
24. David, John, Mary, Paul, Paula, Vincent, William
25. Antony, Henry
26. Gabriel, Mary, Michael, Paula, Robert, Stephen
27. George, Henry, John, Julian, Rosalie
28. Agatha, James, John, Joseph, Julian, Laurence
29. Agnes, James, Julian, Paul, Thomas
30. John, Matthew, Peter, Sebastian, Stephen, Thomas
31. Agatha, Augustine, Dominic, Martin

FEBRUARY

With a few exceptions, saints are commemorated here on the date of their death. SS Cyril and Methodius are properly celebrated on the 14th (the date of Cyril's death), but the date is now synonymous worldwide with the saint whose name means lovers' tokens, so the latter is considered here and the two great missionaries two days later. On the 17th the Martyrs of China have replaced the Seven Founders of the Servite Order (about whose lives, as opposed to the Order, information is scarce). Fra Angelico has been moved forward one day to the 19th to allow the champion of the Celtic cause at the Synod of Whitby, St Colman of Lindisfarne, to be recorded on his anniversary. St Peter Damian actually died on 22 February; his feast-day is the 21st, and he is moved forward a day here to allow St Robert Southwell to feature on the actual date of his martyrdom. St Oswald of Worcester appears on the 29th, the actual date of his death in a leap year, but in other years he would take precedence on the 28th.

1

St Brigid of Kildare (about 452–524)

Ireland's most popular saint after St Patrick (see 17 Mar.) was born around the middle of the fifth century and probably consecrated herself to God as a virgin at an early age. She is said to have founded the monastery at Kildare, about forty miles south-west of Dublin. This later developed into a double monastery of the type not uncommon in Britain and on the Continent. They usually contained nuns of a high social standing, who needed monks to perform liturgical services and carry out heavy manual work. It was therefore normal for the abbess to be in charge of both. There is, however, no evidence that Kildare developed into such a foundation in Brigid's time. Abbots and abbesses tended to exercise considerable local power in Ireland, which had never been colon- ized by the Romans and therefore did not have the system of bishoprics, derived from Roman civil administration.

Beyond these basic facts, what was built up into several Lives of Brigid dissolves into myth and legend. The root of her name, *Bríg*, is that of the Druidic goddess who was responsible for knowledge and life, for fire, wisdom, and hearth, the mother of poets. She had two sisters of the same name, who were patrons of healing and of metalwork, and her feast was *Imbolg*, the first day of the pagan spring—our 1st of February. Her cult had been observed by female priestesses on the very spot where Brigid built her church at Kildare. So she inherited their qualities and began to "live" in different ages: she was led by Druids to assist in the birth of the Holy Child; she will come again to wash Christ's feet in a future incarnation; she is "Mary of the Gael" as the result of a vision in which a priest attending a synod at Kildare was told that the Virgin Mary would appear among them: Brigid arrived the following day and was hailed as "the Holy Mary whom I saw in my dream." When the Vikings invaded Ireland in the eighth century, she was also assimilated to their goddess Brigantia. Her mother, it was said, gave birth to her with one foot inside and one foot outside her house, making Brigid a symbolic bridge between pagan and Christian cultures.

Brigid's association with fire—symbolizing living in the presence of God—was carried on for many centuries after her death. A sacred fire was kept burning in the church at Kildare, each of the twenty nuns taking turn at a night's vigil to tend it. After Brigid's death, "When the twentieth night comes, the nineteenth nun puts the logs beside the fire and says, 'Brigid, guard your fire. This is your night.' And in this way the fire is left there, and in the morning the wood, as usual, has been burnt and the fire is still alight" (Gerald of Wales, writing in the twelfth century). Stories told of her emphasize her kindness to people and animals, her wisdom in dealing with personal—especially marital—problems, her generosity rather than austerity in interpreting rulings. "Brigid's cross," which she is supposed to have made out of rushes to protect a pagan chieftain who was sick, is still made today and hung in houses and outbuildings on the eve of her feast, to protect against fire and also to help sheep with lambing.

Her fame was spread across western Europe by Irish pilgrims and missionaries, and many churches were dedicated to her, as far afield as Piacenza in Italy. Pilgrimages are still held in her honour in Brittany. She has an ongoing significance for women in Ireland today, "Catholic, post-Catholic, Protestant, and pagan" (Mary T. Condren), and her feast-day has recently been proclaimed a national holiday for women.

You who turned back the streams of war
whose name invoked stilled monsters in the seas
whose cross remains a resplendent, golden sparking flame
come again from the dark bog
And forge us anew.

Anne Kelly, poem for the Millennium gathering of the Institute for

Feminism and Religion, held in Belfast on 1 February 2000, on the theme of "Brigid: Soulsmith for the New Millennium."

2

St Théophane Vénard (1829–1861)

St Thérèse of Lisieux (see 1 Oct.) called him another "little saint" and saw him as a kindred spirit. This, combined with his startling good looks, preserved in a number of photographs, and the remarkable letters he wrote from his mission and then from captivity in Vietnam, helped to make Théophane the best-known martyr of the nineteenth century. He stands here both for his own story and for that of the many martyrs who suffered in Vietnam, mainly between 1745 and 1862, who have been beatified in several groups and of whom one hundred and seventeen were canonized by Pope John Paul II in 1988.

Théophane was the second of six children born to a village schoolmaster and his wife in west-central France. He studied at the major seminary in Poitiers and, once he had been ordained sub-deacon, entered the seminary of the Paris Society for Foreign Missions, where he was ordained priest in 1852. He was to have been sent to China but was diverted and reached the western Tonkin area of Vietnam in July 1854, to find a fresh wave of persecution holding sway after new decrees against Christianity issued by the emperor Tu Duc some years earlier. Missionaries appealed to France for protection; France used warships rather than negotiation, and so the missionaries were seen as colonial lackeys in a conflict that dragged on for several years, during which sixteen Vietnamese and six European Christians, clergy and lay, met their deaths.

Théophane was prevented for some time by sickness from carrying out an effective mission, but he learned the native language and was eventually cured and appointed district head of missions in the Hoang-Nguyen district, where there were some twelve hundred Christians. In June 1858 an attack, of which they had been warned in advance, forced the missionaries underground—often literally, as they had to take refuge in pits infested with spiders, toads, and rats. "This is how I have lived for about three months. . . . Three missionaries, one of whom is a bishop, lying side by side, day and night, in a space of about one and a half yards square, our only light and means of breathing being three holes, the size of a little finger, made in the mud wall," he wrote to a priest friend. Under these conditions, he translated the New Testament into Vietnamese.

He was betrayed to the authorities, arrested, and taken to Hanoi in a bamboo cage, in which he was kept for two months, during which he managed to write eleven letters to his family. Everyone seems to have treated him kindly, expressing regret (sincere or not) at what the laws were forcing them to do to him. He remained resolutely cheerful throughout, as his letters show, and aroused the admiration of the crowds who came to stare at him in his cage. He expressed his undying love for the local people in one of his last letters: "I have loved and still love this Annamite people with a burning love. If God had given me long life, I believe I would have devoted myself completely, body and soul, to building up the Church of Tonkin." He was beheaded on 2 February 1861.

His Life and letters were published in 1864, and some years later a missionary gave a copy to Thérèse of Lisieux. She was so inspired that she tried to have herself sent to the Carmelite convent in Hanoi. She copied out some of the letters and composed a poem "To the Venerable Théophane Vénard" for the thirty-sixth anniversary of his death, in 1897, and in her last illness she clung to a relic and a picture of him.

Théophane's severed head has remained in Tonkin, but his body was brought back to Paris. He was beatified with nineteen other martyrs from Tonkin in 1909 and canonized as one of one hundred and seventeen Martyrs of Vietnam in 1988.

> *Ah, may the Lord see me, too, as a flower—*
> *A flower of spring he'll gather soon, then you*
> *May come down here to me, at my last hour—*
> *O Blessed Martyr, I beseech you to!*
> *And, from your love, your purity that glows,*
> *May I, on earth, be set alight by you!*
> *Then I can fly up Heavenwards, with those*
> *Who'll make up your eternal retinue!*
> St Thérèse of Lisieux, *To the Venerable Théophane Vénard*, last stanza, translated by Alan Bancroft

3

St Blaise (died about 316)

Virtually nothing can be known with certainty about the life of St Blaise, but as long as people continue to suffer from sore throats, devotion to him is likely to live on. The new Roman Martyrology calls him "bishop and martyr, who for the name of Christian suffered at Sebastea in Armenia under the emperor Licinius," and anything more than this has to be treated as legend. He is said to have been put to death by having his flesh torn by metal wool combs, which has made him the patron saint of woolcombers.

Legendary Lives written in Greek and Latin make him the son of wealthy parents who became a bishop at an early age. In order to escape persecution he took refuge in a cave, where his only companions were wild animals, which he cured of various ailments so that they flocked to receive his blessing. Hunters following the animals were amazed at the scene but nevertheless took Blaise away to be interrogated by the governor of Cappadocia. On the way they met a woman whose pig had been carried off by a wolf; she appealed to Blaise for help and he commanded the wolf to give up the pig, which it did, whole and unharmed. Blaise was imprisoned, and this same woman brought tapers to light his cell. Before his death, Blaise promised that anyone who lit a taper in his memory would be free of infection.

His association with sore throats perhaps originates in the fact that (at least in Europe) his feast-day comes at the time of year when people are most likely to be suffering from these. It is also said that while he was in prison he cured a boy who had a fish bone stuck in his throat. This and the story of the pig produced the ceremony in which two crossed candles or tapers are held under people's throats, while the priest says the words, "Through the intercession of St Blaise may God deliver you from ills of the throat and other ills." This practice arose in the sixteenth century, when Blaise's popularity was at its peak as one of the "Fourteen Holy Helpers." Their cult, despite being discouraged by the Council of Trent, lasted with a collective feast-day on 8 August until it was abolished in 1969.

Parson Woodforde describes processions in his memory in his *Diary of a Country Parson,* and in the late nineteenth century bonfires were still lit on the night of his feast, at least in England and Germany, where the day was sometimes called "Little Candlemas Day" on account of these fires. His patronage of woolcombers produced a festival held every five years in Bradford, main town of the Yorkshire wool industry, but as the industry declined, so the festival disappeared from memory. He was extremely popular in France, where many places claim to possess relics of him—remarkably, considering how far away Armenia is.

4

St Gilbert of Sempringham (about 1083–1189)

The dates given for his life may not be entirely accurate, but it does seem certain that Gilbert, born in Lincolnshire, lived to extreme old age by any standards. This was despite the fact that he was born with a physical disability—which at least prevented him from following the knightly career that otherwise would have been his lot. Instead, he pursued clerical studies in

France, returned to England in minor orders, and opened a school for girls and boys, at a time when co-educational schools were most unusual.

He could have enjoyed a comfortable "plural" living on the revenues from two parishes belonging to his father's estates but chose to live in poverty, while his pastoral care and teaching made his parish a model of observance and sobriety. In 1122 he was appointed household clerk to the bishop of Lincoln. He was ordained priest and offered a rich archdeaconship, but he refused this and returned as priest to one of his parishes, giving all the revenue from the other to the poor. When his father died he found himself squire as well as parish priest.

Among his parishioners was a group of seven young women who wanted to live a communal religious life. They asked for his guidance, and he had a house built for them next to the church, where they lived in strict enclosure under an adaptation of the Rule of St Benedict made by him. The community grew, and lay sisters and then brothers were added, to help work its land. Gilbert went to Cîteaux, seeking to have the house placed under Cistercian rule, but the Cistercians had taken on other new commitments and refused. Pope Eugenius III, who was also at the general chapter at Cîteaux, persuaded Gilbert to retain responsibility. Bernard of Clairvaux (see 20 Aug.) helped him to draw up instruments of government, and the pope appointed him first master of the Order of Sempringham, generally known as the Gilbertines. It was the only medieval religious Order that originated in England.

Monasteries were double, for women and men, the men divided into canons regular for the liturgy and lay brothers for manual work. Discipline was strict and the way of life austere. The liturgy was chanted in monotone rather than the more elaborate plainchant, and Gilbert had a "plate of the Lord Jesus" on the table, on which the tastiest morsels were placed and then given to the poor. By the time of Gilbert's death there were thirteen houses, of which nine were double monasteries and four for canons only.

The Order came into conflict with King Henry II (who reigned from 1154 to 1189) over Thomas Becket (see 29 Dec.). At a council held in Nottingham in 1164, Thomas had been condemned for opposing the king on matters of church prerogatives. He was to be arrested but disguised himself as a Gilbertine lay brother and took refuge in the Order's houses in Lincolnshire, from where he escaped to France, where he spent six years before returning to Canterbury and his death at the hands of the king's men. Henry summoned Gilbert to explain his part in the affair but pardoned him and granted the Order immunity. When he was nearly ninety, two of the brothers made slanderous accusations against him, which were supported by prominent figures in both Church and State, but the pope decided for Gilbert, who forgave the rebels and took them back. The Order doubled in size over nearly three hundred and fifty years, but then all its houses were dissolved by Henry VIII, and it was never revived.

Gilbert had provided a remarkable witness to the value of poverty and austerity, following the example of the recent Cistercian reform. He had also shown great personal enterprise, tenacity, magnanimity—and longevity. A widespread cult developed soon after his death, and he was canonized only thirteen years later, by Pope Innocent III.

5

St Agatha (dates unknown)

St Agatha remains one of the best-loved saints in Christian devotional life, despite the fact that nothing is known of her life. There is, however, good evidence of an early cult, which suggests that she cannot be dismissed as a mere fiction. She stands for the long tradition in Christian devotion of exalting female virginity. This can be read in a number of ways, and traditional interpretations are now widely challenged by Christian feminist approaches. One fact that emerges is that virginity is chosen, not imposed, so that it represents self-empowering against the dominant culture. (A less positive aspect of the cult of virgin martyrs is a dwelling on sexual mutilation that is never encountered in accounts of male martyrs.)

Agatha is presented as the daughter of wealthy parents who dedicated her virginity to Christ. This, rather than her life, is, then, presented as her most precious possession. She is said to have been born in either Catania or Palermo in Sicily and to have died at Catania, which has an older and stronger claim to be her birthplace. The story is that a consul named Quintianus tried to take her virginity by force. He is described in *The Golden Legend* as "base-born," thus adding an element of class-desecration to his attempted crime. He used the imperial edict against Christians to have her placed in a brothel run by the aptly named Aphrodisia, aided by her six (or nine) daughters (or assistants). When all manner of tricks and assaults fail to make her succumb, she is handed over to be tortured. The tortures culminate with her breasts being cut off and placed on a platter. The same shocking image is also presented in accounts of the martyrdom of other women, which may make it a stock image in what has been described as "religious pornography" (Margaret R. Miles). An illustrated manuscript version of her passion, produced in Burgundy around the end of the tenth century, helped to perpetuate the image.

Her tortures gave her an elaborate and interlocking assignment of patronages in the Middle Ages. She was also said to have been rolled over live coals, so she is invoked against fire, but this may be an extension of her protection against volcanic eruptions. This comes from her association with Sicily and the claim in her legend that after her death flows of molten lava from

Mount Etna could be miraculously diverted when her silk scarf was held up on a staff in their path (a miracle claimed as relatively recently as the 1840s). This was also extended to claiming her protection against earthquakes. As bells were used to warn against volcanic eruptions and fire, she has long been the patron saint of bell-founders. Appropriately, she is also invoked against diseases of the breast. Her breasts on the platter were often mistaken for loaves, which led to the custom of blessing loaves brought to the altar on a dish on her feast-day.

Pope St Damasus I composed a hymn to her in the late fourth century, and two churches were dedicated to her in Rome in the sixth. Pope St Gregory the Great had rich shrines made for her relics in Rome, then moved them to the island of Capri. Other relics were venerated in Catania but moved to Constantinople in 1840, leaving her veil, which is still carried in procession in Catania on her feast-day. Her story remains compelling, whatever attitude is taken to its origin, purpose, dissemination, and details.

6

St Paul Miki and Companions (died 1597)

Just as Théophane Vénard in this work represents all the martyrs of Vietnam, so the Japanese Jesuit Paul Miki and those killed with him here represent many thousand missionaries and Japanese Christians cruelly put to death for their faith between 1597 and 1640. Little is known about them individually, and so their story has to be a brief summary of Christianity in Japan.

Christian missions began effectively with St Francis Xavier (see 3 Dec.) in 1549. He attempted to convert the emperor, following Jesuit practice, but found that the emperor ruled in name only, with most of the country in the hands of local lords. Some of these were converted, with their people following in tens of thousands. Then power shifted to a national military commander, known as the *shogun*. In the early 1580s the emperor appointed Hideyoshi as his regent, and he turned against the Christians, having previously tolerated them. In 1580 Spanish missionaries joined the Portuguese, not always on a cooperative footing, and in 1593 Franciscans were sent to establish a mission, which produced some hostility with the Jesuits.

These divisions were exploited by Hideyoshi, who was then given a more definite pretext for action when the captain of a Spanish ship driven on to an unauthorized part of the coast of Japan by a storm is supposed to have told him that the Spanish and Portuguese were both using missionaries to prepare the country for conquest. He seized six Franciscans, three Japanese Jesuits, sixteen other Japanese (and one Korean) Christians, had part of their left ears cut off, and marched them through various towns with blood streaming down their faces to warn others of the consequences of being Christian. They were finally led to a hill outside Nagasaki, where they were tied to crosses with chains and cords and then run through with lances—indicating that their executioners too had become familiar with the New Testament. Their clothes were collected as relics, and miracles were attributed to their intercession. They were canonized as a group by Pope Pius IX in 1862. Paul Miki was the most prominent among the Japanese Jesuits (who were not yet ordained priests), coming from a noble family and known as a distinguished preacher.

This first martyrdom in fact led to an increase in missionary activity and conversions, with Spanish Dominicans and Augustinians coming from the Philippines. Hideyoshi died in 1598, and a new national leader, Ieyasu, emerged victorious from wars among local lords and established the "Tokugawa shogunate," a military regime that was to last until the Meiji restoration of 1865. Like Hideyoshi, after a period of toleration of Christianity, he turned to persecution, which reached its peak with a savage decree issued in 1614, banishing all foreign missionaries (by now Protestant as well as Catholic) and threatening all Japanese who had any dealings with Christians with death by burning. In 1617 one hundred missionaries and native converts were executed. The usual method was by burning at the stake. Five others suffered in this way in 1619, a further twenty-two in 1622, thirty Japanese were beheaded the following year, and others in 1627, bringing the number in this period to 205, who were all beatified in 1867.

From 1623 all Japanese had to make a public show once a year of rejecting Christianity. This took the form of trampling on *fumie*, plaques imprinted with the image of the Virgin and Child. Many refused, even though they were told that all they had to do was brush the plaque lightly with their feet. The authorities, however, began to see that making martyrs of the missionaries was not achieving their ends. They had to be made to apostasize. To this end, appalling means of torture were devised, including *ana-tsurushi*, "the pit," in which victims were tightly bound with ropes and hung from a gallows head down over a pit. Death through suffocation was agonizing and could take up to three days. It was designed specifically to make priests apostasize, and some did. Laurence Ruiz and fifteen companions did not; they died in this way between 1633 and 1637 and were canonized as a group.

Persecution reached its peak after the Shimbara Revolt of 1637–38, which developed from a protest against excessive taxation into a manifestation of Christian faith, with insurgents carrying banners of the Blessed Sacrament and shouting the names of Jesus and Mary. It resulted in some twenty-five thousand Christians being put to death and the country being closed to all foreign contact. Christianity went into hiding for two centuries, but when the country was reopened in 1865, thousands emerged speaking a smattering of Latin and Portuguese and asking for statues of Jesus and Mary. Christianity is now tolerated and intellectually understood, but it remains a Western construct for Japanese minds and has still not found a way to become culturally accepted in Japanese society. This is regarded as the reason why there are still under half a million Catholics in the country.

7

Bd Mary of Providence (Eugénie Smet; 1825–1871)

Many religious Orders for women were founded in the nineteenth century, largely in response to changing social conditions, which brought new classes of needs, and many of their founders have been beatified. Bd Mary of Providence, born Eugénie Smet in Lille in northern France, is one of the most determined and remarkable of them.

She was the third of six children born to a relatively prosperous couple. As a child she became almost obsessed with the thought of the suffering of souls in purgatory, failing, not unnaturally, to see that the poor of newly industrialized Lille were suffering hardly less. Eugénie was insulated from them as a pupil at a boarding school. Her parents suffered a reversal of fortune and were forced to sell their house in Lille and move to what they had built as a small country house a few miles outside. There, during the school holidays, Eugénie discovered human suffering in this life and set out to remedy it by the sort of direct action that was to be characteristic of her for the rest of her life. This ranged from taking her father's windfall apples (some being encouraged to fall) to the poor to collecting so much money for missions to China that she received a personal letter of thanks from a bishop in Rome.

She had had what she called a "conversion" as a result of a retreat preached at her school by a Jesuit, and in 1850 she took a vow of perpetual virginity and set about founding an Order dedicated to relieving the suffering of souls in purgatory. She was encouraged in this by the bishop of Lille and also indirectly by the Curé d'Ars (St John Vianney; see 4 Aug.), but she typically demanded five signs from Divine Providence to seal her determination. All were granted within five years. She then heard that a priest in Paris had started a small community dedicated to the souls in purgatory, so she took a train there.

The beginnings were chaotic: she disagreed with the priest on methods and aims and could find nowhere tolerable to live, let alone anywhere suitable for a community. She went back to her family to think things over and returned to Paris with her younger sister, Juliette. The archbishop of Paris had told her that if faith could move mountains it could surely build houses. She found one for rent, at a price she could not possibly afford: she persuaded the owner's lawyer to let her have it on the promise of money one day. Other young women came to join her, the parish priest of Saint-Merry took charge of forming them into a Congregation, and a well-wisher sent money for a down payment against the rent. All the members took names in religion, with Eugénie becoming Mary of Providence – appropriately, given her unbounded faith in Providence.

It was, though, one thing to be called the Helpers of the Holy Souls and to be dedicated to the souls in purgatory, but what did this actually involve day to day? The answer came in the form of a woman who knocked on the door and asked if they would care for a sick woman of the locality who refused to see a priest or a nun. Mary heard an inner voice saying, "This is how you will love me." From then on, her Helpers went out to meet every sort of need. With Paris growing rapidly and the grandiose rebuilding schemes of Baron Haussmann reducing former communities to rubble, they found alcoholism, prostitution, destitution, and overcrowding on a scale they could not have imagined. They plunged into this situation, caring for the suffering and the sick, preaching the gospel as they did so. They had found that love for the souls in purgatory was to be expressed in works of love carried out for those suffering in this world.

The Institute was blessed by the pope and in 1859 adopted a Constitution based on that of the Society of Jesus. Numbers grew rapidly; a wealthy supporter bought the house for the community, and a postulant from a well-to-do family provided actual furniture. A second house was opened in Nantes in 1863. Mary's health was declining by this time, but as superior she was responsible—initially against her judgment but in response to a direct plea—for sending six Helpers to China. These recruited Chinese Helpers from the start, and a hundred of a later generation of these were to carry out their mission faithfully during thirty years of the Communist period when foreign missionaries were expelled. By 1869 Mary was desperately ill with cancer. In 1870 the Franco-Prussian war broke out, and her last months were spent in besieged Paris, forced to take refuge in the cellars and in intolerable pain. She died, with her faith in Providence undimmed, on 7 February 1871. The Helpers now work with the neediest on four continents, in twenty-five communities.

We believe that there are no boundaries to love and that we are in solidarity with all those who follow Jesus Christ in his Paschal Mystery, whether they are on earth or have already passed through death. We support them through our prayer, action, and communion with them in their trials, knowing that God's transforming love is a gratuitous gift.
  from the Constitutions of the Helpers of the Holy Souls

8

St Josephine Bakhita (1869–1947)

The extraordinary early life of this Sudanese girl, kidnapped into slavery, rescued, and finally a Canossian Sister in Italy for fifty years, was dictated by her to another Sister in 1910. She did not know her original name but did recall that she came from a large and loving family. Internal evidence places her birth in the Darfur region of western Sudan, as a member of the Daju tribe. When she was seven or eight, she was seized at knife- and gun-point by a pair of the slave-traders who roamed the area. Her eldest sister had been kidnapped some two years earlier. She was asked her name but was too frightened to remember it, so one of her captors ironically dubbed her Bakhita, meaning "lucky one."

She and another girl of about the same age were taken to a town with a slave market. They managed to escape when their door was left unlocked one evening but were recognized as escapees and tricked back into captivity. After a long forced march eastward they reached the town of El Obeid (Al-Ubayyid, the capital of Kurdufan), where they were sold to an Arab chief and assigned to his daughters as maids. The daughters liked them, but Bakhita somehow offended the son, who beat her unconscious, from which she took a month to recover. She was then sold to a general in the Turkish Army (most of Sudan being then under Turkish–Egyptian military control), where she was harshly treated by his mother and his wife, including being tattooed with some one hundred and forty cuts made on her chest, belly, and arms, into which salt was then rubbed to keep the wounds open. This was a traditional mark of ownership, and again it took her a month to recover.

Some three years later, in mid-1882, the general and his family decided to return to Turkey. In Khartoum he let it be known that he had some slaves for sale, and Bakhita was purchased by the Italian consul, Signor Calisto Legnani. She was freed, employed to help his maid, and treated far more kindly. Late in 1884 the consul was summoned back to Italy, in fact escaping from Khartoum shortly before it was taken by the Islamic revolutionary leader known as the Mahdi (responsible for General Gordon's death there the following year). Bakhita begged to be taken with the family. They sailed from the Red Sea coast to Genoa, where Bakhita was given to the owner of the hotel in which they stayed, who was a friend of the consul's. His name was Augusto Michieli. There are conflicting accounts of dates and journeys between Italy and Africa, but it is known that Bakhita became nanny to the Michielis' daughter, Alice, born in February 1886. Later that year she accompanied the family to Suakin, on the Red Sea coast of Sudan (developing rapidly after the opening of the Suez Canal), where Michieli bought a hotel, returning to Italy a year later. Then, when the parents went back to Suakin in 1889, they left Bakhita and Alice in Italy.

It was at this time that she was introduced to the Christian faith, through the agency of a remarkable man named Illuminato Cecchini, who, besides being a writer and a populist local politician, was the Michieli family's business administrator. He gave her a crucifix and began to tell her about Jesus. It was he who persuaded Signora Michieli to leave Bakhita and Alice in the care of the Canossian Sisters at their Institute of Catechumens in Venice. Signora Michieli returned a year later to settle some business affairs, proposing to take Bakhita back with her to work in the hotel. Bakhita flatly refused on the grounds that it would compromise her new faith, but it took Cecchini and an appeal to the cardinal patriarch and through him to high government officials, who told Signora Michieli that slavery did not obtain in Italy, to make her give in. Bakhita received Baptism, First Communion, and Confirmation at the Institute on 9 January 1890. Three years later she joined the novitiate, and she was professed in 1896, after being examined by the new cardinal patriarch, the future Pope (and Saint) Pius X, who was also a long-standing friend of Cecchini. So the slave girl from Sudan began a life as a religious in Italy, which was to last fifty years. Echoing the sense of inferiority drummed into her by life and society, she exclaimed at her luck, as she saw it, that this should happen to her: *Mi, povera negra, povera negra!*—"Me, a poor black girl, a poor black girl!"

The remainder of her life was relatively uneventful. She was transferred to the Canossian house at Schio, north of Padua, where the Canossian Sisters ran a school. There she held various offices, all of which she carried out with care, including helping nurses when the convent was requisitioned as a military hospital in the Great War. An African skin was a rare possession in northern Italy at the time, and she undoubtedly became something of a pet, known as Mother *Moretta*, "Little Brown Mother," as well as being regarded as a saint for her transparent goodness. In 1929 she again dictated episodes of her life to a Sister, and this brought her wide renown when episodes began to appear in the Canossian Yearbook as "A marvellous life." In the 1930s she longed to be a missionary, but her health would not allow this, though she did spend several years spreading the missionary ideal to other Canossian convents and two years at the Order's missionary novitiate in Milan. She spent the years of the Second World War at Schio (where the nuns were convinced that her saintly presence protected them from bombing) and died of pneumonia on 8 February 1947.

She was beatified by Pope John Paul II on 17 May 1992, at the same ceremony that brought two hundred and fifty thousand Opus Dei supporters to Rome for the beatification of their founder, Mgr Josemaría Escrivá de Balaguer. The Sisters thought she might be overshadowed by this, but came to the

65

conclusion that it had helped to spread her message and simple way of holiness. Pope John Paul II handed a casket of her relics to the archbishop at a huge open-air Mass in Khartoum in 1993. She has become a symbol of resistance and hope for Christians in Sudan, persecuted by the Islamic fundamentalist regime, and for women and oppressed people in general on a continent where children as young as she was are still being sold into slavery. She was canonized on 1 October 2000.

❖

Bakhita learned from tragic events in her life to have complete trust in the One who is present everywhere. Using religion as a pretext for injustice and violence is a terrible abuse and must be condemned by all those who have genuine belief in God.
Pope John Paul II at the open-air Mass in Khartoum, 10 February 1993

9

St Miguel Febres Cordero (Francisco Febres Cordero Muñoz; 1854–1910)

The first canonized saint from Ecuador was born into a family prominent in politics and education in Cuenca on 7 November 1854. Known as Panchito in the family, he was born with crippled legs, which made his father regard him as always likely to be a burden on the family, though his mother always believed he would grow strong. At the age of nine he went to the new school opened in Cuenca by the Institute of the Brothers of the Christian Schools ("Christian Brothers" in the USA, "De La Salle Brothers" elsewhere). He distinguised himself at school and soon decided that his future lay with the Brothers. There was fierce family opposition: the Brothers were French, poor, and had none of the cachet of the older Orders. Francisco persevered and, when it was obvious that his health was suffering from the controversy, his father gave his permission. Francisco was only fourteen—this being before the minimum age for admission to religious Orders was set at sixteen—and he took the name Miguel in religion.

After only a year of novitiate, he was sent to teach in the capital, Quito. There he embarked on an outstanding career that was to last with mounting distinction for thirty-eight years. He prepared boys for First Communion (then made in the early teens), being noted for the individual attention he gave to each pupil. His academic speciality, though, was the Spanish language, and he was not yet twenty when he published a Spanish grammar so good that within a year it was prescribed for all schools in Ecuador. The fortune of the Brothers' school waxed and waned with the toleration or anticlericalism of successive governments, but Brother Miguel's reputation grew as he published more excellent textbooks. In 1887 he was chosen to represent the Ecuadorian branch of the Institute at the beatification of its founder, Jean Baptiste de la Salle, finding himself, "an unknown brother from Ecuador," in Rome: "Being there, I felt I had been carried up into the third heaven!"

His reputation soon spread beyond Ecuador. He was elected to the Academy of Ecuador in 1892, and this brought automatic corresponding membership of the Royal Academy of Spain. In 1900 he was awarded the diploma of the French Academy. In 1895 another revolutionary government seized power in Ecuador and cut off the grant that enabled the Brothers to run their school. They opened a free school, supported by the archdiocese, and Miguel, refusing prestigious posts offered by the government, went back to elementary teaching there. He also distinguished himself as master of novices from 1896 to 1905 and as head of the school, which had grown to over a thousand pupils, from 1902.

The Order then summoned him to Europe, to the motherhouse in Belgium. He travelled via Panama and New York, from where he sailed to Le Havre and went on to Paris, where he caught a chill that nearly killed him and where the Order wasted his talents by making him translate French textbooks into Spanish. He moved to Belgium in July 1907, but by autumn the Belgian climate was causing him recurring bouts of fever, and the following summer he was sent to Premià del Mar, on the coast north of Barcelona, where the Order had opened a junior novitiate. He taught there and wrote and translated more textbooks.

The following summer he was caught up in the "tragic week" of Barcelona, beginning with the declaration of a general strike on 26 July 1909. The strike was against right-wing policies in which the Church was deeply implicated, and the novices were warned to be ready to flee. Churches were set on fire, as was the nearby railway station, and on 30 July the Brothers were evacuated by sea, in boats provided by the government. They returned about a week later to find a statue of the Virgin that Miguel had placed in the window for protection still there and nothing disturbed. The incident, however, led to the final collapse of Miguel's health, and after an autumn and winter of recurrent pneumonia he died on 9 February 1910.

His personal devotional life, meticulously recorded in a spiritual diary and detailing the love of God that inspired all he did and wrote, underpinned his international reputation as a writer and teacher. He was very much of his time in having a deep devotion to the Sacred Heart, to which the President had dedicated Ecuador in 1873. In Ecuador it was soon felt that he should be the country's first official saint. His remains survived the sacking of the chapel at Premià by left-wing militia in 1936, and the following year the Ecuadorian consul in Barcelona was given permission to have them transported back to his native country. They were carried in triumphant procession from the port of Guayaquil to Quito, with massive crowds along the route and many cures being reported. In 1950 great celebrations marked the centenary of his birth, and a massive memorial was erected to him in Quito in 1955. He was beatified by Pope Paul VI on 30 October 1977 (with another De la Salle Brother, Mutien-Marie Wiaux) and canonized by Pope John Paul II on World Mission Sunday, 21 October 1984. Ecuador had given the Church a saint totally devoted to the love of God, and the world a teacher totally devoted to his pupils.

❖

I do not know anyone writing in Spanish, whether in Spain or in South America, who can rival him in clarity, methodology, precision, ease of expression, and that special attentiveness that understands the workings of the young mind.

Dr Honorato Vásquez, Ecuadorian ambassador to Spain, writing of Miguel after his death

10

St Scholastica (died 547)

St Benedict's twin sister has become a universally loved and revered figure, yet it has to be said that there is no information about her that can be called historical in the modern sense. The same might be said of her brother, but she left no Rule to exert such influence on Western civilization. Information on both their lives depends on the *Dialogues* of St Gregory the Great, written in Rome some forty years after Benedict's death and reputedly relying on information supplied by abbots who had known him. But the name Benedict means simply "the blessed man" and Scholastica "the learned woman," so the information may be manufactured to fit the depiction of a type. Little matter: the type or personality assigned to Scholastica emerges delightfully from one famous episode.

She is said to have dedicated herself to God from an early age and to have settled near Monte Cassino when Benedict moved there, supervising a community of women under Benedict's direction. She would visit her brother once a year, the two meeting in a house outside his monastery, since as a woman she was not allowed in. These visits were devoted to conversations on spiritual matters and praise of God.

After many years of such meetings, Scholastica had a premonition that the current one was going to be her last. She begged her brother to stay the night so that they might continue their conversation. He replied that his Rule made this absolutely impossible and that he had to return to the monastery. Scholastica bowed her head in prayer, whereupon such a violent thunderstorm broke out that Benedict could not leave the house. He accused her of provoking this, to which she replied: "I asked a favour of you, and you refused it. I asked it of God, and he has granted it." So they spent the night discoursing on the joys of heaven, and three days later Benedict, sitting in his cell, saw her soul rising to heaven in the form of a dove. He sent some monks to collect her body, which was placed in a tomb he had had prepared. When he died four years later, he was buried with her.

The tomb still survives at Monte Cassino, despite the destruction of the monastery by Allied bombardment in 1944, but it is not certain that it contains relics of either brother or sister: as with so many early saints, there are places in France that lay claim to them. Scholastica is the patron saint of Benedictine nuns (who to this day can provide convincing demonstrations of bowing one's head and getting one's way).

11

St Caedmon (died 680)

As with St Scholastica, there is only one source for what we know about St Caedmon, but this is the Venerable Bede's *Ecclesiastical History*, which can be credited with a good deal of factual accuracy. The story he tells is that Caedmon looked after livestock on lands belonging to the double monastery of Whitby. One night, when he was already an old man, he had followed his usual practice of leaving the table when the singing started on feast-days. He fell asleep with his animals in the stables and in a dream saw a man standing beside him, who called him by his name and asked him to sing a song. Caedmon protested that it was because he could not sing that he was there, but the man insisted and told him to make up a song about the creation, whereupon Caedmon sang verses in praise of God the creator that he had never heard before.

He told "his superior the reeve" about this dream, and the reeve took him to the abbess, Hilda, who quoted a verse from scripture to him and asked him to put it into verse. He returned the next morning with "excellent verses," so Hilda persuaded him to enter the monastery, learn the scriptures, and use his gift in the service of the Church. This he did. His poems would have been learned by heart and would have been a powerful aid to preaching. Bede quotes some lines (see below) from the Creation song referred to in the story of the dream. Caedmon is said to have foreseen the hour of his death and to have asked for the Eucharist, even though he appeared to be in good health. He then died peacefully, having waited until the monks began chanting the night office.

Bede wrote in Latin, but the verses he quotes appear in various early dialect translations of him and in a separate eighth-century Northumbrian manuscript. Bede lists the books of the Bible on which Caedmon composed poems, and this was apparently supported by a manuscript dating from around 1000, containing poems on Genesis, Exodus, Daniel, and Christ and Satan and attributing them to Caedmon (presumably on the authority of Bede). They have, however, since been shown to date from after his death and to be by different hands. The attribution led to Caedmon being hailed as "the father of English sacred poetry." Bede writes, "These verses of his have stirred the hearts of many folk to despise the world and aspire to heavenly things. Others after him tried to compose religious poems in English, but none could compare with him; for he did not acquire the art of poetry from men or through any human teacher but received it as a free gift from God." All that can confidently be claimed now is that there is enough evidence to indicate that Caedmon did compose verses based on scripture in the tradition of the time, and that some magnificent religious poetry was produced in the age of Bede, as evidenced by the surviving *Dream of the Rood*.

Now we must praise the ruler of heaven,
The might of the Lord and his purpose of mind,
The work of the glorious father.
For he, God eternal, established each wonder,
He, holy creator, first fashioned the heavens
As a roof for the children of earth,
And then our guardian, the everlasting God,
Adorned this middle earth for men.
Praise the almighty king of heaven!
    Caedmon, in Bede, *Ecclesiastical History of the English People*, book 4, chapter 24

12

St Benedict of Aniane (751–821)

This great reformer rescued Western monasticism from the many abuses and the variety of observances that had crept into it over the two centuries since the death of St Benedict himself (see 11 July). His reforms endured for centuries and then provided an example and basis for later reforms, such as those of Cluny (see St Odilo; 1 Jan.). He also steered a skilful diplomatic course in his relations with the "Holy Roman" Empire at a time when ecclesiastical affairs were very much the business of emperors.

He came from a noble family and as a young man served at the imperial court during the reigns of Pepin and his son Charlemagne. He even fought in the imperial army, distinguishing himself at the siege of Pavia in 774, after which he underwent a religious conversion and tried to withdraw from the world. He became a monk near Dijon and applied a very strict rule of life to himself, going back beyond the Rule of Benedict to that of St Basil (see 2 Jan.). He refused to become abbot, knowing that not all monks would be able to follow this way of life, and instead retired to a family property on the banks of the river Aniane in Languedoc, where he lived for some years as a hermit. Others came to live under his direction, and they gradually evolved a simple and strict way of life.

The community outgrew its original premises and moved to where a monastery could be built. His influence grew too, and he was appointed overseer of all monasteries in southern France. Charlemagne inherited the imperial throne in 800 and approved Benedict's reforms. When he died in 814, his successor, Louis the Pious, wanted Benedict near the capital, at Aachen, on the Rhine near the eastern frontier of the empire. He built Benedict a monastery at Kornelimünster, just five miles from Aachen, which in 817 was consecrated as an imperial foundation, with a palace school attached. From there, Benedict directed the course of monastic reform throughout the empire, while also becoming one of Louis' most trusted advisers on secular affairs.

His reforms imposed the Benedictine observance on all monasteries. By making observance the same for all, he intended to remove motives for jealousy and to encourage charity. More emphasis was placed on scholarship, spiritual reading, study of the scriptures, and liturgical observance. Lay people were banished from monastic enclosures. Measures of food and drink for monks were regulated. The overall aim was to enable monks to pass "from faith to sight"—for understanding to blossom into contemplation of God. Inevitably, compliance was patchy, particularly as it depended on the unity of the empire, which began to crumble about the time of Benedict's death. Nevertheless, these reforms marked the greatest turning-point in Western monasticism since its foundation. Benedict was personally extremely austere and worked incessantly. He suffered various illnesses in his final years but died peacefully in his monastery at the age of seventy-one.

13

Bd Jordan of Saxony (about 1177–1237)

Jordan was elected master general of the Dominicans in succession to St Dominic (see 8 Aug.) himself, having been clothed as a Dominican for a little over two years only. Knowledge of his early life is uncertain: he appears to have come from a wealthy family in Saxony and is known to have been a "bachelor" of theology at the university of Paris in 1219. By then he must have been forty years old, so what had he been doing before then? A probable answer is that he was the brilliant mathematician known as Jordanus Nemorarius, whose treatises lasted several centuries and were used by Leonardo da Vinci. This was certainly claimed by the English Dominican chronicler Nicholas Trivet, writing some eighty years after Jordan's death: "Brother Jordan, by nationality a Teuton of the diocese of Mayence, was made successor to Blessed Dominic ... being held to be great in the secular sciences and particularly in mathematics. ..." If he was a famed recruit to the Order, this makes his meteoric rise in it more understandable.

Dominic had held several long conversations with him in the spring of 1219, and he made his profession to Reginald of Orleans, sent by Dominic to Paris from Bologna, the following spring. Two months later he was chosen as one of four "definitors" from Paris to attend the chapter summoned in Bologna to prepare a Constitution. He was elected prior provincial of Lombardy the following year. This was the major province of the new Order and included the university of Bologna, then the most important legal school in Europe. Under Jordan, the Dominican house of studies there was soon attracting students of the highest calibre. He enthusiastically embraced Dominic's initiative of making academic circles a particular focus for the Dominican apostolate. In 1223 he established a Dominican house in Padua, another great university city. Increasing numbers of students in Paris required a new building, which was financed by the queen, Blanche of Castile, who also provided the Dominicans with a house in Chartres, where they soon founded a church, priory, and school. (The bishop objected, but the pope overrode him with a Bull.)

There followed long years of ceaseless travel, preaching, and exhorting young men of high intellect to join the Order. Jordan succumbed to "marsh fever," probably malaria from the swamps along the river Po, which was to recur for the rest of his life. He went to Paris via Milan and Besançon; there he preached the Advent sermons and welcomed forty new recruits. Then to northern Europe: Lille, Brussels, Trier; south to Provence the following year, and so back to Bologna. After the general chapter of 1225, he headed off to Germany after being delayed in Verona for some time with his fever. Returning via Venice the following year, he was nearly killed in Rome when a mentally unstable friar whom he had released from captivity slashed his throat with a razor. Fortunately, the wound was superficial, and he was back preaching and recruiting within a few days. In 1227 a new pope, Gregory X, who as Cardinal Ugolino had been a close friend of Dominic, gave the Dominicans the right to preach everywhere, regardless of permission from local bishops (such as the bishop of Chartres). In 1228 Jordan discussed with him the agenda for the general chapter, held in Paris, which opened up new mission provinces in the

Holy Land, Greece, north-central Europe, and Poland—a decisive move into "heathen," or at best schismatic, territories.

Houses of study were Jordan's main concern during these years. The Dominicans were granted a chair of theology at Paris in 1229. Jordan became known as "the Siren of the Schools" for his ability to attract academics to the Order. He was at the formal opening of the university of Toulouse in 1229 and in Oxford the following year, preaching the Lent course of sermons. His visit produced three Dominican priories in England and another three in Scotland over the next few years. Then he was in Paris, Milan, Bologna for the general chapter of 1233, Strasbourg (where he received the news of Dominic's canonization), and Zurich the following year. Somewhere along the road he lost an eye, and he was unkindly referred to as "one-eye" from then on.

Throughout all this, there was another side to his life, which sets him apart from other heroic activists. On Dominic's death, Jordan had been left responsible for founding a convent for women in Bologna. This convent, named St Agnes, started with five Sisters, including Diana d'Andalo, the lively daughter of a prominent family of the city. She and Jordan were obviously drawn to one another, and over the years his letters to her (her replies have been lost) show the development of a great spiritual friendship, on a par with that between Francis and Clare of Assisi or Francis de Sales and Jane de Chantal. He visited the convent whenever he returned to Bologna, sent suitable novices from his travels, and secured a Bull from the pope to bring the convent under direct Dominican control when internal tensions threatened it in 1226. It became the motherhouse of the Second Order and the starting point for the development of the Third, the Tertiaries.

The "Most General Chapter" held in Paris in 1236 decided that he should visit the four Dominican priories he had established in the Holy Land, which he did that winter. He preached to the Knights Templar in Jerusalem, asking them to excuse his "mediocre French." From Palestine, he wrote his last letter to Diana: "O Diana, how miserable is the present state which we must endure since we cannot love one another without sorrow or think of one another without anxiety." They did not have to endure much longer: on his return journey, Jordan's ship was wrecked in a storm, with the loss of everyone on board, on 13 February 1237; Diana died probably before this last letter reached her. Jordan's body was washed up on the shore at Acre and buried in the priory there, but the Saracens sacked the town a few years later, and his remains were lost for ever. So their bodies were kept apart even after death, but their longed-for spiritual union in God was sealed: "In him, who is our bond, my heart is always united to thine..."

Jordan was popularly hailed as a saint immediately after his death but was not officially recognized in just a few years, as Dominic had been. Too much of an academic and activist, were his letters to Diana too capable of mis-interpretation (unlikely, as she was also beatified, though not till 1891), or were the relevant popes somewhat cooler toward the Dominicans? He was not actually beatified till 1827 and has never been canonized.

❖

Bees collect from earthly flowers an earthly honey, carrying it into their hives and keeping it there for the future. If your spirit is not refreshed with spiritual honey, it will die. ... Send your spirit then, my dear, toward the flowers of the celestial meadows which never fade, so that it there may gather honey on which to live.
from a letter from Bd Jordan to Bd Diana

14

St Valentine (possibly Third Century)

Despite his popularity, virtually nothing is known of the historical Valentine. For a long time there were apparently two, one a martyr in Rome, the second a bishop and martyr at Terni, some sixty miles north of Rome. The new Roman Martyrology has at last (accepting the general rule that if two saints of the same name are commemorated on the same day, the chances are that they are one and the same person) decided on one: "At Rome on the via Flaminia by the Milvan Bridge, saint Valentine, martyr." The comment in previous editions that he is also claimed by Terni has been dropped, so we are left with just a martyr in Rome.

There is evidence of an early cult in Rome, and a basilica was built, possibly as early as 350, on the spot where he is supposed to have been martyred. A catacomb was formed there to hold his remains, which were later transferred by Pope St Paschal I to a special chapel he had built on to the church of St Praxedes to hold them. But the early story of his martyrdom is actually borrowed from another martyrdom story now known to be fictitious, so the most that can be said about him is that details are uncertain.

There are also various possibilities connecting his feast-day with lovers. It could have been a Christian takeover of the Roman feast of Lupercalia, to (as Butler originally put it) "abolish the heathen's lewd superstitious custom of boys drawing the names of girls, in honour of their goddess Februata Juno ..." Chaucer suggests that it was because birds choose their mates on this day. Or it could be that the association should be with another Valentine, bishop of Genoa, whose feast-day was 2 May, and that this Valentine's association is accidental. It had certainly happened by 1447, as is shown in *The Paston Letters*, a collection preserved by a wealthy family from Norfolk, where Elizabeth Drew writes to John Paston, who was due to marry her daughter, "And, Cousin, upon Friday is St Valentine's day, and every bird chooseth him a mate," and Margery, the daughter, boldly addresses John as "my right well beloved Valentine."

The eighteenth-century *Diary of a Country Parson*, by James Woodforde, refers to a rather different custom associated with the day, apparently more reminiscent of the "trick or treat" now associated with Hallowe'en: "To 36 Children being Valentine's day and what is customary for them to go about in these Parts [also Norfolk] this Day gave 0. 3. 0. [three shillings, each of twelve pence] being one penny apiece to each of them." The massive card and flower industry of today may seem to have been with us for ever, but in the 1950s edition of Butler's *Lives*, the association of the day with lovers was referred to as "at the present time ... hardly more than a memory." Perhaps—dare one say?—its revival is more commercial than devotional, and the Roman Lupercalia may have regained lost ground.

15

St Claude La Colombière (1641–1682)

For English Protestants, Claude was a classic scheming foreign Jesuit, out to make Britain Catholic again through court intrigue; for Catholics he was an entirely innocent, non-political, preacher and chaplain devoted to the Sacred Heart. Recent research suggests the Protestants may have had a point, which makes both him and his canonization in 1992 considerably more interesting.

He was born near Lyons, educated at the Jesuit college there, joined the Society, and returned to teach grammar and humanities at the college. Before he was ordained he proved his abilities as a preacher, at convents of the Visitation nuns (see St Francis de Sales; 24 Jan.) in Avignon, which was still papal territory. He then went to complete his theology studies in Paris, where he was chosen as tutor to the sons of the famous finance minister Colbert. This came to an abrupt end when he was found to be the author of a satirical article attacking Colbert. Back in Avignon, he worked on a course of sermons to justify Jesuit defence of free will against the strict tendency known as Jansenism, which the Jesuits saw as bringing Luther and Calvin's teaching on predestination into the Church. One weapon the Jesuits used was the doctrine of God's unconditional love and forgiveness, exemplified in increasing devotion to the Sacred Heart of Jesus.

Claude, after a retreat in which he dedicated himself to the Sacred Heart, was appointed superior of the Jesuit house at Paray-le-Monial in Burgundy. There he became the confessor to the nuns of the Visitation Convent, including Margaret Mary Alacoque, who had received a series of visions in which, she claimed, Jesus had instructed her to see that an annual feast of the Sacred Heart should be instituted. Claude came as a godsend to her, and he saw her as a buttress to his own devotion.

He was then appointed preacher to the duchess of York, Mary of Modena (wife of the future king, James II), at the Queen's Chapel in St James' Palace in London. He arrived in lay dress, but his reputation as a preacher had preceded him, and Protestants as well as Catholics crowded the chapel to hear him. They cannot have been delighted by what they heard: Claude had taken over Margaret Mary's theme of the world's ingratitude for God's love poured out through the Sacred Heart of Jesus, and he equated this ingratitude with heresy. After a final sermon on England, attacking the "irreverence and sacrilege" of the Protestant Church, he declared an annual Feast of the Sacred Heart as a means of appeasing God. When the duchess of York's third child died, he virtually attributed the death to God's punishment for the continuance of Protestantism in England.

He was obviously not at all afraid of speaking his mind, and it was almost inevitable that he would fall foul of the authorities. His early biographers made him out to be far more timid and retiring than he actually was, presumably so as to make him seem obviously innocent of any of the charges made against him. It was even said that he never looked out of the windows of St James' Palace for fear of being contaminated by the wicked city. Yet he seems to have been in touch with underground Catholic cells, to have sent potential converts to France for instruction, and to have looked out for priests who might be sent to Virginia. He was arrested for his supposed complicity in the "Popish Plot" to assassinate King Charles II. He was tried by the House of Commons in 1679, but King Louis XIV of France intervened to save him from execution, and after three weeks in prison he was banished back to France. But prison had fatally undermined his health; he lived an invalid life for a further three years and died at Paray-le-Monial on 15 February 1682.

Many of his sermons survive, as do a number of spiritual letters. His "institution" of the feast of the Sacred Heart was copied in Poland a century later and then officially extended to the whole Church in 1856, celebrated on the third Friday after Pentecost, leading to a huge outpouring of devotion in the shape of new churches and statues dedicated to the Sacred Heart. Claude was beatified in 1929 and canonized by Pope John Paul II on 31 May 1992.

16

SS Cyril and Methodius (827–869 and 815–884)

These two brothers have long been venerated in the countries they evangelized as apostles to the southern Slavs and as the fathers of Slavonic literature. The

Orthodox Church celebrates their feast on 11 May. Their feast was extended to the universal Church in 1880, and Pope Paul II has nominated them as patrons of Europe. They are also regarded as patrons of ecumenism—a patronage still needed as much as ever today in the troubled areas of south-eastern Europe they evangelized. In their day, too, the region was torn between Western and Eastern influences.

Cyril studied the secular sciences at Constantinople, becoming known as "the philosopher." He then retired to a religious house for a time, before being sent by the emperor on a mission to Ukraine in 860. Methodius, twelve years his senior, also seems to have combined religion with imperial politics, as a provincial governor and then an abbot. In 862 Duke Ratislav of Moravia asked the eastern emperor to send missionaries to evangelize his lands, stipulating that they must speak Slavonic (so countering German influence, which brought allegiance to the western empire). Cyril and Methodius both spoke Slavonic from childhood, and the emperor chose them to lead the mission. They set about translating the Bible, Greek liturgical texts, and the Roman Mass into Slavonic, for use as a liturgical language. It was at the time a popular spoken language only, so they had to devise a written alphabet for it: the result is known as the Glagolitic script, based on Greek with the addition of some specially devised characters. This developed into the Cyrillic (after Cyril) script used by Russian and other Slav languages today, and their Southern Slavonic became the Old or Church Slavonic used in the liturgies of Eastern Catholic and Orthodox Churches to this day.

Their mission in Moravia was a great success, but they were not bishops and could not ordain priests and so leave a native clergy behind them. The Bavarian (so Western) bishop of Passau took advantage of this by refusing to ordain their candidates, so in 867 they set out for Constantinople to seek help. When they reached Venice they were invited to Rome by the pope, not so much as a gesture of reconciliation as because Cyril was carrying the supposed relics of St Clement, the early Roman martyr, which he had miraculously retrieved from the bottom of a lake in the Ukraine. So they changed course, but by the time they reached Rome there was a new pope. Hadrian II supported their liturgical innovation—strongly criticized by others—and even had the liturgy celebrated in Slavonic in some Roman churches. Cyril died in Rome, and the pope insisted that he should be buried in San Clemente, where the relics he brought had been interred.

Methodius returned to his mission field, and the prince of Slovenia petitioned the pope to have him appointed to the revived archbishopric of Sirmium (now Mitrovitsa, near Belgrade). He was consecrated in Rome by Pope Hadrian in 870. His province, covering the mission territories of Serbia, Croatia, Slovenia, and Moravia, thus became effectively the eastern outpost of the Western Church. But the Bavarian authorities did not see him as an ally and arrested him. The next pope, John VII, eventually secured his release, but he countermanded Hadrian's approval of the use of Slavonic in the liturgy. It took Methodius ten years to persuade Pope John to reverse this latter decision. He spent the last four years of his life translating almost the entire Bible into Slavonic, which may suggest that he was prevented politically from exercising a full-time ministry. He died in what is now the Czech Republic in 874. His achievement as "Apostle to the Moravians" had been great, but his death brought about a crisis in his mission territory, with political and liturgical factions tearing it apart in a manner all too reminiscent of the quarrels, political and religious, still dividing a region in which the map has so often been redrawn by the conflicting powers of West and East—with their attendant Churches.

17

The Martyrs of China (from 1748 to 1900)

Systematic missions to China began in the late sixteenth century. Jesuits arrived in 1583, followed by Dominicans, Franciscans, Augustinians, and, later, Paris Foreign Missioners and Lazarists. The first Chinese priest was ordained in 1658. All missionaries came up against the problem of how to explain and apply Christianity in a civilization with its own ancient religious tradition— what is now known as "inculturation." The Jesuits tried to produce an "inculturated" liturgy, incorporating the notion of filial piety, but were contested by others and eventually overruled by Pope Clement IV in 1704, putting an end to the "Chinese Rites Controversy" and to any significant progress that might have been made. Christianity was from then on under a cloud of suspicion as inherently foreign, and foreigners were "barbarians."

Persecution was sporadic rather than systematic, determined by the attitude of local mandarins and provincial governors. Six Spanish Dominicans were executed in Fukien Province in 1748. There was then a lull, and the next to suffer was Bishop Gabriel Dufresse, beheaded in the capital of Szechwan Province in 1815, despite the respect in which he was held locally. The Italian Franciscan John Lantrua was brutally treated before being executed the following February. Two Chinese laymen, Paul Lieu and Peter Lieu, were executed in 1818 and 1834 respectively, and in 1820 the distinguished Lazarist priest Francis-Régis Clet was strangled after being horrifically tortured, ending a ministry in China of over thirty years, during which he had struggled heroically against climate, opposition, isolation, and the language in the depths of the interior. A new wave of persecution in 1840 led to the torture and execution of another Lazarist priest, John Perboyre, who became the first missionary to China to be beatified, in 1889. In 1856 a priest of the Paris Foreign Missions, Augustus Chapdelaine, was brutally tortured, together with a Chinese convert,

Agnes Sao Kuy, whom he had engaged to teach. She died from her tortures on 28 February, and he was executed the following day. These and others, Chinese and European, were beatified in groups in 1900 and 1909.

European expansion into China increased after the second Opium War, in which France joined England on account of the death of Fr Chapdelaine. Territorial concessions were won from China in treaties of 1858 and 1860, which also gave missionaries unprecedented rights. They were allowed to preach freely and also to purchase land on which to build churches. They saw themselves as distinct from European imperialism and working to improve the lot of the impoverished population, building hospitals, schools, leprosaria, orphanages, and dispensaries. Hundreds of thousands of converts were made, but there was a widespread accusation that many of these were "rice Christians," converting only for the material benefits. Individually, most of the missionaries, Catholic and Protestant, worked in a spirit of heroic self-sacrifice, but there was also a tendency to become involved in local politics. By 1898 the Chinese feeling of national humiliation led to the first uprising by a nationalist secret society called *Yi Ho Chuan*, "Righteous Harmony Fists," known in English as the Boxers. These were encouraged to turn their violence on to foreigners and Christians, and this resulted in massacres during the winter of 1899–1900 in which some two hundred and fifty European missionaries, most of them Protestant, were killed, together with some twenty-five thousand Catholic and two thousand Protestant converts.

Catholic missionaries killed include two Italian Franciscan priests, Cesidio Giacomantonio and Joseph Gambaro, and two bishops, Antony Fantosati and Gregory Grassi. The latter was the leader of the largest group to suffer together, under a notorious governor in Shansi province, together with the coadjutor, Francis Fogolla, two other Franciscan priests and a lay brother. Five Chinese seminarians and nine catechists and servants of the mission, and seven Sisters of the Franciscan Missionaries of Mary under their superior, Hermina Grivot, whom Mgr Fogolla had persuaded to come to China also suffered. They were all imprisoned in a mandarin's house known as the Inn of Heavenly Peace, from where they were taken before a court and condemned to immediate death, the governor himself killing Bishop Grassi and Mgr Fogolla with a sword. The others were either run through with a sword or had their throats cut. They were all beatified together in 1946, followed in 1955 by four French Jesuits and over fifty Chinese lay people, also killed by the Boxers. Thousands of other Chinese victims are still possible candidates for beatification.

The governor, Yu Hsien, had himself produced a document claiming that the "European religion," which he called "wicked and cruel … perverse," was what the Boxers hated. This enabled the deaths to be seen as martyrdoms and not political.

Lessons were learned by the missionary Churches, Catholic and Protestant: numbers of Chinese priests, ministers, nuns, and lay helpers were built up, so that Christianity came to wear a much more indigenous face during the first half of the twentieth century. After the Communist victory in 1948, foreign missionaries were imprisoned, then expelled, but when China was again opened to the outside world forty years later, there were more Christians than in 1948, and their numbers have grown rapidly in the last decade, even though they still make up only some two per cent of the population. Pope John Paul II has (in 2001) publicly apologized for mistakes made in the past, and relations between the Chinese government and the Vatican are improving.

18

St Colman of Lindisfarne (died 676)

Colman does not feature in the new Roman Martyrology, which does not mean that he is unhistorical or that his holiness is in doubt but means rather that he should not be venerated universally, though he can be locally. His omission is perhaps not surprising in view of the fact that he was the chief "anti-Roman" protagonist at the Synod of Whitby in 663 or 664, which makes him significant enough in the development of Christianity in the British Isles to be considered here. Our knowledge concerning him derives mainly from Bede's *Ecclesiastical History of the English People* (Book 3, Chapters 25 and 26), and Bede, though fully supportive of the "Roman" arguments at Whitby, praises him for the austerity and simplicity of his way of life.

He came from Ireland and was a monk at Iona before being appointed third bishop of Lindisfarne in 661, a post he held for three years only. The debate at Whitby concerned the date of Easter, styles of monastic tonsure, and outward signs of the differences between Iona and its (northern) Irish satellites on one hand and Southern Ireland and the rest of western Europe on the other. Observance of Easter was indeed chaotic, with King Oswy of Northumberland, instructed and baptized by the Irish, following the Iona date and finishing his celebration days before his queen, schooled in Kent, started hers. King Oswy presided at the synod and asked Colman to put his point of view first. He claimed that the Iona observance had been faithfully handed down and derived ultimately from the community of St John the Evangelist. The spokesman for the Roman side, St Wilfrid (see 24 Apr.), was as dismissive as the English have been of the Scots and Irish ever since: "The only people who stupidly contend against the whole world are those Irishmen and their partners in obstinacy the Picts and the Britons, who inhabit only a portion of these the two uttermost islands of the ocean." Colman again appealed to St John, but Wilfrid cited the tradition deriving from SS Peter and Paul in Rome, which he claimed also fulfilled the Jewish Passover rules. Eventually the king obliged Colman to accept that authority had been given to Peter.

He did not, however, signal his agreement to the Roman customs but took some followers and returned to Iona. From there he went back to Ireland and founded a monastery on an island off the coast of Galway. This contained both Irish and English monks: "But a dispute arose among them because in summer the Irish went off to wander on their own around places they knew instead of assisting at harvest, and then, as winter approached, came back and wanted to share whatever the English monks had gathered" (Bede, 4:4, sounding not unlike an English Victorian statesman at the time of the Irish potato famine). Colman eventually solved this by founding a new monastery on the mainland and sending all the English monks there, to live "devoutly and austerely by the work of their own hands."

Colman remained abbot of both communities until his death, which different chroniclers place on various dates from 672 to 676. His cult was confirmed in 1898 (so he has never been officially beatified or canonized). His feast is observed in some parts of Ireland on 8 August, but on today's date in Argyll and the Isles.

19

Bd John of Fiesole (Fra Angelico) (Guido di Piero; about 1400–1455)

The painter known to the world as Fra Angelico, beatified by Pope John Paul II and declared patron of Christian artists in 1982, spent his adult life as a Dominican friar. He was born near Florence, probably closer to 1400 than the previously accepted date of 1387. He was a painter before he became a friar: his name is listed as a member of a painting fraternity in 1417, and he joined the Dominicans in 1420.

He entered the convent of St Dominic in Fiesole, just outside Florence, becoming Brother John in religion and the disciple of a painter known as Lorenzo Monaco (the monk), who painted in the bold and generous tradition of Andrea Orcagna. The community moved into the convent of San Marco in Florence around the time Brother John took major orders. San Marco was then enlarged and rebuilt over a fifteen-year period under the patronage of the Medicis, and John undertook the unique series of murals on which his fame rests.

His work bridges the Middle Ages and the Renaissance, combining the religious intensity of the former with the love of beauty of the latter. As Bernard Berenson has written, his work shows "Perfect certainty of purpose, utter devotion to his task, a sacramental eagerness in performing it." The spirit of the new humanism shows in his naturalism, his introduction of landscape, and his sense of nature as a place to be enjoyed rather than feared. At home with the new understanding of perspective, he used his skills to tell the sacred stories that were the subject of his work. At San Marco he painted a sacred scene in each friar's cell and at the end of each corridor. These were not for decoration but aids to meditation and devotion. These scenes form the bulk of his work, and they have been preserved in their original setting.

His approach is simple and narrative, with large areas of flat colour. Details are kept to a minimum, with none of the "extraneous" elements often introduced in devotional works painted at the time for lay people. The inclusion of the figure of a friar or a nun in many of the paintings enables those whose cells they are in to see themselves in the scene. His art is a means of preaching, in accordance with the Dominican spirit: he shows people what should be adored. As his work progressed, his compositions became simpler, as evidenced in *St Dominic adoring Christ on the Cross*. *The Annunciation*, dating from about 1449, demonstrates his knowledge of classical architecture, but this is kept as a background, not allowed to intrude on the story.

He also painted several altarpieces outside San Marco, usually depicting the Madonna and Child with a group of saints, a theme that was to become known as a "sacred conversation." His fame spread to Rome, and Pope Eugenius IV commissioned him to decorate two chapels in the Vatican, only one of which, showing scenes from the lives of St Stephen and St Laurence, survives. In 1447 he began work on a huge fresco cycle depicting the Last Judgment in Orvieto Cathedral, but he was unable to complete this. He was called back to Rome, to work in St Peter's and in the pope's private study. He was active in the affairs of his Order, especially as prior of the convent in Fiesole from 1450 to 1452. It is said that Pope Eugenius wanted to appoint him archbishop of Florence, but he suggested his friend Antoninus (canonized in 1523; see 4 May), preferring the lesser role for himself. His legacy is in his paintings, which earned him the title of "Angelic Brother" soon after his death. He integrated his artistic gifts totally into the ideals of his life and devoted his life to expressing the state of beatitude. Ruskin was right to call him "not an artist, properly so called, but an inspired saint." The official Church was slow to give him this recognition but has now made amends.

One has to believe that this good monk has been allowed to visit paradise and been allowed to choose his models there.

Michelangelo on Fra Angelico

Clinging always to Christ, he expressed in pictures what he contemplated inwardly, so as to raise people's minds to the highest things.

Roman Martyrology (new)

20

St Peter Damian (1007–1072)

Peter was a hermit and scholar who became a bishop and a cardinal, has been declared a Doctor of the Church, and was one of the great reforming figures of the Middle Ages.

He was born into a large family in Ravenna. His parents both died when he was young, and he was placed in the care of one of his brothers, who treated him more like a slave. An elder brother, then archpriest of Ravenna, rescued him and sent him to study, at which he excelled. In due course he returned to Ravenna as a professor, already dedicated to an extremely ascetic way of life. He then joined a group of Benedictine followers of St Romuald who were living as hermits at Fonte Avellana in northern Italy. Peter was soon outdoing them all in austerities, to the point where he developed near-permanent insomnia and was forced to modify his penances somewhat. After the abbot died in 1043, he was made superior of the community, but he refused to accept the title of abbot. He studied the scriptures and the Church Fathers and wrote a Life of St Romuald, in which he set out his ideals for reform of the clergy, many of whom at the time were reluctant to accept disciplines such as celibacy.

His reputation grew, and Pope St Leo IX (1049–54) employed him to preach against simony at a series of synods held throughout Italy. In 1057 another reforming pope, Stephen IX (1057–58) persuaded him to become cardinal-bishop of Ostia, the seaport of Rome. This brought the hermit movement into the heart of the official Church. Peter constantly begged to be allowed to return to Fonte Avellana, but his voice was too important, and successive popes found further missions for him. He managed to prevent a popular reform movement in Milan, whose lay leaders, the *Patares*, were trying to persuade the urban clergy to be celibate, from breaking away into schism. He was eventually allowed back to his hermitage, but Pope Alexander II (1061–73) took him out of retirement for a diplomatic mission to Germany, where, as papal legate at the Synod of Frankfurt, he persuaded the emperor not to divorce his wife. Three years later he was sent on another mission to restore order in Ravenna after the wrongdoings of the then archbishop had split the town into factions. He died on his way back to his hermitage.

He saw the central authority of a reformed papacy as the key to order in the Church and helped further the imposition of the Roman liturgy in place of local rites as a means to this end: only Milan held out, clinging to the Ambrosian Rite. He gave the hermit movement a firm theological and organizational base and sought to extend monastic ideals of poverty and sharing to canons regular and the rest of the clergy. The idea that they should "imitate the primitive Church" proved original and shocking to many but had a permanent influence on clerical spirituality. He considered the classical learning of his earlier years unsuited to his hermits, who were to concentrate absolutely on the love of God, while allowing lay people and other clergy a sound intellectual formation, provided they kept their priorities right. It was he who propounded the idea that philosophy had to be the handmaid of theology.

He taught his hermits the ideals of the Desert Fathers, told bishops that they should pray without ceasing, and suggested to the abbot of Cluny that its monks should use the discipline and fast more. To this the abbot replied by asking him to try the life there first before making such suggestions: "Eat with us first and then say whether you think our food needs more seasoning." He had a great devotion to the image of Christ on the cross and to the motherhood of Mary, prefiguring the "modern devotion" of the later Middle Ages. He also wrote many hymns, including one celebrating Gregory the Great's sending of St Augustine and other monks to convert the English. He was declared a Doctor of the Church in 1828 for his preaching and writing in the cause of church reform.

21

St Robert Southwell (about 1561–1595)

Robert Southwell was as influential in his life for his writing as he became through the martyrdom he expected and received. His poetry and his death both left indelible marks on the age in which he lived. Born in Norfolk, he was sent abroad to study at the English College at Douai in northern France, where his master was the Jesuit Leonard Lessius. From there he moved on to Paris, and at the age of seventeen he announced his intention of joining the Society of Jesus. He was refused as being too young, but a few months later he was admitted to the novitiate at Sant' Andrea in Rome. He wrote of the life for which he was preparing himself: "How great a perfection is required in a religious of the Society, who should ever be ready at a moment's notice for any part of the world and for any kind of people, be they heretics, Turks, pagans or barbarians...."

He was ordained in 1584 and sent to England two years later, by which time it was high treason for a Jesuit trained abroad to enter the country. Surely knowing what his probable end would be, he professed himself eager to embrace it: "Nor do I so much dread the tortures as look forward to the crown." He attended a remarkable meeting in the Thames Valley, held to map out the future strategy for the survival of Catholicism in England, and managed to preach a sermon in the Marshalsea prison in London. This led to his being recommended as a suitable priest to bring the sacraments to Anne, countess of Arundel and Surrey, the wife of the imprisoned Philip Howard (see 22 Oct.), and to his taking up residence in her house in the Strand, an absurdly prominent location for someone in hiding. Yet he lived there in secrecy for six years, his presence known to only a trusted few.

He wrote during the day and emerged after dark to minister to Catholics. He produced *An Epistle of Comfort,* based on letters to Philip Howard and published in England with Anne's help. (The "comfort" offered to Catholics suffering in prison is that everyone will eventually be brought to the same end in death.) He travelled outside London and, despite the secrecy of his life, became a considerable figure in English literary circles. His *Peter's Plaint,* a long narrative of the closing stages of Jesus' life put into the mouth of repentant Peter, was addressed to the earl of Southampton, Shakespeare's patron, and arguably brought about a change in the moral tone of the latter's work. Shakespeare and Southampton could both have fitted into the category of prominent people whom the Jesuits sought to "reconcile" to their faith, though evidence that Shakespeare had been a Catholic is still disputed.

His charmed life could not last for ever, and he was eventually tracked down by the notorious "chief pursuivant," Robert Topcliffe, who used torture and rape to bring about his betrayal. Topcliffe tortured him dreadfully at his own house, which he had had equipped as a torture chamber. He was put to the newly devised "wall torture"—hanging from a wall by manacled wrists, which Sir Robert Cecil described as "not possible for a man to bear"—ten times. He was then imprisoned for nearly three years without any charge being brought against him. His eventual trial brought about a revulsion against the barbarity of the torture and execution methods then employed. Topcliffe first denied torturing him, then—Eichmann-like—whined that he was only obeying orders: "I had authority to use him as I did. ..." The judge finally demanded that he be silenced, bringing his five-year reign of terror to an end.

The verdict was inevitable and the sentence mandatory: Robert was to be hanged, drawn, and quartered at Tyburn. His friend and fellow-Jesuit Henry Garnet was an eyewitness to his death. When the rope by which he was hanged was about to be cut so that he could be butchered before he was dead, there was uproar from the crowd, and the hangman pulled on his legs until he felt the body go limp. His head was cut off and held up to the crowd with the usual declaration, "Here is the head of a traitor," but there was no answering roar of "Traitor!" from the crowd, just silence. Robert Southwell was beatified in 1929 and canonized as one of the Forty Martyrs of England and Wales (see 25 Oct.) in 1970.

❖

And so it fares with man's life, he comes into the world with pain, begins his course with pitiful cries and is continually molested with divers vexations; he never ceases running down till in the end he falls into the sea of death. Neither is our last hour the beginning of our death but the conclusion; for then is come what has been long in the coming, and fully finished what was still in the ending.

St Robert Southwell, *An Epistle of Comfort*

22

St Margaret of Cortona (1247–1297)

Margaret was the daughter of a poor farming family from Laviano in Tuscany. Her mother died when she was seven, and her father married again. His new wife treated Margaret, who seems to have been the only child, with such hatred and violence that she eventually felt driven from the family home. She took refuge with a young nobleman from Montepulciano named Arsenio, and the two lived together openly and faithfully as lovers for nine years. This caused a great scandal, even though the only reason they did not marry was the impossibility of doing so imposed by society owing to the difference in their social rank.

One day Arsenio failed to come home from a hunting expedition. The next afternoon his dog returned and dragged Margaret to a pile of leaves by an oak tree, where it scratched and revealed his body in a shallow pit. Margaret saw this as a judgment on her for her sin. She put on penitential dress and went to beg her father's forgiveness. He would have taken her (and her son) back, but her stepmother persuaded him that this would bring social disgrace on him and refused to allow her in. She took refuge with the Franciscans at Cortona, who became her spiritual guides. They tried to dissuade her from the course of extreme penitential practices on which she embarked, but with little success. "Between me and my body," she told her confessor, Friar Giunta, "there must needs be a struggle till death." She deprived herself of sleep and of practically all food and mutilated herself in ways that would now be seen as cries for help.

As a recognized "penitent," she had a certain place in society: she nursed the sick poor and lived on charity. After three years the worst of her excesses moderated, and the Franciscans agreed to her joining the Third Order, which had come into being largely to keep secular penitents within bounds and under some sort of control. She formed a group of women tertiaries into a nursing community, which eventually developed into a hospital. Perhaps not surprisingly in view of her physical deprivations, she saw visions and—according to the account compiled by her confessor—claimed that Christ on the cross was calling her the "third light" of the Order (for the Third Order, after Francis for the First and Clare for the Second). For a time she was accused of improper relations with the Franciscans, and Friar Giunta was moved away from Cortona. For seven years she had little contact with them, but her convictions and her prayer life remained as strong as ever, and eventually they came back to support her. Despite being envied as well as admired, her reputation as a holy woman spread; she began to speak in public, and soon people were coming from all over Italy and even from France and Spain to seek healing at her hands.

Worn out by years of penance, despite the best efforts of the Franciscans, her health gave way, and she died at the age of fifty. She was popularly acclaimed as a saint on the day of her death, and the citizens of Cortona immediately began building a church in commemoration of her. Her feast was approved for the diocese in 1522, and she was formally canonized in 1728. If she had been treated kindly after her mother's death; if she had been pitied and cared for after the shock of her lover's death instead of condemned as a sinner; if her penitential practices had been understood instead of being either admired as heroic or condemned as hypocritical, who knows what her life might have been? At least the Franciscans of Cortona showed her what care and understanding the society of the time allowed them.

23

St Polycarp (about 69–about 155)

Polycarp was bishop of Smyrna in the first half of the second century. He was martyred, at a date about which there is some uncertainty, by the pagan population of the town, and his congregation wrote an account of his death in the form of a letter to a nearby Christian community and, through this, to the whole Church. This document, the *Martyrium Polycarpi*, established the essential elements of the cult of martyrs, who for several centuries were the only Christians recognized as saints after their death. It founded the custom of observing the date of death, the *dies natalis*, meaning "birthday into heaven," as the day on which the martyr was commemorated, when the Christian community would gather and celebrate, as opposed to the pagans, who celebrated the anniversary of birth into this world. It also provides the first evidence of the veneration of relics and makes a careful distinction between the adoration due to Christ and the love and respect accorded to martyrs, which they deserve "for their unsurpassable devotion to their own King and Teacher."

Little is known of Polycarp's life, but he is generally accepted as being one of the "Apostolic Fathers," meaning those who had personally known the apostles themselves. He is referred to as a disciple of St John the Evangelist, who is traditionally regarded as the youngest of the apostles, dying in around 100, so if Polycarp was born in around 69, it would be perfectly possible for him to have known John. In a surviving pastoral letter he quotes from the First Letter of John. Polycarp's letter was still being read in churches in Asia in the fourth century. It shows what concerns were urgent to a church leader at an early date and contains an attack on Marcion for refusing to accept the God of the Old Testament as the Father of Jesus Christ. His discipleship of John is confirmed by St Irenaeus of Lyons (died 203) in a letter: "I remember how he spoke of his intercourse with John and with others who had seen the Lord; how he repeated their words from memory; and how the things that he had heard them say about the Lord ... were proclaimed by Polycarp in complete harmony with scripture. ..." As Irenaeus learned from him, Polycarp stands at the source of the transmission of the faith to the West.

The account of his martyrdom is to a large extent "harmonized" with the passion of Jesus as described in the Gospels, and in this became a pattern for virtually all subsequent accounts of martyrdoms and then of saints' lives. He waits at a nearby farm for his arrest (the agony in the garden); he invites his captors to a supper (the Last Supper); he is taken into the city riding on a donkey on a great sabbath (Jesus' entry into Jerusalem at Passover); he is questioned by Herod the chief of police (Jesus before Pilate); the crowd call out for a lion to be set on him ("Crucify him! Crucify him!"). After fire fails to kill him he is executed by a sword-thrust to the neck, whereupon his blood spurted to put out the flames ("There came forth blood and water"). His body was burned, so that only the bones remained to be taken away as relics, to prevent the Christians from having "communion with his holy flesh." His final prayer expresses confidence in the fact of redemption and shows that various elements that were to develop into Eucharistic Prayers had already come together.

The custom of celebrating the "birthday into heaven" developed first in the East and is recorded in Rome only in the third century. This may be because it was not until then that Christians were allowed their own cemeteries, in which they could gather to celebrate. The account of Polycarp's martyrdom established the connection between devotion to the martyrs and imitation of Christ: martyrs are the authentic disciples of the Lord, and their finest example is Polycarp.

24

St Ethelbert of Kent (about 552–616)

Ethelbert's life is recorded by the Venerable Bede (see 25 May). He was the first Anglo-Saxon king to be converted to Christianity. He had the title of *bretwalda*, meaning overlord, of England, which meant that nominally his rule extended over all of present-day England south of the river Humber. He became king as a young child, in 560, and sometime before 588 he married a Christian princess named Bertha, daughter of King Charibert of Paris. One of the conditions of the marriage settlement was that she should be free to practice her own religion and to bring over a chaplain with her. This was Bishop Luidhard, who was possibly to have some influence on Ethelbert's conversion.

Christianity had been present in the British Isles for some time; the process in which Ethelbert's conversion played a part was its introduction into Anglo-Saxon England. He was the local king to whom St Augustine (of Canterbury; see 27 May), sent by Pope Gregory the Great (see 3 Sept.) in 597, sought to explain his purpose. Ethelbert's reaction was initially cautious: "After some days the king came to the island [Thanet] and, sitting down in the open air, summoned Augustine and his companions to an audience. But he took precautions that they should not approach him in a house; for he held to an ancient superstition that, if they were practitioners of magical arts, they might have opportunity to deceive and master him." He recognized that their words were "fair indeed," but they were also "new and uncertain," and he did not feel able immediately to "accept them and abandon the age-old beliefs that I have held together with the whole English nation"—an attitude that has still not disappeared from English reactions to innovations from the Continent.

Ethelbert did, however, treat the new arrivals well, giving them a house in Canterbury and permission to preach and make converts. Then he himself was converted, probably in 601. From then on the monks "had greater freedom to build and restore churches everywhere," but the king would not allow any sort of compulsion to be brought to bear on his subjects, saying that he had been taught that Christ must be accepted freely. His approach is in marked contrast, it must be said, to a letter he received from Pope Gregory, urging him to "Press on with the work of extending the Christian faith among the people committed to your charge. Make their conversion your first concern; suppress the worship of idols, and destroy their shrines. . . ." He arranged for Augustine to meet the bishops of the Britons, in whose territories, to the north and west, the "old" date of Easter still prevailed. Augustine was not able to persuade them to change. He also helped to bring about the conversion of King Sabert of the East Saxons, which led to bishoprics being established in London and Rochester. The church in London, dedicated to St Paul, was to develop later into St Paul's Cathedral.

In the secular sphere, Ethelbert introduced a code of law, resembling the Salic law introduced by King Clovis of the Franks, though Bede claims it was based on Roman law. He died in 616 and was buried next to his wife in the monastery of SS Peter and Paul in Canterbury. His son Eadbald failed to carry on his work in support of the Church. Ethelbert's cult was confined to Canterbury until the Middle Ages but was then extended to the universal Church.

25

St Walburga (died 779)

Walburga was a distinguished abbess at the time when women often had charge of double monasteries (that is, those for men and women); a custom that generally reflected the fact that women of high social rank often became nuns. She was one of a family of English missionaries from the west of England associated with the evangelization of Germany by St Boniface (see 5 June), who was her mother's brother and came from Crediton in Devon. She came to Wimborne in Dorset as a child to attend the monastic school attached to the double monastery there. Such schools then offered virtually the only education available to women, while the adjoining establishment for men afforded them some protection in a violent age. Boniface asked Abbess Tatta of Wimborne for nuns to found a convent in newly evangelized German territory. Tatta sent Walburga and others to a former nun of Wimborne, Lioba (also a saint), who had been sent to help Boniface two years earlier. Walburga spent her first two years in Germany with Lioba and became skilled in medicine there.

Her brother Winnibald (another saint, as was the other brother, Willibald; see 7 July) had established a double monastery, the only one of its kind in Germany, at Heidenheim (to the east of modern Stuttgart), and he asked Walburga to govern the nuns while he governed the monks. After his death in 761, she was appointed superior over both parts by Willibald, who was by then bishop of Eichstätt in Bavaria. Little is known about her rule, as no contemporary Life of her was written, but the new Roman Martyrology claims that *optime rexit*, "she ruled very well."

She became extraordinarily famous after her death. Winnibald died in 776, and his remains were interred in the church of the Holy Cross in Eichstätt. Walburga died three years later, and her body was moved after a year to lie beside her brother's. For some reason an aromatic fluid with undoubted healing qualities began to flow (and still flows) from a fissure in the rock on which their tomb stands. Its healing powers were attributed to her, and the fluid became known everywhere as St Walburga's Oil. In a gruesome attempt to spread her cures, her remains were disinterred in 893 and divided between other parts of Germany, France, and Flanders. Legend then associated her alive with at least some of these places.

An even more unlikely development was to follow. A German variant of her name is Walpurgis, universally associated with witches as a result of Wagner's *Walpurgisnacht* music, describing the witches' sabbath supposed to take place at Blockberg in the Hartz mountains. This concept derived from a spring fertility rite, and it seems that the unsuspecting English nun from Dorset gave it her name because a feast of the "translation" of her relics was observed on 1 May and because her name sounded like that of the earth goddess Walborg. In art she is sometimes shown holding three ears of wheat, which has reinforced the association with fertility rites, though it more probably refers to her medicinal use of wheat—she had studied medicine in her early years in Germany—to cure a girl afflicted with an eating disorder. She is more often depicted holding a phial of her healing oil. There are churches dedicated to her all over Europe and also in America. She is the patron saint of the diocese of Eichstätt and, at least locally, of midwives, builders, and domestic animals.

26

St Porphyry of Gaza (353–421)

Porpyhry was a native of Thessalonika in Macedonia. When he was twenty-five years old he followed the example of many of his contemporaries and went to be a monk in the desert of Skete in Egypt, seeking the "flight from the world" exemplified by St Antony (see 17 Jan.) and his followers. He stayed there for five years—there were no lifelong "vows" attached to the decision in his time—and then moved to Palestine, where he spent a further five years as a hermit, living in a cave near the river Jordan. He developed a crippling illness, perhaps some form of arthritis, which forced him to abandon this way of life. He moved into Jerusalem, where, walking with the aid of a stick, he made daily visits to the Holy Places.

A young man named Mark saw him struggling up some steps and offered to help. The offer was refused, but Porphyry evidently befriended Mark, as he asked him to go and arrange the sale of his family estate in Thessalonika, so that the proceeds could be given to the poor. Mark did this and returned three months later with the money. To his surprise, he found Porphyry walking unaided. He listened with amazement as Porpyhry told him that he had had a vision of Christ, who asked him to carry his cross. He did so for "some way," after which he had been free of pain ever since. The money from the sale of the estate was distributed to the poor, leaving Porphyry nothing on which to live, so he taught himself to make shoes, which brought in a small income. Mark earned a little more from copying books and offered to share his income, but Porphyry refused this offer, saying that St Paul had earned his living from making tents.

He was ordained priest in 393, when he was forty years old. The bishop of Jerusalem entrusted the great relic of the Holy Cross to his care. Three years later, he was secretly elected bishop of Gaza in southern Palestine and was deceived into going there by being told that John, the bishop of Caesarea, wished to discuss some matters of scripture with him. He was still reluctant to go, but in another vision Christ told him that he wished him to "marry ... a wife, poor indeed and lowly, but of great piety and virtue"—words that were to be quoted many centuries later by St Francis de Sales (see 24 Jan.), when he refused the king of France's invitation to stay in Paris on the grounds that his duties lay in less glamorous Geneva. Porphyry, uncertain what the words might mean, set out. In Caesarea he was effectively kidnapped by the townspeople of Gaza and forcibly consecrated as their bishop. When he arrived in Gaza, after a terrible journey as the local pagans had broken up the roads in an attempt to prevent him from coming, he was accused of bringing a drought on the area, as foretold by the pagan god Marnas. No rain fell for two months. The Christians gathered to pray in the church of St Timothy, outside the town walls, and were locked out. They redoubled their prayers, and the heavens opened. The pagans opened the gates with cries of "Christ alone is God! He alone has overcome!" Many of them were converted.

Those who remained pagan tried to debar Christians from important posts in the town's trade and civic affairs. Porphyry, accompanied by the ever-faithful Mark, journeyed to Constantinople to seek the emperor's permission to destroy the remaining pagan temples, which was granted. Eight were burned, and houses were ransacked for idols. Porphyry was almost killed in the ensuing riot. (Architectural historians might argue that this would have served him right for destroying the temple of Marnas, which Emperor Theodosius I had previously spared on account of its beauty.) He lived for a further thirteen years, a zealous bishop respected above all for his generosity to the poor. His companion Mark is generally taken to be the author—though his authorship is now disputed—of the near-contemporary Life, written in Latin, which is the main source for the details of Porphyry's life.

27

St Anne Line (around 1565–1601)

Anne was born into an Essex family of fervent Calvinists. She decided to become a Catholic before she was twenty, as did her brother William. Their father, William Heighman, disinherited them both. She married Robert Line, who came from the New Forest area of Hampshire and had also been disinherited for converting. He was forced into exile in Flanders for attending Mass and died there in 1594. Anne was left virtually destitute and in continual ill health. Despite this, she determined to devote the rest of her life to helping her persecuted fellow-Catholics.

She asked the Jesuits what she could do and was placed in charge of the "safe house" operated in London by Fr John Gerard. She took voluntary vows to help increase her dedication, and she organized the house, found other safe houses for priests passing through, and even had time to teach children. Fr Gerard described her tasks, in his famous *Autobiography of a Hunted Priest*, as being "to manage the finances, do all the housekeeping, look after the guests, and deal with the enquiries of strangers," adding that "She was full of kindness, very discreet, and possessed her soul in great peace."

Fr Gerard escaped from the Tower of London in 1587, one of very few ever to have done so, and took refuge on the Continent. The house came under suspicion, and Anne was forced to move. But her new residence was also tracked down by the authorities, and she was arrested on 2 February (Candlemas Day) 1601, just as Fr Francis Page, another Jesuit, was vesting to say Mass. He escaped. Anne was accused of sheltering priests, an offence punishable by death. She was tried at the Old Bailey on 26 February. She was so ill that she had to be carried into the courtroom on a chair. The main evidence against her was the altar found in her house, which by most standards would not be compelling evidence of the presence of priests, but the judge, Lord Chief Justice Popham, had other criteria and directed that she should be found guilty and, despite her condition, be executed the following day.

She spent her last night in prayer and was taken to Tyburn to be hanged. An eyewitness wrote of her: "She behaved herself most meekly, patiently and virtuously to her last breath. She kissed the gallows and, before and after her private prayers blessing herself, the cart was drawn away; and she made the sign of the cross upon her, and after that never moved."

Anne Line was beatified in 1929 and canonized in 1970 as one of the Forty Martyrs of England and Wales (25 Oct.). She was one of three laywomen in the group, the others being Margaret Clitherow and Margaret Ward.

Often she would say to me "I want more than anything to die for Christ, but it is too much to hope that it will be by the executioner's hand. Possibly our Lord will let me be taken one day with a priest and be put in some cold filthy dungeon where I won't be able to live very long in this wretched life."

Fr John Gerard, writing of Anne Line

28

BB Mark Barkworth and Roger Filcock (1601)

Two priests were executed immediately after Anne Line. Mark Barkworth, venerated as the first English Benedictine martyr, is reported to have kissed the hem of her dress and her hand as she hung from the gallows, saying, "Ah, sister, you've got ahead of us, but we'll soon catch you up." The other priest was Roger Filcock, a Jesuit, who had been her confessor. It is possible that Anne and the two priests were executed in haste because Queen Elizabeth's former favourite the earl of Essex was executed for treason on the same day: the death of the Catholics was planned to draw attention away from an unpopular decision.

Mark Barkworth was born near Searby in Lincolnshire in 1572 and brought up as a Protestant. There is a story that his parents, shocked when a woman reputed to be a seer told him that he would die on a scaffold, sent him to Oxford University to confirm his faith, but there is no record that he actually studied there. While travelling on the Continent, he visited the English College at Douai, where he was converted to Catholicism. He entered the seminary there, probably in the autumn of 1593, but the following year was moved to Valladolid to escape an outbreak of plague. He was ordained there in 1599 and despatched on the English mission. The English College in Valladolid was run by the Jesuits, but he apparently became the leader of a group of students who were considering becoming Benedictine monks, which displeased his tutors.

In England he was soon arrested and imprisoned in the Bridewell prison in London. By this time it was treason to be a priest in England who had been ordained abroad, and three fellow-students who had apostasized gave evidence that he was a priest, so he was condemned to death. He claimed to have had a vision of St Benedict, who told him that he would die a martyr and a monk, and he had acquired a Benedictine habit and tonsured his head in the Benedictine fashion. At his execution he reminded the crowd that Pope St Gregory had sent Benedictine monks to evangelize their heathen forebears and claimed to be dying "as a Catholic, a priest, and a religious of the same Order." He was hanged, drawn, and quartered in the usual barbarous manner, but his body was claimed by some Catholic onlookers, and at least part of it reappeared in Hampshire in 1613.

Roger Filcock, from Sandwich in Kent, had also studied at Douai and Valladolid, one of the first ten students to be sent to the latter when it was acquired in 1590. He was ordained there as a secular priest and sent on the

English mission as such, even though he wanted to join the Jesuits, as the Jesuit superior, Fr Henry Garnet, thought that he should prove his mettle on the mission before being accepted into the Society. This he did for two years, and he was duly accepted, but he was arrested before he could leave to join the Jesuit novitiate in Flanders. He was imprisoned in Newgate and tried on 23 February 1601, when he was condemned for treason without any evidence being brought against him. Mark Barkworth, who had known him well at Valladolid, described him as "A man exceedingly humble and of extraordinary patience, piety, and charity." Roger's last words, uttered as he watched Mark die, were, "I desire to be dissolved and to be with Christ."

29

St Oswald of Worcester (died 992)

Oswald was one of the major figures responsible for carrying out the reforms of the Church in England associated with the collaboration between King Edgar of Wessex and St Dunstan of Canterbury (19 May). He was of Danish descent and was a nephew of St Oda, archbishop of Canterbury from 942 to 959, from whom he received his early education. He was then a canon of Winchester cathedral for some years, after which he decided to become a monk and crossed over to France to study at Fleury-sur-Loire (the monastery that claims to house the relics of St Benedict). When he heard that Oda was dying, he returned to England as a monk and an ordained priest.

About two years later, in 961, Dunstan advised Edgar to appoint him to the bishopric of Worcester. From there he founded a monastery at Westbury on Trym, near Bristol, later transferring most of its monks to the new and larger foundation he made at Ramsey in Huntingdonshire. At Worcester he supplanted the secular canons with monks, as St Wulsin (8 Jan.), another protégé of St Dunstan, was to do at Sherborne in 998. The change at Worcester may have been an equally abrupt process, but local tradition tells that he had built a church next to the then cathedral and staffed it with monks. Their services so outshone those of the cathedral that the faithful deserted the latter. The canons were obliged to follow them, so the new church, St Mary's, became the cathedral.

Oswald established a great musical tradition at Worcester (which continues, especially in the shape of the Three Choirs Festival, drawing on the talents of Worcester, Gloucester, and Hereford Cathedrals). He encouraged learning of all sorts, bringing learned masters over from the Continent, including Abbo of Fleury, a noted mathematician and astronomer, who spent two years at Ramsey Abbey.

In 972 Oswald was promoted to be archbishop of York, but, at the king's request and with the pope's permission, he combined this with remaining bishop of Worcester. This seemingly strange (and unreformed) arrangement, finally abolished in 1061, was possibly in the interests of sharing resources between the rich and powerful southern see of Worcester and the poor and turbulent northern one of York. Oswald's Scandinavian descent combined with his loyalty to Edgar may have indicated him as the person best able to unite the northern and southern provinces. He built up the wealth of Worcester by acquiring large tracts of land in the fertile Severn valley and may not have appreciated his times of residence in his northern fastness, but he administered both dioceses until he died and gained a great reputation for his love of the poor.

He showed this love by washing the feet of twelve poor men not just on Maundy Thursday but every day throughout Lent. It was on Leap Year Day in 992 that he died just as he had washed the feet of the last of the twelve, so his feast falls on 29 February in leap years. His death is said to have produced "such lamentations that merchants left their bargaining and women their distaffs and their weaving"—which may be meant to express that both men and women were diverted from what mattered to them most.

Other Familiar English Names for February

1. Andrew, Anne, Antony, Barbara, Henry, John, Mary-Ann, Paul, Peter, Raymund, Reginald
2. Andrew, Catherine, Joan, Laurence, Mary, Nicholas, Peter, Simon, Stephen
3. John, Mary
4. Joan, John, Joseph, Laurence
5. Adelaide, Elizabeth, Frances, Jerome
6. Alexander, Charles, Dorothy, Francis, James, John, Leonard, Martin, Matthew, Paul, Peter, Philip, Thomas
7. Antony, Giles, James, John, Juliana, Laurence, Luke, Philip, Richard, Thomas, William
8. Jerome, Josephine, Paul, Peter, Stephen
9. Miguel *is Spanish for* Michael; *there are no other familiar English names for today*
10. Arnold, Clare, Hugh, Katherine, Louise, Mary-Anne, Peter, William
11. Gregory, Mary *(for the apparitions at Lourdes)*, Peter
12. Antony, Felix, George, James, John, Thomas
13. Christina, Gilbert, Paul, Stephen
14. Luke, Vincent
15. *There are no familiar English names among those venerated today*
16. John, Joseph, Nicholas, Philippa
17. Agnes, Andrew, Anne, Clare, Francis, Gabriel, Gregory, James, Jerome, John, Laurence, Luke, Mary, Natalie, Paul, Peter, Thomas
18. Gertrude, John, Martin, William
19. Elizabeth, George, Peter
20. Leo *is the only other familiar name among those venerated today*
21. George, James, Mary, Maurice, Noel, Peter, Timothy
22. Isabel, Vincent
23. John, Josephine, Nicholas
24. Mark, Peter, Robert
25. Anne, Daniel, Dominic, Frances, Laurence, Robert, Sebastian
26. Andrew, Robert, Victor
27. Basil, Gabriel, Gregory, Luke, Mark, Mary, Roger
28. Antonia, Daniel

MARCH

Fourteen out of the fifteen saints in the Universal Calendar in March are retained here, the only exception being the 16th, the anniversary of the martyrdom of St John de Brébeuf, canonized in 1930 as one of the martyrs of North America. In this work he is included with his companions on their joint feast-day of 19 October, as in the new Roman Martyrology. St Clement Mary Hofbauer died on the 15th, a crowded day on which pride of place has to go to Louise de Marillac, and he is here moved forward one day. Rebecca Ar-Rayes is moved to the 24th from the 23rd, the actual anniversary of her death, as Turibius of Mogrovejo features in the Universal Calendar on that date and cannot be displaced, while Rebecca, canonized in 2001, the first woman saint from the Lebanon, also deserves an entry (if largely as indicative of Pope John Paul II's expressed desire to see more women saints and more saints from outside Europe). St John Climacus is moved back one day to the 29th, to allow an entry for the delightful Bd Restituta Kafka, the only nun beheaded under the Third Reich and surely the only Blessed known to have ordered "a pint of my usual" at the end of a day's work.

1

St David (about 520–589)

There is no contemporary account of the patron saint of Wales—Dewi in Welsh. He is mentioned in lists of saints dating from around 800, but the only "biography" was written about five hundred years after the supposed date of his death. This claims to have drawn on older accounts, but these have disappeared—if they ever existed. The author was the son of a bishop of St David's, so he was concerned to bring out the importance of the see. All later accounts rely on this one source, so basically they tell the same story, with various embellishments.

He is said to have been the son of Prince Sandda (or Sant, which means saint) and of St Non, commemorated on 3 March. His father dreamed that he would receive three gifts—a stag, a fish, and a swarm of bees. The stag represented his son's power over the tempter serpent, the fish his abstinence, and honey from the bees his holiness.

David was ordained priest and founded many monasteries (traditionally twelve, after the tribes of Israel and the apostles and perhaps to show that he converted the tribes of Wales), settling finally at Mynyw (Menevia, in Latin) in the south-western peninsula of Wales, now Pembrokeshire, where he and his community lived a life of extreme austerity, based on the practices of the monks in the Egyptian desert. They drank virtually only water from the local river, the Honthy, from which David was nicknamed *Aquaticus*, "waterman," and ate only bread and vegetables—including, if not exclusively, the local leeks. Their life was divided between hard physical work—including ploughing without the help of oxen—and prayer. They kept a strict vigil from Friday evening to Sunday morning, with only an hour's rest after Matins on Saturday. The verdict of St Gildas the Wise was that they were more abstemious than Christian!

David is supposed to have ruled this monastery until he was a very old man. Gerald of Wales, writing in the twelfth century, calls him "the great ornament and example of his age." A later version of his story, by Geoffrey of Monmouth, attributes these last words to him: "Be joyful, brothers and sisters. Keep the faith and do the little things you have seen and heard with me."

March 1st has always been the traditional day of his death, and his cult had spread beyond Wales to other regions of southern Britain by the tenth century. More than fifty churches were dedicated to him in South Wales before the Reformation. His emblem is a white dove descending, with a mound of earth below; a reference to the legend that while he was speaking at a local synod (at Brefi in Cardigan) a white dove came down on to his shoulder, while at the same time the earth rose up so that he could be heard more clearly. This is a poetic expression of his speaking with such conviction (against Pelagianism) that he was unanimously proclaimed head of the Church in Wales. Leeks are traditionally worn on St David's day to commemorate his eating of them. Glastonbury at one time claimed his relics, probably to encourage pilgrims from Wales to stop there on their way to Canterbury, where his feast-day was promulgated, but his shrine remains in St David's Cathedral, and his life is represented in mosaics at the east end of the church.

2

St Chad (died 672)

Chad came from a Northumbrian family that produced four priests, two of them, Chad and his brother Cedd, distinguished bishops. He was educated for a time by St Aidan at Lindisfarne, then crossed to Ireland, where he lived as a monk. He returned to England at some point, and it is probably there that he was ordained priest, but little or nothing is known of his life before Cedd died in 664, when King Oswy of Northumbria sent Chad to Canterbury to be consecrated as bishop of York (there being no bishops available nearer to hand to perform the consecration). On his arrival, Chad found that the archbishop of Canterbury had died, and he had to continue west into the kingdom of the West Saxons, where he was consecrated in a ceremony that seems to have been of somewhat dubious form.

He returned to Northumbria and began to evangelize the region energetically, showing humility by travelling on foot rather than on horseback. A complication arose when St Wilfrid (see 24 Apr.) returned from Gaul, where he had been sent by another king to be consecrated bishop. The new archbishop of Canterbury, Theodore, upheld Wilfrid's claim to the see of York, and Chad retired gracefully to the abbey of Lastingham, saying that he had never thought himself worthy of being a bishop anyway.

Others thought differently, however, and he was soon reappointed bishop in Menevia, with a see covering a huge area of the Midlands. Theodore reconsecrated him canonically and ordered him to use a horse for long journeys, helping him up on to one when he demurred. Chad established his see at Lichfield and was by all accounts an outstanding bishop for two and a half years. Plague was stalking the land in 672, and Chad fell victim to it. There is a delightful story told by Bede that a week before his death, angelic singing was heard coming down from heaven and filling the oratory in which Chad was praying. Chad opened the window and summoned his brethren to tell them to live in peace and in accordance with all he had taught them, for "The welcome guest who has visited many of our brethren has come to me today, and has deigned to summon me out of this world. Therefore return to the church and ask the brethren to commend my passing to our Lord in their prayers."

His bones were placed in the church of St Peter, where the present Lichfield Cathedral stands. Miracles were reported at his tomb, and his cult spread, with many churches dedicated to him in the Midlands in the Middle Ages. By the nineteenth century, Birmingham had emerged as the major industrial city of the region. It had a rapidly growing Catholic population and was made a Catholic bishopric (later archbishopric) when the Catholic hierarchy was restored. A cathedral was built on the site of a chapel dedicated to Chad, and he became the patron saint of the archdiocese. Some bones long claimed to be his relics and kept in the cathedral were radiocarbon dated to the seventh century in 1996, and some of these may be his.

God stirs the air and raises the winds; He makes the lightning flash and thunders out of heaven, to move the inhabitants of earth to fear Him and to remind them of judgment to come. He shatters their conceit and subdues their presumption by

recalling to their minds that awful day when heaven and earth will flame as He comes in the clouds with great power and majesty to judge the living and the dead. Therefore we should respond to His heavenly warnings with the fear and love we owe Him.

St Chad, in Bede, *Ecclesiastical History of the English People*, IV, 3

3

St Katharine Drexel (1858–1955)

Katharine was born into a family that had moved from being poor Austrian immigrants to wealthy bankers in two generations, typical of the American success story in the nineteenth century. She was the second of three sisters, brought up to a society life in Pennsylvania but devoutly Catholic. Their stepmother's example (their mother died when Katharine was born) showed the girls that their social status brought charitable duties with it. Katharine was carefully educated, including a tour of Europe—which did not impress her greatly—when she was fifteen. She "came out" in 1878, referring casually to the event as "a little party the other night where I made my debut." In the summers the sisters taught in a small school near the family country home.

The pastor of the local church there was Fr James O'Connor, who impressed Katharine by his concern for the American Indians. He saw that they were being forced to war by the injustice of continually broken treaties and by having their territories ever further reduced by the white settlers' drive westward. Katharine's stepmother died in 1883, and her father took the girls to Europe again. Katharine was fascinated by learning about her namesake St Catherine (see 29 Apr.) in Siena, and she returned determined to become a contemplative nun. Fr O'Connor counselled her to wait. Her father died in 1885, leaving the then enormous sum of $15 million, most in trust to the three daughters, the share of each one to pass to the surviving sister(s) on her death. Katharine lived longest and so eventually inherited the whole fortune. She was to use the income to remarkable effect.

Still searching for a vocation and more than ever concerned for the American Indians, with whose plight O'Connor (by then bishop of Nebraska) kept her in touch, Katharine went to Europe again, this time with the definite purpose of consulting Pope Leo XIII as to what her mission in life should be. "Why not become a missionary yourself, my child?" was the pope's reply. On her return, O'Connor invited her to visit missions in the north-west. She toured by rail (in a private coach) and met Chief Red Cloud. She had by now decided to found a new religious Order, but first she had to be trained in an existing one, so in 1888 she entered the convent of the Sisters of Mercy in Pittsburgh. By the time she took her vows in 1891, her intentions were becoming known, and postulants joined her. She took her final vows in 1895 and wanted to start work in the west immediately, but she was advised to wait. So the first convent of the new Congregation, Sisters of the Blessed Sacrament for Indians and Negroes, was in a conversion of the family's former summer house in Pennsylvania. Katharine was already helping twenty-six dioceses financially, giving money for schools, missions, and orphanages. She insisted that her own Congregation should be self-supporting and gave it no money. Requests for help poured in from mission territories. She travelled (now in a public rail coach) to Arizona to visit the Navajo Indians and financed the building of a mission for them. She braved racial prejudice to found a school for African-American children in Nashville, Tennessee.

When the Constitutions of her Congregation were due for revision in 1907, Mother Frances Xavier Cabrini (see 22 Dec.) advised her to go to Rome herself if she wanted any progress. This she did, and she received approval within a month. New schools and missions were financed all over the country. At the request of the archbishop of New Orleans, Katharine bought the former Southern University campus to start a training college for teachers to teach the African-American population. This became Xavier College and then Xavier University, the first Catholic university in the South for Indian and black students. Some years later she was able to see Xavier graduates helping to meet the increasing demand for education all over the South. She drove herself to speak in public, which she disliked, openly condemning segregation years ahead of her time. She was the main beneficiary of an Act of Congress exempting the income of anyone who gave more than 90 per cent of it to charity from taxes, and she was able to give away ever-increasing sums, including $650,000 for new premises for Xavier University in New Orleans.

Katharine continued with her travels and new foundations until, at the age of seventy-six, she suffered a stroke, which forced her to adopt something more like the contemplative style of life to which she had once aspired. The entire income from the Drexel trust came to her when her sister Louise died in 1945, and it all went on new foundations. The capital, however, was left to charities specified in her father's will, and when she died, aged ninety-seven, she had nothing to leave. For some seventy years, however, she had given all her great energies and income to the causes in which she so passionately believed. She died in the 1950s, the decade that saw American society begin to take seriously the human-rights issues she had pursued for so long. She was beatified by Pope John Paul II on 20 November 1988 and canonized by him in St Peter's Piazza on 1 October 2000.

4

St Casimir (1458–1484)

Casimir was the third of the thirteen children born to King Casimir IV of Poland and his wife, Elizabeth of Austria. He was their second son, born on 3 October 1458. He was educated with his two brothers by a distinguished historian from Cracow, a canon named John Dlugosz, who became something of a second father to the boys.

He is known to his countrymen as "The Peacemaker" for refusing to wage an unjust war, but the circumstances suggest that he was motivated by prudence rather than a sense of justice, and to his father his actions were more those of a coward. The nobles of Hungary had risen in revolt against their king, Matthias Corvinus, and appealed to Casimir IV to be able to make the young Casimir their king in his place. The Polish king sent his son, aged only fifteen, to lead an army into Hungary. Casimir then found that the Hungarian nobles were not going to fight for him against their king's considerable army and that his own troops had no stomach for the fight—hardly surprisingly, as their pay was in arrears—and were deserting in some numbers. Wisely, if not exactly in the heroic stamp expected of young princes of his time, he consulted his officers, who advised him to call off the expedition and retreat. In the meantime, Pope Sixtus IV had appealed to King Casimir to order his forces to withdraw, and the king agreed to discuss peace with Hungary. But when he found that his son had already ordered a retreat, he banished him to the castle of Donzki for three months.

Casimir vowed that he would never take up arms again against another Christian country (the only likely beneficiaries of such a war being the "infidel" Turks) and devoted himself to prayer and good works. He gave away everything he had to the poor, who in return called him "Defender of the poor." He pleaded with his father to redress whatever he saw as injustice being done to the poor and to pilgrims and captives. He lived most austerely and spent much of his time in church, at the office or Mass, and much of the night outside locked church doors waiting for them to reopen. Gentle and friendly with individuals, he was harsh on schismatics and persuaded his father not to restore churches they used.

He also vowed never to marry, even though a royal marriage had been arranged for him, with a daughter of Emperor Frederick III, and though doctors told him that his precarious health would be improved by married life. He replied that he knew no other life than Christ and predicted that he would soon be joined with Christ. This came true as he died of tuberculosis at the age of twenty-six. He was buried in Vilna (now Vilnius, capital of Lithuania), and miracles were soon reported at his tomb. The cult became so popular that King Sigismund petitioned Pope Leo X for his canonization, which was proclaimed in 1521. He had had a great devotion to the Blessed Virgin, and the popular hymn known in English as "Daily, daily sing to Mary" has often been called "St Casimir's hymn" and attributed to him. (It was in fact composed much earlier, by Bernard of Cluny in the twelfth century.) He often recited it, and a copy of it was buried with him. His protection was invoked by the Lithuanians in their conflicts with the Russians during the sixteenth and seventeenth centuries, and he was formally decreed patron saint of Lithuania in 1914: eight years later, such being the complications of eastern European politics, he was appointed one of the chief patrons of Russia. In 1948, in response to widespread local demand, it was claimed, Pope Pius XII proclaimed him, in addition, patron of the young people of Lithuania, then under (Soviet) Russian occupation. His cult still has a strong following among Polish and Lithuanian immigrants to the USA and Canada.

5

Bd Placide Viel (Victoire Eulalie Jacqueline Viel; 1815–1877)

Placide was born in Normandy, the eighth of eleven children. Her education in the local town was somewhat minimal, but she was devout and took catechism classes in her parish. Then, through a cousin of her father's, Sr Marie Viel, she was introduced to the community of the Sisters of the Christian Schools and their foundress, St Marie-Madeleine Postel, and was immediately drawn to both. So at the age of eighteen she left home to join this new religious Congregation, of which Sr Marie was bursar.

It was housed in the ruins of the abbey of Saint-Sauveur-le-Vicomte, once a great Benedictine abbey (suppressed at the time of the French Revolution), which Marie-Madeleine Postel had bought but had not yet been able to restore. Fourteen professed nuns and nine novices lived there in conditions of extreme poverty. Victoire loved the life and embraced every hardship with enthusiasm; she was clothed as a novice two years later, taking the name Placide in religion. The foundress reciprocated the admiration the novice felt for her and gave her a rapid succession of new posts, causing Sr Marie to become distinctly jealous. Placide was sent to Paris to beg for funds with which to restore the abbey church. She asked the queen and various ministers for grants and spent four years begging from door to door, weary, lonely, and often rebuffed. The foundress died in July 1846, and Placide found herself elected superior general as her successor. Sr Marie was one of only two who did not vote for her, thinking herself best qualified for the post.

Placide, horrified at her appointment, told the chapter that she needed to complete her fund-raising and proposed that Sr Marie should take charge of the day-to-day running of the house while she continued her travels. This was agreed for a year, but the situation was somehow extended over ten, during which she toured provincial France on foot. Whenever she returned to Saint-Sauveur she was humiliated by Sr Marie, who (aided and abetted by the chaplain) occupied her rooms, read her mail, and gave her orders in front of the community. It was a bizarre situation, which Placide was either unwilling or unable to resolve. She was freed from it only by Marie's death, which took place soon after the restoration of the abbey church had been completed.

For a further thirty years Placide was then able to behave as a true superior general. New foundations were made, schools, nursing homes, and orphanages built. By the time of her death there were over a thousand nuns, in one hundred and five convents. Placide had entirely justified the confidence the foundress had placed in her at a very early age, showing the total dedication that St Marie-Madeleine had seen in her, together with an organizational ability that she had perhaps not seen. Placide herself attributed all the achievements to the intercession of her revered foundress, whose beatification process she started. Marie-Madeleine was canonized in 1925, and Placide was beatified in 1951.

6

St Agnes of Bohemia (died around 1280)

Agnes spent the first twenty-eight years of her life being moved around by other people on the chessboard of the dynastic ambitions of the royal houses of Bohemia and Hungary in central Europe. She eventually decided that Christ was the only bridegroom for whom she cared, devoted herself entirely to him for the rest of her life, and was able to use her position to advance the cause of religious life in what is now the Czech Republic.

Machinations for an advantageous marriage began when she was only three years old. Her father, King Ottakar I of Bohemia, and mother, a sister of the king of Hungary, engaged her to Boleslaus of Silesia. He was the son of St Hedwig (see 17 July), who seems to have been influential in taking Agnes away from her parents and placing her in a monastery that she (Hedwig) had founded, where she could be suitably educated. This plan came to naught when Boleslaus died when Agnes was six. Three years later she was engaged again, this time to Henry, son of the emperor Frederick II. She was sent to the

Austrian court to learn German and other necessary accomplishments, but this plan was foiled by Duke Leopold of Austria, who arranged for his own daughter to marry Henry instead. Agnes was sent home, by now convinced she must live a life of consecrated virginity.

Two more attempts were made to marry her to royalty. The first suitor was King Henry III of England, but the arrangement failed. The next was Henry's widowed father, the emperor himself. He was supported by Agnes' brother, Wenceslaus, now king of Bohemia. Agnes appealed to Pope Gregory IX, pleading her lack of consent and long-felt desire to consecrate herself to Christ. He wrote to Agnes supporting her, and in the end Wenceslaus showed the letters to the emperor, who declared that he would have challenged any other suitor, but "I cannot take offence if she prefers the King of Heaven to me."

Agnes was finally free to devote herself and her possessions to God. Her father had brought the Franciscans to Prague, and she now built a friary for them, followed by a hospital and then a convent for Poor Clare nuns, the Second Order of Franciscans. The foundation was begun with five nuns sent from San Damiano by St Clare (see 11 Aug.) herself. Agnes took the veil there in 1236, and Clare adopted her as a spiritual daughter, writing, "I hold you more than any other in the greatest affection." Agnes spent some forty-four years as a Poor Clare, living a life of prayer and works of charity of the most menial sort she could find. She died, aged around eighty, some time after 1280. Her canonization had to wait seven hundred years, until in 1989, on the eve of the Czech "velvet revolution," Pope Paul II, always eager to inspire Catholics living under Communism, proclaimed her a saint.

Love with your whole heart the One who offered himself with his whole heart for you ... There is nothing greater than a person who is faithful. She is greater than the heavens, for no creature is capable of containing the creator, whereas she is his dwelling-place, his seat, and his throne'
from a letter from St Clare to St Agnes

7

SS Perpetua and Felicity (died 203)

Vivia Perpetua was a nursing mother from Carthage in North Africa, aged twenty-two when she was arrested, together with a slave girl named Felicity, who was pregnant and near to full term, and several others. The account of their subsequent interrogation, sentencing, and martyrdom has been preserved in an absolutely authentic account, part by Perpetua herself and part by an eye-witness, which is one of the great treasures from the early age of persecution.

Perpetua tells how they were baptized after a few days in captivity, how she agonized over whether to hand her infant son into the care of her mother and brother but was then allowed to keep him in prison, and how she resisted her father's renewed entreaties to renounce her new faith. She and the others were charged simply with being Christians and condemned to be thrown to wild beasts for refusing to sacrifice to the pagan gods. Their ordeal was set for the festival of Geta, whom the emperor Severus had proclaimed Caesar four years previously. Perpetua concludes her journal on the eve of their execution, writing, "Let whoever has a mind to do so write down what will take place at the actual games."

The eyewitness who takes up the story records that Felicity prayed that she would have her baby, as pregnant women could not be physically punished, and gave birth to a baby girl a month prematurely. The baby was taken away and nursed by "a certain sister." When Perpetua and Felicity were brought to the arena they were to be clothed as priestesses of Ceres, but Perpetua opposed this, and they were allowed to keep their own clothes until they were stripped. Perpetua's youth and the evidence that Felicity had obviously recently given birth so shocked the crowd that their tunics were put back on them. They were tossed by a savage heifer—it being thought inappropriate, apparently, for male beasts to be set on them—but Perpetua seemed not even to have noticed the attack and went to help the winded Felicity to her feet. The two women and their companions, who were also still alive despite encounters with a leopard and a somewhat reluctant bear, exchanged a kiss of peace and went to the place where they were to be finally despatched with the traditional Roman sword-thrust to the neck. The gladiator's sword struck Perpetua on a bone, and she screamed in agony, then guided the sword to the right place: "perhaps such a woman, feared as she was by the unclean spirit, could not die unless she herself had willed it," the eyewitness comments.

The bodies of the martyrs were buried in the Basilica Majorum in Carthage, where an ancient inscription was found in 1907. They were commemorated in all early calendars and martyrologies, and Perpetua and Felicity figure in the Procession of Martyrs in the great mosaic fresco decorating the nave of the basilica of San Apollinare Nuovo in Ravenna. Their feast was for some time celebrated on 6 March to make way for that of St Thomas Aquinas, but his has now been moved to 28 January and theirs has been restored to its original date.

Christ's martyrs feared neither death nor pain. He triumphed in them who lived in them; and they, who lived not for themselves but for him, found in death itself the way to life.
St Augustine

8

St John of God (1495–1550)

John was born in Portugal but spent most of his life in Spain. He typifies the extraordinary zeal and energy that filled the country after Columbus' "discovery" of America, but he became a *conquistador* in the service of the poor. His sobriquet "of God" derives from a vision he had of the child Jesus, who held up a half pomegranate (*granada* in Spanish and an emblem of charity) and a cross, saying to him, "John of God, Granada will be your cross."

Nothing in his early life indicated the direction his life was eventually to take. He seems to have been abducted from his native village by a visiting priest when he was eight. The priest left him in the Spanish border town of Oropeza, where the count's bailiff fostered him and gave him a sound education. He progressed from shepherd to estate manager and then joined the army of the emperor Charles V, who was at war with Francis I of France. A fall from a horse led him to implore the Virgin for his safety. He was then accused, unjustly, of helping himself to the army's booty and was to have been executed, but a sympathetic officer enabled him to escape. After four more years in Oropeza, he joined the count in an expedition to Hungary to fight the Turks.

After the expeditionary force had been disbanded on its return to Spain, John went back to the village of his birth. He was told that his mother had died of grief two weeks after his disappearance and that his father had then become a Franciscan. He resolved to follow his father's example and devote himself wholly to God. He resolved to work for Christians enslaved by the Moors in North Africa, and embarked from Gibraltar to Ceuta with a Portuguese family exiled to this enclave, where he undertook menial work to help feed this family when the father fell ill. He hoped for martyrdom but was eventually advised to go back to Spain.

He became a travelling seller of religious books and images, and this brought him to Granada in 1536, by which time he was forty-two. There he heard Bd John of Avila (see 11 May) preach on the joys experienced by those who suffer for Christ. He threw himself into a paroxysm of repentance, crying and tearing his hair and clothes. He ran around the streets doing this until he was eventually locked up in the lunatic asylum. The prescribed treatment for his condition was flogging and solitary confinement, but months of this failed to cure him. John of Avila heard of his plight, came to visit him, and told him firmly that he had done enough penance and that it was time to do something useful. John immediately became calm and was released, but he stayed on to minister to the other inmates as well as visiting the sick in other hospitals.

He went on pilgrimage to the shrine of Our Lady of Guadalupe, where he had a vision of the Virgin holding out clothing, which he was to use to clothe the child Jesus. The meaning was clear to him: he was to clothe the naked Christ, feed the hungry Christ, visit the sick Christ—wherever he was to be found. Back in Granada he took on an empty house, somehow acquired forty-six beds and mattresses, and in no time was running a highly efficient hospital, with all the beds occupied. He introduced standards of hygiene virtually unknown in his day but was even more concerned with his patients' spiritual hygiene, with daily prayers and Mass and Confession and the last rites available as needed. John spent his days nursing and his nights begging, preparing vegetables, and praying, reducing his sleep to an hour a night. The inhabitants of Granada told him he could not possibly keep the hospital going by begging, and they then found themselves caught up in his miracle of loaves and fishes as they realized they had to provide food, clothing, medicines, and what professional services they could. John was soon moving the hospital into a larger building and setting up a night shelter for the homeless and a refuge for prostitutes.

His work came to the notice of the bishop of Túy. John came before him dressed in the rags of a beggar to whom he had just given his own clothes. The bishop gave him a religious habit, which he kept for the rest of his life. Helpers began to join him in increasing numbers, some of them former sceptics who were converted by apparent miracles showing them the error of their ways. John's heroism single-handedly achieved the rescue of the inmates of the royal hospital during a serious fire. His own hospital again became too small, and this time the archbishop of Granada persuaded leading citizens of the town to buy a disused monastery for him and the civic authorities to pay the medical expenses.

By now John had been working unstintingly and begging for thirteen years. His reputation reached the Spanish court at Valladolid, where he was received kindly and showered with gifts—which he gave to the poor of Valladolid. After a madcap episode trying to gather firewood for the poor from a flooded Genil River in Granada and then trying to rescue a drowning helper, his health finally collapsed. Despite his protests, he was taken by a lady who had been a generous helper to be cared for in her house, where he died on his fifty-fifth birthday, kneeling before an altar set up in his room. His body was buried in the church of the Minims, and the whole of Granada accompanied the funeral procession. In 1586 Pope Sixtus V established the Brothers of St John of God, which is still active throughout the world, and of which he is regarded as the founder. He was canonized in 1690 and is the patron of hospitals and the sick and also of booksellers, in memory of his itinerant bookselling mission.

9

St Frances of Rome (Francesca Busso; 1384–1440)

Francesca was born in the Trastevere district of Rome, to parents who were both wealthy and deeply religious. With the Benedictine spiritual director her mother chose for her, Francesca planned an ascetic religious life for herself, but her parents had already chosen a husband for her, and at the age of thirteen she became the wife of Lorenzo Ponziano. He never treated her with anything except love and respect, but she was not happy. Her sister-in-law, Vanozza, found her weeping one day; Frances confided her longing for a life devoted to God and found a kindred spirit. Together they planned how to reconcile their wishes with married life.

They began visiting the sick and distributing alms and set up an oratory in the family palace, where they could pray once their day's duties were done. Frances gave birth to her first son in 1400 and the following year was appointed head of the household on the death of her mother-in-law, despite her protests that the post should be Vanozza's. She was loved and respected by the whole household. At about this time, however, outside events began affecting the family and Rome. A war over the kingdom of Naples brought famine and disease. Frances distributed the family's supplies to the hungry, and when there was nothing left (except provisions for the family's basic needs, which her father-in-law insisted on keeping in the cellar), she went out begging.

Struggles between pope and antipope following the Great Schism of the West reduced Rome to a battleground in 1408, by which time Frances had had another son. The elder son was seized as a hostage, and Lorenzo was stabbed. Frances' son was given back to her when two horses on which he was to have been taken away refused to budge, and she gradually nursed her husband back to health. The son was taken once more and exiled with his father. The family palace was ruined, but Frances and Vanozza opened a hospital in what remained for victims of the plague that was ravishing the city. Her infant second son caught this and died; Frances was very ill with it for several months but survived.

She developed remarkable powers of healing (which she attributed to a guardian angel visible to her), and the fame of these spread all over Rome. She also predicted the end of the Great Schism, and once Martin V had been elected sole pope and peace was restored, Lorenzo and the elder son returned from exile. Lorenzo's health was broken, but he willingly took second place in his wife's concerns as she set about forming a group of like-minded women into a religious community. This was known first as the Oblates of Mary and then as Oblates of Tor de Specchi, after the tower into which they moved in 1433. They were not religious Sisters and did not take vows, but they were committed to living in common (which Frances could not do while her husband was still alive) and devoting their lives to works of mercy. Frances refused to be called foundress and ensured that all were loyal to the first superior, Agnes de Lellis, but when Lorenzo died she entered the community, whereupon Agnes insisted on resigning and compelled her to become superior. Frances' visions and ecstasies increased as her health failed. She died in the evening of 9 March 1440, uttering the words, "The angel has finished his work. He is beckoning me to follow." Her body was buried in the chapel of the oblates in Santa Maria Nuova, which was later renamed Santa Francesca Romana after her. She was canonized in 1608.

10

St John Ogilvie (1580–1615)

Urbane, cultured, witty, and fearless, John Ogilvie was in many ways typical of both the higher echelons of Scottish society, from which he came, and of the Society of Jesus, which he joined. His father, a baron, embraced Presbyterianism; his mother, who died when he was only two, had been at least sympathetic to Catholicism. John was brought up as a Calvinist but sent to both Catholic and Reformed Europe for his continued education. The open intellectual climate he found there led him to ponder Catholic claims and eventually to ask to be received into the Roman Catholic Church.

He studied at the Scots College in Louvain for two years, then at Regensburg, then at the Jesuit College in Olmütz, entering the Jesuit novitiate in Bohemia in 1599. He was ordained in Paris in 1610, the year before the last two Jesuits working in Scotland were obliged to leave as persecution intensified. Ogilvie was determined to return to Scotland, but it was three years before the Jesuit general, Aquaviva, could be persuaded to let him face such risk. He arrived there in November 1613, ministering first in his home county of Banffshire and then in Edinburgh, with an interruption for a visit first to London and then to his superiors in France, the purpose of which remains a mystery. He returned to Scotland in April 1614 together with a fellow-Jesuit and a secular priest, and they made converts in Glasgow and Edinburgh. In October he was betrayed to the Episcopal archbishop of Glasgow by a potential convert, seized by his waiting servants, and taken to the provost's house.

The archbishop, John Spottiswoode, punched him in the face, saying, "Sir, you are overbold to say your Masses in a reformed city," to which Ogilvie replied, "You act like a hangman, not a bishop, in striking me." Saying Mass was a treasonable offence, and when a former benefactor handed Ogilvie's Mass kit to the authorities, his fate was effectively sealed. The archbishop, who was also a privy councillor, presided at his trial, which became a personal contest between the two. Ogilvie refused to incriminate himself, saying it was up to witnesses to prove that he had said Mass. After a day's interrogation, he became feverish and was left in peace for two days. He then spent two months with a heavy iron bar tied to his feet, so that he could not move around, and was brought back to trial. This time he was asked to reveal the names of other Catholics, but he steadfastly refused, saying, "In betraying my neighbour I should offend God and kill my own soul."

He was then deprived of sleep for nine days in an attempt to weaken his mind, being prodded with pins and daggers and then dragged to his feet and dropped again. This brought him so near death that he was allowed two days' rest before being brought back to court. He continued to refuse to name names and responded to all threats with such good humour that his persecutors eventually found themselves joking and drinking with him. Even Spottiswoode relaxed to the point of showing him round his house and garden—and sent his wife away to Edinburgh, suspecting her of being too fond of the charming Jesuit. After two months of a relatively easier prison regime, during which the fame of his courage and wit spread all over and beyond Scotland, he was brought back to court and, inevitably, found guilty of treason. The sentence was hanging and quartering, but the crowd at his execution the following day was so sympathetic that he was allowed to hang until he was dead. He was beatified in 1929 and canonized by Pope Paul VI in 1976.

11

The Martyrs of Córdoba (between 822 and 859)

In 711, Moors from North Africa overran most of Spain, imposing Islam on the people of a country with a flourishing and orthodox Christian Church. Córdoba became the capital from which a vastly more sophisticated civilization spread across the land. There were irrigation systems, public schools and baths, sumptuous palaces, paved roads, and a great flowering of art and literature. None of this, however, could be achieved without control of the subject population. There was not outright persecution of Christians, but they were subject to discriminatory taxes and restrictions. Some, including even bishops, thought this a price worth paying for the benefits of living and working within the system. Others could not see very much difference between the two monotheistic faiths, Christianity and Islam, and there was a good deal of intermarriage. Gradually, though, a more principled, even fanatical, resistance began to take shape, as people saw their most cherished values and beliefs being threatened.

Resistance began in Córdoba itself, and its leading figures were priests. A priest at the basilica of St Zoilo, Eulogius, was appointed head of the school attached to it. From there he fired a generation of young Christians with ideals of resistance—to the point of martyrdom if need be. Such a radical concept was inconceivable to the Moors, who even called a council of bishops in the hope that they would put a stop to the movement. But Eulogius, learned in the scriptures and early church history, could quote examples to kindle the enthusiasm of the radical Christians.

Two brothers, Adulphus and John, had been executed in 822 for insulting Islam. After that there were no more martyrdoms for twenty-eight years. What the Moors could not tolerate was hearing Mohammed called a false prophet. A priest named Prefectus was accused of doing just this in 850. He at first denied the charge, but in prison he admitted it, and he was beheaded. Isaac, from a wealthy Christian family, fluent in Arabic, had held a high post in local administration but had abandoned it and joined a monastery three years earlier. He now came out of the monastery and began to attack those he had worked with previously. He was accused of insulting the Prophet and was also beheaded. His body was then burned to ashes and thrown in the river Guadalquivir, so that no relics could be kept. Far from ending the movement, this savagery encouraged it, and eight more Christians, mostly priests or deacons, openly insulted Mohammed and were executed over the next few weeks.

Two women, Flora and María, daughters of mixed marriages and therefore expected to follow Islam, publicly protested their Christianity in the face of persecution by Flora's brother and were imprisoned. To encourage them, Eulogius, himself imprisoned in the autumn of 851, wrote a long letter, known as the *Documentum Martyrii*, a passionate statement of the value of absolute loyalty to Christ. The two women again refused to recant and were finally beheaded. Other groups—priests, monks, hermits, and married couples, and unmarried lay men and women—were put to death in January, August, and September of the following year.

In October 852 a new and far more severe Moorish king, Muhammad I, came to power in Córdoba. Far from seeking to calm things down, as his predecessor had tried to do, his solution was to increase financial and other penalties on Christians. Some abjured their faith, but others still came forward seeking martyrdom, and many were executed, singly or in groups, over the next three years. Eulogius, seen as the instigator of the movement, was eventually persuaded to discourage Christians from actively seeking martyrdom. Then he himself was arrested, for sheltering an "apostate" young woman, whom he had encouraged to run away from her family. He had by now been elected archbishop of Toledo and was widely respected, even by the

Moorish palace officials who formed a tribunal to try him. In the face of his repeated affirmations of faith, they had no alternative but to sentence him to death, and he was beheaded on 11 March 859. It is his execution that establishes the commemoration of all these martyrs on today's date. Lucretia, the young woman he had helped, was herself martyred four days later.

Do you think you are going to destroy my body with a whip? If you want to return my soul to God, you had better whet your sword. I am a Christian, just as I have always been. I confess that Christ, son of Mary, is the true Son of God.

Eulogius, rejecting the lesser but ignominious penalty of whipping

12

Bd Aloysius Orione (1872–1940)

This great social activist may be seen as following in the footsteps of St Francis de Sales (see 24 Jan.), John (Don) Bosco (see 31 Jan.), and others who worked in the northern Italian region of Piedmont where he was born. He was the fourth child of working-class parents from the village of Pontecurone, in the Po valley due north of Genoa, and was christened Luigi after an elder brother who had died. His father was a road-mender and subscribed to the prevailing anticlericalism; his mother was deeply devout and was delighted when he tried his vocation as a Franciscan. A bout of pneumonia led to his rejection, and he went instead to the Salesian college at Valdocco in the suburbs of Turin, where he was personally received by Don Bosco. Following possibly bad advice, though, he did not join the Salesians but went to the diocesan seminary at Tortona.

He flourished academically there and also began seeking out the underprivileged of all sorts—the sick in hospital, prisoners, and orphans. His ministrations included playing the mandolin outside the prison walls and organizing sports for boys in the cathedral, to which the bishop, unsurprisingly, put a stop. He then determined to start a school for boys, a risky venture at a time when education was firmly in the hands of a secular State, but permission was granted and the Collegio Santa Chiara opened with one hundred and fifty pupils in 1891. Luigi was still a seminarian, four years from ordination, but already pursuing the sort of visions that were to inspire the rest of his life.

The decade after his ordination in 1895 was one of progress and conflict. He was invited to Sicily, where the bishop of Noto offered him buildings and land for a school and an agricultural training centre for less academic pupils—a course he had already followed at Santa Chiara. He gathered followers, though not yet a regular Congregation, and put them to work wherever he saw a need. He became a popular preacher, in demand all over the place. His bishop tried to bring all this activity under diocesan control—and to persuade Luigi (by now known as Don Orione) that he was right, to which Don Orione's reply was that if he tried to stop the Lord's work in this way he should not in conscience say Mass the next day. Don Orione and his helpers, organized and approved in 1903 as the Congregation of the Little Work of Divine Providence, had become an unstoppable force.

He was a great admirer of Pius X, with whom he had a first audience in 1906. But his charity extended to offering a home to priests dismissed on suspicion of Modernist tendencies, and a second audience in 1908 might have been more difficult. In the event the pope sent him away with a blessing. He went to Messina in Sicily to organize relief and rebuilding work after a devastating earthquake in December 1908, but he was resented as an interfering northener and eventually resigned. In 1915 he was exhausting himself once more trying to care for five thousands orphans following another major earthquake, this time in the Abruzzi.

He had long wanted to send helpers out to South America to minister to the huge numbers of Italian immigrants, particularly in Brazil and Argentina. He was able to send the first of these in 1913, but he himself did not visit the continent until after the First World War, in 1921. Hospitals, orphanages, and agricultural schools were established, and he returned in 1934 to see substantial progress. In Italy, the coming of Mussolini brought State intervention in everything, but Don Orione would have nothing to do with the Fascists, declaring that "Our spirit and theirs have nothing in common." His spirit was one of total reliance on what he—with complete confidence—saw as "the Lord's way." He foresaw a terrible future, but this did not lessen his confidence in the eventual triumph of good. He died before the full horrors of the Second World War had engulfed Italy. He was beatified by Pope John Paul II in 1980, and some four thousand members of his Congregation carry on his work of uncompromising charity throughout Italy and all over the world.

Let us be truly sons of Divine Providence and trust wholly in God. We are not amongst those doom-sayers who think that the world will end tomorrow. Corruption and evil are indeed rampant, but I still maintain that God will triumph in the end.
  Bd Aloysius Orione

13

Bd Agnellus of Pisa (about 1194–1232)

The future founder of the English Franciscan province was recruited into the Order by St Francis (see 4 Oct.) himself when Francis visited Pisa, probably in 1211. Six years later the chapter decided that the Friars Minor should expand into France, and Francis appointed Agnellus, then a deacon, as leader of the group entrusted with making foundations there. They opened a first house at Saint-Denis, on the outskirts of Paris, soon followed by others in the region. Agnellus then took the significant step of opening a friary for Franciscan students at the university of Paris, thereby associating the Franciscans with the most influential seat of learning at the time. This in some sense was an early departure from the founding spirit of the Order, as Francis himself had a certain distrust for learning, which he saw as possibly leading to ambition and away from the overriding ideal of holy poverty. Agnellus, however, kept the commitment to poverty at the forefront of all his works.

After seven years in France, Agnellus was designated leader of a group entrusted with crossing the Channel and making foundations in England. This group, eight strong, including three Englishmen, landed at Dover in September 1224 and moved on to Canterbury, where four of them stayed, lodged in a building known as the Poor Priests' House. This was used as a school by day, so they could emerge from one cramped room only at night. Despite cold, damp, and a miserable diet, they remained cheerful and impressed the archbishop of Canterbury, Stephen Langton, with their apostolic spirit.

Four of the friars had moved to London, where Agnellus joined them later. Two of these, both English, then pressed on to Oxford, probably with the original intention of seeking recruits among the students. Agnellus established a school of theology at the university, repeating the association between the Order and learning that he had brought about in Paris. The English province soon had the highest academic standard in the entire Order, but Agnellus kept a steady focus on poverty throughout the debates that troubled the Order during the years after Francis' death in 1226. He engaged the great scholar Robert Grosseteste as lecturer at the Oxford school, and he was to be followed by other intellectual giants including Roger Bacon, Duns Scotus (now Bd; see 8 Nov.), and William of Ockham. From Oxford, the friars spread to Cambridge, where they helped to establish the faculty of theology, though they were never as prominent there as they were at Oxford.

Agnellus himself was concerned primarily to live the Franciscan ideal of poverty and to communicate the Franciscan spirit to all with whom he came into contact. He inspired those he received into the Order, and his reputation spread to the court, where King Henry II became a friend and engaged him to use his qualities of gentleness and tact to negotiate with the rebel leader Earl Marshall. (This is related by the chronicler Matthew Paris.) He undertook an exhausting last journey to Italy and on his return died from a prolonged bout of dysentery on 3 March 1232, at the early age of not yet forty. He was never formally beatified, but his cult was confirmed by Leo XIII in 1892. The English Franciscans celebrate his feast on 10 September.

Where there is poverty and joy, there is neither covetousness nor avarice.
Where there is patience and humility, there is neither anger nor worry.
Where there is love and wisdom, there is neither fear nor ignorance.
St Francis of Assisi

14

St Matilda (about 895–968)

Matilda both enjoyed and was imprisoned by her status in life. Her father was a count of Westphalia and her mother a member of the royal house of Denmark. Her upbringing was entrusted to a grandmother who was abbess of Erfurt. From there she emerged beautiful, learned, and devout, and in due course she married Henry, son of Duke Otto of Saxony. Henry's chief interest was falconry, from which he derived his nickname of "The Fowler," but the marriage seems to have been a happy one. By 919 Henry had become king of Germany and was engaged in constant wars. The piety of the time had no difficulty in attributing his successes as much to Matilda's prayers as to his prowess. When he died in 936, she immediately took off all her jewels as a sign that she renounced the trappings of her position.

She had already been living more like a religious than a queen, noted especially for the generosity of her almsgiving, which was to threaten the royal revenues. Her five children included a son nicknamed "the quarrelsome" and a future canonized archbishop of Cologne. The elder son, Otto, succeeded to the throne on his father's death, but Matilda encouraged her younger son, Henry, to oppose him. The uprising was defeated and Otto generously acceded to his mother's request and made Henry duke of Bavaria. Both these sons agreed that their mother's scale of almsgiving had to be reduced and urged her to take the veil. She wryly remarked that it was good to see them united, if only to prosecute her, and retired to her birthplace.

The affairs of the kingdom immediately took a turn for the worse, and Otto, prompted by nobles, clergy, and his wife, eventually persuaded her to forgive him, to return to court and resume her almsgiving. When he journeyed to Rome to be crowned Holy Roman Emperor, he left the kingdom in her hands. Henry, on the other hand, never asked her forgiveness, treated his subjects badly, and died, to her great distress, in what she could only consider a state of mortal sin.

After Easter 965, when a great family gathering was held in Cologne, Matilda spent most of her time in her monastic foundations. By late 967 she was seriously ill at Nordhausen, where a former lady-in-waiting, Richburga, was abbess. She gave orders that she should be moved to Quedlinburg, where it had been agreed between her husband and herself that they should both be buried. She was moved there in January 968, and on the way her grandson, now Bishop William of Mainz, heard her Confession. She wanted to give him a present, but there was nothing left except the shroud, or winding-sheet, intended to wrap her body. "Give it to William," she ordered; "He will need it before I do." Indeed he did, dying twelve days before her. She also said she would prove the truth of the proverb that families will always find something for a wedding or a funeral, and as her body lay in church, her daughter Gerberga arrived with a gold-embroidered cloth with which to drape the casket.

Matilda was venerated locally as a saint from the moment of her death. She is often shown in statues and paintings with a church or a bag of money in her hands to indicate her generosity to the poor and the religious foundations she made.

15

St Louise de Marillac (1591–1660)

The foundress of the Daughters (now Sisters) of Charity came from a complicated background, which eventually helped her relate to all levels of society. Her father was Louis de Marillac, who came from a distinguished family in the Auvergne region of south-central France, and she was born between his first and second marriages. He recognized her as his daughter, thereby removing a great deal of the stigma attaching then to illegitimacy. He also made financial provision for her upbringing and education, but after his death she was removed from a fashionable convent and placed in the care of a "poor spinster"—possibly her natural mother—who ran an informal orphanage. Louise wanted to become a nun but was discouraged by her spiritual director on the grounds of chronic ill health. Marriage was the only remaining option.

A "suitable" husband was found in the person of Antoine le Gras, secretary to the queen's household. It seems to have been a fairly loveless marriage, though Louise was a dutiful wife in every way. Then misfortunes piled in on her: the son born to them proved slow-witted and awkward; the queen was banished and Antoine was left without an income; a rash attempt to help a family to whose children he became tutor deprived him of all his assets; his health collapsed. Louise saw all this as punishment for abandoning her wish to become a nun and was plunged into years of agonizing self-doubt. Antoine died in 1625, and Louise made a vow never to marry again, to which she added the religious vows of chastity, poverty, and obedience. She consulted St Francis de Sales (see 24 Jan.) and his friend and disciple Pierre Camus, bishop of Belley, who asked St Vincent de Paul (see 27 Sept.) to take care of her. But Vincent never did things without due reflection, and Louise's spiritual life remained locked in observance and scruple until she was in her late thirties.

Then Vincent found the way to unlock her potential. She had moved close to the seminary where his Mission Priests were working. They were funded and helped by "Ladies of Charity," mainly aristocratic women who carried out charitable works in parishes following outline schemes proposed by Vincent. But they lacked impetus and organization, as well as tending to send their maids rather than get their own hands dirty. Vincent gave Louise the task of surveying their activities and proposing improvements. It was something positive she discovered she could do and which she found rewarding. She came out of her depression and flung herself into the work. She and Vincent soon found that they needed a different class of women to penetrate where social deprivation was at its worst. Vincent proposed (in terms that might sound patronizing today) "country girls," as being artless, open, not stubbornly attached to their opinions, egalitarian in spirit. ... Louise set about recruiting and training such. The first four were housed in her own apartment in 1633; three years later numbers had increased to fifteen and they had to find a larger house. And so it went on: foundations spread into the suburbs of Paris and then into the provinces.

This was the time when no "gadding about" was allowed to female religious (as the contemporary Mary Ward found to her cost), so the Daughters could not become a religious Congregation as such, since the essence of their work was to be wherever they were most needed. Vincent told them: "Your convent will be the house of the sick; your cell, a hired room; your chapel, the parish church; your cloister, the streets of the city or the wards of the hospital; your enclosure, obedience; your grating, the fear of God; your veil, holy modesty." So they simply lived in communities and took annual vows of poverty. Louise controlled the expansion with ability and prudence, starting with careful selection. Certain qualities were needed for carrying out such physically and emotionally exhausting work, and cheerfulness was essential. She was as much concerned with the Sisters' spiritual formation as with their activities She and

119

Vincent fostered their development through monthly "conferences," at which even the newest and shyest recruits were invited to contribute their thoughts. The two worked together in firm friendship until by 1659 both were becoming infirm. Louise, feeling herself dying, asked Vincent to come and see her one last time, but he was too ill to cross the road and sent the simple message, "Go in peace." She died on 15 March 1660 and was canonized by Pope Pius XI in 1934. The Sisters of Charity, for centuries familiar as "butterfly Sisters" on account of their distinctive headdress (that of French seventeenth-century peasant costume), are still active all over the world and have inspired a whole family of Congregations modelled on their principles.

When we are set free from all attachment to this world and to the senses, from all attachment to our own self-love and our own free will and even from attachment to our delight in Christ and in his presence, when we have created a complete void within ourselves, the Holy Spirit will come into it and make us live with a divine life.
Louise de Marillac

16

St Clement Mary Hofbauer (Johannes Hofbauer; 1751–1820)

Born in Moravia (now the eastern part of the Czech Republic, then in the Habsburg Empire), Johannes Hofbauer was the ninth of twelve children. His father died when Johannes was six, and at the age of fifteen he was apprenticed to a baker as he lacked the means to attend the diocesan seminary. He became a solitary for a time, but the emperor banned all hermitages, and Johannes was forced to return to the bakery trade, this time in Vienna. This was his first encounter with the doctrine of "Josephinism" (named after Emperor Joseph)—that the State should have control over religious institutions—of which he was to become a leading opponent.

He went on three pilgrimages to Rome and on the third joined the Redemptorists, founded some fifty years earlier by St Alphonsus de'Liguori (see 1 Aug.). He had by then abandoned further attempts at being a hermit and realized that his true vocation was that of missioner, the purpose of the Redemptorists. After his profession, at which he took the names Clement Mary, and ordination he was sent to Lithuania, the first member of the relatively new Congregation to be sent north of the Alps. He went with one of his old pilgrimage companions, who had been professed with him, and they were joined by another, who abandoned his hermit's life to become a novice. They never reached Lithuania, as the papal nuncio held on to them in Warsaw to minister to its several thousand Germans, there being no other German-speaking priests owing to the suppression of the Jesuits in 1773. They established a mission at St Benno's Church, where they acquired a Polish novice and were soon preaching in both German and Polish and making converts. The mission grew, opening an orphanage and a school for boys, starting confraternities and other associations, and sending missioners elsewhere, including to their original destination in Lithuania. But in 1808 this was brought to an end when Napoleon suppressed religious Orders. Clement Mary and his companions were arrested and imprisoned in a fortress on the banks of the Oder. The influence of their hymn-singing on their fellow-prisoners and crowds that gathered outside soon forced the authorities to send them away, each back to his native country. Clement Mary returned to Vienna after being imprisoned once more on the Austrian frontier.

There he ministered in the Italian quarter and then became chaplain to the Ursuline nuns and rector of the church attached to their convent. From there his preaching and ministry in the confessional and visiting the sick initiated a religious revival in the city. Through his friendship with Prince Ludwig of Bavaria he exercised influence at the Congress of Vienna to prevent the establishment of a German national Church independent of the papacy. This was his victory over the "Josephinism" that had cut short his earlier career as a hermit. He also founded a Catholic college, the students of which became influential in many religious and secular fields. While he obviously worked to spread the "true faith," he was, for his time, unusually broadminded in outlook, writing to a friend in 1816: "If the Reform in Germany grew and held its ground, it was not due to heretics and philosophers but to men who truly aspired to interior religion."

He became the object of popular admiration in the city, but he had his enemies, supporters of Josephinism, who tried to have him prevented from preaching or even expelled from the city, and who called him a Vatican spy. The new emperor, Francis I, however, supported him and even hinted at formal recognition of Redemptorist houses in German-speaking territories, which Clement Mary prophesied would come about soon after his death. He died on 15 March 1820, and the Viennese crowded the streets as his body was taken to the cathedral. He was canonized in 1909 and declared patron saint of Vienna. The Redemptorists regard him as the second founder of their Order.

17

St Patrick (about 390–about 450)

The patron saint of Ireland left precious indications of his life in two surviving works from his hand, the *Confessions*, written toward the end of his life in response to apparent criticism, and the *Letter to the Soldiers of Coroticus*, a protest to a British warlord at the piratical seizure of some of his Irish converts. Between them they provide a self-portrait of some depth, possibly unique to the period. Later Lives, loaded with wonder-working of a boastful nature, in competition with Druids and set against a totally unhistorical background, rather detract from the picture he himself has provided.

His origins lay in the Carlisle district of north-western Britain, in the last decades of Roman rule there. He gives a name to the village of his birth, but it has never been identified convincingly. His family was one of relatively wealthy clerics: his grandfather had been a priest, and his father was a deacon (clerical marriage being permitted at the time) as well as an alderman of Carlisle. The household seems to have been more formally than devoutly Christian. When not yet sixteen, Patrick was captured by a marauding band from northern Ireland, together with some of his father's slaves, and spent six years there, either in the north-west or possibly herding sheep on Mount Slemis in Co. Antrim in the north-east. The experience changed his personality: in adversity he learned to cast himself on God's mercy and to rely on the power of prayer. He describes being guided by a series of vivid dreams and feeling the Spirit working within him.

He escaped and after a long trek found a ship that landed him on some desolate shore after three days. This might have been Wales or Cornwall. The crew all left the ship and wandered for many days without finding any trace of human habitation. Patrick told them that God would provide, and they came upon a herd of wild pigs and found wild honey. Patrick found his way back to his family, who begged him never again to leave them. At some stage he was ordained deacon and then priest, and he visited Gaul during the time he spent back with his family. But another guiding dream told him to go back to Ireland. He spent some years considering this, and in the end was certainly sent by "seniors" (bishops) in the British church, who consecrated him and sent him as missionary bishop. He sold his patrimony to finance the expedition, prudently deciding not to rely on the bishop financially. It is possible that Pope Leo the Great either commissioned him directly to go to Ireland or did so through the British bishops.

He spent the rest of his life evangelizing Ireland. He was not the first to attempt this: Palladius had preceded him in 431, but his mission seems to have had little lasting impact. Tradition places Patrick's mission in the north, with Armagh as its focus, but Patrick himself provides virtually no geographical clues, and associations with Croagh Patrick and Lough Derg arose through later legend. What Patrick does provide, in the manner of St Paul, is a personal account of his character and mission. Determined yet tender, resolute yet relying entirely on God, he obviously loved his converts deeply. This led to his fury when some were kidnapped by the soldiers of Coroticus: he feared that their vows of virginity would be broken by force and excommunicated the soldiers, something he was probably not entitled to do. This may have induced the British bishops to conduct an investigation into the activities of this lone missionary, thereby producing his apology for his actions in the *Confessions*.

What can we know about the nature of his mission? The Romans never conquered Ireland, and society there had not been urbanized, as it had in Britain. It revolved around largely nomadic tribes or clans. The people worshipped several gods and goddesses, though their religious beliefs are difficult to reconstruct. Patrick, who converted many thousands to Christianity, accused them of worshipping "idols and filthy things" and would have regarded them as uncivilized. He would have led a nomadic life, and he encouraged many of his converts to settle as monks or nuns, or simply to embrace celibacy in their own homes. He thus laid the foundations of the dominant influence of the monastery rather than the diocese (impossible with no settled society) in the Irish Church. He preached a simple but compelling trinitarian doctrine of God's love and providence, redemption through Christ, and the dwelling of the Spirit in people's hearts. The only book he knew was the Latin Bible, and he would have passed on the basic education this gave him to sons of kings and lesser chiefs who were "fostered" with him as his influence grew, in accordance with custom.

We do not know where or when he died, and his burial place is unknown. Even when the monks of Armagh were propagating his cult some two centuries later, they laid no claim to his relics. He died of natural causes, not martyred as he had aspired to be. He is not mentioned in annals or chronicles until 632, but his works were certainly copied and remembered, and they tell us enough to secure his lasting title of "Apostle to the Irish People." Irish missionaries have since taken his spirit, along with legends of him, all over the world.

You can see that we are witnesses that the gospel has been preached as far as the point where there is no one beyond.
St Patrick, *Confessions*, 34, trans. R. P. C. Hanson

18

St Cyril of Jerusalem (about 315–386)

Cyril was appointed bishop of Jerusalem in 350 or 351. Before that, virtually nothing is known about his life, except that he was ordained priest in 345. As a priest he delivered the influential series of Lenten and Easter sermons for catechumens and the newly baptized on which his reputation rests and which earned him the title of Doctor of the Church as relatively recently as 1882. He held office at a time of controversy and conflict over the human and divine natures in Christ, in which he tried to seek peaceful resolutions while upholding orthodox doctrine against the Arians.

His appointment as bishop of Jerusalem must have had the approval of Acacius, bishop of Caesarea and metropolitan of Palestine, with whom he was later to come into conflict over doctrine and precedence. The relationship between the two sees had been rather ambiguously defined at the Council of Nicaea in 325, with Jerusalem called a "succession of honour." Acacius was certainly not going to have Cyril's bishopric being accorded more honour than his and summoned a local synod to judge Cyril. Cyril refused to attend and in his absence was found guilty of insubordination, of selling church property to feed the poor in a time of famine, and finally of being a *homoousian*. This last meant that he upheld the Nicene teaching that Christ was "of one substance" with the Father and so had a fully divine as well as a fully human nature, as opposed to the Arians (the dominant party at the synod), who denied that Christ had a divine nature. Cyril was exiled and went to Tarsus, where he was warmly received. He was eventually reinstated by the Council of Seleucia two years later, to the fury of Acacius.

Acacius did not give up his vendetta and made fresh accusations against Cyril to Constantius, son of Constantine, emperor over the whole empire from 350 to 361. Cyril had addressed a strange letter to Constantius in 351, describing a vision of a huge blazing cross in the sky, seen by the whole population of the city, and suggesting that it was a sign of divine support for Constantius in his civil war against Magnentius. Despite this earlier flattery, if such it was, Constantius believed Acacius' accusations and exiled Cyril once more. Julian, who succeeded him as emperor in 361, reversed the decision and recalled him to Jerusalem.

Julian attempted to rebuild the Jewish temple in Jerusalem. Cyril warned him that it would come to nothing: all sorts of strange happenings, attributed to divine intervention, ensured that the warning came true. Julian lasted only two years as emperor, and in the eastern empire the Arian sympathizer Valens acceded in 364. He reversed all Julian's reinstatements, and Cyril was exiled once more. He spent fifteen years in exile, in some unknown place, until he was finally recalled by Theodosius I, an orthodox Catholic, who took over the eastern empire in 379. By this time Jerusalem was a chaos of heresy and crime, which Cyril seems to have been unable to remedy. He asked the Council of Antioch for help: they sent Gregory of Nyssa (see 10 Jan.), but he seems to have done little more than express his horror at the morals prevailing there, in his *Warning against Pilgrimages*.

Cyril attended the second ecumenical council of the Church, held at Constantinople in 381. This added extra phrases (here in italics) to the Nicene

Creed to make the two natures in Christ plain: he was "begotten from the Father *before all ages*"; "he came down *from the heavens*," and "was incarnate *from the Holy Spirit and the Virgin Mary*"; he "*sits on the right hand of the Father, and will come again with glory* to judge living and dead, *of Whose kingdom there will be no end*." It also reaffirmed the phrase *homoousion to Patri* (of one being with the Father), orthodox doctrine from then on, to which Cyril gave his assent. The date of his death is generally put at 386, which means that he had been bishop for thirty-five years, of which sixteen were spent in exile. He was a gentle man, conciliatory by nature, who had the misfortune to live in turbulent times.

19

St Joseph (died First Century)

Nothing is really known with any certainty about St Joseph, yet he has been a figure of popular devotion and interest—and sometimes of fun—since very early times of the Church. The infancy narratives in Matthew's and Luke's Gospels, though not intended to be "biographical" in a modern sense, kindled interest in Jesus' early life and encouraged the production of a number of apocryphal works, beginning with the *Protevangelium of James*, written in about 150, which purported to flesh out the details missing from the Gospel accounts. This and several other apocryphal Gospels provided most of the details found in medieval devotion and art.

Matthew alone presents Joseph's dilemma when he hears that Mary, to whom he was betrothed, or engaged (which gave him considerable rights over her), is expecting a child. He traces Joseph's descent from Abraham and calls him "the husband of Mary, of whom Jesus was born," thus from the start excluding him as Jesus' human father. Mary's pregnancy was obviously a threat to his good name, and he could either have exposed her to public shame or repudiated her privately. "[B]eing a righteous man" (Matt. 1:19), he was inclined to take the latter course, but an angel told him in a dream that he should "not be afraid to take Mary as your wife, for the child conceived in her is from the Holy Spirit" (1:20). After the visit of the wise men, Joseph is warned in another dream to "take the child and his mother, and flee to Egypt" (2:13) as Herod is seeking to destroy him. After Herod's death, a third dream tells him that it is safe to take his wife and child back to Israel. And there Joseph fades from Matthew's Gospel, apart from the question asked about Jesus in 13:55: "Is not this the carpenter's son?"

Luke, who composes his infancy narrative from Mary's viewpoint, merely remarks that she was "engaged to a man whose name was Joseph, of the house of David" (1:27), has her "much perplexed" by the angel's greeting, but makes no mention of Joseph's feelings on the matter. He then records Joseph going to Bethlehem to be registered, repeating "with Mary, to whom he was engaged and who was expecting a child" (2:5). After Jesus' birth, the shepherds find "Mary and Joseph, and the child lying in a manger" (2:16). After this, Luke tells of Jesus' "parents" taking him to the Temple to be circumcised, making the poor people's offering of "a pair of turtle doves or two young pigeons" (2:24), and then returning to Nazareth. He then adds the later incident of Jesus being lost and found in the Temple when he was twelve years old, when Mary says to him, "Look, your father and I have been searching for you in great anxiety" (2:48). Jesus is then recorded as being "obedient to them." Luke refers to Joseph once more by name, in the genealogy he provides when describing the start of Jesus' public activity: "He was the son (as was thought) of Joseph son of Heli" (3:23). After the parables of the sower and the lamp, "his mother and his brothers came to him" (8:19), which has been taken as implying that Joseph was dead by this time—and, further, that he was therefore relatively old.

So the two Gospels that mention Joseph at all provide mere hints at a portrait, which later devotion was to flesh out considerably. References to "Jesus' brothers," which seemed to conflict with the teaching of Mary's perpetual virginity, were taken to show that Joseph was a widower with children. Matthew's comment that "he had no marital relations" with Mary (1:25) led to the idea of his being an old man and also to portrayals of him holding a lily, symbol of chastity. Mary's surprise pregnancy led, not unnaturally, to a certain amount of ribaldry in portrayals of him in the dramas that grew out of familiar liturgical texts and developed into the cycles of mystery plays. The *History of Joseph*, dating from the fifth or sixth century, portrays him dying in the presence of Jesus and Mary, which led to him becoming the patron of a holy death. The *Golden Legend* presents an account of his "espousals" to Mary in which he is told that the Holy Spirit has chosen him for his role. By the fourteenth and fifteenth centuries, devotion had become more serious owing to the increasing popularity of representations of the Holy Family, deriving from the "new devotion" with its emphasis on the humanity of Christ. The Church in Rome instituted his liturgical feast in the fifteenth century, and this was extended to the universal Church in the sixteenth. With the growth of scientific biblical criticism, the accounts provided by Matthew and Luke began to be seen as more theological than biographical in intent, part of a view of the divine plan.

Saints were intercessors before they were examples, and Joseph is (after Mary) perhaps the supreme intercessor—maybe because there is so little definite information to limit him. St Teresa of Avila said that she knew from experience that he helped "in every need." Devotion to him was spread by the missionary religious Orders of the Catholic Reformation: his first patronage was that of Mexico in 1555. Pius IX declared him Patron of the Universal Church at the close of the First Vatican Council in 1870. A feast of "St Joseph the Worker" on 1 May was instituted in 1956, to counter "socialist" Labour Day. His name was inserted into the Roman Canon (first Eucharistic Prayer) in 1962, and so the official liturgy of the Church now venerates him as much as popular religious feeling always has done.

20

St Cuthbert (about 634–687)

The most revered saint of northern England, born into a fairly wealthy Anglo-Saxon family, began his monastic life in 651 by riding up to the abbey of Melrose in Northumbria armed with a spear. His life is summarized in the last six chapters of the Venerable Bede's *Ecclesiastical History of the English People*, written in 731, and Bede there refers to earlier accounts he had written, in prose and heroic verse. Cuthbert chose Melrose rather than the more prominent Lindisfarne because he knew and admired the prior, Boisil, whom Bede calls "a priest of great virtues and prophetic spirit" (4:27). Boisil persuaded the abbot, Eata, to accept him into the community, and Cuthbert was soon noted for his exemplary and enthusiastic observance of monastic life.

Eata chose him as part of a team to establish a new house at Ripon, to the south in what is now North Yorkshire, on land donated by King Alcfrith. Cuthbert was guestmaster, a task he seems to have carried out with ease and charm. The foundation was made in 660, three years before the Synod of Whitby was to decide the issue of the date to observe Easter and other matters of debate between Roman and Celtic traditions. Eata and his monks followed the tradition brought over from Ireland by Columba (see 9 June) to Iona, from where northern England had been evangelized. The king had been won over to Roman ways, perhaps directly by Wilfrid (see 24 Apr.), but Eata would have none of them and withdrew his monks back north to Melrose rather than comply.

Boisil died of the plague, which Cuthbert caught but recovered from, though it affected his health for the rest of his life. He was appointed prior in Boisil's place and combined a life of strict monastic observance with preaching missions to hamlets in the mountainous surrounding area. Bede tells of his preaching being so effective that people rushed forward to confess their sins and amend their way of life. Eata had become abbot of Lindisfarne, and he persuaded Cuthbert to accept appointment as prior there. The persuasion was needed because Cuthbert's mind was turning more and more to a solitary life. He obediently spent twelve years as prior at Lindisfarne, during which he did much to clarify and impose the Rule under which the monks were to live: this was either the Rule of St Benedict or a revised version of the older Rule of St Columba.

Eata then gave him permission to adopt the solitary life, which he did first on the nearby "Cuthbert's Isle" and then on Inner Farne, one of the more remote and barren Farne Islands to the south-east of Lindisfarne. There, with initial help from other monks, he built a cell for himself, with lowered floor and high walls so that he would not be distracted from his prayers by the sight of the sea, and a shelter for visitors. He found that wheat would not grow but barley would, and with this and a freshwater well he declared himself self-sufficient. There he lived for nine years in a solitude broken only by monks coming to seek his advice and spiritual counsel. By 684, however, the fame of his holiness was such that he was elected bishop of the new diocese of Hexham. King Egfrith of the Northumbrians himself led a delegation to Inner Farne to per-suade Cuthbert to accept, which he eventually did. Eata, by then bishop of Lindisfarne, knowing that this would be more familiar to Cuthbert, exchanged bishoprics with him, going himself to Hexham and leaving Cuthbert at Lin-disfarne. As bishop he carried out an active and charismatic ministry for two years, especially to the poor, sick, and bereaved, then took leave of his diocese and community at Christmas 686 and retired to his cell to prepare himself for death.

He died on 20 March 687, or, as Bede says, entered into "that life which alone may be called life." In Cuthbert's case, though, his earthly remains then embarked on a long and extraordinary new pilgrimage. He was buried in the church at Lindisfarne, but eleven years later, by which time crowds were flocking to his tomb as many miracles of healing had been reported, the monks exhumed his body to place it in a more accessible shrine above ground. It was found to be incorrupt, was placed in fresh clothes, and reinterred in a wooden casket, placed above ground in the sanctuary. What is known as the *Anonymous Life* of Cuthbert was written shortly after this. The body stayed there for nearly two hundred years. In 875 the monks fled Lindisfarne to escape a Viking invasion, taking Cuthbert's body with them. They wandered over northern England with it for seven years, then settled it at Chester-le-Street for over a hundred, after which it was moved to Ripon in 995, and then to Durham, again to escape the Vikings, in 999. It was taken to Lindisfarne for a time, out of fear of William the Conqueror, but returned to Durham in 1070. Benedictine monks built a new church (later the cathedral), in which the body was interred, in a triple casket and in a new shrine, in 1104. There it stayed until the dissolution of the monasteries. The caskets were opened in 1539 and the body found to be still incorrupt. The shrine was destroyed, but the body was reburied in the same place. The grave was opened again in 1827, when a single skeleton was found at the lowest level. It was assumed to be that of St Cuthbert and was reburied after some precious objects found with it had been removed. The grave was opened again in 1899; the bones were examined medically and stated to date from before the eleventh century and to be those of a man aged about fifty. Pieces of fabric still adhering to them were dated to the seventh century. Is this

Cuthbert's body? Old Catholic families in northern England claim to pass down "secrets" showing that the true relics are elsewhere, removed by Catholics at the dissolution, but no alternative claims of this nature have been substantiated, and the balance of evidence still suggests that it is. Cuthbert is the subject of the first fully illustrated Life of a saint produced in England; he is featured in a fifteenth-century stained-glass window in York Minster, and over a hundred churches are dedicated to him in England alone. He is the patron saint of Durham, and a dense fog that saved the city from the threat of bombing in the World War II was attributed to his intercession.

21

Bd Benedicta Frassinello (1791–1858)

Benedicta, from a simple peasant farming family in Liguria, was one of those indomitable nineteenth-century women who perceived a social need, saw it as God's will that they should do something to remedy it, and set about doing so, often in the teeth of opposition from prejudiced ecclesiastical authorities.

When she was sixteen, Napoleon annexed Liguria. Her family left their land and opened a greengrocer shop in the main street of the university town of Pavia, south of Milan. She was much given to reading Lives of the saints and very taken with the asceticism of the Desert Fathers. She ran away from home and lived in a cave on nuts and berries for a week before being found and taken back. She realized this was a fantasy but still craved the religious life, and in the meantime she indulged in excessive penitential practices. Her parents decided that marriage was the only solution and found a husband; a kind, skilful, intelligent though illiterate young man named Giovanni Battista Frasinello. They were married in February 1816.

Giovanni proved his essentially Christian nature by agreeing to take Benedicta's terminally ill sister, Maria, into their house after her husband had abandoned her. She was to live for another nine years in their care. Meanwhile, after two years of marriage, Benedicta and Giovanni decided to live in celibacy and to devote themselves to rescuing young girls who hung around the university, offering themselves as prostitutes to the students. Both the bishop of Pavia and Benedicta's confessor effectively told her that such prostitution was inevitable and that she should forget the venture. After Maria's death in 1825, wife and husband entered religious life, she in a Capuchin convent and he as a lay brother with the Somaschi Canons.

After a time of peace, enjoying the prayerful silence of the convent, Benedicta again felt the call to an apostolate for young people. The community tried to dissuade her, and the conflict made her ill. The bishop had her sent home, apparently in response to a dream. Benedicta, seemingly at death's door, retaliated with a more powerful guiding dream in which St Jerome Emiliani told her to dedicate her life to young girls in moral peril. This was plainly what she wanted to hear: she recovered her health and set about the task, gathered seven desperate young girls and, with others interested in the work, settled with them in a run-down house. Her parents regarded this as an insult to the family and persuaded the bishop to get Giovanni back to dissuade Benedicta. But he joined her in the venture, and the number of girls soon reached one hundred. A rich layman helped them buy another house.

Benedicta organized her helpers like a monastic community, with shared ideals underpinned by a Rule. Chronically short of funds, they threw themselves on divine providence, and benefactors appeared in the nick of time to show the efficacy of this. Bishop Tosi, now aged and infirm, appointed an administrative committee to help him run the diocese. Many of its members did not like what they found at "Benedicta's Hospice" and were soon spreading gossip to discredit her. The bishop believed this and forced her to leave not only the hospice but the town as well. Giovanni and five co-workers went with her, and they set up a similar venture in his birthplace, Ronco Scrivia, north of Genoa. There the community prospered, opening a school and an orphanage and growing into a Congregation, which received official approval in 1845. Its Rule matured on the basis of the one devised earlier in Pavia and was approved by the archbishop of Genoa in 1856. Two Sisters started another house at Voghera in Piedmont in 1847, housing and educating young people, especially girls in danger of being forced by poverty into prostitution. This was given considerable freedom from the start and became a separate Congregation in 1905.

Bishop Tosi of Pavia died in 1851, and Benedicta was asked to go back there. She opened a school for girls and an orphanage in a former Benedictine monastery. Once more, calumny gathered force and she was asked to leave the city and her work. On her way to another school for girls, she had a heart attack at Ronco Scrivia and died there on 21 March 1858, the feast of St Benedict, after whom she had been named. The Benedictine Sisters of Providence continue to work in Italy, Spain, and Peru. Benedicta's remains were destroyed by Allied bombing in World War II, and she was beatified by Pope John Paul II in 1987.

22

St Nicholas Owen (died 1606)

English and Welsh Catholics who were killed for their faith, mainly in the reigns of Elizabeth I, James I, and Charles I (so between 1533 and 1649) have been beatified and canonized in groups. The largest group was beatified in 1929, with a feast-day on 4 May. Forty were singled out for canonization in 1970, celebrated on 25 October. There are general entries on both these dates in the full edition of *Butler's Lives* as well as many individual entries on the martyr's actual date of death. Here a relatively small selection can be treated this way, of whom Nicholas Owen, the master craftsman of priests' hiding-holes, is one.

His date of birth is not known, but he was one of four sons of a carpenter from Oxford. Of the other three, two became priests and the other printed and distributed Catholic books, so the family showed an extraordinary dedication to keeping the Catholic faith alive in times of persecution. Nicholas was short and walked with a limp as a result of a packhorse having fallen on him, breaking his leg. It is possible that he was the servant of Edmund Campion (see 1 Dec.): he spoke up for him at his trial and as a result was himself imprisoned in 1581. The conditions of his imprisonment were hideous, but they did not prevent him from going back to work for priests, especially the Jesuits, after his release. He spent the twenty years from 1586 to his death in the service of the Jesuit provincial, Fr Henry Garnet.

His life was one of constant travel, staying in the houses of prominent Catholic families under the guise of carrying out repairs to the house by day, while working on the hiding-holes by night. He worked alone on these, to prevent others revealing their secrets under torture; only he and the owner of the house knew where the entrance to each was. They were of quite extra-ordinary ingenuity, often involving removing whole walls, designed to house one or two men for several days in a minimum of discomfort, with access to light and air and storage for food. They saved hundreds of priests from arrest and death and the owners of the houses from having their property confiscated.

In 1594 Nicholas went to London to help the celebrated Fr John Gerard to buy a house. They were betrayed and arrested. Nicholas was severely tortured, hanging in the air from iron bands round his wrists for three hours at a time. He revealed nothing and eventually a bribe secured his release. He continued to see Fr Gerard, who in 1597 was sent to the Tower of London, from where he made a spectacular escape, which Nicholas may have helped to plan. Nicholas became a Jesuit lay brother in the same year.

The Gunpowder Plot in November 1605 produced a fresh wave of anti-Catholic feeling, and Fr Garnet, another Jesuit priest, Nicholas, and another lay brother took refuge in Hindlip Hall in Worcestershire. The Secretary of State, Robert Cecil, knew they were there but made no move to arrest them until all the Gunpowder Plot conspirators had been arrested. Nicholas had constructed two hiding-holes, one for the two priests, the other for himself and the other lay brother. The local magistrate set one hundred men to search the house; after a week they had not found the hiding places. But the refugees were running out of food. Nicholas gave himself up, hoping that the searchers would then go away and leave the priests. They did not, but searched the house for another week, after which the second hiding-hole was found.

Fr Garnet and Nicholas were taken to London; the other two were hanged, drawn, and quartered in Worcester. Fr Garnet was tried and executed in London. Nicholas was not sent to trial but simply tortured without mercy in an attempt to gain information about the hiding-holes he had made. He revealed nothing. Eventually an old hernia caused his abdomen to burst open, despite having an iron band fastened round it to prevent this from happening, and he died in agony on 22 March 1606. A cover-up story was put about to the effect that he had committed suicide, but no one believed this, and his jailer let slip the truth: "The man is dead; he died in our hands."

23

St Turibius of Mogrovejo (Turibio Alfonso de Mogrovejo y Morán; 1538–1606)

This great figure in the history of the Church in Latin America, the second archbishop of Lima, was born in Spain, in the province of León. He was a brilliant law student and then became well known as a teacher of law, acting at the same time as a counsellor to the Inquisition in Granada. He was chosen by Philip II (actually his second choice, as his wife vetoed his first) to succeed Jerónimo de Loaiza, the first archbishop of Lima, who died in 1575. The fact that it fell to the king to make the choice is indicative of the control exercised by the State over the Church in Spain and even more so in the viceroyalty of New Spain, of which Lima was the administrative capital. Turibius was not even a deacon and had to be hurried through the ordination and consecration processes.

He arrived in Lima in May 1581, to take possession of a metropolitan see with ecclesiastical jurisdiction over the whole of Spanish South America. Two

Councils of Lima had been held, and a third was planned. On his arrival, Turibius convoked it for the following year and then set off on a visitation of the southern and eastern parts of his archdiocese. In his archdiocese, the population spoke either Aymara or Quechua as their first language, which it was vital for the clergy to learn. Most of the local population felt that they had merely exchanged the Incas for other rulers and acted with docility toward the new rulers and their religion. On the periphery, outside the old Inca Empire, they were more rebellious.

Turibius returned from his visitation fifteen days before the council opened. This passed a number of administrative measures and then had a stormy passage involving the openly simoniacal bishop of Cuzco, resolved only by his death. Its most important measures concerned pastoral care of the Indians: all parish priests had to learn the appropriate local language; a new catechism was to be produced in Aymara and Quechua; rites surrounding the sacraments and native practices were to be made uniform; Indians could be admitted to minor orders, though not yet to the priesthood. The catechism was published in Spanish as well in 1584 and proved to be the council's greatest achievement.

The Laws of the Indies, promulgated in 1542, had laid down that the Church's apostolate was to be directed first and foremost to the Indian population. Turibius spent the next twenty years trying to make this a reality. He criss-crossed the vast area of his diocese, with its tropical jungle, mountains, and deserts, four times, staying in presbyteries where they existed, in the primitive huts of the Indians where they did not. He learned Quechua and really tried to come to understand the Indian mind. Inevitably, he never stayed long enough in one place to dig beneath the surface and may have heard more of what the Indians thought he wanted to hear than their real feelings about their situation.

When he was back in Lima in the intervals between his apostolic journeys there were problems to be faced, stemming mainly from the competing claims of civil and ecclesiastical powers in the persons of the king of Spain and the pope. Turibius tried to manage both by providing a stream of information. The rivalry was repeated on the local level, with conflicts between the viceroy and the provincial and diocesan church hierarchies. Turibius summoned a series of synods (too many for some people) to try to resolve matters. He also summoned two further councils of Lima: the fourth and fifth. They failed to live up to the third: relatively few bishops attended the fourth, but it did reinforce some of the provisions agreed at the third. The fifth was held despite the opposition of the viceroy: it decided little, and the king, who had not been informed of it in advance and so had not sent a representative, disapproved.

He also had trouble with the viceroy and the civil council over the establishment and running of a seminary for the archdiocese. The viceroy objected to his order that seminarians and professors should leave their arms at the door. Eventually the king ordered the viceroy not to interfere, and Turibius, who had closed the seminary in protest, reopened it. He founded a home for separated women, a hospital for sick priests, and a convent of Poor Clares, where he died on Holy Thursday in 1606, in the middle of another marathon visitation of his territory. His body was initially buried there but was later brought back to Lima and now rests in the cathedral (which was still being built). He was canonized in 1672 and is the patron saint of Peru. While the actual scale of his achievements may be debatable, there is no doubt about his apostolic zeal or his concern for the Indians, a concern by no means always shared by the civil authorities or some sectors of the Church. He personally baptized and confirmed about half a million people, including South America's two best-known saints, Rose of Lima and Martin de Porres.

24

St Rebecca Ar-Rayes (Boutroussieh Ar-Rayes; 1832–1914)

Rebecca came from a poor family of Maronite Christians living in the town of Himlaya. (The Maronites, named after St Maro, a friend of St John Chrysostom, originated around the seventh century when their local church disagreed with Rome over doctrine and they were excommunicated. They were brought back into communion after contact with the Crusaders in the twelfth century and have been in continuous communion ever since.) Her mother died while she was still a child, and as soon as she was old enough she went to work as a domestic servant for a Christian Lebanese family living in Damascus. Her father summoned her home when she was fourteen, thinking it time she was married. She had no desire to marry and fled after hearing her stepmother and aunt discussing who her husband should be.

She made her way to a convent of the Mariamette Sisters, a new teaching Order founded by the Jesuits for local women, where the superior immediately accepted her and then turned away her parents when they arrived to take her home. She never saw them again. She was clothed in 1855 and professed the following year as Sr Agnes. She studied Arabic, writing, and arithmetic, and was able to start teaching in 1860. That year the Druze, a fanatically anti-Christian Lebanese tribe, carried out a terrible massacre of some eight thousand Christians. An Arab hid the Sisters in a stable, even though the Druse did not normally kill women. After the trouble was over, Sr Agnes spent ten more years teaching in various locations.

In 1871 the Jesuits wanted to merge the Mariamette Sisters with the Daughters of the Sacred Heart and suppressed both Institutes when they could not agree on certain points. Many of the Sisters returned to secular life, but Sr Agnes sought entry to a monastery. The Maronite Order of Lebanon had split into two monastic Congregations in 1770, one of which was the Baladite Order, and she was admitted to their monastery of St Sé'man El-Qarn, where she was professed in August 1873. This time she took her mother's name, Rafqa (Rebecca in English), in religion. As a nun she was noted for her hard work, cheerfulness, and charity to all. She, however, felt that God was not with her in every way as he had not come to her in the suffering of illness. She prayed to be made ill, and it seems that her prayer was immediately answered. She felt a violent pain in her head and her eyes. She gradually lost the sight of her right eye, which was then gouged out by a quack doctor, concentrating the pain in her left eye.

She was sent to the monastery of Saint Joseph at Jrabta, nearer sea level and so warmer, with no need for the wood fires that made the pain worse. But she soon lost the sight of her remaining eye, and the pain from what may have been a cancer of the bone became even worse. She was soon paralysed except for her hands, with which she knitted or said the rosary, and she spent seventeen years in this agony, never complaining but saying only that her sufferings were as nothing compared to the agony of Jesus. On one occasion some movement was mysteriously restored for a short time, enabling her to attend Mass on the feast of Corpus Christi, and on another she could see the other Sisters for an hour. She died on 23 March 1914 at the age of eighty-two and was beatified by John Paul II in 1985 and canonized by him on 13 March 2001.

25

St Margaret Clitherow (about 1553–1586)

This lively and attractive housewife from York is one of the best documented and best loved of the Forty Martyrs of England and Wales. Born into a respected and even distinguished Protestant family of York, she was married at the age of eighteen (or possibly younger) to John Clitherow, a widower with children, who was considerably older than she was and ran a successful butcher's business in the Shambles, the butchers' quarter. He was wealthy and held various civic posts in the city. He adhered, probably more out of convenience than conviction, to the established Church, but a brother, William, was a Catholic (later ordained and a Carthusian) and may have had some influence on Margaret.

Three years after they were married, Margaret became a Catholic and refused to attend Reformed services with her husband, thereby making him liable to fines, which he paid with cheerful tolerance. The 1559 Act of Supremacy had declared Elizabeth head of the Church of England and made attendance at Sunday worship compulsory, though its application was far from strict. Large numbers of Catholics conformed outwardly while keeping their true beliefs to themselves. The situation changed when Pope Pius V formally excommunicated Elizabeth in 1570, the year before Margaret's marriage. The English Parliament responded with an Act that effectively made it high treason, punishable by death, to take part in or aid any propagation of the "old" faith. Catholics now had to conform or risk the direst consequences.

Margaret blithely served periods of imprisonment for refusing to attend services at her parish church. She used these times to teach herself to read, and when she came out she started a small school at her house, where children were taught the Catholic faith. She came into contact with Dorothy Vavasour, who became leader of the Catholics in York after her husband's death. Her eldest son had trained for the priesthood with John Mush, who became Margaret's confessor in the last two years of her life and then wrote her biography. Margaret had a secret room built into her house to shelter priests, and Mass was said there often, with John Clitherow apparently conniving. He was arrested in 1586 for sending their son Henry to a Catholic college on the Continent. The authorities used his absence to search the house and eventually extracted information about the secret room and who attended Mass from an eleven-year-old Flemish boy, whom they stripped and threatened with a beating. Margaret was arrested and charged with sheltering priests.

She would normally have been imprisoned for this, but she was determined to be a martyr. She was brought to trial before two judges from Westminster and a whole panoply of officials from the city of York, but she refused to plead either guilty or not guilty. This saved her from naming anyone else involved in the York Catholic network. It also incurred the barbarous medieval penalty of *peine forte et dure* (being crushed, first almost to death in order to extract a confession, then to death if this was not forthcoming). At least one of the judges did his best to persuade her to consider her husband and family and avoid this fate, but she was determined and was accordingly sentenced for not pleading, rather than on the original charge of sheltering priests.

Her husband spoke despairingly of losing the "best wife in England, and the best Catholic also." Judge Clinch made further efforts to save her, offering her a reprieve if she would only hear one Protestant sermon and then trying to find out if she were pregnant. Midwives said she probably was, but it was too late: sentence had been passed. The first crushing was skipped, as she was obviously not going to confess. A sharp stone was placed under her spine, a door on top of her, and heavy weights on this. She died after fifteen minutes of agony. She had kept her wit and spirits to the last, sending her husband her hat, as he was "her head," and her daughter Anne her shoes and stockings, so that she might "follow in her footsteps." Her body was buried secretly by the authorities, but Catholics discovered it six weeks later, exhumed it, and reburied it in such a secret place that it has never been found since. Margaret was beatified in 1929 and canonized in 1970, the first woman martyr of the north of England.

❖

They persecuted her and she thereby learnt patience; they shut her up into close prison, and she learned thereby to forget and despise the world; they separated her from house, children and husband and she thereby became familiar with God; they sought to terrify her and she thereby increased in most glorious constancy and fortitude ...

from the *True Report on the Life and Death of Mrs. Margaret Clitherow* by Fr John Mush, her confessor

26

St Ludger of Münster (about 742–809)

Ludger was a major figure in bringing the faith to the peoples of Frisia (covering what are now parts of the Netherlands and north-western Germany), following in the footsteps of the great St Boniface (see 5 June), whom he saw briefly while he was a student at the abbey school of Utrecht. As part of an arrangement to secure a new bishop to relieve the abbot of Utrecht, Gregory, from having to serve as both abbot and bishop, Ludger went to York with two companions. Connections between York and Frisia went back a century, to 678, when St Wilfrid (see 24 Apr.) had spent a year there on his way to Rome to protest to the pope about the actions of Theodore of Canterbury, and the English mission there bore lasting fruits with St Willibrord (see 7 Nov.) in the last decade of the seventh century. Ludger was ordained deacon in York and there came under the influence of Alcuin, the great scholar who was to play such a prominent part in the restoration of learning at the court of Charlemagne. Ludger stayed for a year in York initially and then obtained Abbot Gregory's permission to return there, when he spent a further three and a half years in Alcuin's school.

Gregory's successor as abbot, Alberic, sent Ludger to Deventer to rebuild a wrecked church, and from there he went on a mission to the frontiers of Friesland, where he made many converts. Alberic then took him to Cologne, where he was ordained priest. He was put in charge of Ostergau, at the mouth of the River Ems, which was still occupied by pagan tribes. He built a church at Dokkum, where St Boniface had been martyred, and his mission prospered until all his work was undone by a Saxon invasion. Wars with the heathen Saxons were a constant feature once Charlemagne had become sole high king of the Franks in 771. His aim changed over the years from keeping them under control to making them a subject people and then to making them a subject Christian people, with baptism enforced by law and tithes payable to the Christian clergy.

After the destruction of his church at Dokkum, Ludger went on pilgrimage to Rome and to the great monastery of Monte Cassino, where he spent some two years studying the Benedictine Rule, with a view to establishing a monastery at Werden on his return. The Saxon leader who had previously destroyed his community, Widukind, was defeated by Charlemagne in 785 and (forcibly) converted to Christianity. Ludger was able to return, to rebuild his mission on a more permanent basis, and to extend his evangelizing efforts eastward. Charlemagne asked him to go still further afield, into the newly subjugated province of north-west Saxony, where his gentleness and powers of persuasion achieved far more than the forced baptisms previously enjoined by the emperor.

He settled and built a monastery at Mimigerneford, from which the modern Münster takes its name, and where, in 804, he finally agreed to be ordained bishop. His brother, Hildegrim, who had previously accompanied him to Rome, joined him, and together they evangelized Westphalia and Eastphalia. They even had plans to travel farther north into Scandinavia, but Charlemagne restrained them. At one point the emperor summoned Ludger to explain why he was giving away so much church property in alms. Ludger not only failed to apologize but kept the emperor waiting until he had finished his prayers, saying that the service of God should come before that of any man—as Charlemagne must have intended to convey by appointing him bishop.

Ludger died peacefully on Passion Sunday, 26 March 809, having preached in the morning and afternoon of that day. He was buried in the monastery he had built at Werden, where his body remained until 1984, when it was transferred to Münster, of which he is patron saint. The church of St Ludger there, founded in 796, contains the "Ludger-chalice," considered the oldest chalice in Germany. There are many representations of Ludger in the diocese, some showing him holding a church and some with geese, as he was believed to have delivered the diocese from a plague of wild geese. He had been a zealous missionary priest and bishop; he was also an accomplished teacher and writer, producing Lives of his two abbots at Utrecht, Gregory and Alberic. Besides and perhaps above these qualities, his study of the Benedictine Rule instilled a deep love of the regular life of prayer, as his reproof to Charlemagne showed.

27

St Rupert (died about 718)

Rupert, like Ludger, was a great missionary bishop, working further south, where evangelization had come by different routes, mainly from Aquileia in northern Italy, and a century earlier. The early part of his life is largely unknown. Tradition has tried to make him an Irishman, one of the many voluntary exiles who did so much to bring monasticism and learning to western Europe in the sixth and seventh centuries. He is also associated with the monastery of Luxeuil in Burgundy, founded by St Columban about 692. Neither can be proved, but the fact that he followed the Irish custom of combining the offices of abbot and bishop seems to indicate Irish influence.

He is first heard of as bishop of Worms, from which he seems to have been expelled. Whether his expulsion was brought about by political enemies, warring pagans, Arians, or a combination of all three is not clear. He was then invited by Duke Theodo II of the Bavarians to work in his dukedom, which covered modern Bavaria and parts of Austria. Rupert agreed, seeing the invitation as a sign from God, and met the duke at Regensburg, on the River Danube in Bavaria. His first mission was eastward along the Danube, travelling as far as modern Hungary, preaching and teaching in towns and villages. The population was part pagan, part Arian, part orthodox, mixed with Arianism and superstition. Rupert therefore had to undertake a mission of initial conversion and re-evangelization. He returned by land and established his headquarters on the site of the once elegant Roman town of Juvavum, then ruined (now Salzburg), on land given to him by the duke. He built the first church there, which he dedicated to St Peter, a monastery for monks (also St Peter's) and another for nuns, and a school.

Needing more helpers, he undertook a journey of recruitment—either to Worms or to Luxeuil, it is not known which—and returned with twelve companions. These assisted him in missionary work and became the nucleus of the monastery for monks. His niece Ermentrude became the first abbess of that for nuns. He was then free to travel all over his territory, preaching and founding new churches and monasteries. He returned to Salzburg when he felt death approaching and died there one Easter Sunday, probably between 710 and 720. He was buried in St Peter's monastery there; in 774 his relics were moved into the then cathedral, and in the seventeenth century they were moved again into the new cathedral.

In 716 Duke Theodo petitioned Rome for Bavaria to be raised to the status of ecclesiastical province, but he died and his lands were divided before this could be put into effect. The tradition of abbot-bishops lasted at Salzburg for some three hundred years after Rupert's death. He is credited with discovering salt mines near Salzburg and has been depicted, most commonly on coins, holding a container of salt.

28

St Stephen Harding (died 1134)

Stephen was one of the three co-founders of the Cistercian Order. The Cistercians emerged as part of a widespread monastic reform movement seeking greater detachment from the powers of the world, inspired by love of poverty and solitude. Together with the Carthusians, they have survived and flourished to the present day. Stephen's other co-founders were Alberic (died 1109) and Robert of Molesme (died 1110).

Stephen was born in south-west England and became a monk or at least a pupil with the Benedictines of Sherborne Abbey in Dorset, where St Wulsin (see 8 Jan.) had installed the monks in 998. He seems to have left the monastery for a time and returned to lay life—or he may never have intended to become a monk. He went to study first in Scotland and then in France. There he underwent a conversion experience that made him decide to lead the religious life. He went on pilgrimage to Rome and on his return joined the monastic community at Molesme in the Burgundy region of eastern France.

Life in the monastery there was apparently too easy for Alberic, Robert, and Stephen, and in 1098 they left, taking a number of supporters, and went to Cîteaux, described as "a place of horror, a vast wilderness." They were given land by the lord of nearby Beaune and authorized by the archbishop of Lyons to make a new monastic foundation. Robert became the first abbot, with Alberic prior and Stephen sub-prior, but after some disagreement among them, Robert was ordered back to Molesme by Pope Urban II and Alberic was appointed abbot in his place. He died nine years later and was succeeded by Stephen, who called him "a father, a friend, a fellow-soldier and a principal warrior in the Lord's battles ... who carried us in his heart with affectionate love."

Stephen was abbot for twenty-three years and saw the new Order firmly established. Initial hardships and worries about numbers came to an end when thirty young noblemen rode up to the monastery and asked to be admitted as novices. They were led by Bernard (of Clairvaux; see 20 Aug.), whose amazing energy was to spread the Order and its influence far and wide in his lifetime. Stephen was mainly responsible for the foundational documents, which established the particular nature of the Order. The "Charter of Charity" laid down that the abbot of the founding house should visit each of its dependent abbeys every year, while the abbots of all the houses assembled at Cîteaux itself for an annual assembly to legislate to safeguard the original spirit and observance. This bound all the monasteries of the Order together in a formalized fashion not envisaged in the original Rule of St Benedict.

The Cistercians denied themselves all personal luxuries and also rents from dependent churches and other properties. This, together with the remote sites they deliberately chose, forced them to develop techniques of self-sufficiency. They took in large numbers of lay brothers to do the necessary agricultural work, in which the Cistercians soon became technical pioneers. Their water supply and land-reclamation schemes mark the landscape around the ruins of their monasteries in England to this day. The choir monks were thereby left relatively free to pursue the contemplative life of public and private prayer and "divine reading." They developed into scholars, theologians, and spiritual writers, though scholarship was not part of their way of life as originally planned. Despite renouncing any sort of luxury, they also produced beautiful manuscripts, and those produced or collected under Stephen's abbacy can still be seen at Dijon.

By 1119 there were eleven abbeys dependent on Cîteaux, including Clairvaux, where Stephen appointed Bernard abbot, and the organization provided for in the Charter proved its worth. Stephen resigned as abbot in 1133, as he was by then old and blind. By the time of his death the following year, the Order had spread beyond France. It later opened houses for women, and, with its Trappist reform houses, is now present on all five continents. Bernard was the prime mover in its early expansion, and he somewhat ungraciously never made any mention of what he owed to Stephen, who nevertheless stands as a sort of calm father-figure behind him and as the most influential of the three founders. An early history calls him "an ardent lover and staunch champion of religious life, poverty, and regular discipline."

29

St John Climacus (Seventh Century)

John was first known as John the Scholar, but the sobriquet Climacus, from *Klimax*, the Greek for "ladder," came into universal use from the first word of the title of his famous treatise *Ladder to Paradise*. This still has immense influence, particularly in Orthodox monasteries, where it is read every Lent.

Relatively little is known about John's life, but he belonged to the tradition of eastern monasticism and experienced both its solitary (eremitical) and communal (cenobitical) forms. He also embodies its tradition of extreme physical asceticism to a marked degree. He is first heard of at the age of sixteen, when he joined the community of monks on Mount Sinai. These led a semi-eremitical life, living singly in huts around a church and relying for spiritual growth on the teaching of an *abba*, a spiritual father. John received the tonsure there from his *abba*, named Martyrios, before moving on at the age of about thirty-five to lead the life of a complete solitary at Thole. He would still have received visitors, as his reputation as a spiritual counsellor was considerable. In fact he did so much counselling that other monks called him a "chatterbox." Taking this as a reprimand, he did none for a year, until he was persuaded to take it up again.

After forty years of this way of life he was elected *igumen* (leader) of the cenobitical community of Mount Sinai, where he remained for four years before retiring once more to his hermitage and dying at an unknown age. It was in his later years that he was asked to write a treatise on the spiritual life, to which he brought a wealth of wisdom and experience. Today the work may seem to have an overemphasis on sin and punishment: he was always conscious of fallen human nature as a hurdle that continually has to be overcome in order to arrive at the outpouring of love that can be achieved only through humility and poverty of heart. John knew the works of earlier spiritual writers, including Origen (of whom he disapproved), but taught that experience, not reading, was the true guide. He had imbibed three centuries of Eastern monasticism, and so the experience he passed on was more than just his own.

The *Ladder* was translated into Syriac not long after John's death, then into Arabic, Georgian, Armenian, and Slavonic in the tenth century, so enabling it to penetrate into virtually all Eastern Churches. It had to wait until the fourteenth century for a complete translation into Latin, by which time its stress on imitation of Christ, insofar as that is possible, would have appealed to the spirit of the "new devotion" most typically embodied in Thomas à Kempis' *Imitation of Christ*. John also wrote a short treatise titled *To the Shepherd*, a guide for the spiritual father, *abba*, of monasteries, who has to be a teacher but above all to lead by example.

Get rid of sin, and tears will become superfluous. Adam did not shed tears before the fall, and after the resurrection there will be no more . . .

God does not expect us to mourn from motives of sorrow [but rather] to rejoice for love of him with the laughter of the soul . . .

Love of its nature is a likeness to God insofar as it is humanly possible to attain it.
from the *Ladder to Paradise*

30

Bd Restituta Kafka (Helene Kafka; 1894–1943)

Victims of the Nazis now recognized as martyrs are quite numerous, but this little nun of Czech descent has the distinction of being the only nun to have been beheaded under the Third Reich.

Helene Kafka was born in Brno in Moravia, then part of the Austro-Hungarian Empire, now the eastern province of the Czech Republic. Her father was a shoemaker, and both he and his wife came from Catholic families. They emigrated to Vienna when Helene was two and settled in a working-class district with thousands of other Czech immigrant workers. Helene attended local schools until she was fifteen, when she went into domestic service for four years. Her ambition, though, was to work for "those who are suffering and desperately in need of help," and she planned to join a nursing Order. In 1913 the German Hartmann Sisters were asked to provide the nursing staff for a new hospital in the Lainz district of Vienna, and Helene started work as an unskilled general assistant at the hospital so that she could observe the Sisters at close hand.

She asked her parents for permission to join the Order, but they, for some reason (perhaps anti-German sentiment), refused, with her mother protesting more vigorously against the notion. Helene ran away from home to the Hartmann motherhouse, and after some months her parents relented and gave their consent. They were too poor to provide the dowry required, but this came in the form of a bequest from the diocese. Helene took the name Restituta in religion, for Restituta of Sora, beheaded for her faith under Emperor Aurelian. She was a novice at the outbreak of the First World War in 1914. Casualties were soon pouring into the hospital, and she began work in the operating theatre. After the war she volunteered to work for a surgeon, known to be moody and difficult, in the market town of Mödling, south of Vienna. She soon became a highly skilled theatre Sister and anaesthetist, nicknamed "Sr Resoluta" for her strength of will and much loved for her sense of fun. Short and stout, she was fond of "a goulash and a pint of my usual" after a hard day's work.

She worked there throughout the inter-war period. In 1938 Hitler annexed Austria, and all religious activity in hospital wards was forbidden. The surgeon for whom she worked was a fanatical Nazi, but he valued her skills so highly that he turned a blind eye to her continuing to pray with the dying. When she put up crucifixes in the wards he could no longer do so and called in the

Gestapo. She was held in prison for over a year, during which she gave most of her rations to others, saving the lives of a pregnant mother and her baby and losing half her own weight in the process. Then Martin Bormann, Hitler's secretary, decided to make an example of her and sentenced her to be guillotined. On 30 March 1943 she was led out wearing only a paper shirt and with her hands tied behind her back. A prison chaplain was allowed to accompany her to the door of the death chamber. He then heard a "dull thud" as the blade fell. Her body was thrown into a mass grave and has never been recovered.

It was some years before the political situation in Austria allowed the process for her beatification to go forward, but it finally gathered momentum, and she was beatified in Vienna by Pope John Paul II on 20 June 1998. The only relic that could be found to present to the pope was a small piece of her habit. The district hospital in Mödling now has a large maternity unit, and in 1995 the street in which it stands was renamed "Sister Restituta Street," so her name appears on the birth certificates of all babies born there.

31

St Stephen of Mar Saba (about 725–794)

We owe our knowledge of Stephen to an account of his life written in Latin by his disciple Leontius. He was a nephew of St John Damascene (see 4 Dec.), declared a Doctor of the Church for his great work *The Fount of Knowledge*, and was a defender of images against the Iconoclasts. John took his nephew into the *laura* of Mar Saba, founded some two centuries earlier by St Sabas (see 5 Dec.). This was a monastery in the form of a group of huts, in which monks lived largely solitary lives, grouped around a church, where they came together for communal worship. Stephen was only ten at the time, and his admission seems to have been somewhat unusual, as "unbearded" boys were not generally allowed to join; it was perhaps a special dispensation reflecting John's prestige.

For the next fifteen years Stephen received a thorough education and training from his uncle. John died in 749, and Stephen spent the next eight years passing on the benefits of his education and experience to the community. One of the distinguishing features of the monastery was its composition and singing of hymns, and Stephen, amongst other functions, held the office of cantor. He then told his *igumen* (abbot), Martyrios, that he wanted to lead a hermit's life. Martyrios persuaded him that he should not deprive others of the benefits of his learning and counsel, so Stephen agreed to a compromise whereby he spent Monday to Friday in solitude but received visitors at weekends, pinning a notice on his cell door: "Forgive me, Fathers, in the name of the Lord, but please do not disturb me except on Saturdays and Sundays." He followed this way of life for five years, then embraced complete solitude for the next fifteen, after which he admitted disciples once more.

This last period may be when he earned the title "Wonder-worker": he seemed, indeed, to have a preternatural gift for sensing the sufferings of others and for saving them from all sorts of spiritual and material troubles. Monks from other monasteries as well as his own came to him for healing, as did lay people from far and wide. He was, as he saw it, but an instrument, and an unworthy one at that, of the healing power of God: "I am no more than a dead, dry stick, sterile and full of bitterness." His compassion extended to the animal kingdom: like an earlier St Francis, he is portrayed with his shoulders and arms covered with birds—ravens, doves, starlings—which he fed and then told to be off when they had had enough. He also fed gazelles and was even concerned that no one should tread on the worms he collected from the floor of his cell and carefully placed outside, saying that those who were careless of "irrational nature" would soon become equally careless of their fellow-humans.

Stephen died on the Monday of Low Week, 794, after doling out final counsels, some kind, some strict, to the Brothers of Mar Saba. His biographer obviously regarded him as a Christ-like figure and includes an account of what seems to be an echo of the Transfiguration, witnessed by another monk, named Christopher, who had begged him to say Mass in his cell. Stephen, characteristically, prayed to be spared further special graces until the next life, asking only: "When I pray for my fellow-men, heal them and build them up"(a prayer that seems to have been granted throughout the remainder of his life).

To know the Lord is the principle of good. Abide in this knowledge and you will draw close to God. There is nothing of value except the soul's gain, but the soul's gain is to be found only in the love of God.
St Stephen, quoted in the Life by Leontius, trans. Teresa Rodrigues, OSB

Other Familiar English Names for March

1. Christopher, Joanna, Leo
2. Angela, Charles
3. Frederick, Michael, Peter, Samuel, Teresa
4. Alexander, Christopher, Nicholas, Peter
5. Adrian, Christopher, George, Gregory, Jeremy, John, Joseph, Mark
6. Colette, Julian, Rose
7. Basil, John, Paul, Teresa
8. Bernard, Cyril, Felix, Humphrey, Peter, Simon, Stephen, Vincent
9. Bruno, Catherine, Dominic
10. Alexander, John, Matthew, Peter, Mary
11. Benedict, Dominic, George, John, Mark, Peter, Thomas, Vincent
12. Bernard, Jerome, Joseph, Paul, Peter
13. Frances, Joan, Peter
14. Alexander, Eve, James
15. William *is the only other familiar English name today*
16. Gregory, Hilary, John, Julian
17. Gabriel, Gertrude, John, Paul
18. Edward, John, Martha, Roger
19. Andrew, John, Mark
20. Ambrose, Francis, John, Martin, Mary, Paul
21. James, John, Nicholas, Matthew, Thomas
22. Basil, Francis, Paul, Peter
23. Edmund, Joseph, Peter, Rebecca
24. Catherine, John
25. James, Lucy
26. Peter *is the only familiar English name for today*
27. Francis *is the only other familiar English name for today*
28. Christopher, Cyril, Joan
29. John, Mark, William
30. Antony, John, Leonard, Peter
31. Benjamin, Guy, Jane

APRIL

April spaces its saints in the Universal Calendar quite conveniently, but several substitutions have been made this month with other dates. St Gemma Galgani's actual date of death is the 11th, but she is considered here on the 9th, a day with no really major figures, as St Stanislaus has a place in the Universal Calendar on the 11th, while Gemma deserves consideration as a remarkable example of what have been called "the physical phenomena of mysticism." Several English martyrs are grouped together on the 20th, all of whom except one, who died on the 19th, are actually commemorated on this day. St Adalbert of Prague is moved forward one day to the 22nd, as the 23rd has to belong to St George. St Wilfrid is included here on the date of his death, the 24th, as in the new Roman Martyrology, rather than on his traditional feast-day of 12 October. Marie Guyart (Bd Mary of the Incarnation) died on the 30th, a day crowded with major figures; she deserves consideration here, not only for the sake of North American readers, and so is moved to the relatively empty 26th. Gianna Beretta Molla, an interesting modern "Blessed," is moved forward one day to the 27th to leave her date of death to St Peter Chanel, who is in the Universal Calendar. St Joseph Cottolengo features on the 30th, a day when readers might have expected to find St Pius V, but the new Roman Martyrology has moved him on one day to 1 May, where he will be found.

1

Bd Vilmos Apor (1892–1945)

Vilmos was born in Transylvania, the mountainous region of northern Romania. His father was Baron Gabor Apor, his mother was Countess Palffy, and he was the seventh of their eight children. His mother was very devout and ensured that the children had a thorough religious education. Vilmos was educated by the Jesuits from the age of ten and in 1910 went to study theology at Innsbruck University in Austria. He was ordained priest in 1915 and served as a curate in the Hungarian town of Gyula, near the present Romanian border. In the First World War he was sent to the Italian front, where his already strong commitment to the poor was strengthened by the suffering he saw.

He returned to Gyula after the war and became parish priest. Romania went on fighting against Hungary and Romanian soldiers occupied the town, deporting Hungarian prisoners inside Romania. Vilmos interceded successfully with Queen Mary of Romania for their release. More lasting problems he set out to tackle were a decline in church attendance (often through poverty), unemployment during the depression of the 1930s, and relations with other churches. He improved the latter so significantly that when he was appointed bishop of Győr in 1940, the dean of the Reformed Church in Gyula spoke of the "golden age of denominational peace" he had created and upheld for twenty-five years.

As bishop, he saw at once that the persecution of the Jews in Hungary was the worst problem facing him. He protested constantly against their deportation and sheltered refugees. In 1944, when Jews were being sent to death camps in their thousands, he wrote to the minister of the interior: "I protest before God, Hungary, and the world against these measures, which are in contradiction to human rights." He went to German headquarters to protest; he wrote to the prime minister and heads of local authorities, asking to be allowed to visit the Jews held in captivity. Everything was refused, and he was threatened with imprisonment.

On Whitsunday of 1944 he preached again against the treatment of the Jews, saying that everyone who allows torture must be regarded as a pagan, "even if he boasts of being a Christian." Writing to a fellow-bishop, he declared, "One cannot tolerate anti-Semitism. It must be condemned from the Pope down to the least of the bishops. ... One must state openly that nobody must be persecuted for the blood in his veins. What Jews are undergoing is genocide. ..." Again his protests fell on deaf ears, and more Jews were deported to their deaths.

When the Russians advanced into Hungary in autumn 1944 he gathered some three or four hundred refugees in the cellars of his vast bishop's palace, which he equipped with food supplies and generators. It was not until Holy Week 1945 that the Russians engaged the Germans in Győr. He personally welcomed the Russian troops but would not allow them to molest his refugees. On the evening of Good Friday some drunken soldiers started to abuse a young woman. She called to the bishop for help, and he stood in front of her. The soldiers fired at him and wounded him seriously. He could not be taken to hospital in time to prevent his wounds from becoming infected, and he died on Easter Monday. He was buried in the Carmelite church, as the cathedral was too badly damaged. Devotion to him spread quickly, especially among refugees, and in 1986 the authorities allowed his body to be moved to the rebuilt cathedral. He was beatified by Pope John Paul II in November 1997 and remains an outstanding example, a martyr to the cause of racial harmony and the plight of refugees, issues that once more trouble and disfigure the world.

2

St Francis of Paola (Francesco Alessio; 1416–1507)

Francis was born in Calabria, southern Italy, to a long-childless couple who had prayed to St Francis of Assisi (see 4 Oct.), promising to name any son born to them after him. He had a devout upbringing and was famous for his holiness while still in his teens. Horrified by the worldliness and wealth of Rome, where his parents had taken him on pilgrimage, he retired to live as a hermit in a cave not far from his home town of Paola, resolving to live according to the ideals of poverty set out by St Francis.

By the time he was twenty, several like-minded companions had joined him, and the group called itself "the hermits of Brother Francis of Assisi." Local people built them a church and monastery, and by 1474 they had received papal recognition as a new Mendicant Order. Their reputation for holiness spread, and other towns in the region and in Sicily appealed to them to open new houses. Francis had drawn up a Rule for them, which included an extra vow to observe a perpetual Lenten fast so that they lived without eating meat, eggs, or dairy products. Their way of life was extremely austere, apparently modelled on the Desert Fathers as much as on the Franciscans. Francis himself was very conscious of moral laxity in the Church and constantly stressed the need for penance.

His fame spread, and King Louis XI invited him to the French court. He would not have gone had he not been ordered to do so by the pope. He travelled barefoot on a long journey that became a sort of march for humility. He lived his usual life of extreme simplicity and austerity at the court, but the impression he made was evidently a powerful one, as while he was there he was invited to open houses of his Order in France, Spain, and Germany. The previous year he had changed its name to the Order of Minims, the name *minimi* indicating that they wished to be regarded as the least of all. Under this name, which it still keeps today, the Order expanded rapidly in the first half of the sixteenth century, playing an important part in the Catholic reform movement.

Francis never returned to Italy and died in France on 2 April 1507, Good Friday. His reputation for holiness and reforming zeal was such that he was beatified just six years after his death and canonized a further six years later. Various versions of his Rule, the later ones somewhat less strict, are still extant, as are some letters and a manual of penances for those who broke the Rule. This austere character evidently struck a chord with the popular spirituality of his day, as he was regarded as one of the major miracle-workers of the age. So many of his wonders were performed at sea or on behalf of those at sea that he was declared patron of Italian seafarers by Pope Pius XII in 1943. The Order of Minims declined in numbers and locations from the end of the eighteenth century and now has houses in Italy and Spain only.

3

St Richard of Chichester (about 1197–1253)

Richard was born at Wyche (now Droitwich) in the English Midlands. His family were landowners, but his parents died when he was young, and the family fortunes declined. Refusing to take the land offered by his elder brother, Richard went to study at Oxford and then at Paris. He returned to Oxford, gaining such a reputation as a scholar and a teacher that he was made chancellor of the university, a role he helped to enhance through his able administration. This came to the notice of Edmund of Abingdon, who had previously been his tutor and was then archbishop of Canterbury. He invited Richard to become his diocesan chancellor.

Edmund's upholding of the rights of the Church against the throne led to a number of quarrels with King Henry III and eventually to his voluntary exile in France. Richard went with him, and after Edmund died there in 1240 he studied for the priesthood with the Dominicans at Orleans and was ordained in 1243. He returned to England and worked as a parish priest until the new archbishop of Canterbury asked him to resume as his chancellor. The new archbishop also quarrelled with the king: he appointed Richard to the see of Chichester when the king had proposed his own candidate. Pope Innocent IV upheld Richard's appointment and consecrated him bishop at Lyons in 1245, but King Henry confiscated all the property of the diocese, leaving Richard homeless, as the king had decreed that no one should give him shelter. For two years he lived in the house of one of his priests and visited his diocese on foot, after which Henry relented.

Richard was then able to administer his diocese in freedom for seven and a half years and showed himself to be a great reforming bishop. His personal life was marked by austerity and charity, and his administrative powers led to increased revenues for the diocese, which enabled him to provide suitable vicarages for his clergy. He also insisted on the formation of his priests: they were to instruct the people on the meaning of the sacraments, say Mass clearly and unhurriedly, stay clear of personal gain, and observe the rule of celibacy. His biographer wrote of him: "Towards his clergy he desired to be as a master to his disciples, to his household as a father to his children, to the people as a kindly nurse to her children."

He preached for the purpose of raising volunteers for a crusade toward the end of his life, but he emphasized the spiritual aims of showing devotion and enabling pilgrims to visit the Holy Places once again rather than conquest or religious hatred. He was still engaged in this when he died in Dover on 3 April 1253. He was quickly canonized, in 1262, and his shrine in Chichester Cathedral became a focus of pilgrimage, but his popularity was never widespread.

❖

Thanks be to thee my Lord Jesus Christ for all the benefits thou hast given me, for all the pains and insults thou hast borne for me. O most merciful redeemer, friend and brother, may I know thee more clearly, love thee more dearly, and follow thee more nearly.
Prayer composed by Richard of Chichester

4

St Isidore (560–636)

The family of the "last Father of the Western Church" came from Cartagena in south-eastern Spain, but he was born probably in Seville, where his family had moved to escape an invasion by the Byzantines. His elder brother, Leander, was a friend of Gregory the Great, became a great archbishop of Seville, and is venerated as a saint, as are another brother, Fulgentius, bishop of Ecija, and their sister Florentina, a distinguished abbess. Leander oversaw Isidore's education, probably in one of the episcopal or monastic schools, which formed him into the most learned person of his generation and a leading authority on a whole range of subjects throughout the Middle Ages.

Isidore succeeded Leander in the see of Seville in 599. At this time most of Spain was ruled by the Visigoths, who gradually took over and absorbed the old Roman provinces and other tribal areas. Their king, Recared, had converted to orthodox Catholicism from Arianism thirteen years earlier. He summoned the Third Council of Toledo, the first national council of the Spanish Gothic Church, which declared the purpose of converting the Visigothic kingdom, which in turn was the springboard for the unification of Spain. Politics and religion were inseparable in its formation: while the king appointed the bishops, these contributed greatly to the political ethics and system of justice. Isidore's vast intellectual work was undertaken in order to provide a cultural and historical framework for this new Catholic kingdom.

He has left a word picture of the ideal bishop: "He who is set in authority for the education and instruction of the people for their good must be holy in all things and reprehensible in nothing. ... Every bishop should be distinguished as much by his humility as by his authority. ... He will also preserve that charity which exceeds all other gifts, and without which all virtue is nothing." (This definition is known to have inspired Pope John XXIII.) Not much is known about his diocesan pastoral work, but his ability as a thinker and administrator is shown in the achievements of the provincial council over which he presided in Seville in 619 and the national Fourth Council of Toledo in 633. This defined a creed based on Isidore's theology of the Trinity, which largely established the acceptance in the Western Church that the Spirit "proceeds from the Father *and* the Son." Isidore also played a major part in the composition of the Mozarabic liturgy, which this council decreed should be observed throughout Spain.

He was a compiler of popular knowledge rather than an original thinker, claiming that his works contained all that the clergy of future generations needed to know. He left a storehouse of knowledge that was extensively quarried for a thousand years. His most encyclopedic work was the "Etymologies" (from the number of words whose meaning he explained) or "Origins" (because explanations of words led to origins of things). Its twenty volumes set out to cover the then sum total of human knowledge, from grammar and mathematics to God and the Church, the earth, living beings, and even domestic management. Its divisions established the seven liberal arts that formed the basis of medieval education. He also wrote on the books of the Bible and the Fathers of the Church, as well as on pagan classical literature, and he passed on his own spiritual and pastoral guidance in another major work, *The Book of Sentences*. The extent of his influence can be seen in the fact that there are more manuscript copies of his works than of those of any other writer from the pre-printing age.

He prepared himself most carefully for death, giving away all his possessions and publicly asking forgiveness for any faults. He was carried into his church, dressed in sackcloth and with ashes on his forehead. After confessing to the people and receiving Communion, he was taken back to his room, where he died a few days later, on 4 April 636. All this is attested by a deacon who wrote an eyewitness account. He was not really accounted a great saint until his remains were transferred to León in 1063. This was on the pilgrimage route to Santiago de Compostela, and his shrine became a major attraction. His cult was officially approved in 1598, and he was declared a Doctor of the Church in 1722. There are numerous paintings, including one by Murillo in Seville Cathedral, and statues of him in Spain, most dating from the sixteenth and seventeenth centuries, but little representation outside Spain. At the time of writing he is the foremost candidate for being declared the patron saint of the Internet, on account of the vast scope of his writings and the similarity between the structure of his "Etymologies" and modern databases.

❖

If we want to be always with God, we ought to pray often and to read often as well. For when we pray, it is we who talk to God, whereas when we read, it is God who speaks to us.

Isidore, from *The Book of Sentences*

5

St Vincent Ferrer (Vicente Ferrer Miguel; about 1350–1419)

This brilliant and fiery Dominican preacher represents a later and very different period of Spanish history from that of Isidore of Seville. His surname is English, as his father was an Englishman, William Ferrer, who had settled in Spain and married a Spanish woman, Costanza Miguel. Academically brilliant and devout, Vincent joined the Dominicans at an early age and by the time he was twenty-one was teaching philosophy at Lérida University in Catalonia. After his ordination in 1374 he taught in Barcelona, then moved to Toledo to study theology and Hebrew. In 1379 he was appointed prior of the Dominican house in Valencia, the only office he was to hold. Totally dedicated to the good of his Order and of the Church, he inevitably shared the views of his age, including anti-Semitism. He was successful in converting a number of Jews, including a Rabbi Paul, who later became bishop of Cartagena.

His close friendship with the great canon lawyer Cardinal Pedro (Peter) de Luna led to his involvement in the ecclesiastical political upheavals surrounding the rival claims to the papacy that produced the Great Schism of 1378 to 1417. De Luna supported Cardinal Robert of Geneva, one of those who initially voted Urban VI as pope but then declared his election invalid. Elected in his stead as Clement VII, Robert established a rival papal court at Avignon. Vincent accompanied de Luna, Clement's legate, on various missions to rally support in Spain and Portugal. On Clement's death in 1394, Peter de Luna became (anti-)pope as Benedict XIII and appointed Vincent as his adviser and confessor. Happy at first, Vincent soon became convinced that his friend was hindering attempts at a solution and defending his own position rather than trying to promote unity. In 1399 he left Avignon to work as a roving missioner and preacher.

For the next thirteen years he preached repentance and conversion in various parts of France, Spain, and Italy. He had considerable success, with large crowds flocking to hear him, many of whom were moved to penance (often taking excessive forms) and to enter the religious life. Several distinguished postulants went to La Grande Chartrese, where his brother was prior. Then he was drawn back once more into efforts at healing the Great Schism. By 1409 there were three rivals for the papacy, of whom Benedict was still one. Vincent preached a famous sermon before him and a great assembly of bishops and nobles, beginning, "You dry bones, listen to the word of the Lord." He condemned their pride and urged the need for unity, but it was only when Ferdinand of Aragon withdrew his support that Benedict gave way and the Council of Constance was able to restore unity in 1417.

Vincent returned again to his roving preaching for three years, in Brittany and Normandy. He died at Vannes in Brittany in 1419 and was immediately popularly venerated as a saint. His cult spread rapidly, with many accounts of miracles through his intercession, and he was canonized in 1455. He wrote two treatises of philosophy, a book on the Mass, and an account of the Great Schism. These, with many sermons and letters and other spiritual treatises, have survived. There is a painting of him in the National Gallery in London and a series of murals in Vannes Cathedral depicting his life.

6

Bd Michael Rua (Michele Rua; 1837–1910)

Michael was one of the first associates of Don Bosco (St John Bosco; see 31 Jan.) in his educational work in northern Italy and in the establishment of his Salesian Congregation. He was born in Turin and educated first by the Brothers of the Christian Schools (see next entry) and then at a grammar school. At Don Bosco's suggestion, he entered the Turin Oratory after his schooling. He took his religious vows in 1854 and worked as a catechist. His gifts were such that he was appointed the first spiritual director of the new Congregation while he was still a sub-deacon.

He was ordained in 1860 and three years later obtained a teaching diploma at the university of Turin. In 1865 he was appointed Don Bosco's official vicar and worked constantly with him at the task of spreading and guiding the Salesians. In 1884 Don Bosco asked the pope to declare Michael his successor as their superior, or "rector major," and he was confirmed in this position on the founder's death in 1888. Over the next twenty-two years he oversaw a huge expansion: from sixty-four to three hundred and forty-one houses; from seven hundred and sixty-eight members to over four thousand; from an Italian Congregation to a presence in twenty-three countries.

The main purpose of the Oratories was the rescue and education of poor children, especially those who would be called street children today. After one of his many missionary journeys Michael was able to say, "I have seen poverty everywhere, and yet, thank God, I have also seen thousands of children taken off the streets and changed into honest citizens and good Christians." Part school, part chapel, part club, the Oratories were a matter of approach first, of resources second: "If you wish to save a poor neighbourhood, open an Oratory. Even without grounds and buildings, if you are real Salesians, the Oratory will be in you."

Most of Michael's life was spent as an administrator, and as such he was a perfectionist and perhaps overscrupulous. His attention to all details of the Rule earned him the nickname "the living Rule." But he showed a wider vision in the developments he brought to the Oratories: he introduced high schools and vocational and commercial courses, and set up social circles and hostels for boarders. He faced various trials and difficulties: the Salesians were driven out of Ecuador by an anticlerical government in 1896 (see St Miguel Febres Cordero; 9 Feb), and out of France in 1902. In 1907 there was an orchestrated press campaign against them in Liguria; this was eventually shown to be a fraud, and its perpetrators fled, but a great deal of damage had been done, and the strain it placed on Michael probably shortened his life. There was a further burden placed on him the following year, when nine Salesians and thirty of their pupils were killed by an earthquake in Sicily.

Michael died of heart disease in Turin on 6 April 1910 and was buried beside Don Bosco, with the words "The Second Father of the Salesian Family" inscribed on his tomb. He was beatified in 1972 by Pope Paul VI, who called him "the continuation" of Don Bosco.

7

St Jean Baptist De La Salle (Jean-Baptiste De La Salle; 1651–1719)

This great champion of the education of the poor was born into and for a time embraced a life of comfort that gave no indication of the direction in which a chance encounter was to steer him. His family, from the cathedral city of Reims in northern France, was wealthy and aristocratic. He studied in Reims and then at the seminary of Saint-Sulpice in Paris, in the meantime inheriting a comfortable post as a canon of the cathedral. His parents died while he was in Paris, and he returned to Reims, completing his theology studies there and being ordained in 1781. He seemed destined to be a successful "career cleric," giving no hint of any particular inspiration.

In 1679 a layman named Adrien Nyel, who had opened four free schools for poor children in Rouen (a comparable cathedral city further to the west, in Normandy), asked him for help in opening a similar school in Reims. He initially took charge of the administration, but soon found himself paying for teachers and premises. Then, seeing that many of the teachers were incompetent, he took them into his house so that he could train them. This, to his family, was class treason on a major scale: his two brothers were ordered to leave the house. Eventually he and the teachers moved into a rented house to counter ongoing criticism, leaving the family house to other members of his family. This took place on the feast of the birthday of St John the Baptist, 24 June 1682. Two years later he had given away his fortune, mainly on famine relief, and resigned his cathedral canonry.

A new and then revolutionary concept was taking shape in his mind: a community devoted to Christian teaching but not ordained priests. He and twelve teachers took a simple vow of obedience and called themselves "Brothers of the Christian Schools." Their success was immediate and considerable, to the extent that they were seen as a threat by fee-paying schools. Despite this and other problems, many new schools were founded. Jean Baptist opened a novitiate in 1694, but official recognition of the Congregation by the Church was not forthcoming. Jean Baptist composed a Rule, needed for recognition. This borrowed from monastic Rules but set out a new vision: the apostolate of teaching was to be a means of achieving holiness through total dedication; the teachers had to "put on Christ" in order to become his "ambassadors to the young." To be able to do this, they had to be steeped in the scriptures and were to take a New Testament with them everywhere. And, as teaching was wearying enough in itself, they were not to undertake any extra form of mortification.

Jean Baptist followed the Rule with a series of manuals on Christian education and character. An aristocrat by birth, working with the poor, he was sometimes unable to shed his class background and so tended to try to impose an upper-class culture on the working classes rather than redeeming their own culture. The value he placed on good manners would have come across as alien, but it was at least based on solidly Christian foundations: the notion that every human being was worthy of respect as being made in the image of God. In *The Duties of a Christian*, published in 1695 and addressing a wider audience, he encouraged silent prayer and frequent Communion—the latter a radical suggestion in his day. All that he wrote about education was based on experience, tried and tested. He encouraged whole-class teaching, stressed that Christian schools must be communities, planned the curriculum, and insisted on regular monitoring of each pupil's progress, with as much care taken of those who are kept back as of those who achieve steady promotion.

The expansion of the Congregation continued, with more schools opening in Paris and other French towns. When James II of England was exiled to France after the "glorious revolution" of 1688, his Irish supporters who had fled with him asked the Brothers to educate their children, and this led them into secondary education. Hostility from some ecclesiastical quarters also continued, with suspicion arising from the fact that the Brothers were not priests and were not under the control of priests. In Paris an "ecclesiastical superior" from outside was appointed, but he failed to defend the Brothers against resentful lay schoolmasters, and several of their schools there had to close. Jean Baptist moved his centre of operation and the novitiate to Rouen. The Brothers opened their first boarding school outside Rouen, teaching a more modern and commercial curriculum. They also established a reformatory school for difficult and delinquent children, an area in which they were later to specialize.

By 1714, when he was sixty-three, Jean Baptist was ready to lay down some of his responsibilities, but he was forced to become superior general under his vow of obedience. Three years later a successor was appointed, and he was allowed to relinquish responsibilities apart from helping to revise the Rule. He retired to Saint-Yon, outside Rouen, where a new novitiate had been established some years earlier, and taught the students. He continued to write, devoting the rest of his time to prayer and meditation. He personally undertook penitential practices that he had discouraged his teachers from adopting, and generally lived a life as different from that suggested by his origins as would be possible to imagine, content to be guided in all things by what he experienced very directly as the will of God.

He died on 7 April 1719, which was Good Friday that year. His Congregation received official approval in 1726 and expanded greatly until it was suppressed under the French Revolution. It had a massive revival in the nineteenth century, when a thousand new foundations were made, and was still strong worldwide by the end of the twentieth. Jean Baptist was beatified in 1888, canonized in 1900, and in 1950 declared the principal patron of all teachers of young people.

I will often consider myself as an instrument which is of no use except in the hands of the workman. Hence I must await the orders of Providence before acting and be careful to accomplish them when known.
Jean Baptist De La Salle

8

St Julie Billiart (Marie Rose Julie Billiart; 1751–1816)

The foundress of the Institute of Notre Dame, later the Sisters of Notre Dame de Namur, came from a relatively wealthy family in Picardy, north-eastern France. When she was sixteen, her parents lost their money and she was forced to take on heavy manual work to help the family survive. Some years later, worse disaster struck: she was sitting in a room with her father when someone attempted to shoot him through the window. The shock of this left her with a nervous paralysis that gradually worsened and eventually, exacerbated by an incompetent doctor, left her unable to move.

She had been a devout child, encouraged by her parish priest to teach children the catechism and to visit the sick. She continued to teach and to give spiritual advice from her bed and developed a circle of wealthy ladies who visited her regularly. This led, on the outbreak of the French Revolution in 1789, to accusations of being a friend of the aristocracy and of sheltering priests. She was smuggled away in a haycart and spent three years in hiding. When the Terror had abated somewhat, she moved to Amiens, where she met a viscountess named Françoise Blin de Bourdon, who became her companion and co-foundress of the Institute and was later to write the first biography of her. They then met Fr Joseph Varin, who, convinced that Julie was being called to do special work in the Church, encouraged the foundation. Its main aims were the education of poor children and the formation of teachers. Fr Varin devised a provisional Rule, and the first Sisters took religious vows in 1804. During a parish mission in Amiens, in which the new Sisters were preparing women to receive the sacraments, one of the priests involved organized a novena to pray for Julie's recovery. Encouraged by him, she took her first steps in twenty-two years; her recovery lasted for the remaining twelve years of her life.

From then on she travelled all over France, opening convents and schools and centres for the training of teachers. Her Sisters had to be mobile and so there was no enclosure. She also did away with the traditional (usually class-based) division into choir and lay Sisters. All were to pray and meditate, and all were to share in manual work: they were all to lead "an interior life in the midst of external work," as without the first element, she saw, they would not have the strength to carry out the second. The poor remained her first care, but she saw the whole of society as de-Christianized in the wake of the French Revolution and also founded more select schools for the daughters of the wealthier classes. Like all pioneers, she met opposition from both civil and church authorities. As with the De La Salle Brothers (see previous entry), priests wanted to bring her Sisters under closer control. A dispute over this with the bishop of Amiens led Julie to move the motherhouse to Namur, hence the change of name for the Institute. Her most serious setback was the temporary closure of all her convents and schools in France after a number of allegations had been made against her. She dealt with all setbacks by keeping a complete trust in God's providence.

Her own education had been fairly minimal and she constantly stressed her ignorance and deferred to those she saw as more learned. She did not write any manual setting out her educational principles, but these can be gathered from her letters and from notes made at the many conferences she gave. Her schools were not to be just places where learning was acquired: they were for the formation of "good Christians who know how to manage their household, their family, their affairs." After a good grounding in religious instruction and the three Rs, pupils could take other subjects, but these were not to extend to such non-essentials as "dancing and drawing, elocution and deportment." She wanted a practical curriculum to give children "an education for life," and to this end she was willing to give her teachers considerable liberty in approach and choice of material.

Despite her lack of education, she developed a spirituality considered worthy of a "doctor or director of souls," as one parish priest who heard her give advice stated. Its essence was complete dependence on God, which produced a "simplicity" she urged on her Sisters. This was to be achieved through "care to look only to God and to his good pleasure," and involved learning detachment from material things even when dealing constantly with the material world.

Julie died after a few months illness on 8 April 1816. Françoise took over the direction of the Institute, and by the time she died in 1838 it was firmly established and widely respected. Julie had created a system that was flexible enough to meet the new demands of post-revolutionary society. By the end of the nineteenth century the Sisters were working in the United States, Britain, and several African countries; by the end of the twentieth they had spread to China, Japan, and Latin America. Julie was beatified in 1906 and canonized by Pope Paul VI in 1969.

May Jesus Christ live within us, and as for me may I no longer live but for his pure and holy love. May this love consume me every instant of my life so that I may become a victim of love. Praised be Jesus Christ! Praised be Mary!
favourite prayer of Julie Billiart

9

St Gemma Galgani (1878–1903)

Gemma was born near Lucca in Tuscany. Her mother died when she was eight, and her father when she was nineteen. She had suffered poor health from childhood, with a number of ailments including tuberculosis of the spine. Her health prevented her from joining the Passionist Sisters, which was her chief desire in life. For a time she seemed to have been cured, apparently as a result of supernatural intervention, attributed variously to the intercession of St Gabriel Possenti, a Passionist who had died at the age of twenty-four from tuberculosis, or of St Margaret Mary Alacoque, the visionary promoter of devotion to the Sacred Heart (see 16 Oct.). The cure, however, was not to last.

She left over 230 letters to her spiritual director and her confessor, which reveal a humble and devout young woman, willing to suffer anything in imitation of Christ's passion and constantly aware of the presence of God. All the while she was writing these perfectly balanced letters, she was subjected to extreme physical and psychical phenomena, the origins of which have remained a subject of controversy ever since. For almost two years she regularly showed the stigmata from Thursday evening to Friday afternoon, and sometimes her body also bore the marks of Jesus' scourging at the pillar. She would go into visionary trances, during which she could be heard talking to those she saw in her visions. Blasphemous language could cause her to sweat blood. If these seemed to show some sort of divine possession, she also showed more alarming symptoms of diabolic possession, which once caused her to spit on a crucifix.

"Possession" might have been the verdict in an earlier century, but this was at the turn of the twentieth century, at a time when psychoanalysis was making its way, and "chronic hysteria" was the more common diagnosis. Such a judgment, though, had to overcome the level-headedness she showed in her letters and in her actions for most of the time. Her spiritual director, Fr Germano, was inclined to accept a divine cause, while her confessor, Bishop Volpi, remained more doubtful, saying it would be difficult to believe that all her experiences came from God.

Gemma died from her illnesses at the age of twenty-five, leaving the verdict open. Today people would have less difficulty in accepting a mixture of psychosomatic and other causes, some not understood. She left an impression of saintliness on all who knew her, and the cause of her beatification was soon introduced. She was beatified in 1933, and the decree carefully stated that she was declared Blessed because of her heroic virtue, with no opinion implied as to the origin of her experiences. She was canonized in 1940, and her letters were published the following year, enabling a wider public to appreciate her good humour and common sense, along with the intense piety deriving from her love of God and her appreciation of the sufferings of Christ so strangely replicated in her life.

10

St Magdalen of Canossa (Maddalena Gabriella di Canossa; 1774–1835)

A contemporary portrait shows her at the age of fifteen as a fashionable society beauty, but Magdalen knew only loss and rejection from her aristocratic family, and then did all she could to reject her origins. Her father died when she was five, and her mother married again and abandoned her and her four brothers. After a serious illness when she was fifteen, she declared that she intended to become a nun, to the horror of her relatives. But an attempt to try her vocation with the Carmelites failed, as she felt she could not do what she wanted, which was to serve "Jesus Christ in his poor," as a member of an enclosed Order. She returned to the family estates and administered them while at the same time doing what she could to help poor girls in her native city of Verona.

Encouraged by her spiritual director, she gradually increased the range of her apostolate, working in hospitals, giving alms extensively, instructing parishioners in the catechism, and visiting the sick and the destitute in their homes. Her brothers were horrified, but she still felt she was not doing enough to save herself from damnation, and her spiritual director (who cannot have been popular in the family) advised her to devote her entire time to the work she had undertaken. She lodged two poor girls in her own house, opened a refuge and a school in the poorest part of the city, and recruited teachers with a view to forming them into some sort of religious community. In 1808 she took over a disused (because suppressed) monastery and moved the school and the community into it. The school prospered, offering girls practical subjects as well as numeracy and literacy, all underpinned with sound religious instruction (not unlike the initiatives of St Julie Billiart; see 8 Apr.).

A new religious Congregation took shape, as she had wished, and she wrote a first Rule for what became known as the Congregation of the Daughters of Charity, or the Canossian Sisters of Charity. This was given provisional approval by Pope Pius VII on his return journey to Rome from exile in France in 1816. She was soon asked to open a similar house in Venice, and over the next twenty years the initiative spread to most major cities in northern Italy. She devised a scheme for training young women from rural areas as primary school teachers, giving then a seven-month course in one of the Canossian houses. She sought the advice of Antonio Rosmini, founder of the Institute of Charity (the Rosminians) in connection with extending the work to a men's Congregation and schools for boys, and in 1831 founded the Institute of the Sons of Charity.

Magdalen's practical work was sustained by an intense personal spirituality, with mystical experiences, which she tried to describe, with their joyous rewards and their periods of dryness, in her *Memoirs*. She had a special devotion to Our Lady of Sorrows, seeing Mary as becoming "mother of charity" as she stood at the foot of the cross, an example of strength she constantly put before her Sisters. Her inspiration was the gospel, especially through her identification with Christ crucified, and she described the religious life as "only the gospel translated into practice." In accordance with the vision of the kingdom of God set out in Matthew 25, she always saw the crucified Christ in the poor, the sick, and the suffering.

Pope Leo XII gave the Congregation formal approval in 1828, and Magdalen died seven years later. Her cause was introduced in 1877 but made relatively slow progress; she was eventually beatified by Pope Pius XII in 1941 and canonized by Pope John Paul II in 1988. The Congregation continues her work in twenty-one countries around the world, carried out by some four thousand Sisters. The men's Institute has remained smaller, with some two hundred priests and lay brothers working in Italy, Brazil, and the Philippines.

11

St Stanislaus of Cracow (around 1030–1079)

Stanislaus is one of the patron saints of Poland and particularly venerated in the city of Cracow, of which he was bishop and where most of his relics are preserved in the cathedral. No biography of him was written for some four hundred years after his death, when the historian John Dlugosz produced one, compiled apparently from earlier fragments and oral traditions. It cannot be termed historical as now understood, and, beyond a basic outline, little is known of his life, and there has to be some question over whether his death was a martyrdom or simply political.

He was born into a noble family to, it is said, long-childless parents, on (possibly) 26 July 1030. He was educated first at Gnesen (now Gniezno in west-central Poland) and then possibly at Liège in what is now Belgium—the biography says Paris, but there was no university there at the time. He was ordained priest and appointed canon of Cracow Cathedral. He proved himself a great preacher, responsible for reform among the clergy, to the extent that Bishop Lampert Zula, who had ordained him, wished to resign so that Stanislaus could be appointed in his place. But he refused to contemplate this, becoming bishop only on Lampert's death in 1072, when the people acclaimed him and Pope Alexander II formally appointed him.

Gregory VII succeeded to the papacy the following year and took a keen interest in the mission territories of eastern Europe. Poland was ruled by Boleslaus II, who, despite his characterization in earlier editions of *Butler's Lives* as "a prince whose finer qualities were completely eclipsed by his unbridled lust and savage qualities," paid tribute to the papacy and welcomed Gregory's reforming initiatives, in 1075 accepting Roman legates who were to improve the organization of the Polish Church. Boleslaus therefore also on principle supported the reforming new bishop of Cracow, but then they quarrelled, for reasons that remain unclear. The traditional story is that Stanislaus infuriated him by rebuking him for kidnapping a nobleman's beautiful wife, when no other prelate or courtier had dared to protest. Boleslaus refused to give the lady up, and in the end Stanislaus excommunicated him.

The king determined to have him executed and ordered his guards to kill him in the chapel of St Michael, outside Cracow, where Stanislaus was saying Mass. The guards refused, claiming, it is said, that he was protected by a heavenly light shining all around him. The king had no such fears and rushed in and killed the bishop himself. His body, the story tells, was then cut into pieces and put out to be eaten by wild beasts, but it was protected by eagles, and the pieces were collected and buried at the door of the chapel. There were certainly enough relics to be reinterred in the cathedral in 1088. Pope Gregory placed the whole country under an interdict, which contributed to Boleslaus being deposed. Stanislaus was canonized by Pope Innocent IV in 1253. In the early twentieth century a historical work was published claiming that Stanislaus had been plotting to overthrow Boleslaus and should therefore be regarded as a traitor rather than a martyr; this was strongly denied by other historians. Perhaps all that can be said is that it was virtually impossible to separate religion and politics in Poland at the time—as indeed it has been in far more recent times. Many churches are dedicated to Stanislaus in Poland and in areas of the USA where Polish immigrants have settled.

12

St Joseph Moscati (Giuseppe Moscati; 1880–1927)

Joseph Moscati was a distinguished doctor who saw medicine as a vocation and practised it as though he were exercising a priesthood. He was born in Benevento, east of Naples, into an old aristocratic family. His father was a distinguished judge, and the family moved as he was promoted, until he died in Naples when Joseph was seventeen. He began studying at the faculty of medicine there the same year and after six years of study was awarded a congratulatory degree and joined first one of the local hospitals and then that of Santa Maria del Popolo, known as the *Incurabili*, for those with incurable diseases.

It was a time when the religious concept of what it meant to be a human being was battling against a more materialist concept typical of much nineteenth-century science. Joseph's deep faith led him to take a holistic approach well before such a theory became widespread, seeking always to treat the whole person and not just the disease. He wrote to a pupil: "Remember that you must take care not only of bodies but also of souls, through counselling and by seeking out their spirit, rather than with cold prescriptions to be sent to the chemist." He was above all a caring doctor, inspired by seeing Christ in person in each suffering patient. He showed his deep care when he risked his life to evacuate patients from a subsidiary hospital on the slopes of

163

Mount Vesuvius when the volcano erupted in 1906. He found that most of the staff had fled but, with those who had stayed, just managed to get the last patients out before the roof collapsed under the ash that had fallen on it.

In 1908 he was appointed professor of clinical chemistry in the Naples Institute of Physiological Chemistry. This academic phase of his career lasted only three years, with commitments to teaching and research, and resulted in the publication of at least thirty-two papers. His main area of research was chemical reactions to glycogen in the human body. He was then promoted to director of the *Incurabili* in 1911, a year that also saw him showing deep devotion to his patients during a cholera outbreak. He retained direct responsibility for some departments as well as being in overall charge, but still found time for daily Communion. He treated poorer patients free of charge and even paid personally for medicines they could not afford.

In February 1927 Joseph went to listen to a conference talk by an eminent doctor and politician, Professor Bianchi, who had previously taught him. Bianchi was also an anti-Christian Freemason, not the sort of person Joseph would naturally have gone to hear. He said afterwards that he had felt impelled to go by some outside force. At the end of his speech, the professor collapsed on the platform as the applause was still sounding. Joseph rushed to his aid. Bianchi seemed to recognize him and squeezed his hand in response to Joseph's urgent recommendation of repentance and trust in God. Less than two months later Joseph himself died suddenly during a home visit to a patient. He had, as usual, been to Mass and visited his parents that morning. He was only forty-seven.

A huge crowd of mourners attended the funeral of the man generally known as "the good doctor." One old man spoke for all: "We mourn him because the world has lost a saint, Naples has lost an example of every virtue, and the sick poor have lost everything." Public pressure caused his remains to be moved in November of the same year from the municipal cemetery to the Gesù Nuovo church inside the city. Joseph was beatified by Pope Paul VI on 16 November 1976 and canonized by Pope John Paul II on 25 October 1987.

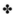

Love truth; show yourself just as you are, without dissimulation, fear, or precautions. And if truth means that you are persecuted, accept it; that you are tormented, bear it. And if you should have to sacrifice yourself and your life for truth, be strong in that sacrifice.

Joseph Moscati, from a personal notebook

13

St Martin I (died 655)

Martin was pope at the height of the political and doctrinal dispute between orthodoxy and the heresy known as Monothelitism. The debate was over whether Christ had both a human and a divine will, so two wills, or a divine will only, so one. (The word comes from the Greek *monos*, one, and *thelein*, to will.) The Monothelite teaching that there was one will only resembled the Monophysite doctrine that Christ had only one nature, a divine one, as opposed to the orthodox view that he had two, divine and human. Monothelitism was in fact an attempted compromise, designed to reconcile the Monophysites, who were causing division in the Roman Empire at a time when it was facing outside threats from the Persians and from nascent Islam. It had, however, been condemned by successive popes.

The emperor Constans II, Roman emperor from 642 to 688, embraced a derivative of Monothelitism to rally political support. Martin, who came originally from Todi in Umbria, had served for a time under the emperor in Constantinople. He was elected pope in 649 and showed his opposition to Constans and his doctrine by having himself consecrated without the emperor's approval. In retaliation, Constans refused to recognize him as pope and issued a decree forbidding discussion of any of the issues involved. Martin summoned a synod at the Lateran in Rome to condemn both Monothelitism and the emperor's decree and wrote to Constans insisting that he accept the synod's pronouncements. Constans' response was to send a legate, Olympius by name, to Italy to arrest Martin and bring him back to Constantinople to be tried for treason. Olympius, however, was won over to Martin's side; Constans sent a second envoy, Theodore Calliopas, in 653, and this time Martin, by now bedridden from illness, was taken to the imperial capital, spending a year as a captive on the Greek island of Naxos on the way and not reaching Constantinople till December 654.

He was kept in solitary confinement and treated harshly for three months, then brought before a court, which refused to take any account of the real issue, the doctrinal differences between him and Constans, but condemned him to exile and had him publicly scourged. The patriarch of Constantinople intervened, and the sentence was commuted to banishment to the Crimea (then called Chersonesus). Churchmen in Rome seem to have forgotten about their pope and done nothing to attempt to secure his release—worse, they went ahead and elected a new pope while he was still alive. He sent them a number of—not unsurprisingly—complaining letters from prison, where conditions were so harsh that within six months he was dead from starvation and brutal treatment. He was venerated as a martyr—the last pope to be so regarded—though it might be claimed that his own Church of Rome should bear at least some of the responsibility for the death of its bishop. He has always been commemorated on today's date in the Eastern Church, and his former feast-day of 12 November in the West has now been moved to accord with this.

14

Bd Lydwina of Schiedam (1380–1433)

Lydwina presents a most disturbing case of apparent acceptance of grotesque suffering on the advice of a spiritual director—what might be termed "victimhood" today. But since her physical sufferings were in fact so extreme and since at this distance in time it is impossible to judge exactly what their causes were, it may be that the advice she was given was for the best.

Her family, from Schiedam, near Rotterdam in Holland, was poor. She lived a normal life to the age of fifteen, though her position as the only girl in a family of nine may have meant that she was overworked as a child. Then she had an accident while ice-skating. She appeared at first to have just broken a rib, but it seems that some severe internal damage must have been done, as she began vomiting and suffering other painful symptoms. She gradually became able to do less and less. The parish priest was asked to counsel her, as she was refusing to accept her situation, and he told her that identifying her sufferings with the passion of Christ might prove to be a special sort of religious calling.

She came to see herself as a sacrificial victim, taking on the sins of other people, and as her physical condition deteriorated, her reputation for holiness increased, and people began to come to her to seek spiritual advice. By the time she was nineteen her face was grossly disfigured, her limbs were contorted, she suffered recurring heart attacks that left her able to move only her left arm, and she was blind in one eye. She was frequently unconscious for long periods of time, and these were interpreted as ecstasies. For the last nineteen years of her life she seemed to take no food except for the communion wafer—a condition that can be faked, but in her case there seem to have been a number of reliable witnesses to confirm it.

Not everyone accepted her saintliness. A new parish priest attributed her sufferings to diabolical possession and would not let her take Communion. Others thought she was a sham and a hypocrite. An inquiry was held and found her innocent and to be acting in good faith. She was once again allowed to receive Communion, once a fortnight. That she lived under these conditions for some thirty-four years can only be termed astonishing, whatever the details of her symptoms and their causes. By the time she died on 13 April 1433, a cult had already developed. Three contemporaries, including Thomas à Kempis, the author of the *Imitation of Christ,* wrote Lives of her, but it was not until 1890 that her cult was officially approved, and she has not been canonized. Her life, like that of Gemma Galgani, presents puzzles on which the official Church wisely refuses to comment, but popular religious culture usually finds extreme suffering quite devoid of meaning if it is not referred ultimately to God.

15

Bd Damien De Veuster (Joseph De Veuster; 1840–1889)

The apostle to the lepers was born in Belgium into a modest and pious farming family. Two of his sisters became nuns and one brother a priest. Joseph himself, the seventh child, was also determined to pursue a religious vocation, and followed his brother into the Fathers of the Sacred Hearts of Jesus and Mary, joining the community at Louvain and taking the name Damien in religion. At first he was considered too uneducated to be allowed to study for the priest-hood, but his brother taught him Latin and the decision was reversed. He made his vows in Paris in 1860 and studied philosophy there, then theology at Louvain.

His life's work began by accident: his brother was due to be sent on the Order's mission to Hawaii but was taken ill with typhus, and Damien offered to go in his place. This was accepted, and he sailed for Honolulu in November 1863, arrived after a five-month voyage, and was ordained there. He worked at two mission stations on the islands for nine years, then volunteered to go to the leper colony on Molokai. The bishop planned a rotating team of missionaries, each spending no more than three weeks at a time, to minimize risk of infection, but Damien said he would go and stay there. There was no cure for leprosy, and lepers were simply removed from all normal human contact and herded together under dreadful conditions. When Damien arrived on Molokai there were some eight hundred lepers, confined to one end of the island, and more were continually arriving.

A hospital had been built for them, and they received occasional visits from a government doctor, but there was nothing for them to do except sit around and drink. This and the fact that leprosy was thought to be spread mainly through sexual contact gave them a terrible reputation, and the place was referred to as "the Devil's paradise." Damien simply loved them as souls redeemed by Christ and was prepared to do anything for them. Paraphrasing St Paul, he wrote, "I have made myself a leper with the lepers, to gain all to Jesus Christ." On the practical level, he tried to improve their living conditions, begging clothes from other missions and introducing at least rudimentary standards of hygiene. His work became known around the world, though he did not publicize it, and a lot of money was raised to support it, including £2,000 (around half a million dollars at current rates) from an Anglican clergyman who organized subscriptions through *The Times*. He set up an orphanage, improved roads and the harbour, enlarged the hospital to make new forms of treatment possible, and generally turned the "human jungle" he had found into a viable community. From 1878 he was helped by another priest, and then the Hawaiian authorities provided more material help and two schoolteachers, so he was not working entirely alone.

Like so many pioneers, he met with disapproval, which he partly brought upon himself, as he was convinced he knew best in every field and became distinctly autocratic. There was also envy in government and church circles at the amount of money that was flowing to his mission compared to other projects. He had worked with the lepers for nearly twelve years when he was diagnosed as having the disease. This brought accusations, because of current beliefs, that he must have had sexual relations with leper women, and he was submitted to humiliating medical examinations, as well as being forbidden to leave the island. Visitors stopped coming, and he was deprived of the consolation of Confession. He was filled with fear and desolation for a time but then became completely reconciled to God's will, describing himself in 1887 as "the happiest missionary in the world." His only worry was that he would become too disabled to say Mass.

Attitudes to him suddenly changed: he was allowed off the island to spend a week in hospital on Honolulu, where the king, the prime minister, and the bishop visited him. Money flowed in from the United States and England. More assistants joined him, including an American layman, Joseph Dutton, who was to stay for forty years. But Damien's leprosy was advancing inexorably, and he died on 15 April 1889, aged forty-nine. Controversy continued after his death: he was attacked by a Protestant clergyman from Honolulu named Dr Hyde, which prompted a famous riposte in the form of an open letter by Robert Louis Stevenson. His remains were transferred to the Sacred Hearts Congregation's church in Louvain in 1936, which led to a whole spate of European books about him. A new tomb was built in the crypt in 1962, and he was beatified in 1995 for the heroic virtue of a life, however controversial, dedicated out of love of God to the poorest of the poor.

16

St Bernadette (Marie Bernarde Soubirous; 1844–1879)

This famous visionary seemed destined to a life of total obscurity. She was the eldest of six children born in Lourdes, on the French side of the Pyrenees, to a family sinking ever deeper into poverty. She was also small and sickly; she suffered from asthma and caught cholera in the epidemic of 1854. Her family called her Bernadette, "little Bernarde." She was also considered mentally dull, and by 1858, when she was fourteen, she still had not been allowed to make her First Communion. In that year, however, her life and that of her little town were totally changed.

She insisted that she experienced a series of visions of "a Lady" in a natural cavity in a rock-face, known as Massabielle, across the river Gave de Pau from where she was. The Lady spoke to her and told her to dig in the ground; she did so and water began to flow, a trickle at first, then a stream (which has been flowing ever since). Bernadette told her family about the first vision, and when she went back to the grotto, on days indicated by the Lady, increasing numbers of people went with her, but they saw or heard nothing out of the ordinary. Bernadette, however, continued "receiving" messages, urging people to do penance and to visit the place on pilgrimage. She was urged to ask the Lady who she was and was told, in the local dialect, *"Que soy era Immaculada Conceptiou,"* "I am the Immaculate Conception." This had been defined as a dogma binding on all the faithful just four years earlier, so it is quite possible that Bernadette would have had some understanding of what the words signified, but they have been taken as having been put into her mouth by local clergy in an attempt to make the dogma better known.

At first the clergy and people were sceptical, but Bernadette clung to the authenticity of her experiences. She was obviously sincere and showed no signs of hysteria, so gradually opinion swung round—helped, no doubt, by the crowds and attendant revenue as the fame of her visions spread. A chapel was built by the grotto in 1862, and, aided by the end of the Franco-Prussian War in 1870 and the rapid spread of the railways, Lourdes became the most popular pilgrimage place in Europe. The Lady had not promised cures, but people began bringing their sick, and over the years a large number of cures still inexplicable to medical science have been recorded and meticulously documented. They now seem to be on the decrease, but millions still flock to Lourdes every year, and few come away without feeling spiritually refreshed, despite the inevitable commercialization of the town.

Bernadette, the vehicle for all this, hated the publicity it brought her and refused to claim any special powers. She boarded in a hospice run by the Sisters of Charity for five years and was then, in 1866, accepted as a novice in the convent of the Sisters of Notre Dame at Nevers, well away from Lourdes. She adopted the Latin form of her names, Maria Bernarda, in religion. She spent the rest of her life there and did not even leave the convent to attend the ceremonies marking the opening of a new basilica at Lourdes in 1876. She was unwilling to be seen or to draw attention to herself in any way. She sought the straightforward holiness of a religious through obedience to the Rule of her Order. She saw herself as someone who had been used in an extraordinary way and then "put back in my corner," like a broom, and she was happy to stay there.

Her health continued to worsen, with tuberculosis of the bones added to increasingly severe asthma. She bore all her sufferings with great patience and resignation, for the sake of "the heart of Jesus, with all its treasures." She died on 16 April 1879, having led a completely uneventful life but one full of unquestioning obedience to the will of God ever since the last apparition. She was canonized as St Maria Bernarda in 1933. As with all visionaries, the Church upheld its principle, defined by St Thomas Aquinas, that any special experience "is received by the recipient according to the manner of the recipient," that is without presuming to pass judgment on its origin. Her saintliness consisted in her life of prayer, simple devotion, and steadfast obedience. Her legacy lives on at Lourdes in an outpouring of communal charity that would be hard to find paralleled anywhere else on earth.

O Jesus, keep me under the standard of your cross. Let me not just look at you crucified but have you living in my heart.
Prayer of St Bernadette

17

Bd Kateri Tekakwitha (Tekakwitha; about 1656–1680)

The first Native American to be beatified was the daughter of a Christian Algonquin woman and a pagan Mohawk chief. The Mohawks were at the time part of the "Five Nations Confederacy," a sort of non-aggression pact among the tribes occupying the territory of the "Longhouses," the land running north–south between the Hudson River in New York and Lake Erie. There were some twenty-five thousand inhabitants of this territory, and they were able to muster an army of three or four thousand braves. The Mohawks occupied the eastern strip and were in themselves a powerful deterrent against white incursions from the colonized coastal area.

Kateri's mother had been raised as a Christian, captured by the Mohawks, and taken to Ossernenon in their "longhouse" area (now Auriesville, in New York State), where she was married to a chief. They named their first child Tekakwitha, meaning "she who puts things in order," and had another child, a son, three years later. The village was the site of the martyrdom of St Isaac Jogues and his companions (19 Oct.) some ten years earlier. In 1660 the Mohawks were struck with smallpox, the "white man's disease," against which they had no immunity. Tekakwitha's parents both died, as did her infant brother, and she was left disfigured and partially blind. An uncle was elected war chief in her father's place, and she was welcomed by his family, staying with them when the tribe moved to Gandawague, taking the bodies of her dead parents and brother with them. She could see close up and became an expert at decorative embroidery.

In 1667 Jesuit missionaries came to the settlement and lodged with her uncle. This was her first contact with Christian missionaries, and she seems to have been impressed by the Blackrobes, as the Jesuits were known. She attended their festivals but made no move to seek instruction or ask to be baptized. At about this time she also appears to have made a private vow never to marry, and she refused a number of young Mohawk braves, something inexplicable in their culture and which exposed her to a good deal of mockery and derision. Some eight years after the first missionaries, Fr Jacques de Lamberville, a Jesuit who knew the Mohawks well, whom they called "Dawn of Day," came to the mission. Tekakwitha asked him for Baptism, which made a deep impression on the village, as her status as daughter of the chief was high. He baptized her on Easter Sunday 1676, when she took the baptismal name Catherine, Kateri in her language. She seemed already to have a deep understanding of prayer and the sacramental life.

Her uncle made no objection to her conversion but was anxious that she should not leave the village to live near the Jesuit mission station, as many converts were doing. She stayed, but her situation became increasingly difficult, with threats of violence on account of her continued refusal to marry. Fr de Lamberville sought a means by which she could get away, and help came from an Oneida chief, a Christian, known as "Hot Ashes" or "Hot Cinders" for his ferocious temper. One of his companions was an Algonquin related to Kateri's mother, and he and some others engineered her escape. Her uncle was furious and made determined attempts to have her brought back, but these proved in vain, and she eventually reached the Sault St Louis mission near Montreal, on the site where the Portage River flows into the St Lawrence (*sault* being French for rapids). Fr de Lamberville had given Kateri a message for the priests: "Here is a treasure, guard it well."

171

There were three priests in charge of the mission, which was a compound of some size, with well over a hundred Native American converts living within its stockade. Kateri settled into a life of intense religious observance, with two Masses every day, starting at 4 a.m., recitation of the Rosary, and Vespers and Benediction in the evenings. She was allowed to make her First Communion on Christmas Day 1677, having been through the long probationary period since her Baptism on which the missionaries insisted. She was befriended by an older woman named Marie Thérèse Tegaiaguenta, and they inspired each other to fresh heights of devotion, even asking if they could become nuns. The missionaries, true to their time, laughed at the idea of Native American women as nuns. Kateri consoled herself by making a private vow of perpetual virginity.

Her health, never robust since her childhood smallpox, began to fail, not helped by her fasting on Wednesdays and Saturdays and other acts of penance, and she was confined to her bed, a thin stuffed mattress. She spent hours staring joyfully at holy pictures given her by the missionaries when she was no longer able to go to the chapel. She died on 17 April 1680 and was buried beside the river. The message, "The saint is dead," spread rapidly, and a cult developed immediately after her death, with reported cures and apparitions and stories of her supernatural understanding of other people's problems. She was declared venerable in 1947 and beatified in 1980.

18

Bd Mary of the Incarnation (Barbe Acarie; 1566–1618)

The name of Barbe Acarie is associated with several great reforming figures in French religious life during and after the religious wars in France in the latter half of the sixteenth century, but she is a significant figure in her own right. She was born Barbe Avrillot, the daughter of Nicholas Avrillot, who was financial counsellor to the Paris Parliament and became chancellor to Queen Margaret of Valois (who married the future King Henry IV). She was educated at the Franciscan convent at Longchamps, where her aunt was prioress. This was usually reserved for girls destined to enter the religious life, and Barbe was determined to do so, but her mother was even more determined that she should make a fashionable marriage. Barbe resisted her and was shut in her room for two years with no heating, in an apparent attempt by her mother to show her what convent life was really like. She lost a toe from an infected chilblain as a result.

When she was sixteen, Barbe agreed to marry. The husband chosen for her was Pierre Acarie, viscount of Villemore, a young, witty, wealthy lawyer and a devout Catholic. She could hardly have asked for a more suitable husband and may well have been attracted to him; he could certainly not have had a more devoted wife. He was active in helping English Catholic refugees from persecution under Queen Elizabeth. She consented at last to wear fashionable clothes and to join fully in the social life that went with her position. Her charm brought her the nickname of "la belle Acarie." The couple had six children, to whom Barbe devoted an unusual amount of attention for her social class at the time. Pierre thought she had become too worldly, as she read novels, which he then replaced with devotional works, but it gradually emerged that she was leading an intense inner spiritual life, subject to ecstasies that lasted for hours and were at first diagnosed as illness and treated with blood-letting. An English Capuchin, Fr Benet of Canfield, reassured her that the experiences came from God.

Their comfortable social life was overturned when Henry IV, a Huguenot by conviction (despite one conversion to Catholicism, which he later revoked), acceded to the French throne in 1589. He besieged Paris in the winter of 1590–91, reducing the population to starvation. Barbe did all she could to help the sick, the starving, and the dying. When Henry took Paris, Pierre, a member of the Catholic League, was exiled from the capital. He had spent vast sums of money supporting the League, and the family was suddenly heavily in debt. Bailiffs seized all their possessions. It fell to Barbe to negotiate with creditors and do all she could to rebuild the position, which she gradually achieved, showing the immense practical capability that often goes with mystical experience—as witness St Teresa of Avila (see 15 Oct.), who influenced the rest of Barbe's life. She moved out of the family house, boarding the children at the convent at Longchamps and herself lodging with a cousin, Madame de Bérulle. She regularly rode the sixty-plus miles to Soissons, where Pierre was exiled, and once broke her leg falling off her horse. She was to break it again twice in other accidents; it was badly reset, and she endured great pain and could walk only with the aid of a stick.

In 1593 Henry IV became a Catholic again, and when he issued the Edict of Nantes in 1598, granting religious toleration to Protestants, France was united. The following year Pierre was allowed back from exile, returning, without wealth or office, to find that his house had been turned into a spiritual salon. Barbe had become well known in devout circles, and many people came to her seeking advice and asking for her prayers. The group of women who gathered in the salon read the works of St Teresa of Avila together. (Barbe was unable to do more than listen: if she attempted to read out loud, she went into ecstasy.) Barbe determined to establish the Discalced Carmelites of Teresa's reform in Paris and was encouraged by both Francis de Sales (see 24 Jan.) and her cousin Pierre de Bérulle, later the founder of the French Oratorians. The matter required delicate diplomatic negotiations with Spain and the papacy, but the foundation was eventually authorized in 1602, and the deserted priory of Notre-Dame-des-Champs was acquired for the first house. Barbe devoted her energies to rebuilding and refitting it, and to recruiting and training French novices. Six Spanish nuns, including Teresa's close companions Anne of Jesus and Anne of St Bartholomew, arrived by coach in October 1604, expecting martyrdom at the hands of French heretics but receiving a splendid and warm reception.

There were difficulties of communication and cultural differences between the Spanish nuns and the French novices, and eventually the nuns moved on to the Spanish Netherlands, but by that time the movement had taken root in France, and Barbe was busy organizing new foundations. She also helped Fr de Bérulle establish the Oratory, to "supply the bishops with good parish priests and curates," and encouraged St Vincent de Paul (see 27 Sept.), who was beginning his work for the destitute of Paris. Somehow she managed all this while hobbling about on her stick and caring for her husband and children. Her three daughters all became Discalced Carmelites; of the three sons, one became a priest and two married.

Pierre died in 1613, nursed assiduously to the last by his wife. She disposed of the family property and entered the Discalced Carmelite convent at Amiens as a lay sister, taking the name Mary of the Incarnation in religion. She went into ecstasy during her clothing ceremony and as soon as she had recovered went to the kitchen to prepare the nuns' dinner. She spent the last four years of her life seeking obscurity, sometimes misunderstood and bullied as a result. She was moved to the convent at Pontoise as a result of this, though ostensibly "for her health's sake." She was warmly welcomed and put her organizing talents to work to build up the community, with the help of money from the many people who came from Paris seeking her spiritual advice. She died on 18 April 1618, which was Easter Sunday, and was widely hailed as a saint. Her son Pierre tried to introduce her cause in 1627, but Pope Urban VIII had issued a decree that at least fifty years must elapse between a person's death and beatification procedures, and the cause lapsed. It was reintroduced one hundred and fifty years later by King Louis XIV and his sister, who was a Carmelite prioress, and she was beatified, not on account of her ecstasies but specifically for her work "in the world," a rare endorsement of a married woman's life, on 5 June 1791.

19

St Leo IX (Bruno of Toul; 1002–1054)

This reforming pope was born in Alsace and christened Bruno. His father was a count and closely related to the family of the Holy Roman emperors in the west. Bruno was educated at Toul (just west of Nancy in eastern France) and became a canon of the cathedral there, though his disposition seemed more that of a warrior than of a cleric—not that there was necessarily a distinction in his day. He led an expeditionary force consisting of troops provided by the bishop into Italy to help put down a Lombard rebellion against his relative Emperor Conrad II. The bishop of Toul died while he was in Italy, and Bruno was appointed to succeed him. As bishop for twenty years he proved an energetic reformer, attacking abuses such as simony and nepotism as well as clerical marriage. He also reformed the monasteries in his diocese.

In 1048 Pope Damasus II, who had been elected the same year, died, and Bruno was chosen by the emperor, by then Henry III, Conrad's son. It is interesting that a pope who is regarded as pioneering the Gregorian Reform, essentially aimed at securing the separation of Church and State, was appointed bishop and then pope not only by the imperial power (which still saw itself as "Holy Roman") but also by an emperor who was a relative. But Leo in fact was still prepared to work closely with rulers, without being overawed by them. The manner of his appointment certainly did nothing to mar the way he set about his papacy: he entered Rome dressed as a pilgrim and took the name Leo, a name not used for a century and chosen to hark back to times when the Church was purer. He held a reforming synod in Rome and then journeyed to other prominent European cities, holding twelve synods in all.

These were important tools for reform, and Leo was not afraid of deposing some bishops permanently and making others, including those in whose diocese the synod was being held, resign and be reappointed by him, significantly making them accept a new crozier. He insisted that new bishops should be elected by the clergy and people of their diocese, in an effort to curb secular power over the Church—despite the manner of his own appointments. He was aided in his reforms by advisers he chose from outside the Roman Curia, including two future popes: Hildebrand, who became the great St Gregory VII (1073–85; see 22 May), and Frederick of Liège, who became Stephen IX (1057–58). He also took advice from the austere reforming monk Peter Damian (see 20 Feb.), but fell out with him over an ill-judged venture that marred the last year of his papacy, when he seemed to revert to the warrior days of his youth.

He personally led an army against the Normans, who invaded papal territories in southern Italy, and was defeated and held captive for several months. Peter Damian firmly told him that battles should be fought by emperors, not by popes. The defeat led to worse for the whole Church: the break known as the Eastern Schism. The Church in the east, under the headship of the patriarch of Constantinople, claimed jurisdiction over some parts of southern Italy. Leo had annoyed the current patriarch, Michael Cerularius, by holding a synod in what Michael regarded as his territory in 1050. Leo's incursion made matters worse. He wanted help from the Eastern Church against the Normans and sent Humbert, former abbot of Moyenmoutiers (one of the abbeys in the diocese of

Toul), whom he had appointed archbishop of Sicily, as legate to ask for this help. But the patriarch was enraged by the appointment to a place over which he also claimed jurisdiction; Humbert was intransigent, and the patriarch eventually pronounced an excommunication against both him and the pope. By this time Leo was dead. The quarrel became theological, and the two Churches finally split over the famous *filioque* clause in the Creed—the question of whether the Holy Spirit "proceeds from the Father *and* the Son" of "from the Father *through* the Son." This is still unresolved.

Leo was brought back from his captivity in March 1054, already ill. He had his bed and his coffin placed side by side in St Peter's and there awaited death. He died on 19 April 1054 and was immediately acclaimed as a saint, with many miracles reported at his tomb. The popular cult was confirmed when his relics were placed in a new shrine in St Peter's in 1087. His legacy seems a mixed one now, but despite his errors he set the Church on a course of reform guided from the centre, and he can at least be seen as a link between the age of the papacy under the control of the emperor and the Church in control of its own destiny that was to emerge under his former adviser, Gregory VII.

20

Some English Martyrs (from 1584–1602)

There are two dates in the year when those who died for the Catholic Faith, mostly in the reign of Queen Elizabeth I (1558–1603), are commemorated in groups: the Martyrs of England and Wales (those beatified on different occasions between 1874 and 1987) on 4 May and the Forty Martyrs of England and Wales (those canonized in 1970) on 25 October. In the full *Butler's Lives* there are general accounts on both those dates, as well as individual entries for all on the actual dates of their deaths. In this volume a few outstanding figures are chosen (see St Robert Southwell; 21 Feb., for example) for the day's commemoration. Several died on today's date in various years (and there is no other figure who demands an entry for today), and each is given a paragraph below, as is one who died the previous day.

James Bell was born in Lancaster in about 1525 and studied at Oxford University. He was ordained priest during the reign of the Catholic Queen Mary (1553–58) but then conformed to the "new" religion reimposed by Elizabeth and worked as a reformed minister in various parishes. In 1570 Pope St Pius V (see 1 May) excommunicated Elizabeth, which technically made all English Catholics traitors by removing them from their allegiance to the queen and making it their duty to work to depose her. The English Parliament responded with Acts in 1571, 1581, and 1585 that made it treason to deny any of the queen's titles, including that of Supreme Head of the Church in England. James Bell reverted to Catholicism in 1581, itself a treasonable offence under the 1581 Act, and began practising once again as a priest. He was arrested in January 1584, imprisoned in Manchester, taken to Lancaster, and tried and found guilty. He suffered the barbaric punishment of being hanged, drawn, and quartered (meaning that the rope was cut before he was dead, his body taken down, his entrails cut out, and the body hacked into quarters) on 20 April 1584.

John Finch was a layman who suffered the same fate with Fr James Bell. He was a Lancashire farmer who first adopted the new religion but was then "reconciled" to Catholicism. He tried to convert others and sheltered priests working in the area until he was betrayed by one of his brothers. He was kept in prison, in dreadful conditions, for most of two years before being found guilty of upholding the pope's claim to jurisdiction over England and sentenced to death. These two were beatified in 1929.

Richard Sergeant came from Gloucestershire and was educated at Oxford. He then went to the English College founded at Douai in northern France in 1568 by Cardinal Allen (which after a few years moved to Reims) and was ordained at nearby Laon in 1583. He returned to England in the same year and worked for some two and a half years before he was arrested and tried at the Old Bailey in London in 1586. Laws enacted the previous year made it a treasonable offence for priests ordained abroad to come back to England, so he was found guilty of treason and executed in the same barbarous fashion on 20 April 1586.

William Thompson was another Lancashire man and another priest educated at Reims—some four hundred priests were to be ordained there and at other colleges on the Continent and return to work on the "English mission" by the end of Elizabeth's reign. He was ordained in 1584 and worked as a chaplain to St Anne Line (see 27 Feb.) until he was arrested in 1586. He was condemned on the same charge as Richard Sergeant and suffered with him on the same day, at Tyburn in London. He was only about twenty-six years old.

Antony Page was born in Middlesex around 1563 and studied at Oxford before going to Reims, where he was ordained in 1591, leaving for England the following year. He worked as a priest in Yorkshire but was soon arrested and imprisoned. He is said to have held his own in debates with Protestant ministers while he was in prison, but a trial and its inevitable verdict followed. He was charged with treason on the same grounds as the previous two and executed at York in the same way on 20 April 1593. The above three were all beatified in 1987.

Robert Watkinson was born into a Catholic Yorkshire family in about 1579. He studied at Douai (where the college had moved back) and at the English College in Rome, but in Rome his health declined and he had to return to Douai. He was ordained in 1602 and returned to England, more to seek medical help than to practise as a priest. He was betrayed by a government spy who had been allowed to study for a while at Douai and so obtain the names of all newly ordained priests from there. Robert too suffered the fate of hanging, drawing, and quartering, about a month after his ordination, on 20 April 1602, apparently without having been able to carry out any ministry.

Francis Page was probably related to Antony (above) but had been born in Antwerp. Brought up a Protestant, he fell in love with his employer's daughter, who was a Catholic. She introduced him to the famous Jesuit John Gerard, who was in prison in the Tower of London at the time. Francis visited him there often and decided to become a Catholic and a priest. He was arrested on account of these visits, but purchased his release and went to Douai, being ordained in 1600. He returned to London and was caught some months later in Anne Line's house, imprisoned in Newgate Jail (where he was received into the Jesuits), tried on the usual charge, and executed at Tyburn with Robert Watkinson. They were both beatified in 1929.

On the previous day, Tyburn had seen the execution of a London bookseller named James Duckett (whose name survived at Duckett's bookshop in the Strand until the 1970s). He came from Cumbria, had been brought up a devout Protestant, but turned to Catholicism while apprenticed to a publisher and bookseller in London. He was twice arrested for not attending church; his employer paid the fines but was unwilling to pay more, so James set up in business on his own. He became a Catholic and married Anne Hart, a Catholic widow. They were married for twelve years, much of which time James spent in prison for supplying Catholics with books upholding their faith. He was eventually arrested on a charge of possessing forbidden books and condemned (after a jury had acquitted him and the judge ordered the verdict to be over-turned) on the evidence of a single witness, a Catholic bookbinder who hoped to save his own life by giving evidence against him. In this he failed, as he too was condemned and butchered with James, who forgave him from the scaffold. James' son John, who became a Carthusian prior, wrote an account of his life and death, and he was beatified in 1929.

21

St Anselm (about 1033–1109)

This towering and complex figure—great abbot, archbishop, statesman, defender of the rights of the Church, theologian, and philosopher—has been described (by Dom David Knowles) as the most luminous and penetrating intellect between St Augustine (see 28 Aug.) and St Thomas Aquinas (see 28 Jan.).

His early years gave little indication of his later achievements. Born into a land-owning family of Aosta in Lombardy (in present-day northern Italy), he was a brilliant pupil but seems to have been persuaded by his father, Gundulf, to abandon the idea of a monastic calling and involve himself in worldly affairs, leading a life he later bitterly regretted as dissipated. But when his mother died he quarrelled with his father's family and went to study in Burgundy, living with his mother's family. He then moved on to the great abbey of Bec in Normandy and after some years spent as a secular student there reverted to his earlier intention of becoming a monk. The prior was Lanfranc of Pavia (also from Anselm's native Lombardy), later to be William the Conqueror's reforming archbishop of Canterbury. He was appointed bishop of Caen, and Anselm, despite his youth, succeeded him as prior.

In 1078 he was elected abbot by a unanimous vote of the monks. This meant becoming a great temporal as well as spiritual lord, and Anselm was successful in expanding the abbey's lands and prestige while at the same time being a loving father to his monks. Lanfranc died in 1089, and William Rufus, who had succeeded his father as king two years earlier, refused to make a new appointment—this being still in his power—so as to keep the revenues of the archdiocese for the crown. Anselm was the obvious choice to succeed Lanfranc, and the king, frightened by an illness in 1093, named him archbishop-elect. There is considerable debate about whether Anselm accepted the post willingly, seeing himself chosen by God to deal with the problems it brought, or most unwillingly, being essentially a contemplative monk at heart. However he approached it, it brought him endless trouble.

William Rufus clung on to his revenues, refused to allow Anselm to hold a reforming synod, and even asked the pope to depose him. Anselm left England in 1097, spent some time at Cluny and then in Lyons, and then proceeded to Rome to consult the pope, who wrote to William threatening to excommunicate him if he did not allow Anselm back, but to no avail. Then William died suddenly in 1100, and the new king, Henry I, invited him to return. For a time it seemed that king and archbishop could work harmoniously together, but the question of lay investiture (the claim by lay rulers to invest abbots and bishops with the symbols of their office) led to him being exiled for a second time in 1103. Anselm had supported papal decrees, passed by a synod he had attended in Rome in 1099, forbidding lay investiture, and felt in conscience bound to oppose Henry when the king insisted (with some justification) that if abbots and bishops were in fact also temporal lords, they should take the same oath of allegiance to their sovereign. Anselm promoted the papal case from Rome, to such good effect that by 1106 Henry gave up his right of investiture and allowed him back. He returned in triumph, and his three further years as archbishop increased the prestige of Canterbury as the primatial see, with its jurisdiction extended to the Church of Wales.

The above outline of Anselm's complex public life shows only one side of his nature. Throughout his struggles, triumphs, and defeats, he had been producing a stream of letters, devotional works, and, above all, the theological and philosophical treatises that were to earn him the title of Doctor of the Church. His guiding principle was the Rule of St Benedict; he lived in obedience to it and strove to create a community of love based on it, as prior and later abbot of Bec. To these years belongs a series of letters, written to be read within the monastery, which express friendship and love for his monks in emotional terms that prefigure the later medieval tradition of courtly love (and which have led to questions about his suppressed homosexuality), though for him the love is in community and in the service of God. Collections of his prayers and meditations were widely circulated and as widely imitated, so that it is now impossible to decide what is authentically his (which was not a concern in his time). His famous motto, *Fides quaerens intellectum* ("Faith seeking understanding") underpinned his theological inquiries, such as *Cur Deus homo?* ("Why did God become man?"), which produced a theory of Christ's atonement that dominated Christian thinking on the subject for many centuries. He also produced the equally famous and durable "ontological argument" for the existence of God: that if we mean by God "that than which nothing greater can be conceived," then the concept must include existence, since if it did not, one that did would be greater. Faith for him was the precondition of the right use of reason, but we are bound to use reason, informed by faith, to help us to understand revealed truth.

Anselm died on 21 April 1109, and a cult developed locally, later eclipsed by that of his martyred successor Thomas Becket (see 29 Dec.). Becket had tried to have him canonized in 1163, but papal deliberations on the subject have been lost, and it seems that he has never officially been made a saint, despite which he was declared a Doctor of the Church in 1720. In art he is shown as monk, abbot, or archbishop, sometimes holding a book or a pen, and sometimes with a ship, indicating his many journeys across the English Channel. Some paintings depict him as a supporter of the doctrine of the Immaculate Conception, strongly upheld in England while still debated on the Continent.

Come now, little man, put aside your business for a while, take refuge for a little from your tumultuous thoughts; cast off your cares, and let your burdensome distractions wait. Take some leisure from God; rest awhile in him. . . . Say now to God with all your heart, "I seek thy face, O Lord, thy face do I seek."

St Anselm, addressing himself at the beginning of one of his treatises

22

St Adalbert of Prague (Wojciech of Libice; 956–997)

Adalbert was born in Bohemia (now the western part of the Czech Republic), the youngest son of Duke Slavnic of Libice, and sent to be educated by Archbishop Adalbert of Magdeburg, who gave him his name when he confirmed him. Adalbert returned to Prague nine years later and was ordained by its bishop; in 982 he succeeded as bishop, although he was still under canonical age. Described as amiable and somewhat worldly, he was not expected to trouble the secular powers by making excessive claims for the Church. But he began to take his religion and duties far more seriously once he was a bishop (as Thomas Becket was to do some two hundred years later). He entered Prague barefoot to an enthusiastic welcome from Duke Boleslaus II, the clergy, and the people.

Once he started to propose reforms, however, he met opposition from the secular powers and the clergy. He left Prague in 990 and went to Rome. The reasons behind this seem to have been mainly political: his family refused to support Boleslaus in an unsuccessful war against Poland, and he was no longer welcome. His early biographers (who were monks) give the impression that he longed to become a monk, but in fact he spent some time in Rome before becoming one, under the influence of St Nilus. Boleslaus then asked the pope to order his return, so that he could influence his powerful family to support him. He did so, making it a condition that the civil authorities should support his reforms, but was soon again exiled, this time for good. The occasion was seemingly a plot against him: a noblewoman caught in adultery had fled to a convent and been killed there; Adalbert, upholding the Church's right to give sanctuary, excommunicated her killers. The incident was probably engineered by enemies of his family.

He returned to Rome and was again ordered back to Prague by the pope, but he suspected that he would not be allowed back and asked the pope to give him a roving missionary brief. He went instead to consult Willigis, his metropolitan, and the German emperor Otto III in Mainz. After long deliberations he settled in Poland, from where he planned a mission to the Prussians to the north. He set out with two companions to preach there in the spring of 997, escorted as far as Gdansk by soldiers of Poland's new ruler, Boleslaus I "the Brave." The Prussians regarded them as Polish spies, and when they refused to abandon their mission, they were murdered, somewhere east of Gdansk. Adalbert's body was recovered and buried at Gniezno, which in 1000 became the first permanent Polish bishopric, when the emperor visited his shrine. It was forcibly moved from there to Prague in 1039.

His cult spread quickly through western Europe, as well as in his native Bohemia and farther east. His life had been marked by the blurring of the roles of Church and State in medieval Europe that so marked those of Anselm, Pope Leo IX, and Stanislaus of Cracow, all considered in this month. He had been a major player on the political scene of central Europe and an interesting combination of monk and bishop. He seems to have shared the emperor's desire to renew the Roman Empire, and he had great missionary aspirations for eastern Europe, cut short by his death. He was venerated, nevertheless, as a monk and a martyr. The twelfth-century bronze doors of Gniezno Cathedral depict scenes from his life and his murder.

23

St George (died about 303)

This renowned martyr, of whom virtually nothing historical is known, is Protector of England, patron saint of Italian cavalry, and a patron of Venice, Genoa, Portugal, Catalonia, and Istanbul. He also has the honoured title of "prophet" in Islamic hagiography. Great offence was caused in England by the calendar reform of 1969, which demoted him from saint of the Universal Calendar to one who *could* be venerated by national Churches. The new Roman Martyrology places him first on the day's list, in the large type reserved for universal saints, above St Adalbert of Prague. No explanation is given for this apparent *volte-face*. Most of his story is that of the extraordinary spread of his popularity, and even that is difficult to be certain about.

There are good grounds for believing that he was a genuine martyr, who was killed at Lydda (now Lod, in Israel), probably during the persecution under Diocletian, which started in 303. Detailed Acts of his martyrdom exist in many languages and versions, dating from around the end of the fifth century, but they are all so full of fable and magic that they were treated with suspicion even by those who dealt in this sort of exaggeration. The legend of the slaying of the dragon is a medieval introduction, possibly deriving from the Crusaders misinterpreting an image in Constantinople of Constantine destroying a dragon representing the devil. It was popularized by the *Golden Legend*, written about 1260.

He was described by the earlier Acts as an officer in the Roman army. This is probably why he was invoked as a protector by the armies of Byzantium, from which his protecting role spread more widely. The cult of his shrine at Lydda was attested by pilgrims to the Holy Land in the seventh and eighth centuries, despite Coptic claims that his remains had been taken to Egypt—possibly a confusion with the Arian George of Cappadocia. He was known in Britain and Ireland before the Norman Conquest, but it was the Crusaders who really spread his renown, after he and St Demetrius, a fellow-martyr, "appeared" to help them at the siege of Antioch in 1098. They were then known as "the martyr knights." King Richard I (1189–99) a century later placed himself and his armies under his protection and brought back stories of his power. The battle-cry "St George for England" was introduced in the fourteenth century, and he was still protecting English armies in the Hundred Years' War, when his feast was made a national festival in England after the battle of Agincourt in 1415—"Cry England, Harry, and St George!" In 1348 Edward III had founded the Order of the Garter with St George as its patron. His feast-day was a holiday of obligation for English Catholics in the seventeenth and eighteenth centuries, and Pope Benedict XV (1740–58) recognized him as Protector of England. His patronage of Istanbul dates from 1914, and of the Italian cavalry from 1937, confirmed in 1956, by which time he was protecting soldiers in armoured cars rather than on horses.

Artistic representations are legion and usually feature the legend of the dragon, as in the works by Uccello in the National Gallery, London; by Raphael in the National Gallery of Art, Washington, DC, and in the Louvre, Paris; and by Rubens in the Prado, Madrid. The earliest known was a sixth-century fresco in Egypt, now flooded by the Aswan Dam. He is usually shown as a very young man and is sometimes paired with Michael the Archangel, with whom he shares patronage of England.

24

St Wilfrid (634–709)

Wilfrid, upholder of Roman customs at the Synod of Whitby in 663/4 and therefore a hero to Bede (see 25 May), has more pages devoted to him in the *Ecclesiastical History of the English People* than any other individual. Born in Northumbria in 634, he joined St Aidan's (see 31 Aug.) monastery at Lindisfarne at the age of fourteen. This was still run according to Celtic customs, and Wilfrid seems to have developed his antipathy to them there. After four years he went to Rome, staying at Lyons on the way there and back, where he was taught by Bishop Annemund. In Rome he was instructed in the "proper" way of doing things by Boniface, a papal secretary. In Lyons he learned that bishops had to become involved in politics if they were to uphold order in the Church (even if this got them murdered, as happened to Annemund).

On his return he was appointed abbot of a new monastery at Ripon in Yorkshire, with a brief to turn the monks from Celtic to Roman ways. The main difference was in the manner of calculating the date of Easter: Bede makes much of how the debate was handled at the Synod of Whitby, but the universalization of the Roman method was already in progress and had been adopted in southern Ireland (Bede's "Irish" are northern Irish and Scots in modern terms). Wilfrid carried the day with his appeal to the supreme authority given to Peter, and he was appointed bishop of Northumbria as a reward. He went to Paris to be consecrated bishop with due ceremony, but, having spent a year there, he returned to find that King Oswy had appointed Chad (see 2 Mar.) to the see. Chad had been consecrated in the "Irish" way, and Theodore (see 24 Sept.), archbishop of Canterbury and determined to introduce uniformity, declared him uncanonical and appointed Wilfrid in his place. (Chad departed meekly to Lichfield.)

The diocese of York was immense, which Wilfrid (rather in the manner of a modern corporate executive) saw as necessary for development, supplying the resources needed to build churches and monasteries. Theodore, however, had been schooled in the Mediterranean notion of a bishop being the pastor of a small area around a town, and chosen for holiness, not to be a quasi prince or tribal leader. He would have preferred a divided diocese, but the decision was taken for him when Wilfrid quarrelled with King Egfrith, who somewhat resented him counselling his wife to become a nun and expelled him from Northumbria in 678. Theodore took the opportunity and divided York into three, later into five smaller dioceses. Furious at this demotion, Wilfrid set off for Rome to appeal to the pope. Blown off course in the Channel, he landed in Friesland and there showed the better, pastoral side of his nature, preaching to the people and effectively founding the English mission later carried on by St Willibrord (see 7 Nov.).

He eventually reached Rome, but the pope, while upholding his claim, also supported the division of the diocese, allowing Wilfrid to choose suffragan bishops. Egfrith, though, would not have him back, accused him of bribing the pope, clapped him in jail for nine months, and expelled him once more. This time he did not have to cross the Channel to find another outlet for his preaching abilities—in Sussex and Wessex, where he converted the people and built a monastery. Egfrith died after he had been there about five years, and Theodore persuaded his successor to take Wilfrid back, but he quarrelled with the new king and was exiled again, this time for eleven years. He appealed again to Rome and was eventually restored, but to the much smaller diocese of Hexham. He founded several more monasteries outside his diocese and died at one of them, Oundle in present-day Northamptonshire.

He may seem triumphalistic and arrogant, but he had to operate in a climate where kings and princes could appoint and dismiss bishops (as they did with him), and his view of the bishop's office was formed by his conviction that the

Church had to be strong to be independent, not by desire for personal aggrandisement. He was venerated initially in Ripon and Hexham; his relics were later transferred to Canterbury and Worcester, and his cult spread across the country.

25

St Mark (First Century)

Mark is the name given to the author of the second Gospel in canonical order, generally accepted as the earliest to be written. Any details of his life belong to tradition rather than to history: he is not one of those disciples whose doings are recorded in the New Testament, so any account of him has to be drawn from the Gospel itself.

By the second century Mark was apparently being referred to as St Peter's "interpreter," who had accurately written down all that Peter remembered, but this tradition is recorded only in the late third century, by the historian Eusebius. There are several references to a Mark or John Mark in the Acts of the Apostles and one in the Letter to the Colossians, stating that he was in Rome when Paul was in prison there, and these have all been taken as referring to the same person, though without any real evidence. There is also the passage in his own Gospel where a young man flees naked when Jesus has been arrested (Mark 14:51–2). This young man has been held to be Mark himself, as he is the only evangelist who mentions the incident. The tradition that makes him one of the original seventy-two disciples sent out by Jesus starts after the second century.

Internal evidence from the Gospel suggests that he did not come from Palestine. He writes fluent Greek and makes topographical mistakes about Palestine. He is at pains to explain Jewish customs, suggesting that he is writing for a non-Jewish audience. He may have written in Rome (as per the tradition that places him there with St Peter), in which case the date of the composition would be around 65, or possibly in Alexandria (the sort of popular Greek he writes was the common language of the eastern Mediterranean), in which case a date of around 70 is indicated, before the destruction of the Temple in Jerusalem.

Long held to be the simplest, most historical, and least theological of the four, Mark's Gospel is now viewed by scholars rather differently. He drew on oral and probably also written traditions already circulating and wove them into a deliberate pattern. The fact that he devoted a third of his text to the last week of Jesus' life would seem to show that he is stressing a theology of the cross, showing Christians of his time (when persecution had perhaps already begun) that they too must expect to suffer and die for their faith. This emphasis also distinguishes Jesus from other wandering preachers and wonder-workers (who were common in Palestine) and makes him someone unique, whose nature is difficult to grasp: a "king" whose "kingdom" is not of this world, as Mark records him as saying to Pilate, "a son of God," as he has the centurion confess after Jesus' death.

The principal cult of Mark developed in Venice after his supposed relics had been taken there from near Alexandria (where he was said to have been martyred) in the early ninth century to prevent them being desecrated by Arabs. There is also a claim that his remains were then moved to Reichenau on Lake Constance in 890. St Mark's Cathedral in Venice has twelfth- and thirteenth-century frescoes showing supposed scenes from his life, and his symbol, a winged lion (which dates back to the fourth century and is based on the visions in Ezekiel and Revelation), was adopted as that of the Republic of Venice and used increasingly as its prosperity grew. His other patronages include Egypt, notaries, basket-weavers, glass-workers, and opticians. Venetian painters depicted him as saving the city from plague and as protector of justice and the law; virtually all allegorical depictions of the glory of Venice include him in one role or another.

26

Bd Mary of the Incarnation (Marie Guyart; 1599–1672)

Marie Guyart was born in Tours, in west-central France, the daughter of a baker. She decided in her teens that she had a religious vocation, but her parents had other plans and arranged her marriage at the age of seventeen to a master silk-worker named Claude Martin. He died, leaving her with a one-year-old son and heavy debts. She took over the business and made it prosper sufficiently to pay the creditors, then worked for a time in her brother-in-law's transport business. Refusing to re-marry, despite pressure to do so for the sake of her son, she took a vow of perpetual chastity. In the midst of her busy life, she began experiencing visions, of the Trinity and of Our Lord, including the mystical experience of "spiritual marriage." In 1632 she entered the Ursuline convent in Tours, where she was professed as Mary of the Incarnation, leaving her son, Claude, who was twelve, in the care of her sister.

This was the heroic age of French Jesuit missions in North America (many were to be martyred in the 1640s), and the Ursulines, dedicated to education, planned to set up convents and schools there to consolidate the work of the missionaries. Marie responded to an offer of money to educate children of Native American converts and volunteered to go to Canada, where she landed in August 1639, the first missionary Sister to go there. She settled in Quebec, opening a convent and then a school, which flourished despite various problems including sickness, lack of money, and opposition from Native Americans, particularly the Iroquois, who threatened Quebec itself in 1648. Marie and her companions decided to stay, and they survived despite her increasing ill health and further wars with the Iroquois. She studied Native American languages and compiled dictionaries, enabling the scriptures and the catechism to be translated into them. Thousands of letters poured from her pen, encouraging missionaries to persevere despite persecution.

She continued to experience mystical union with God, combining this, in the manner of St Teresa of Avila (see 15 Oct.) and St John of the Cross (see 14 Dec.), with a life of almost superhuman activity. She saw an essential unity between contemplation and action: this "mixed life," she wrote—with some understatement—"has its difficulties," but she saw it as inspired "by the Spirit of him who regulates it" and found herself "closer to God when I leave the peace and quiet for the sake of his love" to perform some work of love for others. Her son Claude became a Benedictine monk and wrote the first account of her life. She herself wrote two "Relations" of her spiritual experiences, the first shortly after she joined the Ursulines and the second (apparently at her son's suggestion) in Quebec some twenty years later. Together they form a sort of spiritual autobiography and, with a book of notes made during her retreats, give considerable insight into the wellsprings of her spirituality.

The combination of austere devotion in her personal life and endless work for others, carried on for many years despite a severe illness in 1654, resulted in her being regarded as a saint by the time of her death, and the cause for her beatification started almost immediately. It ran, however, into a climate of suspicion of mystical experiences and was suspended. She had to wait until the twentieth century for the process to restart, and it was not until 1980 that she was finally beatified, by Pope John Paul II.

27

Bd Gianna Beretta Molla (1922–1962)

The reasons for the beatification of this twentieth-century married woman have been debated in the context of the "mother and child" issue and how female "self-sacrifice" is viewed in the Church. As time has moved on, however, she is seen more as a person in her own right and as one who lived her whole life attempting to follow God's will as expressed in the gospel and made the decision that probably led to her early death in the light of this.

She was the tenth of thirteen children born to a devout Catholic family in Milan. Two children died in infancy and three more in the outbreak of Spanish influenza that swept Europe at the end of the First World War, causing more deaths than the war itself. The family moved to Bergamo when Gianna was three and then to Genoa when she was fifteen. She became involved in Catholic Action and went to Mass daily, so that the nuns of her convent school saw her as a potential novice. She had not seemed particularly bright at school, but when she was twenty, both her parents died, and she subsequently resolved to study medicine. She studied in Milan and then in Pavia, keeping up her involvement in Catholic Action and developing an interest in mountain walking and skiing that remained with her for the rest of her life.

She qualified in 1947 and opened a clinic in Milan, beginning to specialize in paediatrics three years later. One of her brothers had become a Capuchin and was working as a missionary in Brazil, and Gianna gave much thought to whether she too should enter the religious life and use her medical skills on the missions. She made a pilgrimage to Lourdes in 1954 to ask Our Lady's guidance on making a decision. With or without this guidance, shortly after her return she met an engineer named Pietro Molla, fell in love with him, and married him the following year. They had a son a year later and a daughter in 1959. Both parents combined their careers with devoted parenthood in a happy and fulfilled life, finding time to pursue their hobbies of mountaineering and skiing.

In September 1961 Gianna, two months pregnant with her third child, had a tumour detected in her womb. Medical science counselled either a complete hysterectomy or the removal of the growth and the foetus. The teaching of the Catholic Church was that nothing should be done directly to abort or harm the unborn child, despite risk to the mother. This was also Gianna's view, and she directed that nothing should be done to harm the foetus. The tumour was removed and the pregnancy continued successfully to full term, when the baby was delivered by Caesarean section in April 1962. She had said to her husband, "I beg you, if you have to decide between me and the baby, decide in favour of the baby and not me," and to a friend, "The birth will be difficult; they must save one or the other; what I want is for my baby to live." In the event it appeared that no heart-rending choice needed to be made, as both mother and baby survived the birth, but Gianna developed peritonitis and died a week later.

She had in fact made the vital decision seven months earlier that the baby should be saved at all costs. This was fully in accordance with Catholic teaching, as were her words to her husband and to her friend recorded above. She was prominent in Catholic Action, and her death was widely reported in church circles as a "sacrifice" voluntarily made to uphold a principle, though she had not actually had to make a deliberate sacrifice: she had simply been obviously prepared to do so. She was beatified in 1994, chosen as a suitable candidate in what was designated the International Year of the Family. By that time, her whole life was seen as exemplary, and this was the tenor of the official announcement of her beatification: she was "a woman of exceptional love, an outstanding wife and mother, a witness to the power for good of the gospel in everyday life. In holding her out as an example of Christian perfection, we wish to praise all courageous mothers of families, who give themselves totally to the family, who suffer in bearing their children, who are ready for any labour, any sacrifice, in order to hand on to others something better than they had themselves."

28

St Peter Chanel (Pierre Louis-Marie Chanel; 1803–1841)

This Marist missionary to Western Oceania was born into a peasant farming family in eastern France. He was given a place in a local school started by a priest for bright boys who might be destined for the priesthood, from which he progressed to the junior and senior seminaries in Belley. He was ordained priest in 1827 and given charge of a parish at Crozet, near Geneva, where in three years his devotion to his parishioners, especially the sick, transformed what had been a neglected parish. His underlying desire was to be a missionary, and in 1831 his bishop, who had refused to spare him earlier, allowed him to join the clerical branch of the new Society of Mary, the Marist priests, dedicated to missionary work. They, however, appointed him to teach in the junior seminary at Belley, where he remained for five years, becoming vice rector.

In 1833 he went with the founder of the Marist priests to Rome, seeking papal approval for their Rule. This was granted three years later, and Peter's superiors then allowed him to go on an overseas mission, giving him the islands of the South Pacific Ocean, geographically a somewhat vague term, as his territory. A group sailed from Le Havre via Valparaíso to Tonga. Their ship put in at the French-owned island of Futuna, and Peter's superior suggested he might like to stay and work there. He agreed, and was put ashore with a Marist Brother and a European trader who was to act as their interpreter. They were told to pass themselves off as interested travellers, which was a mistake, as it made the inhabitants suspicious when they learned their true intentions.

Progress, as recorded in Peter's diary, was slow and difficult, but by 1840 they were preaching openly and carrying out some baptisms. They were not aided by their contempt for the native religion, the product of their education, typical of its day, or by general Western policy, gunboat diplomacy supporting greed and exploitation. The islanders associated them with this approach and began a campaign of harassment of their catechumens. When the king's son asked to be baptized, opposition became violent, the royal family was outraged, and the king ordered the missionaries to be killed. Peter was clubbed and hacked to death on 28 April 1841. This, shortly followed by the king's own death, produced a dramatic change, and within a year virtually the whole population of the island had been baptized. How much this was due to conviction and Peter's example and how much to fear of French reprisals for his killing is a moot point. A French frigate collected his remains the year after his death.

Peter was venerated mainly in Australasia until he was canonized in 1954 as the proto-martyr of Oceania and of the Marists. When the calendar reform of 1969 moved St Paul of the Cross from today's date to the anniversary of his death in October, Peter became the only saint of the day in the Universal Calendar, with the rank of optional memorial.

29

St Catherine of Siena (Caterina di Giacomo di Benincasa; 1347–1380)

Mystic, activist and reformer, extreme ascetic, Doctor of the Church: Catherine is one of the most extraordinary figures in Christian history. Born a twin into a family of comfortable means, already with twenty-two children, she soon showed herself both devout and determined—inheriting, it has been said, the first quality from her father and the second from her mother.

In her teens she made a vow of virginity and retreated into a regime of penance and austerity when her favourite sister died suddenly in 1362. When her mother tried to persuade her to marry, she cut off all her hair to make herself unattractive. Her mother, the determined parent, treated her like a household servant rather than a daughter. Another sister died, and Catherine virtually gave up eating for the rest of her life. By the time she was twenty-one her spiritual life had developed to the point where she experienced "mystical espousals" with Christ, accompanied by a call to abandon her private penitential way of life and become active on behalf of others. At first she did not understand why she could not have Christ to herself, but the link between loving God and doing his work was to become the cornerstone of her belief and actions.

She became a member of the *Mantellatae*, devout women members of the Dominican Third Order (who took a great deal of persuading to admit this troublesome fierce girl into their matronly ranks). She combined years of intense mystical inner life with devotion to the sick and the poor, especially during a famine in 1370 and an outbreak of plague in 1374. When she felt called to preach, even she felt that God was asking the wrong thing of her as a woman. She had acquired a sensible confessor (later her first biographer), Raymund of Capua, who reminded her that Jesus had chosen the weak and despised to teach the mighty and proud. Convinced that she was truly inspired by the Holy Spirit, she preached to huge effect, despite objections from civil and church authorities: "I *will* go and I *will* do as the Holy Spirit inspires me," she told the authorities.

She preached and acted against the evils of poverty, and she preached and acted against corruption in the Church. The sinful world had to be refashioned according to God's purpose for it, and if no one else would undertake the task, she would, alone if needs be. Her politics were not always as clear as her aim, and she saw a Crusade against the Turks as a way of distracting Christian States from waging war on each other. She wrote a series of letters to Pope Gregory IX, often addressing him as though he were a naughty boy, urging him to return from Avignon: "I am *telling* you: come back and conquer our enemies. ... Be a courageous man for me and not a coward." She went to Avignon in 1376, trying to mediate between him and anti-papal forces in Florence, but these were not going to be bound by her. Gregory did return, possibly spurred on by her prodding, but failed to resolve matters, and two years later he died. Catherine was almost killed by anti-papal forces—she lamented her escape—and the Great Schism began with the election of an antipope to oppose Urban VI.

Urban summoned her to Rome to support him, and there she gathered a "spiritual family" with whom she lived in community. She tried to assemble a "council" to promote unity and reform, but politically wiser heads than hers regarded her support for Urban (who did nothing to repay it) as misguided. Her reaction to apparent failure was to make herself into a living sacrifice to persuade God to save the Church. She went on a complete hunger strike and collapsed after a month. She then took minimal nourishment, mainly frequent Communion, but she had done her body too much damage and died at the age of thirty-three. How far she was responsible for her own death and how far she was suffering from what we now know as *anorexia nervosa* are questions that can be debated for ever. She certainly used fasting to control her will, but she was pursuing not some deluded self-image but that of the suffering Christ. All that she did stemmed from her sense of union with Christ: her mysticism was never a break from her activities but the constant wellspring of them.

We know of her inner state from *The Dialogue* (which she called "my book"), dictated between 1377 and 1378 to instruct and help her "spiritual family." She expounds the idea of Christ as the bridge between heaven and earth, the only way by which sinful human beings can cross over the abyss opened up by sin. She praises the Mystic Body of the Church while condemning clerical abuse and immorality. She is discerning, insightful, and theologically informed and orthodox to a degree remarkable in view of her relative lack of education and the fact that she learned to read and write only in her adult years. It is a key work of mystical theology and enables her worthily to stand alongside St Teresa of Avila and St John of the Cross and to share their dignity as a Doctor of the Church.

Raymund of Capua finished his biography of her in 1395. It was intended to promote the cause of her canonization, but the divisions in the Church she had tried and failed to heal prevented this from taking place for a further sixty-six years. In the twentieth century she was declared patron of women involved in Catholic Action and joint patron of Italy with Francis of Assisi, in 1939. Finally, Pope Paul VI proclaimed her a Doctor of the Church in 1970, the only lay woman to receive the title in the history of the Church.

You must love others with the same pure love with which I love you. But you cannot do this for me because I love you without being loved by you . . . you cannot repay me. But you must give this love to other people, loving them without being loved by them. You must love them without any concern for your spiritual or material profit, but only for the glory and praise of my name, because I love them.

Jesus, speaking to Catherine, in *The Dialogue*

30

St Joseph Cottolengo (Giuseppe Benedetto Cottolengo; 1786–1842)

Joseph Cottolengo is one of the many great socially active saints who did so much to help the victims of poverty, sickness, social injustice, and the industrial revolution in the nineteenth century. He was the eldest of twelve children born to a devout middle-class couple in Piedmont, now in the north-west of Italy. He began studying for the priesthood at home when he was sixteen, the local seminary having been closed by the Napoleonic War, and was ordained priest in 1811. His mother had instilled the ideal of caring for the poor and the sick into him from an early age, and after taking a degree in theology and spending eight or nine years as a canon of the Corpus Domini basilica in Turin, he found a way to make this ideal his life's work.

He had long been an admirer of "Monsieur Vincent" (St Vincent de Paul; see 27 Sept.), and it was appropriately a French family who showed him how his ideal might be achieved. This family was passing through Turin on its way home, with no money and with the mother desperately ill from tuberculosis and pregnant. The city hospital refused to take her in because she was pregnant; the maternity hospital refused because she had tuberculosis. The city authorities put her in a room reserved for sick vagrants, where her plight came to the notice of "the good canon," as Joseph was known, and he stayed at her bedside until she died. He decided to open a house to take those rejected by everyone else, starting by renting two rooms near the basilica and with no great plans other than reliance on God's Providence.

Soon more rooms were needed, and he acquired a group of young women helpers. But he was also accused of spoiling a "good" neighbourhood and of endangering other people's health, especially during an outbreak of cholera. So he moved the undertaking to a derelict area on the outskirts of the city, named Valdocco. Its dwellings were a few scattered hovels, many operating as drinking dens. Joseph rented one, but soon needed another building as sick people came to him. He called the establishment the "Little House of Divine Providence" and placed it under the patronage of St Vincent de Paul, adopting the motto *Caritas Christi urget nos* ("The love of Christ drives us forward"). The "little house" gradually grew into a small town, with different buildings for different needs: the terminally sick, the mentally ill, abandoned children: no one was turned away. Schools and workshops were added to the primary care, and Providence still appeared to take care of the financial needs and provide the necessary human help and skills.

Joseph founded a Congregation of lay Brothers to do the manual work, one of priests to attend to the patients' spiritual needs, and several separate ones of nuns, each dedicated to some aspect of nursing, education, and other caring functions. He made Our Lady patroness of the Little House and claimed that it was prayer and devotion to her that kept it going. He insisted on reverent performance of the liturgy and encouraged daily Communion, long before Pope Pius X recommended the practice to the whole Church. His work gained the official approval of the pope, Gregory XVI, and the civil ruler, Charles-Albert, duke of Savoy and king of Sardinia, who made him a knight of the Order of SS Maurice and Lazarus, but Joseph continued to live like the poorest of the poor to the day of his death, 30 April 1842.

He was buried under the Lady Altar of the main chapel in Valdocco and was beatified in 1917 and canonized in 1934. The Cottolengo Charitable Institute continues his works in several parts of the world, as do the Sisters of Vincent, also known as *Cottolenghine*.

Other Familiar English Names for April

1. Gilbert, Hugh, John, Mary
2. John, Leopold
3. *There are no other familiar English names for today*
4. Benedict, Joseph, Peter
5. Gerald, Mary
6. Catherine, Michael, Peter, William
7. Alexander, Edward, Henry, Ralph
8. Dominic, Julian, Walter
9. Antony, Thomas
10. Antony, Mark, Michael
11. George
12. Teresa
13. Edmund, John, Margaret
14. Bernard, Peter
15. *There are no other familiar English names today*
16. Benedict, Joseph
17. Clare, Henry, James, Robert
18. Alexander, Andrew, James
19. Bernard, Conrad, James
20. Agnes, Antony, Francis, James, John, Hugh, Richard, Robert, William
21. Conrad, John
22. Francis, Theodore
23. Gerard, Giles, Helen, Mary, Teresa
24. Benedict, Mary, Wilfrid
25. Peter, Robert, William
26. Stephen
27. James
28. Cyril, Louis
29. Hugh
30. Benedict, Francis, Mary, Miles, Pauline

MAY

In Britain, 4 May is the feast of the Blessed Martyrs of England and Wales, who will be remembered in this work on 25 October with the forty who were canonized in 1970 and whose feast-day that is; Antoninus of Florence is "borrowed" from the 2nd, which has to be devoted to Athanasius. On the 8th, Bd Mary-Teresa of Jesus Gerhardinger is brought forward by one day. John of Avila is postponed by one day to the 11th. The 18th is properly the feast-day of Pope John I, martyred in 526, while St Peter Celestine is commemorated the following day, when he would have had to make way here for St Dunstan; the story of the only pope ever to have abdicated is of considerable interest, so he is moved forward a day. The choices for the latter part of the month are complicated by the fact that five saints who deserve entries all died on the 25th: Bede the Venerable, Gregory VII, Aldhelm, Mary Magdalen de'Pazzi, and Madeleine Sophie Barat. By contrast (and luck) there are nearby days without major figures. Bede is here kept to the 25th; Gregory VII is moved forward to the 22nd (on which the Roman Martyrology gives pride of place to St Rita of Cascia, still widely invoked, like St Jude, in desperate situations and for lost causes); Mary Magdalen de'Pazzi to the 23rd; Madeleine Sophie Barat to the 24th; and Aldhelm back to the 28th; allowing St Philip Neri and St Augustine of Canterbury to appear on their correct dates of 26th and 27th respectively. Augustine has the peculiarity of being commemorated in the new Roman Martyrology on the 27th even though it recognizes that he actually died on the 26th: *Die vero vigesima sexta obiit.*

1

St Pius V (Antonio Ghislieri; 1504–1572)

During a papacy lasting a mere six years, Pius set the course of the Church for the next four hundred. His origins were humble, and he worked as a shepherd near Alessandria in northern Italy before joining the Dominicans at the age of fourteen (when he took the name Michael in religion). He showed a remarkable aptitude for learning, was ordained priest in 1528, and spent the next sixteen years lecturing in philosophy and theology at the university of Pavia. He was also a zealous inquisitor, rising through the ranks of the Roman

Inquisition and finally being appointed Inquisitor General by the severe and harsh Pope Paul IV (1555–59) in 1558, by which time he was also a bishop and a cardinal. He was not zealous enough for the pope, who at one point accused him of Lutheranism and threatened to imprison him in Castel Sant'Angelo.

Paul IV was succeeded by Pius IV, who showed the same tendency to promote nephews to prominent positions, and when Michael protested at this, he was encouraged to spend more time in his diocese, where he proved a strict reformer, leading by his own ascetic example. Pius IV died in 1566, and St Charles Borromeo (see 4 Nov.) led a reforming party, which successfully supported Michael's election. Taking the name Pius V, Michael set out to implement the reforms laid down or suggested in the decrees of the Council of Trent, which Paul IV had suspended three years earlier. He started in Rome itself, drastically reducing the overblown papal court, virtually cutting out family appointments to the College of Cardinals, imposing strict sexual morality on the clergy (and attempting to do the same for the whole city), reforming the structure of the Curia, and finally imposing Trent's reform principles on the religious Orders, most of which welcomed them.

From Rome, he spread his reforming zeal over the Papal States and other substantial parts of Italy, which he ruled as pope. Some of his measures were aimed at reducing social abuses, but he was more concerned with spiritual ones. Trent had produced a "Catholic Reformation" designed to roll back the Protestant one, but Protestantism was a State and not just an individual reform, so reconquest of lost territory involved just that, in political and military as well as spiritual terms. Pius was inevitably dependent on Catholic rulers to achieve his aims, and they had their own national agendas first and foremost. Philip II of Spain saw himself and not the pope as the true champion of Catholicism and simply ignored Pius unless their plans coincided. Essentially a spiritual reformer, Pius was no match for politicians and was led into several errors. Probably the worst of these was the Bull of 1570 excommunicating Queen Elizabeth I of England and releasing her Catholic subjects from any oath of allegiance to her. This attempt to reassert medieval papal authority over a sovereign made it easy for the government to brand active Catholics as traitors and greatly increased the severity of persecution.

Worse than Protestant "heretics," in Pius' view, were Islamic "infidels." He persuaded Spain and Venice to join him in a "holy league" against the Ottoman Turks, who were ravaging the Mediterranean. The league won a great sea victory at Lepanto in 1571, when its forces under Don John of Austria routed the Turkish fleet. Pius became a hero throughout Catholic Europe. He attributed the victory to the intercession of Our Lady, and this led to a cult of Our Lady of Victory and the establishment of the feast of Our Lady of the Rosary. The members of the league, however, then quarrelled among themselves and failed to follow up their victory.

It was in Church life rather than on the political scene that Pius' influence was so lasting. He effectively designed the centralized "Tridentine Church" that remained the dominant model for pastoral care, the liturgy, catechetics, canon law, theology, and missionary work until the Second Vatican Council (1962–65). His reforms were as thoroughgoing in his day as those of John XXIII were to be in the twentieth century, and if they outlasted their relevance to changing times, he cannot be blamed retrospectively for the perpetuation of a "fortress Church" through the nineteenth century and beyond.

Pius died in 1572; his remains were moved to a magnificent tomb in Santa Maria Maggiore in 1588. He was beatified in 1672 and canonized in 1712.

2

St Athanasius (295–373)

Athanasius was the great defender of orthodox Christianity against the Arian heresy, which denied the divinity of Christ. He insisted that Jesus was truly God and truly man. With the adoption of Christianity as the state religion of the Roman Empire, persecution of Christians as such had ceased, but theological debates were not just an intellectual matter. Emperors had armies, and if they were persuaded of a particular belief they were quite prepared to use them to persuade others of the rightness of this belief. Athanasius was repeatedly exiled from his see by powers holding Arian beliefs.

He was born in Alexandria and when he was in his early thirties was promoted, partly by popular acclaim, to be the city's metropolitan patriarch, ranking in prestige with those of Antioch and Jerusalem. He had been the secretary and companion to his predecessor, Alexander, at the Council of Nicaea, in 325, at which orthodox belief in Christ was defined, in the shape of the statement of belief we know as the Nicene Creed. Alexandria had been the site where Arius first preached his doctrine that Christ was created out of nothing and was therefore a creature and not God. Bishop Alexander had condemned this teaching at a synod in 320, so Athanasius had long known the dangers of Arianism and been its energetic and even impetuous opponent.

The Nicene Creed had been accepted by three hundred and eighteen out of the three hundred and twenty bishops who attended the council, but in Alexandria some diocesan clergy refused to accept it. Athanasius' followers included some extremists, who set upon these dissenters and killed some of them. Accusations made to the emperor suggested—wrongly—that he himself was responsible, and Constantine exiled him to Trier (now in western Germany). St Antony of Egypt (see 17 Jan.) wrote to the emperor in his defence, but Constantine would not relent, and it was not until after his death in 337 that Athanasius was able to return to his flock, with whom he had remained in contact through letters. Two years later he faced a series of stratagems orchestrated by Bishop Eusebius of Nicomedia, who had reverted to support for Arianism after signing the Creed at Nicaea. A council in Rome, which Eastern bishops refused to attend, upheld Athanasius; a rival one at Antioch deposed him; a mixed one at Sardica was inconclusive but enabled him to return to his diocese in triumph.

He spent the next ten years working to improve the spiritual life of his diocese. The number of monks and nuns increased, and he chose sensible and mature bishops from among the monks. Athanasius' own preaching and spiritual writings sustained the revival, and he left attendance at the imperial court to others. Further trouble came from there in 356, however, when Constantius (Constantine's younger son, emperor in the East), who championed Arianism, led a revolt and used his army to depose Athanasius once more. Athanasius escaped from a church surrounded by imperial troops and fled to monastic cells in the desert of the Thebaid. His flock underwent a reign of terror, ended only with the death of Constantius in 361. Under Constantius' successor, Julian the Apostate, who at first adopted a stance of not interfering in religious controversies, Athanasius and other exiled bishops were able to return to their sees. He attempted reconciliation with Antioch, but his violent partisans prevented any lasting peace or truce. Julian turned against him and ordered him to leave Alexandria once more, with a "wanted dead or alive" proclamation against him. He took refuge in the desert once again.

The see-saw of imperial theology continued: Julian died suddenly in 363, and Athanasius returned in triumph once more. Then Julian's successor, Valens, reverted to the policies of Constantius, and Athanasius was exiled again, this time hiding in the suburbs of the city. Valens, made aware by the populace of the unpopularity of his decision, reversed it and invited Athanasius back. He ruled his see in peace for the last seven years of his life. By the time he died in the night of 2–3 May 373, he had been a bishop for forty-six years. He was venerated as one of the first "confessors," those worthy of veneration as saints even though they had not been martyred. He has been regarded mainly as a champion of orthodoxy in the West, while the Eastern Church has laid more stress on his ascetic and mystical writings and teachings. He was universally regarded as a Doctor of the Church from early times. He wrote a Life of Antony of Egypt, which became a classic. In its Latin translation it was the first work to introduce the Desert Fathers to the West; it was found in virtually all monasteries and became a model for hagiography in the Middle Ages as well as spreading the ideal of the ascetic life. His emblem shows a stole draped over a triangle, symbolizing his office as bishop and his upholding of orthodox teaching on the Trinity.

❖

There is one form of Godhead, which is also in the Word; one God the Father, existing by himself in respect that he is above all, and appearing in the Son in respect that he pervades all things, and in the Spirit in that he acts in all things in him through the Word. Thus we acknowledge God to be one through the Trinity.
St Athanasius

3

SS Philip and James (First Century)

These two apostles, whose actual dates of death are not known, are commemorated on the same day because a basilica in Rome, later known as the Twelve Apostles, was originally dedicated to them. Virtually all reference to them is found in the New Testament—never intended to be a biographical source.

Philip came from Bethsaida: "The next day Jesus decided to go to Galilee. He found Philip and said to him, 'Follow me.' Now Philip was from Bethsaida, the city of Andrew and Peter" (John 1:43). His name is Greek, meaning "lover of horses." After his call by Jesus, he goes to find Nathanael, evidently a Jew who has been waiting for the Messiah, and says to him, "We have found him about whom Moses in the law and also the prophets wrote, Jesus son of Joseph from Nazareth" (1:45), to which Nathanael makes the famous rejoinder, "Can anything good come out of Nazareth?" and Philip answers simply, "Come and see" (1:46).

His faith in Jesus is put openly to the test in John's account of the feeding of the five thousand: "Jesus said to Philip, 'Where are we to buy bread for these people to eat?' He said this to test him, for he himself knew what he was going to do. Philip answered him, 'Six months' wages would not buy enough bread for each of them to get a little'" (6:5–7). As so often, the disciples start by doubting and have to be convinced by Jesus' actions. Some Greeks come to Philip asking where they can find Jesus when he is in Jerusalem for the Passover: "They came to Philip, who was from Bethsaida in Galilee, and said to him, 'Sir, we wish to see Jesus.' Philip went and told Andrew; then Andrew and Philip went and told Jesus" (12:21–2). At the end of Jesus' discourse at the Last Supper, when he tells the apostles that those who know him will know the Father also, it is Philip who wants proof: "Lord, show us the Father, and we will be satisfied" (14:8). This earns something of a rebuke from Jesus: "Have I been with you all this time, Philip, and you still do not know me? Whoever has seen me has seen the Father. How can you say, 'Show us the Father.'? Do you not believe that I am in the Father and the Father is in me?" (14:9–10a). It would probably be unfair to Philip to think of him as particularly lacking in faith: the apostles are often shown in this light, and the evangelist may be using

Philip's Greek origins to make him seem something of a rationalist. In any case, his faith would have been confirmed with that of the other apostles at Pentecost. After that his destiny is uncertain.

Today's James is James the Less, not the Greater (whose feast is on 25 July), "son of Zebedee" in Matthew's list of the twelve apostles (their title is changed from "disciples" when they are given authority to heal and to cast out unclean spirits). This James is "son of Alphaeus" (see Matt. 10:1–4) and the "brother" ("cousin" in modern usage) of the Lord, who came to rule the Church in Jerusalem. Paul names him as the special object of Jesus' third post-resurrection appearance: "Then he appeared to James, then to all the apostles" (1 Cor. 15:7), just before he appears to Paul himself. When Paul and Barnabas return from their missionary journeys and argue (against Pharisee converts, at what is known as the "Council of Jerusalem") that Gentile converts should be welcomed for their faith and not be subjected to Jewish circumcision and other laws, it is James who produces a compromise solution, speaking with personal authority: "My brothers, listen to me … I have reached the decision that we should not trouble those Gentiles who are turning to God, but we should write to them to abstain only from things polluted by idols and from fornication and from whatever has been strangled and from blood" (Acts 15:13b, 19–20).

In his letter to the Galatians, Paul confirms the outcome of the "council" and the authority held by James, equal to that of Peter and John: "and when James and Cephas [Peter] and John, who were acknowledged pillars, recognized the grace that had been given to me, they gave to Barnabas and me the right hand of fellowship, agreeing that we should go to the Gentiles and they to the circumcised. They asked only one thing, that we remember the poor, which was actually what I was eager to do" (2:9–10). The poor of the Christian communities are the protagonists of the Epistle of James, but this was written some time after James' death, which took place, according to the Jewish historian Josephus, in the year 61, and was a martyr's death. The "of James" is therefore an example of "pseudepigraphy," attribution to an authority, a common device at the time, rather than an indication of actual authorship. With its upholding of the poor and stress on the importance of works of charity, the letter is a radical and significant text and conveys a message with which James could be proud to be associated.

But be doers of the word, and not merely hearers who deceive themselves. For if any are hearers of the word and not doers, they are like those who look at themselves in a mirror; for they look at themselves and, on going away, immediately forget what they were like.

But those who look into the perfect law, the law of liberty, and persevere, being not hearers who forget but doers who act—they will be blessed in their doing.
James 1:22–5

4

St Antoninus of Florence (Antonio Pierozzi; 1389–1459)

Small of stature, like Francis of Assisi (see 4 Oct.) and John of the Cross (see 14 Dec.), but great in achievements, he was known as "little Antonio," *Antonino*. He was the son of a notary from Florence, named Niccolo, and his wife, and was born on 1 March 1389. He joined the Dominicans at the age of fifteen, at the convent of Santa Maria Novella, where the reformer John Dominici was prior. He served his novitiate at Cortona, where the great painter Fra Angelico (beatified in 1982; see 19 Feb.) was a novice at the same time. After his profession he joined the house at Fiesole and began his spectacular rise in the Order; he was successively prior of the Dominican houses at Cortona, Fiesole, Rome, Naples, Gaeta, Siena, and Florence, carrying through reforms in each. In Florence he engaged the architect and sculptor Michelozzi (court architect to Cosimo de Medici, the founder of the Medici dynasty and ruler of what was then the republic of Florence) to convert the former Sylvestrine monastery into the Dominican convent of San Marco. Fra Angelico painted some fifty murals in the friars' cells and in the corridors, with a magnificent *Annunciation* on the main staircase, so the whole building became a visual aid to devotion.

In 1446 Antoninus was consecrated archbishop of Florence by Pope Eugenius II, recommended, it is said, by Fra Angelico. He was an exemplary archbishop, personally austere in his way of life, cutting his household down to six members and virtually doing without personal possessions: everything possible was given to the poor, including the bulk of the furniture and most of his clothes. His bravery and charity during an outbreak of plague in 1448 and an earthquake in 1453 earned him the admiration and affection of his people. He carried out a visitation of his diocese every year, preaching tirelessly against such abuses as usury and magic. In 1447 Nicholas V succeeded to the papacy, and he valued Antoninus as a counsellor. In 1458 the great Renaissance scholar Aeneas Silvius Piccolomini was elected as Pope Pius II. He too appreciated Antoninus' qualities and appointed him to a commission established to reform the Roman Curia. Antoninus also enjoyed the confidence of Cosimo de Medici, who employed him as an ambassador.

In addition to his pastoral and wider church and civic activities, Antoninus was a considerable scholar in several disciplines and produced a number of significant works, including a *Summa Theologica* (reissued in 1958), a history of the world (reissued as *Chronicles* in 1933), a summary of moral theology, and several treatises on the Christian life, one of which was published in one hundred and two early printed editions. Although he preached against usury, meaning the lending of money at interest, which the Church traditionally condemned, he made an important distinction between this and the investment of capital in a business, on which he said that a moderate return was permissible. He thereby made a major contribution to the Church's adjustment to the modern financial and industrial world, in which the Republic of Florence played a pioneering part.

Antoninus died in 1459 and was canonized in 1523. There is a contemporary bust of him in Santa Maria Novella, a statue in the Uffizi Gallery, and a series painted by Antonio del Pollaiuolo illustrating his life in San Marco. Pius II paid this tribute to him in his memoirs:

> He conquered avarice, trampled on pride, was utterly unacquainted with lust and most abstemious in food and drink; he did not yield to anger or envy or any other passion. He was a brilliant theologian, he wrote several books which are praised by scholars; he was a popular preacher though he inveighed against sin with the utmost energy; he reformed the morals of clergy and laity and strove earnestly to settle quarrels; he did his best to clear the city of feuds; he distributed the revenues of the Church to the poor, but to his relatives and friends (unless they were very needy) he gave nothing. He used only glass and clay dishes; he wished his household (which was very small) to be contented with little and to live according to the precept of philosophy. When he died, he was given a splendid funeral. At his house was found nothing except the mule on which he used to ride and some cheap furniture: the poor had had everything else. The whole state believed that he had passed to a life of bliss—nor can we think their belief unfounded.

Seldom can a more eloquent tribute have been paid—or so richly deserved.

5

St Hilary of Arles (about 401–449)

Hilary was a relative of the better-known Honoratus of Arles and followed him into the great and influential monastery of Lérins. Honoratus, who died twenty years before Hilary, is commemorated on 16 January but does not have an entry in this work, so some account of him and the foundation of Lérins is needed here to set the scene for Hilary.

Their family was from the Roman consular class and had settled in Gaul, where Honoratus was educated as a pagan but became a Christian. He was inspired by the example of St Caprasius to lead a hermit's life and tried this, taking his elder brother Venantius on the same course, first in Greece (to escape their father's wrath) and then in southern Gaul (in the coastal hills above what is now the French Riviera). Caprasius lived on the Iles de Lérins, off the south coast of France opposite the modern Cannes. Honoratus had become acquainted with the Rule of St Pachomius (see 9 May), outlining a communal way of life, and seems to have persuaded Caprasius to adopt this. In around 410 they settled on the more seaward of the two islands (now called Saint-Honorat after him) and established what in twenty years had grown into an *ingens fratrem coenobium*, a "great community of brethren," as John Cassian called it. It attracted large numbers of recruits from leading families of Roman Gaul, many of whom became bishops and so extended the influence of Lérins throughout Gaul. Honoratus himself was appointed metropolitan bishop of Arles in 426.

Hilary, also educated as a pagan at a school of rhetoric and then a convert, joined the ranks of monks at Lérins. He had not been there long when Honoratus was appointed to Arles and took Hilary with him. When Honoratus died three years later, Hilary set out to return to Lérins, but messengers followed him from Arles to tell him that he had been chosen to succeed his relative as bishop there. He was then twenty-nine and was probably promoted too young through family influence or at least prestige. As bishop, he lived as far as possible like a monk, saying the Office at stated times and undertaking manual work (for wages, which he then gave to the poor). He also built and visited several monasteries in his diocese.

Arles was (or at least claimed to be) a metropolitan see, which gave its bishop the right to appoint others in the area under its control—a large part of southern Gaul. As metropolitan bishop, Hilary presided over important gatherings, such as the First Council of Orange in 441 and the Council of Vaisson in 442. He also claimed the right to depose bishops of whom he disapproved, and did so with Chelidonius of Besançon in 444. Chelidonius appealed to Pope Leo I (St Leo the Great; see 10 Nov.), who decided that Hilary had exceeded his authority and reinstated him. Hilary went to Rome to appeal in his turn, but Leo's response was to ask Emperor Valentinian to give him direct authority over the Church in Gaul. He allowed Hilary to remain in office but stripped him of the title of metropolitan (giving this to the bishop of Fréjus) and forbade him to consecrate any more bishops. Leo and Hilary seem to have been reconciled later, as Leo referred to him as "of blessed memory."

Hilary wrote a Life of Honoratus, which survives, as do some letters and poetry by him. The Life is a panegyric, but for a time it set a style of writing saints' Lives that generally discarded miracles as irrelevant and concentrated instead on personal virtues and affecting death scenes. Lérins survives, with some parts dating back to the seventh century and a twelfth-century cloister, though most of the buildings date from the sixteenth and seventeenth centuries. It was reopened as a monastery by the Cistercians after the Second World War.

6

Bd Francis of Quebec (François Montmorency-Laval; 1623–1708)

Francis was born in the Eure region of north-western France into one of the country's leading families. He was educated by the Jesuits at their school of La Flèche and at an early age began an ecclesiastical career suited to his high birth when he was appointed canon of Evreux Cathedral by the bishop, who was his uncle. This was before he was ordained priest. He studied for the priesthood at Clermont College in Paris, but he was called away from his studies when his two elder brothers both died and he was summoned to take charge of family business.

Resuming his interrupted studies, he was ordained in 1647 and took up an appointment as archdeacon of Evreux. This post meant that he had administrative authority delegated by the bishop over a part of the diocese, in which he was responsible for administering church property and appointing the clergy. Francis spent several years carrying out effective visitations of his area and was then appointed vicar apostolic of the missionary territory of Tonkin (the northern part of what is now Vietnam). Evangelization there was recent, begun in 1623 by a brilliant French Jesuit named Alexandre de Rhodes, who trained native catechists and so made the local Church virtually self-managing. In fifty years of mission, the number of Christians in Tonkin reached three hundred thousand. It was, however, a period of wars between warlords of north and south, and Francis never actually went there.

After a time away from church duties looking after nieces and nephews, he resigned the post and spent four years effectively in retreat, at a school of spirituality in the Hermitage at Caen, near the Normandy coast. He was obviously still an important figure in church circles, whether on account of his family connections or his personal qualities or both, and in 1658 Pope Alexander VII (1655–67) appointed him vicar apostolic of the newly established apostolic vicariate of New France, as the French settlements in North America were then known. He sailed for Canada the following year and reached Quebec in June 1659. France had entered the race for the conquest and evangelization of the New World after Spain and Portugal (between which Pope Alexander VI had divided all new discoveries, either side of an imaginary line drawn down the west Atlantic), but in 1534 Jacques Cartier had taken possession of Canada in the name of France. In 1598 King Henri IV of France (1589–1610) secured the right to annex territory north of an east-west line drawn through the Canary Islands, but exploitation of the vast tracts of Canada was slow, and when Francis arrived conditions were still pioneering and harsh. The mission in Quebec, the first to take root in New France, had been founded by Samuel de Champlin in 1608. By the time Francis was appointed, all overseas missions were controlled by the Roman Congregation for the Propagation of the Faith, not simply by the kings of the colonizing powers. Established in 1622, *Propaganda fidei*, as the Congregation was known, set about wide-ranging reform designed to eliminate international rivalry and that between bishops and religious Orders and to prevent missionaries regarding their territories as a source of personal wealth. It also overturned the ethos of the Churches of the "patronage powers" (Spain and Portugal) by encouraging the ordination of native clergy.

This was the spirit of the mission Church to which Francis devoted the next thirty years of his life. Quebec was a little settlement of fewer than two thousand inhabitants, desperately poor, and constantly threatened by the English colonists on the eastern seaboard. Francis founded parishes, defended the Native tribes from exploitation by European merchants, and struggled to preserve the Church from French royal control—monarchs were, not unnaturally, unimpressed by *Propaganda*'s reforming ideas. His social activities included attempts to limit sales of alcohol and to regulate the fur trade. Francis returned to France in 1662 and obtained many privileges for the Church in Canada from King Louis XIV (1643–1715). On his return he founded a seminary in Quebec, and when in 1674 Quebec was raised to the status of diocese, he was appointed its first bishop. He was an active bishop for ten years, but the many years of intense activity in harsh conditions had taken their toll on his health, and he resigned the see in 1684. He spent the last twenty-four years of his life in retirement in the seminary he had founded and died there at the age of eighty-five.

By 1712 the see of Quebec extended over the whole territory of New France, covering Canada and most of the present United States, excluding the English colonies in the east and the Spanish territories in the south. As the population increased, new dioceses were formed from it, until there are now more than one hundred and fifty in modern Canada. The war with England in the late eighteenth century at first threatened the position of Catholics, with the Church playing a leading role in assuring the survival of the French-speaking population, but their position has long been stabilized. Francis, the father of the Church in Canada, was beatified in 1980.

7

St John of Beverley (died 721)

The Venerable Bede (see 25 May) devotes five chapters in Book 5 of his *Ecclesiastical History of the English People* to John of Beverley, but unfortunately they are almost entirely taken up with hearsay accounts of rather conventional (if charming) miracles of healing. The chief source of the stories is Abbot Berthun, "a most reverend and truthful man, formerly John's deacon." The most interesting is a version of "the dumb speak," related in detail that suggests that John really did carry out a form of speech therapy, making a dumb boy repeat simple sounds after him, gradually building up into words and then sentences, until he was able to express his thoughts for the first time in his life. It is possible that he had grown up "wild," with no consistent contact with human speech. His reaction to his cure is reminiscent of some of those healed in the Gospels: "In his joy at this recovery, he declined an offer from the bishop of a permanent place in his household, preferring to return to his own home." John also cures the daughter of an abbess from a swollen arm brought on by bleeding "when the light of the moon and the pull of the tide is increasing," a *thegn*'s wife of a forty-day complaint, a servant from paralysis, and one of his clergy from death after a fall from a horse.

Of his actual life, the outline is known, but little detail. He was born at Harpham in Yorkshire and studied at the famous school in Canterbury established by St Theodore, where he was taught by St Adrian of Canterbury (see 9 Jan.). From there he returned to Yorkshire and became a monk in the double monastery at Whitby, ruled by St Hilda (see 29 Oct.), which, Bede tells us, produced five bishops, including John, "all of them men of outstanding merit and holiness." John was consecrated bishop of Hexham, replacing St Wilfrid (see 24 April). He conferred both the diaconate and the priesthood on Bede, who writes in the "Autobiographical Note" at the end of his *History*, "I was ordained deacon in my nineteenth year, and priest in my thirtieth, receiving both these orders at the hands of the most reverend Bishop John."

John used to retire frequently for periods of prayer and devotional reading with a few companions in "an isolated house surrounded by open woodland and a dyke [that] stood about a mile and a half from the church at Hexham across the River Tyne, and had a burial-ground dedicated to St Michael the Archangel." He found "some poor person who was either infirm or in dire want" to stay with them and be cared for. This was the setting for the cure of the dumb boy. In 705 he was appointed bishop of York, and Wilfrid was restored to Hexham. He founded a monastery at Beverley, to which he retired in old age and where he died. An official cult developed, and by the eleventh century pilgrims were going to his tomb, where many miracles were reported.

He aroused the admiration of more than Bede. Alcuin also wrote of him in the eighth century; King Athelstan did in the ninth; St John Fisher (see 22 June) did in the sixteenth. King Henry V invoked him at the Battle of Agincourt in 1415, the date of which he selected to fall on his feast-day. Julian of Norwich, in her fourteenth-century *Revelations of Divine Love*, chapter 38, describes being shown examples of how those who have "fallen" in life have their sins "transformed to their glory" in heaven. After seeing King David, St Peter, and others, she is shown John of Beverley as someone closer to her in place and time (though his "fall" is not specified):

> And for the sake of familiarity, our Lord showed Saint John of Beverley in comfort, most clearly, reminding me that he is a neighbour near to hand, one whom we know. And God called him Saint John of Beverley plainly, just as we do, and did so with a most glad, sweet expression, showing that he is a very high, blissful saint in heaven in God's sight.
>
> With this showing God made mention that Saint John of Beverley, in his youth and tender years, was a most valuable servant to God, extremely good, loving and reverencing Him. Nevertheless, God allowed him to fall, mercifully preserving him from perishing or losing time. Afterwards God raised him to grace many times greater, and by the contrition and humility he practised in his living, God has given him joy in heaven many times surpassing what he would have had, had he not fallen. And God shows on earth that this is the truth, by means of abundant miracles, performed continually around the body of Saint John of Beverley. And all this was shown and done to make us glad and merry in love. (*Trans.* M. L. del Mastro)

8

Bd Mary-Teresa of Jesus Gerhardinger (Karolina Gerhardinger; 1797–1879)

Karolina was the only child of a boatman, born in the Stadtamhof suburb of Regensburg in Bavaria. She was educated by the Canonesses of Our Lady, but they were suppressed and the school secularized in 1809 on the orders of Napoleon, who had invaded Bavaria. She worked there as a teacher from the age of fifteen, under the sympathetic direction of Fr George Wittman, a priest at the cathedral and later bishop of Regensburg. He encouraged her to form a Congregation of teachers to take charge of the education of the poor, especially the rural poor, in Bavaria. When he died in 1833, Karolina was befriended by Fr Francis Job, chaplain to the empress of Austria, who asked her to start a local school in his home area of Neunburg vorm Wald. Fr Job died the year after Bishop Wittman, and Karolina proceeded with the foundation with little support, financial or otherwise.

She obtained permission from King Ludwig I of Bavaria and the approval of the new bishop of Regensburg, Francis Schwäbl, and wrote a Rule for the new Congregation the following year, based on that of the Canonesses of Our Lady. She made her profession to the bishop, taking the name Mary-Teresa of Jesus in religion. The purpose of the Congregation was to provide Sisters who would work in pairs in rural schools, so they were to be unenclosed. It expanded rapidly, and in 1837 Archbishop von Gebsattel of Munich gave permission for a motherhouse to be established in what had been a convent of Poor Clare nuns. The Congregation grew, taking the name of School-Sisters of Notre Dame, and ten years later it had fifty-two houses in Bavaria. Foundations followed in other German provinces, in Austria, and in England.

Mary-Teresa was chosen as superior in 1839 and was to remain in that post for the rest of her life, a further forty years. In 1847 she and five Sisters travelled to America in order to staff schools founded by Fr John Nepomucene Neumann (see 5 Jan.), then vice-provincial of the Redemptorists in the USA. His mother had been Czech, and Czech was one of the eight languages he spoke. The School-Sisters of Notre Dame extended their mission to health and social care to serve the Czech immigrant communities, providing the same sort of services as Frances Xavier Cabrini (see 22 Dec.) was later to provide for Italian immigrants. Mary-Teresa returned to Munich the following year and concentrated on receiving official papal approval for the growing Congregation and its Rule. This was granted in 1854, when Pope Pius IX also confirmed her as superior general for life.

Mother Mary-Teresa was forceful and outspoken by nature and saw to it that her ideas were put into practice. She had a talent for spotting different educational needs and started the first kindergartens and the first technical high schools in Bavaria. Some bishops expressed concern at such an extended Congregation having just one motherhouse and being in effect so dependent on one woman, but she gradually won the respect of all church and civic authorities as well as the love of parents of her schoolchildren. She was seriously ill in 1877 and seemed to be on the point of death, but she had, with her usual determination, declared that she would die in 1879, and so she did. By then her Congregation numbered over three thousand, working in three hundred houses spread throughout the world. Her cause was introduced in 1952, and she was beatified by Pope John Paul II in 1985. Her School-Sisters still work extensively in the USA, organized in seven Provinces, teaching in schools and with a continued apostolate in health care and social services, as well as providing prison chaplains, spiritual directors, and parish and diocesan administrators. There are also foundations in South and Central America, Europe, Africa, Asia, and the Pacific Islands.

9

St Pachomius (about 292–346)

Pachomius, a contemporary of St Antony of Egypt (see 17 Jan.), founded Christian community monasticism, whereas Antony established the solitary form, for hermits. Pachomius came from a relatively wealthy family from upper Egypt and served, apparently unwillingly, in the Roman army before becoming a Christian when he was released in 316. He spoke and wrote Coptic and later learned some Greek. After his army service he became a disciple of the hermit Palamon for seven years, during which his ideas for community took shape. He then founded a monastery at Tabennesi, on the west bank of the Nile in the Thebaid area of lower Egypt (the Roman province known as Thebais II). At first the villagers flocked to join him, but they proved incapable of accepting his discipline, and he sent them away.

Recruits then came from farther afield. Pachomius organized them into groups of houses each accommodating some forty monks; up to forty of these houses made up a monastery, so they were large settlements, making, as the title of a modern book on the movement claims, "the desert a city." The monks had to work at agriculture and basic crafts, including mat-making, weaving, and pottery, to earn a modest living. There was a central church and kitchen to serve the whole monastery and an infirmary with its own kitchen attached. Each house was governed by a dean and his assistant, who regulated and accounted for the sales of produce and assigned monks to liturgical and kitchen duties.

Life was simple and austere, with one main meal a day, plus an optional supper on all except Wednesdays and Fridays, which were fast days. Pachomius himself is said to have eaten virtually nothing, relaxing to the extent of three meals a week in winter. The day was organized around liturgical observance, interspersed with manual work and devotional reading, which took the form of learning the Psalms and other passages of the Bible by heart. The Psalms were repeated often, just as their repetition still forms the basis of the daily monastic office today. Pachomius wrote a Rule for the monastery, containing two thousand five hundred quotations from the Bible.

The movement grew rapidly, and by the time of Pachomius' death there were nine such monasteries for men and two or three for women. Pachomius, a great organizer, appointed a superior to each monastery but kept a personal oversight of all his monks. Said to know the secrets of their hearts, he was quite ready to transfer them from one foundation to another. The superiors met twice a year, at Easter and in August, to celebrate the liturgy together and to present the accounts for their individual monasteries, a mixture of the "divine" and the practical that has been a mark of monasticism ever since.

In 336 or 337 Pachomius moved across the Nile to the second monastery he had founded, at Pboou, leaving a monk named Theodore as superior at Tabennesi. When Pachomius was taken ill a few years later, Theodore was presumptuous enough to remark that he was quite ready to take over as superior general of all the monasteries if Pachomius were to die. Pachomius heard of this, recovered, and stripped Theodore of all his responsibilities, making him do penance for two years. Individual ambition was not part of the monastic agenda. Theodore's turn came later, when the first successor to Pachomius died quickly and the second soon resigned after a rebellion by some of the monks; Theodore was appointed and ruled till his death in 368.

Pachomius' Rule and a collection of letters by him were found by St Jerome (see 30 Sept.) at the monastery of Canope, founded in 391. He translated them into Latin, thus ensuring the lasting influence of Pachomius in the West, where his Rule strongly influenced that of St Benedict, though in this the exceptional austerity was moderated considerably. St Benedict of Aniane (see 12 Feb.) referred to his Rule (known only through Jerome's translation, as the original Coptic version had been lost) in his study of pre-Benedictine monasticism. In the East, his Rule served as a model for the monastic foundations made by St Basil (see 2 Jan.) later in the fifth century. His influence was thus considerable and widespread, and the austerity of his life, like that of Antony's, must have served as a pattern for later Lives of saints from the East.

10

St Comgall of Bangor (516–602)

The "outstanding father of the monks of Ireland" was the founder and first abbot of Bangor Abbey, on the south side of Belfast Lough. He was a pupil and close friend of St Columba (see 9 June), who took Irish monasticism to Scotland, and the teacher of St Columbanus (see 24 Nov.), who took it into western Europe. There are references to him by Columba's biographer, Adomnán, and that of Columbanus, Jonas (source of the quotation above), which tend to deal with visions and praeternatural powers (as when Columba, on Iona, sees some of Comgall's monks drowned on Belfast Lough, with angels successfully battling demons for their souls). He is also mentioned in early Annals, but the earliest surviving Life dates from the thirteenth century.

He was born at Dal Araide in Antrim, the son of a soldier, who hoped his son would follow in his footsteps. He went, instead, to study with a cleric (reputed to keep a mistress) and then at a monastic school, probably that run by St Finian of Moville. He seems to have been prey to at least the usual adolescent doubts and temptations, but after confessing these to his abbot, he settled into monastic life and was ordained priest. He started a small monastery on Lough Erne, where his extreme austerity (perhaps modelled on that of St Pachomius, above), which included praying standing in freezing rivers, had to be modified for the sake of his monks' health. He is called "a founder of monasteries" by Adomnán: other foundations may not have survived for long, including one on Rathlin Island, off the north coast of Antrim.

He founded Bangor in about 558, on a site well placed for sea travel to both Scotland and Gaul. It was said to have three or four thousand monks, but this may refer to the number who passed through it during the time Comgall was abbot—precisely defined in the Martyrology of Tallacht as fifty years, three months, and ten days. His pupil Columbanus in turn taught Gallus, who founded the great monastery of Saint-Gall (or Sankt Gallen) in Switzerland. There Bd Notker composed a Martyrology nearly three hundred years after Comgall's death, which makes the link between Comgall and the monastery, saying of St Columba, "[He] had many pupils or comrades his equal in sanctity, but one, like Isaac, was the sole heir of his virtues and merits. This was Comgall, distinguished by the Latin name Faustus, teacher of St Columbanus, who was in turn the master of our learned father Gallus." Comgall himself never went to the Continent, but he did visit Scotland, travelling with St Columba to obtain authorization for a monastery on the island of Tiree in the Inner Hebrides and permission for his monks to preach in areas ruled by King Brude of Inverness.

There is a monastic Rule attributed to him, which survives in Irish, in metrical form, and an Antiphonary of Bangor, in Latin, is now in Milan. The Rule defines its "essence" as, "Love Christ, hate wealth: piety … toward the king of the sun and smoothness toward men." The three rules by which the monks are to live are "patience and humility and the love of the Lord in your heart." Any sufferings they may face are as nothing compared to "those of the King who sent them." The Antiphonary shows that Bangor's liturgy had three night offices (Vespers, Vigils, Lauds) and three day (Terce, Sext, None), to which Prime and Compline were added a century later. It includes the earliest Eucharistic hymn known in the West, which translates as, "Come, you who are holy, receive the body of Christ, drinking (also) the blood of Christ by which you are redeemed." The spirit of the monastery is perhaps reflected in the saying attributed to Comgall: "My soul-friend has died and I am headless; you too are headless, for a man without a soul-friend is a body without a head." He died in 601 or 602 after a long illness to which his austerities probably contributed. He was certainly over eighty, perhaps ninety if the duration of his abbacy given in the Annals is correct.

❖

Good the rule of Bangor, correct and divine; strict, holy and constant, excellent, just and admirable. Happy the family of Bangor, founded on a sure faith; graced with the hope of salvation and made perfect in love.

from the Antiphonary of Bangor

11

St John of Avila (1500–1569)

Born eight years after Columbus' "discovery" of America in 1492, John lived in an age of Catholic reformation, an age of saints and, in Spain, of a crusading, triumphalist faith. He was a friend of St Ignatius of Loyola, the founder of the Jesuits (see 31 July), and an adviser to St Teresa of Avila (see 15 Oct.), the reformer of the Carmelites. He was an outstanding preacher, known as the "Apostle of Andalusia," and was responsible for the conversion of St John of God (see 8 Mar.) and of St Francis Borgia. He has to a large extent been overshadowed by these and others from among the wealth of outstanding religious figures of Spain's "Golden Age," and he was beatified only in 1894. There was then a fairly lengthy gap before his canonization in 1970, since when interest in him has revived.

He was born in the town of Almodóvar del Campo, in the province of Ciudad Real in south-central Spain. His parents were wealthy and converts from Judaism. They sent him to study law at Salamanca University. He refused to take this up as a career, however, and spent three years at home doing penance and praying, which cannot have answered his parents' expectations. He came into contact with a Franciscan, who pointed him in the direction of Spain's other great Renaissance university, Alcalá de Henares. Founded by Cardinal Ximénez de Cisneros and opened in 1508, this was where the great Hebrew, Greek, and Latin Bible known as the Complutensian (from the Latin name for Alcalá) Polyglot, compiled by the cardinal, was published in 1522, during John's period of study there. He studied philosophy and theology from 1520 to 1526; for part of the time his master was the great Dominican theologian Domingo de Soto (1495–1560), later professor of theology at Salamanca and confessor to the emperor, Charles V.

While John was studying at Alcalá, both his parents died. He was ordained priest in 1525 and gave most of his family inheritance to the poor. He developed a great gift for preaching and wanted to put this to use on the mission in Mexico, where, following the conquest by Hernán Cortés, the first Franciscans had arrived in 1524, followed two years later by Dominicans and in 1533 by Augustinians. But the archbishop of Seville pressed him to preach instead in

Andalusia, where the conversion of Muslims and Jews following the conquest of the last Moorish kingdom, Granada, in 1492, was still in progress. John preached there from 1529 to 1538, with great success in making converts, but in terms that were not to everyone's liking. He was accused of being too rigorous in denying that the rich could enter the kingdom of heaven and was denounced to the Inquisition. He was acquitted of the charges and released to general rejoicing, continuing his preaching in the former Moorish capitals of Seville, Córdoba, and Granada.

His sermons survive only in the form of notes made by some of those who heard them, but spiritual letters he wrote are still extant in their original form (and were published in an English translation by the Benedictine nuns of Stanbrook Abbey in 1914). He is also the author of a systematic treatise, *Audi, filia* ("Hear, O daughter"), enjoining strict following of the way shown by Christ himself, with the emphasis on humility and suffering and avoidance of worldly pomp and wealth, as well as an insistence that all progress in the spiritual life is a gift from God and cannot be achieved by or attributed to our own efforts. In this he was teaching in much the same vein as St John of the Cross, and of his first biographer, the spiritual writer Luis de Granada—who were both suspected of "illuminism" (false mysticism) for a time and had their works investigated by the Inquisition. (Luis de Granada's two main spiritual treatises were actually placed on the Index of Forbidden Books for several years until they were approved by the Council of Trent.)

John of Avila was one of the few saints of his time in Spain who did not belong to a religious Order. He had expressed a desire to join the Society of Jesus, but the Jesuit provincial of Andalusia dissuaded him. The last fifteen years of his life were spent in constant pain, though this did not deter him from preaching. He died on 10 May 1569 and was buried in the Jesuit church in Montilla, in the province of Seville.

Christ tells us that if we wish to join him, we shall travel the way he took. It is surely not right that the Son of God should go his way on the path of shame while the sons of men walk the way of worldly honour.
St John of Avila

12

St Epiphanius of Salamis (about 310–403)

This doughty and outspoken champion of orthodoxy in the intense theological controversies over the nature of Christ that racked the Church in the fourth century was born into a Jewish family in Palestine. Convinced of the truth of Christianity, he and his sister, Callithrope, were baptized together. He then joined the monastery founded by St Hilarion (known for claiming that it was pointless to wash a hair shirt), the equally ascetic disciple of St Antony of Egypt (see 17 Jan.), in the desert south of Gaza. He then moved to Egypt to study and to stay with a group of hermits who were ardent partisans of St Athanasius (see 2 May). On his way there he met another great figure of the time and opponent of Arianism, Paphnutius, who is said to have foretold that Epiphanius would one day become "a hierarch in Cyprus," as indeed he did. In Egypt Epiphanius came across a group of monks and nuns whose Gnostic beliefs led them to regard chastity as pointless; he had them expelled from their monasteries.

He returned to Palestine, founded a monastery near Eleutheropolis in Judaea, and lived there for thirty years. In 367, Paphnutius' prophecy was apparently fulfilled when the bishops of Cyprus, impressed by Epiphanius' determination and talent for organization, elected him as their metropolitan, with his see at Salamis, to the north of Famagusta. Like so many who lived a very frugal life in the climate of the Middle East, Epiphanius lived to a great age, and he was to complete thirty-six years of devoted service to his diocese. He remained an outspoken champion of orthodoxy, castigating opponents with little attempt to understand, let alone sympathize with their position. He was involved in debates over the date of Easter, the relationship between the three Persons of the Trinity (in what was known as the Schism of Antioch), the rightness or otherwise of venerating images (to emerge later as the Iconoclast conflict), and the tendency toward Neoplatonism evidenced in the theology of Origen.

Epiphanius, who besides his native Greek knew four Eastern languages as well as Latin, was immensely learned, despite his lack of judgment. His writings provide an overview of the controversies of the early Church, especially the *Panarion*, or "Refutation of all heresies," the Greek word meaning "medicine-chest." In this he described and attacked every heresy known to him from the beginning of the Church. Origenism features as the sixty-fourth heresy. He went to Rome in 392, where he met St Jerome (see 30 Sept.), who had previously been a supporter of Origen but changed his views and supported Epiphanius in his attacks on him. Epiphanius visited Jerome again in Jerusalem in 395, resulting in Jerome attempting to persuade Bishop John of Jerusalem to condemn Origenism. John refused and even tried to have Jerome exiled from Jersualem, but the secular authorities did not put the sentence into effect.

In 400 he travelled to Constantinople to express support for Bishop Theophilus of Alexandria, who had initially tried to reconcile him and Jerome with the Origenists but had then expelled the Origenist monks from his see. In 403 he was involved in a struggle with no less a personage than St John Chrysostom (see 13 Sept.), who had fallen foul of the emperor, Arcadius, and empress, Eudoxia. They convened a synod of bishops known as the "Oak Tree Synod," from the name of the suburb of Constantinople in which it was held. The straightforward version of what happened then is that Epiphanius realized that he was being used as an imperial pawn in their struggle against Chrysostom and set out to return to Salamis, dying on the way back. A more dramatic version is that Chrysostom threatened him prophetically, saying, "My brother Epiphanius, I hear that you have advised the emperor that I should be banished: know that you will never again see your episcopal throne." This of course proved true, but Epiphanius replied, "John, my suffering brother, withstand insults, but know that you will not reach the place to which you are exiled," which proved equally true, as Chrysostom died on his way into exile in Armenia.

Besides the *Panarion*, Epiphanius wrote the *Ancoratus*, "anchor," or "Good anchor of faith," surviving manuscripts of which provide what is probably the earliest documented form of the Nicene-Constantinopolitan Creed (the version still used in the Mass), though since this was not adopted till 451, whereas the *Ancoratus* dates from 374, it must have been added in place of the Nicene Creed of 325 in later copies of the work. His many other works include a treatise on weights and measures and one on gems, in which his appetite for controversy was presumably curtailed.

13

St Andrew Fournet (André Hubert Fournet; 1752–1834)

One of André's schoolbooks contains the refreshing, if mistaken, declaration: "This book belongs to André Hubert Fournet, a good boy, though he is not going to become a priest or a monk." This was produced in reaction against his pious and overbearing mother, whose effect was to make him declare himself bored by religion, to refuse to pray, and to amuse himself in every way possible. He might in fact have been an early subject of one of Hilaire Belloc's *Cautionary Tales*: he ran away from school and was thrashed on being brought back; he was sent to study law and philosophy at Poitiers but did no work; he even joined the army but was bought out; his mother tried to find him a post as a secretary, but his handwriting was too bad. Finally, he was sent to an uncle who was a parish priest in an obscure rural parish. Reduced to this from a relatively wealthy background, he seemed to have reaped a just reward for his unruly youthful behaviour.

This low point in his career proved to be a turning point. The uncle was a far more tactful influence than his mother and eventually steered him to the study of theology. He contradicted his early declaration of non-intent in 1776, when he was ordained priest. He served first in his uncle's country parish, then in a nearby town, and in 1781 was appointed parish priest in his home town of Maillé. So changed was his character that he was even reconciled to his mother, who, with his sister, came to live with him and his curate in their simple presbytery. He was generous to the poor, giving away what he regarded as surplus family possessions, and generally highly regarded in the town.

The outbreak of the French Revolution brought this simple, stable, and fruitful way of life to an abrupt end. In July 1790 the Civil Constitution on the Clergy attempted to make the clergy into civil servants, requiring them to swear an oath of loyalty to the State and its laws. About half of them, including Andrew, refused and were removed from their posts. Persecution began in earnest in 1791; a new "Liberty–Equality" oath was required in August 1792, and massacres of bishops, priests, and religious who refused to swear to this began the following month. Andrew continued to minister to his flock, but his life was in danger, and his bishop sent him to Spain for his safety. He spent five years there but returned in secret in 1797, to lead a life of constant evasion of Pursuivants. On one occasion a housewife pretended he was her herdsman, boxed his ears, and told him to go and mind the cattle; on another he was covered by a shroud and played dead. This state of affairs lasted for four years, after which Napoleon's Concordat with Pope Pius VII brought the terror to an end and the clergy were allowed to resume their ministry.

Andrew returned to his parish and set about restoring the people's disrupted religious life, preaching missions and spending long hours hearing Confessions. The parish church had been destroyed, but he used a barn as a church. During this period he acquired a disciple in the person of a young woman who had collected a group of peasants into a prayer group during the persecution, named Elizabeth Bichier des Ages (canonized in 1947). Andrew dissuaded her from becoming a Trappistine nun and devised a Rule of life for her and some friends who came to join her. He was rebuked by the vicar-general for approving of her dressing in coarse peasant mourning clothes. Undeterred, he went on to suggest that she should head a new community of nuns dedicated to good works in the area. She spent six months learning about the religious life, then gathered a larger group around her to teach children and to shelter the sick, aged, and poor. By 1811 the community, grown to twenty-five, moved into a larger house in Maillé. In 1816 they received diocesan approval of the Rule devised for them by Andrew and became the Daughters of the Cross, though Elizabeth preferred to call them the Sisters of St Andrew.

Andrew looked after his parish until fatigue and illness forced him to resign at the age of sixty-eight. He lived for a further fourteen years, in semi-retirement at the new Congregation's house at La Puye, from where he helped in nearby parishes and acted as spiritual director to a number of clergy and lay people. He died on 13 May 1834 and was beatified in 1926 and canonized in 1933.

14

St Matthias (First Century)

Matthias was the one chosen to replace Judas to make up the number of apostles to twelve once more. This is described in the first chapter of the Acts of the Apostles, taking place "in those days" after the eleven had witnessed Christ's Ascension on Mount Olivet and before the Spirit came down on the new twelve at Pentecost. Peter stands up "among the believers," describes Judas' death as fulfilling scripture, and sets out the criterion that is to govern the choice of a replacement: "So one of the men who have accompanied us throughout the time that the Lord Jesus went in and out among us, beginning from the baptism of John until the day he was taken up from us—one of these must become a witness with us to his resurrection" (1:21–2).

Two candidates are then proposed and a vote is taken:

> So they proposed two, Joseph called Barsabbas, who was also known as Justus, and Matthias. Then they prayed and said, "Lord, you know everyone's heart. Show us which one of these two you have chosen to take the place in this ministry and apostleship from which Judas turned aside to go to his own place." And they cast lots for them, and the lot fell on Matthias; and he was added to the eleven apostles (1:23–6).

(This prompt and democratic election has been criticized by some cha-rismatically inclined theologians, who would have preferred the apostles to have waited for the promised coming of the Spirit—which seems somewhat churlish, as the apostles invoked the authority of the risen Lord and were presumably not to know how soon the Spirit would come.)

With this brief but important appearance in the New Testament, definite information about Matthias begins and ends. Early tradition places him preaching in Judaea, and somewhat later Greek accounts claim that he preached in Cappadocia (southern Turkey) and near the Caspian Sea. Another tradition links him with Ethiopia, and a fictitious *Acts of Andrew and Matthias* became very popular, though in some versions he is replaced by Matthew. Clement of Alexandria makes him one of the seventy-two disciples sent out to preach throughout the known world. How, when, or where he died is not known. Some legends state that he was crucified, but the tradition that became incorporated in his emblem is that he was beheaded: this shows an axe superimposed over an open book on which appear the words *super Matthiam*, "upon Matthias," from Acts 1:26. His claimed relics were taken to Jerusalem and at least some of them were later sent to Rome by the empress Helena (see 18 Aug.) when she went to the Holy Land to find the true cross. Matthias' feast was moved from 24 February to today in the calendar reform of 1969.

15

St Isidore the Farmer (about 1070–1130)

This humble farmworker, which is what he appears to have been (in Spain he is *San Isidro, labrador,* and the Spanish word *labrador* means farmer, farm labourer, ploughman, or peasant), shared a magnificent canonization ceremony, in 1622, with four great figures of the Catholic Reformation: St Philip Neri (see 26 May), St Ignatius Loyola (see 31 July), St Teresa of Avila (see 15 Oct.), and St Francis Xavier (see 3 Dec.). The other four had been prominent founders or reformers of powerful Orders or Congregations or had initiated great missions; all had also died relatively recently. Why was a humble peasant of whose life virtually nothing was known with any certainty, who had died in obscurity five hundred and fifty years earlier, added to their number? And what is the appeal of the patron saint of Madrid that still plunges the capital of Spain into ten days of bullfights and other celebrations leading up to his feast-day?

The cynical answer is that in about 1615 King Philip III of Spain (1598–1621) had been mortally ill until Isidore's shrine was carried into his sick room, whereupon he made a seemingly miraculous recovery and in return petitioned the pope for Isidore's official canonization, so his name was added to the distinguished list. And the fact that his feast-day is the subject of such celebration can be attributed to more than Madrid waking out of its cold winter in the mood for a party. Both these may be true, but the Church has always had an instinct for celebrating ordinary as well as extraordinary people's lives, the humble alongside the magnificent—beginning, it might be said, with Mary the mother of Jesus.

The outline of Isidore's life is that he spent all his working life on an estate called Torrelaguna, near what in his lifetime was the very modest settlement of Madrid. He married a woman much younger than himself, and they had one son, who died young. His piety must have been such as to make a deep impression on people, since in 1170, forty years after his death (and five years before his wife's), his body, incorrupt or mummified—as it remains to this day—was transferred into a beautiful shrine, which at the time was the equivalent of canonization. This was over a hundred years before his Life was written, by the Franciscan Juan Egidio de Zamora, so it is not an example of a biography and then a shrine being manufactured to attract pilgrims (as happened with not a few saints along the road to Compostela in northern Spain).

Miracles of multiplying food for the poor and even for birds were related in the biography, and he was credited (like James the Greater; see 25 July) with helping in battles against the Moors, in his case by appearing in a vision to King Alfonso of Castile and showing him a secret path. So attempts were made to add extraordinary elements to his ordinary life.

Whether to enhance this tendency or out of people's deep sense of justice, Isidore's wife was also venerated, making them possibly unique in the history of the Church—in that both were popularly acclaimed as saints soon after their death, and then, much later, one was officially canonized and the other had her cult officially confirmed. Her story is that she was named Toribia and that after the death of their son she and Isidore took a vow of permanent continence: this idea comes from the thirteenth-century Franciscan biography, trying to make their condition approach that of religious. When a skull was discovered at a shrine of Our Lady by the Jarama River it was declared to be hers and she was venerated as a saint, called *Santa María de la Cabeza*, because of the shrine and the fact that it was a head (*cabeza*) that was the venerated relic. The rest of the body was found in the same place in the sixteenth century and a formal process for her beatification was begun; she was described as the perfect counterpart of her husband and was beatified as Bd María de la Cabeza in 1695. Her remains were moved to Torrelaguna, where Isidore had worked, in 1615, but a continuing cult of her in her own right is evidenced in paintings depicting her in at least seven towns, all of which claim to be her birthplace. The new Roman Martyrology restores the name Toribia (*Turibia* in Latin), thereby upholding early popular tradition, as an alternative to María de la Cabeza, and she is commemorated separately from her husband, on 9 September.

Whatever the ecclesiastical processes and motivations, Isidore and Turibia stand as an extraordinary affirmation of the holiness of the ordinary, the humble, and the humdrum in the lives of countless men and women throughout the world and down the ages.

16

St Brendan of Clonfert (484–577)

This Brendan (or Brenainn) is "Brendan the Navigator" or "the Voyager," famous from *The Voyages of Brendan* or *The Navigation of St Brendan*, a hugely popular medieval romance written in Germany, in Latin, by an exiled Irish monk and translated into all the main European vernaculars. Its diffusion can be gauged by the fact that one hundred and sixteen medieval manuscripts of it still survive.

Though his fame derives from the *Navigation*, Brendan was nevertheless a historical personage, and at least the outline facts of his life are known. He was born near Tralee in western Ireland and educated by Erc, the bishop of Kerry, who both baptized and ordained him. He became a monk and later an abbot and founded several monasteries in the west of Ireland. The best known of these is Clonfert (Cluain Fearta), in Co. Galway, which he is said to have founded in 559 or 561; others are Annadown, Inishadroun, and Ardfert. His name is commemorated in Mount Brandon on the Dingle Peninsula, the most westerly point in Europe, and his cult was strong in Scotland, Wales, and Brittany, all of which he may well have visited. The churches of Brendon in Devonshire and Brancepeth in Co. Durham are dedicated to him. The dates of his birth and death vary by a few years in different sources, but all concur in making him around ninety years of age at the time of his death.

The *Navigation* is basically a quest story, telling of marvels encountered on journeys in search of the Island of Paradise. There may be a basis in reality, as Irish monks did travel to the Hebrides, or round the northern tip of Scotland to the Orkneys and Shetlands and Faroes, and even to Iceland, but most of the story seems to be the product of a lively imagination, mixed in with snatches of earlier Christian apocryphal writings and episodes from the Gospels. After recounting wonderful signs associated with Brendan's birth, it tells of his education by Erc, who encourages him to learn the "canon" of the Old and New Testaments and then the "rules" of the Irish saints, which instil in him a desire to leave his native land (this was written after several centuries of emigration by Irish monks to continental Europe), so he begs the Lord "to give him some unknown country to visit, far removed from humankind." An old holy man comes to see him and tells him of "The Land of the Saints," which he had visited with his son.

Brendan collects fourteen monks to go with him to find this land, and after fasting for forty days and forty nights they sail west from the Aran Islands. They find an island with a holy man and celebrate Easter on it, returning again the following year. From there they go on to "the paradise of Birds," where a bird sings to them from the prow of their boat, telling them how they are to organize their future journeys according to the liturgical seasons: "On this journey four seasons have been determined for you; that is, the day of the Lord's Supper with the holy man, Easter on the island, which is really the back of a sea monster, and from Easter to Pentecost with us on Paradise Island, and Christmas on the Island of Ailbe up to Mary's feast of Candlemas. At the end of the seventh year you will reach the land you are seeking, and you will be there forty days and then be borne back to your homeland."

The monks accordingly return to Ireland after four years, and Ita, Brendan's foster-mother, tells him that they will never find the land they seek in a boat made of skins but that they need a timber one. So they have a larger, wooden boat made in Connaght and set sail again. They find the Land of Promise in the middle of the western ocean, and again there is a holy man to welcome them to a land of flowers and angels. They stay there for a while, marvelling at the "wonders of God and his power," then return to a great welcome in Aran, where they stay for a month before going on to Limerick on the mainland of Ireland. After this Brendan sails to Britain, having an adventure with sea monsters on the way, which leads him to make a mutual confession with St Brigid (see 1 Feb.), who proves to him that he forgets God more often than she does (which is not for a moment). Finally, after "traversing the great perils of sea and land, after raising dead men, healing lepers, the blind, deaf, and lame, and all kinds of sick folk, after founding many cells, monasteries, and churches, after pre-eminence in pilgrimage and ascetic devotion, and after performing mighty works and miracles too numerous to mention, Brendan drew near to the day of his death." He goes to visit his sister, Brig, in his last days and gives instructions for his body to be taken to Clonfert on a "small chariot" so that "the tribes" will not notice and quarrel over it. A single brother accompanies his body, and it is buried at Clonfert "with great honor and reverence, with psalms and hymns and spiritual songs in honor of the Father, and of the Son, and of the Holy Spirit."

17

St Paschal Baylon (1540–1592)

This Spanish Franciscan lay brother, little known in his lifetime, which was spent mainly in prayer in a convent of Reformed Franciscans, became the patron of Eucharistic Congresses. These spectacular international celebrations, designed to increase devotion to the Blessed Sacrament of the Altar, were a prominent feature of the Church in the late nineteenth and twentieth centuries, developing out of a more local event organized by Bishop Gaston de Ségur of Lille in northern France in 1881. One was held in London in 1908, providing the first occasion when a papal legate had set foot in England since Cardinal Pole in the sixteenth century. Others in English-speaking countries (or where English is a common language) have been in Chicago in 1926, Sydney in 1928, Dublin in 1932, Bombay in 1964, Melbourne in 1973, and Philadelphia in 1976. Paschal's Life was written by his religious superior, Fr Ximénez, and this portrayed him spending long hours kneeling unsupported in prayer before the Blessed Sacrament, thus establishing his claim to become patron of the congresses.

Paschal was born in the little town of Torre Hermosa ("beautiful tower") on the borders of Castile and Aragon on Whitsunday 1540. His family lived on the land as peasant farmers, which meant hard work for all its members and little time for education. He is said to have taught himself to read while looking after flocks of sheep belonging to his own family and others. The contemporary biography tells that he was scrupulous in repairing damage done to other people's vineyards when his sheep broke in.

He was attracted to the religious life—and to a severe form of it. At the age of twenty-one he joined the Franciscans of the Observance of St Peter of Alcántara. Peter was an extremely austere reformer, admired by St Teresa of Avila (see 15 Oct.). His Rule of life could hardly have been more severe: the friars had cells only seven feet long, took no meat or wine, and went barefoot. They engaged in three hours of mental prayer every day and relied completely on alms for their support, being forbidden to accept stipends for saying Masses—this inspired St Teresa's insistence on absolute poverty for her reformed Carmelites. Each community was limited to eight friars. They were an extreme development of the Observant Franciscans, the branch of the Franciscan family to which they belonged (except for a short period at their origin). Paschal joined the community of Loreto, two hundred miles from his home town. He found the life far from joyless: he was once seen performing an elaborate solo dance before a statue of the Blessed Virgin placed over the refectory door. His prayers before the Blessed Sacrament were additional to those prescribed in the Rule. He distributed alms and food to the poor who came to the convent for help with exemplary devotion and good grace.

During the religious wars in France he was sent to Orleans, carrying letters for the minister general of the Observants. Why he was chosen for this dangerous mission is not clear. Despite his lack of French and being repeatedly attacked by Huguenots on the way, he reached Orleans and duly delivered the letters. He spent the rest of his life in pain from a shoulder injured when stones were thrown at him. Despite all this, he made his way safely back to his convent and resumed his life of prayer and charity to the poor. He died at the age of fifty-two, and miraculous cures were attributed to him even before he was buried. The sound of blows or knocking (*golpes* in the Spanish account) was said to come from his tomb for two hundred years. He was beatified in 1618, a year before Peter of Alcántara himself, and canonized in 1690. His tomb was devastated and his relics burned during the eruption of anti-Catholic revolutionary zeal at the outbreak of the Spanish civil war of 1936–39.

18

St Peter Celestine (Pietro da Morrone; about 1215–1296)

Peter was born not far from the great monastery of Monte Cassino. He was the eleventh child of a peasant family from the Abruzzi region and at the age of seventeen became a Benedictine monk before deciding to embrace the life of a hermit. He was ordained priest in Rome and then lived for several years in a cave on Mount Morrone. He began to accept disciples, whom he formed into a religious Congregation, known initially as the Hermits of St Damian, then as Poor Hermits of Celestine. In 1274 they were incorporated into the Benedictine family as Celestines, when Peter obtained confirmation of their status from Pope Gregory X, whom he travelled to see at the Council of Lyons. Peter lived by an extremely harsh regime, wearing a hair shirt and chains that bit into his flesh. In 1276 he became abbot of Santa Maria di Faifula, his original monastery, and prior of Maiella, where he had held the first general chapter of the Congregation. In 1293 he laid down his appointments and retired to his hermitage near Maiella.

Meanwhile, in Rome, Pope Nicholas IV had died in April 1292, after a papacy lasting four years. The College of Cardinals was dominated by three families, the Orsini, the Colonna, and the dukes of Anjou (to which King Charles of Sicily belonged), and they spent twenty-seven months scheming to elect their chosen candidate, without success. Filled with holy rage, Peter wrote to them, threatening divine punishment if they could not agree. Out of repentance or vengeance, they promptly chose him. He was almost eighty years old, saintly but totally unworldly, and in poor health after a long lifetime of rigorous asceticism. The choice was a disaster.

A procession of cardinals and a huge, enthusiastic crowd, expecting this to be the onset of the Age of the Holy Spirit foretold by Joachim of Fiore, set out to break the glad news to him. They found him in his cave, wearing his hair shirt and with shoes made of donkey skin. He tried desperately to refuse, but he eventually had to agree, and was mounted on a donkey. Escorted by King Charles II of Naples and his son (who were not going to let him fall under Anjou influence), the procession stopped at Aquila, where Peter was forced to exchange his hair shirt for papal robes and tiara. He took the name Celestine V. He was in effect a pawn of the king of Naples, who made him move to Naples, pack the College of Cardinals and the Curia with his supporters, and make other religious Orders subject to the Celestines. Charles II was in effect ruling the Church in his own interests, and the pope had little idea of what was being done in his name.

The cardinals regretted their choice, and Peter himself wanted to resign. The question was: Could he? It had never been done before, so a commission of theologians and canon lawyers was set up to study the case. This gave an affirmative answer, and Peter announced that the Roman Pontiff could therefore lay down any of his responsibilities when he desired to do so. This seems to have been a free decision on his part, though Cardinal Gaetani, whose advice he sought and who was then elected as Boniface VIII (1294–1303), has often been charged with forcing him to take it. The cardinals did not oppose him, and on 13 December 1294 he formally resigned, giving his poor health, desire for solitude, and lack of knowledge and experience as reasons.

But he still had popular support, and his successor was unwilling for him to become a focus that might lead to a schism in the Church. Peter tried to leave Italy across the Adriatic Sea, but Boniface had him seized and interned in the castle of Fumone, where he died on 19 May 1296. He was buried at nearby Ferentino, and then on the occasion of his canonization his remains were transferred to the church of Santa Maria di Collemaggio in Aquila, where he had been crowned pope.

Differing judgments have been passed on his abdication. Dante's *Inferno* (3:59–60) speaks of "him who made the great rejection out of cowardice," whereas Petrarch celebrated it as the action of a saint. What was obvious was that devotion and asceticism were not sufficient qualities to make a successful pope. Boniface had many of these: prudence, experience, authority, and a willingness to make decisions. All he lacked was saintliness. His successor but one, Clement V (1305–14), canonized Peter Celestine on 5 May 1313, partly from pure recognition of his personal holiness, at least partly as an adverse political judgment on his predecessor Boniface.

19

St Dunstan (909–988)

In England monasticism declined for two hundred years after the "golden age" of Bede (see 25 May) until by the early tenth century there were no surviving monasteries for men. It was Dunstan's great achievement to restore the monasteries with a structure and a spirituality to make them last another six hundred years, until the dissolution under King Henry VIII. He was also an outstanding archbishop of Canterbury, presiding over far-reaching reforms in both Church and society.

He was born in Somerset to a family connected by marriage to the kings of Wessex. He was educated at Glastonbury, then apparently consisting of a group of Celtic clerics "exiled for Christ." He was a devoted scholar and a gifted artist and musician. His drawing ability can be seen in a famous addition to an illustration of Christ as the Wisdom of God, now in the Bodleian Library in Oxford. It depicts a small cowled figure kneeling at Christ's feet, bowing his head to a sloping piece of ground that might represent Glastonbury Tor. Above him is a Latin inscription, saying, "I Dunstan, beg the merciful Christ to protect me, lest the storms of the underworld swallow me up." His learning was seen as more than natural, and he was expelled from the court of King Athelstan on suspicion of witchcraft.

He returned to Glastonbury and lived as a hermit, by now ordained priest and probably privately vowed to a monastic life. In 939 Edmund became king of Wessex, and he gave Glastonbury to Dunstan, appointing him abbot in 940 and charging him to create a genuine Benedictine monastery there. Dunstan brought in the Benedictine Rule and began adding new buildings. His fortunes took another turn for the worse in 955, when he rebuked Edmund's successor but one, Edwy, for licentious conduct at his coronation feast and consequently had to flee to Ghent, where he would have seen how the reformed monasteries on the Continent were operating. Edwy died in 959, and Dunstan was recalled by his successor, Edgar, and appointed to the bishoprics of Worcester in 957 and London before becoming archbishop of Canterbury in 960. He went to Rome to receive the *pallium* from Pope John XII the following year.

Edgar, still only sixteen, had been a pupil of Dunstan and was to collaborate with him in the project of monastic renewal. His coronation was delayed for many years—possibly on account of his scandalous personal life—until 973, when he was crowned in Bath Abbey in a ceremony largely devised by Dunstan, which still forms the basis of the British coronation ceremony today. The king was required to respect the liberty and integrity of the Church, act against theft and violence, and rule with justice and mercy. This was before he was crowned and anointed, thus establishing the principle that he has to account for his authority to God and the people. The Church was to advise the king, giving it an established place in British political life that it has nominally retained ever since. Edgar died prematurely in 975; Dunstan secured the throne for his son, Edward, but Edward was murdered a year later by supporters of his half-brother, Ethelred, who became king (known later as "the Unready") in 978. Relations between him and Dunstan alternated between stormy and cool for the remaining ten years of the archbishop's life.

The monastic way of life defined by Dunstan was distinguished by close dependence on the royal family for protection and support, so protecting the monasteries from the territorial and other ambitions of local lords. The monks added special prayers for the royal family to their regular ones. This was laid down in the *Regularis concordia*, the manual for monastic life produced under Dunstan's guidance and with personal contributions by him. This, besides producing a common way of life among the monasteries, made them answerable in part to the king as well as to the Church. This was largely to defend them against the secular clergy, many of whom were married and passed on church lands to their families; they resented the reforms and the new prominence of the monks.

Learning flourished in the monasteries, and a high standard of integrity ensured that many abbots were promoted to be diocesan bishops—as with Dunstan's disciple Wulsin at Sherborne (see 8 Jan.), his friend Ethelwold, abbot of Abingdon and bishop of Winchester, then capital of Wessex, and Oswald, who moved from the revived abbey of Westbury-on-Trym to be bishop of Worcester (see 29 Feb.). Church reforms inspired by Dunstan included observance of marriage laws and those of fasting and abstinence; he also made all priests take up some craft work. He influenced civil laws, especially those relating to payment of tithes and other church taxes. His theology, especially his view of Christ as the focus of prayer and the source of all authority, is illustrated in a remarkable series of four drawings of Christ—crucified, as King, as herald of the gospel, and risen—in the *Sherborne Pontifical*, a magnificent liturgical book produced at Canterbury under Dunstan and presented to Wulsin at Sherborne.

Dunstan was widely regarded as a saint immediately after his death. His cult, like that of most Anglo-Saxon saints, was downplayed by Archbishop Lanfranc after the Norman Conquest but soon revived. Two early Lives were written, the first largely anecdotal, with many visions and signs of divine grace, the second to provide readings for the monastic office commemorating him in the early eleventh century; this contains a dramatic account of his death. A slightly later third Life was designed to persuade Lanfranc to recognize his importance. St Anselm (see 21 Apr.) raised his commemoration to the level of a nationally observed feast with an octave. His memory was later somewhat eclipsed by that of St Thomas Becket (see 29 Dec.). The fact that his remains were at Canterbury, not Glastonbury, which also claimed them, was confirmed in 1508. Nationally, his memory was revived in the twentieth century: in 1998, the millennium of his death, the site of his burial place was again marked in Canterbury Cathedral and the place of his birth, Baltonsborough, near Glastonbury, was also marked. Because of his personal skills, he is patron of goldsmiths, jewellers, and locksmiths.

20

St Bernardino of Siena (1380–1444)

This great preacher and reformer was able, it would seem, to project his voice, without benefit of amplification or an enclosed stadium, so that he could be heard by up to thirty thousand people at a time in the open air. He was also responsible for instituting the feast of the Holy Name of Jesus, for which he adopted the IHS monogram—an abbreviation of the Greek form of Jesus' name, though later adapted to fit Latin phrases such as *Jesus Hominum Salvator* ("Jesus, Saviour of mankind") or *In hoc signo* ("in this sign [you shall conquer]") and used by the Jesuits and others.

He was born on 8 September 1380 in the town of Massa Marittima, of which his father was governor, in the Republic (as it then was) of Siena, some thirty miles south-west of the capital. Orphaned at the age of six, he was brought up by an aunt in Siena, where by the time he was twenty he had studied grammar and rhetoric and taken a degree in law at the university. He cared for plague victims in the local hospital during a severe outbreak in 1400 and then nursed his bedridden aunt until she died. He joined the Franciscans in 1402, was ordained priest two years later, and then went on to study ascetical and mystical theology, as well as the Fathers of the Church and the Franciscan masters, at Fiesole, where his cell can still be seen.

He adhered to the Observant movement of the Franciscan Order, made up of those who wished to return to the original simplicity and absolute poverty enjoined by St Francis (see 4 Oct.), from which subsequent adjustments, mainly in the direction of common ownership of property, backed up by papal definitions, had removed it. In 1350 Pope Clement VI allowed hermits in Umbria to observe the Rule according to its original letter; this was soon disallowed and then allowed again, causing bitter conflict that was to last for two hundred years. Early Observants were generally lay brothers of rustic origins, with little education. In the early fifteenth century they were given provinces free from jurisdiction of the minister general, and Bernardino became the provincial vicar for Tuscany. This post was later abolished and then re-instated; by 1438 the Observants had virtually split completely from the Conventuals, and Bernardino was appointed their first vicar-general. They counteracted the solitude of their hermitages by preaching, and this was the tradition that Bernardino upheld and developed.

Beginning in 1417, Bernardino accepted invitations to preach all over northern and central Italy, travelling everywhere on foot. He preached against abuses of his day, including gambling, usury, witchcraft and superstition, urging the need for personal prayer and penance and for ethics in commerce to be based on peace and justice. His voice and his style were full of human warmth and joy; he could mimic and act, reducing his audiences to tears or laughter as required. People amended their lives after hearing him and restored stolen or otherwise misappropriated property. He was denounced for preaching false doctrine three times, but on none of these occasions could the accusation be upheld: he may have been extreme in some ways, but he was totally orthodox in his teaching and beyond reproach in his personal life.

In 1430 he began writing theological works, which have survived along with many of his sermons, most of these written down by those who heard them. He wrote on mystical and ascetical theology, on moral and doctrinal matters, and on the Blessed Virgin Mary, devotion to whom was always a prominent part of Franciscan spirituality. He was offered three bishoprics, but he refused them all. He was vicar-general of the Observants from 1438 to 1442, during which time their numbers increased dramatically. He moved his friars away from the "holy rusticity" of their early days, insisted on education, and involved them in teaching as well as preaching.

He resigned as vicar-general in 1442 and resumed his itinerant preaching, making the concession to his age of travelling on a donkey. His reputation was such that he was reckoned the most influential religious in Italy. In 1444 he preached on fifty consecutive days in his native town and then set out for Naples, farther south than he had been before, but he died at Aquila on the way. He was buried there, and miracles were soon being reported in great numbers at his tomb. He was canonized in 1450, just six years after his death.

The Feast of the Holy Name was extended to the universal Church by Pope Innocent XIII in the early eighteenth century. Bernardino's collected works first appeared in four volumes in 1591; they were reissued in nine volumes in the 1950s and 1960s. There are many fine portraits of him, mainly in Siena and elsewhere in Tuscany. El Greco (1541–1614) produced a striking version of him preaching, with three baroque mitres at his feet, representing the three bishoprics he had refused.

21

St Godric of Finchale (about 1070–1170)

Godric was never formally canonized (dying before the official process had been introduced) and does not appear in the new Roman Martyrology, but his cult is ancient in England; he has some of the most attractive animal stories of the Middle Ages told of him; he led a most remarkable life, having been peddler, sailor, and ship's captain (and possibly pirate), and bailiff before spending fifty years as a hermit: on many counts he deserves to be better known.

He was born into an Anglo-Saxon peasant family in Norfolk but instead of working the land earned his living as a peddler in Lincolnshire, to where his family had moved. He then set out on a series of voyages of pilgrimage and commerce. He made a first pilgrimage to Rome, then traded by sea, visiting Scotland, Denmark, and Flanders. This enabled him to buy a quarter share in one ship and a half share in another, becoming captain of the latter. In 1101 he went on pilgrimage to Jerusalem, and the following year he may well have been the *Gudericus pirata* who took Baldwin I (Crusader and first king of Jerusalem) to Jaffa. He returned from the Holy Land via the third great medieval pilgrimage destination, Santiago de Compostela in north-western Spain. He then went on a second and a third pilgrimage to Rome, taking his aged mother on the third.

On his return he decided to become a hermit and sold all his possessions. He started in a forest near Carlisle, then joined another hermit near Durham. Then he was seized with another urge for penitential pilgrimage and returned to the Holy Land. There he spent some time with other hermits in the desert and worked in the great hospital in Jerusalem. One of his early biographers, Reginald of Durham, tells that on coming out of the Jordan he looked down at his feet and made a vow: " 'Lord,' he said within himself, 'for love of thy name, who for our salvation didst walk always barefoot through the world, and didst not deny to have thy naked feet struck through with nails for me: from this day I shall put no shoes upon these feet.'" And he kept this promise for the remaining fifty years and more of his life, no mean feat in winter in northern Britain.

He came back to Durham, took up his peddling again for a time, then put himself to school at the choir school of St Mary-le-Bow in London—writing music was another of his talents. He went back north and eventually settled into a hermit's life at Finchale on the River Wear. At first he made his own rules by which to live; later Prior Roger of Durham provided him with a Rule and associated him with the monastic community there. He received visitors and was known as a good listener and wise counsellor, though his life was dedicated mostly to prayerful solitude—so prayerful that he forgot mundane tasks and the monks sent a succession of boys to perform these for him. He spent nearly sixty years in this astonishingly austere way of life, with his fame increasing and his health declining as he approached his hundredth year. Near the end of his life he received a letter of encouragement from Pope Alexander II (which still survives). He died on 21 May 1170.

He wrote verse, the earliest person to do so in Middle English, which he set to music in a style close to Gregorian chant. Several hymns exist in a fourteenth-century manuscript, from which a recording of them was made in 1965. Both early biographies, one by Geoffrey of Durham and the more picturesque one by Reginald, recount delightful stories of his dealings with animals: he told the cow that gave him milk when to go out to pasture and when to return for milking, as his boy-helper at the time was forgetful; he led a stag that was eating his young apple trees out of the orchard with his belt and made a herd of deer kneel while he told them those trees were for humans and not for them; he produced a salmon to feed two monks, sent to him "by St John the Baptist" at a time when they could not possibly have swum up the river; he sheltered a stag pursued by hunters, which for years after would come back to lie at his feet; he tied a bunch of vegetables round the neck of a hare that was stealing them and sent it off telling it that he was growing them for the poor. ...

22

St Gregory VII (Hildebrand; about 1021–1085)

Secretary to several relatively short-lived popes before his own election by acclamation, then champion of the liberty of the Church during his twelve-year pontificate, Gregory has been hailed as a great reformer and, in some traditions, reviled as an obscurantist tyrant. This latter view has now declined, though historians would not entirely condemn the secular rulers who opposed him and would attribute some of the reforms known as "Gregorian" to his predecessor, Leo IX.

He was born at Rovaco in Tuscany and christened Hildebrand. He was educated in Rome under John Gratian (not the great canon lawyer Gratian but the future Pope Gregory VI). It was this Gratian who persuaded the dissolute and simoniacal Benedict IX to abdicate, for the second but not the last time, in 1045, by offering him a large sum of money. He was then elected in his place, but this made his offer of money seem like buying office for himself, and he was deposed and exiled the following year on the orders of the emperor Henry III. Hildebrand followed him into exile at Cluny. He returned to Rome in 1049 to serve the newly elected Leo IX (1048–54) as papal treasurer. He became a deacon and prior of the monastery of St Paul outside the Walls and was a major influence on the pontificates of the next four popes. On the death of Alexander II (1061–73), he was elected by popular acclaim.

He began his reform process by holding a series of synods, designed to do away with abuses such as clerical marriage, the buying of offices (simony), and the appointment to clerical office by secular rulers (lay investiture). This last practice reduced the Church to a subservient role in the State, whereas Gregory was determined that it should have authority over the State. He required bishops to take an oath of obedience and threatened to depose those who would not carry out papal decrees. His principal targets were Philip I of France, the German (or Holy Roman) emperor, Henry IV, and William I (the Conqueror) of England, who all resisted the abolition of lay investiture, the first two for mainly discreditable reasons, the last on firmer principle—that the pope was not going to become the feudal lord of England.

Gregory's aim was not so much political power for the papacy as its authority to impose reform, on clerics and lay people alike. It was to become the supreme spiritual authority in Western Christendom, and this authority was to be imposed first by the pope in the name of Christ the King, then by all who supported him, clerical or lay, using force if necessary. His greatest struggle was with Henry IV, who was used to appointing bishops, even Bishops of Rome. Three years into Gregory's pontificate, Henry assembled "his" bishops at Worms and insisted that they declare Gregory deposed. Gregory was made of sterner stuff than to accept this: he excommunicated Henry and declared his subjects freed from allegiance to him. Henry gave in and travelled to Canossa in January 1077 to ask Gregory's pardon and absolution—which he could hardly refuse, though he kept the emperor waiting for some time in the snow before granting them.

Gregory's "victory" was not to last. Henry rallied his forces, invaded Italy, and again declared Gregory deposed, having the antipope Clement III elected in 1080. He besieged and captured Rome, forcing Gregory to take refuge in

Castel Sant'Angelo. Gregory was relieved by Norman forces under Duke Robert de Guiscard, whom he had invited to his rescue, but the Norman troops behaved so badly that the population of Rome turned on Gregory for inviting them in, forcing him to retire first to Monte Cassino and then to Salerno. He died there, his last words being, "I have loved justice and hated iniquity; that is why I die in exile."

He had in many ways set the course of the papacy in the Middle Ages, including its reliance on force—the First Crusade started just ten years after his death—and the collision course with secular rulers that was eventually to spread the Reformation. His influence was undoubted, but his holiness was proclaimed only in a climate of Catholic Reformation centuries later. He was beatified in 1584 and canonized in 1606. His feast was extended to the universal Church in 1728, causing fury among proponents of Gallicanism (effectively, denial of the temporal powers of the pope) in France and to a lesser extent elsewhere. He was later seen as a precursor of the First Vatican Council (1869–70), whose proclamation of papal infallibility seemed a logical expression of his views and made Gallicanism incompatible with orthodox Catholicism. The various tyrannies of the twentieth century may be said to prove the value of his insistence on the freedom of the Church, though not through fighting force with force.

23

St Mary Magdalen de'Pazzi (Caterina di Geri de'Pazzi; 1566–1607)

Born into one of the wealthiest families in Florence, Caterina showed an exceptional interest in religion from an early age and experienced her first ecstasy at the age of twelve. This happened in her mother's presence and set the pattern for well-documented extraordinary experiences that marked the remainder of her relatively short life.

Her family had naturally planned for her to make an advantageous marriage, and her beauty added to her wealth made her an outstanding prospect. Instead, she determined to enter the religious life, and after an another ecstatic experience when she was sixteen she entered the Carmelite convent in Florence. The first two years of her novitiate were relatively uneventful, but then she was stricken by a mysterious illness and was thought to be dying. Anxious that she should make her profession before she died, the nuns took her to the chapel. She was able to make her profession and then had an ecstatic experience in which she felt herself united to the Holy Trinity, which she described as giving her heart to the Trinity and receiving it back together with a gift of purity like that given to the Virgin Mary. She went on to describe her "mystical marriage" with Jesus in graphic terms: "Then Jesus, caressing me gently like a newly-wed, united me to him and hid me in his side, where I tasted sweet repose. The Lord then seemed to take away from me my will and all my desires, so that I can no longer wish or desire anything except what he wills." The experience left her in tears, but she recovered from her illness.

A whole series of similar experiences followed, all documented and carefully dated: on 8 June 1584 she saw Jesus' passion; two days later she and Jesus made an exchange of their hearts; on 28 June she received the stigmata; on 6 July she felt the crown of thorns being pressed on her head, and she was to feel the pain of this for the rest of her life. These were particular experiences, but she was liable to go into ecstatic trances every day, whether she was praying or doing anything else. More particular manifestations affected her the following year: on 15 April she had a vision of the five wounds of Jesus; on 28 April she was given a ring as a sign of her mystical marriage to Jesus. She was then "told" to live on bread and water except on Sundays in reparation for the sins of the human race. Her confessor suspected that she was being deluded and countermanded the instruction, but when Mary Magdalen tried to live on the normal convent regime she was physically sick, and when she tried to resist her ecstasies, she was thrown to the ground. This persisted for five years.

She was also "told" that she would be plunged into a "dark night of the soul," an experience common to most mystics, when she would feel deprived of all divine help. This indeed happened, and she was prey to all sorts of temptations, even to suicide, when she went so far as to carry a knife, which she eventually left at the feet of a statue of Our Lady. "Hysteria" springs to mind, but she was able to use her ecstasies to produce perfectly sensible advice for the younger nuns. Her confessor was cautious, and she relied on the prioress, to whom she turned constantly for advice, so there seems to have been no evidence of the hysterical atmosphere that can grip an enclosed community. Her ecstasies continued for many years, but they did not prevent her from progressing in responsibility in the convent. She was made novice-mistress in 1598 and subprioress in 1604. She counselled the novices in poverty and obedience and self-abandonment to the will of God, but shortly after her appointment as subprioress she relapsed into the kind of spiritual desolation and physical suffering she had known earlier. She was bedridden for the last three years of her life and died, exhausted, on 25 May 1607.

She was far from being an "untutored" mystic and sought inspiration in her spiritual life from the Bible, St Augustine, and the letters and *Dialogue* of St Catherine of Siena (see 29 Apr.). The essence of her doctrine was that the soul must strip itself of everything except God and become a "nothing" (the *nada* of St John of the Cross) in order to be united with God. She believed firmly in the value of suffering for the salvation of souls and certainly suffered to an intense degree as well as experiencing the blissful heights of mystical union. Her teachings, collected by her spiritual directors and the other nuns in her convent, were published in seven volumes from the 1960s onward. Her cult began almost immediately after her death, and she was canonized in 1669.

24

St Madeleine Sophie Barat (1779–1865)

Madeleine's birth was dramatic and her education exceptionally severe; surviving both, not to mention the French Revolution, as she did, proved a good preparation for founding and leading a great religious Order.

She was born two months prematurely during a fire that swept through the timber houses of her home town, Joigny in Burgundy. She was not expected to survive and was handed to her ten-year-old brother, Louis, to be rushed to church and christened. The men of the town were fighting the fire, so the priest made Louis act as godfather. The solemn promises he made under such conditions made a deep impression on him. He went away to study for the priesthood and returned to Joigny after the seminary to teach mathematics and wait until he was old enough to be ordained. Assuming his responsibilities as her godfather as he saw fit, he set about educating his sister, who by then was ten. He put her through long days of Latin, Greek, mathematics, history, and botany, never praising or encouraging her, endlessly finding fault and correcting. She flourished under this regime, which lasted for the first four years of the Revolution, and carried on studying on her own when Louis was ordained. At first, Louis took the oath to the Civil Constitution of the Clergy, then retracted, went to Paris, was thrown into prison, and escaped the guillotine only because a former schoolmate kept his name off the daily lists of those condemned to die.

He was released in 1795, when Madeleine was sixteen and determined to enter a religious Order. These had all been suppressed and there was nowhere she could join. Louis took her back to Paris, determined that she should now embark on theological studies. The outcome was a unique person—a woman with the education provided by the seminaries, closed to women. She was still diffident, however, and wanted to become a Carmelite lay Sister. Then, through Louis, she met the Abbé de Varin, who was planning an Order of the Sacred Heart, based on the Jesuits (who had been suppressed in 1773) but with an equivalent Order for women. He saw that Madeleine had the qualities to lead such an Order, telling her that her gifts and education were not meant to be kept in a cloister. She seems simply to have followed all his proposals.

In 1800, by when the ban on religious Orders had been relaxed, she and three others were clothed as nuns; the following year they took over a school in

Amiens, which soon acquired a high academic reputation and attracted daughters of émigrés returning after the Revolution. By the time Madeleine was twenty-three she was appointed superior. Growth was immediate and rapid: the new Order converted abandoned abbeys and convents and took in former members of other Orders, including Philippine Duchesne (see 18 Nov.), who was to bring the Order to the United States. Madeleine—by now Mother Barat—had to abandon teaching and spend her time interviewing new applicants and overseeing new foundations, of boarding schools for those who could pay fees and of day schools for those who could not. She was in the happy position of being able to take only first-class teachers. For the first few years her Order had no name, though initially the Sisters were known as Ladies of Faith, but in 1807 Napoleon, under pressure from his devout mother, gave it official recognition as the Society of the Sacred Heart of Jesus.

There were years of internal strife, with divisions opened up by the personal ambitions that seem to dog all rapidly growing institutions, but Mother Barat's technique of waiting and praying usually (because she was usually in the right) caused opposition to her to collapse. She guided through a revised Constitution, with a new Rule and a new habit (the original white-frilled cap, with a black gauze veil worn over it, was perhaps not very practical for teaching) in 1815, when the Church in France regained some of its autonomy after Napoleon's defeat at Waterloo. The following year she opened a new motherhouse in Paris, where she received royal visitors and an increasing number of aristocratic parents who wanted their girls to be educated in Sacred Heart schools. "Bishop after bishop" came to her, wanting schools in their dioceses. Mother Barat managed to remain her simple, though capable, self through all this. The Society was formally approved by the pope in 1826 (despite lingering Vatican opposition to unenclosed women religious) and opened houses in Rome and Turin as well as those in the United States that grew out of the first foundation at St Charles on the Missouri River in 1818.

Her health grew worse, not helped by accidents, and she was unable to visit most of her overseas foundations, though she continued to travel all over France. She resisted an attempt radically to overhaul the Constitution in 1839, but she was always looking for ways to keep the educational approach attuned to changing times, revising the study-plan in the Society's schools every six years. The coming of the railways made her constant travelling far easier. She gradually slowed down, finding time to talk to children and befriend animals, but it was not until she was eighty-five that, having threatened to resign, she was given a vicar-general to help her. But it was too late for any real retirement, and she died less than a year later, on Ascension Day 1865. She lived well into the age of photography but refused to have her picture taken, so all likenesses of her are based on a photograph taken after her death. She had been in charge of the Society for sixty-four years, and it had grown to eighty-six houses (which would have been more had not hostile governments closed a further twenty-five) and three thousand five hundred Sisters. Today, they still teach world-wide, as well as caring for the poor, doing pastoral work in hospitals, parishes, and prisons, and acting as spiritual counsellors and retreat-givers. Madeleine Sophie Barat, one of the Church's great innovators, was beatified in 1908 and canonized in 1926, when St Peter's Basilica was filled with thousands of girls and women who had been educated in Sacred Heart schools.

25

St Bede the Venerable (673–735)

Bede is the only Englishman ever to have been declared a Doctor of the Church. This title was conferred on him in 1899 by Pope Leo XIII, in recognition of his scholarship in several disciplines, most notably history. He is remembered above all for his *Ecclesiastical History of the English People*, from which virtually all we know of the Church in England up to the time in which he wrote is derived.

He was, as he tells us toward the end of that work, sent by his family to be educated first by St Benedict Biscop and then by Abbot Ceolfrith. His education was based firmly on the Latin Bible, of which Ceolfrith made three fine copies, a work to which Bede may have contributed as a scribe. His native language was Old English, but his books, written in Latin, show how great a command of that language he acquired. He then joined the monastery of Wearmouth-Jarrow in Northumbria and spent the rest of his life there. He was ordained deacon in his nineteenth year and priest in his thirtieth. He describes his "chief delight" as being always in "study, teaching, and writing." He finished his *History* in 731 and provided a list of his earlier works, mostly "short extracts from the works of the venerable Fathers on Holy Scripture," to which he added his own comments "on their meaning and interpretation."

He wrote during the period after the Synod of Whitby in 663/4, by which time Roman customs were firmly established in northern England. Bede sympathized entirely with the Roman order and had little sympathy for the Celtic method of calculating Easter, though he did admire the monastic saints produced by those Churches. He was concerned with the Anglo-Saxon Church, which was united by its use of the Latin language and its devotion to Rome. His concerns were pastoral as well as historical and in some ways remarkably modern: he saw the lives of some lay people as so blameless that they should be allowed to receive Holy Communion every week or even every day. He wanted more bishops in Northumbria, and he wanted remote rural communities to receive instruction, so that everyone should know at least the Lord's Prayer and the Creed by heart.

In the centuries following his death, his scripture commentaries were the most widely read of his works. St Boniface (see 5 June), the other great Anglo-Saxon saint of his period, asked for copies of them to be sent to Germany to help in his mission there. They remained influential throughout the Middle Ages, especially the commentaries on books of the Bible on which little else had been written. Soon after his death they provided a basis for teaching the scriptures to people living in a largely illiterate province on the edge of the known world, where pagan survivals were strong and Christianity at best half-understood. His historical work was intended to do for the Anglo-Saxon Church what Eusebius had done for the whole Church four hundred years earlier, and on the whole it succeeded, providing his local Church with knowledge of its own past and so a basis on which to cohere and understand itself.

His death was described by his pupil Cuthbert, a future abbot of Jarrow. His final illness was short, and he kept busy with teaching, reciting the Psalms, and meditating until virtually the end. Unable owing to ill health to finish writing his final work he urged a pupil to complete it for him. When he heard this was done, on the feast of the Ascension, he asked this pupil to hold his head in his hands as he sat on the floor of his cell, and so he died, having taken leave of his fellow-monks in the afternoon, leaving them all "very sad" and weeping at hearing that "they would not see his face much longer in this world." His cult spread rapidly, with relics taken to York Minster and to Fulda in Germany. A Greek and Latin copy of the Acts of the Apostles in his hand survives in the Bodleian Library in Oxford, while the earliest known copy of the *Ecclesiastical History* is in St Petersburg, though this is not his own manuscript.

I pray you, noble Jesu, that as you have graciously granted me joyfully to imbibe the words of your knowledge, so you will also of your bounty grant me to come at length to yourself, the fount of all wisdom, and to dwell in your presence for ever.

Final prayer added by Bede to the end of his *Ecclesiastical History of the English People*

26

St Philip Neri (1515–1595)

The "second apostle of Rome" was a great reformer distinguished from many others by the joy that was a hallmark of his life and his message. He lived in a Rome shaken by the neo-paganism of many aspects of the Renaissance and the shock of the Reformation, against which the Vatican reacted at least in part by putting up the shutters in the shape of the Inquisition and the Index of Forbidden Books. Philip's approach was far more open and not always appreciated by the Church authorities.

He was born in Florence, one of four brothers living at their mother's death when Philip was five. He was educated by the Dominicans at the convent of San Marco, where Fra Angelico's (see 19 Feb.) paintings were a continual inspiration to study and meditation. In the last decade of the fifteenth century, the reformer Girolamo Savonarola had been prior of San Marco, preaching increasingly vehemently against humanism and abuses in both Church and State until he was condemned as a heretic and burned at the stake in 1498. Philip and his father both revered his memory, and Philip would have taken much from his legacy, though not his fiery spirit.

He left Florence in 1532 and never returned there. After a year spent with a merchant uncle at San Germano, between Naples and Rome, during which he acquired a longing for solitude and the conviction that he was not destined to be a merchant, he left for Rome, where he became tutor to the two sons of a customs agent from Florence. He lived as simply as possible, studied philosophy and theology, and spent nights in prayer. In 1544 he was praying in the catacombs when "he suddenly felt himself filled with the power of the Spirit with such force that his heart began to palpitate within his body and to be inflamed with such love that . . . he indicated that he was completely unable to bear it," as his first biographer put it. The experience left him with violent sensations of burning in his heart, and, whether from a physical phenomenon attributable to mystical experience or from other causes, his heart was enlarged to such an extent that several of his ribs broke to allow it to expand, as was discovered at his autopsy.

He was ordained priest in 1551, when he was thirty-six, and joined an association of secular priests known as San Girolamo. Its members lived together without taking vows or following the strictly ordered regime of an established religious Order, paying for their food and board from their private means. Philip said Mass late in the morning, spent long hours in the confessional each day, preached, and ministered to the sick in hospitals. He saw the guidance given to penitents in the confessional as an important means of securing the conversion of personal life that had to be the basis for reform of both civil and ecclesiastical public life. This was also the view of St Ignatius Loyola (see 31 July), who befriended Philip in Rome, and of the group who had formed the Jesuits some twenty years earlier.

Philip encouraged those he had instructed to pray together, attending Vespers as a group or visiting one of Rome's "station" churches together, and it was from these beginnings that the Oratory developed. Groups began meetings with spiritual reading, prayed together, and visited ancient Roman basilicas as pilgrims. The movement had soon attracted hundreds from all social classes and walks of life, who were all expected to serve in hospitals and to beg with and for the poor. The novelty of this way of life was soon proving too much for the religious authorities. Philip was first forbidden to preach by the autocratic, inquisitorial Paul IV and was later threatened with the closure of the Oratory. This was averted by St Charles Borromeo (see 4 Nov.), who had influence over Pope Pius V (see 1 May), having supported his election to the papacy. The next pope, Gregory XIII (1572–85), successfully introduced a whole range of reforms, broke the power of wealthy elites in Rome, and put a stop to the envy and jealousy that were damaging Philip's venture. He officially approved the Oratory in 1575, by which time they had a church of their own, rebuilt as the Chiesa Nuova two years later and soon attracting huge crowds.

Volunteers to join the Oratory became so numerous that some had to be turned away. New houses were started in Naples and Bologna and elsewhere in Italy, numbering seven by the time of Philip's death. Daily reading and preaching from the scriptures and frequent reception of the sacraments were at the heart of the new apostolate. A contemporary wrote of him: "With the word of God he miraculously enkindled in many a holy love of Christ. He had nothing else in mind but to put them on fire with the desire for prayer, for frequentation of the sacraments, and for works of charity." He aimed for a return to the apostolic simplicity of life, as his early hero Savonarola had, but encouraged people to embrace this without using hell-fire sermons and without deliberately upsetting the church establishment. For forty-five years, from his ordination to his death, as the great Oratorian Cardinal Newman wrote, "Philip was every day and almost every hour ... restoring, teaching, encouraging, and guiding penitents along the narrow way of salvation."

He celebrated the Eucharist and heard confessions up to the last full day of his life, dying early the following morning, 26 May 1595, beloved by all Rome. He was immediately acclaimed as a saint by the people and was canonized in 1622. The Oratory movement, in common with others, was almost destroyed by the French Revolution and its aftermath, but it recovered and has since spread to many countries, in the New World as well as the Old. It was established in England at Old Oscott (later moved to Edgbaston in Birmingham) by John Henry Newman in 1847, and in London two years later. Besides their preaching and hearing Confessions, Oratorians have concentrated on providing attractive music at their services, and the "oratorio" form was named after the original Oratory. Palestrina, who composed many oratorios, had been a penitent of St Philip's.

If you want to be obeyed, don't make commandments.
It is easier to guide cheerful persons in the spiritual life than melancholy ones.
Be good if you can.

One should not wish to become a saint in four days but step by step.
Some maxims of St Philip Neri

27

St Augustine of Canterbury (died about 604)

Augustine, born in Italy and prior of a monastery in Rome, was the pioneer builder of the conversion of the Anglo-Saxons, a complex and difficult project of which Pope St Gregory the Great (see 3 Sept.) was the architect. Christianity was established in the western parts of the British Isles, but the nearest Church, that of Wales, had done nothing to try to convert the newer arrivals in the east. During ten years work in the south-east of England, Augustine laid the foundations, converting the king, establishing a see and building a cathedral and monastery at Canterbury, and founding the dioceses of London and Rochester. The long task was finished by those who came after him. The history of the enterprise is known mainly through Gregory's letters and Bede's *History*, for which he was able to draw on at least some of Gregory's letters.

Gregory may have wished to lead the expedition, especially after seeing Anglo-Saxon slaves for sale in the Roman Forum and being impressed by their fair good looks, inspiring his famous comment: *Non Angli sed angeli* ("Not Angles but angels"). As pope, however, he had to delegate the mission. He selected a group of monks and appointed Augustine as their abbot. The party sailed from Rome to Provence, where some wanted to abandon the expedition as being too perilous. They were firmly told by Gregory to trust in God and Augustine, by now consecrated bishop, so the party set off across Gaul, picking up some Frankish clergy on the way to act as interpreters. The group that sailed for England probably numbered about forty. The new mission was effectively to till virgin soil, since although Christianity had come to England earlier with the Romans and some remnants could be found, it was one hundred and fifty years since the Romans had left, and successive waves of Angle, Saxon, and Jute immigration/conquest had re-established paganism.

They landed on the Isle of Thanet (which is a promontory rather than a true isle) in eastern Kent and soon met the king, Ethelbert (St Ethelbert; see 24 Feb.), who received them courteously but insisted on meeting them in the open air, in case they should cast spells on him. They told him that they were bringing the good news of eternal salvation, and he granted them land in nearby Canterbury and freedom to preach. His wife, Bertha, was a Christian, but she does not seem to have taken active steps to convert him. Eventually the example of a holy and simple life set by Augustine and his monks prevailed, and Ethelbert became a Christian. The conversion of the king was a decisive

239

step and must have implied the support of his noblemen. From about 601, Augustine, supported by extra clergy and letters of guidance on many points from Gregory, was able to expand the administration of the Church throughout the kingdom. He received the archbishop's, or metropolitan's, sign of juris-diction, the woollen *pallium*, from Gregory, and was instructed to form one metropolitan see in the south (which Gregory assumed, from Roman records, would be London, but was in fact Canterbury), with twelve suffragan bish-oprics, and another in the north at York, again with twelve suffragans. The latter was not established for over another hundred years, but the provinces of Canterbury and York make up the Church of England to this day.

Gregory, who warned Augustine not to let the miracles attributed to him go to his head, also wrote to Ethelbert, congratulating him on his conversion and asking him to listen carefully to Augustine, as he "has been trained under monastic Rule, has a complete knowledge of holy scripture, and, by the grace of God, is a man of holy life." He should therefore "listen to his advice ungrud-gingly, follow it exactly, and store it carefully in [his] memory" (Bede 1:32).

Augustine seems from the start to have seen a need for two establishments at Canterbury, the cathedral and a monastery close by it. One would serve as the main focus for mission, the other for liturgy and learning. The clergy from both came together for the daytime offices, and Canterbury became known for its "Gregorian" (that is, as developed in Rome in Gregory's time) liturgical chanting. Augustine concentrated on the eastern side of the country and (even making allowances for Bede's pro-Anglo-Saxon prejudices) never established good relations with the Welsh. He founded a cathedral in London, on the site of what is now St Paul's, which had to be abandoned for a time owing to London resistance to being ruled by the Kentish Ethelred.

By the time he died, ten years after the start of his mission, Augustine had some fairly substantial, if relatively local, achievements to his credit, but there was still a lot of work to be done by his successors, who proved in the main worthy of the task and followers of his example. He was buried in the mon-astery of SS Peter and Paul in Canterbury (later to be renamed St Augustine's and to become a great school—see next entry). His remains were ceremonially reinterred in the east end of a rebuilt monastery church in 1091. His time at Canterbury marks an era of harmony between pope and archbishop, so in the ecumenical movement he is seen as an important figure.

28

St Aldhelm (639–709)

Aldhelm, an outstanding figure in the English west country in the seventh century, was related to the kings of Wessex. He became the first abbot of Malmesbury and the first bishop of Sherborne. He was also the first Anglo-Saxon writer of distinction (though only his writings in Latin, not those in Old English, survive) and an accomplished musician. Bede (see 25 May, above) gives a brief account of him and praises his writings, but Wessex was a long way from Northumbria, where Bede wrote, and he displays no great knowledge of conditions there.

Aldhelm was educated first at Malmesbury ("Maelduib's Town" in Bede) and then at the great clerical school at St Augustine's in Canterbury, which he claimed was superior to anything Ireland could offer at the time. There he learned, according to William of Malmesbury, "metre-craft, star-craft and ecclesiastical arithmetic" in addition to music and theology. He also mastered Latin and possibly Greek, as well as Hebrew—the first Englishman, it is said, to learn the latter. He had "wonderful hands," which made him "the best of all lute players," and wrote poems to be sung to a harp accompaniment, designed as aids to preaching. He was ordained priest, by Hlothere, bishop of Winchester, during his time at Canterbury and returned to Malmesbury as abbot in about 675, the first abbot there of which anything historical is recorded.

The background to his ministry in Wessex was the gradual westward advance of Saxon armies into the lands of the British, pushing the boundaries of the kingdom farther from its capital, Winchester. There was a considerable physical barrier formed by Selwood Forest, a huge belt of woodland extending south from Malmesbury to the Dorset heath, making the parts to the west of it far more remote than they are today. There was therefore a need for a new diocese, separate from Winchester, to cater for the western parts of the kingdom. Sherborne was chosen as the new see, and Aldhelm became its first bishop in 705, in charge of a diocese extending nominally from Wiltshire to Land's End. He was by now sixty-six years old and reluctant to take on such a huge task, but "bishops, clergy, and a great multitude of the laity, according to ancient custom, chose this holy man." He was taken to Canterbury to be consecrated by Archbishop Bretwald, a fellow-monk and former fellow-student with him at St Augustine's.

He built or rebuilt a church in Sherborne to serve as the cathedral, on the site where the abbey now stands. William of Malmesbury claims to have seen it, but this would in fact have been the replacement built by St Wulsin (see 8 Jan.). William also tells the story that Aldhelm rode all the way to Dover on hearing of a ship landing there, to see if it had brought any books he might acquire for his churches. His eye fell on a magnificent complete Bible, for which he made an offer. The sailors wanted more, and when he refused, they put out to sea again rather than let him have it at his price, whereupon a great storm blew up. The ship was saved by Aldhelm's prayers for its safety, which showed the sailors that he was a holy man, so they brought it back into port and let him have the Bible at his original offer price.

As bishop, Aldhelm was assiduous in visiting his huge diocese, going from village to village and from one religious house to another. These would have been small missionary outposts at the time. It was said of him that "by his preaching he completed the conquest of Wessex," helping to assimilate the British people into the new Saxon ecclesiastical and civil order. (The latter was enshrined in an important code of laws made by King Ine [688–726], which reflect a settled society in which Church and State and Saxons and Britons worked in harmony.) As a writer, he is best known for his treatise *On Virginity*, which he composed in two forms, one in verse and one in prose, and of which an illuminated manuscript survives—with Old English explanations written between the lines of Latin: Aldhelm's style was not of the simplest, and even the nuns for whom this manuscript was prepared would have found it difficult. He also wrote a series of riddles, a very popular form at the time, and accounts, in Latin verse, of the building of several churches in Wessex, as well as what Bede calls "a notable treatise against the errors of the Britons in observing Easter at the wrong time and doing other things contrary to the orthodoxy and unity of the Church." This was commissioned by "a synod of his own people" and was responsible for persuading "many of those Britons who were subject to the West Saxons to conform to the Catholic observance of our Lord's resurrection."

He died at Doulting, a village near Shepton Mallet in the present county of Somerset. Sensing that his end was near, he asked to be carried into the little wooden church to die. His body was taken back to Malmesbury Abbey, in a procession the stages of which were marked with a series of stone crosses, no longer standing. A cult developed at Malmesbury, interrupted for a time by Norman dislike of Anglo-Saxon saints but restored at the end of the eleventh century. Though his many achievements are perhaps not sufficiently appreciated, his name lives on in St Aldhelm's Head (often wrongly called St Alban's) on the Dorset coast. When a Catholic mission—later parish—was reestablished in Sherborne at the end of the nineteenth century, its church was dedicated to St Aldhelm and the Sacred Heart.

29

St Germanus of Paris (about 500–576)

Germanus was lucky to survive beyond childhood. He was born in Burgundy and sent to be educated in the house of a cousin named Stratidius. His aunt cast an envious eye on the legacy he would inherit and put poison in his cup. But her son drank it instead, ruining his health for the rest of his life. Germanus presumably left the household after this incident and is known to have spent the next fifteen years in a semi-monastic way of life. He was then ordained priest by the bishop of Autun and appointed to be abbot of the monastic church of St Symphorien there. This followed the Rule of Lérins (on which see St Hilary of Arles; 5 May) and owned widespread properties, of which Germanus was a competent administrator.

He was then caught up in the wars and political intrigue of the period. The kingdom of the Franks, a northern Germanic people, had expanded under their king Clovis (ruled from 481 to 511), from a territory covering parts of (modern) northern France, the Low Countries, and north-west Germany. He first overthrew the Gallo-Romans to the south and extended his kingdom to the line of the River Loire. He then conquered the Alemanni to the south-east, in a battle that at first went against him but turned to his advantage when he called on Jesus, the God of his Christian wife, Clotilde, for help. As a result he and thousands of his warriors were converted. He conquered the Visigothic kingdom in south-western France at the battle of Vouillé in 507. The Burgundian kingdom in which Germanus lived, occupying roughly the south-eastern quarter of France, was conquered by Clovis' grandson, Theodebert. Germanus appears to have stood firm with the Burgundians and to have prophesied that Theodebert would meet an early death, as indeed he did.

Clovis had established his capital at Paris and instituted a system of national episcopal synods or councils—replacing the previous regional or provincial ones. His grandson Childebert was king of Paris at the time of Theodebert's death, and he invited Germanus to Paris for a council. This was called to depose the bishop, Saffaracus, for a fault that seems to have been more political than doctrinal or moral. Saffaracus retired to a monastery, and Germanus was appointed bishop in his place. With Childebert's support he built the cathedral of St Stephen and the basilica of St Vincent and the Holy Cross. Childebert was succeeded by Charibert, who took a very different attitude to the Church, pillaging its property and leading a notoriously dissolute life. When he married two sisters at once, Germanus could tolerate his way of life no more and excommunicated him. In 573 another king who refused to take Germanus' advice met an early death: Sigebert attacked Childebert for killing his sister-in-law; Germanus warned him to seek a peaceful solution, but Sigebert refused and was assassinated.

Germanus died in Paris on 28 May 576, already with a reputation for miracle-working and widely regarded as a saint. He was credited with healing blind people, sufferers from paralysis (especially of the hands), epileptics, and those possessed by evil spirits. The accounts of his cures are interesting for the light they shed on maladies current at the time and on his generally common-sense remedies, such as the application of oil. He was also known for his devotion to the poor and to prisoners and slaves. He was buried in the basilica he had built, which was later renamed Saint-Germain-des-Prés (St Germanus in the Fields) after him. His relics, after a series of elevations to more prominent places in the church, were destroyed in the French Revolution, but his name lives on in that of the *quartier* of Paris best known for literary, artistic, and student life.

30

St Joan of Arc (Jeanne d'Arc; 1412–1431)

At the beginning of the fifteenth century France was torn by civil war between the houses of Burgundy and Orleans. In addition, England claimed jurisdiction over most of the northern half and parts of the south-west. In 1415, when Joan was only three, King Henry V of England won the battle of Agincourt and claimed the throne of the French king, Charles VI, "the Foolish," who had been subject to fits of madness since 1392. His son, the Dauphin (meaning "eldest son"), succeeded to the throne in 1422, the year in which Henry V died, leaving an infant son aged one, Henry VI, in whose name the Protector, the duke of Bedford, continued the claim to the French throne. Charles (still known as the Dauphin) could not be crowned at the traditional site of Reims, which was in English hands. The Burgundians sided with the English after servants of the Dauphin murdered their duke, and Bedford captured city after city while the Dauphin devoted himself to frivolous amusements at his court.

This was the background to the extraordinary, at first triumphant, finally tragic career of *Jeanne la Pucelle*, "the maid of Orleans." She was born into a substantial peasant family at Domrémy in the Meuse region of eastern France and had a happy childhood, learning traditional feminine pursuits but not how to read or write. When she was fourteen, she began to "hear voices" telling her that it was her mission to "save France." She made no mention of these at home but persuaded an uncle to take her to Robert Baudricourt, commander of the royal forces in the nearby town of Vaucouleurs. He laughed at her and sent her home; her voices insisted her mission was "God's command," and she went back to Baudricourt. Shaken by a defeat she had foretold on her first visit, he accepted her and sent her with an escort to see the king, then residing at Chinon. She asked to wear male dress for her protection on the journey. On 6 March 1429 the party reached Chinon, and two days later she greeted the king, despite his having adopted a disguise to test her. She asked for troops to go to relieve the siege of Orleans and was, not surprisingly, opposed as a mad visionary.

A panel of theologians was set to examine her and after three weeks' interrogation could find no fault, so they recommended that Charles should make prudent use of her. Wearing a white suit of armour and carrying a standard bearing the words "Jesus, Maria," she rode from Blois to Orleans at the head of an expeditionary force. Two days later the city was in royalist hands and two weeks later the English forts surrounding it had been dismantled. Despite advice to the contrary from the king's adviser, La Trémouilee, and the archbishop of Reims, she was allowed to campaign along the Loire with the duke of Alençon, who believed in and supported her. They were successful and finally inflicted a crushing defeat on the English at Patay, after which the English surrendered Troyes, south of Reims. The way to Reims and the Dauphin's coronation was now open. Charles and his court hesitated, but eventually moved, and on 7 July he was crowned, with Joan standing beside him holding her standard.

This marked the high point of her success, and she had carried out the mission enjoined on her by her voices. She carried on campaigning, however, and was wounded in an unsuccessful attempt to take Paris. Hostilities were adjourned for the winter, which she spent fretting and under suspicion at Charles' court. In the spring of 1430 she was campaigning again against the Burgundian forces. She rode into the besieged city of Compiègne on 23 May and immediately led a raiding party out of the gates. This was forced to retreat, but the drawbridge was raised too soon, and Joan was left outside the walls. She was dragged from her horse and made prisoner of the duke of Burgundy. Charles made no attempt to rescue or ransom her, but the English, smarting under their defeats at her hands, paid the Burgundians to hand her over, planning to exact their revenge by trying her for witchcraft.

She spent the winter in wretched conditions in a prison in Rouen, and in February 1431 was brought before a tribunal. Its president was Bishop Cauchon of Beauvais, an unscrupulous prelate with his eyes on the archbishopric of Rouen, which the English could deliver to him. She was accused of being in league with the devil, wearing men's clothes, and disobeying the Church. She defended herself valiantly, showing a sharp mind and an excellent memory, but the outcome had to all intents and purposes been decided in advance. Her voices were declared diabolical and she was condemned as a heretic. When she still refused to recant, she was handed over to the secular authorities for punishment. She seems to have made some sort of part recantation but then changed her mind, declared once again that her voices came from God, and accepted her fate. Early on 30 May she was burned at the stake in Rouen, unflinching to the last and calling on Jesus in her last moments. Her ashes were thrown into the Seine. Among the spectators was one of King Henry VI's secretaries, John Tressart, who is reported as saying, "We are lost. We have burned a saint."

Joan's mother and brothers appealed for the case to be reopened, and in 1456 a commission appointed by Pope Callistus III quashed the original verdict and completely rehabilitated her. Another four hundred and fifty years elapsed, however, before she was beatified, in 1910, and then canonized, in 1920. She has since been the subject of books, plays, and films, but there is no real consensus about what makes her holy as opposed to simply heroic. She has been made a patron of France and has been hailed by Protestants, nationalists, and feminists for fighting against a corrupt Church, an invading power, and male oppression. The Church has not claimed her as a martyr for the faith, and there is the problem that two of the saints whose voices inspired her, Margaret of Antioch and Catherine of Alexandria, have been found to have no historical existence. Her own identity has recently been called into question with the suggestion, based on some historical evidence, that she was in fact Jehanne, the illegitimate daughter of Queen Isabeau of France and Louis, duke of Orleans, the king's brother. In the end, all theories have to take second place to the fact that, like the Virgin Mary, she answered a call she saw as coming from God and followed the course it dictated to the bitter end. Her integrity shines out from a corrupt world, and no greater example than that can be asked of anyone.

(Two interesting recent discoveries have been: 1. what appears to be her suit of armour, with marks corresponding to the wounds she received, in the attic of a French country house in 1996; 2. a fresco on the wall of a medieval chapel at Domrémy showing her as a typical peasant girl of the region—blonde, blue-eyed, and chubby—in 1998. The latter has been carbon-dated to the early fifteenth century and so may well be contemporary with her death.)

As for the Church, I love her and I should wish to support her with all my strength for our Christian faith. And it is not me who should be prevented from going to Mass. ... I agree with God, who sent me, and with Our Lady, and with all the saints who are in heaven. And it seems to me that it is the same for God and for the Church and that there is no need to make this into a problem.

Joan of Arc at the tribunal hearing

31

Bd Christopher Magallanes and Companions (died between 1915 and 1937)

The majority of the twenty-two Mexican priests and three laymen beatified as martyrs in 1992 lost their lives in the *Cristero* ("for Christ") uprising between 1926 and 1929. This was a reaction against the "Calles laws," enacted in 1926 under President Plutarco Elías Calles, which severely limited the civil and political rights of the clergy and the Church's right to hold property. They had been proposed as part of a new constitution in 1917 and accorded well with the policies of the revolutionary government that took power in 1920. The hierarchy reacted against them by declaring a sort of ecclesiastical strike, involving the suspension of all public worship. This hardly affected the wealthy elites, who had their private clergy (whom they regarded as servants), but the peasants in the countryside were left deprived of the sacraments, and many took up arms against the government, with the slogan, "Long live Christ the King and the Virgin of Guadalupe!" The official Church did not support this revolt, but clerics and lay people were involved in it at many levels. Many rural priests disobeyed the bishops' instructions to hide in the cities and remained to minister to their people, many undoubtedly taking up arms with them. Any priest found in rural areas was automatically suspected of supporting the revolt and liable to be shot, as some ninety were. Those beatified are known not to have resorted to armed violence but to have lost their lives in non-violent pursuit of their cause.

One of today's martyrs was shot in an earlier exchange between supporters of Carranza and those of Pancho Villa, in 1915, when he went to assist some wounded men lying in the street. The three laymen among today's group, with one priest, were the first to die in the *Cristero* uprising itself. All were members of the Catholic Action of Mexican Youth (ACJM), a militant movement supporting the National League for the Defense of Religious Freedom, which formed around the revolt and of which one of the three, Manuel Morales, was president. Fr Luis Batiz was chaplain to the ACJM. All four were arrested on 14 August 1926 and shot by soldiers who were supposed to be taking them to prison.

Eight of the priests were killed between January and May 1927, including Christopher Magallanes, who gives his name to the whole group. He was born into a poor family and worked on the land before entering the seminary of Guadalajara at the age of nineteen. He was ordained in 1899 and in 1910 was appointed parish priest of Totalice, where he established catechetical centres and schools in the villages that made up the parish, built a dam to provide a water supply, and enabled peasants to buy small plots of land. Between 1914 and his death he had pioneered the re-evangelization of the Huichole Indians, who had effectively been cut off from the Church since the Jesuits were expelled in the late eighteenth century. He found himself in the middle of a battle between *Cristeros* and government soldiers on 27 May 1927 and was arrested, accused of supporting the uprising, and shot four days later. He died hoping that "my blood may serve to bring peace to divided Mexicans."

A further six priests met their deaths between June and the end of the year. They included more former students of the Guadalajara seminary, and most were from poor peasant backgrounds. All were continuing to minister in rural areas, were discovered in one way or another, most in private houses, and arrested—one, Miguel de la Mora, when a woman asked him to perform a marriage ceremony for her daughter. Five more were killed in 1928, of whom two were educated at Guadalajara and two were of Indian descent. All were devoted parish priests or assistant priests. The body of one, Jesús Méndez Montoya, was placed on a railway line after he had been shot, so that it would be cut to pieces, but was taken away by federal officers' wives and given a proper wake and burial.

The last of the group to die was involved in a renewed outbreak of persecution in 1937. He was Pedro de Jesús Maldonado, born in Sacramento in 1892. He was ordained at El Paso in Texas, after his studies for the priesthood in Mexico had been interrupted by the revolution. He served as parish priest in Santa Isabel in the province of Chihuahua, surviving the years of intense persecution, but was then arrested in 1931, when churches were closed once more, released, and again arrested and released in 1932 and 1934, when he was exiled to El Paso. He returned in 1937, only to be falsely accused of starting a fire in the public school and seized by a group of armed drunks, who beat him unconscious. He died in hospital in Chihuahua on 11 February 1937.

The cause for the canonization of these Mexican martyrs is under active consideration.

Other Familiar English Names for May

1. Augustine, John, Julian, Richard
2. Antony, Joseph, Nicholas, William
3. Alexander, Edward, Emily, Mary, Timothy
4. Augustine, John, Richard, Robert
5. *There are no other familiar English names for today*
6. Antony, Edward, Francis, James, Mary
7. Albert, Antony, Augustine, John, Rose
8. Louis, Mary, Victor
9. Joseph, Mary, Thomas
10. Beatrice, Henry, John, Nicholas, William
11. Francis, Gregory, James, John, Matthew, Walter
12. Cyril, Dominic, Joanna, Philip
13. Gemma, Madeleine
14. Mary, Michael, Victor
15. Andrew, Paul, Peter, Rupert
16. Adam, Andrew, Simon
17. Antonia, Paul, Peter, Victor
18. Eric, Gerard, John, William
19. Augustine, John, Mary, Peter
20. Hilary, Guy
21. Charles, John, Timothy
22. Dominic, John, Julia, Mary, Matthew, Michael, Rita
23. John, Gilbert, Michael
24. Agatha, Augustine, Joan, John, Philip, Vincent
25. Christopher, Gregory, James, Leo, Madeleine, Mary, Peter
26. Andrew, Augustine, Francis, John, Joseph, Mary, Matthew, Peter
27. Barbara, Bruno, Edmund, John, Richard
28. John, Margaret, Mary, Paul, Robert, Thomas, William
29. Gerard, Joseph, Richard, Ursula, William
30. Basil, Hubert, Joseph, Luke, Matthew, Richard, William
31. Felix, James, Robert, Thomas

JUNE

Departures from the dates proposed by the new Roman Martyrology in this month are as follows: Pope John XXIII, beatified in 2000, has the entry for the date of his death (3rd), and the Martyrs of Uganda are moved to the following day. St Marcellin Champagnat, founder of the Marist Brothers, canonized in 1999, is preferred to St Norbert on the 6th. St Columba of Iona shares a crowded day (9th) and has displaced St Ephraem to the 10th and Bd Anne Mary Taigi—one of unusually few women to be found this month—to the 12th. St Germaine of Pibrac is moved back a day to leave St Vitus, known for his dance, on the traditional day of his death (15th). St Juliana Falconieri is moved forward two days to the 17th. The 22nd is one of those crowded days the major figures of which have to be spread over several days: SS John Fisher and Thomas More have outweighed the protomartyr of England, St Alban, who appears here on the 24th, which is the feast of the birthday (into this world, not into heaven) of St John the Baptist in the Universal Calendar, but his one entry in the present work is on the date of his death, 29 August. One of the scarce women this month, St Etheldreda, can then occupy her correct date of the 23rd. St Paulinus of Nola, who leads the list for the 22nd in the Universal Calendar, is moved to the 25th. St John Southworth actually shares his anniversary with St Irenaeus of Lyons on the 28th and is here moved forward two days.

1

Bd John Baptist Scalabrini (Giovanni Battista Scalabrini; 1839–1905)

This great apostle to the Italian immigrant communities in North and South America was born near Como in northern Italy on 8 July 1839. His father, a wine merchant, actively provided for the Catholic education of his children. After completing his elementary schooling in his home town, Giovanni was sent to high school in Como. His parents were delighted when he expressed a desire to study for the priesthood. After junior seminary at Sant' Abbondio, he progressed to the theological seminary and then the major seminary, coming first in his class in both "academics" and "disposition." He was ordained on 30 May 1863. In the early years of his ministry he was a professor at and then rector of Sant'Abbondio. He then became pastor of San Bartolomeo in Como, where he involved himself in ministering to young people and textile and other factory workers. He founded a kindergarten, for which he wrote his first catechism, which he dedicated to the memory of his mother, who had died in 1865.

In 1875, at the age of thirty-six, he was consecrated bishop of Piacenza. He proved to be a tireless and dedicated pastoral bishop, making five visitations of the three hundred and sixty-five parishes under his care, half of which could be reached only on foot or on mule-back, during his twenty-nine years as bishop. He organized and personally supervised three diocesan synods and worked to remove superstition and restore the Eucharist to a central position in the popular piety of the time, dedicating two hundred churches in the process. He reorganized the diocesan seminaries and used his theological expertise to reform their curriculum. Wherever he went, he administered the sacraments, taught the Faith, and devised educational programmes. His charity was both abundant and discreet: he ministered to victims of cholera; visited the sick and prisoners; aided both the poor and noble families who had lost their wealth; sold his own belongings and opened the bishop's residence as a dispensary. He founded an institute for those with hearing and speaking difficulties; organized protection for the young women employed in the rice fields, who were often subject to sexual as well as economic exploitation; and established mutual aid societies, worker's associations, rural banks, cooperatives, and Catholic Action centres.

His pastoral visitations showed him that emigration, particularly from the rural parishes, was turning into an exodus. The young men were deserting the region in great numbers, leaving behind them villages populated only by the elderly and young women. He became a passionate champion of the welfare of emigrants. Inspired by the sight of them cramming the Milan railway station, he gave an address in Piacenza in 1887 in which he spoke of "the vast waiting room filled with three or four hundred individuals, poorly dressed ... marked by premature wrinkles drawn by privation. They were emigrants. They were leaving. They belonged to the various provinces of northern Italy and they were waiting ... for the train to the Mediterranean ... from where they would embark for the Americas ... to find less hostile fortune." From 1887 to 1892 he forced the phenomenon of emigration into the arena of national debate. He worked and corresponded with many other great figures deeply concerned with this and other social issues, including Frances Xavier Cabrini (see 22 Dec.), whom he persuaded to work in the United States rather than go to the Far East.

Bishop Scalabrini saw the need for an organized body to care for the pastoral needs of the migrants and founded the Missionaries of St Charles, who were to be migrants with the migrants. The community was formally recognized by Pope Leo XIII (1878–1903), who actively supported its aims, in November 1887. Eight years later Scalabrini founded a parallel Society for women, the Missionary Sisters of St Charles.

In the last ten years of his life he made two pastoral visits to his missionaries. His first was to the eastern United States from 3 August to 12 November 1901. His three-month itinerary was covered by both the Italian and the American press, and his visits to Italian immigrant ghettos brought reporters into neighbourhoods that previously had received publicity only for crimes. By his own account, given during an interview in New York City, Scalabrini's travels took him to New Haven, Boston, Utica, Syracuse, Buffalo, Cleveland, Detroit, Canada, Chicago, St Paul, Kansas City, St Louis, Cincinnati, Columbus, and Washington, DC, where he was received by President Theodore Roosevelt. The tour afforded him the opportunity to speak out against injustice toward Italian immigrants and to defend them to the President. His second international visit was to his missions in Brazil, starting on 13 June 1904. Here too he was received as the personal envoy of Pope Leo, and in later years he would reflect on these visits to Cardinal Merry del Val, the Secretary of State of Pope Pius X, asking him to encourage the pope to establish a Commission or a Pontifical Congregation for the pastoral care of immigrants.

All his activity was nourished by a deep devotion to Christ in the Eucharist and to the Blessed Virgin, as his homilies and pilgrimages testify. He died in the early hours of 1 June 1905, which that year was the feast of the Ascension. His last words were indicative of a life lived for others and in the service of God: "My priests, where are my priests? Let them come in; do not make them wait too long ... God's will be done." He was beatified by Pope John Paul II on 9 November 1997.

2

The Martyrs of Lyons and Vienne (died 177)

This important group of martyrs and the details of when and how they died are known in some detail from a contemporary letter. This undoubtedly authentic letter was written to Churches in the East by witnesses who survived the persecution. It also provides the earliest evidence of organized Christian communities in Gaul, referred to as dioceses. It was preserved, presumably copied many times, and almost one hundred and fifty years later came into the hands of Eusebius, bishop of Caesarea and the historian to whom we owe much of our knowledge of the first three centuries of the Church's existence. His method was to include documents at length, setting them in their historical and geographical context. He included the whole letter in his *Collection of Martyrs*, of which no trace has survived, but fortunately he also included long extracts from it in his *History of the Church*, which did survive and which is generally available in good modern translations.

The cities of Lyons and Vienne, on opposite banks of the River Rhône, were then, according to Eusebius, joint capitals of the Roman province of Gaul, and "famous and held in higher repute than any in the land." They were the terminus of the trade route from the East, the Rhône being broad and navigable as far as Lyons, the more northerly of the two. Persecution began with the exclusion of Christians from "houses, baths, and the forum," and indeed from any public place. They stood up to angry mobs, which seized them and took them before the authorities, who imprisoned them and brought them to be interrogated by the ferociously anti-Christian governor. Some remained steadfast and accepted martyrdom; others wavered, and ten denied their faith—"proved stillborn." Their pagan servants were either tempted or cajoled into bringing all sorts of heinous charges against them—"things we ought never to speak or think about, or even believe that such things ever happened among human beings." The rumours spread, and even their relatives turned against them: "Even those who because of blood-relationship had previously exercised restraint now turned on us, grinding their teeth with fury."

After selective interrogations, all the Christians in the two dioceses were hunted out. The letter singles out Sancturus, the deacon from Vienne; the young, newly baptized Maturus; Attalus, a "pillar and support"; Blandina, a young slave girl who was dreadfully tortured, maintaining throughout, "I am a Christian: we do nothing to be ashamed of"; Sanctus, who steadfastly refused to give even "name, rank, and number" but replied only "I am a Christian" to every question. Sanctus was tortured by having "red-hot copper plates [pressed] against the most sensitive parts of his body," leaving him doubled up and virtually unrecognizable; he was then racked, which straightened him out again. A woman named Biblis, who had previously denied Christ, was accused of slander and racked: this "brought her to her senses," making her insist that she was a Christian. Many of the younger martyrs, who had not previously had to undergo torture, died from suffocation in filthy prison conditions. So did Pothinus, aged over ninety, who had been mercilessly assaulted after telling the governor that "if he were a fit person" he would know who the God of the Christians was.

Then those who had originally denied Christ were rounded up again and imprisoned with those who had stood firm and been tortured; the former were "tormented by their conscience" and "dejected, downcast, ill-favoured and devoid of charm," whereas the faithful "stepped out with a happy smile, wondrous glory and grace blended on their faces." Their resolution affected the waverers, who then "unhesitatingly declared their faith without one thought for the devil's promptings."

Maturus and Sanctus died after a whole day of suffering in the arena—being whipped, mauled by wild animals, and placed in red-hot iron chairs. Blandina was "hung on a post and exposed as food for the wild beasts"; they refused to touch her, and she was taken back to prison. So was Attalus, as he was thought to be a Roman citizen, whose fate should be decreed by the emperor. He and any others thought to be citizens were beheaded; the rest were thrown to the wild beasts. Attalus was apparently not included with the Roman citizens, as he faced a full day of ordeal at the games, dying with Alexander, a doctor from Phrygia, accused of encouraging others to confess their Christianity. On the last day of the games, Blandina was exposed to the full ordeal of whips, wild animals, and roasting, plus being dropped in a basket and thrown to a bull. A boy of about fifteen, Ponticus, suffered with her, inspired by her example.

What remained of the martyrs bodies was finally burned to ashes and swept into the Rhône, so that no relics could be collected and in the belief that this would deprive them of the possibility of "resurrection—the belief that has led them to bring into this country a new foreign cult and treat torture with contempt, going willingly and cheerfully to their deaths." The dungeons in which they were kept and the ampitheatre in which they died can both be seen to this day.

3

Bd John XXIII (Angelo Giuseppe Roncalli; 1881–1963)

Regarded as *un papa di passaggio*, a "transitional" (in the sense of "stop-gap") pope, when he was elected at the age of seventy-seven in 1958, John proved transitional in quite an unexpected way. Through his calling of the Second Vatican Council, he steered—or pushed—the Church through transition from what Karl Rahner called its "second age," the European Church begun by St Paul's mission to the gentiles, into its "third age," that of being a truly "universal Church." Like other great figures of the modern age—Archbishop Romero falls into the same category—there was apparently little in his earlier life to suggest what was to come.

Angelo Roncalli was born at Sotto il Monte, a village in the foothills of Piedmont near Bergamo, on 25 November 1881. From a peasant background, he was educated first at the village school, then the diocesan seminary, and finally the San Apollinare Institute in Rome, where he gained a doctorate in theology in 1904. After his ordination, he was appointed secretary to the reforming bishop of Bergamo, Radini-Tadeschi. He served in the Italian army in the First World War, achieving the rank of sergeant and growing an impressive handlebar moustache. After the war he was given a roving brief to modernize the Church's methods of fund-raising and then taught a course on the Fathers of the Church at the Lateran seminary in Rome, where he acquired a reputation for rambling somewhat in his lectures and advancing some fairly revolutionary (for the time) ideas, such as that mixed marriages might sometimes be admissible. He researched into the life of St Charles Borromeo (see 4 Nov.) at the library of the Ambrosianum in Rome, where the librarian was Cardinal Ratti, who became pope as Pius XI in 1922. As pope, Ratti appointed Roncalli archbishop and sent him on diplomatic missions to Bulgaria in 1924 and Turkey and Greece in 1934. He had thus spent twenty years in not very glamorous Vatican diplomatic postings when Pius XII appointed him papal nuncio to France in 1944. He handled the post-war recriminations over collaborationists (including some bishops) with tact and skill and progressively endeared himself to the French over nine years. He was rewarded by being made a cardinal in 1953 and being appointed patriarch of Venice the same year.

He had, then, had long experience of the world outside the Vatican by the time he was elected pope. He was aghast at his election: *"Horrefactus sum,"* was his reaction, quoting from the Book of Job. He could see that the Church, though well preserved by recent popes as a "perfect society" (meaning one "sufficient unto itself" rather than "perfect" in the usual sense), was inward- rather than outward-looking. His "horrifying" task would be "to love the world in a special way, to minister to it, and to serve it" (Robert Kaiser). He had to make the message of the Church acceptable to the whole world, to take it to a world in need of Christ. The vision of the Church as above the world, dominant throughout the nineteenth century and the first half of the twentieth, had to be replaced by something more positive and more biblical. Significantly, Roncalli chose the name John.

He refused to change his easy-going ways to the aloof manners expected of popes and was soon hugely popular in Rome, where he walked about freely and visited the sick and prisoners—telling these that two of his cousins had been in prison and survived. The wider world gradually realized that something rather remarkable was happening to the papacy. His conventionally pious spiritual writings were published as *Giornale d'un anima* (*Journal of a Soul*) and became a worldwide bestseller. But he still felt imprisoned by the narrow, traditional world of the Vatican government, the Roman Curia—as he famously remarked to Cardinal Richard Cushing: *"Sono nel sacco qui,"* ("I'm in a bag here"). The way out, for himself and for the Church, came to him, at the instigation of the Holy Spirit, he claimed, when he was receiving reports on the problems of the Church around the world and on the state of the world itself from Cardinal Tardini, his pro-Secretary of State: "A council." Tardini is variously reported as accepting the idea enthusiastically and as telling curial officials that John would soon forget about it.

John did not forget about it and told the curial cardinals of it after celebrating Mass at the basilica of the apostle to the Gentiles, St Paul's outside the Walls. The idea was first received with some incredulity within the Church and largely with incomprehension outside, but it gradually came to be seen as a serious attempt to respond to a world in crisis. John had proclaimed an "ecumenical" council; a word understood differently by Reformed and Orthodox Churches and hardly known in Roman Catholic circles. It suggested that the council would have to address the historic splits in Christianity between East and West, between Catholic and Reformed traditions. This indeed was John's intention: "Let us come together. Let us make an end of our divisions." The Catholic press generally interpreted this as proposing a "return" to the "one true fold," but this was not what John had said.

Despite obstruction and the slow ways of the Curia, preparations went ahead, the media gradually became better informed about what was proposed, and worldwide interest in Pope John's project grew. In March 1960 John took a major step forward when he approved the establishment of a Vatican Secretariat for Promoting Christian Unity, proposed to him by the scholarly Jesuit cardinal Augustin Bea. Also in 1960, he openly refused to countenance any sort of "crusade" against Communism; in November of that year Nikita Kruschev sent him a birthday greeting, calling him a "man of peace." The following year he revolutionized the Church in Africa by calling for the immediate consecration of thirteen indigenous bishops. He set his face against centuries of anti-Semitism by asking Cardinal Bea to prepare an outline document that would remove the age-old charge of "deicide people" against the Jews. His encyclical letter *Mater et Magistra* (*Mother and Teacher*) dealing with the Church and social issues was accused in Franco's Spain of fomenting strikes. His next encyclical, *Pacem in Terris* (*Peace on Earth*, published in April 1963) again avoided condemnation of any political system. In every sphere, Pope John was reaching out to the whole world, breaking down barriers, trying to show the relevance of Christ to the world as it was.

In the Vatican, the Central Commission formed to digest all the suggestions sent in from bishops and others all over the world was trying to do the opposite, but this story and that of the reaction of the Council Fathers at the first session belong now to general history. John himself broadcast his vision in a radio message "to the world," delivered on 11 September 1962. It began, "The world indeed has need of Christ, and it is the Church that must bring Christ to the world," and it ended by recalling Jesus' wish "that they all may be one" in John 17. Pope John lived to see only the first of the council's four sessions completed. When it closed on 8 December 1962 he described it as "an introduction, slow and solemn, to the great work of the Council." He saw the difficulties but remained hopeful, trusting in the Holy Spirit. His health declined during the first half of 1963, and he died on 3 June. He had gathered his Roman cardinals on the last day of May, told them that he was "on the point of leaving," and expressed his final wish: "that the great work will be crowned with success." He was beatified by Pope John Paul II (who took the two names to express his desire to carry on the work of "good Pope John" and his successor, Paul VI) on 3 September 2000.

His body was exhumed early in 2001, to be moved from the grotto under St Peter's to an altar in the basilica itself. It had been injected with formaldehyde, to enable the faithful to venerate it after his death, but not embalmed, and it was found to be perfectly preserved. The preservation of his face "intact and smiling" was described by the Vatican Secretary of State as "a gift from God," but great care was taken not to claim anything miraculous about the body's incorrupt state, which could naturally be attributed to the formaldehyde and the traditional triple coffins.

4

St Charles Lwanga and Companions (died 1885 and 1886)

The martyrs of Uganda are venerated as the protomartyrs of Black Africa. Killed with members of other Christian Churches, they were directly victims of an exceptionally cruel ruler but indirectly of the fear of loss of a way of life felt by native societies faced with an influx of white missionaries and colonizers.

The White Fathers, the first Catholic missionaries to the people of southern Uganda, the Baganda, arrived in 1879 and were well received by the king, Mtesa. The mission flourished until his death in 1884, when he was succeeded by his eighteen-year-old son, Mwanga. He had attended the mission school, but whether from lack of ability or failure of attention had not learned to read or write, which seems to have left him with a feeling of inferiority. His traditional counsellors—witch doctors and fetishists—advised him that his ancestors were angry at the way foreigners were taking over the country, and he embarked on a systematic persecution.

Owing to an accidental failure to learn that the land of the Masai tribesmen was closed to white people, the newly appointed Anglican bishop, James Hannington, tried to make his way to Baganda by that route and was seized and killed. The White Fathers immediately realized that this was only the beginning of Mwanga's persecution. The young king was drinking heavily, smoking hemp, and given to homosexual practices, which he is said to have learned from white traders. His court contained a number of young pages, many of them Christian converts, who infuriated him by refusing his advances. Their master was Joseph Mkasa, a Catholic convert and catechist. He defended them against Mwanga and openly accused him of debauchery and of responsibility for the murder of Bishop Hannington. For this he was beheaded on 15 November 1885, the first of the martyrs to suffer. He was followed by Denis Sebuggwawo, a Christian page accused of giving instruction to another. Charles Lwanga, another Catholic, took Mkasa's place as master of the pages. He and all the pages were rounded up and the Christians separated from the others. They were asked if they intended to remain Christians, and when they declared that they did, Mwanga ordered, "Then put them to death!"

They were taken to a traditional place of ritual sacrifice, named Namugongo. Three pages were killed on the way there; the others were forced to construct a huge pyre. Charles Lwanga was the first to be burned to death, on 3 June 1886, which was Ascension Day. The others followed, including the son of the chief executioner, whom his father ordered to be killed first by a blow to the neck. The persecution spread sporadically, embracing other Christian denominations and also Muslims, and it ended only with Mwanga's death in 1888. There is some doubt about the exact number killed in the mass execution at Namugongo, but the list kept there includes some killed elsewhere and names twenty-two Catholics and twenty-four Anglicans or Protestants.

The massacre led to a great increase in converts, and by 1890 there were some ten thousand Christians in Baganda. Catholic and Protestant shrines were set up at Namugongo, and both have become great focuses of pilgrimage on the martyrs' feast-day. The Catholic shrine is built in the shape of a pyre and has the story of the martyrdom carved on its bronze doors. The Catholic martyrs were beatified in 1920 and canonized by Pope Paul VI on 8 October 1964, on the Mission Sunday preceding the opening of the third session of the Second Vatican Council, further demonstrating the Church's new determination to nourish native African roots of the Church in Africa (see the previous entry). Five years later, continuing this process, Pope Paul VI became the first pope ever to visit Africa, making a pilgrimage to Namugongo in the course of that visit.

A well that has many sources never runs dry. When we are gone, others will come after us.
Ugandan Martyr Bruno Serúnkuma

5

St Boniface (about 675–754)

The great apostle of Germany was born in Devon, probably at Crediton. He went to a monastery school near Exeter and then studied under Abbot Winbert in the school at Nursling, in the Winchester diocese. A brilliant pupil, he was made director of the school after finishing his studies. His lectures were so popular that copies of students' notes were circulated far beyond the monastery, and he was the first person in England to compile a Latin Grammar.

He felt called to mission work overseas and in 716 sailed with two companions for Friesland (now northern Netherlands), where St Wilfrid (see

24 Apr.) and St Willibrord (see 7 Nov.) had been pioneering missionaries some decades earlier and where Willibrord had stayed to become bishop of Utrecht. This first expedition ended in failure when the local ruler, Radbod, declared that he had no wish "to go to heaven with a handful of beggars" and forced them to return to England. The monks at Nursling elected him abbot in an attempt to keep him there, but he refused to accept the appointment, going instead to Rome to ask the pope to appoint him directly to a mission in Germany, which he did. On hearing that Radbod had died, he went north to help Willibrord in Utrecht. His preaching there was so successful that Pope Gregory II consecrated him bishop with jurisdiction over Germany.

Fortified by a sealed letter of support from Charles Martel, the leader of the Franks, he set energetically about his mission. He braved the wrath of the old Norse gods by splitting an oak tree sacred to them with four blows of an axe (as is claimed), using the wood to build a chapel when, to the people's amazement, he was not struck dead on the spot. Starting in the southern province of Bavaria and then moving northward to Hesse and Thuringia, he founded monasteries and made many converts. Pope Gregory III elevated him to the rank of archbishop on his accession in 732. In a famous letter Boniface appealed to England to provide the teachers needed to instruct the mass of new converts; the English monasteries responded generously, sending groups of missionaries—many of whom are venerated as saints, including two cousins of his, Lull and Lioba—as well as regular gifts of money, books, vestments, and relics.

Boniface made a further visit to Rome and was appointed papal legate. Returning to Germany, he convened a synod to establish permanent bishoprics, which he entrusted to followers of his from England. In 741 he was asked to reorganize the Frankish Church, which had become lax and uneducated. Boniface set about the needed reform with energy and learning, remedying abuses and introducing the Rule of St Benedict into monasteries. He crowned Charles Martel's son, Pepin, sole king of the Franks in 751, after Carloman, Charles' other son, had joined a monastery. When he considered his work among the Franks finished and could delegate its bishoprics, instead of retiring at the age of nearly eighty he returned to evangelizing the Friesians. His efforts extended eastward into hostile tribal territory, and there he met a martyr's death when his camp was attacked and he refused to allow any armed resistance. The book he was reading survives, dented with sword-cuts and apparently stained with his blood.

His body was taken to Fulda, his last monastic foundation, where, in a letter to the pope, he had earlier expressed his wish to be buried. It is still there, the focus of widespread veneration from Germany and the Netherlands. It has been said of him that "he had a deeper influence on the history of Europe than any Englishman who ever lived" (Christopher Dawson, *The Making of Europe*). An English synod declared that he should be regarded as patron of England alongside Gregory the Great (see 3 Sept.) and Augustine of Canterbury (see 27

May), but his cult has not been as great in England—ever mistrustful of deeds done on the Continent of Europe. Many of his letters survive, providing first-hand evidence of his power and influence as administrator and teacher but also of more personal qualities of simplicity, kindness, and holiness.

6

St Marcellin Champagnat (1789–1840)

The founder of the Marist Brothers of the Schools was born barely two months before the outbreak of the French Revolution. In the troubled years that followed, he received practically no schooling until he was fourteen, when a diocesan recruiter found that he had an interest in becoming a priest. His teacher brother-in-law declared that he lacked the capacity to study for the priesthood, but despite this verdict he entered the minor seminary of Verrières two years later. After one year the seminary authorities recommended that he should not return after the holiday break, but his mother employed means both spiritual (a pilgrimage) and material (influential friends) to have him re-admitted. After eight years he moved on to the major seminary of St Irenaeus in Lyons, where he came into contact with a charismatic student, Jean-Claude Courveille, whose eloquence, drive, and enthusiasm led to the formation of a group dedicated to forming a Society bearing the name of Mary. This would have three branches: a Society of priests, an Institute of religious Sisters, and a Third Order for lay members. One persistent voice, that of Champagnat, held out for a fourth branch, an Institute of teaching Brothers. His own lack of early education and awareness of the country's dire need for Christian educators clearly showed him this need. His companions finally agreed that he should found the teaching Brothers' branch.

On 23 July 1816, immediately after their ordination ceremonies, twelve of the companions placed their written and signed pledge on the altar at the shrine of the Black Virgin at Fourvière while Courveille celebrated Mass. Then the new priests went to their respective placements as clergy of the archdiocese of Lyons—not to come together as priests of the Society of Mary for twenty years. Champagnat became a village curate; he carried out his parish duties with zeal but remained conscious of the unborn Society of Mary. He found a prospective candidate to whom he started to give the first elements of a formal education. Then, after attending to the spiritual needs of a dying youth whose knowledge of religion was abysmally poor, he determined to act. A second recruit providentially came his way.

Early in 1817 Champagnat brought these two followers to a house he had acquired, forming the infant Society of Mary. It met resistance from the parish priest, who opposed the project and influenced other priests against his curate. Despite this, they founded a number of primary schools. The vicar-general of Lyons, Mgr Bochard, wanted the group of Brothers to be absorbed into his own Congregation, the Society of the Cross of Jesus, but a sudden influx of vocations convinced Champagnat that he had to "stiffen the sinews, summon up the blood," and resist the threat to his Institute. He was rescued when a new pope, Leo X, removed Cardinal Fesch from the archdiocese of Lyons, soon followed by Bochard. The new archbishop encouraged Champagnat in his work, but then internal troubles arose. Courveille, the charismatic inspirer of the would-be Marists, sought to have himself elected as superior of the Brothers, but he could not convince them to accept him, and they voted for the man they knew and admired, Marcellin Champagnat.

The Marist Society of priests was approved in 1836, having agreed to be the Church's missionaries in the south-west Pacific. Ten of the twenty-one who first took their vows had been influenced by Champagnat in the archdiocese of Lyons. He was also instrumental in sending young women to the incipient Congregation of Marist Sisters. By this time some among the Brothers were expressing disaffection in regard to educational method and other matters. Champagnat, who had suffered a long illness and period of convalescence, induced them to change to a modern, more effective method of teaching reading—the "simultaneous method" used by the De La Salle Brothers. He believed that the Brothers should be with the young, should love them, should lead them to Jesus, and should form them to be good Christians and good citizens. In a circular letter to the Brothers (19 January 1839) he said, "I desire and wish that, following the example of Jesus, you have a tender love for the children. With holy zeal break for them the spiritual bread of religion."

A major difficulty was that of obtaining official government recognition of the Institute as French governments became increasingly anticlerical. At one point there was a threat of compulsory military service for his Brothers, and government recognition finally came only after the founder's death, when Louis Napoleon granted the long-sought authorization. Champagnat's cause was hardly furthered by some clerical friends who tried to solve his lack of government recognition by attempting to amalgamate his Institute with other groups that possessed the vital authorization. Progress continued, despite the problems, and by the time of his death his Institute of Marist Brothers numbered forty-eight establishments and two hundred and eighty Brothers. Champagnat himself had become a priest of the Society of Mary in 1836 and to the end of his life believed in an integrated Society, all four branches under the leadership of one man, though with different functions. He wanted the Brothers to run schools and to live in community. But he was also enthusiastic about the apostolate of the missions and sent his Brothers to Oceania under the superiorship of Marist priests.

Champagnat perceptibly declined in health in 1839, dying at the comparatively early age of fifty-one on 6 June 1840. During the twenty-year generalate of his successor, Br François Rivat, the Institute expanded vastly, at a rate of one new primary school opening every three weeks. In 1856 the Marist Brothers entered the field of secondary education, and at the beginning of the Third Millennium some five thousand Marist Brothers were working not only in primary, secondary, and tertiary education but also in many mission situations and in other apostolates associated with young people. Marcellin Champagnat was beatified in 1955 and canonized on 18 April 1999.

7

Bd Baptista Varani (Camilla Varani; died 1527)

Camilla came from a social background of magnificence totally at variance with the life she was to choose. Her father, Prince Julius Caesar Varani, was lord of Camerino and commander-in-chief of the papal army during the reigns of Popes Nicholas V (1447–55) and Sixtus IV (1471–84). Her mother was the daughter of the lord of Rimini, Sigismund Malatesta. Their aim for their daughter was a brilliant marriage, for which "music, dancing, driving, dress, and other worldly amusements" were seen as suitable preparation. She seemed quite prepared to concur in this, declaring that she "could not bear the sight" of monks or nuns.

There was, however, a different current of influence at work in her life. When she was only eight she had heard the Franciscan Mark of Montegallo (Bd, commemorated on 20 Mar.) preach on the passion of Our Lord. The sermon had made a deep impression, and she had continued to meditate on Christ's sufferings throughout her schooldays. Then, after three years of worldly adult life, another sermon by a Franciscan, Fr Francis of Urbino, had an effect "like flashes of lightning," going "right against my natural inclinations and my attachment to the world." She wrote to the preacher, actually commending others to his pastoral care, but his reply reinforced the message to her personally, telling her to "guard yourself from the seduction of the world, and strive to overcome yourself." She made a general confession and started to entertain serious thoughts of entering the religious life, to the disgust of her father, who spoke of imprisoning her to prevent her doing any such thing.

She persevered, helped by gifts, which she saw as coming from God and called her "three lilies": hatred of the world, a sense of her own unworthiness, and willingness to suffer. After two years her father accepted her resolve, and she was clothed at the convent of Poor Clares in Urbino in November 1481, taking the name Baptista in religion. She spent two years at Urbino, during which, at the request of her superior, she wrote down her meditations under the title *The Sufferings of the Agonizing Heart of Jesus*. Her father, who had previously forbidden the foundation of any religious houses on his lands, now saw that there was only one way to keep in contact with her, obtained the pope's approval for a Poor Clare convent at Camerino, and had it built at his own expense. Baptista, with several other members of the family who had also joined the Poor Clares, were transferred there.

Whether she welcomed the move is not known, but she continued to lead an intense spiritual life, the fruits of which matured in another book, on the mental sufferings of Jesus. This was widely read in many different editions and was influential in forming devotion to the Sacred Heart of Jesus. She also wrote a history of her own spiritual life—couched in the form of a letter to the preacher who had inspired her meditations, Mark of Montegallo—and a course of instruction on seeking spiritual perfection. This was written in response to a request from a Spanish priest but could well be a manual for any Christian, with touches of humour and shrewdness reminiscent of Teresa of Avila. She suffered a great personal sorrow when her father and her three elder brothers were murdered in an uprising provoked by Cesare Borgia. Pope Julius II (1503–13) asked her to open a Poor Clare convent in Fermo, where she spent about a year. She then returned to Camerino and was superior there until she died in 1527.

8

St William of York (William Fitzherbert, or of Thwayte; died 1154)

William's story is a complicated one and his life seems to have been lived tossed about by political and religious storms beyond his control. A brief account of him has to be largely a short lesson in medieval English history, and the main testimony to his holiness is the high regard in which the people of York held him when he was finally able to take up his post of archbishop—for two months only.

The political storm was the feud between the house of Normandy and the house of Blois over the throne of England. Henry I (1100–35; Normandy) had left the throne to his daughter Matilda and made all the nobles swear to support her, but another Henry, brother of Stephen of Blois and bishop of Winchester, used his seizure of the royal treasury to promote Stephen's accession. Civil war broke out when Matilda landed from Normandy to claim her inheritance. William was inevitably involved as he was the son of Stephen's (and Henry of Winchester's) half-sister Emma and so seen as an ally by Stephen.

In 1140 William was treasurer of York Minster, and when the archbishop died, Stephen appointed him (as an ecclesiastical counterweight to the archbishop of Canterbury, who supported Matilda) and made sure of his election by sending the earl of York to sit in on the election process conducted by the chapter of York Minster. Theobald of Canterbury refused to consecrate William, who had been accused of simony, so Henry of Winchester did so, without papal approval. Pope Innocent II died in 1143, and after four years of bitter debate—over the papacy as well as over York—Pope Eugenius III, through the agency of the Council of Reims, deposed William (who went first to Sicily and then to Winchester for six years) and consecrated Henry Murdac, abbot of Fountains Abbey some thirty miles from York, in his stead. When Murdac tried to take possession of his see, the clergy of York refused to admit him. In 1153 a new pope, Anastasius IV, conferred the archbishop's *pallium* on William, giving him papal approval for the first time, and he entered York in some triumph in April 1154. (He had actually had the *pallium* conferred on him by Lucius II, Eugenius' predecessor, in 1146, but had failed to collect it.)

The clergy generally supported him, but they were prey to the religious storm, which was the feud between the supporters of Cluny (moderately reformed) and those of Cîteaux, led by St Bernard of Clairvaux (see 20 Aug.; severely reformed). Pope Innocent II had placed the influence of Cluniac monks behind Stephen's claim and so indirectly behind his brother Henry's tenure of Winchester and William's appointment as archbishop of York. But Eugenius III had actually been a monk at Cîteaux under Bernard and took a very different line. So had his nominee for York, Murdac, who as abbot of Fountains had led the Cistercian abbots on the York chapter in opposing William's first nomination. (The accusations of simony made against William came from Cistercian sources.) William's relatives attacked and severely damaged Fountains Abbey. Murdac's death in 1153 helped to swing the balance back to the supporters of Cluny and so of William.

When William returned to York in April 1154 he was welcomed by such a great crowd of people that the bridge over the River Ouse collapsed under their weight. The fact that no one was killed was seen as a miracle. On Trinity Sunday he was celebrating Mass when he was suddenly taken ill. His archdeacon, Osbert, was suspected of putting poison in his chalice, but this was never proved. William died on 8 June.

He had been accused (by the Cistercian faction) of being worldly and lax, fond of sport and good living. His supporters saw him as kind-hearted, liberal in giving to the poor, and personally austere. He was canonized in 1227 after an inquiry conducted, interestingly, by two Cistercian abbots, the religious as well as the political storms of the previous century having died down. His remains were placed in a shrine behind the high altar in York Minster, but this was demolished during the Reformation, and his relics are supposed to be in a sarcophagus under the altar (donated by the Catholic diocese of Leeds) in a chapel dedicated to him in the crypt. The great fifteenth-century north choir transept window commemorates his life and the miracles attributed to him in one hundred and ten panels.

9

St Columba of Iona (Columcille, Colm, or Colum; about 521–597)

Columba came from royal families of Ireland: his father was a great-grandson of the overlord of Ireland and his mother was descended from a king of Leinster. Columcille, as he is more generally known in Ireland, is, according to Bede, a compound of "Columba" and "cell." His Life was written some decades after his death by Adomnán of Iona, a successor as abbot of his best-known foundation, which remains a great place of pilgrimage and retreat for Christians of all denominations and people of other faiths and none.

He studied the scriptures under a bishop, according to Adomnán, though other sources associate him with various monastic schools. When he was ordained priest, his family gave him a fort at Daire Calgach, now Derry to the Irish (and northern Irish nationalists) and Londonderry to the English (and Unionists). This became his first monastery, and he founded many others as he went about Ireland preaching for the next fifteen years. His voice was said to carry for a mile. His love of books and learning involved him on one occasion in an early "breach of copyright" case: he borrowed a copy of St Jerome's Psalter (the first to reach Ireland) from St Finnian of Moville and made a copy of it; Finnian claimed the copy as his, took his case to King Diarmid, and won, with the judgment, "To every cow her calf, and to every book its son-book."

He then became involved in a sanctuary dispute, which turned into a massacre: a man who had fatally injured an opponent in a hurling match took refuge with Columba, but Diarmid's men literally tore him from Columba's arms and killed him. Columba's clan went to war with Diarmid's followers, and three thousand died in battle. Columba was held responsible and would have been excommunicated if St Brendan of Clonfert (see 16 May) had not interceded for him. It may have been a feeling of guilt over this affair that led him to leave Ireland, or he may have been invited to Scotland by the king of Scottish Dalriada, who was related to him. He and twelve relatives sailed for Scotland in a coracle in 561. They landed on a small island off the south-west corner of Mull and there set about building the monastery that was to become known throughout the world as Iona.

From there he taught the people of Scottish Dalriada (to the south and west of the Grampian mountains), who were of Irish descent and already had some knowledge of Christianity. He then crossed the mountains to the castle of the northern Pictish king, Brude, or Bride, at Inverness. Having initially been forbidden entry, Columba raised a mighty arm and made the sign of the cross, after which he and his party were admitted and treated with respect. It was Brude who confirmed his possession of Iona. Bede's version is simply that Columba "converted [the northern Picts] to the Faith of Christ by his preaching and example, and received from them the island of Iona on which to found a monastery." The northern Picts had a Druidic form of religion, and their conversion was no easy task, made harder by the terrain Columba had to cross to reach them; he seems to have made the journey two or three times.

He returned to Ireland several times, but Iona became his headquarters for the remainder of his life. In his later years he transcribed books and wrote poetry, and he seems to have mellowed somewhat from the extreme austerity of his earlier life—which he had been as ready to impose on others as on himself. Adomnán describes him as "an angel in demeanour, blameless in what he said, godly in what he did, brilliant in intellect . . . loving to all people." He is said to have made three hundred copies of the Gospels, and he was transcribing the Psalms the day before he died, leaving the task to his cousin and designated successor, Baithéne, to finish.

His final blessing on Iona was prophetic: "This place, however small and mean, will have bestowed on it no small but great honour by the kings and peoples of Ireland, and also by the rulers of even barbarous and foreign nations with their subject tribes. And the saints of other churches too will give it great reverence." Columba's influence dominated the churches of Ireland and northern Britain for many years after his death. Bede, who was no friend to the "Celtic" side in the disputes over the date of Easter and other observances that formed the subject matter of the Synod of Whitby, held sixty-six years after Columba's death, still testified to the holiness of the way of life stemming from Iona, whose monks were "distinguished for their purity of life, their love of God, and their loyalty to the monastic Rule."

10

St Ephraem (about 306–373)

Declared a Doctor of the Church by Pope Benedict XV in 1920, Ephraem "the Syrian" is the only Syrian Church Father to have been so distinguished. Poet, preacher, orator, known as the "Harp of the Holy Ghost," his influence lives on above all in the Orthodox liturgy, in which monks repeat the "Prayer of St Ephraem" three times during the Lenten offices while bowing their foreheads to the ground in the gesture known as *metanoïa*, meaning "conversion of life."

He was born in the Roman province of Mesopotamia, to parents variously described as Christians and as opposed to Christianity. He was baptized at the age of eighteen and became a pupil of Bishop James of Nisibia, his place of birth; he probably went with him to the Council of Nicaea the following year (325). Back in Nisibia he became head of the cathedral school and in that capacity composed many hymns, several of which reflect the conditions under which they were written, with the Persians besieging the town. They were repulsed, but it was ceded to them in 363, when Christians left the town and Ephraem withdrew to a cave overlooking Edessa. Here he lived extremely frugally, but not as a hermit, preaching often in Edessa, where his oratory could reduce crowds to tears.

Most of his spiritual works date from this period. St Jerome (see 30 Sept.), reading a work of his "On the Holy Spirit" in Greek translation, "recognized, even in translation, the incisive power of lofty genius." He was concerned to refute the teachings of a Gnostic sect called the Bardesanes. They made their teachings known by setting maxims to popular tunes, a technique Ephraem copied, writing his own words to be sung to the same tunes and training a choir (of women, interestingly) to sing them in church. So, ironically, the use of hymns as a means of instructing the people may be said to originate with an heretical sect.

Jerome refers to Ephraem as "a deacon of the Church of Edessa," and he was certainly ordained deacon, late on in his life. Whether he was also ordained to the priesthood is less certain. He is known, from his own writings and from those of Gregory of Nyssa (see 10 Jan.), to have visited the latter's brother, St Basil the Great (see 2 Jan.) in 370. Basil is said to have greeted him with the words, "Are you Ephraem, who follows the way of salvation so well?" to which he replied, "I am Ephraem, who walks unworthily in the way of salvation." He is heard of two or three years later, when he managed the distribution of supplies of grain and money to the starving during a winter famine: those with the food and money would trust no one else to distribute it fairly. Having earned widespread praise for his actions, he returned to his cave, where he died a few months later.

His writings have survived to a large extent, some in the original Syrian, others in early Greek and Armenian translations. His works were not translated into Latin until the 1730s, which may help explain why he was not declared a Doctor of the Western Church until 1920. Besides poems, hymns, sermons, and treatises, he produced commentaries on the Old and New Testaments. His insights into Christ's suffering and sacrifice are early and insightful expressions of the doctrine of the Eucharist: "The Lord himself became true altar, priest, and bread and chalice of salvation. . . . Altar he is, and lamb, victim and sacrificer, priest as well as food."

❖

Lord and master of my life,
take from me the spirit of laziness, of dejection,
of domination, of empty words;
grant to me your servant
a spirit of chastity, of humility, of patience and love;
Yes, Lord King, permit me to see my sins
and not to judge my brother,
for you are blessed, world without end. Amen.
Prayer of St Ephraem used in the Orthodox Lent liturgy

11

St Barnabas (First Century)

The story of Barnabas is told in the Acts of the Apostles. He appears in the context of the early believers sharing all their possessions, so that "[t]here was not a needy person among them, for as many as owned lands or houses sold them and brought the proceeds of what was sold. They laid it at the apostle's feet, and it was distributed to each as any had need" (4:34–5). Barnabas was not one of the original apostles but a Levite from Cyprus, originally named Joseph but renamed "Barnabas (which means 'son of encouragement')" by the apostles. "He sold a field that belonged to him, then brought the money, and laid it at the apostles' feet" (4:36–7).

When the disciples were scattered during the persecution that followed the stoning of Stephen (see 26 Dec.), some of them went to Antioch and began to preach not only to Jews but to Greeks, many of whom were converted. News of this reached Jerusalem, and the leaders of the Church there saw the need for someone to go and instruct them. They sent Barnabas, who "[w]hen he . . . saw the grace of God . . . rejoiced and . . . exhorted them all to remain faithful to the Lord with steadfast devotion; for he was a good man, full of the Holy Spirit and of faith" (11:23). He then went on to Tarsus, found Paul (still referred to as Saul, who had earlier persecuted believers) and took him back to Antioch, where the two preached for a year, teaching a great many people and forming the first community to be called "Christians" (11:26).

He continued to work with Paul—and indeed for a time was given the leading part—in taking the message to the Gentiles. The two were responsible for taking money from the relatively wealthy community of Antioch to help the apostles in relieving a famine in Judea (11:28–30). After the persecution by King Herod (during which Peter miraculously escaped from prison), they returned to Jerusalem once again, having gained more followers in Antioch, where "the word of God continued to advance" (12:24). They were then back in Antioch, where they were singled out from among the "prophets" there by the Holy Spirit: "Set apart for me Barnabas and Saul for the work to which I have called them" (13:2b). Taking John Mark with them, they sailed from Seleucia to Cyprus, where they preached in the synagogues of Salamis and then went over the whole island (13:5–6a). The Roman proconsul, "an intelligent man" who was being led astray by a "Jewish false prophet, named Bar-Jesus," asked to hear the word of God and after some very fierce words from Paul was converted (see 13:6–12).

Barnabas, Paul, and John Mark sailed from Paphos to Perga in Pamphylia, where John Mark left them and returned to Jerusalem. Barnabas and Paul went on to another Antioch, in Asia Minor, where they were invited to preach in the synagogue and, after an inspiring address from Paul, invited back the following week, when many converts were made. But resistance then increased, and Barnabas and Paul were forced to leave the city—famously shaking its dust from their feet in a gesture of protest—and move on to Iconium (see 13:42–52). There again they made converts but also roused some of both the Gentiles and the Jews to such fury that they were about to stone them. Warned in time, they moved on to other cities and the surrounding countryside, "and there they continued proclaiming the good news" (14:7). In Lystra Paul healed a crippled man; the pair were then taken for Greek gods come down to earth in human form, with Barnabas cast as Zeus and Paul as Hermes, "because he was the chief speaker" (14:12b). They protested vehemently that they were just ordinary mortals bringing good news but "[e]ven with these words, they scarcely restrained the crowds from offering sacrifice to them" (14:18). But then some zealous Jews from Antioch and Iconium turned the people against them. Paul was stoned, rescued by some followers, and went, with Barnabas, to another city, Derbe. They preached the gospel there, making many converts, then returned to Lystra, Iconium, and Antioch, establishing settled communities with elders in charge as they went. Retracing their steps further, they returned to the original Antioch in northern Palestine from which they had set out. There they "called the church together and related all that God had done with them, and how he had opened a door of faith for the Gentiles" (14:27b).

They stayed there for some time, but when other disciples came and preached that no one could be saved without being circumcised, they went to Jerusalem to confront the apostles and leaders on the question, in what has become known as the Council of Jerusalem. There they were accorded respectful attention "as they told of all the signs and wonders that God had done through them among the Gentiles" (15:12b). James, the leader of the church in Jerusalem, was won over, and the Church, thanks to Barnabas as well as to Paul, was set on its missionary course. Paul and Barnabas returned to Antioch, taking other disciples who had been assigned to them as helpers, as well as the message to the converts there that leading an upright life was more important than observing many rituals, at which "they rejoiced" (15:31b).

Paul then proposed to Barnabas that they should revisit all the cities they had preached in originally. Barnabas wanted to take John Mark with them, but Paul refused, saying he had deserted them on the first journey. This unfortunately led to a disagreement "so sharp that they parted company" (15:39a). Barnabas took John Mark with him "and sailed away to Cyprus" (15:39b). Acts then follows Paul's journeys, and so Barnabas largely disappears from our view. He and Paul seem to have been reconciled and to have worked together again in about the year 56 or 57, as Paul asks the Christians of Corinth, "[I]s it only Barnabas and I who have no right to refrain from working for a living?" (1 Cor. 9:6). Barnabas is thought to have been stoned to death in Cyprus; he was buried near Salamis, and his body was later taken to Constantinople, where a church was built with a shrine to house his remains. Later apocryphal *Acts*, purporting to be written by John Mark but actually dating from the fifth century, add an account of his supposed later life, but the only true source is the Acts of the Apostles, which should be seen as conveying a message rather than as a historical account in the modern sense. Even allowing for this, Barnabas obviously played a major part in the missionary expansion of the early Church.

12

Bd Anne Mary Taigi (Anna Maria Gesualda; 1769–1837)

The story of this humble wife and mother who never learned to read or write but became the spiritual confidante of great figures in secular society and the Church is a remarkable one by any standards. It is also known in unusual detail, thanks to the abundant testimony given by her husband and many eminent churchmen when her cause was first introduced.

She came from a moderately wealthy family of apothecaries in Siena, but the business failed when she was six. The family had to move to Rome, and she grew up in real poverty, with her parents working as domestic servants. After some schooling she could recite most of the Psalms by heart but scarcely write her own name. The family situation improved when her father found a post in the household of Signora Serra, a relative of the prominent Chigi family, then positions there for Anne's mother and for Anne herself, as Signora Serra's personal maid. Prince Chigi's kitchen porter, who brought meals from his palace, was attracted to her, and after a confessor had advised her that she had no real calling to the religious life, she agreed to marry him. His name was Domenico Taigi; he was twenty-eight and she twenty years old.

Married life was hard but not desperate. Domenico was rough but steady and could supplement his modest earnings with pickings from the great house. Like other young couples, they could find leisure to stroll on the Corso in the evening. Their positions as domestic servants provided rooms in which to live, but Domenico kindly invited Anne's mother to move in with them after she had quarrelled with her husband; she proved an ungrateful and interfering lodger. The greatest cause of friction, however, came from Anne's spiritual development. Around the time her first child (of seven) was born, she began to feel she was called to make expiation for the sins of the world and to undertake exceptional penances—as though life had not provided her with enough. After one confessor had dismissed her as hysterical, she was advised by a Servite friar to become a tertiary of the Order of the Trinity. She then gave up all worldly pleasures, however small. She was sustained by a constant vision that she called her "sun," in which she saw (according to the deposition of Cardinal Pedicini at her process), a dazzling globe surrounded by a crown of thorns, from the middle of which Eternal Wisdom showed her "the world [as] an open book, consisting of one word, God."

Domenico, with no such inner consolation, became increasingly demanding and bad-tempered, though he never showed her violence and was indeed physically protective. In 1799 the French invaded Italy and Prince Chigi and his family fled, leaving Domenico unemployed. Anne earned a little money from sewing, but they had a terrible two years, losing a child, before Chigi returned, employed Domenico again, and found them better living quarters. Anne's influence began to spread out from the home, in practical charitable works, starting with battered wives, moving on to the sick and dying in hospitals, and extending to stray cats. People began coming to her for counselling, including great ladies such as Marie-Louise de Bourbon, daughter of the queen of Spain, whom Anne is said to have cured of epilepsy, and "Madame Mère," otherwise Letitzia Buonaparte, Napoleon's mother, who was brought from Corsica by her half-brother, Cardinal Fesch, to live near the Chigi Palace after Napoleon had been exiled to Elba. They became part of a Confraternity which met every Friday for Stations of the Cross and prayer. Anne was part of this, and the cardinal became her disciple. Letitzia lived on to 1836, given a last message by Anne at the cardinal's request: that she should meditate on "what she had been, what she was, and what she would be soon."

By this time Anne's own health was failing, and she died quietly on 9 June 1837, after talking to Domenico and each of her children. There was a cholera epidemic in Rome at the time, so people avoided large gatherings, and she was buried very simply in the public cemetery. Her friends and disciples began gathering testimonies to the holiness of her life almost immediately. Because she had no position in public life, everything had to be gathered from people who had known her. They included cardinals, nobles, perhaps even the pope. It still took almost a hundred years for the beatification process to come to fruition; at the ceremony in 1920 Pope Benedict XV held her up as an example to wives and mothers, saying she had been "a soul quite different from that of the virgins, nuns, and widows canonized by the Church" and calling her "the glory of this Rome of ours." Perhaps only in Rome would such a combination of normality and mysticism, and of obscurity and prominence among nobility and higher clergy, have been possible.

13

St Antony of Padua (Fernando Bulhon; 1195–1231)

Antony, one of the most popular saints in the Calendar and closely associated with St Francis of Assisi (see 4 Oct.), was in fact Portuguese, born into a noble family from Lisbon and baptized Fernando. He was educated by the cathedral clergy in Lisbon and joined the Augustinians at the age of fifteen. Two years later he asked to be moved to the priory of the Holy Cross at Coïmbra, where he would be less distracted by visits from friends. There he spent eight years studying and meditating, acquiring a deep knowledge of the Bible.

The course of his life was changed when the king of Portugal brought relics of Franciscan missionaries martyred by the Moors back from Morocco. Antony longed to be a missionary and perhaps a martyr like them. But the Augustinians were not a missionary Order, and he asked to be released from his vows to them so that he could join the Franciscans. This was arranged, and he sailed for Morocco to preach to the Moors, but he soon became seriously ill and was sent home. His ship was blown so far off course that it landed in Sicily instead of in Portugal. He made contact with Franciscans in Messina, who told him that a general chapter of the Order, open to all its members, was about to be held in Assisi. So he set out for Assisi, attended the chapter, met Francis, who impressed him deeply with his humility, and was then sent to a hermitage, where he carried out menial tasks and devoted himself to prayer. No one seems to have appreciated his learning and preaching powers, perhaps because he was too humble to demonstrate them, perhaps because the early Franciscans tended not to value erudition.

An ordination service for both Franciscans and Dominicans was held in Forli. It emerged that no one had been appointed to preach: the Dominicans expected a Franciscan to do so, as they were the hosts; the Franciscans assumed a Dominican would, as they were the Order of Preachers. Antony was asked to preach and, after protesting that he was not fit, delivered a sermon that became "a flood of divine eloquence" (as an early Life called it) and astonished all who heard it. He was removed from his retreat and sent to preach all over Lombardy. He drew such crowds that the churches were not big enough, and he preached to thousands gathered in town squares, moving sinners and criminals to repentance with his charisma and the power of his words.

His learning was also then appreciated, and in 1222 Francis, whose friend and close disciple he had become, personally appointed him lector in theology, the first person in the Order to hold such a post. His letter of appointment shows Francis still slightly suspicious: "I am well pleased that you should read theology to the friars, provided that such study does not quench the spirit of holy prayer and devotion according to our Rule." He taught first at Bologna and was then sent to southern France to assist the "crusade" against the Albigensians. He taught at Montpellier and Toulouse and became known as the "hammer of the heretics." He held posts at Puy and Limoges, then was recalled to Italy when Francis died in 1226. He may have been the provincial in Emilia or Romagna, but he was released from office by Pope Gregory IX in 1227 to devote himself to preaching, spending the last few years of his life in and around Padua. He had a remarkable effect on both the religious and the civic life of the town, reducing crime, reconciling enemies, denouncing usury, and freeing debtors from prison. His fragile health gave out when he was only thirty-six, and he died on 13 June 1231. He was immediately hailed as a saint by the masses and was canonized the following year. At the ceremony, the anthem *O doctor optime* was sung, but he was not formally proclaimed a Doctor of the Church till 1946.

Legends grew up around him over the centuries, and works of art abound, focusing mainly on his gentleness and kindness, which extended, in the true spirit of St Francis, to animals, birds, fishes, and flowers. He was later often depicted holding an open book on which the infant Jesus stands or sits. The origin of this is a story that a friar saw a bright light shining under the door of Antony's room; he looked through the keyhole and saw a child of rare beauty standing on an open book on the desk, with his arms round Antony's neck. Velázquez, Murillo, and Raphael all painted scenes showing his miracles or his emblems. Others refer to his attacks on usury, one painting, by Pesillino, showing him plucking a miser's heart out of a money chest. A lily and a book feature regularly, symbolizing his purity and learning. In Padua a bas-relief shows an ass kneeling in front of the saint who is holding up the Blessed Sacrament. His popularity increased hugely in the late nineteenth century (spread largely through the [by then] cheap colour-lithography prayer cards), when he became patron of the poor—with the collection for the relief of hunger known as St Antony's Bread—and of lost causes articles: "St Antony, St Antony, where art thou?" was a familiar phrase in Catholic households until recently. This seems to stem from an incident in which a novice ran off with a Psalter on which Antony was working; he prayed for its return, and the novice saw an alarming apparition on the opposite bank of a river he was about to cross ordering him to take the book back, which he did.

14

St Methodius of Constantinople (died 847)

This patriarch of Constantinople is venerated by the Greek Orthodox Church for the part he played in the overthrow of Iconoclasm. This movement, the "breaking of images," was supported in the eighth century by the Eastern emperor Leo III, the Isaurian, and again in the ninth by Leo V, the Armenian. It was inspired partly by Monophysite denial of the separate human nature of Christ, partly by Gnostic belief that all matter was evil, and partly by the Islamic ban on portrayal of human images. Leo III saw the (by then excessive) use of images as an obstacle to the conversion of Jews and Muslims and in 726 published an edict declaring that all images were idols and must be destroyed. He persecuted the monks, who were the main defenders of images; John Damascene wrote "apologies" for images, and Pope Gregory III held two synods in Rome condemning Leo.

Leo's son, Constantine V, continued his father's policy, and many monks were martyred. A synod called in 753 declared that images of Christ, because they could show only his human nature, either denied the unity of his two natures (so were Nestorian) or confused them (and so were Monophysite). It also ordered the destruction of all images of the Virgin Mary and the saints. Constantine's son, Leo IV, followed after his death by his wife Irene, regent for his young son Constantine, reversed the policy and sought a compromise with the pope, achieved at the Seventh Council of Nicaea in 787, which defined the degree of veneration to be paid to images and ordered their restoration. The imperial army, however, remained on the side of the Iconoclasts, and when it proclaimed one of its generals emperor, as Leo V, the struggle broke out again.

This was the point at which Methodius became involved. Born in Sicily, he became a monk on a Greek island and was called from there to Constantinople by the patriarch, Nicephorus. He argued that statues and pictures were an aid to devotion and a vital part of the Church's tradition. Nicephorus was deposed and exiled by Leo, and Methodius went to Rome armed with a letter informing the pope of the situation. He stayed there until Leo V was assassinated in 820 and then returned to Constantinople with a letter from the pope to the new emperor, Michael II, "the Stammerer," requesting Nicephorus' reinstatement. But the supporters of Iconclasm siezed him and threw him in prison, where he remained, in inhuman conditions, for seven or nine years. He emerged broken in body but not in spirit. Michael's son, Theophilus, continued the persecution and had Methodius thrown back into prison and his jaw broken, but

Theophilus died in 842, and Theodora, regent for her son Michael III, reversed the policy once more and had Methodius appointed patriarch in place of the Iconoclast who had succeeded Nicephorus. On the first Sunday of Lent, 843, a great feast was held to celebrate the restoration of icons, still observed as the "Festival of Orthodoxy" in the Greek Orthodox Church. Methodius, the hero of the restoration, still had a bandaged jaw.

He was patriarch for four years. He ordered Nicephorus' remains to be brought back and suitably re-interred and had the lawfulness of venerating images reaffirmed at a synod. The unity that appeared to have been achieved at his accession was not to last, however. Rivalry between emperors and popes, exacerbated by theological misunderstandings, prolonged the Iconoclast Controversy as the final stage of the quarrels between the Churches of West and East that led to their separation in 1054.

15

St Vitus (died about 303)

Known for "St Vitus' Dance" and so, by extension, the patron saint of actors and dancers, Vitus appears to have been martyred in the persecution under Diocletian, emperor from 284 to 305, when he abdicated. Diocletian had made the Roman Empire into an absolute monarchy, with all power concentrated on the emperor as semi-divine ruler. He then divided the empire into four administrative parts, appointing Galerius as "Caesar" of the north-central area. It seems to have been Galerius who was the moving spirit in instigating the "Great Persecution," which took place between the years 303 and 312, when Constantine defeated Maxentius (emperor of Italy and Africa) at the battle of the Milvian Bridge. This enabled him to declare himself joint emperor, with Licinius, and to agree with him on the terms of the "Edict of Milan," establishing equal toleration of all religions, the following year.

Vitus, according to tradition, was the son of a Sicilian senator. He was entrusted to a tutor named Modestus and a nurse named Crescentia, who between them brought him up as a Christian. Vitus' father discovered this and tried to reconvert him to paganism, but without success. He and his mentors escaped to Lucania in southern Italy by boat and made their way to Rome, where Vitus healed Diocletian's son, who was suffering from demonic possession. Diocletian regarded this as sorcery, and condemned all three to torture and death. How much of this is true is impossible to discover: there is evidence that there was a relatively early cult of a St Vitus, but this may have been someone else of the same name, from Lucania. Whoever he was, he was associated with bodily health as early as the sixth or seventh century, as this is stated in the earliest known version of the Roman Missal, the Gelasian Sacramentary. Medieval legends developed stories of angelic liberation from death, and Modestus and Crescentia were added to the cult at a later date, but they never achieved the same renown as Vitus, and their names have now been removed from today's commemoration, which was formerly of all three, as martyrs.

The cult of Vitus spread far and wide in the Middle Ages, when the story of his healing of the emperor's son made him the patron saint of those suffering from "St Vitus' dance," a popular name for the condition that causes twitching and convulsions, medically known as Sydenham's chorea. This appeared among soldiers of King Roger II's army in Sicily, where Vitus came from. This outbreak is now thought to have been caused by bites from poisonous spiders, but there are other causes, such as rabies, snakebite, food poisoning, or epilepsy. Ergotism, common in the Middle Ages and caused by eating infected rye bread, also produced similar symptoms (but those suffering from it invoked St Antony of Egypt). There were therefore many people with good reason to call on St Vitus, who became especially popular in Italy, Germany, and the Slav countries. In Germany he became one of the Fourteen Holy Helpers, a devotion based in the Rhineland and discouraged, though not ended, by the Council of Trent.

Then Jesus summoned his twelve disciples and gave them authority over unclean spirits, to cast them out, and to cure every disease and every sickness.

Matthew 10:1, the closing verse of the Gospel assigned to the feast of St Vitus

16

St Germaine of Pibrac (Germaine Cousin; about 1579–1601)

Had Germaine become a nun, her short life of suffering patiently might have become almost as well known as that of Thérèse of Lisieux, another victim of tuberculosis who died young. As it is, her memory was kept alive through the respect and sorrow felt by local people in her remote French village, but they kept it alive enough for her to be declared a saint by Pope Pius IX over two hundred and fifty years after her death, when he declared that she "shone like a star not only in her native France but throughout the world-wide Church." Stripped of picturesque accretions, her life can be briefly told, though a book-length biography of her exists.

She was born in the village of Pibrac, in southern France near Toulouse, where her father was an agricultural worker. Her mother died shortly after her birth. She had a paralysed right arm and suffered from ugly swellings on her neck, probably tubercular in origin but designated as "scrofula" at the time. Her father married again, and her stepmother treated her even more unkindly than stepmothers are generally supposed to, making her sleep in the stable or under the stairs, feeding her on scraps, and keeping her away from her healthier brothers and sisters. As soon as she was old enough, she was sent to mind the sheep. She never complained and gradually developed "the practice of the presence of God," to whom she would speak directly while she was out in the fields. She had a great rapport with children younger than herself, who would have accepted her physical disabilities more easily, and gave them simple religious instruction. She went to Mass as often as she could, and gradually stories began to circulate that whenever she did so she could leave her sheep in the fields without them straying or being attacked by wolves, which were common in the region.

The adults of the village stopped seeing her as useless and deformed and began to think they had a saint in their midst. It was said that a stream in spate parted like the Red Sea to allow her to cross it on her way to Mass; that once when her stepmother chased her with a stick, accusing her of stealing bread, she let her apron fall and summer flowers fell out, even though there was snow on the ground. Her father and stepmother eventually shared the village change of mood and invited her to live like the others in the house, but she continued as before until one morning she was found dead on her pallet under the stairs. She was twenty-two years old.

She was buried in the village church, and a considerable local cult developed, with many miraculous cures reported down the years. She was beatified in 1854 and canonized in 1867. Her remains are still in the church, and an annual pilgrimage to her shrine still takes place. She was a victim of misfortune who refused to be a victim, an outcast who came in from the cold, an apparent example of patient suffering who would probably have seen her life as happy and fulfilled. In worldly terms she was simple and ignorant, but, as the bishop of Poitiers said in his eulogy at her beatification ceremony, "What she learned under the rule of divine grace, in the school of the Savior's cross, took the place of all the other kinds of knowledge."

17

St Juliana Falconieri (1270–1341)

Juliana was a niece of one of the Seven Founders of the Servite Order, or Order of the Servants of the Blessed Virgin Mary, and the second member of the family to be canonized. The seven were wealthy young men of Florence who, disenchanted with the city's worldly ways and in reaction against the Catharism that was affecting its religious life, joined the Confraternity of the Blessed Virgin, whose members were known as *Laudesi*, "Praisers." Inspired by the confraternity's chaplain, James of Poggibonsi, they increasingly renounced the world (even though two were still married) and devoted their lives to service of the Blessed Virgin. Inspired by a vision of Our Lady on the feast of the Assumption, they withdrew first to just outside Florence and then, when they were still disturbed by visitors, to the wilderness of Monte Senario north of Florence, where they built a simple church and lived lives of extreme austerity (those who had dependants having provided for them financially). They initially refused to accept recruits, but when Cardinal Castiglione told them they were living like wild animals, they asked him to devise a Rule for them and began to accept recruits. Another vision of Mary showed them a black habit, accompanied by an angel bearing a scroll with the words "Servants of Mary" on it. The seven founders were canonized jointly in 1888 and are commemorated in the Church's Universal Calendar on 17 February.

Juliana's uncle, Alexis Falconieri, was the only one of the seven not to be ordained priest, pleading his unworthiness. He was also the only one to live to see the official approbation of the Order in 1304, dying six years later at the reputed age of one hundred and ten. Juliana's parents, who were extremely wealthy, had built the church and convent of L'Annunziata in Florence for the Order, which had grown rapidly during the thirteenth century. Her father had died when she was young, and Alexis had shared her upbringing with her mother. In 1285, when Juliana was fifteen, Philip Benizi (canonized in 1671), the Order's greatest promoter, became prior general. He clothed Juliana in the habit that year, and the following year she became a tertiary. She continued to live in the family house, though observing the Rule. Her mother was so impressed by her conduct that she gave up planning her marriage and eventually placed herself under her daughter's direction.

Other tertiaries were recruited from among the young women of Florence, and Juliana installed them in the Grifoni Palace, near the church. When her mother died, in 1304, she went to the palace and asked to be admitted as a servant but was elected abbess. They adopted a habit with short, wide sleeves, leaving their hands free for work, and became known as the *Mantellate* Sisters, as it looked as though they were wearing mantles. Their principal devotion was to Our Lady of Sorrows and their main activity was caring for the sick. In due course they were fully recognized as nuns, but remained the Third Servite Order, as the Second was a congregation of contemplative nuns started by two disciples of Philip Benizi. Juliana, who is regarded as the foundress even though she was not the first to join, drew up a Rule, which was not formally recognized for another hundred years.

She remained as superior, described as conscientious and hardworking, until she died, having lived to the age of seventy-one despite excessive penances and fasting. She was buried below the altar in L'Annunziata. By the time of her death she was unable to take any solid food, even the communion wafer. On her deathbed, she begged to be able to worship the Blessed Sacrament one last time. A host was brought and placed over her heart, and it was reported that she died at that moment and the host vanished from sight, with other reports adding that the image of Jesus crucified was found impressed on her flesh at that very spot. This was referred to in the Collect prayer of the (Tridentine) Mass for 19 June: "God, who wast pleased miraculously to restore thy virgin blessed Juliana on her deathbed with the precious body of thy Son, grant . . ." She was canonized in 1737.

The Congregation has houses on mainland Europe, and in the nineteenth century it spread to England, the USA, and Canada, with the Sisters involved in education at all levels as well as providing parish ministries, hospital and prison chaplaincies, counselling services, and care of cancer and AIDS sufferers. They also provide support for single mothers, care for those with mental and physical disabilities, and support missions in Jamaica and Zaire.

18

Bd Osanna of Mantua (Osanna Andreasi; 1449–1505)

Like Catherine of Siena (see 29 Apr.) a century earlier, Osanna had her first significant religious experience at the age of five; like her she experienced a "Spiritual Espousal" to Christ; and like her she lived when the Church was going through troubled times and the papacy was hardly facing up to its responsibilities. Unlike her, however, she did not engage in public pleading about the state of the Church but confined her concerns to her prayers. Her active ministry was devoted service to others, particularly to her siblings and the ducal family.

Her parents both came from noble families, and her mother was related to the dukes of Mantua. Osanna was the eldest of many children and was still caring for some of them when she died aged fifty-six. When she was five, she precociously understood the message "life and death consist in loving God," which came to her in a vision and which led her to surrender her whole life to carrying out God's will as revealed to her day by day. She spent long hours in prayer and penitential exercises, often going into alarming trances. Her father refused to allow her to learn to read and write, occupations he considered dangerous for young ladies, but she seems to have learned all the same, probably from her brothers. He wanted her to marry, but she told him that she was to become a member of the Third Order of St Dominic. He allowed her to wear the habit for a time but not to make her profession, which she was not do for a further thirty-seven years.

When she was eighteen she had a vision in which Our Lady made her a Bride of Christ, who placed a ring on her finger. As in the case of St Catherine of Siena, this ring could not be seen but she said she could always feel it. When she was in her late twenties she had further visions, including repeated painful ones of Christ as a crucified child and sublime ones of heaven. She was also able to share in the pain of Christ's passion. She tried to conceal these experiences, but the visions came to her suddenly and she could not always conceal what was happening to her. She attended local meetings of Dominican tertiaries. They were scornful and accused her of shamming or even of being possessed by a devil. By this time her parents were dead and she was continuing to live in the family palace, devoting herself to caring for her brothers and their children.

Duke Frederick of Mantua (related to her mother) appreciated her qualities and asked her to look after his wife and their six children while he was away campaigning in Tuscany. She divided her time between care of her own family and this new responsibility, which seems to have involved acting more as major-domo than as simple housekeeper or nanny, making important decisions and becoming a valued and trusted friend of the family. She continued in the same role with Frederick's son, Francis II, and his wife, Isabella D'Este. She managed to combine all her duties with extensive charitable works, never refusing anyone who came to her for help. Her life—known from many surviving letters—was as regulated as that of a nun, austere and penitential, with long periods devoted to prayer. She was deeply distressed by the state of the Church under the dissolute Borgia pope Alexander VI and prayed to Our Lady and the saints for his salvation, but it seems that he was beyond even their intercession, for "God ever kept motionless, with aspect and countenance of wrath, and he gave no reply to anyone who prayed: not to the Madonna, not to the apostles, not to my soul."

Osanna was finally professed as a Dominican tertiary in 1501 and died four years later. The ducal family gave her a magnificent funeral and exempted her family from paying taxes for twenty years in recognition of her services.

19

St Romuald (about 950–1027)

Romuald came from a family of wealthy noblemen, the dukes of Onesti. Though used to the ways of the world in violent times, he was so distressed by seeing his father kill a relative in a dispute over property that he fled to a monastery. This followed the moderately reformed Benedictine Rule of Cluny (see St Odilo of Cluny; 1 Jan.), but Romuald embraced a far more austere way of life, to the irritation of some of the other monks. This did not prevent him from being elected abbot, but the communal way of life did not appeal to his rather prickly character: he read the Desert Fathers (see St Antony of Egypt; 17 Jan.) and decided that a solitary monastic life was the best way to achieve holiness, so he left the monastery, placed himself under the direction of a hermit near Venice, and set up hermitages in various places in northern Italy and southern France.

The rugged mountain terrain of northern Italy lent itself well to this ideal. Romuald gathered disciples, including Peter Damian (see 20 Feb.). The two founded a monastery at Campus Maldoli, or Camaldoli, named after the local lord, Maldolo, near Arezzo. The monastery was built on the lines of the foundations in the Egyptian desert, as a collection of hermits' huts in which the monks lived alone except when they came together for the liturgy and for some meals. The huts were built of stone and each had a chapel and a garden for growing subsistence produce. But Romuald provided an alternative, with a monastery developed from a villa some two miles below the hermits' huts, so the monks could choose either a solitary or a communal way of life. He devised a Rule that was a stricter version of Benedict's, with almost perpetual silence, but not intended to mark out a separate Congregation, though this came about after his death. After further years of wandering and making new foundations he died alone in his cell at Val-di-Castro on 19 June 1027.

The Camaldolese, as his followers became, divided over the years into five provinces: Romuald's original Congregation continued to embrace both the solitary and the communal monastic life, with hermitages as well as rural or urban monasteries; a new foundation was made on Cemetery Island, between Venice and Murano, in 1212, but split into hermits and communal monks; a more strictly eremitical one was made at Monte Corona in the fifteenth century; another was made in Turin in an attempt to stop the spread of plague in 1487, eventually merged with Monte Corona; the last was made in France in 1631, became tainted with Jansenism, and was suppressed at the end of the eighteenth century. The remaining four Camaldolese Congregations were reunited in 1935. There are monasteries and hermitages in Italy, Poland, France, India, Brazil, and the USA, where a monastery was established at Big Sur, California, in 1958.

20

The Martyrs of the Titus Oates "Plot" (died 1678–1680)

Titus Oates (1649–1705) was the son of an Anabaptist preacher. He studied for Anglican orders at Cambridge but was dismissed from his curacy for misconduct. He pretended conversion to Catholicism and attended various Jesuit seminaries on the mainland before being expelled, which enabled him to gain knowledge of Jesuit names. In 1677 he claimed to have uncovered a "Popish Plot" to murder King Charles II of England and place his brother, the Catholic convert James II, on the throne in his place. The supposed plot caused panic in the country for three years: James, who had been forced to resign as Lord High Admiral of England when he became a Catholic, had to retire to the Continent, and many innocent men were put to death before Oates was suspected, tried for perjury, and imprisoned for life. The whole plot was a complete fabrication, but Titus Oates was listened to at a time when people who had prospered under Cromwell's Commonealth and been impoverished at the restoration of Charles II in 1660 were ready to inform for money. There was also lingering suspicion of Jesuits and the apparent possibility that James, on his accession to the throne, would effectively undo the whole work of the Reformation in England and the establishment of the national Church. In the event, he succeeded his brother in 1685 but was overthrown in the "Glorious Revolution" of 1688 by Prince William of Orange, who had been invited to invade by leading Anglican clerics and landowners. This revolution led to the pardoning and pensioning of Titus Oates.

The martyrs who are commemorated today are five Jesuit priests: Thomas Whitbread, William Harcourt, John Fenwick, John Gavan, and Antony Turner. Fr Whitbread was the provincial superior. They were arrested and tried at a time when scurrilous broadsheets concerning Jesuits were circulating and widespread public panic made it impossible for them to receive a fair trial. The first three named were accused of plotting in Fr Fenwick's rooms to kill the king. They spent months in prison, probably because of lack of evidence, before being brought to trial with the last two. The witnesses against them, Oates and two others, were all of bad character, and Fr Whitbread was able to point to Oates' expulsion from a Jesuit college as a motive for his vindictiveness. There was no way an independent-minded judge and jury could have condemned the defendants, but Lord Chief Justice Scroggs was totally prejudiced against them and effectively ordered the jury to bring in a verdict of high treason. The five were condemned to death.

They were taken to Newgate Gaol, where the chaplain tried to convert them to Protestantism but found them "very obstinate" in their faith. On the way to the scaffold, Fr Whitbread "put off his hat" to him, a gesture he appreciated. After their execution, on 20 June 1679, the priests' friends were allowed to take away the bodies and bury them in the churchyard of St Giles in the Fields. Other victims of the plot venerated as martyrs (in order of date of death) include Edward Coleman (3 Dec. 1678); William Ireland and John Grove (24 Jan. 1679); Thomas Pickering (9 May 1679); Richard Langhorne (14 July 1679); John Plessington (19 July 1679); John Kemble (22 Aug. 1679); Thomas Thwing (23 Oct. 1680); William Howard (29 Dec. 1680); and Oliver Plunkett (1 July, 1681). Even Judge Scroggs had to see that the evidence given at the trials was a complete fabrication and began to say so, but in all some forty-five Catholics lost their lives before the Popish Plot hysteria died down. Those named here were all beatified, with many other martyrs of England and Wales, by Pope Pius XI in 1929.

21

St Aloysius Gonzaga (Aloysio Gonzaga; 1568–1591)

After a short life apparently totally dedicated to getting out of it and into heaven, this at once extremely popular yet equally "difficult" saint died of the plague at the age of twenty-three. He has been declared "patron of Catholic youth," but what is valid in his example needs some disentangling from what might seem to encourage self-destructive tendencies. Even his spiritual director, the future cardinal Robert Bellarmine (see 17 Sept.), not exactly a "liberal," who checked and revised the first Life written of him, declared his example too extreme for others to follow. So does he simply represent an outmoded notion of holiness—priggish, naïve, angular, and unattractive are adjectives that have been applied to him, to which the sentimentality of the images (still) widely found should be added—or can he convey a valid message to us today?

He needs to be understood in relation to his background, which was that of the higher nobility of most of Europe—wealthy almost beyond imagination (until recently), vicious, feuding, fond of "fraud, the dagger, poison and lust" (Fr C. C. Martindale, S.J.), for whom military prowess was the highest virtue. Aloysio, the eldest son, was brought up to play with guns and parade with troops. When he was seven he turned against the whole panoply and sought a different sort of heroism: the conquest of heaven through mortification, prayer, and complete self-denial. His family were not best pleased.

At the age of about twelve he became very ill at the great Gonzaga palace in Mantua, where he and his younger brother Ridolfo had been sent to stay. His digestion never recovered from what was diagnosed as kidney disease but may have been a psychological effect of conflict with his family. He made up his mind to cede his inheritance of the marquisate of Castiglione to Ridolfo, and dramatically increased the severity of the penances he inflicted on himself, including a total rejection of women, to the extent that he was to say he could not recognize any of his female relatives as he had never looked at them. When he was thirteen, he and Ridolfo had to accompany their father in the escort of Empress Maria of Austria to Madrid. They were made pages to the *infante* Don Diego at the court of Philip II, but even in that austere environment his austerity was seen as extreme.

It was at this time that he determined to enter the Society of Jesus, and although his mother supported him, his father was horrified at this abdication of family responsibility and set numerous relatives, clerical and lay, on him in a campaign to make him change his mind. He railed at Aloysius, sent him on tours, produced possible brides, but to no avail: Aloysius was more determined and, despite his physical frailty, had a will of steel. When finally his father locked him in his room, spied on him, and saw him kneeling on the floor, holding a crucifix and scourging himself with a whip, he gave in. On 25 November 1585, at the age of seventeen, Aloysius entered the Jesuit novitiate, where he found his superiors taking almost the same line as his family, urging him to eat more, to be sociable, to pray less.

He moved on to the years of study that mark Jesuit training, philosophy followed by theology, but saw learning as yet another worldly distraction from his quest. So the plague that struck Rome in 1589, when he was in minor orders, presented itself as a great opportunity. The Jesuits opened a hospital, and Aloysius begged in the streets for food for the sufferers and nursed them in the hospital. He caught the plague, was very ill for a time, then seemed to recover, only to relapse again in the humid Roman summer of 1590, survived the winter, and relapsed again in the spring. Significantly, he came to see his longing for death and heaven as itself sinful, and prayed to be delivered from this too. He died at around midnight in the night of 21–22 June 1591, with Fr Bellarmine reciting the prayers for the dying at his bedside.

He was a totally single-minded young man, destined for one extreme way of life, who rejected this completely and threw himself into the opposite extreme. Seeing "the world" as the first extreme and Christ as the second, he had, as he saw it, no choice. The Church proved to be almost on the side of the world, so he pursued his heroic course virtually alone. From an early age he was faced with opposition to his will, especially from his father, but the eldest son of the Gonzagas was not expected to be second best at anything, and he proved best in the contest of wills. He was canonized in 1726, over a century after his death, which suggests differing views on his holiness, and proclaimed patron of

Catholic youth three years later, a title confirmed by Pope Pius XI in 1926. He is certainly an example to young people of not being indifferent to the sin of the world.

22

SS John Fisher (1469–1535) and Thomas More (1478–1535)

These two great English martyrs did not both die on the same day, but they were canonized together in 1935, and their joint feast is celebrated on the anniversary of the death of Fisher, the first to die. This joint commemoration has been enshrined in the new edition of the Roman Martyrology and is followed here.

John Fisher rose from a modest background, being the son of a draper from Beverley in Yorkshire, through academic distinction at Cambridge. Ordained by special dispensation at the early age of twenty-two, he progressed through senior posts in the university to become vice-chancellor. In 1502 he resigned this post to become chaplain to King Henry VII's mother, Lady Margaret Beaufort. This did not sever his connection with Cambridge, as Lady Margaret was a great benefactress of that university and also of Oxford. Fisher administered her bequests in Cambridge, which produced new colleges, the teaching of Greek and Hebrew, and a huge increase in the size and scope of the library. He also brought the great Dutch Christian humanist Erasmus (1466–1536) there to teach and lecture.

In 1504 he was appointed chancellor of the university, an appointment he held till his death, and later in the same year Henry also appointed him bishop of Rochester. Though reluctant to be parted from academic life, he proved a caring and thorough bishop, later refusing larger and wealthier sees. King Henry VII and Lady Margaret both died in 1509, and he preached classic orations at their funerals. His personal life was austere in the extreme, collecting books being his only pleasure. In middle age he learned first Greek and then Hebrew. The new king, Henry VIII, declared him to be the most distinguished prelate in any kingdom.

In ecclesiastical affairs he was a reformer, but he saw reform as necessarily organic and from within. He produced the first English refutation of Luther in four large volumes. He protested against abuses but was adamant that unity had to be preserved. Inevitably, his eminent position involved him in "the king's matter" of his nullity suit against his queen and first wife, Catherine of Aragon. Fisher's integrity compelled him to support her case, and he was her most eloquent champion at the hearing of the suit. He argued passionately against the king's attempts to make himself supreme governor of the Church in

285

England and began to suffer persecution as a result. By the time the pope decided for Catherine, he had twice been imprisoned and attempts had been made on his life. When the Act of Succession of 30 March 1534 required all the king's subjects to recognize the children of Henry and his new wife Anne Boleyn as successors to the throne, Fisher's fate was sealed. He refused to take the Oath and was imprisoned in the Tower of London, charged with treason.

Exhausted, ill, and emaciated, he survived in the Tower for over a year. The pope sent him a cardinal's hat, which prompted Henry to declare that he would not have a head to put it on. He went through a farce of a trial and was condemned to death on 17 June 1535. Five days later he had to be carried in a chair to the place of execution on Tower Hill, though he summoned the strength to walk the final steps to the scaffold. He told the crowd that he was dying for the faith of Christ's Holy Catholic Church. His head was impaled on London Bridge until, fourteen days later, it was removed to make way for that of Thomas More.

Thomas was the only surviving son of a barrister, Sir John More, and went to school in London, where at the age of thirteen he joined the household of the archbishop of Canterbury and Lord Chancellor of England, John Morton. Morton sent him to Oxford, from which his father removed him after two years (when he was only sixteen), thinking he was coming under dangerous humanist influences. He made his son study law in London, but Thomas' enthusiasm for Greek and the new learning continued, helped by his friendship with Erasmus, which began in 1497. Together they sought ways of reconciling Catholic tradition with Greek classical scholarship.

More spent four years living at the London Charterhouse, considering whether to join the Carthusians or the Franciscans or to become a diocesan priest. But then he married Jane Colt, who died four years later, leaving him with four children. A month later he married Alice Middleton, seven years his senior. He managed his household as part monastery and part school, sleeping only four or five hours a night in order to combine a secular career as lawyer with observance of much monastic discipline and pursuit of learning. He took care over the education of his daughters together with that of his son. The household met for daily prayers, and there was reading from the scriptures at meals. Hospitality was extended more to poorer acquaintances than to the wealthy and noble who might advance his career.

More earned the favour of Henry VIII, who came to the throne in 1509. He was appointed reader at Lincoln's Inn and under-sheriff of London, then knighted and given other public offices, including Speaker of the House of Commons and High Steward of both Oxford and Cambridge Universities. In

1515 Cardinal Wolsey sent him with a trade delegation to the Netherlands, where the negotiations failed to make progress, enabling him to write the second part of *Utopia* while staying with a humanist friend, Peter Gilles. This account of an ideal state—"no where"—was largely a learned frolic, though it owed a lot to monastic ideas of communal living. The first part was added on his return to London and was a savage attack on the current state of the criminal law. The king might well have enjoyed the book; in any event More was drawn closer into his circle, as both friend and adviser. His public career advanced further, and in 1529 he was appointed Lord Chancellor of England in succession to Wolsey.

Like Fisher, he was inevitably drawn into the question of the king's divorce. Ever the subtle lawyer, he tried to avoid expressing a personal opinion on the matter, confining himself to expounding the law, but he could not avoid counselling against Henry's marriage to Anne Boleyn and was forced to resign as Lord Chancellor after only three years in the post. He refused to attend her coronation ceremony. Reduced to poverty, he lived quietly with his family until, like Fisher, he was summoned to take the Oath required by the Act of Succession. He refused, still giving no personal reasons, in the belief that he was safe as long as he said nothing that could be construed as treasonable. He was first put under the custody of the abbot of Westminster and then, when he again refused to take the Oath, imprisoned in the Tower.

There he steadfastly upheld his duty to his conscience, refusing all his family's efforts to seek reconciliation with the king and consequently reducing them to absolute penury. His absolute acceptance of his cross imposed suffering on others, but his love for his family—and theirs for him—remained constant, if strained, as shown in his letters to his eldest daughter, Margaret. He was tried on 1 July 1535 and finally declared that no "temporal lord could or ought to be head of the spirituality." This was accounted treason, and he was executed four days later, famously joking on the scaffold and declaring that he died "the king's good servant, but God's first."

More's position as Lord Chancellor, the classic status of his *Utopia*, the evident complexity of his character, and the frequent portrayal of him and his family by his friend and contemporary Hans Holbein have combined to make him a far more familiar figure than Fisher. Their witness and integrity are equal, however, and both died for standing in the way of a monarch bent on imposing his absolute will on the religious and civil life of his country.

Give me, good Lord, a longing to be with thee: not for the avoiding of the calamities of this wicked world, nor of the pains of hell neither, nor so much for attaining the joys of heaven ... as even for a very love of thee.
Prayer of St Thomas More

23

St Etheldreda (died 679)

This most popular of early English women saints was the daughter of royalty and sister of three other saints, Sexburga, Ethelburga, and Withburga (only the second of whom—who became a nun—features in the new Roman Martyrology). Etheldreda's marriage portion was the Isle of Ely, given by her first husband, Tonbert, who died after some three years of (unconsummated) marriage. She retired there after his death and led a solitary life of prayer for five years, but then her family persuaded her to marry Egfrith, son of King Oswy of Northumbria, a boy of fifteen at the time. He too agreed at first that their marriage should be continent, but later he wanted them to live as man and wife. Ethelburga refused and appealed for advice to Wilfrid of York (see 24 Apr.), who decided that her vow of virginity should be respected; so she left Egfrith and went to live in the convent at Coldingham, where her aunt was abbess. Egfrith married again and took his revenge on Wilfrid by dividing his huge diocese and exiling him from York.

In 673 Etheldreda founded a double monastery at Ely, where she remained as abbess for the rest of her life, which was to amount to only six years. Personally very austere, she ate just one meal a day, wore wool rather than the fine linen more usual for "ladies," religious included, and spent the time from Matins to dawn in prayer vigil. She died from plague, which produced a tumour in her neck—maliciously said in some quarters to be a punishment for her youthful vanity in wearing necklaces. When her body was moved to a stone shrine provided by Sexburga seventeen years later, it and the simple wooden coffin were found to be incorrupt, and the tumour—which had been lanced by a doctor—had healed. Her body was later moved again, first into the new choir at Ely built in the early twelfth century, then into a new shrine (with supposed relics of St Alban). This was destroyed by Reformers in 1541, but some relics are claimed by St Etheldreda's church at Ely Place in the City of London. The popular version of her name is Audrey, and the cheap necklaces and other trinkets sold at the great annual St Audrey's Fair held in her honour gave rise to the term "tawdry," hardly a fitting epithet for one of her grandeur and austerity.

24

St Alban (Third Century)

Alban is the first recorded martyr of Britain. The earliest surviving account of his death is provided by the Welsh abbot Gildas, writing in about 540, and the Venerable Bede (see 25 May) gives a fuller account in Book 1, Chapter 7 of his *Ecclesiastical History*, written in about 730. Bede dates his martyrdom to "the twenty-second day of June" and gives the place as "near the city of Verulamium, which the British now call Verlamacaestir or Vaeclingacaestir"—now Saint Albans after the martyr.

According to Bede's account, Alban was not yet a Christian when he gave shelter to a priest fleeing from pursuers. Over some days, the priest instructed him, and he "sincerely accepted Christ." Rumour of the priest's hiding place reached the "evil ruler", but when soldiers arrived to take him away, Alban donned his cloak and offered himself in his place. He was taken before a judge, who "happened to be standing before an altar, offering sacrifice to devils." The judge told him that he would suffer all the tortures planned for the priest unless he renounced his Christianity, but Alban refused, refusing also to give any details about his family, other than that his parents had named him Alban and that "I worship and adore the living and true God, who created all things." The judge ordered him to be flogged and, when this failed to shake his resolve, to be beheaded immediately.

Bede then pursues the narrative with an interesting mixture of miracle and naturalistic detail. The place appointed for the execution was an arena some five hundred yards outside the city wall, separated from the city by a fast-flowing river spanned by a bridge. The dense crowds on the bridge made it impossible for Alban, "who desired a speedy martyrdom," to reach the place, so he prayed, and the river dried up, enabling him to cross. When the man appointed to behead him saw this he threw down his sword and asked to die in his place. Another man eventually picked up the sword and beheaded both Alban and the man who had refused to kill him. But, Bede recounts, he "was not permitted to boast of his deed, for as the martyr's head fell, the executioner's eyes dropped out."

Bede and Gildas before him describe the place in some detail, even allowing for the symbolic aspects of the water: "This hill, a lovely spot as befitted the occasion, was clad in a gay mantle of many kinds of flowers. Here was neither cliff nor crag, but a gentle rising slope made smooth by nature, its beauty providing a worthy place to be hallowed by a martyr's blood. As he reached the summit, holy Alban asked God to give him water, and at once a perennial spring bubbled up at his feet—a sign to all present that it was at the martyr's prayer that the river also had dried in its course … but the river, having performed its due service, gave proof of its obedience and returned to its natural course." Neither Gildas, a solitary on an island in the Bristol Channel, nor Bede, a monk in even more distant Northumbria, could have known the topography of Saint Albans (which is accurately portrayed, except for the size of the River Ver), so it seems likely that they were both drawing on an earlier source—possibly one with a Celtic origin, in view of the appreciation of natural beauty it expresses.

There was in fact no persecution in the West at the time to which Bede dates the martyrdom, and there has long been debate about the actual date. Some scholars have suggested a time almost a century earlier, around 209, under Severus, but the consensus now appears to place it during persecutions under Decius or Valerian I, so in the mid-third century. The fact that he was killed with a sword implies that Alban was a Roman citizen, and that he could shelter a priest suggests he owned a house of some size. His name is unusual for a Romano-Briton and may indicate that he came from the Albanus region of Italy, so he could have been a Christian escaping persecution on the Continent.

Devotion to St Alban extended, not unnaturally, to attempts to identify the priest whom he sheltered, and a mistranslation of an early document, embellished by later pilgrim-seeking abbots and chroniclers, may have given rise to the creation of "St Overcoat." Severus was accompanied on his Scottish campaign by his son Antoninus, who wore an overcoat of a type known as a *caracalla*, which led to him being nicknamed Caracalla. So *"et Caracalla"* (meaning "and his son") came to be understood as "with his overcoat." Later, the term *caracalla* dropped out of common usage, and an overcoat became an *amphibalon*. A copyist mistakenly moved the "with his overcoat" two lines down, to a reference to Alban and his priest companion, who thus became known as *Amphibalus*. Remains "discovered" four miles from St Albans in the twelfth century were declared to be his; this was taken up by the chronicler Geoffrey of Monmouth, and "St Overcoat" was established. The problem with this delightful theory is that it suggests the less likely dating of 209, under Severus, for Alban's martyrdom.

An earlier account than Gildas or Bede, the *Vita S. Germani*, written by Constantius of Lyons in about 480, helped to spread the story of Alban beyond Britain and to allow his fame to survive the collapse of the Roman Empire. When Pelagianism was rife in Britain, the British bishops sought help from France and invited Germanus of Auxerre and Lupus of Troyes to come and refute its proponents. This they did, in 429 (surviving a sea whipped up by demons), and after the "abominable heresy" had been (temporarily) put down, Germanus visited Alban's tomb, "to return thanks to God through him." He deposited relics of "all the Apostles and several martyrs" in the tomb, and took away some earth from the place where Alban had been killed: "This earth was seen to have retained the martyr's blood, which had reddened the shrine." After campaigning with the Britons and winning a victory over the Saxons and Picts through great shouts of "Alleluia!," Germanus returned to France, his voyage kept smooth by his merits "and the prayers of the blessed martyr Alban" (Bede, 1, 17–21).

25

St Paulinus of Nola (about 354–431)

Wealthy but not attached to his wealth, a man of deep culture but not given to making much of his scholarship, a fine administrator but prepared to abandon high office in order better to serve God, Paulinus seems in many ways to embody the sophisticated world-weariness characteristic of the latter days of the Roman Empire. He was born in Bordeaux, son of the prefect of Gaul, and was tutored by the great poet Ausonius, the master of fleeting life and initiator of the "gather roses while ye may" theme. His family owned lands in Italy and Spain as well as in Aquitaine, the province of which Bordeaux was the principal city. He trained as an advocate and acquired a great reputation for eloquence. He travelled extensively and held several posts in the imperial administration.

He married a Spanish woman named Therasia, but the marriage was childless for some years. Resigning his public offices, Paulinus and his wife retired to their Aquitaine estates, where he devoted himself to leisure and literature. Under the influence of Bishop Delphinus of Bordeaux, he was baptized, after which the couple moved to their Spanish estates near Barcelona. There a son was born, but he died in infancy. This may have been the spur for Paulinus to give away most of his money to the poor of Barcelona. They responded by clamouring for him to be ordained priest, and the bishop obliged them on Christmas Day 393. (He was not ordained to any particular "charge"; the same was true of his pen-friend Jerome [see 30 Sept.], and their cases may have been in the minds of the Fathers at Chalcedon in 451 when in their canon 6 they declared that "No man is to be ordained without a charge … but whoever is ordained must be appointed particularly to some charge in a church of a city, or in the country, or in a martyry or monastery.")

Paulinus did not reward the people of Barcelona by staying among them but moved to Italy. He had supported Jerome's candidacy for the papacy, which led to a frosty reception from Pope Siricius, Jerome's rival, who had been elected, though he was warmly welcomed by Ambrose (see 7 Dec.) in Milan. He and his wife settled on their estate at Nola, near Naples. There they engaged in philanthropic works to provide for the most needy and also engaged in public building works, including an aqueduct. Both Paulinus and Therasia lived like hermits, he in a cell near the tomb of St Felix of Nola, though they still received numerous and distinguished guests. Refusing pleas by numerous friends to return to public life, Paulinus continued his reclusive life until about 409, when the bishop of Nola died and he was chosen to succeed him.

As bishop he is said to have been wise and liberal. Unlike many bishops at the time, he stayed almost continually in his diocese, making just one annual journey to Rome for the feast of SS Peter and Paul (29 June). He continued his scholarly pursuits, consulting both St Jerome and St Augustine (see 28 Aug.) on matters such as obscure points of biblical interpretation. He lacked the grand sweep and passion of both these giant figures, and Jerome was somewhat dismissive of his "many short works in verse." He was the recipient of Jerome's letter complaining about the throng of pilgrims making Jerusalem a worse place to live than the western cities he had escaped from: "Men rush here from all quarters of the world, the city is filled with people of every race, and so great is the throng of men and women that what you used partially to escape elsewhere, you must here put up with in its entirety" (Letter 58.4). Paulinus must have felt grateful for the relative tranquillity of Nola. He died there and was buried in a new church he had built in homage to St Felix, richly adorned with mosaics. His remains were moved to Rome but restored to Nola by Pope Pius X in 1909. Some thirty poems, fifty letters, and some other fragments of his writing survive, enough to show him to have been one of the best Christian poets of his age, comparable to Prudentius.

26

St John Southworth (died 1654)

John came from a Lancashire family that remained staunchly Catholic through long years of persecution and as a result had been impoverished by payment of heavy fines for not attending official Church of England worship. The date of his birth has been put as 1592 (by Challoner) or as early as 1584. He was sent to Douai in 1613 to train for the priesthood and was ordained at Cambrai in 1618. In December the following year, after some six months trying his vocation with Benedictines, he embarked on the English mission. Little is known of his first years there, except that he worked around London, and in 1624, perhaps in poor health, he returned to Douai. After some months there he was sent as confessor to the Benedictine nuns in Brussels.

In 1626 he was back in England, this time in his native Lancashire. He was arrested after about a year's ministry and formally condemned to death for being a priest, but the sentence was commuted to imprisonment in Wisbech

Castle. Charles I's queen consort, Henrietta Maria (daughter of Henri IV of France), had been allowed to continue practising as a Catholic by the terms of her marriage settlement and had brought many French Catholic nobles with her. This was not generally popular, but her influence was such as to prevent the law from being enforced strictly. John seems never to have been sent to Wisbech but to have remained in prison in Lancaster. Three years later he was sent to London and, with fifteen other priests, released at the queen's insistence.

He was ordered to leave the country but seems not to have done so; in 1632 he was in the Clink jail in London, where his conditions of imprisonment allowed him "full liberty to walk abroad at his pleasure", as a Puritan fellow-prisoner complained, and to sign numerous petitions. In the summer of 1636 the plague struck London, and John, with Fr Henry Morse, helped to bring relief (mostly supplied by the queen) to suffering Catholics, who were denied any other aid. Priests known to be saying Mass in London (as John was) were generally left alone for a time, then arrested and briefly imprisoned. John spent some weeks in the Fleet prison in the summer of 1640.

In the Civil War, which broke out in 1642, the parliamentarians regarded all Catholics as royalists, but John seems to have remained at relative liberty until he was arrested in 1654. Cromwell, who came to power after the execution of Charles I in 1649, was more inclined to fine Catholics than to kill their priests. Priests for their part were often more involved in collecting money to keep the mission going than in proselytizing. John was appointed collector for London and Middlesex in 1653. A year later, against the general trend of the time, he was indicted for practising as a priest and condemned to death, despite the efforts of the judge to get him to plead "not guilty" and determined efforts by the French and Spanish ambassadors to save him. The full brutal sentence of hanging, drawing, and quartering was carried out before a huge crowd, who listened respectfully as he declared that he died "for Christ's law, which no human law, by whomsover committed, ought to withstand or contradict."

His history after his death is rather more remarkable than his life. The pieces of his body were bought by the Spanish ambassador, sewn together at the expense of a member of the Howard family, and smuggled out of the country to Douai. There they were greatly venerated and at some date enclosed in a lead coffin. To save the body from profanation when the college was seized in 1793 during the French Revolution, it was buried under the refectory floor and escaped discovery. When the foundations of the building (no longer a Catholic seminary) were being excavated in 1927, the coffin was discovered, and the remains were identified and brought back in triumph to St Edmund's College at Ware, which was carrying on the work of Douai. John was one of the English Martyrs beatified in 1929, and the following year his body was moved to Westminster Cathedral and solemnly enshrined there. He was canonized as one of the Forty Martyrs of England and Wales in 1970. There is an almost contemporary account of a conversation he held shortly before his arrest with the president of Douai, Dr George Leyburn, who was in London. John asked to be allowed to return with him to the college, on the grounds of his advanced age (seventy or seventy-two). Leyburn refused his request, saying he was too "zealous a missioner" to be spared. "Well, sir," John replied, "if you will not let me go with you, at least I'll follow you." As indeed he did.

27

St Cyril of Alexandria (376–444)

Cyril was the leading champion of orthodox doctrine in the theological debates over the nature(s) of Christ that led up to the Council of Ephesus in 431, at which his formulations carried the day. His methods earned him what must be the most vitriolic "obituaries" of any saint. A nephew of Patriarch Theophilus of Alexandria, he seems to have supported his uncle in deposing and exiling St John Chrysostom (see 13 Sept.) from Constantinople on what can only be described as frivolous charges. He succeeded his uncle as patriarch in 412 and proceeded to drive out the Jews and shut the churches of the schismatic Novationists in the name of preserving orthodoxy. The atmosphere of violence and intolerance whipped up by his supporters, if not by Cyril himself, led to the murder of a Neoplatonist woman philosopher named Hypatia, which led to a quarrel between Cyril and the imperial prefect, Orestes.

Theologically, his principal enemy was Nestorius, who became archbishop of Constantinople in 428. He taught that Christ's human body was only the "temple" of his divine spirit, and that Mary was the mother of the human person of Christ alone, so could be called *Christokotos*, Christ-bearer, but not *Theotokos*, God-bearer. Cyril saw this as undermining the doctrines of the incarnation and redemption and referred the question to Rome. Pope Celestine I upheld his teaching and charged him with forcing Nestorius to retract. When Nestorius refused, Cyril convened the Council of Ephesus. He started the debates before the archbishop and forty-one bishops of Antioch, many of whom would have supported Nestorius, had arrived, let alone the papal legates. Nestorius refused to plead before the council and was eventually condemned and exiled, though not until at one point both Cyril and he had been arrested on the emperor's orders. From exile, Nestorius wrote: "Cyril is therefore pro-secutor and accuser, and I the defendant ... I was summoned by Cyril, who assembled the council, by Cyril who presided. Who was judge? Cyril! Who was accuser? Cyril!! Who was Bishop of Rome? Cyril!!! Cyril was everything."

For Cyril it must have been a question of the end justifying the means, and the end for him was vital. He saw how central the *Theotokos* definition was to the whole structure of faith, as an essential affirmation about Christ. If Mary could not be said to be Mother of God, then Christ could not be said to be true God and true man. He wrote to Archbishop John of Antioch, two years after the council, setting out the essence of his position:

> We confess, therefore, our Lord Jesus Christ, the only-begotten Son of God, perfect God and perfect Man, consisting of a rational soul and a body begotten of the Father before the ages as touching his Godhead, the same, in the last days, for us and for our salvation, born of the Virgin Mary, as touching his Manhood; the same of one substance with the Father as touching his Godhead, and of one substance with us as touching his Manhood. For of two natures a union has been made. For this cause we confess one Christ, one Son, one Lord. In accordance with this sense of the unconfused union, we confess the holy Virgin to be *Theotokos*, because God the Word became incarnate and was made man ... You ought, I say, to be aware that almost the whole of our contention for the faith has grown out of our affirmation that the holy Virgin is *Theotokos*.

Cyril had undoubtedly grasped the essence and the importance of the argument, but there is room to doubt the impossibility of finding some way of extending the sense of the Nestorians' "moral union" of the two natures in Christ to embrace the orthodox position. But the definition of "truth" was then the equivalent of today's political and religious disputes in the Middle East, and no compromise was sought or found. Nestorius and his followers became a schismatic Church; Cyril was eventually declared a Doctor of the Church in 1882. The kind of feeling he provoked is illustrated by a letter (attributed, possibly correctly, to Theodoret) written shortly after his death: "At last and with difficulty the villain has gone. ... His survivors are indeed delighted at his departure. The dead, maybe, are sorry. There is some ground of alarm lest they should be so annoyed at his company as to send him back to us. ... Great care must then be taken ... to tell the guild of undertakers to lay a very big heavy stone upon his grave, for fear he should come back again and show his changeable mind once more." And there is more in the same vein, prompting one scholar, G. L. Prestige, to comment: "It affords striking testimony to Cyril's greatness. Small men do not earn such heartfelt obituaries, even from deeply indignant saints."

28

St Irenaeus of Lyons (about 125–202)

Irenaeus, a Greek from Asia Minor, belonged to the generation that learned from those who had learned directly from the disciples. In his case, his teacher was the martyr Polycarp (see 23 Feb.), who had been a disciple of St John the Evangelist (see 27 Dec.). Irenaeus had clear and detailed memories of Polycarp's teaching. He then spread the apostolic tradition he had received to Gaul.

In the second century Lugdonum, now Lyons, became the main trading port of western Europe and the first city of Gaul, expanding on trade from the East conveyed by boat up the River Rhône. Missionaries followed the traders, and Irenaeus was one of the earliest of these. By the year 177, Christians in Lyons were being subjected to fierce persecution (see The Martyrs of Lyons and Vienne; 2 June). Irenaeus escaped because the first bishop of Lyons, Pothinus, had sent him on a mission to Rome concerned with another matter. He stayed in Rome for probably some years and returned to Lyons as its second bishop, spending the next twenty years rebuilding the Church in the Rhône valley and evangelizing the adjoining areas. He seems to have been devoted to his people and spoke to them in their vernacular rather than his native Greek.

Irenaeus is remembered mainly for his major treatise, *Against Heresies*. In his time Gnosticism was widespread. This took many forms, but its chief tenet was that the world was under the control of angelic beings, good and evil, while God remained aloof from it. This directly contradicted the doctrine of the incarnation. Another feature was that it spread as a form of secret knowledge reserved to initiates, who regarded themselves as better than anyone else. This ran counter to Christ's command that the gospel was to be taught to all. Irenaeus refuted both these doctrines: "God sustains the universe in being. His nature and greatness cannot be seen or described by any of the creatures he has made. But he is known to all of them. The Word proclaims to all that there is one God, the Father, who holds all things in being and gives being to all creatures." *Against Heresies*, written in Greek, was soon translated into Latin and effectively destroyed Gnosticism as a serious threat (though it has resurfaced in various guises in later centuries). The full text survives in Latin, whereas another work by Irenaeus, *Proof of the Apostolic Teaching*, was lost and came to light only in 1904, showing him to have produced a comprehensive and systematic Christian theology.

In about 190 he was asked to mediate between the pope and a group in Asia Minor known as the Quartodecimans, who followed their own tradition, not the Western usage, in calculating the date of Easter. Irenaeus persuaded the pope that this was not a matter on which the Church should be divided and so averted a schism. He died in about 202, probably a natural rather than a martyr's death, and his body was buried in what was then the church of St John in Lyons, later St Irenaeus. The shrine was destroyed by Calvinists in 1562.

The Father is above all, and he is the head of Christ, but the Word is through all things, and he is himself the head of the Church, while the Spirit is in us all; and his

is the living water which the Lord gave to those who believe in him and love him and know that there is one Father above all things and through all things and in all things.

St Irenaeus on the Trinity

29

St Peter (died about 64)

Liturgically, today's feast is that of St Peter and St Paul, remembered together in Rome from very early times, but Paul has been considered here on 25 January, the feast of his conversion, so today is reserved for St Peter, who has always had a more prominent part in its liturgy. Peter is known to us from the texts of the New Testament, which tell his story up to the "Council of Jerusalem" in the year 50 or 51. His subsequent life and association with Rome are the subjects of tradition, strongly supported by archaeological evidence.

Peter came from Bethsaida in Galilee, and was Andrew's (see 30 Nov.) brother. They were fishermen, working with the sons of Zebedee, James (the Greater; see 25 July) and John (see 27 Dec.). Peter and Andrew were the first to be called by Jesus to follow him, and "Immediately they left their nets and followed him" (Matt. 4:20; Mark 1:18). Peter was married, and Jesus cured his mother-in-law of a fever (Mark 1:30–31). His original name was Simon, or Symeon in the local Aramaic, but Jesus said he should be known as *Cephas* (Greek for rock). *Petros* was another Greek word for rock, hence Peter, or Simon Peter, as he is often referred to in the New Testament, and the famous (though probably later) saying, "You are Peter and upon this rock [*tu es Petrus et super hanc petram*] I will build my church."

He is given a leadership role in the New Testament texts, and it is he who makes the supreme confession of faith in Jesus: "You are the Messiah, the Son of the living God" (Matt. 16:16). His name comes first in lists; he asks questions on behalf of the others; he is named first in key incidents such as the raising of Jairus' daughter, the transfiguration, and the agony in the garden. Yet he is no mere figurehead: his character comes across strongly from the texts: enthusiastic, as when he wants to make tents so that they can stay at the scene of the transfiguration; impulsive, as when he tries to walk across the waters of the lake to Jesus; with a streak of weakness, as shown by the triple denial after Jesus' arrest. This character is supported by an artistic tradition, firm from early times, which represents him as burly and thickly bearded, often contrasted with a thin, ascetic, sparsely bearded Paul.

After the resurrection, his triple denial is forgiven and, in Jesus' final speech in John's Gospel, mirrored in a triple commission: "Feed my lambs . . . tend my lambs ... feed my sheep." At Pentecost he is the first to address the crowds, astonishing them by the transformation from the cowed group hiding in an upper room, and telling them that God had poured out his spirit "that you see and hear" (Acts 2:33). He performs the first cure worked in the name of the risen Lord (Acts 3:6); faces up to the learned members of the Sanhedrin (Acts 4:5–22); confirms the first mission outside Israel, that of Philip the Deacon (Acts 8:14–17); and is convinced that the good news must be taken to the Gentiles, through the dream related in Acts 10:9–16, in which God effectively overturns the Jewish purity laws in which he has been educated. He puts his new conviction into effect by baptizing the Roman centurion Cornelius and the members of his household. He then leaves James in charge of the Church in Jerusalem and undertakes a series of missionary journeys.

As the Church grew, so it aroused fears in the empire and incurred persecution. King Herod Agrippa had James killed and Peter arrested and imprisoned. He was dramatically rescued (see Acts 12:1–11), after which he seems to have withdrawn to safety for a time. He is heard of in Antioch and probably in Corinth. The First Letter of Peter is written from "Babylon" (meaning Rome), and this is generally taken to be authentic (though the Second Letter is much later), indicating that he was in Rome. It is generally accepted that he was martyred there under Nero (emperor from 54 to 68), but no written account has survived. The tradition that he was crucified, head down at his own wish so as not to be seen imitating Jesus, can be traced back to the early third century, and there is evidence from the catacombs that there was devotion to him and Paul in Rome by the same date.

Constantine built a basilica in the fourth century to house his tomb, holding bones moved from the catacombs. The present basilica was built on the same site in the sixteenth century, and excavations in the twentieth century seem certainly to have uncovered his tomb, even if they cannot prove that the bones it contains are his. If they are, the traditional representation of him as a man of heavy build, quite elderly by the time he died, is confirmed. Whatever his status was in Rome, it now seems that the tradition that he was martyred there is correct. This, added to the way he is portrayed in the New Testament, keeps his name at the head of lists of Bishops of Rome. He is patron of fishermen and regarded as holder of the keys to the kingdom of heaven.

When they had finished breakfast, Jesus said to Simon Peter, "Simon son of John, do you love me more than these?" He said to him, "Yes, Lord; you know that I love you." Jesus said to him, "Feed my lambs." A second time he said to him, "Simon son of John, do you love me?" He said to him, "Yes, Lord; you know that I love you." Jesus said to him, "Tend my sheep." He said to him the third time, "Simon son of John, do you love me?" Peter felt hurt because he said to him the third time, "Do you

love me?" And he said to him, "Lord, you know everything; you know that I love you." Jesus said to him, "Feed my sheep."
 John 21:15–17

30

Bd Raymund Lull (Ramón Llull; 1232–1316)

Raymund Lull has never formally been beatified (and indeed had his major work condemned by a pope), but he is patron of Majorca and led an extra-ordinary life amply documented in a contemporary account known to have been related by him to his followers at their request. His life's work was an attempt to reconcile Christians and Muslims, which gives him an exeptional degree of contemporary relevance.

He was born in what was then the independent kingdom of Majorca in 1232 (or possibly 1235), at a time when the island had just been reconquered from the Moors in a military campaign in which his father took part. He was a page at court, then marshall and high steward to King James. He enjoyed his wealth more than prudence counselled and the company of women more than his marriage vows permitted. The society in which he grew up was a mixed Moorish and Christian one—more cultured and sophisticated than most as a result. When Raymund was thirty, he had a sudden vision of Christ crucified; this was repeated five times and finally convinced him that it was telling him to renounce his current way of life and devote all his energies to converting the Moors.

He threw himself into this endeavour as enthusiastically as he had thrown himself into the culture, leisure, luxury, and lust of court life. He went on pilgrimage to Santiago and then to Rocamadour, home to a twelfth-century black Virgin. Thus fortified, he returned home, provided generously for his family, and then sold his other possessions and gave the proceeds to the poor. He spent the next nine years learning Arabic and planning a missionary college in Majorca for the conversion of Muslims. This did not seem such an impos-sible task theologically: both faiths shared belief in the one God of the Hebrew Scriptures; Muslims regarded Jesus as the greatest prophet before Muhammad, though Christians were less complimentary about Muhammad; in Spain and the Balearic Islands, despite wars, Christians and Muslims had lived together and exchanged a great deal of their cultures.

The climate of the times was more one of crusade than of conciliation, however, and Raymund found little support for his great plan. He was a lay-man, for a start, with no bishop or religious Order to back him. He tried to promote his ideas in Rome, in Paris, and in Genoa, but with scant success. The

Franciscans eventually accepted him as a tertiary—St Francis himself (see 4 Oct.) had, after all, gone to the Holy Land in an (equally unsuccessful) attempt to convert the Saracens. He succeeded in getting to Tunis and preaching in the streets, but he made little impression and was beaten and deported to Naples. He appealed in vain for help to Pope Boniface VIII in Rome and to his rival claimant, Clement V, in Avignon. He then made an equally ineffectual journey to Cyprus, followed by a return to Africa, where he was once more beaten and deported. This time he was shipwrecked on his way back to Naples. Further appeals to the papacy, to the Council of Vienne in 1311, and then to the university of Paris went unheeded. A lesser man would have despaired long before now, but he went back to Africa. At Budia in Algeria he was stoned so severely that he was left for dead. Some Genoese sailors rescued him and brought him back to Majorca, but he finally died from his injuries within sight of Palma harbour on 29 June 1316 (though some local accounts say it was in winter). His shrine is in the church of San Francisc in Palma.

In the midst of all his travels and travails, Raymund wrote (in Catalan) many theological and philosophical works, the mystical treatise *Book of the Lover and the Beloved*, and a romance, *Blanquerna*. His *Ars magna* was condemned by Pope Gregory XVI in 1376 for trying to show that all knowledge could be deduced by reason from first principles (so denying the need for revelation). Seldom can anyone's great ideals have generated less recognition: the fact that he came from Majorca, so recently under Muslim rule, cannot have helped; nor can his lay status and trenchant criticisms of church abuses, making him too independent by half. He had to wait till 1928 for any positive papal comment, when Pope Pius XI praised him in his encyclical *Orientalium rerum*. In Majorca he is venerated as the Enlightened Doctor, and a society of followers, the Lullists, devote themselves to studying the most esoteric aspects of his works, such as mysticism and alchemy.

Other Familiar English names for June

1. John, Justin
2. Dominic, John, Nicholas, Peter
3. Charles, Isaac, John, Kevin, Olive
4. Francis, Nicholas, Philip
5. Dominic, Luke
6. Alexander, Laurence, Peter, William
7. Anne, Antony, Mary, Paul, Peter, Robert
8. James, John, Mary, William
9. Andrew, Anne, Joseph, Robert, Richard, Vincent
10. Diana, Henry, John, Thomas, Walter
11. John, Mary, Mary-Rose, Paula, Stephen
12. John, Laurence, Stephen
13. Augustine, Gerard, Nicholas
14. *There are no familiar names today*
15. Barbara, Bernard, Louis, Peter, Ralph, Thomas
16. Andrew, Dominic, Guy, Mary, Thomas, Vincent
17. Paul, Peter, Philip, Teresa
18. Elizabeth, Gregory, Mark
19. Humphrey, Sebastian, Thomas, William
20. Antony, Dermot, Francis, John, Margaret, Thomas, William
21. James, John, Joseph, Ralph
22. Mary
23. Joseph, Mary, Peter, Thomas
24. John, Joseph
25. Dominic, Dorothy, Francis, Henry, John, William
26. David, Frances, Joan, John, Joseph, Madeleine, Teresa
27. George, John, Margaret, Thomas
28. Jerome, Luke, Mary, Paul
29. Emma, John, Judith, Madeleine, Mary, Paul
30. Bertrand, Peter, Philip, Vincent

JULY

There are relatively few departures from the Roman Martyrology this month, though some saints have been chosen as more interesting than those featured there for the day: SS Antony and Theodosius Pechersky (Russian Orthodox) on the 10th and St Veronica (legendary) on the 12th. Martyrs of the Spanish civil war have been beatified in groups, and the process is still continuing. The main wave of killing took place in late July and early August 1936: if all the priests and religious who died are considered to have died for their faith, not for political reasons, they will become the biggest group of martyrs in history. They have a joint entry here on the 20th, with an individual entry on the 28th.

1

St Oliver Plunkett (1625–1681)

Oliver came from a wealthy landed family, with aristocratic connections on his mother's side, from Co. Meath in Ireland. Several relatives were prominent in the Confederation of Kilkenny, which led the Irish rebellion of 1641. Through the Confederation, Oliver met the Oratorian papal envoy, Fr Pierfrancesco Scarampi, who paid for his training at the Irish College in Rome. A brilliant student, he was ordained in 1654, when the penal laws in force in Ireland prevented him from returning there. He became chaplain to an Oratorian house in Rome, followed by an appointment to the missionary college of *Propaganda Fidei*, where he lectured in theology and apologetics, and also by a post at the Congregation of the Index, where he considered books of supposedly doubtful orthodoxy. He also held the post of procurator of the Irish bishops.

He was appointed archbishop of Armagh and Primate of all Ireland in 1669, probably at his request and through the intervention of Pope Clement IX. He was consecrated at Ghent on his way back to Ireland, which he reached in March 1670. With Cromwell dead for twelve years and Charles II on the throne and more sympathetic to Catholicism, there was relative peace in Ireland, but penal laws were still in effect, and Oliver still thought it safer to adopt the alias "Captain Brown" and to wear a sword and carry pistols to match his new persona. In 1670 a new viceroy proved more tolerant, and he was able to travel freely and without disguise. He found the people full of faith but lacking in instruction and organization. Very few had been confirmed, and he had soon carried out ten thousand confirmations. There was rivalry and dissension among the religious Orders and the secular clergy; Oliver set about tackling these and other deficiencies through diocesan synods and tireless pastoral activity.

In 1673 the religious climate changed for the worst once more, with bishops and religious banned from Ireland. Oliver was forced into hiding until the worst of the persecution was over, after some seven months. Even then, he had to lead a semi-clandestine life for several years. Then the revelations of the "Popish Plot" against the king's life led to a fresh outbreak of persecution. A price was put on the Irish bishops' heads, and Oliver, careless of the danger, was arrested and placed in Dublin Castle in December 1679. The following July he was tried on a trumped-up charge of trying to bring seventy thousand French troops into Ireland to overthrow English rule. In Ireland he was respected by Catholics and Protestants alike, and the charge could never have been made to stick. So the authorities moved him to London and put him on trial for treason. The English courts had no jurisdiction; the "statute of limitation" on the time between the supposed crime and the indictment had run out; the witnesses were a mixture of known criminals and apostate priests. Even a travesty on this scale, however, made no impression on the judge, Sir Francis Pemberton, for whom "endeavouring ... to alter the true religion" in Ireland was Oliver's real crime. He was found guilty, condemned to death, and hanged, drawn, and quartered at Tyburn on 1 July (by the Julian calendar) 1681.

His body was taken to a Benedictine abbey in Germany in 1684 and his head to Rome, where Cardinal Howard eventually gave it to the then archbishop of Armagh, who in turn gave it to the Dominicans in Drogheda; it is now in the memorial church built to him there. The rest of his remains spent almost two hundred years in Germany and were then brought to Downside Abbey in Somerset, where they are to this day. Some two hundred and thirty letters written by him, mostly about official diocesan business, survive. Later ones, written from prison, show an extraordinary willingness to accept the brutal way of death facing him: Tyburn was but a "flea biting" compared to the sufferings of Christ. He was the last Catholic to be martyred there. He was beatified in 1920 and canonized in 1975, the first Irishman to be canonized since St Laurence O'Toole in the thirteenth century.

Happy are we who have a second baptism, nay a third; water we received, the sacrament of penance we got, and now we have ... the baptism of blood.
St Oliver Plunkett

2

St Bernardino Realino (1530–1616)

Bernardino was born in Carpi, near Modena in northern Italy. His father sent him to study at the academy of Modena, for which he expressed his gratitude in a letter that has been preserved. He progressed from there to Bologna University, where he studied arts and medicine. He considered taking up medical practice but seems to have been steered instead toward the law by a lady with whom he fell in love. He regarded his legal studies as a route to advancement in civil administration and gained his doctorate in law in 1556.

Helped by the position of his father, who was serving in the household of Cardinal Madruzzo, prince-bishop of Trent and governor of Milan, Bernardino advanced through a series of posts to become auditor and general superintendent for the marquis of Pescara in the kingdom of Naples. His mind, however, was already moving beyond worldly position: "I have no desire for the honours of this world but solely for the glory of God and the salvation of my soul," he wrote to his brother. In Naples he came into contact with the Jesuits and decided to join them, writing to his father to tell him that he had been called to serve the Lord in a "flock of the most dear souls God has on earth, that is the Society of Jesus." He became a novice in 1564 and was ordained three years later. He was soon acting as novice-master, an early promotion indicating the respect he had earned from his superiors. The Jesuit novitiate was then moved away from Naples, but he stayed there, devoting himself to the care of the poor and of Muslim slaves. He preached, heard confessions, and directed a lay confraternity with an aristocratic membership; then in 1574 he moved to Lecce in Apulia, where he established a new Jesuit house and college and remained for the rest of his life.

He served as teacher, vice rector, and rector of the college, but was known and loved outside it for his work among the poor. As in Naples, he preached (which was not his strongest suit), counselled individuals (with greater success), and cared particularly for prisoners and slaves. He helped to reform the secular and the religious clergy of Lecce and became known as the "father of the city." Miracles began to be attributed to him during his lifetime. St Robert Bellarmine (17 Sept.), who had been his provincial, wrote of him that he had never heard a single complaint about him, that even those who disliked the Jesuits (of which there have usually been a fair number) made an exception for him, and that "everyone knows that he is a saint."

He died in 1616, but even if everyone knew he was a saint, he was not beatified till 1895 and was canonized as relatively recently as 1947. His cult shared the Neapolitan tradition of St Januarius (see 19 Sept.), though to a lesser and less apparently convincing extent, of his blood liquefying in a phial. The phenomenon, if it ever really existed, seems to have stopped some time before his beatification, and a biography produced in the year he was beatified admitted that it may not have had anything to do with his holiness, having been described only as an example of "prodigies [that] raise an interest and excitement out of all proportion to their importance or significance." The real significance of Bernardino was that such an accomplished "Renaissance man," with the world and wealth open to him, chose "the better part."

3

St Thomas (First Century)

Thomas is known from three episodes in John's Gospel, in which he appears as an individual. In the first, "Thomas, who was called the Twin, said ... 'Let us also go [to Lazarus' house], that we may die with him'" (11:16). In the second, at the Last Supper, "Thomas said to [Jesus], 'Lord, we do not know where you are going. How can we know the way?'" Jesus replies that he is the way, the truth, and the life (14:5–6). In the third, one of the best-known episodes in all the Gospels, "doubting Thomas," hiding with the other disciples in a locked house, one of the twelve, was not with them when Jesus came [to show them his wounds and thus convince them of the truth of the resurrection]. So the other disciples told him, "We have seen the Lord." But he said to them, "Unless I see the mark of the nails in his hands, and put my finger in the mark of the nails and my hand in his side, I will not believe." A week later his disciples were again in the house, and Thomas was with them. Although the doors were shut, Jesus came and stood among them and ... said to Thomas, "Put your finger here and see my hands. Reach out your hand and put it in my side. Do not doubt but believe." Thomas answered him, "My Lord and my God" (20:24a–8). He is mentioned once more as one of the disciples gathered on the shore of the Sea of Tiberias when Jesus appears and directs them to the miraculous catch of fish (21:1–14).

The disciple who questions and then doubts without the evidence of his senses becomes the only one to make a full confession of faith in Christ's divinity. His cameo role is therefore one of vital importance, and it has been suggested that he and not John should be seen as the "beloved disciple."

After this, all is tradition and conjecture. The church historian Eusebius supports the tradition that he went to preach to the Parthians, one of those

305

many nations whose people heard and understood the disciples after Pentecost, in what is now Iran. The most persistent tradition is that he went to
southern India, and the Syriac Christians of Malabar still call themselves
"Christians of St Thomas." They claim that he was martyred there in 72 and
that his body is still in Mylapore, near Madras, where he was buried. Others
claim that it was moved to Damascus and then to Italy in the late fourth
century. The Indian tradition is supported by many early authorities; Marco
Polo reported that both Christians and Saracens went on pilgrimage to his
tomb; when the Portuguese first landed in India, in 1498, they found established Christian communities.

Unfortunately, the only purported account of his work in India is an apocryphal *Acts of Thomas* dating from the third century. According to this, he
initially refused to go, pleading that a Hebrew could not teach Indians, and was
persuaded only when Christ, appearing to a merchant named Abban, sold
Thomas to him as a slave. Abban took him to his king, Gundafor, and Thomas
went with nothing but his purchase price, twenty pieces of silver, which Christ
himself had given to him. His fame increased with the discovery of the Coptic
manuscript of the *Gospel of Thomas*, much given to miracles worked by Jesus,
though it may contain some genuine sayings, in the 1940s. The *Infancy Gospel
of Thomas* tells of miracles worked by Jesus as a child, but they are completely
out of character, with no healing purpose. These works helped to make Thomas' cult very strong in the West, where his feast was traditionally celebrated
on 21 December until recent calendar reform moved it to today's date, thereby
agreeing with the Syro-Malabar traditional dating of his death. He is the patron
saint of builders, architects, and now Italian quantity surveyors, thanks to a
story in the *Acts of Thomas*, repeated in *The Golden Legend* of James of Voragine
(see 13 July), that he built a palace for a local king in India. He is also patron of
blind people, on account of his spiritual blindness.

4

St Elizabeth of Portugal (Isabel; 1271–1336)

Elizabeth was a great-niece of St Elizabeth of Hungary (see 17 Nov.), who died
forty years before her birth, and the daughter of King Pedro III of Aragon. She
was married at the age of twelve to Diniz, king of Portugal, who tolerantly
allowed her to pursue the practices of piety to which she inclined in preference
to court life. She bore him a daughter, Constanza, in 1590, and a son, Alfonso,
the following year. He was not inclined to imitate her pious way of life and
fathered a number of illegitimate children, whose care and education Elizabeth

took upon herself and who were also to play a large part in the fate of the nation.

Diniz was an able ruler, famed for the justice of his laws, but seemingly unable to deal with his own household as justly. His legitimate son Alfonso, jealous of the preference he saw being given to an illegitimate half-brother, took up arms against his father. Elizabeth attempted to make peace, but her husband resented her apparent support for Alfonso and banished her from the court for a time. She used this period of exile to pattern her life on a strict rule, with hours set apart for prayer and almsgiving. She gave generously to the sick and poor, cared for pilgrims, provided marriage dowries for poor girls, and set up hostels for repentant prostitutes. She also employed her peacemaking skills in mediating between her son-in-law, Fernando IV of Aragon, and other princes. She finally, after Alfonso had laid siege to Lisbon in 1323, succeeded in making peace between him and his father.

Diniz then fell seriously ill, and Elizabeth personally nursed him for two years, until he died. After his death Elizabeth resolved to lead a religious form of life and devote herself to works of mercy. She went on pilgrimage to Santiago de Compostela (see St James the Greater; 25 July) dressed as a Franciscan tertiary and then lived simply in a house alongside a convent of Poor Clare nuns (the second Order of St Francis) that she had founded in Coimbra. She did not take religious vows until she was on her deathbed in Estremoz, where she had gone, despite illness, on another peacekeeping mission, this time between her son, now Alfonso IV of Portugal, and the king of Castile. She died on 4 July 1336, and miracles were soon attributed to her intercession. Her cause was begun in 1576, and when her body was exhumed in 1612 it was found to be incorrupt. She was canonized in 1625 and is one of the patron saints of Portugal.

In art she is often depicted with her great-aunt, Elizabeth of Hungary. Both are sometimes shown carrying roses, from the story that when their husbands tried to prevent them giving alms to the poor the money they were carrying turned to roses. They are also shown caring for sick people with repugnant skin diseases, but the story of the dying leper placed in the marital bed, who turned into Christ when discovered by her husband, belongs to Elizabeth of Hungary, not of Portugal.

5

St Antony Zaccariah (1502–1539)

Born in Cremona in northern Italy, Antony studied medicine at the university of Padua and worked for a time as a doctor in Cremona. He then discovered that his healing vocation extended to souls as well as bodies, and, under the influence of the Dominicans, he became a priest, being ordained in 1528. Two years later he moved to Milan, where he helped Countess Louisa Torelli of Gusatalla, whose spiritual director he had become, found a women's Congregation dedicated to helping women in danger of falling into prostitution. He also founded several lay groups active in trying to improve the morals of the city.

With two Milanese noblemen, members of the Congregation of Eternal Wisdom, he then decided there was a need for a new Congregation of priests, devoted to regenerating "a properly Christian way of life by frequent preaching and faithful ministering of the sacraments"—indicating that the practice of many of the clergy left quite a lot to be desired, this being the period just before the reforms brought in by the Council of Trent. The Congregation started with five members and soon gained a reputation for preaching, with stress on Our Lord's redeeming passion, and pastoral work, including ministering to plague victims. Brought to the notice of the pope, Clement VII, it was granted formal recognition as an Order in 1533, taking the name of Clerks Regular of St Paul when the approval was confirmed two years later. (They were "of St Paul Beheaded" for a few years but then dropped the "Beheaded.")

The reforms they sought to introduce were far from popular with the regular clergy, and the Clerks were twice delated to Rome for heresy but were exonerated both times. Antony, refusing the title of provost general, set up a second house in Vicenza. He introduced the custom of ringing church bells on Friday afternoons to mark the death of Christ, spread the Milanese practice of exposing the Blessed Sacrament for three days of devotion, preached in the open air, cared for the sick, organized conferences for the clergy, and formed groups of married couples "devoted to St Paul." His spirituality was firmly Pauline, and in some ways he shared the approach of the Protestant reformers, with emphasis on a return to the New Testament and to the texts of St Paul in particular. Members of the Order lived austerely in strict poverty.

In 1539 he established the Order's headquarters at the church of St Barnabas in Milan, so its members became better known as Barnabite Fathers. He himself died the same year after a short illness, but the Order survived, growing steadily but never becoming very large. Its priests work among the poorest of the people, especially those who would now be called "excluded," mainly living in big cities. Their work spread to France, Germany, Belgium, South America, and a small missionary presence in Africa. They opened their first house in North America in Buffalo in 1952. The impetus for their foundation was not a reaction to the Protestant Reformation but a similar realization in Catholic circles that reform was needed. Some of Antony's letters and sermons survive. There are contemporary portraits, but in art he is usually portrayed holding a chalice and a host to show his devotion to the Blessed Sacrament. A statue of him as a founder of a religious Order was erected in St Peter's in 1909.

6

St Maria Goretti (1890–1902)

Seldom can any child's story have evoked such passionate interest as that of Maria Goretti, her defence of her virginity against a young male attacker, her forgiveness of him before she died as a result of the attack, and her assailant's subsequent repentance.

She was the third child born to a family of peasant farmers near Ancona in Italy. When she was eight the struggle of making the farm pay became too much and they moved into the Pontine Marshes as tenant farmers. Two years later, when Maria was ten, her father died. Marietta, as she was known, had to look after the house and the younger children while her mother worked ever longer hours in the fields. She received no formal education, but of her own accord went to the local town to receive special lessons to enable her to make her first Holy Communion, which she did in May 1902, becoming a weekly communicant (at a time when this was not usual). The family shared accommodation above an old barn with the Serenelli family, who had moved with them and worked the farm as partners. Their son Alessandro, nearly twenty years old, had formerly related to Maria rather as an elder brother, but he then began to make sexual advances to her, threatening to kill her if she told anyone. On 5 July she was alone in the house when he came back there. He dragged her inside and tried to rape her; she resisted, and he stabbed her and then fled.

She was taken to hospital but died from her wounds the next day. She was able to receive the Last Sacraments and declared that she forgave Alessandro "for the love of Jesus," adding that she hoped God would also forgive him. He was apprehended, found guilty of her murder, and—being too young for the death penalty—sentenced to thirty years in prison. He expressed remorse for what he had done, apparently after a dream in which Maria appeared to him and offered him lilies. He was released in 1929, when the process for her beatification began, and testified that at the time Maria had begged him to think of his soul and not commit such a grave sin. Maria was beatified in 1947 and canonized in the Holy Year of 1950, following a number of miracles attributed to her intercession.

It was perhaps a very Mediterranean crime, echoing a society in which a woman's "virtue" was prized above her life. The sexual aspect predominated in people's minds: she had of course done the right thing in refusing him, even at the risk to her life. Alessandro was behaving as any hot-blooded young Italian male might be expected to in attempting to "conquer" her, and rape was often the prelude to marriage, yet if she had yielded she would have been seen as guilty of grave sin. Therefore she saved her soul at the expense of her life. The fact that he was armed with a knife and had done the ultimate violence to another human being seemed to be secondary. This has more recently caused considerable disquiet, at least in Christian feminist circles, where Maria has been seen more as a martyr to a patriarchal society, which the Church has done little to condemn or attempt to change. Her canonization took place at a time before such views were expressed and drew the biggest crowd ever to attend a canonization ceremony in Rome. She has been declared the patron of the Children of Mary and of teenage girls.

7

St Willibald (about 700–786)

Willibald's life—which proved far longer than could have been expected when he was a child and is unusually well documented for the period—falls into two phases, the pilgrim and the bishop. He came from a prominent West Saxon family, and his father, brother, and sister were also all venerated as saints. His mother was St Boniface's (see 5 June) sister, and this determined the course of the second phase of his life.

As a child he was so sickly that he was not expected to live. After an apparently miraculous recovery he received a monastic education. When he was twenty years old, he embarked with his father and brother on a pilgrimage to the Holy Land, then in the hands of the Saracens. Of the three, Willibald was the only one to arrive. His father died on the way at Lucca in Tuscany (where he is still venerated as St Richard the King, even though he was not a king—his real name is unknown, and his sainthood was inferred only from that of his sons). His brother became too ill to continue once they reached Rome and stayed there.

Willibald, travelling with two other companions, progressed to Sicily and embarked from there for the Holy Land. They were twice arrested as spies in Syria, but each time seem to have been treated with common sense—if a certain amount of incomprehension—as people from unknown lands who had strange customs, and they were allowed to continue. The group, grown to seven, made its way from Damascus to Jerusalem and visited all the holy sites—Cana, Mount Tabor, Capernaum, Nazareth, the Jordan, Bethlehem— their wonder growing as they did so. Willibald also visited the monasteries of the area and learned about the Eastern monastic tradition. After a long stay in Constantinople he returned to Italy in 730. He spent the next ten years at the monastery of Monte Cassino, where his experiences of monasticism in the East enabled him to contribute to the restoration of the original Benedictine Rule.

The second phase of his life began in 740, when the pope sent him to Germany to assist St Boniface in his mission: Boniface, being his uncle, may well have asked for him personally. He was ordained priest and set about evangelizing the people of Franconia, in the upper Rhine valley. In 742, Willibald was consecrated bishop of Eichstätt, and he devoted the remaining forty-four years of his life to the pastoral care of his diocese. He founded a double monastery at Heidenheim and installed his brother Wynbald (who had survived his earlier illness) as abbot and his sister Walburga (summoned from the double monastery at Wimborne in Dorset; see 25 Feb.) as abbess. It was there that he dictated his memories of his pilgrimage to a nun: the resulting book, the *Hodoeporicon*, is effectively the first piece of Anglo-Saxon travel writing.

His body was enshrined in his cathedral in Eichstätt, where his tomb can still be seen. Walburga had also been buried there. The healing oil that flowed (and still flows) from the rock by her tomb helped to make Eichstätt a great place of pilgrimage, and attempts were made to have their father's body transferred there from Lucca to complete the picture. But the people of Lucca had no intention of parting with remains that had become so holy and famous by association: all they would send was "a little dust" collected from near the tomb.

8

Bd Eugene III (Pietro Pignatelli; died 1153)

Little is known of his early life, but he was apparently a canon in Pisa by the time he met St Bernard (see 20 Aug.) in 1137. Bernard persuaded him to become a monk at Clairvaux, where he took the name Bernard in religion. From there he moved back to Italy as abbot of the Cistercian monastery of SS Vincenzo and Anastasio outside Rome, and from there, to everyone's amazement and St Bernard's fury (more because it was something he, personally, had not planned than on account of any disapproval of Eugene), he was elected pope in 1145. He took the name Eugene and set about his task with seriousness and resolution.

He inherited a situation of warfare between the papacy and the senate of Rome over who should control the city. This had accounted for the death of his predecessor, who died of wounds received while attempting to storm the Capitol. Refusing to recognize the authority of the senate, Eugene was consecrated at Farfa and set up his court at Viterbo. He proclaimed the Second

Crusade, going to France to help Bernard, whom he had appointed to preach it there. After its complete failure, he wisely refrained from following Bernard's advice to start another and this time take Constantinople. While in France, Eugene had held three synods to examine matters of doctrine and discipline, which included examining the works of Hildegard of Bingen (see 4 Sept.), to which he gave guarded approval, though tempering this with a word of caution against pride. He became involved (again through St Bernard, without whom it was difficult for anyone to make a decision in the twelfth century) in the quarrel between Archbishops Theobald of Canterbury and William of York, leading to the latter's (possibly unfair) dismissal, and he also approved the Rule drawn up by St Gilbert of Sempringham (see 4 Feb.) for his Order of Gilbertines.

He believed that popes were given supreme temporal as well as spiritual authority, so saw to it that the reforms he proposed were accompanied by a strengthening of ties between local Churches and the papacy. He applied this policy in Ireland and in Scandinavia, where he sent Nicholas Breakspear (the future—and only – English pope, Adrian IV) as papal legate. St Bernard wrote a treatise setting out how he saw the pope's role in worldly and spiritual affairs, causing some members of the papal court to complain that he, rather than Eugene, was effectively pope, but this was unfair to Eugene, who was quite capable of acting independently of his great counsellor.

The time he spent in France had not helped his position in Rome. He required military assistance from Roger of Sicily to enable him to re-enter the city and was soon forced to leave once more. He spent three years in exile from his see and died in July of the year he was able to return. His papacy may not seem to have been great in achievements, but his personality drew some memorable tributes. Roger of Hoveden, an English chronicler, called him "worthy of the highest dignity of the papacy," and Peter of Cluny wrote to St Bernard: "Never have I known a truer friend, a more trustworthy brother, a kinder father. ... There is in him no arrogance, no domineering, no royalty: justice, humility, and reason claim the whole person." He was buried in St Peter's and miracles were soon attributed to his intercession. He was never formally beatified, but his cult was confirmed in 1872.

9

St Veronica Giuliani (Orsola Giuliani; 1660–1727)

This initially worldly daughter of a wealthy northern Italian family became a Capuchin nun and exhibited what Fr Herbert Thurston, S.J., has called "perhaps the most remarkable known" case of physical phenomena of mysticism. These were so carefully examined that there can be no question of their reality, and they caused her more than physical suffering for most of her life.

She seems to have been drawn at an early age to contemplation of Our Lord's passion, despite her enjoyment of her wealth and status. At the age of seventeen she had a vision of Our Lady, as a result of which she entered the Capuchin convent of Città di Castello, in Umbria, taking the name Veronica in religion. Three of her sisters had already become nuns, and her father was extremely reluctant to see yet another chance of a brilliant marriage escape his family. The bishop at her clothing ceremony made the psychological error of calling her a future saint, with the result that the nuns made her novitiate as harsh as they could.

She began to experience visions of Christ in his passion, and as these intensified marks of the passion began to appear on and in her body. These started with the imprint of the crown of thorns on her head; then after an experience of "mystical marriage" her heart was pierced with an arrow: the wording may be fanciful, but, whatever happened, she was left with a wound that bled frequently. On Good Friday 1697 Christ's five wounds appeared, and she carried the marks for the rest of her life. The convent superiors viewed all this with the greatest suspicion, ensuring that she was watched night and day and reporting her to the bishop, who made her wear sealed gloves so that she could do nothing to the wounds in her hands.

Eventually they relented, accepted the phenomena, and allowed her to lead a normal life within the convent. The fact that Veronica showed absolutely no sign of mental imbalance and was totally sensible and practical in everyday life must have helped: indeed this had long been recognized, as she was appointed novice-mistress in 1688, so cannot have been regarded as a bad example. Though she herself read mystical writers avidly, she would not allow her novices to do so, instilling into them that charity and obedience were the foundations of a religious life. In 1717 she was elected abbess, and she was re-elected at three-year intervals until she died ten years later. As abbess she continued to act as novice-mistress, while administering the physical and economic structure of the convent with great ability, even having piped water brought in. Over two hundred letters she wrote to the local bishop on administrative matters survive.

She died on 9 July 1727. Long before her death she had told her confessor that the instruments of Christ's passion were imprinted on her heart and even drawn a sketch showing exactly where. A post-mortem examination found a number of tiny objects in the right ventricle of her heart, in exactly the position she had sketched. Her confessor had also ordered her to keep an account of her mystical experiences, and by the time of her death this ran to twenty-two thousand pages. Her state of mind over a long period is thus known in great detail, and if the account does not amount to a systematic treatise on the journey to union with God, it provides abundant psychological and theological insights. She never claimed to have received extraordinary revelations but simply an increasing sense of the love of God, to which she responded with total dedication to suffering, which she saw as the "key to love." This unlocked the door to union, which she experienced in what she called "visions" and in the Eucharist, which she called "that great invention of love."

The mass of documentary evidence made the process of her beatification and canonization a lengthy one, and it was eventually completed over a hundred years after her death, in 1839.

10

SS Antony (Antipa; 983–1073) and Theodosius (about 1002–1074) Pechersky

These two great figures in the establishment of Russian Orthodox monasticism were not related: the name "Pechersky" derives from the monastery of Kiev-Pecierskaya, meaning the Caves of Kiev, of which both were abbots.

Antony came from the Ukraine, began to live a solitary life in imitation of the Desert Fathers at an early age, and went on pilgrimage to Mount Athos in Greece in search of training. He spent several years there, changing his birth name, Antipa, to Antony in homage to St Antony of Egypt (see 17 Jan.). He would have stayed there, but his abbot told him that the time had come for him to lead, not to learn. Finding Russian monasteries too lax, he settled in a cave in a cliff above the River Dnieper by Kiev. Disciples began to gather around him, and further caves had to be excavated, including large ones for use as the chapel and refectory. Eventually this troglodytic establishment could not hold the monks, and a new monastery was built on the hill above the cliff. Antony eventually retired from the abbacy, handing it over to a monk named Barlaam, and founded another monastery at Chernihiv (near where he had been born) some hundred miles north-east of Kiev. He returned to his cave toward the end of his life and died there at the age of ninety.

Theodosius had been one of Antony's first disciples in the monastery of the caves. He came from a wealthy background but was determined to serve the poor, working for a time as a baker to supply them with bread, to his mother's distress. She tried to discourage him from becoming a monk, but he fled to the caves in 1032. After thirty-one years as a monk, he took over the abbacy from Barlaam and proceeded to organize the monastery on more communal lines, with less emphasis on personal austerity than Antony had enjoined. He established a hospital for sick and disabled people and a hostel for travellers. His service to the poor was continued by sending a cartload of food to the local prison every week: "Mindful of the commandment of the good Lord, it is good for us to feed the hungry and the tramps with the fruit of our labours," he told his monks. The monastery was to be totally integrated into surrounding society, while at the same time serving as an example to it. Theodosius' extant letters and sermons saw that he took human nature and the whole of creation as they were, rather than cutting religious life off from them. He has been compared to St Francis of Assisi (see 4 Oct.) in this respect.

Theodosius was a typical figure of Russian spirituality, a *Staretz*, a holy man who exercised great influence, counselling prominent people in public life and reproving them when necessary. He died in 1074 and was buried, as he had requested, in one of the caves, but his body was moved to the hilltop church in 1091, and the bishops of the province of Kiev canonized him in 1108. The monastery grew in importance (and wealth) over the centuries, despite being sacked by invaders three times. Under the Soviet Communist regime it became a museum and scientific research establishment, but it has since been restored to use as a monastery.

[God] sought us out, found us, carried us on his shoulders, and set us at the right hand of the Father. It was not we who sought him, but he who sought us.
St Theodosius Pechersky

11

St Benedict (about 480–547)

Benedict is one of the most formative influences on Western society through the Rule he wrote for his monks, but he himself remains a shadowy figure. He never speaks of himself in his Rule, and no mention of him by contemporary writers has survived. The earliest account appears in *The Dialogues*, a four-book work by Pope St Gregory the Great (see 3 Sept.), written in Rome in 593–4, some fifty years after Benedict's supposed date of death. Gregory claims to have acquired much of his information from abbots of Monte Cassino, from the abbot of the Lateran monastery in Rome, and from the then abbot of Subiaco.

The story he tells is that Benedict was born in the province of Nursia, in the Sabine hills east of Rome (present-day Norcia). He was sent to study in Rome with his nurse in attendance, which suggests that his family must have been of some social standing. He was disillusioned by the decay and immorality he found in Rome, three times sacked by barbarian tribes from the north and reconquered by imperial troops of the eastern empire. He escaped, still taking his nurse with him, to a village named Enfide, where he first joined a group of pious Christians, seeking solitude, though not at first finding it, and "leaving the world, becoming knowingly unknown and wisely unlearned." Being unknown seems to have proved problematic, as he was in danger of becoming celebrated as a local wonder-worker, so he moved away from the group to live as a hermit in the wild country around Subiaco in about 500.

Helped by a monk named Romanus, who found him a cave and kept him supplied with food, Benedict lived in solitude for some three years. He kept a young man's temptations at bay by rolling in brambles and nettles. Then disciples, in the form of monks living in the area, asked him to be their abbot. He finally agreed and left his cave, but they would not submit to the sort of life he proposed for them and attempted to poison him. He returned to Subiaco, but again disciples gathered around him. He organized them into twelve "deaneries" of about ten monks each, but they still lived more as hermits than in community. The parish priest became jealous of this influx, not subject to his control, and Benedict withdrew, moving south to Monte Cassino, near Naples, toward 525. It was there that he produced the final form of his Rule. The monastery grew, with a school attached, to which Roman senators began sending their boys. Benedict's sister, Scholastica (see 10 Feb.) used to visit him once a year. She died three days after one of these visits and was buried in a tomb prepared for her at Monte Cassino. When he died, Benedict was buried with her, and the tomb has survived all vicissitudes of history, including heavy bombardment by the Allies in the Second World War.

Benedict did not invent the monastic Rule and was clearly far from unlettered, drawing on previous works by the Desert Fathers, St Basil (see 2 Jan.), St Augustine (see 28 Aug.), and St John Cassian, as well as the anonymous "Rule of the Master." He made a synthesis of the best parts of these and then moved on. His Rule was eminently practical, physically moderate, and spiritually uncompromising, setting up a way of life to counter the decay of secular society in his time. The work was addressed to monks, but monks were not clergy, and the way was open to all who applied—provided they proved capable of keeping its rules. This life revolved around the Divine Office, manual work, and *lectio divina*—spiritual reading, mainly of the Bible. It required obedience to the father-figure of the abbot, but obedience as love: "If you love me, you will keep my commandments" (John 14:15). It enjoined stability, meaning attachment to one community, remaining under the control of one abbot, even on travels. This was to counter the disorder and instability of the way of contemporary life outside the monastery. Its aim was *conversatio morum*, a "conversion of manners" by which acceptance of the monastic way of life becomes second nature. The outcome was the building of a community in which people could live together in harmony, in "right order" with one another and with God. To achieve this, each had particular duties in the community, and Benedict enumerates these and the qualities required to perform them, so that monks can live in love of each other and of God. To do this, they were required to take vows of celibacy, poverty, and obedience—in other words, to submerge personal ambition into the greater good of the community.

The Rule existed alongside others for several centuries, but successive reforms gradually made it almost universally applied in the West. Communities of nuns began to adopt it from about the seventh century. Monks tended to be ordained priests and to concentrate more on the liturgy, with lay brothers to do most of the manual work, a distinction not originally envisaged. Successive reforms in the Middle Ages led to new Orders, such as the Cistercians, seeking a stricter way of life. More recently, Anglican and Lutheran communities have adopted the Rule, while communities of Benedictine Sisters have adapted it for an apostolate based on charitable work outside the monastic enclosure. Many influential modern works portray the Rule as applicable (with some modifications) to business corporations and lay life in general.

Benedict is supposed to have died on 21 March, the date on which the Order celebrates his feast-day, but the Roman Martyrology and Universal Calendar place his commemoration on today's date, which marks the "translation" of his relics, so that he can be celebrated by the universal Church outside Lent.

Those who wish to grasp his character and life better will find in the layout of the Rule a complete statement of the abbot's way of life, for the holy man cannot have taught otherwise than as he lived.
St Gregory, *The Dialogues*, Book 4, Chapter 36

12

St Veronica (nominally First Century)

"As Jesus proceeds on the way, covered with the sweat of death, a woman, moved with compassion, makes her way through the crowd and wipes his face with a handkerchief. As a reward of her piety, the impression of his sacred countenance is miraculously imprinted upon the handkerchief." This "sixth station" of the Way of the Cross popularized in the nineteenth century has made Veronica one of the best known of all saints, but it seems certain that she is a legend springing from an understandable desire to know what Jesus actually looked like. An actual image of him would be proof of his true humanity and historical existence. Images were then devised to supply the need, and in the process Veronica became an embodiment of what Christ showed by his life and death: *compassio*, suffering with, to an extent that renders her historical existence unnecessary.

Plausibility, however, required that Veronica be identified with one of the women mentioned in the New Testament. The earliest known attempt to do this was in the *Acts of Pilate*, dating from the fourth or fifth century, which makes her the woman whom Jesus cured of hemorrhages (Matt. 9:20–22). A French tradition has her as wife to Zaccheus (Luke 19:2–10), while another identified her with Martha of Bethany (see 29 July). She has also been made out to be a Syrian princess, the wife of a Roman officer on duty in Jerusalem, or the tormented daughter of the Canaanite women in Matthew 15:22–8.

The best-known claimant to be the "true image" of Christ was the *mandylion* (towel or handerchief) from Edessa in Syria, supposed to have been given by Jesus himself to King Abgar of Edessa. This was moved to Constantinople and was known to be there in the tenth century but disappeared after the sack of the city in 1204. Devotion to the Holy Face became so popular that Pope Innocent III authorized a Mass and Office in 1216. "Veronica's veil" (supposedly taken to Rome by Veronica and left by her to Pope Clement) in St Peter's became an object of great veneration in the late Middle Ages, mentioned by both Petrarch and Dante. Seeing it was regarded as a foretaste of seeing Christ in glory, but the idea that it held a miraculous image was not developed before the thirteenth century. It became a rival pilgrimage attraction to the image kept in the Lateran Basilica, claimed to be a portrait of Jesus painted by St Luke. It disappeared after the emperor Charles V's forces sacked Rome in 1527, and it was said to have been auctioned in a tavern by Lutheran soldiers, but in the seventeenth century it was found hidden in a relic chamber built by Bernini into one of the piers supporting the dome of St Peter's. It has no image on it. In the sixteenth century a more historical approach to relics gained ground in the wake of the Protestant Reformation and the Catholic response at the Council of Trent, leading St Charles Borromeo (see 4 Nov.) to suppress the Mass and Office of the Holy Face in Milan.

The name Veronica has been supposed to be made up of the Latin for "true," *vera*, and the Greek for "image," *eikon*, but is more probably a Western version of the name Berenike, given in early traditions to the woman suffering from hemorrhages. The name was then applied to images of Our Lord's face. By extension, it is the name of a "pass" in the first phase of a bullfight, in which the matador "wipes" the bull's face with his cape.

O Jesus! May the contemplation of thy sufferings move us with the deepest compassion, make us to hate our sins, and kindle in our hearts more fervent love to thee. May our image be graven on our minds, until we are transformed into thy likeness.

Nineteenth-century prayer at the Sixth Station of the Cross, from *The Golden Manual* (Burns & Lambert, 1850)

13

Bd James of Voragine (Jacopo da Voragine; about 1230–1298)

James' fame, like that of St Benedict, rests not on his life but on his work. He did more than anyone else to set a style for Lives of the saints that lasted through the Middle Ages and beyond. His *Legenda Sanctorum*, better known as the *Legenda aurea* (the *Golden Legend*), was written between 1255 and 1266. More than a thousand manuscript copies of the Latin survive; the invention of printing made it the first printed bestseller, with over a hundred editions by 1530. It was translated into German, Italian, French, and Czech by 1480, and then into English, printed by Caxton in 1483.

James was born in Voraggio (now Varezze) near Genoa and joined the Dominicans when he was fourteen. He gained a reputation as a powerful preacher, taught theology and scripture, and became prior of the house in Genoa, then prior provincial of Lombardy. In 1286 the cathedral chapter of Genoa chose him as their bishop, but he refused the appointment. Six years later, the chapter chose him again, and this time he accepted. He inherited a city torn between two rival factions, the Guelphs, who supported the papacy, and the Ghibellines, who supported the empire. He failed to reconcile them but did have a number of achievements to his credit, endowing hospitals and monasteries, repairing churches, giving generously to the poor, and restoring clerical discipline. He was obviously seen as a holy man, as a cult started straight after his death, though it was not officially approved by the Vatican.

His view of what constitutes sainthood is certainly not one that scholars would accept today, though it has proved virtually impossible to eradicate from the popular idea of what makes a saint. He made much of holy childhoods, following Pope Innocent IV's declaration, made some twenty or thirty years earlier, that to be canonized a person needed to have led a life of continuous and uninterrupted virtue. (Modern understanding tends more to a significant period of heroic virtue, which allows for youthful indiscretions and the possibility of conversion, but the emphasis on devout childhood, with or without historical basis, persisted—in English saints' Lives—until the 1995–2000 new full edition of *Butler's Lives* consciously downplayed it.) James also reflected the new emphasis on monastic saints, with a consequent reduction of stress on practical works of charity (indicated by Matthew 25 to be the essence of being Christian) and increased attention given to learning, contemplation, mysticism, and supernatural heroism. So why did *The Golden Legend* become so popular? Possibly because it was so engagingly written, but mainly because it was designed to be read by preachers, to provide examples for use in their sermons. Most preachers were members of religious Orders, and they welcomed the book for showing sainthood attaching more to their condition of life than to that of lay people—or of their rivals, the secular clergy.

The book declined in popularity in the sixteenth century, attacked by reformers and humanists as exemplifying much that was wrong with medieval religion, especially "magical" rewards to be obtained through the intercession of certain saints (largely those subsequently shown to be purely legendary). It was unhistorical and uncritical, but then if James had been asked why he had not been more historical and more critical, he would not have understood the question. His purpose was to edify, not to instruct, and a more valid approach to the book is to ask whether it does edify in an acceptable fashion. Inevitably, James' examples of sanctity, in the choices of lives he makes and in the choices of elements in those lives he stresses, are no longer all ones we might choose, but he wrote, at least partly, to provide his readers—and their audiences—with examples. This aim was carried on, with modifications suited to the Age of Enlightenment, by Alban Butler in the eighteenth century: "Example instructs without usurping the authoritative air of a master. ... In the lives of the saints we see the most perfect maxims of the gospel reduced to practice." This aim, supported by a belief that it is best achieved through historical truth, is still valid today.

God shows [us] in a vivid way his presence and his face in the lives of those companions of ours who are more perfectly transformed into the image of Christ.
Vatican II, *Constitution on the Church*, n. 50

14

St Camillus of Lellis (1550–1614)

Camillus is an excellent example of a saint who cannot be claimed to have led a pious life from childhood (see previous entry). Six feet six inches tall and strongly built, he put his youthful physical energies into soldiering, fighting, and gambling. The last of these reduced him to ruin when he lost even the proverbial shirt off his back in Naples, which reminded him of a vow he had once made to join a religious Order.

He went to do manual work at the new Capuchin friary in Manfredonia, but he had contracted leg ulcers at some stage in his earlier life, and when he applied to become a Franciscan novice he was rejected on account of this infirmity. His ulcers had previously put him in the San Giacomo hospital for incurables in Rome as a patient, and he now returned there to nurse the sick. Proving himself an efficient administrator as well as a devoted nurse, he rose to become bursar of the hospital. He was horrified by both the condition of the patients and the approach of the nurses, whom he found uncaring and immoral. He decided that only "men of good will who would consecrate themselves to the sick purely out of love of God and would wear a cross as their badge" could provide the incurably sick with the sort of care—spiritual as well as physical—they needed. He moved away from San Giacomo and set up house with two like-minded companions, with whom, backed financially by a wealthy patron and encouraged spiritually by St Philip Neri (see 26 May), he worked in the hospital of Santo Spirito.

Camillus also set himself to study for the priesthood and was ordained in 1584. By the following year more helpers had joined the original group; Camillus rented a larger house and began to think in terms of a religious Congregation. He drew up a provisional Rule, which was approved in 1586. Two years later he opened a new house in Naples, and here two of his Ministers of the Sick, as they were now known, died nursing plague victims. Several formed the first recorded medical field unit, nursing the wounded from battles in Croatia and Hungary. The Rule was formally approved in 1591, with members of the Congregation given the status of Clerks Regular. Besides the three vows of chastity, poverty, and obedience, they would take a fourth, of "perpetual physical and spiritual assistance to the sick, especially those with the plague."

Camillus' approach to the sick was eminently practical: he insisted that hospitals should be well insulated, provide a good diet, isolate those with infectious diseases, and always seek a cure, not writing anyone off as incurable. He equally insisted that his ministers should see the face of Christ in their suffering patients. He himself had mystical experiences of the crucified Christ; these inspired his approach, but he did not see such experiences as things that should be sought: what mattered, rather, was service in practical charity: "I don't like this talk about mystical union ... [we should] do good and help the poor ... since we'll have plenty of time to contemplate God in heaven." He anticipated modern practice by insisting that nurses should nurse and not be distracted by becoming involved in administration, which should be left to others. For him, "the least of my brethren" really was Christ himself. The red cross on the breast and cape of the Order's habit was to remind ministers always to have Christ before their eyes.

Camillus himself, despite suffering from a number of long-term illnesses, personally continued to nurse as long as he was able. He died in the motherhouse in Rome on 14 July 1614. Miracles had already been attributed to him during his life, and many more were after his death. He was canonized in 1746. In the late nineteenth century Pope Leo XIII made him patron (with St

John of God; see 8 Mar.) of hospitals and the sick; in the twentieth century Pope Pius XI added the patronage of nurses. The Order of St Camillus, variously known otherwise as Agonizants, Camillans, Clerks Regular Ministers of the Infirm, Fathers of a Good Death, and Order of the Servants of the Sick is active worldwide, with female branches started in the nineteenth century and a Secular Institute of Missionaries to the Sick established in 1948.

15

St Bonaventure (Giovanni di Fidanza; 1221–1274)

Born near Orvieto in Umbria five years before the death of St Francis (see 4 Oct.), Giovanni joined the Franciscans in 1243, taking the name Bonaventure. He studied in Paris and by 1253 was a doctor of theology and master of the Franciscan school there. Four years later he was elected master general of the Order, and it was only then that he was made a fellow of the university of Paris, having been excluded till then by the influence of the seculars, who resented the rise of the new Orders.

He inherited a situation of conflict in the still-new Order, revolving mainly over how strictly to observe Francis' teachings on poverty. On one side were the Spirituals, who insisted that poverty had to be the absolute mark of the Order, not just of individual friars, and rejected any corporate ownership of buildings or even books. On the other were the Conventuals, who argued that the huge growth in numbers required a greater degree of organization, which meant communal living, requiring places in which to live. There was also debate about how far the Franciscans should engage in the universities, rapidly emerging as the main focuses of learning. Francis had appeared to despise learning, but without a presence in the universities how was the Order to exert influence in formative sectors of society, and if its members refused high office in the Church how was it to effect the reforms it saw as so necessary?

Bonaventure, seeking a middle way, supported specialist Franciscan houses in university towns, at which friars would be equipped to become preachers and spiritual directors. He wrote a Life of St Francis, known as the *Legenda Maior*, and all other versions were ordered to be destroyed, even though not everyone agreed that his interpretation of the founder's mind was always correct. He succeeded in adapting the ideal to a new situation, and by his personal simplicity and frugality of life showed how this could be done without departing from the ideals of St Francis. He refused the archbishopric of York, offered to him by Pope Clement IV, but then Gregory X (elected in 1271, largely thanks to Bonaventure's influence) appointed him cardinal-bishop of Albano, including a condition that he could not refuse. In 1274 he played a prominent part in the Council of Lyons, called by the pope to bring about the reunion of East and West, to liberate the Holy Land, and to tackle general moral reform in the Church. Reunion was agreed (though it was not to last more than a few years) and Bonaventure preached at the Mass of Reconciliation to celebrate the event. This council was to see the deaths of the "twin summits of medieval theology" (David Knowles): Thomas Aquinas (see 28 Jan.) died on his way to it, and Bonaventure died while it was still in session.

He is best remembered as a theologian, the founder of the Franciscan school, as Thomas Aquinas was of the Dominican. Bonaventure was more conservative, relying largely on St Augustine (see 28 Aug.) and St Anselm (see 21 Apr.) and suspicious of the new currents of thought deriving from Aristotle, which Thomas was happy to employ. For Bonaventure, all learning had to further the "Journey of the Mind toward God," as his most influential spiritual writing was titled. Even though he counted the powers of human reason and emotions as little in comparison with the illumination granted by God, and so can be seen as a mystical writer rather than a systematic theologian, he nevertheless produced the first great medieval synthesis of thought and doctrine. His model was St Francis and his ultimate aim the union with God achieved by Francis on Mount Alverna. In his "On the Triple Way" he set out three stages on the way to achieving this ideal: active purification from sin, bringing the "calm of peace"; the way of illumination, leading to the "splendour of the truth"; and finally union with God, producing "the sweetness of love." This "purgative, illuminative, and unitive" way was to become the basis for virtually all future mystical writing.

It has been said of him that reading his theology makes us imagine that St Francis has become a philosopher and is teaching at the university of Paris. There was no early cult after his death, but he was canonized in 1482 and declared a Doctor of the Church in 1588—usually referred to as the "Seraphic Doctor," as Franciscans have been called the "Seraphic Order" in memory of the founder's experience on Mount Alverna. He is often referred to as the "second founder" of the Order.

And may you ever, O devout soul, say to the Lord with all your heart:
I seek you, I hope for you, I desire you, I raise myself up toward you,
I lay hold on you, I exult in you, at last I cleave to you.
St Bonaventure, "On the Triple Way," Part 2, chapter 3

16

Bd Anne Marie Javouhey (1779–1851)

Anne Marie was known in her large family by the quite unsuitable diminutive of Nanette, and "Nanette," her mother declared, "will always be a trouble to us." She was not wrong. Born the fifth of nine children into a bourgeois farming family in Burgundy, Anne Marie was an extraordinarily strong-willed child who soon had her siblings organized into a sort of junior religious Congregation, keeping periods of silence and reciting the Hours of the Divine Office. Her father, who would rather have had them working on his farms, removed the weights from the clock.

She was twelve when anticlerical revolutionary activity was at its height. She rescued people from a chapel that had been set alight, warned priests of local spies, and misdirected a mob hunting for them. She taught local children the catechism and prepared them for First Communion, which they had to receive in one of her father's barns. This led her to decide to devote her life to the education of the poor. When religious Orders were allowed to function again in France she joined the Sisters of Charity at Besançon, but decided just before her clothing that this was not the right life for her. Seeking a practical outlet for her ideals and energies, she took three of her sisters and started a school for girls in a nearby village. But the local farmers saw little point in educating girls, and the school failed. She tried her vocation again with Trappist nuns in Switzerland, but again fled home on the eve of her clothing—trouble to her parents. She had a dream (or just imagined, she was happy to admit) of a crowd of children, "poor, sick, weeping. ... What especially struck me was a multitude of Blacks, men, women, and children, calling me 'Dear Mother.'" She probably had no knowledge of the existence of black races, and women at the time could not be missionaries, but the dream was to prove remarkably prophetic.

After other attempts to establish schools, which reduced her and her sisters to near starvation, from which her father had to rescue them—more trouble to her parents—Anne Marie met Pope Pius VII in Chalon as he was returning from Napoleon's coronation in Paris. She firmly asked for an audience, and Pius told her and her sisters to persevere. This produced support, first modestly from the local priest and then more substantially, in a grant and premises, from the mayor of Autun. With her brother Pierre, two of her sisters, and other helpers, Anne Marie was soon running a school for eighty boys and another for one hundred and twenty-three girls, including boarders.

With the necessary permission from the civil authorities, she formed herself, her sisters, and five other women into a "religious association formed in the diocese of Autun and called by the name of St Joseph." Its object was to form "children of either sex for work, good morality, and Christian virtue." The first members were clothed in May 1807. Anne Marie had soon started so many new ventures—workshops, a hostel, another boys' school, a seminary, houses in other dioceses—that her father had to come to the Association's financial rescue—yet more trouble to her parents. He bought them a disused Franciscan convent in Cluny, from which they later became known as the Congregation of St Joseph of Cluny. In 1814 Anne Marie opened a school in Paris where pupils were taught according to the "Lancastrian system" (pioneered by Henry Lancaster), in which teachers taught monitors who then taught the younger pupils. Many Parisians objected (more because the system was English than on account of its results, which were good), but the authorities supported her and the school carried on.

The minister of the interior introduced her to the deputy governor of Réunion (an island east of Madagascar, then the French colony of Bourbon), who asked for Sisters to develop education there, especially for newly freed slaves. Anne Marie agreed, and four Sisters left for Réunion in 1817 and started a school; this prospered, and they were joined the following year by a further four, who started another school. Word spread, and they were asked to do the same in Senegal, in West Africa. They found a "desolate scrub" with no resources, but stayed. For eighteen months they had no priest, but then one arrived, with equally welcome crates of potatoes. Anne Marie saw this overseas expansion as her main task, sent other teams to Guadeloupe and Guiana, and in 1822 went to Senegal herself. The governor of the British colonies of Sierra Leone and the Gambia asked her to work there as well, which she did, helping to run hospitals. She had to contend with poor health and with a move by a Sister in Réunion to form a breakaway Congregation, which was eventually settled in Anne Marie's favour by the archbishop of Paris. The superior in Guiana was killed by a building falling during a cyclone; this was followed by an outbreak of yellow fever, but still the Sisters stayed.

More houses were founded in France and overseas. Anne Marie oversaw rapid expansion with determination: for some, she was too much of a martinet, and she made enemies. She was ahead of her time in sending Guianese students to France to study for the priesthood, but the cultural difference was too great for most of them, and they abandoned their training. She was forced into a prolonged battle with a new bishop of Autun, a former brilliant army officer, who ran his diocese like a military command and was not having women running Congregations, believing that they needed a man's hand and "that hand was his." He even deprived her of the sacraments for a time and told the Sisters it was a sin to obey her. But he had met a commander as determined and skilful as himself, and she would not surrender. Eventually the papal nuncio prevented the bishop from closing the house at Cluny and the archbishop of Paris confirmed her as superior. She charitably ordered all her correspondence with the bishop to be destroyed before she died. He died a month before her, and her only comment was, "So he's gone, that good bishop. God rest his soul." She was proposing a visit to Rome to obtain full papal approval for the Congregation but died at Senlis before she could set out.

She was one of the most remarkable of a remarkable generation of women and men who produced fresh initiatives to meet the rapidly changing social conditions of the early nineteenth century. Combining vision with outstanding organizational ability and determination, she made a huge contribution to education and other areas of need. In Guiana the governor called her Sisters "the consolation of this land," and the same could be said in many other places. She was beatified in 1950, nearly a century after her death, by which time her Congregation was working in thirty-two countries.

17

St Hedwig of Poland (Jadwiga; 1374–1399)

Hedwig spent her childhood as a pawn on the dynastic chessboard of eastern Europe and her short adulthood making the sort of mark on Polish nationhood that Joan of Arc (see 30 May) did on that of France.

The daughter of the king of Hungary and Poland, she was betrothed to Wilhelm, the Hapsburg heir to the grand duchy, when she was one and he was five. She was sent to Vienna to be educated in the ways of the Austrian court but had to return to Buda when her eldest sister, Catherine, died and her father chose her as his heir to the throne of Hungary. He died when she was eight, but the Hungarians preferred her sister Maria, who had already been accepted as queen of Poland by the nobles. Diplomatic intrigue then caused Maria to be rejected in both countries, and Hedwig was crowned in 1384, aged ten. The Polish nobles set aside the vows made by proxy between her and Wilhelm and decided she should marry Jagiello, grand duke of Lithuania and Ruthenia (thereby forming a powerful buffer State between Germany and Russia), who promised to become a Christian if the marriage went ahead. Despite contrary pressure from the Hapsburg camp, she agreed to marry Jagiello, and the wedding took place in Cracow Cathedral in February 1386, shortly after Jagiello, his brothers, and the leading Lithuanian nobles had been baptized. She was twelve (the accepted age of maturity at the time) and he was thirty-six.

The Hapsburgs, not surprisingly, were outraged and began to circulate stories that she and Wilhelm had consummated a marriage when he had visited her to persuade her to marry him, so the queen of Poland was an adulteress and a bigamist. These slanders were spread in the influential chronicles of the Teutonic Knights and were even repeated in the following century in the works of the great scholar Aeneas Silvius Piccolomini, who became Pope Pius II. At the time, the pope stood by Hedwig and Jagiello, but great damage was done to their reputation outside Poland.

Jagiello embarked on the Christianization of Lithuania. While not actually employing force, he decreed that people should be baptized, though the fact that none of his missionaries spoke Lithuanian rendered their instruction problematical. Nevertheless, a diocese was established in Vilnius, the capital, and Hedwig sent church plate and vestments for the cathedral there and for other churches. Her ambition was to unite Latin and Orthodox Christians in her lands. She brought monks from Prague, who used a Slavonic rite in an attempt to build bridges between the communities, and introduced perpetual adoration in Cracow Cathedral, with a "college of psalmists" taking turns to sing the Psalms without interruption except for services.

The Teutonic Knights invaded Lithuania. Hedwig persuaded them to withdraw through skilful diplomatic negotiation. In dealing with other rebellious elements in Poland she always sought a compromise aimed at restoring peace. In 1399 she was expecting a baby and retired from public life, but the baby was born prematurely and died after three weeks, and Hedwig died four days later. In her will, she asked that all her possessions should be sold and the money used to help restore Cracow University. Many miracles were soon being attributed to her intercession, and a list of these was kept in a special register. The cause for her canonization was opened in 1426 and she was popularly called "Blessed," but the official Church did not confirm the cause until the first Polish pope was elected in 1978. Pope John Paul II then beatified her in 1986 and canonized her on a visit to Cracow in 1997.

18

St Leo IV (died 855)

Leo was an outstanding pope who, in the manner of his time, defended Rome against the Saracens and helped to organize naval campaigns against them. He also defended the universal rights of the Roman Pontiff against political interference by Western emperors, but he moved in the world of power politics with no thought of personal gain or hint of corruption.

Born in Rome, he was brought up and became a monk in the monastery of San Martino, near the city. He then entered papal service, first as a curial subdeacon, then as cardinal priest of the church of the Four Crowned Martyrs, appointed by Pope Sergius II (844–7). When Sergius died, he was unanimously elected to succeed him. The electors did not consult the emperor, on the grounds that a strong leader was needed immediately to enable Rome to resist Saracen raids. In 846 the Saracens had sailed up the Tiber, raided the city, and desecrated the tombs of SS Peter and Paul. Leo set about strengthening the city walls to prevent a recurrence of this. He built new walls around St Peter's and the Vatican Hill, creating what is known as the "Leonine city," still visible today. The emperor, Lothair I, helped financially, but the initiative was Leo's and showed the independence he sought for the papacy, besides being an amazing feat of organization.

With three fleets combined, also through his organizational skills, he defeated the Saracens in a decisive sea battle off the coast of the Roman seaport of Ostia in 849. This and other works of reconstruction and restoration led the people of Rome to regard him as their saviour, and this enhanced the standing of the papacy. He acted just as decisively against "enemies" in the Church, denouncing prelates whom he thought were abusing their power to the detriment of the papacy, such as Hincmar of Reims, who wanted to declare himself vicar apostolic of France. He even excommunicated a cardinal who had the backing of the emperor; he supported the bishops of Brittany against their duke, and refused to recognize the emperor's appointments in France, where he forced the Synod of Soissons (853) to be held afresh, annulling its previous decrees because papal legates had not presided at it. In all these actions, he was refusing to allow the Western emperors to dictate Church policy, but he was sensible enough to ask them to confirm appointments he made. He took the same unbending approach to the Eastern Church, summoning the patriarch of Constantinople to Rome for deposing a Sicilian bishop without having consulted him.

He made an enormous number of gifts to individual churches, to enable the liturgy to be celebrated with due ceremony, which for him meant being sung in the "sweet chant of St Gregory," which was not only beautiful but also a unifying factor among "all who use the Latin tongue to pay their tribute to the King of Heaven," as he reminded an erring abbot. He insisted on strict clerical discipline and upheld recent reforms in the areas of clerical education, Sunday observance, simony, and marriage. Personally, he was known as patient, humble, a scripture scholar and lover of justice, a "nourisher of the poor contemptuous of himself." He died on 17 July 855 and was buried in St Peter's. He was said to have extinguished a dangerous fire in Rome by his prayers, and this is the subject of a painting in the Vatican by a pupil of Raphael.

19

St Macrina the Younger (about 330–379)

Macrina came from a most remarkable family: her parents were St Basil the Elder, a celebrated teacher of rhetoric, and St Emmelia (jointly commemorated on 30 May); three brothers became bishops and saints: St Basil the Great (see 2 Jan.), St Gregory of Nyssa (see 10 Jan.), and St Peter of Sebaste (commemorated on 26 Mar.). Her paternal grandmother, St Macrina the Elder (commemorated on 14 Jan.) had studied under St Gregory the Wonder-worker (commemorated on 17 Nov.), who is said to have found Caesarea in Palestine with only seventeen Christians and to have left it with only seventeen pagans, converting the inhabitants largely through the observance of feast-days and much rejoicing.

Macrina, and much about the Church in Asia Minor at the time, are known largely through the account of her by her younger brother Gregory of Nyssa, who referred to her as "the Teacher" and recorded their discussions in a treatise, *On the Soul and Resurrection*, which is also known as the *Macriniae*. Macrina was the eldest daughter and possibly the eldest child of the ten born to Basil and Emmelia. She was born some years after Constantine had ended the persecution of Christians and moved the imperial capital to Byzantium (later named Constantinople after him). Her grandmother died when she was ten or eleven, and much of the upbringing of her younger brothers and sisters would have fallen on her shoulders. She is said to have inspired both Basil and Gregory to their religious life.

Basil was close to her in age (she is said to have been betrothed to a brother of Gregory Nazianzen, commemorated with Basil on 2 Jan.), and after he had finished his studies they discussed taking a vow of celibacy, and both did so. He went on to become bishop of Caesarea, whereas she led the life of a consecrated virgin in the family home. Gregory, five years her junior, married and taught rhetoric, then (after his wife either died or became a nun) became a monk and was appointed bishop of Nyssa in 371. When Macrina was about forty, her father died, and her mother established a religious community near Pontus, on the banks of the River Iris. Macrina joined her there, later becoming a nun and a spiritual director.

Basil died in 379, and a grieving Gregory visited his sister, whom he had not seen for eight years, on his way back to Nyssa from a synod in Antioch. He found her mortally ill but seems to have spent more time pouring out his grief at Basil's death than in concern for her health. She roused herself and comforted him, and in his account it is she who provides the answers to his questions; she consoles him with thoughts of the resurrection: he is therefore right to call her his teacher. She reminds him of Jesus' words that "unless a grain of wheat falls into the earth and dies, it remains just a single grain; but if it dies, it bears much fruit" (John 12:24), quotes St Paul on the mortal body putting on immortality, and adds her own vision of everlasting life: "The divine power, in the superabundance of Omnipotence, does not only restore you that body, once dissolved, but makes great and splendid additions to it."

Some (male) commentators have suggested that Gregory is attributing his own thoughts to her, but Macrina was a scholar like her mother and grand-mother, and there is no reason to assume she was not capable of such rea-soning, even when virtually on her deathbed. She was also Gregory's elder sister, and he naturally turned to her for consolation in his grief at the death of his brother. Macrina died so denuded of any possessions that Gregory had to provide a shroud in which to bury her.

20

Martyrs of the Spanish Civil War

The Spanish civil war lasted from July 1936, when General Franco led a "Nationalist" uprising against the Republican Government, to his final victory in April 1939. The Nationalist side adopted a Catholic banner and defined itself as a "crusade." The uprising led to the formation of "revolutionary commit-tees" in towns and villages and unleashed an immediate wave of hatred against Catholic priests, religious, and lay people. During the war, six thousand eight hundred and thirty-two priests, and religious were put to death. If they and many more lay people are all to be seen as martyrs, then this becomes by far the largest collective martyrdom in the history of the Church. Most of those already beatified or whose causes are still being pursued died during the latter days of July and August 1936. They have been beatified (and some canonized) in groups by Pope John Paul II since 1987, and the process is still continuing, with a further hundred groups covering over a thousand individuals still under consideration. The beatification of two hundred and thirty-three martyrs on 21 March 2001 was the largest group beatification in history, exceeding that of two hundred and six Japanese martyrs by Pope Pius IX in 1867.

In the years leading up to the war, the causes of which are complex, the Catholic Church had either adopted or been forced into a generally ultra-conservative position, and this, combined with its virtual monopoly of the education system, produced resentment. In 1931 the abdication of King Alfonso XII led to the creation of a Republic by default. A series of democratically elected governments, tending generally further toward the political left, failed to resolve the country's problems and heal the age-old split between conservatives and liberals, and this led to the uprising of July 1936.

Before the outbreak of war, eight De La Salle Brothers and a Passionist priest were "shot like rabbits" (according to the postulator of their cause) during social unrest in the mining area of Asturias. The De La Salle Congregation was prominent in providing the sort of "practical education"—teaching boys carpentry and similar skills, and girls sewing and the like, and then selling the products of the school workshops as a means of providing free education—that provoked most resentment as this competed with local workers. This seems to have been the underlying reason for their execution. The nine were canonized in 1999 as St Cyril Bertrand Tejedor and Companions, becoming the first saints of the Spanish persecution; one of them came from Argentina and is the first native-born Argentinian saint.

Elections in February 1936 produced a Popular Front government made up of Communists and left-wing Republicans (the Socialists refusing to join), which led to an outbreak of destruction of churches across the country, though not yet of slaughter of priests. This began in reaction to the Nationalist military uprising and had soon led to the deaths of one in seven of Spain's diocesan priests plus over two thousand monks and almost three hundred nuns. Violence was generally worst in areas seized by anarchists. In the Aragonese diocese of Barbastro, seized by Catalan anarchists, eighty-eight per cent of the diocesan clergy, including the bishop, Florentino Asensio Barroso, a great worker for social justice and unity, were killed. This same outbreak of violence also wiped out the entire Claretian community in Barbastro, with the priests shot on 21 July and the students in three groups in early August. They were all beatified as Bd Felipe de Jesús Munárriz and his Fifty Companions in 1992.

The Order of Hospitallers founded by St John of God (see 8 Mar.) suffered seventy-one dead in various places between July and December 1936, many in the panic caused by General Franco's advance on Madrid in November. Most worked in children's or psychiatric hospitals. Hatred of the idea of religious Orders seemed to prove stronger than recognition of the fact that they carried out practical caring roles in society that no one else was prepared to take on. These were also beatified in the same 1992 ceremony. Religious Sisters were forced to leave their convents in Barcelona, where teaching Sisters were especially singled out. One such was María Mercedes Prat y Prat, seized in the street on the night of 23–4 July 1936, shot, and left to die in agony. She was beatified with the Asturian martyrs of 1934. In the province of Toledo, forty-eight per cent of the diocesan clergy were killed; in the rural province of Ciudad Real, forty per cent, together with twenty-six members of the Passionist Order, some students still doing their training. They were divided into groups; some were killed immediately, others maltreated for some days first. A few were wounded, spent some time in hospital, and were shot later. They were all beatified as Nicéforo Diez Tejerina and Companions in 1989.

To the north of Madrid, three Carmelite nuns from the convent of St Joseph in Guadalajara were shot, after initially escaping in secular dress, on 23 July 1936. They were the first martyrs of the Spanish civil war to be beatified, on 29 March 1987. Two Sisters of Charity—one aged eighty-three—shot in Madrid in July, seven Visitandine nuns from the Order's house there shot in November, and a Carmelite prioress shot on 15 August were all beatified in 1998.

In the south-easter province of Almería, revolutionary committees rounded up everyone they suspected of not supporting the revolution, starting with priests and religious. The bishops of Almería and Guadix were both shot during the night of 29–30 August, followed by seven De La Salle Brothers and two Teresians (see 28 July); all these were beatified in 1993. Seven Augustinian recollects and a parish priest were shot in the south-coast town of Motril in July and August; they were beatified in 1999. A further forty-five martyrs from eastern provinces, including the bishop of Teruel, Alonso Polanco Fontecha, were killed during the course of the war. They included members of the Congregation of Diocesan Workers, Piarists, Marianists, Sisters of Christian Doctrine, and a prominent layman, Vicente Vilar David. These were beatified in 1995. The only exception to the rule that the Church sided with the Nationalists was the Basque Country, which tended to produce priests dedicated to solving the social problems of Spain's most industrialized provinces. Fourteen of these were shot by the Nationalists (their causes have not been promoted) and a further sixty imprisoned.

Most of the parish priests, who bore the brunt of the persecution, were as poor as most of their parishioners and innocent of political prejudice. But they were identified with an institution that represented privilege, and they suffered for this. Pope John Paul II has taken pains at the beatification ceremonies to stress that the martyrs died for their faith and not for a political cause. Of the two hundred and thirty-three new martyrs beatified on 21 March 2001, he said, "They were men and women of all ages and conditions: diocesan priests, men and women religious, fathers and mothers of families, lay youths. They were killed for being Christians, for their faith in Christ, for being active members of the Church. . . . The new blessed raised to the altars today were not involved in political or ideological struggles, nor did they wish to enter these. They died only for religious reasons." He added the hope that "Their blessed memory may remove any form of violence, hatred and resentment for ever from Spanish soil" (where violence by the Basque separatist movement, ETA, still continues). In July 1986 the Spanish bishops attempted to draw a line under the whole conflict in their document "Constructors of Peace":

> Although the Church does not pretend to be free from every error, those who reproach her with having ranged herself on the side of one of the contending parties should bear in mind the harshness of the religious persecution suffered in Spain from the year 1931. Nothing of this kind, on either side, should ever be repeated. May forgiveness and magnanimity provide the climate for our times.

21

St Laurence of Brindisi (Giulio Cesare Russo; 1559–1619)

Laurence, as he became when he joined the Capuchins in Verona in 1575, came from a wealthy Venetian family and went on to become a distinguished scholar and one of the most eminent preachers of the Catholic Reformation, declared a Doctor of the Church in 1959.

His studies led to an exceptional command of ancient and modern languages, with an extraordinary knowledge of the scriptures. He was ordained in 1582 and was soon preaching with great success in the major towns of northern Italy. He was called to Rome in 1596, appointed definitor general of the Capuchins, and charged by Pope Clement VIII with special responsibility for the conversion of the Jews. He was then posted to Austria and Bohemia and founded houses in Vienna, Prague, and Graz. The general chapter of the Order appointed him minister general in 1602; he refused to serve a second term though re-elected three years later. In 1606 he became commissary general and in 1613 and 1618 was again definitor general.

This steady progression within the Order was coupled with political and even military distinction. The Turks were threatening Hungary, and the Holy Roman emperor, Rudolf II, enlisted Laurence's help in persuading the German princes to unite against them. He was successful in this and was appointed chaplain general of the army. At the battle of Szekes-Fehervar in 1601 he personally led the Christian forces into battle, holding a crucifix aloft. Their success was widely attributed to him. Rudolf then sent him to Spain to persuade King Philip III to join the Catholic League, and he opened a Capuchin house in Madrid. His next appointment was an ecclesiastical one, as papal nuncio in Munich, where he negotiated with Maximilian of Bavaria, the head of the Catholic League, as well as administering two Capuchin provinces. Throughout his dual careers he continued his work of preaching and conversion. By 1618, elderly and exhausted, he retired to the friary in Caserta, intending to devote what time was left to him to prayer. But he was summoned for a further diplomatic mission to Philip III of Spain. He found that Philip had gone to Lisbon and followed him there, negotiating successfully over the status of Naples. The journey in the summer heat finally sapped his strength, and he died in Lisbon on 22 July 1619. His body was taken to Villafranca del Bierzo in northern Spain and buried in the Poor Clares cemetery there.

It was not until the twentieth century that his numerous writings were printed and scholarly study of them could be made. Besides a total of eight hundred and four sermons, they consist of a commentary on Genesis, some anti-Lutheran treatises and one on the place of Mary, an autobiographical account of his time in Austria and Germany produced at the request of his superiors, and some eighty surviving letters. His exaltation of Mary as sharing in the divine plan of creation and redemption and as mediatrix of all graces foreshadowed later devotional schemes, but stemmed from his devotion to the person of Christ (as does her title of Mother of God and all subsequent balanced devotion to her). His teaching was strongly based on his exhaustive knowledge of the scriptures; his humanist background is evident in his teachings, and he shows an optimistic belief in the possibility of perfection achieved through the imitation of Christ.

His personal spirituality was intense. He had the "gift of tears" and was often so rapt in ecstasy that it took him three hours to celebrate Mass. This, rather than his public activities, made his cult very popular (he died shortly before the papacy forbade a cult preceding beatification), with great reverence paid to "second degree" relics, such as the handkerchief he used to wipe away his tears during Mass. He was not beatified for over one hundred and fifty years after his death, in 1783. This led to numerous representations of him by major Italian artists, who usually show him saying Mass in ecstasy or writing about Mary. He was canonized nearly a hundred years later, in 1881, when images of him inspiring Christian troops in battle became very popular. The publication of his works undoubtedly led to his title of Doctor of the Church in 1959. The new Roman Martyrology keeps his feast on today's date, while noting that he actually died on the following day.

22

St Mary Magdalene (First Century)

> Soon afterwards [Jesus] went on through cities and villages, proclaiming and bringing the good news of the kingdom of God. The twelve were with him, as well as some women who had been cured of evil spirits and infirmities: Mary, called Magdalene, from whom seven demons had gone out, and Joanna, the wife of Herod's steward Chuza, and Susanna, and many others, who provided for them out of their resources. (Luke 8:1–3)

This is how we are introduced to Mary Magdalene in the Gospels, and she goes on to be a constant companion of Jesus, as it is the women who remain faithful to him at times of crisis when the male disciples become discouraged and abandon him. She and the other women are present at Jesus' crucifixion and burial: "Mary Magdalene and the other Mary were there" (Matt. 27:61a);

"There were also women looking on from a distance; among them were Mary Magdalene ... Mary Magdalene and Mary the mother of Joses saw where the body was laid" (Mark 15:40a, 47) "The women who had come with him from Galilee followed, and they saw the tomb and how his body was laid" (Luke 23:55); "Meanwhile, standing near the cross of Jesus were his mother, and his mother's sister, Mary the wife of Clopas, and Mary Magdalene" (John 19:25b).

Finally, on the morning of Easter Sunday, she (alone, in John's Gospel: 20:1–18) goes to the tomb, finds that the stone has been rolled away, and runs to tell Peter, "They have taken the Lord away, and we do not know where they have laid him." Peter and the disciple "whom Jesus loved" look into the tomb and then return to their houses, but Mary stays there, weeping. Two angels ask her why she is crying, and she repeats what she had said to Peter, but then turns round and sees a figure, whom she does not recognize as Jesus but takes to be the gardener. He asks why she is weeping, and she replies, "Sir, if you have carried him away, tell me where you have laid him, and I will take him away." Jesus replies by speaking her name, whereupon she recognizes him and exclaims (in Hebrew) "Rabbouni!" (teacher). He tells her not to hold on to him but to go and tell the disciples. In Luke's Gospel (24:1–12) it is "the women who had followed him from Galilee" (a group always headed by Mary Magdalene) who go to the tomb. They are told by "two men in dazzling clothes" not to look for the living among the dead and to go and remind the disciples that Jesus told them he would rise again on the third day. The women are then named: "Now it was Mary Magdalene, Joanna, Mary the mother of James, and the other women with them who told this to the apostles." Luke then specifically adds, "But these words seemed to them an idle tale, and they did not believe them." The words seem idle because they are women's words—and women, for example, could not give witness in court—yet Luke (no feminist) specifically makes the women the bearers of the most important message of the gospel. Mark, in the longer ending to his Gospel, makes the same point (16:9–11): "Now after he rose early on the first day of the week, he appeared first to Mary Magdalene, from whom he had cast out seven demons. She went out and told those who had been with him, while they were mourning and weeping. But when they heard that he was alive and had been seen by her, they would not believe it." Matthew has "Mary Magdalene and the other Mary" going to the tomb, and provides a rather more dramatic account of the commission from Jesus to go and tell the apostles (28:1–10). So Mary Magdalene is the one constant in the four accounts. She is thus singled out as the first witness to the risen Christ and on account of this has been called the "apostle to the apostles."

She then passes from canonical text to legend. In the East, she is said to have accompanied Our Lady and St John to Ephesus and to have died there. In the West, she had a more dramatic time: turned loose in an oarless boat with Martha, Lazarus, and others, she landed in southern France, where she spent her last years in a cave, living as a hermit and clothed only in her long hair (a touch borrowed from St Mary of Egypt). Fascination with her was increased by her identification (in the West only) with the woman "who was a sinner" who anoints Jesus and dries his feet with her hair. This woman is not named, whereas Mary Magdalene always is, and there is no real reason for the identification other than that the story immediately precedes her first appearance, with her seven demons, in Luke's Gospel (see 7:36–50). So she became the repentant prostitute familiar from countless works of art. But there is no necessary connection between demonic possession and immoral conduct, and the seven demons should rather be seen as indicating severe (the number seven indicating completeness) psychological disturbance, from which Jesus releases her. She has also been identified with Mary, Martha's sister, who sits at Jesus' feet, and it is seemingly as her that she would have sailed to Provence with Martha. Yet the Gospels distinguish her clearly as Magdalene, meaning that she came from Magdala, a town on the west bank of the Sea of Galilee, where Jesus spent much of his early public life. In the East, the three women have always been kept separate: St Jerome (see 30 Sept.) and St Gregory the Great (see 3 Sept.) upheld the tradition in the West that they were one and the same, but this was rejected by St Bernard (see 20 Aug.), and the three separate identities are now generally agreed.

Medieval pilgrimage routes had more to do with claims to her remains than any possible historical basis. Her cave was identified at La Sainte-Baume in Provence, and she is said to have been miraculously transported to nearby Saint-Maximin before she died, to be given the last sacraments by St Maximinus, who was claimed to have been one of the seventy-two disciples sent out to preach, to have sailed in the boat with her, and to have become the first bishop of Aix-en-Provence. In the eleventh century Vézelay in Burgundy claimed her relics and became an important place of pilgrimage. Saint-Maximin retaliated with the "discovery" of her body in the crypt of the Benedictine monastery there. Her cult became associated with certain guilds, which led the French government to discourage it, and scholarly opinion in the Church has discounted the legends, but pilgrimages to La Sainte-Baume and Saint-Maximin still take place. Mary Magdalene is a saint with whom popular devotion counts for more than official teaching, but the prominence she is given in the Gospels should be enough to ensure her an equally prominent place among the saints.

❖

Dic nobis, Maria,
quid vidisti in via?
Sepulchrum Christi viventis,
et gloriam vidi resurgentis.

Angelicos testes,
sudarium et vestes.
Surrexit Christus spes mea;
Praecedet suos in Galileam.

Tell us, Mary, what did you see on the way? I saw the tomb of the now living Christ. I saw the glory of Christ, now risen. I saw angels who gave witness; the cloths too, which once had covered head and limbs. Christ my hope has risen. He will go before his own into Galilee.

from the Easter Sunday hymn *"Victimae Paschali laudes"*

23

St Bridget of Sweden (1303–1373)

Bridget is known above all for her astonishing "revelations," taken down carefully by her confessors and filling several books. Their graphic accounts of biblical scenes, especially the nativity and the crucifixion, have inspired much of subsequent artistic imagery and popular piety. It is, however, for her religious foundation and her works of practical charity that she was canonized, not for her private revelations—which had some very harsh things to say about popes.

The daughter of a Swedish provincial governor, Bridget married Ulf Gudmarsson when she was thirteen or fourteen; they lived happily together for twenty-eight years and had eight children. In about 1335 she became lady-in-waiting to Blanche of Namur, the new queen of King Magnus II of Sweden. Her visions were already known, as was her care of the sick, but the royal family were content to admire her piety rather than follow her example. Her youngest son died in 1340, and she and her husband went on pilgrimage together in sorrow. He died shortly after their return from Santiago de Compostela, and her visions increased in number and intensity, leading her to wonder whether they were diabolic delusions. Christ assured her that they were not and that she was to be his bride and his mouthpiece.

His "voice" in her visions became more and more specific, even dictating the details of the Rule for a new religious Order. The Order of the Most Holy Saviour, or Brigettines, started with a double monastery at Vadstena. Even the numbers of nuns, priests, deacons, and lay brothers were laid down, as was the disposition of income—any surplus to be given to the poor and to provide books for study. Through her, Christ also admonished the popes for not returning to Rome from Avignon, but even calling Clement VI (1342–52) "a destroyer of souls, worse than Lucifer, more unjust than Pilate, and more merciless than Judas" failed to persuade him. She also used her visions to enjoin peace on King Edward III of England and King Philip IV of France, but they were not sufficiently impressed to call off the devastating Hundred Years War. Nor was King Magnus inclined to call off his "crusade" against pagan neighbours, which was clearly no more than a land-grab. Disillusioned with the lack of effect her increasingly apocalyptic prophecies were having, Bridget left Sweden, even though her continuing charitable works kept her popular with its people, and went to Rome.

There she attended the Jubilee of 1350, to which an indulgence was attached, but she also sought papal approval for her religious foundation and still hoped to influence the pope to return from Avignon. She was given a house by a cardinal, and there wrote her *Sermo Angelicus* from revelations dictated to her by an angel. In the form of a long hymn of praise to the Virgin, its overall theme is God's omnipotence and justice tempered with mercy, with which Mary is associated from the beginning of time. She still tried to admonish worldly churchmen and, with help from her daughter Catherine, also a saint, reformed a lax monastery in Bologna. In 1367 Pope Urban V returned to Rome from Avignon. Bridget was able to get her Rule approved by him, but he failed to listen to her warnings that his death was close and that he should not go back to Avignon. He did, and he died four months later. Her pleadings to his successor, Gregory XI, to return to Rome went unheeded. Her warnings of dire consequences for the people of Rome if they failed to mend their ways did not help her popularity there: she fell into debt and was forced to leave her house.

Directed in a vision to go on pilgrimage to the Holy Land, she set out in 1371 with Catherine, two of her sons, and other followers. Her son Charles died in Naples on the way (after an affair with the notorious Queen Joanna), and they were nearly shipwrecked, but Bridget ploughed resolutely on. In the Holy Land, she experienced detailed visions of episodes in Jesus' life in the places where they were said to have occurred (with some variants on the biblical accounts). She took time on the return journey to denounce the people of Cyprus and Naples for their immoral ways as she passed through, but with little or no effect. She arrived back in Rome early in 1373 already ill and died there on 23 July. Her remains were taken in triumph back to Vadstena four months later. She was canonized in 1391 and is the patron saint of Sweden.

Her revelations were soon translated (from the Latin in which her confessors had compiled them from her verbal accounts, checking their version carefully with her) into several languages, including English by 1415. They had a wide influence on the devotional life of the fifteenth century. King Henry V of England had a great devotion to her and founded the great Brigettine abbey at Syon, halfway between Windsor and Westminster. This was dissolved by Henry VIII but has a descendant at South Brent in Devon. There are now three branches of the Brigettine Order in existence, with some thirty houses in Europe, the USA, and India.

❖

Because [Mary] had proved to be the most humble among angels and humans, she was raised above all that was created and is most beautiful of all and more like God than any other can be.
St Bridget, *Sermo Angelicus*

24

St John Boste and other English and Welsh Martyrs (died between 1588 and 1598)

This group of English martyrs suffered during the period when anti-Catholic feeling in England was intensified as a result of the defeat of the Spanish Armada in July 1588, after which it became more logical, as well as official policy, to see Catholics as supporters of an overseas power and therefore as traitors. It had also become a capital offence to be a priest working in England who had trained on the Continent. Most of those recognized as martyrs from these years fall into this category. Those noted here, in chronological order of their date of death, died on various days in July between the above dates; St John Boste gives his name to the group as a canonized saint whose anniversary actually falls today.

Robert Ludlam, Nicholas Garlick, and Robert Sutton suffered in July 1588. Ludlam was born in Derbyshire and attended St John's College, Oxford, but left after two years without taking a degree. After some time spent teaching, he went to the English College at Reims (the seminary founded originally by Cardinal William Allen at Douai and later moved to Reims) in 1580, was ordained in 1581, and returned to the English mission the following year. He was arrested in his home county and condemned at Derby. Garlick had a similar background: Derbyshire, a short spell at Oxford, teaching, Reims. Ordained in 1582, he was back in England the following year, was betrayed, arrested, banished, went back to Reims for two days only, and set out for England once more. He took part in a famous series of exorcisms at the house of Lord Vaux in Hackney (east London) in 1585–6, from which he was known to the spies of Elizabeth's secretary of state, Sir Francis Walsingham, as "Garlick the demonite." He was arrested with Ludlam in Derbyshire and tried with him. Both were condemned for being seminary priests working in England and were hanged, drawn, and quartered on the 24th. Three days later Sutton suffered the same barbarous fate at Stafford. Born in Staffordshire, he had also been at Oxford, where he took an MA at Trinity College. He was given a living in the queen's gift and ordained deacon (in the reformed Church) in

1576 but resigned and went to Douai, where he was ordained the next year. Back in England, he worked for some years before being arrested in London and banished. He too soon returned to England, and he was arrested in July 1588, by which time the climate had changed and he was tried and condemned to death. These three were beatified in 1987.

The following year two priests and two laymen were executed together at Oxford on 5 July. George Nichols went to Reims after studying at Brasenose College, Oxford. Ordained in 1583, he returned and worked in the Oxford area, bringing several people back to the old faith. A regular meeting place for Catholics was the Catherine Wheel Inn, where Nichols was arrested. Richard Yaxley had been ordained at Reims in 1585 and then worked in Cornwall. He was arrested with Nichols, as were Thomas Belson, who had studied at Reims but without being ordained and who was at the inn to make his confession to Nichols, and the inn's pot-boy, Humphrey Pritchard, who helped Catholics on the run or in hiding. The two priests were condemned to death for working as priests and the two laymen for helping them. These four were also beatified in 1987.

Three more seminary priests and two laymen died in July 1591. Roger Beesley, from Lancashire, was ordained at Reims in 1587, returned to England the following year, and worked near Lancaster. He was arrested in London in late 1590 and tortured in the Tower, then moved to Newgate, and hanged, drawn, and quartered in Fleet Street on the 1st. Montford Scott studied at Cambridge before going to Douai, was arrested once when he returned to England as a sub-deacon and again after his ordination in 1577, being exiled both times. He was back in the early 1580s, working in East Anglia and widely revered for his holiness. He was arrested again in December 1590, sent to London, examined, condemned, and executed with Beesley, with whom he was beatified in 1987. Roger Dickenson, from Lincolnshire, went to Reims in 1582 and was ordained and returned to England the following year, by the end of which he had been arrested. He seems to have been exiled in 1585 but came back and worked with the poor in Winchester, helping a Fr Thomas Stanney and also caring for Catholics in prison. There he met an illiterate farm worker named Ralph Milner, who had become a Catholic as an adult and been arrested as he made his First Communion, released, but imprisoned several times. Both were arrested in January 1591, examined in London, and sent back to Winchester for trial. Milner refused to give up "his God" for the sake of his wife and nine children and was condemned for sheltering Dickenson. Both were executed on the 7th. Laurence Humphrey was a young layman who had become a Catholic after conversations with Fr Stanney, who praised him for his piety and his charity. He had the misfortune to catch a fever and in his delirium call the queen a whore and a heretic. This was treason, even though he had no memory of it, and he was executed in Winchester (the exact date is not known), aged twenty. These three were beatified, as part of a large group, in 1929.

July 1592 saw the death of one seminary priest, Joseph Lambton, who came from Malton in Yorkshire. After studying at Reims he went on to the English College in Rome, where he was ordained in 1592 and left for England. He was arrested almost as soon as he landed at Newcastle upon Tyne by the town clerk, who suspected this stranger of being a priest. Condemned for being a seminary priest working in England, even though he had not done any work, he was hanged, drawn, and quartered—spending longer in agony than usual, as the hangman botched the job—in Newcastle on the 24th. He was beatified in 1987.

In July 1593 the first Welshman in this group, William Davies, was executed in Anglesey. Born in North Wales in about 1558, he was ordained at Reims in 1585 and was arrested on landing two months later. He spent over three years in the Tower but was then released for some reason, despite the increase in persecution following the defeat of the Armada. He worked in North Wales before he was arrested again, at Holyhead as he was about to embark for Ireland with four students destined for the English College at Valladolid. All five were condemned to death, but the students were reprieved when the judge found them guilty of the lesser crime of refusing to attend church. William, who seems to have refused several offers of help to escape from prison, was hanged, drawn, and quartered at Beaumaris on the 27th.

St John Boste, who gives his name to the group considered here, was one of four known as the Durham martyrs. He was born in Westmorland and educated at Oxford, serving for a time as a Protestant minister. He then became a Catholic and went to Reims in 1580. Ordained and back on the English mission the following year, he ministered in the north of England and occasionally in Scotland, becoming the most wanted priest in the country. He was eventually captured after being betrayed by a renegade priest, sent to London, then to Windsor for questioning by the infamous Topcliffe, then taken to the Tower and tortured so severely that he was left permanently crippled. In July 1594 he was sent back to Durham for trial. Tried with him were John Ingram and George Swallowell. Ingram came from Herefordshire and appears to have been expelled from Oxford for becoming a Catholic. He went to Douai and moved to Reims in 1582, being captured on his way there by a group of Calvinist soldiers but managing to escape. He moved on to the English College in Rome in 1584 and was ordained in 1589. The English authorities were waiting for his return, but he evaded them by sailing to Scotland, where he served as chaplain to a knight before being forced to move to England when persecution broke out in Scotland. He was captured immediately, tortured in the Tower, and sent to the July 1594 Durham assizes. Swallowell, born in County Durham, served as a Protestant minister and then announced to his congregation that he was becoming a Catholic. He was arrested and imprisoned in Durham with John Boste, who helped confirm him in his new faith. Boste was executed on the 24th, Ingram and Swallowell on the 26th. The fourth Durham martyr was John

Speed, who was not executed till 4 February in the following year. The Durham martyrs were beatified in 1929, and John Boste was canonized in 1970 as one of the Forty Martyrs of England and Wales.

Three years later another convert seminary priest and three laymen were executed at York. William Andelby was brought up a Protestant in Yorkshire and graduated from Cambridge in 1572. In Flanders, on his way to join Dutch Protestant forces to fight against the occupying Spaniards, he visited Douai and, after conversations with Cardinal Allen, decided to become a Catholic. He was ordained in 1587 and sent back to England early the following year. Known for the austerity and prayerfulness of his life, he evaded capture for an unusually long period. Eventually caught—it is not known how or when—he was sentenced for being a seminary priest working in England and martyred on 4 July 1597. The three laymen executed with him were Thomas Warcop, who had sheltered him, Edward Fulthrop, who had been reconciled to Catholicism by him, and Henry Abbot, who seems to have had no connection with him. They were all beatified in 1929.

The following July another Welshman, John Jones, was executed in London. Born in North Wales and brought up a Catholic, he studied for the priesthood in France, joining the Friars Minor of the Observance. There is some confusion about his identity and whereabouts for several years, but he made his final profession in Rome in 1591 and returned to England the following year. He was sheltered in London by Anne Line (see 27 Feb.) for a time, then worked in various parts of the country until he was arrested in 1597. He was severely tortured in prison and tried on 3 July 1598. He asked to be tried by judges rather than an "ignorant jury" and protested his innocence of treason, but the judge told him that working in England as a priest trained abroad was treason by statute. He was hanged, drawn, and quartered in the Old Kent Road on the 12th. He was beatified in 1929 and canonized in 1970.

25

St James the Greater (First Century)

James the Greater (as opposed to the younger apostle of the same name) was called by Jesus with his brother John immediately after Peter (see 29 June) and Andrew (see 30 Nov.): "As he went a little farther, he saw James son of Zebedee and his brother John, who were in their boat mending the nets. Immediately he called them; and they left their father Zebedee in the boat with the hired men, and followed him" (Mark 1:19–20). With Peter, James and John form a privileged trio in the Gospels, a reflection of the position they held in the early Church. They are singled out to be present at the cure of Peter's mother-in-law (Mark 1:29–31), at the raising of Jairus' daughter (Mark 5:35–43; Luke 8:49–56), most significantly as witnesses to the transfiguration (Matt. 17:1–8; Mark 9:2–8; Luke 9:28–36) and then called to keep watch during Jesus' agony in the garden (Matt. 26:36–46; Mark 14:32–42).

Jesus nicknamed James and his brother *Boanerges,* meaning "sons of thunder," an indication of the temper they show when they want to call down fire from heaven to destroy a Samaritan village that would not welcome Jesus (Luke 9:51–6). According to Matthew, their mother is ambitious for them to sit on either side of Jesus in his kingdom; in Mark's account they make the request themselves (Matt. 20:20–24; Mark 10:35–40). Jesus asks if they can drink the cup that he is to drink, they answer that they can, and he promises them that they will—in other words that they will suffer martyrdom. James was in fact the first of the apostles to be martyred, in the persecution started by King Herod Agrippa in about the year 44: "About that time, King Herod laid violent hands on some who belonged to the church. He had James, the brother of John, killed with the sword" (Acts 12:1–2). Nothing else is known about his death, though there is a tradition that he was buried in Jerusalem.

After that, legend takes over, as it did with Mary Magdalene (see 22 July), and James became the patron saint of Spain, the "moor-slayer" who led the Reconquest as a mounted knight, and the focus of one of the three great pilgrimages of the Middle Ages (and indeed of our own times), the others being Rome and Jerusalem. Santiago de Compostela means "St James of the Field of Stars," its name deriving from a story that a shepherd was guided to discover his bones by stars shining on a particular spot. This is in fact the site of an early Christian *martyrium,* indicating that there was an early cult of a saint associated with it. But the cult of James there began in the eighth century, after the Moorish invasion had rapidly pushed the Christian forces into the northwestern corner of Spain, and there is no documentary evidence of it before the ninth century. The cult then grew with the growth of pilgrimages, and his image became more warlike as the Crusades (not just the Reconquest of Spain) developed. This version depended on his remains being transferred to Galicia some time after his death. An earlier version based the cult on the story that he had preached in Spain, which is even less likely. As the pilgrimage grew, with routes starting in various places in France, abbeys and churches were built along the routes, acquiring their own background stories (such as the association of El Cid with San Pedro de Cardeña near Burgos) to impress pilgrims.

St James himself acquired the attributes of a pilgrim: a floppy hat, staff, water bottle, and scallop shell. The "Road to Santiago" has recently been restored with funds from the European Community and attracts hundreds of thousands of pilgrims each year. The *botafumeiro,* the six-foot-high incense censer hung from the crossing vault of Santiago Cathedral, introduced to counteract the stench of the pilgrim crowds, is still swung across the transepts, almost brushing the floor of the crossing, on the saint's feast-day each year.

26

Bd Titus Brandsma (Anno Sjoerd Brandsma; 1881–1942)

Born into a staunchly Catholic family in the mainly Calvinist Netherlands province of Friesland—his three sisters all became nuns and his brother a Franciscan—Anno entered the Carmelites, taking the name Titus in religion. He was ordained in 1905 and spent three years in Rome studying philosophy.

Returning to the Netherlands, he taught philosophy at the Carmelite seminary for fifteen years. He also started a journal of Marian devotion, edited a Catholic newspaper, set up a Catholic library, and founded a Catholic secondary school specializing in the sciences—all this in addition to translating the works of St Teresa of Avila (see 15 Oct.) into Dutch. In 1923 he was appointed professor of philosophy and of the history of mysticism at the Catholic University of Nijmegen. He became an internationally recognized expert on mysticism, writing, organizing congresses, and lecturing widely on the subject. He also worked to promote Christian unity and became national spiritual adviser to Dutch Catholic journalists.

In 1935 Hitler promulgated new marriage laws restricting the rights of Jews. Titus protested against this in the press and on a lecture tour undertaken to explain its evil. He also drew up plans to evacuate Dutch Jews to a Carmelite mission in Brazil, but he was never able to put this into effect. Germany occupied the Netherlands early in the Second World War, and Titus issued guidelines to the Dutch Catholic press, telling them that newspapers could not carry Nazi propaganda or advertisements and still call themselves Catholic. He was warned that he was liable to arrest but dismissed the threat saying he had always wanted a cell of his own. The arrest came shortly after his warning to Catholic journalists, and he spent several months in various prisons. He used the time to write a biography of St Teresa and kept a journal. He maintained a consistent charity toward the prison guards, however strict, telling his fellow-prisoners that they should pray for them—even though "You don't need to pray for them all day long. God is quite pleased with a single prayer"—and that there might still be hidden good in them.

He was moved to the concentration camp at Dachau, in Bavaria near Munich, where he was regularly beaten but still urged prayers for his persecutors. He risked worse punishment by distributing hosts consecrated by German priests in the camp, who were allowed to say Mass. After five weeks in the camp his health broke down under the forced physical work and he was sent to the hospital. There, a number of inhumane medical experiments were carried out on him before he was put to death by lethal injection on 26 July 1942. The nurse who gave the injection was Dutch and a lapsed Catholic, and Titus had tried to persuade her back to the Faith. She refused to try to pray, but he gave her his rosary, saying, "Surely you can say, 'Pray for us sinners'?" After the war she did return to Catholic practice, and she gave evidence that he accepted death with the words, "Not my will, but thy will be done." His body was cremated. His prison writings were published in the Netherlands and his popularity led to his cause being introduced in 1973. He was beatified in 1985.

27

St Simeon Stylites (390–459)

Stylite means "pillar," and this Simeon (the Elder) was the first to adopt the extraordinary penitential life of spending his entire time on top of a pillar. His motive for doing so was to find solitude, and in this he failed: as the fame of his holiness spread, he was surrounded by increasing crowds.

He was the son of a shepherd from Cilicia (southern Turkey), near the northern border of Syria. As a young man he had a dream or vision in which he was exhorted to dig the foundations of a house ever deeper. He seems to have interpreted this as meaning that he had to adopt a life of increasing penance and mortification. He joined a nearby monastery as a servant, then moved to another, from which the abbot expelled him for excess after a rope of twisted palm leaves he had wound round himself became so embedded in his flesh that it had to be cut out with careful softening and incisions.

Moving on to another site as a hermit, he is reputed to have spent his first Lent entirely without food or water. At the end, he was found unconscious and was coaxed back to life with a few lettuce leaves and the Eucharist. The loaves and water left earlier by a kindly priest were untouched. After three years he moved to the top of a mountain, where he chained himself to a rock. The vicar of the patriarch of Antioch told him that his will and God's grace were enough to keep him free from temptation, so he sent for a blacksmith to cut him free. Even on his mountain-top, he could not find the solitude he craved, so he came down, built a pillar some nine feet high, and established himself on top of it, on a platform about six feet across. He spent the rest of his life on top of pillars of increasing height. Accounts vary (and may all exaggerate) but it seems that he spent four years on this first pillar, three on a second, eighteen feet high, ten on a third, thirty-three feet high, and finally twenty on a fourth, sixty feet high.

He spent his days and nights in prayer, bowing over twelve hundred times daily, and fasting totally in Lent, of which he spent the first two weeks standing, the second two sitting, and the last two lying down from exhaustion.

Obviously there was some rope system to carry food and other absolute necessities up (and waste down) for the rest of the year, and this supposed other people. As he might have foreseen, people came in increasing numbers, and he started preaching twice-daily homilies. These had none of the extremism of his way of life but, in moderate and gentle terms, encouraged people to act with justice and sincerity, to pray, and to avoid usury and swearing. He was a firm upholder of the doctrines of Chalcedon (451), so he was by no means completely detached from what was happening in the wider Church. Three eastern emperors, Theodosius II, Marcian, and Leo, were among those who came to listen to his advice. His was a unique form of challenge to the debased values of his age. For some it was clearly excessive and repellent: some Egyptian monks sent him a writ of excommunication; they were then told of his charity and good sense and withdrew it.

Simeon died on top of his pillar, bowing in prayer. The bishops of the province of Antioch bore his body there for burial. The date of his death was 1 September, on which his feast is celebrated in the East, but the new Roman Martyrology assigns him to today. His extreme way of life was inevitably copied, and two stylite successors, Simeon the Younger and Daniel, are commemorated on 24 May and 11 December respectively. The remains of a church and monastery built near his pillar can still be seen.

28

Bd Peter Poveda (Pedro Poveda Castroverde; 1874–1936)

Peter Poveda was beatified as a martyr of the Spanish civil war (see 20 June) but is considered here mainly as a distinguished educator and founder of the Teresian Association. Born in Linares in south-eastern Spain, he came from a solidly Catholic family and entered the seminary in Jaén at the age of fifteen. His parents could not maintain him there, but the bishop of Guadix (further south) offered him a scholarship, and he moved to the seminary there, where he was ordained in 1897. The outskirts of Guadix consisted (and still consist) of caves cut out of hillocks, and their inhabitants were then desperately poor (most of the caves sprouted TV aerials in the 1960s). Peter, after studying theology in Seville, worked among them for three years, building schools for the children and workshops for the adults to give both some chance in life.

His evident success made him very popular among the cave-dwellers, and the town council named a street after him, but some more conservative-minded Catholics became envious of his success. Some of his fellow-priests conspired against him to the point where he felt he had to leave the town. After a period of being unattached to any diocese, he was "promoted" to the post of canon at the shrine of the Virgin Mary in Covadonga, in the north-western province of Asturias, about as far from Guadix as it is possible to go in Spain, and equally far in terms of function from his previous social apostolate. At the age of thirty-two, full of energy and crusading zeal, Peter found himself in vast buildings, surrounded by elderly canons. Covadonga, however, was known as the place where the Reconquest of Spain from the Moors had begun, and Peter decided to use it as the springboard for a new crusade.

His chosen field was education, concentrating on the professional formation of teachers. He opened a student residence in the nearby large town of Oviedo and named it the St Teresa of Avila Academy. This became the start of the Teresian Association, whose members, initially all women involved in education at all levels, encouraged young women into higher education—an aim quite distinct from the fostering of the domestic virtues of "piety, duty, and domesticity" that characterized Spanish Catholic education of the time. Inspired by the teaching of Pope Leo XIII's *Rerum Novarum* and spurred on by his experiences of the poverty of Guadix, Poveda made sure that the educational principles of his Association included social justice.

In 1913 he returned to Andalusia when he was appointed canon of Jaén Cathedral. The Teresian Association gained both ecclesiastical and civil approval, and he opened a hall of residence for women students in Madrid, followed by more in other major cities. In 1921 Poveda was appointed chaplain at the royal palace and moved permanently to Madrid. He took part in all major initiatives and debates throughout the 1920s. The Association continued to grow and received papal approval in 1924. He personally oversaw the establishment of new branches in Chile and Italy.

On the outbreak of the civil war he was warned that his life was in danger because of his part in Catholic education, resented by the revolutionary committees, even though he propounded a thoroughly liberal educational creed. He refused to leave Republican-held Madrid, however, and was arrested by militiamen on 27 July 1936. After a series of interrogations, he disappeared, and his body was found by the eastern cemetery the following morning. Another member of the Teresian Association was beatified with him on 10 October 1993. She was Victoria Diez y Bustos de Molina, born in Seville, a dedicated teacher who also saw educated women as the great hope for Spain's future. She was in charge of a school some twenty miles west of Córdoba when she was seized in the evening of 11 August 1936, marched to an abandoned lead mine, and shot at dawn the next day.

29

SS Martha, Mary, and Lazarus (First Century)

According to the Gospels, Martha and Mary were sisters living in Bethany, near Jerusalem, where their brother Lazarus (either a blood-brother or a cousin like "Jesus' brothers") lived with them. The new Roman Martyrology accords Martha the leading "memorial" for today, on account of her confession of faith in Jesus as the Christ, with Mary and Lazarus sharing a "commemoration," but their stories and legends are inextricably linked.

According to Luke, Martha welcomes Jesus into their house, and there follows one of those vignettes that stamp personages in the Gospels with an indelible character, so that "a Martha" is instantly recognizable:

> [H]e entered a certain village, where a woman named Martha welcomed him into her home. She had a sister named Mary, who sat at the Lord's feet and listened to what he was saying. But Martha was distracted by her many tasks; so she came to him and asked, "Lord, do you not care that my sister has left me to do all the work by myself? Tell her then to help me." But the Lord answered her, "Martha, Martha, you are worried and distracted by many things; there is need of only one thing. Mary has chosen the better part, which will not be taken away from her." (Luke 10:38b–42)

Luke makes no mention of the raising of Lazarus, which is told by John (in chapter 11). Jesus, told that Lazarus is ill, makes a point of not going to Bethany until he knows he has died, "so that you may believe" (v. 15b). When he does go to Bethany, again it is Martha who comes out to meet him, saying, "Lord, if you had been here, my brother would not have died" (v. 21b). Jesus tells her he will rise again, to which she replies that she knows about the resurrection on the last day, but Jesus tells her that he is "the resurrection and the life" and asks her if she believes that. She answers, "Yes. Lord, I believe that you are the Messiah, the Son of God, the one coming into the world" (v. 27b). Martha summons Mary, who had stayed in the house with numerous mourners who had come from Jerusalem, and Mary also tells Jesus that if he had been there, Lazarus would not have died. Jesus, who had earlier seemed almost hard-hearted over Lazarus' death, is moved by Mary's tears, so that people remark on how much he loved Lazarus. He goes to the cave in which Lazarus has been placed and asks for the stone to be rolled away. The ever-practical Martha warns him, "Lord, already there is a stench because he has been dead for four days" (v. 39b). Jesus urges faith, calls on his Father, and summons Lazarus, who emerges with "his hands and feet bound with strips of cloth, and his face wrapped in a cloth" (v. 44a)—an image that has fascinated artists down the centuries.

Lazarus makes a brief further appearance as one of those "at table" when Jesus eats with Martha and Mary, when John relates that Mary "took a pound of costly perfume made of pure nard, anointed Jesus' feet, and wiped them with her hair" (12:3a). Judas rebukes her for the waste, saying (hypocritically) that the nard could have been sold and the money given to the poor, leading to Jesus' (problematical) rebuke that "[y]ou always have the poor with you, but you do not always have me" (12:8). This is the episode that led to the confusion of Mary of Bethany with the woman who performs a similar anointing in Luke 7 and hence with Mary Magdalene and the repentant prostitute (see 22 July).

None of the three makes a post-resurrection appearance in the New Testament, leaving them open to legendary development. In the East, Lazarus and his sisters were put to sea in a leaking boat but reached Cyprus, where Lazarus became bishop of Larnaca, dying peacefully about thirty years later. The (later) Western tradition has the boat drifting to the south coast of France and Lazarus becoming first bishop of Marseilles. Martha and Mary (as Mary of Bethany, though not as Mary Magdalene) then disappear, leaving the man Lazarus to do the preaching and converting, but he takes on the persona of the other Lazarus in the Gospels, the poor man in the parable of Dives and Lazarus. It was this Lazarus who gave his name to the charitable hospitals, *lazarettos*, of the Middle Ages, and to the Saint-Lazare prison in Marseilles. To add to the confusion, a fifth-century bishop of Aix-en-Provence was buried in Saint-Victor's crypt in Marseilles; his relics were then confused with those of St Nazarius, supposedly discovered by St Ambrose (see 7 Dec.). Processions to the place where Lazarus was raised from the tomb were drawing great crowds by the fourth century, and "his tomb" is still shown to pilgrims today (though some maintain it is a grain silo).

30

St Leopold Mandic (Bogdan Mandic; 1866–1942)

Bogdan (in English Theodore, meaning "God-given") was the youngest of twelve children born to a devoutly Croatian Catholic couple in Dalmatia (the eastern coast of the Adriatic Sea, now in Croatia). He grew to be less than four foot six inches tall, and later developed a bad limp from arthritis as well as a speech impediment. At the age of sixteen he entered the Seraphic Seminary of the Capuchins at Udine, close to the border in northern Italy, from where Capuchins evangelizing in Dalmatia had made a deep impression on him. Two years later he joined the Capuchin novitiate at Bassano, taking the name Leopold in religion.

He came from a region where Catholics and Orthodox lived alongside each other, not always in harmony, and he resolved to make the return of those he termed "dissident Orientals" to the true Church his life's work. He dedicated himself to this special calling as best he could for the rest of his life. Ordained priest in 1890, he spent seven years in the Capuchin monastery in Venice, where he devoted most of his time to hearing Confessions. He was then posted back to Dalmatia to take charge of the monastery at Zara. In 1909 he moved to Italy once more and spent the rest of his life in Padua. What he called his "headquarters" was a confessional, roasting in summer and freezing in winter, where he heard Confessions for between ten and fifteen hours a day. He was given other jobs from time to time but was usually relieved of them quite quickly and returned to his confessional.

His brethren, who tended to despise him on account of his physical short-comings, accused him of lacking moral theology and being too lenient with his penitents, calling him "Brother Absolve-all." He pointed to the love Jesus had shown on the cross for sinners. He continued to strive for reunion with the Orthodox Church, but his superiors saw this as a stupid obsession and pre-vented him from taking any appointment that would allow him to carry out practical work toward its achievement. It seemed such a post might come his way when he was appointed in 1923 to Fiume, a town on the border with Dalmatia recently annexed by Italy (now Rijeka in Croatia). But the bishop of Padua revoked the appointment, wanting to keep such an assiduous confessor. From then on, after a personal revelation that "every soul he helped in the confessional would be his East," Leopold confined his thoughts on reunion to his private writings. He treated every penitent with extreme attention, as though the conversion of each sinner were a decisive contribution to the conversion of Eastern "schismatics."

He was already regarded as a saint in his lifetime, with claims of miraculous cures being obtained through his prayers. On 30 July 1942 he collapsed and died just as he was about to begin his morning Mass. The sort of popular cult that the Vatican now tries to discourage began immediately, intensified when the church and monastery were destroyed by Allied bombing in 1944 but his confessional, his "cell," as he called it, remained intact. He had prophesied to a friend before his death that this would happen, claiming that so many souls had been saved in his cell that it had to stay undamaged. A statue of the Mother of God that stood next to it was also preserved, symbolizing the intense love of Mary that pervaded Leopold's spirituality and counsel. A special chapel was later built next to the confessional; his body was reburied there, and it became a popular place of pilgrimage. He was beatified in 1976 and canonized on 16 October 1983.

31

St Ignatius of Loyola (1491–1556)

The founder of the Society of Jesus was born in Loyola in the Spanish Basque Country to parents who both came from distinguished families in the area. At the age of about fifteen he left home to become a page in the household of the treasurer to the king of Castile, a prominent Castilian nobleman, named Juan Velázquez de Cuellar, living at Arévalo, between Avila and Valladolid. Here Iñigo (the form of his name familiar in the Basque region) received a courtly education, learned to read books of chivalry and romance, gambled recklessly, became involved with women, quarrelled, and duelled. In 1515 he was brought to court for carrying out an ambush on some clergy: as he was dressed in armour and carrying a dagger and a sword, this was premeditated assault, not a spur-of-the-moment brawl.

His career as a non-idealistic Don Quixote was cut short in 1516 when King Ferdinand died and was succeeded by his distant cousin Charles of Burgundy. Velázquez de Cuellar lost his position and retired heavily in debt. Iñigo went north to Pamplona and spent five years serving in the army of the viceroy of Navarre, to whom he was related. In 1521 the French invaded Navarre and besieged Pamplona. Iñigo rashly refused to surrender and was hit by a cannon ball, which badly broke one leg and injured the other. He was taken prisoner by the French, who set his leg and eventually allowed him home to Loyola. He had promised to devote his life to being a knight for St Peter if he recovered, which he did after nine months of convalescence. He asked for novels of chivalry to read during his enforced inactivity, but instead was given a copy of *The Golden Legend* by James of Voragine (see 13 July) and began to dream of becoming a "knight of Christ," pursuing the ideals of saints he came to admire, such as Francis and Dominic, instead of the impossible dream of some high-born lady. Doing penance was the starting-point of the knightly quest, sacred and secular, and he planned a pilgrimage to Jerusalem.

One wakeful night (knight-errants are not much given to sleeping) he had a vision of Our Lady, which filled him with intense joy and (he later wrote) permanently removed all temptations of the flesh. Setting off for Jerusalem by way of Barcelona, he stopped at the monastery of Montserrat, where he made a general confession and seems to have been dissuaded from going on to Jerusalem, perhaps until he had become more settled in his converted life. He became a hermit at nearby Manresa, praying, studying the spiritual life, meditating on the Trinity, and fasting and doing penance. He emerged after ten months at peace with himself and with the germs of the *Spiritual Exercises* in note form. Designed as a practical manual for those teaching seekers after perfection, not simply an account of the mystical way, this became his greatest contribution to Western spirituality. Their goal was personal conversion and individual salvation, forcing those who carried out the prescribed systematic examination of conscience to choose either Christ or the world.

Iñigo then proceeded on to Jerusalem, staying about three weeks and learning that dreams of converting the Muslims were simply not practicable. Back in Barcelona, he set himself to learn Latin and study theology, and he began to guide others through early forms of the *Exercises*, which led him to counsel moderation in penance. Moving on to the university of Alcalá de Henares, he began to gather a group of "disciples" around him and to wear clerical dress. This aroused the suspicions of the Inquisition; the *Exercises* were examined and found orthodox, but he was told not to ape a religious Order. The same happened at Salamanca University, to which he had progressed, and he decided to leave Spain in order to be able to study while carrying on his apostolate. He moved to Paris in 1528 and spent six extremely formative years there. A group of those who were to be the first members of the new Society gathered around him; he took them through the *Exercises* and started organizing them to make a real contribution to reform in the Church as well as carrying out works of practical charity among the sick and the poor. After a period of rest in Spain and a further two years of study in Venice, Ignatius (as he now called himself in the more familiar Latin form) gathered his companions there, and they decided to form themselves into a "Company of Jesus." Between 1537 and 1539 the group re-formed in Rome. Ignatius had a momentous spiritual experience on the way there, which showed him "clearly that God the Father had placed him with his Son Christ," which he saw as divine confirmation of the course he was following. The group offered their services to Pope Paul III and proved their practical charity when Rome suffered a famine. Rulers began to ask them to go to other cities and on missions to the new colonies. They saw the need for closer organization and asked Ignatius to draw up an outline that would confirm their way of life. Ignatius aimed for flexibility in action and did not prescribe the saying of the traditional Office. After some objections the new foundation received papal approval in September 1540, with the revised name "Society of Jesus." Its aims were directed more to converting the Muslims and evangelizing distant countries than to combating the Protestant Reformation, in which Jesuits were in fact to play such a prominent part.

Ignatius spent the rest of his life in Rome, directing the Society and starting many charitable institutions. He wrote some seven thousand letters to members on distant missions and to kings and queens and others who asked him for spiritual guidance. He was no autocrat, relying on members' good judgment after they had been formed by the *Exercises*. At the same time, total obedience was owed to regional superiors. It was an army composed of officers, with God in command. Ignatius drew up a formal Constitution between 1544 and 1550, which confirmed the lines of delegation of command and the lack of formal division of time; it also enjoined exceptionally long courses of study, as Ignatius saw the need for highly educated clergy on the basis of his personal experience. Colleges were soon opened in major Italian cities, followed by the Gregorian University in Rome. Less than a decade after his death, there were Jesuit colleges in Spain, Portugal, France, Germany, India, Brazil, and Japan. The influence of the Society on the Church worldwide has been incalculable ever since. It has been called (by Prof. H. Outram Evennett) "the most powerful, active, modernizing, humanistic, and flexible force in the Counter-Reformation." Ignatius' insistence on "visualizing" the subject matter of a meditation as intensely as possible also had a huge influence on Western theatre, literature, and painting.

Ignatius died suddenly on 31 July 1556, and his remains were enshrined in what is now the church of the Gesù in Rome. He was canonized in 1622, on an extraordinary occasion when two other great religious founders, Teresa of Avila (see 15 Oct.) and Philip Neri (see 26 May) were also canonized, together with the first great Jesuit missionary, Francis Xavier (see 3 Dec.), and the humble Spanish farmer Isidore (see 15 May).

❖

May it please him through his infinite and supreme goodness to deign to give us his abundant grace, so that we may know his most holy will and perfectly fulfil it.
from one of the last letters written by Ignatius

Other Familiar English Names for July

1. George, John, Justin, Peter, Thomas
2. John, Peter
3. Joseph, Leo, Mark, Mary, Peter, Philip, Raymund
4. Andrew, Antony, Bertha, Catherine, Edward, Henry, John, Patrick, Peter, Thomas, Valentine, William
5. Edward, George, Humphrey, Matthew, Richard, Robert, Rose, Teresa, Thomas
6. Mary, Peter, Susannah, Thomas
7. Benedict, Felix, John, Joseph, Laurence, Mary, Peter, Ralph, Roger
8. Adrian, John
9. Adrian, Francis, Gregory, Joan, Nicholas, Pauline, Veronica
10. Antony, Philip, Victoria
11. Anne, Bertrand, John, Mary, Thomas
12. David, John, Leo, Peter, Rose
13. Henry, James, Joseph, Paul, Thomas
14. Francis, John, Richard, Vincent
15. Andrew, Anne, Bernard, David, Donald, Edith, Felix, James, Joseph, Peter, Philip
16. John, Mary, Paul, Simon, Teresa
17. Leo, Peter, Teresa
18. Bruno, Dominic, Frederick, Simon
19. Elizabeth, John, Peter
20. Bernard, Joseph, Margaret, Paul
21. Gabriel, Joseph, Victor
22. Andrew, Anne, Augustine, James, John, Laurence, Philip, Walter
23. Joan, John
24. Antony, Christine, John, Joseph, Louisa, Mary, Nicholas, Richard, Robert, Teresa
25. Antony, Christopher, Francis, John, Paul, Peter
26. Anne, Camilla, Edward, George, Hugo, John, Peter, Robert, Vincent, William
27. Felix, George, Mary, Natalie, Robert, William
28. James, Victor
29. John, Joseph, William
30. Edward, Joseph, Richard, Thomas
31. Helen, John, Justin, Peter

AUGUST

August is a month crammed with major saints, to the point where several days have more than one who should ideally have an entry here. There are also few relatively "empty" days, and so moving names to dates close to that of their commemoration has not been easy. The 1st is a particularly crowded day: St Ethelwold has been moved from there to the 5th and St Julian Peter Eymard from there (he is already moved to the 2nd in the new Roman Martyrology) to the 3rd. Bd Mary McKillop, who deserves an entry as a most remarkable woman and Australia's first blessed, has been moved from the 8th, which has to belong to St Dominic, to the 12th. The Feast of the Assumption, the 15th, is taken as the "birthday into heaven" of the Blessed Virgin Mary and contains the only entry on her in this volume, restricted almost entirely to a consideration of what the New Testament tells us of her life. St Louis of France and St Joseph Calasanz both feature in the Universal Calendar on the 25th, and both deserve an entry, so the latter has been moved to the 26th.

1

St Alphonsus de'Liguori (Alfonso Maria de'Liguori; 1696–1787)

The founder of the Redemptorists was the eldest child of the captain of the royal galleys of the kingdom of Naples. By the age of sixteen he held a doctorate in civil and canon law; he practised as a barrister for eight years, during which it is claimed that he never lost a case, but then he did lose in a major land dispute. Interpreting this as a sign that God did not wish him to practise law, he also abandoned any intention of marrying. To his father's initial distress, he placed his sword on an altar and asked to join the Oratory.

He was ordained at the age of thirty and spent two years in preaching missions all over the kingdom of Naples, gaining a reputation for being effective without pomposity or undue severity. He organized the unemployed and petty thieves into prayer groups and encouraged them to look after their physical as well as their mental health, which aroused mistrust among more traditionally zealous elements. He was then appointed chaplain to a college that trained missionaries to go to China. During his time there he became friendly with an older priest, Thomas Falcoia, who had started a convent for

Visitandine nuns near Amalfi. One of these, Sister Mary Celeste, had a vision of a new Rule, which corresponded closely to one Falcoia (now bishop of Castellamare) had had twenty years earlier. He asked Alphonsus to investigate the nun's claim, and Alphonsus decided it came from God. The convent was reorganized according to the new Rule, which then became the basis for a new Congregation for men, to evangelize the neglected poor of Naples. This was named the Congregation of the Most Holy Redeemer in November 1732. After some initial arguments and difficulties, Alphonsus and his postulants enjoyed growing success and were able to open a second house.

Alphonsus preached missions in villages and hamlets throughout the kingdom for twenty-six years. A formal Rule and Constitutions were approved, Alphonsus was elected "rector major" (superior general), and despite political and anticlerical opposition the missions continued to flourish and more foundations were made. Over the years Alphonsus had made a deep study of moral theology, and he published a book with this title in 1748. It was an immediate success and was to go through seven more editions during his lifetime. Its approach, avoiding both the rigorism of Jansenism and laxity, gave rise to the term "probabilism," by which an opinion tending to freedom may be held if there are solidly probable grounds to hold it, even if a more likely interpretation suggests that an opposite view is upheld by the law. The arguments were of course far more subtle, and Alphonsus qualified this position over the years. He also opposed the Jansenists in upholding the value of devotion to Mary, most notably in his book *The Glories of Mary*, published in 1750, which was widely influential at least till the end of the nineteenth century.

He led an extremely active life at the head of his Congregation until around 1752, when his health began to decline and he had to spend less time on missions, which enabled him to spend more time writing. He was widely regarded as an obvious candidate for sainthood. When he was sixty-six, the pope appointed him bishop of Sant' Agata dei Goti, a diocese of thirty thousand souls in a state of religious decay. After trying to refuse the bishopric, Alphonsus recruited a band of priests (from all Orders except his own Redemptorists, so as not to appear to favour them) to evangelize the diocese, with a mission to start by reforming the clergy, many of whom lived on benefices, did virtually no work, and were, in Alphonsus' words, "just mountebanks earning their livelihood by their antics," saying Mass so fast and carelessly that "even pagans would be scandalized." When famine and plague broke out in the diocese (as he had predicted they would), he sold everything to buy food for the populace. Yet he had no time for persistent sinners and made the courts turn them out of the diocese for the common good.

In 1767 he developed severe rheumatic fever and was not expected to live long. He made a partial recovery and endured eight more years as bishop, during which time the Redemptorists were often attacked as "Jesuitical" (the

Jesuits having been suppressed in Spanish territory, which included Naples, in 1767), before being allowed to retire in 1775. His Rule had received ecclesiastical but not civil approval, vital under an absolutist regime. Alphonsus—old, crippled, and partly blind—was betrayed into signing a version of the Rule for presentation to the authorities that was in fact a travesty of it. The king of Naples approved this version, but the Redemptorists in the Papal States would not and could not, as the previous version had been approved by the pope, and the pope refused to accept any amendments or to recognize those who did as true Redemptorists. Alphonsus found himself effectively excluded from the Order he had founded. He accepted this with humility but endured a terrible "dark night of the soul," assailed by every sort of temptation, for eighteen months, after which his mood seems to have changed to one mainly of exaltation. He died in the early morning of 1 August 1787, and Pope Pius VI, who had unintentionally excluded him from his Order, personally introduced his cause. He was beatified in 1816, canonized in 1839, and declared a Doctor of the Church in 1871. Eventually the divided Congregation was reunited and spread to become the spearhead of mission in Europe, America, and elsewhere.

2

St Eusebius of Vercelli (died 371)

Several prominent fourth-century churchmen were named Eusebius, and this saint should not be confused with the church historian Eusebius of Caesarea, the Arian bishop Eusebius of Nicomedia, or St Eusebius of Samosata. He was born in Sardinia to parents who suffered for their Christian faith, with his father claimed as a martyr. His widowed mother took him to Rome, where he was educated and became a lector. He ministered in the town of Vercelli in Piedmont, where he became so popular that the people chose him as their bishop—he is the first recorded bishop of Vercelli. He instituted a semi-monastic rule of life for his clergy, which he shared with them.

From 354 he was concerned mainly with defending the orthodoxy of the wider Church, threatened by the Arian heresy (denying the true divinity of Christ). Pope Liberius asked him to persuade the emperor, Constantius, to summon a council to decide the question. This met in Milan in 355, with orthodox Catholic bishops in the majority but a large Arian faction with powerful secular backing. The Arians tried to persuade the bishops to sign a condemnation of Athanasius (see 2 May), the protagonist of the doctrine of the two natures in Christ agreed at the Council of Nicaea in 325. Eusebius placed a copy of the Nicene Creed on the table and required all the bishops to sign that, declaring that Athanasius should not be condemned unheard and that doctrinal questions should not be subject to influence by secular force. This infuriated the emperor, who at first threatened to put him and two others to death but then commuted this to banishment, and Eusebius was sent to Scythopolis (modern Beisan) in Palestine and handed into the care of an Arian bishop. At first he had an orthodox protector in the town, Count (and St) Joseph, but when Joseph died he was severely maltreated in an attempt to make him conform to Arian belief. He started a hunger strike and was freed but then robbed before being sent on to continue his exile in Cappadocia and later in the Upper Thebaid in Egypt. He described his sufferings in various letters.

Constantius died in 361, and his successor, Julian ("the apostate") allowed the exiled bishops back to their sees. Eusebius, though, spent some years still attempting to resolve the Arian question in the East. He travelled to Alexandria to consult with Athanasius and devise a formula for receiving ex-Arian bishops back into the fold; he then went to Antioch, where he found that his former companion, ally, and fellow-exile, Lucifer of Cagliari, had made a complex situation worse. Lucifer broke off communion with him and others who had agreed to the formula devised at Alexandria, thus producing what is called the Luciferian schism. After further travels in the East, rallying the orthodox faithful as he went, Eusebius returned to Italy. In Milan he worked with St Hilary of Poitiers (see 13 Jan.) to oppose Bishop Auxentius, an Arian supporter. He regained his diocese, where his people were delighted to see him again after an absence of many years, and he died there on 1 August 371.

He was a scholar of distinction, as his three surviving letters show. The composition of the earliest surviving Old Latin (pre-Vulgate) version of the Gospels, known as the Vercelli Gospel Book, has been attributed to him, as has the composition of the Athanasian Creed, though both are doubtful. He has been regarded as a martyr, but, though he certainly suffered for the faith, he did not die for it. His life is an example of the consequences of upholding belief at a time when reputations, lives, local Churches, and even empires were determined by theological controversies.

3

St Peter Julian Eymard (Pierre-Julien Eymard; 1811–1868)

The "priest of the Eucharist," as a late-nineteenth-century study called him, was born in the diocese of Grenoble, in south-eastern France. He worked mainly at his father's trade of cutler, studying Latin in his spare time, until he entered the seminary in Grenoble at the age of twenty. Ordained in 1834, he served in parishes for five years and then applied to join the Marists, the Congregation recently founded by Jean Colin, St Marcellin Champagnat (see 6

June), and others. He served his novitiate, became spiritual director of the junior seminary at Bellay, and in 1845 was appointed provincial in Lyons.

The focus of his devotion was the Blessed Sacrament, and he was haunted by the thought that "Jesus in the Blessed Sacrament has no religious Institute to glorify his service of love." He vowed to Mary that he would remedy this. Encouraged by Colin and even by Pope Pius IX, he eventually submitted a proposal for an Institute of Priest-Adorers of the Blessed Sacrament to the archbishop of Paris, who approved it and placed a house at his disposal. The Blessed Sacrament was exposed in its chapel for the first time on 6 January 1857, when Eymard preached to a large number of people who had come for the occasion. At first the idea of a vocation revolving around this form of devotion was slow to bear fruit: the two original members had to move to a small house in the suburbs. But then Pope Pius IX issued a brief praising the venture, and its fortunes changed. A second house was soon opened in Marseilles, followed by a third in Angers in 1862. Vocations multiplied, and a regular novitiate was established. Priests took turns with lay brothers to maintain perpetual adoration of the exposed Blessed Sacrament, besides singing the Office in choir and performing normal clerical duties. Eymard planned a wider Union of Priest-Adorers, which was approved after his death, and established the Servants of the Blessed Sacrament, a Congregation of Sisters to carry on the work of perpetual adoration as well as practical work among the poor. These were followed by a Priests' Eucharistic League, approved in 1905, and the Archconfraternity of the Blessed Sacrament, encouraged in every diocese by the 1917 Code of Canon Law. By the mid-twentieth century and up to the liturgical reforms and the Second Vatican Council of the 1960s, Eymard's ideas and Congregation directly inspired a large part of Catholic devotion.

He was part of a movement to re-Christianize France (and the wider Church) in the wake of the widespread falling away from popular practice in the wake of the growing industrialization of society in the early nineteenth century, together with the spread of "scientific" opposition to belief. Like others at the time, he developed a piety based on the humanity of Jesus, as shown in devotions to the Holy Child, the Sacred Heart, and the Holy Face, as well as practices such as the Stations of the Cross. He faced difficulties, largely brought about by the fact that he had left the respected Marists, and spent his last years suffering from depression as well as rheumatism and insomnia. His health gave way in the extreme heat of July 1868, and he died on 1 August. He was beatified in 1925 and canonized during the first session of the Second Vatican Council in 1962.

4

St John Vianney (Jean-Marie Vianney; 1786–1859)

The model priest of the nineteenth century and future patron of parish clergy, known universally as the *Curé d'Ars*, was born into a peasant family near Lyons. His childhood was spent during the changes and terrors of the French Revolution, but his childhood games revolved more around "church" than soldiers. He made his first Communion in secret at the age of thirteen, and five years later he told his father that he wanted to be a priest. His father, who had hardly been able to afford to pay for any education, kept him working on the farm for a further two years, after which he went to the nearby school at Ecully, where the priest ran a "presbytery school." He was not a natural student and found Latin very difficult. In 1809 he was mistakenly—he should have had exemption as a student for the priesthood—called up to join the army, but he was taken ill, sent to hospital in Lyons, and missed his draft. Called up again in January 1810, he was praying in a church when his draft once more left without him. He tried to catch it up but was picked up and sheltered by a sympathetic deserter. He worked on a farm and taught the children there for a time; he was then free to return home following the amnesty declared by Napoleon in 1810.

He studied at a minor seminary and then at the major seminary in Lyons, where instruction was in Latin, with which he found it impossible to keep up. Nevertheless, the vicar-general set his obvious goodness above his lack of learning and allowed him to go forward to the priesthood. He was ordained in 1814 and posted as curate to Fr Bellay, who had earlier taught him at Ecully. He soon showed his qualities in the confessional, serious and attentive to his penitents. In 1817 he was appointed parish priest of a depressing little village named Ars-en-Dombe. He refused to accept this as a dead-end posting and steeled himself through great personal austerity to carry out a plan of converting Ars wholly to a religious life. He visited and preached (usually on hell) assiduously and forced the occasional wine-shops in the village out of business; he banned all swearing—even quoting the banned words in the pulpit so there could be no mistake—and dancing, and he forced everyone to attend Mass and Vespers on Sundays and not to work.

Vianney was attacked by some and revered by others for this strict moralizing. In 1824 two young women whom he had sent to a convent for training returned and opened a free school in the village. Known as *La Providence*, this provided shelter for all who called on it; it survived on alms, sometimes so precariously that actual miracles in keeping its occupants fed were attributed to the *curé*. He was for years assailed by poltergeist-type manifestations, which he attributed to the devil: on one occasion, his bed was even set alight. Some thought him mad and delated him to the bishop, who told them he wished all his clergy were as mad. He developed an intense devotion to St Philomena, the child-martyr product of mistaken identity of some bones found in a Roman catacomb in 1802 (whose cult was encouraged by several popes until it was suppressed as unhistorical in 1969). Modestly, he attributed the extraordinary growth of his mission to her intervention.

The railways spread in France in the 1830s and 1840s, and a special ticket office had to be opened in Lyons to cope with the rush of pilgrims to Ars, averaging three hundred per day. People took eight-day return tickets to ensure their turn in the confessional, where Vianney was spending up to twelve hours in winter and sixteen in summer. He also gave a public instruction every day in the church at eleven o'clock for the last fifteen years of his life. He developed a truly remarkable insight into people's problems—and an equal gift for swift dismissal of frivolous requests, as when he told a future nun who asked for some relics to make them herself. He really wanted to be a monk, and he effectively ran away three times to do so, being persuaded back only by the authority of the bishop.

He was made an honorary canon in 1852 but never wore the cape, which he eventually sold for charity. He was also made a Knight of the *Légion d'Honneur*, but he refused to wear the imperial cross. By the late 1850s the strain of over a thousand pilgrims per week had become too much for a man in his seventies who had never spared himself in any way. By late July 1859 he knew he was shortly to die and sent for a local priest to bring him the last sacraments, still hearing Confessions as he lay on his deathbed, to which twenty priests and hundred of lay penitents flocked. He died peacefully on 4 August, having remarked that it was sad to receive Communion for the last time. Intransigent moralist he may have been, but he produced a phenomenon in nineteenth-century rural France: a parish totally devoted to religion. Pope Pius XI canonized him in 1925, and in 1929 declared him patron of parish clergy throughout the world.

5

St Ethelwold (or Aethelwold; about 912–984)

Ethelwold was a friend of St Dunstan (see 19 May), was ordained priest on the same day as him, and played a major part in the monastic reform in England led by him. Born in Winchester, he spent his youth as a courtier before asking for ordination. When Dunstan became abbot of Glastonbury in 940 and introduced strict Benedictine observance, Ethelwold joined the Order there, soon being appointed prior. His own manner of life went way beyond any reformed ideal and was so penitential that Dunstan had to order him to eat meat once every three months.

In about 954 King Edred appointed him abbot of Abingdon, which prevented him from going to Cluny, as he had wanted, to study the source of reform at first hand. Abingdon was then derelict, and Ethelwold not only oversaw but actually took part in restoration work until prevented from doing so by falling off a scaffold and breaking several ribs. He designed a new church on a double rotunda plan and brought monks from Glastonbury to re-establish regular monastic life and a music-master from Corbie in France. He sent a disciple, Osgar, to France instead of going himself, to learn the reformed discipline from the monks of Fleury, so that Abingdon could become a model for English monasticism.

In 963 he was consecrated bishop of Winchester by Dunstan. He ejected the cathedral canons and replaced them with monks from Abingdon, creating the first monastic cathedral, a model unique to England and copied in other cities or towns, such as Sherborne by St Wulsin (see 8 Jan.). Together with Dunstan, appointed archbishop of Canterbury in 960, and Oswald (see 29 Feb.), bishop of Worcester, Ethelwold embarked on a great course of monastic foundation and renewal. He rebuilt formerly great monasteries destroyed in Danish invasions, such as Ely and Peterborough, replaced secular priests at Newminster in Winchester, restored and endowed others. Peterborough became an "ecclesiastical franchise," which meant that it, not the king, received revenues from the local courts (and so began to build up excuses for the dissolution of the monasteries centuries later).

Ethelwold's personal skills extended to organ-building: the great organ at Winchester had four hundred pipes and thirty-six bellows and needed two monks to play it. He wrote the earliest known polyphonic chant, preserved as the *Winchester Troper*. He was also a skilled bell-founder and metalworker, as well as introducing a new style of manuscript illumination. Winchester Cathedral, consecrated in 980, became a major school of translation from Latin and of vernacular writing. The consecration was a great occasion, as was the transfer there of St Swithun's relics in 971. Ethelwold could be intransigent, to the point of being nicknamed *Boanerges*, "son of thunder," but he was also known as "the benevolent bishop" and "the father of monks" and was a wise counsellor to the kings of Wessex. He was probably responsible for the composition of the *Regularis Concordia*, an agreed statement of observance for thirty major monasteries in southern Britain, which was promoted at a congress he summoned in about 970. The details of his death are not known, but he was undoubtedly one of the great figures of pre-Norman England.

6

St Sixtus II and Companions (died 258)

Sixtus spent just one year as pope. He is known from documentary evidence of the part he played in the controversy between the papacy and churches in Africa and Asia over whether Baptism administered by heretics was valid. This dispute had begun under his predecessor, Pope St Stephen I. Sixtus was advised to tread gently in the matter, which he did, avoiding a break with St Cyprian, bishop of Carthage (see 16 Sept.), the leader of the more severe faction, which held that the sacrament was invalid if administered by heretics, schismatics, or apostates.

Sixtus became the victim of a change of attitude toward Christians by the joint emperor Valerian (253–60), who had originally been friendly but in the fourth year of his reign began to persecute them, possibly on advice that confiscating their property would be a good means of replenishing the depleted imperial treasury. He issued a decree, addressed to "eminent men" and "Roman knights"—thereby targeting prominent Christians, whom he may genuinely have seen as posing a threat to the stability of the empire by undermining its belief system from within at a time when it was under military threat from outside. He required them not to abandon their beliefs but merely to conform outwardly by sacrificing to the Roman state gods. Some laymen complied, but many others and most of the clergy refused. Valerian was left with little alternative but to make an example of the leaders and to go on to try to eradicate Christianity.

In 257 many clerics and lay people lost their lives, and the use of cemeteries and liturgical worship was forbidden. Sixtus was consecrated pope in secret. The following year persecution intensified even further, and Sixtus was arrested. Cyprian wrote to tell his fellow-bishop in Africa what then happened: "Sixtus suffered in a cemetery on the sixth day of August, and with him four deacons." He went on to warn them to be prepared to accept the worst, but added that death meant not so much being "killed as crowned." He himself was martyred a few weeks later. Sixtus had been seized while addressing a congregation in the cemetery of Praetextatus and apparently refused to take a chance to escape, in order to prevent a massacre of the people. He was buried in the nearby cemetery of Callistus, on the Appian Way. A cult soon developed, and he became the most venerated martyr-pope after St Peter. Four sub-deacons were executed on the same day: Januarius, Vincent, Magnus, and Stephen. Two deacons, Felicissimus and Agapitus, were probably taken with

Sixtus, killed with the sword, and buried in the cemetery of Praetextatus. These two are, strictly speaking, his "companions" in today's commemoration (which the new Roman Martyrology moves to tomorrow, presumably to avoid a clash with the feast of the Transfiguration). The seventh deacon of Rome, St Laurence (see 10 Aug.) was executed a few days later.

He appears in Raphael's *Sistine Madonna* (the *Sistine* meaning "of Sixtus," not referring to the Sistine Chapel), otherwise called *Our Lady and Child with SS Sixtus II and Barbara*, one of the best-known and most reproduced paintings in the world, painted in 1512–13. In it, Sixtus (who has the features of Raphael's patron, Pope Julius II) points out of the picture to its viewers, whom he commends to Our Lady's care and protection, thus forming a connection between the world of heaven, from which Mary, carrying the infant Jesus, is descending, and the earth on which we stand.

7

St Cajetan (Tommaso de Vio Gaetano; 1480–1547)

Tommaso was the son of the count of Thiene and his wife and was born in Vicenza in northern Italy. He studied law and philosophy at the university of Padua, became a senator of Vicenza, and received the tonsure, indicating his intention of being ordained priest. He held an appointment in the Roman Curia under Pope Julius II for seven years, then resigned on Julius' death, and spent three years studying for the priesthood, being ordained in 1516.

Two years later he returned to Vicenza, where he scandalized his friends by joining an organization normally open to men from the lowest orders in society, the Oratory of St Jerome. He cared for incurables in their hospital and responded to accusations of betraying his family by claiming that he "actually found God" in those he treated in hospital. In 1523 he went back to Rome, where he and some companions had previously refounded the Oratory of Divine Love, which they now sought to expand into an Institute of secular priests who by their learning and strict way of life would counteract the indifference and laxity widespread among the clergy at this time, when the fundamental challenge posed by the Protestant Reformation was not generally appreciated. They chose the Augustinian Rule as their structural basis and the lives of the apostles as their inspiration, and the first four members were professed in St Peter's on 14 September 1524. They were known as "Theatines," from the bishopric held (and resigned) by John Peter Caraffa, elected first provost general—and later to become the forbidding Pope Paul IV. They were to preach, serve the sick, restore sacramental life, and generally reform the clergy. They rejected all ownership of property (the issue that had split the

Franciscans three centuries earlier), relying solely on gifts to provide for their needs.

They were given a house in Rome but were forced to flee to Venice when Charles V's army sacked Rome in 1527. There Cajetan took over from Caraffa as superior and worked valiantly to help plague and famine victims. He tried to introduce reforms in Verona and did so to a large extent in the kingdom of Naples some years later, but he met resistance. He was also seen as exceptionally severe—a reputation enhanced by his close association with Caraffa. One lasting achievement on behalf of the poor was his establishment of *montes pietatis*, "benevolent pawnshops," where they could borrow cheaply. He welcomed the Council of Trent, of which he had been a precursor in many ways, and was distressed when it was suspended in 1547. He died worn out by his efforts to bring about religious peace in Naples, choosing bare planks as a sickbed in imitation of Christ's cross. In the year of his death Thomas Goldwell, who became bishop of St Asaph under Queen Mary and was the last member of the old (unreformed) hierarchy of England and Wales, became a Theatine Father at the house in Naples.

The Theatines flourished in Italy under Pope Paul VII and expanded into Austria, Bavaria, and other parts of central Europe in the seventeenth century, but they never achieved the sort of worldwide expansion that the Jesuits, founded with similar aims, did. They opened overseas missions in Borneo, Peru, Sumatra, and the Near East, including Iran. Now more reduced in numbers, they still have a seminary in Denver, Colorado, providing priests who have a special ministry to the Hispanic population of the USA and who also provide missions in Latin America and Africa.

8

St Dominic (Domingo de Guzmán; about 1170–1221)

The founder of the Dominicans was born twelve years before the other great founder of the Mendicant Orders, St Francis of Assisi (1182–1226; see 4 Oct.), and died five years before him. His birthplace was Calaroga (now Calaruega) in Castile, and he studied theology at Palencia University. He was made a canon of Osma Cathedral while he was still a student, partly because he sold his books to help the needy, was ordained priest, and rose to become prior of the cathedral chapter in 1201.

In 1203 Dominic and the bishop of Osma, his friend Diego de Azevedo, were sent by King Alfonso VIII of Castile to northern Germany (or possibly Denmark) to negotiate a marriage for his son—which eventually foundered when his betrothed decided to become a nun. On their way there and back they were made aware of the strength of the Albigensians or Cathars in Languedoc. Diego was at first less concerned with them than with the Cuman pagans he had encountered in Germany, and took Dominic to Rome to ask Pope Innocent II's permission to mount a mission to preach to them. The pope encouraged them to turn their evangelizing zeal to the Albigensians, already condemned as heretics, since they were seen as threatening to become a rival Church rather than just a reform movement (*Cathari* meaning "perfect ones") within the Church, of which there were many at the time. Heresy was a crime, and so the pontifical legates leading the "crusade" against these heretics were responsible for handing them over to the civil authorities for punishment. Dominic realized that for missionaries to be associated with secular power would only make martyrs of people whose way of life was based on admiration of the poverty and strictness of their own "perfect ones" and was locally based, in opposition to outside power of any sort.

He and Diego persuaded the papal legates that all their trappings of power should be abandoned, and they embarked on a course of preaching allied to a radically poor way of life: travelling on foot, without money, begging for food. Their method was based on persuasion by argument, not power. The Cistercian chapter approved the venture and in November 1206 the pope allowed volunteer monks to join the campaign. One of the Cathars' strengths was their education of women, and Diego founded a convent to provide a rival Catholic education. He then returned to Spain, leaving Dominic in charge of a growing community of young women and converts at Prouille. In 1207 a large group of Cistercians arrived in Languedoc to preach a concerted mission, but this approach was not successful: Dominic and a small group of full-time preachers seemed to provide a better answer.

His peaceful, persuasive route was then blocked when the pope reverted to the use of secular power, asking the king of France to put down the heresy by force. A servant of the Cathar count of Toulouse assassinated one of the papal legates, Peter of Castelnau (venerated as a saint), and in 1209 Simon de Montfort led a savage crusade against the Cathars. Toulouse was beseiged and fell in 1214. Dominic took the "orthodox" side, though there is no evidence that he took part in the actual crusade, confining his contribution to preaching. Living when he did, he undoubtedly saw heresy as intolerable, though he sought the conversion, not the death, of heretics. As he told the warrior Bishop Fulk of Toulouse, the arms employed should be prayer and humility, not the sword and fine clothes. His methods had some limited success but were seen as slow by the authorities; he made a number of converts, but most relapsed. After his death, the Inquisition employed sterner methods, but he cannot be held responsible for the fact that the Dominicans were charged with administering the Inquisition, despite petitioning to be released from this charge in 1243.

Dominic refused three offers of a bishopric, preferring to head a small band of preachers with no canonical status. They followed the Augustinian Rule, but

Dominic was gradually taking them in the direction of a new foundation combining the contemplative life with study, preaching, and teaching. In 1215 an Institute of preachers was approved in Toulouse by Bishop Fulk, whom Dominic then accompanied to the Fourth Lateran Council. This recognized the importance of preaching but forbade the founding of new religious Orders. The pope, however, wanted heresy reduced and asked Dominic to draw up a Rule for what was effectively to be a new Order devoted to preaching. In 1216 the first Dominicans began to lead life in community in Toulouse, under a modified Augustinian Rule, which developed as need arose in the early years. The following year Dominic sent four friars to preach in Spain and seven to Paris, where they could study if trouble threatened the house in Toulouse. A papal letter secured them a property in Paris in 1218, part of a series of papal communications that rapidly gave the new Order status throughout the Church. A foundation was also made in Bologna; with Paris, this was to form the intellectual powerhouse of the Dominicans. It also saw the first foundation for nuns, under Diana d'Andalo (see Bd Jordan of Saxony; 13 Feb.). In 1219, Pope Honorius III declared the Order "necessary," which obliged diocesan bishops to cooperate with its members in their dioceses.

Expansion was rapid over the next few years, and the Rule was modified to make travelling freer and more practicable. The university cities provided stable conditions for study and teaching, but itinerant preaching remained the prime purpose. Papal Bulls encouraged growth beyond Italy and France, and there were soon houses in Poland, Scandinavia, Germany, Hungary, Palestine, Morocco, and England, where foundations were made in Canterbury, London, and Oxford. By the summer of 1221 Dominic was tired. He had travelled and preached incessantly, in Italy's summer heat and Germany's winter cold, and had overseen all the work of the Order in Italy. Returning to Bologna knowing that his death was near, he was taken to the convent of St Mary in the Hills to escape the city heat, where he was put to bed "in Brother Moneta's bed because he had none of his own, in Brother Moneta's habit because he had no other to replace the one he had worn for so long." He died after telling his brethren that he would be more use to them dead than alive.

He was canonized in 1234, by which time a popular cult was already strong. His Order went on growing for many centuries. It provided many of the best scholastic minds of the later Middle Ages and, after the Reformation, remained, with the Jesuits (and often in bitter opposition to them), one of the great intellectual forces in the Church, besides remaining true to its historical calling to preach and convert. By the end of the second millennium it comprised some six thousand six hundred friars, four thousand four hundred enclosed contemplative nuns, and thirty-eight thousand Dominican Sisters engaged in a huge variety of apostolic works, besides some seventy thousand lay members in the Third Order, inspired largely by the ideals of discipline and intellectual work.

✤

Nothing disturbed his equanimity except a lively sympathy with any suffering. A person's face shows whether he or she is really happy. Dominic's was friendly and joyful. You could easily see his inward peace.

Bd Jordan of Saxony' describing Dominic in a letter

9

St Teresa Benedicta of the Cross (Edith Stein; 1891–1942)

Born into an Orthodox Jewish family in Breslau (then in Germany, now Wroclaw in Poland), Edith became a convinced atheist in her school and early university years, though never ceasing to seek truth. After first studying experimental psychology at Breslau University, she moved on to Göttingen to read philosophy. There she became a pupil of Edmund Husserl, a baptized Christian from a Jewish background. She began to realize that study of human experience must include religious experience. She was also influenced by Max Scheler, another pupil of Husserl's, who introduced her to contemporary Catholic thought, and she felt her "rationalist prejudices ... lifted to reveal the world of faith."

She acted as Husserl's assistant, but this involved a lot of menial work and no recognition. She gained her doctorate *summa cum laude* in 1919 and left the university to seek academic work in her own right. This proved difficult: in shattered post-war Germany there were few positions available for men and none for women. She found the autobiography of St Teresa of Avila (see 15 Oct.) in a Lutheran friend's house, read it at a sitting, and declared, "This is the truth!" She resolved to become a Christian and was baptized into the Catholic Church on 1 January 1922, making her profession of faith in Latin. Her mother wept when she heard the news, but Edith did not see her Christianity as a rejection of Judaism, which she had after all abandoned for atheism at the age of fourteen. She wanted to become a Carmelite, but her spiritual director told her she was of too much value to the Church as an academic writer. He found her a post teaching German to the upper forms in a school run by Dominican Sisters. Stiff and humourless and unable to see why her pupils failed to understand what was obvious to her, she was not a success as a teacher.

The Jesuit scholar Fr Erich Przywara persuaded her to translate Newman into German, but her approach was too literal and the result almost unreadable. She was more successful with works of Thomas Aquinas (see 28 Jan.) and began to immerse herself in Thomism—from the source, not the arid neo-Thomism ruling official Catholic thought at the time. In 1928 she began to lecture on Thomist thought and the position of women in society. She was still trying to obtain an academic post, but either her Jewishness or her forbidding manner or prejudice against women, or a combination of all three, made her unsuccessful. In 1932 she did find a post in the Educational Institute in Münster, and she began to express herself trenchantly on the position of women in the Church, arguing against the dominant view that women should be wives and mothers and pointing to the number of careers—teaching, nursing, social work—that the Church had previously opened up for women.

By October 1933, with Hitler in power as Chancellor and anti-Semitism mounting, Edith knew that it was time for her to enter Carmel. She saw this as her way of embracing the cross of Christ, which she saw being imposed on the Jewish people. She was forty-two years old and had no dowry except her library of books, which the nuns jumbled up. The Carmelite nuns had none of the Benedictine or Dominican tradition of scholarship and hoped she was good at sewing, but she had learned abandonment to the will of God from St John of the Cross (see 14 Dec.) and was perfectly happy to set aside her intellectual life and become a simple postulant. Then the provincial of the Order told her to take up writing again, which she did. Two relatively minor works were followed by *Endliches und Ewigers sein* ("finite and eternal being"), arguing that there could be no philosophy without revelation. It was becoming virtually impossible for works by Jews to be published in Germany, and though one brave publisher took it as far as proof stage, he was forced to abandon it, and the work was not published in her lifetime.

She made her final vows in 1937, by which time Jewish shops and houses were being sacked, Jews murdered, and synagogues burned. She was not safe even inside convent walls, and at the end of the year she was sent to Echt in Holland for her protection. It was not a happy move: the Dutch nuns had less respect for her intellect than her German Sisters, and she was forced to speak Dutch, which she found imprecise. She accepted such deprivations as part of the cross she was called to bear. She immersed herself in study of St John of the Cross, which was to result in her last, unfinished, book, *The Knowledge of the Cross*, and took little interest in plans to transfer her to Switzerland for her safety.

In July 1942 all the Christian Churches in the Netherlands protested to the Nazi authorities about the persecution of the Jews. The Nazis responded by rounding up all non-Aryan Christians and deporting them to eastern Europe for "resettlement"—meaning the death camps. Sr Teresa Benedicta and her sister, Rosa, who had also taken refuge in the convent, were taken away in a Gestapo van on 2 August. She took her sister's hand, saying, "Come on—we are on our way to our own people." She was briefly spotted at a camp in Germany, where she "walked about among the women, comforting, helping, soothing like an angel." After the appalling experience of travelling across Europe in a cattle truck, she was murdered in Auschwitz on 9 August 1942.

She was beatified by Pope John Paul II in 1987 and canonized the following year, on 12 October. Some Jewish groups protested at what they saw as a death for being Jewish being "taken over" as a Catholic martyrdom, but her acceptance of "sufferings endured with the Lord" was for people of all faiths and none.

I spoke to Our Lord and told him that it was his cross that was being laid on the Jewish people. Most of them did not know that, but those who did ought to embrace it willingly in the name of all. This I desired to do. He should only show me in what way.

Edith Stein, on her prayer for guidance before entering Carmel

10

St Laurence (died 258)

Laurence was one of the seven deacons of Rome under Pope St Sixtus II (see 6 Aug.), and the only one not to die on the same day as the pope. He was martyred four days later, probably by the usual Roman method of a sword-thrust to the neck, and was buried in the cemetery of Cyriaca on the Via Tiburtina. This is essentially all that is known of his life and death. After that, story-telling takes over, his death becomes roasting on a gridiron, and a vast artistic representation makes Laurence one of the most venerated of all the martyrs.

The deacons of Rome were responsible for looking after the Church's goods and for giving alms to the poor. This responsible office produced the story that, when Sixtus told Laurence he would follow him to a martyr's death in a few days, Laurence sold the sacred vessels in his keeping and gave all the money in his charge to the widows, the poor, and the sick of the city. When asked to produce the Church's treasures, he summoned all these and showed them to the prefect, saying that they were the only true treasure of the Church. For this insult the prefect condemned him to die a slow death, and the gridiron was laid over glowing coals. Laurence asked to be turned when one side was done, and told the onlookers that they could eat when his whole body was "done to a turn." The story of the gridiron seems to have been borrowed from St Vincent of Zaragoza (martyred in 304). One suggestion is that it derives from a scribe missing the initial "p" in *passus est* (he suffered), leaving *assus est* (he was roasted).

His death was said to have put an end to idolatry in the city, and very soon the power of his prayers had converted all the inhabitants to Christianity.

Constantine built the first church to his memory on the site of his burial, now St Laurence-outside-the-Walls. His story was told by such eminent writers as Prudentius, Ambrose, and Augustine, and his cult became most popular in Spain and North Africa. It spread northward too, and Pope St Vitalian gave King Oswy of Northumbria relics. A charred bone, supposedly his forearm, is in the abbey church of Ampleforth in Yorkshire. The earliest representation of him, dating from about 450, is in Ravenna and shows him with a gridiron. Because he did not sell the books in his care, he is the patron saint of librarians.

He became one of the great subjects for Renaissance painters. Fra Angelico produced a cycle of frescoes depicting his life and death for the chapel of Nicholas V in the Vatican. King Philip II of Spain named his vast monastery-palace at El Escorial after him (he was supposedly Spanish by birth), built it on a gridiron plan, and commissioned Titian to paint a *Martyrdom of St Laurence* for its church. In the painting he looks up through a sinister darkness lit by blazing coals to the faint light of heaven, seen by him alone as a source of hope. Another version by Titian in the Jesuit church in Venice is given a deliberately antique setting. Among many others, Tintoretto painted a version of this scene derived from Titian's in the Escorial, and Zurbarán, early in the seventeenth century, twice painted him holding a shining gridiron.

11

St Clare of Assisi (about 1193–1253)

Some ten years younger than Francis (see 4 Oct.), with whom she was to form one of the great partnerships of history, Clare was born into an aristocratic family in Assisi. Her father, Faverone Offreduccio, died when she still young but old enough for her persistent refusal to marry to be a cause of severe annoyance to her surviving male relatives, who could not marry off her two younger sisters before her. When she was eighteen she heard Francis preach the Lenten sermons at the church of San Giorgio. His message of abandoning the world and serving God in total poverty inspired her to ask to see him and learn more about this way of living. On Palm Sunday, after the bishop, probably inspired by Francis, had gone to her pew to give her a palm branch, she went to the Portiuncula, a mile outside the city, where Francis and his small community were living. In front of the altar she exchanged her fine clothes for a simple dress of sackcloth; Francis cut off her hair, and she made her vow to become a nun. As the Franciscans then had no accommodation for women, she was lodged with the Benedictine nuns at nearby Bastia.

This dramatic episode must have been planned in the conversations she had had with Francis, and her mind was certainly already made up. It also seems likely that she had told her female relatives what she planned to do. Her male relatives were outraged, broke into the convent, and tried to drag her out of the church as she clung to the altar cloths. Francis showed them her shorn hair and persuaded them to leave her with the only husband she wanted, Christ. They seem to have admitted defeat. Francis moved her to another convent on the slopes of Monte Subasio, overlooking Assisi, and it was not long before her sister Agnes and her widowed mother joined her there. Francis then found them a small house by the church of San Damiano, on the southern edge of Assisi, and other women, including members of the aristocratic Ubaldini family of Florence—turning their backs, like Clare, on their background and wealth— came to join her.

Clare was appointed abbess of the small but growing community, despite her attempts to resist the appointment. Francis drew up a rudimentary Rule, and the nuns vowed obedience to the friars, who at first came and went freely. But then contact between the two groups was severely restricted by the ecclesiastical authorities, afraid of scandal. Only Benedictine monks were allowed in to give them the sacraments. There followed long years of inter- ference by successive popes attempting to impose a Rule on them—generally involving acceptance of rents or property—or to force them to live enclosed lives as Benedictine nuns, but Clare clung to her conviction that their first calling was to poverty and that they had to be free to beg outside the convent. She worked on her own Rule throughout her life and succeeded in having it approved only just before her death. This allowed the Sisters to own no property, either individually or as a community, and imposed responsibility on all. It was the fruit of long meditation on what Francis' intentions really were. She was the first woman founder of an Order to write her own Rule—an indication of her considerable independence of mind.

The poverty combined with relative freedom of movement at San Damiano was soon being copied in other foundations in Italy and beyond—in France, Germany, and also Bohemia, where Agnes, daughter of King Ottakar I, formed a convent on similar lines in Prague, after a longer struggle than Clare's not to marry. Clare and Agnes corresponded assiduously, and Clare called Agnes her "second half." The way of life was austere: the nuns went barefoot, slept on boards, never ate meat, and never spoke unless doing so was absolutely necessary. Clare was even harder on herself, wearing a hair shirt (with attendant vermin), and fasting to extremes. This probably damaged her health, and in later years she moderated her penances and advised Agnes to do the same, since women's bodies "are not of brass."

Clare governed the convent at San Damiano for forty years and is said never to have left it. She was the servant of the other Sisters, up first in the morning to ring the bell for prayer, washing their feet when they came back from begging trips, waiting on them at table, tending them when they were sick. This life took its toll, and she was often ill. She was, though, the convent's "tower of strength," and this quality probably inspired the story of her saving it—and Assisi—from attack by the emperor's Saracen troops by exposing the Blessed Sacrament on the walls and praying in front of it, at which the army melted away. During her final illness Pope Innocent II twice visited the convent to give her absolution, saying as he did so that he wished he needed it as little. She died on 11 August 1253, was buried the next day, and canonized just two years later.

Known originally as Poor Ladies of San Damiano, then Poor Ladies of St Clare, her Sisters eventually became universally known as Poor Clares. They were troubled by the same sort of disputes over observance as were the Franciscan friars after Francis' death, but the Second Order of St Francis spread rapidly, with over four hundred convents by the end of the fourteenth century and almost a thousand, on five continents, by the end of the twentieth. Clare is supposed to have seen the crib and heard singing as though in church when confined to her bed one Christmas, and this inspired Pope Pius XII to declare her the patron saint of television in 1958.

Go forth in peace, for you have followed the good road. Go forth without fear, for he that created you has sanctified you, has always protected you, and loves you as a mother. Blessed be Thou, O God, for having created me.
St Clare, speaking to herself on her deathbed

12

Bd Mary McKillop (1842–1909)

The bishop of Queensland called her "an obstinate and ambitious woman"; she herself wrote that "bishops and priests think me some extraordinary and bold woman." Seldom can any religious Sister have suffered so much at the hands of clergymen more concerned with their own positions than with the work of the Church as Australia's first blessed.

Born to somewhat feckless Scottish immigrant parents, Mary spent her childhood moving from place to place, generally to escape her father's creditors. He, a former seminarian, nevertheless gave her a good education. This enabled her to become a governess in Penola, in present-day South Australia. There she met a charismatic priest named Julian Tenison Woods, who was to play a large and ambivalent part in her life. He encouraged her in her ambitions to become a teacher: her first venture, in a large rented house in Portland, Victoria, failed because her large and improvident family mopped up any money available. She returned to Penola and started again, in a dilapidated stable, which her brother restored for her. Fr Woods helped to disperse the non-productive members of the family, and several young women came to offer their services as teachers.

Fr Woods optimistically saw them as the kernel of a new teaching Institute, produced a Rule and a first version of a habit, but caused them serious problems with his complete lack of financial or any other sort of planning. He was transferred to Adelaide and summoned Mary and a companion, Rose Cunningham, there. The plan was that they should be formally professed and take over a private school in the city. This they did, and there were soon some two hundred children, most from desperately poor families. Mary was aiming to provide a fully Catholic (fee-paying) education at a time when the Australian States were beginning to introduce free and compulsory state education, so she required a special sacrifice from parents who preferred her system. Despite the difficulties, the Sisters' obvious commitment and poverty of life attracted both postulants and pupils. Fr Woods had devised an elaborate profession ceremony, and Mary was now Sister Mary of the Cross in the Institute of Sisters of St Joseph, but he insisted on being director of the Institute and was becoming a liability, especially when he began to encourage two over-enthusiastic Sisters to believe they were great mystics.

Within two years the schools in Adelaide had grown to seventeen, and Mary was beginning other ventures: she visited the sick, caring for Catholics and others alike; a house for homeless women and a refuge for unmarried mothers had to be financed entirely from begging. In 1869 Fr Woods promised to send Sisters to Queensland, and the bishop of Adelaide assumed that he would lead a small party of them, but there was no money provided, and Mary departed alone, with enough money to take her only as far as Sydney by coastal steamer. She eventually arrived in Brisbane, only to be told that the diocese had accepted the state provision for religious education and there was accordingly no need for the Institute. Mary stayed, found parents willing to pay for Catholic education, and founded three schools. When she returned to Adelaide, she found Fr Woods ill and vague, the affairs of the Institute in financial chaos, and Bishop Shiel of Adelaide drinking heavily and blaming her for quarrels between him and Fr Woods. He even formally excommunicated her but managed to bungle the ritual. Mary stayed outside Adelaide, but her Sisters were disbanded in the diocese. Bishop Shiel died in January 1872 (having rescinded the excommunication), and an Apostolic Commission set up by the archbishop of Sydney recognized the value of the Institute and made it self-governing, with Mary as superior and Fr Woods forbidden to have anything to do with it.

The schools reopened, and the clergy were now friendly, but the Institute still had no formal canonical status, for which approval from Rome was needed. Mary embarked on the long sea voyage, travelling disguised as a widow, landed at Brindisi, crossed Italy by train, and arrived in Rome in the heat of the summer to find everyone she needed to see away. She visited churches, prayed at shrines, waited, and caught the dreaded Roman fever. The Jesuits came to her rescue and sent her to England to seek postulants while she was waiting. This was not a success, and after going on to Scotland, where she met with a friendly reception, she returned to Rome. The Rule was approved about a year after her first arrival there. She then went to Ireland in search of postulants, and after an initially shocked reception from clergy unused to such an independent female figure, she found friendly support and eventually returned to Australia with fifteen postulants and two priests. She found almost a hundred new postulants waiting for her at the motherhouse.

What might have been a triumphant culmination to her work was marred by more disputes with bishops over whether the Institute should be subject to the diocesan clergy. The Rule approved in Rome made her superior "in Australia," but Rome was a long way away, and two bishops refused to accept this. She was supported by Cardinal Moran of Sydney, who in 1885 obtained a statement from Rome giving the Institute extra-diocesan status provided Mary resigned as superior, which she willingly did, but the following year a council of the bishops of Australia and New Zealand made their houses subject to diocesan control. Two years later Pope Leo XIII formally made the Institute a canonical Congregation. Mary was appointed superior of the motherhouse in Sydney, trained the novices for a time, and then made visitations of all the houses. The superior (now mother general) appointed in her place died suddenly in 1898, and Mary was unanimously chosen to succeed her. Despite a stroke in 1901, she worked tirelessly until she died peacefully on 8 August 1909. Her Institute then had one hundred and six convents and seven hundred and fifty nuns. Her cause was opened in 1973, and she was beatified by Pope John Paul II in Australia in 1995, at a ceremony presented as a cause for celebration for all Australians, just as she had made no distinctions in her charitable works.

13

St Radegund (518–587)

Radegund came from the area of present-day central Germany then called Thuringia, between the rivers Weser and Elbe. Her father was a pagan prince who was murdered by his brother. Invading Christian Franks from the west invaded Thuringia in about 531 and Radegund was captured and taken to the court of Clotaire I, the eldest son of Clovis, the founder of the Frankish dynasty. He is said to have instructed her in the Christian faith, but he also finally persuaded her to marry him, which she did when she was about eighteen. The marriage was childless, for which he blamed her.

She took refuge from his anger in charitable works, caring for the poor and starting a leper hospital. Clotaire complained that he was married to a nun and that she was turning his court into a monastery. He murdered her brother in 550, and she fled, veiling herself as a nun, to lands she owned near Poitiers. There she founded a double monastery, to which she retired in about 561. Clotaire was planning to seize her, but she appealed to St Germanus of Paris (see 29 May), who persuaded him to leave her alone—so successfully that Clotaire even asked her to forgive him and made gifts to the monastery, which became known as the abbey of the Holy Cross when Emperor Justinian II sent it a relic of the true cross. She spent thirty years there, praying, studying, and carrying out good works. Women of high social rank and considerable intellectual stature joined the monastery, which became an oasis of culture and refinement in a collapsing society.

The monastery acquired a friend and eventually chaplain very much to Radegund's taste in the person of Venantius Fortunatus, better known as a poet than as a saint (commemorated on 14 Dec.). He had set out from northern Italy on a pilgrimage of thanksgiving to Tours, to thank St Martin (see 11 Nov.) for curing him of incipient blindness. A scholar and a gentleman, he was welcomed in grand houses along the way and never returned to Italy, which was in any case being laid waste by the Lombards. There were not many places to his refined Roman taste in brutal Gaul, and Holy Cross must have seemed a heaven-sent haven to him. It had Roman baths and gardens and an excellent kitchen. Radegund herself led a very austere life, but the monastery's interpretation of the Rule she chose—that of St Caesarius of Arles—seems to have been fairly relaxed. Fortunatus, the most accomplished poet and hymn-writer of his day, could "sing for his supper" by writing flattering poems about the monastery in exchange for dainty meals sent to his lodging by the admiring Radegund and the abbess, her friend Agnes, whom he called "dear mother and dear sister." He was also able to put his extensive contacts to work on behalf of the abbey. The reception of the relic of the cross inspired his first great hymn, *Vexilla regis prodeunt* ("The royal banners forward go"), followed by *Pange lingua, gloriosi* ("Sing, my tongue, the glorious battle"), which he wrote for Passiontide. Both have graced the liturgy for centuries. He was taken from the monastery when he was elected bishop of Poitiers, which proved such a rude shock that he died a year later.

Radegund died peacefully on 13 August 587 and, with the help of a Life written by Fortunatus, developed into a great miracle-worker and champion of Christianity against the pagans. On one occasion, it was claimed, she had repulsed an army of Franks simply by holding up the cross she had with her. She also became the patron saint of prisoners, because she had been taken captive; of shoemakers, because she cleaned the other nuns' shoes; and of potters, because she cleaned the convent's earthenware dishes. She was frequently portrayed in art, shown either as a queen or as a nun holding an open book. A nineteenth-century mural showing her listening to Fortunatus' poems, painted by Puvis de Chavannes, adorns the staircase of Poitiers Town Hall.

14

St Maximilian Kolbe (Raimund Kolbe; 1894–1941)

Raimund was born in what was then Russian Poland, into a family of Bohemian origin, though they were Russian citizens. His parents were poor, deeply devout, and probably both Franciscan tertiaries. Raimund was kept at home to work to enable his brother, Frank, to go to middle school and thence to study for the priesthood, but the local chemist discovered his knowledge of Latin scientific names, gave him lessons, and entered him for the examinations to middle school, which he passed easily. Both brothers were accepted into the Minorite junior seminary at Lwow in 1907. By 1910 Raimund had decided that he had no vocation and was about to tell his provincial so when his mother announced that the youngest brother had also decided to become a religious. Having no more responsibility for their children meant that the parents could both pursue a religious vocation: Raimund's mother became a Benedictine nun for a time and his father a Franciscan. (He later left to run a religious bookshop and was hanged as a traitor after being captured by the Russians during the First World War.)

In autumn 1912 Maximilian (the name Raimund had taken in religion) went to study at the Gregorian University in Rome. He became interested in how the Church's message could be spread and also a passionate devotee of "Mary Immaculate" (who had apparently miraculously cured an abscess on his right thumb). The Catholic Church in Poland made Mary a national symbol, defending Poland against all forms of foreign domination and internal dissension, including—it has to be said—the large Jewish population. Maximilian and a group of seminarians took vows as Knights of the Queen of Heaven in the Militant Order of Mary the Immaculate. He returned to Poland in 1919 with doctorates in theology and philosophy, but his main concern was to find ways of disseminating the Knights' ideas in a crusade aimed at reversing the de-Christianization he saw affecting Europe. He begged money to start a magazine, and the first issue of *Knights of the Immaculata* appeared in January 1922. His superiors, thinking he should have other priorities, transferred him with a few other Brothers to remote north-western Poland, but he took the printing-press bought with a donation from an American priest with him and was soon printing increased numbers of the magazine. His popularity grew, and after a little while the community needed larger premises.

He had already lost the use of one lung from the tuberculosis that was to dog the rest of his life. A year in a sanatorium had enabled him to return to work, but the pressure associated with the growing community brought on renewed symptoms, and he had to spend a further eighteen months in the sanatorium. Seemingly miraculously, negotiations to buy a site near Warsaw on which to build his projected *Niepokalanow*, or "town of the Immaculate," had been suddenly concluded, and Maximilian joined his brethren there. They built in simple barrack-like style, but with accommodation for the latest printing machinery, and magazines and papers in several languages were soon rolling off their rotary presses. A meeting with some Japanese students inspired him to start a similar venture in Japan, and he and three other Brothers arrived in Nagasaki in 1930. They overcame the huge problem of learning and hand-setting 2,000 *kanji* (Japanese ideograms) and were soon producing their magazine there. Then he was off to India, where a similar operation was soon underway. Back in Nagasaki, he built a "Garden of the Immaculata," which, sheltered by a hill, was to survive the 1945 atom bomb. In 1936 he was recalled to Poland, and by the outbreak of the Second World War he had a broadcasting station and was building a Catholic film studio and an airfield—his plans to spread the message of the Knights to the entire world seemed well on course.

The invasion of Poland in September 1939 changed everything. Maximilian sent all but forty-eight of his Franciscans back to their families, instructing them to join the Polish Red Cross but not armed resistance groups. He and the forty-eight were marched off to a camp on 19 September, transferred to another on the 24th, and unexpectedly released less than three months later. The reason for this became apparent when three thousand Polish refugees were sent to them, followed by fifteen hundred Jews. The Brothers made them all welcome and accommodated them as best they could in the *Niepokalanow*, which the Germans had ransacked. Throughout 1940, persecution of the Catholic Church in Poland (identified with nationalism) intensified, and in February 1941 Maximilian, who had refused an offer of German citizenship, was arrested with four companions and eventually transferred to the forced labour and extermination camp complex of Auschwitz-Birkenau.

There he ministered to the other prisoners, encouraging them to hope in the eventual triumph of God's justice and to feel the comfort being offered to them by Mary Immaculate. In July he was transferred to a labour block from which one prisoner escaped. The guards chose ten men to be starved to death in reprisal. They did not include Maximilian, but he stepped forward and offered himself in the place of one man who had a wife and children. Instead of shooting him directly, as was the usual fate of those who "stepped out of line" in any way, the deputy commandant asked what his profession was and, when he replied "Catholic priest," agreed to his request. He and the other nine were stripped and taken to a death bunker, to be left without food or water until they died. By 14 August all except Maximilian were dead, and he was dragged out and killed by lethal injection to make way for the next batch. His body was burned in the camp ovens the next day.

Pope Paul II beatified Maximilian in 1971, calling him a "typical Polish hero," and eleven years later he canonized him; the man whose life he had saved was present at the ceremony. The churches at his "towns of the Immaculata" in Poland and Japan are places of pilgrimage, and the death bunker at Auschwitz is always filled with flowers. Maximilian literally showed the greatest possible love in laying down his life for another. Calling him "the martyr of Auschwitz" should in no way detract from the four million other martyrdoms, mainly of Jewish people, inflicted in that truly awful place.

15

St Mary, the Blessed Virgin (died about 63)

In Matthew's Gospel, the genealogy of Jesus in chapter 1 ends with Mary: "and Jacob the father of Joseph the husband of Mary, of whom Jesus was born, who is called the Messiah" (v. 16). Her unique place in the history of salvation is thereby asserted, while the birth of Jesus is set into the history of the Israelites, fourteen generations after the deportation from Babylon (v. 17). Matthew then relates the familiar story of Jesus' birth more from Joseph's point of view (vv. 18–25). He then tells of the visit of the wise men, who "On entering the house ... saw the child with Mary his mother" (2:11a), followed by the story of the flight into Egypt and the return, both guided by Joseph's dreams.

Luke alone of the evangelists tells of the events that precede the birth of Jesus in Mary's life: the visit from the angel Gabriel to tell her she is to bear a son, ending with Mary's agreement, "Here am I, the servant of the Lord; let it be with me according to your word" (1:38a), and her visit to her cousin Elizabeth, pregnant with John the Baptist, to whom she speaks the *Magnificat* and with whom she stays "about three months" (1:56) and then returns home. Luke's chapter 2 tells of the nativity, with "no place for them in the inn" (v. 7b), the choir of angels, the shepherds telling Mary what the angels have told them, so that "Mary treasured all these words and pondered them in her heart" (v. 19). Later, Mary goes with Joseph and Jesus to Jerusalem to be purified in the Temple, making the poor people's offering of "a pair of turtle-doves or two young pigeons" (v. 24b). There Simeon makes an enigmatic prophecy about Jesus to Mary: "This child is destined for the falling and the rising of many in Israel, and to be a sign that will be opposed so that the inner thoughts of many will be revealed—and a sword will pierce your own soul too" (vv. 34b–5). Luke does not tell the story of the flight into Egypt, which, taken with the *Magnificat* and the offering proper to the poor, serves to dignify poverty, humility, and oppression through Mary. Matthew has Joseph settle the family in Nazareth in response to another dream; Luke adds Jesus growing in wisdom and the story of him staying behind in the Temple, his parents searching for him, and Mary's protest when they find him: "Child, why have you treated us like this?" (v. 48b). Not surprisingly, she does not understand Jesus' reply: "Did you not know that I must be in my Father's house?" (v. 49b). Despite this apparent insolence, Jesus returned to Nazareth with his parents and "was obedient to them." And Mary, once again accepting her place in events beyond her understanding, "treasured all these things in her heart" (v. 51b).

Mary appears next, in John's Gospel only, at the wedding in Cana, placed by John on "the third day" after he had called his first followers. The wine runs out, and Mary points this out to Jesus. His reply, "Woman, what concern is that to you and to me? My hour has not yet come" (John 2:4b), is not as sharp as it sounds: "Woman" is a correct form of address, and the subsequent events show that Mary knew her son would still take notice of her. After this she apparently suffers another rebuke when Jesus, told that his "mother and brothers" are looking for him, declares that "Whoever does the will of God is my brother and sister and mother" (see Mark 3:31–5; Luke 8:19–21). Mary is here incorporated into the community, and later devotion interpreted this saying as meaning that Mary is the mother of the whole Church. She next appears standing at the foot of the cross, listed first among the women by John (19:25). From the cross, Jesus entrusts her to "the disciple whom he loved standing beside her ... 'Woman, here is your son' ... [and] to the disciple, 'Here is your mother'" (vv. 26b–7a). She reappears briefly in chapter 1 of Acts, as part of the early community at prayer, "together with certain women, including Mary the Mother of Jesus" (1:14b).

Apart from these few episodes, most as much theological as historical, the New Testament is silent about Mary. However, as Christian feminist writers have pointed out, the New Testament was written by men in a patriarchal society, and to understand the true place of women, one has to make an "exegesis of silence" (Carla Ricci), to tease out the likely truth from behind the words. Women were Jesus' most faithful companions from the early days in Galilee to Calvary, and his mother may have played a part in his public life, as her presence at the foot of the cross suggests.

Devotion to Mary as Mother of God began in the second century, with several influential works, notably the *Protevangelium of James*, supplying details of her "life" missing from the New Testament. The tradition of her Dormition (in the East) or Assumption (later dogma, in the West) seems to have begun in the fourth or fifth century and to have taken various forms until the idea of her being taken body and soul into heaven became generalized in the ninth century. It was, nevertheless, still possible to portray her death in art in the sixteenth century, and the dogma was not proclaimed until Pope Pius XII made it the crowning act of the Holy Year of 1950. Her title of "Mother of God" came out of the great controversies in the early councils over the nature of Christ, and what it asserts is that the child to whom she gave birth is truly God and truly human. As we are all "sons and daughters" in Christ, Mary thus becomes our mother too and as such our protector and intercessor with God, who can seem more remote than this humble girl who said "Yes" to the most important request ever made of a human person.

Mary is celebrated throughout the Church's year, her main feasts being 1 January, Solemnity of the Mother of God; 25 March, the Annunciation of the Lord; 31 May, the Visitation of the Blessed Virgin Mary; 15 August, the Assumption of the Blessed Virgin Mary; 22 August, the Queenship of Mary; 8 September, the Birthday of Our Lady; 8 December, the Immaculate Conception.

❖

Surely, from now on all generations will call me blessed;
for the Mighty One has done great things for me,
and holy is his name.
　　Luke 1:48b–9

16

St Stephen of Hungary (Vaik; about 965–1038)

Stephen is venerated in Hungary as a national hero and as the most important of Hungary's Christian kings, and most of what is known about him falls into the realm of public policy. This did not prevent miracles being attributed to him after his death and his early canonization.

He was the son of Geza, the third duke of the Magyars, who had swept westward from north of the Black Sea in the ninth century and plundered much of central Europe before settling into the great plain between the Alps and the Carpathian mountains. They became at least nominally Christian, and Vaik was baptized with the name Istvan (or Stephen) at the age of about ten. He married Gisela, sister of Duke Henry of Bavaria, when he was about twenty and two years later inherited his father's Magyar dukedom (*Magyar* being the word the Hungarians use to describe themselves).

Having quelled various insurrections, Stephen set about establishing a formal ecclesiastical structure in his territory, sending his intended first archbishop, Astrik, to Rome to ask for papal approval of his plans from Pope Silvester II. He also asked Silvester to grant him the title of king. This was granted, and Silvester is said to have had a crown made, with which Stephen was crowned king in 1001. The religious foundation ensured independence from the Bavarian Church to the west and the Greek Church to the east, and he promoted this by founding bishoprics only as Magyar clergymen became available. Vesprem and Esztergom, which became the primatial see, can claim to be founded by him, as can the monastery of St Martin, still the motherhouse of the Hungarian Benedictines. He made Christianity the religion of the State by using royal power: he prohibited marriages between Christians and pagans, ordered all except the clergy and religious to marry, and severely punished adultery, murder, blasphemy, and theft. Every tenth town had to build a church, and tithes had to be collected. He defended Hungarian independence of Church and State fiercely, especially against the German emperor, driving out invading Bavarian nobles and in 1030 taking Vienna, which he held for a year. He promulgated a code of laws, reducing the power of the nobles and establishing regional administration through governors and magistrates. Hungary became a feudal kingdom, but Stephen's achievements in both Christianizing and unifying the country were not to last.

He promoted his son, Emeric (venerated as Blessed on 4 Nov.) to a greater share in the running of the kingdom, but then Emeric was killed in a hunting accident in 1031. Stephen fell ill for the last years of his life and died on 15 August 1038. Disputes over the succession broke out, with several claimants to the throne, including his nephew, Peter, the son of his widow, Gisela, and the son of his ambitious sister, also named Gisela. Peter succeeded to the throne but lost it after unsuccessful raids on Germany. The Magyar chiefs took control once more and elected a new king, who supported a revival of paganism. Stephen, who was said to have been generous in giving alms to the poor in disguise, to the extent of once risking his life when his purse was snatched, was canonized by Pope St Gregory VII (see 22 May) in 1083, and his relics were enshrined in the church of Our Lady in Buda.

17

St Joan of the Cross (Jeanne Delanoue; 1666–1736)

Joan's story is an extraordinary one of conversion by unlikely means and an illustration of the fact that a holy childhood is not necessary for sainthood.

She was the last of twelve children born to parents who owned a small draper's shop in Saumur, in the Anjou region of France. The shop was near the shrine of Notre Dame des Ardilliers in the town and developed a profitable sideline in selling religious souvenirs to the many pilgrims who visited the shrine. Joan's father died when she six, and she had to help in the shop. When her mother died in 1691, she took it over and proved a hard-headed businesswoman. She offered accommodation to pilgrims, in the shape of unsanitary caves in a cliff behind the house, and sent her niece (whom she had made a partner in the business) out to buy food just before meals, so that at any other time she could truthfully tell beggars there was no food in the house. She offended the local clergy by opening on Sundays and feast-days.

Early in January 1693 a shabby old widow from Rennes appeared as a pilgrim and asked for lodging. Joan acted out of character and let her stay in the house for very little money, and the widow, Madame Souchet, began passing on some enigmatic communications she claimed to be receiving direct from Jesus. Disturbed by these, Joan contacted the local hospital chaplain, who was known for wise counselling. As a result, she stopped opening the shop on Sundays and began to fast three days a week. Madame Souchet came back at Whitsun with more delphic sayings. The townspeople thought she was mad, but Joan took her seriously as a messenger from Jesus and declared that she was going to devote the rest of her life to the poor.

God, through Madame Souchet, found for her six poor children living in a stable to care for. Joan took a cartload of food and clothing to them and their parents and devoted almost half her time to them. Others in need started coming to her, and in 1698 she closed the shop. Two years later she turned the house and the caves into a lodging house for the poor and orphans, but when the cliff collapsed, killing a child, she had to find somewhere else. For a time the local Oratorians lent her a house, but the type of person she was caring for did not appeal to their more aristocratic tastes, and they forced her to leave. She found another house with three rooms and a cave, but this was soon too small. Her niece helped her, and then two other young women joined them. There was thus the germ of a new Congregation, which Joan had heard from Jesus that she should start. They were clothed as Sisters of St Anne in 1704. Two years later the Oratorians rented them a large house, but they increased the rent dramatically when they saw (and no doubt smelled) its occupants. They also tried to take over the running of the Congregation, but Joan successfully resisted this. The bishop of Angers formally approved its Rule in 1709, a year of famine in which the Sisters were caring for over a hundred sick people. In 1715 she opened the first hospice in Saumur. The governor of Annecy and other benefactors bought her a large house and other buildings and renovated them, so that in 1717 she was able to move from what was known as Providence House into Great Providence House. Soon there were forty helpers.

Joan had by this time taken to excessive personal mortifications, despite suffering for years from toothache, earache, and rheumatism. Her spiritual director eventually persuaded her to modify her penances, but her health did not recover, and she died after almost a year of final illness on 17 August 1736. She had founded twelve communities, hospices, and schools and was already being called a saint. Her Congregation, finally known as Sisters of St Anne of

Providence of Saumur, now has some four hundred Sisters working for orphans, old people, and the destitute in France, Madagascar, and Sumatra. Joan was beatified in 1947 and canonized on 31 October 1982—a founder of a women's religious Order, like so many beatified and canonized women, but one with a difference.

18

St Helena (died about 329)

The mother of Constantine is best known for something she is unlikely actually to have done—finding the true cross. Even without this, she is regarded as a saint because of her many gifts to help facilitate the building of new churches, her work in liberating prisoners and helping the needy, and the influence she exerted over the man who ended persecution of Christianity in the Roman Empire.

Despite a medieval claim that she was the daughter of an English king ("old King Cole," no less), she was born in Asia Minor. She married a Roman general named Constantius Chlorus, and Constantine was born in what is now Serbia in 274. Constantius became western emperor, and he and his son were campaigning in Britain when Constantius died at York and Constantine was immediately acclaimed as his successor. He later showed his appreciation of his mother by giving her the title Augusta, or empress, and having medals struck with her portrait. She became a Christian in 312 and was known for being devout in prayer and going to church and for her generosity to the poor. This was the year in which Constantine, at the head of a mainly Christian army, raised the *chi rho* symbol for Christ at the battle of the Milvian Bridge, at which he defeated his rival Maxentius and entered Rome as emperor. The following year he proclaimed the Edict of Milan, tolerating Christianity throughout the empire.

Helena's and Constantine's roots were in the east. In 324 he defeated Licinius and became sole emperor. He invited the bishops of the Church to the first ecumenical council, held at Nicaea in what is now north-western Turkey, in 325, and planned and built a splendid new capital for the empire in the East, at Byzantium, also called Constantinople after him. He stressed the importance of Palestine, the setting for Christ's life on earth, as a cohesive force in the newly Christian empire, and in 326 Helena went to Jerusalem. Her purpose seems to have been to investigate the places where Jesus was born and lived, and to oversee Constantine's project to demolish the temple of Venus built on the site of Calvary by Hadrian and build a basilica in its place. The only contemporary account of her visit, by the historian Eusebius, says that "though now advanced in years, yet gifted with no common degree of wisdom, [she] had hastened with alacrity to survey this venerable land." She spent the last three or four years of her life in the Holy Land, founding the church of the Nativity at Bethlehem and another on the Mount of Olives, helping the poor. She lived humbly in a convent, where she did the housework. Her presence there inspired a great increase in pilgrimage and a quest for relics. She fell ill in Palestine but reached the imperial court at Nicomedia before she died. Constantine, according to Eusebius, was with her at her death, "caring for her and holding her hands."

Any actual part she played in the "discovery" of the true cross is probably impossible to establish. (The new Roman Martyrology has abandoned any explicit claim that she did so, saying only that "venerating the manger and cross of the Lord she honoured them with basilicas.") Constantine certainly instituted a quest for the cross on Mount Calvary: he wrote to the bishop of Jerusalem commissioning him to look for it. Any actual finding and identification are known only from later accounts, usually involving a miracle of healing, revealing which of the three crosses found was that of Jesus. Less than twenty years later, St Cyril of Jerusalem refers to the fact that fragments of the true cross had been distributed everywhere, so that "they nearly filled the world." (The popular belief that, if all the known relics were put together, they would make up many crosses, is not actually true: they would make up only a small fraction of one.) Relics of the cross were certainly being venerated in Jerusalem by the end of the fourth century. It became a very important image in the Iconoclast debate over the veneration of images in the eighth century. Two feasts of the cross, the Invention (discovery) of the Cross on 3 May and the Exaltation of the Cross on 14 September, were celebrated until the 1969 Calendar reform removed the latter.

Helena's body was taken to Rome, and her tomb was later attached to the church of SS Peter and Marcellinus, the first church built as a memorial to martyrs. By the ninth century, it was claimed to be in the abbey of Hautvillers, near Reims. St Helen's in Lancashire and the Atlantic island of St Helena, where Napoleon died in exile, are named after her. There are many churches dedicated to her in north-eastern England, on account of her association with York.

19

St John Eudes (1601–1680)

Born in Normandy, where he spent most of his life, John was one of the great reforming figures of seventeenth-century France. His journals show that from an early age he was aware of the effective de-Christianization of large parts of rural France. The newer religious Orders, such as the Jesuits, were attempting to combat this, but the bulk of the diocesan clergy remained ignorant and apparently apathetic. John's parents were deeply religious, and they sent him, aged fourteen, to be educated at the Jesuit college in Caen. He received the tonsure and minor orders but did not seem inspired either to become a diocesan priest or to join an Order. In 1622 he came across the Oratorian house in Caen, a branch of the Paris Oratory founded by the great spiritual writer Pierre de Bérulle on the model of the Rome Oratory started by St Philip Neri (see 26 May). He was drawn to their structure of community without religious vows, dedicated to the spiritual and pastoral education of priests, and became a devoted follower of Bérulle. In 1623 he joined the Paris Oratory, and he was ordained two years later.

John then fell seriously ill and had scarcely recovered when the plague struck the part of Normandy he came from. He went there and spent two months nursing and comforting the sick. At the end of 1627 he joined the Oratorian community in Caen, acting as preacher, confessor, and spiritual director. In 1630 the plague broke out there, and again he risked his life to help the sick and dying. To avoid contaminating his fellow-priests, he adopted the bizarre expedient of living in a wine vat in fields outside the town belonging to a convent of Benedictine nuns, who brought him food. He was seriously ill but recovered. The following year he began a long course of preaching missions in parishes. Each lasted between six and eight weeks, and they were aimed primarily at bringing adult Catholics to "conversion" to a life in which they really knew and cared about their faith (efforts to convert Protestants who had not fled France in the devastating religious wars proving less successful). He used visual devices and physical involvement as much as possible, with processions, plays, and mimes as well as traditional devotions. The missions ended with penitents making a general Confession.

The work was exhausting—John preached over a hundred such missions—but he also produced his own theory to buttress his work. *The Life and Kingdom of Jesus in Christian Souls*, published in 1637 and running into sixteen editions in his lifetime, provides the essence of his devotional thinking. Adapting mysticism and theology to daily life through a dual structure of exercises and thoughts set alongside meditations on Jesus' life, it is a practical manual for making Christian life a living relationship with Jesus. His thoughts were later developed in *Meditations*, which emphasized the humanity of Jesus, dwelling on the generosity of his heart. John was influential in spreading devotion to the Sacred Heart of Jesus, without turning it into a matter of physical symptoms and reward.

Seeing that the education of priests was central to the reforms he was trying to effect, John left the Oratory in 1643 and opened a new seminary at Caen, forming a new body, the Congregation of Jesus and Mary (generally known as Eudists), to run it. He followed this with five other seminaries in Normandy and Brittany, but an attempt to extend the work to Paris failed. His break with the Oratory had caused bitterness, and he had to contend with harsh opposition, with enemies in the Church invoking State sanctions against him. It took him fourteen years to obtain full approval for the seminary at Caen. Even when he seemed about to receive royal approval (essential in absolutist France, where Louis XIV was constantly in dispute with the pope about influence over the national Church), he was frustrated by the production of a document, dating from a decade earlier, which promised his Congregation's support for the pope in all circumstances. Furious, Louis banished him from the capital. This aroused suspicion in Rome rather than the support that might have been expected, and some possibly unwise associations—mainly with women, involving mysticism and care of prostitutes—and some elements in his teaching were expanded into a huge dossier compiled by a Cistercian abbot, which concluded that he should be burned at the stake as a heretic.

Though weakened by such attacks, which continued despite detailed refutations by his followers, John still persisted in preaching his missions and with attempts to have feasts of the Sacred Heart of Jesus and of the Holy Heart of Mary accepted by the universal Church. He wrote several offices for these feasts, but in the event only the first was to be approved, and that not until nearly a hundred years after his death. He appealed desperately to the king, whose continued opposition was threatening the very existence of his Congregation, and was eventually granted a royal audience in 1679, at which Louis said he knew that John was doing good work. This assured the future of the Eudists, though they were nearly to disappear during the French Revolution. John appointed a new superior in June 1680 and died peacefully two months later. He was beatified in 1909 and canonized in 1925. The Eudists now work mainly in secondary education, in the Americas as well as in Europe.

The union of Father and Son is the model for our union with God through baptism. The Holy Spirit is the link uniting One with the Other and you and me with God, enabling us to be with Jesus and relate to him perfectly as long as we live.
St John Eudes, in *The Life and Kingdom of Jesus in Christian Souls*

20

St Bernard (1090–1153)

Statesman, churchman, incomparable letter-writer, preacher of Crusade, devotee of Mary, Bernard was an extraordinary, multifaceted personality who "bestrode" his world "like a colossus," as Shakespeare said of Caesar. For much of the twelfth century it seemed that no one, from popes and kings downward, could do anything without his permission or at least approval—and as his verdict was sometimes inspired by charity and gentleness and sometimes by a spirit of domination and relentless sarcasm, these could be counted on with some difficulty.

He was one of seven children born to Burgundian aristocrats: of these, only two failed to become saints or blessed. In 1112 he and thirty-one other young noblemen rode up to the monastery of Cîteaux (see St Stephen Harding; 28 Mar.) and asked to be admitted. He had decided on being a knight of Christ and characteristically took his friends and relatives with him. Three years later Stephen asked him to found another monastery, which he did at Clairvaux. This became a major focus of the rapid expansion of the strictly reformed Cistercians. Twenty-four other foundations were made from Clairvaux within a few years. Bernard directed virtually every aspect of every foundation: ethics, discipline, architecture, art. Simplicity and severity were to be the pattern in all of these.

His reputation spread beyond monastic confines, and he was soon travelling all over Europe advising bishops, dictating letters to popes, kings, and anyone, however humble, who wrote to him for advice. A steady stream of letters, rich in metaphor, always to the point, even if they now seem mannered, poured out of him, dictated several at a time to secretaries. He was secretary to the Synod of Troyes in 1128, where he approved (and perhaps wrote) the Rules of the Knights Templar; he settled the succession to the see of York; he rallied the Church behind Innocent II against the antipope Peter Leontius, refusing the emperor rights of investiture in the process—all this while directing his own community, overseeing others, and suffering constant stomach pains, perhaps from an ulcer. When one of his Cistercian pupils was elected pope as Eugenius III in 1145, his influence increased still further.

True to the spirit of his age, Bernard was implacably opposed to anything that smacked of unorthodoxy or heresy. His famous quarrel with Peter Abelard was motivated by his dislike of an approach to the mysteries of faith different from his own: Abelard was logical, speculative, intellectual; Bernard, though by no means lacking in intellect, was passionate, intuitive, mystical, allegorical. Even worse than Abelard were the Albigensians (see St Dominic; 8 Aug.), against whom he preached a vehement (and quite unsuccessful, though he would not admit this) crusade. When the Turks captured Edessa, in the Latin kingdom of Jerusalem, Pope Eugenius asked Bernard to preach the Second Crusade. He began this at Vézelay in 1146, and the following year the emperor, Conrad, and King Louis of France set out at the head of their armies. The result was a disastrous failure, mainly owing to the appetite of the Christian knights for plunder, and Bernard, who had—unsurprisingly—his enemies, found himself widely, if unfairly, blamed for its failure.

Besides his thousands of letters, Bernard wrote major theological treatises and an impressive series of sermons. His writings show him to be a profound mystic, convinced that contemplation must result in action: "love in action" (which might be a fitting motto for his teaching), as exemplified in the life and death of Jesus, should bring us closer to God and therefore reconcile what we are with what we ought to be. He also promulgated devotion to Mary, whom he saw as the dispenser of love from heaven. His followers and biographers certainly over-elaborated some aspects of this devotion, largely through false attribution and legend. Dante chose him as the culminating poet in his *Paradiso*, putting into his mouth the daring concept that Mary conceives the Father and bears him as her Son; his Canto 33 has been translated as a hymn by Mgr R. A. Knox: "Virgin, yet a mother, / daughter of thy Son."

As he travelled about Europe preaching, counselling, founding, arbitrating, Bernard acquired a huge popular following as a healer. He could not escape from the crowds who flocked to him, begging for his help. He had to allocate "consultation times"—in the most extreme case, he stood at an upper window in the bishop's palace in Cologne, and petitioners were allowed up a ladder one at a time. Practising what he preached of following Christ, he could not turn people away; his charity had to take precedence over his instincts, and he was careful to attribute cures to people's faith rather than to his own personal qualities.

In 1153, already showing signs of his last illness, Bernard was called on by the archbishop of Trier to settle a dispute between the duke of Lorraine and the inhabitants of Metz. He made both sides lay down their arms, then returned to Clairvaux, where he died on 20 August. He was quickly canonized (though not so quickly by the standards of the time), in 1174, and he was widely regarded as a Doctor of the Church, though this title was not formally granted till 1830. Called *Doctor mellifluus*, (honey-tongued doctor), he is the patron saint of beekeepers. His remains were buried at Clairvaux but were scattered during the French Revolution.

Is it possible to burn with greater fervour than in meditating on [God's] love? Can we show more patience and perseverance in love than in wholehearted longing for this everlasting love? Yes, our perseverance is a kind of prefiguration of this eternity. It is the sole virtue that will be granted eternity, or rather that will allow human beings that state of eternity which they have lost.

St Bernard, in his five-volume work *De Consideratione*, written for the guidance of Pope Eugenius III

21

St Pius X (Giuseppe Sarto; 1835–1914)

Giuseppe (Joseph) was the second of ten children born to a poor family in the upper Venetia region of north-eastern Italy. He entered the seminary in Padua at the age of fifteen, was ordained priest at twenty-three, and progressed steadily if unspectacularly up the ecclesiastical ladder: chaplain, archpriest, canon, then bishop of Mantua in 1884, and cardinal and patriarch of Venice in 1893. In 1903 he was elected pope, seemingly against his will, after political interference by the Austrian emperor had gradually eroded the vote for the initial front-runner, Cardinal Rampolla. He had thus taken a purely pastoral route to the papacy.

He took the name Pius in memory of previous popes of that name (such as Pius V, who had excommunicated Queen Elizabeth I) to signal that he intended to carry on their fight "against sects and rampant errors." He disliked the pomp and ceremony of the Vatican but was determined to uphold the temporal as well as spiritual power of the papacy, seeing it as the one remedy for a sick society and demanding obedience "from man and beast." The background to this was the occupation of Rome by Italian forces that had put a premature end to the First Vatican Council in 1870. This had produced a ban on Italian Catholics voting in parliamentary elections: Pius revoked this but still insisted that lay Catholics should be guided by the hierarchy on how to vote.

In 1904 a diplomatic dispute with France led to the breaking off of diplomatic relations between the "eldest daughter of the Church" and the Vatican, followed by separation of State and Church in France the following year, ending the Concordat signed in 1801. Some French bishops saw this as advantageous to the Church, since it prevented the civil powers from nominating candidates for bishoprics. Pius, however, protested vehemently against the abrogation of the Concordat in two encyclical letters (a weapon of which he made prolific use). Further political and social encyclicals condemned social democratic movements in the Church, non-denominational trade unions, and any liberalizing tendencies, while he did not condemn the right-wing *Action Française* movement, with which prominent Catholics were associated. He was deeply mistrustful of the wealth of historical research that had inspired first Protestant and then Catholic biblical and other scholars during the nineteenth century, seeing it as serving merely to undermine the basic truths of faith (which he collected and published in a simple catechism). The outcome was his blanket condemnation of "Modernism" in two encyclicals, known from their first words as *Lamentabili* and *Pascendi*, issued in 1907. Their targets included the French scholars Maurice Blondel and Alfred Loisy and the Anglo-Irish Jesuit George Tyrrell. Using the Index of Forbidden Books and other forms of censorship, Pius and the Vatican network he created to root out Modernism prevented many scholars from publishing and effectively put an end to their careers. The effect, it has to be said, was to set the course of scholarship in the Church back by over half a century.

Other aspects of Pius' pontificate were more positive. He ended the right of Catholic monarchs to veto candidates for the papacy. He helped to draft the new Code of Canon law, issued in 1917. He encouraged daily reading of scripture, reformed the Breviary, promoted the restoration of Gregorian chant in the liturgy, laid down guidelines for the teaching of doctrine and the duties of bishops, and above all introduced the habit of frequent, even daily, Communion by the laity and lowered the age for first receiving Communion to seven. Until then, most Catholics had tended to abide by the minimum laid down in the Catechism for Confession and Communion: once a year, "and that at Easter or thereabouts." This was a real revolution in lay spirituality and might be said to have paved the way for the understanding of the Mass as a shared meal that developed with the liturgical reforms of Vatican II.

As canon and bishop, he had promoted practical works of charity, and he continued these as pope, acting on behalf of victims as widespread as Peruvian mineworkers and those made homeless by an earthquake in Messina. He was extremely popular with the people, sought after as a healer (like St Bernard), and widely regarded as a saint in his lifetime. Various unsubstantiated accounts show him either trying to prevent the onset of the First World War or supporting the Austrian emperor-king, Franz Joseph. The onset of the war certainly depressed him, perhaps even to the extent of hastening his death, which came rapidly on 20 August 1914. He was beatified in 1951 and canonized in 1954 by Pope Pius XII, who shared many of his concerns in the areas of uniformity of thought and the central power of the papal office. His motto, "To restore all things in Christ," taken from Ephesians 1:10, is cited in his entry in the new Roman Martyrology.

22

Bd Thomas Percy (1528–1572)

The northern rebellion of 1569 against Queen Elizabeth I, of which Thomas Percy, seventh earl of Northumberland, was one of the leaders, was inextricably political and religious. It originated in an area that was still largely Catholic, but its originators included Protestants as well as Catholics. After its failure, those arrested were required to abjure the Catholic religion, and those who refused to do so were executed, so Thomas Percy and others can justly be said to have died for the Faith.

Thomas was the son of Sir Thomas, who had played a prominent part in an earlier northern uprising, known as the Pilgrimage of Grace, a protest against King Henry VIII's assumption of the title of supreme governor of the Church in England in 1536. This was forcefully put down, and Sir Thomas was executed at Tyburn for his part in it. His sons were taken from their mother for a time but then restored to her, and the family enjoyed royal support when the Catholic Queen Mary came to the throne in 1553. Thomas was made earl of Northumberland and high marshal of the army in the north. When Elizabeth replaced Mary as queen in 1558, his fortunes fluctuated: he was first forced to resign as marshal but was then made a Knight of the Garter in 1563; two years later Elizabeth's chief secretary of state, William Cecil (later the first Baron Burghley), who had earlier served under him, reported him to be "dangerously obstinate in religion." He was reputedly sympathetic to the cause of Mary, Queen of Scots, whom he interviewed in Carlisle on her way south to imprisonment.

The rebellion was planned mainly by Thomas Markenfield and the earl of Westmorland, but Thomas Percy, reflecting the widespread discontent felt in the north with Elizabeth's reign and the new religion, joined it willingly. Known in advance to the royal forces, it was forced into action without adequate preparation. A force that at one point amounted to five thousand foot soldiers and over twelve hundred horsemen marched south from Durham to Ripon but then turned back and faded away. In Durham they had ceremonially burned the Protestant Bible and the Book of Common Prayer and celebrated the last Mass in Durham Cathedral. So their purposes were overtly Catholic, though they included the restoration of "the ancient nobility of the realm" as well as overthrowing the "new found religion and heresy contrary to God's word." Those arrested in Durham and Yorkshire after the failure of the uprising were mostly its poorest followers: eight hundred were executed and a further thousand heavily fined. The queen's soldiers ruthlessly plundered northern England.

Thomas went into hiding and then took refuge in Scotland. His wife, Anne, née Somerset, took their daughter Mary (a son had died in infancy in 1560) to Antwerp, then in the Spanish Netherlands, to try to raise money to ransom her husband and enable him to escape, but he was arrested by the Calvinist regent of Scotland in 1572 and sold to Elizabeth's officers for £2,000. He was taken to York for trial, refused to deny his religion, and was beheaded on 22 August. The earldom passed to his brother Henry, one of whose daughters, Lady Mary Percy, was to found the English Benedictine abbey in Brussels. Thomas was beatified in 1895.

23

St Rose of Lima (Isabel de Flores y del Oliva; 1586–1617)

The first canonized saint from the New World is a disturbing figure and becomes more so when saints are seen more as models than as intercessors. Born in the capital of Peru on the feast of Pentecost 1586 and christened Isabel (Elizabeth), she became known as Rosa when an Indian maid declared her to be *"como una rosa"*—as beautiful as a rose. At the age of fourteen she was confirmed by the archbishop of Lima, Turibius of Mogrovejo (see 23 Mar.), and seemed set for the marriage market to which her parents' wishes and society's norms destined her and in which her beauty seemed to assure a dazzling success.

She, however, was quite determined not to marry. Inspired by the Life of St Catherine of Siena (see 29 Apr.) to dedicate herself to God, she apparently also imitated Catherine's extreme means of making herself unattractive to any suitor, rubbing her face with pepper to bring on blisters and blotches. She developed the symptoms of what we now call bulimia, and she cut herself. The more she was admired, the more drastic her remedies became: when a woman remarked on her fine skin, she rubbed lime on her hands, rendering them virtually useless for a month. She wanted to enter a nunnery, but her parents refused to allow this. She was caught in a complete dilemma: she owed a duty of obedience to her parents but a higher duty to what she saw as the will of God, which her parents seemed to be disobeying. Admiration of her gradually turned to ridicule.

When her parents lost money in a mining speculation, she stood by them, growing flowers in their garden and selling them as well as working as a seamstress deep into the night. For ten years they went on trying to persuade her to marry and she went on resisting and torturing herself. She wore a "crown of thorns," a garland of flowers held together with metal spikes, and lived as a near recluse in a "hermitage" she had earlier built in the garden, where she slept on a bed of broken tiles. Like St Catherine, she became a member of the Third Order of St Dominic. She knew states of mystical exaltation and of near despair in which she was strengthened by hearing Christ's voice telling her that his cross was even more painful than anything she endured. Gradually she opened out to other people: she turned a room in her parents' house into an infirmary, especially nursing destitute children and sick elderly people. It is hard to know the scale on which this eventually operated, but she became extremely popular in Lima, and the venture has been called the beginning of social services in Peru.

Rose died at the age of thirty-one. The actual date was 24 August 1617, though she is commemorated today. The ordinary people of Lima regarded her as a saint, though the religious authorities were more suspicious of her experiences (as they were of all forms of "illuminism," or what we would now call charismatic religion, in Spain at the time). Such crowds thronged the route along which the dignitaries of the city took turns to carry her coffin that it was several days before she could be buried. She was beatified in 1668 and canonized (together with St John of the Cross; see 14 Dec.) by Pope Clement X in 1671. She is patron of Peru, of all Latin America, of the Indies, and of the Philippines.

Her legacy is clearly a difficult one to assess. She cannot be seen as a model for young women in her self-inflicted suffering, but neither can she be judged by the accepted standards of a later and very different society. How she would have behaved if her parents had allowed her to enter a convent when she first expressed the desire to do so is impossible to determine, as is the whole balance between her personal disposition and the conditions inflicted on her by society. In some sense she is a feminist martyr to a patriarchal and *macho* world, a model of resistance and independence: for some this aspect will outweigh symptoms we now class as sick or at best a cry for help; for others it will not. She lived in a confusing and violent world. She died the year after Cervantes, whose Don Quixote started as a figure of ridicule and ended standing in judgment on the "sane" world.

24

St Bartholomew (First Century)

Bartholomew, one of the twelve apostles, is mentioned only a few times in the Synoptic Gospels. In Mark 3:18 he is one of the twelve whom Jesus calls to be with him and names as apostles: "and Andrew, and Philip, and Bartholomew ..." Luke has a parallel calling, with him in approximately the same place in the list: "... Andrew, and James, and John, and Philip, and Bartholomew ..." (6:14). Matthew's chapter 10 gives the same account of the summoning and naming of the twelve: "James son of Zebedee, and his brother John; Philip and Bartholomew ..." (10:2b–3a). His name means "son of Tolmai" and so is a patronymic rather than an actual name. John does not mention Bartholomew, but he does list a Nathanael in his account of the gathering of the apostles, stating that he is found by Philip (1:45), after whom Bartholomew's name appears directly in the three Synoptic accounts, so there is a strong possibility that the two names designate the same person. Nathanael it is who asks the cynical question, "Can anything good come out of Nazareth?" (1:46a), to which Philip answers simply, "Come and see." He goes, and Jesus welcomes him with the words, "Here is truly an Israelite in whom there is no deceit!" Evidently surprised (and doubtless flattered), Nathanael asks, "Where did you come to know me?" and Jesus tells him, "I saw you under the fig tree before Philip called you" (1:48–9). Nathanael then makes an early profession of faith, in which John puts later titles of Christ into his mouth, in terms that do not seem to be called for by Jesus' simple statement: "Rabbi, you are the Son of God! You are the King of Israel!" Jesus promises him that he will see "heaven opened and the angels of God ascending and descending upon the Son of Man" (John 1:49, 51b).

The New Testament, though, is silent on what he may have seen or done later and makes no further mention of him, leaving legend to take over. According to this he went east and preached variously in India, Armenia, Mesopotamia, and Persia, or south to Egypt, and elsewhere. The fourth-century church historian Eusebius says that when St Pantaneus went to India late in the second century, "he appears to have found that Matthew's gospel had arrived before him and was in the hands of some there who had come to know Christ. Bartholomew, one of the apostles, had preached to them and had left behind Matthew's account in the actual Hebrew characters . . ." (*The History of the Church*, 5, 10). This sounds very precise, but Eusebius' geography was not necessarily very accurate, and he could be using "India" for almost anywhere in the Near East.

His death is said to have been the horrific one of being flayed alive and then beheaded, but this is almost certainly copied from the Greek myth of the flaying of Marsyas by Apollo. This made him the patron saint of tanners, and he is most often portrayed in art with his skin draped over one arm while he holds the flensing knife in his hand. His relics are supposed to have been sent to Rome for safekeeping and are claimed by St Bartholomew-in-the-Tiber as well as by Benevento, through which they passed on the way. An arm was presented to Canterbury in the eleventh century, and he was widely venerated in England, where over one hundred and fifty churches were dedicated to him.

25

St Louis of France (1214–1270)

King Louis IX of France, the son of Louis VIII and his half-Spanish, half-English wife, Blanche of Castile, was born at Poissy, near Paris. His father died when he was twelve; he was crowned the same year, but his mother acted as regent of France until he came of age. Before this he was active in the field against rebellious nobles, leading three campaigns when he was only fifteen. At the age of twenty he married Margaret, daughter of the count of Provence, an alliance that extended his kingdom to the Mediterranean. (King Henry III of England married Margaret's sister, Eleanor, but that did not prevent the two kings going to war.) They had eleven children: five sons and six daughters, the eldest of whom was born in 1240.

In 1239 Louis further extended the royal domains into Burgundy and then south-westward by defeating the count of Toulouse. Henry III of England landed in western France with an army in 1242 to support his stepfather, Hugh of Lusignan (who was rebelling against his feudal overlord), and try to win back formerly English territory in the Anjou region. Louis defeated him in battle and forced him to flee southward to Bordeaux and then to sign a truce. Two years later he (and the whole of Europe) were faced with a greater threat than territorial disputes between Christian monarchs. The Saracens had defeated the Christians of Palestine in Gaza and threatened all of the Holy Land. Louis, against all advice, decided that he would lead a Crusade. It took four years to raise the necessary funds; he sailed for Cyprus in June 1248 and was joined there by two hundred English knights led by the earl of Salisbury. They sailed to the Nile Delta and captured Damietta, into which Louis walked barefoot, preceded by the papal legate.

For him the Crusade was a pilgrimage to the place of Christ's birth and death, not a war of extermination against Muslims. He gave orders that no Muslim should be killed if he could be taken prisoner. Louis did not, however, have the power to extend his ideals to the crusading knights, who were more concerned with booty—or often with simple survival as disease and the heat took their toll. His force was defeated at Mansourah in April 1250, and he was taken prisoner. He was released a month later, after handing back Damietta and paying a huge ransom. Despite this disaster, he did not return to France but went on to Syria, aiding the Crusaders there to strengthen their positions, and then to Caesarea in Palestine, visiting those Holy Places that were not in Muslim hands. After further stays in Jaffa and Sidon, he returned to France only when news of his mother's death reached him. He took with him a number of converts from Islam and their families, whom he supported for the remainder of their lives.

He now turned his attention to the state of his own kingdom and embarked on a major course of reform, as if to compensate for the failure of the Crusade. Between 1254 and 1270 a series of measures was enacted designed to form French society according to a moral order, imposing a complex structure of responsibility and accountability at all levels of public life. Louis also saw the need to devalue the coinage as a measure against growing inflation, in which he was many centuries ahead of his time. He took steps to secure his borders through dynastic marriages, and ceded parts of south-west France to Henry III in exchange for Henry's renunciation of any claim to areas farther north. He was criticized for this but defended it on the grounds that it was designed to secure a lasting peace between England and France—in which he failed, as the Hundred Years War broke out less than a century later.

In 1267 he turned his attention to the Muslims once more and planned another Crusade, in response to the capture of Caesarea in 1265, which was followed by that of Jaffa three years later. He set sail in July 1270 but had reached no farther than Tunis when he succumbed to an attack of dysentery, dying on 25 August. Since he regarded all Christians who died fighting the Muslims as martyrs, he would have regarded his own death as a martyrdom. His body was chopped into pieces and boiled in wine to separate the flesh from the bones. These, together with his heart, were brought back to France and buried at Saint-Denis in 1271. After a number of pontifical inquiries into his holiness he was canonized by Pope Boniface VIII in 1297. Philip "the Fair" divided up the bones in 1308, giving some to other major churches and to important people. Those that remained at Saint-Denis were solemnly enshrined, but they were scattered during the French Revolution.

His legacy has been a complex one, his reputation resting on different aspects of his personality as various forms of government have succeeded one another. His goal was to be a perfect Christian prince: on a personal level, he set an example of frugality and austerity unusual in a monarch of his time, so that he was said to embody Christ as both Suffering Servant and King; as a statesman, he achieved only mixed success, while his attitude to the Muslims—certainly not bloodthirsty or contemptuous of individuals—has been seen as sowing the seeds of the "colonial" approach of the West in general and the resentments this still provokes. The same has to be said for his attitude to the Jews in France, who were subjected to increasing restrictions throughout his reign and obliged to abandon usury or leave the country. He was, like St Bernard, widely regarded as a healer in his lifetime and drew crowds of people wanting to touch him. His legal and structural reforms, coupled with his extension of universities and monastic foundations, made France admired throughout Europe, and he was responsible for one of its greatest artistic and architectural treasures, the Sainte-Chapelle in Paris, built to house the supposed crown of thorns sent from Constantinople in 1239.

26

St Joseph Calasanz (José Calasanz y Gastonia; 1556–1648)

Born into an aristocratic family in Aragon, Joseph's career followed a smooth path until he was sixty-five. He studied at the universities of Lérida, Valencia, and Alcalá. The bishop of Urgel ordained him priest in 1583, then promoted him to vicar-general of the Trempe region in the north of his diocese. As such he visited remote parishes in the Pyrenees, including Andorra, with the aim of rekindling the religious enthusiasm and sense of duty of the local clergy. On his return to Trempe he was appointed vicar-general of the whole diocese. In 1592 he resigned his post and benefices, divided his inheritance among his sisters, the poor, and certain charitable institutions and moved to Rome.

There he became friendly with Camillus of Lellis (see 14 July) and with him nursed the sick and the dying during an outbreak of plague in 1595. He joined the Confraternity of Christian Doctrine, which instructed children and adults on Sundays and Holy Days, but found that homeless and abandoned children were virtually beyond the reach of any existing religious institution. He campaigned for parishes to admit poor children to their schools without having to pay fees, but the clergy rejected this. He appealed to the Jesuits and Dominicans for help, but they were fully committed, so he started a school himself, the first free school in Rome. Three other priests joined him; within a week they had a hundred pupils. Larger premises had to be found, as well as more teachers, who were soon living on the premises as a community: this was to develop into a recognized Institute. By 1602 the number of pupils had grown to seven hundred, and again larger premises were needed. There began to be complaints that some parents who could well afford fees were sending their children there, but an "inspection" by Pope Paul V brought the venture under papal protection, with a doubled grant. The next move was in 1612, to the Torres Palace, now with twelve hundred pupils. Further schools were founded, the Institute was formally approved as a religious Congregation, with Joseph as its superior general, and it seemed that he could rest on his laurels.

This was not to be, and instead he found himself delated to the Holy Office of the Inquisition. The source of the accusations was a former colleague named Mario Sozzi, who had joined the Institute in Naples, then been sent as provincial to Tuscany, where he had proved unsatisfactory. Joseph had a friend at the Holy Office in the person of Cardinal Cesarini, and he ordered Sozzi's papers to be seized. They included some documents belonging to the Inquisition, but Sozzi had some strange hold over the authorities and managed to blame this on Joseph, who was arrested and paraded through the streets and would have been imprisoned but for Cesarini's intervention. Sozzi persuaded the members of the Institute that Joseph was senile, had him removed as superior general, and took over himself, aided by a friendly apostolic visitor. Sozzi died in 1643, twenty-two years after first making his accusations, but the truth did not prevail for two more years. Then a committee of cardinals examined the affair and recommended that Joseph, then nearly ninety, should be reinstated. He had suffered many years of humiliation patiently telling himself, "The Lord has given and the Lord has taken away. Blessed be the name of the Lord." Sozzi's successor, who had continued the persecution for two years, was eventually charged with maladministration and had to leave Rome in disgrace.

Joseph died on 25 August 1648. His cause was introduced in 1728, when Cardinal Lambertini called him "a perpetual miracle of fortitude and another Job." He was beatified in 1748, canonized in 1767, and declared the patron of Catholic schools by Pope Pius XII in 1948. There are famous paintings of his last Communion by Valdés Leal and Goya. The Congregation became the Clerks Regular of the Pious Schools, or Piarist Fathers, in 1669 and spread through Italy, Spain, and South America. They now also work in the USA, with a special mission to poor families in the Appalachian Mountains. Besides teaching at all levels, they undertake counselling, run drug-dependency clinics, and provide pastoral care.

27

St Monica (332–387)

St Augustine's mother was a very powerful influence on his life, just as he was a huge concern in hers. He embraced heresy and had a son by his mistress; she would not let go of him. Their relationship is described in Augustine's *Confessions* in detail and with his total honesty, with the result that we know far more about her than we do about most saints' mothers, even if from Augustine's point of view rather than hers. Inevitably, any account of her is equally one of him up to the time of her death.

She was born to Christian parents in present-day Algeria (in Thagaste, now Souk-Ahras) and married at thirteen or fourteen to a man named Patricius, who was neither wealthy nor Christian and about whom Augustine has little good to say, except that he did not actually beat her. In addition she had to contend with her mother-in-law living with them and constantly criticizing her. Monica obviously saw her prime duty as obedience to her husband, but her emotional refuge was in prayer and her children, of whom three, Augustine, a brother, and a sister, survived: there may have been two others who died in infancy. After twenty years of marriage, Patricius became a Christian, perhaps looking to the afterlife, as he died the following year. By this time Augustine was a student in Carthage, keeping bad company and immersed in "a cauldron of illicit loves." He took a young Carthaginian woman as his mistress, perhaps seeking a steadier life, and stayed with her for fifteen years. Monica prayed constantly for his morals and his faith, but the first faith he found was as a Manichee, whereupon she banned him from her house, despite advice from a sensible bishop (a convert from Manichaeism) that he should be allowed time to find his own way to the truth.

In 328 Augustine left North Africa as a renowned teacher, though still under thirty, and disillusioned with Manichaeism. Monica was determined to go with him; he was determined to leave her behind and tricked her into believing he was only visiting the port when in fact he was embarking. He saw the separation as necessary for God to bring him to faith, but she evidently had different views and after some time followed him to Rome. By this time he had moved on to Milan and come under the influence of Ambrose (see 7 Dec.), the archbishop. Monica followed him to Milan, found him seriously depressed, and for a time tried to arrange a wealthy marriage for him. (The faithful mistress left their son with him and went back to Carthage.) Augustine took another mistress, then engaged himself to a wealthy young woman, but then abandoned her and decided to take a vow of celibacy. Monica, son, and grandson found a house in the country near Milan, where they lived in community with some of Augustine's friends and his brother, Navigius, with Monica acting as housekeeper. She herself was deeply influenced by Ambrose, whose teaching was constantly discussed in the community. Augustine was baptized by him at Easter 387.

He then tired of teaching and resolved to go back to North Africa. Monica went with him, and they reached the port of Ostia, the seaport for Rome. There they achieved peace together, in a (possibly visionary) conversation recorded by Augustine. They discussed silence and listening to the word of God. For Monica, Augustine's conversion and baptism had fulfilled her deepest desires, and she saw little point in undertaking the long journey back to Africa: "I do not know what there is now left for me to do, or why I am still here, all my hopes in this world being now fulfilled." As if in answer to prayer, she fainted a few days later and was clearly mortally ill. She abandoned her earlier desire to be buried with her husband and asked Augustine to bury her anywhere but always to remember her in his prayers. She died in Ostia and was buried there. There was no real cult of her as a saint until the Middle Ages. In 1430 her reputed remains were transferred by Pope Martin V to a shrine in the church of Sant'Agostino in Rome. She is the patroness of wives and mothers.

In his *Confessions* Augustine moves beyond the tribulations she had caused him and recognizes his double indebtedness to her: addressing God, he says, "I shall not pass over whatever my soul shall bring to birth concerning your servant, who brought me to birth both in her body so that I was born into the light of time, and in her heart so that I was born into the light of eternity."

28

St Augustine (354–430)

Born, like his mother (see the previous entry), at Thagaste in Roman North Africa, Augustine was taught by his father, Patricius, to admire the Latin classics, and both parents struggled to find the money to send him to Carthage to study law and rhetoric. He turned away from these and from a steady academic career, to run his own courses in philosophy and theology, his endlessly questing mind already looking for ultimate truth. For a time he thought he had found this in Manichaeism, with its belief in dual powers of light and darkness, good and evil. His struggles with temptations of the flesh are universally known from his *Confessions*. After moving to Rome and then to Milan with his concubine and their son, Adeodatus, he became convinced of the truth of orthodox Christianity and dismissed the concubine (to whom, in the accepted practice of the time, he had no permanent responsibility), eventually deciding on celibacy.

He had been a catechumen in his youth, but was not baptized until his adult convictions allowed him to seek Baptism. By that time he had been through possibly the most anguished personal quest ever described: longing for belief yet fearing to believe untruth, he could not take the plunge into faith until, lamenting "How long, how long shall I go on saying tomorrow and tomorrow? Why not now?," he heard a voice chanting "Take and read. Take and read" and turned to the Bible, learning to surrender himself to Christ in the manner of Eastern monks whom he saw in Milan. He was thirty-three when Ambrose baptized him at Easter 387. This was shortly followed by his proposed return to Africa, postponed in the event to the following year by his mother's death at Ostia.

Back in Thagaste, he collected a group of like-minded companions and lived with them in community in his house. Using the Bible as well as philosophical arguments, he began to write against the Manichees, putting faith in Christ forward as the necessary condition for understanding the world and affirming that belief in an absolute power of evil was mistaken. He was ordained priest in 391 and appointed coadjutor bishop of Hippo in 395. He succeeded Bishop Valerius there the following year, and was bishop of Hippo for the remaining thirty-four years of his life. He set a personal example of frugal living and required his clergy to do the same. He cared for the impoverished and unfortunate in an era of wars and disasters, using first his own inheritance and then church revenues and property to provide for them. He founded a community of women, with his sister as its first abbess: when she died, he wrote them a letter on the religious life that, together with two sermons, became the Rule of St Augustine. He preached daily, often moving vast congregations to tears, and conducted an enormous correspondence.

As bishop, he was a political figure. He became a spokesman for the North African Church and was drawn into the major controversies then dividing the universal Church. He saw heresy as an evil to be rooted out and defended state coercion to bring heretics back to the true faith—this being preferable to their eternal damnation. His writings were to be used in the Middle Ages to support the view of the State as the executive arm of the Church. When the Visigoth

King Alaric sacked Rome in 410, Augustine produced *The City of God*, contrasting the societies of "Jerusalem" and "Babylon," the heavenly city to which human beings aspire and the earthly city to which they are bound by original sin. This was a response to pagans who saw Alaric's victory as the revenge of their gods for the imposition of Christianity on the Roman Empire. Over a period of some twelve years he refined his views on grace and free will, concluding that humans could not choose salvation without God's grace. He maintained this against Pelagius, who had fled to North Africa after the sack of Rome and argued that people could achieve perfection through freedom of choice. This view was condemned by Pope Zosimus in 418—leaving Augustine's thinking on grace (with its concomitant of some form of predestination) and free will an inescapable component of virtually all major controversies ever since, not least the Protestant Reformation. It is also the reason for his title as a Doctor of the Church, "Doctor of Grace."

His thinking on sex—inevitably formed by his own experiences—has been just as influential, partly owing to subsequent failures to separate what is time-conditioned from what is of permanent value in his teaching (as with St Paul, on whom he relied). The (still official) teaching on the primary purpose of marriage as procreation and the inadmissibility of women to the priesthood rely largely on Augustine, though no mainstream Churches still hold his views on the impossibility of salvation without Baptism. Against this negative legacy must be set his emphasis on the Church as the Mystical Body of Christ, his concept of the unity of all believers, and his constant stress on the love of God. His linking of the three powers of the soul—memory, understanding, and will—to the three Persons of the Trinity has been present in all subsequent doctrinal discussion of the Trinity. Perhaps even more influential than his theology, the self-examination most evident in the *Confessions* has inspired and informed Western consciousness as expressed in fiction, autobiography, philosophy, psychology, and the theory of knowledge.

His last years were beset by political troubles, and he died in the midst of a Vandal siege of Hippo, the result of feuds within the empire's ruling families, which produced slaughter, devastation, famine, and a flood of refugees from the countryside. One of his disciples, Posidius of Calama, wrote an account of his life shortly after his death; this is of real historical value. His cult began at an early stage, and there are images of him dating from the sixth century. His usual attribute in representations is a fiery heart to represent his burning love of God.

Understanding is the reward given by faith. Do not try to understand in order to believe, but believe in order to understand.
Augustine, *On the Teacher*, 11, 37

29

St John the Baptist (First Century)

All that is known of the "forerunner of Christ" comes from the New Testament and the Jewish historian Josephus. Luke alone of the evangelists tells, in his first chapter, the story of his elderly father Zechariah and barren mother Elizabeth (elderly and barren being attributes often used in the Bible to point to divine intervention), who are told by the angel Gabriel that they will have a son. Zechariah is struck dumb for not believing Gabriel's words; Elizabeth conceives, as does her "relative" Mary (see 15 Aug.) some months later; Mary visits Elizabeth, who later gives birth to her son and declares that he is to be called John. This is confirmed by Zechariah, still dumb, writing on a tablet, "His name is John" (1:63), after which he is able to speak again and pronounces the hymn of blessing (see 1:68–79).

All four evangelists then have a virtually similar account of John appearing preaching in the wilderness. Matthew 3 provides a physical description: "Now John wore clothing of camel's hair, with a leather belt around his waist, and his food was locusts and wild honey" (v. 4). Mark 1 gives a parallel account of his preaching, calling to repentance, and baptizing, then mentions his arrest. Luke 3 tells of his arrest before relating the baptism of Jesus and precisely dates the time of his baptizing to the "fifteenth year of the reign of Emperor Tiberius" (v. 1a); that is, 29 AD. These three accounts have an objective description of Jesus' baptism by John and the Spirit descending on him, but in John 1:19ff it is John the Baptist himself who sees the Spirit descending and points Jesus out as the "Son of God" and "Lamb of God." (John is using theological titles that would not have been in use at the time.)

John told those who came to see and hear him to repent and begin a new life, not relying on having Abraham for a father. They are told to share their clothing and food with the poor. He even baptized tax collectors, telling them to collect no more than they should, and soldiers of the hated army of occupation, telling them not to exploit the people and to be happy with their wages (see Luke 3:10–14). He announced that the kingdom of God was at hand, when everyone would be judged, and he proclaimed his message from "the wilderness," a place for self-examination far removed from the central places of Jewish ritual and worship. The fact that Jesus (who, being without sin, had no need of John's baptism of repentance) accepted baptism from John raises the question of how Jesus actually saw himself. John too, is a puzzle: some take him for Elijah come back; on the other hand, some say Jesus is John the Baptist back from the dead, and it takes Peter to define him as the Messiah. Jesus himself is typically gnomic about John: he is great, but "the least in the kingdom of heaven is greater than he," pointing up the contrast between "the world" and "the kingdom."

John then rebuked Herod Antipas, who married ten times, for his latest marriage, to Herodias, who was not only his niece but had also been his brother's wife, his brother being still alive. He was therefore violating Jewish law, besides all the other evil things he had done. Herodias was the more offended at John's criticism and persuaded Herod to have him arrested. In Matthew, Jesus hears of John's arrest after his own forty days in the wilderness. The news is presumably a shock, since he "withdrew to Galilee," where he takes up John's message: "Repent, for the kingdom of heaven has come near"(4:17b). In prison, John was still able to communicate with the outside world, since he sent his disciples to ask Jesus whether he was the Messiah. Josephus states that Herod had John killed for political reasons, but the New Testament (Matthew 14 and Mark 6 have the fullest accounts) gives the familiar, far more exotic account of Herodias' daughter, known as Salome, dancing before Herod and pleasing him so much that he promises her anything she asks for. Prompted by her mother, she asks for the head of John the Baptist on a platter, and Herod, though distressed, obliges her and has John beheaded immediately. When he hears this news, Jesus again withdraws into the wilderness. John's death is generally dated to two years before Jesus' crucifixion.

According to Josephus, John's death took place in the fortress of Machaerus, close to the Dead Sea. He was supposedly buried at Sebaste in Samaria. His followers were still influential twenty years after his death. From the fact that he preached near the Dead Sea, it is reasonable to suggest that he could have been associated with the Qumran community, whose rites, as revealed in the Dead Sea Scrolls, place a similar stress on baptism and repentance. The idea expressed by some of the Fathers that John was given a special prenatal grace led to his physical birth being celebrated (on 24 June) as well as—and in popular religion more than—the anniversary of his death. St John's Eve took over many rituals associated with the summer solstice, the most persistent being St John's Fires, showing that John was a light to the people: these survived in Britain to the late nineteenth century and are still lit in some parts of France. The image of his appearance provided by Matthew and the dramatic story of Salome (to which various sexual interpretations have been added) have ensured that the figure of John the Baptist has fascinated painters and writers down the ages. He is the patron of the city of Florence, of tailors (because of his coat) and farriers, of the Order of Knights Hospitallers, of spas (from his—spiritually—health-giving baptism with water), and—more recently and still unofficially—of motorways: "Make straight the ways of the Lord."

30

St Margaret Ward (died 1588)

Margaret, one of the very few English Catholic martyrs to be canonized, was a victim of the renewed persecution that broke out with the defeat of the Spanish Armada in July 1588 and of her association with a remarkable priest named William Watson. Her story is largely part of his.

Born in Cheshire, Margaret was in service in London—perhaps as house-keeper or companion, as she is described as a gentlewoman—when she decided to help Watson, who was undergoing one of his frequent spells of imprisonment in the Bridewell prison. Margaret became friendly with the gaoler's wife, took food to Watson, who was almost starved to death in an attic, and then smuggled in a length of rope. She arranged for two Catholic watermen to wait in a boat on the Thames below the prison walls one night. Watson doubled the rope instead of tying one end securely, fell from a con-siderable height, breaking an arm and a leg, and was picked up by the watermen, who rowed him to a safe hiding place.

He left the rope hanging, and it was traced to Margaret, who was arrested, tortured by being hung by her hands and beaten for eight days, and then brought to court, charged with aiding a traitor to escape. An Irishman named John Roche, who was either one of the watermen or her servant, was also arrested and tried with her. They were offered release if they asked the queen's pardon and agreed to worship in the established Church, but both refused. It was not quite clear what their crime was, and the death penalty was usually imposed only on priests who had been ordained on the Continent and had come back on the English mission, who could therefore be said to be abetting a foreign power. Those aiding and abetting them were also liable to the death penalty, but Watson (who had indeed been ordained at Reims) was not acting as a priest at the time of his escape and had indeed been persuaded to attend Protestant services. Nevertheless, both Margaret and John were condemned to death, essentially for refusing to conform to the established Church. They were hanged at Tyburn on 30 August 1588. Both were beatified in a large group in 1929, and Margaret was canonized as one of the Forty Martyrs of England and Wales by Pope Paul VI in 1970.

William Watson, who prior to the escape had become a thoroughly con-troversial figure, attacking his fellow-Catholic Antony Babington for plotting to murder Elizabeth and release Mary, Queen of Scots, attending Protestant worship, reclaiming his Catholicism and receiving absolution from another priest, was captured, escaped again, spent two years in Liège, then returned to England. He was fanatically opposed to the Jesuits, who were leading the "hard-line" Catholic approach to the reconversion of England, and he sought, with other clergy, some accommodation that would enable Catholics to take an oath of allegiance to Queen Elizabeth. Despite this, he spent three more spells in prison, escaping from two, and was released finally when Elizabeth died in 1603. In prison he wrote his autobiography and a polemical work attacking the Jesuits. He somehow secured an audience with King James VI/I but then plotted with other Catholics to kidnap him and replace his Protestant ministers with Catholic ones, among which he appointed himself Lord Chancellor. The Jesuits had their revenge on him by revealing the plot to the king. He was arrested, tried, and finally condemned to death and executed—a martyr, as it were, to the Jesuits, to whom he added insult to injury by asking their forgiveness.

31

St Aidan (died 651)

The story of Aidan, one of the great missionary saints of northern Britain, is told by Bede in his *Ecclesiastical History of the English People*. He came to England at the behest of St Oswald, king of Northumbria (d. 642), who had fled to Scotland when his kingdom was invaded by the then pagan (later St) Edwin, been converted to Christianity at Iona and wished his kingdom to become Christian when he won it back in 634. His kingdom extended from the Firth of Forth to Yorkshire. He asked the monks of Iona to send him a bishop and assistants for the work of conversion. Their first choice proved too austere for the people to listen to, and their next was the monk Aidan, "a man of outstanding gentleness, holiness, and moderation," whom they consecrated bishop and who proved a better choice, even though Oswald himself had to translate from his Gaelic for some time.

Oswald gave Aidan the island of Lindisfarne off the Northumberland coast (connected to it by a strip of sand at low tide) as his episcopal see. Aidan was either of Irish origin or actually born in Ireland, and he was followed by "many Irishmen [who] arrived day by day in Britain and proclaimed the word of God in all the provinces under Oswald's rule." They built churches, the king gave land and funds to build monasteries, and "the English, both noble and simple, were instructed by their Irish teachers to observe a monastic way of life." Bede's only criticism of Aidan is that he kept the date of Easter according to the northern Irish and Pictish calculation, not the Roman (which was to prevail at the Synod of Whitby in 663). Aidan and his followers "lived as they taught," so the English learned "self-discipline and continence," the habit of fasting on Wednesdays and Fridays, and the practice of meditation and praying the Psalms daily. Aidan gave away any money he was given to help the poor and took an especial interest in the ransoming of slaves. Many of those freed in this way became his disciples.

Oswald was killed in battle against the pagan King Penda of Mercia in August 642. Penda dismembered his body and put pieces on stakes as a sacrifice to his god, Woden. Bede devotes several chapters to the miracles attributed to him after his death. He was succeeded by Oswy and then in the southern province of Deira by Oswin, also a saint, who reigned for seven years and who also treated Aidan as a close friend. He gave him a splendid horse, which Aidan promptly gave with all its royal trappings to a beggar, "for he was most compassionate, a protector of the poor and a father to the wretched." Oswin remonstrated, saying he had less valuable horses that could have been given away, to which Aidan retorted, "What are you saying, Your Majesty? Is this child of a mare more valuable to you than this child of God?" The king pondered this before dinner, then took off his sword, knelt, and asked Aidan's forgiveness, promising never again to question anything he gave away.

Aidan, saying he had "never before seen a humble king," prophesied that he would not live very long. Shortly afterwards Oswin, who was at war with Oswy, ruler of the northern province, Bernicia, decided not to risk a battle against superior forces but to take refuge in the house of his friend Hunwald. But Hunwald betrayed his whereabouts to Oswy, who ordered him to be killed. Aidan died only eleven days later, on 31 August 651, when he was staying at Bamburgh Castle. He had been bishop for sixteen years. His body was taken to Lindisfarne and buried in the monks' cemetery. Later a larger church was built and his remains were transferred there and buried "at the right side of the altar in accordance with the honours due to so great a prelate." Bede insists that, "as a truthful historian [he has] given an accurate account of his life," despite his reiterated disapproval of his manner of observing Easter. Aidan, he says, "cultivated peace and love, purity and humility; he ... was above anger and greed, and despised pride and conceit. ... He used his priestly power to check the proud and powerful; he tenderly comforted the sick; he relieved and protected the poor."

Other Familiar English Names for August

1. Dominic, John, Leo, Mary, Peter, Timothy, Thomas
2. Joan, Peter, Stephen, Thomas, Walter
3. Augustine, Conrad, Martin, Peter
4. Cecilia, Frederick, William
5. Margaret, Oswald, Peter
6. Anne, Dominic, Mary
7. Albert, Conrad, Edward, John, Nicholas, Thomas, Vincent
8. John, Margaret, Mary, Paul, Robert
9. James, John, Julian, Mary, Peter, Richard
10. Augustine, Hugh
11. Alexander, John, Nicholas, Susanna
12. Antony, Charles, James, Michael
13. John, William
14. Antony, Dominic, Elizabeth, Felix, Francis
15. Philip, Rupert
16. Beatrice, James, John, Laurence, Ralph, Rose, Simon, Thomas
17. Clare, Francis, James, John, Luke, Martin, Mary, Michael, Nicholas
18. Leonard, Paula
19. Andrew, Antony, Hugh, James, John, Louis, Mark, Michael, Thomas, Timothy
20. Anna, Christopher, John, Lucy, Mary, Teresa
21. Bernard, Grace, Joseph, Mary, Victoria
22. Bernard, James, John, Philip, Richard, Timothy, William
23. *There are no other familiar names for today*
24. Andrew, Emily, George, Joan, Mary
25. Gregory, Michael, Peter, Thomas
26. Adrian, Alexander, Elizabeth, John, Margaret, Mary, Teresa, Victor
27. David, Dominic, John, Luke, Roger
28. Alexander, Edmund, Henry, Hugh, James, Julian, Robert, Thomas, William
29. Edmund, Mary, Peter, Richard, Victor
30. Edward, John, Peter, Richard
31. Andrew, Benedict, John, Joseph

SEPTEMBER

September has several days with too many saints to choose from and several with no major figures. This has resulted in some shifts far from correct dates, the farthest moved being St Hildegard of Bingen, from the 17th (occupied of right by St Robert Bellarmine) to the 4th. St Thomas of Villanova moves from the 8th to the 5th; St Ambrose Barlow from the 10th to the 11th; Bd Anton Schwarz from the 15th to the 12th; St Theodore of Canterbury from the 19th to the 24th; St Lioba from the 28th to the 29th. Another feature of September is the greater than usual shortage of women: the inclusion of only four does not imply any prejudice against them in selection—rather the reverse, in view of the fact that several men who feature in the Universal Calendar are not included here.

1

St Giles (or Gilles, or Aegidius; died about 710)

Giles became one of the most widely known and most popular saints of the Middle Ages on the strength of a Life written in the tenth century, based on legends that grew up around him and drawing freely on other saints' Lives. According to this, he was born in Athens and became famous for giving alms to the poor and working miracles. The miracles place him in the Western rather than the Eastern tradition, in which holiness depended more on asceticism.

In order to escape from his fame as a miracle-worker, he set sail from Athens and reached Marseilles, and after spending two years with St Caesarius of Arles (which he could not have done, as Caesarius died over one hundred and fifty years earlier) he became a hermit near Nîmes. While he was living alone in the wood, the story goes, a hind fed him with her milk. The local king led hunting parties into the wood, but the hind escaped by hiding in Giles' cave; one of the huntsmen shot an arrow at it as it disappeared into some bushes, and when the king, accompanied by a bishop, went to see where it had gone, they found Giles wounded by the arrow. The king offered money in compensation, which Giles at first refused; he eventually accepted on condition that it should be used to build a monastery, to which the king agreed provided Giles became its first abbot.

The monastery was supposedly built near the site of Giles' cave, and a large community developed. Charlemagne (who actually lived too late rather than too early for it to have been him) sent for Giles to ask his spiritual advice but was too ashamed to confess a particularly serious sin. When Giles was saying Mass, an angel "laid upon the altar a scroll on which was written the sin the king had committed." At the end of Mass Giles showed the scroll to the king, who repented and did penance. Giles later visited Rome, where he obtained a number of recommendations and privileges from the pope (known not to be true from the fact that the documents referred to can be shown to be forgeries).

The bare bones of known fact behind the legend are that Giles was probably born in the first half of the seventh century and that he built the monastery of Saint-Gilles on land given him near Arles in Provence by King Wamba. This was on the pilgrimage routes to Compostela and the Holy Land, and so the legends were developed to give the monastery importance and attract pilgrims. Saint-Gilles was far from being alone in using this technique in the Middle Ages, though the forgery of papal Bulls might have been going farther than most. Giles was included in the list of Fourteen Holy Helpers, the only one of them not to have been martyred. He became the patron saint of beggars, blacksmiths, cripples, lepers, and woods. He was invoked against cancer, epilepsy, sterility in women, and night terrors. His cult spread all over Europe, as far north as St Giles' Cathedral in Edinburgh, of which city he is the patron saint, and his name lives on in the street of St Giles in Oxford and St Giles, Cripplegate, in London. Every county in England except Westmorland and Cumberland (Cumbria) had churches dedicated to him. The monastery of Saint-Gilles suffered at the hands of the Albigensians (see St Dominic; 8 Aug.) in the thirteenth century and never really recovered. Most of Giles' bones were taken for safety to Sant-Sernin in Toulouse, the rest being sent to other places.

2

Martyrs of the French Revolution (died 1792)

Today's commemoration is not a general one of all those who were martyred in the terror of the French Revolution but of four specific groups who all died in Paris on 2 and 3 September 1792. Three were bishops, most were priests, but they included some laymen; they died in the context of widespread and uncontrolled violence that claimed the lives of many thousands.

In July 1790 the ruling body of the revolutionary forces, the Constituent Assembly, had promulgated the Civil Constitution on the Clergy, declaring all clergy to be French civil servants with no allegiance to Rome. All were required to take an oath of allegiance to the Constitution; many agreed, but the majority refused and were therefore declared enemies of the State. The hierarchy condemned the Constitution, but the Vatican took ten months to back this condemnation. Many rural priests, known to their parishioners, took refuge in Paris, where they could be anonymous. By April 1792, with France at war against a coalition supported by the pope, all priests who had not taken the oath were declared to be enemies of the Revolution, so traitors and liable to execution or at least deportation.

On 2 September, after Marat had declared that the enemy was at the gates of Paris and all "enemies" in the city should be removed, a group of captive priests marked for deportation was being taken from the town hall to the prison of L'Abbaye in Saint Germain des Prés. A crowd gathered, headed by a group of militiamen led by Stanislaus Maillard, a notorious bully. They demanded that the priests take the oath there and then and, when they refused, began to hack them to death on the spot. Twenty-one died, known (in the new Roman Martyrology) as Pierre James Mary Vitalis and twenty companions. One of these had been the king's confessor. Five escaped and provided an eyewitness account. The prison has since been demolished.

The crowd, possibly encouraged by Maillard, now turned to the Carmelite convent in the Rue de Rennes, where a larger group was being held captive. The leaders of the mob broke into the garden and killed the first priest they saw. The archbishop of Arles and the bishops of Beauvais and Saintes (who were brothers) were saying Vespers in the church with a number of priests and came out when they heard the disturbance. The archbishop was shot as soon as he said who he was; the bishop of Beauvais' legs were broken. The mob then appointed a "judge" to pass sentence "properly." He asked each cleric to take the oath, and when he refused he was hacked to death. By the end of the day ninety-six had been killed in this way. They are commemorated as Jean Marie du Lau d'Alleman (the archbishop), François Joseph de la Rochefoucauld-Maumont, Pierre Louis de la Rochefoucauld-Bayers, bishops, and ninety-three companions. The Carmelite convent is now the Institut Catholique.

The next day seventy-two people were slaughtered at the Lazarist seminary of Saint-Firmin, which had been turned into a prison. They included seven former Jesuits (the Order had been suppressed in France in 1759), the superior of the seminary, and the vice-chancellor of the university of Paris. Later in the day three clerics held in La Force prison were also killed. These groups are commemorated respectively as André Abel Alricy, priest, and seventy-one companions and by the three names of those who died in La Force: Jean-Baptiste Bottex, Michel François de la Gardette, and François Hyacinthe Le Livec de Trésurin. Saint-Firmin is now an office building, and La Force prison no longer exists.

All these martyrs were beatified on 1 October 1929.

3

St Gregory the Great (about 540–604)

Only three popes have been accorded the title "the Great," Leo I (440–61) and Nicholas I (858–67) being the other two. Gregory seems to have been a reluctant pope, but his extremely active and influential papacy set the course for Church–State relations that was to last for centuries and introduced internal reforms that lasted even longer.

He came from a wealthy Roman family of senatorial rank, received a thorough education, and served for a time as administrator of the city of Rome. His father died in 573, leaving him vast estates in Italy and Sicily. He handed these over to the Church and founded seven monasteries, most in Sicily but including one in the family house on the Coelian Hill in Rome, which he dedicated to St Andrew and in which he became a monk. He led a peaceful monastic life there for four years (though he ruined his health through excessive austerities) and was then called out of the monastery to become one of the seven deacons of Rome, with the rank of cardinal, by which time he had also been ordained priest. The pope then sent him on an expedition to Constantinople to try to persuade the emperor to provide help to the Romans, who were under siege from the Lombards. He spent five or six years there, developing an extensive knowledge of the Eastern Church that was to stand him in good stead as pope—though he was not impressed by the Eastern way of life in general. He was not very successful in obtaining military help from the emperor.

Recalled to Rome in 585 or 586, he was elected abbot of his former monastery, where he observed the Rule of St Basil. He became involved in a complicated doctrinal and political dispute, involving a schism in northern Italy, known as the Three Chapters (the chapters being in fact writers), which even his theological and diplomatic skills could not resolve. In 589 the Tiber burst its banks in Rome, destroying the city's grain store and producing an outbreak of plague. Gregory organized practical help and led public prayers to combat the plague, while trying to resist his election to the papacy. In the end, he had to give in to popular demand, and he was consecrated on 3 September 590.

His first tasks were in the realm of civil affairs. He assured Rome's food supply by reorganizing the estates owned by the papacy in Europe and North Africa known as the "patrimony of Peter," appointing managers to make sure they were efficiently, productively, and fairly run. He saved Rome from the threat of invasion by the Lombards from the north, though at the cost of paying the Lombard king an annual tribute. The Lombards were Arians, and he sought their conversion as well as peace. In the ecclesiastical sphere he centralized administration, established generally good relations with local Churches, rooted out corruption, and imposed strict celibacy on the Italian clergy. In Constantinople he had become a close friend of Leander of Seville, younger brother of St Isidore (see 4 Apr.) and his successor as archbishop, who assured good relations with Spain, where the Visigothic kingdom had converted from Arianism in 589. He had trouble with Donatists in North Africa. He memorably initiated Augustine of Canterbury's (see 27 May) mission to England after having Anglo-Saxon slaves, whose blond beauty impressed him— hence the famous saying, *"Non Angli sed angeli"* ("Not Angles but angels")— liberated so that they could be trained as missionary monks. He continued to keep a watchful eye on the progress of the mission, giving the English Church a very close relationship with the papacy and leading to him being called "apostle of the English" by Bede (see 25 May) and other writers.

As a monk, Gregory took a keen interest in the liturgy; he composed at least some of the prayers in what is known as the Gregorian Sacramentary and oversaw the musical development that is still called Gregorian Chant. He wrote extensively, explaining the Fathers in accessible terms, producing a manual on pastoral care that set the tone for the best practice by bishops throughout the Middle Ages, and providing posterity with the only record (or account) of the life of St Benedict (see 11 July) in his *Dialogues*. He also left eight hundred and fifty-four letters, to people in all walks of life on a huge variety of topics, and these provide the best insight into his character. He was strongly influenced by the *Rule of St Benedict* and did more than anyone to pass its spirit on to medieval monasticism.

Gregory died aged about sixty-five and was buried in St Peter's. (The actual date of his death was 12 March, but his feast has always been on the anniversary of his consecration as pope.) He was given the epitaph "God's consul" and was quickly acclaimed as a saint and widely venerated in West and East. Many churches in England, Ireland, and elsewhere were dedicated to him, and he is widely represented in art, beginning with medieval illuminations, in which he is shown as pope writing at the dictation of the Holy Spirit. In the fifteenth and sixteenth centuries, the "Mass of St Gregory" became a popular subject, showing the crucified Christ appearing while he is saying Mass, as a confirmation of his faith in the real presence. He is the patron of Ecuador and also of masons, musicians, scholars, singers, students, and teachers, reflecting his encouragement of the arts, especially of music.

In the position I now occupy I am so battered by the waves of life that I despair of bringing safely to port the weather-beaten old barque of which God, in his hidden

wisdom, has given me charge. .... Weeping I remember that I have lost the peaceful shore of my retreat, with a sigh I look at the land on to which I am prevented from stepping by the violence of the winds.

St Gregory on exchanging the life of a monk for the papal throne

4

St Hildegard of Bingen (1098–1179)

Hildegard has in recent years become something of a cult figure through the wide dissemination of her music, which was only one of the accomplishments of this most remarkable woman of any age. The daughter of a German nobleman, she was sent to an "anchoress" named Jutta for her education, which included learning to read and sing Latin. As more girls or young women were sent to Jutta, she formed them into a religious community under the Rule of St Benedict, with herself as abbess.

From the age of three, Hildegard had been receiving revelations or visions or hearing voices, which initially terrified her while totally absorbing her interest. When Jutta died in 1136, she was appointed to succeed her as abbess, having been a nun for seventeen years. She eventually told her confessor about the revelations, and he encouraged her to write them down and submitted the results to the archbishop of Mainz. They had often caused her terrible head-aches and depression, but—possibly due to the relief of expressing them or simply to her time of life—the headaches and spiritual aridity disappeared, and she was left feeling like "a feather on the breath of God" (a phrase since used as a title for the most popular CD of her music).

The archbishop consulted a panel of theologians, and they decided that her revelations were "from God" and encouraged her to go on dictating them, which she did to a monk named Volmar (and sometimes to others when he could not keep up). The result was a three-volume work, known as *Scivias*, a shortened version of *Nosce vias Domini* ("Know the ways of the Lord)". Her constant theme is the life-giving power of God, which she saw as the Spirit's "greening" effect on individuals and institutions. Often verging on pantheism, she has an obvious appeal to modern "deep ecology" spirituality. She had clearly read deeply in scripture and earlier Christian writers, but she absorbed them and never used them as authorities, perhaps because claiming direct divine inspiration was a better way of stressing the urgency of her message. The archbishop gave her work to the pope when he was visiting nearby Trier, and he appointed a commission including the redoubtable Bernard of Clairvaux (see 20 Aug.) to examine them. Again the verdict was favourable, though the pope warned her against pride—to which she, no respecter of rank, retaliated by warning him against machinations in his own household.

One of her visions had been of a place on a hill, the Rupertsberg, near Bingen on the Rhine, and the pope told her to follow the vision and move the community (which had outgrown its present premises) there. This caused a conflict with the abbot and monks of the nearby monastery of St Disibod, which relied on Jutta's relics and Hildegard's growing fame to attract pilgrims and therefore revenues. Hildegard became ill with the strain, and when the abbot saw that this was genuine, he agreed to the move. Within a few years there was a flourishing community of fifty nuns on the bleak hillside. Hildegard's practical side showed in having "water piped to all offices," and her artistic genius produced words and music for hymns and canticles as well as a cantata for the nuns to perform. She wrote Lives of St Disibod and St Rupert, used her leisure time (which she somehow found) to devise an early form of Esperanto, collected herbal remedies, and wrote a book on natural history and another on medicine, which described the circulation of the blood with considerable accuracy, five centuries before Harvey established it as fact. She illustrated the *Scivias* herself, in a style that anticipates William Blake: the originals have not survived, but careful copies have. *The Book of Life's Merits* continued her account of her visions, as did the later *Book of Divine Works*.

On top of this she wrote to everyone from the pope and kings downward, delivering homilies and warnings about the evils of the age, not afraid of rebuking anyone. Many people came to consult her; others denounced her as mad or fraudulent. Convinced that God was using her as a mouthpiece, she also preached publicly—something unknown for a woman of her age. She became a sort of consultant to other monasteries and convents, bearing down hard on any evidence of laxity. She had a final dispute with the archdiocese of Mainz when she buried the body of a young man who had once been excommunicated in the convent cemetery. The vicar-general told her he could not be buried in sacred ground; she replied that he had received the Last Rites and therefore could, so if he wanted his body dug up he could come and do it himself. The bishop sent a team of men to do so, but Hildegard had hidden the site and they failed to find it. He placed the convent under an interdict, which meant that the nuns could not receive the sacraments or have music in church for some months; she wrote him a long letter on sacred music, with a sting in the tail: "Those therefore who, without good reason, impose silence on churches in which singing in God's honour can be heard will not deserve to hear the glorious choir of angels that praises the Lord in heaven." The interdict was lifted.

She died peacefully on 17 September 1179, aged over eighty and so frail that she had to be carried everywhere, but writing, counselling, advising, and admonishing to the last. Miracles were reported at her tomb, and a cult developed; this was given public approval by Pope John XXII in 1324, and although she has never been officially canonized (a later exhaustive process might well have found at least some of her views heretical), she has an entry as

"Saint" in the new Roman Martyrology. She is the patron of philologists and Esperantists.

I am the supreme and fiery force who has kindled all sparks of life and breathed forth none of death, and I judge them as they are. I have rightly established that order, encircling it with my upper wings, that is, embracing them with wisdom. I, the fiery life of the divine substance, blaze in the beauty of the fields, shine in the waters, and burn in the sun, moon, and stars.

The Holy Spirit, described by Hildegard in her *Book of Divine Works*

5

St Thomas of Villanova (Tomás García y Martínez de Castellanos; 1486–1555)

Thomas was known in his lifetime as "the model of bishops," "the almsgiver," and "the father of the poor." He was in many ways a precursor of the Council of Trent, which he did not attend. He was born in Old Castile and at the age of sixteen went to the new university started by Cardinal Cisneros at Alcalá de Henares. He then joined its staff and was made professor of philosophy at the early age of twenty-six, but two years later he left to join the Augustinians in Salamanca. He was ordained after two years, then appointed prior, subsequently becoming prior of the houses in Burgos and Valladolid, the capital at the time, and vicar-general and, in 1534, provincial of Castile. He was noted for his concern for each friar in his care, especially any who were sick.

As provincial he was responsible for sending the first group of missionaries to Mexico. The king-emperor, Charles V, nominated him to the archbishopric of Granada, but he succeeded in declining this. In 1544 the archbishopric of Valencia became vacant. Charles proposed to respect his wishes and nominate someone else, but the secretary to whom he dictated the letter heard the name Thomas of Villanova and addressed the letter to him. Charles took this as a sign and sent the letter. This time Thomas accepted and was consecrated in Valladolid. He set out across more than half of Spain to take possession of his new see on foot, dressed in an old monastic habit and the hat he had worn since his profession. In Valencia he went straight to the Augustinian house and spent several days in prayer and penance to prepare himself. The cathedral canons gave him four hundred crowns to furnish his house, but he gave the money to the local hospital, asking what a poor friar like him wanted with furniture. His poverty was a frank embarrassment to an establishment with different ideas about clerical dignity, but in the end all he would accept was a new hat.

Valencia had been without a resident archbishop for seventeen years. Thomas made a visitation of all its churches, preaching so fervently as to change many people's lives and also discovering various clerical abuses. In 1548 he convened a provincial synod at which he presented his bishops with guidelines for abolishing these. His plans amounted to an advance summary of the Council of Trent, which had begun its intermittent sessions three years earlier. He poured all his energies into pastoral care of his people: every day several hundred would be given a meal and some money at his door. When warned that some of these were taking advantage of him, he replied that that was a matter for the police; his duty was simply to "assist and relieve those who come to my door." He gave his porters a crown for each foundling they brought (who would otherwise have died) and helped poor brides. When pirates sacked a nearby coastal town he sent money to ransom their captives and cloth for new clothes. He founded a college for children of converts from Islam (*moriscos*) and persuaded the emperor to provide funds for priests who worked to instruct converts—who were otherwise liable to fall foul of the Inquisition for lapsing.

Not all bishops attended the Council of Trent, at which he was represented by the bishop of Huesca. He may have taken the view that Valencia needed his presence more, while he could express his views by proxy. These were that the Church needed internal reform at least as much as a response to Luther. He proposed that a benefice should always go to a local priest and that bishops should not move from one diocese to another. Neither was adopted, but the ideas typify the bond he felt with the place for which he was responsible. He fell ill in August 1555, distributed all his money to the poor, and gave all his possessions to the rector of his college—except his bed, which he donated to the prison but borrowed back for as long as he should need it. He died in it on 8 September. He was beatified in 1618 and canonized in 1658. His relics are in a chapel dedicated to him in Valencia Cathedral. His sermons and other writings had a deep effect on Spanish literature and spirituality. He was known as "the Spanish Bernard", and universities have been named after him in Australia, Cuba, and the USA. In art he is usually shown as a bishop surrounded by poor people, as in the earliest representation, by Juan de Juanes, who knew him personally.

6

St Magnus of Füssen (died about 722)

Like St Giles (1 Sept.) Magnus is a saint whose *Life* (the account written of him in the Middle Ages, associated with an important monastery) is better known than his *life* (what he actually did). Nonetheless, according to what appear to be more reliable parts of the Life, he seems to have been a missionary of some importance.

He cannot have been the disciple of St Columbanus (see 24 Nov.) named Magnoald, as the Life claims, as this would make him over one hundred and fifty years old at the time of his death. The claim is made to identify him with the great monastery of Saint-Gall (in Switzerland; Sankt-Gallen in German), which developed on the site of the hermitage of St Gall, one of the twelve monks who accompanied Columbanus on his missionary journey to Gaul in about 590. (The monastery was closed in 1805, as part of a general suppression of religious Orders, but it was not destroyed: its church is now the cathedral, and its great and ancient library is housed beside it.)

Magnus became a monk at Saint-Gall, from where he was sent at the request of, or with the support of, Bishop Wichpert of Augsburg to preach to the pagan people of the Allgäu region of Bavaria. He set out with two companions, who remained with him for some years; one, Theodore, preaching in Kempten (now the principal town of the Allgäu), then returning to Saint-Gall, the other staying in a place they had evangelized to found a church. Magnus established a hermitage at Füssen (now on the border between Bavaria and Austria, south-west of Munich), which became the focus of his missionary activity. Wichpert sent some young clerics to assist him, and they formed the basis of a monastic community, which was later known as Sankt-Mang, built on land donated by King Pepin the Short of the Franks. Magnus' mission was practical as well as spiritual, as he showed the local inhabitants how best to clear land for cultivation and started mining for minerals in a nearby mountainside.

He died after twenty-six years of missionary work, and a cult developed. A church was built in the mid-840s over his tomb, and a synod in 847 decreed that his relics should be exposed. They were moved to Saint-Gall in 980. By the thirteenth century his cult had spread beyond Bavaria to the rest of Germany and beyond. His name began to appear in calendars, and by the fifteenth century he was often named as one of the Holy Helpers, invoked against storms, insects, dragons, and other dangers and disasters. The Life from which information, legendary or otherwise, about him derives was once thought to have been written by his companion Theodore and embellished about a century later, but scholarly opinion now inclines to the view that it was written wholly in the tenth century, presumably to support the move of his relics to Saint-Gall, with some stylistic amendments carried out in the eleventh century. Magnus is usually represented treading on serpents and other harmful beasts, to indicate his victory over paganism.

7

Bd John Duckett and other English, Welsh, and Scottish Martyrs (Sixteenth and Seventeenth Centuries)

This entry covers a number of those martyred on various dates during the month of September. They are considered in chronological order of the year of their death. St Ambrose Barlow has a separate entry below, on the 11th.

Thomas Johnson was a priest at the London charterhouse and one of the earliest martyrs in the Tudor persecution. The prior and three monks were executed in May 1534, and three more monks in June, after the prior had told all his monks that they could not assent to the Act of Supremacy, making Henry VIII supreme head of the Church in England. Thomas, with nine others, refused and was arrested, imprisoned in the Marshalsea prison, and left to starve to death. They seemed to stay alive for a surprisingly long time; this was found to be due to St Thomas More's adopted daughter Margaret Clement bribing the gaolers and bringing them food. She was prevented from further visiting, and one by one the ten died, Thomas on 20 September 1534.

George Douglas was a Scotsman born in Edinburgh. He was ordained abroad, but does not feature in the Douai lists, which has been taken to suggest that he was a Franciscan, but he does not feature on lists of Franciscan *beati*. . . . Whoever he was, he was hanged, drawn, and quartered at York on 9 September 1587 for persuading the queen's subjects to embrace the Catholic faith.

William Way, born in 1562, studied at Douai and joined the English mission in December 1586. He was arrested some six months later in London and imprisoned in the Clink Street jail. He was taken before a magistrate charged with being a priest ordained abroad and exercising his ministry in England, but he refused to be tried by a layman and so was referred to the bishop of London; he refused to recognize him as a valid bishop; the authorities lost patience and condemned him at the next quarter sessions. He was executed in the usual brutal fashion on 9 September 1588.

The following year William Spenser, ordained at Reims in 1583, was hanged, drawn, and quartered at York on 24 September. Nothing is known of his ministry before his arrest. Robert Hardesty, a layman arrested for sheltering him, was arrested and executed at the same time. They and the two previously named were all beatified among Eighty-Five Martyrs of England, Scotland, and Wales on 22 November 1987.

A layman named William Brown was hanged, drawn, and quartered at Ripon on 5 September 1605, but apart from the fact that he came from

Northamptonshire and was arrested with two others—executed that August for "being zealous Catholics, and industrious in exhorting some of their neighbours to embrace the Catholic faith"—nothing is known about him.

John Duckett (or Ducket) was born in Yorkshire in 1613, studied at the English College at Douai, and was ordained there in 1639. He studied for a further three years in Paris, where he became known for his cheerful disposition, then prepared to go on the English mission in Flanders, where he was directed by a "kinsman", Fr Duckett, who was the son of Bd James Duckett, a bookseller whose bookshop in the Strand survived until the 1970s. He was arrested after a year's mission in Co. Durham, admitted to being a priest to save two lay helpers from further interrogation, and was sent to London for trial and imprisoned in Newgate. He was condemned to death for being a priest ordained abroad and ministering in England and was executed at Tyburn on 7 September 1644.

Ralph Corby, who was sent to London, imprisoned, tried, and executed with Duckett, was born near Dublin but came to England when his Durham-born family returned there when he was five. Every member of the family entered the religious life: his father with the Jesuits, his mother and two sisters with Benedictine nuns in Belgium and his two brothers, like himself joining the Jesuits. He studied and was ordained in Flanders and was sent back to England in 1632 and so had ministered for twelve years by the time he was arrested in Newcastle. The English Jesuits tried to exchange him for a Scots colonel held prisoner in Germany; he offered the reprieve to John Duckett on the grounds that he was the younger man, but the death sentence passed on both of them put an end to the negotiations.

8

Bd Frederick Ozanam (Antoine-Frédéric Ozanam; 1813–1853)

The Ozanam family had long been Christian but were still proud to trace their ancestry back to Samuel Hosannam, a Jew converted by St Didier of Nevers during the seventh century. Frederick was one of four (out of fourteen) children in his family to survive infancy. His father had been an officer in Napoleon's army but then left the army to become a doctor in Milan, where Frederick was born. After Napoleon's final defeat they moved back to Lyons. Frederick studied with distinction at the Collège Royal there, nearly lost his faith at the age of fifteen, but was coaxed back into it, and left convinced that his life's work was to dedicate himself to "the service of the truth."

He went on to study law, and his father hoped he would become a lawyer; he, though he did not abandon his studies, found himself increasingly more interested in the history of literature. Soon after the Revolution of 1830 he became involved with a group of liberal Catholic intellectuals, which included such famous names as the Dominican Lacordaire and the historian Montalembert. He also became friends with Chateaubriand, passionate historian of France, and Lamartine, Romantic poet. The greatest influence on him, however, was Emanuel Bailly, who since 1819 had been directing a group of young men whom he saw as the spearhead of a Christian renewal in France: they were convinced that apostolic activity had to spring from sound thinking, which in turn had to lead to right action. This produced the Society of St Vincent de Paul, in which Frederick, with four other young men and a Daughter of Charity named Rosalie Rendu, who had more practical experience of working with the poor, played a founding role. The Society was (and is) an Institute for lay people dedicated to caring for the physical and spiritual well-being of the poor.

He took his doctorate in law in 1836, and shortly after this his father died. After much heart-searching, he decided that he must follow his inclination, which was to be "a missionary of the faith to science and society." He turned to literature and three years later gained a doctorate with a thesis on Dante's philosophy. Nevertheless, he then returned to Lyons, where for a year he was professor of commercial law at the university. He devised a course that included his ideas on what the social teaching of the Church should be: ideas that in some respects antedated the Communist Manifesto of 1848. He was then offered a post as assistant professor of foreign literature at the Sorbonne in Paris, which he saw as a call from God. He moved to Paris, married, and in 1845 his wife, Amalie, gave birth to a daughter. With her love and support he was able to combine an academic career with lecturing to the *Cercle catholique*, visiting the poor, and being permanently "at home" to his students, who respected him as much for his example of principled Christian living as for his academic abilities. Promoted to full professor, by 1846 he was planning a "literary history of the Middle Ages from the fifth century to Dante," which he saw as being above all a study of "the work of Christianity." It was a vast plan, but he was still only thirty-three and proficient in German, English, Spanish, and Italian, besides classical Greek and Latin and Sanskrit. He produced nine volumes, but he was suffering from tuberculosis and his health began to fail.

In 1848 he stood for the "Popular Party" against Louis Philippe but did not win a seat in the Assembly. With Lacordaire he started a journal expounding their Christian socialist principles. In 1853 he went to Italy, partly for the sake of his health, partly to collect a prestigious academic award for his work on Dante. He collapsed on his way back and died in Marseilles on 8 September. Pope John Paul II, in accordance with his desire to see more married saints, beatified him in August 1997, praising all that he had accomplished for family life, society, and the Church. He had indeed, with the manic energy that often accompanies tuberculosis, accompanied an extraordinary amount in a tragically short life. The Society of St Vincent de Paul has over a million members in thirty-two countries, so his legacy lives on in practical social action, even if his ideas have not yet met with full acceptance.

9

St Peter Claver (1580–1654)

The "saint of the slaves" was born in Catalonia to deeply Christian working parents. He graduated brilliantly from the Jesuit university in Barcelona and was determined to join the Jesuits. He joined their novitiate in Tarragona, took his first vows there in 1602, and was sent on to Majorca, where he was deeply impressed with St Alphonsus Rodríguez, the humble porter who "kept the door" for thirty years, who also suggested to him the idea of becoming a missionary in the New World. His superiors told him that it was up to them to decide where he went, but in 1610 they sent him to New Granada (the northern part of South America, now mainly Colombia). Landing at Cartagena, he went to the Jesuit house in Bogotá to continue his training and carry out various duties, and in 1615 he returned to Cartagena, where he was ordained. He was never to return to Spain.

Cartagena was one of the main entry ports for slaves from Africa. The trade was well established by this time, supported even by Catholic monarchs such as Charles V, despite the fact that several popes had condemned it as a great crime, to which the traders responded by having their slaves baptized and carrying on. Some ten thousand live slaves reached Latin America each year, with half that number dying in the appalling conditions of the voyage. Peter, under the guidance of the great Jesuit missionary Alfonso de Sandoval, dedicated himself to their welfare, calling himself *"Aethiporum servus"* ("slave of the Ethiops [Africans]"). He developed teams of assistants who were waiting whenever a slave ship docked. They took medicines, food, brandy, lemons, and tobacco to the sick, dazed, and filthy slaves, who were herded into sheds. Most were too frightened to accept what was being offered, but Peter persevered, learning Angolan to help him make contact. He and his helpers baptized those who were dying and babies born during the crossing and ministered as they could to the rest.

He set about trying to convince them that God's love for them was greater than the abuse they were suffering at the hands of God's supposed children, which must have been an uphill struggle. He used pictures devised by himself and taken from an illustrated life of Our Lord to try to give them an idea of a loving God, but at the same time the theology of his time told him that they were in error as "heathens" and had to repent, so any message the slaves received of their worth in the eyes of God was bound to be somewhat mixed. Nevertheless, he prepared them for Baptism and Penance at the rate of some five thousand a year. The slaves were then put to work in mines or on plantations, and this was the last Peter saw of most of them, though he paid an annual visit to those on plantations within reach of Cartagena, sharing their accommodation and saying Mass for them. Spanish law laid down one humane consideration lacking in the English system by allowing slaves to marry and stay with their families. Peter did what he could to ensure this was obeyed. None of his efforts endeared him to slave-owners—or indeed to many churchmen.

In Cartagena he regularly visited the sick, who suffered dreadful conditions in two hospitals, especially the one reserved to those suffering from leprosy and erysipelas. The sick included several Protestant traders and sailors, whom he treated with equal care, with an eye to their conversion; he made many converts, including, it seems, an archdeacon of London. He treated Muslims with the same kindness but was less successful in making converts among them. His mission extended also to prisoners and then to anyone who arrived in the port, to whom he would preach in the main square. He saw no form of human wickedness or squalor as being beyond his reach.

In 1650 he was preaching a Jubilee Year mission when he was struck down with a virulent form of plague. He was brought back to Cartagena, seemingly dying, but he lived on in a weakened state, shaking and in constant pain. His Jesuit colleagues treated him with neglect and contempt. Confined to his cell, he was nominally looked after by a young African, who often left him for days on end. A few Spanish penitents came to him, and he was occasionally able to get out to visit a sick person or administer Baptism. He was accused of rebaptizing Africans and forbidden to baptize any more. He bore all this with the patience of the "dumb ass" he compared himself to. In 1654 he knew he was dying, but he had the consolation of knowing that the king of Spain had sent another priest with a special commission to work among the slaves. In the evening of 6 September he lapsed into a coma. People flocked to strip his cell of everything that might be claimed as a relic. He died two days later, and the authorities who had neglected him and hindered his work now did all they could to reverence his memory. He had a great official funeral, and the slaves organized their own Mass, to which they invited the Spanish authorities. His fame gradually spread, and he was canonized in 1888 by Pope Leo XIII, who named him patron of all missionary work among the black peoples. Alphonsus Rodríguez, his early mentor, was canonized in the same ceremony.

If being a saint consists in having no taste and a strong stomach, I admit I may be one.
St Peter Claver

10

St Nicholas of Tolentino (Nicolà dei Guarutti; 1245–1305)

His parents named him in thanksgiving to St Nicholas of Myra (see 6 Dec.), to whose shrine they had made a pilgrimage after being childless for six years of marriage. They promised the saint that, if they had a son, he would serve him faithfully. He joined the Austin Friars in Castel Sant'Angelo and was professed shortly before his eighteenth birthday. He did his theological studies at a monastery, where his duties included distributing bread to the poor, which he did with such enthusiasm that the prior accused him of squandering the community's resources. Even at this early stage he began to acquire a reputation as a healer: he placed his hand on a sick child's head, said, "The good God will heal you," and the child recovered.

He was ordained in 1269 and spent several years moving from one friary and monastery to another. He was in one that was distinctly more comfortable than the others and was tempted to stay there, when he heard a voice saying, "To Tolentino! To Tolentino!" Shortly afterwards, he was posted there. Tolentino (in the Marches of Ancona region of east-central Italy) had suffered from the rival pro-papal (Guelph) and pro-imperial (Ghibelline) factions. Nicholas set about restoring peace and unity by preaching in the streets; he was a great success with most of the population, but a few held out and heckled him. When the most prominent of these begged his forgiveness, his reputation was made.

His ministry, which in practical terms was to the poor while he reminded the rich of their social obligations, was so effective that it was seen as miraculous. The most extraordinary story is of a man waylaid in hills near Padua, killed, and thrown in a lake without being able to make his confession. A man in an Augustinian habit (supposedly Nicholas) rescued him from the lake a week later and returned him, alive, to his family. As soon as he had been able to receive the last sacraments, he died again and was given a Christian burial. It has to be said that there is not much to connect this with Nicholas, but it was the fashion of the times (this was written in about 1380, long after Nicholas' death) to make the extraordinary supernatural. What is certain is that Nicholas was a deeply perceptive confessor and counsellor, an assiduous visitor of the sick and the poor, for whom he set up a special fund, and that he had an ongoing reputation as a healer. But what the people of Tolentino saw and loved in him were above all the religious virtues of humility and obedience, his kindness and gentleness, and his unfailing good spirits.

He was ill for a year before his death but hid the evidence from people as far as possible. He died peacefully on 10 September 1305, and a commission was soon set up to inquire into his holiness, so it took evidence from those who had known him. This was interrupted when the papacy moved to Avignon, and he was not canonized until 1446. Some thirty miracles were accepted as evidence, but his "heroic virtue" over a long period of years was obvious. His cult spread throughout Europe in the sixteenth century, by which time he had become a frequent subject for Italian Renaissance painters, including Piero della Francesca.

When his superiors ordered him to take up the public ministry of the gospel, he did not try to display his knowledge or show off his ability, but simply to glorify God. Looking at his audience, you could see the tears and hear the sighs of people ... repenting of their past lives.
St Antoninus of Florence, writing of St Nicholas in the fifteenth century

11

St Ambrose Barlow (1585–1641)

Ambrose Barlow was the son of a knight, Sir Alexander Barlow, and was born near Manchester in 1585. He seems to have conformed to the Church of England in his youth, but in 1607 he was reconciled to the Catholic Church and went to study for the priesthood at Douai. He returned to England before being ordained and spent a year in prison for some unknown reason. He then joined the English Benedictine community of St Gregory (now at Downside Abbey), where his brother was prior, in Douai. Ordained in 1617, he was sent on the English mission and worked in Lancashire (always a Catholic stronghold) for twenty-four years. He was based at Morleys Hall in the parish of Leigh, and was noted for his "great zeal in the conversion of souls and the exemplary piety of his life and conversation." He lived a simple life, preferring to lodge with poor people than great families. His "mild, witty, and cheerful ... conversation" earned the comment from one Catholic that "of all men I ever knew he seemed most likely to represent the spirit of Sir Thomas More."

In 1628 he took the Last Sacraments to St Edmund Arrowsmith, who was in prison in Lancaster awaiting execution on the charge of being a seminary priest, and Edmund is said to have warned him in a dream that he would suffer in the same way. He was arrested four times but released, but then in 1641 King Charles I was pressured by parliament into passing a law rendering any priest who did not leave the country a traitor. The vicar of Leigh armed his congregation and rode to Morleys Hall on Easter Sunday. They seized Ambrose, who had suffered a stroke, as he was preaching after Mass, and handed him over to a magistrate, who imprisoned him in Lancaster Castle, where he was held for four months without trial. Eventually he was interrogated: asked why he had not left the country, he pointed out that his stroke had rendered him incapable of travelling. He also said that the law referred to Jesuits and seminary priests and that he, a Benedictine monk, was neither. He refused to promise not to "seduce" anyone else from Protestantism and was condemned to death.

He was hanged, drawn, and quartered at Tyburn on 10 September 1641, beatified in 1929, and canonized as one of the Forty Martyrs of England and Wales in 1970 (see 25 Oct.).

12

Bd Anton Schwartz (1852–1929)

Born near Vienna, Anton was educated at a famous choir school and then at a Benedictine grammar school. He joined the Piarists (founded by St Joseph Calasanz; see 26 Aug.) for a time, admiring their social principles, but left on the advice that the Order was likely to be disbanded and entered the diocesan seminary in Krems. His family had fallen on hard times with the death of his father, and when he came to be ordained he had to borrow a chalice and vestments. He also suffered from a serious lung infection and was not expected to live long beyond his ordination.

He survived, and his health improved. After a time as curate in Marchegg, east of Vienna, he was appointed chaplain to a hospital run by the Sisters of Mercy in Vienna's 15th district. Here he saw the dreadful conditions in which apprentices and young workers were forced to live. He asked the archbishop if he could leave his chaplaincy to concentrate on ministering to poor apprentices, but this was refused. He continued to help them out of his own resources, building up considerable debts in the process. The mother superior at the hospital eventually collected enough money from a group of wealthy aristocrats to pay off his debts and fund his continued work.

While hierarchies tended to deplore the moral degradation of the working classes, Anton (long before *Rerum Novarum*, let alone the liberation theology of the late twentieth century) saw that their moral state would not be rectified without a drastic improvement in their physical living conditions. He founded a Catholic Apprentices' Association and urged workers to form their own associations. His apprentices were given a good meal on Sundays, followed by drama and music before a final prayer. In 1886 he added a refuge, where apprentices from outside Vienna could stay. In 1889 he and five religious Brothers founded the Congregation for the Devout Workers of St Joseph Calasanz. He served as father superior for the final thirty years of his life. The Brothers combed the streets of Vienna searching for homeless apprentices, whom they fed and housed; they found good Catholic employers for them, started savings associations, and promoted social insurance. Anton supported strikes for fair wages and shorter working hours and foresaw a time when the Church would be seen as the natural ally of the working classes.

Others in the Church saw things differently, and he and his Brothers came under frequent attack until, in 1913, the then cardinal archbishop of Vienna expressed public support for what he was doing and actively befriended and helped him. From 1908, Anton had devoted all his energies to helping young workers. He died on 15 September 1929 and was buried in the church he had built, Our Lady Help of Christians, on what is now Father Anton Schwartz Street. His cause was introduced twenty years after his death, and he was beatified by Pope John Paul II in Vienna on 21 June 1998.

13

St John Chrysostom (about 350–407)

Preacher, bishop, theologian, moralist, controversialist, John, later called "golden tongue" (*chrysostomos*), lived, suffered, and died for ideals that were not those of the ruling society of his day. Born in Antioch, he was brought up by his mother after the early death of his father, which gave him a respect for women—demonstrated in his lifelong collaboration with St Olympias—and an excellent education.

He was baptized and studied doctrine and scripture as well as law. The monastic life appealed to him, and at the age of about twenty-three he joined a group of hermits living according to the Rule of St Pachomius in the mountains. He lasted there for seven years before returning to Antioch with his health broken by personal austerities and the dampness of his cave. Ordained in 386, he threw himself into the christological debates consuming the Church at the time. The bishop of Antioch made him his assistant with special care of the poor. He preached constantly, expressing orthodoxy succinctly and even sharply, and always concerned to bring peace in controversies.

His reputation as a preacher and as a commentator on scripture spread beyond Antioch, most notably through a series of twenty-one sermons preached to prevent reprisals in the affair of "the Statues"—statues of the emperor, his father, and sons, which had been broken. As a result, when the archbishopric (or patriarchate) of Constantinople became vacant in 397, the eastern emperor (the Roman Empire had divided into eastern and western parts in 395 on the death of Theodosius I) wanted John to be appointed. He had John smuggled out of Antioch for fear that the people would hold on to him. As archbishop, John proceeded to try to reform everyone from the empress downward. His own household he could reduce drastically. More controversial were his excessively severe reforms of clergy and his attacks on the empress, Eudoxia, whom he is supposed to have called a Jezebel. She had a silver statue of herself erected outside the cathedral church of Santa Sophia and ordered games to be held around it.

Much of John's support, financial and spiritual, came from a group of deaconesses headed by Olympias. A great heiress, she had evaded remarriage after one elderly husband died and had come under the protection of John's predecessor, Nectarius. She used her wealth to build a large hostel and hospital, caring for the poor, the sick, and travellers, a venture that John supported. Other single women came to help staff the institution; they were so generous that John warned them to be on their guard against spongers—among whom Theophilus, the patriarch of Alexandria, was not the least.

In 402 Olympias gave shelter to four monks, known as the Tall Brothers, whom Theophilus had expelled and who had come to appeal to John for redress. John appealed to the emperor, who convened a synod, summoning Theophilus to attend. Theophilus, at the head of a group of bishops who supported Eudoxia in her battles with John, turned the tables on him and made the synod (known as the Oak Tree Synod after the suburb of Constantinople in which it was held) into a tribunal judging John on various more or less absurd charges: carrying out irregular ordinations, eating alone, bathing alone, receiving women without adequate chaperoning. ... John refused to defend himself and was condemned and exiled. His exile provoked a popular outcry and—apparently—an earthquake that frightened even Eudoxia, and he was recalled. He made no attempt to moderate his attacks on her, and Theophilus engineered his banishment once more, on the grounds that he had returned to a see from which he had been "lawfully deposed." His supporters protested vigorously, and there was a riot at Santa Sophia, during which it caught fire. Olympias and others were accused of starting the blaze. She was arrested, and despite her protests that her judge was really her accuser and that she used her money to build churches, not to destroy them, she was fined, held under house arrest, and then exiled.

John was taken first to Armenia and then held in the fortress of Arabissos, from where he wrote a stream of protesting letters to the pope and others. The pope expressed support but did nothing practical. John and Olympias comforted one another in a regular correspondence—of which seventeen of his letters have survived but none of hers. To avoid further publicity, his captors moved him to Pontus, forcing him to travel hundreds of miles on foot in bad weather, which led to his death on 14 September 407. Seven years later he was posthumously rehabilitated by order of Pope Innocent I. His body was taken back to Constantinople and enshrined in the Church of the Apostles in 430. (His relics were later taken to Rome, possibly by Crusaders.) Three years later the Council of Chalcedon recognized him as a Father of the Church, and some eleven hundred years later Pope Pius V proclaimed him a Doctor of the Church, one of the four Greek Doctors, alongside SS Athanasius (see 2 May), Basil, and Gregory Nazianzen (both 2 Jan.). He is the patron of Christian orators and preachers, as well as of Istanbul (formerly Constantinople).

If the prayer of a single person is so powerful, much more so is the prayer that is offered with many other people. The sinewy strength of such a prayer and the confidence that God will hear it is far greater than you can have for the prayer you offer privately at home.

St John Chrysostom, "On the Incomprehensible Nature of God," 5, 10

14

St Peter of Tarentaise (about 1120–1174)

This Peter of Tarentaise (there are two blesseds and one other saint who have been known by the same name) was born in the diocese of Vienne (on the Rhône, south of Lyons). His parents were known for the hospitality they showed to travelling monks, including Cistercians from the new monastery of Bonnevaux, which Peter joined when he was twenty-one—following his elder brother and to be followed by his father and youngest brother, while his mother and sister became Cistercian nuns.

In 1132 Peter was appointed abbot of a new foundation made from Bonnevaux. He stayed there for eight years, building a guest house and hospital for travellers and becoming known for his holiness and care of the needy. In 1140 the archbishop of Tarentaise (a mountainous district of the Savoie in eastern France, close to the Italian border) died; an unsuitable successor was removed by the pope, and Peter was asked to take his place. Persuaded by St Bernard (see 20 Aug.) and other Cistercian abbots, he eventually accepted, and for the next fifteen years he worked at reforming his clergy and people. He brought in Augustinian Canons to replace the existing cathedral chapter, appointed exemplary priests to parishes, supported them by visits, and founded schools and hospitals.

Several popes came to rely on his skills as a mediator, and his success in resolving one dispute earned him a reputation as a miracle-worker, which horrified him and led him to flee from his archdiocese in secret, going northward into Switzerland, where he enrolled as a lay brother in a Cistercian monastery. He was discovered a year later and forcibly restored to his archdiocese. He resumed his care for pilgrims and travellers, shared his meals with the poor, and generally resumed his pastoral care. He felt obliged to take a public stance when the death of Hadrian IV in 1159 produced a disputed election result, with an antipope supported by the emperor's party. Peter preached tirelessly throughout eastern France in support of Alexander III, the pope for whom the majority of electors had voted, pleading for unity, but without success, as the schism lasted for eighteen years.

In 1173 the pope asked him to mediate between the English king, Henry II, who controlled substantial parts of France and had his court at Limoges, and the French king, Louis VII. In Limoges he was looked after by the English chronicler Walter Map, on whom he made a great impression and who recorded his opinion of him: "A man of such virtue and distinguished by so many miracles that he might very properly be proclaimed equal to the old fathers whom we reverence in the Church." The following year he returned to Tarentaise, but the pope then asked him to go and resolve differences among monks at the abbey of Bellevaux. He caught a fever on the way, died there on 14 September, and was buried in front of the Lady Altar in the abbey church. He was canonized less than twenty years later, in 1191, after Geoffrey of Auxerre, who knew him well, had written a Life extolling his virtues and miracles.

15

St Catherine of Genoa (1447–1510)

Catherine was born into the great Fieschi family of Genoa, who counted two popes among their members. Her uncle was a cardinal; her father, who died when she was in her teens, was viceroy of Naples. She seems to have wanted to follow her elder sister, Limbania, into religious life when she was about thirteen, but her confessor told her she was too young. When she was nearly sixteen her male relatives organized her marriage to Giuliano Adorno. Her family were Guelphs (supporters of the papacy), his were Ghibellines (supporters of the emperor), so this was a dynastic arrangement presumably aimed at reducing conflict and so preserving wealth. Catherine's only part in it was to obey.

She was intense and somewhat morose by nature; he was wayward and hot-tempered, had several affairs, and was seldom at home. They had no children, and she spent ten years in a state of depression. She kept up her religious practices and one day prayed for relief, asking that God would make her "stay three months sick in bed." The prayer was not answered in this form, but two days later she was suddenly filled with a sense of God's love and shortly after that she had a vision, "in the spirit," of Christ's passion. The aridity she had felt for ten years left her, she became a daily communicant (very rare for lay people at the time), and her life was changed. This more of less coincided (it is not clear which came first) with a sudden change for the worse in Giuliano's fortunes, which also changed his character. They moved out of their *palazzo* into a small house and devoted their lives to looking after the inmates—nearly all terminally ill—of the hospital of Pammatone. He became a Franciscan tertiary. Six years later they moved into the hospital, where Catherine became matron. She proved capable and devoted, especially during an outbreak of plague in which she nearly died herself.

She expended more energy than her austere regime and what would now be called eating disorders gave her strength for, and her health collapsed in 1496, forcing her to abandon administering the hospital. Then she had to nurse her husband, who died after a painful illness. She did this with patience and devotion, perhaps with some real affection that she had not been able to feel for him earlier. "My tender Love [that is God] assured me of his salvation," she said. She expressed this devotion by continued care for a long-standing mistress of his and their daughter, then in her twenties.

Between 1473, when she had her experience of the love of God, and 1497, she had led an intense spiritual life, learning of the mystics either from books or conversations and developing her own spiritual doctrine, but with no formal direction and no real contact with the institutional Church other than daily Mass and Communion. She never went to Confession, which was ordered "at least once a year," either because she simply could not think of anything she had done wrong or because she felt no confessor could understand her or due to some deeper malaise. Then, however, she met a sympathetic priest who had just been made rector of the hospital. She turned to him after Giuliano died and made a general Confession, which he said showed her to be blameless in every way, and he became her spiritual director for the remainder of her life. He and Ettore Vernazza, a young lawyer who had become one of the group of "disciples" she gathered around her in Genoa, encouraged her to dictate (or at least relate) her mystical and spiritual insights: she herself has left nothing in writing. These resulted in a treatise on Purgatory, originally a chapter in an account of her *Life and Doctrine,* and a book of *Dialogues* between the body and the soul. These were later pronounced sufficient evidence of her sanctity.

For the last three years of her life she was seriously ill, though no doctor could determine what was wrong with her. Henry VII's (of England) chief physician took refuge in pronouncing it "a supernatural and divine thing." No doubt the term *anorexia* would feature in a retrospective diagnosis. She died at dawn on 15 September 1510 and was buried in the church of the Annunciation at the Pammatone Hospital. It was over one hundred and fifty years before her cult was approved, followed by beatification in 1737 and "equipollent" canonization shortly after that.

Her enigmatic personality was the central study in Baron von Hügel's massive two-volume study, *The Mystical Element of Religion as studied in St Catherine of Genoa and her Friends*, of which the first volume was published in 1908. Some of the psychological terms he uses (such as "neurasthenia") are no longer in use today. He found her "excessive," lacking in any sort of sensuousness, however innocent, "highly nervous, delicately poised ... and impressionable," and concluded that "she became a saint because she had to ... to prevent herself going to pieces," that "she literally had to save, and actually did save, the fruitful life of reason and of love, by ceaselessly fighting her immensely sensitive, absolute, and claimful self." A more recent analysis (1979, by Fr Benedict J. Groeschel) asks whether she would now be classed as psychotic, possibly schizophrenic, and anorexic, and concludes that she had a healthy personality, "exceptional but not eccentric," and had to adjust to great stress. Another (1999, by Kathleen Jones) suggests looking deeper into her relationship with her husband, largely ignored by von Hügel. There seems to be nothing so traumatic in the known outward events of her life as to force her to abandon houses and wealth (the reverses were not that catastrophic) and live unsupported; her marriage under obedience to a wayward husband was hardly unique. Was there something deeper, perhaps concerned with the Guelph–Ghibelline feud, that kept her away from Confession for so many years, perhaps because she would have had to reveal something about her husband? There are hints in her *Life and Doctrine* at some "secret sin," but she may have been bound up with it without having committed it.

16

St Cyprian (Thascius Caecilianus Cyprianus; died 258)

In the Universal Calendar, today's memorial is jointly that of SS Cornelius, pope and martyr, died 253, and Cyprian. Their lives are bound up together, and they are mentioned together in the First Eucharistic Prayer (the Roman Canon) of the Mass, but Cornelius' claim to martyrdom is frankly dubious, and Cyprian is the more influential figure, so he is given today's entry here, with due mention of Cornelius.

He was born in Carthage in about 200 and became an orator, teacher of rhetoric, and advocate. In about 245 a priest named Caecilian influenced him to change his life completely; he was baptized, took a vow of celibacy, abandoned his beloved pagan writers for scripture and the Fathers, and was shortly ordained priest. Three years later he was named bishop of Carthage. He administered his diocese with a mixture of kindness and firmness. The next year, an edict from the new emperor, Decius (249–51) ordered all the inhabitants to sacrifice to the pagan gods; most Christians apostasized and did so out of fear. Cyprian went into hiding, for which he was extensively criticized, but he was able to continue to administer his diocese through a steady stream of letters, urging unity in the face of persecution.

He allowed those who had lapsed and then repented back into communion after a period of penance, but in his absence a priest named Novatus began receiving them back without any penance and started a schismatic group of clerical and lay supporters. Cyprian denounced him in uncompromising terms once he was able to return to Cyprus, and Novatus took his group to Rome. There the lull in persecution had made it possible to hold papal elections after an interval of fourteen months since the death of Pope St Fabian in January 250. A priest named (confusingly) Novatian seemed the right choice (a more obvious candidate having died), as he had been one of the leaders of a council in the interval, but the electors chose a Roman patrician (also preferred by Cyprian) instead. Novatian declared himself a bishop and took a group into schism, gradually hardening his line on the readmission of the lapsed—so occupying the opposite end of the spectrum from Novatus, while Cornelius, supported by Cyprian after a certain amount of mistrust, held the middle ground. Cornelius convened a synod and excommunicated Novatian and his followers. Cyprian's firm but compassionate stance eventually became the norm.

From 252 to 254 Carthage was struck with plague. Cyprian organized the practical relief effort and also wrote a treatise "On Mortality" in an attempt to comfort his people. He became involved with the next pope, Stephen I (Cornelius having died in June 253, banished to [modern-day] Civitavecchia after an outbreak of plague in Rome had caused Christians to be blamed for angering the gods), over the question of whether Baptism was valid if administered by heretics, schismatics, or apostates. He took the view that it was not, but in this case the opposite view prevailed, though not until after his death, and then more as an assertion of Roman authority over local Churches than on theological grounds. There was a fresh outbreak of persecution under Valerian in 257; Cyprian was exiled for refusing to participate in official pagan worship, brought back the following year, kept under some sort of house arrest, tried again for the same offence, and put to death by the sword on 14 September 258. His writings are his great legacy—letters, sermons, treatises, and some biblical commentaries. His main concerns are in the area of what would now be called pastoral theology: Church unity, the role of the bishop, the value of the sacraments. Much of what he wrote was of such permanent value that he is quoted in the documents of Vatican II (1962–5).

17

St Robert Bellarmine (Roberto Francesco Romolo Bellarmino; 1542–1621)

Robert was born in Montepulciano in Tuscany. His father was chief magistrate of the town; his mother was sister to a short-reigned pope, Marcellus II (1555). He received a broad education, including playing the violin and composing Latin verse. After three years at the new Jesuit school in the town he determined to join the Society, and at the age of eighteen he set out for Rome, where he was accepted by the Jesuit superior general, Diego Laínez. His ten-year training included teaching classics, and after studying theology at Padua and Louvain he was ordained priest in 1570 at Louvain, where he remained for the next seven years.

He saw the need for an adequate theological response to the Protestant Reformers and developed "controversial theology," focusing on the current divisions. Because the Reformers emphasized the biblical basis of their claims, he learned Hebrew and even wrote a Hebrew grammar. He preached to congregations of over two thousand on Sundays and saw preaching and theology as mutually necessary for effective spreading of the word of God. Recalled to Rome in 1576, he lectured in "controversial theology" at the Gregorianum, founded by St Ignatius of Loyola (see 31 July) twenty-five years earlier. His lectures formed the basis for his great work, "Disputations on the Controversies of the Christian Faith against the Heretics of this Age," which he spent three years preparing. It was banned in England, but copies of its three volumes were smuggled in.

While he gave up teaching to prepare this work, he acted as spiritual director to students at the Gregorianum and also at the English College, where he encouraged several of those who would be martyred on the English mission. Other tasks were given to him: he helped to revise St Jerome's (see 30 Sept.) Vulgate Latin Bible; he contributed to the Catechism of Christian Doctrine, the basis for the religious instruction of most Catholics for over three hundred years; he served on the commission arbitrating between King Henry of Navarre and the Catholic League over Henry's accession as king of France. In 1594 he was appointed provincial of the Jesuit province of Naples and added pastoral care of his priests there to his many duties. This appointment lasted only three years, until in 1597 Pope Clement VIII summoned him to Rome as his personal theologian. This plunged him into the bitter dispute between Jesuits and Dominicans over the nature of grace; he tried to steer a middle course but failed to put an end to the dispute.

He was made a cardinal in 1599 and managed to live simply while accepting the trappings of the office. Three years later he was appointed archbishop of Capua, which took him away from Rome (where perhaps his outspokenness was not to everyone's taste). He was concerned to reform the clergy, insisted on the importance of instructing adults, gave an example by preaching every Sunday and on feast-days, and took an active interest in the welfare work of the archdiocese. Three years later he was nearly elected pope in a year of three popes (there was to be another in 1978). To his relief, he was not, but the new pope, Paul V, appointed him prefect of the Vatican Library and asked him to serve on a number of curial congregations. He was obliged to resign from his see and live in Rome once more.

He became involved in the Galileo affair. Galileo was a friend of his, and Bellarmine probably thought the Copernican theory that the earth revolves around the sun correct, but it was still only a theory, and he begged Galileo not to assert it as proven truth. He succeeded in saving him from prosecution once, but in the end he subscribed to the Church's official acceptance of the Ptolemaic view that the earth is the centre of the universe. As he aged, he moved away from controversy and wrote devotional books, including an "Art of dying well." He kept up a massive volume of correspondence and received hundreds of visitors. In August 1621 he retired to the Jesuit novitiate on the Quirinal Hill, but he fell ill almost as soon as he arrived. After three weeks receiving all those anxious to see him for a last time, he died on 17 September. He was buried in the Lady Chapel of the main Jesuit church in Rome, the Gesù.

He had one of the best minds of the Catholic Reformation and applied his talents polemically. Perhaps because of this, or perhaps because the Jesuits were suppressed in various places in the eighteenth century, he had to wait until the twentieth century (which produced greater enemies than each other for all Christian churches) for recognition of his holiness. He was beatified in 1923, canonized in 1930, and declared a Doctor of the Church the following year.

18

St Joseph of Copertino (Giuseppe Desa; 1603–1663)

Joseph appears to present the most extraordinary example of physical phenomena recorded among saints, but his early years gave little indication of what was to come. His birth had elements of Luke's Gospel: his father, a carpenter, had had to sell the family home to pay debts, so Joseph was born in a shed. His father then died, so his mother was left with a desperate struggle to bring him up, not helped by the fact that he was absent-minded and forgetful, wandering round the village with his mouth open, which earned him the nickname *Boccaperta* (Gaper). After failing as apprentice to a shoemaker, he tried to enter religious life; the Conventual Franciscans refused him, then the Capuchins accepted him. After he had served them incompetently for some months, they threw him out; after some persuasion the Franciscans made him a tertiary and gave him a job as a servant, working in the stables.

He thrived on this degree of confidence shown in him, carried out his duties with competence, and became generally more cheerful, besides showing a remarkable spirit of prayer and penance. The friars admitted him as a novice and set him to train for the priesthood: he had no real scholastic aptitude, but he did manage to learn to read the Breviary and the Missal, and in the event his candidature was waived through. For the next thirty-five years he served his community as best he could. He was given to supplementing his prayer with extreme austerities, and these may have been the route by which other forces soon apparently began to take control of his life. Two years after his ordination he first found himself raised off the ground—"levitated." He responded to these "seizures" with redoubled prayer and austerities but was increasingly subject to fits of complete ecstatic abstraction, from which his brethren would try to wake him by hitting or pricking him. His levitations were observed by numerous and seemingly sober and reliable witnesses, and inevitably his fame spread.

In 1638 the Neapolitan Inquisition witnessed an episode and accused him of doing it on purpose, working wonders on the ignorant and behaving like "a new Messiah." It certainly brought him no advantages, in fact in human terms it could be said to have ruined his life. Even though the Roman Holy Office and Pope Urban VIII exonerated him of any deliberate fraud, the friars at Grottella found him too embarrassing and sent him to Assisi, where he spent an unhappy thirteen years, forbidden to say Mass in public or to take part in any public rites. People came from far and wide to consult him, but if he could give them advice it was from a heavy heart and a feeling that God had deserted him. The Spanish ambassador to the papal court met him and described him as another St Francis (the pope was later to say that one was enough), and his wife asked to meet him. As he came into the church to see her, he looked up at the statue of Our Lady and was suddenly whisked through the air to its feet, where he prayed for a moment, then uttered "his customary shrill cry" and was brought back to earth. This was seen by the ambassador as well as by his wife and their large retinue, who were all "speechless with astonishment."

The Franciscan minister general eventually realized that Joseph was being treated with a complete absence of understanding and called him to Rome, where his sense of God's presence returned. In 1653 the Inquisition of Perugia decided for some obscure reason that he should be transferred to the Capuchins. They kept him in virtual seclusion for three or four years, forbidden to say Mass or communicate with anyone other than the friars. He was then allowed back to the Conventual Franciscans, with whom he led an only slightly less restricted life. He died at their friary in Osimo on 18 September 1663, and there was an immediate popular upsurge of veneration, though official reactions were muted. His cause was put forward in the following century, when the "devil's advocate" (objector) was Prosper Lambertini, who formalized the grounds for beatification in his treatise "On the beatification of servants of God." He examined Joseph's case with extreme care and, without pronouncing on the objective phenomena (which the Church never does) beyond commenting on the trustworthiness of the eyewitnesses, declared Joseph worthy of sainthood on the strength of his exceptional humility, gentleness, and patience. Lambertini then became Pope Benedict XV and beatified Joseph in 1753. He was canonized in 1767. Because of his academic struggles he is the patron of students and those taking exams; he is also—for obvious reasons—patron of aviators and of astronauts.

19

St Januarius (died about 305)

What Januarius is known for is the "miracle" of the liquefaction of his blood rather than his life, so it might be asked why he is given an entry in a book that claims to be about saints' lives. The answer is that such cultural manifestations are significant and that saints' lives are in a sense carried on in their legacies. If such unlikely devotions are alien to enlightened Anglo-Saxon religious experience, are we in a position to cast stones? If Januarius' blood is (somehow) a scandal, it is a relatively harmless one.

A bishop named Januarius did die for his faith near Naples, and he was venerated from an early date. In 431 St Paulinus of Nola (see 25 June) was said to have been comforted on his deathbed by a vision of St Martin of Tours (11 Nov.) and of St Januarius, "bishop and martyr and glory of the church of Naples": this was written by a priest the following year. There is a "catacomb of St Januarius" in Naples, in which he is shown with a nimbus, in a wall-painting dating from the fifth century. He is also mentioned in the Martyrology of St Jerome (see 30 Sept.), so there is quite a wealth of relatively early testimony to him. He is said to have been born in Naples and to have been bishop of Benevento (to the east of Naples) during the persecution of Diocletian in 303. He went to visit two deacons and two laymen who had been imprisoned and, with his deacon and a lector, was himself arrested, questioned, and tortured. The three were then imprisoned with those they had gone to visit and condemned to be thrown to wild beasts. In the arena none of the beasts would attack them, so they were beheaded.

Januarius' relics were moved first to Naples, then to Benevento, then to Monte Vergine (farther east) before being returned to Venice in 1497—when he is credited with saving the city from plague. His blood somehow preceded him, as the liquefaction has been taking place since 1389, though legend places the first occasion when the body was brought to Naples in the time of Constantine. He is the principal patron saint of Naples, and is celebrated there on three feast-days: the Saturday before the first Sunday in May, the anniversary of the translation of his relics; 19 September, the anniversary of his death; and 16 December, the day on which he averted a threatened eruption of Vesuvius in 1631 (as he subsequently did in 1698, 1767, and 1779). The blood (or whatever it is) is made to "work" six times on each of these days. It consists of a dark, solid, opaque mass, and is held in a phial kept in the treasury chapel of Naples cathedral. Brought out together with a reliquary said to contain his head, it is held and turned by a priest, as the people pray. After a period that varies between two minutes and an hour or more, it appears to become reddish and liquid and sometimes to bubble—or sometimes it does not. If it does, the priest proclaims that the miracle has happened, and a *Te Deum* is sung in thanksgiving.

Endless investigation (short of breaking the phial) has produced no natural explanation. It is not something that melts in heat: it has sometimes failed to liquefy in temperatures in the nineties and done so below freezing. Sometimes it is sluggish, sometimes apparently boiling. It is a mystery: it can hardly be authentic, and there is "blood" of other saints in the Naples area that behaves in the same way, but no one can explain it. It also seems to be a somewhat pointless happening, except, presumably to confirm the people in their faith in their patron—but he could, like others, do some useful healing. It can also be political: it liquefied during a visit by Cardinal Terence Cooke of New York in 1978 but refused to do so when Naples elected a communist mayor.

20

The Martyrs of Korea (died between 1839 and 1867)

The full title of today's memorial in the new Roman Martyrology is SS Andrew Kim Tae-gon, Paul Chong Ha-san, and Companions. Their total number is one hundred and three, made up of three bishops, eight priests, and the rest lay people, described as "married or unmarried, old, young, and children ... [who] with their blood consecrated the beginnings of the Church in Korea." This "beginnings" causes some problems, as it dates the Church there to the establishment of an apostolic vicariate at Choson, staffed by European missionaries, in 1831, whereas Catholicism was actually brought to Korea by a Korean layman fifty years earlier.

After centuries during which Buddhism, Confucianism, and then Neo-Confucianism had been the dominant religion or culture, contact with Catholic missionaries in China in the eighteenth century began to interest Korean intellectuals looking for new cultural values. Jesuits in Beijing lent Korean diplomats books, which they took back with them. A young man named Yi Sung-hun began to promote the new faith among his friends and was baptized by a French priest when he went to Beijing with his father, taking the name Peter. He returned laden with books, rosaries, and crucifixes and baptized several of his friends, who lived together as the first Christian community in Korea. The authorities, however, were not tolerant, and they dispersed the group, arresting the man in whose house they gathered, Kim Bom-u, torturing and then exiling him. He died in exile and—were it not for the burden of proof required that martyrs died directly from persecution—should be considered the first martyr of Korea.

In 1791 several Korean Catholics died for their faith, denounced as heretics by members of the nobility. In 1794 a Chinese priest finally arrived, after the first one sent had failed to link up with his guide and never found his way there—and after Peter and his companions had had a brief flirtation with appointing themselves priests; which they later abandoned. Queen Chong-sun became regent for her great-grandson in 1800 and unleashed a wave of persecution that saw some three hundred Catholics, including the Chinese priest, martyred in 1801 alone. Many fled into the mountains, where they kept the Faith alive in small communities. Paul Chong Ha-san, a nobleman whose father and elder brother had died in the 1801 persecution, made no less than nine journeys to Beijing in an effort to get priests, and (with others) wrote to Pope Pius VII asking for missionaries, saying that there were some ten thousand Catholics in the country.

The apostolic vicariate was entrusted to the Paris Foreign Missions Society. The first vicar apostolic appointed died in Mongolia before he could reach the country. His successor was Bishop Laurence Imbert, who crossed the Yalu River from China on the last day of 1837, hidden under the traditional mourner's basket worn over the head. Two priests joined him, and there were nine thousand lay Catholics, on whom the missionaries were entirely dependent for shelter, food, and safety. They formed a group of tight-knit communities, drawing members from all levels of society from the court down. As long as they could, they stayed where they were and worked at their various occupations, with some acting as full-time catechists. When danger threatened, they moved, with members of the community helping those who were impoverished by doing so.

A new wave of persecution broke out in 1839. Bishop Imbert and the two priests were betrayed by informers and gave themselves up in the hope of deflecting attention from the lay people. They were beheaded on 21 September, and many lay Catholics were arrested and subjected to extraordinarily cruel tortures in prison before finally being beheaded. Paul Chong Ha-sang was executed the day after Bishop Imbert and the two French priests. Sixty-seven of the ninety-two lay people commemorated today died between May 1839 and April 1841. Imbert had managed to send three young Korean men to Macao to be trained for the priesthood. The first to be ordained was Andrew Kim Tae-gon, in Shanghai in 1845. He returned to Korea that August but was arrested the following June and finally beheaded after three months in prison, on 16 September 1846. Between then and 1867 at least two hundred and fifty Koreans are known to have died for their faith, though only twenty-five are named among the martyrs, together with seven French priests. In 1886 France signed a treaty with Korea, and persecution stopped. There was a fresh local wave in 1901, when over seven hundred Catholics were killed on Cheju Island. During the Korean war of 1950–53 many priests, nuns, and lay people were killed or expelled. In today's still divided Korea, the Church flourishes in the South both in terms of numbers and intellectually, but it remains underground in the North.

21

St Matthew (First Century)

In the list of the apostles in the Gospel attributed to him, Matthew is called "the tax-collector" (10:3); in the parallel lists in the other two Synoptic Gospels he is simply Matthew (Mark 3:18; Luke 6:15). Reference to him as the tax collector identifies him with the Levi whose call is related in Mark 2:13–14, in which he is also called "son of Alpheus," and in Luke 5:27–8: "After this [Jesus] went out and saw a tax-collector named Levi, sitting at the tax booth, and he said to him, 'Follow me.' And he got up, left everything, and followed him." Tax collectors, or "publicans," were despised tools of the Roman occupation, so the account indicates a sudden political as well as religious conversion. The name Matthew means "gift of Yahweh," and it is possible that he was given this name when he followed Jesus. This happened in the Roman garrison town of Capernaum, and it is the only time Matthew is mentioned individually in the Gospels. He appears after the resurrection, but only in the list of the apostles in Acts 1:13–14.

The first Gospel in the canonical order, attributed to him from an early date, is unlikely to have been the first written. It appears to have been put into its present form in about the year 80, written in Greek in Syria or Phoenicia, using material from Mark and also from an earlier source (referred to as Q) known also to Mark and Luke. It is obviously addressed to a Jewish audience, constantly showing Jesus fulfilling the promises made in the Hebrew scriptures. This is the aspect of him stressed in his entry in the new Roman Martyrology: "he composed a Gospel, in which Jesus Christ, son of David, son of Abraham, is proclaimed to fulfill the prophecies of the Old Testament."

As with most of the apostles, legend takes over to fill the gaps left by history as to what happened to them after Jesus' earthly life. He is reputed to have preached in various locations, mostly in the Middle East but also in Ireland. There is no certain record of his death, and though he has been venerated as a martyr, early writers, including Clement of Rome (see 23 Nov.), assume that he died a natural death. His supposed relics were taken from Ethiopia to Brittany and then to Salerno in Sicily in the eleventh century, and he is patron of the diocese of Salerno, where the relics are enshrined in the cathedral church, dedicated to him. He is also patron of accountants, bankers, tax collectors, and customs officers, officially confirmed by curial decree as patron of Italian accountants in 1954, with customs officers added in 1957 and the Portuguese "tax police" in 1964. His symbol as an evangelist is a man, since he started his Gospel with a genealogy of Jesus, thus emphasizing his human family. In art he is represented with a book or scroll and often an angel dictating to him. In the Middle Ages he was sometimes depicted wearing reading glasses. He may also be holding a bag or box of money, referring to his original profession.

22

St Emily de Rodat (Marie Guillemette Emilie de Rodat; 1787–1852)

Born in comfortable circumstances near Rodez, in the Midi-Pyrénées department in south-central France, Emily was sheltered from the terrors of the French Revolution, which broke out when she was two, in a remote château belonging to her maternal grandmother. She seems to have been a "normal" young woman without any special religious ambitions—she shunned the company of "nuns and pious females"—until at the age of seventeen she had a spiritual experience that gave her a lasting impression of God's presence to her.

The next year she went as a teacher to her old school in Villefranche, the Maison Saint-Cyr, staffed by nuns from various communities dispersed by the Revolution. She looked after the children at recreation, prepared them for First Communion, and taught geography—with a religious slant, as she was expected to tell the stories of saints associated with places the children marked on maps. Her aim had been to join the community, but the nuns, mostly elderly and not a coherent community, were unwelcoming. She found a friend in the chaplain, Abbé Marty, and he suggested she try her vocation elsewhere. She did so three times, but each time failed to settle and returned to the school.

In 1815 she was visiting a sick woman and heard her discussing the impossibility of educating her children as she was too poor to pay fees. Emily immediately saw a new vocation for herself, teaching poor children. Within a few weeks she had forty children and three assistant teachers crammed into a small room. Abbé Marty supported the venture, though many priests and lay people thought it absurd, and the parents of one of the assistants tried legal action to get their daughter back. In May 1816 Emily took larger rented premises. Then the Saint-Cyr community broke up, and Emily, who by then had eight companions and a hundred pupils, took over the school buildings. She made public vows, and the Congregation of the Holy Family of Ville-franche effectively came into being.

By the end of 1819 she had been able to buy a disused monastery, but then the whole venture was threatened when several Sisters died mysteriously. There were those who saw this as the work of the devil, and Emily was prepared to abandon the idea of a separate Congregation. The Sisters refused any idea of amalgamation, however, and she decided to carry on. She herself then developed cancerous growths in her nose and a condition that left her with permanent ringing in her ears (tinnitus). She consulted a doctor in the town of Aubin, and this raised the possibility of a second foundation there; Marty counselled against it, but she decided to go ahead and then reproached herself for going against his wishes. Further expansion followed over the next two decades, with some houses of enclosed nuns and some of unenclosed Sisters, who moved into nursing as well as teaching and then into rescue homes for women, caring for prostitutes, and visiting prisoners. Emily controlled all this growth firmly—some said arrogantly; she received many abusive letters, to which she always managed to send a courteous reply. She felt guided by the constant presence of the Holy Spirit and remained forever grateful to Abbé Marty for assuring her concerning this, even though their ways had diverged.

In April 1852 the cancer spread to her left eye and she realized she did not have long to live. She endured five months of increasing weakness and suffering and died on 18 September. She was canonized in 1950. Her Congregation now has houses in France, England, Switzerland, Spain, the Near East, Africa, Bolivia, and Brazil. Their main activities are running orphanages and health-care centres.

23

St Pius of Pietrelcina (Padre Pio) (Francesco Forgione; 1887–1968)

Finally canonized amidst mass rejoicing in June 2002, the stigmatist universally known as Padre Pio was born in Pietrelcina, in the Benevento region north-east of Naples, on 25 May 1887. His parents were agricultural workers. He entered the Capuchin convent in Morcone at the age of sixteen and was ordained priest in 1910. He then began to experience pains in his hands and feet and confessed that he had had "invisible stigmata" for over a year and that he also felt the pain of Christ's crown of thorns and his scourging. Priests in Italy were not exempted from military service (usually as medical orderlies) in the First World War, but he had trouble with his lungs and spent most of the war on convalescent leave. Early in 1918 he contracted double pneumonia and was sent to the convent of San Giovanni Rotondo, where he stayed for the rest of his life.

On 5 August 1918 the wound of the spear with which Jesus' body was pierced (see John 19:34) appeared in his side; this bled for the rest of his life. A month later the stigmata in his hands and feet became visible; they remained so for fifty years and two days, until he celebrated his last Mass on the day before he died (which was filmed by the journalist Patrick O'Donovan for a BBC documentary). In the twentieth century, news spread far faster and wider than in the thirteenth, when St Francis of Assisi (see 4 Oct.) received the stigmata. The Capuchins made no attempt to hide his condition, and the convent was soon being besieged by thousands of pilgrims. The Vatican, as always with "private" revelations and gifts, was more cautious and had him examined by a series of doctors, without making any official pronouncement on the "genuineness" or otherwise of the phenomena. Attempts to make him say Mass in private and to move him to another convent had to be abandoned in the face of mass protest. Pius himself claimed no more than that he was "a mystery to himself" and asked that his gifts should be put to use to help others.

This became possible as offerings from pilgrims and from more distant admirers began pouring in. In January 1925 he opened a twenty-bed hospital in a disused convent, which remained operational for twenty years. The Vatican continued more than suspicious: in 1931 he was forbidden to hear Confessions and suspended from all priestly functions except saying Mass, which he had to do in private. This lasted two years, after which public pressure again forced a retreat. He was suspected of being too close in relationships with women (all allegations of impropriety being later proved fraudulent), but his care of a dying American woman in 1929 led in 1940 to a large bequest from her daughter that enabled him to embark on a far more ambitious medical project—a wholly new hospital complex to be built in the remote countryside near San Giovanni Rotondo. Though it was delayed by the Second World War and widely criticized as a folly, work started in 1947, and it was inaugurated in 1957. Padre Pio (supported far more by Pope Pius XII than by his predecessor) was given personal control and put in place a unique regime of prayer and science, with space for an international study centre, a hospice, and a hermitage for spiritual exercises. Confounding the widespread doubts, the venture flourished from the start—and still does. At the pope's suggestion, international prayer groups were set up to support its work.

In 1959 Padre Pio's health worsened—until he was apparently miraculously cured when a statue of Our Lady of Fatima was brought into the hospital: there was no inquiry into this. He broadcast his spiritual thoughts twice daily, after the Angelus, on the hospital radio. In 1966 a huge convention of the prayer groups gathered to celebrate the hospital's tenth anniversary. Two years later, huge crowds gathered for Padre Pio's Mass on the fiftieth anniversary of the stigmata becoming visible: when he raised his hands, members of the congregation noticed that they had vanished. He died the next day, and doctors found his hands and feet completely unmarked.

Pressure for his canonization soon built up, and the process was set in motion in 1969. He was beatified on 2 May 1999, in front of crowds that overflowed St Peter's piazza, so that many watched the ceremony on huge television screens set up in the square by the Lateran basilica. Pope John Paul II—as always in such cases—stressed not his "gifts" but the massive charitable effort into which he had channelled them. He made the same points at his canonization on 16 June 2002, when crowds of three hundred thousand (in a temperature of ninety-seven degrees) again overflowed the piazza and watched on TV screens placed down the Via della Conciliazione.

Padre Pio had bequeathed the hospital, know as the House for the Relief of Suffering, to the Holy See, but it operates within the Italian national health system, highly ranked and respected. Whatever the explanation for his physical symptoms (which is unlikely ever to be conclusive), Padre Pio had "poured [his charity] like balm on the sufferings of his brothers and sisters" (Pope John Paul II), and had been led "to see Christ in the sufferings of others" (Cardinal Casaroli).

24

St Theodore of Canterbury (about 602–690)

Theodore, the seventh archbishop of Canterbury, is known from Book Four of Bede's indispensable *Ecclesiastical History of the English People*. His appointment was a roundabout affair: the previous archbishop, Deusdedit, died in 655, on the same day as King Earconbert of Kent, and the see was left vacant for nine years; King Egbert of Kent and King Oswy of Northumberland then settled on a priest named Wigbert, and he went to Rome to be consecrated, but died there of the plague; Pope Vitalian asked a learned abbot named Hadrian to accept the post, but he excused himself and suggested a monk named Andrew, who refused on grounds of ill health; the pope asked Hadrian to think again, and he suggested Theodore. Theodore was Greek, a native of Tarsus, "learned both in sacred and secular literature, in Greek and in Latin, of proved integrity, and of the venerable age of sixty-six." The pope agreed and consecrated Theodore subdeacon—he seems to have been a monk but not in holy orders. He had to spend four months in Rome waiting for his hair to grow so that he could receive the Western circular tonsure. Vitalian then consecrated him bishop and despatched him on the long journey to Britain, sending Hadrian to accompany him, as he had made the journey before and—presumably unnecessarily—to make sure he did not introduce any strange Greek customs.

They set out in May 668, by sea to Marseilles then overland via Arles to Paris, where they were welcomed by Bishop (St) Agilbert and where they spent the winter. By the time they reached the north coast of France, Theodore was exhausted and rested for a time before crossing the Channel; he reached England a year to the day after leaving Rome. Hadrian was detained for a while by the Frankish king Ebroin, but then allowed to follow. Theodore appointed him abbot of St Augustine's (formerly St Peter's) monastery in Canterbury.

As he was by then sixty-eight, Theodore's time in office might have been expected to be relatively short and not too demanding, but he was to remain in the see for over twenty-one years and to carry out a thorough reorganization of the Church in England. He set out on a visitation of as many churches throughout the land as possible. He had begun learning English in Paris but still needed to take Hadrian with him as interpreter. He saw that everyone used the Roman date of Easter (to Bede's delight), introduced plainchant (previously known only in Kent), and filled vacant sees. He adjudicated in a complex dispute between the irascible Wilfrid (see 24 Apr.) and the meek Chad (see 2 Mar.) over the archbishopric of York, ruling for Wilfrid, but reconsecrating

Chad canonically and appointing him bishop in Menevia, where he established his see at Lichfield. There was later criticism of how Wilfrid administered the vast see of York, and Theodore divided it into three, ignoring Wilfrid's storming off to Rome to protest to the pope. In the end, and after much diplomacy by Theodore with reluctant kings, they compromised, and Wilfrid accepted the reduced see of York.

In 672 Theodore summoned a council of all the English bishops at Hertford. Exercising more authority than later archbishops of Canterbury were to be able to do, he charged the bishops with their duty of promoting church unity and peace and established canons dealing with the date of Easter, bishops' residence in their sees, the independence of monasteries, the submission of diocesan clergy to their bishop, the indissolubility of marriage, and questions of seniority and precedence among bishops. A second synod held at Hatfield seven years later confirmed the doctrinal orthodoxy of the English Church in matters of theological debate at the time. With this organization and the famous school he founded at Canterbury, where he and Hadrian taught Latin and Greek, science and mathematics, Roman law, verse composition and music, Theodore left the Church in England in a far more developed state than that in which he had found it. When he died, on 19 September 690, he was buried next to St Augustine of Canterbury (see 27 May), the first archbishop. Bede's "brief summary" remains entirely valid: "The churches of England made greater progress during his pontificate than they had ever done before."

25

St Sergius of Radonezh (Bartholomew; about 1315–1392)

The most popular of all Russian saints was brought into the calendar of the Roman Catholic Church in 1940, through the introduction of a liturgical calendar for Russian Christians in communion with Rome. He was born into a wealthy aristocratic family near Rostov, some hundred miles north-east of Moscow (not the better-known Rostov-on-Don) and then a considerable centre of power. Muscovite expansionism forced the family to flee and work as peasants when Bartholomew (his baptismal name) was about fifteen. He was not as bright as his brothers but became literate enough to study the Bible, and he developed a longing for the solitary life.

After his parents' death he and his brother Istvan (already widowed) chose a site for a hermitage in a wild forest location and built a wooden hut and chapel. A priest from Kiev dedicated the settlement to the Holy Trinity—an unusual dedication in Russia at the time. Istvan tired of the solitary life and left to join a community in Moscow, but Sergius (the name he took when he received the monk's habit) stayed on. He lived a life of prayer and austerity reminiscent of the Desert Fathers, with the additional discomfort of Russian winters. His reputation spread, and disciples came to join him, each building a hut for himself. Sergius agreed to be their abbot and was ordained priest. He chose a communal way of life for the monastery that had come into being, and in 1354 chose the Rule of St Theodore the Studite. This was a change from the hermit's life many of the monks had come expecting to follow, and it caused dissension. Theodore slipped quietly away and settled alone near another monastery, but some of his monks followed him, and Holy Trinity was threatened with decline. The metropolitan of Moscow asked Sergius to return, which he obediently did, to the delight of the monks who had remained there.

His reputation for wisdom grew, and princes came to consult him on political matters, including Prince Donskoy of Moscow, threatened by Tartar forces from the east under Khan Mamai. He asked Sergius whether he should retreat tactically or risk all on an offensive; Sergius reminded him of his duty to protect his people, entrusted to him by God, and sent him away with two monks (former soldiers) to advise him; Donskoy attacked and won the great victory of Kulikovo (1380), which permanently removed the Tartar threat. The following year he reconciled Donskoy with Prince Oleg of Riazan, his last intervention on the political scene. He resigned as abbot, designating Nikon as his successor. Several of his other disciples became monastery founders and well-known Russian saints. In 1392 he sensed that he was soon to die and became ill for the first time in his life. He died on 25 September and was buried in the principal church of the monastery of the Holy Trinity. This immediately became a place of pilgrimage and has remained one ever since, except for 1917–45, when the Communist authorities closed the monastery and removed his relics to an "anti-religion museum."

Sergius is the prime example of "men of the wilderness" (*pustiniky* in Russian) who helped restore Russian society after the Tartar invasions in the thirteenth century, and who have had an influence on Russian spirituality ever since. He was canonized in 1448 and is regarded as the founding father of Russian monasticism. He appears in many icons, and the great icon painter Andrei Rublev was a monk in his Holy Trinity monastery.

26

SS Cosmas and Damian (late Third Century)

These brothers, supposedly doctors and martyrs, are among the best-known names in the whole calendar, included in the Roman Canon (the First Eucharistic Prayer), but very little, if anything, is known about their actual lives.

The basis for their extraordinarily popular cult is that they were born in Arabia, brought up as Christians, and went to Syria to study medicine. They practised medicine without charging fees for their services, so becoming known as *anargyroi*, "moneyless ones" or "silverless ones." They were accordingly widely known and loved for their charity, but during the persecution under Diocletian, which was most severe in the eastern part of the Roman Empire, they were denounced for being Christians and brought before the governor of Cilicia (now south-eastern Turkey), who ordered them to be tortured and beheaded. Their legend embroiders on their suffering, claiming that they were first ordered to be drowned in the sea but were saved by an angel; they were thrown into a fire, which failed to burn them; then they were bound to crosses and stoned, but the stones recoiled on those who threw them; only after all this were they beheaded.

The earliest reference to their martyrdom places it at Cyrrhus, north of Antioch in Syria. A basilica built to them was certainly there by the year 400, when a wealthy pagan named Rabboula is recorded as praying to them. Bishop Theodoret of Cyrrhus, who died in 458, called them "illustrious athletes and generous martyrs." Many other churches dedicated to them were built, including one in Constantinople in the fifth century and Santo Cosma e Damiano in Rome in the sixth, to which their relics were transferred by Pope St Felix III (526–30). These became popular places of healing, and the church in Constantinople originated the practice of "incubation," sick people staying in the church overnight for the saints to come to them in dreams and heal them in various spectacular ways (some of which are also attributed to other saints). Perhaps the most extreme of these was a man with a diseased leg, who had it amputated in the night and replaced by a new one, sealed in place by precious ointment.

Three of their brothers, named as Anthimus, Leontius, and Euprepius, were previously said to have been martyred with them, but these have been dropped from the new Roman Martyrology. Another complication was that two other pairs of martyrs with the same names were venerated in the East, but they are now generally agreed to be the same person. Cosmas and Damian are the patron saints of doctors and nurses, of barbers (formerly also "curers") and pharmacists, and of confectioners (perhaps because they put different pieces together?). Cosimo de Medici, the ruler of Florence in the fifteenth century, was named after Cosmas and had a great devotion to him, adopting the brothers as protectors of the Medici family. As patron of Fra Angelico (see 19 Feb.), he commissioned a cycle of frescoes depicting their lives, which is in San Marco in Florence.

27

St Vincent de Paul (or Depaul; 1581–1660)

"Monsieur Vincent," as he became generally known, was born into a peasant family near Dax in the Gascony region of south-western France. At the age of fourteen he was accepted into the Franciscan college in Dax to train for the priesthood. He made exceptionally rapid progress and, despite being taken out of college to act as a private tutor, he was ordained just before he was twenty, in 1600. He went on to study theology at Toulouse, taking his degree in 1604. There then follows a mysterious period during which letters, undoubtedly written by him, claim that he was captured by pirates and taken to Tunisia, where he converted his third owner and sailed back to southern France with him, after which he went on to Rome. He certainly went to Rome, but there are records of him acting as a court chaplain during this period. Why he invented the story—if indeed he did—remains a mystery.

After his stay in Rome he joined a group of priests in Paris gathered around Pierre de Bérulle, who in 1611 formed them into the Congregation of the Oratory. He advised Vincent to become a parish priest at Clichy (now the terminus of a north–south Paris Métro line), then to serve the powerful Gondi family as tutor to the eldest son, Pierre (whose father was general in command of the infamous galleys in which criminals were condemned to row, and whose brother Paul went on to become the scheming Cardinal de Retz). He stayed with the Gondi family for about twelve years, during which he came to know and be influenced by St Francis de Sales (see 24 Jan.). He acted as chaplain to the peasants on the Gondi estates, which probably helped develop his instinctive responses to needs of all kinds, but it was during a period as acting parish priest that he began to organize his special brand of charity. Realizing that an appeal for help could produce a generous immediate response but not long-term care for those in greatest need, he brought together a "Charity," a group of individuals (all women) who would take turns to look after the sick poor. He gave them a Rule, embodying his principle of seeing Christ in the poor, and founded other groups on the Gondi estates when he returned to Paris.

There he also formed a group of priests dedicated to preaching missions in villages, which proved so successful that, with financial help from Madame Gondi, he was able to place the venture on a permanent canonical footing as the Congregation of the Mission, otherwise known as Vincentians, with premises in the rue Saint-Victoire, later moving to larger premises in the priory of Saint-Lazare (so adding "Lazarists" to its names). Dedicated to preaching in villages, care of the poor and of convicts, and training of the clergy, the priests lived in common, taking no titles and initially making no vows, though these were introduced in 1651. The archbishop of Paris asked him to train diocesan seminarians there, to which he agreed, and Saint-Lazare became one of the great focuses of spiritual renewal in France.

The women members of the "Charities," originally known as "Servants of the Poor," became the "Ladies of Charity" when the movement spread in Paris, but then its "ladies" began finding some of the tasks beneath them, so Vincent recruited simple country girls to help them. He invited Louise de Marillac (see 15 Mar.) to help him train them; she asked four of them to live with her; the number soon grew to twelve, and this developed into a movement that needed to be formalized in some way. All women religious had to be enclosed, and Vincent was determined that his Sisters should not be, as they had to be free "to leave God for God," to move from conventual prayer to the homes of the sick. So the Sisters of Charity (as they became) had a special Constitution—still in effect—by which each Sister makes private vows every year. This was approved by the archbishop of Paris in 1646 and by the pope eight years after Vincent died.

In 1633 Vincent began a series of Tuesday conferences in response to demands from young priests for a follow-up to the Spiritual Exercises he had led for them; these were to last until he died, twenty-seven years later. His impact on clergy training was immense, through his own conferences and through the courses given in seminaries by his Vincentian priests. He was drawn into the appointment of bishops as a member of the "Council of Conscience" established in 1643 by Cardinal Mazarin, but he quarrelled with Mazarin, who used the Council for political ends, and was dropped from it. Politics and theology were also intertwined in the dispute over Jansenism—the narrow view of grace and predestination held by Cornelius Jansen and his followers in France. Vincent was friendly with the abbot of Saint-Cyran, who introduced the doctrine into France, but he disagreed profoundly with his views and was instrumental in petitioning the pope to condemn five basic Jansenist propositions. The pope did so, and Vincent campaigned to have his decision accepted in charity, but this was an uphill struggle that continued after his death.

After suffering from a fever in 1656, Vincent developed worsening leg ulcers and was unable to walk. He died at his hospital of Saint-Lazare on 27 September 1660, and a cult developed almost immediately. He was beatified in 1729 and canonized in 1737. Through his simple and practical spirituality he had, as the bishop who preached at his funeral stated, "changed the face of the Church," establishing a pattern of charity at grassroots level that is still operating. In his lifetime the Vincentians had extended their mission beyond France, and in the nineteenth century they expanded to South America and

Australia as well as England and the USA, where their original seminary at Perryville, Missouri, is now the motherhouse of the Congregation. The Daughters of Charity of St Vincent de Paul also work worldwide, as does the lay confraternity of the Society of St Vincent de Paul (established by Frederick Ozanam; see 8 Sept., and others) at parish level. In May 1885 Pope Leo XIII named Vincent universal patron of all works of charity. The movie *Monsieur Vincent*, first shown in France in 1947, made him one of the most widely known of all saints.

28

St Wenceslas (Václav; about 907–929)

Wenceslas (whose name means "greater glory") was the eldest son of Duke Ratislav of Bohemia and the nominally Christian Drahomíra and was born near Prague. The area had been evangelized by SS Cyril and Methodius (see 16 Feb.) in the previous century, but there were still tensions between their Slav Christianity and the Germanic strain based on Regensburg to the west, as well as with residual paganism. Wenceslas was educated by his grandmother, Ludmilla, a convert (venerated as a saint), and given an excellent grounding in Latin and Slavonic.

His father was killed in battle against the Magyars (Hungarians) in 921, when Wenceslas was only fourteen, and the family split into warring factions. His mother, backed by anti-Christian factions, appointed herself regent, but Ludmilla tried to persuade him to assume power for the sake of the survival of Christianity. She was murdered by two of Drahomíra's supporters. Wenceslas gained increasing support, and the following year he was proclaimed duke. His mother was banished, and he brought Ludmilla's body to St George's church in Prague. He had control of the western and southern parts of Bohemia, but his brother Boleslas, who had supported their mother, was building a power base in the east. Wenceslas, however, felt secure enough to recall Drahomíra from banishment, and she made no further attempt to oppose him.

Despite his youth, Wenceslas was a strong ruler: he strove to establish the rule of law (which meant curbing the power of the nobles), to improve education, and to build up Christianity among the people. He also wanted to improve Bohemia's connections with western Europe and accepted the German king-emperor, Henry I (known as the Fowler), as his overlord, which angered many resentful nobles. They grouped behind Boleslas, and when Wenceslas married and had a son, thus depriving Boleslas of his place in line of succession to the dukedom, a plot was hatched. Wenceslas was invited to visit Boleslas, nominally to celebrate the dedication of a new church of SS Cosmas and Damian (see 26 Sept.) on their feast-day (which was then the 27th). Despite warnings, he went, and the morning after the celebrations he was attacked on his way to Matins by Boleslas and a group of his nobles. He died murmuring, "Brother, may God forgive you."

While this sordid tale of intrigue does not seem to have much to do with the life of a saint, Wenceslas did maintain a consistently upright and Christian stance. He was venerated as a martyr (and still is), even though his death cannot be directly attributed to his defence of the faith (the usual condition for the title). His mother took charge of his body, which was later enshrined in St Vitus' church in Prague—perhaps by a contrite Boleslas. Legends soon made him the ideal Christian prince, though not in the style of the "Good King Wenceslas" of the nineteenth-century carol, which does not relate to any known incident in his life. He was regarded as the patron saint of Bohemia from the eleventh century, then of Czechoslovakia when this was formed out of the provinces of Bohemia, Moravia, and Slovakia after the First World War, and now of the Czech Republic (without Slovakia), whose charismatic first president, Václav Havel, was named after him. Series of pictures depicting his life, such as those in the metropolitan church at Prague Castle, tend to concentrate on the nationalist aspirations associated with him.

29

St Lioba (Trhûtgeba or Liobgetha; died 782)

Lioba was one of the redoubtable group of women from the west country of England who supported St Boniface (see 5 June; himself a Devon man) in the evangelization of Germany. Her mother, Aebba, was related to Boniface, though how closely is not known, and he had been a friend of her father, Dynna. It was this kinship that later inspired Lioba to contact him and so led to her mission. Baptized Trhûtgeba, but known as Liobgetha, abbreviated to Lioba, meaning "dear one," she was educated by nuns, first in Kent and then at Wimborne in Dorset, where at some stage she was fully professed.

In 722 Boniface was consecrated bishop and sent to preach the gospel in what are now the Low Countries and north-western Germany. News of his work reached Wimborne, and Lioba wrote to him, asking for his prayers, reminding him of her existence, saying she regarded him as a brother and trusted him more than any of her other relatives, and asking him for a word in reply. He gave her more than a word, entering into a correspondence that lasted for years. Twenty-six years later, he wrote to the abbess of Wimborne asking her to send Lioba and some other nuns to him to help in the evangelization of Germany by founding monasteries for women. The abbess, St

Tetta, sent no less than thirty nuns, including Walburga (later of healing fame: see 25 Feb.) and Lioba, who became abbess at Tauberbischofsheim (meaning the bishop's house at Tauber, so perhaps Boniface's own house) near Aachen, the capital of Charlemagne's Holy Roman Empire. This flourished, and Lioba was soon sending her nuns out to found other houses and to help others not directly founded from there.

The monasteries followed the Rule of St Benedict, with its sensible divisions of the day into prayer, manual work, and "divine reading," with adequate rest. Lioba insisted that her nuns take their rest periods and not indulge in excessive austerity, though she herself spent her hour having a novice read the Bible to her—and correcting her pronunciation when necessary, so apparently depriving at least two people of the siesta she commended. Her fame spread, and prominent statesmen and clerics came to consult her. Boniface came to say farewell to her before setting out on his last mission in 754, perhaps suspecting the fate that was in store for him. She herself retired, after twenty-eight years as abbess, to the monastery of Schornsheim near Mainz. She died in 782 and was buried in the abbey church at Fulda; her relics were moved twice, finally to the church of Mount St Peter.

Her character as well as her movements can be described with some confidence, thanks to a Life compiled by Rudolf of Fulda from recollections of four of her close companions and mercifully free from conventional exaggeration. She is said to have been striking in appearance and patient, warm, and kind by nature. She had a deep love of books and was devoted to learning—she certainly had no need to dictate her letters. She provides the best evidence of the prominent part played by women in missionary work at this period of the Church's history.

30

St Jerome (Eusebius Hieronymus Sophronius; about 345–420)

Jerome, translator of the Bible into its official Latin version (the Vulgate), classical scholar, monk, traveller, teacher, ascetic, polemicist, and letter-writer is one of the towering figures in the history of the Church. Seeing a picture of him holding a stone, supposedly his instrument of penance, a Renaissance pope remarked that without it he would hardly be considered a saint. He was reviled by many but revered and loved by those close to him, particularly the group of women he called the "matrons of Rome," who studied the scriptures with him and most possibly helped him in his translation work.

He was born into a wealthy and probably Christian family near Aquileia, north of Venice, between 340 and 347. His father sent him to study in Rome, and he soon became fluent in Latin and Greek (his native language was Illyrian) and passionately devoted to the classical writers. He then decided he needed to travel to broaden his mind and spent three years moving around western Europe with his friend Bonosus. At this stage he was more superficially than devotedly Christian, but he had a conversion experience in Trier and decided to become a monk. He joined a community in Aquileia in 370, meeting many of those who were to become his close friends—and enemies: the step from one to the other was difficult to guard against. A quarrel split the group, and Jerome, through a chance meeting with a priest from Antioch, decided to go east. There he fell seriously ill and in his delirium found himself before the judgment-seat of Christ, who called him a liar when he protested he was a Christian, and told him he was a Ciceronian, rather, "for where your treasure is, there also is you heart." (He described this years later in a letter to St Eustochium.) He retired to the desert region of Chalcis, south of Antioch, where he began to learn Hebrew, partly as a distraction from recurrent visions of "young Roman women dancing." He hated Hebrew, calling it "this language of hissing and broken-winded words," so far from the sonorities of Quintilian, Cicero, and Pliny, but he persevered, equipping himself to become a translator of and commentator on the Bible.

Antioch had three rival claimants to the see, and Jerome (instead, for once, of plunging headlong into the fray) wrote to Pope Damasus I for guidance on whom to support. Damasus must have chosen Paulinus, as it was he who ordained Jerome when he returned from his desert after four years there—not that he seems ever to have celebrated Mass. He then moved to Constantinople, where he studied the scriptures under St Gregory Nazianzen, an experience for which he remained profoundly grateful. He translated some of Origen and Eusebius from Greek into Latin and wrote an original commentary on Isaiah. Pope Damasus called a council in Rome to discuss the schism in Antioch, and Jerome went as interpreter to two Greek-speaking bishops. Damasus asked him to stay on as his secretary, a post the duties of which included writing biblical commentaries; besides these, he decided to embark on a complete translation of the Hebrew and Greek scriptures into Latin.

It was a long mental as well as physical journey from the deserts of Syria to the city of Rome, and Jerome was not one to keep quiet about what he saw, from women who "enamel a lost youth on the wrinkles of age and affect a maidenly timidity in the midst of a troupe of grandchildren" to priests whose "one concern is to know about the names, the houses, and the activities of rich women." While Pope Damasus was alive he was protected, but once he died (in 384), he was vulnerable. Fortunately, at this point he became acquainted with (St) Marcella, whom he was to call "the glory of the ladies of Rome," who after being widowed very early had turned to a life of asceticism and gathered around her a group of like-minded women determined to imitate the life of St Antony of Egypt (see 17 Jan.). Jerome became their spiritual director and agreed to help them study the scriptures. The group was joined by Paula—a wealthy widow who had earlier offered the Greek bishops hospitality and so met Jerome—and by her daughter Eustochium. Both were looking for theological and spiritual guidance, and a close relationship developed; they questioned him about everything—and proved more adept than Jerome at learning Hebrew.

Jerome could hardly inveigh against priests concerned only with "rich women" and then expect his closeness to these rich women to go unnoticed. Allegations that he and Paula were lovers circulated: they were proved false and malicious, but they probably cost him the nomination to the papacy when Damasus died, and he was forced to leave Rome. He went to the Holy Land in search of peace and quiet in August 385, but his women disciples, including Paula and Eustochium, followed him nine months later after a pilgrimage via Cyprus and Antioch. Jerome met them in Jerusalem and helped them tour the Holy Places. The party then travelled south to Egypt, where the women consulted the monks living in the deserts of the Thebaïd and Nitria. After a year of exhausting travels, they returned to Jerusalem, where Jerome settled in a cave close to the church of the Nativity in Bethlehem. The women established themselves in three communities nearby. Paula built a separate monastery for monks, then a hospice for pilgrims. Jerome worked on his translations, "creeping slowly through the darkness of the idioms" as he worked on the Old Testament; Paula and her companions returned to their studies of Hebrew and helped shed light on his darkness. They all lived simply, but with as much of pastoral idyll as desert austerity, growing their own vegetables, with supplies of bread and milk, trees to give them shade in summer and firewood in winter as well as providing shelter for songbirds. ...

Controversy, never far from Jerome's life, reared its head again, this time over the perpetual virginity of the Virgin Mary, on which he had earlier written a treatise, attacking a certain Helvidius, who claimed she had had other children by Joseph. This idea was then taken up by Jovinian, whose writings were sent to Jerome. He replied in a typical blast and was then accused of belittling marriage, so he wrote a treatise supposedly in support of that institution—not to general satisfaction. He then turned to defending celibacy and the veneration of relics against attacks on both from Rome. A more vital and damaging dispute was over the works of Origen, whom Jerome admired in himself (and had translated), but whom he felt was being distorted by some Eastern groups to the detriment of their orthodoxy. Jerome's friend from the days of the community in Aquileia, Rufinus, was then living in Jerusalem and translating and expressing admiration for Origen. Jerome attacked both him and Origen, destroying an old and valued friendship. He nearly did the same with St Augustine (see 28 Aug.) of all people, but Augustine's tact saved the situation.

Paula died in 404, saying she felt "a supreme peace." Jerome, who had said of her and Eustochium that they were "mine in Christ, whether the world likes it or not," grieved greatly and wrote an epitaph calling her "first in the series of noble Roman matrons, [who] preferred the poverty of Christ and the humble fields of Jerusalem to the splendours of Rome." He was further saddened by the sack of Rome by Alaric the Goth in 410, when a stream of refugees came to him; he set aside translation for works of charity, saying, "Today we must translate the words of scripture into deeds, and instead of speaking saintly words we must act them." In 416 the monastic complex was attacked by a gang of ruffians, who set fire to the buildings. Eustochium never recovered and died the next year. Jerome's own great heart, dealt another blow by this, was failing by then, as was his eyesight. He died peacefully on 30 September 420 and was buried close to Paula and Eustochium in the church of the Nativity. His remains were later taken to Santa Maria Maggiore in Rome. He had written no Rule, and the monasteries around Bethlehem did not last for long, but several eremitical and communal foundations took his name in the fourteenth century, of whom the Jeronimite Monks survive in Spain, though not in the numbers they once achieved.

His main legacy to the Church has been his scholarship, to which the greatest monument is the continued place held by the Vulgate in the Latin Church. His *De viris illustribus* (On Illustrious Men) was a major early contribution to the writing of saints' Lives. He has long been recognized as one of the four Latin Doctors of the Church. There are countless representations of him in art: those showing him as a cardinal are anachronistic, as cardinals did not exist in his day, but Renaissance painters assumed that as secretary to Pope Damasus he must have been one, as he would have been in their day. He is most often shown as an ascetic in his cave, gazing at a skull or holding a stone. The lion often shown at his feet (because he had pulled a thorn out of its paw, after which it minded his donkey out of gratitude) is actually a borrowing from the legend of St Gerasimus.

Tell them [his detractors in Rome] *that we shall all stand before the judgment seat of Christ, and then the spirit in which each of us has lived will be plain for all to see.*
St Jerome, in a letter passing on greetings to Paula and Eustochium

Other Familiar English Names for September

1. Joan, Victor, Vincent
2. Albert, Ingrid, William
3. Andrew, Antony, Charles, George, James, John, Michael, Nicholas, Paul, Peter, Phoebe, Vincent
4. Catherine, Joseph, Mary
5. John, Joseph, Peter, William
6. *There are no familiar names for today*
7. Claude, Francis, John, Mark, Stephen, Thomas
8. Antony, Dominic, Francis, John, Joseph, Louis, Lucy, Matthew, Michael, Peter, Thomas
9. Francis, George, James, Mary
10. Francis, James, Sebastian
11. Daniel, Francis, John, Laurence, Louis, Peter
12. Dominic, Francis, Guy, Peter, Thomas
13. Claude, Julian, Mary
14. Albert, Claude, Gabriel
15. Jeremy, Roland
16. Alexander, Andrew, Dominic, Edith, Felix, John, Louis, Martin, Michael, Paul, Victor
17. Francis, Mary, Peter, Reginald
18. Charles, Dominic
19. Charles, Emily, Mary
20. Francis, John, Joseph, Laurence, Thomas
21. Alexander, Francis, James, Mark, Michael, Peter, Thomas
22. Augustine, Charles, Joseph, Maurice, Paul
23. Andrew, Antony, Christopher, Elizabeth, Helen, John, Peter, William
24. Antony, Robert, William
25. John, Mark, Paul
26. Lucy, Sebastian, Teresa
27. John, Laurence
28. Antony, Dominic, Francis, James, Laurence, Luke, Simon, Thomas, Matthew, Michael, Peter, Vincent, William
29. Charles, Gabriel, John, Laurence, Michael, Nicholas, Raphael, William, Vincent
30. Francis, Frederick, Gregory, John, Simon, Teresa

OCTOBER

Even more noticeably than September, October has some overcrowded days and some periods with no major figures. This has resulted in several shifts of dates within the month: St Denis from the 9th to the 10th; St Lull from the 16th to the 12th (formerly St Wilfrid, who is now on his date of death, 24 Apr.); St Paul of the Cross from the 19th to the 20th; St Gerard Majella from the 16th to the 21st; Bd Louis Guanella from the 26th to the 27th to allow St Cedd his traditional feast-day. Bd Contardo Ferrini, an inspiring modern lay Blessed, occupies a relatively blank day on the 7th, moved from his actual date of death, the 17th, which is given to St Ignatius of Antioch in the Universal Calendar. There are also some transfers from outside the month, partly as a form of positive discrimination to bring up the number of women (scarce in this month but too many on some days in others): St Francis Borgia has been moved from 10 October to 30 September (the same day as St Jerome) in the new Roman Martyrology but is featured here on the 2nd; St Teresa Couderc is brought in from 26 September to the 3rd; St Hilda of Whitby from 17 November to the 29th; St Winifred from 2 November (redated from the 3rd in the new Roman Martyrology) to the 30th. St Edward the Confessor (13th) and the Forty Martyrs of England and Wales (25th) are important dates in the English calendar and are retained here even though they do not feature on these dates in the new Roman Martyrology (where Edward is on 5 January and the martyrs are on their individual dates of death).

1

St Thérèse of Lisieux (Marie Françoise Thérèse Martin; 1873–1897)

The best-loved saint of modern times was born in Alençon in Normandy, the youngest of five surviving children of a devout and relatively prosperous couple, Louis Martin, a watchmaker, and Azélie-Marie Guérin. Her mother died when Thérèse was only four, and she turned to her eldest sister, Pauline, as a second mother. Pauline entered the Carmelite convent at Lisieux (to where the family had moved) when Thérèse was nine, plunging her into years of nervousness and search for security. A second sister, Marie, then entered the same convent, and Thérèse longed to do the same. She was rejected by the convent authorities and the local bishop as she was still only fourteen. She accompanied her father on a journey to Rome and appealed to Pope Leo XIII, who gave her an enigmatic papal reply: "You shall enter if it be God's will." This crushed her immediate hopes but brought out the toughness at the core of her character: "God cannot try me more than I can bear."

The bishop allowed her to join the Carmelites the following year; she took the name Thérèse of the Infant Jesus, to which she later added "and the Holy Face." She was convinced that everyone is called to holiness and that she, a "little soul," needed to find a "little way" to achieve it. She did not indulge in any extraordinary mortifications but sought to perform every least task for the greater glory of God. The "little" was a correction to temptations to pride, not an indication of childishness. She read the great Carmelite mystics St John of the Cross (see 14 Dec.) and St Teresa of Avila (see 15 Oct.), *The Imitation of Christ*, and St Francis de Sales (see 24 Jan.), learning to reject advice that made perfection something for the chosen few and to turn back to the scriptures, where, "perfection seems easy." She never claimed that it was a prerogative of priests and religious. In many ways her years in the convent were hard: the prioress was severe, the community was divided in some ways, and she had doubts about her vocation.

Her father suffered a series of strokes and spent three years in an institution, on account of which Thérèse's clothing ceremony and profession of vows had to be postponed. He died in 1894, and another sister, Céline, freed from nursing him, entered the convent. Thérèse was appointed assistant to the novice-mistress, the only official position she held. She began to write poems and plays to mark pious commemorations in the convent, while continuing to write vivid and copious letters, then began to set down her "little way" in her *Story of a Soul*, the autobiographical account that was to lead to her immense popularity. She consecrated herself as a victim to God's merciful love, in a variant of a traditional Carmelite spiritual tradition of taking on themselves punishment due to sinners, asking that God consume her entirely, that she become "a martyr of your love, O my God."

In 1864 she was brought a copy of the Life and letters of Bd Théophane Vénard (see 2 Feb.), martyred in Indochina (Vietnam) in 1861, and was inspired by his example to volunteer for the new Carmelite monastery in Hanoi. But her health was already declining, with the tuberculosis that was to kill her becoming evident, and in the event the closest she could get to him was to clutch a relic as she lay dying. She wrote a series of moving letters to two missionaries in Vietnam during the last two years of her life. Her last months were a real "dark night of the soul," which she described in graphic terms: "God allowed my soul to be overrun by an impenetrable darkness, which made the thought of heaven, hitherto so welcome, a subject of nothing but conflict and torment." She suffered increasingly from Holy Week 1896 to the end of

September 1897, with no drugs given to relieve her pain or oxygen for her breathlessness, dying on 30 September.

The Carmelites published her autobiography (in a somewhat doctored version) a year after her death, and popular devotion gathered pace, hundreds of thousands of copies being rapidly sold. Many cures through her intercession were claimed, and her cause was introduced in 1914; Pope Benedict XV beatified her in 1923; Pope Pius XI canonized her in 1925 and proclaimed her a principal patron of all missionaries. Her image was sentimentalized in a flood of devotional aids, but recently the underlying strength of her character and the original power of her message have been recognized. This was confirmed when Pope John Paul II declared her a Doctor of the Church as part of the celebrations marking the centenary of her death in 1997.

❖

I will spend my heaven doing good upon earth ... I shall not be able to take any rest until the end of the world as long as there are souls to be saved.
St Thérèse, in a letter to a missionary in Vietnam

2

St Francis Borgia (Francisco de Borja y Aragón; 1510–1572)

Francis was born into high estate, a great-grandson of a pope, Alexander VI (born Rodrigo Borgia), and of a king, Ferdinand of Aragon, cousin to the emperor Charles V, and eldest son of the duke of Gandia (on the east coast of Spain). He joined the imperial court in 1528, married the following year, was created marquis of Llombay the next, and appeared to be set on a brilliant career in public life. He was appointed viceroy of Catalonia in 1539, where he set about eradicating corruption in public affairs and at the same time began to develop more spiritual concerns in his personal life.

In 1543 his father died and he succeeded him as duke of Gandia. His public career seems to have suffered a setback when his reforms were opposed, as a result of which he retired to devote himself to his estates and his family. He had met the first group of Jesuits to visit his part of Spain and been impressed by them: he founded a hospital and a university for the Society. He was a devoted family man, but when his wife died in 1546 he decided to give up public life altogether and joined the Jesuits in secret. After making provision for his eight children, he embarked for Rome to meet Ignatius of Loyola (see 31 July).

His administrative abilities and his name meant that from the beginning of his life as a religious he was involved in major projects, such as the foundation of the Roman College (which became the Gregorian University), whereas his personal desire was for a more hermit-like life. He was ordained in Spain in 1551 and managed to devote some time to quiet prayer and spiritual writing, though Charles V sought him out for various missions and made him one of his executors. To avoid being made a cardinal he took the simple vows of a professed Jesuit, renouncing all titles. While in Spain he founded twelve colleges and a novitiate. Philip II, who became king of Spain when Charles abdicated and retired to a monastery in 1555, consulted him on state matters, which led some to accuse him of exercising undue influence. In 1559 he fled to Portugal to avoid further involvement in politics, but two years later he was summoned to Rome to act as vicar-general of the Jesuits while their general, Fr Laínez, attended the Council of Trent.

Four years later Laínez died, and Francis was elected to succeed him as general of the Society of Jesus. As such, he concentrated mainly on the spiritual training of his priests and the expansion of the Society's missionary work, especially in countries affected by the Protestant Reformation, above all Poland and Germany. He established the first Jesuit missions in the Spanish colonies in America, and in 1571 the pope sent him to Spain and Portugal to help build the alliance against the Turks that produced the great naval victory of Lepanto the same year. This was to be the last public mission of his life; his health was failing, and he died on 30 September 1572, only three days after returning to Rome.

His legacy consists as much in his writings as in his activities. During his period of relative quiet as duke of Gandia he was already writing spiritual works for lay people, based largely on contrasting God's generosity with sinners' selfishness: perhaps because of his position, he saw himself as a great sinner and had carried out excessive self-mortification until the Jesuits persuaded him to modify it. His major work as a Jesuit priest was a treatise on prayer, written for members of his family and of the Society. As general he wrote a series of *Meditations*, embodying Ignatius' structured approach to prayer. He wrote in the vernacular, not in Latin, and partly for lay people: both these aroused the suspicions of the Inquisition, and he was in the anomalous position of being general of the Jesuits while several of his works were on the Index of Forbidden Books, on which they remained until after his death. The Jesuits were a source of controversy in the Church virtually from their inception, which may have been part of Francis' motivation in choosing them rather than one of the more established Orders. An outstanding example of someone who renounces great wealth and worldly position for Christ, he was beatified in 1624 and canonized in 1671.

Christ was crucified and I am without a single wound ... I desire to shed my blood for the love of Jesus whenever it may be for service.
Final entry in St Francis Borgia's *Spiritual Diary*

3

St Teresa Couderc (Marie-Victoire Couderc; 1805–1885)

Teresa Couderc is one of many indomitable French women who contributed greatly to the huge task of re-Christianizing the country, especially the rural areas (in which the bulk of the population still lived), after the horrors and depradations of the French Revolution, which had involved a massive effort to rid the nation of its religion. Like many others, she was to suffer more setbacks from rivalries within the Church than from hostility among the people.

She came from the Ardèche region of south-central France and grew up in a farming family, with little formal education. Despite parental opposition, she went to a boarding school run by the Sisters of St Joseph (see Bd Anne Marie Javouhey; 16 July) and then, as a result of hearing a Lent mission preached by a Fr Jean Terme, joined a new community he proposed to form to teach in his parish. She was one of its first members, in 1826. Fr Terme then invited her and two others to help with pilgrims who flocked to the shrine of St John-Francis Régis (30 Dec.), where there was evident need of a hostel for women pilgrims. A building was acquired, and two years later Fr Terme appointed Teresa, still only twenty-three, superior of the community, known as the Daughters of St Régis. Inspired by a Jesuit retreat, Fr Terme then divided the work of the Sisters into running the hostel and giving retreats to women. This was a novel idea at the time and proved an immediate success.

Trouble began with the death of Fr Terme in December 1834. Teresa lost not only a valued friend and counsellor but also the community's treasurer. Jesuits took over the parish and the shrine and separated the teaching Sisters from the retreat-givers, who became known first as Sisters of the Retreat and later as Religious of the Cenacle. They learned the Ignatian method of giving retreats and at first were so popular that another house and church had to be built. But they overspent and built up debts. The Jesuit parish priest, Fr Renault, humiliated Teresa by giving her a bunch of bills as a "spiritual bouquet" on her birthday. In distress, she resigned as superior, seeing a wealthy aristocratic widow, who had joined the community only a month before, installed in her place and styled "foundress." The latter failed to halt the debts and was soon replaced by a more experienced but equally high-handed religious, Charlotte Contenet, who dismissed nine of the original Sisters but had to keep Teresa as she was joint owner of the house in which they lived under the terms of Fr

Terme's will. She forced her to do heavy manual work, which Teresa accepted with good grace. Her true financial ability was revealed when she bought a house in Lyons at half the market rate.

Charlotte died in 1851, and the Congregation virtually split into halves under the new superior general and her assistant, who refused to accept the result and took half the Sisters to Paris. Teresa was sent to mediate and succeeded in bringing some Sisters back, though some left altogether. She was then returned to humble work, but her place was recognized when the bishop of Viviers confirmed that she and Fr Terme were the only true founders. She helped with one or two new foundations, but remained generally in the background, discreetly helping the Congregation to progress and never showing the least bitterness. As she aged she suffered from deafness, rheumatism, and arthritis, and the Franco-Prussian war added mental sufferings to her physical ones. She united all her pains to those of the souls in purgatory, which brought her spiritual solace. She died on 26 September 1885, by which time there were nine Cenacles in France and three in Italy. She was beatified in 1951 and canonized in 1970, and there are now over sixty Cenacles, spread over fourteen countries.

4

St Francis of Assisi (Giovanni Francesco di Bernadone; 1182–1226)

Francis's baptismal name was Giovanni (John), but his father, a cloth merchant who was trading in France when he was born, added the unusual Francesco to mark his love of France. Francis grew up learning the trade and leading the life of a prominent young man about town. When he was twenty, Assisi rashly waged war on nearby Perugia. Francis joined the town's army, which was defeated, and he was held prisoner for a year. He was then ill for a further year but still saw himself as a soldier and set off southward to join the papal forces. On his way he was struck by a dream in which a voice told him to "follow the master, not the man." He interpreted this as a call from Christ, turned back to Assisi, and began to care for the poor and the sick, especially lepers.

A further call came in a dream in 1205, when he was praying in the church of San Damiano, outside Assisi, and heard a voice telling him to repair the church, "which as you can see is in ruins." He applied this literally and sold some of his father's cloth to raise money for repairs to San Damiano. His father, already disturbed by the course his son's life was taking, took him to the bishop's court, where he was ordered to pay back the money. He did so with a dramatic gesture, renouncing his inheritance and handing his fine clothes over as well. Dressed only in a workman's smock, he left the town and spent the next two years as a hermit, vowed to complete poverty and dedication to God. He begged alms for food and worked manually at restoring three churches. In one of these, a chapel named the Portiuncula, he was listening to the Mass reading about Jesus sending out the disciples, without money or "two tunics, or sandals, or a staff" (see Matt 10:5–23) when he realized that this was to be, quite literally, his vocation. Keeping only a rough shepherd's tunic, he began preaching repentance in the streets of Assisi.

He soon attracted a group of disciples, whom he called the "lesser brothers"—hence Friars Minor, as they became known. They lived together in a primitive cottage, and Francis devised a rule of life for them based on the evangelical counsel of perfection. They were to own nothing personally (like the traditional Orders) and nothing in common (unlike these). In 1210 He obtained papal approval for this Rule, together with the grant of clerical status (tonsured but not ordained) and a licence to preach. They travelled about Italy doing so, attracting huge numbers of penitents and also many recruits. Francis was ordained deacon but never aspired to priestly ordination out of respect for the office. He had not envisaged a large movement but now found himself having to organize one. He divided his friars into provincial groups, with a superior general in charge of each, and held annual general chapters from 1217. His preaching had attracted a wealthy young woman, Clare (see 11 Aug.), followed by others, who became a Second Order, based initially at San Damiano and leading a life of penance and strict enclosure.

Francis turned his mind to missionary work outside Europe, especially among the "infidel" Muslims. His own first attempts to preach in the Holy Land and Morocco were defeated by shipwreck and illness. He did reach Egypt, where he was received courteously by the Sultan of Damietta, on the Nile Delta, who allowed him to preach. He realized that the "Christian" Crusaders were as much in need of conversion as the Muslims. The missionary activity of the friars did spread, and the Order had its first martyrs as early as 1227, when a group was executed in Morocco. They soon reached as far as Mongolia and China, where they established a Christian community that flourished for over a century.

In 1220 Francis opened up the practice of his ideals to lay people through the Third Order of Penitents, better known as tertiaries. By then the number of friars had grown to some five thousand, and tensions were becoming evident. One cause of these was the contribution the Order was making to the new universities, which involved the need for books and buildings. Francis, largely uneducated himself, worried that "Lady Learning" would become a rival to "Lady Poverty" and had not included study in his original Rule, but he saw the value of this learned apostolate, and a new Rule he submitted for papal approval in 1223 made the necessary concessions. He later approved the foundation of a Franciscan theological school in Bologna, appointing St Antony of Padua (see 13 June) its first lecturer. He himself had resigned as minister general in 1220 and three years later he moved to a hermitage at Grecchio (where he built the Christmas crib that was to make that devotion universally popular) and then to a more remote place, La Verna, in the mountains above Arezzo. He famously tamed a wolf at Gubbio and preached to the birds—symbolic, perhaps, of his concern to remove all causes of strife from people's lives and to preach the unadorned gospel everywhere.

It was at La Verna that he received the marks of Christ's wounds known as the stigmata, the closest possible mark of his self-identification with the suffering Christ. However one seeks to explain their origin, the wounds were physically there: they bled, and they hurt, and they were clearly visible despite Francis' attempts to keep them hidden. (He is the first recorded stigmatic in history: others followed as devotion to the physical sufferings of Christ spread—and as the popularity of Francis himself increased.) His health was failing in the last two years of his life, with a painful eye infection, made worse by attempted surgery, and acute stomach disorders. He came down from La Verna, paid a last visit to Clare at San Damiano, the occasion for the composition of the *Canticle of the Sun*, and was taken back into Assisi, where he dictated his *Testament*, and then out to the Portiuncula, where he was laid on the ground. Having broken bread with those present, he died in the evening of 3 October 1226. Brother Elias of Cortona, whom he had appointed to succeed him, began the building of a large basilica in Assisi (surely the last thing Francis would have wanted) and his remains were transferred there in 1230, by which time he had already been canonized for two years, an extraordinarily rapid process indicative of the huge impact he and his movement had made on the Church.

His was not the only radical movement embracing poverty at a time when the Church was widely seen as wealthy and corrupt. What he did was to live and promote a spirituality rooted totally in the Gospels—which could therefore not be attacked as unorthodox—and to make his movement grow in union with the institutional Church—even though there were to be frictions between the two—so that it could not be written off as some deviant enthusiasm. His message was radical to the point of fanaticism and could not be accepted fully except by a few—hence the early split into the strict "observants" and the more compromising "conventuals," and the permanent tendency to take from Francis what each person wants rather than the whole of his example. But different aspects of him can be more relevant at different periods, and his proclamation in 1979 as patron saint of ecology and ecologists certainly relates him to one of the world's most pressing concerns. His movement, with its First, Second, and Third Orders and some eighty separate but affiliated Congregations has spread worldwide and always been one of the Church's great missionary spearheads. Assisi has recently become a major focus for ecumenical pilgrimages to pray for world peace. A fresco series by Giotto illustrating Francis' life, on the walls of the upper basilica (completed in 1253, built on top of the original basilica containing his relics), was badly damaged by an earthquake in September 1997. Francis, who refused to let his friars live in stone buildings, might have permitted himself a heavenly smile.

Most high, omnipotent, good Lord, all praise, glory, honour and blessing are yours; to you alone, Most High, do they belong, and no one is to pronounce your name.
    Opening of St Francis' *Canticle of the Sun*

5

St Mary Faustina Kowalska (Helena Kowalska; 1905–1938)

Mary was born on 25 August 1905 in Glogowiec in Poland, the third of ten children of a poor and devout family of peasants and baptized with the name Helena in the parish church of Ðwinice Warckie. She made her first Communion when she was nine and attended school for three years. At the age of sixteen she left home and went to work as a housekeeper in Aleksandrów, Lodi, and Ostrówek in order to support herself and help her parents. She had thought of a religious vocation from the time she was seven and sought to enter a convent after she finished school, but her parents would not give their permission.

On 1 August 1925 she had a vision of the suffering Christ, after which she entered the Congregation of the Sisters of Our Lady of Mercy, taking the names Mary Faustina in religion. She spent the rest of her life, a mere thirteen years, in the Congregation's houses in Krakow, Plock, and Vilnius, where she worked as a cook, gardener, and porter. She carried out her tasks dutifully, outwardly recollected, very natural, serene, and outgoing. This exterior hid an extraordinary union with God. Her spirituality was based on contemplation of the mystery of the Mercy of God, which she saw in the word of God as well as in the everyday activities of her life. Her contemplation was to issue in practical mercy shown to those in need. She wrote in her Diary: "O my Jesus, each of your saints reflects one of your virtues; I desire to reflect your compassionate heart, full of mercy; I want to glorify it. Let your mercy, O Jesus, be impressed upon my heart and soul like a seal, and this will be my badge in this and the future life". Prompted by a direct revelation, she dedicated herself to cooperating with God's mercy in the task of saving lost souls.

She experienced extraordinary "gifts" throughout her years in the convent: revelations, visions, hidden stigmata, participation in the passion of Jesus, apparent bilocation, the reading of minds ("infused knowledge"), foretelling the future, and the rare experience of mystical engagement and marriage. Her relationship with God, the Virgin Mary, the angels and saints, souls in purgatory—with the entire supernatural world—was as real to her as the outer world, but she retained a clear-sighted appreciation of the nature of holiness: "Neither graces, nor revelations, nor raptures, nor gifts granted to a soul make it perfect, but rather the intimate union of the soul with God. These gifts are merely ornaments of the soul, but constitute neither its essence nor its perfection. My sanctity and perfection consist in the close union of my will with the will of God" (Diary). She recorded very precise messages "received" from Jesus, who called her the Apostle and "Secretary" of his mercy and charged her to tell the world of his message: "In the Old Covenant I sent prophets wielding thunderbolts to my people. Today I am sending you with my mercy to the people of the whole world. I do not want to punish aching mankind, but I desire to heal it, pressing it to my merciful heart" (Diary). Her three tasks were to be reminding the world of God's merciful love for every human being; entreating God's mercy for the whole world and particularly for sinners; and initiating the apostolic movement of the Divine Mercy, which undertakes the task of proclaiming and entreating God's mercy for the world. This movement was to strive for Christian perfection by following precepts she laid down: to display an attitude of child-like trust in God, which expresses itself in fulfilling his will, and to show mercy toward one's neighbours.

Today, this movement involves millions of people throughout the world, comprising religious Congregations, lay institutes, religious brotherhoods, associations, and various communities of Apostles of the Divine Mercy, as well as individuals. Sister Mary Faustina recorded this "mission" in her Diary, which she kept at the specific request of her confessors. She set down all of the wishes revealed to her as though dictated to her. The Diary is accessible to simple and uneducated people but also used by scholars, who look upon it as an additional source of theological research. It has been translated into many languages, including English, German, Italian, Spanish, French, Portuguese, Arabic, Russian, Hungarian, Czech, and Slovak.

Mary Faustina, suffering from tuberculosis and other ailments, died in Krakow at the age of just thirty-three on 5 October 1938, already regarded as a saint. Pope John Paul II beatified Sister Mary Faustina on 18 April 1993 and canonized her on 30 April 2000. Her remains are preserved in the Sanctuary of the Divine Mercy in Krakow-Lagiewniki. At a huge open-air ceremony for the beatification of four Poles in August 2002, the pope said that from the beginning of its existence the Church has preached the mercy of God, but that

[n]onetheless, it would appear that we today have been particularly called to proclaim this message before the world. We cannot neglect this mission, if God himself has called us to it through the testimony of St Faustina Kowalska. ... God has chosen our own times for this purpose perhaps because the twentieth cen-

tury, despite indisputable achievements in many areas, was marked in a particular way by the "mystery of iniquity." With this heritage both of good and evil, we have entered the new millennium.

6

St Bruno (about 1035–1101)

The founder of the Carthusians was born in Cologne and studied in France, first at Reims and then at Tours, where he read philosophy but was renowned for his brilliance in all subjects. He returned to Cologne to study theology and was ordained there in 1055. He was then appointed rector of the cathedral school in Reims, at which he had studied and remained there for some twenty years, seemingly destined to remain and progress in academic life. One of his pupils was the future Pope Urban II (1088–99).

He then became chancellor of the diocese of Reims, where the archbishop had obtained the post by simony and lived a life of scandal and wealth. Bruno and a number of other priests opposed him but failed to have him deposed. Bruno returned to Cologne, and the quarrel with the bishop led him to begin to think that a simple, solitary life would be preferable to high office with its rivalries. Instead of agreeing to become the next bishop of Reims, he gave up all his possessions and positions and moved with a few companions to Molesme, the first Cistercian foundation (see St Stephen Harding; 28 Mar.).

Even living in a hermitage separate from the monastery proved too easy for Bruno, and in about 1084 he took his companions south to the mountainous area of Grenoble, where the bishop (another former pupil from Reims) gave them a remote valley known as La Chartreuse. There they built an oratory and small cells and lived a mainly solitary life, coming together for Matins and Vespers, for Mass on Sundays and feast-days only, and for a main meal on major feasts. The part hermit, part community pattern was modelled on the monks of the Egyptian desert centuries earlier, and was not intended to constitute a new Order. They wore hair shirts, ate no meat, and ate fish only if it was given to them. The day was divided into periods for prayer, reading, and manual work, largely copying manuscripts (once there were enough lay brothers to carry out the necessary agricultural tasks).

After six years of this life Bruno's past caught up with him when Urban summoned him to Rome as his counsellor in various matters, the most pressing of which were reform of the clergy and a quarrel with an antipope, Gilbert of Ravenna. Gilbert forced Urban to flee from Rome, south into Calabria, and he took Bruno with him. Refusing the offer of the bishopric of Reggio, Bruno founded a second monastery at La Torre, modelled on Chartreuse, and five years later another, St Stephen's, as the number of disciples had outgrown the first. He kept in touch with the monks of the motherhouse by letter, writing of the joys of the solitary life in sensible and balanced tones, and through a visit to La Torre by the prior. He also wrote on the Psalms and on the Epistles of St Paul, as well as corresponding with eminent political figures. He left no written Rule, but the basic inspiration for the way of life he advocated can be found in his letters and what is claimed to be a final "testament;" a profession of faith made to his monks just before his death.

He died at La Torre on 6 October 1101 and was buried at St Stephen's. His body was transferred back to La Torre in 1513, when it was found to be incorrupt. His cult developed quickly, and he acquired a great reputation as a protector against diabolic possession. He was never formally beatified or canonized, but became both "equivalently" when his cult was approved for the Carthusians in 1514 and extended to the universal Church in 1623, by which time several other Carthusians had been canonized.

Carthusian monks first came to England in 1173, and the number of houses, known as "charterhouses" had grown to nine by the time of the Reformation, when Carthusians were some of the earliest martyrs. The Order has the unique distinction of never having had to be reformed.

7

Bd Contardo Ferrini (1859–1902)

The leading historian of his day, Contardo inherited his intellectual curiosity from his father, who had graduated in architecture and engineering, and taught mathematics and physics. He was fortunate to be well guided in his religious and scholarly development by three learned priests, one of whom taught him Hebrew, in addition to his Greek, so he could read the Bible in its original languages. In 1876 he won a scholarship to study law at the Borromeo College in Pavia. He was almost as devout as he was precociously learned, for which he earned a fair amount of mockery from his fellow-students, though they generally remembered him later with great respect. He also developed a love of poetry and became a keen and able mountaineer.

In 1880 he was awarded a bursary to study in Berlin. Terrified at the thought of entering this hotbed of Protestantism, he found when he arrived that there was an active body of Catholics involved in social and charitable work and joined the local branch of the St Vincent de Paul Society (see Bd Frederick Ozanam; 8 Sept.). His thesis from Pavia had been on penal law in the works of Homer and Hesiod, and he returned to Pavia in 1883 as lecturer in Roman Law. Besides his classical languages, Latin, Greek, Hebrew, Syriac, and some

Coptic, he was at ease in German, English, Dutch, French, and Spanish. He had been taught by his priest mentors early in life to go to primary sources, and he researched in major libraries across Europe. He held several chairs in the 1880s and early 1890s before returning to Pavia as professor of Roman Law, on which he was the world's leading expert. He published hundreds of articles, several textbooks, and numerous contributions to collective works.

Toward the end of his time in Berlin he had made a vow of lifelong celibacy, but he did not believe he had a vocation to the priesthood. He joined the Third Order of St Francis and developed a spirituality based on devotion to the Blessed Sacrament, prayer, and meditation. The simple Franciscan approach to God appealed to him, and his love of poetry combined to give him a somewhat Romantic approach to the finding of God in the beauty of creation, with echoes of Wordsworth or Gerard Manley Hopkins: "For the spirit of God by which nature lives is a spirit forever young, incessantly renewing itself, happy in its snow and rain and mist, for out of these come birth and life, spring ever renewed and undaunted hope." He kept up his concern for social work and became a city councillor of Milan in 1895. Opposed to socialism and a vigorous upholder of the Church at a time when it was under widespread attack in Italy, he nevertheless deplored the papal ban on Catholics taking part in Italian politics. He publicly upheld the indissolubility of marriage and the value of Catholic elementary education, and he was instrumental in bringing the University of the Sacred Heart in Milan into being, though it opened only after his death.

He caught typhoid fever while staying on Lake Maggiore and died on 17 October 1902, at the early age of forty-three. He had accomplished an astonishing amount: above all he had shown true dedication to work, making it not an end in itself but a "hymn of praise to the Lord of all learning." He was beatified in 1947, when Pope Pius XII held him up as a model of the Catholic layperson and an example of how holiness can be achieved in modern times.

8

St Pelagia the Penitent (possibly Fourth Century)

The name Pelagia is given to both a historical personage, a young woman from Antioch who escaped rape and murder at the hands of Diocletian's soldiers by jumping off the roof of her house into a river and drowning, and to a very different character, a courtesan from Antioch, living a century or so later. The first Pelagia was venerated in Antioch on today's date at least from the fourth century, as is recorded by both St John Chrysostom (13 Sept.) and St Ambrose (7 Dec.) in his *De Virginibus*. She is regarded as a martyr, but her "death before dishonour" choice kept many a medieval disputation going.

John Chrysostom is also the source of the story of the second Pelagia, though in fairly summary form compared to its later elaboration, confining it to an incident of sudden conversion and not giving his penitent a name. It was elaborated in a Greek Life claimed, probably wrongly, to be the work of one James the Deacon, who worked for Bishop Nonnus. It has been described as a masterpiece of storytelling, but it may have some basis in fact. Nonnus had been a monk in the desert of Tabbenesi, from where he was summoned to be bishop of Edessa; he is known to have attended the Council of Chalcedon in 451, together with some other bishops mentioned in the story. Pelagia was a celebrated dancer and actress (which implies worse) who one day passed, with her troupe, in front of the basilica of St Julian in Antioch, where Nonnus and eight bishops who had been summoned by the metropolitan for a synod were sitting in the shade while he expounded the gospel to them. At the sight of her jewelled, perfumed, and partly uncovered body all the bishops except Nonnus turned their heads away and groaned. He gazed at her and then burst into tears, struck by the thought that she lavished more time and care on preparing her body to please men than he did on preparing his soul to please God. That night he dreamed of a filthy, smelly black dove, which he eventually caught and dipped in the baptismal font, from which it emerged pure white and flew away.

The next day was Sunday, and Nonnus preached in a crowded church. To the astonishment of the congregation, Pelagia came and wept tears of penitence with the rest of them at Nonnus' words. Afterwards, she asked to see him; he prudently agreed only if he were in the company of other bishops. She came, flung herself at his feet, washed his feet with her tears, and dried them with her hair (as sinful women should: see Luke 7:38) and asked for baptism. Nonnus exorcised her and then baptized her with the name of Pelagia, which she said her parents had given her, though the townspeople called her Margarita (meaning "pearl"—hence St Margaret of Antioch). She was put with other women catechumens, while the devil (or perhaps Pelagia's manager?) cursed Nonnus from the city gates for depriving him of such a prize. She gave Nonnus all her wealth, which he handed on to the widows and orphans. A week later he seems to have given her his tunic and cloak, in which she disappeared.

Three or four years later, the person calling himself James the Deacon went on pilgrimage to Jerusalem, where Nonnus had asked him to visit the recluse Pelagius, living in a cell on the Mount of Olives. He knocked on a little shutter, which was opened; a haggard face looked out, with eyes "like trenches" that seemed to recognize him. He said he came from Nonnus, and Pelagius asked Nonnus, "a saint of God," to pray for him. Some time later James went back but twice received no answer. He sealed the shutter with clay and went and told the monks in Jerusalem that Pelagius was dead. They recovered the body and, when they laid it out for burial, discovered it was a woman's. The story spread rapidly, and her funeral was a fine affair of torches and chanting. It was too good a story to be kept to one person, so elements from it produced not only Margaret of Antioch, but "saints" Marina, Mary, Apollinaria, Euphrosyne, and Theodora, all literary replicas of "James'" story—of which at least certain details, such as sealing of the shutter, ring rather true . . .

9

St John Leonardi (1542–1609)

John Leonardi was one of the more important reformers of church life in Italy following and implementing the Council of Trent. He was brought up in Lucca, a Tuscan walled city west of Florence. He joined a lay confraternity, studied for the priesthood, and after being rejected by the Franciscans was ordained in 1572. He became increasingly concerned for the welfare of prisoners and hospital inmates and gathered a group of like-minded companions to work to improve their situation. This group lived in common and prayed as well as worked together. John saw the Church going through a period of great crisis: there was apathy and corruption combined with pockets of enthusiastic devotion, but much of the latter was among followers of charismatic but unorthodox reformers. He saw preaching and education as the main planks of a thoroughgoing reform process. The bishop of Lucca supported him and gave him permission to preach in all the city's churches, but many of the leading families were among those influenced by unorthodox figures, and they resented his preaching.

This opposition intensified when John proposed to form his followers, many of whom wished to be ordained priests, into a regular religious Congregation. Again the bishop of Lucca supported him, and in 1583, with approval from Pope Gregory XIII, the group took simple vows and became a recognized association of secular priests. John, though, was forced to leave Lucca and was able to visit it only with special papal protection during the rest of his life. St Philip Neri (see 26 May), the founder of the "oratories," which had comparable objectives, gave him premises in Rome (and his cat to look after), and St Joseph Calasanz (see 26 Aug.) also helped him, associating his group with his own Piarists for a time. In 1595 John's priests were formally recognized as a religious Congregation by Pope Clement VIII.

The pope also commissioned John to reform a number of monasteries and to help in planning a new seminary for training students for overseas missions, a subject in which John had a great interest (which took shape later as the "College for the Propagation of the Faith"). He wrote on aspects of theology and education, but little of this was published, despite the prominent place he occupied within Catholic reform movements. He was particularly associated with the growth of the Forty Hours devotion and with the move towards frequent Communion.

John died of the plague, caught from his continual visiting of the sick, in 1609. Twelve years later his Congregation was formally recognized as a religious Order, which meant that his priests took solemn (as opposed to simple) vows. They adopted the name Clerks Regular of the Mother of God. John never wanted a large association, and membership has stayed select, its priests still working in hospitals and prisons, with a motherhouse in Rome and other houses in Naples and Monte Carlo. John was beatified in 1861 and canonized in 1938; his feast-day (formerly a "double," now ranked as an optional memorial) was added to the Universal Calendar in 1941.

10

St Denis (died about 258)

Denis (or Dionysius in Latin) is a name given to several personages, though in this case the confusion is not just the result of the spreading of a popular story (as with Pelagia) but of deliberate falsification. This was carried out by Abbot Hilduin of Saint-Denis (in Paris) in the ninth century, with the purpose of fostering the cult at his abbey and so increasing the number of pilgrims and therefore the revenues.

The original "Denis" appears in chapter 17 of the Acts of the Apostles. Paul, forced to leave Thessalonica by hostile crowds, has been taken to Athens, where, distressed at the number of idols all over the city, he preaches to the population, telling them he can put a name to their "unknown god," to whom he has seen an altar. His reception is mixed, but some are impressed by his message of the risen Christ, including a woman named Damaris and "Dionysius the Areopagite" (indicating that he was a member of the judicial council that met on the Areopagus hill) and become believers. Dionysius is not mentioned again but is referred to later variously as a martyr and as first bishop of Athens.

By the seventh century his name was being confused with that of Denis, the first bishop of Paris, seemingly in an attempt by the "eldest daughter of the Church" to push her association with Christianity back to apostolic times. Writing in the previous century, St Gregory of Tours had provided the basic elements of the story of this Denis. He was Italian by birth and became a missionary bishop. In about 250 he and five companions were sent to evangelize Gaul and established a mission centre on an island in the Seine (now in central Paris). Their success disturbed the local authorities to such an extent that Denis, a priest named Rusticus, and a deacon named Eleutherius were arrested, imprisoned for a long time, and finally beheaded. Their bodies were thrown into the Seine but were recovered by some of their converts and buried in a chapel, which developed into the abbey of Saint-Denis, built by the Frankish king Dagobert in the seventh century. His relics were enshrined there in 626, and it later became the burial-place of French kings.

Hilduin not only conflated these two historical Denises into one person but added to "his" prestige with a third identity by attributing a series of spiritual treatises of a mystical nature, actually written about 500 by an unknown writer, to him. In this he was following (perhaps not totally ingenuously) the author, who sought to give his works greater apostolic authenticity by "signing" them "Denis the Areopagite." The first bishop of Paris was now not only a famous convert of St Paul's but an influential spiritual writer as well. (The writer is now referred to as "Pseudo-Denis" or "Pseudo-Dionysius" and has been extremely influential in his own right.) The cult of such a major personage spread rapidly in the Middle Ages, and in England alone over forty churches were dedicated to St Denis.

11

St Philip the Deacon (First Century)

Today's Philip is not the apostle (commemorated with James the Lesser on 3 May) but one of the seven deacons, "men of good standing, full of the Spirit and of wisdom," chosen by the apostles to take over the task of distributing food so as to leave the apostles free to preach. The Greeks had complained that their widows were being neglected in favour of the Hebrews, so the work that had to be done was obviously beyond the capacity of the twelve. Philip comes second to Stephen in the list. His name implies that he was Greek, as was Stephen, so the apostles were clearly taking pains to assuage the Greek Christian community (see Acts 6:1–6).

The deacons' work soon extended beyond mere helping at the common tables, and in Acts 8:4–13 Philip preaches and heals in Samaria, where "[t]he crowds with one accord listened eagerly to what [he] said ... hearing and seeing the signs that he did" (8:6). They had previously been as impressed by Simon the magician, seeing the power of God in him, but even he was converted by Philip and "stayed constantly with [him] and was amazed when he saw the signs and great miracles that took place" (8.13b). He had not quite seen the point of his new faith, however, as he then tried to buy the gift of giving the Spirit through the laying on of hands, to which Peter replied, "May your silver perish with you ...!" (8:20a).

Philip then felt inspired (was told by an angel, in the text) to take the road south through the wilderness from Jerusalem to Gaza. On the road he met the chief treasurer of the queen of Ethiopia, a eunuch, who had been up to Jerusalem to worship and was on his way back south. He was seated in his chariot reading Isaiah when Philip came upon him. Philip asked him if he understood what he was reading, which was 53:7–8, about the sheep being led to the slaughter, and the treasurer replied that he could not see if the prophet was describing himself or someone else unless someone explained it to him. So Philip did, "and starting with this scripture, he proclaimed to him the good news about Jesus" (8:35b) showing how the prophecy had been fulfilled in his life, death, and resurrection. They came to some water, and the treasurer asked why he should not be baptized in it. Philip agreed and baptized him. Then the "Spirit of the Lord snatched [him] away," and the eunuch never saw him again but still "went on his way rejoicing." Philip "found himself" at Azotus and proceeded on his way, preaching as he went, until he reached Caesarea, which may have been his home town (8:39–40)).

This episode shows that Philip understood, before the apostles, that the good news had to be proclaimed beyond Israel. The treasurer was a man of high rank in Ethiopia, and his return as a baptized Christian may have marked the birth of the Church there. The last we hear of Philip is later, when Paul and his companions stay with him in Caesarea after sailing back to Palestine from Ephesus: "and we went into the house of Philip the evangelist [a higher title than he has been given before], one of the seven, and stayed with him" (Acts 21:8). The narrator adds that Philip had four unmarried daughters, "who had the gift of prophecy." They are not named, but it is an interesting aside on the way charisms were distributed in the early Church. No more is known about his ministry, though a later Greek legend makes him bishop of Tralles in Lydia.

12

St Lull (about 710–786)

Lull was yet another of the relatives of St Boniface (see 5 June) from Wessex who joined him in his work of evangelizing in Germany. He was a monk at Malmesbury Abbey before joining his cousin. Boniface ordained him priest and sent him to Rome to consult Pope St Zachary. He was consecrated bishop on his return from Rome and appointed bishop of Mainz when Boniface went north to Frisia. He was responsible for collecting Boniface's body after he had been martyred in 755 and for burying it in the abbey Boniface had built at Fulda.

His time as bishop was beset by a long-running quarrel with the abbot of Fulda, St Sturmi, who had been appointed by Boniface and claimed independence for the abbey from the diocese—which Lull, ironically, may have helped negotiate on his visit to Rome. He deposed Sturmi at one point but then found that he, the bishop, was not independent of the secular power, as King Pepin reinstated him. He was an active and energetic bishop, founding two monasteries and attending a number of regional councils. He wanted an educated clergy and sent to England and other places for books to help in this process. He obviously felt his position as an exile keenly, as his letters show: he wrote to the archbishop of York complaining of the "insults and tribulations [by which the Church] is daily afflicted, burdened, and harassed." Much of his complaint relates to having to remain in this life while longing for the glories of heaven, but phrases such as "incessant sickness of body and anxiety of mind" seem to convey a real indication of his feelings.

The letters also show his care for enforcing canon law, as well as containing orders for prayers and Masses to be said for saving the harvest. He wrote to other bishops and abbots, including the abbot of Wearmouth in Northumberland, telling them who had died and asking for prayers to be said for them, receiving similar information and requests in return. This seems to have been a regular custom in the eighth century. In 781 Mainz was restored to the status of archbishopric, which it had held under St Boniface, and Lull received the *pallium* from Pope Adrian I. He made a written profession of faith, which has survived, the only one to do so from the period. As his health failed he retired to the monastery he had founded at Hersfeld, where he died on 16 October 786. He had been a faithful follower of Boniface and is regarded as the greatest of his disciples.

13

St Edward the Confessor (1005–1066)

Edward, son of Ethelred the Unready and king of England from 1042 to his death just before the Norman Invasion, became an extremely popular saint in England in the later Middle Ages, but it is quite difficult to disentangle his actual saintliness as shown in his life from motives of royal and ecclesiastical prestige urging his canonization. Like so many saints of the period, he was the subject of a Life written mainly to promote the interests of an abbey, in this case by Osbert of Clare, prior of St Peter's, Westminster, which Edward had founded and where he was buried. This made him out, in the manner of the times, to be a great miracle-worker and generous (especially to monks), kind, and chaste. The Normans had an interest in his sainthood because William the

Conqueror claimed to have been nominated by him as his successor; for the Anglo-Saxons he was the last king of "their" line. Nevertheless, his reputation for holiness started in his lifetime.

Edward was born in a troubled England in 1005 (or possibly 1003 or 1004), educated first at Ely, then sent to Normandy for his safe upbringing when he was about ten. He did not return until Harthacnut (Harold "Harefoot") chose him as his successor in 1041, and he was acclaimed king the following year. In Normandy he seems to have acquired most of the qualities he demonstrated as king: mainly patience, caution, and a typically English pragmatism. As king he protected the country from overseas threats, building up a strong army and navy to repel invasions, and defended royal authority against overambitious lords, especially Earl Godwin of Wessex. He married Godwin's daughter, Edith, in an attempt to secure his loyalty, but Godwin still threatened rebellion in 1051, so Edward banished him overseas and Edith to a convent (which could provide some basis for the legend that they lived chastely, though there is no evidence or plausible reason for this). He had to relent and recall Godwin, who, however, posed no further threat. In general, he left the country to his successor, Harold, in a more stable and united state that it had been in on his own accession. There seems no reason to doubt his generosity to the poor.

In his dealings with the Church he exercised his right of appointment wisely, sometimes appointing foreign priests, in order to diminish the near monopoly power of monastic bishops. He strengthened links with Rome, sending bishops to councils and receiving papal legates, and introduced a number of important local reforms. His reputed generosity does not seem to have been extreme, and his foundation (actually re-foundation) of Westminster Abbey seems to have been in fulfilment of a vow rather than out of deliberate policy: in Normandy he had vowed to go on pilgrimage to Rome if his family fortunes were restored; when he became king he was unable to leave the country, so he asked the pope to release him from his vow, which he did on condition that he endow an abbey dedicated to St Peter. There was an existing house at Thorney, just west of the city of London, and Edward chose this, gave it grants of land and money, and built a great romanesque church, three hundred feet long. He was too ill to attend its consecration, dying on 5 January 1066.

His remains were buried in the abbey and moved to a new site in 1102, when his body was found to be intact. Moves were made to have him canonized after the writing of Osbert's Life in the 1130s but were interrupted by the political troubles of Stephen's reign (1135–54). In 1161 King Henry II persuaded Pope Alexander III that his support against rival papal claimants might well be rewarded with the canonization of Edward, and it went ahead. His body was moved twice more within the abbey, first on 13 October 1163, when a sermon was preached by St Aelred of Rievaulx (who wrote a miracle-packed Life of him) in the presence of St Thomas Becket (see 29 Dec), since when 13 October has remained as his traditional feast-day, and again in 1269, into a magnificent new shrine in the new gothic choir built by Henry III. His relics survived the Reformation and are still in Westminster Abbey. The new Roman Martyrology restores his commemoration to the anniversary of his death, 5 January.

He became a patron of England for a time, together with St George, who had taken over by the fifteenth century. He is represented in the Bayeux Tapestry as tall, with a long face and blond hair and beard, and this has remained the tradition in later representations, which include the Wilton Diptych of around 1390 in the National Gallery, London, where he is shown presenting King Richard II to Our Lady. One of his most popular legends has him giving a ring to an old beggar in Westminster; two years later English pilgrims in the Holy Land meet an old man who says he is the apostle John, gives them the ring, and asks them to return it to Edward, warning him he has not long to live. This features in stained glass in York Minster and elsewhere and in tiles in West-minster Abbey.

14

St Callistus I (died 222)

Callistus has the unusual distinctions for a pope of having been born a slave and of having served a sentence of forced labour as a common criminal. The main source of information about him is in a work titled *Philosophoumena*, by Hippolytus, a bitter rival for the papacy and theological opponent, who cannot be called an unbiased commentator. He was also attacked by Tertullian for the laxity of his teaching, so there has to be some interest in trying to find out what he actually did and taught.

He was a slave of a Christian master named Carpophorus, who put him in charge of monies deposited by other Christians. Either through malice or incompetence he managed to lose these. He was then involved in a brawl in a synagogue, arrested, and condemned to work in the mines in Sardinia. On his release—through the good offices of Marcia, concubine of the emperor Commodus—he returned to Italy and settled at Anzio.

When Zephyrinus became pope in 199 his fortunes changed for the better. He was ordained deacon and made manager of the Christian cemetery on the Via Appia, a task he carried out very well, so that his prestige increased to the point where he was elected to succeed Zephyrinus eighteen years later. Hip-polytus, who had wanted the papacy for himself, had himself elected Bishop of Rome by a group of followers, thereby effectively gaining the distinction of becoming the first antipope. He criticized Callistus for his weakness toward heretics in allowing them back to the sacraments if they recanted and for his views on the Trinity. Callistus refrained from condemning him, thereby making him a self-induced schismatic, but Hippolytus was later reconciled with the papacy and died a martyr's death in 235.

During his short papacy of five years, Callistus condemned a theologian named Sabellius and his followers, who upheld that the distinction between the Persons of the Trinity was only in their modes of operation (the heresy of "modalism"), not as separate persons. In the moral sphere, he readmitted previously married persons to the sacraments, upheld the validity of marriages between citizens and slaves (against Roman law) in order to prevent clandestine unions between Christian women and slave men in which the children would not be brought up Christian, and declared that the Church had the power to remit all sins, even murder and adultery, so could be merciful toward the gravest sinners. Tertullian (the first great Latin Christian writer; about 155–220), who had a convert's zeal and hated pagans, Jews, and heretics, was not impressed and accused Callistus of being tainted with adultery and fornication, but it was he who broke with the Church (in 213), while Callistus' views accorded better with later tradition.

Callistus died in 222 (or possibly) 223, victim of a ferocious pagan uprising against Christians. The story—unhistorical—of his death is that he was thrown from a window of his house in the Trastevere district of Rome down a well. His body was recovered and buried secretly in the cemetery of Calepodius on the Via Aurelia, where his tomb, with sixth-century frescoes depicting his supposed martyrdom, was discovered in 1960. His relics were taken in the mid-fourth century to Santa Maria in Trastevere, claimed to be the oldest church dedication to Our Lady in Rome—predating the peace of Constantine—and to be built on the site of the well in which he drowned. The little church of St Callistus nearby (now closed) may be on the site of an even earlier church built by Callistus himself, the result of Emperor Alexander Severus deciding that a disputed plot of land should be given to Christians rather than to tavern-keepers, saying. "I prefer that it should belong to those who honour God, whatever be their form of worship." As virtually every other building in the *piazza* (and in most of Trastevere) is now either a bar or a restaurant, the tavern-keepers have perhaps had the last word: the district fountain, supposed to represent its interests, features a barrel, a vat, and two wine measures.

15

St Teresa of Avila (Teresa de Cepeda y Ahumada; 1515–1582)

The greatest of Spanish religious reformers, perhaps the most impressive woman saint of all time, Teresa was born into a wealthy family in Avila, in Old Castile, the third of nine children born to Don Alonso Sánchez de Cepeda and his second wife, Doña Beatriz de Ahumada. The family was respected, but Don Alonso was the son of a convert Jew and so could not boast the "old Christian" blood essential for social advancement and freedom from suspicion in sixteenth-century Spain.

She had an ordinary and happy childhood, including the famous episode of running away (but not far) with her brother Rodrigo to seek martyrdom at the hands of the Moors and then settling for building hermitages in the garden. Her mother died when she was fourteen, and she turned to reading romances and other normal teenage frivolities, for which she was later to reproach herself unduly harshly. Her father sent her to be "finished" at a local Augustinian convent, but the idea of marriage, with its submission to the will of a man and risk of early death from excessive childbearing, did not seem ever to appeal to her, leaving the alternative of a religious life, which could offer more freedom and comfort. She took this seriously and, despite her father's refusal, entered the Convent of the Incarnation just outside Avila, which a close friend had already joined. Life was fairly comfortable, with her own oratory, kitchen, and guest room; those nuns who could afford them took their servants with them. But there was regular community prayer, Confession once every two weeks, discipline, and fasting: it was far from a life of scandalous ease.

She made her solemn profession but then fell seriously ill; her father took her away to recuperate. She read *The Third Spiritual Alphabet* by the Franciscan Francisco de Osuna, which opened up a whole spectrum of personal advancement in mental and contemplative prayer. Her illness worsened, to the point where she was thought to have died, but then she gradually recovered, over a period of three years, and returned to her convent and external practices of religion, judging herself unworthy and physically unfit for mental prayer. The twelve years between 1543 and what she called her "second conversion" in 1555 seemed relatively barren, but she persevered and began to return to the practice of mental prayer, occasionally experiencing moments of real intimacy with God.

She felt that she was too dependent on human relationships and also that any deep spiritual life was impossible amid the distractions afforded in a community of over one hundred and eighty nuns. She began to envisage a poor, small community of about a dozen nuns, living in strict enclosure—at the Incarnation, comings and goings for nuns and visitors were free—and following the strict Carmelite Rule. There was reform in the air all around her, this being the age of Ignatius of Loyola (see 31 July), Peter of Alcántara, and Francis Borgia (see 2 Oct.), not to mention John of the Cross (see 14 Dec.) in her Order, but Carmelite convents were generally places for unmarried women of good family to live regular and reasonably comfortable lives, and her extreme ideas aroused fierce opposition. She was also by now subject to frequent visions and ecstasies, and these were viewed with the gravest suspicion by the Inquisition, which had placed the works of her mentor Osuna on the Index and did the same with those of Francis Borgia. Poverty, however, was an essential for her: Christ hanging naked on the Cross had nothing, so why should his true followers be attached to possessions? Overcoming (reasonable) objections that there were already far too many convents in Spain for extra ones depending solely on alms to have a chance, she persevered, opening her first Discalced (her nuns wore no shoes) Carmelite convent, St Joseph's, in Avila in 1562.

The nuns, four at first, then thirteen after five years, relied on voluntary alms and lived a life of poverty and penance, though without excessive mortification and certainly not in any spirit of holy misery: Teresa disliked "long-faced saints that make both virtue and themselves abhorrent." The father general of the Carmelite Order visited St Joseph's in 1567, was impressed by what he found, and gave Teresa permission to found two more convents for women and two for friars on the same strict reformed lines. She spent the next nine years travelling all over Spain, in all weathers and in bad health, and made twelve new foundations. A constant stream of letters gives a very vivid impression of her life, her character, and her spiritual experiences, and shows her unique gift for illustrating spiritual advice with the most homely examples from everyday life: as she said, "God walks among the pots and pans." Her own experience of God advanced to the point of mystical union, with raptures that she could not control, though in general she showed that it is possible to combine the highest flights of contemplation with a busy practical life.

The "unreformed" or Calced (shod) Carmelites resented her reforms. They captured and imprisoned her friend and ally John of the Cross, put the superior of the Discalced under house arrest, and excommunicated nuns at the convent of the Incarnation who voted for Teresa to be prioress. The papal nuncio called her a "restless, disobedient and contumacious gad-about woman, who ... has left the enclosure ... and gone about teaching, contrary to the injunction of St Paul ..." But she had powerful protectors too, including King Philip II, whom she went to see. Peace was made with the nuncio, and in 1580 the Discalced Carmelites were given the status of a separate province. Teresa founded four more convents in the next two years, but her health was failing further and she realized she could not go on. She asked to be taken back to Avila but died on the way, at her convent at Alba de Tormes, on 4 October 1582. There was an unseemly scramble for relics, and her cult spread rapidly in Spain, where she had been seen as exceptional in an age of outstanding reformers. She was beatified in 1614 and canonized in 1622 at the extraordinary ceremony that also included Ignatius of Loyola, Francis Xavier, Philip Neri, and the humble peasant Isidore the Farmer. She was the first woman not a "virgin martyr" to have her feast extended to the Universal Calendar, in 1688, and in 1970 Pope Paul VI declared her a Doctor of the Church.

This last title recognizes that she found time in her hectic life to produce a considerable and remarkable body of writing. Her autobiography has been a bestseller in many languages, as have her major mystical treatises *The Interior*

Castle and *The Way of Perfection*. She was one of the great letter writers of all time. The first woman to write systematically and at length on the spiritual life, she continually stresses the humanity of Christ. She is of equal interest to theologians and "ordinary" lay people, largely because she lived what she writes about: she might be taken as the supreme example of Alban Butler's claim that "[i]n the lives of the saints we see the most perfect maxims of the gospel reduced to practice."

Nada te turbe;	Let nothing worry you;
Nada te espante;	Nothing dismay you;
Todo se pasa;	Everything passes;
Dios no se muda.	God does not change.
La paciencia	If you have patience
Todo lo alcanza.	You can do anything.
Quien a Dios tiene	Those who have God
Nada le falta;	Want for nothing;
Sólo Dios basta.	God alone is enough.

"St Teresa's bookmark," lines found in her breviary after her death

16

St Margaret Mary Alacoque (1647–1690)

One of the most famous visionaries among saints, largely responsible for popularizing devotion to the Sacred Heart of Jesus, Margaret Alacoque was born in the town of Janots in the Burgundy region of eastern France. Her father, a prosperous notary, died when she was eight, and she was sent to school with Poor Clare nuns. The following year she developed a rheumatic illness that kept her bedridden, at the convent school, for six years. When she recovered and returned home, she found the family home under the control of relatives of her father, who treated her and her mother harshly. After some consideration of marriage, she decided at the age of twenty to become a nun, helped, she later revealed, by a vision of Our Lord. She joined the Visitation, or Visitandine, nuns (founded by St Jane Frances de Chantal; see 12 Dec.) in their convent at Paray-le-Monial.

She had already progressed to a stage of contemplative prayer where she was aware of Christ as a sensible presence and found it difficult to follow the more basic methods taught to the novices. She had difficulty in following the "humiliations and mortifications" asked of her by Our Lord in her visions in the mundane tasks to be performed in the convent—at which she was slow and clumsy and so was often rebuked. Shortly after her profession, her personal revelations began to be more distinct. She heard Our Lord telling her that she was to be the instrument for spreading love of his Sacred Heart throughout the world. (This devotion seems to have originated with the "modern devotion" to the humanity of Jesus that spread particularly in the Rhineland area in the thirteenth century, and is promoted in the *Revelations* of St Gertrude of Helfta.) The instructions became even more specific: a special feast of the Sacred Heart was to be established on the Friday after Corpus Christi; the faithful were to receive Communion on the first Friday of each month and to spend an hour in prayer every Thursday evening in memory of the Agony in the Garden. ... Such specialized "revelations" were bound to be treated with suspicion, and Margaret Mary was generally dismissed as delusional, but she found a supporter in the new confessor appointed to the convent, Claude de la Colombière (canonized in 1992; see 15 Feb.). When asked in a vision to offer herself in reparation for the ingratitude of some of the nuns toward the Sacred Heart, her troubles with them understandably increased, and she was also plagued with alternate vanity and self-doubt.

Matters resolved themselves more in her direction when she was appointed assistant to a new superior and also novice-mistress, at which she proved most effective; she was also able to inspire her novices with devotion to the Sacred Heart and so spread the message. It was accepted in other Visitandine convents in France, and then more widely, spread by the writings of St Claude and St John Eudes (see 19 Aug.), another influential disciple. Under obedience, Margaret Mary wrote an account of her revelations about five years before her death. She was serving a second term as assistant superior when she was taken ill. She died as she was being anointed on 17 October 1690.

The devotion spread hugely in the Catholic Church at least up to the mid-twentieth century, with excessively pious images proliferating in the nineteenth. The feast was established for Poland in 1765 and for the universal Church in 1856; Pope Leo XIII dedicated the world to the Sacred Heart, and Pope Pius XI ordained that this dedication should be renewed on the feast of Christ the King every year; the "nine first Fridays" practice was widespread at least until Vatican II. Margaret Mary's legacy has been immense, but official suspicion lingered, and she was not canonized until 1920.

This divine heart is an ocean full of all good things, wherein poor souls can cast all their needs; it is an ocean full of joy to drown all our sadness, an ocean of humility to drown our folly, an ocean of mercy for those in distress, an ocean of love in which to submerge our poverty.
St Margaret Mary

17

St Ignatius of Antioch (about 37–107)

Ignatius was born in Syria and may have been a Roman citizen. Virtually nothing is known of his life until he was appointed bishop of Antioch in 69 and very little of his episcopate except that he was arrested for being a Christian and taken to Rome under military guard. He is said by some to have been a disciple of St John the Evangelist and therefore a direct link between the apostles and the next generation. He describes himself as *theophoros*, "bearer of God." Knowledge of him comes from the "Letters to the Seven Churches" that he wrote during the journey to Rome, where he was put to death. The escort does not seem to have been too restricting, as he was able to visit Churches on the way, and he also met St Polycarp (see 23 Feb.).

The letters are addressed to Polycarp, the Church in Rome, and five Churches in Asia Minor—at Ephesus, Magnesia, Tralles, Philadelphia, and Smyrna. He exhorts the Churches to preserve unity through obedience to their bishop, speaks of the Eucharist as a bond of peace, warns against any dealings with schismatics and heretics: "Avoid heretics like wild beasts; for they are mad dogs, biting secretly" (to the Ephesians). He points to Christ as the fulfilment of the prophets, so that Christians cannot still live according to Judaic practices; he stresses the true humanity of Jesus Christ, "who was of David's line, born of Mary, who was truly born, ate and drank; was truly persecuted under Pontius Pilate, truly crucified and died ... who also was truly raised from the dead" (to the Trallians).

He tells the Romans that he longs for martyrdom: "Let me be given to the wild beasts, for by their means I can attain to God. I am God's wheat and I am being ground by the teeth of the beasts so that I may appear as pure bread." In an indication that he was writing before the cult of relics had developed, he continues, "Rather coax the beasts, that they may become my tomb, and leave no part of my body behind, that I may not be a nuisance to anyone when I have fallen asleep." His letters provide the earliest Christian theology of martyrdom, based on the Christian imitation of Christ, including becoming one with him in his passion—which does not mean sharing in all the physical details but rather an attitude of welcome to suffering and death.

Legend tells that the Christians of Rome went out to meet him hoping that they could still save him from death, but he asked them not to stand in the way of his attaining God. He was taken to the Colosseum, thrown to the lions, and died almost immediately. The date is variously given as 107, 110, or as late as

115. His "birthday into heaven" was always celebrated in Antioch on 17 October, and the Western Church has fallen in line with this in the calendar reform of 1969, though the Eastern Churches keep to 20 December, the supposed date of his arrival in Rome. He is often represented in art, usually in full episcopal regalia, as in mosaics in Santa Sophia and statues at Chartres; sometimes his heart is shown being removed, bearing the word Jesus to show his dedication to the humanity of Christ, or he holds his heart in his left hand.

18

St Luke (First Century)

The name given to the third evangelist and the author of the Acts of the Apostles was a fairly common one at the time, probably derived from the Latin Lucanus or Lucius. Early traditions make him unmarried, a doctor, coming from Antioch, one of the seventy disciples sent out by Jesus, one of the two disciples on the road to Emmaus, writing in Greece (he writes in classical Greek), and dying in Boetia, but the truth is that we know next to nothing about his life. Paul writes of "Luke, the beloved physician" (Col. 4:14a) and says that "only Luke is with me" (2 Tim. 4:10a), and it is usually assumed that he is referring to the same Luke who wrote the third Gospel and Acts, but this is not definite. Paul never calls his companion Luke a writer, but the "we" in Acts 16:10 suggests that the author accompanied Paul on at least some of his journeys. What is certain is that the same person wrote Luke's Gospel and Acts and that he intended them as "Books 1 and 2" of the same work. What we can deduce about Luke is contained in these two works. They are generally accepted as being written between the years 70 and 85—which leaves the ending of Acts, with no mention of the death of Paul, as something of a mystery.

The Prologues to the Gospel and Acts are written in a contemporary classical Greek, but he also shows himself capable of using a more popular version for narrative as well as the style of the Septuagint, the version of the Old Testament used by Jews living outside Palestine. Unlike Matthew, he is writing for a non-Jewish audience. He is a brilliant storyteller and adept at making his stories sound like history. His detailed narrative of Jesus' birth and infancy led to suggestions that he got his information directly from Mary; a more plausible scenario is that he learned from some of the women he mentions in his Gospel: he pays more attention to the group who followed Jesus from Galilee to Jerusalem than do the other evangelists. He has, however, an overall theological scheme running through his writings, and "historical" incidents and portraits should be judged in the light of this. Central to this scheme is the importance of Jerusalem, from where the evangelization of the world must start. He builds up a long account (9:51–19:44) of Jesus' journey to Jerusalem to emphasize this. After Jesus' death, he situates Pentecost and the birth of the Church's missionary work in Jerusalem (Acts 2).

Writing outside Palestine and with a view to the acceptance of the new religion within the Roman Empire, he absolves the Roman authorities of blame for the crucifixion. He stresses Jesus' concern for the weaker elements in society—for women, sinners, outcasts—and he is kinder to the apostles when they misunderstand than Matthew is, for example. He gives a continuing place to the action of the Holy Spirit, from the Incarnation through Pentecost and continued guidance to the Church. He dwells on the importance of prayer in both Jesus' life and the lives of Christians. He gives prominence not only to the group of women who follow Jesus (8:1–3) from the early days of his preaching, but also to Mary from the Incarnation and infancy narratives to his mention of her being with the apostles at Pentecost (Acts 1:14), and he relates several other instances of Jesus' dealings with women: the widow of Nain, the woman "who was a sinner" (7:37), the woman in the crowd who blesses his mother, the women of Jerusalem on the road to Calvary. . . . (This does not make him a very early feminist, but it does seem to indicate that women may have been among his sources, and his Gospel provides more—often hidden—evidence of the radical nature of Jesus' association with women in the context of his age than do the others.) In Acts 4 he paints the famous picture of the apostle's sharing all things in common and providing for the needy from community funds. Whether this is an ideal or an actual picture, it does show Luke's concept of what following the "Way" of Jesus involves for the life of disciples. Of all the evangelists, he most stresses the need for detachment from material things and preaches what we would now call a spirituality of liberation.

He is the patron saint of the medical profession, since he is referred to as a physician. He is also the patron of painters, stemming from a long tradition that he painted an icon of the Virgin Mary, which later became a popular subject for painters. A more obscure patronage is that of butchers, perhaps derived from the fact that his evangelist's symbol is an ox, which may be based on his mention of temple sacrifice in his infancy narrative. Finally, he is the patron of notaries, on account of the careful detail in his writings. His supposed relics were taken from Thebes to Constantinople in the mid-fourth century.

There was not a needy person among them, for as many as owned lands or houses sold them and brought the proceeds of what was sold. They laid it at the apostles' feet, and it was distributed to each as any had need.
St Luke, Acts 4:34–5

19

The Proto-Martyrs of North America (Jean de Brébeuf, Isaac Jogues, Jean de la Lande, René Goupil, Gabriel Lalemant, Antoine Daniel, Charles Garnier, Noël Chabanel; died between 1642 and 1649)

These eight missionaries, six Jesuit priests and two helpers, brutally put to death, mainly by members of the Iroquois and Mohawk peoples, were canonized in 1930, and in 1969 their feast-day was fixed at 19 October and extended to the universal Church.

The first Jesuits to arrive in North America were Jean de Brébeuf and two companions, who landed in Quebec to help the Franciscan missionaries in the area in 1615: an earlier group had been driven back by English pirates. Brébeuf, trained in Rouen, seems to have suffered from tuberculosis yet was to survive thirty years of appalling physical hardships—travelling by canoe for hundreds of miles, bitten by fleas all night, choked by smoke in log cabins. He called these "minor martyrdoms" compared to the passion of Christ. He spent the first winter among the Algonquins, learning their language and customs, and was then sent into Huron territory, on the eastern shore of Lake Huron, where he had no success in making converts before the English drove him out and forced him to return to France. He went back to Canada in 1632 and joined Antoine Daniel in a second campaign to evangelize the Hurons. They knew the language and could understand the Huron religion, but progress was still slow and they realized that the way forward was to train young Hurons for the priesthood. Daniel took several back to Quebec to start a seminary.

Brébeuf was joined by five more Jesuits, including Isaac Jogues, from Orleans, and Charles Garnier, from Paris. The attitude of the Hurons changed: the Jesuits were invited to villages, listened to with respect, and carried out over two hundred Baptisms. Brébeuf was then transferred to Sainte-Marie, a French settlement and mission centre, with a fort, a hospital, and a cemetery. Gabriel Lalemant, the last of the martyred missionaries to reach Canada, took over his mission and a new one at Teanaustaye. The missionaries began to express desire for martyrdom—known from their letters sent back to France as part of the package of "Jesuit Relations," information about the mission designed to raise support and funds in France. Perhaps they saw this as the only way to give the missions a real boost. It came first to Isaac Jogues and his lay medical assistant René Goupil. They were seized by a group of Iroquois, sworn enemies of the Hurons, and horribly tortured. Goupil was hacked to death with tomahawks on 29 September 1642, but Jogues, with his fingers cut off, was kept as a slave, then rescued and returned to France. He was back in Canada in 1644, only to be enticed by Mohawks to a meal, seized, and beheaded on 18 October 1646. A new assistant, Jean de la Lande, died in the same way the following day.

The mission to the Hurons was now showing signs of success, but the Iroquois attacked Teanaustaye, where Antoine Daniel was in charge of the mission. He tried to get his converts to safety and pleaded with the attackers but was shot with arrows and thrown into the chapel, which was then set alight. He died on 4 July 1648. The following year the Iroquois captured Brébeuf and Lalemant and tortured them horribly before killing them on 16 and 17 March respectively. Later that year the Iroquois attacked the Tobacco nation, where Charles Garnier, the only priest with them at the time, was shot, then tomahawked to death on 7 December 1649. His companion Noël Chabanel was killed the following day by an apostasized Huron Christian who believed the missionaries had brought misfortune to his family.

These missionaries were men of their time in their views of "heathens," though more enlightened than some in their efforts to learn American Indian languages and at least something of their culture, if not to appreciate it. They were convinced of their cultural superiority as Europeans and Christians, but at the same time they saw the conversion of "pagan lands" as essential service to Christ and were prepared to share in his sufferings to a possibly unparalleled degree to play their part in achieving it.

How I grieve, my God, that you are not known, that this savage country is not yet wholly converted to faith in you, that sin is not yet blotted out.
Jean de Brébeuf, writing in his spiritual diary

20

St Paul of the Cross (Paolo Francesco Danei; 1694–1775)

The founder of the Passionists came from a noble but impoverished family from Genoa. As a young man he fought for a time against the Turks, but then he abandoned soldiering as a career and devoted himself to a solitary life of prayer. A vision of Christ's passion in 1720 inspired him with the idea of founding a religious Congregation devoted to the passion. He wrote a Constitution for this and with his brother John began accepting novices in 1725. Both brothers were ordained priest by Pope Benedict XIII two years later, and they established a first house in the mountains above Genoa.

From the start he aimed to combine meditation with practical work, which in the Passionists' case was to be preaching to the poor and ministering to the sick. The way of life he proposed was too austere for many of the novices, and eventually the pope persuaded him to modify the Rule, which then received papal approval in 1741. The concept prospered and there were three houses by 1747. The Rule and Constitution received final approval, with the privileges of a religious Order, in 1769. Its full title was Discalced Clerks of the Most Holy Cross and Passion of Our Lord Jesus Christ. Its members wore a black habit with a large badge bearing the motto *Jesu XPI Passio*. Paul, who was elected superior general in 1747, and his priests were soon in demand for preaching missions and retreats throughout Italy.

Their message was an exaltation of suffering and sorrow, which Paul, himself an ascetical theologian of distinction, equated with love. Bearing the image of Christ crucified was to be a visible way of life, not just a badge. Paul insisted on poverty above all: "The spirit of prayer, the spirit of solitude, and the spirit of poverty" were to be the qualities that would make his priests "shine before God and before the world." A contemplative at heart, Paul spent long hours in prayer, but he proved that this could be combined with an active ministry and, in his own case, with a significant body of spiritual writing. He produced a stream of letters, over two thousand of which have been published. Two key works were neglected or lost (or perhaps hidden from the Inquisition) for a long time after his death: a Diary written during a long retreat in 1720 was published only in 1964, and a work on "Mystical Death" in 1976. His letters are easy to read, simply and often humorously written. A further book of forty short meditations on the passion and death of Christ was directed at uneducated lay people. In 1765 the pope gave Paul (whose brother John had died) the basilica of SS John and Paul, and when the Congregation received its final approval in 1769, Paul spent most of his time in Rome. He founded a Congregation of enclosed nuns also devoted to meditation on the passion, gained a considerable reputation as a healer and miracle-worker, and died in October 1775. He was canonized in 1867.

The Passionists did not spread outside Italy until the mid-nineteenth century, first to Belgium in 1840, then to England in the following year, where they became a major force in preaching and ministering to the largely Irish immigrant workers in the industrialized areas of the north-west and Midlands, with Fr Dominic Barbieri as provincial superior. Overcoming taunts at his poor English and bedraggled appearance, and ridicule for his "hell-fire and repentance" preaching, he won respect by showing just the quality that Paul asked of his priests: an embodiment of the suffering Christ in his own person. His poverty was obvious to all, and yet somehow he was endlessly distributing alms. He became famous—infamous in many circles—when the outcome of a letter written by John Henry Newman to his friends became known: "Littlemore, October 8th, 1845. I am this night expecting Father Dominic, the Passionist, who ... has had little to do with conversions. ... He does not know of my intentions; but I mean to ask of him admission into the One Fold of Christ. ...." Barbieri received Newman into the Catholic Church that night. The Congregation spread to the United States in 1852 and has since spread to most European countries and to South America and Australia.

[Christ crucified] is the pattern of all that is gentle and attractive. ... Bury yourselves, therefore, in the heart of Jesus crucified, desiring nothing else but to lead all men to follow his will in all things.
St Paul of the Cross, in a letter

21

St Gerald Majella (1726–1755)

Gerald became famous in his lifetime as a "flying saint," much given to bilocation and ecstatic levitation (see also St Joseph of Copertino; 18 Sept.), and then after his death acquired—for no obvious reason—a growing cult as the patron saint of women in childbirth. In 1955, the second centenary of his death, this grew into a worldwide petition for his patronage to be extended to all women. The true nature of his holiness lies in rather more down-to-earth aspects of his short life.

He was born south of Naples and apprenticed to a tailor, which had been his father's trade, after his father died. He was treated badly by other workers and left. He then applied to join the Capuchins, but they rejected him on the grounds of his youth and delicate health. He became a servant in the household of the bishop of Lacedogna, but this proved to be a move from the frying pan into the fire, as the bishop had a foul temper and treated him worse than his co-workers had done. He returned home, lived with his mother and sisters, and worked as a tailor in the town. He gave away some two-thirds of the money he earned, while living an increasingly austere life and spending hours each night in prayer.

After attending a mission given by Redemptorist priests (see St Alphonsus de'Liguori; 1 Aug.) he applied to join them. After some hesitation because of his health, he was admitted as a lay brother in 1752, and put to work as gardener and then as sacristan. He was so self-effacing that it was said of him that he was "either a fool or a great saint." St Alphonsus recognized his qualities and, far from regarding him as a fool, shortened the period of his novitiate. He began working on missions with Redemptorist priests and soon showed an extraordinary gift for reading people's hearts, seeing their faults, and bringing them to repentance. He also worked as tailor and infirmarian for the community. His ecstatic trances and levitations (including one reported instance of being carried through the air for half a mile) became known, as did instances of bilocation, as when he was seen attending to a sick man in a cottage while talking to a friend in the monastery at the same time.

His reputation for holiness increased, so that he was appointed spiritual director to several communities of nuns, even though he was not an ordained priest. As his fame as a miracle-worker increased, people flocked to the monastery to see him in greater numbers than could be accommodated, so he was moved to another house. He worked there as porter, and it was said that only he knew where the food and clothes he found for beggars every day came from. He suffered from consumption and had only three years of religious life. He forecast the time of his death, toward midnight on the night of 15–16 October 1755. He was beatified in 1893, when Pope Leo XIII called him "one of those angelic youths whom God has given to the world as models," and canonized in 1904. His fame as "the greatest wonder-worker of the eighteenth century" (whatever the authenticity of many accounts) led to the production of a great many religious images of him. In some he is shown carrying a cross and a skull, and this, through an interesting process of syncretism, may be the explanation for the demand for him to be declared patron of women: a Central American Voodoo underworld figure who protects women in childbirth carries the same symbols. (Or perhaps he is simply the answer to every mother's problem—"I can't be expected to be in two places at the same time!")

22

St Philip Howard (1557–1595)

Philip was the eldest son of Thomas Howard, fourth duke of Norfolk, which made him heir of England's leading aristocratic family. His father abjured his Catholicism on Elizabeth's accession to the throne in 1558, so Philip was brought up as a Protestant, with no less a personage than John Knox, the founder of the Church of Scotland, as his tutor. The fourth duke then brought disgrace on the family in 1570 through his part in the plot devised by Roberto di Ridolfi to marry him to Mary, Queen of Scots, and depose Elizabeth from the throne. Ridolfi was abroad when the plot was discovered, but Thomas Howard was executed. Philip did not share in the blame attaching to his father and was made the ward of Lord Burghley, Elizabeth's chief minister, who sent him to Cambridge, where the tone of teaching was firmly Protestant. He graduated in

1576 and became a court favourite, with a reputation for high living. He succeeded his uncle as earl of Arundel in 1581, but Elizabeth never made him duke
of Norfolk.

When he was only twelve Philip had been married to Anne, the daughter of
Lord Dacre, but he had lived apart from her. In the early 1580s they came
together again. He began to take an interest in religious matters when he
attended an enforced disputation in 1581 between the Jesuit priest Edmund
Campion (see 1 Dec.), then in prison, and some Protestant theologians, in
which he felt that Campion had the better of the argument. Anne had been
brought up a Catholic and in 1582 was secretly reconciled to the Church. The
queen discovered this and placed her and Philip under house arrest; Philip
followed her into the Roman Catholic Church in 1584. By then laws against
Catholics were becoming more stringent, and Philip and Anne tried to escape
to the Continent. They were arrested by government agents at sea—leaving the
country without the queen's permission was an offence in itself—and Philip
was thrown into the Tower of London. He was tried on a charge of treason but
cleared: he was ordered to pay the then huge sum of £10,000 as a fine and to be
detained at the queen's pleasure. In 1589 he was again accused of treason, for
having prayed for the success of the Spanish Armada the previous year, but
the sentence was never carried out, and he died in the Tower after a long illness
in 1595.

He employed much of his time in prison (where conditions for someone of
his rank could be quite lenient) in writing hymns and meditations and translating devotional works, the best known being *The Epistle of Jesus Christ to the
Faithful Soul* by John of Landsberg (1489–1539). Published in Latin in 1555, this
quickly became one of the most popular of all works of devotion, and Philip
Howard's translation, first published clandestinely before his death, was widely
read in England for three hundred years. He made his condition harsher by
fasting three days a week and imposing on himself a rigorous regime of prayer
and penance. A great deprivation was not being allowed to see his wife or the
son conceived before his capture. He wrote to Anne shortly before he died,
begging her to forgive him for all the wrongs he had earlier done her and
assuring her that if had been allowed more time he would have been "as good
a husband … by [God's] grace, as you have found me bad before."

On the wall of the room in the Beauchamp tower in which he was imprisoned he scratched a crucifix and the words (in Latin), "The more suffering for
Christ in this world, so much the more glory with Christ in the next." These
can still be seen. He was beatified in 1929 and canonized as one of the Forty
Martyrs of England and Wales (see 25 Oct.) in 1970.

❖

What creature, O sweet Lord,
From praising thee can stay?
What earthly thing but, full of joy,
Thine honour doth bewray?
Let us, therefore, with praise
Thy mighty works express,
With heart and hand, with mind, and all
Which we from thee possess.
last verse of a hymn written by Philip Howard in the Tower

23

St John of Capistrano (1386–1456)

John was one of the leading figures in the Observant reform movement within the Franciscan Order, seeking a return to the primitive Rule. Born in the Abruzzi region of south-central Italy, he studied law at Perugia with such distinction that he was appointed governor of the city in 1412. He married a daughter of one of Perugia's leading families and was involved in the wars between cities endemic at the time. He was captured, and in captivity he seems to have had a vision of St Francis, who appealed to him to enter religious life. He was dispensed from the "impediment" of marriage (presumably with his wife's consent) and rode to a convent sitting backward on a donkey, inviting children to pelt him with muck as he passed. In this state he was admitted as a novice in 1414.

John studied under Bernardino of Siena (see 20 May), the great protagonist of Observant reform. At the Council of Constance in 1415 the Observants were granted the right to establish separate convents, with their own superiors, in all Franciscan provinces, giving the movement a great boost and largely destroying the hierarchical pattern of government that had developed when the opposing Conventual party was in the ascendant. The Conventuals resisted this, and in 1430 Pope Martin V convened a general chapter at Assisi and gave John the task of drawing up new Constitutions to restore unity to the Order. These were known as the *Martiniae* and were published as a Bull. They seemed to promise unity for a while by requiring substantial concessions from both parties, but the Conventuals proved unable to give up their privileges and revenues, while the Observants would not sacrifice their independent superiors, which were restored by the Council of Basle in 1434. The split extended to liturgical practice, with the Conventuals chanting the psalms and the Observants reciting them. John proposed a compromise whereby there was singing at Vespers and at the daily conventual Mass, with plain recitation at the other "hours" of the daily Office.

The Observants tended to live in small groups in remote places, but their vocation was not to be hermits. What kept them rooted in social activity was their dedication to preaching, and John became one of their most effective voices. He was also concerned with care of the sick, especially of lepers, and was involved in the foundation of the Hospital of Santa Maria della Scala and the Consortium of Charity in Milan. In 1451 Pope Nicholas V appointed him inquisitor general in Hungary and Bohemia, with a mission to convert or subject the Hussites (followers of John Hus, the Bohemian reformer burned at the stake at the Council of Constance) and other heretical groups. His methods were those of his time and would now be seen as brutal, though he seems to have been more enlightened than most on the subjects of witchcraft and the use of torture. The banner under which he preached was the Name of Jesus, which the Franciscan Observants did much to have incorporated into the liturgy with its own office. He was also a leader in promoting use of the Franciscan rosary of the "Seven Joys of Mary."

His mission in Hungary was brought to an end when the Turks captured Constantinople in 1453 and he was asked to preach a crusade to rally support against the Islamic threat. He preached with little success in Bavaria and Austria, then returned to Hungary, where the threat was more direct and he was more successful, even leading some troops himself to defend Belgrade and being largely responsible for the victory over Mohammed II in 1456. The battle, however, led to his death, as thousands of bodies were left unburied and he died in the resultant outbreak of disease. He was canonized in 1724, one of many fifteenth-century Observant Franciscans to be raised to the altars.

24

St Antony Mary Claret (Antonio Juan Claret i Clará; 1807–1870)

The founder of the Claretians or Congregation of Missionary Sons of the Immaculate Heart of Mary, to give them their full title, was born in Catalonia and entered the seminary at Vic after working as a weaver. He was ordained into the diocesan clergy in 1835 but longed to join a religious Order. He went to Rome to offer his services to the Congregation for the Propagation of the Faith as a missionary and became a Jesuit novice. His health forced him to leave the Society, and he returned to Spain, advised by his superiors to work for evangelization of his own country and furnished with the title of Apostolic Missionary to help him to do so.

He spent ten years preaching missions and giving retreats in Catalonia, then fifteen months in the Canary Islands. The mainstay of his preaching was devotion to the heart of Mary, and he set up many groups of parish women to further this work. In 1849 he founded the Congregation usually called after him, dedicated especially to this aim. A notable aspect of his mission was the use of the printed word, using the new techniques of powered printing presses to achieve mass diffusion of books, pamphlets, and leaflets. He had studied printing before entering the seminary and was able to oversee all aspects of production. He was mainly responsible for the Religious Library, a publishing enterprise that produced over five million books and booklets in twenty years.

In 1850 his life took a completely new turn when he was appointed arch-bishop of Santiago in Cuba. Despite his unwillingness to accept the post, once there he set about a vigorous reform of his archdiocese, which had been without a pastor for fifteen years. He added the name Mary at his consecration, taking her as "my Mother, my Protector, my Teacher." He visited all parts of his diocese three times in six years, establishing many new parishes, restoring the seminary, gaining a reputation for personal involvement in pastoral work at all levels—visiting hospitals, attending the sick and dying in earthquakes and epidemics. He was an initiator rather than an administrator, able to expend vast physical energy in setting up projects but then happier if others oversaw their further progress.

After seven years in Cuba he was recalled to become confessor to Queen Isabella II of Spain, involving a way of life at court completely alien to his restless nature. He found outlets for his energy when the court travelled around Spain: he preached, founded the Congregation of Catholic Mothers, and set up religious libraries in furtherance of his belief that the laity needed to be edu-cated in the faith. He became rector of the Royal Monastery of the Escorial, where he established a science laboratory, a museum of natural history, and music and language schools. He founded the Academy of St Michael, for writers and artists willing to pursue an active apostolate through writing and disseminating books and acting as a Christian elite in society. He wrote a second set of Constitutions for his Congregation, stressing catechetics, spiritual direction, and the training of seminarians. He imposed his own structure on his life at court, with long hours of prayer in addition to the Divine Office, fasting, and taking the discipline.

A liberal revolution forced Isabella off the throne in 1868. Already the object of anticlerical hostility, Antony went into exile with her. The Claretian houses in Spain were forced to close, and their occupants took refuge in France. He was in Rome for the First Vatican Council and was a strong supporter of papal infallibility. He suffered a stroke there, and his general health began to fail, although he recovered from the stroke. Spanish anticlericals prevented him from staying with his own priests in France, and he was obliged to take refuge with the Cistercians at Fontforoide, near Narbonne. He was accused of collecting weapons destined for the overthrow of the new Spanish government, but this could not be proved before his death on 24 October 1870. He was beatified in 1934 and canonized in 1950. The Claretians carry on his apostolate worldwide through publishing, a recent major venture being their *Christian Community Bible*, published in the Philippines in Spanish, Engish, Tagalog, and Chinese, which has sold many millions of copies, with revenues from licences in developed countries helping to subsidize sales in poor areas of the world.

25

The Forty Martyrs of England and Wales (died between 1535 and 1679)

The forty commemorated today are those canonized by Pope Paul VI in 1970. Larger groups have been beatified over the years, many in 1929 and the latest batch in 1987: these are all commemorated together on 4 May (when the first died, in 1535), but here today's date has been chosen for a brief overview of the history of persecution of Catholics in England and Wales from the time when Henry VIII was declared supreme head of the Church in England to the "Popish Plot" in the reign of Charles II. Each Church now proudly celebrates its own martyrs in a more ecumenical climate than in earlier times, and in a Roman Catholic book it is necessary to place on record the fact that more Protestants—some two hundred and eighty—were killed for their faith under the five-year reign of Mary Tudor (1553–8) than were Catholics during the long reign of Elizabeth I (1558–1603). They have their own tributes, most famously in "Foxe's Book of Martyrs."

In 1534 the Act of Supremacy was passed by Parliament, declaring that Henry was "the only Supreme Head on earth of the Church in England," and it became high treason to deny this. Three Carthusian monks were executed the following year at Tyburn in London for refusing to comply. Although Protestantism of an evangelical stamp increased its hold during the reign of Edward VI (1547–53) there were no executions of those faithful to the "old religion," and then it was the turn of Protestants, mostly lay people living in and around London, to suffer under Mary Tudor. The first acts of Elizabeth's reign restored the sovereign as head of the Church in England, but persecution did not become severe until the government's hand was forced by the Northern Rebellion of 1569, aimed at restoring Catholicism; the excommunication of Elizabeth by Pope Pius V (see 1 May), which had the unfortunate effect of making all Catholics technically traitors; and the Ridolfi Plot of 1571, aimed at deposing Elizabeth (see St Philip Howard; 22 Oct.). Subsequent acts made it treasonable to be a priest in England ordained abroad and to shelter or help any priest. Most of the one hundred and ninety who suffered martyrdom between 1570 and 1603 were caught by these laws, including twenty of today's forty. The Spanish Armada in 1588, which Catholics were suspected of supporting, though most of them certainly did not, further increased the tempo of persecution.

During this period, colleges for training priests were established on the Continent, at Douai in northern France and also in Rome, Valladolid, and Seville. These sent some four hundred priests on the "English mission," and these "seminary priests" were the main target of legislation. From 1580 Jesuits also began to make their appearance and quickly became the most hated and feared of all. They were singled out in the 1585 "Act against Jesuits, Seminary Priests and other Suchlike Disobedient Persons," which ordered any priests ordained abroad after 1559 to leave the country within four weeks or be prosecuted for treason. Most declined to leave, and one hundred and twenty-three of the one hundred and forty-six persons condemned between the passing of this act and the end of Elizabeth's reign suffered on account of it. Most of the priests were not traitors in any real sense of the term, seeing the restoration of the old religion as necessary for the well-being of their country, but the government could not make distinction between them and those on the Continent, including Philip II of Spain and several popes, who were working for the overthrow of Elizabeth.

Throughout the first half of the seventeenth century, under James I and Charles I, and then under the Commonwealth, persecution was more sporadic, with a total of thirty-seven deaths before 1660. There was a final outbreak under Charles II as a result of the "Popish Plot" concocted by Titus Oates (see 20 June), which produced a national outbreak of anti-Catholic feeling and led to eighteen people being martyred in 1679 and three more the following year. After that, with the exception of the execution of the Irish archbishop Oliver Plunkett (see 1 July) at Tyburn in 1681, persecution became a matter of taxation and discrimination, enforced less strictly as time wore on, so that Catholicism increased in strength during the eighteenth century, paving the way for the Catholic Emancipation Act of 1829 and the restoration of the hierarchy and the end of most forms of discrimination (though some remain).

Veneration of the martyrs began early as private devotion but received official sanction when portraits of them were added to those of earlier martyrs, from St Alban onward, on the walls of the English College in Rome in the late sixteenth century. Three hundred years later, Cardinal Manning sent a list of three hundred and sixty names to Rome for possible beatification. Leo XIII examined these and decided that fifty-four had already been "equipollently" beatified by Gregory XIII (1572–85); a further one hundred and thirty-six were beatified in 1929, Manning's original list having been added to in the meantime; eighty-five more were beatified in 1987. The forty singled out for canonization, in a campaign started by Cardinal Godfrey of Westminster in 1960, were all well known, already beatified, and the object of devotion. The list excludes the best known of all English martyrs, John Fisher and Thomas More (see 22 June), as they had been canonized in 1935. The forty names, grouped by the year of their death, are given below.

1535	4 May	John Houghton, Robert Lawrence, Augustine Webster
	11 May	Richard Reynolds
1539	12 May	John Stone
1577	30 Nov.	Cuthbert Mayne
1581	1 Dec.	Alexander Briant, Edmund Campion, Ralph Sherwin
1582	2 Apr.	John Paine
	30 May	Luke Kirby
1584	15 Oct.	Richard Gwynn
1586	25 Mar.	Margaret Clitherow
1588	30 Aug.	Margaret Ward
1591	10 Dec.	Edmund Gennings, Polydore Plasden, Swithun Wells, Eustace White
1594	24 July	John Boste,
1595	21 Feb.	Robert Southwell
	7 Apr.	Henry Walpole
	19 Oct.	Philip Howard
1598	12 July	John Jones
1600	21 June	John Rigby
1601	27 Feb.	Anne Line
1606	22 Mar.	Nicholas Owen
1608	23 June	Thomas Garnet
1610	10 Dec.	John Roberts
1612	3 Dec.	John Almond
1628	28 Aug.	Edmund Arrowsmith
1641	10 Sept.	Ambrose Barlow
1642	21 Jan.	Alban Roe
1645	1 Feb.	Henry Morse
1654	28 June	John Southworth
1679	19 July	John Plessington
	22 July	Philip Evans, John Lloyd
	22 Aug.	John Kemble
	26 Aug.	John Wall
	27 Aug.	David Lewis

❖

The martyr tradition is one in which all have shared and from which all may draw strength, even across ecumenical boundaries.

British Council of Churches, on the occasion of the canonization of the Forty Martyrs in 1970

26

St Cedd (died 664)

Virtually all that we know about St Chad's (see 2 Mar.) brother Cedd comes, as usual for England in this period, from Bede's *Ecclesiastical History of the English People*. He was a monk at Lindisfarne (see St Aidan; 31 Aug.) for some years and was sent, with three others, to evangelize the Middle Angles when their king, Peada, became a Christian after King Oswy of Northumbria had told him he could not marry his daughter unless he did so. Oswy then persuaded King Sigbert of the East Saxons that gods made of wood or metal were no match for the ruler of the world and universal dispenser of justice, and he too became a Christian and asked for priests to teach his people. Oswy sent Cedd and one other from the Midlands to what is now Essex. They preached and baptized, and then Cedd returned to Lindisfarne to report to the bishop, St Finan, who was so impressed by the reports Cedd gave him that he summoned two other bishops and consecrated him bishop of the East Saxons.

Cedd returned to what was now his diocese and "used his increased authority to promote the work already done." He built churches and ordained priests and deacons to carry out the work of preaching and baptizing. He established communities in minster churches at Bradwell-on-Sea (where the church, built on the Roman basilica plan, survives in modified form) and at Tilbury, on the Thames Estuary, teaching his priests there "to maintain the discipline of the regular life so far as these untutored folk were then capable of doing." He excommunicated a nobleman for contracting an illicit marriage and forbade anyone to enter his house. The king disobeyed him and accepted an invitation to a feast. Cedd met him as he was leaving the house, touched the king, who had fallen at his feet and begged forgiveness, with his staff, and told him that the house would prove to be the place of his death. The king was later murdered by his own kinsmen, apparently for being too Christian in forgiving his enemies, a death that Bede believes "atoned for his earlier offence and increased his merits."

Cedd returned often to Northumbria to preach, and on one of his visits the king of the southern part (now Yorkshire) granted him a piece of land on which to found a monastery where he could come to pray and where he would be buried, thus assuring himself of the prayers of many holy men for his salvation. Cedd chose a place in the wild hills of the North Yorkshire moors, at Lastingham, near Whitby, and dedicated it according to Lindisfarne custom by spending Lent there fasting. Ten days before the end of Lent he was summoned away by the king and so asked his brother, a priest named Cynibil, to complete the fast for him, which he willingly did. The monastery was founded in 658 and the monks followed the Rule observed at Lindisfarne. It was later destroyed by Danish invaders.

He was present at the Synod of Whitby, supporting the "Irish" (or Celtic) cause, together with St Hilda of Whitby (29 Oct.), but acting as "a most careful intepreter for both parties at the council." He was persuaded, it seems, by the claims of the Roman (or Catholic) party and went back to his diocese "having abandoned the Irish customs and accepted the Catholic." He then returned to Lastingham, where he died on 26 October 664 during a plague epidemic sweeping northern England. He was buried first in the open, but then a stone church was built and his body was interred to the right of the altar. He bequeathed the abbacy to his brother Chad. When his Essex monks heard of his death, about thirty of them went to Lastingham seeking "either, God willing, to live near the body of their Father, or else to die and be laid to rest at his side." Their wish was granted in the latter form, as they all died in the same outbreak of plague. Cedd's relics were later venerated at Lichfield, where Chad had been bishop. Of four brothers, all had been priests and two bishops, "a rare occurrence in one family," as Bede remarks.

27

Bd Louis Guanella (1842–1915)

Born near Lake Como in northern Italy, Louis was at school for six years with the Somaschi fathers in the town of Como before entering the diocesan seminary. He was ordained in 1866 and put in charge of a parish, where he built an elementary school and started to teach, besides organizing a branch of Young Catholic Action and various charitable works for the poor. This was a period of widespread anticlericalism in Italy, in which the Freemasons played a prominent and powerful role. They objected to all this social work being done by a churchman and had him blacklisted by the government, which meant that he could not be a parish priest.

In 1875 he went to Turin to work with St John Bosco (31 Jan.) and joined his Congregation; three years later he obeyed his bishop's order to return to his diocese. He opened one school for poor children but again had to close it because of opposition from the Freemasons. The civil authorities moved him to a tiny parish in the mountains, where he found an orphanage and a hospice, recently founded by a priest who had previously been a revolutionary in 1848 and then secretary to Garibaldi's collaborator Giuseppe Mazzini. He joined enthusiastically in the work involved and, together with Sister Marcellina

Bosatta, one of the original nuns there, organized a transfer to Como, where they could serve more people. By 1890 the hospice was caring for over two hundred elderly and sick people. To ensure continuity, Louis formed a Congregation of religious Sisters. Known as the Daughters of Mary of Providence, they received formal approval from the Holy See in 1917. Louis insisted that care must be given to those in dire need "without exceptions": these included disabled, sick, and poor people, and also victims of natural disasters, such as major earthquakes in 1905, 1908, and 1915, when he, aged seventy-three, went to help survivors.

Men too came to join in the work, and in 1908 he formed another Congregation for them, the Servants of Charity, taking religious vows with its first members. He was a great admirer of his near contemporary Fr John Baptist Scalabrini (beatified in 1997; see 1 June), with whom he had served as prefect of discipline at the seminary, and of his mission to Italian immigrants in the United States. He sent one of his first priests to help in Scalabrini's mission, and in 1912 he went there himself to see the situation at first-hand. In 1913 he organized a worldwide crusade of prayer for the dying, for which he established the Archconfraternity of St Joseph for the Dying, which grew to have some ten million members in the 1960s.

Charitable work formed only part of his boundless ideas and initiatives. He also opened day, evening, and vocational schools; he took a particular interest in preparing young people for the world of work; he helped with a plan to drain the malarial Spagna Plain; he sent members of his Congregation into Switzerland to preach missions to the Protestant population of the southern valleys; he wrote books of history and social commentary as well as some short devotional works. During the First World War he worked for the wounded, for which he was awarded a gold medal by the authorities in Como. After suffering a stroke, he died in Como on 24 October 1915. His cause was introduced in 1939 and he was beatified by Pope Paul VI in 1964. His Congregations now work in nineteen countries throughout the world, caring for the disabled, sick, and needy of all sorts.

28

SS Simon and Jude (First Century)

Very little is known about these two apostles, traditionally celebrated together in the West, though they have separate feast-days in the East.

Simon is called "the Cananaean" (or Canaanite) in the list of the apostles' names in Matthew 10:4 and Mark 3:18. In Luke's corresponding list (6:15) he "was called the Zealot": both terms could mean that he was a member of the sect that later rose up against the Romans, leading to the destruction of Jerusalem in AD 70. He is also referred to as "Simon the less," to distinguish him from Simon Peter. Apart from being named as one of the twelve, he plays no special part in the New Testament.

Jude is usually taken to be the Thaddeus in the lists given by Matthew and Mark. His name can also be Judas, and he is differentiated from Judas Iscariot, "who became a traitor," by Luke, who calls him "Judas son of James" (some translations have "Judas of James," which could indicate a brother). John calls him "Judas (not Iscariot)" (14:22) in his account of Jesus' discourse after the Last Supper, when Jude asks him, "Lord, how is it that you will reveal yourself to us, and not to the world?," to which Jesus replies, "Those who love me will keep my word, and my Father will love them, and we will come to them and make our home with them" (14:23). The Epistle of Jude claims to be written by "a servant of Jesus Christ and brother of James," but it makes no claim to direct apostolic authority: it refers to the apostles in the past—"they said to you" (v. 18)—and is now thought to have been written possibly in the last decade of the first century.

Neither appears after Pentecost, so there is nothing but tradition and legend on which to base any account of their later lives, and these vary. In the East, Simon is said to have died a peaceful death at Edessa; in the West he is supposed to have preached in Egypt, then gone with Jude, who had been working in Mesopotamia, to Persia, where they were both martyred together. They were venerated before this account became current in the sixth century. Not surprisingly, their relics are claimed by several places: Rome, Toulouse, and Reims. Simon's emblem contains a fish, and Jude's a boat, and artistic representations often show both with a fish, this reflecting the assumption that they were fishermen in Galilee when Jesus called them to follow him.

29

St Hilda of Whitby (614–680)

"The Life and death of Abbess Hilda" forms the subject matter of Chapter 23 of Bede's fourth Book in his *Ecclesiastical History*, which is the principal source of information about her. Her life, he says, fell into two equal halves, thirty-three years spent "most nobly in secular occupations" and thirty-three dedicated "even more nobly to our Lord in the monastic life."

She was the daughter of King Hereric, a nephew of Edwin of Northumbria, and was baptized, together with Edwin, by Archishop Paulinus of York, when she was thirteen. Bede provides no details of the next twenty years of her life, before she decided to become a nun. She then went to East Anglia, where a cousin was king, intending to sail from there to Gaul, to learn the monastic life at Chelles, where her sister Hereswitha was a member of the community. She spent a year in East Anglia, and was then summoned back north by Aidan, bishop of Lindisfarne (see 31 Aug.), who, evidently unwilling to lose her from his province, gave her a plot of land on the north bank of the river Wear, where she gathered some companions and "observed the monastic life" for a year.

She was then elected abbess of the monastery at Hartlepool, which the previous abbess, Heiu, had left to move to Tadcaster. Hilda worked to establish a regular way of life there. It was a double monastery, with monks and nuns coming together for choral liturgy but otherwise living separately; this was a fairly common arrangement at the time, under the general control of an abbess, who was usually of noble birth. She "followed the instructions of learned men" in establishing a Rule, which was probably an Irish form based on that of St Columbanus (see 24 Nov.). After some years at Hartlepool she established another double monastery on the coast of Yorkshire at Streanaeshalch (meaning "bay of the beacon"), modern-day Whitby. She applied the same Rule there (this being before the Rule of St Benedict was in general use), and Bede finds it worth commenting that its effect was to mirror the life of the early communities, so that "no one was rich, no one was needy, and nothing was considered to be anyone's personal property." Hilda remained abbess there for the rest of her life.

She encouraged study of Latin and of the scriptures, as well as charitable works: five of Whitby's monks went on to become bishops—"all of them men of outstanding merit and holiness," according to Bede. It was probably owing to the prestige of the abbey that it was chosen as the site for the Synod of Whitby in 663/4. Hilda, brought up in the Celtic tradition, acquiesced in the decision, promoted by one of "her" five bishops, Wilfrid (see 24 Apr.), to adopt the Roman date of Easter and other customs, but fifteen years later she agreed with the decision to divide Wilfrid's huge diocese into three (two parts going to two other bishops also trained at Whitby), so she may not entirely have forgiven him.

She was generally known as "Mother" on account of her "wonderful devotion and grace," and her influence spread far and wide. Kings and others came to seek her advice, and knowledge of her became an inspiration to others living at a distance. For the last seven years of her life she was seriously ill, racked with what Bede calls a "burning fever," but she did not allow this to interfere with her activities, until in the final year "the pain passed into her innermost parts." She made her last Communion and instructed all her nuns to keep the peace of the gospel among themselves and with others. The date of her death was probably 17 November 680. Bede tells how a devout nun named Begu, in a monastery Hilda had founded, thirteen miles from Whitby, had a vision in which she heard a passing bell and saw Hilda's soul being carried up to heaven surrounded by angels. She summoned all her companions to gather in choir to pray at the very time of her death.

The original abbey at Whitby was destroyed by Danish raiders in the eighth century, refounded in the eleventh, rebuilt in the thirteenth in Gothic style, and dissolved by Henry VIII in the 1530s. Considerable ruins of the church remain, providing a prominent landmark for sailors.

30

St Winifred (Gwenfrewi; possibly Seventh Century)

The only surviving accounts of Winifred, the Welsh saint most widely venerated outside Wales (described as English, to Welsh fury, in Cardinal Baronius' original Roman Martyrology of 1584) date from some five hundred years after her death, supposedly in about 650. They work back from the famous spring associated with her, and their central element is her death at the hands of a would-be husband and resuscitation by her uncle, St Beuno.

The story is that she was the only child of a noble and wealthy family in Clwyd and was educated (rare for a girl at the time), possibly by Beuno, who was her mother's brother. Her father, in need of a male heir, wanted her to marry, and she was courted by a young chieftain named Caradoc. To put him off, she rather unwisely told him she was engaged to another man (possibly meaning Christ?) and fled to her uncle's oratory. Before she could enter it, Caradoc galloped up behind her and cut off her head. Beuno came out, cursed Caradoc, who melted like wax, and placed Winifred's head back on her body and prayed; her soul returned, and only a thin scar showed at her neck. Where her head had fallen, a stream sprang from the ground. Beuno gave her his oratory, where she became abbess over eleven other virgins who came to join her. She later joined a nunnery at Gwytherin, became abbess there, and died fifteen years after her miraculous reheading. (Another version has her going to Rome, but this seems to have been written in support of an argument about hermits and communities.)

Her supposed relics were enshrined at Gwytherin and transferred with great ceremony to Shrewsbury Abbey in 1138. In 1348 her feast was decreed to be observed (on the traditional date of her beheading, 22 June) in the diocese of Canterbury, about the same time as she first appears in Welsh calendars. There is no doubt that St Winifred's Well—at Holywell in English, *Tre Ffynnon* in Welsh—is the most venerated of many "miraculous" springs in Celtic sites, with cures reported continuously from the early Middle Ages to the present. King Henry V visited it to give thanks after the battle of Agincourt in 1415; King Henry VII's mother, Lady Margaret Beaufort, and a group of Welsh nobles were responsible for the buildings that enclose it; in 1629, after nearly a century of discouragement of veneration of saints, fourteen thousand pilgrims were reported there on her feast-day. The Jesuit mission named after St Beuno was already established there during penal times; it was handed over to the diocesan authorities in the 1930s. The well was of sufficient importance for mining activities in the area in 1917 to be referred to Parliament, which imposed restrictions in case these caused the spring to run dry. They did, but fortunately another underground supply was found, and the water still flows. There is a stone mentioned in 1729 as being Winifred's gravestone in the church at Gwytherin, and in 1991 a section of an oak reliquary for her remains, dating from about the ninth century, was discovered there. Gerard Manley Hopkins (see also next entry), who was at St Beuno's in the 1870s, began a verse drama on her but completed only fragments. He also produced a short poem celebrating the fact that water from the spring not only worked miraculous cures but also produced water for baths and for turning a mill.

31

St Alphonsus Rodríguez (about 1533–1617)

Born into a well-to-do wool merchant's family in Segovia, north of Madrid, Alphonsus spent nearly forty years trying and failing to make a success of life "in the world" and the remainder of his relatively long life as a Jesuit, most in the humble position of door-keeper but acquiring widespread respect for the quality of his spiritual life and the counselling that he was able to give from his inner resources.

He was given his first Communion by the Jesuit Peter Favre, who was preaching a mission in Segovia and stayed at his parents' house. He went to study at the Jesuit school in Alcalá but had to return home after only a year when his father died and he was needed to help his mother run the family business. She retired when he was twenty-three, leaving him in charge of it, but he could not make it prosper. He married María Suarez, but then she, their young daughter, and his mother all died within a space of three years, leaving him questioning the purpose of his life. He sold the business and moved in with his two devout unmarried sisters, who introduced him to the habit of regular prayer and meditation. Some years later, his son died, and he applied to join the Jesuits. They rejected him as being too old at nearly forty and insufficiently educated. He set himself to learn Latin and tried again. This time the provincial appreciated at least his determination and admitted him as a lay brother in 1571. Six months later he was sent to the college of Montesión in Majorca, where he was appointed door-keeper, a position he kept for the remaining forty-five years of his life.

He spent the time not occupied by his duties in prayer, forcing himself to carry out regular spiritual exercises even in periods of spiritual aridity and desolation, trusting that God would bring him comfort. Some reward came when he was allowed to take his final vows in 1585. His quiet, constant, determined spiritual quest became well known; priests and lay people began coming to him for advice, and he was made spiritual director of students at the college, including Peter Claver (see 9 Sept.), whom he advised to go to America on the mission that made him "saint of the slaves." He produced some short, simple works of spiritual advice, but he was not the composer of the Little Office of the Immaculate Conception often attributed to him on account of his deep devotion to the Immaculate Conception.

His health eventually declined, and his last years were spent in considerable pain. He died just after midnight on 31 October 1617. His funeral was attended by crowds of poor and high-ranking people, and sixteen years later he was declared patron of Majorca, in a gesture of canonization by popular acclaim. This preceded his official canonization by some two hundred and fifty years; it came in 1888, in the same ceremony as that of Peter Claver. The occasion inspired another Jesuit who suffered agonies of spiritual desolation, the poet Gerard Manley Hopkins (who died the following year), to compose his sonnet "In honour of St Alphonsus Rodriguez," in which he expresses the truth that a "hidden" life of humble activity is as significant before God as lives filled with glorious exploits. Its final sextet reads:

Yet God (that hews mountain and continent,
Earth, all, out; who, with trickling increment,
Veins violets and tall trees makes more and more)

Could crowd career with conquest while there went
Those years and years by of world without event
That in Majorca Alfonso watched the door.

Other Familiar English Names for October

1. Christopher, Edward, Gerald, John, Ralph, Robert
2. Andrew, Antony, Francis, George, Louis
3. Gerard, Luke, Paul, Peter
4. *There are no other familiar English names for today*
5. Anne, John, William, Mary, Matthew, Peter, Robert
6. Francis, Joseph, Mary
7. John, Mark, Martin
8. Felix, Hugh, John, Robert
9. Bernard, Cyril, Louis
10. Daniel, John, Samuel, Sophia
11. Alexander, Bruno, James, Kenneth, Mary
12. Thomas
13. Gerald, Gerard, Luke
14. Dominic, James
15. *There are no other familiar English names for today*
16. Gerard
17. Gilbert, James, John, Mary, Peter, Richard
18. Paul, Peter
19. Luke, Matthew, Philip, Thomas
20. Andrew, James, Mary
21. Peter
22. Benedict, Mark,
23. Arnold, Benedict, Gregory, John, Josephine, Mary, Paul, Thomas
24. Joseph, Louis, Martin
25. Bernard, Hilary
26. Damian
27. *There are no familiar English names for today*
28. Francis, John, Roderick, Vincent
29. James
30. Claude, Gerard, John, Terence
31. Christopher, Dominic, Thomas

NOVEMBER

The calendar for November presents a number of days with two or more saints in the Universal Calendar and several others with more than one major figure. This has resulted in the following date changes: Bd Joan de Maillé moves back one day, from the 6th to the 5th; Bd Eugene Bossilkov, beatified in 1998, has an entry on the 13th, two days after his actual date of death; St Hugh of Lincoln leaves the 17th to St Elizabeth of Hungary and moves forward two days; St Edmund of Abingdon gives way to royalty in the person of St Margaret of Scotland on the 16th and moves to the 20th; St Columbanus and Bd Michael Pro, who share the 23rd with St Clement, are moved on one and two days respectively; St Cuthbert Mayne is brought forward from the feast of St Andrew on the 30th to the 27th, and other English martyrs who died in November are mentioned with him; finally, the first martyrs in Latin America to be beatified, St Roque González and Companions, are moved from the 15th to the 28th.

1

The Solemnity of All Saints

On this day the Church venerates all those, known and unknown, whose virtues and efforts in this life are considered to have earned them an eternal reward with God. In doing so, we, the Church on earth, traditionally give thanks for their lives, consider their example and strive to emulate them, ask for their intercession in the trials of this life, and glorify God through the multitude that have gone before us, remembering that we too are all called to be saints. Veneration given to saints is giving glory to God in them and through them; their graces are God's gifts to them, and their example is our hope. This feast also reminds us that great saints, who have their own feast-days, like lesser ones who have not, have come from all states and walks of life: clergy and lay, married and single, humble and mighty. If in past centuries emphasis seems to have been placed on members of religious communities, this is not surprising, since those communities were the chief keepers of society's records as well as its conscience. Today, beatifications and canonizations are of people from a greater variety of backgrounds and countries, and it is possible to form a more comprehensive view of what constitutes the universal holiness of the

Church, "distinguished by the eminent holiness of so many thousands of its members," in the words of the once-familiar Catechism.

In the early centuries, martyrs alone were venerated as saints, and a feast of "the martyrs of all the earth" was celebrated in Edessa and elsewhere in Syria by the middle of the fourth century. Its usual date was the first Sunday after Pentecost—our Trinity Sunday. In the West, the origin seems to have been later, possibly traceable to 13 May 610, when the Pantheon in Rome, given by the emperor to Pope Boniface IV for use as a church, was dedicated to "St Mary and all the Martyrs." Toward the middle of the eighth century, a chapel in St Peter's basilica was dedicated to Christ, the Virgin Mary, and all the saints. All the saints of Europe were celebrated on 20 April, with all the saints of Africa on 23 December. The first mention of 1 November seems to come from England in the eighth century, and by 799 Alcuin of York, then in France as abbot of Tours, could write of his "most solemn" celebration of All Saints, which he held on 1 November, preceded by a three-day fast. In this case, Rome seems to have followed the practice observed in England and France.

The date was formally fixed as 1 November by Pope Gregory IV (827–44), who moved it from May on the practical grounds that Rome in summer could not accommodate the great number of pilgrims who flocked to it. ("Roman fever" was a great killer in the hot summers, and there may have been public health considerations affecting the decision.) By the twelfth century, the date was generally fixed throughout the Western Church. Its traditional English name, All Hallows, produced the festival of Halloween, All Hallows' Eve, which has acquired a connection with ghosts more appropriate to tomorrow's commemoration of all the faithful departed.

2

Commemoration of All Souls

The belief that prayers offered and rituals performed for the dead can somehow affect their fate in "the next world," however that is conceived, is universal in human culture, and the fact of death is surrounded and dignified with ritual everywhere. For Christians this is not a day of grief and mourning but of hope and prayer that God will deliver all those who may still be suffering in some form and bring them to everlasting happiness.

The belief in some form of resurrection for everyone—a denial of the ultimate power of death over life—takes various forms. It evolved, though not in any systematic fashion, in Old Testament times, and receives its fullest pre-Christian expression in 2 Maccabees 12:44–5, where it is said of Judas Maccabeus that if he were not expecting that those who had fallen would rise again, it would have been superfluous and foolish to pray for the dead. But if he was looking to the splendid reward that is laid up for those who fall asleep in godliness, it was a holy and pious thought. Therefore he made atonement for the dead, that they might be delivered from their sin.

The idea that all the dead, not only those classed as "saints," should have a day devoted to prayer for them developed out of the doctrine of purgatory, the intermediate state when the souls of the dead had not reached a final destination and could be supposed to be open to help from those still on earth. Two great monasteries, Saint-Gall and Reichenau, made an agreement in about 800 to pray for each other's dead, who might have "pass[ed] out of this world without at once being admitted into the company of the blessed," on 14 November each year. Then in 998 St Odilo of Cluny (see 1 Jan.) directed his congregation to set aside the day immediately following All Saints for prayer for the dead, since it seemed "desirable that at Cluny they [the monks] should also keep with joyous affection the memory of the faithful departed who have lived from the beginning of the world until the end." The idea spread rapidly, if sporadically, owing to the influence of Cluny, though without any official endorsement. Within some thirty years of Odilo's death, Archbishop Lanfranc of Canterbury was instructing his monks to observe a solemn commemoration of all the dead on 2 November, but later Canterbury calendars do not mention it.

It became extremely popular in Spain, where the custom of saying three Masses was introduced by the Dominicans in Valencia in the early fifteenth century, in response to demand. From Spain it spread to the New World, where it chimed with the veneration given to ancestors in pre-Colombian religion, and the *día de los muertos*, the day of the dead, has remained a key feature of popular Catholicism, especially in Mexico, with many families spending the night in vigil, with lights, food, and drink, alongside their dead in the cemeteries. It was first officially made a feast for the whole of Spain, in 1748, and was not extended to the universal Church until 10 August 1915, when the vast numbers of dead in the First World War gave it a special poignancy, as Pope Benedict XV recognized in his Apostolic Constitution extending the privilege of having three Masses (otherwise reserved to Christmas Day only). The hymn *Dies irae, dies illa* ("A day of wrath that day will be"), referring to the Last Judgment, sung or said at today's Masses, has been attributed to Thomas of Celano, St Francis' biographer; the attribution is not certain, but it is probably Franciscan in origin and was in existence by the thirteenth century.

❖

When this perishable body puts on imperishability, and this mortal body puts on immortality, then the saying that is written will be fulfilled:
"Death has been swallowed up in victory."
"Where, O death, is your victory?
Where, O death, is your sting?"
1 Corinthians 15:54–5

3

St Martin de Porres (1575–1639)

Martin, the natural-born son of a Spanish father, Don Juan de Porres, and a freed black slave from Panama, was born in Lima. By the time he was born, over forty years since the Spanish conquest of Peru, society in Lima was stratified and hierarchical. Martin had inherited his mother's African features, and his father disowned him, though he did take him and his sister to Ecuador with him to be educated. He was then appointed governor of Panama and sent both children back to their mother.

In Lima Martin was apprenticed to a barber surgeon from whom he received a grounding in current medical knowledge. His mother was a practitioner of herbal medicine, so he acquired knowledge of this as well. Both were to stand him in good stead. He joined the Third Order of St Dominic and was accepted as a lay brother, performing menial tasks in return for board. "Indians, blacks, and their descendants" were at the time barred from becoming full members of religious Orders. The prior of the convent of the Holy Rosary was prepared to make an exception in Martin's case, but he, always conscious of his status as a "poor *mulatto*," refused the offer. He did eventually become a lay brother in 1603, when he was twenty-eight.

He flung himself into all possible works of practical charity: he was "barber, surgeon, wardrobe-keeper, and infirmarian," according to a witness speaking at the early stages of his beatification process, who said that each of these jobs was enough for any one man but that Martin managed them all "with great generosity, promptness, and attention to detail," attributable only to "the effects of divine grace." His dual healing tradition helped him to accomplish some remarkable cures, and he was soon spoken of as a miracle-worker. He extended his work beyond the community into the city, where he helped to establish an orphanage and foundling hospital. He was entrusted with distributing food from the convent to the poor, and this appeared to multiply miraculously. He cared for African slaves, who had been imported into Peru since 1538 and made to carry out heavy work in dreadful conditions. His love extended to all creatures, so that he became known as the St Francis of the Americas.

He was so successful in collecting money that he raised enough to give a niece a dowry in three days, during which he collected at least as much again for the poor. He provided for the most detailed needs of all in his care. When the priory got into debt, he offered himself—as only a poor *mulatto* and the property of the Order—in payment. He longed to be sent overseas on a mission where he could become a martyr, but his racial background and the structure of the Church at the time made this impossible, so he martyred his own body with rigorous penances—which added to his reputation for supernatural powers.

Despite the prejudices of society, all ranks, including prelates and nobles, turned out to carry him to his grave when he died at the age of sixty-three, on 3 November 1639. He had become everyone's saint. Notwithstanding this and the impressive testimony given by his brother Dominicans at the inquiry into his holiness, he was not beatified until 1837 and then waited over a hundred years more—until 1962, the opening year of the Second Vatican Council and what has been called the new "universal" age in the Church—for canonization. He had already been declared the patron of all work for justice, by Pius XII, at the request of the Peruvian hierarchy, in 1935. Thirty years later Paul VI approved him as patron of public education in Peru: the bishops envisaged mass catechesis through television, so he also became the patron of Peruvian television. In 1982 Pope John Paul II added patronage of the public health services of Peru, and he has also been taken as patron of all persons of mixed race. The development of the functions of a "barber" into hairdressing earned him the patronage of Italian barbers and hairdressers in 1966, and his work for social justice caused him to be declared patron of the Spanish "national syndicate for various trades" (a Franco-approved term for a General Workers' Union) in 1973. One way and another, the all-embracing charity of the first *mulatto* saint of the Church is sure to be remembered.

4

St Charles Borromeo (Carlo Borromeo; 1538–1584)

Born into a distinguished family in northern Italy, Charles was to pack an astonishing amount into a short life of forty-six years, becoming one of the chief architects, in theory and in practice, of the Catholic Reformation that took shape around the Council of Trent. He was extremely intelligent but suffered from a speech impediment that sometimes obscured this. He pursued a career that destined him for high position in the Church but used this to work for others, leading an austere life himself. He was given effective lordship of a Benedictine abbey when he was still a boy but insisted that its revenues (administered on his behalf by his father, Count Gilberto Borromeo) were the patrimony of the poor, not a source of personal wealth.

After he had studied in Milan and Pavia and gained a doctorate in 1559, he suddenly found himself pitched into the heart of the Vatican when his mother's brother was elected pope as Pius IV and he became the pope's favorite nephew. Still in minor Orders, he was made a cardinal at the age of twenty-two, then appointed administrator of the archdiocese of Milan. Next, in giddying succession, he was made the pope's Secretary of State; papal legate in Bologna, Romagna, and the March of Ancona; and cardinal-protector of Portugal, the Catholic cantons of Switzerland, the Franciscans, the Carmelites, the Knights of Malta, and other bodies. He took all these as serious tasks, not empty titles. Somehow, his methodical mind and energy enabled him to cope with them all—except the archdiocese of Milan, which his multitudinous tasks in Rome prevented him from visiting. He longed to retire to a monastery, but the archbishop of Braga assured him that God had given him all these tasks for the good of the Church, and he carried on.

The Council of Trent had been suspended in 1552, leaving a great deal of important work uncompleted. Pope Pius IV announced his intention of reconvening it. Charles took on the task with enthusiasm and was largely responsible for the fact that it was able to reopen in January 1562 and complete its work in two years. He helped draft the Catechism it produced (the basis of popular Catholic instruction for almost four hundred years) and to reform the liturgy and church music. Behind the scenes, he was the mastermind shaping most of the Council's decrees—and he was twenty-six years old when it closed. In the same years his own life changed: his elder brother died and he became head of the family. Instead of pursuing the life this would have involved (including marrying), he conferred the position on his uncle Giulio and was ordained priest in 1563; two months later, he was consecrated bishop of Milan.

When he was eventually able to go there, he found the diocese in a deplorable state. It was under Spanish rule, the clergy were generally lazy and corrupt, and the laity had virtually ceased all practice. Charles held a provincial council and ordered the decrees of Trent to be put into effect. He then had to return to Rome, arriving there just in time to be at his uncle's deathbed. The new pope, Pius V, tried to persuade him to stay in Rome, but he saw his uncle's death as his release from Rome and hastened back to Milan. Through a combination of energy, hard work, lack of respect for persons, obvious personal goodness, and intellectual firmness, he set about reforming the great diocese. He started seminaries for the education of the clergy, insisted on the proper performance of the liturgy, founded the Confraternity of Christian Doctrine to ensure that children were taught the catechism, made his priests go on an annual retreat, and instituted a society of secular priests to carry out his reforms over the heads of those, such as the cathedral canons, who refused to cooperate. He turned back the advancing tide of Protestantism in the Alpine valleys in the north of the diocese, survived an assassination attempt in 1569, fed three thousand people from diocesan stores during a famine, and set an example of personal heroism during an outbreak of plague in 1576, organizing care of the sick, burial of the dead, and feeding of the population.

He carried on exhausting his energies and diocesan resources until his health finally gave way in the autumn of 1584, when he was making his annual retreat at Monte Varallo. He returned to the city, took to his bed, and died there during the night of 3–4 November. He was buried in the cathedral and a popular cult developed immediately. This was quickly taken up by the official Church, and he was canonized in 1610. In 1932 Pope Pius XI declared him patron both of those who teach catechetics and of their pupils.

5

Bd Joan de Maillé (Jeanne Marie de Maillé; 1332–1414)

Joan was the daughter of aristocratic parents, her father being Baron Hardouin VI de Maillé and her mother a member of the Montbazon family. They lived in the Touraine region of central France, where Joan grew up exceptionally devout, to the point where her prayers were supposed to have saved a young boy, Robert de Sillé, from drowning. He became devoted to her, and after her father's death, her grandfather arranged for her to marry him. She had wanted to be a nun but felt unable to disobey her grandfather's wishes. He then died on their wedding day. Joan and Robert had sixteen years of happy life together: they lived as brother and sister, adopted three orphaned children, and turned the Château de Sillé into a refuge for the poor of the district.

The Hundred Years War between France and England brought this tranquil existence to an end. Robert enlisted in the service of the French king and was left for dead on the battlefield of Maupertius in 1356. He was in fact still alive and was taken prisoner by the English, who demanded the huge sum of three thousand florins for his release. Joan sold what she could and borrowed the money still needed. He attributed his release to the direct intervention of Our Lady. The couple returned to their good works and self-denial, extending their charity to the ransoming of prisoners.

Robert died in 1362, and his family turned against Joan, accusing her of impoverishing the family, and drove her from the château. With no means of support, she returned to live with her mother for a while. She was still relatively young, and several would-be suitors sought her in marriage. This bothered her so much that she went to live in a little house attached to the church of St Martin in Tours, where she spent her time in prayer, reciting the divine office and caring for the sick. Her total dedication attracted jealousy as well as admiration, and a deranged woman threw a large stone at her one day as she was praying, badly injuring her back. After no surgeon—even a royal one—had been able to effect a cure, she recovered suddenly and apparently miraculously.

Robert's family had relented toward her and restored her family home to her, but she gave all her possessions, including the château, to the Carthusians of Liget and renounced any property that might come to her in the future. This turned her own family against her and she was forced to beg for a living and sleep in unoccupied pigsties or kennels. Even when she found menial work in a hospital she aroused jealousy and was forced to leave. She eventually found a deserted hermitage in the countryside, which she restored. In 1389 she returned to Tours, where some people thought her mad or a witch, while others regarded her as a saint. She probably became a Franciscan tertiary at this time. She found a tiny room near the Franciscan church and from there resumed her care of the sick and needy, including prisoners and captives. She even persuaded the king to release all prisoners held in Tours. She died in 1414 with a reputation for bringing about miraculous cures and conversions, but her popular cult was not approved by the Vatican until 1871. The actual date of her death was 28 March, but the Franciscans commemorate her on 6 November.

6

St Illtyd (Sixth Century)

Relatively early accounts of Illtyd (or Illtut, the name deriving from the Latin *ille tutus*, meaning "the safe one") refer to him somewhat obliquely, being Lives of his pupils, Samson of Dol (died about 565), Paul Aurelian (died about 575), and Gildas (died about 570). These three, from their dates, probably were his pupils, but St David (see 1 Mar.), who was not born until about 605, could not have been, though the Life of Gildas claims that he was. Even allowing for excessive claims—which the author says he is avoiding by not "relating all his wondrous works"—Illtyd is unquestionably one of the great founding fathers of Welsh Christianity.

The only Life of which he is the main subject is much later, dating from the eleventh century. According to this, he came from a princely family living in a Welsh colony in Brittany. His father was a warrior, and Illtyd, despite his excellent education in religious literature, followed in his footsteps. He crossed the Channel to visit "his cousin King Arthur," becoming, in one account, one of the four knights who had charge of the Holy Grail, and married a woman named Trynihid. He then crossed into Wales and entered the service of a chieftain in Glamorgan, earning the title "Illtyd the knight." Then a hunting accident, which led to the death of several of his companions, led him to encounter a "holy man" (and possibly an angel), who told him to leave his wife and his military service, return to the studies he had despised, and become a monk. Marriage did not form part of the austere pattern (modelled on the Desert Fathers) of Celtic spirituality, and the unfortunate Trynihid was simply cast aside as a hindrance, told not to cling to him, and left "cold and trembling." Illtyd walked out on her very early one morning and went to receive the clerical tonsure from St Dyfrig (Dubricius in Latin).

He became a hermit in the Wye Valley, living very simply and growing his own food. Dyfrig then found land on the coast of what is now South Glamorgan that could support a community, and he and Illtyd moved there, gathering increasing numbers of disciples into what became the great monastery of Llantwit Major (*Llaniltud Fawr* in Welsh). The only person not welcome was poor Trynihid, who came to see her husband and found him working in the fields and covered in mud (he was responsible for introducing an improved method of ploughing); she pleaded with him to return to his family, but he refused and turned his back on her. He became, according to the Life of Gildas, "the most learned of all the Britons, both in the Old Testament and in the New, and in all kinds of philosophy—poetry and rhetoric, grammar and arithmetic." He is said to have founded the monastery on Caldey Island, and even to have increased the size of the island overnight by making the monks pray for this.

Much of the Latin Life devoted to him is taken up with accounts of wonder-working, some of a nature called "unsavoury" by a seventeenth-century Benedictine, Dom Serenus Cressy. By no means unsavoury and probably true is the story that he organized corn ships to take grain to Brittany during a famine there. There are various accounts of his death: the Life of Samson gives a moving account of his last days at Llantwit Major; another account gives Defynnog in Powys as the place of his death and claims that he was buried at Bedd Gwyl Illtud (meaning Grave of Illtyd's Feast); other, Breton, accounts claim that he crossed over to Brittany once more and died at Dol. After the Norman Conquest Llantwit Major, by then greatly reduced in numbers, was taken over by the abbot of Tewkesbury, and, at about the time the Life was written, his shrine was moved to Glastonbury and he became one of the figures used to promote pilgrimage there—hence his identification with the legends of Arthur and the Holy Grail.

7

St Willibrord (658–739)

Willibrord, the "apostle to the Frisians" or "to the Low Countries," was the first to take Christianity from Northumbria to the Continent of Europe. Coming as he did from Northumbria and living around the same time as the Venerable Bede (see 25 May), he offers the advantage of a contemporary account of at least the earlier part of his life in Bede's *Ecclesiastical History*. Bede died four years before he did, so was not able to follow his evangelizing through to its final years.

Born in Yorkshire and educated by St Wilfrid (see 24 Apr.) from an early age, he was apparently professed as a monk by the time he was fifteen. When Wilfrid's huge diocese was divided into four, he moved to Ireland, where he spent twelve years studying, returning to England in 690. By then, one of his companions in Ireland, Egbert, had planned to evangelize the Frisians, a Germanic tribe living on the coast of what are now The Netherlands. He was warned in a vision or two to go instead to Scotland, to straighten out the errant ways of monks still observing Celtic practices there. Then another companion in exile, Wigbert, preached to the Frisians for two years but then had to admit defeat and return home. Willibrord took up the challenge and sailed with twelve companions, landing at the mouth of the Rhine and travelling into Frankish territory in Holland.

King Pepin of the Franks had conquered an area between the Meuse and the sea from the Frisian pagan king Radbod, and he encouraged the new missionaries to go there. Willibrord, brought up by Wilfrid to respect Rome in all things, went there to obtain the pope's authority for his mission. He returned armed with this and a large number of relics, to be used in consecrating churches, and led a successful mission for five years. He then made a short return visit to Rome, taking with him Pepin's recommendation that he be consecrated bishop. Pope Sergius I agreed with alacrity, and after no more than fourteen days in Rome he returned graced with the *pallium* and the title of archbishop to the Frisians, having been consecrated on the feast of St Cecilia (see 22 Nov.) in 696. He was charged with establishing a province on the Roman model (exemplified at Canterbury), with a cathedral at Wiltaberg (now Utrecht) and surrounding suffragan bishoprics. He also co-founded the great monastery of Echternacht in Luxembourg.

He was successful in the western part of his mission territory but less so in the east, where Radbod still held sway. He went as far as Denmark but seems to have done little more than purchase thirty boys to take back for instruction. On the return journey their ship was blown off course on to the sacred island of Heligoland, a place of enjoined silence and prohibition to kill any living thing. Willibrord challenged the deity supposed to hold sway there by killing animals and baptizing people in a loud voice. Nothing happened, but Radbod was not going to let this affront go unpunished. He forced Willibrord's companions to cast lots and executed the one who drew the short straw as a sacrifice to the god.

Willibrord suffered a reverse in 714, when Radbod regained the parts of Frisia previously taken by Pepin and undid most of his work there. Radbod was killed five years later, however, and Willibrord returned to both western and eastern Frisia. He was joined in the eastern part by St Boniface (see 5 June), who was on his way to Germany. He asked Boniface to stay and succeed him in the see of Utrecht, but Boniface had received a definite papal commission to evangelize Germany, and after three years of fruitful collaboration he moved on. Willibrord was by now an old man, and he retired to Echternach, where he died on 7 November 739. He was immediately venerated as a saint, and pilgrimages to his tomb in the crypt of the abbey church began almost immediately.

Alcuin, the intellectual force behind Charlemagne's "renaissance," who was born four years before Willibrord's death, wrote two accounts of his life, one in prose and one in verse so that children in monastic schools could memorize it. He does not add much that can be called historical to Bede's account, but he describes Willibrord as striking in looks, cheerful in manner, wise in counsel, and totally dedicated to his ministry, the impetus for which came from a deep interior life. A calendar compiled for his use survives, with a marginal entry in his own hand giving details of his consecration. He is the patron of Holland, and at Echternacht every Whit Tuesday a liturgical dance known as the *Springende Heiligen* (Dancing Saints) has been performed in his honour since at least the sixteenth century, with a break during the French Revolution.

8

Bd John Duns Scotus (about 1265–1308)

The term "Scot" was applied equally to the Irish in the Middle Ages, but John did come from Scotland, being born at Duns, near Berwick-upon-Tweed. Little is known about his early life, though he is supposed to have joined the Franciscans at the age of fifteen and to have studied at their house in Oxford. He is known to have been ordained as a Franciscan priest in Northampton on 17 March 1291, when he was about twenty-five years old. He then went to the university of Paris to study for a master's degree in theology, but seems to have left without one. He returned to Oxford and lectured there and at Cambridge. The standard theological textbook of the time was the *Sentences* of Peter Lombard (about 1100–60), and John commented on these, refining his views from one course to the next.

After four years based in Oxford he returned to Paris, where he was caught up in a dispute between the king and the pope and forced to leave for a while for failing to support the king. He obtained a letter of recommendation from the minister general of the Franciscans, Gonsalvus Hispanus, who had taught him in Paris from 1293 to 1296. Hispanus referred to his "most subtle genius" in the letter, which led to his later being known as *doctor subtilis*, the "subtle doctor." He finally obtained the degree of "ruling master" from the university in 1305 and spent the next two years lecturing there. In 1307 he aroused controversy with his views on what has subsequently become the dogma of the Immaculate Conception: he was one of the first to propound the now orthodox teaching that the redemption had been applied in advance to Mary. In the words of Gerard Manley Hopkins' poem "Duns Scotus' Oxford," he "fired France for Mary without spot." Hopkins called his insight "not rivalled," but France (or at least the university of Paris) was fired with anger as well as enthusiasm, and John was forced to leave and move to Cologne. He lectured there for a year before his early death on 8 November 1308.

His greatness can be seen only in his works, not in the outward events of his life. He lived and worked at a time when philosophy and theology in the West were developing in response to the discovery of Aristotle through great Islamic scholars such as Avicenna (died 1037). Thomas Aquinas (died 1275; see 28 Jan.) had been condemned for over-reliance on Aristotle by the more conservative elements in the university of Paris while Scotus was still a boy. He worked on a new synthesis—these were times when theologians/philosophers could still try to encompass the whole of human knowledge—using the works of St Paul (see 25 Jan.), St Augustine (see 28 Aug.), his Franciscan predecessors Alexander of Hales and St Bonaventure (see 15 July), and Avicenna, though he confined his use of him to what did not conflict with orthodox Christian teaching. The essence of his theology is that God is love and that this love spreads from God through the whole of creation, so that human beings, thanks to the Incarnation, can love God in return. His teaching on Mary, which earned him the title *doctor Marianus*, stems from this doctrine of universal love.

He was buried in the Franciscan church in Cologne, where his body still lies, and immediately venerated as a saint, though official progress toward his beatification was particularly slow: it was not until 1906 that his cult was confirmed for the Franciscans, who were then allowed to venerate him as "Blessed," and it was 1993 before Pope John Paul II extended this to the universal Church.

❧

Yet ah! This air I gather and I release
He lived on; these weeds and waters, these walls are what
He haunted who of all men most sways my spirits to peace;

Of realty the rarest-veinèd unraveller; a not
Rivalled insight, be rival Italy or Greece;
Who fired France for Mary without spot.
Gerard Manley Hopkins, "Duns Scotus' Oxford"

9

Bd Elizabeth of the Trinity (Elizabeth Catez; 1880–1906)

A French Carmelite who lived a short life at around the same time as St Thérèse of Lisieux (see 1 Oct.), Elizabeth invites comparison with her far more famous contemporary. Physically their sufferings were similar—early deaths from wasting diseases that were incurable at the time, which both endured with extraordinary courage: tuberculosis in Thérèse's case, Addison's disease in Elizabeth's. They shared a deep conviction that their destiny lay in heaven, which for Elizabeth was home and rest, for Thérèse a new place from which to work. Both were conscious that their gifts and their sufferings, both coming from God, marked them out for a special destiny.

Elizabeth was born near Bourges in central France and then moved with her family to Dijon, where her father died when she was seven. Her sister Marguerite described her as "a little devil," but from the time of her First Communion and Confirmation in 1891 she seems to have set her heart on becoming a contemplative nun. She had little formal education but became proficient in music, winning several prizes at the Dijon *Conservatoire*, so that her mother hoped she would use this gift to help support the family. She, however, vowed herself to Christ with a private vow of virginity when she was fourteen and decided that her future was in a Carmelite convent. Her mother forbade her to have any contact with the Dijon Carmel and tried to interest her in various young men she produced as potential suitors. In 1899 her mother relented, asking her only to wait another two years, until she was twenty-one, to which Elizabeth readily agreed.

She entered the Dijon Carmel on 2 August 1901, but less than two years later she showed the first symptoms of Addison's disease, caused by a glandular malfunction and with no known treatment. She accepted the news calmly as an opportunity to "conform oneself to the Crucified in love," offering herself as a "prey" to the Trinity. She developed a mystical theology of suffering, written down in two notebooks that the prioress asked her to keep. Christ, her Spouse, she wrote, "wishes me to be the surrogate human being in whom he can suffer again for the glory of the Father and the salvation of the Church. This thought makes me so happy." For the first three years the disease was not especially painful, but it worsened suddenly in the summer of 1906, and though she welcomed even acute pain with joy, she was later afflicted with temptations to despair. In the end she won through these, believing that "Nothing remains but love. Everything must be done for love." After a week of final agony she died in the morning of 9 November 1906. Her final words, quoted in her entry in the new Roman Martyrology, were: "I am going to the light, to love, to life." Four years earlier she had written to a friend: "I feel I have found heaven on earth, because heaven is God and God is in my soul. The day I understood this a light went on inside me. ..."

Like Thérèse, she wrote verse, and in one poem she expressed this sense of being in heaven: "I plunge into Infinity / Dive into my Patrimony. / In this profound immensity / As in eternity, / My soul is blessed. / With the Trinity I rest." She knew Thérèse's works, as her autobiography had been circulated to Carmels in its first (1898) printing and was on its way to becoming a bestseller by the time she died. Asked whether she, like Thérèse, planned to "come back" to earth after her death, she replied: "Certainly not! The moment I reach the threshold of eternity I shall be off like a shot into the heart of the Trinity, where I shall be immovable." She was a mystic in the great Carmelite tradition of John of the Cross (see 14 Dec.) and so many others, but not a revolutionary like her great contemporary. Overshadowed by her after death as well, she was beatified by Pope John Paul II on 25 November 1984, nearly sixty years after Thérèse's canonization.

10

St Leo the Great (died 461)

The earliest of only three popes to have been given the title "great"—the others being Gregory I (died 604; see 3 Sept.) and Nicholas I (died 867)—Leo was born in Rome around the end of the fourth century. He became an adviser to popes at an early age and was involved with negotiations with St Cyril of Alexandria (see 27 June) over whether the see of Jerusalem should be raised to the rank of a patriarchate. He persuaded John Cassian to write his treatise "On the Incarnation against Nestorius," which Cassian dedicated to him. He was mediating between a provincial governor and the commander-in-chief in Gaul when news reached him that he had been chosen as pope by the unanimous vote of the clergy and people of Rome.

He developed and taught the doctrine that the Gospel commission to Peter to be the rock on which the Church is founded means that the Bishop of Rome, as Peter's heir, has universal authority derived directly from Christ. His sermons and other writings are full of the conviction that the pope is the "primate of all bishops," which has had lasting consequences of great importance for the role of the papacy throughout subsequent history. With this view of his office, he wrote letters to the Churches in Africa, Gaul, and Spain expressing the need for uniformity of practice and orthodoxy of belief to oppose the major heresies of his time, especially Manichaeism. He even invoked the "secular arm" against the latter, persuading the government to enact legislation against its adherents. He asserted the doctrine that any bishop had the right to appeal directly to the Bishop of Rome in a dispute with his metropolitan, as when he rebuked St Hilary of Arles (see 5 May) for acting independently of Rome in dealings with his bishops, but he extended the same principle to metropolitans when he saw their rightful authority being disregarded by papal legates.

In the sphere of doctrine, his greatest achievement was to have the doctrine of two natures in Christ confirmed by the Council of Chalcedon in 451. The background to this was that Bishop Flavian of Constantinople had dismissed a monk named Eutyches for preaching that there was only one nature in Christ (Monophysitism). Eutyches appealed to Leo, but Leo asserted the two natures in a letter to Flavian, the *Tomus ad Favianun*, which has come to be known as the Tome of Leo. The human and divine natures exist in Christ and are united, he wrote, "without confusion or admixture." The emperor in the east, Theodosius II, summoned a council in support of Eutyches and reinstated him. Leo called this gathering "a den of thieves" and pressed for a new council. When this met (consisting of six hundred bishops from the Eastern part of the Church and two from Africa), Leo's Tome was read out by his papal legates, and the assembly confirmed its assent by declaring: "This is the faith of the fathers; this is the faith of the apostles. We ourselves believe this, those whose faith is true believe this. Let anyone who believes otherwise be anathema! Peter has spoken through the mouth of Leo. Leo has taught in piety and in truth."

A Roman view had prevailed in the East, but Leo and the council Fathers appreciated that Rome's authority had nothing to do with geography but only with the doctrine of apostolic succession. The imperial power of Rome was coming to an end, and this was reflected at Chalcedon: Leo was powerless to prevent the council from declaring Constantinople a patriarchate. He was more successful in saving Rome from being sacked by Attila the Hun, to whom he offered tribute, in 452, and by Genseric the Vandal three years later. He restored several Roman basilicas, including St Peter's, built new churches, and provided relief for the people of Rome in time of famine. He died on 10 November 461 and was buried in St Peter's.

His surviving writings consist of one hundred and seventy-three letters attributed to him, of which one hundred and forty-three are in his own hand, plus some eighty sermons, elegant in style and rich in doctrine. Most of the sermons follow the readings of the liturgical year. He was essentially a pastor of his flock, concerned to pass on true teaching, rather than an original theologian. The effectiveness of his expression and transmission of orthodox teaching was enough for him to be declared a Doctor of the Church by Pope Benedict XIV in 1754.

11

St Martin of Tours (about 336–397)

Martin became one of the most popular saints of the Middle Ages through a contemporary Life written by Sulpicius Severus, completed a year before his death. This was widely copied over the centuries and found its way into virtually every monastery. It became a pattern for subsequent saints' Lives, and so Martin became in many ways the typical saint. The work contains some idealization and tries to make Martin's life follow that of Jesus, but it is a genuine attempt to portray a real person and to celebrate him for the way he lived, rather than just for the way he died. Sulpicius, who visited Martin frequently during the last four years of his life, evidently saw him as an embodiment of the ideal Christian.

He was born to pagan parents in the Roman province of Pannonia (now western Hungary and parts of adjoining countries) and was forced to follow his father's profession of soldier, even though he was drawn to Christianity and as a Christian would have refused to fight. He was posted to Amiens in northern France, where one of the most famous episodes in Christian history is told of him: on a cold winter day he saw a beggar shivering outside the gates. He cut his own cloak in two and gave half to the beggar. That night he saw Christ in a dream, wearing the half cloak and saying, "Martin, still a catechumen, has covered me with his garment." He immediately sought baptism. An episode when he asked to leave the army, since as "a soldier of Christ" it was no longer lawful for him to fight for the empire, led to a brief imprisonment on a charge of cowardice (he was a member of the imperial guard, from which it was forbidden to resign), but he was soon released and put himself in the hands of St Hilary of Poitiers (see 13 Jan.) who welcomed him as one of his disciples and ordained him to the minor order of exorcist when popular opposition to soldiers becoming clerics prevented him from being ordained deacon.

He then at some point made a return journey to his homeland, over the Alps, where he had a remarkable escape from robbers. He saw his family once more and encouraged his mother and some others—though not his father—to become Christians. He journeyed back across northern Italy, and in Milan he heard that Arians, in the ascendancy in parts of Gaul, had caused Hilary to be exiled. Martin, who had already preached against Arianism on the Dalmatian coast and been scourged as a result, heard of this and decided to stay in Milan, but the bishop, Auxentius, was also Arian and forced him to retire to an island in the Gulf of Genoa, where he stayed until Hilary returned to Poitiers in 360, when he rejoined him.

He felt his vocation was to a solitary life—the desert monks of Egypt, known through Athanasius' (see 2 May) Life of Antony (see 17 Jan.), being a powerful influence at the time. Hilary gave him some land, but others, drawn by his example, came to join him, and what is generally considered the first monastic community in Gaul came into being. He spent ten years there, teaching and preaching, until the people of Tours wanted him as their bishop. He refused, so they tricked him into the city by saying a sick man needed a visit from him and while he was there declared him bishop, despite opposition from some bishops from nearby, who regarded his unkempt appearance as unsuitable. He continued to live a simple monkish life, first in a cell near the cathedral and then outside the city, where he founded the abbey of Marmoutier, which soon grew into a large community and became a focus of evangelization, with the first seminary for the training of priests. Christianity was an urban religion in Gaul, and Martin was a pioneer in spreading it to rural areas, where he established a rudimentary parish system. Sometimes the methods he used were harsh and even illegal, as when he destroyed pagan temples and built chapels on their ruins.

He was unsparing of himself, travelling all over his diocese on foot, by donkey, or by boat. He ventured farther afield and preached in other dioceses, which did not always endear him to their bishops. He became involved in a number of doctrinal disputes, including a major one with the extremely ascetic Priscillianists, condemned as heretics. In a complex series of events involving bishops and the secular powers, Priscillian and some of his supporters were executed, for which Martin, who did not believe heretics should be executed but had given in to pressure, reproached himself for the rest of his life.

He fell ill in a remote part of his diocese, where he died on 8 November 297. His body was taken to Tours and buried there three days later, so the date of his burial has become his feast-day. As Sulpicius' Life spread, so did his cult, and Tours was one of Europe's most popular pilgrimage destinations until the religious wars of the sixteenth century. He became a popular subject in art, with the cloak-sharing episode featuring in mosaic, stained glass, statues, and paintings, including one by Van Dyck in the royal collection at Windsor Castle.

12

St Josaphat (Ioann Kuncewycz; about 1580–1623)

Ioann was born in what is now north-western Ukraine but was apprenticed to a merchant in Vilna (now Vilnius, the capital of Lithuania). Though he worked hard, he was less interested in trade than in learning Church Slavonik (the official language of the Eastern Church), in which he was encouraged by the rector of the Oriental College and two Jesuits who befriended him. Despite this, his master eventually offered him a partnership and his daughter's hand in marriage, but by this time Ioann had decided to become a monk, so he refused both and joined the monastery of the Holy Trinity in Vilna, taking the name Josaphat in religion and going on to ordination, first as deacon and then priest.

When he was fifteen the Orthodox metropolitan of Kiev had sought communion with Rome, which was achieved in the Union of Brest-Litovsk (23 Dec. 1595), in which millions of Ruthenian (Ukrainian and Byelorussian) Byzantine-rite Christians became members of the Roman Catholic Church, with permission to retain their own liturgy. This action produced a long and bitter controversy but deeply impressed Ioann and left him with an abiding concern for Church unity. He persuaded a young man named Venyamin Rutsky, a scholar and a convert from Calvinism, to join the monastery with him, and together they began to look at possible means of bringing about a reconciliation between Orthodoxy and Western Catholicism. They initiated a movement for the reform of Ruthenian monasticism that eventually developed into the Order of St Basil.

Rutsky was appointed abbot of Holy Trinity, which led to an increase in applicants to the monastery, necessitating the founding of new houses, which he sent Josaphat to organize in Poland. Josaphat then succeeded his friend as abbot when Rutsky was promoted to be metropolitan of Kiev. He himself became a bishop soon after and then archbishop of Polotsk. He inherited a situation of decay in his archdiocese, together with widespread suspicion of his desire for union with Rome among his more devout churchgoers, who feared Roman interference in their practices. Josaphat employed monks from Holy Trinity to help him in a process of general reform. He held synods in all the major cities, imposed a catechism he himself composed, laid down rules for the conduct of the clergy, and removed lay control of benefices and other church matters.

By 1620 his reforms had taken effect, but then opposition to the Union of Brest-Litovsk grew, both among the Latin-rite Poles, who regarded the Ruthenians as barbarians, and the Orthodox, who claimed that Roman Catholicism was not the proper Christianity for the people of the region. A rival archbishop was appointed, and although Josaphat had the support of the people of Polotsk, he was not backed by the other Polish bishops, who resented his insistence on retaining the separate rites allowed by the Union. Anti-Roman feeling was strong in the city of Vitebsk, but Josaphat decided to go there in person to preach and attempt to make peace. He fell into a trap set by followers of the rival archbishop and found his followers being attacked and himself threatened by a hostile crowd assembled for the purpose. When he appealed to them to leave his servants alone and take him instead, they murdered him and threw his body in the River Dvina.

Josaphat was canonized by Pope Pius IX in 1867, the first Eastern-rite saint whose cause was processed by the Roman Congregation of Rites. His feast was extended to the entire Western Church by Pope Leo XIII in 1892. He was a great ecumenist three centuries before ecumenism was generally recognized as an essential goal by the major Christian Churches.

13

Bd Eugene Bossilkov (1900–1952)

Eugene Bossilkov was born into a family of Latin-rite Catholics in northern Bulgaria and was given the name Vincent at his baptism. At this time the mission to northern Bulgaria was entrusted to the Passionist Fathers, and he received his secondary education first at the Passionist minor seminary in Oresc and then at the diocesan seminary in Nikopol. In 1914 he was sent to the Order's seminary in Belgium, where he received the habit in 1919, taking the name Eugene of the Sacred Heart in religion. He was ordained on 25 July 1926, at a time when Catholics in Bulgaria numbered less than 1 per cent of a total population of some three and a half million, of whom the great majority were Eastern Orthodox, with a sizeable Muslim minority.

In 1927 he was sent to Rome to study for a degree at the Pontifical Oriental Institute, and in 1932 he gained a doctorate with a thesis on the union of Bulgaria with the Roman Catholic Church in the early thirteenth century (1204). On his return home in 1933 he served first as personal secretary to the Passionist Bishop Damian Theelen and then, having expressed a preference for more pastoral work, as pastor in Bardaski-Gheran, where he concentrated on improving the level of religious education among his flock, with particular emphasis on young people.

The government of Bulgaria agreed to cooperate with Hitler's forces in March 1941, thereby avoiding actual occupation by Germany. This put a stop to all missionary endeavours, though it also prevented the Nazi excesses that took place in other eastern European countries. In summer 1944 the government tried to change sides but did so just too late, three days after Stalin had declared war on Bulgaria on 5 September. A "Fatherland Front" government was installed with partisan participation and Soviet military support, and moves began to control religious activity. All religious feasts were suppressed, any religious manifestation had to be within church buildings, church schools were confiscated, and all Catholic charities were suppressed. A special law passed in 1949 forbade any religious activity not under state control and all contacts with ecclesiastical bodies outside the country.

Bishop Theelen died in August 1946, and Fr Eugene was chosen as apostolic administrator in anticipation of the nomination of a successor. Despite the prohibitions in force he ordered a mission to be conducted in each parish and personally took part in these. He was named bishop of Nikopol by Pope Pius XII on 26 July 1947 and made his *ad limina* visit to Rome in July 1948. He left to go back to Bulgaria on 1 October, despite being advised against returning because of danger of imprisonment or even death, telling a friend, "I am the shepherd of my flock. I cannot abandon the flock."

After his return the political situation deteriorated, and he advised the Passionist provincial in Holland to recall the missionaries; most left in early 1949. He stayed behind, writing to his provincial, "If it comes to the worst, so be it. I have the courage to go on living. I hope I also have the courage to suffer the worst, always remaining faithful to Christ, the Pope, and the Church." Arrests of priests began the following year, and he was under constant surveillance and unable to move around freely: "I can't take a step without my 'guardian angel' always at my heels. What a feeling!" he wrote to his provincial. He resorted to writing in a simple code, with the government his "dentist" and his troubles his "toothache": "My health is fine, but the dentist won't leave me in peace; it's not easy to free oneself of a dentist of this kind, but that's only part of the entire story!" He was nevertheless able to ordain four priests on 18 December 1951.

On 16 July 1952 the state police took action against every Catholic community in Bulgaria, arresting some forty priests, including the bishop, who was staying in a modest holiday home outside Sofia. Until his trial opened on 29 September there was no further news of him, though evidence was to emerge that he had been savagely tortured in prison. After four days during which the authorities failed to extract any confession of anti-Soviet activities from him or any of those tried with him, he, two Assumptionist religious, and a parish priest were condemned to be shot. Relatives were allowed to visit him for the last time on 6 October; they implored him to ask for clemency, but he refused, saying, "No, I know the Lord will give me the strength to accept death in accordance with his will. I have not denounced anyone ... I could have been free to enjoy every possible comfort, if I had wished it." He did ask for blankets, as he was made to sleep on a bare cement floor. His niece Gabriella brought him a basket of food every day until mid-November, the guard returning the empty basket. When it was returned with the food untouched on 18 November, Gabriella was told that he had been executed on the 11th. Confirmation of this reached the Vatican only in 1975, when the Bulgarian Head of State, Todor Zhikov, had an audience with Pope Paul VI, who asked him directly what had happened to Bishop Bossilkov and was told that he had died "in prison twenty-three years ago." His body was thrown into a common grave and has never been found.

He was beatified in Rome on 15 March 1998. The Bulgarian prosecutor general then started proceedings for his posthumous exoneration, and in May 1999 a decree of the Bulgarian Supreme Court of Appeal found that the 1952 trial records contained "glaring violations" of justice and annulled the death sentence.

14

St Laurence O'Toole (Lorcán Ua Tuathail; 1128–1180)

Laurence was born into a chieftain's family in Co. Kildare. At the age of ten he was taken hostage by the king of Leinster and held for two years until his father persuaded the king to give him to the bishop of Glendalough. When his father arrived to take him home, Laurence told him he wanted to become a monk, so his father left him with the bishop. By the time he was twenty-five, he had been appointed abbot. Besides his normal duties he soon had to provide relief for people in the countryside, ravaged by a serious famine. He was widely seen as their saviour, but some people envied him for his goodness, and there were still bandits to be subdued in the Wicklow Hills.

Having refused the bishopric of Glendalough earlier on the canonical grounds that he was not yet thirty, he was appointed second archbishop of the recently created archdiocese of Dublin on the death of the first, Gregory, in 1161. He set about reforming the diocesan clergy, imposing a Rule on the canons of the cathedral and himself setting the example by wearing a religious habit and living austerely. He gave generously to the poor, preached tirelessly, and celebrated the liturgy with dignity.

By 1170 he found himself caught up in wider affairs. The immediately preceding history was that Pope Hadrian IV (Nicholas Brakespear, the only English pope; 1154–9) had effectively invested the English king, Henry II (1154–89) with the right to rule over Ireland—the popes claiming jurisdiction over the western isles—in 1158. He gave Henry an emerald ring in token of this and authorized him to go to Ireland and "subject its people to the rule of law and to root out therefrom the weeds of vice." He can hardly have foreseen the long-term consequences of his action. Then Laurence's former captor the king of Leinster (Dermot MacMurrough) was driven out of Ireland and took refuge in England. He asked Henry II to provide him with volunteers to help him return. Henry raised a force, which landed at Waterford in 1170 and marched on Dublin, sacking the city while Laurence was negotiating with its leader, Richard de Clare, earl of Pembroke, known as Strongbow, who was married to Dermot's daughter, Laurence's niece. Dermot then died suddenly, forcing Strongbow to garrison his forces in Dublin Castle, while Laurence again attempted to arrange peace and to bring supplies and comfort to the people.

Strongbow, contrary to expectations, broke out of the castle and routed the opposing Irish troops led by Rory O'Conor, the high king. Henry himself went to Dublin in 1171 and received the submission of most of the Irish sub-kings. This was the year in which the whole of Christendom had been shocked by the murder of Thomas Becket (29 Dec. 1170), and he was anxious to make amends. He presented his effective conquest as a crusade undertaken to bring Ireland into subjection to the Holy See. He presented the Bull for the first time, and the Irish bishops accepted the imposition of clerical celibacy and the use of the Sarum rite.

Laurence became a mediator between Henry and the Irish rulers. In 1175 he went to England, successfully negotiated a treaty between Henry and Rory O'Conor, and spent a night in prayer at Thomas Becket's tomb—where he survived an attack by a deranged would-be assassin. In 1179 he took part in the Third Lateran Council, where he took the opportunity to give the pope (Alexander III; 1159–81) a full account of the state of the Church in Ireland. Alexander gave him jurisdiction over five suffragan dioceses (two more than today) and appointed him papal legate in Ireland. Later the same year a council held at Clonfert deposed "lay" bishops and generally reduced secular control over church affairs. When Laurence returned from the council he set about using his new powers in a manner that Henry found too reminiscent of Thomas Becket. He refused to see Laurence when he came to Abingdon for further negotiations between the king and O'Conor and sailed for Normandy, refusing Laurence leave to return to Dublin. Laurence followed him and obtained permission to return, but he fell ill on the way and died at the abbey of Eu in northern France on 14 October 1180. He was buried in the crypt of the church of Our Lady there and was canonized in 1225.

15

St Albert the Great (1206–1280)

In the nineteenth century it was said satirically of Benjamin Jowett, the Master of Balliol College, Oxford, that "Whatever there is to know, I know it." Albert's contemporaries said the same of him in all seriousness, calling him "a man no less than godlike in all knowledge."

Little is known of his childhood beyond that he was born into a wealthy and powerful military family, that he was the eldest son, and that sometime before 1222 (so at the age of fourteen or less) he went to study at the university of Padua, and in 1222, having made contact with the Dominicans in Padua, he joined the Order as a postulant. As with his most famous pupil, St Thomas Aquinas (see 28 Jan.), his family tried hard to prevent this, but to no avail. Six years later he was teaching in Cologne, and from there he moved to teach in several German Dominican houses before holding one of the Dominican chairs of theology at Paris. He finally gained his master's degree in 1248 and was sent back to Cologne, where Thomas Aquinas studied with him. His was not purely an academic mind, and in 1254 he was appointed Dominican prior provincial in Germany. As such, he attended a general chapter of the Order in Paris in 1256, where, amongst other matters, it was decided that Dominicans should not be known as "master" or any other title, but only by their names: this was in effect aimed at him, as he was already generally known as "the universal doctor."

The title was apt because of the universality of his learning. He might be less systematic than Aquinas, but he ranged over the whole of philosophy and theology and the natural sciences. Using observation and inexhaustible curiosity, he wrote on physics, astronomy, botany, chemistry (then called alchemy), and biology. He explained that the earth has to be spherical and why latitude affects climate. Before Aquinas, he attempted to reconcile orthodoxy with the teachings of the ancient philosophers, especially Aristotle, whom he read in the Latin translations of Averroes and other Islamic scholars, only recently available in the West, greatly expanding Aristotle's natural science with his own observations. He wrote biblical commentaries, three volumes of commentary on the standard theology textbook of the time, the *Sentences* of Peter Lombard, and an unfinished two-volume *Summa* of theology.

He was attacked (as was Aquinas) by conservative elements in the university of Paris, led by William of Saint-Amour, who produced a treatise "On the Dangers of These Present Times" aimed at those—mainly members of the Mendicant Orders—who were seeking to reconcile Aristotle and Christian orthodoxy. He went to Rome to defend these and became the pope's personal theologian for a while. Then the pope (Alexander IV; 1254–61) appointed him bishop of Regensburg, where both spiritual and temporal affairs were in turmoil. The task was beyond him, and he tried to resign: his resignation was accepted after two years by the next pope, Urban IV. Albert returned to teaching in Cologne, where he remained almost without interruption until 1274, when he was asked to attend the Second Council of Lyons. He was about to set out when news reached him of Thomas Aquinas' death on his way there. Shocked, he carried on and played an active role in the council, particularly on the question of reunion with the Greek Church.

In 1277 he defended Aquinas' writings—in which he had a considerable personal stake—against the bishop of Paris and other theologians. The following year his memory suddenly failed him in the middle of a lecture, and it grew progressively worse, displaying symptoms of what would now most probably be called Alzheimer's disease. He died in the midst of his brethren, suddenly and peacefully, on 15 November 1580. He had to wait even longer than his great pupil (who was declared a Doctor of the Church in 1567) to be fully recognized by the official Church: he was beatified in 1622, which prompted a great increase in devotion to him, but not canonized and declared a Doctor until 1931. Ten years later, Pope Pius XII proclaimed him patron of natural scientists.

16

St Margaret of Scotland (about 1045–1093)

Margaret is one of relatively few medieval saints to have benefited from a near-contemporary Life written by someone who knew her well. It was commissioned by her daughter Matilda from her confessor, Turgot, prior of Durham and then bishop of St Andrews. It conforms to the general pattern of saints' Lives, but her personality comes through. She was the youngest of four children of Edward the Atheling, son of Edmund Ironside, king of Wessex, who had taken refuge in Hungary from the Danish invaders of England. She was born probably in Hungary, and she received a good education there, developing an appreciation of beautiful books and clothes.

In 1057 Edward the Confessor, king of England from 1042 to 1066 (and saint; see 13 Oct.), summoned her father back to England. He planned to make him heir to the throne of England, but Edward the Atheling died soon after arriving back there. This led to the dispute over the succession on Edward the Confessor's death, resolved by the Norman Conquest and the accession of William the Conqueror. Margaret was no longer safe in England and followed her brother to Scotland. There she was welcomed by King Malcolm III Canmore, who married her in about 1070 in the palace of Dunfermline (the capital of Scotland until 1603). They lived happily together until his death (which immediately preceded hers), and she bore him six sons and two daughters. She proved, according to Turgot's "Life of Margaret, Queen of Scotland," a civilizing influence at the somewhat rough Scottish court. She also promoted adoption of Roman practices in such matters as observance of Lent and Easter and keeping Sundays as a day of abstinence from work. She revived the monastery of Iona, which had fallen into decay, and built hostels on either side of the River Forth for pilgrims to St Andrew's. She developed the priory of Dunfermline, founded by Malcolm, which became the royal burial place: it houses the tombs of twenty-two Scottish kings and queens, including Robert the Bruce.

Her life was devoted to the care of her husband, her children, and the poor, but she found time for reading and became an accomplished needlewoman. Malcolm never learned to read, but he appreciated her books as beautiful objects. (A pocket edition of the Gospels, a Life of St Cuthbert that belonged to her, and a Psalter that may have done still survive.) He was killed, with one of their younger sons, at the battle of Alnwick against William II of England. Margaret was terminally ill when she heard the news, despite efforts to keep it from her. She accepted it as the will of God. His body was brought home and she was buried beside him after dying on 16 November 1093.

A popular cult soon developed, but it was a further century and a half—by which time canonizations were reserved to the Holy See—before Pope Innocent IV called for an inquiry into her life and miracles and canonized her in 1250. When Dunfermline was sacked by the English in 1560, her body and Malcolm's were rescued and taken to Philip II's monastery/palace of the Escorial, near Madrid. Her head had been separated, as was often done to allow more widespread veneration, and was taken first to Edinburgh and then to the English College at Douai. She was made a patron of Scotland in 1673.

17

St Elizabeth of Hungary (1207–1231)

Elizabeth's short life is now likely to be seen as raising a number of awkward questions about the Church's traditional attitude to women, but its course was as much dictated by the demands of her position in society and her reaction to this. Born in Bratislava, she was betrothed at the age of four to Ludwig of Thuringia (in central Germany) and sent to live at his father's court. Ludwig's affection for her grew steadily, and their marriage was solemnized when she was fourteen and he twenty-one. She bore him three children, and they seem to have been extremely happy together. He is venerated as a saint in Germany and appears to have shared many of her qualities or at least to have willingly accepted her need for a life of prayer and charity.

The fact that she took the initiative, and went well beyond what might have been expected, is illustrated by the best-known story about the couple. She had taken in a dying leper and placed him in their marital bed. Ludwig was furious when told of this and rushed in and pulled the covers back: when he saw the figure of the leper, he realized he was witnessing a literal embodiment of the Gospel's "just as you did it to one of the least of these who are members of my family, you did it to me" (Matt. 25:40b) and that for him the leper was Christ. (Altering what had been an intuitive leap of faith into a miracle by substituting the crucified Christ for the body of the leper as later versions did, does no service to Ludwig or to storytelling.) Elizabeth gave away what she could spare and more, but, as Ludwig patiently remarked, she never alienated any of his lands. She built a hospital at the foot of the steep hill on which her castle stood, so that the sick would not have to make the climb. She distributed money sensibly, finding work for the able-bodied.

Their happy marriage came to an end in 1227, when Ludwig decided to join the emperor, Frederick II, in a new Crusade. He never reached the Holy Land but died of the plague on the way. Elizabeth had just given birth to their second daughter and was totally grief-stricken. She lost not only her husband but also her position, and she seems either to have been driven from the castle with her children and two attendants or to have left voluntarily. They went to her aunt Matilda, who was abbess of Kitzingen, then on to her uncle, bishop of Bamberg, leaving her elder daughter at Kitzingen. He placed a castle at her disposal and set about making plans for a second marriage for her. She, however, apart from having vowed with Ludwig that neither of them would ever marry again, had decided on a complete renunciation of her position, and on Good Friday 1228, having buried her husband and provided for her children, she joined the Third Order of St Francis.

She settled in a small house she had built just outside Marburg, to which she attached a hospice for the sick, the poor, and the old. Three years earlier, she had taken Konrad of Marburg as her confessor and had (with the pope's approval) vowed obedience to him. He was a fanatic who had gained the pope's approval as an inquisitor, and now, with Ludwig gone, he began to exercise an abnormal degree of control over Elizabeth. He cannot be said to have destroyed her will—she compared herself to sedge, which is flattened by floodwaters but then stands up straight again once the flood has past—but he seems to have set out to do so. In some ways he moderated her impetuosity, teaching her to avoid the risk of contracting leprosy, for example, but he deprived her of normal human support and is said even to have resorted to physical violence against her in his desire for her unquestioning obedience. She imposed extreme austerities on herself, and her health gave way after two years of this way of life.

She died in the evening of 17 November 1231, aged just twenty-four. She was buried in the hospice chapel, and miracles through her intercession were soon widely reported. Konrad collected information on her sanctity to send to the pope but died before her canonization, which took place a mere four years later. Her relics were then moved to a new church of St Elizabeth in Marburg, where they remained until the Reformation, when Lutherans removed them to a destination that has never been traced. She soon became a central figure in devotional art, and there are notable representations of her by Simone Martini, Fra Angelico (London, National Gallery), Piero della Francesca, and Jan van Eyck (New York, Frick Collection).

18

St Philippine Duchesne (1769–1852)

The future first superior of the Sacred Heart nuns in America was born in Grenoble, into a prosperous family, in which she was effectively the eldest of six children, as an elder sister died in infancy. She received an exceptionally good education from the local Visitandine nuns, developed an interest in history and the missions—especially to Louisiana—and at the age of seventeen told her parents that she intended to join the Order. They agreed, but when the time for her profession came, in 1789, her father refused his permission, foreseeing that the coming Revolution would mean trouble for nuns: the Visitandines were in fact expelled from Grenoble two years later. Philippine returned to her family and for the next ten years devoted herself to the care of the sick and of prisoners and the education of children, while living under a simple form of religious Rule.

When Pius VII's Concordat with Napoleon in 1801 re-established Catholicism as the official religion of France, Philippine bought the—now very dilapidated—convent building, which had been used as a prison. With a few other Sisters she tried to lead an enclosed life, but the project headed for failure. She wrote to Mother Madeleine Sophie Barat (see 24 May) offering herself and four other Visitandines, together with the convent buildings, and they were admitted into the Society of the Sacred Heart at the end of 1804. She spent the next twelve years there, longing to be away in mission fields but resigned. Then in 1817 her brother Louis suggested her as a potential missionary to Bishop Dubourg of Louisiana, and Mother Barat agreed, sending five Sisters with Philippine as their superior.

They reached Louisiana on 29 May 1818, after a voyage of over two months, and after some six weeks in New Orleans (where they had cooler cotton habits made to replace their thick woollen ones) proceeded up the Mississippi to St Louis, then a frontier town of some six thousand inhabitants. Bishop Dubourg found them a log cabin in St Charles, on the Missouri, and there they set up the first free school west of the Mississippi, for the poor children of the area, most of whom were at least nominally Catholic. Philippine and the others found English hard to master—and the "docile and innocent Indians" she had dreamed of teaching given to drink and impossible to understand. After a very hard first year, during which they had to become self-sufficient pioneers, the bishop found them a larger house in Florissant, closer to St Louis, where Philippine proposed to open a novitiate. Her first native-born American postulant was enrolled in November 1820. Nothing was easy, and the American way of life—especially its combination of social egalitarianism with slavery—remained strange to her, but her enthusiasm remained high, and in 1821 she was able to open a second house, in Grand Coteau, west of New Orleans. Financial difficulties threatened, but with help from Jesuits from Maryland she made three more new foundations and reopened the house at St Charles over the next six years.

Philippine found the responsibilities of being superior and then provincial of America beyond her capabilities; she was always tired and her health was worsening. In 1840 Elizabeth Galitzin, the assistant general of the Society, visited the American houses. Philippine asked her if she could resign as provincial and her offer was immediately accepted, in a manner that suggested she had made a failure of her exercise of the office over so many years. This caused her great distress, but she accepted the situation and went to live in the house in St Louis, from where she attempted to establish a mission among the Potawatomi Indians in Sugar Creek, to the west of St Louis in Kansas. But she was now over seventy, was unable to make any headway with their language, and was recalled to St Charles. A further cause of distress was the cessation of what had been regular letters from Mother Barat. This may have been caused by a simple misunderstanding, but it lasted four years, until Mother Barat was alerted to the distress she was causing Philippine, wrote again, and asked a niece of Philippines's to deliver the letter in person.

Philippine Duchesne died at the age of eighty-three on 18 November 1852 and was buried in the convent chapel in St Charles, where her body still lies. A contemporary called her "the St Francis of Assisi of the Society." Pope Pius XII beatified her in 1940, and Pope John Paul II canonized her in 1988.

19

St Hugh of Lincoln (about 1140–1200)

Lincoln's greatest bishop was Burgundian by birth and spent the first forty of his sixty years in France, not England. He is one of the medieval saints known from a contemporary biography, by Abbot Adam of Eynsham, who was his chaplain and confessor during the last four years of his life. Completed thirteen years after his death as part of the preparations for his canonization—a relatively early cause to be referred to the papacy for official and universal authorization—this is known as the *Magna Vita S. Hugonis*, the Great Life of St Hugh.

Hugh was educated by the Augustinian canons and made his profession in the Order when he was fifteen. Ordained deacon at nineteen, he began to gain a reputation as a fine preacher. A visit to the monastery of La Grande Chartreuse, tucked away "almost in the clouds and close to the sky" in the vastness of the French Alps east of Grenoble, changed his life. Despite having promised that he would not leave his Augustinian priory—a promise he decided had been made under duress—he did just that and became a Carthusian at La Grande Chartreuse at the age of twenty-three. After ten years of which virtually nothing is recorded except his love of and affinity with animals, he became procurator, which meant that one of his duties was to welcome visitors. In 1180 one of these was the bishop of Bath, sent by King Henry II of England to invite Hugh, of whom he had heard from a French nobleman, to complete the foundation of Witham Abbey in Somerset, which he had promised as part of his reparation for his part in the murder of Thomas Becket (see 29 Dec.) some ten years earlier. After consulting the Carthusian chapter, Hugh agreed.

He found that building work on the abbey had not even begun and that those on whose land it was supposed to have been built had not been compensated in any way. He insisted this was done first, then oversaw the building, persuaded Henry to meet the costs, overcame local prejudice, and attracted suitable candidates as monks. Henry came to depend on Hugh for advice and rewarded him for his forthright views by pressuring the dean and chapter of Lincoln to elect him as bishop. The huge see, extending from the Humber to the Thames, had been without a bishop almost continuously for eighteen years, thanks to Henry's policy of keeping sees vacant to prevent the Church from becoming too powerful. Hugh tried to refuse, but the prior of La Grande Chartreuse told him to accept. He thus became the only Carthusian to have been a bishop in England.

He set about restoring order in the diocese with his characteristic blend of firmness and kindness. He set an example of dedication, travelling ceaselessly, building pastoral care wherever he went. He found the great cathedral of Lincoln in ruins, badly damaged by an earthquake in 1185, and oversaw its restoration and extension. He was responsible for the overall design and sometimes even actually worked on the building himself. He was reputed to be the most learned monk in England, but he was also cheerful, enthusiastic, fond of conversation and even of children. His concern for justice extended beyond his dealings with three kings—Henry II, Richard I, and John—to defence of Jewish communities during an outbreak of anti-Semitism during the Third Crusade. He upheld the Church's right not to pay a levy to help Richard's war against France, rebuking him to his face when he seized the bishop of Salisbury's goods for refusing to pay. His principles involved him in a long dispute with Hubert Walter, archbishop of Canterbury, always inclined to take the king's side, and in mediating in several other long-running ecclesiastical power struggles.

He had followed Richard to France to attempt to resolve the dispute over seizure of church property to finance the war and was staying at a monastery near Angers when news reached him that the king intended to turn against him, closely followed by news that he was mortally ill from an arrow wound. He went to the abbey of Fontevrault, where Richard was to be buried, arriving just in time to take part in the funeral service. Richard's heir, John, was recognized as such in France, and Hugh spent considerable time and effort in counselling him on the duties of a Christian prince—to little avail. He then returned to England, but the following year, shortly after his coronation, John sent him back to France to witness the Peace of Le Goulet, designed to end hostilities between John and Philip of France. By now Hugh's health was failing, and on his return journey he stopped to pray at the tomb of Thomas Becket in Canterbury. He struggled on to London, where he was forced to take to his bed in the house belonging to the bishops of Lincoln in what is now Lincoln's Inn.

He died there after two months of suffering, on 16 November, and his body was taken to Lincoln in a great six-day triumphal procession. His funeral was attended by three archbishops (including his foe from Canterbury), fourteen bishops, the kings of England and Scotland, a Welsh prince, a hundred abbots, and the people of Lincoln, including representatives from the Jewish ghetto. The king and bishops of England pressed for his canonization—the Carthusians did not consider it right to seek such an honour—and he became the first saint of his Order in 1220. His shrine in Lincoln Cathedral was a place of major pilgrimage until the Reformation, when it was dismantled, and his remains have never since been found.

20

St Edmund of Abingdon (Edmund Rich; about 1175–1240)

Edmund (another medieval saint of whom contemporary Lives exist) was born in Abingdon, Berkshire, into a merchant's family of—probably—two girls and four boys. The dominant influence on them was their mother, Mabel, who lived very austerely and gave her children an exceedingly strict religious education. Edmund went to Oxford University at the age of twelve; after studying grammar there for three years he moved on to Paris, where he studied arts. His mother died during this time (his father having died earlier) and he returned in time to receive her blessing. As head of the family, he arranged for his two sisters to join a Gilbertine monastery in Northamptonshire.

He joined the arts faculty at Oxford, where he became a pioneer in adapting the newly discovered classical philosophy (see St Albert the Great, 15 Nov.), especially that of Aristotle, to Christian theology. In 1201 he returned to Paris to teach theology, and it seems likely that he was ordained priest there. After a year spent with Augustinian canons in Surrey, he went back to Oxford to lecture in theology, probably in 1214. As a scholar, he appreciated the historical context in which the books of the Bible came to be written and distinguished between their literal and their spiritual meaning; as a teacher, he is said to have attended carefully to the individual needs of his pupils.

He was taken away from academic life into church administration in 1222, when he was invited to become a canon and the treasurer of Salisbury Cathedral, which was then being built, making his office an onerous one. He made it even more difficult by contributing a quarter of his income to the cathedral building fund. He lectured at the cathedral school and refreshed himself spiritually—away from contemplating costs—with regular retreats at the Cistercian abbey near Calne, where the abbot, Stephen Lexington, had been a pupil of his at Oxford. Eleven years after his appointment to Salisbury, he found himself nominated by the pope to the archbishopric of Canterbury, which had been vacant for two years—King Henry III, like his father before him, being slow to appoint bishops, as the crown collected revenues from vacant sees. Edmund at first protested, but he submitted when ordered to do so by the bishop of Salisbury and was consecrated on 2 April 1234.

Even if he was at heart a reclusive academic, he possessed personal qualities of warmth, integrity, moral courage, and a concern for justice that were to make him a great reforming archbishop. He was also prudent in his choice of helpers, including his chancellor, Richard of Wych, a former pupil (who went on to become a great bishop himself: St Richard of Chichester; see 3 Apr.), and his own brother Robert. He instinctively disliked court life and politics but developed a frank relationship with the king and mediated successfully in disputes between him and his barons, even while he knew Henry was scheming to limit the influence of the Church and undermine his own position. For this he was accused by the bishop of Lincoln, Robert Grosseteste, of compromising vital principles. He was then accused by the monks of Christ Church in Canterbury of abusing his authority in dealing with them. Unable to resolve this dispute, he went to Rome in 1237 to seek the advice of Pope Gregory IX. After further quarrels with the monks on his return, he excommunicated seventeen of them, earning the disapproval of the king, the papal legate (a royal appointee), and some of his bishops.

Two years later his dealings with the king took a decisive turn for the worse over the question of vacant sees and the revenues from them. He obtained from the pope a Brief stating that an election for a new bishop had to be held once a see had been vacant for six months. Henry persuaded the pope to annul this. Edmund set out for Rome once more to try to get the pope to change his mind back again before attending a general council in 1241, but he was taken ill on his way there, decided to return, and died at an Augustinian priory at Soissy on his way back. One of his early (and unsympathetic) biographers, Matthew of Paris, implies that he was simply walking away from an impossible situation, but this does not seem to be supported by the facts. He was buried in the abbey church at Pontigny, where his remains still lie.

Robert Grosseteste (despite his disagreements with him) and a former pupil, the great Franciscan theologian Alexander of Hales, were members of an inquiry into his life and virtues immediately set up by the pope, and Edmund was canonized in 1246. He was the first Oxford master to be canonized and gives his name to St Edmund Hall there. Henry III made amends to some extent with generous gifts of vestments and other objects for the first celebration of his feast.

Edmund left a considerable body of writing, of which the best known is the "Mirror of the Church," a treatise on the way of perfection for monks and nuns, which was also widely read by secular priests and lay people. It helped to spread devotion to the human person of Christ and compassion for his sufferings from a purely monastic to a generalized Christian spirituality.

21

Bd Mary Siedliska (Franciszka Siedliska; 1842–1902)

Born into a family of wealthy landowners in Poland, Franciszka inherited her father's quick temper and her mother's poor health, but she was intelligent, warm-hearted, and sensitive. She received a good education from tutors at home, though this did not include more than a basic grounding in the nationalistic Catholicism current in Poland at the time. When she was nine, her mother became critically ill, and she prayed to Our Lady of Czestochowa for her recovery, an episode she looked back on as the dawning of her religious sensibility.

She then met a Capuchin friar, Fr Leander Lendzian, at her grandparents' house in Warsaw. He prepared her for her First Communion and Confirmation when she was thirteen, and she began to take a serious interest in religion and to think of a life dedicated to God. Her father had planned the conventional "coming out" in Polish society for her, presumably to be followed by an advantageous marriage, and his opposition to the idea of her becoming a nun made both her and her mother seriously ill. His concern for their health got the better of his intransigence, and he took them both on a tour of Europe, which greatly broadened Franciszka's intellectual and spiritual horizons. They visited Bavaria, Switzerland, and France, and while they were in Cannes he consented to her entering religious life.

She then spent several years of prayer, mortification, and recurrent ill health at home, longing to enter religious life but apparently held back by Fr Leander, who, presumably feeling that nothing else was good enough for her, decided that she had to found a new religious Order. Its spirit was to be informed by the "hidden life and virtues of the Holy Family," and the purpose of its members was to "offer their prayers, works, and their entire life for the Church and the Holy Father." She gained approval for the Congregation of the Holy Family of Nazareth from Pope Pius IX and decided (her background evidently meant that she was not obliged to beg) that its first house should be in Rome— conditions in Poland were too unstable following the Polish National Revolt of 1863. She bought suitable premises in the Via Machiavelli, and the Congregation was formally founded on the First Sunday of Advent in 1875.

The Sisters' prime concern, in accordance with the name of the Congregation, was with family welfare. They looked after neglected and abandoned children, taught religion to young people, and organized preparation courses for couples embarking on marriage as well as discussion groups for young women. Franciszka, now Mother Mary of Jesus the Good Shepherd, devised a Rule that would help to prepare her Sisters mentally and enable them physically to undertake this sort of work. "True charity," she wrote, "does not compel or restrict, and no Rule should do so either." There was to be no attempt to mould the personalities of the Sisters according to preconceived notions of what women religious should be: "In Nazareth there should be freedom of conscience, the liberty of the children of God, regard for the psyche of the Sisters, their temperament, and their natural disposition."

Mother Mary was ahead of her time in her psychology and thoroughly in tune with it in her assessment of its needs. Demand for her Congregation's services spread, and she opened a second house in Cracow in 1881, followed by three others in her native Poland. Poles were emigrating in large numbers to more developed industrial countries, and requests for Nazareth Sisters to care for them came from the USA, France, and England. Houses were opened in Chicago in 1885, in Paris—despite initial opposition from the cardinal archbishop—in 1891, and in London, where it took her two years to find enough Sisters to respond to Cardinal Vaughan's request, in 1895. He told her that her Sisters would have "only work and my blessing. I have neither money nor schools. They must obtain everything." Mother Mary went to America three times, despite her poor health, and to Paris and London, where she was shocked by the material squalor she found but even more by the spiritual degradation of people "living like pagans, without the sacraments, in the state of sin and serious transgression."

Mother Mary died after a short final illness on 21 November 1902. Her friend and adviser Fr Lechert, appointed spiritual director of the Congregation at the time of its foundation, was present at her bedside and wrote: "She died as a saint, and we all regard her as a saint." The Informative Process for her cause was started in 1922; in 1940 Pope Pius XII formally introduced the Cause of Beatification; a miracle of healing through her intercession was accepted in 1988, and Pope John Paul II beatified her on 23 April 1989. The cause of eleven

Nazareth Sisters who offered their lives in exchange for those of fathers of families arrested in Nazi-occupied Poland is also going forward. They were all shot and buried in a common grave on 1 August 1943. Their bodies were exhumed and reburied in the cemetery of Nowogrodek after a formal funeral service in March 1945.

22

St Cecilia (supposedly Third Century)

There is unfortunately no historical evidence for the existence of the patron saint of music, only a legend dating from two centuries after her supposed martyrdom. The story derives from a church in the Roman district of Trastevere founded by a Roman lady named Cecilia. It may be based on an actual martyrdom, but scholars now debate this.

It tells of a Christian Roman maiden from a patrician family who wanted to dedicate herself to God as a virgin but was obliged by her family to marry a young man named Valerian. After the ceremony, she told Valerian about Jesus, adding that her virginity was protected by an angel, and that he could choose between seeing the angel if he respected it and being punished by the angel if he tried to consummate the marriage. He went off to find Pope Urban, who was living among the poor along the Appian Way, and asked to be baptized. On his return, he found the angel standing beside his wife, and they both received a crown of flowers. Then his brother Tiburtius arrived, was told the story, and also went off to be baptized. The two then devoted themselves to good works and were arrested for burying the bodies of martyred Christians. Refusing to recant, they were beheaded outside Rome, together with an official named Maximus, who was converted by their example. Cecilia then buried their bodies.

Officials tried to persuade her to sacrifice to the imperial gods, but she converted them to Christianity instead. A crowd gathered at her house, and Pope Urban baptized some four hundred people there, one of whom established it as a church—the detail that reveals the origin of the story. Cecilia was condemned to be suffocated in her bathroom, which failed, and then beheaded, which was bungled, so that she lingered for three days. She was buried in the catacomb of San Callisto.

Moving from legend into history, complications arise in writing off the whole story as a fabrication. Valerian, Tiburtius, and Maximus were actual martyrs, historically identifiable and buried in the catacomb of Praetextatus. In 821 Pope St Paschal I had their remains moved to St Cecilia's in Trastevere, together with her supposed body, which he had been told in a dream was there and not in

San Callisto. He had this enclosed in a cypress coffin in a marble tomb. In 1599 restoration work was carried out on the church and the bodies had to be reinterred. That claimed as Cecilia's was incorrupt and remained so for some days, long enough for the sculptor Stefano Madera to make a likeness of it, before contact with the air caused it to disintegrate. The body was seen by many people, and full descriptions were written of it by such reputable historians as Cardinal Baronius, who had helped compile the 1584 Roman Martyrology and knew the difference between history and legend. But whose body was it? Incorrupt bodies are not a feature of earlier stories of saints, and no mention was made of it in 821; by the sixteenth century they had become quite "fashionable," and the discovery was a great coup for the church of St Cecilia. She was extremely popular at the time, especially as she had become the patron saint of music when the Academia della Musica was founded in Rome in 1584, based on a misunderstanding of the antiphon in the Office for her feast, which adopts the words from her legend that say she "sang in her heart" to distract herself from the events at her wedding: the "in her heart" was later dropped, and so she was shown singing, and later playing the organ, which she is supposed to have invented.

She is the subject of the second Nun's Tale in Chaucer's *Canterbury Tales*. The poets Dryden, Pope, and Auden, amongst others, have composed odes and hymns to her. Handel composed in her honour, and more recently Benjamin Britten set Auden's hymn to music. She appears in paintings by Fra Angelico, Pietro da Cortona, Raphael, and others, and Albi Cathedral together with numerous churches are dedicated to her.

23

St Clement of Rome (died about 100)

Clement, in the traditional order familiar from the "Roman canon" of the Mass, was the fourth Bishop of Rome, after Peter, Linus, and Cletus, though another tradition places him second. He was one of the first generation of Christians after the apostles, and as such a vital witness to the early life of the Church. St Irenaeus (see 28 June), writing in the second century, claims that he received the teaching of the apostles at first hand, and Origen, some decades later, called him a "disciple of the apostles." In Philippians 4:3 Paul speaks of those who have "struggled beside me in the work of the gospel, together with Clement and the rest of my co-workers, whose names are in the book of life." It is possible, though it cannot be proved, that this is the same Clement.

Between 95 and 98, Clement wrote an *Epistle to the Corinthians*, which survives as a complete text. It provides the earliest example of the Church of Rome (it is written as from the whole Church there, not just from the bishop) intervening in the affairs of another Church, spontaneously, not in response to an invitation. The letter urges reconciliation and respect for the tradition of the apostles, but we no longer know what the problem that occasioned it was. It presents a summary of Christian teaching divided into sections on the Person and work of Christ; sanctification–justification; the Holy Spirit and the Trinity; the Church and ministry; liturgy; eschatology; the Christian life; scripture (meaning the Old Testament) and gospel; Peter and Paul, apostles and martyrs. This last section provides a precious early witness to the fact of their martyrdom.

In the Middle Ages Clement was known less as the author of this document (and possibly of a second letter to the Corinthians) than as a martyr, with a rather fanciful Passion written in the fourth century. According to this, he was exiled to the Crimea, put to work in the mines, and eventually thrown into the sea with an anchor round his neck for making too many converts. Angels made him a grave on the sea bed, which was uncovered once a year by an exceptionally low tide. Following this legend, SS Cyril and Methodius (see 16 Feb.) "miraculously" recovered the body and the anchor. The remains were taken to Rome in about 868 and buried in the church of San Clemente, which had been built on the site of a third-century "pastoral centre" named the *titulus Clementis*, itself developed from a first-century place of Christian worship in the house of a man named Clement—which suggests that the legend developed from the place, as in the case of St Cecilia (above).

He became a popular subject in art, shown with an anchor or with a tiara and a three-branched cross. There is a fine series of frescoes in San Clemente depicting his life and legend, dating from the ninth century. The church of St Clement Danes in London (the parish emblem of which is an anchor) is the best-known dedication to him in England, and he is also patron of Trinity House in London, the body responsible for lighthouses and lightships in and around Britain.

24

St Columbanus (about 543–615)

Columbanus was perhaps the greatest of the Irish "exiles for Christ" who did so much to evangelize the Continent of Europe in the sixth and seventh centuries. Born in Leinster, he received a good education in both the Bible and the Latin Fathers and pagan classical authors. He was distracted from his studies for a time by certain "lascivious wenches" (hardly the first or the last to be so) and, on the advice of a woman hermit, took the drastic step of removing himself entirely from such temptations by becoming a monk, to the great distress of his mother. He studied first under a certain Sinell at the island foundation of Cluain Inis and then at Bangor (Bennchorr, in Irish) under St Comgall (see 10 May), spending "many years" teaching there before undertaking his voluntary exile, probably in about 590, though earlier dates, such as 573, are also given.

He travelled with a group of companions by sea and land across Cornwall, the Channel, and Brittany and pressed on in a south-easterly direction into the kingdom of the Franks, by then partitioned (since 561) and thoroughly lapsed from its earlier Christianity under Clovis (died 511) and his queen, St Clothilde. The Irish monks found paganism, witchcraft, magic, and ritual murder rife. On their way they had visited the court of King Childebert II of Austrasia (now approximately the region of Alsace) and been given an old Roman fort at Annegray, in the foothills of the Vosges mountains, where they established their first monastery, soon founding another some eight miles to the west at Luxeuil. Their austere way of life, codified in Columbanus' own Rule, attracted many followers, but their Irish customs, with a bishop subordinate to the abbot, a different date for Easter, and the Irish tonsure across the front part of the head, and some very penitential practices based on those of the Desert Fathers all annoyed the Frankish bishops, who summoned Columbanus to explain himself at a synod. Regarding them as negligent and lax, he refused to attend but wrote them a letter effectively suggesting they were bothering about trifles and should leave him, "a poor stranger in these parts for the cause of Christ," and his monks in peace. But the bishops renewed their attacks, concentrating on the Easter question, and Columbanus wrote to Pope St Gregory I (see 3 Sept.) asking for confirmation of the validity of his tradition. Gregory sent him a copy of his *Pastoral Care* and advised him to consult the abbot of Lérins. A kind of truce ensued for some years, followed by renewed attacks and a fresh appeal for tolerance. The Irish monks introduced the practice of auricular confession, imposing harsh penances in accordance with a book of *Penitentials* compiled by Columbanus.

Columbanus then fell foul of the Burgundian royal family. The king respected him and used him as an adviser, but Columbanus could not tolerate the fact that he kept concubines and refused to bless his illegitimate children. This incurred the wrath of Theodoric's formidable grandmother, Brunhilda, who exercised a matriarchal rule and did not want Theodoric marrying and so introducing a legitimate queen who might be a rival. She harried the Irish monks until they were forced to leave the kingdom, though the Franks who had joined their monasteries were allowed to stay.

Columbanus and his Irish companions first tried to settle in Tours but were forced under military escort to Nantes, to be deported back to Ireland by sea. Their ship ran into a fierce storm and was forced to turn back. They crossed Gaul once more, by a more northerly route, to Metz, where the Austrasian king, Theodebert II, received them kindly. They finally rowed up the Rhine in the depths of winter, hoping to settle at Bregenz on Lake Constance, but the excessive zeal of their preaching made them enemies, and when Austrasia and Burgundy went to war and Austrasia was defeated, Columbanus' position became untenable and he decided to travel farther afield.

By now aged about seventy, he crossed the Alps to Milan, leaving his disciple Gall and some other monks behind, after what may have been a quarrel. He was well received by King Agilulf (or Duke Agilof) of Lombardy, who was an Arian, though his wife and children were Catholics. He found himself caught up in the complex doctrinal issue of the writings (and writers) known as the Three Chapters, about which he knew little. Persuaded by Agilulf's wife, Theodelinda, who was a passionate defender of the Three Chapters, he wrote a letter to Pope Boniface IV, ostensibly in their defence but actually defending the orthodoxy of his own position: "For we are the disciples of Saints Peter and Paul and all the disciples who by the Holy Spirit wrote the divine canon. No one of us has been a heretic, no one a Jew, no one a schismatic ... the Catholic faith is maintained unchanged." He added that he was a "greenhorn" (*glabrum*) in the matter of the Three Chapters, and so there was no reason for anyone to listen to him on the subject.

The royal couple gave Columbanus land and a ruined church at Bobbio, in an Apennine pass between Genoa and Piacenza, and here he built his last monastery. In 613 King Clotaire II of Neustria reunited the Frankish kingdom, and he invited Columbanus to return, but he was by now preparing for death and refused. He died at Bobbio on 3 November 615 and was buried there. The next abbot commissioned a monk named Jonas, who had joined the abbey three years after Columbanus' death, to write his Life, which he did with the help of many who had known him. Over the centuries Bobbio acquired a great library and became a major influence on learning in northern Italy until the sixteenth century. It was finally suppressed by the French in 1803. Luxeuil, which Columbanus had asked Clotaire to protect, equally flourished until the French Revolution.

25

Bd Michael Pro (Miguel Pro Juárez; 1891–1927)

One of the ten children of Miguel Pro and his wife Josefina Juárez, Miguel was born in Guadalupe, in the Mexican State of Zacatecas. A happy and strongly Catholic upbringing was marred only by his recurrent ill health and the fact that his father's job as a government mining engineer forced the family to move often. Miguel was sent to the Jesuit college in Mexico City at the age of ten, but his health did not allow him to stay there long. After a short spell at another college he had private tutors at home until, at the age of fifteen, he embarked on secretarial work for his father. He was cheerful, sensitive, and popular but felt some lack in his life. He identified this when one of his sisters became a nun: in August 1911 he entered the novitiate of the Mexican province of the Society of Jesus at El Llano in the state of Michoacán.

The long-ruling dictator Porfirio Diaz, under whom the hierarchy had recovered much of the Church's property and position lost to earlier liberal governments, had died in 1910. The ensuing confused years saw two rival movements, led by General Carranza and Pancho Villa respectively, struggling for power but both strongly anti-Catholic. A group of Carranza's men ransacked the novitiate at El Llano, forcing Miguel and the other student priests to flee over the border into Texas. He joined the Jesuit community at El Gato in California and then embarked on the long Jesuit course of study in preparation for the priesthood. He studied classics and philosophy for five years in Granada in Spain, took a master's degree after two years in Granada in Nicaragua, then returned to Europe, to Sarria in Spain and Enghien in Belgium, for a four-year theology course. He was finally ordained at Enghien in August 1925, after which his health relapsed and he had to undergo a number of painful operations.

He returned to Mexico in July 1926 to find the country in a state of virtual religious civil war. The Church had been effectively outlawed by the Constitution of 1917, the provisions of which finally became law in 1926. On 25 July, just over two weeks after Miguel's return, the bishops retaliated by declaring a religious strike, banning all public worship. A peasant uprising in several States against the government broke out, using the slogan "Long Live Christ the King and the Virgin of Guadalupe," unleashing the three-year *cristero* war. The Church held back from condoning the violence, but many priests and committed lay people were members of the League for the Defence of Religious Freedom, the umbrella movement backing the *cristeros*. Miguel carried out a clandestine ministry from his family's house: he set up Communion stations across Mexico City, somehow managing to celebrate Eucharists, hear confessions, administer other sacraments, and conduct retreats, always a step ahead of the police, helped by his two brothers, Humberto and Roberto, who were members of the League.

He and his brothers were finally arrested on 18 November 1927. He was accused of plotting to assassinate the president-elect, General Alvaro Obregón. He had not done so, but the car containing the bomb that wounded Obregón had belonged to one of his brothers until he sold it a week before the attempt. There was no evidence against him, and the person responsible for the attempt gave himself up, but Obregón decided to frighten Catholic opposition by executing Miguel without even a semblance of a trial. He assembled a crowd to witness the execution on 23 November, led him out before a firing squad, and ordered them to shoot. Miguel held up his arms in a cross and shouted "Viva Cristo Rey." Humberto was also shot, but Roberto was spared. Obregón had miscalculated the consequences: twenty thousand people attended Miguel's funeral, news of his death spread rapidly around the world, and he was everywhere acclaimed as a modern martyr. Political conditions in Mexico prevented his cause from going ahead until 1952, and he was beatified by Pope John Paul II on 25 September 1988.

26

St Leonard of Port Maurice (Paolo Girolamo Casanova; 1676–1751)

Born into the family of a master mariner at Porto Maurizio on the Italian Riviera, Paolo was sent to live with a wealthy uncle in Rome and studied literature and philosophy there at the Jesuit college. His uncle wanted him to become a physician, but Paolo was convinced he had a vocation as a Franciscan, which led the uncle to turn him out of his house. He was able to stay with another relative, Leonardo Ponzetti, until he received his father's permission to join the Franciscans, whereupon he took the name Leonardo out of gratitude. He studied at the friary of San Bonaventura in Rome and was ordained in 1702. Shortly after his ordination he developed tuberculosis, which put an end to his dreams of being an overseas missionary.

He taught philosophy for some years at San Bonaventura, which belonged to an offshoot of the strict reformed Franciscans known as the *Riformella*, and in 1709 was sent to Florence, where he reintroduced reformed ideals in the convent of San Francesco del Monte, which had been given to the *Riformella* by the grand duke of Florence, Cosimo III de'Medici. It became a major missionary institution, from where Leonard and other friars set out on preaching missions all over Tuscany. His preaching was extremely effective, and people flocked back to the sacraments. He was increasingly called on to preach farther afield, and one mission in Rome lasted so long that Cosimo sent a ship up the Tiber to fetch him back. In 1736, however, he was appointed guardian of San Bonaventura and returned to Rome. From there he again preached missions far and wide, often attracting such large crowds that he had to move out of churches and preach in the open air. He preached to soldiers, sailors, convicts, and galley slaves in the port of Civitavecchia, and at the other end of the social scale acted as spiritual director to Clementina Sobieska, the wife of James Edward Stuart, the Old Pretender.

In 1744, when he was already sixty-eight, the pope sent him to evangelize Corsica, where religion and social order, torn apart by vendettas, were both in a state of decay. Corsica was under the rule of the doge of Genoa, and Leonard was met with some hostility as he was suspected of being an agent of the doge. He persevered, preaching often to congregations in which the men carried guns, but he saw that any peace he could bring would prove temporary without an effective system of justice. After six months he was exhausted and ill, and a ship was sent from Genoa to bring him back. Corsica relapsed into its previous chaos, as he had predicted, and there were no plans to send him there again. He continued to preach and give retreats, but his health was progressively failing, he had a hostile reception in some places, and he was generally less successful than he had previously been. In November 1745 he returned to Rome, in a carriage the pope had insisted on. This broke down, and he had to finish the journey on foot. He was carried to bed on arrival at San Bonaventura and given the last sacraments. The pope sent an affectionate last message, and he died before midnight on 26 November.

His influence on Catholic devotion was wider than the physical scope of his missions. He was one of the first to use the Stations of the Cross as a "preaching aid," and their continued popularity is largely due to him. He also insisted on the importance of the Immaculate Conception as a doctrine, convinced that it should be decreed as a dogma after consultation with the people of God as a whole rather than through a council involving only bishops. This is what happened, a little more than a century after his death.

27

St Cuthbert Mayne and other English Martyrs (died between 1539 and 1610)

Cuthbert Mayne was the first of the "seminary" priests—those ordained abroad at Douai, as opposed to "Marian" priests, ordained in England under Mary Tudor—to be executed for his faith. He was brought up in Devon by an uncle who was a former Catholic priest, ordained a priest of the Church of England at the age of nineteen, and then studied at Oxford, where he met Edmund Campion (see 1 Dec.), who was still a Protestant but soon became a Catholic and went over to Douai. Mayne corresponded with him and became convinced of the truth of Catholicism. One of his letters fell into the hands of the bishop of London, and he was nearly arrested. He was accepted as a student for the Catholic priesthood in 1573, took a BA in theology at Douai and was ordained there, and returned to the West Country in April 1576.

He posed as an estate steward at Golden Manor near Truro in Cornwall, the home of Francis Tregian. On 8 June the following year a posse of a hundred men appeared at the gates and arrested most of the household, including him.

He was incriminated by an *agnus dei* (a devotional article in the form of a wax medallion of a lamb) worn round his neck. He was taken to Launceston Castle and tried for a number of offences against the Act of Supremacy, which required recognition of Elizabeth I as supreme head of the Church in England. He refused this at the trial and the day before his execution. A verdict of guilty of treason was upheld by the Privy Council, despite the reasoned objections of one of the judges, and he was hanged, drawn, and quartered on 30 November 1577, having refused to implicate Francis Tregian in anything other than being "good and pious." Nevertheless, Tregian's lands were confiscated and he was imprisoned for nearly thirty years. Cuthbert Mayne was canonized in 1970 as one of the Forty Martyrs of England and Wales (see 25 Oct.).

Others who suffered in the month of November for their Catholic faith are recorded briefly below, in chronological order of their date of death.

Richard Whiting, the last abbot of Glastonbury, initially took the 1534 Oath of Supremacy enacted by Henry VIII and the following year was assured that the monastery was in such good order that no action would be taken against it. Four years later it was the only monastery remaining in Somerset; commissioners arrived to examine it, found various incriminating documents, and took Abbot Richard to the Tower of London. The case was pre-judged: "Item, the abbot of Glaston to be tried at Glaston and executed there," is stated in Thomas Cromwell's notebook. Richard was condemned, probably in Wells, and taken to the top of Glastonbury Tor, where he was hanged and dismembered, on 15 November 1539. The abbey treasurer, John Thorne, and sacristan, Roger James, were executed with him. Hugh Cook (known as Faringdon from his birthplace), abbot of Reading, had been personally friendly with King Henry VIII and supported most of his measures until the suppression of the greater monasteries, which he resisted. He was then charged with treason and taken to the Tower. He was executed on the same day as Richard, together with John Eynon, a priest from Reading, and John Rugg, a retired prebendary of Chichester Cathedral living in Reading. These six were beatified in 1895.

John Bodey, son of a former mayor of Wells, was born in 1549 and educated at Winchester and New College, Oxford, where he became a fellow but was deprived of his fellowship for being a Roman Catholic. He studied law at Douai but was not ordained and may have married on his return to England. He was arrested for denying the Oath of Supremacy, imprisoned in Winchester for three years, tried twice, and executed on 2 November 1583. He was beatified in 1929.

Hugh Taylor was born in Durham and studied for the priesthood at Reims (where the English College moved from Douai from 1578 to 1593 owing to political troubles). He had been back in England less than a year when Marmaduke Bowes, a Catholic who had outwardly conformed, either sheltered or refreshed him. Then, hearing that Taylor had been arrested, he went to York assizes to see if he could help to free him. Instead, he was arrested, imprisoned, and condemned to death also. They died together at York on 26 November 1585, the first to suffer under the 1585 Act Against Jesuits, Seminary Priests and Other Suchlike Disobedient Subjects, which made it high treason to be a priest ordained since Elizabeth's accession in England and Wales, or for anyone knowingly to harbour such a priest. Both were beatified among the Eighty-five Martyrs of England and Wales in 1987.

Alexander Crow, from south Yorkshire, worked as a shoemaker for some years but then went to Reims and was ordained in 1584. Two or three years later he was arrested while he was going to baptize a child, taken to York, tried under the same 1585 Act, condemned, and executed on 30 November in either 1586 or 1587. It is said that he was tempted to suicide during his last night in prison, but prayer made this "monster" disappear in time for him to face the gallows. He is another of the eighty-five beatified in 1987.

Edward Burden came from Cleveland and became a Fellow of Corpus Christi College and a Master of Arts at Oxford before going to Reims to study for the priesthood in 1583. Ordained at Soissons the following year, he was sent back in 1586 to minister in Yorkshire, where, as he was recovering from a serious illness, he aroused the suspicions of a certain John Constable, who, after robbing him of everything, took him to York, where the Council put him in prison. He was dragged from a sickbed to court, condemned as a priest ordained abroad and therefore a traitor, and executed on 29 November 1588. He too was beatified in 1987.

Edward Osbaldeston, from Lancashire, was sent to be educated at Reims and then went on to study for the priesthood there, returning to Lancashire in 1589. After ministering there for several years, he was betrayed by a former priest, tried for treason under the 1585 Act, condemned to death, and executed on 16 November 1594. He too was beatified in 1987 as one of the Eighty-five Martyrs of England and Wales.

The year 1596 was the first since 1580 in which no priest was executed for the faith "in this kingdom," according to Bishop Challoner. Three laymen were, however: George Errington, William Gibson, and William Knight. All from the north, they were betrayed by a Protestant minister who tricked them into thinking he was interested in becoming a Catholic and then handed them over to the authorities. They were executed at York on 26 November 1596 and are also included among the eighty-five beatified in 1987.

George Napper was born in Oxford in 1550 and expelled from Corpus Christi College as a recusant. He was arrested as such in 1580 and imprisoned for nine years, being released after admitting the royal supremacy. He regretted this and went to Douai, where he was ordained in 1596. Sent back on the

English mission in 1603, he ministered in Oxfordshire for seven years before being arrested, tried, and condemned for being a seminary priest. He had influential friends, who obtained a stay of execution. In prison he reconciled a condemned man to the Catholic Church and was again reprieved, but then he refused to take the oath of allegiance and was finally condemned to death and executed in Oxford on 9 November 1610. He was beatified in 1929.

28

St Roque González and Companions (died 1628)

These three Jesuit martyrs in Paraguay are the earliest from the Americas to have been beatified. Other missionaries were killed before them, from as early as 1516, but not enough is known about the circumstances of their deaths for their causes to be opened.

The Jesuits came relatively late to the missions in the New World, preceded by Franciscans, Dominicans, Mercedarians, and others. This applied in Paraguay, where the governor of the capital, Asunción, and the local bishop specifically asked for them in 1609. When they arrived, they brought a new approach, setting up the communities that came to be known as "reductions." These were villages in which Indians would be instructed as Christians while being protected from European settlers, who were not allowed inside them. They saw themselves as guardians of the Indians, not as their conquerors, and the reductions flourished for a century or more until the Society was suppressed in Latin America for its opposition to Spanish imperialism.

Each reduction was built on a similar pattern, had an average population of about three thousand, and was virtually self-sufficient, with a combination of collective and private ownership of goods and produce. At their height, there were between thirty and fifty of them. They would now be seen as excessively paternalistic, but in their time they were extremely enlightened, not least in their encouragement of the native talents of the Indians (as emerges in the film *The Mission*). Voltaire, no friend of the Jesuits by inclination, wrote that they had achieved "what is perhaps the highest degree of civilization to which it is possible to lead a young people."

Roque González y de Santa Cruz was born into a noble family of Spanish settlers in Asunción in 1576 and from an early age showed qualities that led everyone to expect him to become a priest. He felt he was unworthy, but he was ordained at the age of twenty-three and started seeking out the indigenous peoples in remote areas to preach Christianity to them. He then joined the Jesuits, seeing this as a way to avoid rising up the hierarchical ladder and to have more time for mission activity. He became involved in the reductions from their start, being in charge of the first, San Ignacio Guazú, for three years from its inception in 1611 and then going on to found others. This took him into parts where no Europeans had yet set foot and into considerable danger from animals, insects, the elements, and hostile tribes—dangers that, as the then governor of Corrientes wrote, "No man but a true apostle, who was as holy as this priest was, could have borne with such fortitude." He became a figure of great influence, respected by the Indians and the colonizing civil authorities alike. The latter eventually undermined his work and that of other missionaries by using him as a way of introducing their representatives into the reductions, where they generally behaved brutally.

In 1628 two young but already experienced Spanish Jesuits, Alonso Rodrí-guez and Juan de Castillo, came to join him. Together, they started a reduction near the Ijuhi River, where they left Juan in charge while the other two pushed farther south and started another in Caaró (now the southern tip of Brazil). There a local medicine man, convinced that all Jesuits had to be killed, organized an attack on the mission. On 15 November Roque was hanging a church bell when he was attacked from behind with a tomahawk, from which he died instantly. Alonso emerged from his hut and was immediately attacked and killed. The two bodies were dragged into the wooden chapel, which was set on fire. The attackers moved on to the Ijuhi mission, where they stoned Juan to death. Three more Spanish Jesuits were killed over the next three days.

Moves to have these martyrs beatified began immediately, with witness accounts of what had happened taken down in writing, including a moving testimony from an Indian chief on how the Indians grieved for Fr Roque, "because he was the father of us all, and so he was called by the Indians of the Paraná." These papers were then lost on their way to Rome, and so the process came to a halt. Some two hundred years later, copies of the original documents came to light in Argentina, and the process was restarted and speedily con-cluded. Roque, Alonso, and Juan were beatified by Pope Pius XI in 1934 and canonized by Pope John Paul II in 1988.

29

St Saturninus of Toulouse (or Sernin; possibly Third Century)

This saint gives his name to the great basilica of Saint-Sernin in Toulouse in south-western France, an important stage on the pilgrim route to Santiago de Compostela and so in need of a major saint to compete with other places along the route. The name Saturninus is African, but nothing is really known about his origins or his early life. He is venerated as a missionary and martyr and as the first bishop of Toulouse, but his *passio* dates from some centuries after his life and cannot be counted as a historical document. Nevertheless, the story it tells sheds some interesting light on conditions during the early years of the spread of Christianity in Gaul. He was known to such writers as Sidonius Apollinaris (d. about 479) and Venantius Fortunatus (died about 600), as well as Gregory of Tours (died 594), who shows himself familiar with the text of the *passio*, indicating that it was written before the end of the sixth century.

The story is that his church in Toulouse was on one side of the city's main pagan temple, while his house was on the other side. The temple oracles had fallen silent for some years, and the priests blamed this on the presence of a Christian bishop. They seized Saturninus one day, dragged him into the temple and ordered him to offer ritual sacrifice to the gods or have his own blood spilt to propitiate them. He replied that he could not respect gods who could be silenced by a bishop, while the God he worshipped was the one true one. They tied him to a bull, which was then goaded into rushing down a hill, dragging Saturninus, until his brains were dashed out against rocks. The rope finally broke, and two Christian women hid his body in a ditch. It was later enshrined in what became the basilica.

He is supposed to have preached in northern Spain as well as southern Gaul, and there is evidence of a widespread cult in both areas dating from the third century. His fame spread as Compostela became one of the three great destinations (with Jerusalem and Rome) for pious medieval pilgrims, and many churches along the route were dedicated to him. There is a thirteenth-century cycle of paintings of his life in the Museum of Catalan Art in Barcelona and a sixteenth-century one in Tours. The manner of his death suggests that some sort of bullfighting was carried on in the area at the time, as it still is, and his emblem is a bull.

There is another St Saturninus also commemorated today, and when two saints of the same name have been venerated on the same day, research has usually shown that they are two "variants" on the same person. This does not seem to be true in today's case as there are no points of similarity, the other being a martyr in Rome during the persecution under Maximian from 306 to 308 and the subject of an exactly contemporary *passio* written by Pope St Marcellus I, who was pope for the same years.

30

St Andrew (First Century)

"As Jesus passed along the Sea of Galilee, he saw Simon and his brother Andrew casting a net into the lake—for they were fishermen. And Jesus said to them, 'Follow me, and I will make you fish for people.' And immediately they left their nets and followed him" (Mark 1:16–18). This is the first appearance of Andrew in the New Testament, from which all information about him derives. Mark's account is substantially followed by Matthew (4:18–22) and Luke (5:1–11), though here he is not named and would be simply one of Simon's "partners." John (1:35–42) gives a rather different account of his calling. He is one of two disciples of John the Baptist who follow Jesus when John tells them, "Look, here is the Lamb of God": "One of the two who heard John speak and followed him was Andrew, Simon Peter's brother. He first found his brother Simon and said to him, 'We have found the Messiah' (which is translated Anointed). He brought Simon to Jesus, who looked at him and said, 'You are Simon son of John. You are to be called Cephas' (which is translated Peter)" (vv. 40–42). This, besides its different starting-point, is obviously a sophisticated theological reworking, introducing concepts—Lamb of God, Messiah, Anointed (Christ)—applied to Jesus in the church communities, and anticipating the giving of the title (*Cephas* literally means "rock") that implies pre-eminence to Peter.

Andrew always appears among the first four in lists of the names of the twelve apostles, and in the Greek tradition he is *protoclete*, "first-called." He appears twice individually: in John 6:8–10 "One of his disciples, Andrew, Simon Peter's brother" tells Jesus that there is a boy who has five barley loaves and two fish, asking how they can feed a large crowd; in John 12:22 he relays Philip's message to Jesus that some Greeks wish to talk to him (which elicits a somewhat enigmatic response about a grain of wheat). It has to be said that he fades into the background compared to Peter, John, and James. He does not feature in the Acts of the Apostles, and there is no more than legend about what he did subsequent to Pentecost. One view, supported by the historian Eusebius and others, is that he preached in Greece. A much later account is that he founded the see of Byzantium, later Constantinople, but this is connected with the prestige attached to his claimed relics. Nothing for certain is known about his death either: the tradition of his crucifixion at Patras in Greece on an X-shaped—"saltire" in heraldic terms—cross did not appear before the tenth century.

His supposed relics were taken to Constantinople in 356 or 357 in order to give the new capital of the empire a prestige comparable to Rome, which had the relics of his brother, and enshrined in the Church of the Apostles (though some parts may have remained at Patras—see below). When Crusaders took the city in 1204 they sent his body to Amalfi; his head was separated and taken to Rome in about 1461, remaining there until Pope Paul VI made the ecumenical gesture of returning it to Constantinople in the 1970s. His feast was universally celebrated in the West from the sixth century, and he is one of the patrons of Russia, although there is no viable claim that he ever went there.

His patronage of Scotland derives from the story of a St Regulus, or Rule, who had charge of the relics that remained at Patras after most had been taken to Constantinople. Told by an angel to take these "to the ends of the earth," Regulus obeyed, headed north-west, and reached what were certainly regarded as the ends of the earth at the time (and still are by many Londoners), ending his journey at what is now St Andrew's in Scotland. There he built a church to house the relics and became the first bishop of St Andrew's. There are several different versions of this legend, which a Victorian historian of Scotland considered to be so unlikely as possibly to contain elements of truth.

The Declaration of Arbroath—an appeal by eight earls, various other lords and officers, and "the whole community of the realm of Scotland" addressed to Pope John XXII in 1321, asking him to put a stop to the "deeds of cruelty, massacre, violence, pillage, arson, imprisoning prelates, burning down monasteries, robbing and killing monks and nuns, and yet other outrages without number" inflicted by Edward I of England on the people of Scotland—invokes St Andrew, "the first of [Christ's] Apostles—by calling, though second or third in rank—the most gentle Saint Andrew, the Blessed Peter's brother," chosen by Christ "to keep [the Scottish people] under his protection as their patron forever." This, the document claims, showed that the Scots, "even though settled in the uttermost parts of the earth," had been called "almost the first to His most holy faith." The document, probably composed by Bernard de Denton, abbot of Arbroath and chancellor of Scotland, may be inaccurate in its history of the Scottish people, but it is a fine assertion of human rights and democratic principles, pointing out that the signatories will support their king, Robert the Bruce, for as long and only as long as he does not agree to make his people "subject to the King of England or the English." It has to be said that in later years St Andrew has not been invoked with the same emotional force as warrior leaders such as William Wallace.

Other Familiar English Names for November

1. Mary, Peter, Rupert
2. George, John, Margaret
3. Hubert, Peter, Simon
4. Frances, Helen
5. Bernard, Dominic, Gerald, John
6. Joan, John, Leonard, Paul, Peter, Stephen
7. Antony, Helen, Margaret, Peter, Vincent
8. Elizabeth, Godfrey, Hugh, John, Joseph, Martin, Mary, Paul
9. Gabriel, George, Joan, Louis
10. Andrew
11. John
12. Benedict, Gabriel, John, Margaret
13. Nicholas
14. John, Nicholas, Peter, Stephen
15. Hugh, John, Leopold, Lucy, Richard, Roger
16. Edward
17. Elizabeth, Gregory, Hugh, John, Thomas
18. Andrew, Caroline, Dominic, John, Leonard, Mary
19. James
20. Angela, Francis, Gregory, Mary
21. *There are no other familiar English names for today*
22. Peter
23. Gregory, Margaret, Mary
24. Albert, Andrew, Antony, Dominic, Francis, John, Joseph, Laurence, Martin, Mary, Michael, Nicholas, Paul, Peter, Philip, Simon, Stephen, Thomas, Vincent
25. Elizabeth, Peter
26. Dominic, James, Hugh, Peter, Thomas
27. James, Thomas
28. Andrew, James, John, Joseph, Stephen
29. Edward, Francis, George, William
30. Alexander, Frederick, John, Joseph, Michael

DECEMBER

December has saints who feature in the Universal Calendar on sixteen of its thirty-one days, more in the early and late parts of the month than in the middle. In three cases, more recent saints have been preferred to the main entry in the Roman Martyrology. I have moved relatively few from their correct date: Bd Anuarite Nengapeta from the 1st, which belongs to St Edmund Campion, to the 8th (which is of course liturgically the feast of the Immaculate Conception); the newly canonized Juan Diego comes in on the 13th, the day after the feast of Our Lady of Guadalupe, which is also that of St Jane Frances de Chantal, who is given the 12th; St Thorlac is found a place on the 20th instead of the 23rd; St Melania the Younger is on the 17th, moved forward from an overcrowded 31st; St John-Francis Régis comes forward by one day from the 31st, leaving it to St Catherine Labouré.

1

St Edmund Campion (about 1540–1581)

The first Jesuit to be executed under the Elizabethan statutes in force prior to the 1585 Act aimed specifically at Jesuits, Campion was brilliant, humorous, and daring to the point of folly. Born in London and educated first at Bluecoat School, he won a scholarship to St John's College, Oxford, at the age of fifteen, was appointed a junior fellow, and built a great reputation as an orator.

To progress further in academic life, he had to make his religious allegiance clear. He had grown up in Queen Mary's reign, with its restoration of Catholicism as the state religion, and although he took the 1559 Oath of Supremacy recognizing Elizabeth as head of the Church in England, he was increasingly troubled by this and felt unable to go forward to ordination. In 1569 he left England and went to Dublin, where he produced a *Short History of Ireland* that would have done nothing to help overcome English prejudices concerning the Irish. He could not settle in Dublin, despite its more relaxed religious climate, and returned to England in 1571. By this time Pope Pius V (see 1 May) had issued his Bull excommunicating Elizabeth (which implied that she could not legitimately be queen), to which she had responded with a statute making it high treason to deny her right to be queen or to call her a heretic. The situation for convinced Catholics had become exceedingly difficult.

Campion, who travelled in disguise, attended the trial of John Storey, who was Oxford's first professor of civil law, then chancellor of the dioceses of London and Oxford under Mary, in which capacity he had been responsible for the deaths of many Protestants. He was accused of treason, condemned, and executed. Campion went to the Continent, to the English College at Douai founded two years earlier. He became a bachelor of divinity there and was ordained sub-deacon, then moved on to Rome and joined the Society of Jesus. He was assigned to the Bohemian province (there being no English one), completed his novitiate at Brno and then taught in Prague. Pope Gregory III was persuaded to add Jesuits to the "seminary priests" (secular priests ordained at Douai and elsewhere on the Continent) on the English mission, and at the end of 1579 Campion and Robert Persons (or Parsons) were chosen as the first two. Many English Catholics were uneasy at this move, thinking the Jesuits too zealous and liable to make the situation worse.

Campion's approach to his mission can be seen in the document he produced after his return to London, known as *Campion's Brag*. Addressed to the Privy Council, it spread rapidly and became a manifesto for the mission. It showed that Campion believed he merely had to win the intellectual argument to get a fair hearing. He was forced to leave London and worked for a time in nearby counties, making some distinguished converts. He then went to Lancashire, where his sermons were to be remembered fifty years later by those who heard them. He continued his intellectual assault on Protestantism in a Latin work, *Decem rationes*, ten reasons for challenging the most learned Anglicans to open debate. The work was secretly printed at Stonor Park in Berkshire, the home of Lady Cecilia Stonor. She was arrested later for this and died in prison. It was published by placing four hundred copies on the benches of St Mary the Virgin, Oxford's university church, on Commemoration Sunday, 27 June 1581. This caused an immediate sensation and led to redoubled efforts to catch Campion.

An informer betrayed his whereabouts, near Wantage in Oxfordshire, and an exhaustive search of the house he was staying in eventually uncovered the priests' hiding hole. He and two others were taken to the Tower, where strenuous efforts were made (possibly even by the queen herself) to persuade or bribe him to give up his cause. When these failed, he was ferociously racked, after which Anglican clergymen tried in vain to get the better of him in debate. He was racked again, even more violently, and then accused, with several other priests, of having come to England with the aim of starting an uprising against Elizabeth. He argued on behalf of them all that they had no political aims and that their only offence was their religion. The jury seem to have debated the verdict seriously, but Campion and his fellow-priests were found guilty and condemned to death. Campion told the court: "In condemning us, you condemn all your own ancestors."

His sister was used to try to persuade him back to the Established Church with the offer of a good benefice, which he was never likely to accept. On 1 December 1581 he, Ralph Sherwin, and Alexander Briant (see 10 Dec.) were dragged on hurdles to Tyburn. Campion prayed for the queen, "Your queen and my queen, unto whom I wish a long reign with all prosperity." The three were hanged, drawn, and quartered in the barbarous fashion associated with the name of Tyburn. Campion was beatified in 1886 and canonized as one of the Forty Martyrs of England and Wales (see 25 Oct.) in 1970.

[My mission is] of free cost to preach the Gospel, to minister the sacraments, to instruct the simple, to reform sinners, to confute errors; in brief, to cry alarm spiritual against foul vice and proud ignorance, wherewith many of my dear countrymen are abused.

from *Campion's Brag*

2

Bd John Ruysbroeck (Jan van Ruysbroeck; 1293–1381)

This great contemplative and mystical writer was born in Brussels and at the age of eleven was sent to live with an uncle, named John Hinckaert, who was a minor canon at the church of St Gudula. He was ordained priest when he was twenty-four. Canon Hinckaert was then inspired by a sermon to give away all his spare possessions and to live a life of contemplation. John and another canon, Franco von Coundebourg, joined him in this venture.

The sort of life they were planning was impossible amidst the busy and corrupt life of the city, and they were given a hermitage at Groenendael, in the nearby forest, where they built a new chapel and settled down. They encountered hostility from the chapter of St Gudula's and from other monks, who resented the fact that they did not belong to an established Order, so, when two more canons joined them, they became a regular community of Canons Regular of St Augustine. Canon Hinckaert died the following year, and Franco became provost and John prior, an arrangement that corresponded well to their particular gifts.

John spent hours alone in contemplation of God in the forest and began to write down his thoughts. He wrote in the local dialect of Flemish, which has led some commentators to suggest that he was ignorant of Latin, but it was a deliberate choice so that ordinary people could understand what he was writing. He gave his works no titles, so they have become known from descriptive ones such as *The Seven Degrees of the Ladder of Love*. Some were translated into Latin in his lifetime, but it was a century after his death before a complete edition was produced. He writes simply out of his own experience, using images he knows to be inadequate in an attempt to grapple with the indescribable mystery of God. He has an affinity with other fourteenth-century mystics such as Julian of Norwich, Richard Rolle, and Meister Eckhart, and his writings form a bridge between the prevailing Scholasticism of his day and the Neoplatonism that underlay later mystical and spiritual writing as exemplified in Gerard Groote and the Brothers of the Common Life and Thomas à Kempis.

His influence and reputation increased dramatically during his own lifetime, and pilgrims flocked to Groenendael. John became physically very frail and was unable to leave his cell for the last few years of his life. He dreamed that his mother came to tell him that God would call him before Advent and asked to be taken to the common infirmary, where he prepared himself calmly for death. There was a considerable popular cult after his death, and he was venerated in a procession from St Gudula's to Groenendael every year on the Second Sunday after Pentecost. The monastery there was suppressed in 1783, and his relics were taken to Brussels, where they disappeared in the course of the French Revolution. The official Church was slower to recognize him, perhaps because he did not write in Latin, perhaps because of the singular nature of his writings. Pope Pius X eventually confirmed his cult in 1908.

3

St Francis Xavier (1506–1552)

Francis was born a Spanish Basque, in the castle of Xavier, near Pamplona. He went to the university of Paris when he was seventeen and there met Ignatius of Loyola (see 31 July), like him a nobleman from the Basque country. Ignatius—fifteen years his senior—had been a soldier, been wounded, undergone a conversion experience during a period of enforced inactivity recovering from his wounds, become leader of an apostolic (but unordained group) at the university of Alcalá, and moved to Paris under pressure from the Inquisition. He arrived in Paris the year Francis obtained his licentiate. He must have been a compelling figure, and though Francis did not immediately fall under his spell, he was one of the group of seven who in 1534 vowed together to live in poverty and to devote their lives to the conversion of Muslims or at least to personal service to the pope—the first Jesuits. They were ordained as a group in Venice the same year.

After some years in which they struggled for recognition, they began to be appointed to missions. Francis was to go to the East Indies, then under Portuguese control. He joined Fr Simon Rodrigues, another of the original group, in Lisbon, where they cared for the sick in hospital, preached and instructed, and heard Confessions at court. He required permission from the king, John III, to embark, and this was delayed because John valued the Jesuits' services so highly. He was eventually able to leave in April 1541, taking with him an Italian priest and a Portuguese not yet ordained. He was embarked on the flagship of a convoy carrying a new governor of the Indies to take up his post in Goa, and, despite being constantly seasick on the long voyage around the Cape of Good Hope and across the Indian ocean, ministered to all those on board, from noble passengers to convicts and slaves. They reached Goa thirteen months after setting out.

Goa had been under Portuguese rule for some thirty years and displayed all the worst characteristics of an early colonial settlement. It had a nominally Christian structure, but the gospel values of justice and mercy were con-spicuously lacking from this and from the civil administration. Francis worked with the most deprived among the native population: prisoners, lepers, slaves. He summoned children to catechism by ringing a bell in the streets and used the tunes of popular songs to compose simple verse versions of basic Christian teachings, which were soon sung everywhere. After five months in Goa, he moved across southern India to conduct a mission among the low-caste Paravas, baptized to obtain Portuguese protection but totally ignorant of the faith. He made repeated journeys to them, brought other priests to help, established several mission centres, and protested vigorously in letters about the way the people were treated. He baptized huge numbers and then moved on to Travancore, where the old-established Mar Thoma Church claimed to have been founded by the apostle Thomas (see 3 July). He was enthusiastically welcomed and made many converts, but he was needed more by the Paravas, to whom he returned.

In 1545 he sent a long account of his mission to King John of Portugal, pointing out that the actions of the Portuguese—violent, debauched, and unjust—were such as to encourage converts to relapse. He moved on to Malacca on the Malay coast and spent some time (his movements are difficult to untangle) around the Moluccas and other islands of what is now Indonesia. In Malacca he heard reports of Japan, then closed to Europeans, and decided to start a mission there. In 1549 he set sail, landing on the southern tip of Kyushu on the feast of the Assumption. He and his companions established their mis-sion-centre, and he set himself to learn Japanese, managing to produce a basic version of Christian doctrine. A year later they had made over a hundred con-verts. He then moved on to Miyako (now Kyoto), where, having realized that the appearance of holy poverty produced only scorn, he arrived well dressed, pre-sented himself as the emissary of the king of Portugal, and gave the ruler the presents the king had sent for the emperor of Japan. This produced the desired results: the missionaries were allowed to stay and to teach and were given an empty Buddhist monastery. Some two thousand converts were soon baptized.

Leaving two Portuguese priests in charge, Francis returned to India, where he spent four months correcting abuses that had crept in during his absence and then sailed eastward again, intending to convert China next. He was caught up in a personal dispute in Malacca between the naval commander and the appointed ambassador to the court of the emperor of China; this resulted in him sailing without the ambassador and so with no civil support. With only a convert interpreter to help, he was landed in disguise on the coast near Canton. His plans for a Chinese mission never matured as he was taken ill. His last days were a nightmare: he was taken off by a Portuguese merchant ship but became so ill from seasickness that he was put ashore on a deserted windswept beach, where his faithful convert, Antony, cared for him until he died, on 3 December 1552. Antony later gave the details of his death to his first biographer.

His relics were taken to Malacca and then to Goa, where they remain enshrined in the church of the Good Jesus. He was canonized in 1622, together with Ignatius of Loyola, Teresa of Avila (see 15 Oct.), Philip Neri (see 26 May), and the humble Isidore the Farmer (see 15 May). His efforts had been superhuman, and though the mission to Japan was to be virtually extinguished in bloodshed in the following century, his achievements in many areas were lasting. Not least, he was a prophet raising his voice against the exploitation and injustice of colonial rule. Pope Pius X proclaimed him patron of all foreign missions in 1904; he was proclaimed patron of Outer Mongolia in 1914, of tourism in 1952, of India in 1962, and of Pakistan in 1971. In a gesture to his Basque origins Pope Paul VI granted Argentine players of the Basque game of *pelota* (the fastest ball game in the world) the right to take him as their patron in 1978: Francis is reputed to have played the game himself.

There is danger that when our Lord God calls Your Highness to his judgment Your Highness may hear angry words from him: "Why did you not punish those who were your subjects and who were enemies to me in India?"
 St Francis Xavier writing to King John III of Portugal

4

St John Damascene (about 657–749)

John was born five years after the death of Mohammed, by which time Islam had spread rapidly and Damascus had become a Muslim city, having fallen to the Arabs in 635. Greeks were still tolerated, however, and indeed occupied important administrative posts. One of these was controller of revenues for the caliph; this was held by John's father, and in due course John inherited it from him. Christians paid a poll tax but were free to worship. John was baptized and received a classical Christian education from a monk named Cosmas, whom the Arabs had brought from Sicily as a slave and sold to John's father for a large sum. John gained a thorough knowledge of theology from Cosmas, but he seems to have been content to work at court until a new and less tolerant caliph made his position untenable.

In about 700 John resigned, gave all his money away to relatives, and joined the monastery of Mar Saba outside Jerusalem. Founded by St Sabas (next entry), this was a *laura*, meaning a complex of hermits' huts around a central church. Monks lived solitary lives, coming together for the liturgy and other essential business. Together with a close friend, a poet and singer also named Cosmas, John spent much of his time writing theological treatises and composing hymns, which Cosmas sang. The other monks objected to this disturbance of a quiet life, but Patriarch John V of Jerusalem appreciated the pair: he took them out of the monastery, appointed Cosmas a bishop, and ordained John priest. John, however, did not relish the prospect of another administrative career and returned to Mar Saba.

One of the subjects on which he wrote passionately was veneration of images. Both the Muslims and the Christians known as Iconoclasts were opposed to any representation of a living being. John defended this representation as essential for preserving precious traditions and as a means by which the Trinity could be worshipped. The eastern emperors of the time were doctrinaire Iconoclasts and persecuted anyone who defended the cult of images. John was able to do so in writing from the relative safety of Muslim territory, even though he attacked Islam as strongly on this score. He rejected a religion of pure spirit with an appeal to the sacredness of matter as part of God's creation.

His output covered the whole range of theology and philosophy. He was not an original thinker but a great organizer of thought, and he produced a synthesis of Christian orthodoxy that did much to steady the Eastern Church at a time of crisis and controversy. His achievement is comparable to the later work of St Thomas Aquinas (see 28 Jan.) in the West, but the Eastern and pre-university tradition was not conducive to the foundation of schools, and the spread of his influence was slow. His major dogmatic work, with the overall title *The Fount of Knowledge*, examines the classical concerns of Greek philosophy—being and substance, action and potential, and the like—in Part I; heresies of the Greeks, Jews, and Christians in Part II; and the orthodox faith in Part III, "De fide orthodoxa", consisting of a hundred chapters examining the nature of God, the Creation, the nature of Christ, the purpose of the Church, and finally the Second Coming. He establishes love as the basic purpose of God's plan for the world and sees the Church as the only vehicle for putting this into effect.

Apart from his dogmatic works, John produced sermons, most notably on the Virgin Mary, poems celebrating the principal feasts of Our Lord in the Eastern liturgy, and hymns. He died at Mar Saba in about 749. His works were translated into Arabic, Armenian, and Georgian long before they were translated into Latin: "De fide orthodoxa" not until 1150—in a bad translation—and most of his other works not until the sixteenth century, with no complete edition until the eighteenth. Official Roman recognition was therefore slow to come, but Pope Leo XIII finally proclaimed him a Doctor of the Church in 1890.

Nothing is greater than the peace of the Church. The law and the prophets came to make it possible. For this, God was made man. This is what Christ came to announce; this he gave to his disciples before his passion and after his resurrection . . . he left his peace to his disciples and through them to the Church. This peace is to live according to what is good.

St John Damascene, "De fide orthodoxa"

5

St Sabas (439–532)

Sabas' first experience of monastic life was at the age of eight, when his relatives sent him away to a monastery while they sorted out a family dispute. Like some other boys sent to boarding school, perhaps to relieve family pressures, he was sufficiently taken with the life to feel a vocation to become part of it. At eighteen he was sent to Jerusalem to learn from solitaries, but Abbot Euthymius enjoined a less harsh regime on him in view of his youth. He lived a community life of prayer and manual work until he was thirty, when his abbot gave him leave to spend five days a week alone in a cave, rejoining the community at weekends. He helped the monastery by weaving fifty baskets a week from palm fronds—as Euthymius had done before him.

After the death of his mentor he moved deeper into the desert toward Jericho and spent four years on his own, living on herbs and river water until the local inhabitants brought him somewhat more nourishing offerings. He was pressed to found a community and eventually did so at Mar Saba, near Jericho, which became the "Great *Laura*" (see previous entry), with one hundred and fifty monk-hermits. At first they lived without a priest, as Sabas did not think any religious should aspire to such a privilege, but the patriarch of Jerusalem was eventually persuaded to ordain him, by which time he was fifty-three years old. Monks came from as far away as Egypt and Armenia, and arrangements were made for them to celebrate the liturgy in their own languages.

In 493 Sabas was given authority as archimandrite over all the monks in Palestine living according to this eremitical way of life. In 511 a new patriarch sent him with others as a delegation to the emperor Anastasius in Constantinople. The guard refused to admit him, taking him for a beggar. He sat in a corner praying until the emperor, reading a glowing account of him from the patriarch, asked where he was. This patriarch, Elias, was banished from Jerusalem for his orthodox opposition to the Monophysite heresy, despite Sabas' attempts to persuade the emperor not to support it. After some time spent preaching in Caesarea and Scythopolis (from where his biographer, Cyril of Scythopolis, came), he was sent as an emissary by the new patriarch of Jerusalem, Peter, to the emperor, Justinian, who received him with great respect and offered an endowment to his monasteries. Sabas refused this but asked for the taxes on Palestinians to be reduced, for money for a pilgrim hostel in Jerusalem, and other privileges, to all of which the emperor agreed.

He returned to his *laura* but quite soon fell ill. The patriarch took him to a nearby church and personally cared for him, but as he felt the end approaching he asked to be taken back to the monastery, where he died, aged ninety-four, on 5 December 532. Euthymius, on whom he modelled himself, lived to ninety-five: both (like others mentioned on various dates) are testimony to the benefits of a frugal diet and a dry climate.

6

St Nicholas (Fourth Century)

There is a great deal more tradition than history attached to the original of Father Christmas, but both are worth recording. The earliest hagiographic account was written by St Methodius of Constantinople (died 847) some five hundred years after his death and tells its readers that "up to the present, the life of this distinguished shepherd has been unknown to the majority of the faithful," which suggests that he may not have had very firm sources on which to draw and that he may have been the chief source for the many other accounts that followed his.

What is certain is that he was bishop of Myra, the capital of Lycia, a province of the Roman Empire in Asia Minor. It is also said that he was imprisoned in the persecutions under Diocletian (around 303), which were more severe in the eastern parts of the empire, and that he was present at the Council of Nicaea in 325, where he argued strongly, even violently, against Arius, going so far as to strike him, for which he was thrown into prison. He was a tireless preacher against Arianism and paganism. He was a great champion of justice, intervening with Roman governors and even with Constantine himself on behalf of prisoners who had been unjustly condemned. He died in Myra and was buried there. By the time of the emperor Justinian (died 565) there was a basilica dedicated to him in Constantinople; by the tenth century a Greek biographer could claim that his fame had spread to the ends of the earth, with churches everywhere dedicated to him, panegyrics preached, festivals held, and Christians of all ages reverencing his memory.

Around this tradition, particular legends developed. One of the best known concerns a citizen of his home town, Patara, who lost all his money and whose three daughters, deprived of dowries, consequently failed to find husbands and were to be forced to become prostitutes. Nicholas threw a bag of gold through the window of the man's house, and the elder daughter was married; after a while he threw another for the second, and then again for the third, on which occasion he was recognized as the benefactor. These became the origin of the pawnbroker's three golden balls. The story made him patron of brides and unmarried women. It may also be the origin of the unpleasant story of the three boys killed by an innkeeper and pickled in a tub of brine, whom Nicholas restored to life. Older paintings of the bags of gold may have been mistaken for boys' heads. This made him into the patron of children and associated him with the giving of presents at Christmas.

His shrine at Myra was said to produce a fragrant "myrrh," and this led to his adoption by makers of perfume as their patron. Myra was taken over by the Saracens in 1087, his relics were claimed by Venice and by Bari, which had the better claim, as it had a large Greek colony and Nicholas was already patron saint of its region, Apulia. They were taken there, were housed in a new church specially built for them, and became a focal point for pilgrimage over the years. At least some were handed over by the archdiocese to the Russian Orthodox patriarchate of Moscow in an ecumenical gesture in March 2002, and these now rest in Davidovsky Monastery. His cult was always particularly strong in Russia, of which he became a national patron.

In Dutch he is Sint Niklaas, and as such he was taken to the New World by the (Protestant) Dutch settlers of New Amsterdam (now New York) and became Santa Claus. In Holland presents are still given on his feast-day and not on Christmas day. A legend that he appeared to storm-tossed sailors and brought them safely into port also made him patron of sailors: in some parts of the Mediterranean the phrase "May St Nicholas hold the tiller" is a way of wishing someone a safe voyage. Another legend that he travelled to the Holy Land and Egypt made him patron of travellers and pilgrims. All these are signs of his universal popularity. He featured prominently in medieval drama, and there are over four hundred churches dedicated to him in England alone.

7

St Ambrose (about 340–397)

Ambrose is possibly the only bishop in the history of the Church to have been elected before he was baptized. His background was as a successful advocate in Rome, leading on to his appointment by the emperor, Valentinian, as provincial governor in Liguria and Aemilia (covering parts of modern northern Italy) with his official residence in Milan. This was at a time when large parts of the Church had turned to Arianism (which denied that Christ had a divine nature) or found it inflicted on them by secular and ecclesiastical powers.

Milan had had an Arian bishop, Auxentius, and his death in 374 left the city divided over a successor to the point where supporters of rival candidates were battling in the streets. Ambrose made a speech exhorting the populace to make a choice in the spirit of peace. A voice from the crowd shouted "Ambrose for bishop!" and this became a general cry. Somewhat stunned, Ambrose, who was a professed Christian, accepted. The emperor expressed himself delighted that he had appointed a governor who was fit to be a bishop, and within a week Ambrose had been baptized and consecrated bishop. (The date of his consecration, 7 December, has become his feast-day in the Universal Calendar, rather than the date of his death, 4 April, when he is commemorated in the Book of Common Prayer.)

He completely changed his way of life, gave his lands to the Church and his money to the poor, and began to study the Fathers and the scriptures. He lived simply and worked extremely hard, always at the service of those who wanted to come and see him and careful not to let social life interfere with his duty: he made it a rule never to dine out in his own city in case he got too many invitations—his other sensible rules were never to be involved in marriage settlements, never to advise anyone to join the army, and never to recommend anyone for a place at court. He played a large part in the conversion of St Augustine (see 28 Aug.): with his knowledge of Greek, he taught him about Eastern theology, and he baptized him on Easter Eve 387.

As a former governor he was better able than most bishops to arbitrate in public affairs. He instructed the western emperor, Gratian, in the orthodox faith to protect him against Arianism. When Gratian was murdered in 383 he persuaded Maximus, who had usurped the succession, not to attack Valentinian II and to confine his claims to parts of the empire. He advised Valentinian when a group of Roman senators sought to restore the cult of the goddess Victory, helping him to make a prudent decision and defuse the debate.

The ungrateful empress Justina, Valentinian's mother, supported the Arians and tried to make him hand over churches where they could worship. An edict of January 386 effectively proscribed Catholic worship and authorized Arian assemblies. Ambrose simply disregarded it and refused to give up a single church, preaching on the need to preserve the heritage of Jesus Christ. On Palm Sunday he had to be protected from physical attack by people who crammed into one of the disputed churches to protect him. The imperial troops surrounded the church but abandoned the siege a week later, on Easter Sunday. Ambrose had kept the people occupied by teaching them hymns and how to sing them antiphonally. This is probably the origin of the attribution of the long-lived Ambrosian Rite of Milan to him, but this cannot really be substantiated.

Maximus then used Valentinian's support of the Arians to invade Italy, forcing Justina and Valentinian to seek the protection of the eastern emperor, Theodosius, who then defeated and executed Maximus, becoming effective ruler of the whole empire. He stayed for a time in Milan and induced Valentinian to respect Ambrose. This did not prevent Ambrose from forcing him to do public penance for his part in the massacre of some seven thousand people in Thessalonica in reprisal for the killing of a provincial governor. Theodosius acquiesced, and when he died three years later, Ambrose preached his funeral oration, praising him for his humility in doing so. He was impressed by this, not by his position, and had earlier told his people that "The emperor is in the Church, not over it." His earlier intervention with Maximus, said to be the first time that a Christian prelate was asked to intervene in state matters, was to preserve justice and right order, not to support one imperial faction against another.

Ambrose was a great protagonist of devotion to the Virgin Mary and of virginity as a deliberate choice for women. This did not endear him to the mothers of Milan, who feared that the city would be depopulated if their daughters did not marry, but he told them that war was the great enemy of the future of the human race. He collected his sermons on the subject of virginity into a book, the lasting and widely circulated treatise *De Virginibus*. He compiled many other works, mainly based on his eloquent preaching, and several hymns, including the Breviary hymn *Aeterne rerum conditor*. He wanted to be remembered for "care and diligence" in sacred writings, qualities that did much to preserve Latin as the language of the Church in the West as its general use declined with the weakening of the Roman Empire.

He fell ill in the spring of 397, continuing his studies and instruction—on Psalm 43—till the very last. He died on Good Friday and was buried on Easter Sunday. His relics were moved to the church of Sant'Ambrogio in Milan in 845 and remain under the high altar. His eloquence, "honey-tongued," was ascribed to the fact that a swarm of bees had settled on him when he was a child. Because Lombardy (the region around Milan) provided many of Europe's stonemasons in the Middle Ages, he became their patron. A more esoteric patronage is that of the Commissariat of the French Army (responsible for supplies and administration), granted in response to their request in 1981, on account of the efficiency with which he ran his diocese. He is one of the original four Latin Doctors of the Church. His attributes in art include a scourge, for the penance he inflicted on Theodosius, and a beehive.

8

Bd Anuarite Nengapeta (died 1964)

The background to the martyrdom of this young Congolese nun is the withdrawal by the European colonial powers from Africa after the Second World War and the subsequent attempts by the Western and Eastern blocs to protect their perceived interests. The Belgian Congo became independent in 1960 after disastrously inadequate preparations. There were democratic elections held, as a result of which Patrice Lumumba became prime minister. He was seen by the West as a tool of the Soviet bloc and deposed within three months, then assassinated, with the collusion of UN peacekeeping troops. The West's chief concern was to keep the Congo's rich mineral deposits for the capitalist economies. Lumumba was seen as a martyr to true independence in the East and among large sections of the population. A rebel force loyal to his memory, calling themselves the *Simbas* (Lions), attracted some support from Russia and China and waged war on aspects of the country they saw as "Western."

These included the Catholic missions, French and Belgian in origin. The missionaries had in fact made efforts to "Africanize" the Church since before independence and to disengage from colonial structures. The missions were largely staffed by Congolese converts, but the Simbas regarded these simply as traitors to the cause of Africa and attacked many of the missions. The canonization of the martyrs of Uganda, St Charles Lwanga and Companions (see 4 June), in October 1964 reminded both sides of what could happen to missionaries in Africa. In November 1964 the Simba headquarters in Stanleyville were captured by government forces, aided by white mercenaries and Belgian paratroopers, airlifted in by the United States. Their reasons for hating anything Western were redoubled.

Anuarite (Sister Marie-Clementine in religion) was born in Wamba and baptized with her mother and sisters. She had joined the Congregation of the Holy Family (*Jamaa Takatifu* in the local language) and in November 1964 was a teacher in their school at Bafwabakka, where the diocesan bishop, Wittebols of Wamba, had been murdered a short time earlier. At lunch-time on the 29th a lorry filled with Simba guerrilla fighters drove into the Sisters' compound.

The officer in charge told them that they should not be afraid as he had come to save them from the "Americans"—either meaning the mercenaries or simply fantasizing. They were herded into the lorry and set off on a nightmare journey toward Isiro. They stopped in villages along the way, where the increasingly drunken soldiers looted everything and terrorized the inhabitants. At nightfall they stopped at an abandoned mission, and the Sisters were left for the night.

The next morning they were forced back into the lorry again, and the journey continued. They were stopped by the Simla colonel in a staff car, which produced wild excitement among the soldiers. He was enraged on seeing one Sister saying the rosary and ordered them to be stripped of all devotional articles, which were thrown into the bush. They were told to go back to Bafwabakka and dress like "proper African women," but continued their journey to Isiro. There most of the Sisters were herded into a house, but Anuarite, the youngest, was kept back, to spend the night with the officers. She and her superior, Mother Kasima, clung to one another, with Anuarite protesting that she would rather die than submit to such a sin. They were eventually released, but then a different colonel tried to force Anuarite and another Sister, Bokuma, into his car. Both resisted, and again Anuarite declared she would rather be killed. The colonel beat them both with the butt of his revolver, breaking Bokuma's arm. Anuarite was thrown to the ground, whereupon the officer called on nearby troops to kill her. "*Naivyo nilivyotaka*" ("This is what I wanted") were her last words as she was repeatedly stabbed. The colonel then shot her through the heart.

Anuarite's body was taken back into the house, and after a few days of threats of rape or death by the Simlas, who were probably panic-stricken at what they had done, the rest of the community were rescued by government troops. The body was exhumed in 1980 and ceremonially reburied in Isiro Cathedral. Pope Paul II approved the opening of her cause on his first visit to the Congo (by then Zaire) that year and in 1985, on a return visit, beatified her at a Solemn High Mass in Kinshasa, the capital. Zaire, subsequently Democratic Republic of Congo, has not enjoyed peace since her death, but the Church in Central Africa has made steady progress toward being a truly African Church while remaining in communion with the universal Church.

When the hour of trial comes, this young religious faces it: her faith, her sense of commitment, the primary value she places on virginity, an intense prayer life and the support of her community enable her to remain steadfast. . . . It is the primary value of fidelity that led to her martyrdom. That is precisely what martyrdom means, "To be a witness."

Pope John Paul II in his homily at the beatification ceremony

9

St Peter Fourier (1565–1640)

Peter Fourier was one of the heroic missionaries who did so much to restore religious observance in the largely de-Christianized rural areas of France in the wake of the reforms introduced by the Council of Trent. He was born in Lorraine (which was then an independent duchy) and sent to a Jesuit university there at the age of fifteen. He joined the Canons Regular of St Augustine (Austin Friars) when he was twenty and was ordained in 1589, in the monastery of Chaumousey. The abbot sent him back to university to obtain a doctorate in theology, after which he rejoined the monastery as procurator and vicar of its parish.

He met with opposition in trying to reform the observance of the monastery and then chose the most difficult of three alternative parishes offered to him. Mattaincourt was in a remote mountainous area, and to visit its villages he had to travel on foot and sleep on bare floors. He refused any material help offered by the villagers and showed the example of the life of poverty he had embraced. He never sought any personal advantage, even after his father had become wealthy, and never refused to give any alms to the poor. This was the era of great and often violent tensions between Catholics and Huguenots (French Calvinist Protestants), but he showed them a tolerance in advance of his age.

He decided that the main priority was to provide free education for the children of his parish. After initial failures on his own, he recruited four women, including Alix Le Clercq, had them trained by Canonesses nearby, and placed them in charge of a free school for girls in Mattaincourt, under his close personal supervision. He formed them into a religious Institute, and vocations increased, so that they soon opened four other houses. The Institute received papal approval in 1616 as the Canonesses Regular of the Congregation of Our Lady; it spread from Lorraine to the USA and Canada during the seventeenth century, and Alix Le Clercq was beatified as its co-founder in 1947. Its nuns took a fourth vow, to bind themselves to the free education of children.

In 1622 the bishop of Toul gave Peter the task of re-establishing discipline in the various houses of the Canons in Lorraine and bringing them together in one reformed Congregation. As with his earlier attempts to reform one monastery, he met with opposition, but he then found an ally in the abbot of Lunéville who gave him and his reformed followers his monastery. They occupied this and gradually won over the opposition. In 1629 the Congregation was renamed the Congregation of Canons of Our Saviour. Peter's aim was that it would provide the same sort of free schooling for boys as the Congregation of Our Lady was providing for girls. This, however, was not accepted by the Vatican, but they were able to undertake other kinds of educational work. The Congregation spread from Lorraine into France to the west and Savoy to the south, and took over the Jesuit colleges in Lorraine when the Jesuits were suppressed in the eighteenth century, but, like so many religious foundations, it did not survive the French Revolution.

Peter remained loyal—though far from uncritically so—to the dukes of Lorraine, and when the duchy was incorporated into France, he refused to take an oath of allegiance to King Louis XIII. He fled to still independent Franche-Comté, where he spent the last few years of his life as chaplain to a convent. He managed to establish a free school and teach in it, so carrying his life's dream to its end. He died on 9 December 1640 and was canonized by Pope Leo XIII in 1897.

10

The London Martyrs of 1591 and other English Martyrs (from 1539 to 1678)

In the autumn of 1591 Fr Edmund Gennings celebrated Mass at the London house of a schoolmaster named Swithin Wells and his wife, Margaret. Born in Lichfield, Gennings had studied for the priesthood at Reims and returned to England in April 1590. He had come to London to see his brother John after hearing that their parents had died. John was a staunch Puritan and had warned him that he was courting death. During the Mass Elizabeth's most notorious priest-hunter, Topcliffe, arrived with a posse to arrest Gennings. The men in the congregation kept them out until Mass was ended, but then Gennings, another priest named Polidore Plasden, the host and hostess, and two laymen, John Mason and Sidney Hodgson, were all arrested. The six were sentenced to death: Gennings and Wells were brutally executed at Gray's Inn Field, near the Wells' house; Plasden, Mason, and Hodgson suffered the same fate at Tyburn; Mrs Wells was reprieved and put in prison, where she died eleven years later. Ten days after the executions, which took place on 10 December, Gennings' brother, who had initially rejoiced at his brother's death, had a sudden conversion: he became not only a Catholic but a Franciscan friar and eventually minister of the English Franciscan province.

Two other priests were executed on the same day. Eustace White, from Lincolnshire, was ministering in the West Country when he was indiscreet in discussing religion with a lawyer, who betrayed him to the authorities. He was taken to the Bridewell prison in London, where he was repeatedly tortured by Topcliffe. Brian Lacey, from the same town in Lincolnshire, was betrayed by his brother.

The seven who died, known collectively as the London Martyrs of 1591 (not Mrs Wells, whose cause was postponed for further evidence), were all beatified in 1929, and Gennings, Plasden, Wells, and White were all canonized among the Forty Martyrs in 1970.

A brief account of others who died in December for the Catholic faith in England during the years of persecution is given below, in chronological order:

John Beche was a Doctor of Divinity from Oxford and a friend of John Fisher and Thomas More (see 22 June). Elected abbot of St John's in Colchester, he and his community at first took the Oath of Supremacy, but he was shocked by the execution of Fisher and More, resolved not to participate willingly in the dissolution of his monastery, and spoke publicly against Henry VIII's marriage to Anne Boleyn. There is some debate over how far he recanted and pleaded with the king, but at his trial he stood firm. He was executed at Colchester on 1 December 1539 and beatified, with Richard Whiting and Hugh Faringdon (see 27 Nov.), in 1895.

Ralph Sherwin and Alexander Briant followed Edmund Campion (see 1 Dec.) to the scaffold at Tyburn on 1 December 1581. Sherwin, an Oxford philosopher, was ordained at Douai and moved on to the English College in Rome. He was the first of its members to enlist for the English mission and is venerated as its proto-martyr. He set out with Campion and Fr Persons, arrived in England in August 1581, ministered in various places for some months, but was then arrested in London in November. Tried for fomenting an uprising, he protested that his only cause was religion. The crowd prayed openly with him as he died. Briant, also educated at Oxford and ordained at Douai, ministered in the west country before his arrest in April 1581. He was atrociously tortured in the Tower, despite which he wrote a long letter to the Jesuits in England, asking to be admitted to the Order if he were released, or even in his absence if he were not. He is therefore counted among the Jesuit martyrs. He and Sherwin were beatified in 1886 and numbered among the Forty Martyrs canonized in 1970.

Richard Langley was a wealthy Yorkshire landowner, married with one son and four daughters. He constructed hiding-places for priests, including an underground one at Grimthorpe. This was betrayed to the authorities, and he was arrested with two priests, one of whom was the biographer of Margaret Clitherow (see 25 Mar.), John Mush. He made no attempt to deny the charge of sheltering priests and was hanged at York on 1 December 1586. He was beatified in 1929.

John Roberts, born in North Wales in 1577, studied at St John's College, Oxford, but left without taking a degree as he refused to take the Oath of Allegiance. He went to Douai in 1598, was received into the Catholic Church, and moved on to the English College in Valladolid. He joined the Spanish Benedictine Congregation, whose monks were vowed to perpetual enclosure, but after the martyrdom of Bd Mark Barkworth (who had started Englishmen joining the Benedictines at Valladolid) in 1601, the enclosure was raised for English monks, enabling them to join the English mission. Roberts set out at the end of 1602 and spent an adventurous eight years, being five times arrested and deported, only to return each time. He was an outstanding minister during two outbreaks of plague and was widely called "the parish priest of London." On his third forced return to the Continent, he co-founded a monastery at Douai for English monks from Valladolid, St Gregory's, which moved to England in the French Revolution and is now at Downside Abbey in Somerset. Roberts was finally arrested while beginning to say Mass in early December 1610 and tried for treason with a secular priest, Thomas Somers. The trial was a notable occasion, during which Roberts rebuked the bishop of London for sitting with secular judges. The result, though, was inevitable, and both were condemned to death. Before they died they were guests of honour at a remarkable dinner for twenty Catholics organized in Newgate by a Spanish lady who had come to England to assist priests, Doña Luisa de Carvajal, who after the meal washed the feet of the condemned men. They were executed at Tyburn the following morning. Both were beatified in 1929, and Roberts was canonized in 1970.

John Almond was a "seminary priest," ordained in Rome and sent on the English mission in 1602. He managed to minister for ten years, including one period of imprisonment, before being arrested in 1612. He spent nine months in Newgate Prison before being tried and condemned for high treason. He spoke movingly from the scaffold at Tyburn of death being the pathway to everlasting life for those who use life well. He died on 5 December 1612, was beatified in 1929, and canonized in 1970.

Edward Coleman was one of the last martyrs to die in England, one of the victims of the wave of anti-Catholic feeling produced by Titus Oates' accusations of a Catholic plot to murder King Charles II and put his Catholic brother, James, duke of York, on the throne in his place. The whole thing was a fabrication by Oates, who had been expelled from the Jesuit College at Saint-Omer, but the unexplained death of a Westminster magistrate lent credence to it. Coleman was secretary to Mary of Modena, James' wife, and as such corresponded with the French court. In the atmosphere of panic, this was construed as treason, and he was tried in November (a month that evoked memories of the Gunpowder Plot) 1678 and executed on 3 December. He was beatified in 1929.

11

St Damasus I (died 384)

Damasus was in many respects the first "pope," as the term is generally understood today, as opposed to simply Bishop of Rome. He is also the first of whom we know something prior to his becoming pope. Born in Rome, the son of a priest from Spain, he became a deacon of the church of San Lorenzo. He was chosen to succeed Pope Liberius in 366, when he was about sixty. The Bishop of Rome was at the time chosen by a majority of the citizens of Rome. At Damasus' election, a minority supported another candidate, Ursinus, and provoked a violent uprising. This was put down with even greater violence, causing the deaths of some one hundred and fifty people, in which Damasus was widely held to be complicit. Other bishops were unwilling to support him and he had to defend himself against a charge of adultery brought by Ursinus. It was not an auspicious beginning to his papacy.

For a time St Jerome (see 30 Sept.) was his secretary, and he has left an account of the considerable style in which Damasus lived. If he had an aim in this, it was not personal aggrandisement but to promote Christianity as the appropriate official religion for the Roman Empire after its period of tolerance from the time of Constantine some fifty years earlier. In 380 this goal was achieved, when Gratian the western emperor and Theodosius the eastern emperor proclaimed Christianity, as professed by the bishops of Rome and Alexandria, as the state religion of the Roman power. Damasus obviously could not foresee the major problems that would arise when civil privilege would become domination by secular powers. Thereafter, he concentrated on establishing Rome, rather than Jerusalem or Alexandria, as "the apostolic see." He based this claim on the fact that, although Christianity and the apostles had come from the east, Rome was distinguished by "the blood of the martyrs," which gave it the greater right to claim them as its citizens. Jerome gave Damasus the biblical backing for this claim, telling him that he was "the successor of the Fisherman" and "the rock on which the Church is built."

Damasus showed his veneration for the martyrs by improving the catacombs in which their relics lay. He drained them, widened passages to accommodate crowds of pilgrims, built stairs leading down to the burial chambers, and had these faced with marble; he devised inscriptions and had many engraved by a leading artist in a style that became known as "Damasine script." All this served to identify the papacy with Roman civic and imperial power; it also showed that the glory of Rome lay in its Christian rather than its pagan past.

He put in place a centralized system of administration to support this new eminence of Rome and oversaw a process of formalizing doctrine in response to the numerous heresies that plagued the early years of his papacy. This codification helped finally to eradicate Arianism from the Western Church. He was the first Bishop of Rome to promulgate doctrine in the form of "decretals" sent to other Churches—in effect telling them what was orthodox, rather than advising them of the Roman view when asked. So he told them that the faith proclaimed at Nicaea in 325 was to be held throughout the empire because Rome had collaborated in defining it, whereas the concessions to Arianism made at the Council of Rimini in 359 were invalid because they had not been approved by the Bishop of Rome, "whose judgment should be sought and accepted prior to any other." He was concerned that orthodoxy should prevail also in the East and so preferred the appointment of the orthodox Gregory of Nazianzen (see 2 Jan.) rather than the Arian Meletius to the patriarchate of Constantinople. They, however, with the emperor Theodosius, summoned the Council of Constantinople in 381 to decide the matter. It was attended by some one hundred and fifty Eastern bishops, and Damasus did not send a legate to it. Although it reaffirmed the orthodoxy of the Nicene creed, it also established Constantinople, the new imperial capital, as ranking above Jerusalem and Antioch, equal to Rome, which cannot have pleased Damasus and sowed the seeds for the eventual split between the Greek and Latin Churches.

Damasus continued to encourage Jerome in the revision of the Latin translation of the Bible that was to form the major part of the Vulgate and even helped him on some points of interpretation, indicating that he possessed considerable scriptural learning himself. In a gesture of personal humility he composed a general epitaph for the "papal crypt" part of the cemetery of St Callistus, in which he said that he had wished to be buried there, "but I feared to offend the ashes of these holy ones." He died aged about eighty on 11 December 384 and was buried first with his mother and sister in a small church he had built himself, but his remains were later moved to San Lorenzo, where he had been a deacon for many years.

He who ... was able to loose the mortal chains of death, and after three days could bring again to the upper world the brother for his sister Martha: he, I believe, will make Damasus rise again from the dust.

Part of an epitaph composed for himself by Pope Damasus I, found by the archaeologist G. B. Rossi in the nineteenth century

12

St Jane Frances de Chantal (Jeanne Frémyot de Chantal; 1572–1641)

Jane's father, president of the "parliament" of Burgundy, was left in charge of his children's education when his wife died. They were still small, and he paid particular attention to their religious education. Jane was confirmed, taking the additional name Françoise, and at the age of about twenty married Christophe de Rabutin, baron de Chantal, and went to take charge of his neglected household, which she soon brought back to order. She and her husband were happy together, but they had to bear the deaths of their first three children. Two boys and a girl then survived infancy, but further misfortune struck Jane when Christophe was wounded in a hunting accident and died after nine days of agony.

Jane spent three years grieving and depressed. Her husband's death seemed a blow from God and a question mark over what purpose God might have for her. A priest who suggested himself as her spiritual director made matters worse, burdening her with endless devotions and penances and demanding absolute obedience from her and secrecy about anything he told her: a relationship that would now be called abusive. While she was staying at her father's house near Dijon she heard the bishop of Geneva, Francis de Sales (see 24 Jan.), preach. She immediately felt she was hearing a voice that spoke directly to her; he noticed her rapt attention and knew intuitively that she was in need of help. So began one of the great friendships of all time between saints. They could of course meet only in public, or at least well chaperoned, and at first Jane could say nothing important because of her vow of silence to her spiritual director, but eventually she overcame this and made a general Confession to Francis.

He told her, "Madame ... all these your former vows have not availed save to destroy your conscience," and set her on a fresh course, listening and gently suggesting what she might do, never ordering. She met the reformed Carmelites in Dijon and considered joining them, but she was a widow still responsible for her children, and they would not take her. The same applied to the Poor Clares. She corresponded with Francis, and they came to the conclusion that she should found a new Congregation. Its way of life was to be "not too mild for the strong, nor too harsh for the weak," in Francis' words, and he wrote his treatise *On the Love of God* as a guide for them. In September 1614 work began on the first house, on a plot of land at Annecy given by the duke of Nemours. Jane and a group of aristocratic ladies taught themselves basic skills that they had formerly relied on servants for and managed a simple establishment. Originally they planned for the Congregation to be unenclosed and devoted to charitable work among the sick and the poor, and it was accordingly to be called the Daughters of St Martha. There were problems with this: Jane was neither young nor very fit, and the same applied to the sort of women who would join her. So the objective changed, and a contemplative Order, still unenclosed, was planned, the first aim of which would be to provide a religious life accessible to older women, widows with family responsibilities. The name was changed to Daughters of the Visitation of St Mary, to reflect the spirit of thanksgiving expressed in the Magnificat Mary pronounced at her Visitation of Elizabeth. Now there were ecclesiastical objections, as the time when women's Orders could be unenclosed had not yet come: eventually they settled for "technical enclosure," which allowed the nuns to go outside to attend to family and other matters. Gradually, they found they wanted to stay enclosed and abandon outside "errands." They were also required to adopt a formal Rule.

The Visitandines, as they came to be called, met the needs of the members, prayed for the world, and dispensed counsel to those who came to them for help. Four other houses were soon established in France, followed by a fifth, in Paris, where Vincent de Paul (see 27 Sept.) acted as spiritual director. He described Jane as "one of the holiest souls I have ever met." The humility and simplicity of the nuns' lives—guided by Francis' teaching and Jane's good sense—was a counterbalance to the pomp and wealth of French society. By 1635 the number of houses had grown to sixty-five: Jane had not been able to found them all in person, but she resolved to visit them all and did so.

She suffered further personal tragedies: the death of Francis de Sales in 1622 was a great loss; five years later her only son was killed fighting the Huguenots and their English supporters on the Ile de Ré, on the Atlantic coast, leaving his widow with a baby daughter (who grew up to become the celebrated writer Madame de Sévigné). There was a terrible outbreak of plague in 1628: Jane refused to leave the convent at Annecy but offered its resources for the relief of the sick and chivvied the authorities into making greater efforts on their behalf; a son-in-law of whom she was very fond and a priest who had been a great help to the Visitandines died.

In 1641, when she was sixty-nine, Jane was invited to Paris by the queen, Anne of Austria, and given a distinguished visitor's reception at court—which may not have given her much pleasure as she preferred to work in obscurity. She fell ill on the way home and died at the Congregation's convent at Moulins. Her body was taken to Annecy and buried close to that of St Francis de Sales. She had given lengthy testimony at the process for his canonization, which took place in 1665. Hers followed over a century later, in 1767.

13

St Juan Diego (Cuauhtlatoatzin; 1474–1548)

The story of Juan Diego, beatified in 1990 and canonized on 30 July 2002 at the shrine of the Virgin of Guadalupe outside Mexico City in front of an estimated five million pilgrims, is that of two peoples, the conquered and the conquerors, being brought together by a powerful symbol. This is the figure of *la morenita*, the "little dark girl" apparently miraculously imprinted on a Mexican Indian's cactus-cloth cloak after he had seen the apparition who called herself "the ever-virgin, Holy Mary, mother of the God of Great Truth, Téotl." This took place, according to the tradition, in 1531. There is a relatively early summary account of the events in Juan Diego's language, Náhuatl, and a fuller one, the *Nican Mopuhua* from some thirty years later. This is the work of Antonio Valeriano, one of the few Indian students privileged to study in the College of Santa Cruz in Tlatelolco.

Juan Diego himself, whose Indian name means "talking eagle," is said to have been a childless widower, a very devout convert Christian. He may well have been converted by Spanish Franciscans, who were the first missionary Order to arrive in Mexico, in 1524. On 9 December 1531 he was walking past a sacred hill named Tepeyac on his way to Mass when he heard a voice calling him from the hill. He climbed up and found an olive-skinned girl apparently about fourteen years old. She told him she was the Virgin Mary and told him to go to the bishop, the Franciscan Juan de Zumárraga, and tell him that she wanted a church built on the spot, in which she would show her compassion to all people, "Because I am your merciful mother and the mother of all nations that live on this earth. ... There I will hear their laments and remedy and cure all their misfortunes." He went to the bishop, who was known for his kindness toward the Indians—who were those who had most of the "misfortunes" under the Spanish conquest and colonial rule—but who told him to come back another day. He returned to Tepeyac and had another conversation with the Virgin, going back to the bishop, who was still unconvinced. The next day Juan went to fetch a priest to visit his uncle, who was in danger of death from smallpox. He avoided Tepeyac, but the Virgin came to meet him, promised to cure his uncle, and sent him to gather roses (which did not grow there) from the hill. She wrapped these in his cloak and told him to go back to the bishop, which he did. When he opened his cloak, the roses tumbled out and the Virgin's image, as described in the *Nican Mopuhua*, was instantaneously imprinted on his cloak. The next day he led the bishop to the spot and went on to see his uncle, whom he found cured. The bishop built the chapel and placed the cloak with the image in it, "so that all might see and venerate her precious image."

The importance of the story lies in the message, not the events. It proclaims Mary's central message for all times, that of the Magnificat: that God is on the side of the downtrodden, not the mighty. It shows that at least sections of the Church were seeking to convey this message to the *conquistadores* and their successors. It has made Mary the advocate of the poor and the excluded peoples of the New World and the whole world. Her image, described so precisely, gives dignity to threatened indigenous peoples everywhere: she is one of the conquered, whom the conquerors regarded as savages who had to be converted or killed. She states clearly that she is one of them.

What historical foundations this rests on will inevitably continue to be a matter of debate. The official Church has now pronounced on the historicity of Juan Diego, claiming recent evidence that has come to light. As recently as 1996, however, no less a person than the abbot of Guadalupe called Juan Diego "a symbol, not a reality" and said that the stories "are sincere, but they spring out of a particular historical context and mentality." The main difficulty is that the account as we have it, a masterpiece of storytelling, is Spanish rather than Indian in its approach and appears to be a conscious attempt to transpose the story of the apparition two hundred years earlier at Guadalupe in the Extremadura province of Spain (from where many of Cortés' soldiers came) to the Mexican situation of the time. The original has similar details, including the "going back a different way" and the miraculous cure (of a dead boy). The image on the cloak (however it got there) is Spanish in style and its details have precedents: whether it reflects the story, or the story is elaborated to accord with the image, is impossible to say.

In the end, sceptics will always find grounds for doubt, and the devout faithful will always find motives for faith. In the story of Juan Diego and Our Lady of Guadalupe, the Church proclaims that its faith, if it is authentic, is life-giving for all, especially for the "little ones" of the Gospel, whom Mary dignifies in her Magnificat and in her appearance as the "little dark girl." Her patronage has been extended over the years: of Mexico City in 1737; of all New Spain in 1746; "Virgin Patroness of Latin America" in 1910; "Queen of Mexico and Empress of the Americas" in 1945. Her message still needs to be proclaimed, as it was during the canonization ceremony of Juan Diego, at which the archbishop of Mexico City asked the pope to confer his blessing on the Indians, so that their needs and human rights would be recognized, and the pope said that Juan Diego, "in accepting the Christian message without forgoing his indigenous identity, discovered the profound truth of the new humanity, in which all are called to be children of God."

14

St John of the Cross (Juan de Yepes y Alvárez; 1542–1591)

The greatest poet of the love of God the Church has produced was born in Fontiveros, a small town between Avila and Salamanca, north-west of Madrid. His father had been prosperous but was disinherited for marrying a poor woman and had to turn from being a silk merchant to weaving silk with his own hands. He died when John was about a year old, leaving his widow, Caterina, to bring up three children in dire poverty. John was sent to an orphanage, where he learned to read and write. He was apprenticed to various trades but proved inept at all of them. By fifteen he was performing the most menial and unpleasant tasks in a hospital for sufferers from venereal diseases. The administrator of the hospital then spotted his natural intelligence and sent him to the Jesuit college in Medina del Campo, telling him he could return as hospital chaplain if he became a priest. He studied there for four years but felt that his calling was to the monastic life. He was admitted to the Carmelite priory of Santa Ana and professed the following year as Friar John of St Matthias.

The Carmelites sent him to study theology at the university of Salamanca, the leading theology school in Spain. There he was fortunate to have the great biblical scholar—and poet—Fray Luis de León as one of his tutors. He studied hard—too hard for his fellow-students, who found him priggish. Ordained priest in 1567, he met Teresa of Avila (see 15 Oct.), who was beginning her reform of Carmelite convents. One convent in Avila was living according to her "Discalced" (barefoot) Rule, and she had been given permission to found two more for women and two for men. The prior of the convent in Medina del Campo, Antonio de Heredia (who had introduced John to Teresa), undertook to embrace the reform, and John decided to join him. After a final year of theology at Salamanca, he did so at a small house in Duruelo, near Avila. After a year as rector of a Carmelite study house near Alcalá, which depressed him, Teresa asked him to come as spiritual director to the Convent of the Incarnation just outside Avila, where she was introducing her reform. He became her confessor, and though she may have teased him about his youth, high seriousness, and small stature, he could exert priestly authority over her.

The "Observant" (unreformed) Carmelites did not take at all kindly to what Teresa and John were doing. Spain was at the time full of people claiming special revelations from God—*iluminados* or *alumbrados*—and the Observants had some grounds for suspecting that the reform might be a product of such movements. Teresa had the king's protection, but John did not. An inquisitor general was sent over from Italy, and he was arrested and imprisoned in Medina del Campo, only to be released on the orders of the papal nuncio, then re-arrested after the nuncio died and thrown into prison in Toledo. He was treated unimaginably harshly considering that a religious Order was in charge: only the pervasive fear of heresy could seem to explain it. He had virtually no light and no heating in winter. He was half starved and regularly dragged into chapter, interrogated, and flogged. He was told the lie that Teresa was also in prison in order to break his morale. After eight months, a more lenient jailer allowed him a candle. Under these conditions, he wrote, or at least made notes for, some of his finest poems.

In August 1578 he made a dramatic escape. He had managed to loosen the lock on his door and to make a rope out of strips torn from rugs. Letting himself down the wall, he found himself in the enclosure of the Franciscan nuns. This in itself would have horrified him, but he managed to make his way out and dropped down to the bank of the Tagus near the Alcántara bridge. Staggering with exhaustion, he made his way to the convent of the Discalced Carmelite nuns. When he told the prioress who he was, she let him in on the pretext that a sick nun needed to make her Confession. The nuns bound his wounds and gave him all he could manage to eat—stewed pears with cinammon. He then dictated the poems he had composed in prison, some from a little notebook, some from memory. The next morning a canon of the cathedral, a member of a powerful noble family, took John under his protection and away from Toledo. He was sent as prior to the convent at Beas, where he continued to compose his poems.

He was given increasing responsibilities, which he dreaded but accepted in obedience. By 1581 he was prior of a convent near Granada and deputy vicar-general of the Discalced Carmelites in Spain. He set up new convents, taught, and still managed to write the prose commentaries on his poems, starting when asked by the nuns at Beas for an explanation of his great poem "Dark Night." These commentaries would have been given mainly in lecture form and taken down by the nuns. Fortunately what was written was carefully collected in his lifetime and he was able to see and correct this version, which has become the basis for all future editions. Central to his thought was the concept of *nada*, nothing: by wishing and asking for nothing, the soul engaged on the "ascent of Mount Carmel" gains everything freely from God. As Teresa wrote in her breviary, "God alone is enough." He wrote using the popular verse forms of his age, including the *romance* (ballad), and used the tradition of the Song of Songs, with its imagery of human love, to express the soul's "love affair" with God.

Teresa died in 1582 and left him exposed to opposition not only from the Observants but also from some of the Discalced. He was stripped of all his offices in 1591 and sent as a simple friar to a remote convent—"thrown in a corner like an old kitchen cloth," as he had foretold would happen to him. Attempts were made to collect scandal about him and throw him out of the Order altogether, but there was no scandal and by this time he was too ill to care. He was moved to Ubeda, where his memory is now intensely revered but where at the time a hostile prior treated him harshly. He had open sores that would not heal and was in constant pain. He died very early on 14 December 1591. At least some of the friars must have realized they had lost a remarkable companion, as they had a portrait painted, full length and exactly life-size, immediately after his death, and this has remained the basis for later representations. He was generally shown holding a crucifix, and it was not until the eighteenth century, when his works became increasingly well known, that he was portrayed writing. He was beatified in 1675, canonized in 1726, and declared a Doctor of the Church in 1926.

Olvido de lo criado,	Remember the Creator
Memoria del Criador,	Forget the creation,
Atención a lo interior	Study the life within,
Y estarse amando al Amado.	And reach love's summation.

St John of the Cross, "The sum of perfection" (trans. Kathleen Jones)

15

St Venantius Fortunatus (about 535–about 605)

Born near Treviso, north of Venice, Venantius was educated at Ravenna, where he studied law, logic, and rhetoric. He nearly went blind when he was in his late twenties but recovered, apparently miraculously, through rubbing his eyes with oil from a lamp burning in front of an image of St Martin of Tours (see 11 Nov.). In thanksgiving, he set off to visit Martin's shrine in Tours, managing to leave northern Italy just before it was invaded by Lombards. Evidently "a scholar and a gentleman," Venantius had a comfortable pilgrimage, being received in great houses along the route. He was a talented poet and paid for the hospitality he enjoyed with flowery tributes in verse.

He decided not to return to war-torn Italy but found it difficult to settle among the barbarous—to his mind—Franks. Then he found Queen Radegund, who had taken shelter in the Holy Cross Monastery in Poitiers when her husband, Clotaire I, murdered her brother. The abbess, Agnes, was Radegund's adopted daughter, and they evidently thought this civilized poet would make a good chaplain, which they invited him to become. He was ordained and became chaplain, friend, counsellor, business adviser, and secretary. The convent, though not exactly scandalously luxurious or relaxed, was comfortable enough, with Roman baths and an excellent kitchen garden. The chaplain was treated to delicacies of every sort, exquisitely served, and responded with devotion shown in flowers, letters, and his usual poems. Radegund became "mother," and Agnes "sister." It was a civilized enclave of the late Roman empire in uncivilized surroundings.

Venantius knew all the high officials in Church and State and could actually be very useful in keeping the convent safe both from warring lords and from bishops looking for more authority over it. He was answerable to Bishop Gregory of Tours, to whom he wrote often and in very deferential terms; Gregory's extant replies are much shorter and may hint at some disapproval of "the Italian priest" and his comfortable ways, but he still seems to have encouraged him to write poems for public occasions. Venantius was himself elected bishop of Poitiers when he was sixty-nine, but the work was too much for him, and he died within a year of the appointment. He has been called a flatterer and a parasite, but the fact remains that he served an austere and high-minded woman, Radegund, for some twenty years, and that he was considered worthy to be elected bishop. Canonization in those days was by popular acclaim, so there was no need for his character to be put through a lengthy process of investigation.

His fame and his contribution to the Church reside, in any case, in the Christian poetry he produced. In 569 the emperor Justinian II sent a relic of the true cross to Holy Cross Monastery. Venantius celebrated the occasion with the great hymn *Vexilla regis prodeunt*, "The royal banners forward go." This was sung in the Good Friday liturgy for many centuries. His *Pange lingua gloriosi*, "Sing, my tongue, the glorious battle," for Passiontide, and *Salve festa dies*, "Hail, festive day," for Easter, are as profound. He wrote many other hymns, some based on the rhythms of Roman legionnaires' marching songs, and also Lives of the saints, some in prose and two, including one of St Martin, in verse, to make them more memorable.

16

Bd Philip Siphong and Companions (died 1940)

A catechist, two nuns, three girls, and an elderly woman were killed in Thailand (formerly Siam) near the border with French Indo-China (now Vietnam) for their faith in December 1940. This was an isolated incident in what had long been a tolerant area of south-east Asia, though never one that yielded many converts.

The first missionaries were Portuguese Dominicans who arrived in 1554. Two of them were killed, but incidentally rather than as part of a sustained policy. Siam was a Buddhist kingdom, but Christians were welcomed as bringing new knowledge to a backward peasant nation. By the nineteenth century most Catholic missionaries were from the Paris Foreign Missions Society, and they lived in enclaves exempt from national jurisdiction and taxation. During the 1930s Western influence decreased, and there was a growing sense of crisis as Japan invaded China and threatened south-east Asia. The country's name was changed to Thailand in 1939. The government adopted a nationalistic and anti-Western stance, and Christianity was branded the "foreign religion." Churches and schools were requisitioned, and Thai converts were put under pressure to recant. The Vichy Government established after the fall of France in 1940 allowed the Japanese to set up bases in northern Vietnam, and the Thai government responded by invading French Indo-China.

These martyrs were caught in the army's advance. A police patrol surrounded the village of Songkhon, near the Mekong River, which formed the border. Christians were threatened at gunpoint and forced to recant. The mission priest was expelled. His catechist was Fr Philip Siphong Ouphitah, and he protested at this treatment of Christians. He was told to report to the local police headquarters, but on his way there he was ambushed, tortured, and shot. This happened on 16 December 1940. Villagers recovered his body, and the two nuns, Agnes Phila and Lucia Khambang, continued to teach in the village school, telling their pupils that Philip was a martyr, while police outside fired guns in the air, shouted insults, and told the Sisters to dress as proper Thai women and to stop teaching Christianity.

The two sisters, four of the older girls, and a kitchen assistant named Agatha Phutt wrote to the police in protest. The police, led by a particularly vicious constable known as Luc, responded by leading them out to the cemetery and shooting them. The youngest of the four girls escaped the bullets and was rescued by villagers, but the three elder schoolgirls, Cecilia Butsi, Bibiana Kampai, and Maria Phong, died with the two Sisters and Agatha. The date was 26 December. The only punishment Luc received was to be transferred to another station. Japan invaded Thailand in 1941 in order to secure bases for its advance on Malaya and Singapore, and the Thai government signed an alliance that lasted until the Japanese surrender in 1945.

The six who died on 26 December were buried with Fr Philip Siphong. The remains of all seven were reinterred, in a ceremony attended by thousands, in the church of the Holy Redeemer in the village of Songkhon in 1986. They were beatified by Pope John Paul II on Mission Sunday, 22 October 1989.

17

St Melania the Younger (about 383–439)

This Melania is "the younger" to distinguish her from her father's mother, who was widowed at the age of twenty-two, gave away most of her possessions, took a vow of celibacy, built a monastery in Jerusalem, and devoted herself to charitable causes. Her son, Publicola, anxious to see his family continue and progress, relied on his daughter to produce male heirs. (It seems that she may have had a brother who was led into the celibate life by his grandmother.) When she was fourteen her father arranged a marriage for her with Valerius Pininaus (Pinian), three years her senior. He refused to live in continence with her, and she produced a daughter. Publicola, still pursuing a male heir, prevented her from associating with Christians, who might preach continence to her, and she became pregnant again, this time giving birth to a boy, who died the following day.

Then the daughter died, and Melania became seriously ill. Despite her father's objections, Pinian swore that if she lived they would both be celibate. Publicola died five years later, begging her forgiveness and leaving her all his property, which was vast, with a palace in Rome and estates in many other parts of the empire. With Melania's mother, Albina, the couple, now "brother and sister in the Lord," left Rome and settled on one of these estates. They lived simply, training themselves "in the practice of the virtues," caring for and taking in the needy of all sorts, so that thirty families were soon living in what became effectively a religious house devoted to the exercise of charity. They then decided to sell all their property in Italy, and after much resistance did so with the help of the emperor, freeing eight thousand slaves, selling many more, and devoting the enormous proceeds to endowing monasteries and other charitable works throughout the empire.

They sold at a time when barbarian tribes were threatening Italy, and it has been suggested that the sale was on such a scale that it caused the equivalent of a stock-market crash. It may be that Melania and Pinian foresaw the end of the civilized world as represented by Rome and decided to get out while they could. They moved to family estates in Sicily and then, when Alaric the Goth's forces threatened that, on to Tagaste in North Africa, still exceedingly wealthy and still living on family estates. They met St Augustine (see 28 Aug.), who called them "real lights of the Church." The inhabitants of Hippo wanted Pinian as their priest, but he had no intention of being ordained. Melania founded a monastery for men and another for women, and filled them with slaves she freed from her African estates. She lived with the women, wearing sackcloth, hardly sleeping or eating, and spending long hours transcribing manuscripts, for which she had a real skill.

In 417 they moved to Jerusalem, by now poor but still giving away anything that came in from residual sales of the last estates. The sale of one in Spain brought enough for them to visit the monks in the Egyptian desert. They gave some gold pieces to one monk, who said he had no use for them and threw them in a river. Deeply impressed by such renunciation, they returned to Jerusalem to live a life of solitude and contemplation. St Jerome (see 30 Sept.) was there, working on his Latin translation of the Bible, and his disciple and collaborator Paula was Melania's cousin. She introduced them, and Melania became a close member of Jerome's circle of helpers. They lived in this way for fourteen years, after which Albina died, followed a year later by Pinian. Melania buried them side by side and established a monastery for women nearby, living simply in a cell and refusing to act as superior, though she guided their lives. She then founded another for men on the Mount of Olives, where her first biographer (and great admirer) Gerontius became a monk.

Melania attended dawn Mass in Bethlehem on Christmas Eve 439, after which she told Paula she was dying. Two days later she was still able to read the account of St Stephen's martyrdom to her companions, but she told them this was the last time they would hear her read. She made a farewell visit to the monks, gathered the nuns to ask their forgiveness for any faults, and died in the evening of 31 December. Her cult was extensive in the East from an early date but extended to the Roman Martyrology only in the twentieth century. Pinian is also given the title "saint" there, and perhaps Albina should have it too.

18

St Winnibald (died 761)

Winnibald is one of a remarkable family, with, until recently, a father, two sons, and a daughter all venerated as saints. It is now recognized that the story of the father, known as Richard of Wessex, then "King Richard," who became "Saint Richard, king of the English," is a fiction written to support the verifiable existence and sanctity of his offspring, and he has been dropped from the new Roman Martyrology—doubtless to the fury of the inhabitants of Lucca in Tuscany, which is where he, whoever he was, was buried, and where miracles were reported at his tomb. There remain today's saint, his brother Willibald (see 7 July), who became a missionary with Boniface (see 5 June) and first bishop of Eichstätt, and their sister Walburga (see 25 Feb.), who governed the double monastery at Heidenheim (some fifty miles east of Stuttgart), first with Winnibald and then on her own. Their mother is historically identifiable: she was named Wunna, and she was Boniface's sister, so he had particular reason for calling on this family to help him. The story of "King Richard" originates from Heidenheim.

The father (whatever his name), from a Hampshire family, is known to have taken his two sons on pilgrimage to Rome in 720, sailing from the Hamble River (which flows into Southampton Water) across the channel and up the Seine to Rouen, then overland, visiting various shrines in France on the way. The father died at Lucca before they reached Rome. The two brothers continued on to Rome, "through the deep valleys, over the craggy mountains," according to the Heidenheim nun who wrote the account. They faced dangers from bandits on the way and gave thanks at the shrine of St Peter for their safe passage when they reached Rome. They both caught the Roman summer fever but recovered. Willibald went on to the Holy Land, but the more delicate Winnibald remained in Rome.

He studied there for seven years, returned to England, and then, with a group of companions, set out once again for Rome, where they dedicated their lives to serving God. There Winnibald met Boniface, who encouraged him to come with him and help in the task of evangelizing Germany. Winnibald was ordained priest in Thuringia (the northern area between the rivers Weser and Elbe) and given charge of seven churches around Erfurt. The inhabitants were Saxons, still hostile to Christianity, and they forced him to move south into Bavaria, where he carried on a hard-working mission for some years, after which he went westward and joined Boniface in Mainz.

By this time Willibald was bishop of Eichstätt, and he asked Winnibald to found a monastery, which he did by clearing the ground and building at Heidenheim. He then summoned Walburga, who had been a nun at the double monastery at Wimborne in Dorset and had been sent out to Germany two years earlier, to add and govern a parallel establishment for nuns. This made it a double monastery, the only one of its kind in Germany, devised on the pattern of Monte Cassino. Winnibald introduced the Rule of St Benedict for monks and nuns, and the monastery became a focus of prayer and study as well as of evangelism. He had hoped to spend his final years at Monte Cassino, but his health, never robust, declined further over his last years, and he died in 761 in the arms of his brother and sister. Walburga was then appointed superior over both halves of the monastery. Winnibald's relics were transferred to Eichstätt in 776 and interred in the church of the Holy Cross. Walburga died in 779, and a year later her body was moved to lie beside his, and the healing oil known the world over as St Walburga's Oil soon began to flow from a fissure in the rock below the tomb. Willibald outlived her by seven years and was buried in Eichstätt Cathedral, having been bishop of the diocese for forty-five years. They were indeed a remarkable generation of one family.

19

Bd Urban V (Guillaume de Grimoard; 1301–1370)

The son of a nobleman from Grisac in Languedoc (southern France), Guillaume (William) was educated at the universities of Montpellier and Toulouse and became a Benedictine. He was ordained priest and studied for his doctorate at Paris and Avignon before returning to teach canon law, in which he was one of the great experts of his day, at Montpellier. In 1352 he became abbot of the great abbey of St Germanus at Auxerre and for the next ten years was used as an envoy by Pope Innocent VI.

Since the beginning of the fourteenth century, the Papal States had been in a state of civil conflict, and the cardinals were additionally divided into French and Italian factions. King Philip IV, "the Fair," of France seemed largely to dictate the Church's agenda. Pope Clement V moved his court to Avignon in 1308 to be near Vienne, where he had summoned a council to condemn the Knights Templar and resolve other issues of church reform. The same year, a dreadful fire destroyed Rome's premier basilica, St John Lateran, which was generally taken as divine punishment on the popes for the move to Avignon, but for various reasons—political rather than religious—they were to stay there for around seventy years, while Rome lapsed into further chaos and ruin. Southern France, then, was the focal point of the Church when William was appointed abbot at the basilica of St Victor in Marseilles in 1361. He was acting as papal legate to Queen Joanna of Naples when Innocent VI died. The cardinals were so divided into factions that they were unable to elect one of their number to succeed him and eventually decided that a scholar and diplomat, also a Benedictine of simple and holy life, would be an appropriate choice. William was elected and moved back from Naples to Avignon, where he was crowned, taking the name Urban because "all the popes named Urban had been saints."

In 1366 he received a dramatic letter from his near contemporary the poet Petrarch (1304–74) urging him to return to Rome, asking him how he could sleep "under your gilded beams on the banks of the Rhône, while the Lateran, the Mother of all churches, ruined and roofless [since the fire of 1308], is open to the wind and rain, and the most holy shrines of Peter and Paul are quaking, and what was once the Church of the Apostles is but a ruin and a shapeless heap of stones?" In April 1367, whether swayed by this letter in whole or in part, despite the protests of King Philip and his nobles, and telling the cardinals that unless they fell into line he would appoint new ones, Urban set out for

Rome, taking vital supplies with him in a great fleet of galleys that sailed from Marseilles. Rome was starving and in a state of anarchy. Four months later Urban entered the city in triumph and wept at what he found. He started rebuilding and distributing food to the poor, setting an example of austerity in his own life.

He made a new alliance with the Holy Roman emperor, Charles IV, who came to Rome to do homage—but then returned to Germany, to Urban's dismay, as he had counted on his presence to keep peace in Rome. The eastern emperor, John V Paleologus, came from Constantinople to disclaim the schism between East and West that had existed since 1054 and to ask Urban to support him in war against the Turks. This, however, proved to be a personal gesture by the emperor and was not supported by the Greek hierarchy; also, the papacy's material resources were exhausted, and Urban could offer no material help. The Roman nobles turned against him, factional fighting became rife once more, and, despite pleas from St Bridget of Sweden (see 23 July) added to renewed ones from Petrarch, urging him to remain in the cradle of civilization rather than return to France, from where nothing good had ever come, he removed the curia back to Avignon, where he soon became ill and died on 18 December 1370.

This seemed like a shameful flight, but history forgave him. Petrarch saw that there were "other originators" of his flight, and his other achievements were recalled. These were not inconsiderable: he had introduced reforms of the clergy, encouraged learning, and supported the universities. He founded new ones in Vienna and Cracow and was a considerable benefactor to Avignon, Bologna, Montpellier, Oxford, Paris, and Toulouse. He entrusted the relics of St Thomas Aquinas (see 28 Jan.) to the Dominicans at Toulouse, telling them to do all in their power to promote his teaching as being "true and Catholic." He was buried in St Victor's Abbey. If he had not succeeded in all he set out to do, he had been taken away from the monastic life he desired for himself and always acted with good intentions. The Benedictines have long venerated him as Blessed, and this was eventually confirmed for the universal Church by Pope Pius IX—another victim of Italian unrest—in 1870.

20

St Thorlac (Thorlac Thorhallsson; 1133–1193)

Iceland rates but a few brief mentions in Histories of the Church, but it was Christianized at a relatively early date (in "universal" terms) and may well have been a staging-post for the bringing of Christianity via Greenland to Viking colonies on the eastern shores of North America many centuries before Columbus and the missionaries who followed in his wake. Iceland was "discovered" by the Vikings in 872, and the Vikings dominated Ireland through the kingdom of Dublin until the battle of Clontarf in 1014. They therefore had two routes to Iceland, one from the west coast of Norway via the Shetland Isles and the Faroes, and the other north from Ireland, along the west coast of Scotland, joining the Norway route at the Shetlands. Iceland was then colonized from Norway and Ireland, and in the year 1000 an agreement was reached with the earlier pagan inhabitants whereby the island became Christian—though with some concessions to the pagans. The first diocese, Skalholt, was established in 1056, and the second, Holar, in 1102. In 1152 both were made suffragan bishoprics of Trondheim in Norway (as were the Western Isles of Scotland and the Isle of Man, the ecclesiastical organization following the trading routes).

Thorlac, who came from a poor family but one with powerful connections, was ordained deacon at the age of fifteen and priest by the time he was twenty. He was sent to England to study and returned to Iceland in 1161. He formed a community of Austin Friars, of which he became abbot, and was then elected bishop of Skalholt in 1174. His consecration was delayed for four years owing to political difficulties between Iceland and Norway.

The office of bishop entailed a respected place on the general assembly that administered Iceland, called the Althing. A church tithe was collected, and the bishops were responsible for distributing part of this to the poor. Churches were built in the main centres of population (which were not very large), usually built and paid for by local chieftains, who (not surprisingly) tended to regard the buildings as theirs and the priests as their servants. This involved Thorlac in conflict with landowners who claimed the right to present their own choice of priest to the bishop for assignment to "their" parishes. Thorlac called for the Church to be financially independent—so to own the churches, whoever had built them—and for bishops to have the sole right to select the priests they wanted. One landowner, on being told that he had to make his church over to the diocese, apparently said he would rather use it as a stable; Thorlac refused to consecrate it, but was dragged back from an episcopal visitation by the landowner and his supporters and forced to do so. Reforms that he did manage to introduce included the abolition of simony and clerical marriage and the imposition of marriage between Christians witnessed by a priest. He was not entirely successful in this with his own family, as his sister had a pagan partner, the chieftain of Oddi, by whom she had a son. Somehow, this did not prevent the son, Pall Jonssen, from succeeding Thorlac as bishop.

He was more popular with the people than he was with chieftains; he cared for the poor and needy and was firm yet patient in administering justice. His monastic way of life became known beyond the confines of Iceland, and it is said that monks from other countries came to visit him and to learn. He died on 23 December 1193, not quite sixty, before he could carry out his proposal to resign his see and retire to his abbey. The Althing (which acted as both parliament and church synod) proclaimed him a saint five years after his death, and a cult developed, spreading to Scandinavia, the northern isles, and some parts of Britain and Germany. This was not officially confirmed until 1984, when Pope John Paul II declared that his name should be added to the calendar and proclaimed him patron saint of Iceland, where his feast is celebrated on the anniversary of the translation of his relics, 14 January.

21

St Peter Canisius (Peeter Kanis; 1521–1597)

Peter Canisius played a leading role in the Catholic revival in Germany following the Lutheran revolt against the Catholic Church and has been called its second apostle, the first being St Boniface (see 5 June) eight centuries earlier. He was born in Nijmegen (now in Holland, then part of the diocese of Cologne), where his father was nine times burgomaster, or mayor. He studied Arts at Cologne University, followed by Canon Law at Louvain, then decided the life of a married lawyer was not for him, took a vow of celibacy, and returned to Cologne to study theology.

He joined the Jesuits under the influence of the preaching of Bd Peter Favre and lived with the Jesuit community in Cologne, studying, teaching, and writing. Even before his ordination he had produced editions of the works of St Cyril of Alexandria (see 27 June) and St Leo the Great (see 10 Nov.). He attended two sessions of the Council of Trent and was then summoned to Rome by St Ignatius (see 31 July). After teaching in the first Jesuit school, in Messina, he made his solemn profession and was then sent back to Germany, to the university of Ingolstadt, where Catholic teaching was at a low ebb, as indeed it was throughout Germany. Luther had formed a Protestant movement, but this did not reach the bulk of the population, who had simply drifted away from their traditional Catholic practice and belief under the influence of lazy, uneducated clergy and the new controversies.

The Jesuits offered free tuition to students and were both learned and zealous. Peter soon made a considerable impression on both the students and the faculty, with the result that he found himself promoted to rector of the university for a six-month term. He could in theory have bought his way out of this unwanted administrative role, but he had no money with which to do so. Once his term was finished, he was appointed vice-chancellor, but Ignatius took him away and sent him with a team of Jesuits to Vienna, where the Church was in an even worse state than in Germany and the university had even closed altogether for a time. His mission was more pastoral than academic: he ministered to the poor, to hospital patients, prisoners, and especially men condemned to death. He worked tirelessly with the sick and their relatives during an outbreak of plague in 1552.

His greatest contribution to the Church was as a writer of catechisms. He was first called on by King Ferdinand of Austria to work on a planned vast *Compendium* of Christian doctrine, designed to cover "everything a good Christian ought to know," but he soon found that it was impossible to address such a work to both the learned and the simple. He said as much, and the work was divided into two parts: a learned one, which was entrusted to the great scholastic theologian Fr Diego Laínez, and a primer for students, written by Peter. This became his *Catechism*, completed in 1555. It was couched in simple question and answer form and divided into five chapters: Faith; Hope; Charity; the Sacraments; Justice—under which he included sin, good works, the other virtues, and the gifts of the Holy Spirit. King Ferdinand decreed that it alone was to be taught in both private and public schools. Peter then simplified it into a *Smaller Catechism*, for children and the generality of lay people, and then again into a *Shortest Catechism*, for younger children, and into an even simpler version for those just learning to read, with the words divided into syllables. All versions had illustrated editions and were rapidly reprinted and translated. The catechism became the main tool for re-educating Catholics and teaching them to debate with Protestants. Peter had become the first great Catholic educator to appreciate the power of the printed book.

He was again summoned to found and administer colleges. The teaching in one he established in Prague was so good that Protestants as well as Catholics sent their sons there. He himself always tried to stress common elements rather than what divided the two allegiances. In addition, he was appointed provincial of a new Jesuit province covering southern Germany. He moved to Augsburg, where he spent six years and found time to produce a "Manual for Catholics" and other works besides carrying out his duties as provincial. He was also commissioned to write a series of books designed to counteract a very anti-Catholic History of the Church being produced by a Protestant group in Magdeburg. To his relief, he was dispensed from this as his health was failing, though he continued active pastorally.

A further major achievement was still before him: in 1580 he was sent to Fribourg in Switzerland to establish a Catholic college, which the inhabitants of this Catholic canton had long wanted. He rapidly raised the money, found a site, and oversaw the building of what was to become the university of Fribourg, which still has one of the world's leading theological faculties. Besides this activity he preached regularly in the cathedral and throughout the canton. He suffered a stroke in 1591 but continued writing until shortly before his death six years later, "managing" his infirmities in a true Ignatian spirit of patience and charity. He died peacefully on 21 December 1597, surrounded by members of his community. He had to wait a long time for canonization, but when it came he was proclaimed a Doctor of the Church at the same time, by Pope Pius XI in 1925.

22

St Frances Xavier Cabrini (1850–1917)

Physically small (under five feet tall) and always frail in health, Francesca took her naming after Francis Xavier (see 3 Dec.) seriously, living a life of missionary zeal that equalled his. Born near Pavia in northern Italy, she qualified as a primary school teacher and at the age of twenty-two was in charge of a school in a nearby village. Newly united Italy was experiencing a wave of anti-clericalism, and it was forbidden to teach religion in schools, but she obtained permission to teach doctrine after school hours.

She applied to join two religious Orders, but both rejected her. Her parish priest placed her in charge of an orphanage, and she gathered a team to help her, but the scheme collapsed for lack of funds. Her aim was to follow literally in her patron's footsteps and be a missionary in China. With seven companions she founded a house devoted to foreign missions, but met with resistance in the Church to the idea of women being missionaries. She persevered, and the Missionary Sisters of the Sacred Heart were approved in 1880, with a Rule balancing hard work and spirituality, but they were not able to work outside Italy, where they soon had several houses and a growing reputation. She went to Rome in 1887 and, after some initial resistance, was able to start a house there. The Italian houses were to be training bases for her work on the mis-sions—when she could start that.

The chance came through a meeting with Bishop John Baptist Scalabrini (see 1 June), who was deeply concerned with the plight of Italian migrants to the United States. Unable to make a living in Italy in the economic depression of the 1870s and 1880s, hundreds of thousands were leaving each year in the hope of a better life in the New World. In the United States they gathered in "Little Italies," ghettos in the cities of the eastern seaboard, generally exploited by employers, and bereft of priests, teachers, and any sort of social care. Sca-labrini, looking for "good priests" to go to New York in response to an appeal from Archbishop Michael Corrigan, saw a role for the Missionary Sisters there as well. Mother Cabrini (as she was by then known) had an audience with Pope Leo XIII, who was aware of the plight of Italians in the United States, and he told her their mission was to be "not to the east but to the west."

So she went, with six other Sisters, on a stormy voyage from Le Havre, to a non-existent reception in New York, where they had to find a slum tenement in which to live and to beg for everything. Somehow they won through and began teaching and looking after the sick and orphans. The archbishop did not approve of women and at first gave them no assistance, but it seems that a sharp letter from Bishop Scalabrini convinced him that the orphanage at least merited support. The work just grew and grew: as Italians began to lift themselves out of the direst poverty they gave the Sisters what they could; wealthy American donors came forward with offers of houses. Mother Cabrini travelled to Cincinatti, Pittsburgh, Buffalo, Saint Louis, Missouri, Denver, San Francisco, Seattle—where she took up a pick and showed her Sisters how to clear a building site.

She was then asked to start a hospital in New York. At first she refused, saying she was a teacher and not a nurse, but then she had a dream in which the Virgin Mary was nursing the sick—telling her she had to because *she*, Francesca Cabrini, would not. So, with a few mattresses and bottles of medicine in an empty building, she started a hospital. Again, begging for help brought results: doctors and clinicians offered their services, and she soon had a well-organized hospital with a medical board in charge. She called it the Columbus Hospital, as it was founded in 1892, the four-hundredth anniversary of Columbus' arrival in the New World—and she wanted everyone to know that he came from Genoa, not from Spain as the Hispanics thought.

And on she went: to Nicaragua, where she thought she was having success converting the Indians until she caught yellow fever and they all vanished; to Panama and down the Pacific coast to Valparaíso, then across the Andes to Argentina and Brazil, both experiencing huge waves of Italian immigration. She set up new schools and orphanages as she went. In Rio de Janeiro there happened to be a smallpox epidemic, so she stayed to nurse the sick. She returned to Italy nine times to gather new recruits, and established houses in France and Spain, conscious that Italian Sisters alone could not be effective where other languages were spoken. She extended the work in the United States to care for prisoners, including those on death row.

In 1907 she became a naturalized citizen of the USA in order to have legal claim under American corporation law to all the properties her Order had there. In 1916 she finally awarded herself six months of spiritual retreat. The following year, back at work, she suddenly collapsed when wrapping sweets to give children for Christmas. She died the next day. She was canonized by Pope Pius XII in 1946 and proclaimed "Patroness of immigrants." In the United States she is known as the "first citizen saint," and she features in the Immigration Museum at the foot of the Statue of Liberty.

23

St Margaret d'Youville (Marie-Marguerite Dufrost de Lajemmerais; 1701–1771)

Margaret came from a Breton family that had emigrated to "New France." Her father died when she was seven, leaving her mother and six children in poverty. Her great-grandfather paid for her education at the Ursuline convent of Varennes, after which she returned home to help out by sewing and embroidering, doing some teaching, and helping with her younger siblings. It was therefore with some joy that she became engaged to François d'Youville, a young nobleman from Montreal. They had a Parisian-style society wedding, but it was not long before Margaret found that her husband's long absences from home were spent not farming, as he claimed, but selling alcohol to the Indians in exchange for furs, which was not only immoral but illegal. She remained married to him for eight years, after which the alcohol he had not traded carried him off, leaving her with two boys, François and Charles, surviving from the five children she had borne. She was left with debts and opened a small store to help pay them and raise her two sons, both of whom went on to become priests.

She turned to the Church for consolation, spent long hours in prayer, joined the Confraternity of the Holy Family, and undertook visits to the sick and other charitable works. She was joined in these by three companions, young women who came to live with her in a rented house in a poor district of Montreal. There was no hospital for women in Montreal, and they started taking women in need of long-term care. They were suspected of carrying on the illegal liquor trade with the Indians and aroused a great deal of hostility in the district. Margaret had dressed the four of them in grey habits, so they were known as Grey Sisters—*Soeurs grises* in French, which can also mean "drunken Sisters." The name was hurled at them as a term of abuse, but Margaret would not abandon it. At Mass on the Sunday after All Saints' Day 1737 a priest called them public sinners from the pulpit and refused them Communion. On New Year's Eve they made their profession and adopted a simple Rule.

Gradually they won respect through their hard work with the poor and needy. By 1745 there were ten elderly, sick, or disturbed women living with them. Sparks from a log fire set the whole house ablaze; all but one of the inmates were saved, and a large number of people came forward with offers of help. They found new premises, and the work went on. They were then asked to take over the only hospital for men in Montreal, when two of the three elderly Charon Brothers running it died. The bishop of Quebec had held out for some time against handing it over to women, but now saw he had no choice. So by 1747 the Grey Sisters, now formally the Sisters of Charity of the General Hospital of Montreal, were providing all the hospital and hospice care in Montreal. They took on a huge debt and borrowed more to repair the dilapidated premises, as well as restoring the farms and workshops needed to support it. They dealt with epidemics and extreme poverty and extended the hospital, which in 1753 received Letters Patent giving the royal approbation of King Louis XV of France. In 1755 the bishop formally approved their Rule, and Margaret became mother Margaret as superior.

Canada was suffering terribly from the war between England and France for control of its territories. The Grey Sisters nursed casualties from both sides: as Margaret said, Christ "died for all without distinction of race or color." She ransomed an English prisoner about to be burned at the stake by Indians; he became their interpreter with the English. On one occasion she hid an English officer, fleeing from pursuing Indians with tomahawks, under a tent the Sisters were making for the army. In 1759 General Wolfe stormed Quebec, and Montreal surrendered to the English. The Sisters expected the worst, but a delegation of officers called on them and politely told them they could carry on their work: the officer Margaret had hidden had evidently spoken up for them. They expanded their work into orphanages, schools, and care for prisoners and slaves. In 1765 they again suffered a disastrous fire, but again help came from all quarters—including two Indian tribes, whom Margaret had nursed during a smallpox epidemic, and the English governor—and the hospital was restored.

Margaret worked for a further six years, dying on 23 December 1771. One of the Sisters who had been with her from the beginning spoke a fitting epitaph: "She loved greatly, Jesus Christ and the poor." She was beatified in 1959 by Pope John XXIII, who called her "the Mother of Universal Charity," and canonized by Pope John Paul II on 9 May 1990. She is the first saint of Canadian origin, and the Grey Sisters continue to work with the sick, orphans, and homeless and abandoned people.

24

Bd Bartholomew dal Monte (1726–1778)

Bartholomew was the only surviving child of parents who had become wealthy through virtue: his father had been left a business as a reward for his virtuous way of life and built this up into one of the wealthiest banks in Bologna. Bartholomew was educated by the Jesuits and confirmed by Cardinal Prosper Lambertini, the future Pope Benedict XIV and author of the classic work on beatification and canonization. His father planned to settle him gently into the world of banking, but a devout parish priest, Alessandro Zani, became a major influence in his life and encouraged him to set out a daily agenda for prayer and spiritual exercises more appropriate to a religious than to a wealthy young layman. He heard the great Reformed Franciscan St Leonard of Port Maurice (see 26 Nov.) preach and came away convinced that he had to be a priest and missioner like him. He was ordained in 1749, at the age of twenty-three, and read for a doctorate in theology in a year.

In 1752 his father died, leaving him a considerable fortune. He devoted part of this to founding an Institute in Bologna, the "Pious Work of the Missions," membership of which was limited to the diocesan clergy of Bologna, with an elected director, whose main task was to plan missions in the diocese so that one was preached in each parish every five years. Bartholomew took no part in the running of the bank but began preaching missions as a member of his Institute, while making journeys to Milan, Rome, and elsewhere to hear the finest preachers of the age and learn from them—which he did systematically, making assiduous notes. Over the next ten years his reputation grew as he preached farther afield, in Rome, other great cities in Italy, and in rural areas, where the populace in general had very little idea of the meaning of the religion they observed outwardly. In 1763 he acknowledged the influence of Leonard of Port Maurice by making his profession as a Franciscan in Assisi.

In 1768 he was invited by Cardinal Migazzi to preach to the Italian community in Vienna. He had a terrible time crossing the Alps, then slipped in an icy street in Vienna and broke several bones in his foot. He was unable to preach the Lent course and had to wait three months before he could return to Bologna. The following year he began to be invited by bishops and cardinals and Pope Clement XIV (1769–74) to resolve ecclesiastical and even civil disputes as well as to preach. In Rome he preached a series of sermons in preparation for the Jubilee Year of 1775, speaking for over an hour several times a day yet being cut short by penitents demanding to make a general Confession to him. He applied to join the foreign missions, but was politely told by the Association for the Propagation of the Faith that he was too old and that he was needed in Italy.

The missions he preached owed a good deal to the Jesuits, from whom he had received his education. They were well prepared in advance and lasted several days, which were carefully structured, with visual and theatrical presentations as well as sermons, catechism classes, and processions. "The four last things"—death, judgment, hell, and heaven—featured prominently, with what would now be considered an overemphasis on the pains of hell. They aimed to convince people intellectually, stimulate their wills to follow a new life, and move their hearts to a deeply felt conversion. They were not felt by the people to be an imposition but were hugely popular, even if (or perhaps because) they were designed to strike terror, and they had considerable long-term effects.

The Jesuits had been suppressed in many countries, including Spain and much of the Spanish New World, in 1769, and Bologna offered hospitality to many who had been expelled. Those from Mexico brought the cult of the Virgin of Guadalupe (see St Juan Diego; 13 Dec.) with them. Bartholomew preached to them on her feast-day (12 Dec.) in 1778. He was already seriously ill, and he died twelve days later. He had to be buried behind closed doors to prevent crowds storming the church of San Michele in Bologna and tearing his remains apart for relics. His body was secretly moved to the basilica of San Petronio in 1808, when Napoleon's occupation of Italy had forced many churches, including San Michele, to be closed and deconsecrated. He was beatified by Pope John Paul II in Bologna on 27 September 1997.

25

St Peter Nolasco (died 1256 or 1258)

The founder (or co-founder) of the Mercedarian Order—from the Spanish *merced*, meaning mercy—presents the interesting case of having been canonized, at a time when scrutiny of testimony relating to candidates was already fairly minute, on the basis of documents that have subsequently been shown to be fakes. This does not necessarily invalidate his claim to holiness, but it does mean that a lot less is known about his life than was previously supposed.

The story as presented in the documents is that he was born into a noble family in Languedoc. His father died when he was fifteen, and his mother encouraged him to devote his life to the service of God. He was in the region when Simon de Montfort was carrying out his vicious campaign against the Albigensians, and de Montfort appointed him tutor to James, the son of the king of Aragon, who had been killed in battle, and sent them both to Spain. Peter began to devote his inheritance to ransoming Christian captives from the Moors, who controlled most of Spain at the time, possibly joining a lay Confraternity formed in Barcelona to carry out this work in 1192. This was formed into a religious Order after Our Lady had declared herself to be the patron of the work in an apparition to Peter, to King James of Aragon, and to Raymund of Peñafort (the second general of the Dominicans; see 7 Jan.), who was then archdeacon of Barcelona and the king's spiritual director. The king declared the new Order to be under his protection, and he and Raymund took Peter to Bishop Berengarius of Barcelona, to whom he made his vows, adding a fourth to devote his whole life to the ransoming of captives. Raymund drew up the Rule and Constitutions for what was to be a military Order, with provision in the habit for wearing a sword. Raymund obtained confirmation of the Rule from Pope Gregory IX in 1235, while Raymund, with two other friars, established new houses in Valencia and Granada. The habit was white, as this was acceptable to the Moors, and the friars went out in pairs to arrange ransoms with the Moorish authorities. Peter himself did this in the southern coastal region of Spain and in Algeria, where he was imprisoned for a time. He resigned the office of master general of the Order some years before his death, after which many miracles were attributed to his relics.

This account of his life was presented at the process for his canonization in 1628 on the basis of documents supposedly found in an iron casket discovered behind a wall in the Mercedarian house in Barcelona. The most important of these claimed to have been written by a notary named Pedro Bages in 1260 in order to be submitted to the Holy See as evidence of Peter's holiness. (Many canonization processes were delayed by centuries in the Middle Ages, usually as a result of political disputes.) This was certainly accepted as historical fact by Alban Butler, relying on it as one of the "authentick Documents" he prized, and generally so until 1921, when the Mercedarian Fr Gazulla Galve read a paper to the Literary Academy of Barcelona proving that Bages had certainly died before February 1259, so the date on the document was false. This led to a reaction that therefore all the information in it was false—which is not necessarily the case.

It is now generally accepted that the Languedoc origin is a fiction designed to connect him to the king of Aragon, and that some of the dates may be wrong. However, Peter certainly existed, lived in Barcelona, and devoted himself to the ransoming of Christian slaves. The Mercedarians spread through France, England, Germany, Portugal, and Spain. From Spain they provided a major missionary presence in the New World. Their concerns today, when there are not so many captives to be ransomed, are largely with prisoners and those in need of education. They have a considerable presence in the USA and South America, and also in Italy and Rwanda. They regard Peter Nolasco as their chief founder, while the Dominicans claim that Raymund of Peñafort should take most of the credit. The new Roman Martyrology assigns the foundation to Peter, Raymund, and James I of Aragon "together."

26

St Stephen (died about 34)

Stephen has the double distinction of being the first deacon and the first martyr. All that we know of him (other than by further deduction) is contained in chapters 6 and 7 of the Acts of the Apostles.

The disciples were increasing in number through conversion, and the commitment to look after those in need (here expressed as "widows") was proving too much for the apostles. The Hellenists—Jews from outside Palestine—complained that their widows were being discriminated against, so the apostles asked them to choose "from among yourselves seven men of good standing, full of the Spirit and of wisdom, whom we may appoint to this task" (Acts 6:3b). The first listed is Stephen (in Greek, *Stephanos*, meaning a crown or a king), "a man full of faith and the Holy Spirit." He and the six others chosen stood before the apostles, who laid their hands on them. More converts were made, including some of the Jewish priests.

"Stephen, full of grace and power, did great wonders and signs among the people" (6:8). This caused a group from the "synagogue of the Freedmen" to conspire against him. They found "some men" who would delate him to the council for blaspheming "against Moses and God" by claiming that Jesus would change the customs that had been handed down. He was summoned to explain himself to the council, where the members all looked at him intently and saw "that his face was like the face of an angel" (6:15b). He was asked to justify himself and pronounced a long speech (7:2–53), taking them through the Old Testament from the calling of Moses to the betrayal and murder of "the Righeous One" (Christ), showing how those who had put their faith in existing institutions and particularly in "houses made of stone"—meaning the Temple—had always been proved wrong by a God who was always moving them on to something new. He ended by telling the priest that they were "for ever opposing the Holy Spirit, just as your ancestors used to do" (v. 51b), that they had received the law "and yet you have not kept it" (v. 53b).

The priests were enraged by this condemnation of their whole approach to religion and "ground their teeth at Stephen" (v. 54b), who "gazed into heaven and saw the glory of God and Jesus standing at the right hand of God" (v. 55b). He told him what he had seen, which proved the last straw, and they rushed at him, "dragged him out of the city and began to stone him" (v. 58a). This suggests a spontaneous lynch mob, but as they had summoned witnesses (who "laid their coats at the feet of a young man named Saul"; v. 58b), it was in fact a judicial execution. Stephen "prayed, 'Lord Jesus, receive my spirit.' Then he knelt down and cried out in a loud voice, 'Lord, do not hold this sin against them.' When he had said this, he died" (vv. 59b–60). Saul, it is stated, "approved of their killing him" (8:1a): the great apostle to the gentiles, Paul (see 25 Jan.), is thus introduced in a way that makes his conversion on the road to Damascus even more dramatic and complete.

Stephen's feast was kept in both East and West from the fourth century or earlier. His supposed tomb was discovered by a priest named Lucian in 415, and this greatly increased his cult, which was then spread when his relics were divided up and taken to Constantinople and Rome (with some of the stones said to have been used to kill him). He became the patron of deacons at an early stage, and in the Middle Ages (in what might be seen as a somewhat sick joke) was invoked against headaches. The manner of his death also made him patron of stonemasons and, by extension, all those involved in the building trades. In art he is usually depicted with a book of the Gospels, a stone, and sometimes a martyr's palm. The finding of his relics was formerly commemorated on 3 August.

27

St John (died about 100)

The apostle John is the Galilean John, the brother of James (the Greater; see 25 July) and son of Zebedee. James and John were fishermen, and Jesus called them to follow him just after summoning Peter and his brother Andrew; this they did, leaving "the boat and their father" (Matt. 4:22b). They are portrayed as impulsive and vehement: when a Samaritan village refused to offer Jesus hospitality (because "his face was set toward Jerusalem," whose inhabitants despised the Samaritans), they ask Jesus, "Lord, do you want us to command fire to come down from heaven and consume them?" (Luke 9:54b). Jesus turns and rebukes them, presumably for being vengeful and for having an exaggerated idea of their powers.

John is also identified with "the disciple whom Jesus loved" and the author of the fourth Gospel, the two being taken to be one and the same person from the number of references to this disciple, without naming him, in this Gospel. He plays a prominent part in the passion narrative: he leans against Jesus at the last Supper and asks who will betray him (John 13:23–6); he follows Peter from the garden of Gethsemane and hears his denial before the cock crows (18:15–16); he is the only apostle to stand at the foot of the cross, where he is given charge of Mary (19:26–7); he is the first to reach the empty tomb in response to Mary Magdalene's (see 22 July) dramatic announcement, then stands aside to let Peter enter first (20:2–6); he is with the risen Jesus in the upper room and on the shore of Lake Tiberias (20:19–22; 21:7). At the end of the Gospel, Jesus rather enigmatically seems to imply that the disciple whom he loved would not die until Christ comes again in glory, or that he would not die a martyr's death (21:20–23)—which he did not, the only one of the apostles of whom this can be said with certainty.

There are difficulties with both identifications. Tradition makes John the disciple whom Jesus loves, but the writer of the Gospel never gives his name. The prominence given to him could suggest that he is meant to be a composite figure representing all Jesus' followers. It has also been suggested recently that the disciple whom Jesus loved is Thomas. The tradition that makes him the author of the fourth Gospel (and of the two Letters of John and the Book of Revelation, or Apocalypse) goes back to the second century. There is a fragment of text from the Gospel (the Chester-Beatty manuscript in the John Rylands Museum in Manchester) that proves it existed in written form at least by the early years of the second century. John is generally supposed to have died at the age of ninety-four around the year 100, so the attribution to him is quite possible. The claim that the writer of the Gospel is the same person as the author of the Letters and Revelation raises more problems.

The fourth Gospel is very different from the three earlier Synoptic (describing events from a common point of view) Gospels. It evidently takes events from them but forms them into a theological treatise: John's sobriquet "the divine" means "the theologian." The generally accepted theory is that, while John the son of Zebedee may have been at the origin of a tradition out of which the fourth Gospel grew, it is, in the form in which it has come down to us, the work of several hands, perhaps guided by John in his old age. The Book of Revelation is different in style and purpose, and its precise authorship is impossible to establish. "Authorship" was in any case not a concept understood in the same personal way in the first and second centuries: Revelation could have been dictated by John the Apostle and written out with considerable changes in wording, as it uses a wider and more sophisticated Greek vocabulary than the Gospel.

John was a prominent figure in the early Church. His brother James was martyred in the persecution under Herod, but John, after working with Peter, settled in Ephesus, where an early tradition, handed on to St Irenaeus (see 28 June) by St Polycarp of Smyrna (died 155 or 166; see 23 Feb), says that he lived until the third year of the reign of the emperor Trajan, who came to power in 98. He was most probably the last of the apostles to die. St Jerome (see 30 Sept.) records a tradition that, when he was too feeble to preach, John would have himself carried into the assembly and tell the people, "My little children, love one another." When asked why he always used the same words, he replied, "Because it is the word of the Lord, and if you keep it, you do enough." If this was the same person who at the end of his Gospel added, "But there are also many other things that Jesus did; if every one were written down, I suppose that the world itself could not contain the books that would be written," he had certainly made his own remarkable theological synopsis of Jesus' message by the time he died.

This is the disciple who is testifying to these things and has written them, and we know that his testimony is true.
John 21:24

28

St Gaspar del Bufalo (Gaspare Melchiore Baltasare Quarterione; 1786–1837)

Gaspar owed his three baptismal names to the fact that he was born on the feast of the Epiphany and so given the names of the three Magi. His family came from Rome and was relatively poor. He studied at what had been the Jesuit Collegio Romano, then run by secular clergy as the Jesuits had been suppressed, and entered a minor seminary at the age of twelve. In his teenage years he became occupied in works of spiritual and material assistance to the poor, and after his ordination at the age of twenty-two he extended this mission to the carters and peasants of the country districts around Rome. A friend named Francesco Albertini introduced him to devotion to the Precious Blood, for which he had started a confraternity dedicated to preaching the redemptive power of Christ's blood. (The Roman church of San Nicolo in Carcere then held a relic claimed to be a fragment of the cloak worn by Longinus at the crucifixion, stained with Jesus' blood. This was little known— which suggests that its authenticity was not widely accepted, as it would, if genuine, have been a sensational relic, on a par with the cross and the crown of thorns. There had been an Order of nobles dedicated to its protection, founded by a duke of Mantua in 1608 and abolished along with the duchy in about 1710. The relic itself disappeared in revolutionary upheavals in 1848.) The Precious Blood became the wellspring of Gaspar's spirituality.

Napoleon entered Rome in 1809, deported Pope Pius VII (1800–23), and required all clergy to sign an oath of allegiance to him and adjure the pope. Most of the clergy, including Gaspar, refused and were exiled from Rome. He was exiled to Piacenza and then imprisoned in Bologna and two other towns successively. He spent four years in prison, using his time to plan, with Albertini, what they would do after the downfall of Napoleon. This came about in 1814; Pope Pius returned to Rome, and Gaspar placed himself at his service. Pius asked him to devote his life to preaching missions to restore religion to Italy after the years of deprivation and persecution under Napoleon, and he left Rome to begin a career of itinerant mission-giving, on similar lines to Bd Bartholomew dal Monte (see 24 Dec.).

After he had preached a mission at Giano, in the diocese of Spoleto to the north of Rome, the pope gave him a house there with an adjoining church, where he could realize his aim of establishing a Congregation of missionaries dedicated to the Precious Blood. This was formally approved by Pope Pius VII on the feast of the Assumption in 1815. An early member of the Congregation was Giovanni Ferretti, who was to become Pope Pius IX and issue the encyclical *Redempti sumus* ("We are redeemed") that was to spread devotion to the Precious Blood worldwide. A second and third house were opened quickly, and Gaspar aimed to have one in every diocese in Italy, choosing the most wicked town in each: Pius VII suggested six in the archdiocese of Naples, which may have said something about his view of that region. The main social problem was that of the bands of brigands who were roaming the country. Originally partisan fighters against Napoleon, they had found this a profitable way of life and were preying on the inhabitants, carrying out vendettas and organizing crime. Gaspar faced them armed only with the gospel and had some success in reducing their activities.

His missions were a "spiritual earthquake," leaving him drained and his audiences inspired. He made numerous converts but also enemies, particularly among the Freemasons, whom he attacked directly as atheists and who responded with threats against his life. He became known as the "hammer of the sectarians." He chose Mary de Mattias (now Blessed) to help make a parallel foundation for women, and the Institute of Sisters Adorers of the Precious Blood came into being in 1834. Gaspar preached his last mission in Rome in 1836, then retired to Albano, knowing he had not long to live. He died on 28 December 1837, and his fame soon spread beyond Italy, especially to France, where St Peter Julian Eymard (see 3 Aug.), who spread devotion to the Blessed Sacrament, constantly appealed to his inspiration.

He was beatified by Pope Pius X (see 21 Aug.) in 1904 and canonized by Pius XII in 1954. One of his priests was invited by the bishop of Cincinatti in 1844 to make a foundation in Ohio, and there are now four provinces of the Society in the USA. Its members work in parishes, schools, hospitals, and clinics as well as preaching missions and retreats. The Sisters Adorers spread their mission to the USA in 1870 and undertake a most varied ministry there and elsewhere: they teach at all levels, care for the aged, run retirement villages, give retreats, care for abused children, and look after those with alcohol and drug dependency.

The wholly splendid glory of the Roman clergy, who was the true and greatest apostle of devotion to the Most Precious Blood of Christ in the world.

Pope John XXIII, speaking of St Gaspar del Bufalo to the Roman Synod in January 1960

29

St Thomas Becket (1118–1170)

Thomas once described himself as "a proud, vain man, a feeder of birds and a follower of hounds," who had been made "a shepherd of sheep." There is a fair amount of truth in this self-assessment of a man who may not always have lived like a saint but who died like one.

The son of a sometime sheriff of London, Thomas worked for some years as a clerk after the death of his parents and then found a post in the household of Archbishop Theobald of Canterbury and began to climb the ladder of ecclesiastical preferment. Theobald sent him to Rome on several important missions, and by 1154 he was archdeacon of Canterbury, in rank just below the bishops and abbots of England. He was responsible for getting Pope Eugenius III to agree to Henry of Anjou becoming king of England in succession to the usurper Stephen, and Henry rewarded him by making him his chancellor. The two became close personal friends, and Thomas' influence was clearly behind many of the reforms Henry II put in hand to restore England after long years of civil war. He kept a magnificent retinue and fought for Henry in France at the head of seven hundred of his own knights. Though reproached for dressing more like a falconer than a cleric, he nevertheless did not allow his public pomp to overflow into his personal life, which was blameless and austere. He was destined to be archbishop of Canterbury and dreaded the prospect, knowing that it would lead him into having to choose between the rights of the Church and the king's continued support.

And so it came about. Theobald died in 1161, and Henry resolved to make his chancellor archbishop. Thomas warned him that his actions in reducing the privileges of the Church "make me fear that you would require of me what I could not agree to." Henry paid no attention, but Thomas held out against the appointment until the papal legate pressed him to agree. He left London for Canterbury and was shortly ordained priest and consecrated archbishop. He dramatically altered his outward style of life, wearing clerical dress, rising early to read the scriptures, saying or hearing Mass daily, distributing alms, and imposing a degree of monastic order on his household.

The king was determined to extract the maximum of revenue from church property and to assert the supremacy of his civil law over ecclesiastical jurisdiction. Thomas responded with a mixture of conciliation and resistance. Henry then demanded the bishops' assent to "all royal customs," some of which he did not specify, but when he spelt them out in the sixteen Constitutions of Clarendon, the provisions of a council he had summoned, Thomas exclaimed, "By the Lord Almighty, no seal of mine shall be put to them!" The Constitutions were largely a one-sided pronouncement on disputes that had rumbled on between the crown and the Church since the Norman Conquest. Thomas set himself forty days of penance to make amends for his former conciliation, which infuriated the king, who twice refused him an audience and forbade him to put his side of the dispute to the pope, who was in France at the time. Thomas embarked secretly for France and saw the pope, who declared some of the provisions of Clarendon intolerable. He resigned the arch-bishopric, but the pope refused to accept this, telling him it would be to abandon the cause of God. He spent six years in France, while three-sided negotiations between him, the pope, and the king dragged on.

In his absence, Archbishop Roger of York, having obtained a licence from the pope—who probably did not realize the implications—crowned Henry's son, while his father was alive, to ensure continuity of succession; something not previously done in England. This was a threat to the primacy of Canterbury over York: Thomas persuaded the pope to cancel the licence—though the cancellation probably did not get to England before young Henry's coronation on 14 June 1170—and returned to England to serve notices of excommuni-cation on the archbishop of York and six bishops who had attended the cor-onation, publicly denouncing them from the pulpit of Canterbury Cathedral on Christmas Day. Roger of York and the bishops of London and Salisbury were already in Normandy to protest to the king, who flew into a royal rage and asked (even if not in so many words) who would rid him of this turbulent priest.

Four knights rushed to do what they took to be his bidding, reaching Canterbury on 29 December. They found Thomas in his bedroom and were soon threatening him. His attendants urged him to move to the cathedral for sanctuary. He did so slowly, preceded by his processional cross, but the knights followed him in shouting, "Where is Thomas the traitor?" He identified himself as "no traitor, but priest and archbishop of God." They hacked him to death between the altars of Our Lady and St Benedict and left his body lying there. Crowds came in to see what had happened, and an opportune thun-derstorm broke overhead. This was sacrilege on a scale that left England and much of Europe stunned. Henry, who probably had not intended Thomas' death, shut himself away to fast and grieve for forty days; at Avranches two years later and at Canterbury four years later, he did public penance. In between the two, Pope Alexander III canonized Thomas in a rapid process designed to show the king (and others) that in matters of holiness the pope was the only arbiter.

Thomas' body was solemnly enshrined behind the high altar of his cathedral in 1220, and Canterbury became a major pilgrimage destination, as immor-talized in Chaucer's *Canterbury Tales*. The shrine was destroyed in Henry VIII's crusade against the cult of saints in 1538, but there is again a chapel dedicated to Thomas in the cathedral, at which Pope John Paul II prayed for church unity with Archbishop Robert Runcie of Canterbury on his visit to England in 1982.

30

St John-Francis Régis (1597–1640)

This great Jesuit missioner's superior picked him out as future saint when he was twenty-two: advised by John's room-mate on his theology course that he was spending much of his nights in prayer, Fr Tarbes, the superior replied, "Take care not to disturb his devotions nor to hinder his communion with God. He is a saint, and if I am not greatly mistaken, the Society will some day celebrate a feast in his honour." The Society had to wait nearly a century after his death, but the celebration came.

John was born in the diocese of Narbonne in the Languedoc region of southern France and educated by the Jesuits at Béziers, Cahors, and Tournon, followed by his theology course at Toulouse. He was ordained in 1631, and the rest of his life was devoted to preaching missions in rural areas, part of the great effort to re-Christianize Europe that followed on from the Council of Trent. His mission field was the peasant and other communities of Languedoc and the Auvergne, just to the north. He addressed himself particularly to the poor, but his simple delivery and evident sincerity drew crowds from all social classes. He spent his summers in the towns, as the peasants could not be taken away from the vital task of harvesting, and in the winters went out to the villages and remote farms. He had a special concern for people in trouble, and, after spending his mornings in the confessional or the pulpit, he would visit prisons and hospitals in the afternoons. In Montpellier he established a committee of women to carry out prison visiting, and he concerned himself with rescuing women from prostitution, arguing against those who told him they always relapsed that preventing even one sin was worth the effort.

He was then approached by the bishop of Viviers to help in his diocese, in the remote and mountainous areas of the Vivarais and Velay, where civil and church institutions were in a state of collapse, with nobles acting as brigands and absentee priests. John spent three years, with a Jesuit companion, helping the bishop to make a complete visitation, going to remote villages a day or two in advance of the bishop, to preach and prepare the people, to whom he could usually speak in their own local dialect, which enabled him to win their confidence. The area had become largely Calvinist in the previous century, but most Calvinists and Catholics had fallen away from virtually any knowledge or practice of their religion, leaving little to choose between them. The campaign aroused some opposition, and calumnies were put about, but the bishop supported him, knowing there was no truth in these.

He seemed impervious to the worst conditions: he once slept in a snowdrift for three weeks, unable to make progress and with very little food to sustain him. He was described as spending the whole day preaching from a heap of snow on top of a mountain and then spending the whole night hearing Confessions—this was said by a witness at the diocesan inquiry for his canonization; another described asking what a procession winding along in the distance was and being told, "It is the saint, and the people are following." He spent his last four summers in Le Puy, the principal town of the Velay, where the church could not hold the congregations of four or five thousand he drew. There he established institutions to carry out social services for those most in need, including a refuge for women and girls, which again drew calumny, mainly from the men from whom they were escaping. He made no attempt to defend himself even when a timid superior stopped his work for a time, but popular support, developing into stories that he was a miracle-worker, ensured that his projects continued.

By the autumn of 1640 he knew that his strength was finally failing. After making a retreat at Le Puy he left the town saying he would not return, though his companion would. After a terrible journey, getting lost and held up in the snow, during which he contracted pleurisy, he reached the town where he had agreed to preach an Advent retreat, La Louvesc. He somehow preached three times on Christmas Day and three times the following day, but then fainted while hearing Confessions. He was carried to the local priest's house and died there on New Year's Eve. He was canonized in 1737. La Louvesc, where his body remains, became a great pilgrimage place, which it still is. A notable nineteenth-century pilgrim was St John Vianney (see 4 Aug.), the Curé d'Ars: it was there that he became convinced of his own vocation, and he later wrote a life of St John-Francis Régis, whose work, never finished, he carried on in another remote part of France.

31

St Catherine Labouré (Zoë Labouré; 1806–1876)

The visionary who gave the world the astonishingly popular "miraculous medal" lived a life without outward incident in a convent. The eighth of ten children born to a yeoman farming couple, she never learned to read or write properly. Her mother died when she was eight, and when an elder sister joined the Sisters of Charity she had to look after the household as well as help her father on the farm. One brother had gone to Paris, where he owned a café, and when Zoë said she too wanted to become a nun, her father sent her there as a waitress to take her mind off the idea. The ruse failed, and in 1830 he gave in and allowed her to join the Sisters of Charity. After serving her postulancy at Châtillon-sur-Seine, she was sent to the Order's convent on the rue du Bac, where she was professed, taking the name Catherine in religion.

She arrived there four days before the relics of St Vincent de Paul (see 27 Sept.), the Order's founder, were moved from the cathedral of Notre-Dame to the Lazarist church on the rue de Sèvres, amid great celebrations. On the first day of the festivities she had the first of a series of visions, of various saints, including Vincent de Paul, and then of the Virgin Mary, culminating in "see-ing" Mary standing on a globe with shafts of light coming from her, sur-rounded by an inscription reading, "Mary, conceived without sin, pray for us who have recourse to thee." The figure then turned round, showing a large capital M with a cross above it and two hearts, one crowned with thorns, the other pierced with a sword, below it. She seemed to hear a voice telling her to have these two "sides" struck as a medal. The visions continued until September 1831.

Catherine was not an exalted or hysterical personality. Superiors at various times used the words "matter of fact and unexcitable," "insignificant," "cold and apathetic" to describe her. She had no wish to become the focus of attention, but she did tell her confessor of the visions and the instruction to have the medal minted. He believed her and approached the archbishop of Paris, who authorized one and a half thousand to be struck in 1832. An account of its origins and of its efficacy, written by her confessor, was published in 1834: it was translated into six languages, including Chinese, and sold one hundred and thirty thousand copies in six years. Its popularity mushroomed after 1842, when an Alsatian Jew named Alphonse Ratisbonne agreed to wear one, experienced a similar vision of Our Lady, became a Catholic and a priest, and went on to found the Fathers and Sisters of Zion.

Catherine managed to remain in obscurity, refusing to appear at a tribunal convened in 1836 to inquire into the authenticity of the origin of the medal—which it upheld. She moved to the convent at Enghien-Reuilly, where for forty-six years she acted as porteress, looking after old people in the hospice, and minded the chickens. She told her superior about the visions eight months before she died (on 31 December 1876), but by the time of her funeral the news had spread and crowds came to venerate her. Her body was interred in the convent on the rue du Bac, where it remains incorrupt. She was canonized in 1947. The miraculous medal retained its reputation at least through the 1950s: the present writer—to end on a personal note—was given one by an aunt in 1953 and urged to wear it on military service in Korea, where it never actually had to prove its efficacy as I arrived there just after the cease-fire.

Other Familiar English Names for December

1. Alexander, Antony, John, Ralph, Richard
2. Mary, Raphael
3. Edward, John
4. Bernard, Francis, John, Simon
5. John, Nicholas, Philip
6. Joseph, Peter
7. Charles, John, Martin, Mary
8. *There are no familiar English names for today*
9. Bernard, Joseph
10. *There are no familiar English names for today other than those of the martyrs recorded*
11. Arthur, Daniel, Jerome, Mary
12. Conrad, James, Simon
13. Antony, John, Joseph, Lucy, Peter
14. Frances, Joseph
15. Charles, Mary
16. Mary, Sebastian
17. John, Joseph
18. Paul, Peter
19. Francis, Gregory, Stephen, Thomas, William
20. Dominic, Vincent
21. Andrew, Dominic, Peter
22. Thomas
23. Antony, John, Nicholas
24. John, Paul
25. Albert, Mary, Michael, Peter
26. Agatha, Agnes, Lucy, Mary
27. *There are no other familiar English names for today*
28. Antony, Francis, Matthew
29. Barbara, Elizabeth, Gerard, Peter, William
30. John, Laurence, Margaret
31. John

CHRONOLOGICAL LIST OF SAINTS BY DATE OF DEATH

Notes

The dates given below exclude *circa*, (about), which would apply to a number in early centuries—though not as many as might be thought, as Christians soon distinguished themselves from pagans by celebrating a person's *dies natalis*, "birthday," as the date of his or her "birthday into heaven" or date of death, as opposed to birthday into this world. Especially once martyrs began to appear in large numbers during various persecutions under the Roman Empire, records were scrupulously kept.

Even bearing in mind that the list below is of a selection (and allowing for some prejudice in the selection) amounting to some fourteen per cent of the entries in the new full edition of *Butler's Lives of the Saints*, and under four per cent of the ten thousand and more names in the new Roman martyrology, it throws up some interesting trends. The categories that feature most prominently are "bishop" (83), "martyr" (66), "founder," used here for men and women, (59), and "abbot" (27; some abbots are also bishops, and vice-versa). Considering the relatively small number of religious Orders compared to bishoprics over the centuries, the number of canonized or beatified founders is quite disproportionate. It has been quipped elsewhere that many nineteenth-century Orders seem to have been founded for the sole purpose of getting their founder canonized, after which they become defunct. There is no need to be so uncharitable, but if one can make a single sweeping generalization from this list, it is that in the first millennium the Church was primarily local, while in the second it was dominated by the religious Orders, unconfined to any one locality. Given changing patterns of travel and exploration, this is hardly unexpected. The Orders arose in response to perceived new challenges, in their greatest numbers after the Reformation, and the French and Industrial Revolutions.

Of the bishops listed here, fifty of the eighty-three belong to the first millennium. They become the dominant category of saints from the end of persecution (with the Peace of Constantine in 313) to around the late sixth century. Dioceses were established on the pattern of the provinces of the

Roman Empire, and veneration of bishops who founded them or led them at a later date was an assertion of the holiness of a local church. With the growth of pilgrimage it also became a major part of its revenues, as pilgrims were encouraged to stop at shrines along the routes, the most important of which were to the Holy Land, Rome, and Santiago de Compostela.

Martyrs account for sixty-six entries here, but several of these are groups, so the number of individuals involved is far larger. The first martyr, St Stephen, heads the list, which is entirely appropriate, since "the blood of the martyrs is the seed of the Church" (Tertullian). Martyrs feature heavily from the first century to the fourth and are then relatively scarce until the sixteenth century, when they are over-represented here in universal terms, as a book destined for an English-speaking readership must give priority to the English, Welsh, and Scottish martyrs under Elizabeth I and her successors. They also appear in "mission territories" following the expansion of the Church into the newly "discovered" lands of America, Africa, and Asia. They feature prominently again in the twentieth century (which Pope John Paul II has called the century of martyrs), and the number in some groups is large, with those recently beatified or, in a few cases, canonized as Martyrs of the Spanish civil war heading the list at over two hundred so far, but with a possible six thousand under examination. Martyrs under Fascism and Communism have both been recognized in some numbers, but there is a clamour from Latin America, where "liberation" theologians are asking why those thousands—of archbishops, bishops, priests, religious, and above all lay people—killed in the name of "national security" and other pernicious ideologies are apparently not being considered. The problem for the official Church is that they were killed mainly by and on the orders of people who called themselves Catholic. . . . The paradigmatic figure here is Archbishop Romero, gunned down in his cathedral in October 1980 for his championship of the people against the ruling clique in El Salvador; popularly "St Romero of America" from the time of his death, his cause has yet to make official progress. The point at issue is whether those who are killed for defending "kingdom values"—as Jesus was—are martyrs in the same sense as those killed for defending the interests of the Church.

Religious founders make their appearance with St Benedict, in 550, who is the only one in the first millennium, the next being St Gilbert of Sempringham, in 1189. Reforms leading to new monastic Orders and then the rise of the Mendicant Orders in the Middle Ages boost the number to eleven by 1500; this then leaps to thirty-two by 1800, to forty-nine by 1900, and to fifty-nine by 2000, so seventeen are included here for the nineteenth century and ten for the twentieth: they are far from being the only ones. In addition, a further forty-nine names on the list belong to members of religious Orders.

Monasticism developed in the East, mainly in the deserts of Egypt, taking the "cenobitic" or community and the "eremitical" or hermit forms. Pilgrims brought back accounts of the austerity of life of the desert monks, and Athanasius' *Life of St Antony* (d. 365) set a pattern for monastic holiness that lasted well into the Middle Ages. In places such as Ireland, where the Romans had not penetrated and there were no significant towns, abbots and abbesses rather than bishops were the natural leaders of the local churches. The *Rule of St Benedict* both codified and spread the monastic ideal in the Roman Church of the West in the sixth century, and abbots (and abbesses) make a significant appearance in the list from this time on, with seventeen out of the twenty-seven dying between the years 500 and 1000. They may, admittedly, be somewhat over-represented here, as they, rather than bishops, ruled local churches in Celtic areas, which are of abiding interest to English-speaking readers.

The classification given after each name is mainly into the categories traditionally and still used in the Roman Martyrology, but some have been made more explicit, such as "Carmelite nun" for St Thérèse of Lisieux and others. I have also added "king" or "queen" when this rank seems to have played a significant part in their recognition. Some are blank, indicating that the person's holiness defies simple classification: St Mary the Virgin and St John the Baptist are obviously each one of a kind, but then so is St Melania the Younger, who seems to have supported most of the monastic foundations in North Africa and the Middle East out of her personal fortune for a period. Many of those undefined are women, which partly reflects the fact that I have not used the traditional classification by "state of life"—as virgin, matron, or widow—because this was never applied to men and now seems discriminatory. These women were holy for what they did, as their relevant entries demonstrate. It is a fact that women are under-represented among those officially recognized by the Church as holy: as Kathleen Jones writes in her *Women Saints* (1999), "There have been as many holy women as holy men in the centuries since Christ walked in Galilee; but the numbers of those whose acts have been recorded and recognized by the Church are less. In most of the standard works on the subject, the proportion is about one woman to six or eight men. . . ." This reflects the relative "visibility" of women in society and the Church, which is too wide a subject to embark on here. Their increasing visibility over the centuries is, however, reflected in their relative numbers in this list: of the eighty-four women saints or blesseds, twenty-two died before 1000 and sixty-two between then and 2000; sixteen out of the thirty-three entries for the nineteenth century are women (mainly the founders of new religious Orders planned to meet new social needs), as are thirteen out of the thirty-nine for the twentieth century. So the proportion of women to men here is nearer one to four than to the traditional six or eight. This is a response not only to natural justice but also to the express desire of Pope John Paul II—who at the time of writing has been responsible for over half the canonizations and beatifications pronounced since these were reserved to the Holy See.

34	St Stephen	*martyr*
64	St Paul	*apostle and martyr*
64	St Peter	*apostle, bishop, and martyr*
1st C.	St Andrew	*apostle*
1st C.	St Barnabas	*apostle*
1st C.	St Bartholomew	*apostle and martyr*
1st C.	St James the Greater	*apostle*
1st C.	St John the Baptist	
1st C.	St Joseph	*husband of Mary*
1st C.	St Luke	*evangelist*
1st C.	St Mark	*evangelist*
1st C.	SS Martha, Mary, and Lazarus	*disciples*
1st C.	St Mary, the Blessed Virgin	
1st C.	St Mary Magdalen	*disciple*
1st C.	St Matthew	*apostle and evangelist*
1st C.	St Matthias	*apostle*
1st C.	St Philip the Deacon	
1st C.	SS Philip and James	*apostles*
1st C.	SS Simon and Jude	*apostles*
1st C.	SS Timothy and Titus	*disciples*
1st C.	St Thomas	*apostle*
1st C.	St Veronica	
100	St Clement of Rome	*pope*
100	St John	*apostle and evangelist*
107	St Ignatius of Antioch	*bishop and martyr*
155	St Polycarp	*bishop and martyr*
177	The Martyrs of Lyons and Vienne	*martyrs*
2nd C.	St Agatha	*martyr*
202	St Ireneaus of Lyons	*bishop*
203	SS Perpetua and Felicity	*martyrs*
222	St Callistus I	*pope and martyr*
258	St Cyprian	*bishop and martyr*
258	St Denis	*bishop and martyr*
258	St Laurence	*martyr*
258	St Sixtus II and Companions	*martyrs*
287	SS Cosmas and Damian	*martyrs*
3rd C.	St Alban	*martyr*
3rd C.	St Cecilia	*martyr*
3rd C.	St Saturninus of Toulouse	*bishop and martyr*
3rd C.	St Valentine	*martyr*
?	St Pelagia the Penitent	
300	St Vitus	*martyr*
303	St George	*martyr*
305	St Agnes	*martyr*
305	St Januarius	*bishop and martyr*
316	St Blaise	*bishop and martyr*

329	St Helen	*dowager empress*
346	St Pachomius	*abbot*
365	St Antony of Egypt	*abbot*
367	St Hilary of Poitiers	*bishop and Doctor*
371	St Eusebius of Vercelli	*bishop*
373	St Athanasius	*bishop and Doctor*
373	St Ephraem	*Doctor*
379	St Basil the Great	*bishop and Doctor*
384	St Damasus I	*pope*
386	St Cyril of Jerusalem	*bishop and Doctor*
387	St Monica	
390	St Macarius the Elder	*hermit*
395	St Gregory of Nyssa	*bishop*
397	St Ambrose	*bishop and Doctor*
397	St Martin of Tours	*bishop*
4th C.	St Nicholas	*bishop*
403	St Epiphanius of Salamis	*bishop*
407	St John Chrysostom	*bishop and Doctor*
420	St Jerome	*Doctor*
421	St Porphyry of Gaza	*hermit, monk, and bishop*
430	St Augustine	*bishop and Doctor*
431	St Paulinus of Nola	*bishop*
439	St Melania the Younger	
444	St Cyril of Alexandria	*bishop and Doctor*
449	St Hilary of Arles	*bishop*
459	St Simeon Stylites	*hermit*
461	St Leo the Great	*pope and Doctor*
5th C.	St Patrick	*bishop*
500	St Genevieve of Paris	
524	St Brigid of Kildare	*abbess*
532	St Sabas	*abbot*
547	St Scholastica	*religious*
550	St Benedict	*abbot and founder*
575	St Brendan of Clonfert	*abbot*
576	St Germanus of Paris	*abbot*
587	St Radegunde	*queen and religious*
589	St David	*bishop*
597	St Columba of Iona	*abbot*
6th C.	St Illtud	*abbot*
602	St Comgall of Bangor	*abbot*
604	St Augustine of Canterbury	*abbot and bishop*
604	St Gregory the Great	*pope and Doctor*
605	St Venantius Fortunatus	*bishop*
615	St Columbanus	*abbot*
616	St Ethelbert of Kent	*king*
636	St Isidore	*bishop and Doctor*

642	St Oswald	*king and martyr*
650	St Winifred	*martyr*
651	St Aidan	*bishop*
655	St Martin I	*pope and martyr*
664	St Cedd	*bishop*
667	St Ildephonsus of Toledo	*bishop*
672	St Chad	*abbot and bishop*
676	St Colman of Lindisfarne	*monk*
679	St Etheldreda	*abbess*
680	St Botulf	*abbot*
680	St Caedmon	*monk and poet*
680	St Hilda of Whitby	*abbess*
687	St Cuthbert	*bishop*
690	St Theodore of Canterbury	*bishop*
7th C.	St John Climacus	*abbot*
709	St Aldhelm	*abbot and bishop*
709	St Wilfrid	*bishop*
710	St Adrian of Canterbury	*abbot*
710	St Giles	*abbot*
718	St Rupert	*bishop*
721	St John of Beverley	*bishop*
735	St Bede the Venerable	*Doctor*
739	St Willbrord	*bishop*
749	St John Damascene	*Doctor*
754	St Boniface	*bishop and martyr*
761	St Winnibald	*abbot*
772	St Magnus of Füssen	*monk*
779	St Walburga	*abbess*
782	St Lioba	*abbess*
786	St Lull	*bishop*
786	St Willibald	*bishop*
794	St Stephen of Mar Saba	*monk and hermit*
804	St Paulinus of Aquileia	*bishop*
809	St Ludger of Münster	*bishop*
821	St Benedict of Aniane	*monk and hermit*
822–59	The Martyrs of Córdoba	*martyrs*
847	St Methodius of Constantinople	*patriarch*
855	St Leo IV	*pope*
869	St Cyril	*missionary*
884	St Methodius	*missionary and bishop*
929	St Wenceslas	*martyr*
968	St Matilda	*queen*
988	St Dunstan	*abbot and bishop*
992	St Oswald of Worcester	*bishop*
997	St Adalbert of Prague	*bishop and martyr*
1005	St Wulsin	*abbot and bishop*

1027	St Romuald	*abbot and founder*
1038	St Stephen of Hungary	*king*
1049	St Odilo of Cluny	*abbot*
1054	St Leo IX	*pope*
1066	St Edward the Confessor	*king*
1072	St Peter Damian	*hermit, bishop, and Doctor*
1073/4	SS Antony and Theodosius Pechersky	*abbots*
1079	St Stanislaus of Cracow	*bishop and martyr*
1085	St Gregory VII	*pope*
1093	St Margaret of Scotland	*queen*
1095	St Wulfstan	*abbot and bishop*
1101	St Bruno	*founder*
1109	St Anselm	*bishop and Doctor*
1130	St Isidore the Farmer	
1134	St Stephen Harding	*abbot*
1153	St Bernard	*abbot and Doctor*
1153	Bd Eugene III	*pope*
1154	St William of York	*bishop*
1170	St Godric of Finchale	*hermit*
1170	St Thomas Becket	*bishop and martyr*
1174	St Peter of Tarentaise	*bishop*
1179	St Hildegard of Bingen	*abbess*
1180	St Laurence O'Toole	*bishop*
1189	St Gilbert of Sempringham	*founder*
1193	St Thorlac	*bishop*
1200	St Hugh of Lincoln	*bishop*
1221	St Dominic	*founder*
1226	St Francis of Assisi	*founder*
1231	St Antony of Padua	*Franciscan and Doctor*
1231	St Elizabeth of Hungary	
1236	Bd Agnellus of Pisa	*Franciscan provincial*
1237	Bd Jordan of Saxony	*Dominican friar*
1237	St Sava of Serbia	*monk*
1240	St Edmund of Abingdon	*bishop*
1253	St Clare of Assisi	*founder*
1253	St Richard of Chichester	*bishop*
1256	St Peter Nolasco	*founder*
1270	St Louis of France	*king*
1274	St Bonaventure	*bishop, cardinal, and Doctor*
1274	St Thomas Aquinas	*religious and Doctor*
1275	St Raymund of Peñafort	*religious*
1280	St Agnes of Bohemia	*abbess*
1280	St Albert the Great	*bishop and Doctor*
1296	St Peter Celestine	*pope*
1297	St Margaret of Cortona	*penitent*
1298	Bd James of Voragine	*bishop*

1305	St Nicholas of Tolentino	*Augustinian friar*
1308	Bd John Duns Scotus	*Doctor*
1316	Bd Raymund Lull	*martyr*
1336	St Elizabeth of Portugal	*queen*
1370	Bd Urban V	*pope*
1373	St Bridget of Sweden	*founder and queen*
1380	St Catherine of Siena	*Doctor*
1381	Bd John Ruysbroeck	*Augustinian canon*
1392	St Sergius of Radonezh	*abbot*
1399	St Hedwig of Poland	*queen*
1414	Bd Joan de Maillé	
1419	St Vincent Ferrer	*Dominican prior*
1431	St Joan of Arc	
1433	Bd Lydwina of Schiedam	
1440	St Frances of Rome	*founder*
1444	St Bernardino of Siena	*Franciscan vicar general*
1455	Bd John of Fiesole (Fra Angelico)	*friar and painter*
1456	St John of Capistrano	*Franciscan friar*
1459	St Antoninus of Florence	*bishop*
1484	St Casimir	*prince*
1505	Bd Osanna of Mantua	*Dominican tertiary*
1507	St Francis of Paola	*founder*
1510	St Catherine of Genoa	
1527	Bd Baptista Varani	*Poor Clare nun*
1535	SS John Fisher and Thomas More	*bishop, and martyrs*
1538	St Margaret Ward	*martyr*
1539	St Antony Zaccariah	*founder*
1540	St Angela Merici	*founder*
1547	St Cajetan	*founder*
1548	St Juan Diego	
1550	St John of God	*founder*
1551	St Ignatius of Loyola	*founder*
1552	St Francis Xavier	*missionary*
1555	St Thomas of Villanova	*bishop*
1569	St John of Avila	*priest*
1572	St Francis Borgia	*Jesuit priest*
1572	St Pius V	*pope*
1572	Bd Thomas Percy	*martyr*
1577	St Cuthbert Mayne	*martyr*
1581	St Edmund Campion	*martyr*
1582	St Teresa of Avila	*founder*
1584	St Charles Borromeo	*bishop*
1586	St Margaret Clitherow	*martyr*
1591	St Aloysius Gonzaga	*Jesuit*
1591	St John of the Cross	*Carmelite and Doctor*
1591	The London Martyrs	*martyrs*

1592	St Paschal Baylon	*Franciscan*
1595	St Philip Neri	*founder*
1595	St Philip Howard	*martyr*
1595	St Robert Southwell	*Jesuit and martyr*
1597	St Paul Miki and Companions	*martyrs*
1597	St Peter Canisius	*Jesuit and Doctor*
16th C.	St John Boste and Other English Martyrs	*martyrs*
16th C.	Some English Martyrs	*martyrs*
16–17th C.	The Forty Martyrs of England and Wales	*martyrs*
1601	St Anne Line	*martyr*
1601	St Germaine of Pibrac	
1601	BB Mark Barkworth and Roger Filcock	*martyrs*
1606	St Nicholas Owen	*martyr*
1606	St Turibius of Mogrovejo	*bishop*
1607	St Mary Magdalen de'Pazzi	*Carmelite nun*
1609	St John Leonardi	*founder*
1614	St Camillus of Lellis	*founder*
1615	St John Ogilvie	*martyr*
1616	St Bernardino Realino	*Jesuit rector*
1617	St Alphonsus Rodríguez	*Jesuit lay brother*
1617	St Rose of Lima	
1618	Bd Mary of the Incarnation (Barbe Acarie)	
1619	St Laurence of Brindisi	*Doctor*
1621	St Robert Bellarmine	*bishop and Doctor*
1622	St Francis de Sales	*bishop and Doctor*
1623	St Josaphat	*bishop and martyr*
1628	St Roque González and Companions	*martyrs*
1634	St John Southworth	*martyr*
1639	St Martin de Porres	*Dominican lay brother*
1640	St John Francis Régis	*Jesuit priest*
1640	St Peter Fourier	*founder*
1641	St Ambrose Barlow	*martyr*
1641	St Jane Frances de Chantal	*founder*
1642	St Alban Roe	*monk and martyr*
1642-9	The Proto-Martyrs of North America	*martyrs*
1644	Bd John Duckett and Other English Martyrs	*martyrs*
1649	St John de Brébeuf	*martyr*
1654	St Peter Claver	*missionary*
1660	St Louise de Marillac	*founder*
1660	St Vincent de Paul	*founder*
1663	St Joseph of Copertino	*Franciscan tertiary*
1672	Bd Mary of the Incarnation (Marie Guyart)	*missionary*
1678	The Martyrs of the Titus Oates "Plot"	*martyrs*
1679	St John Plessington (and Others)	*martyrs*
1680	St John Eudes	*founder*
1680	Bd Kateri Tekakwitha	

1681	St Oliver Plunkett	*bishop and martyr*
1682	St Claude La Colombière	*Jesuit priest*
1690	St Margaret Mary Alacoque	*Visitation nun*
1700	St Margaret Bourgeoys	*founder and missionary*
1708	Bd Francis of Quebec	*bishop*
1711	Bd Joseph Vaz	*founder and missionary*
1719	St John Baptist de La Salle	*founder*
1727	St Veronica Giuliani	*abbess*
1736	St Joan Delanoue	*founder*
1748	The Martyrs of China	*martyrs*
1751	St Leonard of Port Maurice	*Franciscan friar*
1755	St Gerard Majella	*Redemptorist lay brother*
1771	St Margaret d'Youville	*founder*
1775	St Paul of the Cross	*founder*
1778	Bd Bartholomew dal Monte	*founder*
1787	St Alphonsus de'Liguori	*bishop, founder, and Doctor*
1792	Martyrs of the French Revolution	*martyrs*
1816	St Julie Billiart	*founder*
1821	St Elizabeth Ann Seton	*founder*
1835	St Magdalen of Canossa	*founder*
1837	Bd Anne Mary Taigi	
1837	St Gaspar del Bufalo	*founder*
1839	The Martyrs of Korea	*martyrs*
1840	St Marcellin Champagnat	*founder*
1841	St Peter Chanel	*martyr*
1842	St Joseph Cottolengo	*founder*
1850	St Vincent Pallotti	*founder*
1851	Bd Anne Marie Javouhey	*founder*
1852	St Emily de Rodat	*founder*
1852	St Philippine Duchesne	*missionary*
1853	Bd Frederick Ozanam	
1858	Bd Benedicta Frassinello	*founder*
1859	St John Vianney	*parish priest*
1860	St John Neumann	*bishop*
1861	St Théophane Vénard	*missionary and martyr*
1865	St Madeleine Sophie Barat	*founder*
1868	St Peter Julian Eymard	*founder*
1870	St Antony Mary Claret	*founder and bishop*
1871	Bd Mary of Providence	*founder*
1876	St Catherine Labouré	*religious*
1877	Bd Placide Viel	*founder*
1878	Bd Mary of Jesus Crucified	*Carmelite nun*
1879	St Bernadette	*religious*
1879	Br Mary-Teresa Gerhardinger	*religious superior general*
1885	St Teresa Couderc	*founder*
1886	St Charles Lwanga and Companions	*martyrs of Uganda*

1888	St John Bosco	*founder*
1889	Bd Damien De Veuster	*missionary priest*
1897	St Thérèse of Lisieux	*Carmelite nun and Doctor*
1902	Bd Contardo Ferrini	
1902	St Maria Goretti	*martyr*
1902	Bd Mary Siedliska	*founder*
1903	St Gemma Galgani	
1905	Bd John Baptist Scalabrini	*bishop and founder*
1906	Bd Elizabeth of the Trinity	*Carmelite nun*
1908	Bd Joseph Freinademetz	*missionary priest*
1909	Bd Arnold Janssen	*founder*
1909	Bd Mary McKillop	*founder*
1910	Bd Michael Rua	*Salesian rector major*
1910	St Miguel Febres Cordero	*religious*
1914	St Pius X	*pope*
1914	St Rebecca Ar-Rayes	*religious*
1915	Bd Louis Guanella	*founder*
1915–37	Bd Christopher Magallanes and Companions	*martyrs*
1917	St Frances Xavier Cabrini	*founder*
1925	St Raphaela Mary Porras	*religious*
1927	St Joseph Moscati	*doctor*
1927	Bd Michael Pro	*martyr*
1929	Bd Anton Schwartz	*founder*
1936	Martyrs of the Spanish Civil War	*martyrs*
1936	Bd Peter Poveda	*founder and martyr*
1938	St Mary Faustina Kowalska	*religious*
1940	Bd Aloysius Orione	*founder*
1940	Bd Philip Siphong and Companions	*martyrs*
1941	St Maximilian Kolbe	*martyr*
1942	St Leopold Mandic	*Capuchin friar*
1942	St Teresa Benedicta of the Cross	*martyr*
1942	Bd Titus Brandsma	*martyr*
1943	Bd Restituta Kafka	*martyr*
1945	Bd Vilmos Apor	*bishop and martyr*
1947	St Josephine Bakhita	*religious*
1952	Bd Eugene Bossilkov	*bishop and martyr*
1955	St Katharine Drexel	*founder*
1962	Bd Gianna Beretta Molla	
1963	Bd John XXIII	*pope*
1964	Bd Anuarite Nengapeta	*martyr*
1964	Bd Cyprian Michael Iwene Tansi	*priest and monk*
1968	St Pius of Pietrelcina	*Capuchin friar*

GLOSSARY

* = *see separate entry*

Acts   From Latin *Acta*. Written account of the suffering and death of a *martyr. Some are authentic trial records, others spurious, written in imitation of authentic ones.

Apostolic Process   Examination of witnesses in the diocese where a petition for *beatification originates, by judges appointed by the Holy See.

Attribute   Feature usually shown in artistic representation of a *saint, such as a palm for *martyrs.

Ascetic (an)   A person who leads a life of systematic self-discipline as a means of advancing in love of God. Typified by the Desert Fathers, but degrees of asceticism can be exaggerated in written *Lives.

Beatification   Declaration by the papacy that a candidate for *canonization has met the requirements and is to be referred to as *"Blessed" (Latin *beatus* or *beata*), entitling him/her to veneration either locally or universally. A stage introduced by Pope Benedict XIV in the eighteenth century as part of the process of reserving the making of saints to the Holy See. There are currently many more beatifications than *canonizations, and many remain Blessed for long periods, possibly for ever.

Blessed   Title accorded to those for whom a declaration of *beatification has been made by the pope, entitling them to veneration but not enforcing it.

Bull, papal   Solemn form of communication from the pope, named from the lead seal (Latin *bulla*) formerly attached to the document. Little used in modern times, when the encyclical letter is preferred.

Canon   Can mean: (1) a member of a cathedral chapter; (2) the eucharistic prayer used in the Roman rite of Mass up to the Second Vatican Council, now Eucharistic Prayer 1, the "Roman Canon"; (3) an article of church law, defined in the *Code of Canon Law*.

Canonization   Declaration of a person's holiness and entitlement to veneration, local or universal. The final stage in the process, reserved to the papacy since about 1200, before which sainthood, involving the inclusion of a feast-day in the *saint's honor in the calendar was a local decision in response to popular demand.

Cenobitic(ism)
Monastic life lived in community, as opposed to the solitary state of *eremiticism.

Confirmation
Of *cult. Several earlier popular *canonizations have been confirmed by popes without a formal decalration of *beatification or canonization.

Cult
Official, liturgical expression of veneration given to *saints. Its original form was a gathering on the anniversary of a saint's *dies natalis*, meaning "birthday into heaven," so date of death, commemorated in distinction to the pagan celebration of the anniversary of date of birth.

Dies natalis
See previous entry. The date of death became the usual date of commemoration in the Church's calendar, and is the date on which the relevant entry appears in this volume—with exceptions noted at the start of each month.

Equipollent
Meaning "equivalent," it is used to denote *canonization by popular acclaim before the formal papal process was established.

Eremitic(ism)
Solitary way of life of a hermit, whether within a monastic Order or apart.

Habit
Distinctive dress worn by *religious. "Receiving [or taking] the habit" means entering the religious life.

Informative process
The first step in the process of *beatification, the original examination of witnesses before ecclesiastical judges in a diocese.

Life
Used with a capital letter denotes a written account. Like *Acts, some are genuine, some legendary and based on earlier examples.

Martyr
Literally means "witness," applied to those put to death for their faith. All those venerated as *saints up to the fourth century were martyrs; after that, those who had lead a holy life but died a natural death were distinguished as "confessors."

Martyrology
Official list, originally local, first of martyrs, later of all *saints. The Roman Martyrology has, since the editions prepared by Cardinal Baronius in 1586 and 1589, listed all those recognized as *saints by the Roman Catholic Church. Its latest edition (2001) extends the list to include *blessed for the first time, bringing the number of entries to over ten thousand.

Miracle
Popularly, an event for which no natural explanation can be

found and which is therefore attributed to divine intervention. In the context of sainthood, one "miracle" is, with rare exceptions, still required for *beatification, and another for *canonization. These are normally inexplicable cures occurring after pleas to a *venerable or *blessed for help. Extraordinary feats said to have been carried out or extraordinary "graces" received during a person's life are not eligible and are generally the subject of official suspicion during the inquiry process, though this is little barrier to popular belief.

Nun	Member of a contemplative, as opposed to active, women's religious Order. Members of the latter are referred to as *Sisters.
Patron(age)	A particular *saint is often held to be the particular guardian or guide of a group of people, an occupation, a town, or a country. The association is usually based on some aspect of the saint's life, but ancient ones can often be quite obscure. In modern times, patron saints are officially appointed by the pope.
Relics	Literally "remains" of *saints, objects of devotion from early Christian times. Divided into "first-class"—bodies or parts of bodies; "second-class"—clothes worn by a saint; "third-class"—any object that has touched the body of a saint.
Reliquary	Container for *relics. A casket or box, often of considerable artistic and financial value.
Religious	Used as a noun to denote members of religious Orders, male and female.
Rule	With a capital, denotes a written guide, officially approved as embodying the way of life to be followed by members of religious Orders.
Saint(s)	Those recognized by the Church as having gained the reward of heaven and suitable to be venerated and followed as examples on earth. The title given after the fourth and final stage in the process leading to *canonization.
Servant of God	Title given to a person who has died with a reputation for holiness for whom a process of inquiry has been instituted. The first step in the four-stage process, followed by *Venerable.
Sister	Member of an active women's religious Order, Congregation, or Institute. Usually with a capital to prevent confusion with siblings (who often entered the same convents).
Venerable	Title accorded to a *Servant of God after a decision that he/she practised heroic virtue and is worthy to pass on to the process leading to *beatification. The second step in the four-stage process.